Brain and Behavior

A Cognitive Neuroscience Perspective

Brain and Behavior

A Cognitive Neuroscience Perspective

DAVID EAGLEMAN
Baylor College of Medicine, Department of Neuroscience
Director, Initiative on Neuroscience and Law

JONATHAN DOWNAR
Department of Psychiatry and Institute of Medical Science, University of Toronto
Toronto Western Hospital, University Health Network

NEW YORK   OXFORD
OXFORD UNIVERSITY PRESS

Oxford University Press is a department of the University of Oxford.
It furthers the University's objective of excellence in research,
scholarship, and education by publishing worldwide.

Oxford   New York
Auckland   Cape Town   Dar es Salaam   Hong Kong   Karachi
Kuala Lumpur   Madrid   Melbourne   Mexico City   Nairobi
New Delhi   Shanghai   Taipei   Toronto

With offices in
Argentina   Austria   Brazil   Chile   Czech Republic   France   Greece
Guatemala   Hungary   Italy   Japan   Poland   Portugal   Singapore
South Korea   Switzerland   Thailand   Turkey   Ukraine   Vietnam

For titles covered by Section 112 of the US Higher Education
Opportunity Act, please visit www.oup.com/us/he for the
latest information about pricing and alternate formats.

Published by Oxford University Press
198 Madison Avenue, New York, NY 10016
http://www.oup.com

Library of Congress Cataloging-in-Publication Data
Eagleman, David.
  Brain and behavior : a cognitive neuroscience perspective / David Eagleman,
Baylor College of Medicine, Department of Neuroscience, Director, Initiative
on Neuroscience and Law, Jonathan Downar, Department of Psychiatry and
Institute of Medical Science, University of Toronto, Toronto Western Hospital,
University Health Network.
       pages cm
  Includes bibliographical references and index.
   ISBN 978-0-19-537768-2
  1. Cognitive neuroscience. 2. Neuropsychiatry. I. Downar,
Jonathan. II. Title.
   QP360.5.E24 2016
   612.8'233—dc23
                                                    2015013925

Printing number: 9 8 7 6 5 4 3

Printed in the United States of America
on acid-free paper

BRIEF CONTENTS

CONTENTS

» **PART III   HIGHER LEVELS OF
                   INTERACTION**

CHAPTER 8   Attention and
                   Consciousness   232

CHAPTER 9   Memory   270

The human brain is the most complex object we have found in the universe. There are more connections in a cubic millimeter of neural tissue than there are stars in the Milky Way galaxy. So it is no surprise that even in the glow of remarkable advancement in recent decades, we find ourselves squinting to find the lay of the land. Even for experts in the field, the brain's complexity can feel daunting at the best of times.

With this point in mind, we set out to write a cognitive neuroscience textbook that would help readers make sense of this complexity by focusing on fundamental scientific principles, patterns, and ways of thinking. Throughout the text, we prize understanding integration of principles over simple memorization of brain structures and scattered findings. As students from all backgrounds become increasingly interested in the brain, we wanted to capture the state of the science while distilling the expansive territory into understandable parts.

Brain and Behavior covers a wide swath of territory critical for understanding the brain, from the basics of the nervous system to sensory and motor systems, sleep, language, memory, emotions and motivation, social cognition, and brain disorders. Throughout the narrative we have sought to emphasize the dynamically changing nature of the brain through the mechanisms of neuroplasticity. In addition, wherever possible, we make reference to elements of neuroscience that are encountered in everyday life. We illustrate key points and concepts using case studies of rare but illuminating brain disorders. *Brain and Behavior* pulls together the best of our current knowledge about the brain while acknowledging our current areas of ignorance and pointing the reader toward our most promising directions for future research.

Brain and Behavior aims to present key concepts as thoroughly as possible, in a reader-friendly style that does not presuppose advanced knowledge of the field. Our intention was to make the topic as accessible as possible to a wide undergraduate audience. However, it is our hope that students at all levels, and in other fields, will find this text to be a helpful introductory guide to the complexities of the human brain.

Whether you are reading this book as an aspiring neuroscientist or whether you are reading it simply as a fellow human being who wishes to better understand the miniature universe we carry inside our heads, we hope that you will come away from *Brain and Behavior* having gained a better understanding both of the human brain and of the human experience.

With best wishes,
David Eagleman and Jonathan Downar

Approach

Brain and Behavior is a new kind of textbook for the emerging field of cognitive and behavioral neuroscience. No other textbook tells the story of the brain in such a logical and meaningful way. Through the use of overarching principles rather than lists or facts, *Brain and Behavior* highlights what we understand about the function of the brain, as well as what we have left to learn and future directions.

Brain and Behavior illustrates current thinking in the field and builds scaffolding for you to learn new concepts. Without compromising important ideas, it covers a wide swath of territory critical for understanding the brain, from the basics of the nervous system to sensory and motor systems, the frontal lobes, sleep, language, memory, drug addiction, and brain disorders. Throughout the book, the narrative emphasizes the dynamically changing nature of the brain (neuroplasticity) using clear and vibrant writing and fascinating real-life examples and applications.

Brain and Behavior presents the concepts of cognitive neuroscience as thoroughly as possible, using an easy and accessible style that does not presuppose advanced knowledge. It features the following:

- *A principles-based approach.* Students of all ages, and especially undergraduates, find themselves frustrated with lists of unrelated facts to memorize. Overarching principles enable you to wrap your head around the big picture and learn how to mine for further details.
- *A progressive structure.* This book unfolds logically, beginning with the basics of the nervous system before moving to the brain's interaction with the world (sensory and motor systems) and then to more complex interactions (attention, learning, sleeping, and dreaming). Building on this foundation, the book introduces still more complex interactions (language, decisions, emotions, motivation, and reward), before exploring the ways that the system can go awry (drug addiction, mental disorders, and neurological disorders).
- *Engaging features.* Several tools and features throughout each chapter help in the preparation for exams and highlight real-life examples and applications of the material.

Chapter Opening

Each chapter opens with a rendering of the human body, emphasizing a key aspect related to the chapter topic, and includes a list of the major sections, features, and learning objectives to be covered.

LEARNING OBJECTIVES provide a guide to what you will read and learn, helping you focus on the most important points. Each learning objective corresponds to a major section of text.

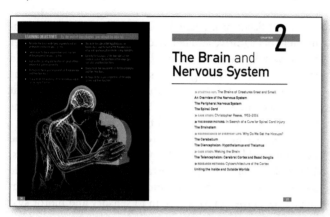

STARTING OUT scenarios begin each chapter with a gripping real-world example of chapter concepts, from hikers on Mount Everest who make a deadly mistake to a boy who functions normally following the removal of half of his brain.

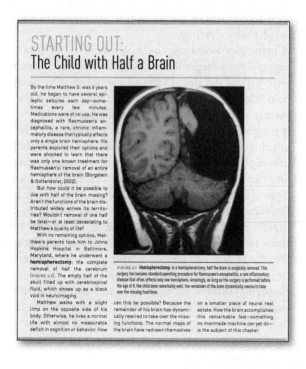

Inside the Chapter

CASE STUDIES interwoven with the text present fascinating human-interest stories that illustrate key content. These clinical cases include a woman incapable of feeling fear and a blind mountain climber who "sees" via electrical signals on his tongue.

Three special features appear throughout each chapter to highlight key themes and concepts:

NEUROSCIENCE OF EVERYDAY LIFE explains how neuroscience directly relates to our daily lives, such as why people have difficulty multitasking.

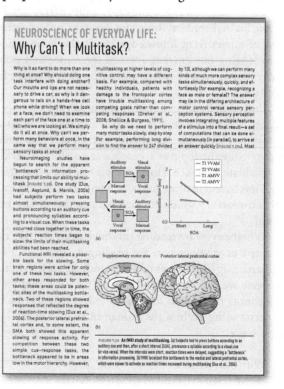

THE BIGGER PICTURE connects neuroscience to larger concepts and questions—social, ethical, legal, and historical. Examples include how neuroscience can help us make better decisions and whether we will one day be able to equip our brains with new senses.

THE BIGGER PICTURE
Neural Implants for Motor Control

Remember the tragic case of Jean-Dominique Bauby from the beginning of the chapter? He had suffered a stroke affecting the medulla and the nearby pyramidal decussations: the outgoing pathway for virtually all of the motor cortex. Locked-in syndrome is the usual result of this kind of stroke. Without any connections to the spinal cord or lower cranial nerves, the cortex is unable to send output to nearly any parts of the body. A few cranial nerves above the injury may be spared, allowing some movement of the eyes and eyelids only. Since these pathways do not easily regenerate, the hopes for recovery are slim.

Yet the motor cortex itself is still intact. What if there were some way to read the activity of the upper motor neurons directly? Could we use them to drive an artificial arm, or a wheelchair, or a computer cursor? Perhaps even a simple speech synthesizer? In fact, for more than a decade, neuroscientists have been using **brain–computer interface** technologies to help locked-in patients communicate with the outside world (Kennedy, Bakay, Moore, Adams, & Goldwalthe, 2000). One strategy involves implanting a set of electrodes directly in the motor cortex, in the part of the homunculus that controls the hand or the mouth. The electrodes may be coated with neural growth factors to encourage the neurons to grow connections to the implant itself.

As one example, in 2006, a research team from Massachusetts General Hospital and Brown University inserted a small electrode array (FIGURE 7.17) into the motor cortex of Matthew N., a 25-year-old who had

FIGURE 7.17 **A neuromotor prosthetic.** A tiny electrode array implanted in the motor cortex of Matthew N. enabled him to control his wheelchair and actions on a screen.

been quadriplegic since a knife attack five years earlier. A successful example of "neuromotor prosthetics" in humans, the sensor was able to read the signals that Matthew's brain was trying to send out to his body, and convert those signals into commands that could direct the movements of a prosthetic arm or a pointer on a computer screen (Hochberg et al., 2006).

Decoding the neural activity into meaningful signals can be difficult. Computer algorithms can learn to interpret the collective activity of a population of neurons as signaling a particular movement, or syllable. The patients themselves can learn to use the prostheses, rewiring the local connections to improve their ability to communicate over time. More

recently, a young man with locked-in syndrome has begun to use this system to produce simple syllables with reasonable accuracy after several years of training for both patient and computer (Guenther et al., 2009).

So far, the technology is still in its infancy. Interpreting the neural signals remains difficult. The signals themselves fade over time as glial cells gradually build up around the implanted electrodes, rendering the electrodes useless. At present, no implant has been able to match the efficacy of the simple blink-coding card used by M. Bauby to write his memoirs. Developing effective brain–computer interfaces will be one of the most important technological challenges of the 21st century.

RESEARCH METHODS shows how we know what we know about the brain, presenting important research techniques and indicating the types of research questions that these techniques have been used to investigate.

RESEARCH METHODS:
Visualizing Neurons and Their Products

The discovery that neurons are discrete, fundamental units of the nervous system was made possible by the ability to stain them. Several techniques allow the visualization of neurons. **Golgi staining** is a technique that impregnates some fraction of neurons with a dark material, allowing the entirety of individual cells to be seen under a microscope (FIGURE 3.10a). This is the method that birthed Ramón y Cajal's neuron doctrine. Another technique, **Nissl staining**, uses a chemical that binds to the RNA in cell bodies, thereby allowing the visualization of somas (FIGURE 3.10b). Nissl staining is most commonly used for judging sizes of cells and their densities.

Several other methods are utilized to obtain detailed pictures of nervous tissue. In the technique of **autoradiography**, a radioactive substance is designed to be taken up by specific cells but not by others (FIGURE 3.10c). Then, when a photographic emulsion is placed over thin slices of the brain tissue, the emulsion is exposed by the radioactivity in the same way that film is exposed by light. In this way, it can be seen which cell types absorbed the substance in question (for example, a pharmaceutical drug).

In the technique of **immunocytochemistry**, antibodies are developed that bind only to specific proteins (FIGURE 3.10d). These antibodies are washed onto a slice of brain tissue, and they attach wherever the protein of interest is being expressed. With some chemical steps, these antibodies can be visualized, revealing the

exact locations of the protein within the cell. A related technique is to use radioactively labeled stretches of RNA or **DNA** that will bind to specific

stretches of messenger RNA (mRNA); this is called *in situ hybridization*, and it reveals which cells have expressed a gene of interest (FIGURE 3.10e).

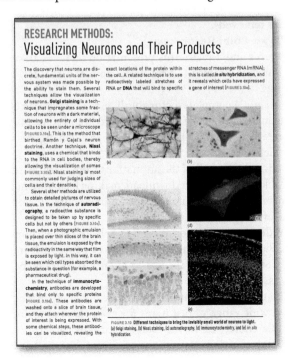

FIGURE 3.10 **Different techniques to bring the invisibly small world of neurons to light.** (a) Golgi staining, (b) Nissl staining, (c) autoradiography, (d) immunocytochemistry, and (e) in situ hybridization.

A CLEAR, MODERN ART PROGRAM provides attractive biological drawings to help convey important concepts and information. Photographs and historical images also connect chapter content to the world around us.

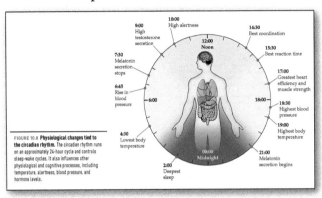

FIGURE 10.8 **Physiological changes tied to the circadian rhythm.** The circadian rhythm runs on an approximately 24-hour cycle and controls sleep-wake cycles. It also influences other physiological and cognitive processes, including temperature, alertness, blood pressure, and hormone levels.

Chapter Ending

KEY PRINCIPLES summarize the main points covered in the chapter—with one principle corresponding to each main heading—to remind you of what you have learned.

KEY PRINCIPLES

- Natural motivations, such as eating, drinking, and reproductive behaviors, help inform the brain what is needed and how to value those needs at the current time.

- The hypothalamus is important for homeostasis and for evaluating internally driven motivation, whereas the amygdala receives input from the external world and evaluates the importance of these outside factors. Dopamine is the neurotransmitter that most commonly conveys these reward and motivation signals.

- The brain learns to predict rewards by comparing the expected outcome of an action to the actual outcome. "Better-than-expected" outcomes increase the motivation toward that action in the future.

- "Liking" and "wanting" are two different things in the brain. Liking refers to the sensation of well-being that is being experienced at that time, whereas wanting refers to a future expectation of well-being.

- Opioids are naturally occurring chemicals in the brain that reduce pain and increase pleasure. These effects can be mimicked by synthetic opioids, such as morphine, heroin, and codeine. Recent research has identified several types of opioid receptors. Stimulation of some of these reduces pain, but stimulation of others produces unpleasant sensations.

- The neurotransmitter dopamine is important for motivation and in learning to predict rewards. It is especially important for assigning value to those

KEY TERMS include all of the chapter's bold glossary terms listed by subsection, with page numbers, for easy exam review.

REVIEW QUESTIONS test your recall and understanding of the key information presented in the chapter to aid with studying.

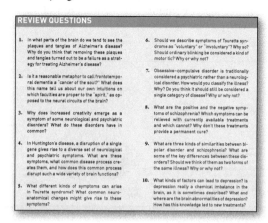

CRITICAL-THINKING QUESTIONS ask you to apply and extend information from the chapter to new scenarios to help you master the material.

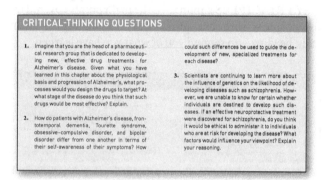

Media and Supplements to Accompany *Brain and Behavior: A Cognitive Neuroscience Perspective*

For Students

Companion Website
Available at no additional cost, the Companion Website provides students with the following review resources:
- **Chapter Outlines:** Detailed outlines give an overview of each chapter.

- **Chapter Summaries:** Full summaries of each chapter provide a thorough review of the important facts and concepts covered.
- **Flashcards:** Interactive flashcard activities are an effective way for students to learn and review all of the important terminology.
- **Practice Quizzes:** Each chapter includes a practice quiz, which students can use as a self-review exercise, to check their understanding.

For Instructors

An extensive and thoughtful supplements program offers instructors everything they need to prepare their course and lectures, and assess student progress.

Ancillary Resource Center (ARC)
For more information, go to www.oup.com/us/eagleman

Available online exclusively to adopters, the Ancillary Resource Center (ARC) includes all of the instructor resources that accompany *Brain and Behavior: A Cognitive Neuroscience Perspective.*

Instructor's Manual: For each chapter of the textbook, the Instructor's Manual includes the following:
- Chapter Overview
- Chapter Outlines
- Key Concepts
- Suggested Online Activities
- Journal Articles and Press Releases

Textbook Figures and Tables: All of the textbook's illustrations and tables are provided in a variety of formats, including high and low resolution, with and without balloon captions, and unlabeled (all balloon captions, labels, and leaders removed).

PowerPoint Resources:
- Figures and Tables: This presentation includes all of the figures and tables (all formats) from the chapter, with titles.
- Lecture: A complete lecture outline, ready for use in class. Includes coverage of all important facts and concepts presented in the chapter along with selected figures and tables.

Animations: All of the animations from Dashboard are available in the ARC for download, making it easy to include them in lecture presentation and online course materials. (Also available in Dashboard.)

Videos: A collection of videos selected to accompany each chapter helps bring some of the key concepts from the textbook to life. Ideal for use as lecture starters or paired with assignments.

Test Bank: A complete test bank provides instructors with a wide range of test items for each chapter, including multiple-choice, fill-in-the-blank, short-answer, true/false, and essay questions. Questions are noted for whether they are factual or conceptual, and for level of difficulty. All questions from the Dashboard and Companion Website quizzes (see below) are also included.

Computerized Test Bank: The Test Bank is also provided in Blackboard Diploma format (software included). Diploma makes it easy to create quizzes and exams using any combination of publisher-provided questions and an instructor's own questions and to export those assessments for print or online delivery in a wide range of learning management system formats.

Dashboard

For more information, go to www.oup.com/us/dashboard

Oxford's Dashboard learning management system features a streamlined interface that connects instructors and students with the functions they perform most often, simplifying the learning experience to save instructors time and put students' progress first. Dashboard's prebuilt assessments were created specifically to accompany *Brain and Behavior: A Cognitive Neuroscience Perspective* and are automatically graded so that instructors can see student progress instantly. Dashboard includes the following resources:

- Quizzes: For each chapter of the textbook, there is a quiz to test student comprehension of important facts and concepts introduced in the chapter.
- A postlecture summative quiz designed to be used as an assessment of student mastery of the important facts and concepts introduced in the chapter, after the student has read the chapter and attended the relevant lecture/class period/discussion section.
- Animations: A set of detailed animations helps students understand some of the book's more complex topics and processes by presenting them in a clear, easy-to-follow narrative.

LMS Course Cartridges

For those instructors who wish to use their campus learning management system, a course cartridge containing all of the Dashboard resources is available for a variety of e-learning environments. (For more information, please contact your local Oxford representative.)

Acknowledgments

Over the past several years, many talented brains have devoted their cognitive powers to making *Brain and Behavior* a reality. We express our heartfelt gratitude for the hard work, patience, and dedication of the team at Oxford University Press, without whom this book would not exist. Special thanks go to editorial director Patrick Lynch, who first saw the project's potential, as well as John Challice, vice president and publisher, who also supported the book at an early stage. Kind thanks to our editor, Jane Potter, who encouraged us steadily onward from deadline to deadline, with patience and gentle persuasion. We are also ever grateful to development editor Anne Kemper, senior development editor Lisa Sussman, and assistant editor Maura MacDonald for their careful attention to detail throughout the manuscript. We also thank the Oxford production team for transforming the unadorned drafts of the manuscript chapters into such an eye-catching and engaging final form: Lisa Grzan, production manager, Jane Lee and Keith Faivre, senior production editors, and Susan Brown, copyeditor. Kudos to art director Michele Laseau and senior designer Caitlin Wagner for their truly beautiful work on the interior and the cover design. Thanks also for the essential efforts of Eden Gingold, marketing manager, Kateri Woody, marketing associate, and Frank Mortimer, director of marketing, for helping to bring this book before a wide audience of curious minds. Grateful acknowledgment is made to the talents of the team at Dragonfly Media for the art program for the book—specifically, art development and art direction by Mike Demaray; art production by Mike Demaray, Craig Durant, Helen Wortham, and Rob Fedirko; and chapter openers and cover art by Craig Durant. Finally, thanks to all of our reviewers, anonymous and otherwise, for their suggestions and insightful comments on the early drafts of this work:

Lewis Barker, Auburn University

Diane E. Beals, University of Tulsa

Patricia Bellas, Irvine Valley College

Annemarie Bettica, Manhattanville College

Christopher Braun, Hunter College

Blaine Browne, Valdosta State University

David Bucci, Dartmouth College

Amanda N. Carey, Simmons College

Cynthia R. Cimino, University of South Florida

Barbara Clancy, University of Central Arkansas

Howard Casey Cromwell, Bowling Green State University

Kelly L. Curtis, High Point University

Deana Davalos, Colorado State University

Scott Decker, University of South Carolina

Dean Dessem, University of Maryland

Vonetta Dotson, University of Florida

Jeffrey Eells, Mississippi State University–Main

Paul Engelhardt, Michigan State University

Joseph Farley, Indiana University–Bloomington

Robert Faux, Duquesne University

Robert P. Ferguson, Buena Vista University

Jane Flinn, George Mason University

Jay Friedenberg, Manhattan College

Jonathan Gewirtz, University of Minnesota

Edward Golob, Tulane University

Kim Gorgens, University of Denver

Jinger S. Gottschall, Penn State University

Jay E. Gould, University of West Florida

Sayamwong E. Hammack, University of Vermont

Valerie Gray Hardcastle, University of Cincinnati

Linda Hermer, University of Florida

Elaine M. Hull, Florida State University

Daniel Hummer, Morehouse College

Mark Hurd, University of Texas

Eric Jackson, University of New Mexico

Daniel Jacobson, Madonna University

Mark Jareb, Sacred Heart University

Penelope L. Kuhn, California State University–Chico

Matthew Kurtz, Wesleyan University

Eric Laws, Longwood University

Ben Lester, University of Iowa

Linda Lockwood, Metropolitan State College of Denver

Jeannie Loeb, University of North Carolina–Chapel Hill

Keith B. Lyle, University of Louisville

Cyrille Magne, Middle Tennessee State University

Kai McCormack, Spelman College

Ming Meng, Dartmouth College

Maura Mitrushina, California State Northridge

Daniel Montoya, Fayetteville State University

Andrea Morris, University of California–Los Angeles

Ezequiel Morsella, San Francisco State University

Andrea Nicholas, University of California–Irvine

J. Ian Norris, Berea College

Jamie Olavarria, University of Washington

Matthew Palmatier, East Tennessee State University

Jim H. Patton, Baylor University

Tadd B. Patton, Georgia Regents University

Richard Payne, University of Maryland–College Park

Michael Sakuma, Dowling College

Haline Schendan, Plymouth University

Lynda Sharrett-Field, University of Kentucky

Robert W. Sikes, Northeastern University

Scott Slotnick, Boston College

Kenith V. Sobel, University of Central Arkansas

Jessica Stephens, Texas A&M University at Kingsville

Jeffrey Taube, Dartmouth College

Sheralee Tershner, Western New England University

Jason Themanson, Illinois Wesleyan University

Lucien T. Thompson, University of Texas at Dallas

Lucy J. Troup, Colorado State University

Jonathan Vaughan, Hamilton College

Sandy Venneman, University of Houston–Victoria

Todd D. Watson, Lewis & Clark College

Douglas A. Weldon, Hamilton College

Robin Wellington, St. John's University

Mark West, Rutgers University

Adrienne Williamson, Kennesaw State University

John L. Woodard, Wayne State University

With special thanks to our Advisory Panel:

Alex Michael Babcock, Montana State University

Peter Brunjes, University of Virginia

Arne Ekstrom, University of California–Davis

Samuel McClure, Stanford University

Juan Salinas, University of Texas at Austin

David Eagleman is a neuroscientist, *New York Times* best-selling author, and Guggenheim Fellow who holds joint appointments in the departments of neuroscience and psychiatry at Baylor College of Medicine in Houston, Texas. Dr. Eagleman's areas of research include time perception, vision, synesthesia, and the intersection of neuroscience with the legal system. He directs the Laboratory for Perception and Action and is the founder and director of Baylor College of Medicine's Initiative on Neuroscience and Law. Dr. Eagleman has written several neuroscience books, including *Incognito: The Secret Lives of the Brain* and *Wednesday Is Indigo Blue: Discovering the Brain of Synesthesia*. He has also written an internationally bestselling book of literary fiction, *Sum*, which has been translated into 28 languages and turned into two operas in Sydney and London. Dr. Eagleman is the author and presenter of "The Brain," an international six-hour series on PBS that poses the question, "What does it mean to be human?" from a neuroscientist's point of view. Dr. Eagleman has written for the *Atlantic, New York Times, Discover Magazine, Slate, Wired,* and *New Scientist* and appears regularly on National Public Radio and BBC.

Jonathan Downar is the Director of the MRI-Guided rTMS Clinic at the University Health Network in Toronto, Canada, and a scientist at the Toronto Western Research Institute. He currently holds appointments with the Department of Psychiatry and the Institute of Medical Science at the University of Toronto.

As a physician-scientist, his clinical work focuses on using noninvasive brain stimulation to treat patients with severe and medication-resistant forms of psychiatric illness, including depression, bipolar disorder, obsessive–compulsive disorder, post–traumatic stress disorder, and eating disorders. His research work focuses on developing a new generation of more effective, more accessible, and less costly techniques for brain stimulation in these disorders. His research laboratory also focuses on developing tests that use functional MRI and EEG to predict the most effective treatment parameters for individual patients.

In addition to his research and clinical work, he teaches undergraduate courses in the neuroscience of social cognition, emotion regulation, decision making, and other forms of complex human behavior. He also teaches medical students and psychiatry resident physicians on the subjects of neuroanatomy, neuroimaging, and therapeutic brain stimulation.

Brain and Behavior

A Cognitive Neuroscience Perspective

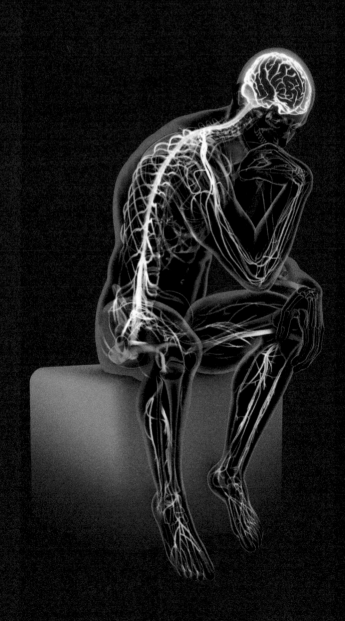

Introduction

STARTING OUT:
A Spark of Awe in the Darkness

On October 9, 1604, a brilliant spark of light grew to life in the darkness of the night sky over Europe. A few days later, the astronomer Johannes Kepler began to gaze up at the new star that had appeared in the void, outshining all its peers, visible for a time even through the brightness of the day. Kepler wrote extensively on the astronomical properties of the new star, or *stella nova*, whose sudden appearance challenged the conventional wisdom that the heavens were fixed and unchanging (Kepler, [1604] 2004). Over the ensuing months, the new star faded gradually back into the celestial background. Nothing similar has appeared in our skies to surpass it since then, even four centuries later.

Today's astronomers would have called Kepler's star a *supernova* and could have told him some astonishing details about the nature of the object that captured his attention on that clear night so long ago (FIGURE 1.1). They could have told him about a star several times more massive than the Sun, reaching the end of a lifespan measured in eons, collapsing suddenly in upon itself to form a core blazing at a hundred billion degrees, then bursting outward again in a cataclysmic explosion that, for a time, shone brighter than the entire surrounding galaxy. The light of that distant explosion was obliged to sear through space to arrive tens of thousands of years later in the night sky over Europe, drawing human eyes upward in wonder.

Yet a supernova, for all its magnificence and rarity, is still outshined

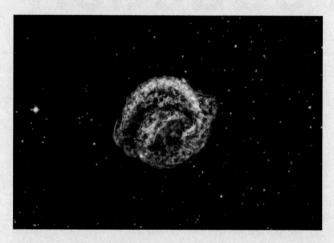

FIGURE 1.1   **SN 1604, also known as Kepler's Supernova, as seen through NASA's Chandra X-ray Observatory in 2013.** This massive stellar explosion was originally observed in 1604 by the astronomer Johannes Kepler. Supernovae of this type are rare and magnificent events: no similar explosion has been seen in our galaxy since Kepler's time, more than 400 years ago. Yet the human brain, a three-pound piece of universe capable of thought, perception, and feeling, is arguably more remarkable than anything it might chance to observe among the stars of the night sky.

by marvels closer to home. As Kepler stood under the stars, beholding the bright spark in the darkness before his eyes, even rarer and more wondrous events were taking place in the darkness *behind* his eyes. In that mysterious vault within his skull, a spark, not of light but of awe, was taking form in the warm, dark passageways of his brain. Where the supernova burned with common light and heat, his mind burned with a rare and incandescent emotion. Where the supernova shed its light blindly in all directions, his mind turned its attention to one tiny facet of the universe beyond, striving to see more clearly. Where the supernova was unaware of its own grandeur, Kepler's mind was capable of reflecting on the curious mystery of its own existence.

Take a three-pound piece of universe, arrange its atoms just so, into the knotty network of a human brain, and the resulting object develops remarkable properties. It is capable of *knowing* that it is a piece of the universe. It is capable of knowing of its own existence, capable of perceiving impressions of the other bits of universe around it, and capable of thrumming with internal feelings of awe, fear, joy, hatred, perplexity, and wonder. There is nothing else we know of, anywhere, that can do these things. Minds are inimitable, mysterious, and precious beyond measure. The very least of us, no matter what our failings or faults, by mere dint of being alive and aware, is more remarkable than any orb in the sky. This is what a mind is worth.

Who Are We?

Take a close look at yourself in the mirror. Beneath your dashing good looks churns a hidden universe of networked machinery. The machinery includes a sophisticated scaffolding of interlocking bones, a netting of sinewy muscles, a great deal of specialized fluid, and a collaboration of internal organs chugging away in darkness to keep you alive. A sheet of high-tech self-healing sensory material that we call skin seamlessly covers your machinery in a pleasing package.

And then there's your brain: three pounds of the most complex material we've discovered in the universe. This is the mission control center that drives the whole operation, gathering dispatches through small portals in the armored bunker of the skull.

Your brain is built of cells called neurons and glia—hundreds of billions of them (FIGURE 1.2). Each one of these cells is as complicated as a major city. And each one contains the entire human genome and traffics billions of molecules in intricate economies. Each cell sends electrical pulses to other cells, up to hundreds of times per second. If you represented each of these trillions and trillions of pulses in your brain by a single spark of light, the combined output would be blinding.

The cells are connected to one another in a network of such staggering complexity that it bankrupts human language. A typical neuron makes about 10,000 connections to neighboring neurons. Given the billions of neurons, this means there are as many connections in a single cubic centimeter of brain tissue as there are stars in the Milky Way galaxy (Nash, 1997).

The three-pound organ in your skull—with its pink consistency of Jell-O—is an alien kind of computational material. It is composed of miniaturized, self-configuring parts, and it vastly outstrips anything we've dreamt of building. So if you ever feel lazy or dull, take heart: you're the busiest, brightest thing on the planet.

Ours is an incredible story. As far as anyone can tell, we're the only system on the planet so complex that we've thrown ourselves headlong into the game of deciphering our own programming language. Imagine that your computer

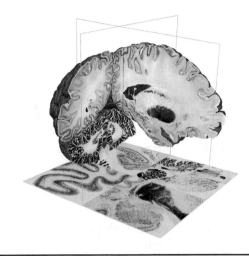

FIGURE 1.3 **BigBrain ultra-high-resolution three-dimensional human brain atlas, reconstructed from 7,404 stained, microscopic sections of a single human brain at a resolution of 20 micrometers.**

began to control its own peripheral devices, removed its own cover, and pointed its webcam at its own circuitry. That's us.

And what we've discovered by peering into the skull ranks among the most significant intellectual developments of our species: the recognition that the innumerable facets of our behavior, thoughts, and experience are inseparably yoked to a vast, wet, chemical–electrical network called the nervous system (FIGURE 1.3). The machinery is utterly alien to us, and yet, somehow, it *is* us.

The Mission of Cognitive Neuroscience

The understanding of the three-pound human brain goes beyond a mere academic interest. Who are we if not our thoughts, decisions, sensations, hopes, dreams, fears, and aspirations? And what are these things if not the products of our brains? The field of **cognitive neuroscience** seeks to determine how the brain processes information, builds memories, navigates decisions, and ultimately produces a human being from trillions of smaller parts.

How are intelligent systems built from simple, senseless parts? How is a great orator constructed from speechless cells? How is a great football player guided in direction by billions of neurons—which by themselves don't know the rules of the game, know what a football is, or understand the concept of winning?

Although at first blush it seems impossible to build an acting, sentient being from neutral, ignorant parts, groups of interacting simple parts can lead to complex **emergent properties**—that is, characteristics of a system that do not belong to any individual component. If you were to decompose your television set into its constituent resistors, capacitors, and transistors, you would see that the comedies and tragedies played out on its screen are not a property of any given piece, but of the system as a whole. The same applies to biology: if

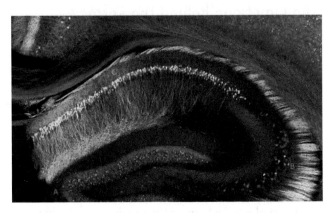

FIGURE 1.2 **A view of the hippocampal neurons of the human brain, visualized using confocal microscopy and fluorescent protein labeling.**

you divided your body into piles of all the different molecules and cells that make you up, you would have an ensemble of uninteresting (and insentient) chemical piles. But rearranging those chemicals into a particular organization, with particular relationships among the molecules, can restore the motivated, dreaming, volitional creature that your friends know and love. The brain's organization, function, and emergent properties are what neurobiology seeks to understand.

To comprehend the connection between mind and brain, it is necessary to ground ourselves in two concrete bodies of data: (1) the way humans behave, perceive, and decide and (2) the biological mechanisms that underlie those behaviors. In this book we will begin at the molecular level and work our way up to larger scales, highlighting the fundamental principles at work at all stages.

From the whirlwind of the brain's great complexity we will glimpse the remarkable mystery that sensations, perceptions, selves, minds, and even consciousness are biological products. After reading this book, it will be easy to understand how, for example, an idea in your head can cause passion or peacefulness, elevate blood pressure and pulse frequency, dispatch a hot upsurge of adrenaline, or make you feel cold with fright. Ideas lead to physical and chemical changes because they themselves are constructed of physical and chemical changes. Neural computations are required at all levels for you to read this page, just as they were required to compose it. Ideas are not incorporeal: they are constructed of parts that are increasingly amenable to description, and that is the journey we will take in this book.

Neuroscience Is a Relatively New Field

How can biological tissue act like a special kind of computer? How do we connect neural function to cognitive capacities? What is the relationship between the brain and the mind, between biology and psychology?

We live in a time of rapid progress in many scientific fields. Neuroscience is no exception. The word *neuroscience* only entered the English lexicon in the 1960s, representing a new understanding that the study of the brain—and the mind—encompasses a field of study in its own right (Schmitt, 1966). Each year remarkable progress is made in understanding the biology of the brain, and much of this progress centers on the detailed biophysical and biochemical processes that attend the operation of the cells comprising the brain. This progress has shone light on the physical mechanisms that permit neurons to organize and operate. The interactions of these neurons give rise to cognitive processes such as attention and memory. These same approaches have yielded important insights into the disease processes that attack the nervous system. These advances, when combined with the revolution in molecular biology, represent a burgeoning picture of the brain and its operations.

Cognitive neuroscience has not always had a distinct name and was once the remote province of visionary thinkers from

FIGURE 1.4 **Every year, nearly 30,000 researchers, fellows, students, and health professionals attend the annual meeting of the Society for Neuroscience.** Their areas of expertise are diverse and include applied mathematics, biophysics, molecular and cellular biology, neuroimaging, electrophysiology, pharmacology, neurology, psychiatry, psychology, and cognitive science.

disciplines as diverse as physics, computer science, biology, psychology, philosophy, mathematics, and engineering. It is now a maturing discipline, and although it continues to draw professionals from those various disciplines, many of them consider themselves "neuroscientists" (FIGURE 1.4). The recent, expansive growth in the field also owes a debt to: (1) unprecedented amounts of detailed biological data, (2) high-speed, low-cost computing power, and (3) rapidly maturing theoretical approaches that have allowed us to see the underpinnings of many frameworks for perception, learning, reasoning, decision making, and disease states.

In Pursuit of Principles

The Functions behind the Form

Although human brains perform feats that seem almost magical, we are, after all, made of biological parts. Somehow these parts run programs that throw balls, walk along uneven paths, detect danger, lift a cup to our lips, phrase a question, communicate with facial expressions, write this sentence, read this sentence, and effortlessly perform the further profusion of sophisticated activities we enjoy each hour. Cognitive neuroscience seeks to determine how the organization and function of the brain's parts engender these everyday, seemingly effortless feats.

The goal is to look under the panels of the machinery of our everyday actions and behaviors to see what's making the engine run. The challenge is that we find a universe of

(a)   (b)

FIGURE 1.5 **(a) The 20 amino acids that make up every protein in your body and (b) a leaf of Sanskrit manuscript.** Knowing only the pieces is insufficient—as insufficient for understanding how biology functions by dint of protein machines as it is for reading a manuscript in an unknown language. The mission of this book is to provide a principles-based approach to understanding what things do.

biological parts and pieces. Many of the operating parts in a cell function for the metabolism, scaffolding, or reproduction of the cell. Many cells may function only in supportive or nutritive roles. Our goal is to avoid a phonebook of detail in favor of teasing out the underlying principles. The details are essential for understanding how the parts of the brain work; however, simply understanding what the parts are, even in detail, is not equivalent to understanding how the parts and their interactions *embody* and *process* information. This latter problem involves understanding what things *do*, instead of simply what they *are* (FIGURE 1.5).

Which Parts Matter?

In modern computers, great care has been taken to separate information content from its physical embodiment. In the brain, the clean hardware/software distinction is misleading. The division of hardware and software in the brain is unclear, if the distinction exists at all. For a complete view of cognitive neuroscience, we will explore topics from the level of single molecules to systems of neurons.

To understand the levels problem, consider the screen on your cell phone. Suppose that no one knew how a cell phone worked, but you were interested in finding out how the components of the screen gave rise to the funny YouTube videos that you watch on it. So you study the personalities of the

characters, why they are sometimes funny and sometimes not, your reaction to their facial expressions, humorous situations, and so on. Through careful study, you may generate a theory of comedy and rules for why it has such powerful effects on humans and not on monkeys or cats. But even at the end of that theoretical work, you are still stuck with a question: exactly what is the relationship between the function of a transistor and the comedy that is displayed on the screen?

You might turn to studying the tiny transistors and the way they are fashioned out of semiconductor materials. This would result in a description of how electrical currents and voltages relate to the detailed structure of the transistor; however, even your complete description of the transistor would give you no insight into why a video was funny.

In the same way, descriptions of cognitive events (such as the perception of a social dilemma in a drama) may require scientific descriptions that are remote from the operation of the underlying biological parts. On the other hand, the two levels, although distant in description, are inseparable: the breaking of a single transistor can kill the display of the funny video. How small parts can unwittingly accomplish functionality at an entirely different level is the surprising and magnificent canvas on which cognitive neuroscience is painted.

Your thoughts, decisions, and moods are underpinned by physical stuff. We know this because alterations to the brain change the kinds of thoughts we can think. During dream sleep, there are unbidden, bizarre thoughts. During the day we enjoy our normal, well-accepted thoughts, which people enthusiastically modulate by spiking the chemical cocktails of the brain with alcohol, narcotics, cigarettes, coffee, or physical exercise. The state of the physical material determines the state of the thoughts.

The physical material is absolutely necessary for normal thinking to tick along. If you were to injure your pinkie in an accident, you'd be saddened, but your normal thinking would be no different than if you had not injured your pinkie. By contrast, if you were to damage an equivalently sized piece of brain tissue, this might change your capacity to understand music, name animals, see colors, judge risk, make decisions, read signals from your body, or understand the concept of a mirror—thereby unmasking the strange, veiled workings of the machinery beneath (FIGURE 1.6). Our hopes, dreams, aspirations, fears, comic instincts, great ideas, fetishes, senses of humor, and desires all emerge from this strange organ—and when the brain changes, so do we. So although it's easy to intuit that thoughts don't have a physical basis, that they are something like feathers on the wind, they in fact depend directly on the integrity of the enigmatic, three-pound mission control center.

What Is the Brain For?

The brain is an evolved biological organ. As such, its products—our thoughts, actions, emotions, moods, fears, etc.—are shaped by evolutionary pressures. As the biologist E. O. Wilson writes,

> The essence of the argument, then, is that the brain exists because it promotes the survival and multiplication of the genes that direct its assembly. The human mind is a device for survival and reproduction, and reason is just one of its various techniques.
>
> —On Human Nature, 1978

A device for survival and reproduction? The surprising character of this observation derives from the fact that what we do think, don't think, and possibly can't think are all *constructions* of a long, undirected evolutionary process. Some of these constructions may have arisen in response to survival pressure; that is, they are psychological **adaptations**—mechanisms that on average enhanced the reproductive success of those creatures that possessed them. Others may have simply arisen as neutral changes and come along for the ride.

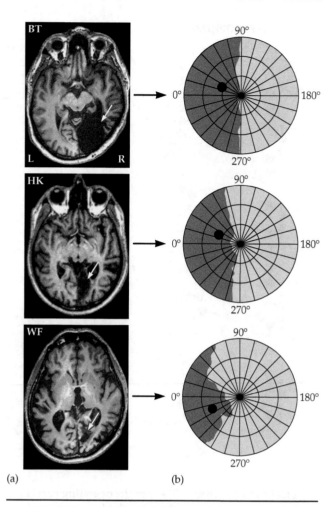

(a)   (b)

FIGURE 1.6   Three patients with deficits in conscious visual perception as a result of injuries to specific regions of the brain. (a) The injured regions of the brain in each patient. (b) The corresponding diagrams show the deficits in each patient's visual field (gray) resulting from the injury. Indicator arrows added by Oxford University Press.

The outcome is that our possible thoughts and actions—the full reach of our cognition—need only to have served the reproductive success of our progenitors. Our possible thoughts and actions do not necessarily equip us with a mental apparatus appropriate to have the right intuitions about the world—or even about our own brains.

Many aspects of neural function are adaptations that were advantageous, given the survival demands placed on our ancestors. Our psychology is no exception to this: it is also an adaptation. It is a construction that made our ancestors reproductively successful and is not simply a picture of the physical world "out there."

There is something strange and immaterial about our thoughts and perceptions. They appear from nowhere; they are vivid while present; and we have no access to where they were before they appeared. Stranger still are the feelings and sensations that attend our thoughts. Our conscious sense of ourselves provides no extra insight into these matters, but only amplifies the foreignness of our internal experience. When we think of our home address, the sensation of eating fine foods, or our feelings during a car wreck, we have no access to the actions of our nervous system associated with the thoughts (Eagleman, 2011). Complicating things further, thoughts are private, and distinct thoughts move about with one body and attend the operation of a particular brain. Although we may recognize that our intact body and brain are required to sustain thoughts, such an insight does not explain them. Upon casual self-inspection, the mind seems quite strange and nonphysical, perhaps resisting modern scientific inquiry. Despite these immaterial qualities, all empirical evidence available today supports the idea that unthinking physical processes in our nervous systems generate our thoughts (Becchio, Manera, Sartori, Cavallo, & Castiello, 2012; Lakoff, 2012; Narayanan, 2003).

The idea that our mental lives arise from the operation of trillions and trillions of unthinking parts is unsettling. It is unsettling because we identify so completely with our thoughts, feelings, and behaviors—but we rarely bother to question their origins. Many people suppose that the rich and subtle cognitive landscape experienced by humans cannot be captured solely in the operation of biological parts. How could the movements of an athlete, the brush strokes of an artist, or the abstract ideas of a philosopher result from the operation of mindless parts? The domain of biological operations using cells and molecules seems so completely different from complex behaviors and mental events that some do not even hope to explain one in terms of the former. To some, it seems presumptuous to try.

Certain qualities of our perceptual experience reinforce the apparent separateness of the physical and mental. For example, although our experiences move around with our body, they don't seem to exist in some specified location. Our experiences also have a kind of special character, feeling to us like independent entities. The effortlessness of perception and action highlights their oddness. When we want to see, we simply open our eyes. We hear, smell, breathe, move, taste, envy, and love without even trying. These observations and their obvious appeal have caused some people to question deeply the physical origins of our mental life, both conscious and unconscious. Perhaps, they say, our psychology arises as a kind of independent property of the material world, not describable by the operation of physical mechanisms. If true, this would place at least part of our minds outside the field of view of modern science (Lakoff, 2012).

Although these ideas may appeal to many levels of our experiences, scientific approaches to the mind–brain problem take the position that *the mind is what the brain generates.* These approaches assume that our experiences do result from the operation of mindless biological parts. This perspective, as unsettling as it may be, has produced a number of different scientific approaches for studying the mind and the brain.

How We Know What We Know

On close inspection, even a single cubic millimeter of brain reveals itself to be a tangle of neural connections more daunting than the alleyways of any medieval city. When taken as a whole, the hundred-billion-neuron labyrinth of the human brain might seem beyond our navigational powers altogether. Yet this is the task before us if we ever hope to answer the Big Questions of neuroscience: to tease out the mechanisms by which we pick a familiar face out of a crowd of hundreds of strangers, regale our friends with stories recounted at 250 words a minute, place ourselves instantly in the recollected scenes of a childhood decades past, choose between life's guilty pleasures and virtuous chores, or smile at the beauty of the morning mist rising from some mountain lake at dawn.

At first glance, it may seem astonishing that we have made any progress whatsoever in linking the rich complexity of human mental life to the even more dizzying intricacy of the human brain. Fortunately, over the past 150 years, we have gradually assembled a whole toolbox of complementary research methods for linking brain and behavior. Although none of these research methods is completely foolproof in isolation, when used together, they have been tremendously useful in helping us to understand how the circuits of the human brain give rise to human abilities.

These tools run the gamut from detailed 19th-century microscopic observations of brain anatomy to far more elaborate 21st-century techniques that involve inserting artificial **genes** into specific types of neurons so that they can be turned on or off with colored pulses of light (as in FIGURE 1.7).

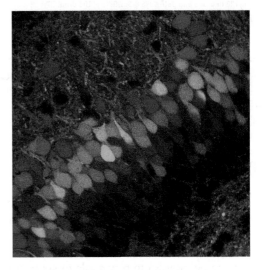

FIGURE 1.7 **Brainbow technique.** The "Brainbow" technique reveals neural circuitry in exquisite detail by causing each individual neuron to produce a slightly different mixture of fluorescent proteins, thus causing them to glow in different colors when illuminated.

CASE 22

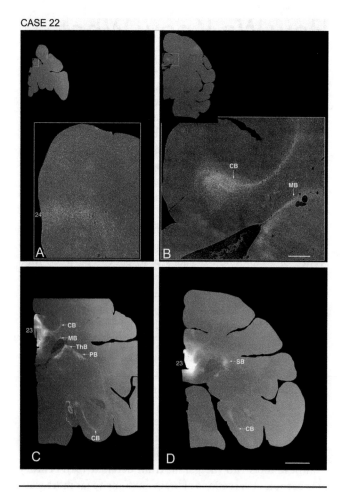

FIGURE 1.8 **Photomicrographs showing connection pathways in the brain of a rhesus monkey.** These are identified by injecting a radioactive tracer substance into one brain region (indicated by the arrow in (D), allowing it to be transported along the input and output pathways of this region, and then examining the neurons and pathways elsewhere in the brain that become labeled by the tracer.

In broad terms, however, all of the tools in our toolbox for linking brain circuits to behavior can be sorted into four categories: connectional methods, correlational methods, lesion methods, and stimulation methods. Let's do a quick overview of each of these approaches.

Connectional Methods

In the social life of neurons, you are who you know. Within the vast network of the brain, the role of any given neuron depends in large part on its inputs and outputs. For example, if a neuron sends direct output to the muscles surrounding the eye, it can be inferred to play a role in controlling eye movements. If that neuron's inputs come from motion-sensing visual regions of the brain, we have a hint that this neuron could help to aim the eye at any sudden movements that might occur in our visual surroundings. In contrast, if its inputs come from auditory regions of the brain, this

might instead suggest that the neuron plays a role in aiming our eyes to spot the sources of sounds that might occur around us. Or, if its inputs come from the movement- and balance-sensing organs of the inner ear, this might give us a hint that the neuron plays a role in keeping our eyes stable as our bodies jostle their way from point A to point B—a sort of camera-steadying mechanism for our visual system.

A wide variety of methods are available for our use in tracing the connections to and from a given neuron or a given region of the brain. Some involve injecting a **tracer** substance into the region. Certain kinds of tracer substances are taken up by the neurons and transported along the input or output **tracts** of neurons until they reach the final input or output terminals of the neurons themselves (FIGURE 1.8). After injecting the tracer substance, we can examine the brain either with the naked eye or under a microscope to see where the tracer has spread, thus obtaining a map of the inputs and outputs to the region we are studying.

This approach has been in use for well over a century and was indispensable to early neuroanatomists who sought to make sense of the vast number of interconnecting pathways within the nervous system (Lassen, 1974). Of course, there was one major drawback to this approach: they had to actually remove the brain to see where the tracers had gone. This meant that connectivity studies had to be performed either in animal species or in anatomical specimens of human brains donated after death. Yet the brains of even the most closely related animal species have important structural differences from the human brain, and postmortem human brains are often affected by disease, decay, or the effects of aging (Buxhoeveden, Lefkowitz, Loats, & Armstrong, 1996; Johnson, Morgan, & Finch, 1986).

A more recent technique, called **diffusion tensor imaging** (FIGURE 1.9), has enabled us to map out connection

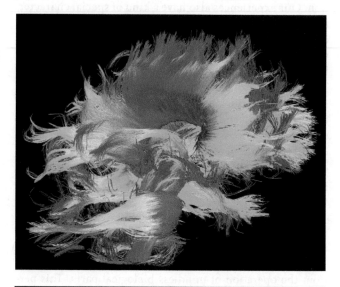

FIGURE 1.9 **Diffusion tensor imaging (DTI).** DTI uses an MRI scanner to create images sensitive to the diffusion of water molecules through the structures of the brain. These images are then reconstructed into maps of the brain's connection fibers.

pathways in living human beings noninvasively. This technique uses a magnetic resonance imaging scanner to create detailed maps of the directions of water diffusion within living tissue. In brains, the connection fibers ("axons," described in Chapter 3) between distant regions of neurons tend to bundle together into tracts, traveling in parallel from region to region like the lanes on a major highway. Water molecules, like the cars on the highway, tend to travel more easily along the tracts than across them. By following the water molecules as they diffuse through the brain, we can create maps showing the most likely routes of the tracts themselves.

Numerous other approaches are available for mapping the connections between brain regions, all of which can provide us with hints as to the functions of the regions themselves. However, for these other connectional approaches to work, we still need to know the approximate functions of the input and output regions in the first place. In addition, the hints provided by connection studies must be confirmed or refuted by more direct observations. For this reason, our toolbox needs additional approaches.

Correlational Methods

Correlational research methods involve making observations of brain activity, through various means, while an individual performs some type of behavior. For example, a correlational study might use a magnetic resonance imaging scanner to map the blood flow and blood oxygenation in the brains of individuals viewing familiar versus unfamiliar faces or rating the attractiveness of different pieces of artwork. By identifying regions and pathways whose activity correlates with the behavior under study, correlational research methods can also offer clues about what brain regions or brain mechanisms are important for specific aspects of human cognition.

More than a dozen different methods are commonly used to measure various aspects of brain activity during behavior. On one end of the spectrum are invasive measures, such as recording the electrical activity of neurons via **microelectrodes** implanted directly in the brain during brain surgery. Other similarly invasive measures include the use of tiny **microdialysis** probes, which are capable of sampling the concentrations of chemical neurotransmitters directly from brain tissue, or **voltammetry** probes, which can detect neurotransmitter concentrations via minute fluctuations in electrical potential within the probes. Less invasive approaches include **electroencephalography**, used since the 1920s to record electrical signals on the scalp that are generated by oscillating electrical activity in nearby brain regions. **Magnetoencephalography**, used since the 1980s, records the even fainter magnetic fields that accompany this electrical activity (FIGURE 1.10).

On the other end of the spectrum, indirect methods can detect the metabolic or neurochemical products of brain activity rather than the activity itself. At the forefront of these

FIGURE 1.10 **Magnetoencephalography.** Two noninvasive scanners are positioned above and below her head. The neuromagnetometer measures magnetic fields produced by the neural activity of the brain.

approaches are neuroimaging techniques, which revolutionized the study of human brain function when they emerged in the 1980s and 1990s. **Positron emission tomography** involves injecting small amounts of radioactively labeled chemical compounds into the body and then mapping out their distribution within the brain. A wide variety of substances can be labeled, ranging from water or **glucose** (a simple sugar) to specially tailored compounds that bind only to a single type of chemical receptor within the brain. **Magnetic resonance imaging (MRI)** lets us view the structure of the brain without exposing the individual to radiation and has become widely used both in clinical medicine and in research (see *Research Methods*, FIGURE 1.11). **Functional magnetic resonance imaging (fMRI)** uses a specific type of rapidly acquired MRI scan to generate whole-brain maps of blood flow and blood oxygenation within the brain. As neurons increase or decrease their activity levels, the changes register as changes in blood flow and oxygenation. Since these changes are quite localized, they can be used to generate maps of the neural activity that accompanies various forms of human cognition or behavior.

A variety of other MRI-based neuroimaging techniques also exist, including magnetic resonance spectroscopy (which can detect subtle changes in the concentrations of certain substances in brain tissue), arterial spin labeling (another method for measuring blood flow in the brain as an indirect measure of neural activity), **voxel-based morphometry** (which can measure subtle differences in the shape or thickness of brain structures), and diffusion tensor imaging (which, as above, can map the pathways of connection tracts within the brain). We will see examples of all of these methods in use throughout the rest of this book.

Studies using correlational research methods, and neuroimaging in particular, have proliferated over the past quarter century. Headline-grabbing studies of the brain regions that activate during romantic love, musical improvisation, or

RESEARCH METHODS:
Magnetic Resonance Imaging

The idea of using magnetic fields for medical imaging is older than you might think. In 1881, Alexander Graham Bell (the inventor of the telephone) hurriedly built a crude metal detector to try to find an assassin's bullet in the dying president James Garfield. Alas, the effort failed. Today, however, millions of people owe their health to a much more sophisticated technique known as MRI. First devised in the 1970s, it is now one of the most powerful technologies for making images of living tissue (De Haën, 2001).

Most medical images are based on the way that different kinds of tissue absorb some kind of radiation (X-rays, or ultrasonic vibrations). But these differences are subtle, and it is often hard to distinguish abnormal tissue (such as cancer) from healthy tissue. However, it turns out that even subtle differences in the properties of a tissue, such as its water or fat content, can create major differences in how the protons in the tissue behave when they are placed in a strong magnetic field. To make images that reveal these differences, we must partially magnetize the body. This is not an easy feat, so every MRI device contains a superconducting magnet powerful enough to make steel furniture or equipment fly across the room in a blur. It turns out that the protons in the hydrogen atoms in your body have a property called

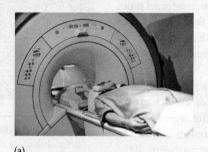
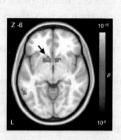

(a)   (b)

FIGURE 1.11 Neuroimaging techniques. (a) A volunteer participant undergoing an MRI scan while performing a cognitive task. (b) An anatomical MRI of the participant's brain (black and white) with a superimposed map of areas showing significant activation on functional MRI during the performance of the task (color).

"spin," as if they were tiny globes spinning around an axis with a north and a south pole. When we put the protons in the strong magnetic field of the MRI device, they tend to reorient themselves, so that their axis of spin align up with the magnetic field, almost like tiny iron filings. Since they are spinning at radio frequencies, millions of times a second, we can use radio waves to knock their spins out of alignment with the field, and radio antennas to record the energy they give off as they come back into alignment. It turns out that the *way* the protons absorb and return energy is exquisitely sensitive to tiny differences in the surrounding tissue: wateriness, fattiness, diffusion rates, even the oxygen content of the blood. We can use these differences to create very clear images of the various

types of tissue within the body, at a resolution of less than a millimeter. Last, powerful computers and many levels of data processing and statistical analysis are used to turn these maps into detailed two- and three-dimensional images for viewing.

MRI is a flexible technique. Using different sequences of magnetic pulses and radio signals, we can generate hundreds of different kinds of scans. Some show gross anatomy clearly, whereas others highlight water-swollen areas of subtle injury or disease that would be invisible to the naked eye. Some black out unwanted signal from fat or fluid to spot hidden abnormalities. Others can even measure patterns of water diffusion or tissue elasticity.

sexual orgasm have brought neuroscience into the spotlight of public awareness. Behind the scenes, an ever-growing cast of less well-publicized but groundbreaking studies have mapped out the hidden crannies of human brain function in unprecedented detail.

However, at the same time, it is important to recognize the inherent limitations of neuroimaging and other correlational approaches to human brain function. Correlation, after all, does not equal causation any more than the crowing rooster calls up the dawn. For example, a neuroimaging study may find an area whose activity correlates with the unpleasant painfulness of a hot probe applied to the hand (FIGURE 1.12). Does this mean that this is a "pain unpleasantness" brain region? What if the region were simply involved in suppressing the urge to move the painful hand away from the probe—an urge that would grow stronger with increasing pain, thus producing an apparent representation of painfulness?

Although careful experimental design can rule out some kinds of spurious correlation, there is always the possibility that a hidden third factor, C, lurks in the background, producing an apparent connection between A and B where in fact none exists. A more reliable approach is to back up the findings of our correlational studies with the results of *causational* studies, which involve actively altering brain activity and observing the effects on behavior. (A closely related approach is the observation of the effects of brain damage as a result of trauma or disease in humans.) These methods find expression in the final two categories of approach: lesion methods and stimulation methods.

Lesion Methods

One of the oldest approaches to mapping out brain–behavior relationships involves studying the effects of brain **lesions**: areas damaged as a result of disease or other injury. A wide variety of events can cause localized damage to a part of the brain's circuitry. **Traumatic brain injuries** from blows to the head, accidents, or wounds from bullets or other weapons can physically destroy a small region of the brain. **Stroke**, meaning either bleeding or blockage of the blood supply into a region of the brain, can also destroy brain tissue within a restricted region. Surgery, performed to remove a **tumor** or correct other abnormalities, often involves removing a part of the brain's structure. Infections from viruses or other microbes can selectively damage certain parts of the brain while sparing others. Degenerative diseases such as dementia can also affect certain areas of the brain preferentially while leaving others more or less intact. In each of these cases, the loss of or damage to specific pathways within the brain often results in specific effects on cognition and behavior, which can be studied experimentally.

One of the oldest and most famous lesion studies was reported by the French neurologist Paul Broca in the 1860s. His patient, nicknamed "Tan," had gradually lost the ability to pronounce any words other than the syllable for which he was named, although his ability to comprehend language remained intact. At autopsy, his brain proved to have a lesion in a specific region of the left frontal lobe—a region that has been known ever since as "Broca's area," which is linked to the production of language (Broca, 1861) (FIGURE 1.13).

Over the next century and a half, lesion studies in animals and in human patients proved useful in identifying areas of the brain with crucial roles in vision, hearing, movement, balance, touch sensation, memory of life events, learning of motor skills, comprehension of language, perception of motion and shape, problem solving, judgment, and decision making. Even today, lesion studies remain useful in understanding the role of specific brain regions in specific forms of cognition and behavior. In the 21st century, lesions are typically mapped out in detail using MRI rather than autopsy, which allows us to draw links between brain lesions and their behavioral effects in living human beings. Several organizations retain large registries of patients with brain injuries so that the

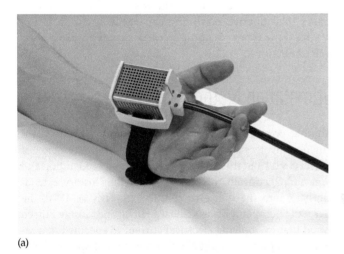

(a)

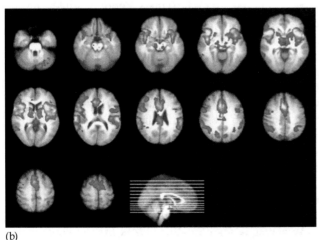

(b)

FIGURE 1.12 Correlation does not equal causation. (a) Hand with thermal probe and (b) activation in cingulate motor area. Brain regions activated during painful stimulation of the hand may reflect pain unpleasantness or other factors such as movement suppression.

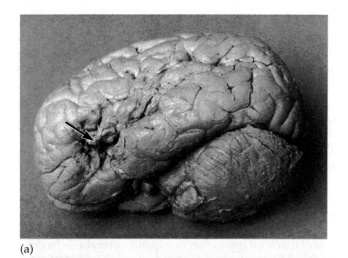

(a)

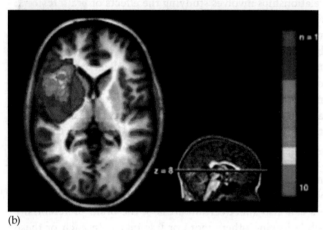

(b)

FIGURE 1.13 **The brain of the patient "Tan," showing (a) the lesion in "Broca's area" of the left frontal lobe and (b) a modern lesion study using MRI to localize the overlap among lesions in a series of 10 patients with damage to this region of the brain (Jakuszeit et al., 2013).**

effects of injuries in different brain areas can be compared across groups of patients, rather than just among individuals.

Today, large-group lesion studies are helping us pinpoint neural pathways involved in addiction, fear, sadness, pleasure, empathy, the knowledge of social conventions, and our ability to understand the thoughts and intentions of other people. When combined with the detailed anatomical maps of neuroimaging and other correlational studies, lesion studies can help to provide evidence for a causal role between a given set of neural circuitry and a specific form of human cognition or behavior.

There are at least three important caveats to lesion studies, however. Lesions themselves are rarely kind enough to map neatly onto just one specific brain structure or circuit, while sparing its neighbors. More commonly, lesions are large, ragged injuries that sprawl across parts of two or three

structures or damage part of one structure while leaving another part intact. When, for example, a patient with such a lesion shows a deficit in, say, the recollection of personal memories, it can be difficult to say exactly which of the several partially damaged brain structures is most crucial for the lost function.

Conversely, if a patient with such a lesion does *not* show an obvious deficit in memory recollection, we might falsely conclude that the damaged structure is *not* involved in this kind of memory. In fact, however, the structure could have had an important role in this kind of memory, but the lesion may have spared just enough tissue to allow it to remain intact.

Finally, in lesion studies, the exact nature of the deficit itself must be assessed carefully or the wrong conclusions can arise. This problem is nicely encapsulated in the old joke about the scientist who trains a frog to jump on command and then removes its legs and tells it to jump. When the frog remains immobile, he writes a paper announcing a momentous discovery: that frogs who lose their legs become deaf! Although the error in the joke is obvious, similar lapses in deductive reasoning can easily occur in lesion studies if the types of cognition we are studying are not yet well understood.

Stimulation Methods

Another powerful approach to understanding human brain function involves actively stimulating a given brain region or neural circuit and then observing the effects on cognition and behavior. Once again, this approach has a long history, extending back into the mid-19th century. As early as 1870, the German neurophysiologists Eduard Hitzig and Gustav Fritsch found that by applying electrical current to specific brain regions in dogs, they could elicit movements of specific body parts on the opposite side (Hitzig, 1900). Similarly, in the 1940s, the Canadian neurosurgeons Wilder Penfield and Herbert Jasper used electrical stimulation to map brain function in patients with epilepsy, producing detailed maps of brain regions responsible for movement, tactile sensation, speech, smell, and other functions (Penfield & Erickson, 1941). Today, studies using intraoperative stimulation of neurosurgical patients continue to reveal new findings about functions such as voluntary control of behavior, the sensation of "willed" action, and the neural circuitry responsible for sensations from inside the body (Lehéricy et al., 2000) (FIGURE 1.14).

In the 21st century, we also have a number of techniques available for stimulating the brain noninvasively in patients or even in healthy volunteers. One such method is called **transcranial magnetic stimulation (TMS)**, first developed in the 1980s and now widely used in both research and medicine. TMS uses powerful electromagnetic coils, held against the scalp, to generate focused magnetic field pulses that pass through the skull to activate neurons directly underneath the

Cortex   Bipolar electrode

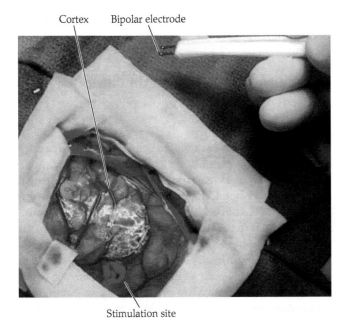

Stimulation site

FIGURE 1.14 A neurosurgical patient undergoing intraoperative mapping of brain function during surgery using a stimulation electrode. Observations during these types of procedures have revealed many important aspects of human brain function over the past century.

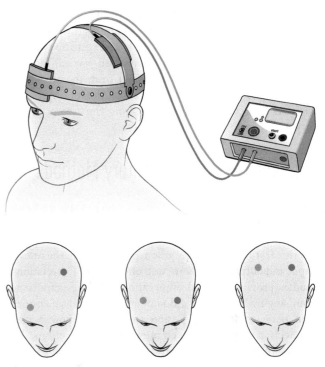

FIGURE 1.16 Transcranial direct current stimulation. Transcranial direct current stimulators can modulate brain activity using mild electrical currents applied to the scalp.

site of stimulation (FIGURE 1.15). TMS coils can be used to generate movements of the body, just as in the studies of Jasper and Penfield. However, they are also being used to study the neural circuitry responsible for a much wider range of functions from vision and hearing to planning, memory, emotion regulation, social cognition, and decision making. Some patients with depression respond to **repetitive transcranial magnetic stimulation (rTMS)**, multiple sessions of TMS.

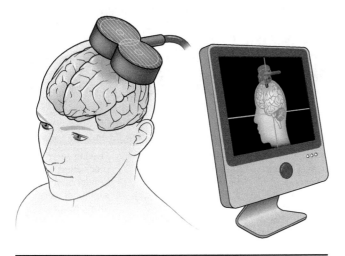

FIGURE 1.15 Transcranial magnetic stimulation (TMS). A TMS device generates a powerful, focused magnetic field pulse that can stimulate the brain noninvasively. The device can be positioned accurately over a target region of the brain using MRI guidance.

Another form of noninvasive brain stimulation, developed more recently, is called **transcranial direct current stimulation (tDCS)**. This technique involves applying two electrodes to the scalp (FIGURE 1.16), each about half the size of a credit card. Once they are attached, a small device passes a weak, constant electrical current across the two electrodes so that the current passes through the scalp and the underlying brain regions. Neurons under the positively charged **cathode** tend to be inhibited by this kind of stimulation, whereas neurons under the negatively charged **anode** tend to become excited. Although the currents are weak, even 20 minutes of tDCS can produce measureable changes in a variety of functions, depending on the site and polarity of stimulation: movement, perception, attention, memory, emotion regulation, impulsivity, and even deception (Fregni, Boggio, Nitsche, & Pascual-Leone, 2005; Nitsche & Paulus, 2000; Nitsche et al., 2008).

As with all the other approaches, stimulation studies have their own caveats. One of the most important is that the effects of the stimulation may spread well beyond the target site into other regions that are physically adjacent or strongly connected to one another. For example, we know that applying TMS to one hemisphere causes effects not only at the site of stimulation, but also at the same site in the opposite hemisphere via connections that cross from one side of the brain to the other. TMS of movement-controlling areas in the brain may also spread via long descending pathways to neurons several feet away, down in the spinal cord. So when we observe an effect from brain stimulation, we still need to clarify whether this is a direct effect from the area being stimulated or a secondary effect from stimulation spreading to areas that can be quite distant from the area originally targeted.

A Toolbox of Complementary Methods

As we have seen, we can use a wide variety of approaches to tease out the complex relationships between brain and behavior. Each has its strengths and also its weaknesses. Connectional studies hint at function, but only when the roles of input and output regions are well understood. Correlational studies provide detailed observations of brain activity accompanying behavior, but do not establish a causal connection between the two. Lesion studies can show a clear connection between lost circuits and lost functions, but finding "clean" lesions of individual structures can be difficult, and interpreting the deficits can be even more difficult, although emerging techniques, including genetic manipulations, offer hope that such clean lesions may be possible soon. Stimulation studies can provide a causal link between brain activity and function, but the stimulation can also spread to distant brain areas, muddying the picture. No approach is perfect. However, the convergent evidence from each of these approaches can help us figure out the specific neural pathways that are important for a given brain function and the mechanisms that operate within these pathways to make that function possible.

Thinking Critically about the Brain

Connection, correlation, lesion, and stimulation approaches form the key components of the methodological toolbox that has allowed us to begin picking apart the Gordian knot of the brain. Just as important, however, are a set of critical-thinking techniques that have been carefully developed over the past several centuries with the emergence of the scientific method of investigation. The scientific method is a toolbox in its own right—a toolbox that has allowed us to repurpose our brains to puzzle out the structure of the solar system, the causes of deadly diseases like cholera or malaria, or the mechanisms of the brain itself. These kinds of problems are far afield from the brain's usual domain of expertise: keeping a vertebrate body alive and healthy long enough to reproduce. Let's take a closer look at the toolbox that allows

our brains to inch their way forward, discovery by discovery, toward understanding their own workings.

Is the Brain Equipped to Understand Itself?

One of the strangest features of the enterprise we call neuroscience is that it is possible at all. Although we rarely think about it this way, the unspoken premise of the neuroscientist is that the three-pound lump of universe within our skulls has the right kind of architecture, mechanisms, functions, and capabilities to construct an accurate, useful model of its own architecture, mechanisms, functions, and capabilities.

But is the brain really equipped to understand itself? Certainly the odds would seem to be stacked against it. After all, the brain is far from a universal, all-purpose computing device designed to crack any problem that falls within its sights. On the contrary, the brain is the end result of millions of generations of careful optimization toward solving three very old, very fundamental, and very specific problems (**FIGURE 1.17**). The first is **homeostasis**: keeping the body fed, watered, and generally within a happy range of survival parameters. The second is **agonistic behavior**: defending its own survival interests against other organisms, fending off challenges from predators and rivals, and chasing down prey that made plans other than being eaten. The third is **reproduction**: making sure that it leaves behind other organisms similar to itself since brains that skip this last task tend to go out of circulation rather quickly.

With the bar for survival being raised every generation, after half a billion years, brains have ended up with exquisitely

Homeostatic	Agonistic	Reproductive
Maintaining the body's balance of energy, temperature, hydration, and other critical parameters for one's own survival	Defending against hostile rivals or predators, establishing territory or dominance over rivals, and seeking out prey to sustain one's own survival	Seeking out mates, procreating, and promoting the survival of one's own offspring
(a)	(b)	(c)

FIGURE 1.17 The critical survival functions of the brain: (a) homeostasis, (b) agonistic behavior and (c) reproduction.

complex mechanisms for meeting these challenges more effectively than the competition. The brain is an organ honed to a specific set of functions, just as the lungs are honed to managing the demands of respiration and the kidneys are honed to managing the balance of water and electrolytes. Imagine how astonished we would be to find a pair of lungs dabbling in metallurgy on the side or a pair of kidneys trying to develop the perfect recipe for chili. After millions of years of vertebrate evolution, it should be no less surprising to find one species of brain taking time off from its usual brainy business to work on a strange new hobby: "decipher your own inner workings."

Even if a brain should for some reason develop a yen for understanding itself, why should there be any guarantee that it is even up to the task? If the sodium-balancing functions of the kidney are ill-suited to cooking up a tolerable chili, then are the food-spotting and threat-escaping functions of the brain any better suited to cooking up a tolerable neuroscience? The bad news is that human cognition is full of biases and pitfalls that make the enterprise of science far from instinctive. The good news is that we *have* managed to develop a reliable toolbox of techniques for making the best of our available cognitive strengths, routing around the worst of the pitfalls, and working our way toward a useful model of our own brain functions.

Biases and Pitfalls in Human Cognition

As we will see in the later chapters of the book, the human brain is prone to an extensive set of biases and pitfalls that lead us to draw erroneous conclusions from our observations of the world. Worse yet, we tend to cling to our mistaken beliefs with a confidence that far outstrips the weight of evidence supporting them. We'll see these biases in more detail in Chapter 12, on human decision making, but let's take a quick look at a couple of common ones here.

The **anchoring bias** describes the human tendency to become overly influenced by a single observation, usually the first observation (the "anchor"), so that it drowns out or even distorts subsequent pieces of information to make them more consistent with the anchor. A bad first impression at a job interview, an inflated price for a house on the real estate market, or a mistaken initial diagnosis in an emergency room all tend to take on a life of their own, becoming hard to erase even when new information comes to light. In one classic illustration, students were asked to write down the last two digits of their Social Security number before being asked to bid on a series of consumer products of uncertain value. Those with higher numbers bid substantially higher prices for the items, under the influence of the irrelevant anchor number (Ariely, Loewenstein, & Prelec, 2006).

Confirmation bias is the tendency to seek out or emphasize information that fits with our existing beliefs, while ignoring or discounting information that contradicts our

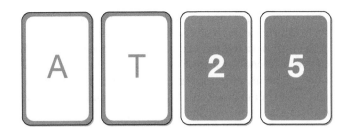

"If a card has a vowel on one side, then it has an even number on the other side."

FIGURE 1.18 The Wason card task. Developed in 1966, this task is a classic example of confirmation bias. Which cards would you need to turn over to test this proposition?

beliefs. Confirmation bias is widespread in human thinking: reinforcing our prejudices about the people around us, shoring up our political and philosophical convictions, feeding our paranoid fantasies, and even leading physicians to develop false beliefs about the effectiveness of the treatments they administer (Downar, Bhatt, & Montague, 2011). It also sabotages our efforts at logical inference. For a classic example of confirmation bias, consider the Wason card task (developed in 1966). Look at the cards in FIGURE 1.18 and decide which card or cards you would have to turn over to test the proposition, "If a card has a vowel on one side, then it has an even number on the other side."

Intuition leads most of us to check the "A" and the "2" card. In fact, our tendency to reach for the "2" card is an example of confirmation bias. If it carries a consonant, it is not relevant to the proposition; if it carries a vowel, this supports the proposition but still does not prove it conclusively because we are still in the dark about the "5." Only by checking the "5" for vowels do we have a chance to refute the proposition by disconfirmation—a point we'll return to soon. The take-home point is that, in checking our beliefs, we all too often cherry-pick the evidence that supports our idea while neglecting the painstaking search for the piece of evidence that would prove us wrong.

The mapping out of human cognitive biases is a major research area in human psychology, with more than a hundred different varieties of bias named in the past half-century alone (Barnes, 1984; Haselton & Nettle, 2006; Mineka & Sutton, 1992). In trying to understand itself, the brain must contend not only with anchoring and confirmation, but also with the **availability heuristic** (where scenarios feel more likely when they are more easily recalled), the **affect heuristic** (where the brain substitutes the easy question "How do I feel about it?" for the harder question "What do I think about it?"), **illusory correlation** (the tendency to perceive a relationship between events that are not actually connected), **belief bias** (in which valid arguments with hard-to-believe conclusions are rejected), and dozens of other kinds of distortion that arise from applying a survival-oriented brain to problems outside its usual scope of operations. Seeing the universe clearly through such distorted lenses is no easy feat. Fortunately, we also have at our disposal a toolbox of critical-thinking techniques that can correct, or at least steer our vision around, some of the worst of the distortions. It is thanks to these techniques, as much as to our microelectrodes and MRI scans, that we have been able to see our own brains with any clarity at all.

A Toolbox of Critical-Thinking Techniques

It is hard to imagine advances in neuroscience, or science of any kind, coming out of a brain whose imagination is driven by what comes first to mind, whose beliefs are driven by illusory correlations and patterns perceived in randomness, whose observations tend to get distorted to confirm what they think they already know, and whose conclusions are rejected when they feel wrong (even when they are actually valid). Yet over the past several centuries, a new tradition of inquiry has gradually emerged to approach the universe's many puzzles in a more systematic way: the **scientific method**.

At its core, the scientific method has four main steps. The first is to begin with an observation of some kind: typically an observation that is puzzling, or novel, or especially salient in some other way. To make further headway, ideally the observation must be well characterized: careful, repeated measurements using standardized techniques and well-defined units of measurement help to improve the richness of the observation and ensure that it holds up against the perils of anchoring, illusory correlation, perceptual errors, and other similar pitfalls.

The next step is to develop a **hypothesis**: a proposed explanation for the observation in question. A good hypothesis should be capable of being verified, or ideally *falsified* (i.e., proven wrong), through some sort of experimental test. Useful hypotheses also tend to be parsimonious (i.e., as simple as possible while still fitting the observation), fit with the existing knowledge base, and be generalizable to other similar classes of observations.

The third step is to generate specific and testable predictions from the hypothesis: if our hypothesis X is true, then we ought to be able to observe other phenomena A, B, and C. Negative predictions are especially helpful: if our hypothesis X is true, we should *not* see phenomena D, E, or F. Finding D, E, or F would disconfirm our hypothesis and force us to reconsider. Generating useful predictions from a hypothesis requires not only the techniques of logical deduction, but also a healthy dose of creativity. Some of the greatest breakthroughs in science involve not merely coming up with a clever hypothesis, but also spotting some key implication of the hypothesis that had eluded everyone else in the field. This implication can then be used as the basis for an experiment.

Experimental testing of the predictions is the last of the four key elements. Here, rather than relying solely on our intuitions about the plausibility of the hypothesis or on our even more distorted intuitions about the plausibility of the predictions, we put them to the empirical test. As with the observation phase, the experimental phase requires careful measurement and comprehensive efforts to control for any additional factors that could influence the observations, thus interfering with the predicted effects. Devising a good experiment also calls for a good deal of creativity, both in terms of the methods of carrying out the experiment and in terms of their execution (FIGURE 1.19). Again, breakthroughs in science often come from spotting an elegant way of testing a prediction that had previously been difficult to translate into an actual experiment.

A key point about the scientific method is that it is *iterative*: the results of one experiment count as observations that can then be fed back into the process to generate new hypotheses, predictions, and experimental tests. The *progression*, or evolution, of scientific knowledge arises from successive iterations of experiments, just as evolution in nature arises from successive iterations of living organisms. Over the generations, as with biological systems, scientific hypotheses can become optimized into intricate, elaborate, and highly effective mechanisms for addressing a given problem.

Outside this core methodology, there are some additional tricks and techniques that have been added to the toolbox to circumvent the biases of our all-too-fallible human brains. An important one is **replication** and extension of findings: confirming preliminary findings with additional observations by other methods, or other groups of investigators, often using more rigorous approaches or more careful controls or a larger number of overall observations. Since individual observations are more likely to be distorted by extraneous factors, seeing the same results consistently across multiple tests can increase our confidence in the findings. The mathematical tools of *statistics* also help us to achieve unbiased estimates of the true values of the phenomena we are observing, of the likelihood that our observations could have arisen by chance, and of the strength of associations or other relationships between different phenomena under observation.

Finally, to circumvent the influences of emotion, expectancy, and other biases upon the brains of individual investigators, the tradition of *peer review* brings other brains into the mix to evaluate scientific work. Independent peer reviewers who lack a personal investment in the work are often in a better position to evaluate the validity of any given study, look for evidence of biased thinking or observation, spot missed assumptions or hidden pitfalls in the interpretation of the data, and steer clear of false implications from any findings that emerge. Traditionally, peer review is a precondition for publication of the results in the larger body of scientific literature. This quality control measure can help to ensure (but certainly does not guarantee) that knowledge disseminated through the scientific literature is less distorted by the common biases and pitfalls of human thought. Although far from perfect, this approach has helped us to make at least some headway toward understanding the workings of our own nervous systems.

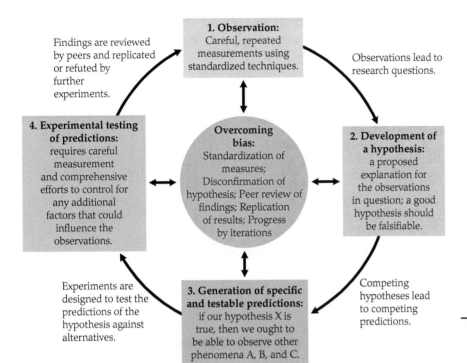

1. Observation: Careful, repeated measurements using standardized techniques.

Findings are reviewed by peers and replicated or refuted by further experiments.

Observations lead to research questions.

4. Experimental testing of predictions: requires careful measurement and comprehensive efforts to control for any additional factors that could influence the observations.

Overcoming bias: Standardization of measures; Disconfirmation of hypothesis; Peer review of findings; Replication of results; Progress by iterations

2. Development of a hypothesis: a proposed explanation for the observations in question; a good hypothesis should be falsifiable.

Experiments are designed to test the predictions of the hypothesis against alternatives.

3. Generation of specific and testable predictions: if our hypothesis X is true, then we ought to be able to observe other phenomena A, B, and C.

Competing hypotheses lead to competing predictions.

FIGURE 1.19 The scientific method helps us to work around the in-built perceptual and cognitive biases of the brain.

The Big Questions in Cognitive Neuroscience

You'll often hear it said that "we still know almost nothing about how the brain works." This isn't strictly true. The fact is that over the past century and a half, thanks to a combination of rigorous scientific study and a versatile toolbox of technical methods, we have learned a great deal about how the brain works. The sum of our current knowledge in neuroscience is already so large that no single human being can any longer claim to keep up with it all. Every year, some 40,000 new studies (more than 100 papers a day) are published in more than 200 different neuroscience journals. Individual neuroscientists can spend their entire careers focusing on the functions of a single neurotransmitter at a single receptor within a single neuron type in a single species. One of the major challenges in neuroscience today is simply finding efficient systems for indexing and organizing all the knowledge that we have already managed to acquire: intricately detailed maps of connections among brain regions, patterns of gene expression at different times during development, chemical signaling pathways within and between neurons, or fMRI images of human brains at work.

That said, for all that we have learned, there remains an even vaster body of knowledge still to be acquired and a lengthy list of questions that remain to be answered. So what are the Big Questions in the cognitive neuroscience of the early 21st century? The list is lengthy, but over the course of this book we'll touch on at least a dozen of them. In this section, we'll take a brief look at what some of these questions are and why the answers are important. As you read through each chapter of the book, try to keep the corresponding questions in mind.

Why Have a Brain at All? (Chapter 2)

As human beings, we are used to working with the assumption that we have a specific body system, the nervous system, that looks after our perception, thought, and behavior. We are also used to the idea that this system is not evenly distributed throughout our body like an immune system or a network of blood vessels, but instead has a "top-heavy" concentration into a single organ, the brain, that lies at one end of the body.

But why should we do it this way? After all, there are entire categories of multicellular organisms that seem to get along fine without a nervous system of any kind: plants, fungi, and many members of the animal kingdom as well (FIGURE 1.20). What is it about our particular branch of the evolutionary tree that makes having a nervous system worthwhile? Furthermore, why concentrate the nervous system into a brain, where its essential functions become vulnerable to strokes, tumors, blows to the head, or other injuries? Other animals like starfish or jellyfish don't have these worries: their nervous systems are distributed throughout their bodies, like a neural net.

In fact, there are some specific advantages to having a nervous system and to concentrating this nervous system at

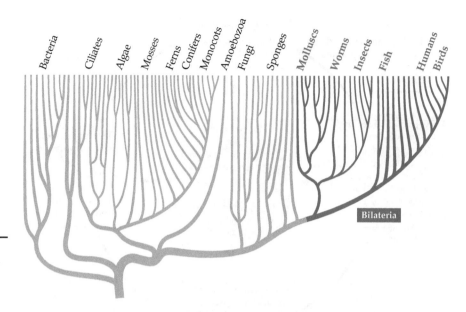

FIGURE 1.20 An evolutionary tree of living organisms. Bilaterians, symmetrical multicellular animals with a head and a tail end, are only a fraction of the whole.

one end of the body. Knowing what these advantages are can give us some clues as to which of life's problems our brains help us to solve. Knowing the brain's to-do list is an essential step in understanding the functions it performs, as well as the mechanisms by which it performs those functions. We'll look at the question of why we have a brain in Chapter 2.

How Is Information Coded in Neural Activity? (Chapter 3)

Neurons, the specialized cells of the brain, can produce brief spikes of voltage in their outer membranes. These electrical pulses travel along specialized extensions called axons to cause the release of chemical signals elsewhere in the brain. The binary, all-or-nothing spikes appear to carry information about the world: What do I see? Am I hungry? Which way should I turn? But what is the code of these millisecond bits of voltage? Spikes may mean different things at different places and times in the brain. In parts of the central nervous system (the brain and spinal cord), the rate of spiking often correlates with clearly definable external features, like the presence of a color or a face (Herrmann, 2001; Singer & Gray, 1995). In the peripheral nervous system, more spikes indicate more heat, a louder sound, or a stronger muscle contraction (Letcher & Goldring, 1968; Woolf & Salter, 2000).

As we delve deeper into the brain, however, we find populations of neurons involved in more complex phenomena, like reminiscence, value judgments, simulation of possible futures, the desire for a mate, and so on—and here the signals become difficult to decrypt (Elliott, Agnew, & Deakin, 2008; Fellows & Farah, 2007). The challenge is something like popping the cover off a computer, measuring a few transistors chattering between high and low voltage, and trying to guess the content of the Web page being surfed.

It is likely that mental information is stored not in single cells but in populations of cells and patterns of their activity. However, it is currently not clear how to know which neurons belong to a particular group; worse still, current technologies (like sticking fine electrodes directly into the brain) are not well suited to measuring the activity of several thousand neurons at once. Nor is it simple to monitor the connections of even one neuron: a typical neuron in the cortex receives input from some 10,000 other neurons (Neff, 1987).

Although traveling bursts of voltage can carry signals across the brain quickly, those electrical spikes may not be the only—or even the main—way that information is carried in nervous systems. Forward-looking studies are examining other possible information couriers: glial cells (the other main cell type in the brain, with functions that are poorly understood at present), other kinds of signaling mechanisms between cells (such as newly discovered gases and peptides), and the biochemical cascades that take place inside cells.

How Does the Brain Balance Stability against Change? (Chapter 4)

The brain is commonly assumed to be like a fixed map, with different regions dedicated to specific tasks. But that assumption misses one of the most fundamental principles and powerful tools of the brain: **plasticity**, or the ability to change and retain the change. The brain is a dynamic system, constantly modifying its own circuitry to match the demands of the environment and the goals of the animal. Whereas your computer is built with hard wiring that remains fixed from the assembly line onward, the brain dynamically reconfigures, ever so slightly, with each new experience. It reorganizes itself from the level of molecules

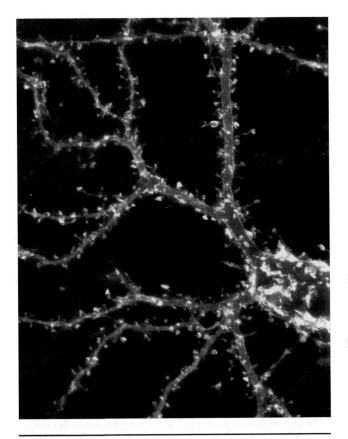

FIGURE 1.21 **Spines.** Structures known as spines, which can be seen here along the dendrites of a neuron from the hippocampus, are important sites of plasticity in neural structure and function.

in the synapses to the level of the gross anatomy visible to the naked eye (FIGURE 1.21). Without this ongoing change, there could be no learning and memory.

The principles of plasticity allow tremendous flexibility: a brain can find itself inside any body plan (four legs, two legs, wings, and so forth), and it will figure out how to configure itself to optimally control the muscles and limbs. The brain can find itself in any ecosystem (e.g., jungle, swamp, mountains), and it will learn how to operate in it. A brain can find itself in any country, and it will absorb the local language and culture.

An open question about change in the brain is known as the stability–plasticity dilemma: how can the brain constantly take in new information without interfering with what it has already stored? In Chapter 4 we will see some potential solutions to this dilemma. For example, some neurotransmitters (chemical messengers in the brain) make plasticity more or less effective so that only the most relevant information is imprinted. Moreover, there are different time scales of plasticity: some brain mechanisms change quickly, whereas others change more slowly. In this way, only the most consistent information works its way deeply into the forest of the brain.

Why Does Vision Have So Little to Do with the Eyes? (Chapter 5)

Vision seems effortless. You open your eyes and *voilà*: there's the world, in all its beautiful shapes and colors. But in fact, vision seems effortless only because of the massive neural machinery that underpins it—about one-third of the human brain. Why all that neural machinery? What is it all doing?

Cells in the back of the eye that sense light—known as photoreceptors—convert light into electrical signals. From there, the signals move through the visual system to the visual cortex. As the signals progress through the anatomy of the visual system, the degree of processing becomes more sophisticated. At low levels, neurons are responsive to spots of light in specific locations; at higher levels, neurons respond to, say, faces or houses in any part of the visual scene. The processing has gone from detail oriented to big picture.

But this picture of a hierarchy of processing—with signals moving from the eyes to some higher level in the cortex—is not the full picture. In fact, it's not even most of it. The story of vision is really about internally generated activity in the cortex. That internal activity is sufficient for visual experience; it is merely modulated by incoming information through the eyes. This is why you can have full, rich visual experience in your dreams, even while your eyes are closed. So the visual system is not like a camera lens that simply reads in a photographic representation of the world. Instead, it is a construction of the brain that is largely built up from expectations.

How Does the Brain Stitch Together a Picture of the World from Different Senses? (Chapter 6)

All senses start out with the same job: converting information sources from the world (say, a beam of light, a sound, a smell, or a touch) into a single, common currency that the brain can use: action potentials. Thus, the mission of the peripheral visual system is to convert (or *transduce*) light into electrical signals. Mechanisms in the ear convert vibrations in the density of the air into electrical signals. Receptors on the skin and in the body convert pressure, temperature, and noxious chemicals into electrical signals. The nose converts drifting odor molecules and the gustatory system converts tastants. Each sense has separate, specialized regions of cortex devoted to processing its inputs: primary auditory cortex, primary visual cortex, and so on.

But there is a surprising property of multisensory experience: despite the extensive division of labor in the cortex (vision, hearing, balance, vibration, temperature, pain, proprioception, and so on), none of that division is apparent perceptually. Instead, we enjoy a unified picture of the world "out there" instead of having a separate visual world, an auditory world, a tactile world, and so on. When you watch a blue bird flying to the left and squawking, the blueness and the motion and the sound do not bleed off one another, but instead appear perfectly bound together. How does the brain produce a unified picture of the seen world given its specialized processing streams? This is known as the **binding problem**.

Although the binding problem remains unsolved, one clue is that the tight coordination of different sensory systems is underpinned by a rich fabric of connections—and these force different regions to "come to agreement" in their firing patterns (Treisman, 1996). As a result of this design, one's final perception does not rely solely on the information coming in through the various channels. It depends partially on the input, but not entirely. Instead, just as we saw with vision, a good deal of what the brain believes it is experiencing depends on its expectations. Sensory information does not simply pour into the body's sensors and flow into a picture of the world (FIGURE 1.22).

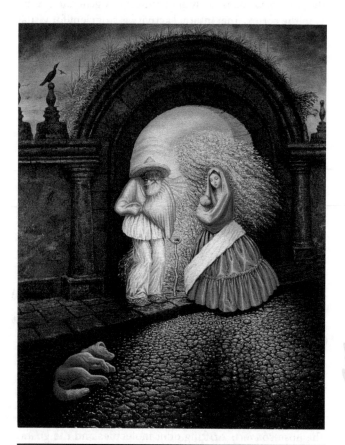

FIGURE 1.22 *La Familia del General* **by Octavio Ocampo.** The same sensory input can generate two different percepts (objects that are perceived), depending on expectations. Do you see an old man clutching his coat lapel or a rustic couple standing under an archway near a dog?

The hopes of early neuroscience—that brain areas would be understood as successive modules in a causal chain—are thwarted by the vast, loopy linkages between brain areas. Through a modern lens, brain areas are dependent for their normal functioning on the interwoven connections they exchange. In the absence of understanding the dynamical loops, drawing conclusions about the function of a brain area from the activity of a single cell is likely to be as doomed as studying the global economy based on one person's credit card report. This is why biology can be more difficult than physics. In physics, isolating a part of the system allows you to understand it directly; this is unlikely to hold true with brain areas.

How Does the Brain Control Our Actions? (Chapter 7)

Next time you reach to pick up a coffee mug, watch your hand carefully. Were you even looking directly at the cup, or did you automatically reach for its approximate location? Are your fingers cupped to grasp the body of the mug or hooked to grasp the handle? Turn the cup 180 degrees and try reaching again: your hand will switch to the opposite grasp, without you having to think about it. Fill the cup with scalding hot liquid: your hand will now automatically switch to hold the cup by the handle, even if this entails an awkward reverse grasp. All of this takes place automatically, even with your thoughts directed elsewhere.

Now try something harder: try to catch the slowly growing urge in your mind just before you decide to reach for the cup. Why did you reach for it at that particular instant? Why not earlier or later? Was there any external signal (such as a friend telling you to hurry up), or was the cue an internal one?

Now look at the larger set of plans into which these simple actions are embedded. What led you to sip on this particular drink in the first place? Why did you choose this particular beverage over the available alternatives? Did you opt for this drink out of personal preference, lack of alternatives, politeness, or longer-term considerations of healthfulness?

Behind even the simplest of actions lies an immense complexity of computations, from choosing how to wrap your fingers around a coffee cup all the way up to deciding on the healthiest (or the tastiest) of available hot drinks to put in the cup itself (FIGURE 1.23). Within the brain, a hierarchy of control regions works to resolve our basic drives into specific desires, goals, strategies, actions, and movements intended to satisfy those drives. In Chapter 7, we will look at this hierarchy in detail and examine the mechanisms by which the brain controls our actions from moment to moment throughout the day.

What Is Consciousness? (Chapter 8)

Think back to your first kiss. The experience of it may pop into your head instantly. Where was that memory before you

FIGURE 1.23 Even the simplest movements are embedded in a rich hierarchy of actions, behaviors, strategies, goals, and evaluations, all under the control of specific neural circuits within the brain.

became conscious of it? How was it stored in your brain before and after it came into consciousness? What is the difference between those states?

An explanation of consciousness is one of the major unsolved problems of modern science. It may not turn out to be a single phenomenon; nonetheless, by way of a preliminary target, let's think of it as the thing that flickers on when you wake up in the morning that was not there, in the exact same brain hardware, moments before.

Neuroscientists believe that consciousness emerges from the material stuff of the brain primarily because even small changes to your brain (say, caused by drugs or disease) can powerfully alter your subjective experiences. The heart of the problem is that we do not yet know how to engineer pieces and parts such that the resulting machine has the kind of private subjective experience that you and I take for granted. If we give you all the Tinkertoys in the world and tell you to hook them up so that they form a conscious machine, good luck. We don't have a theory yet of how to do this; we don't even know what the theory would look like.

One of the traditional challenges to consciousness research is studying it experimentally. It is probable that at any moment some active neuronal processes correlate with consciousness, whereas others do not. The first challenge is to determine the difference between them. Some clever experiments are making at least a little headway. In one of these, subjects see an image of a house in one eye and, simultaneously, an image of a cow in the other. Instead of perceiving a house–cow mixture, people perceive only one of them. Then, after some random amount of time, they will believe they're seeing the other, and they will continue to switch slowly back and forth. Yet nothing about the visual stimulus changes; only the conscious experience changes (Kovács, Papathomas, Yang, & Fehér, 1996). This test allows investigators to probe which properties of neuronal activity correlate with the changes in subjective experience.

The mechanisms underlying consciousness could reside at any of a variety of physical levels: molecular, cellular, circuit, pathway, or some organizational level not yet described. The mechanisms might also be a product of interactions between these levels. One compelling but still speculative notion is that the massive feedback circuitry of the brain is essential to the production of consciousness (Brown, 1970).

In the near term, scientists are working to identify the areas of the brain that correlate with consciousness. Then comes the next step: understanding why they correlate. This is the so-called hard problem of neuroscience, and it lies at the outer limit of what material explanations will say about the experience of being human.

How Are Memories Stored and Retrieved? (Chapter 9)

When you learn a new fact, like someone's name, there are physical changes in the structure of your brain. But we don't yet comprehend exactly what those changes are, how they are orchestrated across vast seas of synapses and neurons, how they embody knowledge, or how they are read out decades later for retrieval.

One complication is that there are many kinds of memories. The brain seems to distinguish **short-term memory** (remembering a phone number just long enough to dial it) from **long-term memory** (what you did on your last birthday). Within long-term memory, **declarative memories** (like names and facts) are distinct from **nondeclarative memories** (riding a bicycle, being affected by a subliminal message), and within these general categories are numerous subtypes. Different brain structures seem to support different kinds of learning and memory; brain damage can lead to the loss of one type without disturbing the others.

FIGURE 1.24 A synapse, or point of communication between two neurons, illustrated in blue and yellow in this image. The three-dimensional structure of these neurons was painstakingly reconstructed by players of an online brain-mapping game known as EyeWire from actual two-dimensional electron microscope images of brain tissue.

Nonetheless, similar molecular mechanisms may be at work in these memory types. Almost all theories of memory propose that memory storage depends on synapses, the tiny connections between brain cells (FIGURE 1.24). When two cells are active at the same time, the connection between them strengthens; when they are not active at the same time, the connection weakens. From such synaptic changes emerges an association (Bliss & Collingridge, 1993). Experience can, for example, fortify the connections among the smell of coffee, its taste, its color, and the feel of its warmth. Since the populations of neurons connected with each of these sensations are typically activated at the same time, the connections between them can cause all the sensory associations of coffee to be triggered by the smell alone (Whitlock, Heynen, Shuler, & Bear, 2006).

But looking only at associations—and strengthened connections between neurons—may not be enough to explain memory. The great secret of memory is that it mostly encodes the relationships between things more than the details of the things themselves. When you memorize a melody, you encode the relationships between the notes, not the notes per se, which is why you can easily sing the song in a different key.

Memory retrieval is even more mysterious than memory storage. When I ask whether you know Alex Ritchie, the answer is immediately obvious to you without your needing to consider every person you have ever met or heard about. There is no good theory to explain how memory retrieval can happen so quickly. Moreover, the act of retrieval can destabilize the memory. When you recall a past event, the memory becomes temporarily susceptible to erasure. Some intriguing recent experiments show it is possible to chemically block memories from reforming during that window, suggesting new ethical questions that require careful consideration (Sara, 2000). We'll look at these issues in Chapter 9.

Why Do Brains Sleep and Dream? (Chapter 10)

One of the most astonishing aspects of our lives is that we spend a third of our time in the strange world of sleep. Newborn babies spend about twice that. It is inordinately difficult to remain awake for more than a full day–night cycle. In humans, continuous wakefulness of the nervous system results in mental derangement; rats deprived of sleep die after approximately two to three weeks (Rechtschaffen & Bergmann, 1995). All mammals sleep, reptiles and birds sleep, and voluntary breathers like dolphins sleep with one brain hemisphere dormant at a time (Goley, 1999). The evolutionary trend is clear, but the function of sleep is not.

The universality of sleep, although it comes at the cost of time and leaves the sleeper relatively defenseless, suggests a deep importance. There is no universally agreed-on answer, but there are at least three popular (and nonexclusive) theories. The first is that sleep is restorative, saving and replenishing the body's energy stores (Adam, 1980). However, the high neural activity during sleep suggests that there is more to the story. A second theory proposes that sleep allows the brain to run simulations of fighting, problem solving, and other key actions before testing them out in the real world (Barrett, 1993).

A third theory—the one that enjoys the most evidence—is that sleep plays a critical role in learning and consolidating memories and in forgetting inconsequential details(Walker & Stickgold, 2004). In other words, sleep allows the brain to store away the important stuff and take out the neural trash. The emerging hypothesis is that information replayed during sleep might determine which events we remember later (Walker & Stickgold, 2004). Sleep, in this view, is akin to an offline practice session, helping to reinforce the learning process.

How Does the Human Brain Acquire Its Unique Ability for Language? (Chapter 11)

In the animal kingdom, human language is unique in its possible methods for expressing intention, signifying identity, and broadcasting social signals. Our small planet contains more than 6,000 human languages, each of which gives speakers the ability to combine symbols in arbitrary,

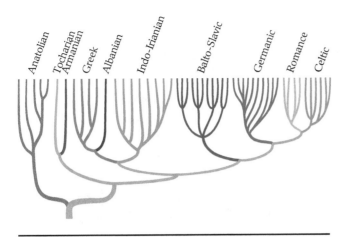

FIGURE 1.25 **An evolutionary "tree of life" for 87 Indo-European languages.**

essentially infinite complexity (FIGURE 1.25). Language—our capacity to translate our inner thoughts into packets of communication—is such a fundamental part of our existence that we typically only appreciate the massive underlying language systems when they stop functioning correctly (Mira & Paredes, 2005).

Centuries of brain damage studies—supplemented more recently by neuroimaging studies—have revealed that a network of brain areas is required to produce the various aspects of language. The complexity of the networks should come as no surprise when we consider all the aspects that comprise language. Take, for example, speech production, comprehension, repetition, semantics, syntax, feedback, and the ability to learn multiple languages that reference the same things.

Given the multifaceted, widespread brain networks, particular regions of brain damage lead to particular deficits: some with the expression of language, some with comprehension, some with recall, and so on. Models exist to explain how these brain areas interact (as we will see in Chapter 11), but these can offer only a general outline and not the particulars of any individual patient's response to brain damage. The detailed story of the emergence of language from the brain remains to be solved.

And there is a related mystery. The two hemispheres of the brain are heavily interconnected, and they appear at first to be mirror images of one another. But surgeries that separate the two hemispheres have revealed that the two sides have important differences (Levy & Trevarthen, 1976, 1977). For example, the left hemisphere is usually dominant for language, whereas the right is dominant for music and spatial abilities. Such division of function between the hemispheres is called **lateralization.** Why the brain is made up of two similar but nonidentical halves is still not clear. Nonetheless, it gives an understanding of why brain damage to identical areas—on the right or left sides—can cause such different results.

How Do We Make Decisions? (Chapter 12)

We human beings are, in the words of one author, "predictably irrational" in our decision making (Ariely, 2009). Offer us a choice between $20 in a week or $30 a week after that and we tend to choose the latter. Yet, offer us a choice between $20 *right now* and $30 in a week and we often choose the former. We pay over the odds for the chance to win large sums of money in the lottery and also pay over the odds to insure ourselves against the chance of *losing* large sums of money to fire, flood, accident, or theft. We spend vast sums to protect ourselves against the remote risks of a terrorist attack, yet feel blasé about the much greater risks of excessive drinking, smoking, driving without a seatbelt, or texting while driving.

What drives the irrational decision making of our species? To answer this question, we must understand the basic mechanisms of decision making in the human brain. Although it is still a new field, the neuroscience of human decision making has already shed some light on what these mechanisms might be, as well as why they sometimes lead us to make irrational choices. In Chapter 12, we will look at some of the more common flavors of irrational decision making in human beings and the neural mechanisms that drive them.

What Are Emotions? (Chapter 13)

We often talk about brains as information-processing systems, but any account of the brain that lacks an account of emotions, motivations, fears, and hopes is incomplete. Emotions involve physical responses to salient stimuli: the increased heartbeat and perspiration that accompany fear, the freezing response of a rat in the presence of a cat, or the extra muscle tension that accompanies anger. They also involve the subjective experiences that sometimes accompany these processes: the sensations of happiness, envy, sadness, and so on. Emotions seem to employ largely unconscious machinery—for example, brain areas involved in emotion will respond to angry faces that are briefly presented and then rapidly masked, even when the appearance is so short that subjects are unaware of having seen any face at all (Winkielman & Berridge, 2004). Across cultures, the expression of basic emotions is remarkably similar (FIGURE 1.26), and as Darwin observed, there are also common elements in the expression of emotions across all mammals. There are even strong similarities in physiological responses among humans, reptiles, and birds when showing fear, anger, or parental love (Ekman & Friesen, 1971; Gosling & John, 1999).

Modern views propose that emotions are brain states that quickly assign value to outcomes and provide a simple plan of action (Stein & Trabasso, 1992). Thus, emotion can

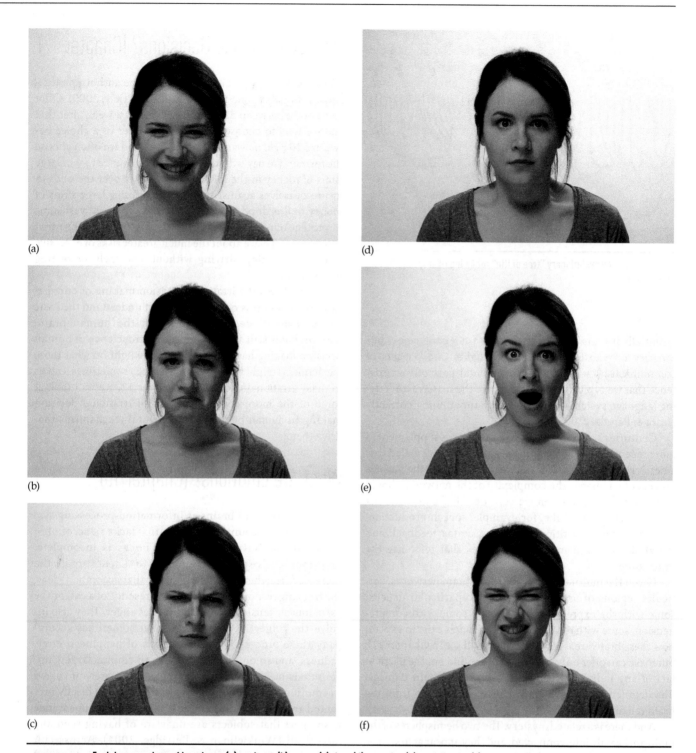

FIGURE 1.26 Facial expressions of happiness (a), sadness (b), anger (c), fear (d), surprise (e), and disgust (f) are recognized universally across human cultures.

be viewed as a type of computation, a rapid, automatic summary that initiates appropriate actions. When a bear is galloping toward you, the rising fear directs your brain to do the right things (determining an escape route) instead of all the other things it could be doing (rounding out your grocery list). Emotions also have a priority-setting function that

colors the landscape of our perceptions and motivations, determining what is most important at any given time and what can be safely relegated to the background. When it comes to perception, you can spot an object more quickly if it is, say, a spider rather than a roll of tape. In the realm of memory, emotional events are laid down differently by a parallel memory system involving a brain area called the amygdala. In the realm of motivation, our emotional state helps to decide, literally, between apples and oranges: a choice that depends on our internal state at the time and thus cannot be resolved by intellectual means alone. Human beings also have elaborate mechanisms for regulating their emotions based on context and current behavior: pathways by which we reassure ourselves of the harmlessness of a rubber snake or understand the threat value of an apparently innocuous piece of paper that on closer inspection turns out to be a court summons.

As recently as 20 years ago, the study of emotions was relegated to the fringes of cognitive neuroscience and often considered lacking in scientific rigor. With the development of new experimental methods, however, so-called "affective neuroscience" has become one of the most active areas of research in the field. One goal of affective neuroscience is to understand the many disorders of emotion, depression being the most common and costly. Impulsive aggression and violence are also thought to be consequences of faulty emotion regulation. In Chapter 13, we will look at what has been learned so far about the neural mechanisms of emotion and how these mechanisms can sometimes go awry in mental disorders, with catastrophic results.

How Do We Set Our Priorities? (Chapter 14)

One of the curious ironies of human existence is the divide between intelligence and priority setting—the so-called "common sense" that is neither common nor, strictly speaking, a sense. Every one of us knows people who are recognized for their cleverness and zip through intellectual puzzles with lightning speed, yet are hopeless at prioritizing activities in their lives. We wonder how someone so intelligent could become so bogged down in irrelevant detail, bury themselves in activities of minor importance while neglecting urgent issues, or procrastinate to the point of failure.

Nor, if we are honest, do we see these qualities only in other people. Every one of us has made a New Year's resolution only to break it later, found ourselves an excuse to put off our homework until the next day, or delayed working on an assignment even when we know it will soon be overdue. Our nearsighted view of life's rewards all too often leaves us with a skewed set of priorities.

Yet how is this possible? For what reason can we know, intellectually, the right thing to do and yet still fail to do it? Why does our alarm clock never fail to activate at the appointed hour, while the vastly greater processing power of our brain all too often finds an excuse to hit the snooze button? What can neuroscience tell us about the mechanisms of reward, motivation, and judgment? How do

reward mechanisms go awry in pathologies of motivation, like addiction? Finally, is there anything we can do to help make sure that we stick to the commitments we have made to ourselves? These are the questions we will consider in Chapter 14.

How Do I Know What You're Thinking? (Chapter 15)

In the children's game of Rock, Paper, Scissors, the trick is to guess your opponent's move ahead of time and choose the move that will beat it (FIGURE 1.27). The winner will reliably choose Paper just when the opponent chooses Rock, or Rock at just the right time to beat Scissors, or a surprise Scissors when your opponent confidently chooses Paper. Of course, your opponent is trying to do the same to you, so the battle of wits quickly escalates into an endless series of outguessing the outguesser: "he knows that I know that he knows I think he'll choose Scissors, so he actually will choose Scissors."

Being able to guess accurately at the thoughts and motivations of others is an immensely valuable faculty. It allows us not only to outfox our opponents, but also to work cooperatively with our friends. Anticipating the thoughts and feelings of others is an essential skill for understanding jokes, avoiding faux pas, making thoughtful gestures, choosing thoughtful gifts, and navigating the complex conventions of human social behavior.

The ability to build models of the thoughts and beliefs of others, sometimes called "theory of mind," is uniquely well developed in human beings. It almost certainly explains why we have been able to organize ourselves into the complex

FIGURE 1.27 **Competitors in the Rock, Paper, Scissors Championships must try to outguess one another's moves at levels consistently above chance.** Although we might expect the outcomes to be random, in fact certain individuals display consistently higher-than-average abilities to guess what their opponents are planning to do.

social structures of modern civilization—structures that, among other things, enable us to take time out from foraging for food and shelter so that we can puzzle away at the workings of our own brains! The neuroscience of social cognition has quickly become one of the most active fields in the modern study of the brain. In Chapter 15, we will look at what we have learned so far about the social faculties of the human brain, which play such a pivotal role in enabling complex forms of human behavior.

What Causes Disorders of the Mind and the Brain? (Chapter 16)

Neurological and psychiatric disorders are among the most prevalent and the most disabling of all illnesses, in the developing as well as in the industrialized world. Major depression, social anxiety, Alzheimer's dementia, stroke, traumatic brain injury, epilepsy, schizophrenia, bipolar disorder, multiple sclerosis, and other brain diseases are not only exceedingly common, but also carry a collective burden of disease and disability that eclipses virtually all other forms of human illness—including perennial killers like malaria, malnutrition, HIV, heart disease, cancer, and death by accident or violence. According to estimates by the World Health Organization, neuropsychiatric diseases will account for fully 14.7 percent of the global burden of disease by 2020 (Murray & Lopez, 1997).

The past century and a half, and in particular the past 50 years, have seen tremendous advances in understanding the neural basis of brain disorders. Traditionally, medicine has divided these disorders into the neurological—diseases of the nervous system—and the psychiatric—diseases of the mind. As we have learned more about these illnesses, the distinction between the two has gradually become blurred. Whether we are looking at the memory lapses and progressive loss of faculties in Alzheimer's dementia or the stubborn persistence of joylessness and despair in major depression, we now have at least some idea of what brain circuitry is involved and how this circuitry might have gone awry.

The hope, of course, is that this new knowledge will lead to new treatments for some of the world's most devastating illnesses (FIGURE 1.28). Although much of this hope has yet to be realized, we do have at least a few hints as to what the next generation of treatments will look like for disorders of the brain. In Chapter 16, we will look at a sampler of illnesses across the spectrum from those traditionally considered "brain diseases" to those traditionally considered "mind diseases." We will look at what seems to have gone awry in each case, as well as what treatments might someday be developed to reverse the underlying causes of illness.

The Payoffs of Cognitive Neuroscience

Neuroscience in general, and cognitive neuroscience in particular, has become one of the most active areas in all of 21st-century science. Worldwide, there are now dozens of health organizations, hundreds of academic institutions, and thousands of private enterprises spending billions of dollars annually to further our understanding of the brain. The scale of these investments gives us at least a rough idea of the size of the anticipated payoffs that are expected to arise from research in cognitive neuroscience over the coming century. In this section, we'll look more closely at what kinds of payoffs we might hope to see from advances in neuroscience over our own lifetimes.

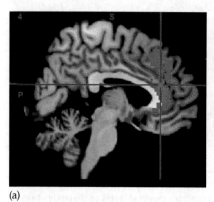 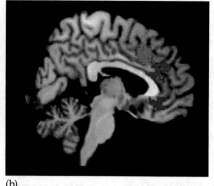 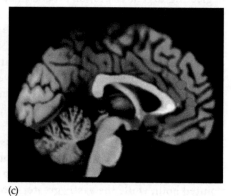

(a)   (b)   (c)

FIGURE 1.28 **Neuroimaging studies are revealing the neural underpinnings of a variety of psychiatric conditions.** Shown here are regions of the brain that undergo a subtle shrinkage of volume in (a) depression, (b) bipolar disorder and schizophrenia, and (c) posttraumatic stress disorder.

Healing the Disordered Brain

Compared to even a century ago, modern medicine has made tremendous strides in its ability to heal common forms of illness. Effective antibiotics and antiviral agents have driven many once-fearsome infectious diseases into the background. Advances in emergency and intensive care have vastly increased the rate of survival from accidents and injuries—even on the battlefield. Safe and effective anesthesia has enabled many once-risky forms of surgery to become routine. In the developed world, death in childbirth has receded from a commonplace tragedy to a rare anomaly.

Yet for many brain diseases, effective treatments remain elusive. For elderly patients with Alzheimer's dementia, a few medications can delay the progression of symptoms, but none can alter the course of the disease. For many other forms of dementia, there are still no effective treatments at all. Patients who suffer strokes can sometimes, with great effort, shift their lost faculties to surviving brain regions. However, the damaged regions themselves are, for the moment, beyond physical repair. The same is true for spinal cord injuries, which leave their victims' bodies partially or totally paralyzed. Schizophrenia is a lifelong condition that appears in early adulthood and leaves patients with hallucinations, delusions, and bizarre patterns of behavior severe enough to preclude normal life in the majority of cases. Although there are medications that can relieve some symptoms, for the moment there is no cure for the illness itself. Depression is one of the most common forms of psychiatric illness, affecting as many as 1 in 10 people in the developed world at any given time (Gonzalez et al., 2010). Although medications and therapy are helpful in many cases, up to one-third of patients do not respond to these kinds of treatment (P. S. Wang et al., 2005). Unfortunately, despite extensive research, no new classes of antidepressant medication have been brought to market in decades. Even our existing antidepressant medications are scarcely more effective than the ones available in the 1950s—although the side effects have improved considerably.

Given this current situation, one of the major payoffs expected from neuroscience research is in the development of new, effective treatments for disorders of the brain. For example, studies of learning and memory have shed light on the cellular and molecular mechanisms that go awry in Alzheimer's disease and other forms of dementia. In the years to come, it may be possible to block or reverse these mechanisms to avert the progression of illness.

The ability to regrow damaged neurons would open up a whole new avenue of treatment for patients with stroke, spinal cord injury, traumatic brain injuries, or degenerative diseases of the nervous system. Rather than simply masking symptoms, neuron-regrowing treatments could replace damaged circuitry and restore lost functions. As it turns out, the brains of many species are capable of regrowing damaged areas, particularly if the damage occurs early in life. Even in human beings, new neurons are constantly produced in the brain throughout adulthood, albeit not in numbers large enough to completely heal large regions of injury (Eriksson et al., 1998; Pérez-Cañellas & García-Verdugo, 1996). If the brain's self-repair mechanisms could be stimulated in adults, whole categories of currently incurable neurological illness might become temporary inconveniences.

Brain stimulation also offers a potentially powerful new avenue for treating neurological and psychiatric disorders. Deep brain stimulators have now been used for several decades to treat movement disorders such as Parkinson's disease (FIGURE 1.29). More recently, these same devices have been used successfully to treat a wider variety of conditions ranging from depression and obsessive–compulsive disorder to the memory dysfunction of Alzheimer's disease (Greenberg et al., 2006; Laxton et al., 2010; Mayberg et al., 2005). Less invasive forms of brain stimulation such as rTMS and tDCS (which we saw earlier in the chapter) are also emerging as treatments for a variety of neurological and psychiatric conditions. To use these treatments effectively, we must be able to target the right area of the brain for each condition. As we'll see throughout this book, ongoing research into the mechanisms of depression and other brain disorders has been helpful in identifying

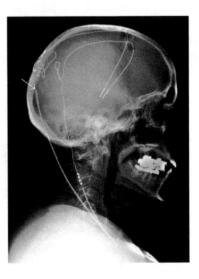

FIGURE 1.29 **Deep brain stimulation.** A skull X-ray of a patient who has undergone surgical implantation of a pacemaker-like device known as a deep brain stimulator. These devices are used to treat an increasingly wide variety of neurological and psychiatric conditions including Parkinson's disease, obsessive–compulsive disorder, and major depression.

effective targets for brain stimulation. The enterprise of mapping out abnormally active circuits in brain disorders and then targeting them for stimulation will likely be one of the more powerful applications of neuroscience in the near future.

Enhancing Human Abilities

Aside from restoring lost functions in disease, cognitive neuroscience research also offers the possibility of enhancing the existing abilities of the healthy human brain. In its simplest and most innocuous form, this may simply involve developing a better science of how to overcome (or at least work with) the predictable irrationalities of human decision making. As we learn more about what induces the brain to cheat on a diet and what induces the brain to stick to a diet, we may be able to find ways of promoting the latter and discouraging the former. Encouraging "the better angels of our nature" could involve a number of different approaches. Brain stimulation techniques such as rTMS or tDCS could be used to strengthen pathways that promote long-term over short-term thinking or to improve our ability to inhibit our counterproductive impulses. New classes of medication might be found to accomplish the same goal pharmacologically rather than electrically. These sorts of tools might make it easier for us to stick by our own commitments: a neural aid to the New Year's resolution.

Another form of enhancement that is currently making the transition from science fiction to science fact is the development of human brain interface devices. Already, we have a long history of enhancing our perceptual and cognitive abilities with simple aids such as eyeglasses or contact lenses for vision, public-address systems or hearing aids for hearing, thesauruses and dictionaries for language, GPS systems for navigation, electronic organizers and reminders

for memory, instructional videos for skills like unplugging a drain or making a crème brûlée, and online reference works for the vast reams of factual knowledge too large to fit inside our heads. In the years to come, neuroscience research will likely lead us to more direct interfaces that allow for more seamless connections between our brain and external devices.

Some such devices are already entering common use (FIGURE 1.30). For decades, cochlear implants have provided hearing to individuals who would otherwise lack it. More recently, retinal implants have provided a modicum of vision to patients who would otherwise be blind. These chips, implanted directly into the central part of the retina, bypass the light-sensing cells of the eye to stimulate the underlying neural pathways directly (Dowling, 2008). Although they are designed to take input from a small, eyeglasses-mounted external camera, they could be easily configured to take input from other sources: a telescope, an X-ray emitter, a night-vision camera, a mass spectrometer, a navigation system, or a Web browser. Such devices might enable whole new classes of human capability: navigating a surgical probe through hard-to-reach areas of the body under visual guidance, sensing the chemical environment of the air by sight, or overlaying "augmented reality" tags on top of the visual scene.

Memory, like any other sense, may also be amenable to interfaces. Already, studies are underway to enhance memory function in Alzheimer's disease through stimulation of the relevant neural pathways. Microelectrode recordings are revealing how memories are encoded and retrieved as patterns of neural activity in brain structures like the hippocampus (Bliss & Collingridge, 1993). These patterns could conceivably be used to index and retrieve externally stored sources of information, such as electronic databases. Interfaces for output devices are also under development. In the motor areas of the brain, implanted electrode arrays are used to allow paralyzed patients to control mouse pointers or

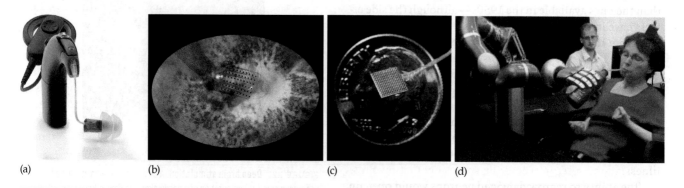

(a) (b) (c) (d)

FIGURE 1.30 **Brain interface devices.** Some such devices already in use include (a) cochlear implants to provide auditory input and (b) retinal implants to provide visual input. Output devices are also entering use. (c) A miniaturized sensor array of 96 microelectrodes, less than a centimeter across, can be implanted in areas of the brain that control movements of the arm and hand. (d) A woman with complete paralysis below the neck uses this implanted device to guide a drink to her lips, using a robot arm controlled by her thoughts, via the implant.

other input devices (Suner, Fellows, Vargas-Irwin, Nakata, & Donoghue, 2005). In animals, interfaces with mechanical effectors (such as robot arms) have been under study for more than a decade, and human applications are emerging (Iáñez, Azorín, Úbeda, Ferrández, & Fernández, 2010).

Making full use of these extended capabilities will require systems that are well designed to tap into the brain's existing functional architecture. For example, why reinvent a memory retrieval system when the brain already has circuitry neatly optimized for this role? Instead, the brain's existing circuitry could be used to index a much larger database of experiences and knowledge. Likewise, the brain's highly efficient action-guidance systems could be used to navigate through databases of information, control external devices with speed and precision, or solve complicated visual–spatial problems like working out the three-dimensional structure of a biological protein—a task that currently requires enormous computational resources. To bring these possibilities to life, we will need to have a detailed understanding of the computational architecture of the brain at the microscopic scale of neural networks and interconnections.

Blueprints for Artificial Cognition

Another payoff from cognitive neuroscience will come from borrowing the brain's best tricks to improve the abilities of our computing devices. There are a large number of problems that are exceedingly difficult for the human-designed architecture of computer hardware and software, but are readily solved by human brains. Recognizing and interpreting speech, balancing a moving body on two legs, recognizing thousands of different classes of objects from a visual scene, distinguishing familiar from unfamiliar faces when viewed from almost any angle, finding efficient routes through a series of destinations, retrieving relevant memories from a large database: for each of these problems, evolutionary processes have endowed the brain with algorithms far more efficient than the best we have managed to engineer in computers.

Borrowing from the brain's architecture has already proved useful in some forms of computation, in which mathematical tools that resemble neural networks can be "trained" to distinguish among different kinds of inputs: for example, to turn written text into digitally encoded words, to predict the words we intend to type into an electronic device, or to spot faces in a photograph so we can remove the "red eyes" induced by a camera flash. The trained networks can be used to categorize new inputs that were not part of the original training set in a non-rule-based way that involves picking out the most relevant "features" within the incoming data, much as in a real neural network (Dony & Haykin, 1995; Golden, 1996; J. Y. Wang & Zhang, 2001).

In a strange, full-circle application of this technique, "neural network" approaches have even been used to classify the complex patterns of brain activity seen in functional MRI scans. In effect, this amounts to us borrowing from the functional architecture of the brain to build tools that help us better understand the functional architecture of the brain. These kinds of techniques are already powerful: in one study, researchers were able to build rough reconstructions of the visual scenes that subjects were viewing simply by analyzing their patterns of fMRI brain activity using an appropriately trained neural network (Naselaris, Kay, Nishimoto, & Gallant, 2011; more on this in Chapter 5).

Despite these advances, there remain many kinds of human cognition whose artificial counterparts are rudimentary at best: understanding the semantic content of human communication, responding to questions posed in natural language, understanding others' thoughts and intentions, self-awareness and self-reflection, creative problem solving, and the generation of emotional states. It is in such areas that an improved understanding of the underlying neural mechanisms within the human brain might lead to the development of artificial mechanisms that perform analogous functions in the realm of machine intelligence.

Brain-Compatible Social Policies

Cognitive neuroscience enjoys increasing payoff in the domain of social policy. Let's consider three examples.

Eyewitness Testimony

At least since 1967, the U.S. Supreme Court has recognized that eyewitness identification evidence is the kind of testimony that "juries seem most receptive to, and not inclined to discredit." And yet they have also recognized that it is "notoriously unreliable" (Young, 1981). In other words, eyewitness testimony is almost certainly the worst "technology" allowed in courtrooms today and yet the one with the most sway on jurors (FIGURE 1.31).

As we will see in Chapter 9, memory is not like a video recorder; instead, it is a reconstruction. More than 30 years of cognitive neuroscience studies have revealed issues that contaminate accurate memory recall, including issues such as weapon focus (concentrating on a weapon at the expense of encoding details about a perpetrator), cue overload (too many things going on too quickly), the other-race effect (it is more difficult to distinguish faces of races other than faces of one's own race), and the detrimental memory effects of general stress and trauma during the event (Chance & Goldstein, 1996; Eakin, Schreiber, & Sergent-Marshall, 2003; Kramer, Buckhout, & Eugenio, 1990). A more general problem is called the misinformation effect: misleading information presented between the encoding of an event and its subsequent recall influences a witness's memory. So if you've seen an event and then are told about it (say, by another witness), the subsequent description will irrevocably alter your own memory.

FIGURE 1.31 **Human brains tend to make rapid judgments about a person's trustworthiness, friendliness, competence, and other personal characteristics based purely on their facial features.** These baseless first impressions are surprisingly influential and difficult to overcome and can affect jury deliberations and election results alike. For example, if you had to trust one of these people to look after your home for the weekend, do you have any "gut feelings" about whom you would choose or whom you would avoid?

As cognitive neuroscience has unmasked these sorts of problems, it has been able to construct real-world solutions. Consider police lineups. Many memory problems plague the accuracy of the eyewitness identification of a person in a lineup, including police suggestibility (in which an investigator influences an eyewitness), co-witness contamination (in which multiple witnesses accidentally influence each other's versions of the details), and contamination of memory by photos subsequently seen in the media (Wells et al., 1998). The illumination of such problems has led to better guidelines for police who conduct lineups—these include using investigators who are blind to the suspects in the case, separating witnesses as soon as possible, and not publishing photos of suspects in the news (Wells et al., 2000).

Attack Demand, Not Supply

Nearly 7 of 10 jail inmates met the criteria for substance abuse or dependence in the year before their admission.

The War on Drugs is utterly unwinnable. Why? Because we are attacking the drug *supply*. When drug enforcement agents attack drug supply in one location, it pops up elsewhere. The right way to deal with drug problems is to address the *demand* for drugs—in other words, the brain mechanisms that drive addiction and make it so hard to overcome (Eagleman, Correro, & Singh, 2010). As we will see in various chapters, a good deal is understood about the circuitry and pharmacology of drug addiction. Addiction may be reasonably viewed as a neurological problem that allows for medical remedies, just as pneumonia may be viewed as an affliction of the lungs. As we progress in our understanding of the underlying circuitry of addiction—how that circuitry leads to drives and how drugs hijack and regulate that circuitry—we have the opportunity to leverage that understanding into more effective drug policy that rests on treatment rather than punishment.

With that understanding in place, promising new technologies relating to emerging knowledge and technologies may provide a bridge between the failed policies of the past and novel solutions in the future. Drug addiction is rooted in the biology of the brain, and society's best hope for breaking addiction lies in new approaches to rehabilitation, not simply in repeated incarceration.

Implications for Criminal Punishment and Rehabilitation

When a convicted criminal stands in front of the judge's bench today, the legal system wants to know whether he is fully *blameworthy* or whether he had mitigating biological problems. In other words, was it his fault or his biology's fault?

But this is the wrong question to be asking. The choices we make are inseparably yoked to our neural circuitry, and therefore there is no meaningful way to tease the two options apart. The more society learns about neuroscience, the more the seemingly simple concept of blameworthiness becomes nuanced, and the more our legal system has to come up to speed with the realities of the brain.

None of this means that lawbreakers will be let off the hook. Instead, neuroscience can contribute to building an evidence-based legal system that will continue to take criminals off the streets, but will customize sentencing, leverage new opportunities for rehabilitation, and better understand how to structure incentives. Discoveries in neuroscience suggest a new way forward for law and order—one that will lead to a more cost-effective, humane, and flexible system than the one we have today (Eagleman, 2011).

As an example, an estimated quarter of the population in American prisons is mentally ill, which means that our prison system has become our *de facto* mental health–care system (Birmingham, Mason, & Grubin, 1996). As we will see in Chapter 16, there are more fruitful ways than incarceration to help those with mental problems.

In all the above examples, decades of cognitive neuroscience research in the lab have the direct chance to inspire real social change.

Conclusion

We experience the world so effortlessly that it is easy to overlook the fact that we are not even remotely aware of the autonomous neural mechanisms that underlie our perceptual capacities and behavior. The world of unthinking biological mechanisms, operating with no apparent intentions or goals, seems at first glance to be insufficient to account for complex behaviors and perceptual capacities. Nevertheless, all empirical evidence available today suggests that the mind is what the brain generates. The human brain has remarkable capabilities that are unmatched by anything else we know of, from subatomic particles to supernovae.

The mechanisms that allow our little three-pound fragments of the Big Bang to think, sense, feel, and act are being explored in greater detail and at a faster pace today than at any other time in human history. Thanks to an ever-expanding kit of neat technical tricks and a trusty toolbox of scientific methods, our brains are making remarkable progress in understanding their own workings. Many big questions remain, and we will be exploring some of them in great detail throughout the rest of this book. If unraveled, these knotty problems may yield solutions with big payoffs, from healthier brains to healthier societies. So, without further ado, let's gather up our enthusiasm, our curiosity, and our critical-thinking skills and dive into one of the last, greatest frontiers of human understanding: the inner workings of the human brain.

KEY PRINCIPLES

- The human brain is one of the most complex and remarkable objects in the known universe.

- Cognitive neuroscience seeks to understand how the brain gives rise to perception, emotion, awareness, memory, planning, decision making, and the many other varieties of human thought.

- We cannot understand how the brain as a whole functions simply by understanding its component parts.

- Studies of the brain's structural connections, brain–behavior correlations, the effects of lesions,

and the effects of brain stimulation all help to unravel the mechanisms behind these cognitive functions.

- The brain is not intrinsically designed to understand its own workings and is subject to built-in cognitive biases that interfere with logical deduction.

- A toolbox of techniques known as the scientific method can help us correct for the built-in cognitive biases that might otherwise frustrate our efforts to understand the workings of our own brains.

- We have learned a great deal about how the brain works using these methods, yet many big questions remain to be answered, including how information is coded in neural activity, how the brain stitches together a picture of the world from different senses, what consciousness is, how memories are stored and retrieved, and how we make decisions.

- Advances in neuroscience may lead to new treatments for brain disorders, enhanced human abilities, blueprints for artificial cognition, and better-informed social policies.

KEY TERMS

Who Are We?
cognitive neuroscience (p. 5)
emergent properties (p. 5)

In Pursuit of Principles
adaptations (p. 8)

How We Know What We Know
genes (p. 9)
tracer (p. 10)
tracts (p. 10)
diffusion tensor imaging (p. 10)
microelectrodes (p. 11)
microdialysis (p. 11)
voltammetry (p. 11)
electroencephalography (p. 11)
magnetoencephalography (p. 11)
positron emission tomography (p. 11)
glucose (p. 11)
magnetic resonance imaging (MRI) (p. 11)

functional magnetic resonance imaging (fMRI) (p. 11)
voxel-based morphometry (p. 11)
lesions (p. 13)
traumatic brain injuries (p. 13)
stroke (p. 13)
tumor (p. 13)
transcranial magnetic stimulation (TMS) (p. 14)
repetitive transcranial magnetic stimulation (rTMS) (p. 15)
transcranial direct current stimulation (tDCS) (p. 15)
cathode (p. 15)
anode (p. 15)

Thinking Critically about the Brain
homeostasis (p. 16)
agonistic behavior (p. 16)
reproduction (p. 16)

anchoring bias (p. 17)
confirmation bias (p. 17)
availability heuristic (p. 17)
affect heuristic (p. 17)
illusory correlation (p. 17)
belief bias (p. 17)
scientific method (p. 18)
hypothesis (p. 18)
replication (p. 18)

The Big Questions in Cognitive Neuroscience
plasticity (p. 20)
binding problem (p. 22)
short-term memory (p. 23)
long-term memory (p. 23)
declarative memories (p. 23)
nondeclarative memories (p. 23)
lateralization (p. 25)

REVIEW QUESTIONS

1. How would you explain the term "cognitive neuroscience" to another person?

2. What categories of research methods are used to study human brain function? What are some examples, advantages, and disadvantages of each?

3. What are three key functions that the brain has evolved to perform as a biological organ?

4. Describe three common forms of cognitive bias in human thinking. Can you think of an example of each type in everyday life?

5. What are the key elements of the scientific method? How might each of these elements help to overcome some of the brain's built-in biases?

CRITICAL-THINKING QUESTIONS

1. What are some of the outstanding questions in cognitive neuroscience? Can you think of two important questions about the brain *other* than the ones that appear in this chapter?

2. In what ways could advances in neuroscience provide benefits for human society? Can you think of two potential dangers posed by advances in neuroscience? How might we address these dangers in a constructive way?

- Describe the basic underlying organization of all vertebrate central nervous systems.

- Summarize the basic organization and structure of the peripheral nervous system.

- Explain the circuitry and function of spinal reflexes and central pattern generators.

- Distinguish the major components of the brainstem and their functions.

- Characterize the anatomy of the cerebellum and its role in motor function.

- Illustrate the role of the hypothalamus in homeostasis and the role of the thalamus as a relay and synchronization center, using examples.

- Identify the locations of the four lobes of the cerebral cortex, the locations of the major gyri and sulci, and their functions.

- Characterize the components of the basal ganglia and their functions.

- Distinguish the major components of the limbic system and their functions.

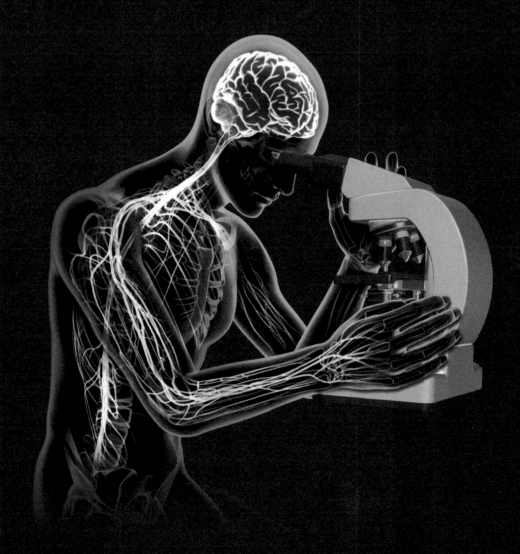

The **Brain** and Nervous System

STARTING OUT:
The Brains of Creatures Great and Small

The smallest mammal on Earth is barely larger than a bumblebee. The hog-nosed bat, which lives in remote areas of Myanmar and Thailand, weighs a mere 2 grams and has a brain that is only a quarter of an inch in length. Yet, this tiny brain can accomplish a remarkable range of feats. It enables the bat to hover and fly, steering flawlessly through three-dimensional space, avoiding obstacles along the way. It equips the bat to pluck insects out of the air and continue onward without breaking its flight. Moreover, it allows the bat to find its prey in total darkness by echolocation: high-frequency sound pulses whose auditory reflections reveal an object's direction, distance, and movement. At the same time, the bat's tiny brain can still process information from our more familiar senses: vision, touch, smell, taste, balance, and position sense. In addition to all of this, the bat's nervous system is highly involved in performing essential tasks of survival, including respiration, hormone regulation, temperature regulation, shelter seeking, mate finding, and rearing of offspring. All in all, this is an impressive set of skills for a nervous system smaller than a raisin.

Another echolocator is one of the largest mammals on Earth: the adult male sperm whale. This 50-ton predator can be found more than a mile below the surface of the ocean, diving for up to 45 minutes at a time, cruising the depths of the ocean in search of the half-ton of fish and squid it must consume every day to survive. Its brain weighs nearly 20 pounds and is the

(a)

(b)

(c)

(d)

FIGURE 2.1 **Common structure.** There is a common structure to the brains of all vertebrate and invertebrate animals, from mammals like the hog-nosed bat (a) or the sperm whale (b), to ancient, jawless fishes like the hagfish (c), to insects like the bumblebee (d).

size of a large Thanksgiving turkey. It continues to function at depths where the water pressure exceeds 3,000 pounds per square inch.

The adult male sperm whale and the hog-nose bat live in vastly different environments, having gone down separate evolutionary paths more than 80 million years ago. However, if we were to assume that their nervous systems are dramatically different from one another in structure and function, we would be wrong.

In fact, the brains of all mammals have a common underlying structure, whether they belong to bats, whales, or humans (FIGURE 2.1). The basic architecture of the nervous system emerged so long ago that we can find much of it even in such distant relatives as the hagfish: a strange, jawless, spineless, deep-water scavenger capable of tying its own body into a knot. Its last common ancestor with the sperm whale lived roughly half a billion years ago, yet its brain has a similar underlying structure. Even the brains of insects have underlying similarities to our own, especially in the genes that guide their development. When the genetic signal that tells a mouse where its eye needs to develop is placed into a fruit fly embryo, the fruit fly will develop an eye in that location (a fruit fly eye, not a mouse eye!).

The underlying similarities of all nervous systems should remind us that the human brain is an old, old heirloom. Although much of this book will focus on the cognitive abilities of human beings, we must keep in mind that these abilities arise from a nervous system whose fundamental organization is ancient and has been highly conserved over time. In this chapter, we will take a first look at the structure and function of the human nervous system from one end to the other. Along the way, we'll point out both the common features and the differences that have emerged between our relatives and us over the past 500 million years.

An Overview of the Nervous System

Why Put Your Neurons in a Brain at All?

The first striking characteristic of the human nervous system is that it is remarkably top heavy. The human nervous system consists of a large accumulation of cells at the top (the brain); a long, thin extension along the body axis (the **spinal cord**); and then still thinner extensions branching out into almost every part of the body. Why is the human nervous system arranged in this way? Doesn't having so many neurons in a central location leave us vulnerable to injury? Wouldn't it be safer to distribute the neurons evenly throughout the body, in a wide network?

In fact, some lower-level organisms do have a more even distribution of neurons throughout the body. For example, jellyfish and sea anemones have no centralized brain, but instead use a distributed nerve net to coordinate the slow, rhythmical contractions they use for movement and feeding. Nerve nets are the usual kind of nervous system for organisms with radial symmetry—that is, organisms with a top and bottom but no front, back, left, or right (FIGURE 2.2a). Although they do possess neurons, creatures like the jellyfish and sea anemones are literally spineless and brainless.

Unlike jellyfish, most animals have bilateral symmetry: the left side and the right side are almost mirror images of each other (FIGURE 2.2b). Bilateral animals have bodies built from a line of segments running from head to tail. You yourself are a segmented, bilateral organism. Your segments may not be as obvious as those of a centipede, but your ribs and the vertebrae of your spine are reminders of the underlying

(a)

(b)

FIGURE 2.2 **Radial versus bilateral symmetry.** (a) Organisms with radial symmetry, like sea anemones, may have distributed "nerve nets" but no centralized brain. (b) Organisms with bilateral symmetry, like dolphins, have a central nervous system running down their body segment. This central nervous system is enlarged at the head end into a brain.

segmental organization of your body. The segmentation of your nervous system is an important feature, as will become more apparent later in this chapter.

For early bilateral animals, having a body of bilaterally symmetrical segments had a significant advantage: the animal could move its streamlined body swiftly through the water to search for prey or to avoid becoming prey. However, the control requirements for a segmented organism with a front and a back are quite different from those of a jellyfish. The nervous system of bilateral organisms has two key features.

The first feature is the presence of local, centralized networks within each body segment. In response to sensory input from the external world, simple circuits within each segment control the local muscles. In response to sensory input from the internal world of the body, similar circuits control the local internal organs. These circuits are capable of simple, localized functions like flexing a muscle when it is stretched.

The second feature is longitudinal transmission of information up and down the body axis between segments. Long connections up and down the length of the nervous system allow the activity of individual segments to be coordinated. For example, many organisms swim through the water by sending waves of alternating muscle contraction down the left and the right sides of the body. These waves of contraction cause the body to undulate back and forth, propelling the organism forward through the water. Longitudinal connections and local, segmental circuits allow the organism to move itself through its environment efficiently.

But how did an early bilaterally symmetrical animal steer itself? The animal's nervous system needed sensory inputs to tell it which way to go. Since the animal had a front end, it made sense to place the sensory equipment there (e.g., receptors for smell, taste, vibrations, light, and electrical currents). The front segments of the body then needed extra circuitry to deal with all of this extra input. Even more circuitry was needed to use this input to alter the ongoing activity of the circuits further back along the spinal cord, so that the animal could use this sensory input to guide what its body was doing. Additional circuitry was needed to drive the local musculature of the mouth for feeding or the head for exploration. All these functions, and more, required extra neurons, and as these neurons were added in the course of evolution, the front end of the spinal cord began to bulge and expand into a top-heavy structure: the beginnings of a brain.

The Common Features of Every Central Nervous System

Neuroscientists are still debating exactly how the evolution of a central nervous system took place or even how many times it took place. It is possible that both neurons and brains arose independently in several different lines of living creatures at different times (FIGURE 2.3). Specialized cells resembling neurons probably appeared more than 600 million years ago, and organized circuits and structures made of neurons probably arose in the

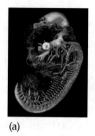
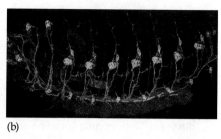

(a)   (b)

FIGURE 2.3 Nervous systems of vertebrates and invertebrates. The nervous systems of vertebrates, as in this mouse embryo (a), have a spinal cord with segments and an expansion of the most anterior segments into a brain. The nervous systems of invertebrates, like this fruit fly *Drosophila melanogaster* (b), are also arranged into segments, with more complexity in the anterior segments (left).

50–100 million years thereafter. We do know that almost all bilateral creatures, from the fruit fly to the mouse to the human, use a similar set of genes and signaling proteins (proteins that serve as chemical messengers between or within cells) to guide the development of the central nervous system. The signaling mechanisms are so similar that, in many cases, the gene of one organism (such as a mouse) can still perform its usual signaling function even when placed inside the nervous system of a distantly related organism (such as a fruit fly) (FIGURE 2.4). This provides evidence that the fundamental mechanisms for building a brain and spinal cord were already present before the ancestors of bilateral vertebrates (organisms with spines, like mice) and invertebrates (organisms without spines, like fruit flies) went down separate evolutionary paths, more than 550 million years ago.

It may seem strange to think of a mammal and an insect as having a common structure to their nervous systems. After all, the nervous system of a mammal runs along its back in a spinal cord, above the digestive tract, whereas the nervous system of an insect runs along its underside, below the digestive tract. However, genetic studies of brain development suggest that the vertebrate nervous system may actually be an upside-down relative of the invertebrate nervous system (Gerhart, 2000) (FIGURE 2.5). For some reason, it appears as if the ancestor of all vertebrates evolved to live with its body flipped upside-down and then

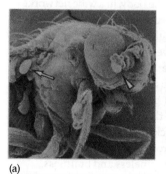
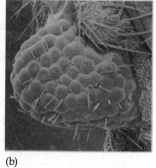

(a)   (b)

FIGURE 2.4 The gene of one organism may still perform its signaling function even when placed inside the nervous system of a distantly related organism. (a) A fruit fly eye can be seen growing near its wing (left arrow), induced by inserting the fly's Pax-6 gene into the local tissue. (b) An eye can also be induced to grow by the Pax-6 gene from a mouse, although fly and mouse diverged half a billion years ago.

compensated by twisting just its foremost segments around 180 degrees, so that its mouth could still face downward toward the ground. The result for its human descendants is a brain whose uppermost parts are crossed over: a left hemisphere that connects with the right side of the body and a right hemisphere that connects with the left side of the body. All vertebrate brains, from those of hagfish to humans, are crossed over in this manner.

Vertebrates also share many other common features. They all contain a **central nervous system** consisting of the brain and the spinal cord. The spinal cord has input and output connections to the rest of the body via the **peripheral nervous system**. The peripheral nervous system connects not only to the skin and muscles, but also to the internal organs of the body.

The developing vertebrate brain itself contains three main bulges or zones of expansion: the **forebrain** (prosencephalon), the **midbrain (mesencephalon)**, and the **hindbrain** (rhombencephalon). Even in the human brain, which grows quite complex at full development, these three fundamental bulges are clearly visible in a developing embryo at about 4 weeks. After this point, further subdivisions occur: the forebrain divides into the **telencephalon** and **diencephalon**, and the hindbrain divides into the **metencephalon** and **myelencephalon**. These structures, in turn, become further subdivided into the many structures of the adult brain, as shown in FIGURE 2.6 and as we will describe later in this chapter.

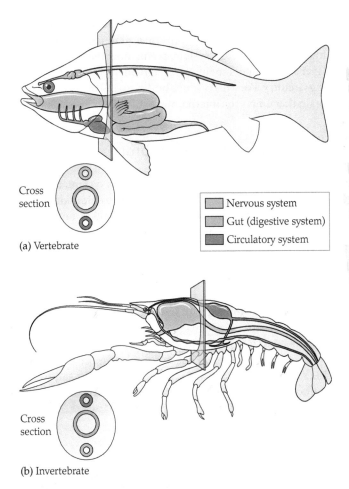

Cross section

(a) Vertebrate

| Nervous system |
| Gut (digestive system) |
| Circulatory system |

Cross section

(b) Invertebrate

FIGURE 2.5 (LEFT) **Vertebrate versus invertebrate nervous systems.** The positions of the nervous system, gut, and circulatory system of vertebrates (a) are upside-down compared to that of invertebrates (b), as is the pattern of expression of major genes guiding body development.

FIGURE 2.6 (BELOW) **Divisions within the developing vertebrate brain.** The forebrain, midbrain, and hindbrain subdivide into all the substructures of the adult brain.

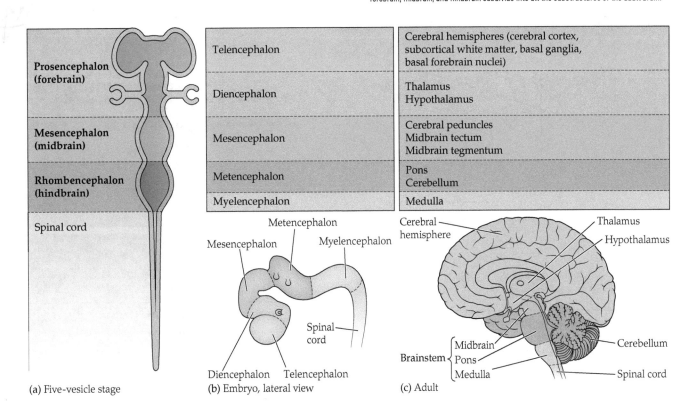

Prosencephalon (forebrain)	Telencephalon	Cerebral hemispheres (cerebral cortex, subcortical white matter, basal ganglia, basal forebrain nuclei)
	Diencephalon	Thalamus Hypothalamus
Mesencephalon (midbrain)	Mesencephalon	Cerebral peduncles Midbrain tectum Midbrain tegmentum
Rhombencephalon (hindbrain)	Metencephalon	Pons Cerebellum
	Myelencephalon	Medulla
Spinal cord		

(a) Five-vesicle stage

Mesencephalon — Metencephalon — Myelencephalon

Diencephalon   Telencephalon

Spinal cord

(b) Embryo, lateral view

Cerebral hemisphere — Thalamus — Hypothalamus

Brainstem { Midbrain / Pons / Medulla } — Cerebellum — Spinal cord

(c) Adult

Neuroanatomists have devised a detailed nomenclature to describe the vast number of structures in the human nervous system. It takes time and practice to become familiar with this nomenclature. However, a few basic principles will help you to understand the functions, rather than just the names, of brain areas.

First, remember that no neuron is an island. All neurons connect to other neurons through circuits, and almost all of these circuits are reciprocal: when neuron A sends output to neuron B, the odds are that neuron B also sends output back to neuron A. Second, remember that the role of a neuron in the nervous system as a whole depends largely on the neuron's inputs and outputs. Knowing who sends input to a neuron and who receives its output can tell you a lot about what that neuron's role is in the nervous system as a whole. Third, remember that when the brain refines one of its functions over evolutionary time scales, it often does so by inserting an additional layer of neurons between the existing inputs and outputs. These additional layers can help to modulate the existing circuit, steering its activity more finely, in context with the circumstances at hand.

As we survey the nervous system, you will see how this process of modulation occurs and how it adds ever-increasing levels of complexity to the resulting behavior in an organism. To keep things simple, we will start with the structure and functions of the simplest circuits, which lie in the peripheral nervous system and spinal cord. Then, gradually, we will move higher in the nervous system, seeing how the brain adds on layer after layer of modulation and refinement to the preexisting circuitry. We will conclude by discussing the system in the brain that unites the internal and external environments.

Getting Oriented in the Brain

When describing locations in the nervous system, neuroscientists use special terminology for anatomical directions (FIGURE 2.7). This terminology can be applied not only in humans, but also in any bilaterally symmetrical organism with a front, back, top, bottom, and sides. **Rostral** means toward the mouth, or the front end; the word comes from the Latin *rostrum*, or "beak." **Caudal** means toward the tail end; again, the word comes from the Latin *caudum*, or "tail." **Dorsal** means toward the top (or back), from the Latin *dorsum*, or "back." **Ventral** means toward the belly, or bottom end, from the Latin *venter*, or "belly."

Anterior and **posterior** also mean toward the front or the back, respectively; **superior** and **inferior** mean toward the top or the bottom, respectively. **Medial** means toward the middle; **lateral** means toward the side. **Ipsilateral** means

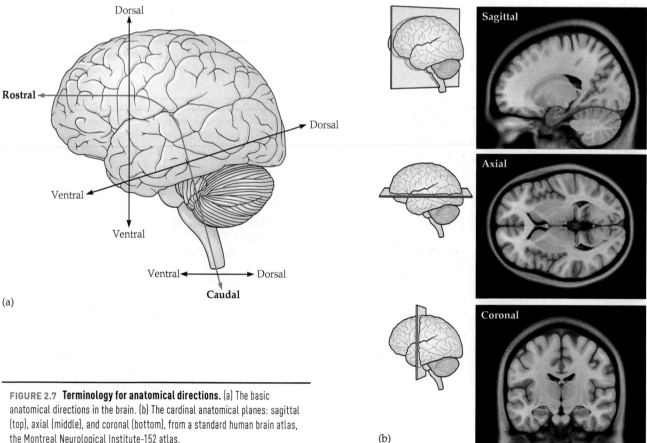

(a)

(b)

FIGURE 2.7 **Terminology for anatomical directions.** (a) The basic anatomical directions in the brain. (b) The cardinal anatomical planes: sagittal (top), axial (middle), and coronal (bottom), from a standard human brain atlas, the Montreal Neurological Institute-152 atlas.

"on the same side"; **contralateral** means "on the opposite side." On a body extension such as a limb, **distal** means toward the far ("distant") end of the limb, whereas **proximal** (from the Latin *proximus*, "nearest") means toward the point where the limb attaches to the body.

Using these terms with respect to the human body can sometimes get confusing because although we keep our body axis vertical, our head still faces forward. Hence, in a human being, rostral can mean "anterior" for structures in the head (since "toward the mouth" will be the same as "toward the front") but superior for structures in the rest of the body (since "toward the mouth" will be the same as "toward the top"). Likewise, dorsal can mean "above" for structures in the head but "behind" for structures in the rest of the body. If this is confusing, you may find it easier to imagine the human body on all fours when thinking about anatomical directions.

Neuroscientists often view the nervous system in planes, or slices: a microscope section, a computerized tomography scan, or an MRI series (see Chapter 1 for a more detailed description of computerized tomography and MRI). Hence, they have developed a set of labels to indicate how the slices are oriented in space. An *axial slice* divides the body along its long axis, into rostral and caudal. A *sagittal slice* divides the body into left and right. The name comes from the Latin *sagittus* or "arrow," as if an imaginary arrow down the spine would pass through this plane. A *midsagittal slice* is a slice through the exact midline of the body or nervous system. A *frontal* or *coronal slice* divides the body into dorsal and ventral. The name comes from the Latin for "crown," as if someone were to place an imaginary crown on the head along this plane.

Now that we have been oriented in the brain and have learned the terminology for anatomical directions, let's begin our exploration of the brain from its outermost extremities, in the peripheral nervous system.

The Peripheral Nervous System

As previously stated, the peripheral nervous system connects the spinal cord and the rest of the body. Let's examine some aspects of its structure and function.

Separate Systems for the Inner and Outer Environments

Sensory neurons have receptors in the skin, muscles, and joints, and through these they convey a multitude of different kinds of sensory input to the body: touch, vibration, pain, temperature, fatigue, itch, stretch, and position. Other sensory nerves extend into the visceral organs of the body: heart, lungs, stomach, intestines, pancreas, kidneys, bladder, uterus, and blood vessels. They are sensitive not only to mechanical stresses such as pain or injury, but also to inflammation, fatigue, and temperature. Depending on the organ to which they provide input, they may also be sensitive to pressure, hormonal or biochemical stimuli, or the local concentration of chemicals that are specific to each organ's function. Sensory neurons have different names depending on what stimulates them: mechanoreceptors for physical movement, nociceptors for injury, thermoreceptors for temperature, baroreceptors for pressure, chemoreceptors for specific chemicals, and so on.

Motor neurons extend to the muscles of the body, making contact at a specialized structure called the **neuromuscular junction.** Electrical activity in the motor neuron causes a release of signaling chemicals called **neurotransmitters** at the neuromuscular junction, and this in turn stimulates the muscle fiber to contract. (You will learn more about this process in Chapter 7 and more about neurotransmitters in Chapter 3.) Low levels of continuous (or "tonic") motor neuron activity exist even at rest, and this activity produces a mild tension known as muscle tone. Higher levels of activity cause a vigorous contraction, which causes a body movement.

The body has two major compartments: the soma, including muscles, skin, and bones, and the viscera, containing the internal organs (FIGURE 2.8a). Other output neurons send signals to the visceral organs of the body. These visceral output signals regulate the activities of the body's *internal* world: heart rate, respiration, blood pressure, temperature regulation, movements of the stomach and intestinal tract, secretion of digestive enzymes, voiding of the bladder and bowels, and sexual organ functions.

The division between the external and the internal world is reflected in the nervous system itself. The peripheral nervous system has two components: the **somatic nervous system** and the **autonomic nervous system.** The peripheral nervous system includes four kinds of neurons for input and output to these compartments: somatic afferent or somatosensory neurons (input), somatic efferent or motor neurons (output), visceral afferent or visceral sensory neurons (input), and visceral efferent or autonomic neurons (output) (FIGURE 2.8b).

The somatic nervous system includes the sensory inputs and motor outputs for guiding voluntary body movements in the external world. When you raise your arm, kick a ball, or withdraw your hand from a hot plate, you are using the somatic nervous system. In contrast, the autonomic nervous system regulates the body's internal world. This process usually goes on automatically (hence the label "autonomic"). When you digest your lunch, or your heart rate speeds up at the sight of an angry dog, or the hot sun causes your skin to sweat, your body's autonomic nervous system is at work.

The autonomic nervous system is itself divided into two subsystems with opposite functions: the **sympathetic nervous system** and the **parasympathetic nervous system** (FIGURE 2.9). These subsystems allow the internal world of the body to operate in two basic modes.

The sympathetic nervous system puts the body in the mode of reacting to threats or opportunities in the external

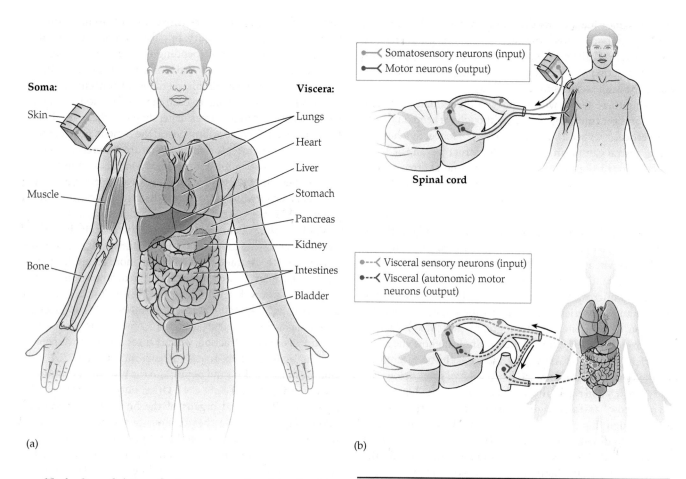

(a)

(b)

world: feeding, fighting, fleeing, or sexual activity. In this mode, the heartbeat quickens, respiration increases, blood pressure increases, and circulation shifts from the digestive organs to the muscles, while the movements of the digestive tract itself slow down or come to a halt. This "fight-or-flight" response system prepares the body to deal with urgent matters in the external world.

In the absence of urgent matters, priorities shift from fight-or-flight to "rest-and-regenerate"—and this latter mode is controlled by the parasympathetic nervous system. In this state, the heart rate slows, respiration decreases, blood pressure falls, muscle tone relaxes, and blood flow shifts to the stomach and digestive organs. The movements of the digestive tract increase as the body rebuilds its stores of energy, protein, and other nutrients. The next time you and a friend or family member are suffering from having eaten too much food in one sitting, you can tell each other, "I parasympathize."

A Nervous System with Segmental Organization

The peripheral nervous system is not an evenly distributed nerve net like that of a jellyfish. As we discussed earlier, the human nervous system has a segmental organization (**FIGURE 2.10**). The segments are easiest to see near the spinal column. Here,

FIGURE 2.8 The body and the peripheral nervous system. (a) The body has two major compartments: the soma and the viscera. (b) The peripheral nervous system includes four kinds of neurons for input and output to these compartments: somatosensory neurons (input), motor neurons (output), visceral sensory neurons (input), and autonomic neurons (output).

the body segments are apparent in the skeleton itself: the line of vertebrae that begins with the cervical spine (within the neck), continues down the thoracic spine (within the ribcage, another segmented structure), continues farther down the lumbar spine (between the ribcage and the pelvis), and ends in humans with the sacral spine (whose segments are fused together into the bony, triangular "sacrum" that forms the back of the pelvis).

The peripheral nerve roots emerge from the spinal cord on either side, near the junction of each vertebra with its neighbor. Hence, every segment of the spinal cord has its own set of peripheral nerve roots on the left and on the right. Near the spinal cord, inputs and outputs are kept separate. All sensory input, somatic and visceral, enters the spinal cord through the dorsal nerve root at the back of the spinal cord. All motor output, somatic and autonomic, exits the spinal cord through the ventral nerve root at the front of the spinal cord.

The segmental organization of the somatic nervous system can also be observed on the outside of the body. Each

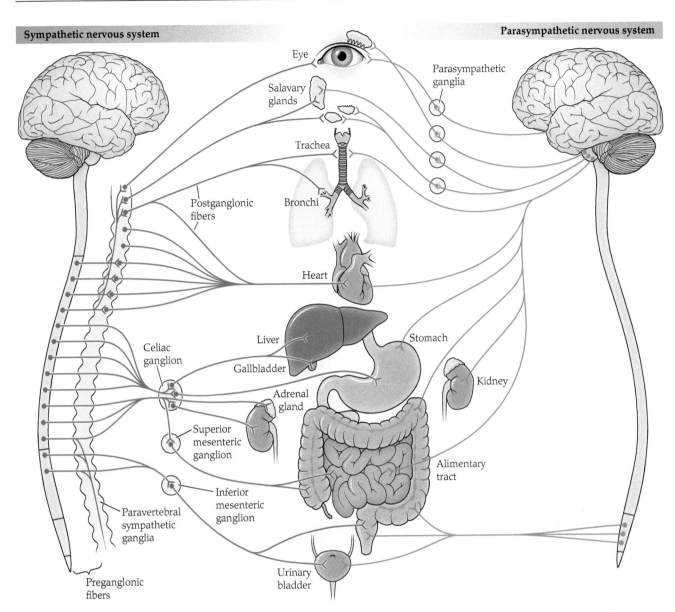

Sympathetic nervous system

Eye

Salavary glands

Trachea

Postganglonic fibers

Bronchi

Heart

Liver

Celiac ganglion

Gallbladder

Adrenal gland

Superior mesenteric ganglion

Inferior mesenteric ganglion

Paravertebral sympathetic ganglia

Preganglonic fibers

Urinary bladder

Parasympathetic nervous system

Parasympathetic ganglia

Stomach

Kidney

Alimentary tract

FIGURE 2.9 **The autonomic nervous system directs the activity of the visceral organs and has two divisions.** The sympathetic nervous system directs activities for fight-or-flight responses, whereas the parasympathetic nervous system directs activities for rest and regeneration.

pair of sensory nerve roots handles input from a narrow stripe on the body surface. The stripes are arranged in a series, from head to tail end, as if the skin were cut up into narrow sections. These stripes are therefore called **dermatomes**, from the Greek words for "skin" and "to cut." Each dermatome corresponds to a different spinal segment and is numbered accordingly—for example, the dermatome of the fifth segment of the cervical spinal cord is known as C5 (FIGURE 2.11a). If the spinal segment or its nerve roots are injured, sensation in the dermatome may be lost. A physician can often determine the site of a spinal injury by carefully testing for areas of sensory loss on the body surface. As one way of visualizing a dermatome, you may be familiar with

shingles, an illness that results from a dormant form of the *Varicella zoster* (chickenpox) virus reactivating itself in one of the nerve roots of a person's body. This causes a painful, blistering skin rash to appear along the dermatome of the nerve root where the virus has reactivated—thus making the dermatome visually apparent (FIGURE 2.11b).

The motor side of the somatic nervous system is also organized into segments. In this case, the segmental "stripes" lie within the musculature rather than the skin and are therefore called myotomes rather than dermatomes. However, they, too, are arranged in a series from head to tail. Spinal injuries can also affect output to the myotomes. For example, an injury to the thoracic spine can block output from the brain to the leg muscles, causing lower limb paralysis (paraplegia). Higher up, an injury to the neck can block output to both the lower and the upper limbs, producing paralysis of all four limbs (quadriplegia). The segmental level of a spinal injury will determine which parts of the body are disabled and which are spared.

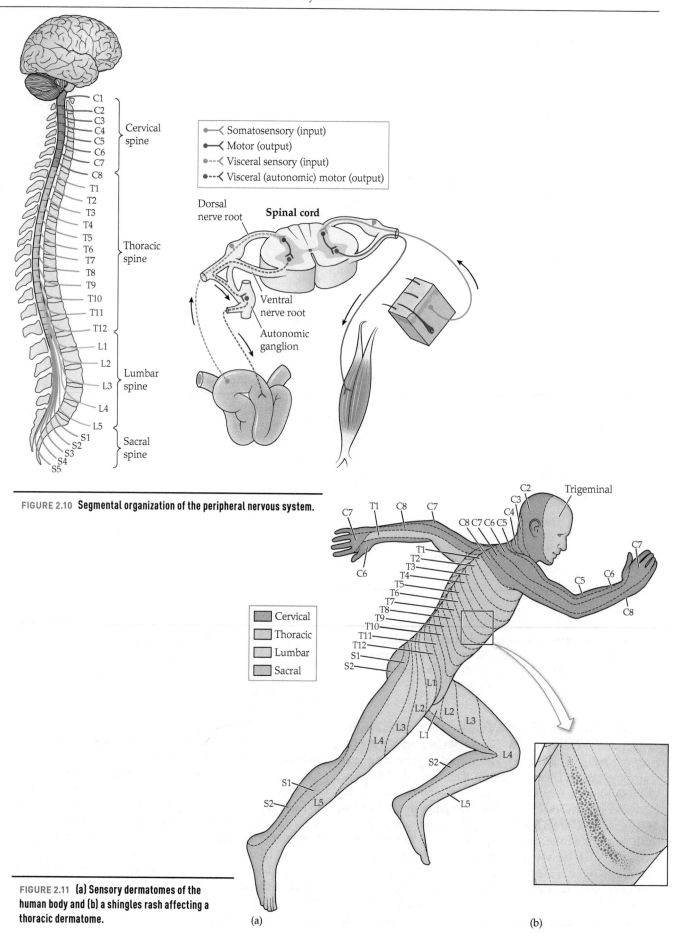

FIGURE 2.10 **Segmental organization of the peripheral nervous system.**

FIGURE 2.11 **(a) Sensory dermatomes of the human body and (b) a shingles rash affecting a thoracic dermatome.**

The neat, segmental pattern of the myotomes and dermatomes is not perfectly preserved at all points in the peripheral nervous system. Sensory and motor neurons take complicated routes from the spinal cord to their final destinations, joining and rejoining neurons from other spinal levels as they reshuffle themselves into peripheral nerve bundles.

The autonomic nervous system is also organized into segments. In fact, the sympathetic and parasympathetic systems exist in completely separate segmental regions. All sympathetic outputs come exclusively from the middle levels of the spinal cord: the thoracic segments and the neighboring, uppermost lumbar segments. All parasympathetic outputs come from either the tail-end segments of the sacral spinal cord or the head-end segments that lie above the spinal cord altogether, in the brainstem.

If this seems complex, just keep in mind some basic principles. The peripheral nervous system has a somatic system for controlling the movement of the "soma," or body, through the external environment and an autonomic system for controlling the "automatic" responses of the internal organs. Both systems have sensory inputs and motor outputs. The autonomic outputs fall into separate subsystems for switching between the body's fight-or-flight (sympathetic) and rest-and-regenerate (parasympathetic) modes. Both systems have a segmental organization of input and output pathways at their point of entry or exit to the spinal cord. However, the input and output pathways often take complicated, tortuous paths between the spinal cord and their endpoints, so that the organization can appear scrambled at intermediate points along the way.

The Spinal Cord

The spinal cord is the meeting place for the inputs and outputs of the peripheral nervous system. Linking sensation to appropriate action is the fundamental method by which nervous systems help an organism to survive and reproduce. In the spinal cord, we find rudimentary circuits that use sensory input to guide motor output. What do these circuits look like, what can they do, and how can they do it? In this section, we'll address each of these questions in turn.

Circuits within a Segment: Spinal Reflexes

If we take a cross-section through a spinal cord, we see a small central canal, surrounded by a butterfly-shaped structure made of **gray matter,** which is itself surrounded by an oval of **white matter.** As throughout the rest of the brain, the central gray matter is home to the cell bodies of neurons and

CASE STUDY:
Christopher Reeve, 1952–2004

The actor Christopher Reeve was known and admired by a generation of moviegoers for playing the role of the fictional hero Superman in the 1970s and 1980s. The character he portrayed was endowed with herculean strength, an almost total invulnerability to injury, and the ability to fly. Tragically, Reeve himself became almost completely paralyzed after being thrown headfirst from a horse during an equestrian competition in 1995. Although his helmet prevented direct brain injury, the force of the impact destroyed the first and second vertebrae of his neck, crushing the upper cervical spinal cord. He was left unable to move his arms or legs and unable to even breathe without mechanical assistance. For the rest of his life, he was restricted to a powered wheelchair, which he steered by puffing air through a strawlike device. The wheelchair had a built-in ventilator to supply his lungs with air.

Undaunted by his injury, Reeve became a prominent activist for spinal cord research. Over the next nine years he traveled the world, making speeches and raising millions of dollars to help fund the search for a cure and improve the quality of life for those with spinal injuries. He urged the U.S. government to support research on using **stem cells** (undifferentiated cells that have the ability to differentiate into several cell types) to regenerate injured neurons. Throughout these years, he maintained an intense regimen of physical therapy and ultimately did regain some sensory and motor function. However, he also battled a series of infections from the bed sores caused by his immobility. In 2004, he died of heart failure at the age of 52. His enduring optimism remains an inspiration to those who live with neurological injuries and illness. Today, the Christopher and Dana Reeve Foundation continues to fund research toward a cure for spinal cord injury.

their local connections, whereas the surrounding white matter is made up of the electrically insulated, long-distance connections between neurons. The overall size of the cord depends on the body segment. If a body segment contains a limb or part of a limb, it will need a larger cord with more gray matter to handle the extra sensory and motor information and more white matter to handle the extra communication with the distant neurons in the brain.

The neurons of the gray matter are stacked in layers, or *laminae*, from ventral to dorsal. As we saw in the last section, sensory input enters the cord from the dorsal side, whereas motor output exits the cord from the ventral side (FIGURE 2.12a). Hence, as you might expect, the neurons in the dorsal layers are mostly sensory neurons, whereas the neurons in the ventral layers (also called the **ventral horns**) are mostly motor neurons. The cell bodies of peripheral sensory neurons live just outside the spinal cord, in the **dorsal root ganglion**. Incoming peripheral signals pass these cell bodies on the way to the spinal cord.

The sensory neurons of the upper gray matter layers lie in two separate columns (perpendicular to the laminae): somatic

and visceral (FIGURE 2.12b). Somatic sensory neurons take input mostly from the skin, skeletal muscles, and joints. This input is useful mainly for guiding body movements with the skeletal muscles: position, stretch, and touch. By contrast, visceral sensory neurons take input from many other tissues as well, including the internal organs. Such input is useful mainly for regulating the internal state of the organism: temperature, pain, inflammation, fatigue, and so on. Sensory neurons are also known as somatic or visceral afferents, the word "afferent" meaning that their information is "carried toward" the central nervous system.

The motor neurons of the spinal cord also lie in separate somatic and visceral columns. Somatic motor neurons send output signals to stimulate the muscles lying in the local myotome. Visceral motor neurons are the output neurons of the sympathetic and parasympathetic nervous systems, sending control signals to the body's internal organs. Motor neurons are also known as somatic or visceral efferents, the word "efferent" indicating that they "carry away" information from the central nervous system.

Now that we have our afferents and efferents in place, what can we do with them? The simplest kind of circuit for connecting inputs to outputs is called a reflex arc. In this kind of circuit, a sensory neuron makes an excitatory connection to a motor neuron so that when the sensory neuron is stimulated, it activates the motor neuron in return. This kind of reflex arc is useful in helping muscles compensate for additional load. If a sensory neuron detects that the muscle is being stretched, it stimulates the appropriate motor neuron to contract the muscle.

The familiar "knee-jerk" **reflex** (properly called the patellar tendon reflex) is a result of suddenly stretching the body of the quadriceps muscle after tapping the attached tendon with the reflex hammer (FIGURE 2.13). The quadriceps makes a powerful, automatic contraction in response to this unexpected extra load. Reflex arcs are just as important for coordinating the activity of the sympathetic and parasympathetic nervous systems: raising the hair follicles in response to cold, producing tears in response to eye irritation, and contracting the blood vessels when standing up so as not to faint from loss of consciousness.

A reflex involving a direct connection between a sensory and a motor neuron is sometimes called a monosynaptic reflex, since the entire circuit involves only one **synapse**, or connection between neurons (we'll learn more about synapses in the next chapter). However, these kinds of circuits are rare. Most reflexes are polysynaptic reflexes—that is, they involve more than one synapse, because an **interneuron** lies between the incoming sensory neuron and the outgoing motor neuron in the circuit.

Compared with monosynaptic reflexes, polysynaptic reflexes allow for more flexibility in the response. For example, imagine you need to contract the biceps muscle of your arm. The problem is that this will stretch the triceps muscle on the other side of the arm. As we saw above, the triceps will automatically compensate by fighting against the stretch. Without some way of turning off the triceps **stretch reflex**, you cannot bend your arm—effectively, you are frozen in place.

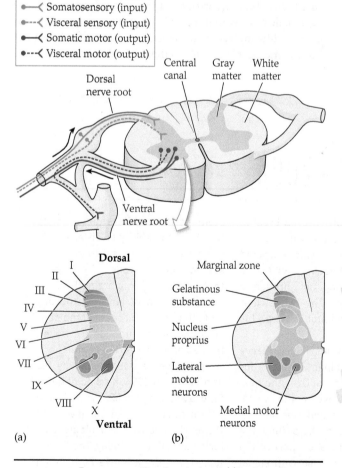

FIGURE 2.12 **Transverse section of a spinal cord.** (a) Laminae and sensory input and motor output through the dorsal and ventral nerve roots as well as (b) the zones for somatic and visceral sensory (upper) and visceral and somatic motor (lower) neuron cell bodies in the spinal cord gray matter.

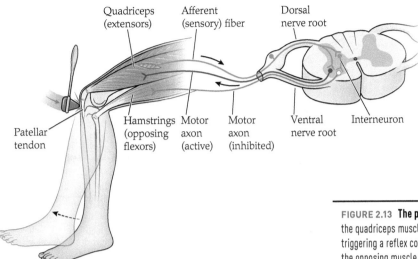

Quadriceps (extensors) Afferent (sensory) fiber Dorsal nerve root

Patellar tendon Hamstrings (opposing flexors) Motor axon (active) Motor axon (inhibited) Ventral nerve root Interneuron

FIGURE 2.13 **The patellar tendon reflex.** Tapping the tendon stretches the quadriceps muscle, sending a sensory signal to the spinal cord and triggering a reflex contraction of the same muscle, along with a relaxation of the opposing muscle.

But what if we add an **inhibitory interneuron (a neuron that transmits inhibitory signals between other neurons)** that connects the biceps motor neuron to the triceps motor neuron? Now the triceps motor neuron has information about the contraction of the biceps and can use this information to override the stretch reflex. You are no longer frozen: you can now bend your arm and wipe your brow in relief.

Visceral and somatic reflexes within a single segment can perform many local functions. However, to execute more complicated actions, we must coordinate activity across multiple body segments. Let's now take a look at the more elaborate circuits that extend across segments and see what feats they are able to accomplish.

Complex Circuits across Segments: Central Pattern Generators

The simple circuits of reflex arcs were among the first to be studied in the nervous system. During the late 19th and early 20th centuries, the British physiologist Sir Charles Sherrington examined how the neural pathways of the spinal cord integrated sensory information to help guide basic forms of movement. He proposed that more complex motor behaviors, such as locomotion (movement from one place to another), could be generated by chains of simpler reflex actions, all driven by incoming sensory input (Burke, 2007).

But was sensory input truly necessary to drive the process, or can the nervous system generate the necessary movements for locomotion all on its own? A few years later, Sherrington's student, T. Graham Brown, found that anesthetized cats could still continue to make stepping movements, even when their spinal cords were completely deprived of all peripheral sensory input. In fact, even when isolated from the brain itself, the spinal cord alone could still drive the stepping movements without sensory input (Brown & Sherrington, 1911; Stuart & Hultborn, 2008).

Brown concluded that the main functional unit of the nervous system was not the reflex arc, but a **central pattern generator** capable of generating movement activity spontaneously (FIGURE 2.14). Input from peripheral sensory neurons of higher brain centers could then adjust these intrinsic patterns of activity as needed. Over the past century, neuroscientists have discovered many different examples of central pattern generators in many species (Barlow, 2009; Frigon, 2012; Konishi, 2010). These circuits drive rhythmical patterns of movement in many different parts of the body: arms, legs, wings, fins, tails, jaws, breathing apparatuses, and visceral organs such as the stomach or intestinal tract.

The basic circuitry of a central pattern generator is surprisingly simple. As in a reflex arc, output comes from a motor neuron that excites the muscle to be moved. The motor neuron is driven by a nearby excitatory interneuron (a neuron that transmits excitatory signals between other neurons), which is spontaneously active even without input. The excitatory interneuron becomes fatigued, and its activity gradually wanes over time. A slightly weaker inhibitory interneuron connects to both of these neurons. As the excitatory interneuron becomes fatigued, the inhibitory interneuron eventually becomes strong enough to shut down the activity of the other neurons, halting the muscle movement. This gives the excitatory interneuron time to recover until it eventually overcomes the inhibition and begins to fire once again.

If we place an identical circuit on the other side of the spinal cord, we can have a pattern of oscillating motor activity on each side of the body. Finally, if we place a pair of inhibitory interneurons reaching across the midline to the opposite circuit, we can ensure that when one circuit is on, the other is off, and vice versa. This kind of pattern will produce alternating movements, such as walking. Alternatively, we can use excitatory interneurons, so that both circuits will turn on and off at the same time. This kind of pattern will produce synchronized movements, such as hopping. We will learn more about central pattern generators in Chapter 7.

FIGURE 2.14 Central pattern generator circuits. These circuits in the spinal cord fire in alternating left–right patterns to drive locomotion in animals as diverse as lampreys swimming (a) or cats walking (b).

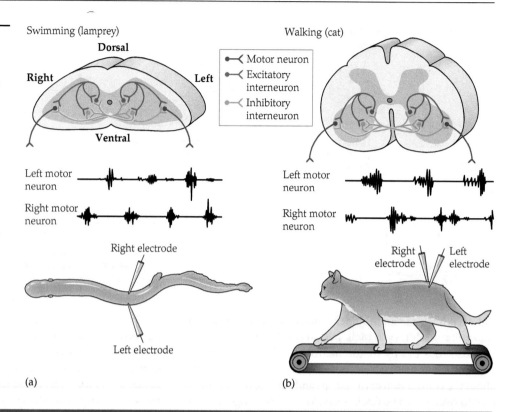

THE BIGGER PICTURE:
In Search of a Cure for Spinal Cord Injury

The *Edwin Smith Surgical Papyrus* is one of the world's most ancient surviving medical texts. Dating from more than 3,500 years ago, it describes with remarkable detail and accuracy the diagnosis and treatment for 48 cases of traumatic bodily injury. Here are its instructions to a physician faced with a patient who has a damaged spinal cord: *Thou shouldst say concerning him: "[This patient has] a dislocation in a vertebra of his neck, while he is unconscious of his two legs and his two arms, and his urine dribbles. An ailment not to be treated."*

Unfortunately, even in today's modern age, the debilitating effects of spinal cord injury remain permanent in most cases. Neither the neurons nor the white matter tracts of the cord regenerate after they are damaged. On the contrary, in the

days and weeks postinjury, the patient's physical condition worsens. The injured area suffers from inflammation, cell death, and the toxic effects of released cell contents from dying neurons. Ultimately, an empty cavity forms, surrounded by a barricade-like scar of glial cells (cells that support neurons), many times the size of the original injury. These physical obstacles prevent neurons from regrowing connections throughout the damaged area.

One potential treatment currently under investigation is to implant neural stem cells into the spinal cord shortly after injury (Li & Lepski, 2013; Mothe, Tam, Zahir, Tator, & Shoichet, 2013). These cells are not yet fully developed into their final forms, and they are therefore uncommonly versatile. Neural stem cells typically proceed to

differentiate into neurons or into cells that support neurons (i.e., glial cells—about which you will learn in Chapter 3). Experimental studies show that neural stem cells may be able to grow new neural pathways to replace those that have been lost (Liu et al., 2013; Saadai et al., 2013). However, the physical barriers of the scar and cavity from the destroyed neural circuits must still be overcome somehow. Potential risks also surround the use of neural stem cells. The embryonic stem cells may activate the patient's immune system (Xu et al., 2010), divide excessively, form pain pathways rather than motor pathways (Macias et al., 2006), or even become a tumor (Kuroda, Yasuda, & Sato, 2013). Many ethical concerns surround the use of embryonic stem cell therapy. The potential for the development of safe and effective neural stem cell therapy holds great promise.

In the meantime, treatment of spinal cord trauma focuses on trying to reduce the inflammation and cell death in the hours and days after injury using medications such as corticosteroids, which have powerful anti-inflammatory and immunosuppressive effects. This may help to limit the damage, but does not heal the neural circuits already destroyed. Finding a cure for spinal cord injury remains a Holy Grail of 21st-century neuroscience.

The Brainstem

The **brainstem,** which is the most posterior region of the brain, acts as a point of communication between the spinal cord and the most anterior structures of the nervous system (FIGURE 2.15). It is composed of three structures: the **medulla oblongata, pons,** and midbrain. The brainstem's most caudal structure is the medulla oblongata. Ahead of it, the brainstem becomes riddled with the additional white matter tracts of the pons or "bridge," which provides connections to the elaborate circuitry of the cerebellum ("little brain") at the same level. Ahead of these two structures lies the midbrain (or mesencephalon) and beyond it the rest of the brain.

Extending out from the brainstem are the **cranial nerves.** Let's take a survey of each one of these structures in turn.

Medulla Oblongata and Pons

The medulla oblongata and pons form the hindbrain. The medulla oblongata regulates involuntary functions that are essential to life, including breathing, heart rate, and blood pressure. The pons relays signals between the cerebellum and the **cerebrum** (the cerebrum is the anteriormost structure of the central nervous system, consisting of the cerebral cortex, basal ganglia, hippocampus, and amygdala. It originates from the telencephalon of the developing embryo). The

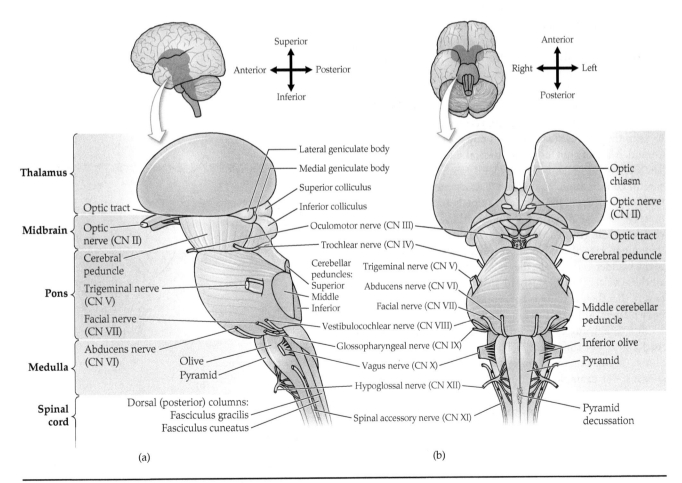

FIGURE 2.15 **Structures of the brainstem, seen in (a) lateral view and (b) ventral view.**

pons is involved in arousal, sleep, breathing, swallowing, bladder control, eye movement, facial expressions, hearing, equilibrium, and posture. In many ways, the hindbrain resembles the spinal cord in structure and function. For example, the hindbrain has incoming sensory neurons and outgoing motor neurons that form peripheral nerves. The hindbrain, too, has a central gray matter with different columns of neurons interacting with the inside and outside worlds: somatic sensory, visceral sensory, visceral motor, and somatic motor neurons. The spinal cord and hindbrain also have some similar kinds of circuits such as reflex arcs.

However, the hindbrain has many important sensory features that the spinal cord lacks. Keep in mind that the head of a bilateral organism has many kinds of special sensory organs not found in the rest of the body. For example, it has light receptors in the eye, sound receptors in the inner ear, odor receptors in the nasal passages, and taste receptors in the oral cavity. In addition, it has pain, temperature, vibration, position, and touch receptors of the head and inside the mouth and throat, as well as the balance-sensing vestibular organ of the inner ear. Many creatures have other sensory systems as well: the shark and the platypus have electroreceptors, pigeons have magnetoreceptors, rattlesnakes have infrared-detecting pit organs below the eyes, and fish have sensitive vibration detectors running down the sides of their bodies. All these extra sensory inputs travel to the brainstem, which needs additional neural circuitry to handle them.

Likewise, the hindbrain has many important motor features that the spinal cord lacks. The tongue, mouth, neck, and head have different forms of movement than the rest of the body, so they need new kinds of circuitry. The eyes cannot form a stable image without expert control. They need an elaborate musculature and an even more elaborate control system to keep themselves steady and on target as the body moves around. Also, let's not forget the visceral side of motor control. The swallowing actions of the upper throat (or *pharynx*) need careful coordination, as do the vibratory movements of the vocal apparatus, or *larynx*, of land animals and the more elaborate *syrinx* of singing birds. Water-breathing animals need to ventilate their gills. Air-breathing animals need to ventilate their lungs. Heartbeat, blood pressure, digestion, the voiding of the bladder and bowels, the functions of the sexual organs: all these visceral functions will also need central control to ensure that their activity is appropriate to the circumstances. For a bilateral animal, steering is complicated.

Brainstem **nuclei** handle these new sensory, motor, somatic, and visceral functional requirements (FIGURE 2.16). Simple brainstem reflex arcs can handle simple, local responses. For example, brushing the sensitive surface of the eye provokes a vigorous, protective blinking movement of the eyelid on the same side. However, most brainstem reflexes are much more complicated. For example, the vestibulo-ocular reflex keeps the eyes steady if the head is suddenly turned or moved. This relatively basic function requires many nuclei to work together. Detecting the sudden movement requires sensory nuclei to process input from the vestibular organ. As

these brainstem nuclei determine the direction and speed of motion, they must pass this information to the motor nuclei controlling each eye's movements. This in itself is complicated because six different muscles and three different nuclei control eye movement. These movements are not even symmetrical: looking to the left means pulling your right eye toward the nose but your left eye away from the nose. Many apparently simple behaviors, like keeping the eyes steady during movement, require a complex circuitry behind the scenes.

Hindbrain circuits also act as central pattern generators for the rhythmical movements of the head and upper body. Chewing, swallowing, yawning, sucking, coughing, sneezing, and hiccuping are examples of rhythmical movements generated by the brainstem. However, the most important central patterns are the movements of breathing. In the medulla oblongata, at least two central pattern generators drive the rhythmical movements of breathing, and either one is sufficient to maintain respiration on its own. Visceral central pattern generators in the medulla oblongata also perform critical functions: the regulation of heart rate and blood pressure. With such heavy responsibilities, the medulla oblongata is essential to survival. Although the body can endure many other kinds of brain injury, destruction of the medulla oblongata is swiftly fatal.

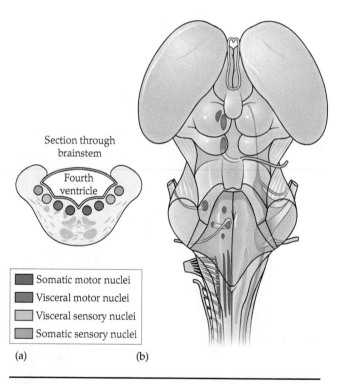

FIGURE 2.16 **Nuclei of the brainstem.** (a) The neurons of the brainstem are arranged into nuclei, which themselves are arranged into columns. There are different columns for visceral and somatic sensory and motor functions. (b) Along each column, different nuclei serve different parts of the head and neck region via the cranial nerves. In this figure, on the left side, only the motor nuclei are shown. On the right side, only the sensory nuclei are shown.

NEUROSCIENCE OF EVERYDAY LIFE:
Why Do We Get the Hiccups?

Most central pattern generators of the brainstem perform functions essential to life: swallowing, breathing, and so on. There is one annoying exception, however: the hiccups. A hiccup involves closing the vocal folds of the glottis and then making a sudden inspiratory movement of the diaphragm. The movement is similar to a cough, except that in a cough the diaphragm makes a sudden expiratory movement, hopefully blasting any obstructions out of the airway. The importance of a clear airway is obvious, but what could be the purpose of a hiccup?

In 2003, researchers at the University of Calgary proposed that the answer may lie with our amphibian ancestors (Straus et al., 2003). These animals possessed simple lungs, but also had gills for respiration in water. When underwater, many amphibians ventilate their gills by pumping water over them with rhythmic contractions of the pharynx. During this gill breathing, the glottis closes forcefully to prevent water from flooding the lungs. You may have seen the rhythmic pulsations of a frog's throat as it rests. These are remnants of movements

from their gill-ventilating youth as tadpoles, although the adult frog has lost its gills. Although we, too, lost our gills long ago, the central pattern generator for gill ventilation may have persisted in our medulla oblongata. Part of this central pattern generator is still useful for controlling suckling behaviors in infants—another function essential to life. Hiccups might therefore be the price we pay for being able to suckle as infants.

Midbrain

The midbrain adds yet another layer of modulation and complexity to the circuits we have seen so far (FIGURE 2.17). Its local inputs and outputs come mostly from the eyes: visual signals from the retina, motor signals to control eye movements, light entry via the iris, and image focus via the lens. To make use of a visual image, the animal must determine where objects are in space.

A midbrain area called the **superior colliculus** (colliculus means "little hill," based on its external appearance) is involved in locating visual stimuli in space and uses this information to direct complex movements, such as turning the eyes to point toward the target. This area can also use visual stimuli to guide movements of other parts including the head, the arm, the tongue (in frogs), or even the whole body. Just below the superior colliculus, the **inferior colliculus** performs parallel functions using auditory rather than visual inputs. These areas are large, important players in motor control in many species such as fish, amphibians, reptiles, and birds. In mammals, many of the functions of the superior colliculus and the inferior colliculus have been transferred to the cerebral cortex, as we will see later in this chapter.

The midbrain also contains so-called command generators capable of starting, stopping, and modulating the activity of central pattern generators in the brainstem and spinal

cord. An example of a command generator is the midbrain locomotor region, a set of nuclei in the midbrain capable of initiating locomotor movements (movements from one place to another) whose nature depends on the species: swimming in aquatic vertebrates or walking in land vertebrates. Placing the command generator in the midbrain allows it to take input from many different sources: visual or auditory input, startle reflexes, and more anterior brain areas responsible for the kinds of behavior that require movement (such as exploring, seeking, and evading).

Some of these types of complex behavior arise from the circuitry of a central midbrain area called the **periaqueductal gray matter**. Here the neurons are again organized into a set of columns, as in the spinal cord. In this case, however, each column handles a different basic class of behavior: not simple behavior like coughing or yawning, but more complex behavior like defense, aggression, or reproduction.

Three major categories of behavior are needed for survival and reproduction. These are appetitive behaviors for finding and consuming essential nutrients, agonistic behaviors for attack and defense against hostile organisms, and reproductive behaviors for courting, mating, and rearing offspring. The midbrain coordinates these behaviors, each of which involves integrating many simpler components, both somatic and visceral. For example, stimulating one of the columns of the periaqueductal gray matter in a cat can elicit a stereotyped defensive reaction: flattening the ears,

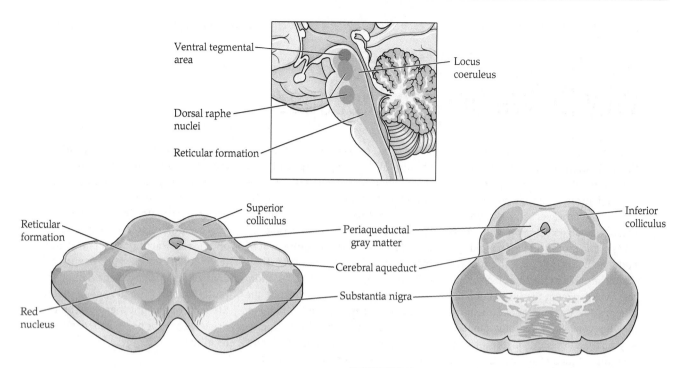

FIGURE 2.17 Structures and nuclei of the midbrain.

narrowing the eyes, baring the teeth, striking out with the forepaw, growling with the vocal cords, and increasing the heart rate and blood pressure (Bhatt & Siegel, 2006). Stimulating other columns can elicit other behavioral patterns: the species-specific responses of courtship, or mating, or freezing, or urinating, or defecating (Drake et al., 2010; Kow, Brown, & Pfaff, 1994; Ohmura et al., 2010; Schimitel et al., 2012). In short, the periaqueductal gray is a sort of central pattern generator that coordinates not reflexes or movements, but other pattern generators themselves.

The midbrain coordinates many important activities not only in the hindbrain and spinal cord, but also in the forebrain. A diffuse network of midbrain cells known as the midbrain **reticular formation** plays a central role in regulating states of consciousness. Depending on its activity, the forebrain will settle into the alertness of the waking state or the unconsciousness of the sleeping state. Another cell group called the **locus coeruleus** (or "blue place" because of its distinctive pigmentation) sends alerting signals to the rest of the brain via a neurotransmitter called **norepinephrine**. Other key neurotransmitter systems are also headquartered in the midbrain. The **substantia nigra** (or "black substance," again because of its color) is the main source of the neurotransmitter **dopamine**, which plays key roles in movement, cognition, motivation, and reward. The substantia nigra is also part of the basal ganglia, about which you will learn later in this chapter. The **midbrain raphe nuclei**, which lie along the seam between the two sides of the brainstem, are the main source of the neurotransmitter **serotonin**. Serotonin has diverse functions in mood, sleep, and social behavior. Each of these neurotransmitter systems is in itself a major topic, and we'll explore each neurotransmitter system in detail in a later chapter.

Most Cranial Nerves Emerge from the Brainstem

Humans have 12 pairs of cranial nerves, which are sometimes numbered with Roman numerals. The cranial nerves transmit sensory and motor information between the brain and the periphery, similar in some ways to the peripheral nerves that connect to the spinal cord. All of the cranial nerves emerge from the brainstem, except for cranial nerves I and II (which emerge from the cerebrum itself). (The cerebrum is the anteriormost structure of the central nervous system). **FIGURE 2.18** shows each cranial nerve, along with its major function(s).

The Cerebellum

As we have seen, the spinal cord and brainstem can produce basic forms of motor activity using reflex circuits and central pattern generators. These basic forms of activity may have been sufficient for the earliest vertebrates that swam in the ocean: jawless scavengers like the hagfish. However, some of these vertebrates gradually developed a new and more active lifestyle. They evolved jaws for capturing and consuming mobile prey, along with improved sensory organs for locating the prey. With this new lifestyle came a need for enhanced motor control.

Shaping the raw motor activity of reflexes and central pattern generators into smooth, efficient movements is a

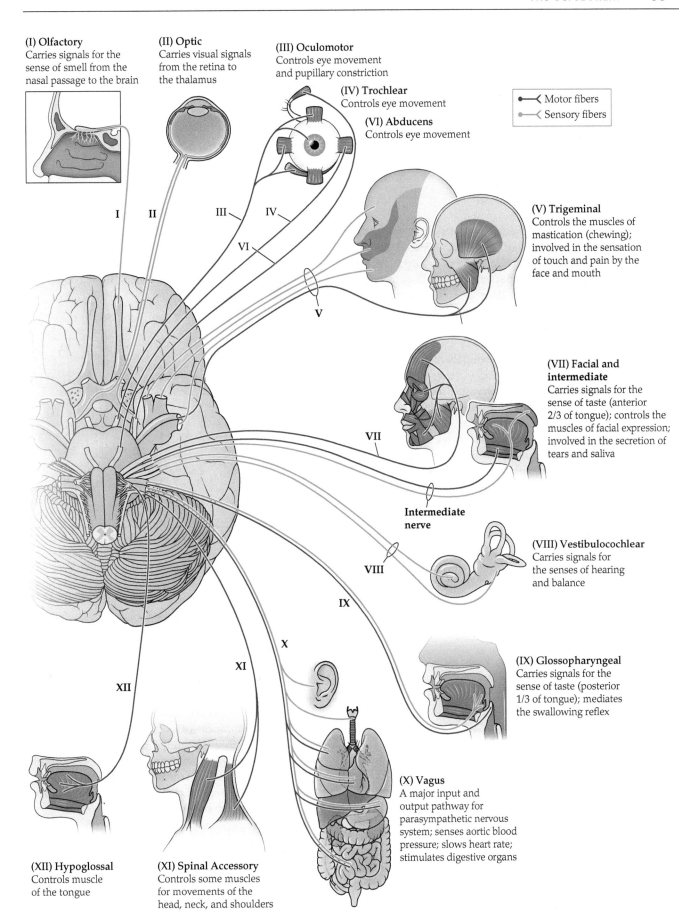

(I) Olfactory
Carries signals for the sense of smell from the nasal passage to the brain

(II) Optic
Carries visual signals from the retina to the thalamus

(III) Oculomotor
Controls eye movement and pupillary constriction

(IV) Trochlear
Controls eye movement

(VI) Abducens
Controls eye movement

Motor fibers
Sensory fibers

(V) Trigeminal
Controls the muscles of mastication (chewing); involved in the sensation of touch and pain by the face and mouth

(VII) Facial and intermediate
Carries signals for the sense of taste (anterior 2/3 of tongue); controls the muscles of facial expression; involved in the secretion of tears and saliva

Intermediate nerve

(VIII) Vestibulocochlear
Carries signals for the senses of hearing and balance

(IX) Glossopharyngeal
Carries signals for the sense of taste (posterior 1/3 of tongue); mediates the swallowing reflex

(X) Vagus
A major input and output pathway for parasympathetic nervous system; senses aortic blood pressure; slows heart rate; stimulates digestive organs

(XII) Hypoglossal
Controls muscle of the tongue

(XI) Spinal Accessory
Controls some muscles for movements of the head, neck, and shoulders

I II III IV VI V VII VIII IX X XI XII

FIGURE 2.18 **The cranial nerves and their major functions.**

complicated process. Movements take place in an environment and hence require steering: toward targets and away from obstacles. Proper steering cannot be blind—it needs sensory input for guidance. When a movement veers off its intended path, it needs correction. If the target tries to flee, the movement needs adjustment. All of these functions require adding on a new kind of circuitry, and lots of it. This circuitry lies in the **cerebellum**.

Circuitry of the "Little Brain"

The cerebellum, or "little brain," contains an enormous number of neurons. The human cerebellum contains more neurons than both hemispheres of our much larger cerebrum combined, and in many species the cerebellum dwarfs all other brain structures. All these neurons are densely packed into leaflike folia, which are themselves packed into larger folds or lobules, which in turn are packed into larger lobes (FIGURE 2.19). This arrangement fits as many neurons into as small a space as possible, allowing them to communicate more efficiently. The cell bodies of these neurons are found in a wrinkly sheet covering the outer surface or cerebellar cortex (not to be confused with the cerebral cortex, which we'll discuss later in the chapter).

The microcircuitry of the cerebellar cortex has a remarkably consistent wiring pattern across the entire sheet, in all species of vertebrates (FIGURE 2.20). Inputs come from

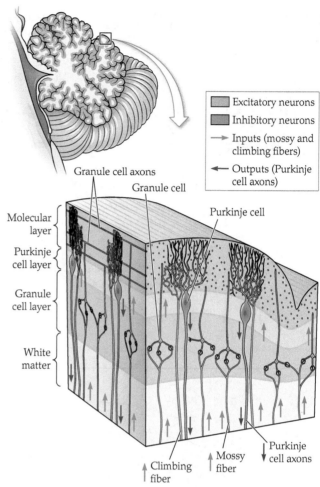

FIGURE 2.20 **The microcircuitry of the cerebellum.**

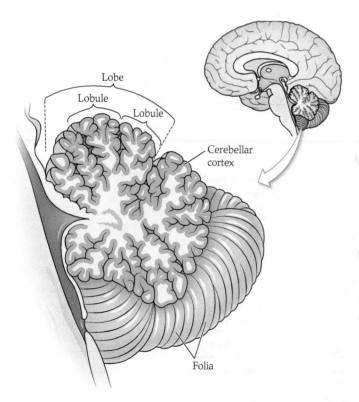

FIGURE 2.19 **The gray matter of the cerebellum is densely packed into leaflike structures called folia, lobules, and lobes.**

dedicated nuclei in the brainstem and connect to small excitatory and inhibitory interneurons in the lower part of the sheet, called the granule cell layer. These interneurons send their output signals to the upper part of the sheet, called the molecular layer. Sandwiched between these two layers lie the giant output neurons, named **Purkinje cells** after the Czech anatomist who discovered them. Purkinje cells have a beautiful, intricate branchwork of input connections that gather information from the molecular layer above them. They integrate this information and send their output back to specialized output nuclei in the brainstem, which pass the information back to the spinal cord and ahead to the cerebral cortex and the rest of the brain.

Functions of the Little Brain

In the brain, function follows circuitry, so the remarkable consistency of cerebellar circuitry across species suggests a common and important function. What could it be? Damage to the cerebellum interferes with the smooth, efficient movements of body parts to their targets in the surrounding environment. Movements become jerky and clumsy. They overshoot or undershoot their targets, occur too early or too late, or are too strong or too weak. Maintaining upright balance becomes difficult or impossible. Learning new motor responses also becomes more difficult.

The cerebellum clearly has an important role in coordinating movements and matching them to their environment, although neuroscientists debate exactly what this role might be. One possibility is that the cerebellum calculates a **forward model** of upcoming movements (Seidler, Noll, & Thiers, 2004). In other words, it makes predictions about the expected sensory outcomes of motor actions and uses these predictions to refine outgoing motor commands. Building a forward model turns out to be incredibly useful for planning fast, precise movements. For example, when you are running, there is not enough time for your brain to send out a motor command to your foot, then wait for the sensory feedback to return to see what happened, and then send out another motor command to adjust the positioning. You would lose your balance and fall over immediately if the system were this slow. Even when you are standing still, the time delay between your vestibular organ sensing how far your legs are from vertical and the motor command arriving at your leg muscles to compensate is too long to maintain balance without a forward model. Likewise, catching a ball or shaking a friend's hand is impossible unless you aim your movements at where the target is going to be, not at where it was a moment ago. By planning ahead, the cerebellum allows a whole new level of sophistication in motor control.

The cerebellum was traditionally considered solely a motor structure. However, more recent research has also found evidence that the cerebellum plays an important role in nonmotor functions such as language, memory, attention, and even emotional regulation (Schmahmann, 2010; Stoodley, Valera, & Schmahmann, 2012; Strick, Dum, & Fiez, 2009). This is an excellent example of how our understanding of brain function is always evolving.

The Diencephalon: Hypothalamus and Thalamus

As we enter the forebrain, the nervous system takes on quite a different structure than we have seen until this point. Here we find few direct inputs or outputs to the body or the outside world. Instead, the neurons of the forebrain can mostly be considered interneurons, whose vast and elaborate circuitry is added on to the simpler circuits we have reviewed so far. Recall that the brain adds complexity to behavior by inserting layers of processing between sensory input and motor output. The additional neural circuits of the forebrain thus tend to have quite complex roles—roles that can be quite flexible over time. We'll begin our look at these circuits with the two main structures of the diencephalon, which lies just forward of the midbrain circuits that we discussed in the section on the brainstem. These structures are the **hypothalamus** and the **thalamus**.

Hypothalamus: A Keystone Structure in Homeostasis

All living organisms have survival needs. The body remains alive only within a narrow range of physical parameters. With insufficient energy supplies, or too little water, or too much water, or too high a temperature, or too cold a temperature, all the delicately balanced biochemical processes that sustain life will grind to a halt. Brains that allow the body's internal parameters to wander too far from the ideal range do not allow the body to survive to reproduce. After millions of generations of experience, the brains of today's living creatures have gotten very, very good at maintaining homeostasis (the process of keeping the body's internal parameters in balance). The neurons that drive homeostasis can be found in the hypothalamus.

Hypothalamic neurons are responsible for the homeostatic control signals we sometimes call "basic drives." Basic drives include hunger, thirst, sexual arousal, temperature regulation, and sleep. These drives serve to maintain the body's balance of energy intake against energy consumption, water intake against dehydration, temperature regulation against overheating and overcooling, and so on. Neurons of the hypothalamus cluster into distinct groups: the hypothalamic nuclei (FIGURE 2.21). Each hypothalamic nucleus has a distinct function, and many relate to a specific drive. For example, one nucleus coordinates feeding; another regulates satiety; others regulate heat-generating behavior, heat-shedding behavior, and mating behavior. Since many drives wax and wane according to the time of day or night, one hypothalamic nucleus acts as a circadian clock to stimulate or inhibit the other nuclei.

To maintain homeostasis, the neurons of the hypothalamus need input about the internal state of the body. They obtain this information from many sources: visceral inputs via the spinal cord, hormonal inputs from other body organs, even direct measurements of the chemistry of the bloodstream. They integrate the information from all of these sources and compare the results against ideal homeostatic **set points**. The set points themselves can be changed when necessary. For example, internal body temperature can be increased to fight infection. Hunger can increase, leading to increased food consumption and storage of energy for the winter months.

When the internal environment deviates too far from the set point, the hypothalamus coordinates the necessary compensatory mechanisms. These compensatory mechanisms fall into three categories: autonomic responses, endocrine

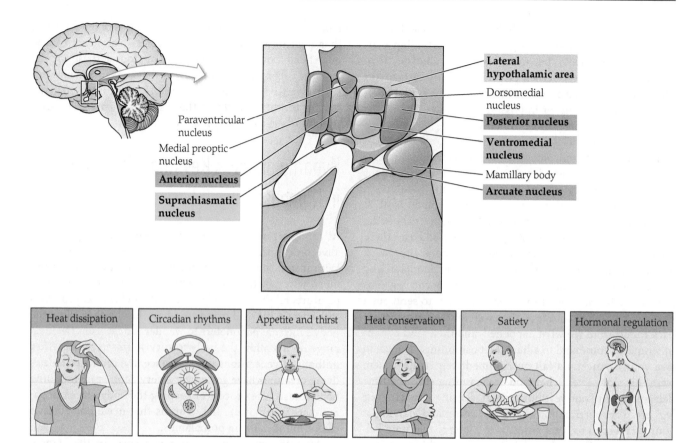

Paraventricular nucleus

Medial preoptic nucleus

Anterior nucleus

Suprachiasmatic nucleus

Lateral hypothalamic area

Dorsomedial nucleus

Posterior nucleus

Ventromedial nucleus

Mamillary body

Arcuate nucleus

Heat dissipation   Circadian rhythms   Appetite and thirst   Heat conservation   Satiety   Hormonal regulation

FIGURE 2.21 **Nuclei of the hypothalamus, with their major functions.**

responses, and behavioral responses. Hypothalamic neurons send outputs via the thalamus to the cerebral cortex, which has the computational power to elaborate basic drives into goals and plans of action. (The next section of the chapter describes the cerebral cortex in greater depth.) The hypothalamus also provides extensive output to the autonomic control centers of the brainstem and spinal cord.

Furthermore, the hypothalamus is considered the master control gland of the body's **hormone**-secreting systems (which are known collectively as the neuroendocrine system) (FIGURE 2.22). It sends control signals down a thin extension to the **pituitary gland**, which in turn releases many kinds of hormonal signals into other parts of the body. One example of a pituitary hormone is growth hormone, which regulates tissue growth throughout the body. Thyroid-stimulating hormone directs the thyroid in controlling the body's overall metabolic rate. Prolactin regulates lactation. **Oxytocin** facilitates maternal bonding, lactation, and social bonding. Antidiuretic hormone directs the kidneys to retain rather than excrete water. These kinds of hormonal responses are essential components of homeostasis. We will learn more about the hypothalamus and its functions in Chapter 13.

How might homeostasis work in practice? Imagine that an organism has not consumed water in several days and becomes dehydrated. The hypothalamus may sense that the blood pressure is dropping and that the osmolarity (a measure of the total concentration of sodium, potassium, and other dissolved chemical constitutents) of its bodily

fluids is increasing to unacceptable levels. It can compensate by sending signals to the autonomic control centers of the brainstem and spinal cord to increase the heart rate and constrict the blood vessels; this will help to maintain blood pressure. It can also stimulate the pituitary gland to produce antidiuretic hormone, which signals the kidneys to stop excreting water. These kinds of physiological compensatory mechanisms will buy the organism some time. However, the autonomic and endocrine responses are not enough to ensure survival without the accompanying behavioral component. The organism needs to find some water, quickly!

By itself, the hypothalamus is not equipped to actually find or consume any water. Foraging for water sources is an extremely demanding task. It requires multisensory input, a repository of past memories, a weighing of possible plans of action, and complex motor behavior. The hypothalamus lacks the necessary circuitry to perform any of these tasks. The **cerebral cortex**, however, is readily capable of performing all the necessary steps for water finding, just as soon as it receives a motivational signal to begin. So the hypothalamus generates a motivational alarm signal and then passes the signal to the cerebral cortex to decide what to do about it. The cerebral cortex is a large and complicated place, however. Getting the signal to the appropriate areas of the cerebral

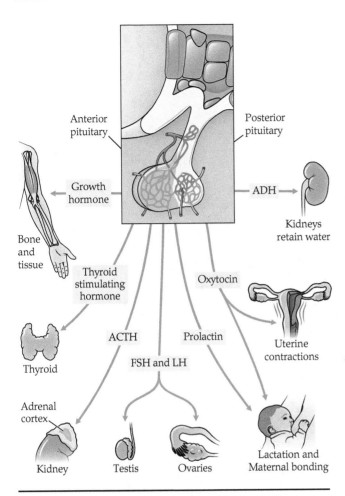

FIGURE 2.22 Hormone-regulating functions of the hypothalamus.
Nuclei in the hypothalamus send signals down to the pituitary gland to control the secretion of a variety of key hormones for controlling the functions of the internal organs of the body.

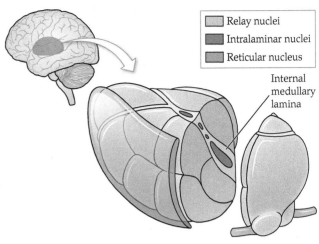

FIGURE 2.23 The thalamus is divided into a number of nuclei. Relay nuclei transmit information to and from specific regions of the cerebral cortex. Intralaminar nuclei connect diffusely to large areas of cortex. The reticular nucleus wraps around the other nuclei and regulates their activity.

Thalamus

The thalamus plays a central role in brain function by acting as a relay station to the cerebral cortex, conveying incoming sensory information to the appropriate cortical areas. It also relays motor signals to the cerebral cortex from other motor control structures like the cerebellum and basal ganglia (which we'll look at in the next section). In addition, the thalamus acts as a relay station between distant areas of the cerebral cortex itself, communicating information from one area to another. Thalamic neurons cluster into a large number of separate thalamic nuclei, which serve different regions and therefore play different roles (FIGURE 2.23). Further, the thalamic nuclei may play an important role in synchronizing neural activity between distant regions, enabling these regions to work together (X. J. Wang & Rinzel, 1993). This role in synchronization may be important for attention, awareness, and the conscious state itself (Bartlett & Wang, 2011; Guldenmund et al., 2013; Schmidt, 2003; Zhang & Bertram, 2002).

The thalamus and the cerebral cortex are tightly interconnected. Each thalamic nucleus serves a different section of the cerebral cortex. For example, the **lateral geniculate nucleus** relays information from the light-sensitive neurons (or **photoreceptors**) of the retina to the neurons of the **primary visual cortex (V1)**, where the first stages of visual information processing in the cortex take place. Another thalamic nucleus, the pulvinar nucleus, conveys the signals from the superior colliculus (which, as you may recall, is involved in moving the eyes to fixate on visual stimuli) to areas of the cerebral cortex that perform similar functions. Other thalamic nuclei convey auditory information from the brainstem to auditory areas of the cerebral cortex, tactile information to the somatosensory cortex, and visceral information (including the sense of taste) to visceral sensory areas of the cerebral cortex.

Still other thalamic nuclei serve motor control regions of the cerebral cortex. Some signals from the cerebellum do not pass to the spinal cord, but instead find their way to the cerebral cortex via relay stations in the thalamus (FIGURE 2.24). This allows the cerebral cortex to use the future-predicting "forward models" of the cerebellum for its own motor functions. Other motor signals pass to the cerebral cortex from the substantia nigra in the brainstem or from the basal ganglia (motor control structures anterior to the thalamus, about which you will learn in the next section). Thalamic nuclei provide the motor cortex with access to all of these diverse sources of motor control information.

Other thalamic nuclei are dedicated to serving **association areas** of the cerebral cortex. The association areas of the

cortex is a job all in itself. The neurons that take on this task lie in the other major diencephalic structure: the thalamus. Let's now turn to this structure and see how it works.

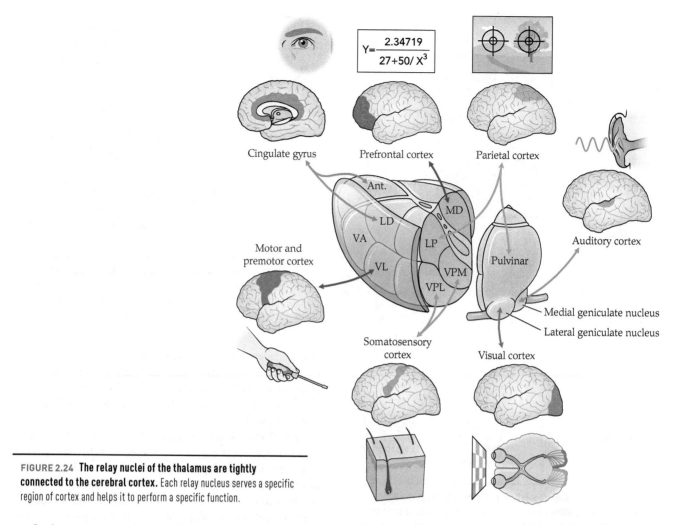

FIGURE 2.24 The relay nuclei of the thalamus are tightly connected to the cerebral cortex. Each relay nucleus serves a specific region of cortex and helps it to perform a specific function.

cerebral cortex are neither purely sensory nor purely motor areas. These areas integrate sensory and motor functions and are important for more complex forms of sensory processing and motor planning.

Additional thalamic nuclei convey information about motivations and drives to the cerebral cortex. Earlier in this section, we saw how the basic homeostatic drives of the hypothalamus must be unpacked into priorities, goals, and action plans so that the organism's behavior meets its essential needs. Specialized nuclei of the thalamus relay information from the hypothalamus and other key motivational structures to the cerebral cortex for behavioral planning.

Other types of thalamic nuclei, called the intralaminar nuclei, provide a more diffuse input to large swaths of the cerebral cortex as a whole. Since they connect to so many areas with such diverse functions, these nuclei are probably not involved in any single type of sensory or motor function (Benarroch, 2008; Van der Werf, Witter, & Groenewegen, 2002). Much of their input comes from brainstem structures involved in alerting and arousal, such as the reticular formation that we discussed in the section on the midbrain, which plays a central role in switching the brain from the conscious to the unconscious state. In addition, these small thalamic nuclei seem to be important in maintaining alertness and

consciousness in general (Edelstyn, Mayes, & Ellis, 2014). Even a small injury to the intralaminar nuclei can produce a profound reduction in the level of consciousness.

The **reticular nucleus** is one final and very important structure of the thalamus. It consists of a thin sheet of neurons that wraps around the entire surface of the thalamus. Unlike all other thalamic nuclei, it has no connections to the cerebral cortex and few inputs from any other outside brain structure. Instead, almost all of the input to the reticular nucleus originates within the thalamus itself. Its neurons, all of which are inhibitory, connect only to other nuclei of the thalamus. Each neuron not only inhibits some of the neurons of a thalamic nucleus, but also inhibits its own neighbors. The effect of this is like changing a babble of uncoordinated neural chatter into a respectful conversation, where other neurons grow silent when one of their neighbors is speaking. The reticular formation may help to organize the communication activity of the thalamic nuclei themselves. The brainstem reticular formation stimulates the activity of the reticular nucleus, so that its activity waxes and wanes over the course of the day and night. As it does so, the level of alertness and the clarity of consciousness increase and decrease. Attention, awareness, and consciousness all critically depend on the information-conveying capacity of the thalamus.

CASE STUDY:
Waking the Brain

Around the turn of the millennium, a young man was assaulted and beaten unconscious while being robbed. He suffered such severe brain injury in the attack that he remained in a diminished state of consciousness for more than two years. He made no signs of verbal communication, rarely responded to commands, and had severely spastic limbs. At that point, with little hope for further recovery, he was transferred from a hospital to a long-term care facility. More than six years after the injury, his condition had not improved much. However, a new series of tests gave some cause for optimism. Brain imaging showed that the network of regions for language function was still intact; other networks might have been similarly spared. Overall, his brain showed much less metabolic activity than a normal, awake brain. Yet perhaps much of his brain was merely dormant rather than destroyed.

In brain injury, the intralaminar nuclei of the thalamus are sometimes damaged to the point of causing unconsciousness although the rest of the brain's circuitry is not as profoundly affected. If the patient could only be "awakened," many brain functions might return. In an attempt to awaken the patient, a team of neurologists and neurosurgeons led by Dr. Nicholas Schiff implanted the intralaminar nuclei of the patient's thalamus with the electrodes of a deep brain stimulator (Schiff et al., 2007; Schiff & Posner, 2007).

Deep brain stimulation involves the surgical implantation of electrodes into the brain. These electrodes send electrical impulses to specified parts of the brain. A pacemaker-like device that is placed under the patient's skin in his or her upper chest controls the amount of brain stimulation. A wire that travels under the patient's skin connects this pacemaker-like device to the implanted electrodes in the brain.

The results of the stimulation were striking. After being virtually unresponsive for nearly seven years, the patient began opening his eyes and turning his head to the sound of a voice. He became able to swallow food placed on his tongue and even began to speak some simple sentences. His condition continued to improve over the following months. He began communicating reliably with his family and the medical staff, watching movies, and even laughing at appropriate times. Since then, other patients in an altered state of consciousness have also undergone the procedure. Although deep brain stimulation is not always so successful, some of these patients have shown similar improvements in their level of consciousness (Giacino, Fins, Machado, & Schiff, 2012). Although resuming a completely independent life is rarely possible after such severe injuries, in some cases deep brain stimulation can return these patients to their families and to the world of waking life.

The Telencephalon: Cerebral Cortex and Basal Ganglia

Cerebral Cortex

The cerebral cortex is the largest part of the human brain and the most quintessential. When we picture a human brain in our minds, we tend to imagine a pinkish, wrinkly organ looking vaguely like an oversized walnut out of its shell. This convoluted structure is actually not the entire brain, but simply the outer covering: the cerebral cortex (*cortex* is Latin for bark, as in tree bark). Present in all mammals but dramatically expanded in humans, the cerebral cortex is critical for all of the most elaborate forms of human cognition: speaking a sentence, reading the words on a page, planning goals for the future, turning those goals into actions, recognizing and using tools, imagining the future and the past, thinking about what other people are thinking, and being aware of our own selves. Since the neuroscience of cognition is the subject of this entire book, we'll have lots of time to consider each of these advanced functions in detail in the chapters ahead. For now, we'll just familiarize ourselves with the different parts of the cerebral cortex and their general functions (FIGURE 2.25).

Early neuroanatomists could only speculate as to the functions of the different parts of the cerebral cortex. They looked at the brain's overall appearance, divided up the structures they saw in front of them, and assigned names to each of them. Of course, the brain was under no obligation to

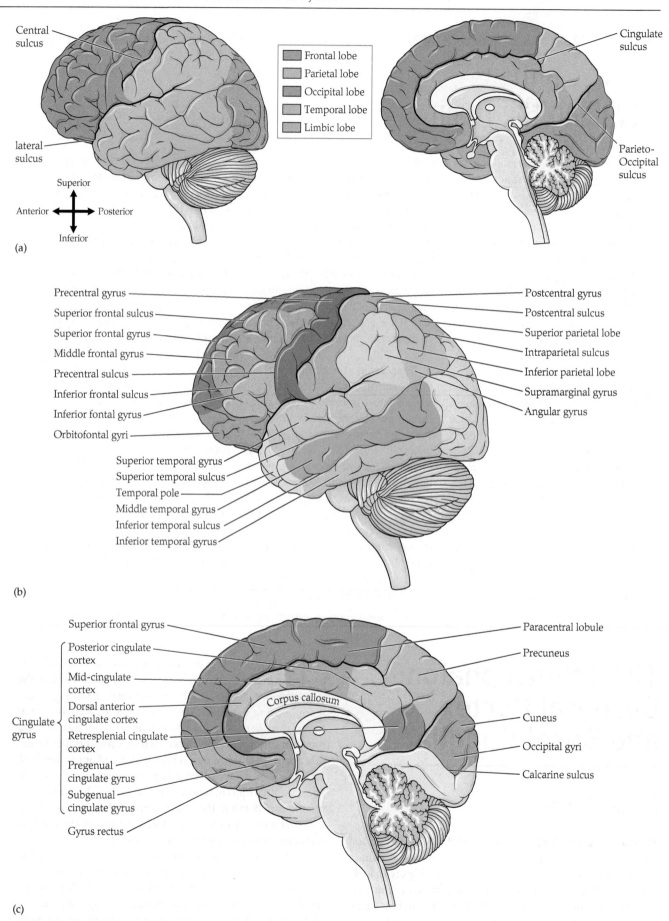

FIGURE 2.25 The major lobes, landmarks, gyri, and sulci of the cerebral cortex. (a) The major lobes and landmarks; (b) lateral view of the left cerebral hemisphere; (c) medial view of the right cerebral hemisphere.

organize its functions in the same way! The result is that we have a long-standing system of anatomical names that does not always map neatly to the functional organization of the cerebral cortex itself. Some structures sprawl across many kinds of functional circuits, whereas others do not map well to any particular function.

The cerebral cortex consists of a layered, outer sheet of gray matter surrounding an inner white matter. As in other parts of the nervous system, the gray matter is composed mostly of the cell bodies of neurons and their local connections, and the white matter is composed of long-distance connection fibers linking neurons that are distant from one another. On the surface, the rounded convolutions of the cerebral cortex are called **gyri** (singular, **gyrus**), and the grooves between gyri are called **sulci** (singular, **sulcus**). As with the cerebellum, this crumpled pattern of gyri and sulci allows the brain to fit a large sheet of cerebral cortex into a small space while minimizing the distance between any two neurons (FIGURE 2.26).

A large midsagittal sulcus (also known as the longitudinal fissure) divides the cerebral cortex into left and right hemispheres, which have a lateral and a medial wall. On the medial wall, you can see the large bridge of white matter connections between the two hemispheres: the **corpus callosum**. The corpus callosum allows the left and right hemispheres to communicate with one another.

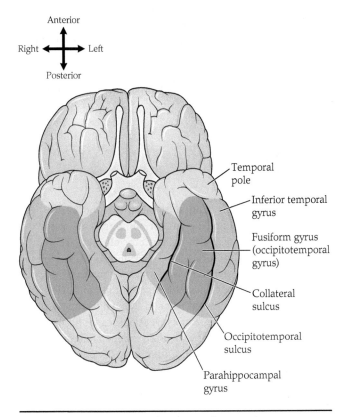

Anterior

Right ◄——————► Left

Posterior

Temporal pole

Inferior temporal gyrus

Fusiform gyrus (occipitotemporal gyrus)

Collateral sulcus

Occipitotemporal sulcus

Parahippocampal gyrus

FIGURE 2.26 **Major structures of the ventral (underside) surface of the cerebral cortex, with brainstem removed.**

Each hemisphere is composed of four smaller lobes: the **frontal lobe, temporal lobe, parietal lobe,** and **occipital lobe.** A large lateral sulcus runs along the side of each hemisphere of the cerebral cortex; below it lies the temporal lobe (under what we call the "temples" of the head). Above it, a vertical **central sulcus** lies between the frontal lobe and the more posterior parietal lobe. Behind the parietal and temporal lobes, at the back of the cerebral cortex, lies the occipital lobe. Each of these lobes has a variety of functions, which we'll consider in a moment. In addition, each lobe has further anatomical and functional subdivisions.

Broadly speaking, the dividing line between the "front" and the "back" of the cerebral cortex is the central sulcus. In rough terms, everything in front of the central sulcus does various forms of motor planning and action, whereas everything behind and below the central sulcus does various forms of sensory processing. Just in front of the central sulcus lies the **precentral gyrus**, which is home to the **primary motor cortex**: a long strip of areas that controls movements of individual body parts. In front of this gyrus are areas involved in planning movements. In front of those areas is the **prefrontal cortex**, which assembles more elaborate sequences of movement and behavior and is a major player in cognition and goal planning. The prefrontal cortex has a superior, middle, and inferior frontal gyrus on its lateral side. The medial prefrontal cortex lies along the medial wall of the frontal lobe. The underside of the prefrontal cortex, above the orbits of the eyes, is called the **orbitofrontal cortex**. It plays an important role in setting priorities and determining how valuable an action or a resource might be, given current needs. The olfactory cortex, which is important in the sense of smell, also lies in this area.

Just behind the central sulcus lies the **postcentral gyrus**, which is home to the **primary somatosensory cortex (S1)**: another strip of areas that handles sensory input from the skin, muscles, and joints of individual body parts. Behind it, the rest of the parietal lobe is divided into the inferior and superior parietal lobules. The dividing line between these lobules is the intraparietal sulcus, in which a large area of cerebral cortex is hidden. Superior parts of the parietal lobe play a key role in locating objects in space, like a more elaborate version of the midbrain's superior and inferior colliculi. This is useful for planning *where* to make movements in space. Inferior parts of the parietal lobe play a role in organizing stimuli according to their form rather than their location. This is useful for planning *what kind* of movements to make. The final part of the parietal lobe lies on the medial wall and is called the **precuneus**. It is one of the most active regions of the brain, even when we are at rest. It is active when we are imagining scenes and when we are navigating: thinking of destinations and finding directions to them.

Behind the parietal lobes lie the gyri of the occipital lobe. The occipital lobe is devoted to processing visual input and contains many different subregions for mapping out the various features of visual stimuli: position, orientation, shape, color, motion, and so on. The primary visual cortex lies on the medial wall of the occipital lobe, mostly tucked away inside the deep calcarine sulcus.

On the medial wall lies the visceral motor cortex of the **cingulate gyrus**, which wraps like a belt (Latin, "cingulum") around the hemisphere-spanning bridge of the corpus callosum. The cingulate gyrus is involved in many different functions, as we'll see in a moment.

Below the lateral sulcus lies the temporal lobe, with a **superior**, middle, and inferior **temporal gyrus** on its lateral side. The superior temporal cortex handles auditory information, with the **primary auditory cortex (A1)** tucked just inside the posterior part of the lateral sulcus. The underside of the temporal lobe has two more gyri: the **fusiform gyrus** and parahippocampal gyrus. These areas are associated with a *ventral visual pathway* that handles the identification, categorization, and evaluation of visual inputs: faces, houses, cars, animals, and other objects in the surroundings (Mahon et al., 2007; Q. Wang, Sporns, & Burkhalter, 2012).

Hidden away within the depths of the lateral sulcus lies a large area of cerebral cortex known as the **insula** (Latin, "island"). The insula is the visceral sensory part of the cerebral cortex. It represents the state of the internal organs and registers internal bodily states like pain, fatigue, hunger, sexual arousal, and so on (FIGURE 2.27). Taste receptors send input to the primary gustatory cortex, which lies in this area.

Basal Ganglia

The **basal ganglia** are a set of closely interconnected gray matter structures beneath the white matter of the cerebral

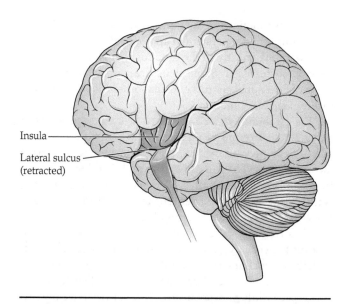

Insula

Lateral sulcus (retracted)

FIGURE 2.27 **The insula region of the cortex is hidden inside the lateral sulcus.** It represents the internal or visceral sensations of the body.

cortex (FIGURE 2.29). They play an important role in initiating and maintaining activity in the cerebral cortex, particularly in the motor control areas of the frontal lobes, which must often be driven by an organism's internal goals and needs. For example, the basal ganglia are involved in a diverse set of functions: limb movements, eye movements, planning and goal setting, motivation, and reward. We will consider the basal ganglia here in a brief overview.

The outermost structure is called the striatum. It consists of a comet-shape structure called the **caudate nucleus**

RESEARCH METHODS:
Cytoarchitecture of the Cortex

Biologists have made tremendous progress in learning about the circuitry of the nervous system. The word *cytoarchitecture* refers to the microscopic structure of the circuits of neurons within a part of the nervous system (FIGURE 2.28). In general terms, the cytoarchitecture of the cerebral cortex has many common features both across areas of the cortical sheet and across mammalian species. Most parts of the cerebral cortex have six layers, each with characteristic connections to other areas of the cerebral cortex, thalamus, cerebellum, and other parts of the nervous system. The relative thickness and appearance of each layer are slightly different in different cortical areas.

The subtle differences in the cytoarchitecture of different cortical regions can help us in mapping the functional anatomy of the brain. In a classic work in 1909, the German neuroanatomist Korbinian Brodmann created a map dividing the cerebral cortex into 52 distinct regions for nonhuman primates (and 43 distinct regions for humans), each with a different characteristic cytoarchitecture (Zilles & Amunts, 2010). He also created similar maps in other species. Although he did not assign different roles to these different regions, later investigators found that the borders often mapped fairly well to specific functions: Brodmann's area 17 corresponded to primary visual cortex, area 4 corresponded to primary motor cortex, and so on (Zilles & Amunts, 2010).

Neuroanatomists have continued to use differences in circuitry to distinguish functional areas in the cerebral cortex. Some maps divide the cerebral cortex into a different zone for each nucleus of the thalamus. Others look at patterns of long-distance connections to other brain regions, at the order in which the areas mature during development, or at the different kinds of receptors and proteins in each region (using immunohistochemical techniques, which employ antibodies as tracers of receptor or protein distribution). The most contemporary methods use an automated process in which the borders between areas are detected by computer algorithms reading microscopic slices of brain tissue. These slices are then reassembled to build maps of the brain. The maps can be compared across many individuals to understand not only the similarities but also the differences in brain architecture. Whatever method is used, cytoarchitectonic maps are based on the principle that the circuitry tells us something important about the function. By understanding these different types of circuits, neuroanatomists hope to unravel the puzzling fabric of the brain's many functions.

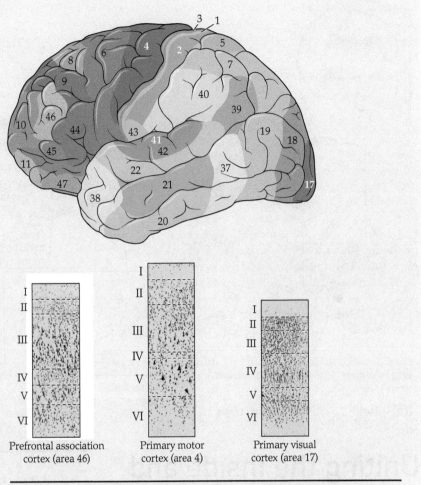

Prefrontal association cortex (area 46)

Primary motor cortex (area 4)

Primary visual cortex (area 17)

FIGURE 2.28 **The cortex can be divided into subregions based on cytoarchitecture: the microscopic appearance of the neural circuitry.** Several cytoarchitectonic maps of the brain are available. The most widely used is the Brodmann atlas, which divides the cortex into about 50 numbered regions.

and a round structure called the **putamen**, sitting within the "C" of the caudate. These two nuclei actually begin as a single structure, but as the brain develops, they become separated by the internal capsule: a massive tract of white matter heading from the cerebral cortex down to the spinal cord, brainstem, cerebellum, and thalamus. By the end of the fetal brain development process, the caudate nucleus and the putamen are connected by only a few thin stripes of gray matter: "striae," hence the collective term "striatum." The ventral striatum contains a structure known as the **nucleus accumbens**—an important player in reward and addiction, as we'll see in Chapter 14. Underneath the putamen lies another ovoid structure called the **globus pallidus** (Latin: "pale globe"), a critical area for regulating voluntary movement.

Other nearby structures work closely with the basal ganglia, even if they are not always considered under that umbrella term. Continuing inward from the globus pallidus, under the thalamus, we find the **subthalamic nucleus**. Below the subthalamic nucleus, we find the midbrain's substantia nigra. These areas are well connected to the basal ganglia, and they participate in the same functions.

The neurons of the basal ganglia are densely interconnected with the cerebral cortex, especially with the frontal cortex. Cortical neurons send connections down to the striatum, which in turn sends connections further inward to the internal and external globus pallidus, sometimes indirectly through the subthalamic nucleus. From here, the circuit continues on to the motor nuclei of the thalamus, which connect back to the original site of the cerebral cortex, forming a complete loop. Different loops or channels serve different regions of the cerebral cortex, which means that they have different functions, as mentioned earlier. We'll take a closer look at these functions in later chapters.

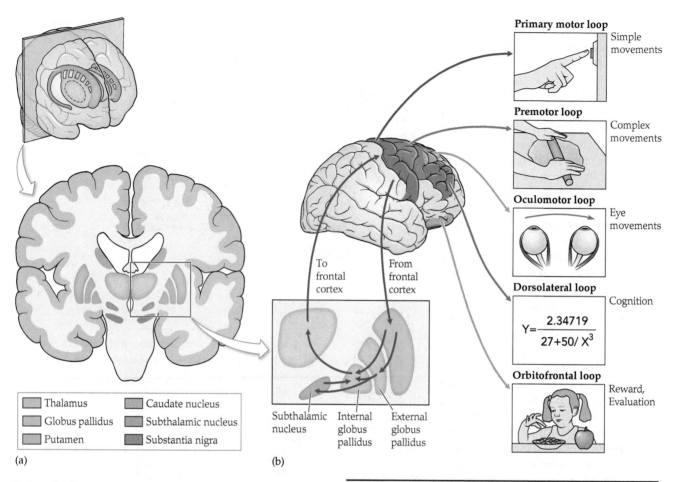

(a)

(b)

FIGURE 2.29 **Major structures of the basal ganglia.** (a) The basal ganglia consist of several gray matter structures beneath the gray and white matter of the cortex. (b) Loop circuits from the cortex through these structures allow the brain to initiate, maintain, and terminate various classes of thought and behavior.

Uniting the Inside and Outside Worlds

The Limbic System

As you have seen throughout this chapter, the nervous system contains distinct input and output pathways for dealing with the external environment and the internal environment. The brain takes input from the external environment via visual inputs from the eyes, auditory inputs from the ears, touch and position inputs from mechanical receptors in the skin and joints, and so on. It also takes input from the internal environment of the heart, lungs, blood and blood vessels, and other visceral tissues via a diverse set of pain, temperature, itch, chemical, and pressure sensors known as interoceptors (Craig, 2002). Likewise, the brain's output pathways include both motor neurons for controlling the muscles, joints, and skeleton to allow the body to take actions within the external environment and the neurons of the autonomic nervous system (both sympathetic and parasympathetic divisions) for controlling the internal environment of the heart, lungs, blood and blood vessels, and other visceral tissues.

The internal environment ("inner world") must, however, interface with the external environment ("outer world") at some point in the nervous system. At every level of the central nervous system, we can find regions where the sensory inputs from both internal and external environments converge to help guide control of the internal environment (Nauta, 1979; Nieuwenhuys, 2008). These areas are sometimes considered as forming their own system, central to motivation and emotion. They are known as the **limbic system**, from the Latin limbus or "border" (FIGURE 2.30).

The very concept of the limbic system is an old one, dating back to the middle of the 19th century (McLachlan, 2009). Over the years, most neuroscientists have agreed that the general concept of a brain system for emotion and motivation is a useful one. However, they have had difficulty agreeing on the details. Rarely do two books on neuroanatomy agree on exactly which brain structures are and are not part of the limbic system. Here we will take a look at some of the most agreed-on structures whose circuits bridge the gap between the brain's internal-environment sensory inputs and motor outputs. These structures have continuously

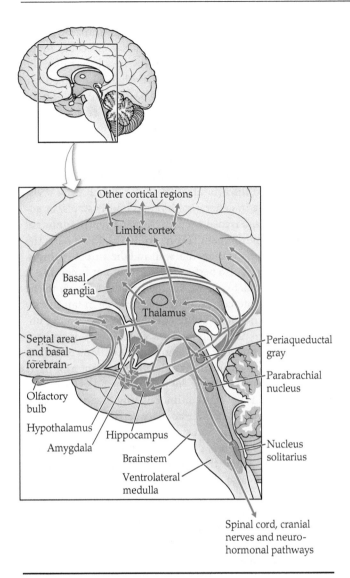

Other cortical regions

Limbic cortex

Basal ganglia

Thalamus

Septal area and basal forebrain

Periaqueductal gray

Parabrachial nucleus

Olfactory bulb

Hypothalamus

Hippocampus

Amygdala

Brainstem

Ventrolateral medulla

Nucleus solitarius

Spinal cord, cranial nerves and neurohormonal pathways

FIGURE 2.30 **The limbic system is a set of regions involved in generating the hormonal, autonomic, and motivational aspects of emotional states.** Core limbic structures include the hypothalamus, amygdala, and hippocampus, as well as some nuclei of the midbrain and brainstem. They also work closely with certain circuits through the basal ganglia and cortex.

proven themselves critical in the regulation of motivation and emotion.

The hypothalamus plays a key role in homeostasis and in motivation, as we saw earlier (for example, the motivation to go find water when thirsty). It is considered a core structure of the limbic system. Parts of the thalamus convey hypothalamic signals to the cerebral cortex; hence, these nuclei are sometimes called limbic nuclei of the thalamus. Certain parts of the midbrain, such as the periaqueductal gray, also link together visceral and somatic functions to produce simple kinds of motivated and emotional behavior. Also in the midbrain, substantia nigra neurons contain dopamine, a neurotransmitter that is central to motivation and reward. Neurons of the raphe nuclei contain serotonin,

a neurotransmitter that is also important for emotion and the regulation of internal states.

In our discussion of the hypothalamus, we saw how internal bodily states are the basis of motivations and drives: they reflect internal needs, but lead to external-world behavior. Emotions, too, are built on a foundation of internal bodily states. Imagine a time when you felt fear, anger, love, friendship, pride, embarrassment, shame, disgust, contentment, or joy: all of these emotions are underpinned by strong visceral sensations. Emotions can be used to assign value to otherwise neutral sensory stimuli from the external environment: a face is suddenly recognized as a friendly face or a house is recognized as one's own home.

In addition, two important limbic structures lie in the medial temporal lobes. The first of these is the **amygdala** (Greek for "almond," whose shape it vaguely resembles). The amygdala is similar to the hypothalamus in its outputs: it, too, can directly drive the internal states of the body through autonomic mechanisms and hormonal signals. It also sends outputs to the cerebral cortex to drive motivated behaviors, prioritization, goal setting, and action planning. However, its inputs are different from those of the hypothalamus. Rather than drawing on the inside world, the amygdala obtains input directly from the external-world senses of vision, hearing, and smell.

The amygdala is a necessary complement to the hypothalamus. After all, an organism whose only drives came from its own internal organs would not react to the external threat of a predator or a rival. Nor would it appreciate the value of an external opportunity like a meal or a mate. The amygdala generates emotions and motivations based on the external sensory inputs of vision, hearing, and smell, rather than internal-environment inputs as with the hypothalamus (FIGURE 2.31a). The amygdala is best known for its role in the "aversive" emotion of fear, but it plays a role in linking external sensory inputs to positive emotional states as well. It is a quick learner of new emotional associations and a key site for emotional memory.

The **hippocampus** is another critically important site for memory and learning. A long, thin structure whose fanciful name means "seahorse," it lies on the medial temporal lobes just behind the amygdala. It is traditionally considered a part of the limbic system, although its role in emotion and motivation is indirect. The hippocampus plays an important role in spatial navigation and **episodic memory**: memory for past personal experiences that occurred at a specific time and place, as opposed to memory for facts (FIGURE 2.31b). It also seems to be crucial for imagining future or hypothetical scenes, such as lying on a beach or going to a restaurant later in the day (Hassabis & Maguire, 2009; Schacter et al., 2012).

How are these functions of the hippocampus related to emotion and motivation? In a natural environment, the means of satisfying our needs are rarely nearby. A thirsty organism probably will not be able to find water in the immediate vicinity. Instead, it must search an internal map of its territory to locate a water source. Its internal map also needs to be kept up to date with past experiences, as new water sources appear and old ones dry up. Emotional associations with different locations are also important: being attacked at one water source might make that place worth avoiding in future, even if it happens to be in a convenient location. The hippocampus therefore has close connections with the

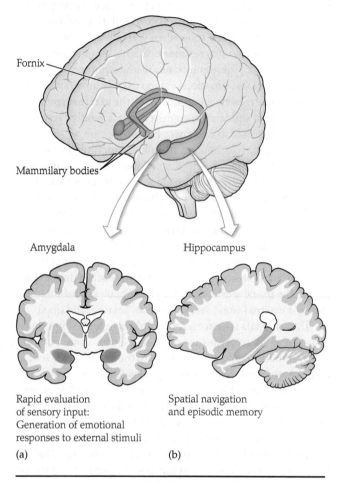

Rapid evaluation of sensory input: Generation of emotional responses to external stimuli

(a)

Spatial navigation and episodic memory

(b)

FIGURE 2.31 The amygdala and hippocampus are key limbic structures. (a) The almond-shaped amygdala uses external sensory input to trigger emotional responses. (b) The hippocampus is a key structure for creating memories of specific locations in space and specific events in time.

amygdala, which helps attach emotional significance to places or events (Richter-Levin & Akirav, 2000; Wells et al., 2011). It also has a major connection pathway via a loop called the **fornix** to a pair of nuclei in the hypothalamus, called the **mamillary bodies**. This circuit may be useful for linking the body's current needs to the organism's knowledge of places and past events (Sutherland & Rodriguez, 1989).

Parts of the cerebral cortex are sometimes considered limbic cortex. Limbic cortex forms a ring that starts with the visceral sensory cortex of the insula. The anterior part of the insula is next to the orbitofrontal cortex, which plays a visceral motor role in generating internal bodily states, or **somatic markers**, based on sensory input from the internal and external environment (Damasio, 1996). From here, the ring continues on to the medial wall and the **anterior cingulate cortex**, which also performs visceral motor functions. It follows the cingulate gyrus over the corpus callosum to the posterior cingulate cortex, which plays a role in familiarity and emotional memory. It then gradually passes to the underside of the medial temporal lobe, whose functions mirror the navigation, memory, and emotional functions of the adjacent hippocampus and amygdala. The most anterior parts of the medial temporal lobe lie next to the anterior insula, completing the ring. This continuous ring of cortex in each hemisphere provides an interface between the internal world and all of the remaining sensory, motor, cognitive, and other functions of the cerebral cortex as a whole. In the chapters ahead, we will see how the limbic system plays an important role in many different types of cognitive functions.

The Ventricular System and Brain Function

Our overview of the brain would be incomplete without describing the critical role of the ventricular system to brain function. The four **ventricles** (cavities) in your brain are

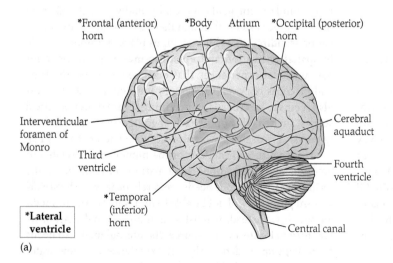

(a)

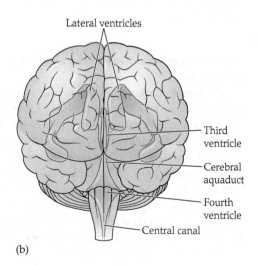

(b)

FIGURE 2.32 The ventricles of the brain.

filled with **cerebrospinal fluid**, not neurons (FIGURE 2.32). Two of these, the lateral ventricles, lie at the center of each hemisphere of the cerebral cortex, inside the white matter. These connect to the third ventricle, which lies along the midline of the brain, between the left and right thalamus. This connects to the fourth ventricle, a small triangular structure tucked between the brainstem and the cerebellum. The ventricles constantly produce cerebrospinal fluid, which circulates through the ventricles and over the surface of the brain and spinal cord. The fluid protects the brain from injury and helps to maintain a stable chemical environment for the neurons.

Conclusion

We began this chapter by exploring the remarkable similarities between the brains of the hog-nose bat and the adult male sperm whale, and we learned how the brains of all mammals possess a common underlying structure. In fact, the cognitive abilities of human beings arise from a nervous system whose fundamental organization has been highly conserved over time.

In exploring the peripheral nervous system, we focused on its segmental organization as well as on its subdivisions into the somatic and autonomic nervous systems. The sympathetic and parasympathetic subsystems of the autonomic nervous system enable the body to operate in "fight-or-flight" and "rest-and-regenerate" modes, respectively. In exploring the central nervous system, we learned about the structure and functions of the spinal cord as well as about the basics of how spinal reflexes and central pattern generators work. Furthermore, we learned about the anatomy and the life-sustaining functions of the brainstem. We explored the complex structure of the cerebellum. Scientists agree that the cerebellum plays a key role in coordinating movement, but they debate its exact role in refining movements and in matching movements to the environment. Moreover, we learned about the role of the hypothalamus in homeostasis and the critical role of the thalamus as a relay station in the brain. Then we arrived at the highest level of the brain: the cerebral cortex. The cerebral cortex is divided into four lobes: the frontal lobe, temporal lobe, parietal lobe, and occipital lobe, each of which contributes uniquely to brain function. We learned how scientists have studied the cytoarchitecture of different cortical regions and have used the differences in circuitry across these regions to map the functional anatomy of the brain.

We learned about the structures of the basal ganglia, which help to initiate and maintain internally driven cortical activity. Finally, we concluded our journey through the nervous system by exploring the limbic system, which unites the internal and external worlds and is the system that modulates motivation and emotions.

As we conclude our survey of the nervous system, let's take a step back once again and look at all of these layers of looping circuits from a broader point of view. We have seen short and simple circuits like reflex arcs, where signals move from sensory input to motor output in only a synapse or two. We have seen the more complex circuits of central pattern generators, command generators, the behavioral programs of the periaqueductal gray, and the still more elaborate homeostatic coordination of the hypothalamus. We have seen the reverberating and refining loops across multiple synapses through the cerebellum, thalamus, cortex, and basal ganglia.

How do we unravel this knot of knots? What is this whole system trying to accomplish, in the most general terms? To solve this problem, we'll borrow a trick from ancient Greek mythology. The legendary hero Theseus used a ball of string to trace his path when he entered the original Labyrinth to battle the half-human Minotaur. After winning the battle, he followed the string through the Labyrinth's twists and turns until at last he was safely back out of the maze.

Let's flatten out all the complex anatomy of the brain into a two-dimensional maze. Now, let's drop ourselves into a randomly chosen neuron in the brain and then follow its connections, synapse by synapse, until we emerge from the maze. What we'll find is that, depending on which neuron we choose and whether we travel backward or forward, we'll end up in one of four places.

We might end up in an external sensory neuron: a photoreceptor in the retina, an auditory receptor in the cochlea, a motion sensor in the vestibular organ, a touch receptor in the skin. External-world sensors make up one "edge" of the nervous system. Alternatively, we might end up at the end of a motor neuron, where it stimulates a skeletal muscle to move the body through the outside world. External-world movements make up a second edge of the nervous system. Sometimes the paths between these two edges are short, as in a reflex arc. Others, through the cerebellum or cortex and basal ganglia, are long and looped in circles along the way. We'll draw these edges as the upper two sides of a square; now we can see the many possible pathways of various different lengths (FIGURE 2.33).

We also might end up at an *internal* sensory neuron: a visceral pain receptor in the stomach, a pressure-sensing baroreceptor in a blood vessel, or an inflammation-sensing histamine receptor in the intestinal tract. These receptors make up a second sensory edge of the nervous system, with its own set of pathways distinct from the external sensory apparatus. Finally, we might end up traveling through the autonomic nervous system and its peripheral ganglia, to end up in a visceral motor neuron, stimulating an internal organ into its fight-or-flight or rest-and-regenerate mode. Again, the pathways between these two edges may be short, as in the simple visceral reflex arcs of the spinal cord. They may also be long, passing through multiple stages and loops, up to the hypothalamus, or even beyond, to the limbic regions of the cortex.

From this perspective, we can see the nervous system as an enormous network, half rooted in the body of the

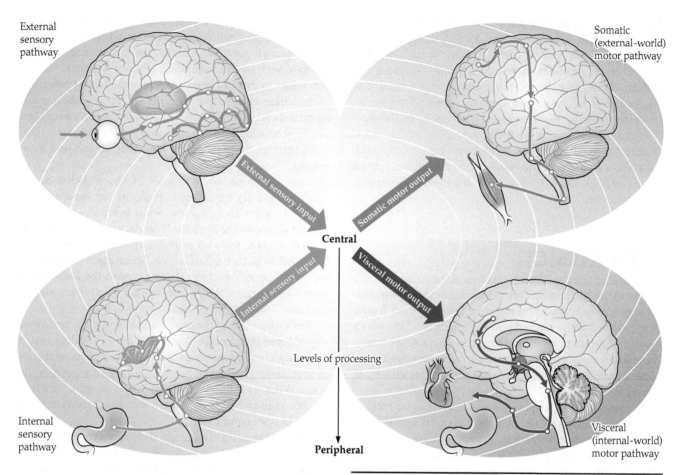

FIGURE 2.33   **The four-sided brain.** We can think of the vast network of all neurons in the nervous system as having four edges. external-world sensory neurons for the major senses, internal-world sensory neurons for internal bodily senses, external-world motor neurons to move the body, and internal-world "motor" neurons to control the internal organs. The many layers of connections among these four edges make up the entirety of the central nervous system, allowing it to answer two key survival questions: "what's going on inside and outside me?" and "what do I do about it?"

organism and half dangling out in the external environment in which it lives. Its pathways carry information back and forth, constantly trying to bridge the gap between these two worlds. To do so, they ask four questions, one for each edge of the network: What is happening out there? What is happening in here? What should I do out there? What should I do in here?

In response to the need for more complex behaviors, the human nervous system has added on longer and longer circuits, inserting more and more interneurons between the input and the output, and building more and more complex circuits. The result is a brain capable of meeting the body's basic needs in astonishingly complex ways. As humans, we plan far ahead to survive and thrive. We deliberately alter our environment over years and even entire generations to better suit our needs. We arrange complex societies in which many can prosper simply by acquiring and using specialized knowledge. We pursue careers or chase lifelong dreams.

In this rarefied environment, many of us could live our entire lives and raise a new generation without ever needing to know how to forage for food, or avoid a predator, or survive a night in the cold. All of these activities are unprecedented

in the 3 billion–year history of life on Earth. As we have seen, the underlying structure of the human brain is not drastically different from that of our nearest living relatives. In fact, we still share many common features with our ancestors of 5, 50, or even 500 million years ago. Yet there is clearly something new and unique about the way that human beings are using the basic machinery of cognition. As we look at this machinery over the rest of the chapters in this book, try to keep this point in mind. Neuroscience is ultimately a concerted, precise effort to understand ourselves using the very brains we study. Neuroscience should tell us a story not only about our nervous system, but also about human nature: who we are and what we are capable of achieving.

KEY PRINCIPLES

- All vertebrates have a nervous system featuring segmental organization and an expansion at the front end for centralized control, using internal and external sensory inputs. Ever-more-complex circuits linking sensory input and motor output are added on top of one another, at multiple levels of the nervous system, to allow more and more complex forms of behavior.

- The peripheral nervous system collects sensory input from both inside and outside the body and transmits it to the central nervous system. The peripheral nervous system carries output signals to the internal organs as well as the muscles of the body.

- Simple spinal reflexes allow sensory inputs to direct motor outputs with minimal involvement of the central nervous system. Central pattern generators allow for more complex, coordinated movements such as locomotion.

- In the brainstem, more elaborate reflexes and central pattern generators operate in the handling of special sensory input and in the control of the special movements of the head region.

- The brainstem includes the medulla oblongata, pons, and midbrain. These regions relay sensory and motor information between the brain and spinal cord and are the point of origin for most of the cranial nerves.

- The cerebellum contains the majority of neurons in the central nervous system, and these are organized as folia, grouped into lobules, which are further grouped into lobes.

- The extensive circuitry of the cerebellum allows for smooth, accurate, coordinated movements.

- The hypothalamus coordinates homeostatic functions, including sleep and eating, to keep the body's internal environment in balance. The thalamus is a relay center that coordinates the flow of sensory information to the cerebral cortex. It also coordinates information flow between distant areas of the cerebral cortex itself.

- The cerebral cortex provides the nervous system's most elaborate circuitry for sensory, motor, and intermediate functions. It is divided into four lobes: the frontal lobe, temporal lobe, parietal lobe, and occipital lobe.

- Circuits of the basal ganglia initiate and maintain internally driven cortical activity, particularly that related to motor control.

- The limbic system includes the hypothalamus, parts of the thalamus, the substantia nigra, the amygdala, the hippocampus, and the limbic regions of the cortex. Collectively, these regions have important motivational and emotional functions.

- Overall, the circuits of the nervous system bridge the gap between sensation and action in the internal and external worlds, linking the questions of *What's happening in here and out there?* to *What should I do in here and out there?*

KEY TERMS

An Overview of the Nervous System

spinal cord (p. 39)

central nervous system (p. 41)

peripheral nervous system (p. 41)

forebrain (p. 41)

midbrain (mesencephalon) (p. 41)

hindbrain (p. 41)

telencephalon (p. 41)

diencephalon (p. 41)

metencephalon (p. 41)

myelencephalon (p. 41)

rostral (p. 42)

caudal (p. 42)

dorsal (p. 42)

ventral (p. 42)

anterior (p. 42)

posterior (p. 42)

superior (p. 42)

inferior (p. 42)

medial (p. 42)

lateral (p. 42)

ipsilateral (p. 42)

contralateral (p. 43)

distal (p. 43)

proximal (p. 43)

The Peripheral Nervous System

sensory neurons (p. 43)

motor neurons (p. 43)

neuromuscular junction (p. 43)

neurotransmitters (p. 43)

somatic nervous system (p. 43)

autonomic nervous
   system (p. 43)

sympathetic nervous
   system (p. 43)

parasympathetic nervous
   system (p. 43)

dermatomes (p. 45)

The Spinal Cord

gray matter (p. 47)

white matter (p. 47)

stem cells (p. 47)

ventral horns (p. 48)

dorsal root ganglion (p. 48)

reflex (p. 48)

synapse (p. 48)

interneuron (p. 48)

stretch reflex (p. 48)

central pattern generator
   (p. 49)

The Brainstem

brainstem (p. 51)

medulla oblongata (p. 51)

pons (p. 51)

cranial nerves (p. 51)

cerebrum (p. 51)

nuclei (p. 52)

superior colliculus (p. 53)

inferior colliculus (p. 53)

periaqueductal gray matter
   (p. 53)

reticular formation (p. 54)

locus coeruleus (p. 54)

norepinephrine (p. 54)

substantia nigra (p. 54)

dopamine (p. 54)

midbrain raphe nuclei
   (p. 54)

serotonin (p. 54)

The Cerebellum

cerebellum (p. 56)

Purkinje cells (p. 56)

forward model (p. 57)

The Diencephalon: Hypothalamus and Thalamus

hypothalamus (p. 57)

thalamus (p. 57)

set points (p. 57)

hormone (p. 58)

pituitary gland (p. 58)

oxytocin (p. 58)

cerebral cortex (p. 58)

lateral geniculate nucleus
   (p. 59)

photoreceptors (p. 59)

primary visual cortex
   (V1) (p. 59)

association areas (p. 59)

reticular nucleus (p. 60)

deep brain stimulation (p. 61)

The Telencephalon: Cerebral Cortex and Basal Ganglia

gyri (singular, gyrus) (p. 63)

sulci (singular, sulcus) (p. 63)

corpus callosum (p. 63)

frontal lobe (p. 63)

temporal lobe (p. 63)

parietal lobe (p. 63)

occipital lobe (p. 63)

central sulcus (p. 63)

precentral gyrus (p. 63)

primary motor cortex (p. 63)

prefrontal cortex (p. 63)

orbitofrontal cortex (p. 63)

postcentral gyrus (p. 63)

primary somatosensory
   cortex (S1) (p. 63)

precuneus (p. 63)

cingulate gyrus (p. 64)

superior temporal gyrus
   (p. 64)

primary auditory cortex (A1)
   (p. 64)

fusiform gyrus (p. 64)

insula (p. 64)

basal ganglia (p. 64)

caudate nucleus (p. 64)

putamen (p. 65)

nucleus accumbens (p. 65)

globus pallidus (p. 65)

subthalamic nucleus (p. 65)

Uniting the Inside and Outside Worlds

limbic system (p. 66)

amygdala (p. 67)

hippocampus (p. 67)

episodic memory (p. 67)

fornix (p. 68)

mamillary bodies (p. 68)

somatic markers (p. 68)

anterior cingulate cortex
   (p. 68)

ventricles (p. 68)

cerebrospinal fluid (p. 69)

REVIEW QUESTIONS

1. Why do vertebrates collect their neurons into a brain?

2. Draw a simple human body as seen from the front and the side. A stick figure will do. Now add labeled arrows illustrating all 14 anatomical directions listed in this chapter. Draw and label three lines showing the angles of an axial, a coronal, and a midsagittal slice through the head.

3. List the components and subcomponents of the peripheral nervous system. Summarize the function of each one in a short sentence.

4. Define dermatomes and myotomes. What are the likely effects of a spinal cord injury at the level of the neck? At the level of the lower back?

5. Explain the mechanism by which a tap below the kneecap can produce a vigorous kick of the leg. Explain how spinal cord circuits can generate simple, alternating movements useful for locomotion.

6. Describe three important functions of the brainstem. Why can an injury to the medulla oblongata be fatal, even if the rest of the brain is unharmed? Describe three categories of behavior coordinated in the midbrain.

7. Describe the homeostatic functions of the hypothalamus. How might your hypothalamus try to compensate when it senses that you are dehydrated?

8. List the four lobes of the cerebral cortex, and give one example of a function contributed by each lobe. What is meant by the term *cytoarchitecture*, and why is cytoarchitecture helpful in understanding brain function?

9. What are the structures of the basal ganglia? How do they contribute to the activity of the cerebral cortex?

10. What is meant by the term *limbic system*? What brain structures are typically considered part of the limbic system? What functions do they perform?

CRITICAL-THINKING QUESTIONS

1. Why do you think that the sympathetic and parasympathetic nervous systems exist in completely separate segmental regions? What functional advantage(s) do you think such segmentation might convey?

2. Imagine that, for one week, you had to suffer from the malfunction of one of three brain structures: your cerebellum, hippocampus, or amygdala. During that week, you had to try to go about your daily routine as much as possible. Which of these three brain structures would you choose to malfunction, and why? In your response, consider the neural pathways in which each of these three brain structures is involved.

3. Imagine that you could choose to have the functioning of one of the four lobes of your cerebral cortex significantly enhanced: the frontal lobe, temporal lobe, parietal lobe, or occipital lobe. Which lobe would you choose, and why? In what specific ways might your everyday life be different if that lobe of your brain were even more powerful in its functioning than it is now?

- Distinguish the major types of cells in the brain.

- Isolate the structures of the neurons that allow neurons to collect, integrate, and output signals.

- Explain how chemical signaling operates at a synapse.

- Describe the mechanisms of an action potential.

- Summarize the type of information carried by action potentials.

- Characterize how the neural code can be distributed across populations of neurons.

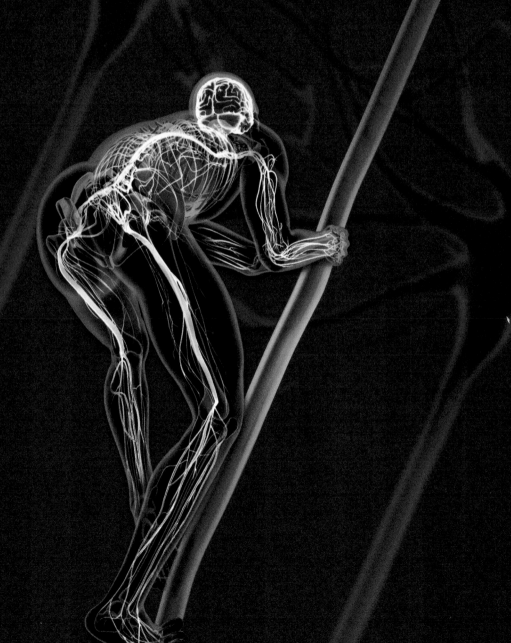

Neurons and Synapses

STARTING OUT:
The Kabuki Actor and the Pufferfish

Bandō Mitsugorō VIII (1906–1975) was one of Japan's most beloved Kabuki actors and was named as a living treasure during his lifetime by the government. In a drunk and pompous display in a restaurant, he claimed immunity from poisoning and demanded four livers of the infamous puffer fish, known in Japanese as *fugu* fish (FIGURE 3.1). The chef, who later claimed to be unable to turn down the request of such a famous celebrity, apprehensively served the livers. Mitsugorō bravely consumed the livers and quickly went into complete paralysis. Since he could not breathe without proper muscle control, he died after seven hours.

Fugu fish contains a molecule called tetrodotoxin, an extremely powerful poison with no known antidote. There is nothing especially striking about the structure of the molecule itself: like all molecules, it is simply several atoms hooked together in a particular way. What makes it *lethal*?

FIGURE 3.1 **The tasty but deadly fugu, or puffer, fish contains tetrodotoxin, which prevents the transmission of action potentials.**

The answer is that tetrodotoxin, like many similar poisons, prevents the transmission of *action potentials*, the electrical signals by which neurons communicate quickly over long distances. In the presence of tetrodotoxin, the brain sends out commands to which the body cannot respond, because the electrical signals never reach their destination. Since the muscles cannot move (and this includes the diaphragm muscles critical to breathing), victims die of suffocation.

In this chapter we will learn about the processes with which tetrodotoxin interferes. We will learn how neurons communicate with one another, what their signals mean, and why getting drunk and claiming that you cannot be poisoned does not accord with your neurobiology.

The overall goal of the nervous system is to enable the organism to move its body appropriately to succeed at the four F's: feeding, fleeing, fighting, and reproducing. To move adaptively, the organism uses information about what is going on inside its body (I am hot; I am thirsty) and outside its body (there is shade under that ledge; there is water at the end of the meadow), so that it can make predictions about external and internal events and act accordingly. Your eyes and ears carry signals about external events by responding to physical stimuli such as light patterns and sound waves. At the behavioral end, motor neurons command the muscles to contract or relax, and this loop constructs an ever-changing decision stream about what is being sensed and what the body should do about it. Complexity emerges as the population of neurons between motor and sensory systems expands to enable more sophisticated prediction. And at the heart of it all is an unimaginably vast network of cells within the nervous system that send lightning-fast signals through a network to allow this all to happen. In this chapter we'll study those cells in detail.

In the previous chapter we learned how the overall structure of the brain allows signals from the periphery (for example, from your eyes and fingertips) to flow in, get processed, and go out to influence in the outside world (for

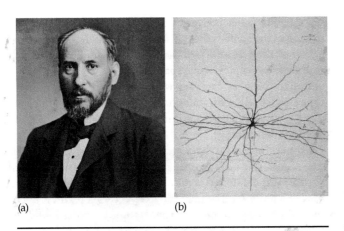

(a)   (b)

FIGURE 3.2 Visualizing brain cells. (a) Santiago Ramón y Cajal (1852–1934). (b) One of Cajal's first renderings of a neuron impregnated with his staining technique.

example, picking up a cup of coffee). But that level of understanding, by itself, does not allow us to understand how pharmaceutical drugs work, why drugs of abuse are self-administered, what happens in diseases like Alzheimer's, how hormones influence your drives, and why people make risky decisions—all topics that we'll be tackling in later chapters. To set the stage for these issues, we'll now zoom in to the individual cells in the nervous system and how they communicate with each other. This chapter will contain many terms that may be new to you, but try to keep in mind a key principle: neurons communicate in a vast network by chemical and electrical signals. We need to appreciate the detailed biology to understand how the signaling carries information and how that information can be modified by pharmaceutical drugs, hormones, drugs of abuse, and disease.

The Cells of the Brain

Imagine how you would think of the brain if you lived 120 years ago. Because the brain has the consistency of slightly hardened mashed potatoes, you would have no idea of what it was actually composed. You might suppose, for

example, that it is made of a continuous series of tubes through which substances flow. And you'd be in good company. Just over a century ago, before the advent of good microscopy, most scientists supposed that neural tissue was a continuous network like the blood vessels (Cimino, 1999; Lopez-Munoz, Boya, & Alamo, 2006). This idea was overturned by the Spanish neuroscientist Santiago Ramón y Cajal, who used new techniques to stain and visualize brain tissue and realized that the brain is built of billions of *discrete* cells (FIGURE 3.2). His "neuron doctrine," which stated that cells in the brain are separate entities, ushered in an important new mystery: the cells somehow need ways to communicate with each other over the tiny spaces that separate them. This chapter is about that signaling. Amazingly, from the enormous symphony of activity of these cells, behavior and cognition emerge.

Neurons: A Close-Up View

The most important type of cell in your nervous system is a **neuron** (FIGURE 3.3). The human brain contains almost 100 billion neurons (Herculano-Houzel, 2012). Neurons are, in most ways, like all the other cells in your body: they have a **membrane**, nucleus, and specialized organelles and they produce, traffic, and secrete chemicals. The cell's membrane separates the cell's components from the environment outside of the cell. Like other cell types, neurons have proteins that are inserted into their membranes, and these proteins allow the cell to interact with its outside environment. But neurons possess an additional property that distinguishes them: because of the particular proteins on their surfaces, they can transmit electrical signals quickly over long distances. And when those electrical signals arrive at their end point(s), they trigger a specialized form of chemical signaling. In the next few sections we will learn how these forms of signaling take place. But first we will turn to the specialized anatomy that gives a neuron its remarkable capabilities.

Neurons have four zones of importance. The first consists of the **dendrites**, which are long, branching extensions from the cell body. Dendritic trees can take on many shapes and sizes—from single branches to large cones, pancakes, or

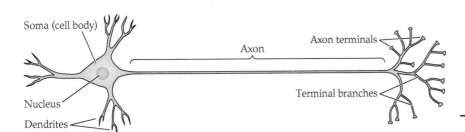

Soma (cell body)

Axon

Axon terminals

Nucleus

Terminal branches

Dendrites

FIGURE 3.3 A typical neuron in the cortex.

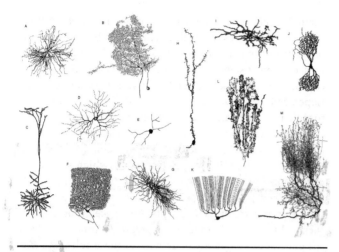

FIGURE 3.4 **Dendrites.** The integrators of thousands of tiny chemical signals come in a variety of shapes.

spheres (FIGURE 3.4). As we will explore in the next section, dendrites are specialized for *collecting* information from thousands of tiny chemical signals that they receive all along their extent.

By responding to chemical messages along their intricate branching patterns, dendrites collect a great deal of information and pass it to the second zone of importance: the **soma**

or **cell body** (*soma* is Greek for "body") (FIGURE 3.5). The key feature of the soma is the cell's **nucleus**, which is the control center of the cell that regulates cell activity, including gene expression. A typical soma spans about 10–25 micrometers, although the sizes can vary widely across different neuron types. As we will see in this chapter, the soma plays a key role in *integrating* (that is, summing up) the signals coming in from the dendrites.

Emerging from the soma is the single, long slender process of the **axon**, or nerve fiber, which is the third zone of importance (FIGURE 3.6). The axon is an extension that reaches long distances beyond the soma, and it is essentially a cable to *conduct* signals rapidly across long distances, as we will see shortly. The axon differs from the dendrites in three ways. First, there is only one axon coming from a neuron, whereas there can be many dendritic extensions. Second, axons tend to remain constant in diameter all along their length, whereas dendrites are tapered. Finally, axons tend to be much longer than dendrites: dendritic trees rarely extend more than 3 millimeters, whereas axons carrying signals from your spinal cord to your big toe (the sciatic nerve) run the entire length of your leg—and in giraffes, axons several meters in length run the entire span of the neck!

A typical axon will branch robustly at its end, typically splitting into about 10,000 **axon terminals** (sometimes called axonal boutons or buttons)—and these terminals constitute the fourth zone of importance (FIGURE 3.7). The terminals are identifiable as small swellings at the end tips and, as we will see, they contain packages of chemicals that can be released into the space between cells. The terminals, therefore, are optimized for the *output* of signals.

Axon terminals are typically found in close proximity to the dendrites and somas of other cells, and such junctions are called synapses (*syn* is Greek for "together" and *haptein* "to clasp"). Santiago Ramón y Cajal poetically described the synapse as a "protoplasmic kiss" between two cells (Ramón y Cajal, 1937). The main location of signal transmission, the synapse links an axon to other neurons (in the central nervous system) or to a neuron, muscle, or gland (in the peripheral nervous system). Although most synapses occur at the axon terminals, they can also exist along the axon itself, and in this case they are known as *en passant* synapses. The typical synapse connects an axon to a

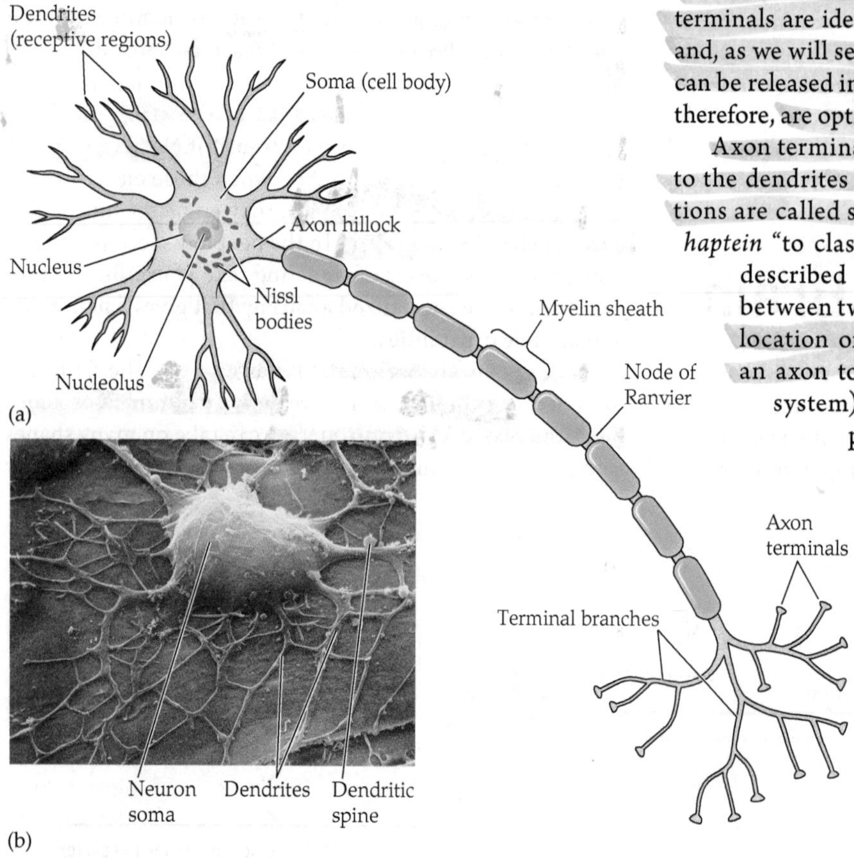

Dendrites
(receptive regions)

Soma (cell body)

Axon hillock

Nucleus

Nissl
bodies

Myelin sheath

Nucleolus

Node of
Ranvier

(a)

Axon
terminals

Terminal branches

Neuron   Dendrites   Dendritic
soma   spine

(b)

FIGURE 3.5 **The cell body, or soma, is the central command center of a neuron.** The dendrites and a single axon grow from the soma, the former for collecting incoming signals and the latter for transmitting outgoing signals over long distances.

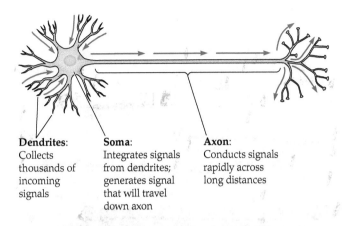

Dendrites:
Collects
thousands of
incoming
signals

Soma:
Integrates signals
from dendrites;
generates signal
that will travel
down axon

Axon:
Conducts signals
rapidly across
long distances

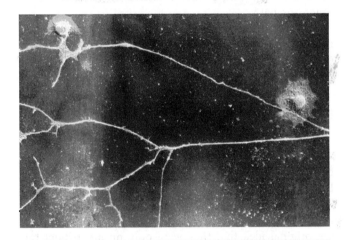

FIGURE 3.6 **An axon is a single, slender extension from the soma.** It is essentially a cable to conduct signals rapidly across long distances.

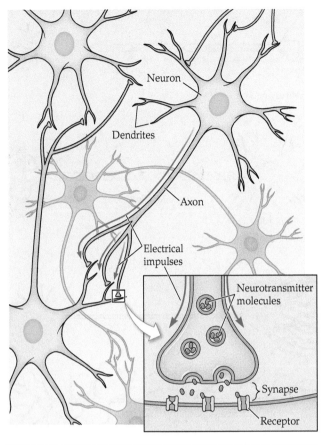

FIGURE 3.7 **Axon terminals are the end points of the axon, where chemical signals are released.**

dendrite or soma. There are also synapses that can join axon to axon or dendrite to dendrite, although these are more rare.

The number of synapses in the brain is boggling: in a three-year-old brain, the total number of synapses is estimated to be a quadrillion (1 followed by 15 zeros) (Alonso-Nanclares, Gonzalez-Soriano, Rodriguez, & DeFelipe, 2008). Synapse numbers decrease with age through a natural pruning process; therefore, an adult brain contains somewhere between 100 and 500 trillion synapses (Drachman, 2005) in a total volume of about 1,200 cubic centimeters (Cosgrove, Mazure, & Staley, 2007). For a typical college student, this means that a cubic millimeter of cerebral cortex contains several billion of these tiny connections—about as many people as exist on the planet.

As we will come to understand in this chapter, the four zones of a neuron foreshadow its critical functions: *collecting* (dendrites), *integrating* (soma), *conducting* (axon), and *outputting information* (axon terminals). The synapses are the point where the axon terminals contact the next cells, and here the chain of signaling continues.

Many Different Types of Neurons

Dendrites, soma, axons, and axon terminals are characteristic features of all neurons, but there is nonetheless a great deal of diversity among neuron types.

The most common way to classify neurons is by their function. Sensory neurons are those that directly respond to signals from the outside environment—for example, light, sound waves, pressure, or odors (FIGURE 3.8a). Motor neurons have direct output to muscles or glands; they are the final step for signals to exit the nervous system and effect change in the body or environment (FIGURE 3.8b). You may sometimes hear the term **afferent neuron** for the incoming (sensory) neurons and **efferent neuron** for the outgoing (or motor) neurons. (These terms can be remembered by associating *afferent* with *arrival* and *efferent* with *exit*). In mammals the vast majority of neurons cannot be classified as either sensory or motor—instead, they are the interneurons between the sensation of a signal at the one end and the action at the other end (FIGURE 3.8c). Primitive animals such

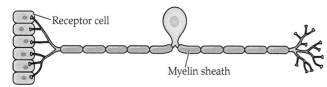

(a) Sensory neuron

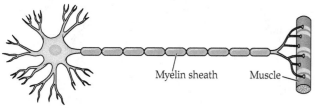

(b) Motor neuron

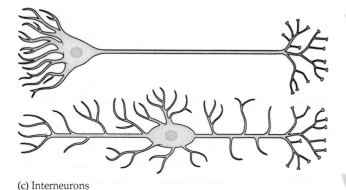

(c) Interneurons

FIGURE 3.8 **Different types of neurons.** Examples of (a) sensory neurons, (b) motor neurons, and (c) interneurons. Interneurons can be of two types: those with long projections to other regions are termed projection interneurons, whereas those that stay within a region are termed local interneurons.

as jellyfish have neurons that contain both sensory and motor qualities in the same cell, but this combination is not found in more advanced species. Evolutionarily, it is thought that mammalian brains have developed by a dissociation of sensory and motor neurons into separate cell types, followed by the gradual insertion of more and more neurons in between (Miller, 2009). By the time we reach the human

brain, almost all the neurons are "in between" the sensory and motor ends.

An alternative way of classifying neurons hinges on their basic shape. In this classification scheme, **multipolar neurons** are those with multiple dendrites (FIGURE 3.9a); these are the most common class. **Bipolar neurons**, on the other hand, are composed of a single dendrite on one end and a single axon on the other (FIGURE 3.9b); these are often found in sensory neurons such as the retina and inner ear. Finally, **monopolar neurons** have only a single extension that leaves the soma and branches in two directions (FIGURE 3.9c). One end of a monopolar neuron receives the information and the other end serves for output. This type of neuron is typically found in sensory neurons that signal touch and pain.

Although there are many types of neurons, it should be noted that they all share in common the feature of being postmitotic—that is, they do not divide like many other cell types in the body.

Glial Cells

Neurons receive the most scientific attention because of their long reach and ability to carry rapid electrical signals. But there is another type of cell that plays a wide range of supporting roles in the nervous system: the **glial cells**, or **glia**. "Glia" comes from the Greek word for "glue," reflecting the original idea that they were only meant to hold the network of neurons together (Kettenmann & Verkhratsky, 2008). Although the full functional capacity of the glial cell is still under intensive study, it is clear that these cells play several roles, providing ways to speed up the signaling from neurons, regulating the concentrations of extracellular chemicals, and determining the extent to which networks of neurons can modify their connections (Allen & Barres, 2009).

Although neurons come in hundreds of forms, glia come in only four basic types. The first is **oligodendrocytes**, large cells whose main function is to wrap a layer of "insulation" around axons—a process known as myelination—similar to the way that a copper wire is wrapped in rubber. The consequence of myelination is the speeding up of electrical signaling by neurons, a topic we'll explore in detail later in the

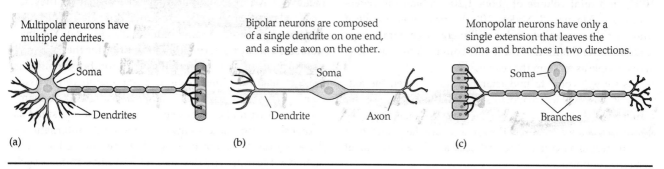

FIGURE 3.9 **Classifying neurons by their shape.** Examples of (a) multipolar neurons, (b) bipolar neurons, and (c) monopolar neurons.

RESEARCH METHODS:
Visualizing Neurons and Their Products

The discovery that neurons are discrete, fundamental units of the nervous system was made possible by the ability to stain them. Several techniques allow the visualization of neurons. **Golgi staining** is a technique that impregnates some fraction of neurons with a dark material, allowing the entirety of individual cells to be seen under a microscope (FIGURE 3.10a). This is the method that birthed Ramón y Cajal's neuron doctrine. Another technique, **Nissl staining**, uses a chemical that binds to the RNA in cell bodies, thereby allowing the visualization of somas (FIGURE 3.10b). Nissl staining is most commonly used for judging sizes of cells and their densities.

Several other methods are utilized to obtain detailed pictures of nervous tissue. In the technique of **autoradiography**, a radioactive substance is designed to be taken up by specific cells but not by others (FIGURE 3.10c). Then, when a photographic emulsion is placed over thin slices of the brain tissue, the emulsion is exposed by the radioactivity in the same way that film is exposed by light. In this way, it can be seen which cell types absorbed the substance in question (for example, a pharmaceutical drug).

In the technique of **immunocytochemistry**, antibodies are developed that bind only to specific proteins (FIGURE 3.10d). These antibodies are washed onto a slice of brain tissue, and they attach wherever the protein of interest is being expressed. With some chemical steps, these antibodies can be visualized, revealing the exact locations of the protein within the cell. A related technique is to use radioactively labeled stretches of RNA or **DNA** that will bind to specific stretches of messenger RNA (mRNA); this is called *in situ* **hybridization**, and it reveals which cells have expressed a gene of interest (FIGURE 3.10e).

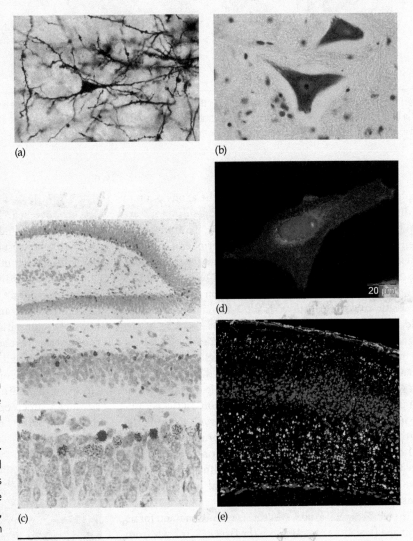

(a)

(b)

(d)

(c)

(e)

FIGURE 3.10 **Different techniques to bring the invisibly small world of neurons to light.** (a) Golgi staining, (b) Nissl staining, (c) autoradiography, (d) immunocytochemistry, and (e) *in situ* hybridization.

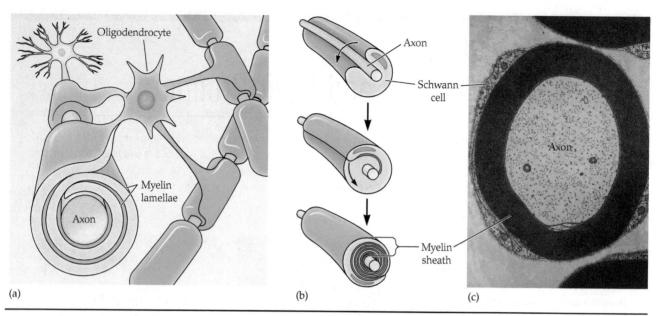

(a)   (b)   (c)

FIGURE 3.11 **Some glial cells myelinate axons.** (a) In the central nervous system, a single oligodendrocyte will wrap up to 50 different axons with myelin sheaths. (b) In the peripheral nervous system, myelination is accomplished by Schwann cells, which wrap around a single axon. Note that the layer of insulation is not continuous, but exists in small sections. (c) Transmission electron micrograph of a myelin sheath.

chapter. A single oligodendrocyte wraps the axons of up to 50 different neurons (FIGURE 3.11a). Oligodendrocytes are found only in the central nervous system; the function of myelination is accomplished in the peripheral nervous system by a second type of glial cell, the **Schwann cells** (FIGURE 3.11b). Schwann cells are quite similar in function to oligodendrocytes, with the minor exception that a Schwann cell wraps **myelin** around only a single axon (Bhatheja & Field, 2006). **Myelin sheaths** are not continuous along the length of an axon, but instead come in short segments (about 100 micrometers), appearing in a microscope like a string of sausages. The gaps between the myelinated segments are called **nodes of Ranvier**, which you will learn more about later in this chapter. Given the length of axons in the peripheral nervous system (recall the sciatic nerve that runs the length of your leg), this translates to an enormous number of glial cells that contribute to the insulation of each axon. Note that many axons do not become myelinated, especially those in the cortex, but most subcortical and peripheral axons do take on myelination.

The third type of glial cell is the **astrocyte**, named for its star shape (FIGURE 3.12a; *astro* from the Greek "star," *cyte* from "cell"). Beyond physical structural support, astrocytes perform critical functions in maintaining the balance of chemicals outside the neurons, the repair of injury in the central nervous system, the contribution of nutrients, the regulation of local blood flow to a region, and the release of chemical signals (Fellin, 2009). The fourth type of glial cell is the **microglia** (FIGURE 3.12b). Making up 20% of the glial cell population, these small cells are the front line of immune

defense in the central nervous system: they are constantly on the move, searching for any infectious agents that might damage normal neural tissue. When they detect a foreign body, they consume and destroy it to prevent disease and inflammation (Kreutzberg, 1995).

When you think about the pieces and parts that make up the brain, don't forget to consider the amazing quality of the big picture: an average desktop computer makes billions of computations in a single second. By contrast, neurons in the cerebral cortex, on average, fire only about 7 times per second and rarely exceed firing rates of 50 times per second (O'Connor, Peron, Huber, & Svoboda, 2010). How can the brain perform feats effortlessly that our most advanced supercomputers cannot, such as finding a path through a forest, recognizing the face of a loved one, or

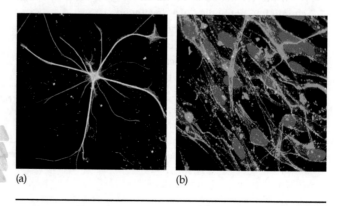

(a)   (b)

FIGURE 3.12 **Two more types of glial cells.** (a) Astrocytes and (b) microglia.

writing a poem? The answer seems to lie in the brain's massive parallelism: the neurons and glial cells may be slow, but they are *massive* in quantity. From the parallel interaction of hundreds of billions of these cells, the magic of cognition and behavior emerges. We now turn to details of that interaction.

Synaptic Transmission: Chemical Signaling in the Brain

In the previous section you learned that dendrites are the first place that signals are received by a neuron. We now turn to this in more detail: what do those signals look like, and how are they collected? In this section, we will describe two of the four critical functions of the neuron that we mentioned before: outputting and collecting information. In later sections, we'll return to the other two functions, integrating and conducting information.

Release of Neurotransmitter at the Synapse

How do neurons communicate across the small spaces that divide them? This was recognized as a problem in the early 1900s, but it was not solved until the 1920s, when a scientist named Otto Loewi performed a simple and elegant experiment (FIGURE 3.13). It was known that electrically stimulating a particular nerve in the frog (the vagus nerve that leads to

the heart) would cause the heart to slow down. Loewi suspected the final mechanism of action was not electrical, but chemical in nature. So he isolated a frog's heart in a bath of salt solution, stimulated the nerve, and then extracted the fluid of the bath. He reasoned that if a chemical had been released by the nerve stimulation, it should still be present in the bath. And indeed, when he pumped the bath solution onto a second frog heart, it immediately slowed the heart rate. He correctly concluded that the signal from the axon was chemical (Zigmond, 1999).

Loewi had just discovered neurotransmission, the trick by which cells of the nervous system communicate across small gulfs of space to each other or to targets such as the muscle cells of the heart. (Loewi was awarded the Nobel Prize in 1936 for this breakthrough.) The released chemicals are called neurotransmitters. The neurotransmitter is released by the presynaptic cell and, by diffusing from its point of release, is felt as a change of chemical concentration at the postsynaptic target (FIGURE 3.14). Note that, in this case, the signal transmission is one way, carrying a signal from the axon to the dendrite, but not the other way around. The **synaptic cleft**—the little space between the pre- and postsynaptic cells—is a mere 20–50 nanometers (billionths of a meter) across, and this small distance allows the concentration of neurotransmitter to rise and decay rapidly. Just inside the membrane of a presynaptic cell, the neurotransmitter molecules are packaged inside small spherical packages called **synaptic vesicles**. The release of the neurotransmitter into the extracellular space occurs when the vesicle fuses with the outer membrane and the molecules spill out into the cleft.

Before we explore what happens when the molecules reach the postsynaptic target, it is important to know that many different chemicals function as neurotransmitters; we will briefly survey these now.

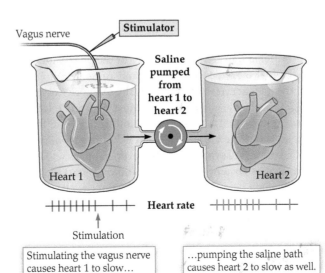

(a)   (b)

FIGURE 3.13 **(a) Otto Loewi and (b) his experimental design that led to the discovery of neurotransmission.**

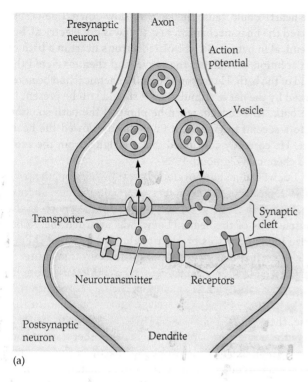

(a)

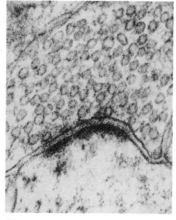

(b)

FIGURE 3.14 **Vesicles carrying neurotransmitter molecules dock with the presynaptic membrane, releasing the signaling molecules into the synaptic cleft.** The neurotransmitters diffuse across the cleft and interact with receptors on the postsynaptic target.

Types of Neurotransmitters

The neurotransmitter discovered in Loewi's experiment was a molecule called **acetylcholine**. This molecule serves as an excitatory neurotransmitter in the peripheral nervous system, causing muscle contractions when released at the junction between the nervous system and the muscular system. Since Loewi's day, dozens more neurotransmitters have been discovered. Because these neurotransmitters will come up again throughout the book, we will briefly cover the different categories—this will be an integral part of everything that comes later. Don't get lost in the details; for now just try to appreciate that there are many different types of molecules that have been capitalized on by neurons to carry signals.

Acetylcholine, the first neurotransmitter discovered, is the only one that stands in a category of its own. Several other neurotransmitters fall under the category of the **monoamines**: examples are dopamine, epinephrine, norepinephrine (all known as **catecholamines**), serotonin, and melatonin. Dopamine, as an example, serves as the critical information-carrying molecule in the brain's reward systems and is the target of drugs of addiction such as cocaine and amphetamines (Chapter 14). It is also the main neurotransmitter implicated in schizophrenia (Chapter 16).

Although the monoamines are large molecules, it is also possible to carry signals with tiny molecules such as **amino acids**, the building blocks of proteins—and these thus comprise a third category of neurotransmitter. The amino acid neurotransmitter **glutamate** is the most common excitatory transmitter in the central nervous system (as acetylcholine is in the peripheral nervous system). Aspartate is another excitatory amino acid neurotransmitter, whereas **GABA (gamma-aminobutyric acid)** and glycine are common inhibitory neurotransmitters.

Beyond these common neurotransmitters, there are also **peptide neurotransmitters** (peptides are short strings of amino acids). Examples of these "neuropeptides" include cholecystokinin, somatostatin, and neuropeptide Y; more than 50 have been found to date.

Finally, signals can also be carried by gases such as nitric oxide and carbon monoxide, which diffuse directly through cell membranes to effect changes at neighboring locations. These soluble gases often work in the opposite way from what we described before, being produced in the dendrites of one cell and crossing the synapse backward, to affect the axons of the presynaptic cell. For that reason, they are often referred to as **retrograde transmitters**. TABLE 3.1 summarizes the categories of neurotransmitters.

Most neurons release one peptide neurotransmitter in addition to one, or a few, of the smaller neurotransmitters (acetylcholine, monoamines, and amino acids). Generally, however, neurons will release the smaller neurotransmitters first and only start to release the larger peptide neurotransmitters after they have been stimulated repeatedly.

Given the long litany of neurotransmitter types, the important point to appreciate is the variety of substances that all serve the function of carrying information between neurons. Through evolutionary timescales, neurons have forged partnerships of presynaptic secretion and postsynaptic detection using chemicals of all types. We now turn to the details of the postsynaptic detection.

TABLE 3.1.	
Types of Neurotransmitters	
NEUROTRANSMITTER CATEGORY	EXAMPLE(S)
Monoamines	Dopamine, epinephrine, norepinephrine, serotonin, melatonin
Amino acids	Glutamate, aspartate, GABA, glycine
Peptide neurotransmitters	Cholecystokinin, somatostatin, neuropeptide Y
Gases	Nitric oxide, carbon monoxide
Organic cation	Acetylcholine

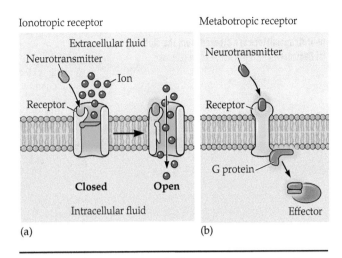

FIGURE 3.15 **Two types of channels allow neurotransmitters to effect target cells.** (a) Ionotropic receptors are opened—or gated—allowing ions to move through a passage in the membrane. (b) Metabotropic receptors relay signals to proteins inside the cell.

Receptors

When the neurotransmitter molecules are released into the synaptic cleft, they exert their effects by binding to **receptors**, specialized proteins in the membrane. Receptors can often be located presynaptically or on neighboring cells, but for now we'll concentrate on the overwhelmingly most common type: *postsynaptic* receptors. There are two main ways in which typical neurotransmitters transmit a signal to another cell: either by causing direct flow of **ions** into or out of the cell (**ionotropic receptors**) or by causing more indirect changes inside the cell by a cascade of signals (**metabotropic receptors**).

Let's first look at the ionotropic receptors. There are different concentrations of ions (charged particles) inside and outside the cells; thus, if you were to poke a hole in a membrane, ions would tend to flow in or out (their direction of flow depends on several factors that we will learn about in the next section). An ionotropic receptor is essentially a sophisticated way of opening a temporary pore in the membrane. In its closed state, the receptor protein blocks the flow of ions; when it is opened, or *gated*, by the right type of neurotransmitter, the protein changes its shape and provides a pore in the membrane (**FIGURE 3.15a**). Many ionotropic receptors allow only a particular type of ion to pass through; thus a receptor that binds the neurotransmitter GABA tends to selectively pass chloride ions, whereas a receptor that binds acetylcholine may selectively pass sodium ions.

The second type of receptor is called metabotropic and is also known as a "second-messenger-coupled" receptor (**FIGURE 3.15b**). To highlight some general principles, consider one well-studied family of such receptors, the **G-coupled protein receptor**. **G-proteins** are associated with the inside face of the postsynaptic membrane, and their function is to relay information from neurotransmitter receptors to other proteins inside the cell. These in turn relay, amplify, and transform the signal. Because so many receptor types are G-protein coupled, this allows the cell to develop sophisticated signaling cascades that integrate several signals from the outside. The **second messengers** triggered by metabotropic receptors can serve many different functions, modulating the activity of neighboring **ion channels**, activating or deactivating enzymes within the cell, or changing which genes are expressed within the cell. These metabotropic receptors are a large and important family of receptors, so important, in fact, that about half of all medical drugs target these receptors. The discovery of these receptors was awarded the 2012 Nobel Prize in Chemistry.

The effects of metabotropic receptors tend to operate on a much slower time scale than ionotropic receptors. For any given neurotransmitter, such as serotonin, there can be literally dozens of different subtypes of ionotropic or metabotropic receptors found in various parts of the nervous system. Thanks to this immense variety, a single neurotransmitter can serve many different types of functions throughout the body.

When neurotransmitters bind to receptors, they do not remain there for long. Instead, the binding is brief, and their presence in the synaptic cleft is quickly and precisely cleaned up. This clean-up occurs by one of three mechanisms: **degradation**, in which the neurotransmitter molecule is broken apart by other molecules; *diffusion*, in which the neurotransmitter moves out of the synapse, down its chemical concentration gradient; or **reuptake**, in which specialized protein **transporters** in the membrane will selectively pull the neurotransmitter back inside the cell, presynaptically, postsynaptically, or, often, into neighboring cells (**FIGURE 3.16**). Of these three methods, reuptake is by far the most common for most small neurotransmitters. Because of this rapid return of the concentration to normal levels, chemical neurotransmission is extremely precise.

FIGURE 3.16 **There are three ways by which neurotransmitters are cleared from the cleft.** (a) Degradation, (b) diffusion, and (c) reuptake.

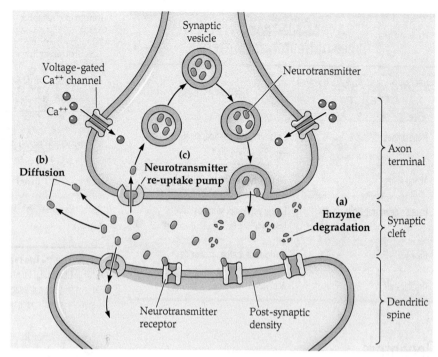

Postsynaptic Potentials

Returning to the ionotropic receptors, what happens after neurotransmitters bind and cause ions to flow in or out of the postsynaptic cell? Because there are different concentrations of ions inside and outside the cell, there is a voltage difference (also known as a potential difference) across the membrane. Normally, the outside of the cell is more positive than the inside, giving a resting **membrane potential** of about -70 millivolts (mV). Depending on the charge of the ions and in which direction they flow, the movement of ions across the membrane can make this potential difference smaller or larger. When positive ions, such as sodium, flow through a receptor into the cell (slightly reducing the difference between inside and outside), this is known as an **excitatory postsynaptic potential**, abbreviated as an **EPSP** (FIGURE 3.17a). Conversely, if neurotransmitter binding causes the potential difference in voltage between the inside and outside of the cell to grow larger (that is, the inside to become even more negative), this change in voltage is known as an **inhibitory postsynaptic potential (IPSP)** (FIGURE 3.17b). This can occur by allowing positively charged potassium to flow *out* of the cell or by allowing negatively charged chloride ions to flow *into* the cell.

Typical postsynaptic potentials are small changes in voltage—about 1 mV—and they are rapid, lasting only a few milliseconds. But recall that a typical cell in the cortex has about 10,000 synaptic inputs, meaning that the postsynaptic cell is receiving a symphony of signals at every moment. These small postsynaptic changes in the membrane potential do not stay where they are, but instead funnel down toward the soma. Remember what you learned about the

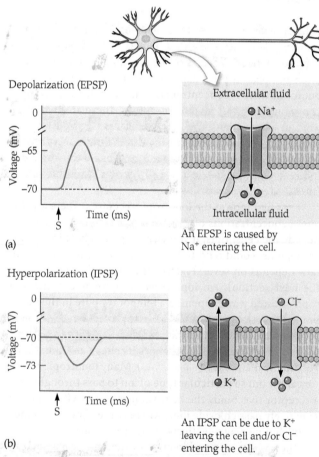

FIGURE 3.17 **Postsynaptic potentials.** (a) An excitatory postsynaptic potential (EPSP) occurs when positive ions flow through an ionotropic receptor into the cell, causing depolarization. (b) An inhibitory postsynaptic potential (IPSP) occurs when positive ions flow out of the cell, or negative ions flow in. This causes the difference in voltage between the inside and outside of the cell to grow larger, known as hyperpolarization.

soma: it *summarizes* the signals, and in the next section we will see how.

But first, one more important point about EPSPs and IPSPs: you will sometimes hear different neurotransmitters referred to as excitatory or inhibitory, meaning that they cause positive or negative changes in the membrane voltage. (For example, "glutamate is an excitatory neurotransmitter, whereas glycine is inhibitory"). But keep in mind that it is not the neurotransmitter molecule itself that is excitatory or inhibitory—it is the action of the receptor that determines the effect. For example, in the developing animal, GABA is considered excitatory because its receptors cause EPSPs by allowing chloride ions to pass *out* of the cell. But as the animal grows older, the receptors allow chloride ions to pass *into* the cell, and GABA now causes IPSPs. Thus, in the adult animal, GABA is considered an inhibitory neurotransmitter. Nothing changes about the molecule, only the consequences it has when it binds to its postsynaptic receptor.

For completeness, you should know one more thing about signaling between cells. Although chemical transmission is the overwhelmingly common form of signal transmission at synapses, another mechanism also exists: **electrical synapses**, also known as **gap junctions**, allow the direct passage of an electrical signal from one cell to the next (Connors & Long, 2004). Such connections often allow the synchronized spiking of groups of neurons. Electrical synapses are far less common, and their function is less understood. For the rest of this chapter, we will concentrate only on chemical transmission, the typical mechanism of signaling at synapses.

THE BIGGER PICTURE:
Psychoactive Drugs

The release of neurotransmitters allows neurons to communicate with one another. Although it may not be obvious at first, this process of neurotransmission is the main target of drugs and medications that effect mood and cognition.

Drugs that affect the brain's communication are known as psychoactive drugs, and these include drugs used to treat dementia and schizophrenia; drugs used to treat depression or anxiety; and recreational drugs such as cocaine, marijuana, and even caffeine. Selective serotonin reuptake inhibitors (in common use as antidepressants) work by preventing serotonin from being transported back into the presynaptic cell. As a result, they are classified as **agonists**, because they cause more serotonin to be present in the cleft. Similarly, attention deficit hyperactivity disorder medications prevent the reuptake of the neurotransmitters norepinephrine and dopamine. Some recreational drugs, such as cocaine, also act as agonists. In this case, cocaine works by preventing the reuptake of dopamine.

Another recreational drug, alcohol, works as an agonist to the neurotransmitter GABA and, as a result of stimulating GABA receptors, decreases overall activity in your central nervous system.

Psychoactive drugs may also be **antagonists**, meaning that they dampen or block normal receptor function. In this class, we find some of the medications used to treat schizophrenia, which prevent dopamine from interacting with a certain type of receptor on the postsynaptic cell. One such medication, risperidone, has a complex profile of effects on many types of receptors. In addition to being a dopamine antagonist, it is also an antagonist for certain serotonin, norepinephrine, and histamine receptors. In terms of recreational drugs, caffeine and alcohol are both antagonists. Caffeine works by blocking a neurotransmitter known as adenosine. Adenosine normally builds up during the day and, in these higher concentrations, causes drowsiness. Caffeine prevents adenosine from binding to its receptors and therefore helps you

stay awake. Alcohol, in addition to the agonist effects we mentioned above, is also an antagonist to the glutamate receptors, which results in memory impairments, among other side effects.

As you've seen here, psychoactive drugs can have many effects on your daily life. However, these descriptions only scratch the surface of a field better known as neuropharmacology. As you saw with risperidone and with alcohol, a single drug can have different effects on different neurotransmitter systems. Furthermore, a drug that is an agonist at one type of neurotransmitter receptor may also act as an antagonist at a different receptor. Because different subtypes of receptors are found in different parts of the nervous system, a given drug can end up enhancing neural activity in one part of the brain, while at the same time damping down activity in other parts of the brain. For these reasons, trying to develop new drugs and understand their effects is a tricky and time-consuming enterprise.

Spikes: Electrical Signaling in the Brain

An electrode placed near a neuron reveals that from time to time the voltage across the neuron's membrane suddenly reverses and then, about a millisecond later, is abruptly restored (FIGURE 3.18). This is known as an **action potential**, often called a **nerve impulse** or **spike** (Rieke, Warland, & Bialek, 1999). Spikes are all or none, meaning that they either happen or they do not, and they are always the same size. In this section, we will see how spikes happen, how they travel, and what they mean.

Adding Up the Signals

The small voltage changes collected in the dendrites (EPSPs and IPSPs) travel along the dendritic membrane to the cell body, where all the branches come together. Although the postsynaptic potentials are small, they can add up with one another in two ways. First, signals that arrive at the soma at the same time (or even close to the same time) will add up when they reach the soma—this is known as **temporal summation**. Second, signals that arrive on different branches of the dendrites will converge at the soma—this is known as **spatial summation**. As a result of both kinds of summation, the soma has the opportunity to integrate signals flowing into disparate parts of the dendrites.

Excitatory and inhibitory postsynaptic potentials add up like a simple math problem. Two EPSPs will sum to a larger voltage change, whereas an EPSP and an IPSP arriving at the same moment will cancel each other out (FIGURE 3.19). Because the soma receives hundreds or thousands of such signals at any moment, the total voltage of the cell is determined not by any one incoming signal, but instead by the overall *pattern* of all the inputs received all over the cell, both excitatory and inhibitory. If the number of

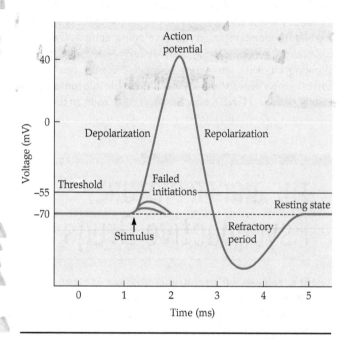

FIGURE 3.18 A neuronal action potential, or spike, is a binary, all-or-none signal. It occurs when voltage across the neuron's membrane suddenly reverses.

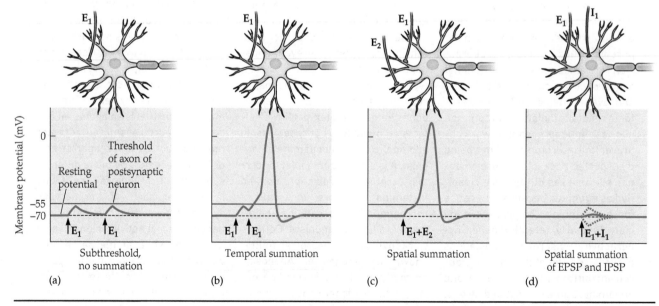

(a) Subthreshold, no summation

(b) Temporal summation

(c) Spatial summation

(d) Spatial summation of EPSP and IPSP

FIGURE 3.19 Temporal and spatial summation. (a) No summation occurs when EPSPs arrive with a delay between them; they, individually, cannot drive the membrane voltage to the threshold for a spike. (b) Temporal summation occurs when EPSPs arrive close in time and their contributions add up at the soma, leading to an action potential. (c) Spatial summation occurs when signals arrive on different branches of the dendrites, converging at the soma. (d) If an EPSP and an IPSP arrive at different locations at the same time, they will cancel each other's effect at the soma.

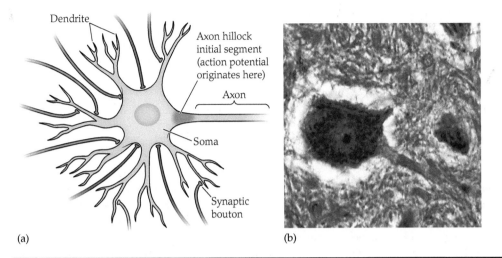

Dendrite

Axon hillock
initial segment
(action potential
originates here)

Axon

Soma

Synaptic
bouton

(a)

(b)

FIGURE 3.20 **Because of its high excitability, the axon hillock serves as the spike initiation zone.**

excitatory potentials overwhelms the number of inhibitory potentials, this can drive the voltage of cell toward more positive values, making it increasingly **depolarized**. If the cell voltage reaches a **threshold**, typically about -60 mV, something special happens: an action potential is generated at the **axon hillock**, the part of the axon that connects to the soma. The axon hillock is the most excitable part of the neuron and therefore the location where spikes are initiated (FIGURE 3.20).

How an Action Potential Travels

Two ions play key roles in making an action potential: sodium (Na^+) and potassium (K^+). (In fact, there are several ions and proteins involved, but we can understand the big picture with only these two). When a cell is at rest, there is a high concentration of Na^+ on the outside of the cell and a much lower concentration on the inside; this is exactly the opposite for K^+ ions (FIGURE 3.21a).

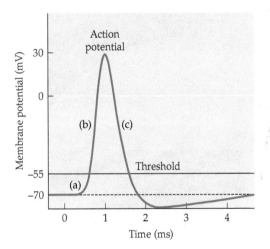

Action
potential

(b)   (c)

Threshold

(a)

Time (ms)

FIGURE 3.21 **The sequence of a voltage spike.** (a) At rest, there are more Na^+ ions outside the cell than inside and more K^+ ions inside the cell than outside. (b) When voltage-gated Na^+ channels open, Na^+ ions rush from the outside to the inside—both because of the concentration differences and because of the electrical field. (c) The depolarization caused by Na^+ influx triggers the opening of K^+ channels, which cause K^+ ions to rush out, thus making the outside more positive again (repolarization).

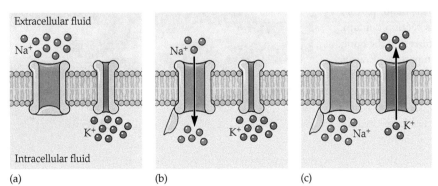

Extracellular fluid

Na^+

K^+

Intracellular fluid

(a)

Na^+

K^+

(b)

Na^+ K^+

(c)

When the membrane potential rises beyond a certain threshold, it triggers the opening of **voltage-gated ion channels**, in this case voltage-gated Na$^+$ channels—ion channels that selectively pass Na$^+$ and are opened only at particular voltages across the membrane. When these channels open, Na$^+$ ions suddenly find a way into the cell. These ions are driven in by both the **concentration gradient** (there are many more on the outside than on the inside) and the **electrical gradient** (the inside of the cell is more negatively charged than the outside of the cell, attracting the positively charged Na$^+$ ions into the cell) (FIGURE 3.21b).

Why doesn't the axon become permanently depolarized and stay there? Because voltage-gated K$^+$ channels are not far behind in their action. The influx of Na$^+$ depolarizes the membrane further, which triggers the opening of the K$^+$ channels (Kang, Huguenard, & Prince, 2000). Now, K$^+$ ions flow down their concentration gradient (that is, there are more on the inside than on the outside, so they will tend to flow out) (FIGURE 3.21c). Because the K$^+$ ions are positive and because they are rushing out of the cell, the inside becomes more negative—that is, it repolarizes. This return to a negative voltage shuts the voltage-gated Na$^+$ channels and ends the swing in voltage.

This exchange of ions causes a voltage spike at the axon hillock, but how does an action potential *travel*? The answer is that the rapid voltage change gives just enough time and spreads far enough down the membrane for neighboring voltage-gated Na$^+$ channels to open up, causing the same cycle of ion exchange to happen nearby. In this way, the cycle of depolarization and repolarization moves down the axon. By analogy, imagine mousetraps arranged in a long line. Each time one trap snaps shut, it gives just enough vibration to trigger the next one to snap and so on down the line. This way of passing the signal along the membrane is the trick by which action potentials propagate, and it is the main reason the nervous system can carry signals quickly across the distant expanses of the brain.

If you're thinking ahead, you may ask why action potentials don't travel in both directions, forward and backward. This is because there is a short **refractory period** after an action potential, during which the Na$^+$ channels are more resistant to opening. (In our analogy, it takes a bit of time to reset the mousetrap.) As a result, the action potential cannot move back to a location where it has already occurred, but can only travel forward.

For completeness we should mention that the full story of an action potential is slightly more complex, involving calcium and chloride ions. These ions contribute to the exact shape of action potentials, but they are not the major players. For our purposes, the level of detail in this section contains the principles you need to understand for the rest of the book.

Now that you understand how an action potential travels, you can understand what happened to the Japanese actor, Bandō Mitsugorō, whose story introduced this chapter. Tetrodotoxin molecules block the pore of the voltage-gated Na$^+$ channel, thereby preventing the channel from opening and passing ions (Lee & Ruben, 2008). When there is no Na$^+$ channel activity, there are no action potentials. Without action potentials, all communication stops. The fact that tetrodotoxin directly interferes with the most basic signaling mechanism of the nervous system—the action potential—explains why it is 100 times more potent than potassium cyanide, the poison of choice for most Hollywood screenwriters.

Myelinating Axons to Make the Action Potential Travel Faster

Remember the myelination of axons that is done by the oligodendrocytes (in the central nervous system) and the Schwann cells (peripheral nervous system)? Now that we've learned about action potentials, we are ready to turn to the function of the myelin sheath.

First, remember that myelination is not continuous along the length of the axon, but instead comes in segments of about 100 micrometers, giving the "string of sausages" look. The small gaps left between the myelin sheaths are known as the nodes of Ranvier, and it is at these points that ions from outside the cell can most easily flow in and out (FIGURE 3.22). In the stretches of myelin-insulated axon, it is difficult for ions to

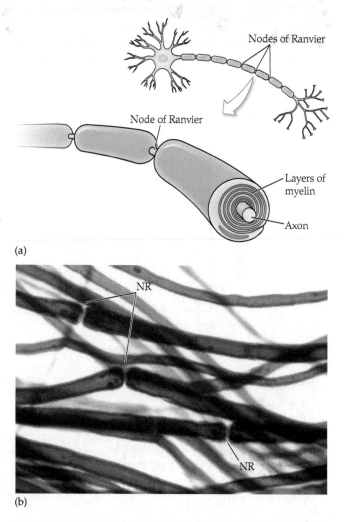

FIGURE 3.22 **The nodes of Ranvier.** (a) Diagram. (b) Microscopic view.

move across the membrane, and the consequence of this is extraordinary: the action potential "leaps" directly from node to node instead of moving smoothly, as it does along an unmyelinated axon. This noncontinuous skipping of the spike is known as **saltatory conduction** ("saltatory" comes from the Latin *saltare*, "to jump"). The action potential is regenerated at each node, but not at the insulated stretches in between. The length of the myelination segments is just short enough that the depolarization at one node will be large enough to open the Na^1 channels at the next node. To return to our previous analogy, this would be like placing mousetraps far enough apart that the snapping of one gives just enough vibration to trigger the next—in this way, the signal reaches the end of the line much more quickly, skipping over a good deal of distance with each event.

The effect of saltatory conduction is to vastly increase the travel speed, or conduction velocity, of the action potentials. In addition to increasing the conduction velocity of action potentials, myelination has the advantage of decreasing energy expenditure: with fewer ions moving around, less energy is needed to replace them (in other words, to "reset" the mousetraps). Most generally, myelination is required for a vast network of neurons to function together properly, as seen by the story of champion speed skater Adam Riedy.

Action Potentials Reach the Terminals and Cause Neurotransmitter Release

Action potentials travel down axons until they invade the axon terminals, and here our story comes full circle. The sudden voltage change in the terminal causes the opening of

CASE STUDY:
Multiple Sclerosis

In 2001, 20-year-old Adam Riedy was a strong candidate for the U.S. Olympic speed skating team. In the World Cup competition, he had just won a bronze medal in the 1,000-meter race and won two medals on relay teams.

But he awoke one morning and discovered his body didn't feel quite right: "I found that the right side of my leg had gotten all tingly and numb. As the day went on, the pain moved all the way up my right side, then back down again" (Puet, 2002). He put down his concerns. The pain soon went away, allowing him to perform at full strength. But just before the Olympic trials in Utah, a more severe attack took place, weakening his right leg. Given his investment of 10 years of training, he tried to skate anyway—but it was to no avail. His body simply wouldn't do what he wanted it to anymore.

Upon visiting a physician, Adam's problems were diagnosed as multiple sclerosis (MS), an autoimmune disease in which the immune system attacks healthy central nervous system tissue. It mistakes the body's own healthy tissues as foreign tissues. The consequence of this self-attack is demyelination: the myelin sheaths become scarred (sclerotic) and are unable to perform their job of insulation. As a result, neurons of the central nervous system cannot properly conduct signals, and the information flow is corrupted. Because the demyelination happens in small, isolated areas, patients often have varied and clinically isolated symptoms. Complaints can include muscle weakness, difficulties with balance, problems with speech or vision, fatigue, and pain (Burks, Bigley, & Hill, 2009). As more areas of demyelination accrue, the symptoms progress. Because the disease is progressive, it results in a gradual deterioration of neurological function.

Despite the ongoing research on MS, the cause of the disease remains unclear and there is no cure.

Strangely, the worldwide incidence of MS shows a clear pattern: the farther you live from the equator, the higher the chances of developing MS; this had led to the suspicion that the disease may have something to do with environmental factors such as climate, sunshine, and vitamin D (Disanto, Morahan, & Ramagopalan, 2012; Pierrot-Deseilligny & Souberbielle, 2013). However, exceptions to this rule—such as the especially low incidence among the equatorially distant Maori of New Zealand or Sami people of Northern Europe—point to genetic involvement as well (Koch-Henriksen & Sorensen, 2010; Lin, Charlesworth, van der Mei, & Taylor, 2012).

Although MS is undergoing intensive study, one point remains clear: the integrity of the myelin sheaths is critical to the functioning of the nervous system. When myelin becomes damaged, the communication networks in the brain become critically compromised.

voltage-gated calcium channels, causing a rapid entry of calcium ions from the outside. The calcium ions cause the vesicles packed with neurotransmitter to fuse with the terminal membrane—and this causes the neurotransmitter molecules to spill out into the synaptic cleft (FIGURE 3.23). At this point we are back to the paradigm presented in the first section of this chapter: the neurotransmitter molecules now diffuse across the synaptic cleft and interact with receptors on the next set of dendrites.

Neurons form dense networks. For simplicity, textbooks often draw a picture of neuron A transmitting a signal to neuron B. But in reality a single action potential traveling down an axon will invade each of its 10,000 terminals, causing chemical release at a vast network of locations.

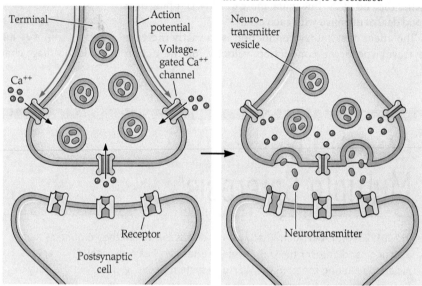

FIGURE 3.23 **Action potentials lead to neurotransmitter release.**

Action potential invades the axon terminal, opening Ca⁺⁺ channels

Terminal —
Action potential
Voltage-gated Ca^{++} channel
Ca^{++}
Receptor
Postsynaptic cell

The entry of Ca^{++} causes the vesicles to fuse with the membrane, allowing the neurotransmitters to be released

Neuro-transmitter vesicle
Neurotransmitter

NEUROSCIENCE OF EVERYDAY LIFE:
The Magic of a Local Anesthetic

Why can the eye doctor put a solution in your eyes and then touch your eyeball without it hurting? How can a dentist extract a tooth while you're awake? Why can a surgeon sew stitches into your leg while you watch? The answer involves the magic of a local anesthetic (an = no, esthetic = feeling). Local anesthetics work simply by blocking action potentials. For example, lidocaine blocks the voltage-gated Na⁺ channels, thus preventing action potentials from spreading along the axon. Touch and pain are signaled to your brain by action potentials traveling up the nerves of your peripheral nervous system to your central nervous system; they are then interpreted by your brain as a sensation (more on this in Chapter 6). When lidocaine is applied to a local area of the body, the electrical signals on the peripheral nerves are blocked at their site of origin, so no sensations can arise. Although the receptors in your eyes, mouth, or skin are being activated, your brain has no way of getting the message. This simple but amazing technique highlights the fact that all of your body's sensations are constructed by the brain, a feat we will discuss in greater detail in later chapters of the book.

What Do Spikes Mean? The Neural Code

If each spike occurring in your brain made a little popping noise, the result would be a cacophony that would blow your ears out. This is because most of your nearly 100 billion neurons are generating spikes somewhere between once per second up to a few hundred times per second. The sending of these electrical signals is the most energy-intensive process your brain engages in. It is costly, from an energy perspective, because the ability to propagate action potentials requires the constant maintenance of chemical gradients (more sodium on the outside, more potassium on the inside). To return to our analogy, the system requires the "setting" of the long line of mousetraps. Once these traps have been snapped, the neuron needs to expend a good deal of energy to reset them. Specifically, it needs to push the Na^+ ions back out and pull the K^+ ions back in, a process that accounts for the majority of the energy expended by the brain (Ames, 2000). The fact that the brain is willing to spend so much of its resources on spikes suggests they carry important information. But what is that information? We will now explore how spikes—and trains of spikes—are thought to carry information.

Encoding Stimuli in Spikes

What do spikes *mean*? It appears that spikes are the binary, all-or-none, fundamental letters of the nervous system, but what are these letters spelling?

It is common to measure the electrical activity of a single neuron in a human or research animal and watch the neuron's electrical response to some stimulus in the outside world (say, showing a visual stimulus, or touching a finger, or presenting a sound). Certain cells are tuned,

or selective, for particular stimuli. For example, imagine using an electrode to record the activity of a single neuron in the human brain (see *Research Methods: Recording Action Potentials with Electrodes* later in this chapter). You show photographs of several different types of animals to the person—say a tiger, an eagle, and a rhinoceros. Let's imagine that none of these pictures seems to "excite" the cell at all—that is, the cell generates no more action potentials beyond its normal background rate of activity. But now you present a picture of a mouse or a rabbit, and the neuron suddenly discharges many more action potentials (FIGURE 3.24; Mormann et al., 2011). In this case, the cell is described as being "selective" for particular stimuli over others. For example, specific regions of the primate brain contain neurons selective for faces ("face cells"; Weiner & Grill-Spector, 2012); other regions contain neurons that respond vigorously to edges, colors, animals, business logos, and hundreds of other stimuli (Bramao, Reis, Petersson, & Faisca, 2011; Kourtzi & Connor, 2011; Ungerleider & Bell, 2011). This is true not only in vision, but also more generally in hearing, touch, smell, vibration, temperature, and so on: neurons are often tuned to particular stimuli and not to others (more on this in Chapters 5 and 6).

It is common to quantify a neuron's response in terms of its firing rate: the number of action potentials that occur per some unit of time (for example, "50 spikes per second"). For example, in FIGURE 3.25, the response of a neuron in visual cortex depends on the orientation of a bar. When the bar is rotated to a different angle, the individual action potentials do not get bigger—rather, they become more frequent. That is, *more* of them occur in the same amount of time.

The idea that neurons encode stimuli by the number of action potentials in a small window of time is called **rate coding**. In this framework, neurons are specialized to detect certain stimuli, and the detection consists of a train of spikes. Because spike trains in a neuron can be elicited as a function

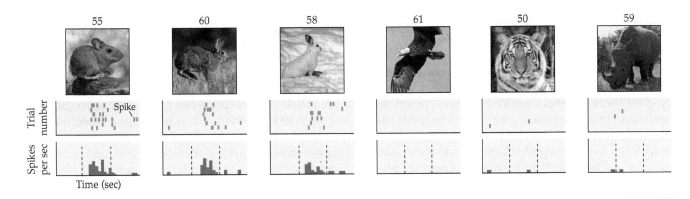

FIGURE 3.24 A selective neuron responds with greater activity to one particular type of stimulus more than to other types. The blue dashes represent individual action potentials; different rows represent individual trials. The red histograms summarize the response of the neuron over many trials.

FIGURE 3.25 The response of a cell depends on the orientation of the stimulus. A horizontal bar in the visual field inspires no action potentials, whereas a diagonal bar excites many action potentials. This cell can thus be said to be selective for diagonal bars.

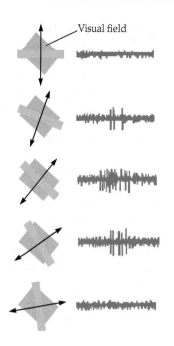

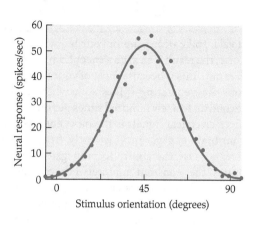

of the specific properties of external stimuli, encoding is based on the average *rate* of firing over some time interval (Adrian, 1928).

Why do neurons need to send a train of spikes? Why can't they simply send off a single spike at exactly the moment when it should occur? This may be for at least two reasons. First, physiologists observe trial-by-trial variability in the number of spikes and their timing when a sensory neuron responds to its preferred stimulus (Butts et al., 2010; Haslinger et al., 2012; Murphy & Rieke, 2006). In other words, the same stimulus results in a slightly different spike train each time. This variability supports the possibility that a neuron's response to a stimulus on any given trial is essentially probabilistic: it is more *likely* to fire at certain moments than at other moments, giving the same general response but with some amount of variability from trial to trial (Knoblauch & Palm, 2005). Second, most neurons spike occasionally even in the absence of a specific stimulus. For example, the neurons that carry visual information out of the retina send out several spikes per second even when it is completely dark (Korenbrot, 1995; Picones & Korenbrot, 1995). This spontaneous activity implies that a single spike is not a reliable sign of the presence of a stimulus and perhaps, by itself, carries little information. Instead, neurons are "noisy": whether a neuron fires at a specific moment or not is probabilistic. In addition, the presence of a baseline firing rate allows the neuron to have a more flexible repertoire of responses, since it now has room to either increase *or* decrease its firing rate from the baseline. If the baseline were zero, the neuron would have no room to further decrease its activity in response to inhibitory stimulation. Given these considerations, it is generally thought that the relevant coding signal

is not a single spike, but the spike train (Ermentrout, Galan, & Urban, 2008).

Although such rate coding provides a good starting point for thinking about neurons, it is not the complete story, at least not everywhere in the brain. For example, animals must react quickly to threatening stimuli (think of how swiftly a fly zips away from a swat). If an animal always needs to count up spikes over some time window, that severely limits how quickly it can decide what to do. Further, rate coding may be the wrong framework for encoding stimuli that change quickly, such as the position of predator or prey: by the time enough spikes have been averaged to tell a story, the message has changed. Reacting rapidly and encoding changing stimuli are two tasks that describe much of what is important in an animal's life. This suggests that the brain has methods of encoding stimuli that can go beyond rate codes.

Many possibilities exist for other coding methods. For example, although the rate coding hypothesis assumes that the exact timing of individual spikes doesn't matter, studies on electric fish reveal that a response to a stimulus can have specific temporal structure (that is, the spikes are arranged precisely in time)—and that the temporal structure could vary as a function of the stimulus properties, even while the total firing rate remains the same (Bullock et al., 2005) (FIGURE 3.26). That is, a neuron might respond with a dense burst of spikes to one stimulus and evenly spread spikes to another; alternatively, the timing of spikes in relation to the stimulus might shift earlier or later. In all these scenarios, the average firing rate remains the same. As a result, rate coding would be too coarse a measure, failing to capture the temporal properties of spiking that carry

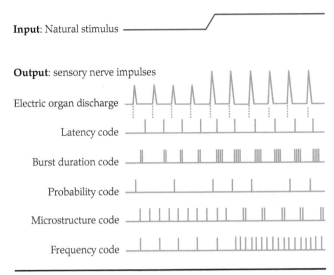

Input: Natural stimulus

Output: sensory nerve impulses

Electric organ discharge

Latency code

Burst duration code

Probability code

Microstructure code

Frequency code

FIGURE 3.26 A palette of coding possibilities for carrying information about a stimulus (Bullock, 1968).

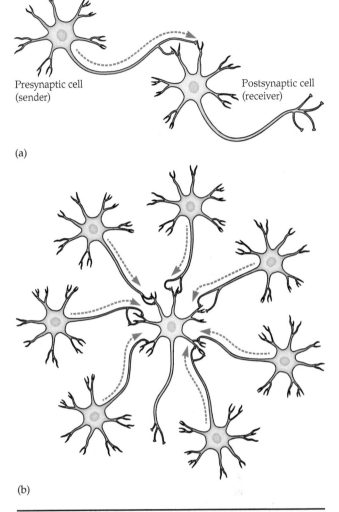

Presynaptic cell (sender)

Postsynaptic cell (receiver)

(a)

(b)

FIGURE 3.27 Are neurons integrators or coincidence detectors? (a) In the "assembly line" view of neurons, neurons pass messages to one another: the cell on the left is the sender, and the cell on the right integrates those signals as the receiver (Konig, Engel, & Singer, 1996). (b) Because neurons receive thousands of inputs, they may be better thought of as coincidence detectors. The cell body of the postsynaptic cell is unable to determine which presynaptic neuron sent which signal—instead, a postsynaptic spike will only signal the coincidence of many excitatory inputs arriving simultaneously.

information. There are several possibilities for coding beyond firing rate, and these may be used in different places and at different times in the nervous system. We will explore some other methods involving populations of neurons shortly in this chapter.

Decoding Spikes

When we consider the neural code—what the spikes *mean*—we must think from the point of view of a single neuron. Because most of the studies about spikes have focused on outgoing spikes from single cells, it is easy to think that those spikes will carry a good deal of information to the neurons they contact. But there's a critical point to keep in mind about the next neurons contacted: a typical neuron in the cortex receives some *10,000* synaptic connections from other neurons. A single input is not sufficient to generate a spike—instead, as we saw earlier, many input signals are needed within a short interval, and they must sum to create a sufficiently large depolarization. This suggests the possibility that a neuron receiving signals is not necessarily analyzing the details of each input line, but instead it is averaging over the population of its inputs. In this way, a neuron acts as a coincidence detector: it becomes activated by enough excitatory inputs coinciding in space and time to send it above threshold (FIGURE 3.27). In other words, an output spike is a response to the coincidence of many excitatory inputs arriving simultaneously (Abeles, 1982).

To envision this, imagine standing outside a sports stadium during a baseball game. You are unable to distinguish the details of any of the individual conversations of the 10,000 chatting fans inside. But when something special happens—like a home run with bases loaded—all of the voices come into a synchronized unison, and you know something important has occurred. The sudden coincidence of the voices is how you can distinguish normal game play from a big moment, and it is presumably the way that neurons operate. Neurons are not driven by other, single neurons, but instead by activity patterns over a population. We are now ready to turn to populations of neurons.

RESEARCH METHODS:
Recording Action Potentials with Electrodes

Action potentials are typically measured in a branch of electrophysiology known as single-unit recording (FIGURE 3.28). In this technique, a fine, thin piece of wire (usually made from tungsten or a platinum–iridium alloy) is inserted into an animal's brain. Because the tip of the electrode rests near one or more neurons, the action potential in the cell will displace ions and generate a signal in the electrode. With this technique, one can detect each time a spike occurs in a nearby neuron. It was by this technique that researchers Torsten Wiesel and David Hubel recorded activity of single neurons in cats and discovered the principles of organization of the visual cortex (we'll get to this in Chapter 5) (Hubel & Wiesel, 1962; Roy & Wang, 2012). For this work, they won the Nobel Prize in 1981.

Although this technique is usually confined to animal research, it is sometimes feasible to implement in humans who are undergoing neurosurgery. In a study by Itzhak Fried and colleagues, an electrode was inserted into the hippocampus of an epilepsy patient (Gelbard-Sagiv, Mukamel, Harel, Malach, & Fried, 2008). As you learned in Chapter 2, the hippocampus is involved in memory. The patient was then shown several short video clips—for example, part of a Martin Luther King speech, a clip from *The Simpsons* television series, a flyover of the Hollywood sign, and more. The hippocampal neuron responded vigorously to certain video clips—in this case,

the *Simpsons* clip—but not to others. Remarkably, when the patient was later asked to *recall* what he had seen, the neuron again fired vigorously when the patient thought about the *Simpsons* clip.

Let's think about what this finding means. First, it does not indicate that this neuron is *the* neuron that encodes *The Simpsons*—instead, it indicates that the neuron is part of a larger network that is activated by *The Simpsons* (either viewing or recalling). Second, it does not mean that the neuron belongs *only* to the "*Simpsons* network" of neurons: instead, neurons can participate in different coalitions at different times, as we will see shortly. At one moment, this neuron may be involved with thousands of other neurons in recalling *The Simpsons*, and the next moment it may be involved in another vast pattern of activity that represents the sight of a cell

phone resting on a chair. In fact, the neuron that responded to the *Simpsons* clip was also found later to respond to a clip of the *Seinfeld* television series.

When thinking about single-unit recording, it is critical to keep in mind that the activity of single neurons merely represents a piece of a much larger pattern. To overcome the limitations in interpretation of single neurons, more recent approaches have implemented multielectrode recording, in which a collection of thin electrodes are bundled together to record the activity of up to hundreds of neurons at once (Whitson, Kubota, Shimono, Jia, & Taketani, 2006). Although this is a move in the right direction, some researchers still lament that there is still no technology at the "sweet spot" level of measuring the detailed spiking activity of tens of thousands of cells simultaneously.

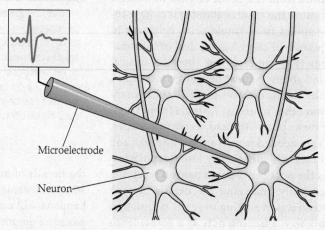

FIGURE 3.28 **A microelectrode for recording from a single neuron.** The tip is usually just a few micrometers wide.

Microelectrode

Neuron

Individuals and Populations

The experimental success in discovering selectivity in individual neurons originally led to a view of the nervous system as a confederation of specialist neurons, in which each neuron encodes some feature of the world. This idea, known as **local coding**, postulates that all stimuli in the outside world become represented uniquely by different neurons (Churchland & Sejnowski, 1992). For example, activity in a given neuron may represent a particular geometrical shape, whereas another neuron might represent a particular animal and another still might represent a more complex stimulus, such as NFL quarterback Ben Roethlisberger throwing a football.

At least some brain areas contain neurons that are highly selective in their representations of sensory stimuli. For example, studies in neurosurgical patients have found individual neurons in the medial temporal lobes that respond specifically to the name or photograph of particular actors, family members, or famous landmarks (Quiroga, Kreiman, Koch, & Fried, 2008). These observations have raised the question of whether the brain might contain a single unique "grandmother cell" for your grandmother and presumably a single unique cell for every other familiar individual in your life experience: a local code of one unique cell to one unique stimulus.

But several difficulties appear to be fatal to the idea of local coding. First, although there are a great number of neurons in the brain, there are almost certainly not enough to recognize all the distinct patterns a person can recognize in a lifetime. Consider all the highly distinctive fonts in which you can read the word "dog." Does the nervous system need a distinct neuron for each one? And consider the comparable issue for the many faces in many orientations in many lighting conditions that are easily recognizable by a single brain over a lifetime. The arithmetic suggests that nervous systems must have evolved a more powerful and flexible strategy than local coding, although it might be used sparingly for special purposes. Consider also how lucky the neurosurgeons would had to have been to find the one unique grandmother cell among the hundreds of millions of neurons in each patient's medial temporal lobe: a task akin to finding a needle in an entire field of haystacks (Waydo, Kraskov, Quian Quiroga, Fried, & Koch, 2006).

Another major problem with local coding is the fact that brain cells die naturally throughout your lifetime, which would leave local-coding memory vulnerable to damage and degradation. If specific individuals were encoded in single cells, you might expect that as you got older and these cells were lost, specific individuals would abruptly vanish one by one from your memory, like photographs dropping out of an old photo album. Yet this is not what happens—instead, memory degrades steadily and "gracefully" over time during the progress of senile dementia (Almor et al., 2009). As with other lines of evidence, the graceful degradation of memory speaks against a grandmother cell strategy for the brain.

But what is the alternative?

Populations of Neurons

A new understanding emerged when researchers began to see that systems of simple units—when strung together properly—could display remarkable emergent properties. For example, the representation of an object, such as a face, can be distributed across neurons in a population, and that distributed representation is both a realistic and a flexible strategy for the nervous system (Lehky & Sereno, 2011; Pasupathy & Connor, 2002; Reddy & Kanwisher, 2006). In the framework of **population coding**, recognition of something—say, your neighbor or college professor—is achieved by a **coalition** of neurons: a group of some hundreds or thousands of neurons temporarily working together as a team (Lehky & Sereno, 2011; Pasupathy & Connor, 2002; Reddy & Kanwisher, 2006). A given neuron might participate in many different coalitions depending on the task and the occasion. As an analogy, consider that a person can at one moment attend a rally for the Democratic Party, at a later moment attend a volunteer group meeting for building homeless shelters, and later on serve on an organizing committee for a fundraiser. The same person is contributing to different coalitions at different times.

Similarly, thinking from the point of view of populations, each neuron contributes its piece to larger patterns at any given moment (deCharms, 1998). If we found a neuron in your brain that reliably responds when you see your grandmother, that neuron would not correctly be described as a grandmother cell—instead, its response would be understood as its standard contribution to the population representing your grandmother. That same neuron will also make contributions (perhaps at different times and with different spike patterns) to the recognition of other, different stimuli, such as nail clippers, balloons, or ducks.

So what does an activity level in an individual neuron mean? In the population view, the neuron's response is simply the piece that the neuron contributes to the pattern of the population as a whole (Lehky & Sereno, 2011). In the case of face representation, for example, a single neuron may not represent anything identifiable (such as a nose or an eye)—it may, rather, be playing a more diffuse and nonintuitive role in the representation. That is, we should not expect that we can describe the individual neuron's representational capacities using the same vocabulary we use to talk about what is perceived in everyday life, such as noses, eyes, mouths, and so on.

Population coding also permits a vastly greater range of representations than could be achieved if each neuron coded for a single property. For a simple illustration, imagine that you had 10 neurons, each of which can have three different levels of activity, or firing rates: low, medium, and high. With this simple system, 1,000 (10^3) different stimuli can be encoded, compared to just 10 stimuli if activity in each neuron simply "stood for" a single stimulus. Population coding is thus much more versatile than local coding (Churchland & Sejnowski, 1992; Lehky & Sereno, 2011). As we will see in Chapter 5, human color vision is a stunning example of how the brain can get by with only three types of color detectors in the eye, but we can nevertheless distinguish upward of 10,000 hues. This is because the representation of color depends on the relative activity of the three types of detectors distributed across the population.

Finally, population coding allows the nervous system to average over the problem of noise in individual neurons. Precision appears to be achieved on any one trial by the activity of many similar neurons. That is, noisy neurons use population coding to achieve precision, and this strategy is more efficient than the use of nonnoisy precise components (Deneve, Latham, & Pouget, 2001). Future computers may shift in the biological direction using a higher number of noisy components rather than a smaller number of precise components.

Forming a Coalition: What Constitutes a Group?

We have seen the advantages of neurons cooperating in a distributed coalition. But how exactly do the neurons form into teams? There are at least two ways this can happen. First, neurons can become active in such a way that each neuron mutually excites the others. The simplest version consists of two neurons releasing excitatory neurotransmitters on one another; scale this up to imagine networks of tens or hundreds or thousands of neurons temporarily maintaining high firing rates because of their mutual connectivity (Koch & Crick, 2001) (FIGURE 3.29). The central idea is that a population that supports one another's high firing rate is a temporary coalition. As you can see, the term "coalition" here parallels the way it is used in political parties, when groups of people support each other for a common cause. Note that in the next moment, any individual neuron may participate in a completely different coalition, contributing to supporting a high firing rate in a new group.

A second possibility for forming a coalition is to use the *time* domain: in this framework, neurons that are members of a temporary coalition fire synchronously, thereby distinguishing them from other neurons that are active for different reasons (Amari, Nakahara, Wu, & Sakai, 2003). In this theoretical framework, those neurons representing a cup of coffee—its smell, its taste, its sight—will temporarily cooperate with each other as a coalition by firing spikes at the same time. As before, a neuron can participate in entirely different coalitions from moment to moment by the synchrony of its spikes with other neurons' spikes.

In one of the first experimental examples of synchrony, investigators found that nearby neurons that encode similar properties (say, the orientation of a bar) tend to fire spikes synchronously (Gray & Singer, 1989). That raised the possibility that neurons at even more distant locations could form temporary coalitions to encode features, simply by firing synchronously. In one demonstration of this principle, researchers found that distant neurons in the visual cortex fire more synchronously when a single bar is presented than a bar broken into two halves with a gap between them—presumably encoding that the first condition represents one single object (Engel, Fries, & Singer, 2001; Engel & Singer, 2001). Note that if a physiologist were averaging spikes over hundreds of milliseconds or so, the subtle details of synchronous firing would be missed—in other words, a typical rate-coding analysis of the data would be blind to the existing synchrony.

Another example of synchrony can be demonstrated in the auditory system. When a tone comes on and stays on, neurons in the auditory cortex give a brief response at the beginning and sometimes a brief response at the offset (FIGURE 3.30a) (Gillespie & Walker, 2001). This left open an important question: how does the brain encode that the tone has come on and *remains* on? The answer turned out to be that although there was no change in firing rate during the continuous presence of the tone, simultaneously recorded neurons change their relative timing, becoming more synchronized with each other while the tone is on (deCharms & Merzenich, 1996) (FIGURE 3.30b).

Again, the fact that these cortical sites change their relative timing without changing their average firing rate is

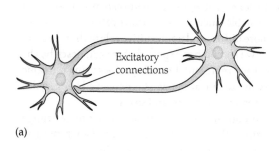

(a)

(b)

FIGURE 3.29 Neurons that excite each other can form coalitions.
(a) Two neurons that mutually excite one another. (b) A larger coalition of excitatory neurons.

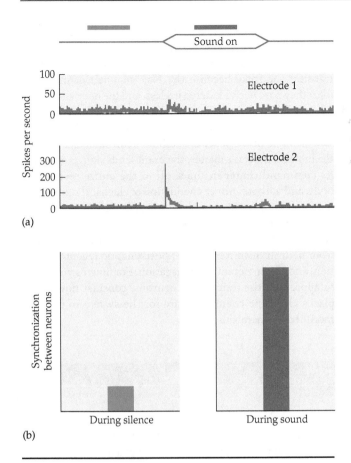

(a)

(b)

FIGURE 3.30 Changes in the mean firing rate and neuronal correlation in the primary auditory cortex of a monkey. (a) A continuous tone (top) was presented while recording from two sites in the auditory cortex. At both sites, the average firing rate showed only a little rise in activity at the onset and offset of the sound. (b) The synchrony of the spikes across the two sites (during an initial silent period, blue, and during the sound, red) reveals that the spikes in the two areas become more synchronized with one another while the sound is present.

something that would have been missed if we thought only about rate coding by single neurons.

Further experiments concerning synchrony across cortical areas have yielded mixed support for this framework, so the full story of synchronous firing is not a closed case (DeWeese & Zador, 2006; Samengo & Montemurro, 2010). But the synchrony framework offers one plausible possibility for how distant groups of neurons form a coalition.

Open Questions for Future Investigation

Even after the 1990s were declared "The Decade of the Brain," you are entering a field in which there are currently more questions than answers. The neural code—that is, the meaning of spikes in the brain—remains unsolved. One issue of confusion for neuroscientists is that neurons seem to exhibit a great deal of seemingly random activity, including membrane voltage fluctuations and spontaneous spikes. The classical paradigm deals with this activity mainly by assuming it is

"noise." However, we suspect neuroscience may someday be able to interpret this ubiquitous activity with more theoretical precision. For example, consider that the brain never starts a task from complete rest, but instead is always active. The level of activity existing when a task begins may be better understood as the context upon which the incoming data arrives, and this context may include information about recent experience, past rewards and punishments, and associated internal and external variables (including feeling ill, well, energetic, bored, irritable, anxious, jumpy, excited, and so on).

Another issue to consider is that current neuroscience concentrates on the details of individual neurons and spikes, as we have in this chapter. But a wider view of "neural activity" includes several other types of activity beyond spikes. For example, there are nonspiking neurons found in such places as the retina and hypothalamus. These generate electrical signals that can have different amplitudes (rather than all-or-none spikes), and they certainly appear to be involved in coding stimuli (Victor, 1999). Next, it remains an open question whether, in addition to neurons, some glial cells have an information-processing role, from allowing neurotransmitters to stay longer in the cleft to encouraging the formation of new synapses (Araque, 2008). Finally, complex biochemical cascades are constantly churning inside of neurons. Although our technologies to examine these interactions are limited, we already know that these intracellular networks are as complex as neural networks—just much smaller.

Next, much is still unknown about spike encoding and decoding, and in part this is because of the historical details of how the problem has been studied. Early ideas about neuronal coding owed much to the details of the canonical experimental setup. First, recording is done from only a handful of cells at a time, and second, a simple, nonbiological stimulus is typically used. A typical stimulus for studying hearing might involve a simple beep; for the visual system, it might be a diagonal bar of light moving from left to right. A natural scene, such as the sounds and sights of forest life, was (and still is) considered filled with confusing variables and has been traditionally avoided (Eggermont & Ponton, 2002; Super & Roelfsema, 2005).

Another feature of traditional experiments, standard even through the 1980s and still around today, was to anesthetize the animal lightly but sufficiently to keep it still, thereby permitting an accurate recording. Although the anesthesia did reduce movement, it was itself a kind of confound, since anesthetic agents change the way cells interact and respond (Alkire, Hudetz, & Tononi, 2008; Andrada, Livingston, Lee, & Antognini, 2012). Moreover, it was problematic that although particular cells displayed a regular response to the stimulus, the anesthetized animal presumably was not really perceiving it (Alkire et al., 2008; Andrada et al., 2012). An additional problem was that in the absence of a behavioral response to the stimulus, it was hard to tell whether the stimulus was significant for the animal's brain as a whole.

Current technologies give us access to spikes from small populations of cells, but much of neural coding might be happening elsewhere—for example, as temporal codes between vast assemblies of neurons throughout the brain. The possibility that information might be encoded in the temporal relationships between neurons is likely, but a better understanding will require new techniques that involve measuring from hundreds, thousands, or eventually millions of neurons at once. This will allow us to finally understand how brain tissue acts as a new kind of physical medium through which signals move. The idea is that as signals spread through this medium, computations are performed by the *interaction of patterns* riding upon the medium. In other words, the individual neurons don't provide the neural code; they provide the surface on which the neural code rides.

Conclusion

We started this chapter with the story of Bandō Mitsugorō, the Japanese Kabuki actor who daringly (and not so wisely) ate the forbidden livers of puffer fish and died. With your new knowledge, you can now understand what happened.

Tetrodotoxin blocks action potentials by blocking the pore opening of the fast, voltage-gated Na^+ channels. Although the soma tries to generate an action potential, the axon cannot transmit the spike because the Na^+ channels cannot pass ions: they have been rendered useless, and the nervous system falls silent. Besides complete paralysis of the skeletal muscles, the diaphragm muscles cannot move, and suffocation ensues. The example of the Japanese Kabuki actor underscores that the molecular details matter: the brain sends signals out from its command center in the skull to the entire rest of the body, and without proper conduction of electrical signals and proper neurotransmission, the system does not operate.

In upcoming chapters we will see how various drugs of abuse interact at all stages of the neural signaling pathways, from neurotransmitter release, postsynaptic receptor function, and action potential propagation. For now, as you come to appreciate the function of neurons, consider how many places along the chain there are for the system to become modified by chemicals.

KEY PRINCIPLES

- Neurons and glial cells are the basic building blocks of the nervous system.

- Neurons consist of four important zones: (1) dendrites, which receive the chemical signals and channel them to the soma, (2) the soma, which summarizes the incoming signals, (3) the single axon, which conveys action potentials away from the soma, and (4) axon terminals, which transmit chemical signals.

- Neurons are linked together in dense networks, connected to each other by synapses, the sites of chemical transmission.

- Glial cells help with breaking down neurotransmitters, wrapping myelin sheaths around axons to speed electrical signaling, and regulating the chemical environment around neurons.

- Neurotransmitters diffuse across the synaptic cleft and bind to receptors on the postsynaptic target.

- Dendrites decode information by responding with small graded voltage changes to neurotransmitter behavior on the membrane; the dendrites and soma sum these signals. Output depends on whether the summed voltage reaches the threshold for initiating a spike.

- A neuron codes information not with single spikes, but instead in its frequency of firing (rate coding).

- Individually, neurons are noisy; collectively, they can be precise.

- Although neurons are traditionally recorded from one at a time, neural coding involves populations of neurons working together in transient coalitions.

KEY TERMS

The Cells of the Brain

neuron (p. 77)

membrane (p. 77)

dendrites (p. 77)

soma (cell body) (p. 78)

nucleus (p. 78)

axon (p. 78)

axon terminals (p. 78)

afferent neuron (p. 79)

efferent neuron (p. 79)

multipolar neurons (p. 80)

bipolar neurons (p. 80)

monopolar neurons (p. 80)

glial cells (glia) (p. 80)

oligodendrocytes (p. 80)

Golgi staining (p. 81)

Nissl staining (p. 81)

autoradiography (p. 81)

immunocytochemistry (p. 81)

DNA (p. 81)

in situ hybridization (p. 81)

REVIEW QUESTIONS

1. How did the discovery that brain cells are discrete lead to new ideas about neural signaling?

2. Action potentials are all or none. Does that mean that brains are like digital computers? Why or why not? In what way are signals between neurons *not* like digital computers?

3. What is the advantage of myelin for an axon?

4. What is the sense in which neurons "make decisions"?

5. Why is it correct to think of a neuron as a pattern recognizer?

6. What are the advantages of having populations of neurons encode stimuli rather than individual "grandmother cells"?

7. What are two possible ways in which neurons might combine to form a coalition?

CRITICAL-THINKING QUESTIONS

1. Given everything that you have learned about the nervous system and the advantages of myelination, why do you think that many neurons are unmyelinated? Do you think that myelination serves a more critical role in some parts of the nervous system than in others? Explain your answer, using examples to illustrate your reasoning.

2. From an evolutionary perspective, do you think it would be better to have cells that functioned more like "grandmother cells" to recognize objects or cells that worked together in coalitions? Explain your reasoning.

3. In what other ways, besides the ones described in this chapter, do you think that neurons could combine to form a coalition? In general terms, describe how you would investigate whether neurons combined to form a coalition in these ways.

- Explain how the brain can reconfigure its circuitry to adapt to changes in sensory input.

- Illustrate how the brain can reconfigure its circuitry to enable new forms of behavior and how neuromodulators control plasticity according to information relevance.

- Describe how the brain adapts to losing neural tissue.

- Explain why the brain has a sensitive period for learning.

- Characterize how genetic factors and experiences interact in brain development.

- Illustrate two biological mechanisms of neural competition.

- Characterize a rapid and a slow mechanism for changing neural circuitry.

- Show how the brain incorporates new forms of sensory input.

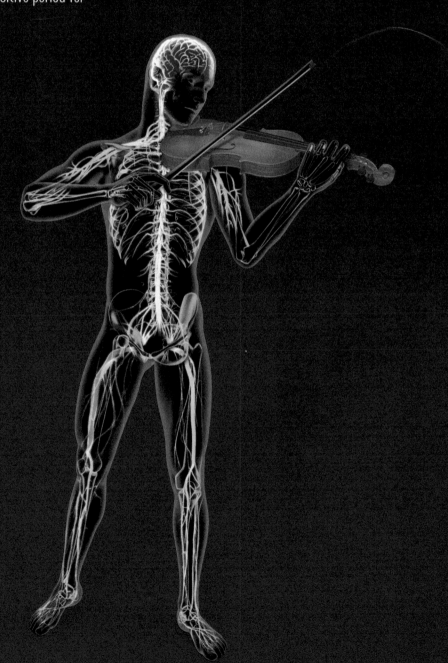

CHAPTER 4

Neuroplasticity

STARTING OUT:
The Child with Half a Brain

By the time Matthew S. was 6 years old, he began to have several epileptic seizures each day—sometimes every few minutes. Medications were of no use. He was diagnosed with Rasmussen's encephalitis, a rare, chronic inflammatory disease that typically affects only a single brain hemisphere. His parents explored their options and were shocked to learn that there was only one known treatment for Rasmussen's: removal of an entire hemisphere of the brain (Borgstein & Gottendorst, 2002).

But how could it be possible to live with half of the brain missing? Aren't the functions of the brain distributed widely across its territories? Wouldn't removal of one half be fatal—or at least devastating to Matthew's quality of life?

With no remaining options, Matthew's parents took him to Johns Hopkins Hospital in Baltimore, Maryland, where he underwent a **hemispherectomy**: the complete removal of half the cerebrum (**FIGURE 4.1**). The empty half of the skull filled up with cerebrospinal fluid, which shows up as a black void in neuroimaging.

Matthew walks with a slight limp on the opposite side of his body. Otherwise, he lives a normal life with almost no measurable deficit in cognition or behavior. How

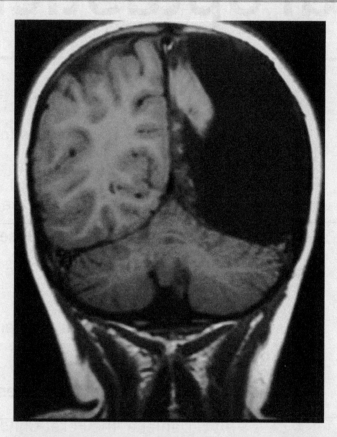

FIGURE 4.1 **Hemispherectomy.** In a hemispherectomy, half the brain is surgically removed. This surgery has become standard operating procedure for Rasmussen's encephalitis, a rare inflammatory disease that often affects only one hemisphere. Amazingly, as long as the surgery is performed before the age of 8, the child does remarkably well: the remainder of the brain dynamically rewires to take over the missing functions.

can this be possible? Because the remainder of his brain has dynamically rewired to take over the missing functions. The normal maps of the brain have redrawn themselves on a smaller piece of neural real estate. How the brain accomplishes this remarkable feat—something no manmade machine can yet do— is the subject of this chapter.

The brain is often thought of as a fixed organ with different regions dedicated to specific tasks. But the brain is better understood as a dynamic system, constantly modifying its own circuitry to match the demands of the environment and the goals of the animal. This ongoing rewiring is the brain's most fundamental principle and the source of its utility. Whereas your computer is built with hardwiring that remains fixed from the assembly line onward, the brain dynamically reconfigures, ever so subtly, with each new experience. It reorganizes itself from the level of molecules in the synapses to the level of the gross anatomy visible to the naked eye. When you learn something new (such as your professor's name), your brain physically changes. This ability to physically change, and to hold that change, is known as *plasticity*—just like the material we call plastic, which can be molded and retain its new shape. Plasticity is the basis of learning and memory, as we'll see in Chapter 9. In this chapter, we will discover how the principles of plasticity allow the brain tremendous flexibility: using the strategy of reconfiguration by experience, a brain can find itself within any body plan (four arms, eight legs, and so forth), and it will figure out how to configure itself to control it optimally. A brain can find itself in any ecosystem (e.g., jungle, swamp, or mountains), and it will learn how to move in it. A brain can find itself in any country, and it will absorb the local language and culture. In this chapter, we'll find out how.

First, we'll examine several examples that unmask the plastic capabilities of the brain by examining how it responds when the sensory input changes. Next, we'll discover how plastic changes are tied into relevant goals for an animal, and we'll see how the brain distributes its functions according to the available territory. This sort of plasticity happens mostly within a time window known as the **sensitive period**. We will then be ready to confront the nature-versus-nurture question to learn how much of the brain is prewired by genetics and how much is plastic. Finally, we'll turn to the mechanics of the reorganization to understand what is happening at the level of the synapses and neurons. The examples we will find along the way are all captured by a single organizing principle: the brain distributes its resources according to what's important for the organism, and it does so by having do-or-die competition at every level, from neurons to brain regions.

The Brain Dynamically Reorganizes to Match Its Inputs

In the sensory and motor areas of the cortex (which we will discuss in the next chapters), neighboring populations of neurons generally represent neighboring parts of the body—that is, the hand is represented near the forearm, which is represented near the elbow, and the upper arm, and so on (Nakamura et al., 1998). This map of the body is known as the **homunculus,** or "little man" (FIGURE 4.2). But how does your brain, encased in its dark vault of silence, know what your body looks like? Is the body plan genetically prespecified? And what would happen if your body changed—say, by the loss of an arm or the addition of two more legs: would the homunculus change?

Changes to the Body Plan

Changes to a body plan—such as the loss of a limb—lead to massive cortical reorganization. In one study with monkeys, the nerves carrying signals from one arm were severed—this is known as **deafferentation**. When the monkeys were tested 12 years later, it became clear that their somatosensory cortex had rearranged: the areas once representing the

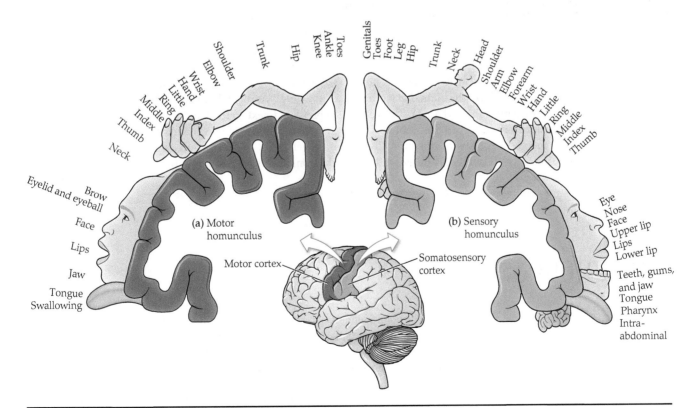

FIGURE 4.2 **(a) Motor homunculus and (b) sensory homunculus.** The body becomes topographically mapped on the precentral gyrus (motor cortex) and postcentral gyrus (somatosensory cortex). Those areas with more sensation, or that are more finely controlled, have larger areas of representation.

Normal somatosensory cortex   **Amputee** somatosensory cortex

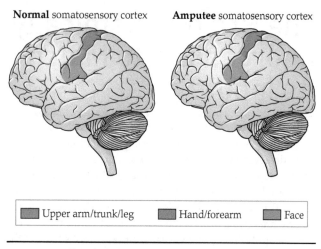

▥ Upper arm/trunk/leg   ▥ Hand/forearm   ▥ Face

FIGURE 4.3 Changes in sensory maps: the brain adapts to changes in incoming activity, even in adulthood. After hand amputation in humans, neighboring cortical territory (purple and green) takes over the territory that previously coded for the hand (orange).

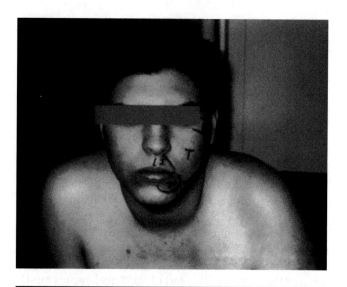

FIGURE 4.4 Phantom sensations in amputee. When an arm is amputated, a touch to the face (represented in neighboring cortical territory) often results in a sensation that the phantom arm is being touched. This 17-year-old man lost his right arm. When a cotton swab was stroked on his face one month later, the area labeled "T" gave rise to sensation in his phantom thumb, "P" to his phantom pinkie, "I" to his index finger, and "B" to the ball of his thumb. Figure from Ramachandran and Hirstein (1998).

arm had been taken over by the neighboring areas, which happened to respond to touch on the face (Pons et al., 1991).

This same phenomenon is observed in humans. When an arm is amputated—say, after a motorcycle accident—the neighboring face representation creeps into the neural territory that used to represent the hand (FIGURE 4.3) (Ramachandran, Rogers-Ramachandran, & Stewart, 1992). In other words, following deafferentation, sensory cortical areas do not go unused; instead, they are taken over by their neighbors (Barinaga, 1992; Flor et al., 1995; Merzenich, 1998). Later in this chapter, we will examine how these changes occur at the level of cells, but here we attend to the bigger picture.

Although the cortex that formerly responded to touch on the arm comes to respond to the face, the takeover is not complete—and this means that parts of the brain that it projects to are "expecting" information about the arm. This can lead to perceptual confusion in the form of a phantom sensation. Almost 150 years ago, S. Weir Mitchell observed Civil War amputees at a hospital in Philadelphia and noted the

curious fact that many of them contended that they could still *feel* their missing limb (Nathanson, 1988).

What could explain these strange aspects of D.M.'s experience? Her story is not uncommon among patients with amputations—this sort of experience happens to the majority. This is because many square centimeters of the cortex that previously responded to the limb now begin to respond to touch on the face, trunk, or the limb stump (Borsook et al., 1998; Cohen, Bandinelli, Findley, & Hallett, 1991; Merzenich, 1998; Pascual-Leone, Peris, Tormos, Pascual, & Catala, 1996; Yang et al., 1994). As a result, touches along the chin and jawline (represented next to the hand in the homunculus) engender the sensation of the missing hand being touched (FIGURE 4.4).

Over time, the distortion of the body—in which the phantom fingers move closer to the stump—is also a common

CASE STUDY:
Phantom Sensation

D.M., a 43-year-old woman, had her right arm amputated just above her elbow. Although her arm was missing, she insisted that she could still *feel* her right forearm, hand, and fingers. She could, in fact, "move" them. When she walked, she felt her missing hand swinging correctly with the motion of her body. She reported that the sensation from her phantom arm felt a bit colder; otherwise, it was mostly indistinguishable from the sensation in her existing arm. When the right side of D.M.'s face was touched, she felt as though her missing limb was being touched at the same time. As the year after her amputation progressed, she felt as though her hand and fingers moved closer to the stump of her arm (Halligan, Marshall, & Wade, 1994).

RESEARCH METHODS:
Mapping Out the Brain

How did researchers know that the homunculus of the monkeys had changed? They inserted an electrode into different parts of the somatosensory cortex and determined what local neurons responded to. By moving the electrode to different locations and touching the monkeys in different places, they could map out the receptive fields of the neurons—in this case, the area of the body that caused the neurons to fire more (FIGURE 4.5). With current technology, researchers can use fMRI with monkeys to determine the responses of different brain regions to different areas on the body—but note that this has lower resolution.

For humans, assessing the brain's map of the body can also be accomplished with fMRI. But the process is otherwise a little different for the humans. Although it's possible to use electrodes to measure individual neurons in the motor cortex, it's rare. But instead there's a different opportunity: just ask them where they perceive the touch! In assessing cortical reorganization in the phantom limb example above (FIGURE 4.4), researchers asked, "where do you feel this?" while touching a cotton swab to different parts of the participant's face, neck, and torso. By noting where the man reported the sensation of the touch, they were able to infer how his homunculus had changed.

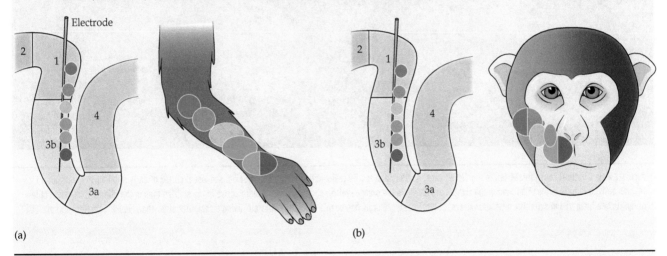

(a) (b)

FIGURE 4.5 **To map out the brain's representation of the body, an electrode is placed in different locations while the animal is touched in different spots.** In the case of the monkeys, neurons in the region of the somatosensory cortex that would normally have encoded touch on the arm (a) now responded to touch on the face (b).

report, and the final sensation of the hand is often perceived as being on or even inside the stump (Cronholm, 1951; Henderson & Smyth, 1948; Merzenich et al., 1984; Ramachandran et al., 1992). The same distortion occurs with phantom feet and toes being felt when higher parts of the leg or genitals are touched, and these phantom feet often move toward the stumps of the amputated leg (Ramachandran & Blakeslee, 1998). Quite commonly, enduring pain parallels these changes and is understood as part of the perceptual consequence of cortical reorganization following arm amputation. The magnitude of this **phantom limb** pain typically correlates with the extent of remodeling recorded in the cortex: the more changes, the more pain (Flor et al., 1995; Karl, Birbaumer, Lutzenberger, Cohen, & Flor, 2001).

The strange phenomenon of phantom limbs illustrates an important point about our perceptions. Although, pain, warmth, and touch feel embodied in our limbs, the fact is that they arise in the brain. You can lose a limb without losing sensation in it. (Conversely, if the brain is injured, you can lose sensation in a limb without losing the limb itself). Experiences are built in the circuitry of neurons. Or, more simply, "no brain, no pain."

Changes to Sensory Input

Cortical reorganization does not require an event as drastic as an amputation—it can instead be induced by a temporary

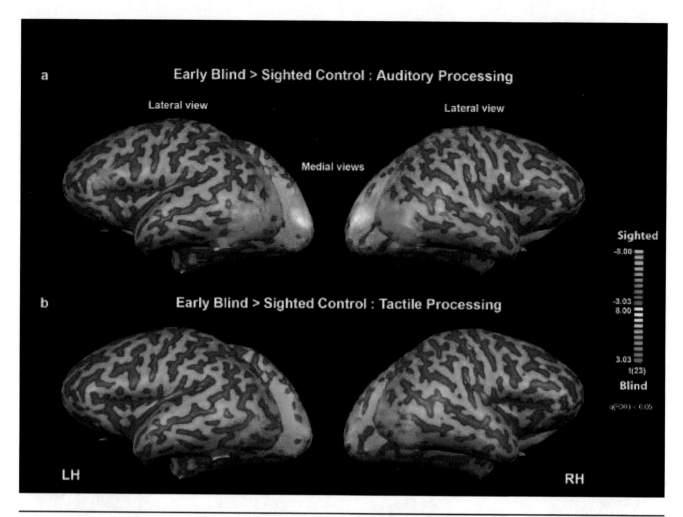

FIGURE 4.6 **Cortical reorganization.** In this fMRI image, auditory and tactile tasks activate the otherwise unused visual cortex of early blind participants. Brain regions activated more in the blind than in the sighted are shown in the orange–yellow spectrum; areas more active in the sighted than in the blind are shown in blue–green. To see the gyri and sulci (the hills and valleys) of the cortex, the brain has been artificially "inflated" using a computer algorithm. Figure from Renier et al. (2010).

change in the sensory input. For example, when a tight pressure cuff is fastened to an arm or the nerves from the arm are blocked pharmacologically, within less than an hour, the human brain adjusts to the loss of sensory input by devoting less territory to that part of the body (Weiss, Miltner, Liepert, Meissner, & Taub, 2004). In another example, if two fingers of the hand of the adult owl monkey are tied together and no longer operate independently of one another, their cortical representation begins to merge into a single area (Clark, Allard, Jenkins, & Merzenich, 1988). In these cases, the brain circuitry adjusts itself to fit the body it is dealing with. The rapidity with which this happens suggests that there does not need to be a large-scale rewiring of these areas, but, instead, that there are connections already in place that are merely unmasked by these changes to sensory input (Clark et al., 1988). This flexible matching to the body plan allows the brain to optimize its allocation of neural resources.

The principles of reorganization go beyond the input from the body to the input of the senses more generally. Have you ever heard that blind people have more sensitive touch and hearing? This is because the brain deploys its space and resources according to the signals that come in. Thus, the visual cortex of the congenitally blind becomes tuned to tactile and auditory input (FIGURE 4.6) (Elbert & Rockstroh, 2004; Pascual-Leone, Amedi, Fregni, & Merabet, 2005). The perceptual consequence of the cortical takeover is increased sensitivity.

Do we need a lifetime's experience to reshape our brains so dramatically? The answer seems to be no. When people with perfectly functioning visual systems are blindfolded for only two days, their primary visual cortex activates when they perform tasks with their fingers or when they hear tones or words (Pascual-Leone & Hamilton, 2001). Removing the blindfold for just 12 hours reverts the visual cortex so that it responds again only to visual input. The brain's sudden ability to take over the visual cortex depends on connections from other areas that are present but unused under normal circumstances, an issue to which we will return later.

Beyond increased sensitivity, another consequence of cortical reorganization can be hallucination. As an example, patients whose auditory nerve is severed may sometimes experience **tinnitus**, a constant ringing in the ears that occurs without any actual auditory input (Lockwood, Salvi, & Burkard, 2002). Similarly, progressive hearing loss can lead to musical and verbal hallucinations (Miller & Crosby, 1979). These symptoms result from cortical reorganization, and they are called auditory phantom sensations (Muhlau et al., 2006).

In short, brains redeploy their territory in the face of changing inputs, a strategy that allows for remarkable adaptability. For example, imagine that you were an animal that ended up near waterfalls in the rain forest, where you could no longer hear other environmental sounds. The parts of your brain devoted to hearing would lose territory and other parts of the system would usurp that neural real estate. Likewise, if you were a fish that evolved to trawl lower depths of the ocean, where shafts of sunlight no longer reached, your visual systems would give up the territory they once commanded. This plasticity gives brains the capacity to find themselves located in a variety of environments and equipped with a variety of senses—and the neural wiring will flexibly adapt to "wrap itself around" the inputs.

The Brain Distributes Resources Based on Relevance

The last section looked at how the brain reorganizes in response to changes in sensory input. We will now learn how an animal's behaviors and actions play a critical role in patterns of change.

The Role of Behavior

Brains appear to employ **adaptive coding**, which means that they allocate more or less neural activity to any given function depending on the needs of the organism (Schweighofer & Arbib, 1998). In other words, if you decide to make a career change to ornithology, more of your neural resources will become devoted toward learning the subtle differences between birds (wing shape, belly coloration, beak size), whereas previously your neural representation with respect to birds may have been crude, such as, "is that a bird or an airplane?" Your sensory abilities refine themselves as required.

This is true not only of sensory representation, but also of motor representation. In one experiment, monkeys were trained on two different tasks. The first task required the monkeys to retrieve small objects via skilled, fine use of the digits. The second was a key-turning task, which required more wrist and forearm use (Nudo, Milliken, Jenkins, & Merzenich, 1996). Then the researchers mapped out how much of the monkeys' motor cortex was devoted to moving each body part. After training on the first task, the cortical representation for digits progressively usurped more territory whereas the wrist and forearm representation shrank (FIGURE 4.7). In contrast, if the monkeys trained on the key-turning task, the amount of neural territory devoted to the wrist and forearm expanded.

These changes demonstrate that the cortex comes to reflect an animal's actions and goals—these become directly reflected in the structure of the brain. We can see these changes in humans as well. For example, learning to play the violin or learning to read Braille both result in increased finger representations in cortical maps (Elbert, Pantev, Wienbruch, Rockstroh, & Taub, 1995; Karni et al., 1995). A different study using structural MRI found that when people learned how to juggle, there was a measurable increase in gray matter volume in visual areas of the brain (Draganski et al., 2004). Three months after the jugglers quit their new hobby, their gray matter volume shrank back to starting levels. (Note that the volume increases may result from many factors, including increases in the size of cell bodies, the birth of new neurons or glia, or changes in the dendrites, all of which can be expressions of plasticity). By devoting more resources to novel tasks, brains can optimize their circuitry based on the goals in front of them.

Knowing how training can reshape the motor cortex has led to a better approach for patients who are paralyzed after a stroke: get the patient to use the paralyzed limb rather than depend on the good one. In **constraint therapy**, a functioning hand or arm is actually bound with a strap device to force the patient to use the weaker one instead. Why does that help? By trying to use the weaker hand, the patient engages the remaining connections in undamaged areas of the brain. These connections can gradually strengthen until new, functional motor control circuits are built. More importantly, restraining the healthy hand prevents its representation from marching in and taking over what few neural resources are left to the disabled hand (Hart, 2005). As in some social circles, the weaker members can survive and even thrive if they are given a little room to succeed.

The Role of Relevance: Gating Plasticity with Neuromodulation

From what we've covered so far, you might think that practicing an act repeatedly is the key to increasing its cortical representation. Although this is part of the story, it is not the whole story: there is a deeper principle at work, and that is whether the actions have *relevance* to the animal. In this

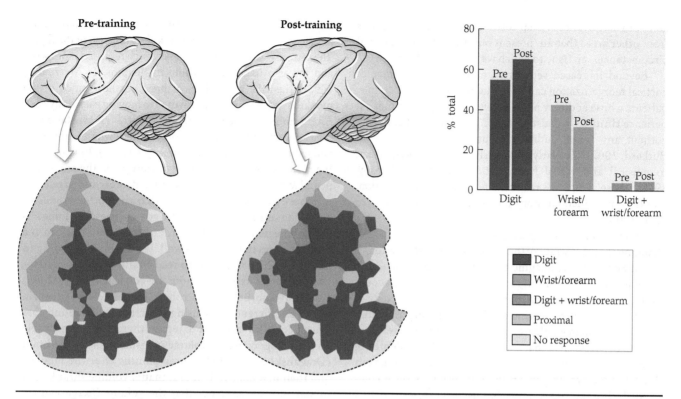

FIGURE 4.7 **Functional mapping of primary motor cortex.** When a monkey trains on a task that requires fine-digit manipulation (such as grabbing small objects), the cortical representation of digits expands. Shown here is a functional mapping of the primary motor cortex, demonstrating an expansion of the digit representation (purple) and a shrinkage of the forearm representation (green).

NEUROSCIENCE OF EVERYDAY LIFE:
Pianists and Violinists Have Different Brains

Because cortical circuitry can come to reflect the behaviors of the animal, the brains of highly trained musicians become measurably different—in a way that can be directly seen by coarse inspection of the brain's surface. In 2006, Bangert and Schlaug examined three-dimensional images of many brains, paying careful attention to a region of the motor cortex involved in hand movement (Bangert & Schlaug, 2006). They found that a particular gyrus in this region was shaped differently for some people than for others, and when the gyrus was puckered up in a particular way, they termed it the Omega Sign (FIGURE 4.8). Independent judges

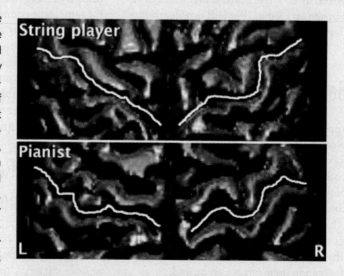

FIGURE 4.8 **Anatomical differences between string players and pianists can be seen with the naked eye.**

compared the brain structures of musicians and nonmusicians and discovered that musicians' brains reliably showed the Omega Sign, whereas nonmusicians' brains did not. Even more strikingly, the type of musician could be distinguished: keyboard players showed a larger Omega Sign in the left hemisphere, whereas string players showed it more in the right hemisphere. Who knew that what you choose to do with your life can end up reflected in the gross anatomy of your brain?

section, we will begin to see how the brain can turn plasticity on and off in particular places and at particular times, according to what is important for the animal's needs. This ability to allow changes to occur only when something important happens is called **gating** (think of opening and closing a gate to allow something to pass through). But how does the brain identify that something important has happened and thereby change to encode it?

One way that significance is expressed, biophysically, is through neuromodulatory systems: widely broadcast neural systems that correlate with reward, punishment, and alertness. We will learn more about these systems in later chapters. For now, you simply need to know that **neuromodulators** are diffusely released chemical signals that can gate plasticity such that changes take place only at the appropriate times, instead of each time activity passes through the network. In other words, reorganization of parts of the cortex only occurs when paired with the release of particular neuromodulators (Bakin & Weinberger, 1996).

One particularly important neuromodulator is the neurotransmitter acetylcholine (Gu, 2003). Neurons that release acetylcholine are called **cholinergic**, and these neurons exist mostly in the **basal forebrain**, a subcortical collection of structures that project to the cortex (FIGURE 4.9). These cholinergic neurons are active when an animal is learning a task, but not once a task is well established (Orsetti,

Casamenti, & Pepeu, 1996). These neurons are driven by both rewards and punishments in proportion to their intensity (Richardson & DeLong, 1991). In this sense, they are using both good and bad outcomes as markers that it is time to change the brain.

Electrical stimulation of these cholinergic neurons increases plasticity in their target areas, whereas blocking the activity decreases plasticity (Hasselmo, 1995). To illustrate this point, let's examine how the auditory cortex of adult rats changes after exposure to auditory tones of various frequencies. The auditory cortex contains maps like those of the motor cortex, but they are **tonotopic** rather than **somatotopic**: they represent adjacent frequencies rather than adjacent body parts. Exposure to a tone does not result in changes to the tonotopic map, but when a particular tone is paired with electrical stimulation of cholinergic neurons, the cortical representation for that tone's frequency massively expands (Kilgard & Merzenich, 1998). In other words, the brain devotes more territory to that tone's frequency because the presence of the acetylcholine indicates that the tone must be important. Parallel results of plasticity-induced effects of acetylcholine have been demonstrated in the visual cortex (Bear & Singer, 1986) and somatosensory cortex (Sachdev, Lu, Wiley, & Ebner, 1998). Similar changes can be imaged with fMRI in humans in an auditory paradigm: plastic changes are blocked by a pharmacological blocker of acetylcholine (Thiel, Friston, & Dolan, 2002).

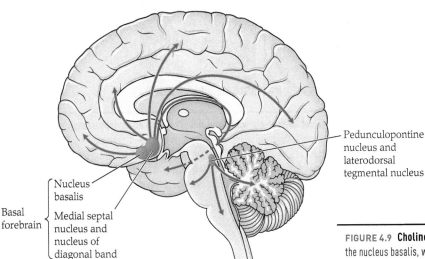

Pedunculopontine nucleus and laterodorsal tegmental nucleus

Nucleus basalis

Basal forebrain

Medial septal nucleus and nucleus of diagonal band

FIGURE 4.9 **Cholinergic pathways in the brain.** Of special importance is the nucleus basalis, which transmits acetylcholine broadly throughout the cortex.

Although it is said that practice makes perfect, practicing a task is not sufficient to change the brain in the absence of the plasticity-enhancing powers of the cholinergic neurons. Consider this study an illustration of that principle: two groups of rats were trained in a difficult task of grabbing sugar pellets through a small, high slot. In one group, cholinergic neurons in the basal forebrain were pharmacologically destroyed. For the normal rats, two weeks of practice led to a 30% increase in the size of the cortical area devoted to the forepaw movement. In parallel, their motor skills and speed improved. By contrast, for the rats without cholinergic modulation, the same cortical area actually *shrank* by 22%, and accuracy for reaching the sugar pellet never improved (FIGURE 4.10) (Conner, Culberson, Packowski, Chiba, & Tuszynski, 2003). So we see that the basis of plasticity and behavioral improvement is not simply the repeated performance of a task: it also requires neuromodulatory systems to encode the relevance of the task.

Reach training

Motor map expands, reaching accuracy improves

Reach training with nucleus basalis lesion

Motor map and reaching accuracy remain unchanged

FIGURE 4.10 **Cholinergic transmission disrupted by lesioning the nucleus basalis.** After lesioning the nucleus basalis, rats do not have an expansion of the motor map associated with the reaching task and do not improve at the task. Figure adapted from Kilgard (2003).

CASE STUDY:
The Government Worker with the Missing Brain

A 44-year-old man in France went to his doctor because of mild weakness in his left leg. After some basic testing, his doctor sent him for routine neuroimaging to investigate the cause. The brain scan revealed something that no one could have guessed: empty space in much of the volume where his brain should reside (FIGURE 4.11) (Feuillet, Dufour, & Pelletier, 2007). To compound the surprising nature of this finding, the man had lived his entire life with his brain in this compressed state and had shown no obvious problems: he was married with two children and worked a white-collar job as a civil servant. His general IQ of 75 did not prevent performance of normal everyday activities, and his verbal IQ was slightly higher, at 84.

To appreciate how amazing this case is, note that our most brilliant engineers have no idea how to build machines that are so resilient to perturbation. Imagine that instead of building a normal digital computer or car, we could harness the principles of dynamic reorganization to build a computer that could survive a truck rolling over half of it or a car that runs just fine after you tear out half its engine.

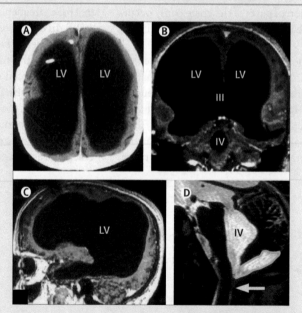

FIGURE 4.11 **Brain scan of 44-year-old white-collar worker with no obvious behavioral abnormalities.** A blockage near the arrow (d) had prevented normal flow of the cerebrospinal fluid since the time he was a child, and his ventricles had filled and expanded as a consequence (known as noncommunicating hydrocephalus). Because of remarkable flexibility in programs of neural development, this did not prevent performance of normal everyday activities. LV = lateral ventricle.

The ancient Greeks knew the importance of relevance, observing that the best learning occurs when one is interested—that is, paying attention (Benson, 1990). Experimental work bears out their observations: attending to one stimulus over another can increase plasticity in the brain region of the first and not the second. For example, in one study a monkey was exposed to simultaneous auditory and tactile stimulation. If the demands of the task required him to pay attention to the touch, the somatosensory cortex showed plastic changes whereas his auditory cortex did not. If he instead was directed to attend to the auditory stimulus, the opposite happened (Burton & Sinclair, 2000). This effect of attention is mediated by acetylcholine: when we attend, more acetylcholine is released (Sarter, Bruno, & Turchi, 1999).

As a side note, the targets of cholinergic transmission tend to be broadly distributed, not precise (FIGURE 4.9). So why doesn't acetylcholine release accidentally cause widespread neural changes? The answer is that cholinergic effects can themselves be modulated by other, inhibitory neurotransmitters. In combination, those neurotransmitters can make local areas less plastic (or not plastic at all), so that the changes occur only in the specific areas where they are intended (Sarter et al., 1999). As a result, the release of acetylcholine gates the brain to reconfigure small, specific regions of circuitry.

The Brain Uses the Available Tissue

We have so far been examining how the brain allocates its resources when sensory inputs or behavioral outputs change. We now turn to a slightly different issue: what happens when the brain's available resources change—that is, when disease, surgery, or brain damage lead to less brain tissue?

Maps Adjust Themselves to the Available Brain Tissue

There are two possibilities that could explain what happens when the brain's available resources change: first, the system might leave out the parts of the map corresponding to the missing tissue or, second, the brain might make the same map of the body on a smaller piece of real estate. Which do you think is the case?

To find out, researchers turned to the frog, in whom nerves from the eye travel directly to the **optic tectum** (roughly analogous to the visual cortex in mammals) (FIGURE 4.12a). There the nerves plug in retinotopically—that is, nerve fibers from the top of the eye connect to the top of the tectum, the left part of the eye to the left part of the tectum, and so on. Essentially, each fiber coming from the eye appears to have a preassigned address where it plugs into the target. To understand the principles of plasticity, researchers removed half of the optic tectum during development, before the optic nerves had arrived. What happened? A full **retinotopic** map developed on the smaller target area (Udin, 1977). The map was compressed in size, but otherwise arranged normally (FIGURE 4.12b).

In a more dramatic demonstration of the same principle, researchers transplanted a third eye in a tadpole (FIGURE 4.12c). This resulted in an unusual situation in which two sets of optic nerves now had to share the same target area of the tectum. What happened? The two eyes shared the territory in alternating stripes, each with its full retinotopic mapping (Constantine-Paton & Law, 1978; Law & Constantine-Paton, 1981). In other words, the retinal fibers once again utilized whatever target area was available. In this case, it was not that one half of the tectum was missing—it was simply being competed for by the fibers from the other eye, leaving less total territory available.

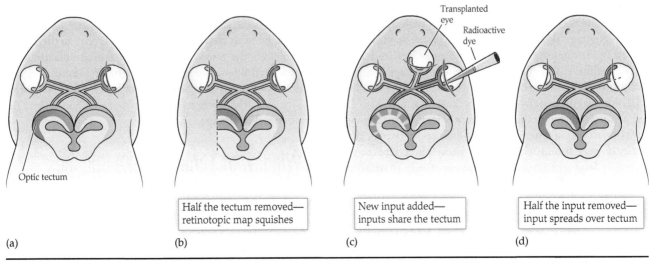

(a)   (b)   (c)   (d)

Half the tectum removed—retinotopic map squishes

New input added—inputs share the tectum

Half the input removed—input spreads over tectum

Optic tectum

Transplanted eye

Radioactive dye

FIGURE 4.12 Plasticity in the development of the nervous system. (a) Fibers from the tadpole's eye map retinotopically onto the tectum. (b) If half the tectum is removed, the complete input fits itself onto the smaller available area. (c) If a third eye is transplanted on one side, the tectum reorganizes to accommodate the additional input. (d) If half the retina is removed, the information from the remaining fibers spreads out to cover the available area of the tectum.

The last two experiments demonstrate that maps can compress, and even alternate when necessary, to fit the space available. But what if *extra* territory is available? Can the maps stretch to fill it? To find out, researchers removed one half of a frog's retina: now only half of the normal number of optic nerves headed out for the normally sized territory of the optic tectum. What happened in this case? The retinotopic map (now coding for only half of the visual space) spread out to utilize the entire tectum (FIGURE 4.12d) (Attardi & Sperry, 1963).

As we will see later in this chapter, neural maps are determined in part from local competitions at the level of neuronal populations, rather than from a prespecified set of blueprints. As a result of these competitions, whatever cortex is available will get used and filled. From an evolutionary point of view, these plastic mechanisms give great flexibility to organisms, allowing a single genetic program to work with innumerable varieties of body types. Remember Matthew S.'s hemispherectomy at the beginning of this chapter? We are starting to understand how his brain could survive losing half its territory: it rewired itself to retain most of the normal function on less than the normal amount of brain territory.

Cortical Reorganization after Brain Damage

The properties of cortical wiring are the best hope after brain damage caused by stroke. It is typical for a patient's symptoms to look the worst immediately after a stroke because of tissue damage and swelling. When tissue damage and swelling subside, typically after a few days, there is often a sharp recovery of some function. But that's when the real work of the brain begins. Over the course of weeks, months, or years, massive cortical reorganization can occur, and functions that were lost can sometimes be regained.

An example of this can often be seen with **aphasia**, in which language skills are damaged or lost following brain injury. In the majority of people, language is localized to the left hemisphere, and after left hemisphere damage language function is impaired. However, with time, language function will often begin to recover—not because of a healing of the left hemisphere, but in theory because of transfer of language function to the right hemisphere. In one report, two separate patients were found who had left hemisphere strokes followed by language impairment and eventually (partial) recovery. But both of these unlucky patients then suffered right-side strokes and showed a worsening of their recovered language, suggesting that the function had transferred to the right hemisphere (Basso, Gardelli, Grassi, & Mariotti, 1989). In recent years, researchers have used fMRI to provide confirmatory evidence for this theory and map this kind of transfer of functions across hemispheres (Hertz-Pannier et al., 2002).

But how can one brain region take over the functions of another? Aren't they in different places, doing different things? How does "visual cortex" stop being visual and assume another role? The answer is that the function of a neuron does not depend on its identity or its location, but instead on its connections. If a neuron is lost, but another neuron manages to get access to the same set of inputs and outputs, it can in time assume the functions of the first. When it comes to the functioning of neurons (as sometimes with people), you are who you know.

In the case of the aphasia patients, some of the neurons in the undamaged hemisphere have similar connections to the ones that were lost. With some adjustments over time, they can learn to perform the missing function. But if these neurons, too, are lost, it may be more difficult to find such well-connected replacements the second time around. At this point, the aphasia becomes much worse (Basso et al., 1989).

To summarize this section, we have seen that the brain's maps can change and adjust to meet the available neural territory. This simple developmental rule allows the brain to build maps that can be stretched and compressed. In a map like this, the hand will be represented near the elbow, which will itself be represented near the shoulder—irrespective of how much or how little territory is available. When large parts of the cortex are removed, automatic rewiring sets into place that can often recreate the functions of the original circuitry. These examples demonstrate that the organizational structure of maps in the brain do not require full genetic prespecification, but instead can unfold naturally with an animal's development and experience.

A Sensitive Period for Plastic Changes

Although brains change quite a bit in response to their interaction with the world, they are not equally plastic at all points in time—instead, they are most plastic during a window of time called the sensitive period. After this period has passed, the system becomes more difficult (but not impossible) to change.

A Window of Time to Make Changes

An understanding of the sensitive period can direct clinical approaches. For example, if a child is born with *strabismus* (misaligned eyes, known colloquially as "lazy eyed" or "crosseyed"), her visual system will not wire up correctly. She will favor one eye and the other eye will develop bad vision, also called *amblyopia*. In terms of visual function, there is nothing physically wrong with the eye on the impaired side; instead, the problem for the child lies in the visual cortex, where the dominant eye outcompetes the misaligned one to take over its territory. If the misalignment is not fixed at an early age (when the eyes are jockeying for control of visual cortex), the vision in the misaligned eye will not be recoverable (Berman & Murphy, 1981).

Just as with the principles of constraint therapy in the stroke patients we saw earlier, the solution is to cover up the dominant eye to give its weaker partner a chance to acquire some cortical territory. Once the sensitive period has passed, the patch can be removed. This clinical knowledge stems from studies of animals with normal vision, in which one eye is covered with a patch to assess the effects on vision. If the patching is done while the animal is young, it changes the balance of activity between two eyes and permanently ruins the vision attainable by that eye. However, the same eye patch applied later in life has no lasting effect because the sensitive period has passed (Issa, Trachtenberg, Chapman, Zahs, & Stryker, 1999).

CASE STUDY:
Danielle, the Feral Child in the Window

In July 2005, police in Plant City, Florida, pulled up outside a dilapidated house to investigate a claim of child abuse. What they found inside caused them to be physically ill. Danielle Crockett (FIGURE 4.13), a girl of almost 7 years of age, had been locked away in a dark closet for, as far as they could tell, her whole childhood (DeGregory, 2008). She was flecked with fecal matter and cockroaches. Beyond basic sustenance, it appeared she had never received physical affection or normal conversation and that she had probably never been let outdoors. She was fully incapable of speech. Police, social workers, and psychologists all reported that she appeared to look right through them; she had no glimmer of recognition or normal human interaction. She could not chew solid food, did not know how to use a toilet, could not nod yes or no, and by one year later had not mastered use of a sippy cup. After many tests, physicians were able to verify that she had no genetic problems such as cerebral palsy, autism, or Down syndrome. Instead, the normal development of her brain had been derailed by severe social deprivation.

As of 2010, Danielle was showing some improvements. She had

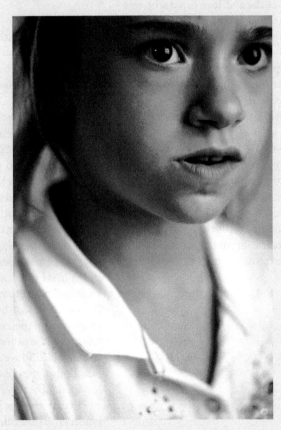

FIGURE 4.13 **Danielle, a feral child discovered in 2005 in Florida.** Although she is a beautiful girl, the expressions and behaviors inherent to normal human interaction did not have a chance to develop properly.

learned how to use the toilet, could understand what people said to her, and could make some limited verbal replies. She was attending prekindergarten and learning to trace letters. Despite these promising signs, however, it is unlikely that she will be able to gain much of the ground lost during her tragic first years of life.

The Sensitive Period in Language

As an example of a sensitive period, consider the acquisition of a second language. You have probably observed that the age at which a child moves to a new country influences how well she will learn the grammar of the new language (Johnson & Newport, 1989) (FIGURE 4.14). If the age of arrival is before 7 years old, fluency is as high as that of a native speaker. An immigrant of 8–10 years of age has a more difficult time reaching that level of facility with the language, and if the child is already past 17 when moving to the new country, her proficiency is likely to remain low. This illustrates that a new language is not equally learnable at all time points—instead, the ability to learn a language declines with age.

During the sensitive period, input from the world is vital for proper development. Infants who are born deaf, for example, will fail to make the proper vocal babbling sounds, even if their vocal cords are perfectly capable of doing so (Oller & Eilers, 1988). Without the auditory input, the rest of the system does not "bootstrap" itself into language acquisition. However, deaf infants with parents who speak sign language will pick up on the ability to express themselves with their hands and will display "manual babbling"—that is, their hands will make resemblances to components of sign language (Petitto & Marentette, 1991).

Note an interesting property of the sensitive period: the opening of some doors often leads to the closing of others. Infants are able to hear all possible sounds of human languages, but with progressive exposure to their mother tongue, they lose the ability to hear foreign sounds. For example, Japanese infants can easily distinguish R and L sounds: if they hear a steady sound like RRRRLLLLL, they will notice the change in the middle. But as they grow slightly older, the sound structure of their own language causes them to lose the capacity to perceive the difference between R and

L; now the change from one to the other is not able to be detected (Kuhl, 2004). The **sensitive period for language sounds** or **phonemes** (perceptually distinct units of sound that distinguish one word from another) is earlier than that for vocabulary, which is why we hear accents in those who acquire our language late in life (Kuhl, Conboy, Padden, Nelson, & Pruitt, 2005).

We have seen that the acquisition of language and the development of vision depend on normal input from the world. More generally, what happens if a child receives none of the proper social input, such as physical touch and social feedback? What impact does severe deprivation have on development? As seen by the tragic case study of Danielle and other feral children (children raised without normal human interaction), the ability to learn language, interact socially, walk normally, chew food, and have normal neurodevelopment is limited to the years of young childhood. After a certain point, these abilities diminish. The brain needs to experience the proper input to achieve its normal connectivity.

Neuromodulation in Young Brains

We have learned that the brain is most spongelike and changeable during the sensitive period. However, this does not mean that brain plasticity is solely the privilege of the young. Neural rewiring is an ongoing process: we can form new ideas, accumulate information, remember people and events, and recover from injury. It simply becomes more difficult to do so. So why do young animals have such plastic brains? Why does learning become harder with age? What is the difference between young and old brains that can account for the drastic change in plasticity?

First, let's consider the situation from a developmental point of view. Species with more plastic brains require longer periods of helplessness. These longer periods allow greater flexibility. For example, the brains of human babies are enormously flexible to learning—but compared to other species, human babies are born with few built-in skills and are unable to survive on their own for a long time (many years!). Human adults, on the other hand, are quite good at specific tasks but less flexible. So we see a trade-off between plasticity and efficiency: as your brain gets good at certain things, it becomes less adaptable to others. What is the mechanism behind this?

Recall what we learned earlier about plasticity in the adult brain: attention causes widespread cholinergic release, which allows change in the tissue—and this is counterbalanced locally by inhibition in the areas that should *not* change. The story appears to be different in the developing brain. Young animals show a generalized plasticity without attentional focus. And this seems to be because young animals have high levels of cholinergic transmitters but not the other inhibitory transmitters, which become available only later (Broide & Leslie, 1999; Gopnik & Schulz, 2004; McKay, Placzek, & Dani, 2007; Torrão & Britto, 2002). As a result, baby brains have a constant flow of cholinergic signaling that enables

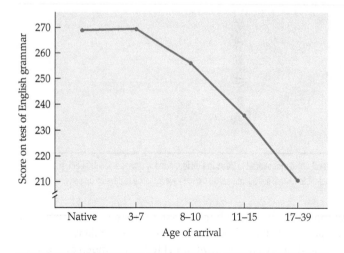

FIGURE 4.14 **Johnson and Newport's study demonstrated the relationship between age of arrival in the United States and total score correct on a test of English grammar.**

generalized plasticity. Their brains are generally flexible, slowly coming into focus all at once like a developing photograph, instead of changing a little at a time like a pointillist artist.

To summarize, adult brains employ the cholinergic system to allow plasticity and local inhibition to keep it from happening at unwanted spots. Young brains, on the other hand, are bathed in chemicals that allow for global change, making babies the "research and development" department of the human species (Schulz & Gopnik, 2004). As a result, flexibility and skill trade off within a single human lifetime. We will learn more about consequences of the cholinergic system and synaptic plasticity in Chapter 14, when we learn how drugs of abuse can tap into the neuromodulatory systems and literally rewrite the circuitry.

Hardwiring versus World Experience

We've shown many examples now in which changes in experience change the brain's wiring. But is there any influence of genetics at all? To what extent does the brain's wiring come prespecified by genetics, and to what extent does it only absorb information from the outside world to change its own wiring? In this section, we'll compare hardwiring to world experience and discover some surprising answers.

Aspects of the Brain Are Preprogrammed

Brains do not come into the world as blank slates; instead, they are born pre-equipped with expectations about the world. Consider the birth of a baby wildebeest: moments after dropping from the womb, it wobbles to its legs and can clumsily run and dodge. In its environment, it simply doesn't have time to spend months or years learning how to move around. Even human infants, who develop much more slowly, nonetheless have basic reflexes for grasping and sucking and will mimic an adult sticking out her tongue, a feat that requires the sophisticated, preprogrammed translation of vision into motor action (Gopnik & Schulz, 2004). And a good deal of work in language demonstrates that we come into the world pre-equipped to pick up on it (as we will learn in Chapter 11).

In the 1960s, Roger Sperry set out to determine just how much of an animal's developmental program is hardwired. He turned to the newt, in which nerve fibers from the eye grow back to the optic tectum and plug in retinotopically, just as we saw with frogs earlier. Sperry wanted to understand why each fiber from the eye appeared to have a preassigned address where it plugs in (FIGURE 4.15a). So he cut the optic nerve of an adult newt and rotated the eyeball upside down (FIGURE 4.15b) (Sperry, 1963). Although a severed optic nerve will not regenerate in a mammal, it will in an amphibian, and that fact

allowed Sperry to examine a simple question: would the fibers from the eye grow back into their original orientation in the tectum or would they twist around to match the world? He discovered that the fibers reconnected to the tectum in their original pattern, as though each fiber retained its original address despite the fact that the eye had been turned (FIGURE 4.15c). But because the eye was rotated, the unhappy newt now saw the world upside down and shot its tongue downward when a morsel of food was dangled above it.

These findings led Sperry to conclude that the newt's optic fibers plug into the tectum in a predefined, addressed manner, the way wires plug into a switchboard with a one-to-one addressing scheme. In his **chemoaffinity hypothesis**, Sperry imagined that each incoming axon might be matched by a particular molecule expressed by each destination cell in the tectum. Later, on realizing that the genome could not possibly code for that many different address molecules, he proposed that gradients of a smaller number of molecules (some repulsive and some attractive) might do the trick, the idea being that each incoming axon will be tuned for a particular combination of concentrations.

Sperry's chemoaffinity hypothesis does not require the animal to have any experience with the world: it is *experience independent*. The axons find their way to their targets based on molecular cues, irrespective of the interactions the animal experiences in the outside world. Sperry's hypothesis was correct (at least, in many places in the brain), indicating that some general aspects of neural connectivity are prespecified and independent of experience. Chemical cues guide the neurons to the right neighborhood, if not their final targets. So, for example, fibers from your retina will always find their way to the visual thalamus; regardless of your experience with the world, they will not wire to your toes.

Experience Changes the Brain

As you've no doubt guessed, preprogramming cannot be the whole story because much of this chapter has been about dynamic rewiring depending on circumstance.

Indeed, even early researchers began to suspect that experience would influence the brain—that is, that brains would not develop exactly the same way every time given the same set of genetic instructions. Two hundred years ago, the physiologist J. C. Spurzheim proposed that the brain (as well as the muscles) could be increased in size by exercise, based on his hypothesis that "the blood is carried in greater abundance to the parts which are excited and nutrition is performed by the blood" (Spurzheim, 1815). Almost 60 years later, in 1871, Charles Darwin wondered whether this same basic idea might explain why domestic rabbits had smaller brains than rabbits in the wild: he suggested that the wild rabbits are forced to use their wits and senses more than the domesticated ones, and their brain bulk reflects that (Darwin, 1871).

By the 1960s, researchers began to study in earnest whether the brain could change in measurable ways as a direct

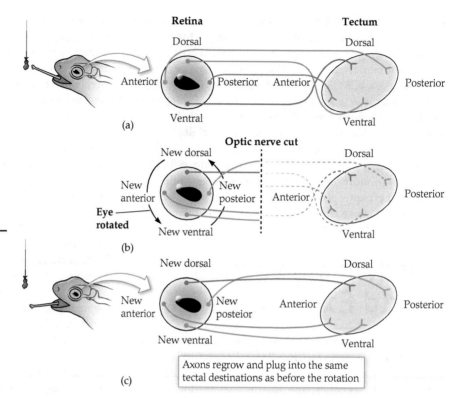

FIGURE 4.15 How the newt's optic nerve makes its connections. (a) Fibers from the retina maintain their organized layout when they plug into the optic tectum. (b) To determine how the fibers find their destinations, Sperry cut the optic nerve and rotated the eye upside down. When the fibers regrew, they plugged into the tectum in their original pattern, (c) This led Sperry to conclude that the fibers do not find their destinations by visual experience, but instead by preprogrammed signaling.

result of experience. The simplest way to examine the question was to rear rats in different environments—for example, a rich environment packed with toys and running wheels or the deprived environment of a solitary cage (Bennett, Diamond, Krech, & Rosenzweig, 1964). The results were clear: the environment altered the brain structure, and this in turn correlated with changes in the animal's capacity for learning and memory. The rats raised in enriched environments performed better at behavioral tasks and were found at autopsy to have lush, extensively branched dendritic trees (FIGURE 4.16b AND c) (Diamond, 1988). By contrast, the rats raised in the deprived environments were poor learners and had abnormally shrunken neurons (FIGURE 4.16d, e, AND f). This same effect of environment was later demonstrated in birds, monkeys, and other mammals (Rosenzweig & Bennett, 1996), making it clear that experience modulates brain development.

Is this effect of environment measurable in humans? Indeed it is (Diamond, 2001). For example, at a Veterans Administration hospital in California in 1993, the brains of college-educated and high school–educated people were compared at autopsy (B. Jacobs, Schall, & Scheibel, 1993). The examiners found that an area involved in language comprehension (Wernicke's area, to which we return in Chapter 11) had more elaborated dendrites in the college-educated people.

The same picture holds true at the level of brain structures. For example, one study showed that taxi drivers in

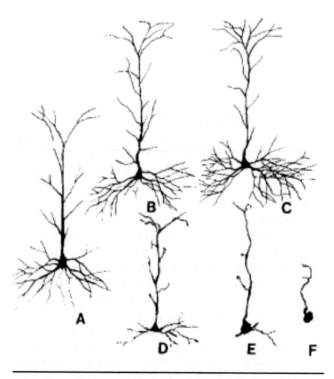

FIGURE 4.16 Neurons in the brain of a rat. (a) A representative neuron in the brain of a rat reared in a normal environment. (b and c) In enriched environments the neurons grow more extensive arborizations. (d, e, and f) In deprived environments the dendrites shrink to the point of total disappearance.

central London, as they gained years of experience on the job, gained volume in their hippocampus, an area involved in spatial mapping (we'll return to this in more detail in Chapter 9) (Maguire et al., 2000).

Brains Rely on Experience to Unpack Their Programs Correctly

The above studies demonstrate that brains reflect the environment to which they are exposed. But we can go one step further: beyond *reflecting* the environment, brains *require* the environment to correctly develop. When the first draft of the Human Genome Project came to completion in 2000, one of the great surprises was that humans have only about 25,000 protein-coding genes (Djebali et al., 2012). How does the massively complicated brain, with its approximately 100 billion neurons, get built from such a small recipe book? Part of the answer turns out to be a clever strategy implemented by the genome: instead of hardwiring everything, a more flexible and efficient strategy is to build a rough draft of the general circuitry required and let world experience refine it. Thus, for humans at birth, the brain is remarkably unfinished, and interaction with the world is necessary to complete it (Ijichi & Ijichi, 2004).

As an example, take the sleep–wake cycle that we will learn about in Chapter 10. This internal clock, known as a circadian rhythm, appears to run on a 24-hour cycle, but if you descend into a cave for several days—where there are no clues to the light and dark cycles of the surface—your circadian rhythm drifts, typically between about 21 to 27 hours. This unmasks the fact that the brain's solution was to build a rather nonexact clock and then pin its period to the solar cycle (Recio, Miguez, Buxton, & Challet, 1997). There is no need to genetically prespecify a perfect clock if the world can help out. So although DNA is often called the secret of life, life's other secret is that there is no need to encode everything if development can exploit the structure of the outside world.

Armed with this new viewpoint, you should now be able to understand why some of the most common problems of vision—such as the inability to see in depth—develop from imbalances in the pattern of activity delivered to the visual cortex by the two eyes. For example, when kittens are raised with artificial strabismus (the two eyes do not look to the same point in space), the activity from the two eyes is not correlated, as it would be in a normal kitten. As a result, cells in visual cortex involved in **binocular** vision do not develop, and the strabismic kittens lack stereo vision (FIGURE 4.17) (Lowel & Singer, 1992). The development of normal visual circuits *depends* on normal visual activity. It is experience dependent.

In a particularly striking experiment in the 1960s, researchers raised a group of kittens in total darkness (Held & Hein, 1963). Then, for one hour a day, the kittens were exposed to light, and during this time one kitten could move around freely in a cylinder with patterns on the wall. The

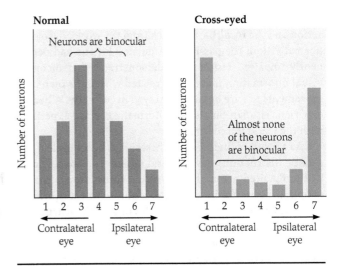

Normal — **Cross-eyed**

Neurons are binocular

Number of neurons

1 2 3 4 5 6 7
Contralateral eye — Ipsilateral eye

Almost none of the neurons are binocular

Number of neurons

1 2 3 4 5 6 7
Contralateral eye — Ipsilateral eye

FIGURE 4.17 **Kittens raised with artificial strabismus.** Histograms show the number of cells in the kitten's visual cortex that respond to input from one eye or the other, along an arbitrary scale of 1 (activity is driven by input to the contralateral eye) to 7 (activity is driven by input to the ipsilateral eye). Neurons in the middle of the distribution (around 4) respond to activity in both eyes equally—in other words, they are binocular. In the kitten reared with strabismus, almost none of the neurons develop binocularly.

second kitten was bound into a gondola that passively carried it so it would have the identical visual stimulation as the first kitten, but would not be controlling its own movements (FIGURE 4.18). The kittens who controlled their own motor

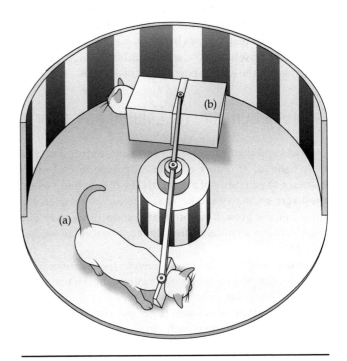

FIGURE 4.18 **Vision only develops correctly when correlated with one's own movement.** In the contraption used by Held and Hein (1963), one kitten controlled the movement—and thereby learned the relationship between its motor actions and the resulting changes in the visual world (a). The other kitten received the same visual input, but was never the one causing it (b). This second kitten had permanently impaired vision.

movements, thus learning the proper relationships between action and the resulting feedback from the world, developed normal vision; the passively stimulated kittens had permanently impaired vision. This demonstrates that incoming visual information must be correlated with one's own body movements to wire up the visual system correctly. When the experience is manipulated, the normal, expected experience with the world is undermined.

As a result of findings like these, it has become clear that genetic instructions have general rather than specific roles in the detailed assembly of cortical connections. That is, neuronal networks require interaction with the world for their proper development. The roles of genetic instructions are simply to guide neurons into the right general areas and to provide them with general mechanisms for adjusting their connections with other neurons. The role of genetics is analogous to the hosts of a social event: they invite the guests and ensure they end up in the same place and speaking the same language, but they do not specify who must befriend whom or what they have to talk about. The result is improvisation rather than scripting and the flexibility to adapt to circumstances.

The Mechanisms of Reorganization

Throughout this chapter, we have seen dozens of examples of the brain's ability to change its own wiring. In Chapter 9 we'll learn the mechanisms by which plasticity occurs at individual synapses; for now, we'll examine the bigger picture of changes at the level of populations of neurons.

Neurons Compete for Limited Space

Neurons and their processes (axons and dendrites) chronically fight for resources to survive, striving to find useful niches in the circuitry of a brain. If they cannot find a role in the larger society of the nervous system, they retract. Deprived of the growth factors that sustain them, they ultimately remove themselves from the conversation altogether, dying out.

One example of this can be seen in the neuromuscular junction, the point where motor neurons in the peripheral nervous system contact muscles (FIGURE 4.19). The neurons release neurotransmitter here to control the contraction of the muscle. In the adult, each muscle fiber is individually controlled by a single motor neuron. However, if you were to look at the situation early in development, you would see that each muscle fiber is innervated by axons from several motor neurons. What happens in between to whittle things down to a one-neuron-to-one-muscle-fiber relationship?

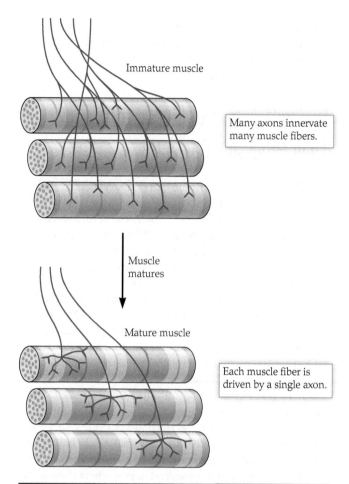

Immature muscle

Many axons innervate many muscle fibers.

Muscle matures

Mature muscle

Each muscle fiber is driven by a single axon.

FIGURE 4.19 Competition at the neuromuscular junction. Early in development, many axons innervate many muscle fibers. As the muscle matures, competition whittles down the playing field until each muscle fiber is driven by a single axon.

The answer is *competition* (Sanes & Lichtman, 1999). Only one neuron can survive on each muscle fiber. They have to find an open niche and chronically defend it.

Although the neuromuscular junction is one of the most studied systems in the peripheral nervous system, let's turn to an example in the central nervous system. **Ocular dominance columns** are alternating stripes in the visual cortex that represent cells responding to signals from either the left or the right eye. During development, axons carrying visual information from the thalamus initially branch widely in the cortex (FIGURE 4.20a) and then segregate into eye-specific patches based on patterns of correlated activity (FIGURE 4.20b). This segregation is activity dependent: if all incoming activity is blocked by an injection of tetrodotoxin in the retinas, the axons in the cortex remain overlapped (FIGURE 4.20c). Under normal circumstances, both eyes carry the same level of activity. But Hubel and Weisel showed that the territory controlled by one eye or the other could be dramatically changed by experience: shutting one

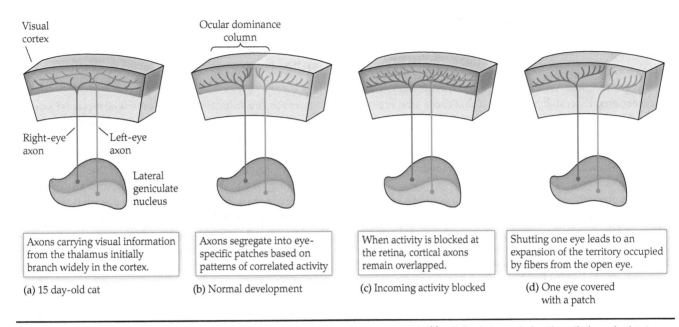

Visual cortex

Ocular dominance column

Right-eye axon   Left-eye axon

Lateral geniculate nucleus

| Axons carrying visual information from the thalamus initially branch widely in the cortex. | Axons segregate into eye-specific patches based on patterns of correlated activity | When activity is blocked at the retina, cortical axons remain overlapped. | Shutting one eye leads to an expansion of the territory occupied by fibers from the open eye. |

(a) 15 day-old cat   (b) Normal development   (c) Incoming activity blocked   (d) One eye covered with a patch

FIGURE 4.20 **Ocular dominance columns in primary visual cortex result from competition for space.** (a) At 15 days in the cat, the input layer of primary visual cortex has approximately uniform input from the left and right eyes. (b) As the animal matures, the connectivity comes to reflect alternating input from both eyes equally. (c) When retinal activity is blocked, the segregation does not occur. (d) When one of a young animal is patched, the inputs from the weak eye progressively shrink as the strong inputs from the other eye successfully fight for the territory.

eye of an animal leads to an expansion of the territory occupied by fibers from the open eye (FIGURE 4.20d) (Gu, 2003; Hubel & Wiesel, 1962; Wiesel & Hubel, 1963b). Just as at the neuromuscular junction, these characteristics result from competition at the synaptic level. Inputs from the strong eye are retained and strengthened, whereas the inputs from the shut eye are weakened and eventually decay (Wiesel & Hubel, 1963a).

Plasticity from world experience also involves a good deal of **pruning** (retraction of axonal branches) and cell death. Cells can die in one of two ways: **necrosis** (in an uncontrolled fashion) or **apoptosis** (in a deliberate, controlled fashion). The controlled process of apoptosis avoids collateral damage to neighbors, and it is a common sculpting mechanism in embryonic development. For example, the process of turning a human embryo's webbed hand into a baby's clearly defined fingers depends on sculpting away cells, not adding them (Kuida et al., 1998). The same principles may apply to the development of the brain. During development, 50% more neurons than needed are produced (Low & Cheng, 2006). Massive die-off is standard operating procedure: neurons die because of failure to compete for chemicals provided by targets. Remember the experiment that removed one-half of the frog's tectum and resulted in a compressed map? Decreasing the available real estate increased the die-off: there was simply not enough room to provide for all the neurons, forcing some to go away. Although the structure of the map was retained, a smaller number of neurons survived.

Competition for Neurotrophins

In 1941, a young Italian woman named Rita Levi-Montalcini fled from her native Turin into a small cottage in the country, where she lived in hiding from the Germans and Italians: her life was in danger because she was Jewish. While in hiding, she set up a mini laboratory in the cottage and worked to figure out how limbs developed in chick embryos (FIGURE 4.21). Her work there led to the discovery of **nerve growth factor**, and for this work she won the 1968 Nobel Prize (Levi-Montalcini & Angeletti, 1968).

What she had discovered was the first example of a class of life-preserving chemicals called **neurotrophins**. These

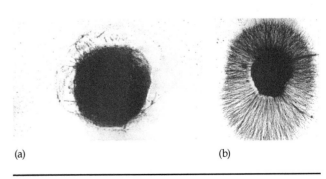

(a)   (b)

FIGURE 4.21 **A ganglion of sensory cells from a chick embryo cultured in the (a) absence or (b) presence of nerve growth factor.**

protein factors, secreted by the neuron's target, allow the survival, development, and function of neurons. Neurotrophins are the currency over which the neurons and synapses compete for real estate; they are what drive neurons to make connections, and the neurotrophins stabilize those connections. Essentially, the rule is that those who are successful at getting these life-preserving chemicals—which promote growth and survival, guide axons, and stimulate the growth of new synaptic connections—live. Otherwise they try elsewhere, or, if they are unsuccessful anywhere, they don't survive.

Neurotrophins work in at least two ways. One is by allowing a cell to differentiate into its next stage of development. The other way, at least early in the development of the organism, is by preventing a cell from initiating suicide by apoptosis. In the intervening years since Levi-Montalcini's initial discovery, many neurotrophic factors have been discovered (Spedding & Gressens, 2008). Additionally, there are several postulated toxic factors—for example, synaptotoxins are thought to eliminate existing synapses (Zoubine, Ma, Smirnova, Citron, & Festoff, 1996). In one model, axons vie to escape the punishing effects of synaptotoxins by remaining active—as soon as they drop below a threshold, the axons are eliminated (Sanes & Lichtman, 1999). Some current research in Alzheimer's disease (Chapter 16) suggests that the amyloid beta molecules that are characteristic of the disease act as synaptotoxins (Klein, 2013). Trophic and toxic molecules provide signals that allow neurons to determine whether they should remain at their posts in the brain's circuitry or remove themselves for the sake of the common good.

We have seen that the constant reorganization of the brain circuitry is underpinned by fierce competition for limited resources in the neural tissue, but how quickly do these changes take place? As we will see, some changes happen rapidly, whereas others happen more slowly.

Rapid Changes: Unmasking Existing Connections

Remember the blindfolded subjects whose visual cortex begins to respond to touch within two days? This rapid time period suggests that the connections were already there (Buonomano & Merzenich, 1998; Pascual-Leone et al., 2005; Pascual-Leone & Hamilton, 2001). A popular model suggests that there are many neural connections that already exist, but they are inhibited so that they have no effect, functionally speaking (Buonomano & Merzenich, 1998). As an analogy, imagine a major disruption to your circle of friends. Because of a socially tragic misunderstanding at a party (where everyone else was acting just as wild as you were), you lose all your closest friends. Suddenly, your social input is less than what it used to be, and now you begin listening for signals from other friends—those with whom you had a tenuous connection but who never had a chance to command your full attention before. Their voices were squelched by the strong relationships you had with your main friends. Now that these peripheral friends can be heard, you begin to fill out your social life by attending to those weak connections and working to strengthen them.

As you can guess from this analogy, the mechanism for unmasking is the release of inhibition that the strong connections had previously provided. That is, when the original connections lose their active input—say, because of an anesthetized arm or a blindfolding—fast changes in receptive fields can result from the disinhibition of covert, existing connections from other sensory regions of the thalamus to the cortex (FIGURE 4.22) (Weiss et al., 2004).

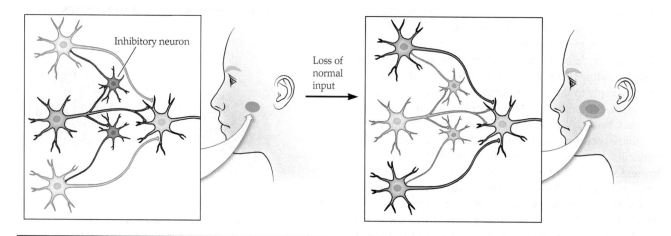

FIGURE 4.22 **Due to disinhibition, the widely spread and previously silent projections from the thalamus begin to play a functional role.** As a result, the receptive field of downstream neurons can expand to contain neighboring structures.

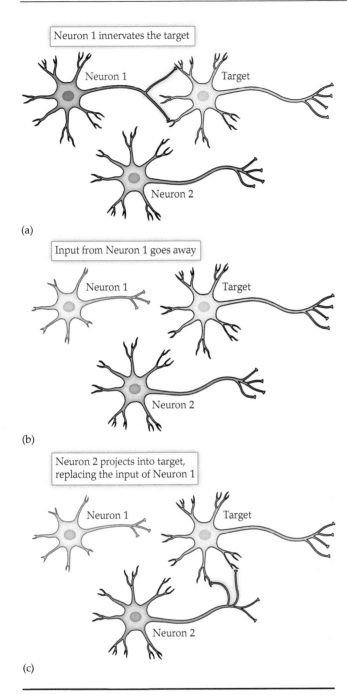

Neuron 1 innervates the target

Neuron 1   Target

Neuron 2

(a)

Input from Neuron 1 goes away

Neuron 1   Target

Neuron 2

(b)

Neuron 2 projects into target, replacing the input of Neuron 1

Neuron 1   Target

Neuron 2

(c)

FIGURE 4.23 **Growth of new neurites into a region after loss of previous input.** (a) Neuron 1 innervates the target; neuron 2 does not. (b) Loss of input to neuron 1 occurs. (c) Neuron 2 projects to target, replacing the input of neuron 1.

Slow Changes: Growth of New Connections

Longer-term changes are thought to involve the growth of axons into new areas and the sprouting of new connections (FIGURE 4.23) (Pascual-Leone et al., 2005). To continue with the social friendship analogy, imagine that you have begun to exchange Facebook messages with those peripheral friends you never paid much attention to before. With time, given the unexpected room in your social schedule, these friends introduce you to *their* friends, and you become open to new friendships that you lacked room for before. You seek out and establish brand new connections that stem from more distant social circles. And so it goes with the brain: with enough time, deafferented areas sprout new connections (Darian-Smith & Gilbert, 1994; Florence, Taub, & Kaas, 1998).

Given the two time scales of cortical remodeling, we can now understand a general principle of reorganization: the brain seems to put into place many "silent" connections that are inhibited during everyday neural conversation—but are there if needed in the future. With these, the brain can respond rapidly to changes in input. However, these silent connections are limited in number, and for longer, more widespread change, a different approach is used. Essentially, if short-term changes (such as unmasking) are found to be useful to the animal, then long-term changes (such as growth of new axons and sprouting of new synapses) will eventually follow (Buonomano & Merzenich, 1998).

Changing the Input Channels

The principles of competition and rewiring that we have learned in this chapter have set us up to understand one of the most striking consequences of plasticity: the brain will allow the incorporation of unusual, new inputs (Hawkins & Blakeslee, 2004; Sharma, Angelucci, & Sur, 2000; von Melchner, Pallas, & Sur, 2000), Consider the **bionic retinal implant** (BRI). The BRI is a gas-permeable patch that is sensitive to light and has miniature electrodes that plug into the back of the eye (Dowling, 2008) (FIGURE 4.24). The implant works well in eye diseases in which the photoreceptors at the back of the eye are degenerating, but the retinal ganglion cells (with which the photoreceptors communicate) are perfectly healthy (more on this in Chapter 5). So the tiny electrodes of the BRI replace the normal functions of the photoreceptor sheet and send out their tiny sparks of electrical activity. Although the signals sent by the implant are not precisely what the rest of the brain is used to, the downstream processes are able to learn to extract the information they need for vision.

Beyond circumventing a broken peripheral sensor, inputs into the brain can be switched around. In a striking demonstration, scientists at MIT redirected inputs from a ferret's eye over to its auditory cortex (through the **medial geniculate nucleus**; FIGURE 4.25). What happened to the auditory cortex? The visual inputs reorganized it, altering its circuitry to resemble circuitry and connectivity in primary visual cortex (Sharma et al., 2000; von Melchner et al.,

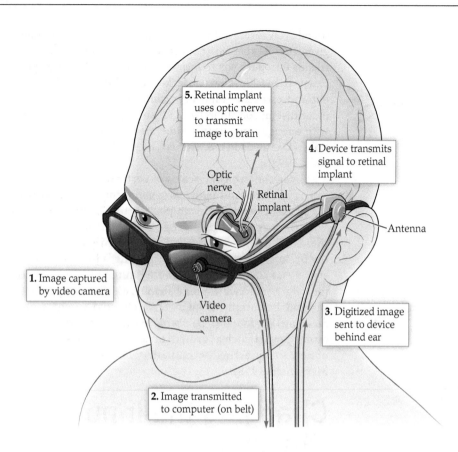

1. Image captured by video camera

2. Image transmitted to computer (on belt)

3. Digitized image sent to device behind ear

4. Device transmits signal to retinal implant

5. Retinal implant uses optic nerve to transmit image to brain

Optic nerve

Retinal implant

Antenna

Video camera

FIGURE 4.24 **The bionic retinal implant.** A camera mounted in front of the eye sends its video feed to an electrode array at the back of the eye.

2000). The rewired animals behaviorally interpreted visual input (now going to the auditory cortex) just as they did with normal vision.

One framework for understanding this result is to think of the **neocortex** as a data-processing engine that accepts whatever input is plugged into it and performs the same basic algorithms on all input (Hawkins & Blakeslee, 2004). The inputs will compete for space, and downstream neural populations will learn how to interact with them. Plug a visual data stream into a patch of cortex, and it will become what

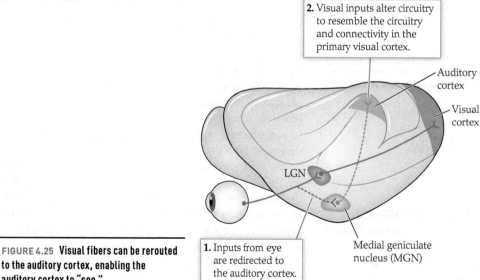

2. Visual inputs alter circuitry to resemble the circuitry and connectivity in the primary visual cortex.

Auditory cortex

Visual cortex

LGN

1. Inputs from eye are redirected to the auditory cortex.

Medial geniculate nucleus (MGN)

FIGURE 4.25 **Visual fibers can be rerouted to the auditory cortex, enabling the auditory cortex to "see."**

3. Rewired animals interpret visual input in the auditory cortex.

CASE STUDY:
The Man Who Climbs with His Tongue

Eric Weihenmayer is a mountaineer who has scaled Mount Everest—a feat made even more impressive by the fact that he is blind. As a child, Eric progressively lost his vision to a rare eye disease called retinoschisis, and he was rendered entirely blind by the age of 13. But that didn't slow his ambition to become a climber. Given his condition, it's captivating to watch Eric scale shear rock faces, holding on to small crevices and protrusions. How does he know where to reach next? How does he do it?

Eric climbs with an electrode grid in his mouth called the BrainPort (FIGURE 4.26). The grid delivers little impulses to his tongue that mirror

 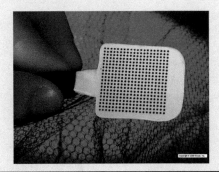

FIGURE 4.26 **BrainPort.** The BrainPort converts a video feed to corresponding electrical activity on the tongue. With this technology, blind users can come to understand their visual surroundings with high accuracy.

the visual signals from a camera attached to his forehead. Eric reports that he first had to think hard about how the tongue stimulation might translate into edges and shapes. But he learned, eventually, to recognize the stimulation as direct perception (Levy, 2008). He is now able to use the device for a low-resolution but effective sense of his visual surroundings.

we think of as a visual cortex; plug an auditory stream into it, and it will become an auditory cortex.

As we have seen so far, the brain has a remarkable capacity to reconfigure itself in the face of new inputs, outputs, neural gains, or neural losses. That versatility opens the door to technologies that can deliver information to the brain through unusual sensory channels. For example, what if a blind person used the data stream from a video camera and converted it into sounds in her headphones? Would she eventually be able to *see* the world by listening? Welcome to the world of **sensory substitution** experiments, in which a deficient sensory channel is circumvented in favor of other routes to the brain (Lenay, Hanneton, Marque, & Genouel, 2003; Maidenbaum, Abboud, & Amedi, 2013; Poirier, De Volder, & Scheiber, 2007).

Why does the BrainPort use the tongue, of all places? Although we normally think of the tongue as a taste organ, it also has the finest sense of touch on the entire body. It can distinguish stimuli only 1.6 mm apart—roughly twice as fine as a typical fingertip (Wilson, Walton, Tyler, & Williams, 2012). This makes the tongue a great site for passing on new kinds of information, even learning to "see." A grid of electrodes, the size of a postage stamp, zaps the tongue, converting the lattice of video pixels into "pixels" in the mouth (Bach-y-Rita, 2004; Bach-y-Rita, Collins, Saunders,

White, & Scadden, 1969). With practice, the tongue learns to interpret the signals that correspond to the visual properties, such as how large an object is, how far away it is, and whether it's moving in a particular direction. With the BrainPort, blind users can learn to navigate complex obstacle courses and throw balls into buckets. For sighted people, the BrainPort can be used to see in the dark. How is any of this possible? Vision isn't about the eyes. It's about the brain (Khoo, Seidel, & Zhu, 2012). Other sensory substitution devices for the blind convert video streams into patterns of touch on the lower back, sound for the ears, or small electric shocks to the skin of the forehead. Similarly, a sensory substitution device for the deaf uses a vest covered in vibratory motors to translate sound into patterns on the skin (Novich & Eagleman, under review). These amazing substitutions are possible only because the brain can dynamically shape itself around whatever input is presented. It even seems possible that in the near future people will feed information streams directly into their cortex.

In conclusion, the rerouting of information and the success of sensory substitution underscores the dynamic plasticity of brains. The principles of competition constantly reorganize the circuitry to optimize their representation of the input.

THE BIGGER PICTURE:
Adding New Peripherals

Note that the plasticity of the brain allows us to think beyond sensory substitution and into the realm of **sensory addition**. For example, researchers have genetically engineered mice to express color photopigments and thus to have color vision when they normally do not (G. H. Jacobs, Williams, Cahill, & Nathans, 2007). Similarly, a third type of color photoreceptor has been genetically engineered into adult monkeys who normally have only two types— this gave them trichromatic instead of dichromatic vision (Mancuso et al., 2009).

Several do-it-yourselfers have begun the movement of sensory addition in humans. One is Neil Harbisson, a man who was

(a)

Name	Color (visual system)	Frequency (auditory system)
Ultraviolet	(invisible)	Over 717.6 Hz
Violet		607.5 Hz
Blue		573.9 Hz
Cyan		551.1 Hz
Green		478.4 Hz
Yellow		462.0 Hz
Orange		440.2 Hz
Red		363.8 Hz
Infrared	(invisible)	Below 363.8 Hz

(b)

FIGURE 4.27   Sonochromatic scale. (a) Colorblind artist Neil Harbisson wears the eyeborg;
(b) his "sonochromatic" scale translates colors detected by the camera into output sound frequencies.
The inclusion of frequencies for ultraviolet and infrared allows the auditory system to surmount the normal limitations of the visual system.

born colorblind. In 2004, inspired by the idea of visual-to-auditory translation, Neil attached a device he calls the "eyeborg" to his head (FIGURE 4.27). The device analyzes a video stream and converts the colors to sounds. The sounds are delivered via bone conduction behind the ear.

Now Neil hears colors. He can put his face in front of any colored swatch and tell you what it is; he's taken to painting colorful paintings this way (Miah & Rich, 2008). Even better, the eyeborg's camera detects wavelengths of light *beyond* the normal spectrum; when translating from colors to sound, he can encode (and come to perceive in the environment) infrared and ultraviolet, in the way that snakes and bees do.

In the not-so-distant future, we may be able to add new kinds of functionality in the brain—for example, by plugging weather data or stock market data into the cortex (Hawkins & Blakeslee, 2004). In line with the principles of plasticity learned in this chapter, the brain should learn how to correlate this with other data and incorporate it into perception. After all, when new peripherals are plugged into the brain, competition does its job so that useful information wins a voice in the system.

Conclusion

Returning to Matthew S.'s hemispherectomy at the beginning of this chapter, we now have the tools to understand how his brain could survive losing half its territory: it rewired itself to retain its overall function on less than the normal amount of brain territory. This was made possible by competition at the level of the synapses and neurons, which allowed both the rapid unmasking of existing cross-hemispheric connections and, with time, the growth of new axons and sprouting of new synapses. All throughout, his desire to move, to walk and talk, and to be like other children his age helped to provide the signals of relevance that allowed plasticity in his brain to express itself fully. This process was helped enormously by the fact that Matthew was only 6 years old—still well within the sensitive period and with lots of extra circuitry to spare. This remarkable property of neural maps to stretch and compress given the available neural real estate expresses a theme that will come up often in this book: the brain is designed quite differently from a conventional digital computer.

Plasticity is found at all levels, from the synapses to whole brain regions. A theme of this chapter is that the constant battle for territory in the brain is a Darwinian competition: each synapse, each neuron, each population is fighting for resources such as neurotrophins. As the border wars are fought, the maps are redrawn in such a way that the goals most important to the organism are always reflected in the structure of the brain. If you drop your career to become a violinist, the neural territory devoted to your left fingers will expand; if you become a microscopist, your visual cortex will reorganize itself to give you higher visual resolution for the small details you search. By examining the key principles of plasticity, we have surveyed a wide swath of territory critical for understanding brain rewiring.

One of the overarching mysteries in neuroscience is how brains are built with so few genes. The fact that we have only 25,000 protein-encoding genes leads us to think about the genome like a compressed file, with the cellular machinery with which it interacts as a decompressor (Marcus, 2004). It was originally hoped that understanding the sequence of the genome would allow us to understand how an organism unpacks itself. But development requires interaction with the world; the genome is like a highly condensed recipe with the label "just add world experience to unpack." However, like all nature-versus-nurture stories, the interplay between experience dependence and experience independence is complex, and in the end what we find is a challenge to the usual belief that flexibility is at variance with genetic control. During development, a careful balance of hard-coded and plastic mechanisms confers tremendous flexibility, allowing an animal to optimize its coding machinery to its body plan and its salient tasks.

Looking to the future, as we learn more about how brains dynamically reconfigure their own circuitry, this suggests new ways to build computers and, eventually, to design cars, space stations, and even the houses we live in as reconfigurable devices. We can build them in such a way that all the details are not prespecified and that they use interaction with the world to complete their own wiring.

KEY PRINCIPLES

- The brain dynamically reorganizes its circuitry to adapt to changes in its sensory inputs.

- The brain reorganizes itself to enable changes in its outputs, distributing resources based on relevance as expressed through plasticity-gating neuromodulators.

- Neural pathways adjust themselves to fit into the available brain tissue. A neuron's function comes from its inputs and outputs, not its identity or location. Neural circuits with similar patterns of inputs and outputs can perform similar functions.

- There is a sensitive period during which brains are the most plastic: young brains are more flexible and less specialized than older brains.

- The very general layout of brain circuitry is programmed through genetic mechanisms. Real-world experiences fine-tune these general circuits into more detailed programs.

- Early in development, neurons and synapses must either compete successfully for growth factors or die.

- Plastic changes use both fast and slow mechanisms.

- The brain wraps itself around useful inputs, opening the door to sensory substitution. The plasticity of the nervous system may allow us to develop advanced devices that connect directly to the brain, to expand human abilities.

KEY TERMS

REVIEW QUESTIONS

1. What mechanisms might have helped Matthew S. to have normal abilities despite the loss of half of his brain? If you were to lose half your brain, would you be able to adapt in any of the same ways? If so, how? If not, why not?

2. Why does a "phantom limb" sometimes persist after amputation? How is it possible to have sensations in a body part that no longer exists? What might be happening in the brain as the phantom limb disappears?

3. How do stroke patients with aphasia regain their use of language? What kinds of changes take place in their brains? If you were their physician, what kinds of treatments would you recommend to help them recover as much function as possible?

4. Why is there a sensitive period for brain functions? Do all brain functions have the same sensitive period? What might determine the sensitive period for a given brain function?

5. What is different about the adult brain that makes it more difficult to learn? What forms of plasticity still exist in the adult? If you had to design a treatment to make the adult brain more plastic, what would you try to do?

6. How do genetic factors influence the wiring of the brain? If you had an identical twin, how might your shared genes give rise to similar talents, interests, and personality quirks? How is it that identical twins can also differ in these areas? How could one identical twin develop a brain-wiring disease such as schizophrenia, whereas the other one does not?

7. How do life experiences fine-tune the brain's circuitry? How much leeway do they have in doing so? Can life experience turn visual cortex into motor cortex? Why or why not?

8. How do neurons compete for survival? Are they like enemy soldiers, battling for victory over one another? Are they like allies fighting for a common cause? Why might a neuron be "willing" to die on purpose if it cannot find a useful function?

CRITICAL-THINKING QUESTIONS

1. If you were somehow born with an extra pair of arms and hands, would your brain be able to make use of them? How might this be possible? How would your brain be different from the brains of other people?

2. How can the brain fit a sensory map into half the number of neurons if necessary? Could it fit the map into only 10% of the original number of neurons? What about 1%? What capabilities might be lost in the process?

3. Sea turtle babies can see, walk, swim, and navigate immediately after hatching. Why do human babies have so much trouble surviving on their own? What advantages do they gain in compensation? Are there advantages for children who learn to walk, talk, or read especially early in life? Could there be disadvantages as well?

4. Imagine inventing a brain-connected device to extend your own abilities or those of someone you know. What kind of device might you build? How would you enable your brain to use it? How long do you believe it will be before we can build such a device in reality?

LEARNING OBJECTIVES   By the end of this chapter, you should be able to:

- Give at least two examples of sensory transduction.

- Trace the path of visual information through the anatomy of the visual system.

- Characterize the hierarchical organization of the visual system.

- Explain how stereo vision works.

- Illustrate the results of damage to primary, secondary, and tertiary areas of the visual cortex.

- Contrast the ventral and dorsal visual processing streams.

- Summarize why we do not see what is actually "out there," but instead the brain's internal model of the world.

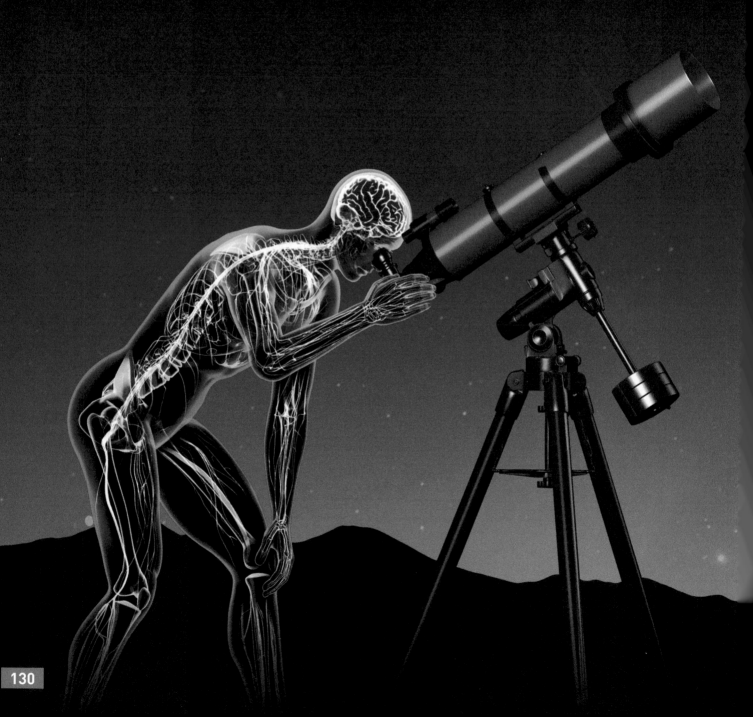

Vision

STARTING OUT:
Vision Is More Than the Eyes

A chemical explosion left Mike May blind at the age of three. The scarring of his corneas prevented light from getting through. Undeterred, Mike grew up to become a family man, a businessman, and a champion blind downhill skier (FIGURE 5.1). Then, when May was in his mid-forties, a new surgical technique emerged that could clear the scarring of his corneas. He signed up, eager to have the possibility of seeing again.

The operation was a success: when the bandages were peeled off, the corneas were clear, allowing light to pass through and onto Mike's retinas. A photographer was there to capture the moment when he gazed into his sons' faces for the first time—faces that he had only known through touch. It was guaranteed to be a very special moment.

But it wasn't. Although light now passed through his eyes, his brain had no ability to interpret the signals racing along the nerves and spattering into his cortex. Mike stared at everything around him in bewilderment. Faces, hallways, doorframes, windows. None of it

FIGURE 5.1 **Mike May (left).** He is guided by his son, Wyndham, while filming *The Movement at the Canyons in Utah.*

made sense to him: he was only experiencing strange visual noise. The pathway from his eyes to his visual cortex was now functioning as it was supposed to, but he couldn't be said to be seeing in the normal sense (Kurson, 2008).

Mike's story illustrates that vision doesn't come for free. Incoming electrochemical signals have to be interpreted by the brain, and that happens only with practice. When Mike's wife drove him home, he

couldn't understand the whizzing cars around them; nor could he tell whether they were going to smash into the looming highway signs. It has required many years of interaction with the world to train up his visual system.

Although vision seems effortless, it isn't. The electrical storms of neural activity in the pitch-blackness of the skull get turned into direct perception only after practice. In this chapter we'll learn how.

Visual Perception

What Is It Like to See?

In the late 19th century, the philosopher and physicist Ernst Mach took notice of something that didn't make sense. If he took several strips of paper—scaled from white to black—and placed them next to each other, an illusion arose (FIGURE 5.2). Each strip, while uniform in color on its own, when placed next to the others appeared to have uneven shading, looking slightly lighter on the side adjacent to the darker color, and slightly darker on the side adjacent to the lighter color (Eagleman 2001).

The illusory color changes at the border are called **Mach bands**; now that you know about these, you'll notice them elsewhere. For instance, look at a corner where two walls meet: although the paint is a single color, it can look darker on one wall and lighter on the other. After we have introduced some of the cell types involved in vision, you'll know why this illusion occurs. But in the meantime, we want you to get better at observing your own experience of vision. Chances

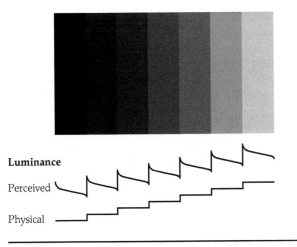

Luminance

Perceived

Physical

FIGURE 5.2 Mach band illusion. To prove to yourself that each vertical strip in the figure is in fact uniform in brightness, cover up all but one. When that same strip is viewed in context with the others, it appears to be darker on the right side and lighter on the left.

FIGURE 5.3 The rotating snakes illusion by Japanese scientist Akiyoshi Kitaoka.

are that although Mach bands have always been in front of you, you have missed them until now. But you shouldn't feel bad. The entire history of painters until the Renaissance failed to notice that mountains look bluer when they're farther away. Once this was pointed out by a careful observer, then it became a standard trick to paint mountains blue. But why had everyone before this missed it entirely, even though the perceptual facts were right in front of them? Do people simply not pay close attention to their own experiences?

Indeed, we are surprisingly poor observers of our own experiences: we assume we know what's out there until it's proven otherwise. In this chapter we'll learn to pay close attention to our experiences, similar to Mach's observation of the illusion with the strips. By doing so, we'll extract clues about the massive visual machinery that lies behind our experiences.

We're going to begin with our perceptions— that is, our experience of the sensory world. Perceptions have a long history of interest, perhaps because of their easy access: all we have to do is open our eyes, and the world seems to be there in all its sensory glory. Vision seems so effortless and seamless that describing it sometimes feels to people as challenging as a fish trying to describe water. Since the fish lives surrounded by water and knows nothing else, it would presumably have a hard time coming to a conceptual understanding of water, that is, until it experiences air for the first time, say from a bubble rising from a vent on the ocean floor. In the same way, insights in the field of neuroscience are often achieved with the help of visual illusions. Illusions highlight "bubbles" in our perception, encouraging neuroscientists to "swim" closer to have a better look. The examples in this chapter will illustrate this point.

For instance, consider the illusion of the rotating snakes (FIGURE 5.3). Nothing on the page is actually moving, yet observers usually report "seeing" the snakes slithering around. What does this tell us?

First, it tells us that the visual system is not like a camera lens that simply reads a photographic representation of the world. This is what one might think from watching a cyborg in a Hollywood movie. As the cyborg stomps around some unlucky city, we occasionally see the world from inside his head. There the world is faithfully reproduced as though his perception were a movie camera, with a heads-up computer display superimposed on the scene for him to read.

But who's doing the reading? What inside his head is watching the display?

In reality, perception is nothing like a movie camera or computer display. Instead, perception is an extraordinarily sophisticated construction of the brain. Sensory machinery is confronted at every moment with a barrage of information, and it is the task of the nervous system to reduce that amount of information to a single, coherent percept, or mental representation of the thing being perceived.

Although this chapter is about vision, keep in mind that the principles we will learn here apply to other perceptual systems as well (e.g., hearing and touch), as we will see in the next chapter. In all cases, the goal of sensory systems is to attend to information-rich energy sources to form a useful idea about objects and events in the outside world.

Signal Transduction

Signals from the outside world—say, a beam of light, a sound, a smell, a touch—are brought into your nervous system by different kinds of sensory receptors. This process of transforming an event from the outside world into electrochemical signals inside your nervous system is called **sensory transduction**. For mammals, this is usually accomplished through pressure-sensitive receptors on the skin, taste buds

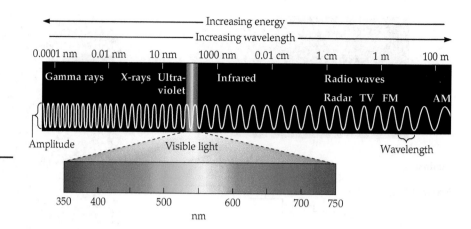

FIGURE 5.4   The electromagnetic spectrum.
The fraction we detect, and thus call "visible light," is approximately one 10-trillionth of the spectrum.

on the tongue, photoreceptors in the eyes, **hair cells** in the inner ear, stretch receptors in the muscle, and so on. These are our windows to the outside world.

We only possess transducers for limited sorts of information. An eyeless animal (say, a worm) does not detect what we call visible light, try as it might. Similarly, the fact that we have no sensors for electromagnetic radiation in the kilohertz and megahertz range means we do not perceive the radio, television, and cell phone signals that pour through our bodies at all hours. Our windows to the world outside are small (although generally good enough for survival).

One of our most prized survival tools is our perception of visible light—as evidenced by the fact that about 30% of the human cortical real estate is devoted to detecting and processing vision, compared with only 8% for touch and 3% for hearing (Grady, 1993). What exactly is visible light? *Electromagnetic radiation* is energy that travels through space in a wavelike pattern. Various frequency ranges of this energy are categorized as radio waves, microwaves, infrared radiation, ultraviolet radiation, X-rays, gamma rays, visible light, and so on (FIGURE 5.4). Our eyes are a sophisticated tool that can detect a small portion of this electromagnetic radiation, wavelengths from about 390 to 750 nm. This frequency range is called *the visible spectrum* or *visible light*. It is surprising that we can survive with only information from this infinitesimally small range, just one 10-billionth of the entire electromagnetic radiation spectrum! Other species, such as bees, butterflies, and some birds, see in the ultraviolet frequency range, whereas some snakes pick up information in the infrared range. However, visible light is traditionally categorized as the range humans can detect (FIGURE 5.4).

Anatomy of the Visual System

Let's examine exactly how our visual system senses and processes information from the outside world.

Sensory Transduction: The Eye and Its Retina

We've just talked about light being a wave, which has a wavelength and amplitude. But light is a strange thing. When we try to measure it as a wave, it acts like a wave. If we think of it as a particle and try to measure it that way, it acts like a particle and has mass and force. These discrete particles of light are called *photons*, which enter the eye through a translucent membrane known as the **cornea** (FIGURE 5.5). It is this cornea that Mike had replaced in the story at the beginning of this chapter.

Light passes through the cornea and is restricted by a ring of colored muscle fibers known as the **iris**, which controls the amount of light that can enter the eye. The light passes through a hole in the middle of the iris known as the **pupil**. From there, the light shines through a **lens** that will focus the image on the **retina**, which is at the back of the eye.

The retina is a layered structure, composed of five layers of cells. From the side closest to the lens to the side furthest from the lens, those cells are the **retinal ganglion cells**, which pass information from the eye to the brain; **amacrine cells**, which allow communication between different parts of the retina; bipolar cells (a type of bipolar neuron), which carry information from the photoreceptors to the retinal ganglion cells; **horizontal cells**, which also allow communication between adjacent parts of the retina; and, finally, the photoreceptors. Light passes through all of those cells, in that order, when it enters the eye. Photoreceptors capture the photons of light and convert the light into neurochemical activity through a biochemical process known as **phototransduction**. In phototransduction, light strikes a pigment molecule, such as rhodopsin, within the photoreceptor, causing it to break into pieces. These pieces act on proteins in the cell to change the resting membrane potential and, thereby, change the neurotransmitter signal the photoreceptor is releasing. With time, an enzyme puts the pigment molecule back together, and the cell is ready to signal again. The information that results from this process flows out of the

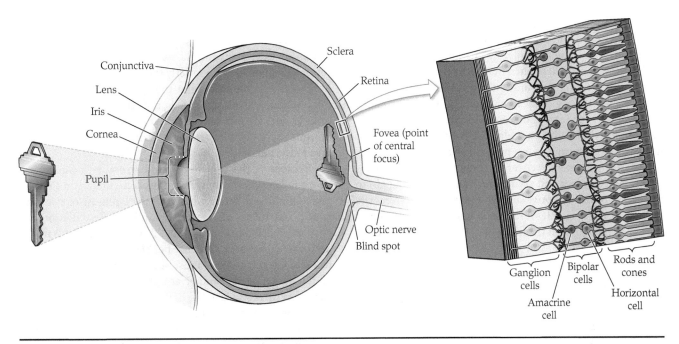

FIGURE 5.5 **The anatomy of the eye and the cellular layers of the retina.**

eye to the brain through those same cells, but in the reverse sequence of the process described just above.

Photoreceptors are of two types: **rods** and **cones**, each of which has a distinct job in the retina. Rods are more numerous, with 90 million cells, compared with only 4.5 million cone cells in the human eye (Mainster, 2005). Rods are highly sensitive to light and therefore ideal for vision in dim environments. However, they are broadly receptive to a wide range of light frequencies. Because they do not respond selectively to a particular frequency of light, they are not more responsive to one color than to another, and they therefore simply detect degrees of light and dark.

Cones, by contrast, are 10 to 100 times *less* sensitive to light than rods. They are best suited for vision in bright environments (e.g., during daylight). Cones come in three types, each of which detects a different distribution of light frequencies that peaks around red, blue, and green (FIGURE 5.6). Eventually, the different activity of these three types of cones in response to objects of different colors will be encoded as color by the brain. Cones are more concentrated in your central vision, a region known as the **fovea**, whereas there are more rods in the periphery. Have you ever noticed on a dark night that it is easier to see a dim star cluster if you don't look straight at it? By looking off to one side, you are viewing the stars with your rods, which have greater light sensitivity. Cones are also more sensitive to the fine details of the stimulus than the rods are. This is for two reasons. First, you may have noticed in FIGURE 5.5 that the fovea looks like a little indentation on the surface of the retina. This is because all those overlying layers of cells are pulled aside and the retinal ganglion cells are literally smaller in this region, to allow light more direct access to the photoreceptors (Hubel, 1995). If this didn't happen, vision would be like looking through several layers of curtains to try to see something; the image would be distorted. The second reason has to do with how the photoreceptors are connected to the bipolar and retinal ganglion cells. Each cone is connected to its own bipolar cell and then to its own retinal ganglion cell. In contrast, many rods connect to a single retinal ganglion cell (Calkins, Schein, Tsukamoto, & Sterling, 1994). For information coming from the cones, this means that when a retinal ganglion cell is activated, the light that caused that activation can come from only one place on the retina. For the information coming from the rods, the stimulus that activates the retinal ganglion cell could come from any one of many (nearby) places. Because of this, we say that the cones have high spatial resolution and that the rods have low spatial resolution.

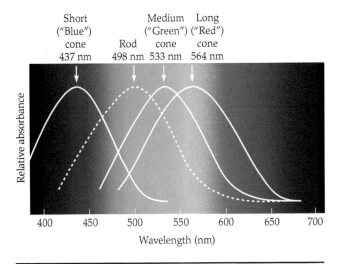

FIGURE 5.6 **Spectral sensitivity of photoreceptors.** This image shows the sensitivity of rods and cones to the visible wavelengths of light.

The signals from the photoreceptors are relayed through the layers of cells in the retina, described above, and then reach the retinal ganglion cells. The pathway from the retina to the cortex is organized such that each retinal ganglion cell responds to stimulation only in a specific location of the visual scene. The region of visual space in which a stimulus will modulate the activity of a particular neuron is called the **receptive field**. Retinal ganglion cells have tiny receptive fields that cover visual space, much like you could use many small tiles to completely cover a floor. Retinal ganglion cells have a **center-surround structure**: a small point of light in the center of the receptive field will maximally activate the cell, whereas a ring of light in the surround (the disk around the center) will inhibit the firing of the cell ("on-center cell,"

FIGURE 5.7). When both the center *and* the surround are stimulated—as by a large patch of light—the excitation and inhibition cancel out and the neuron responds little. Other retinal ganglion cells do exactly the opposite, responding to light in the surround but not the center ("off-center cell"). For both on- and off-center cells, note that a uniform surface of light does little to activate them; instead, these cells are optimized for detecting differences in light levels from one area to the next—that is, *edges*.

Because of the center-surround structure, neighboring neurons can achieve **contrast enhancement**, that is, the amplification of a difference between the lightness of two surfaces. And this is the secret behind the first illusion we encountered, Mach bands (FIGURE 5.2). Receptive fields in the uniform regions have a balance between their excitatory centers and inhibitory surrounds. But a receptive field centered on the lighter Mach band gives a stronger response because part of its surround is in the darker area (and so receives less inhibition from the surround). Conversely, the receptive field over the dark band receives more surround inhibition because part of the surround is in the brighter area.

Here's another example of that concept: five years after Mach had noticed his bands, Ludimar Hermann noticed gray spots between the squares of a grid—and he puzzled over the fact that the spots disappeared when he looked directly at them (Eagleman, 2001) (Hermann grid illusion; FIGURE 5.8). This illusion arises because a retinal ganglion cell receptive field lying at the intersection of the cross has more light falling on its inhibitory surround than a receptive field that lies between two black squares. Consequently, its

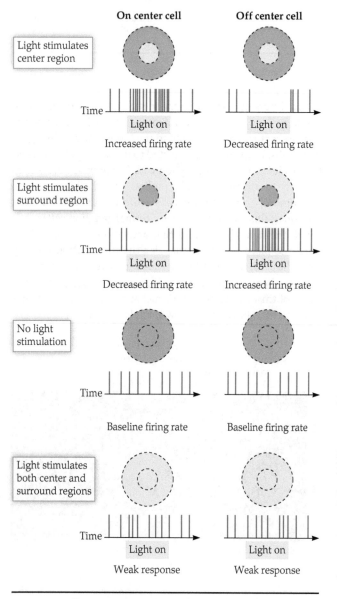

FIGURE 5.7 **The center-surround receptive field of on-center and off-center retinal ganglion cells.**

FIGURE 5.8 **The Hermann grid illusion arises from center-surround receptive fields in retinal ganglion cells.**

CASE STUDY:
The Bionic Retina

Terry Byland lives near Los Angeles, California. In 1993 he was diagnosed with retinitis pigmentosa, a degenerative disorder of his retina. "Aged 37, the last thing you want to hear is that you are going blind—that there's nothing they can do," said Byland (Fleming, 2007).

But then he discovered that there *was* something that could be done, if he was brave enough to try it. In 2004, he became one of the first patients to undergo an experimental procedure: he was implanted with a bionic retinal chip of the type we saw at the end of Chapter 4 (Fleming, 2007). The chip is a tiny device with 16 electrodes that plugs directly into the retina at the back of the eye. A pair of glasses holds a small camera, and the camera wirelessly beams its signals to the chip. The electrodes in the retina give little zaps of electricity to Terry's surviving retinal ganglion cells, thereby sending signals down the previously silent highways of the optic nerve (FIGURE 5.9). Just as with Michael's

case, Terry's nerve functioned just fine: although the photoreceptors had died, Terry's optic nerve remained hungry for signals that it could carry to the brain.

The idea of such a retinal prosthesis had been considered since at least the 1990s (Dowling, 2009). But no one was certain whether it would work. After all, the language of the retina is extraordinarily complex—and to this day remains largely undeciphered. Would a small electronic chip, speaking the dialect of Silicon Valley instead of Mother Nature, be understood by the rest of the brain—or would its patterns of miniature electrical sparks sound like gibberish?

Under the direction of Mark Humayun at the University of Southern California, the research team implanted the miniature chip in Terry's eye. With hushed anticipation, the team turned on the electrodes individually to test them. Terry reported, "It was amazing to see something. It was like little specks of

light—not even the size of a dime—when they were testing the electrodes one by one" (Fleming, 2007).

Terry described his visual experiences over the initial days as small constellations of lights. But, as we discovered in Chapter 4, the brain is plastic—and Terry's visual cortex began to change to extract something out of the signals. After some time, he detected the presence of his 18-year-old son: "I was with my son, walking, the first time—it was the first time I had seen him since he was five years old. I don't mind saying, there were a few tears wept that day" (Fleming, 2007).

Terry has now had the implant for years, and his brain can make better sense of the signals. Although he cannot recognize the details of individual faces, he can see them like a "dark shadow" (Fleming, 2007). The resolution of the retinal chip is only 16 pixels; nevertheless, Terry can touch squares presented at random locations on a computer screen, and he is able to cross a city street by

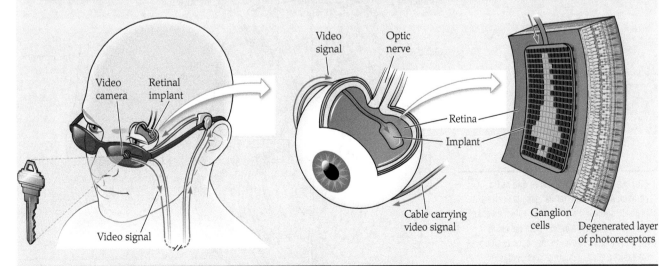

Video camera   Retinal implant

Video signal

Video signal   Optic nerve

Retina

Implant

Cable carrying video signal

Ganglion cells

Degenerated layer of photoreceptors

FIGURE 5.9 **The retinal implant.** In some disorders, photoreceptors of the retina degenerate although the remainder of the visual system remains healthy. In these cases, the diseased photoreceptors can be circumvented by a small chip that speaks directly to the retinal ganglion cells. A head-worn camera captures the scene, and a portable computer worn on the belt converts the input to electrical signals.

discerning the white lines of the crosswalk (Eagleman, 2016). He proudly reports, "When I'm in my home, or another person's house, I can go into any room and switch the light on, or see the light coming in through the window. When I am walking along the street I can avoid low hanging branches—I can see the edges of the branches, so I can avoid them" (Fleming, 2007).

Although incomplete, Terry's transition from blindness to partial sight makes an enormous difference to his quality of life, and this research has continued with other patients. As Dr. Humayun notes, "It's amazing, even with 16 pixels, or electrodes, how much our first six subjects have been able to do" (Fildes, 2007).

excitatory center is suppressed, resulting in weaker activity and the perception of less brightness.

Terry's chip works by sending electrical pulses directly into the retinal ganglion cells. From there, the signals move on toward the brain via the axons of the retinal ganglion cells, which converge to form the **optic nerve** (FIGURE 5.10). There can be no photoreceptors at the point where the optic nerve leaves the eye, so this is known as the **blind spot.**

Both of your eyes are facing forward, and both can see an overlapping part of the world. Therefore, we need to describe what you see not as what comes from your left eye or your right eye, but as what is in the left or right visual field, with the dividing line between them directly in front of you. Each of

your retinas is divided into two halves by an imaginary line running vertically through the eye and located at the boundary between the right and left visual fields. The half closest to your nose is called the nasal hemiretina, and the half furthest from your nose is called the temporal hemiretina.

The optic nerve conducts all of the information from your retina but keeps track of where in the retina the information originated. As you can see in the figure, the optic nerves from the left and the right eye come together at the **optic chiasm**, where half the fibers from the right eye and half the fibers from the left eye cross over (*chiasm* means "crossing"). Specifically, those signals from the right eye that carry information from the right visual field (the right nasal hemiretina)

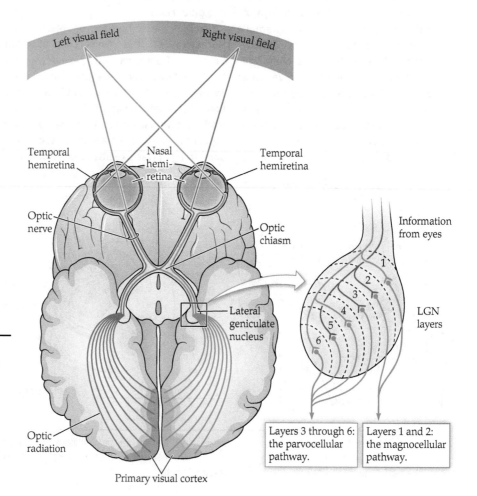

FIGURE 5.10 **The optic nerve and optic chiasm.** Axons of the retinal ganglion cells exit the back of the eye and form the optic nerve. At the optic chiasm, the output from the nasal hemiretina crosses over to the opposite side of the brain, while the information from the temporal hemiretina remains uncrossed. After the chiasm, the nerve bundles carry information about the right or left visual hemifield rather than the right or left eye.

cross over (where they will be processed in the left hemisphere), whereas those fibers from the left eye that carry information about the left visual field (the left nasal hemiretina) cross over (where they will be processed in the right hemisphere). Information from the temporal hemiretinas remains uncrossed and projects to the ipsilateral side of the brain because that information originated in the opposite (contralateral) visual field. The consequence is that the entire right visual field is handled by the left hemisphere (irrespective of whether picked up by your right or left eye), whereas the left visual field is administered by the right hemisphere. After the chiasm, once the fibers have been sorted into the two visual fields, the nerve bundles are now called the optic tracts.

Path to the Visual Cortex: The Lateral Geniculate Nucleus

From the retinal ganglion cell axons, electrical signals carrying information about the visual scene are next processed by a portion of the thalamus known as the lateral geniculate nucleus (LGN). As you recall, the retinal ganglion cells associated with the fovea receive their input from the cones and are smaller than the retinal ganglion cells in other parts of the retina. Based on their size, they are referred to as the **parvocellular retinal ganglion cells**, whereas the others, which are bigger and receive their input from the rods, are known as **magnocellular retinal ganglion cells**. These two different pathways project to different parts of the LGN, which is composed of six layers in human brains: two receive input from the magnocellular retinal ganglion cells and four receive input from the parvocellular retinal ganglion cells. The magnocellular layers process information from the rods, which carry information about *depth, brightness,* and *movement.* The parvocellular layers process information from the cones about fine details of the visual scene including *form* and *color.* Neurons of the LGN have receptive fields similar to those of the retinal ganglion cells: they are slightly larger, but still with a center-surround organization.

From the LGN, visual information travels via axons known as the **optic radiations** to the primary visual cortex.

The Visual Cortex

Axons carrying information from the LGN connect to the primary visual cortex (V1), (FIGURE 5.11). Because the axons are myelinated and most axons within the cortex are not, the massive bundle of inputs is visibly different from the rest of the cortex, making a white stripe visible to the naked eye in layer 4 of cortex. (Remember from Chapter 2 that the cortex is divided into six layers. Layer 4 is the layer that generally receives sensory inputs from the thalamus.) For this reason, you will often hear the primary visual cortex referred to as **striate cortex** (Latin *stria* = stripe).

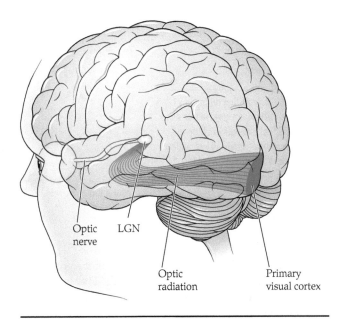

Optic nerve

LGN

Optic radiation

Primary visual cortex

FIGURE 5.11 Pathway to the primary visual cortex, also known as the striate cortex.

Throughout the central nervous system, the brain needs a way to organize the information it receives from the outside world. In many parts of the brain, this is done by topographic organization, which means that there is some orderly mapping from the external world to the internal representation in the brain. We saw the sensory and motor homunculi in Chapter 4 and will see this principle at work again in Chapter 6. Within V1, this topographic organization takes the form of retinotopic organization, meaning that each neuron responds to a particular part of the visual field, and neighboring neurons respond to neighboring parts of the visual field.

The response characteristics of V1 neurons were discovered by accident when David Hubel and Torsten Weisel were recording from a V1 neuron in a cat (Hubel, 1995). They were using a 35-mm projector to show various visual stimuli to a cat, but nothing was making the V1 neuron respond. Then, as they removed one of the slides from the projector, the neuron suddenly responded! As they put the slide back into place, the neuron responded again. After some investigation, they realized that this neuron was responding to the edge of the slide. By moving their electrode forward slightly, they were able to record from a different neuron, which responded to edges at a slightly different angle. They realized that different neurons in V1 responded to edges at different degrees of tilt: some vertical, some at 10 degrees, and so on. These neurons in V1 are orientation tuned, meaning that different orientations of an edge (or simply a line) will maximally activate different neurons. The tuning of a cell refers to the stimuli that activate it (FIGURE 5.12).

In addition to discovering what maximally activates V1 cells, Hubel and Wiesel discovered that the cells were composed of two different types: **simple** and **complex cells** (Hubel & Wiesel, 1968). Simple cells respond to a line at a preferred orientation and particular location in the receptive

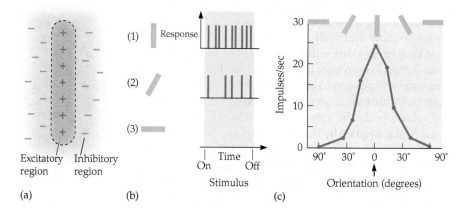

FIGURE 5.12 Orientation tuning in V1 neurons. (a) Particular regions in a neuron's receptive field respond with excitation or inhibition to stimulation. (b) As a result, each neuron can be maximally activated by a particular visual orientation. (c) The response of a neuron to different orientations of a stimulus can be measured—the resultant graph is known as the neuron's tuning curve.

field, whereas complex cells respond to a line of the preferred orientation at any location in the receptive field (FIGURE 5.13).

There are two conceptual points to pay attention to here. First, V1 neurons process more diverse information than LGN cells: they respond to edges of specific orientations rather than simply light and dark spots. This gives us our first glimpse of the hierarchy: as we move farther into the visual system, neurons respond to more abstract stimulus characteristics. Second, *successive stages of the hierarchy are built from parts of earlier stages*: LGN cells gather information from retinal ganglion cells, and simple cell responses in V1 are constructed from the input they receive from several LGN cells, and the response of complex cells is built by combining the input they receive from several simple cells (FIGURE 5.14). This concept of a hierarchy is fundamental to the processing of sensory information, and in the next chapter we will see the same principle at work in the auditory and somatosensory cortex. Although there is a hierarchy, the connections within this hierarchy are reciprocal, meaning that higher levels project back down to lower levels, influencing

processing at the lower levels. The brain also makes use of parallel processing, analyzing different kinds of information simultaneously in different locations. We'll return to these topics in more detail later in the chapter.

Following a series of experiments, researchers realized that there was a two-dimensional grid of neurons within V1 (Smith, Singh, & Greenlee, 2000). Like the rest of the cortex, V1 is organized into columns, with all of the cells within a given column performing similar functions. Along one axis of this grid, the cells differ in their orientation sensitivity. Along the other axis, they differ in the source of their input: one set of columns gets its input from the left eye, and the next set of columns gets its input from the right eye. These columns are known as ocular dominance columns. Within this grid of ocular dominance columns and orientation-tuned columns are clusters of cells known as **blobs**. (Yes, that really is their official name.) These blobs are important for processing the sensory input relating to color. Together, the ocular dominance columns from the left eye and the right eye, the orientation-tuned columns representing a full

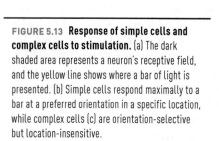

FIGURE 5.13 Response of simple cells and complex cells to stimulation. (a) The dark shaded area represents a neuron's receptive field, and the yellow line shows where a bar of light is presented. (b) Simple cells respond maximally to a bar at a preferred orientation in a specific location, while complex cells (c) are orientation-selective but location-insensitive.

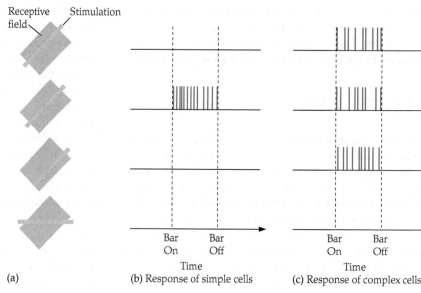

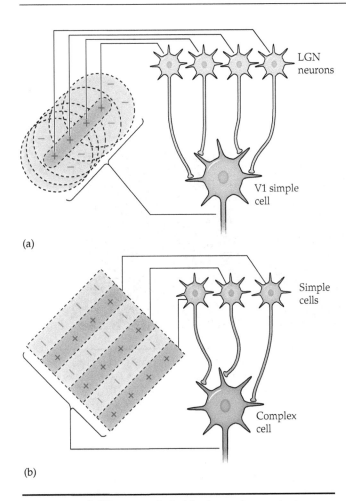

(a)

(b)

FIGURE 5.14 **Building successively richer layers of processing from simple parts.** (a) When several LGN neurons converge on a V1 simple cell, the new receptive field can be tuned to more than spots—in this case, it becomes tuned to oriented lines. (b) When several simple cells converge onto a complex cell, that neuron can respond to the preferred orientation in many locations.

rotation of orientations, and the blobs are called a hypercolumn. This hypercolumn contains all of the information that relates to a single location in the visual field.

Two Eyes Are Better Than One: Stereo Vision

Primary visual cortex is the first stage in the system where information from both eyes comes together for the first time. As we saw in the previous sections, signals from the two eyes remain separated in the LGN and all the way to V1.

Once in V1, the visual system can gain something clever by combining the information from the two eyes. But what does it gain, exactly?

To answer this, take a close look at a pen in your hand. When you close one eye, you see the pen lined up against certain things in the background, and when you close the other eye, you see the pen lined up against a slightly different background. This seems like it should cause problems when both eyes are open. However, it turns out that the visual system constructs a three-dimensional view of the world by taking advantage of this disparity—the difference between the visual images that each eye perceives because of the slightly different angles from which each eye views the world. Because your eyes do not occupy the same position in space, but instead are offset by about 6 centimeters, the visual system can gather useful information from two different points of view. The visual system has evolved sophisticated methods to compute the best three-dimensional answer from two flat images on your retinas.

Consider FIGURE 5.15, which shows two side-by-side photographs taken from a few inches apart. If you cross your eyes, the two photos will drift and eventually lock together to produce a single image. There's something special about this new image: it appears genuinely three-dimensional. This simple demonstration of stereoscopy unmasks something profound: you only need to feed the system the correct inputs, and it constructs a convincing reality for you.

(a)   (b)

FIGURE 5.15 **Stereo vision.** The two eyes receive slightly different images. Because light from the two subjects falls on different parts of the two retinas, (a) the left eye sees one image of the world and (b) the right sees another. This slight informational difference from the two eyes does not confuse the visual system. Instead, it uses the differences to extract depth information.

NEUROSCIENCE OF EVERYDAY LIFE:
Random-Dot Stereograms

The amazing capacity of the visual system to take two slightly different images and match them up led some researchers to ask a simple question: does stereo vision rely on object recognition? In other words, does your visual cortex have to recognize the images above as street scenes before it puts the right- and left-eye images together? The answer came as a surprise to many: recognition is *not* necessary for stereo matching. To elegantly prove this point, psychologist Bela Julesz created random-dot stereograms to demonstrate that the percept of depth can be generated from disparity alone. In his stimuli (FIGURE 5.16), there is nothing recognizable to the naked eye—and yet, when you fuse the images together, a shape in depth is clearly seen (Julesz,

FIGURE 5.16 **Depth information from disparity.** These images can be viewed by crossing your eyes until the images overlap. If you find that difficult, try holding a long envelope down the middle of the visual field (right between your eyes), such that each eye sees only one side of the image. These random-dot images demonstrate that object recognition is not necessary for perceiving depth from differences between the eyes.

1986). These simple images demonstrate that depth computation from disparity is low level. One only needs to trick the system with appropriate input, and it automatically computes its answer—and we experience depth on the completely flat page.

Higher Visual Areas

We've traveled from the retina to the primary visual cortex and are now ready to begin the real story of vision.

Secondary and Tertiary Visual Cortex: Processing Becomes More Complex

V1 feeds its information into a neighboring area known as **secondary visual cortex (V2)** (FIGURE 5.17). V2 receives direct connections from V1, and (like V1) it is laid out in a map of the visual world: it is retinotopic. Neurons in V2 have slightly larger receptive fields than in V1 (Gattass, Gross, & Sandell, 1981). Given the lessons we learned about hierarchy, it should come as no surprise that V2 receptive fields are built from receptive field information coming from V1. Most neurons here are still tuned to relatively simple stimuli (for example, orientation and color), but we can also detect a slight increase in

perceptual complexity as we continue up the hierarchy: for example, neurons in V1 do not respond to the orientation of illusory lines, but neurons in V2 do (Qiu & von der Heydt, 2005). Consider a Kanizsa figure (FIGURE 5.18): the square in the middle does not actually exist, yet observers usually report "seeing" the square there, as well as differences in brightness outside and inside its illusory edges (Sterman, 1994). Many neurons in V2 show an active response if their receptive fields are positioned where the line would be—in other words, they respond as though a real line were actually there. Only half as many cells in V1 do this, and their response is much weaker (Lee & Nguyen, 2001; Zeki, 1996). The response of V2 neurons, therefore, is slightly closer to our final perception of the visual scene, rather than simply a reflection of the world.

V2 projects to several other areas, which are collectively called **tertiary visual cortex** and often summarized as containing areas V3, V4, and V5. Scientists disagree as to what should be included in tertiary cortex, but that's immaterial to the main point: as we move past secondary areas, we are now climbing to higher levels of the hierarchy. Cells begin to respond to more and more abstract stimuli in their receptive

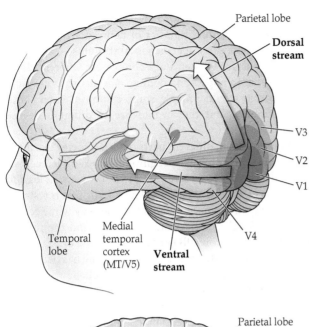

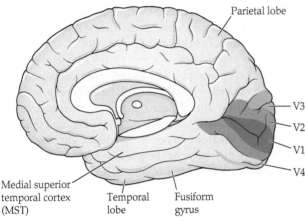

FIGURE 5.17 Lateral and medial view of the brain, highlighting higher visual areas, including V2, V3, V4, and V5/MT.

FIGURE 5.18 Kanizsa figure. Although the four pie shapes are separate objects, the visual system fills in illusory lines to form a square.

fields—such as houses, faces, and movement, as we will see in a moment.

The plot thickens here. Remember how the information from the cones and rods stayed segregated in the LGN in the parvocellular and magnocellular pathways? That separation of function holds true as one moves up the hierarchy. Even as visual information becomes more abstracted, the information moves in two distinct processing "streams" (Mishkin & Ungerleider, 1982). One, the **ventral stream**, deciphers *what* objects are—in other words, how to identify and categorize them. The other, the **dorsal stream**, is focused on *where* objects are and how to interact with them. We meet these two streams in more detail now.

Ventral Stream: What an Object Is

From the parvocellular cells in LGN through V1, visual information flows through V2 and V4 into the inferior temporal

lobe (known as **inferotemporal cortex**). This is the ventral stream of information processing, known sometimes as the *"what pathway"* (Rauschecker & Tian, 2000).

As information progresses from posterior regions (near the back of the head) toward the anterior tip of the temporal lobe, neurons go from encoding features (such as lines, curves, and angles) (Hubel & Wiesel, 1968) to specific objects (faces, cars, logos, and so on) (Martin, Wiggs, Ungerleider, & Haxby, 1996; Martin, Wiggs, & Weisberg, 1997). Specifically, as we saw above, V1 neurons have small receptive fields and encode simple features of visual stimuli, such as oriented lines. In V2, the size of receptive fields increases by about threefold. Neurons in V2 respond to more complex features of visual stimuli, such as curves, angles, and the borders between textures (Foster, Gaska, Nagler, & Pollen, 1985; Martin et al., 1996, 1997). In V4, receptive fields are even larger, and the stimuli they respond to are more complex, such as gratings and line crossings (Gattass, Sousa, & Gross, 1988). Each of these areas (V1, V2, V4) is laid out in a retinotopic map, representing the outside world in the brain (Dougherty et al., 2003).

The complexity of the shapes encoded increases as we pass from V4 into inferior temporal (IT) regions, and it continues to increase as we move from posterior IT cells toward anterior IT cells (FIGURE 5.19) (Kobatake & Tanaka, 1994). By the top of the hierarchy, we find IT neurons selective for complex shapes such as tools and animals (Hung, Kreiman, Poggio, & DiCarlo, 2005; Kanwisher, McDermott, & Chun, 1997). One part of the IT lobe, the fusiform gyrus, seems to be selective for recognizing faces (Kanwisher et al., 1997).

The receptive fields of IT neurons are much larger than those found in early visual cortex, which means they can respond to relevant stimuli almost anywhere in the visual field and gives them the property that they are not focused on *where* exactly an object is—instead they are focused on *what* it is. In other words, changes to the object itself (such as a change in shape) will change the firing rate of IT neurons,

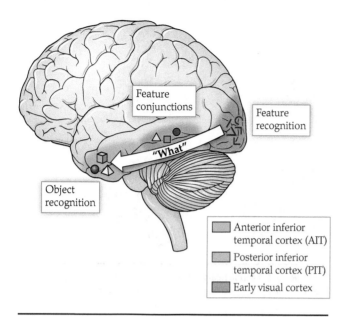

FIGURE 5.19 The ventral stream in inferior temporal cortex. The inferior temporal cortex is subdivided into several areas, and the complexity of information processed increases from the posterior inferior temporal cortex (PIT) to the anterior inferior temporal cortex (AIT). Each of these areas has a full representation, or map, of the visual world. In the progression from posterior to anterior, the response of neurons evolves from specific visual features to generalized understanding of objects.

but a change in the position or size of the object will not (FIGURE 5.20) (Sary, Vogels, & Orban, 1993). A response that remains the same irrespective of the position or size (this is called **position invariance** or **size invariance**) is critical to recognizing an object in different contexts: you want to recognize your mother's face no matter where it is or how close or far she's standing from you.

Given that neurons in IT show size- and position-invariant responses, it is not surprising that these neurons are no longer organized in retinotopic maps (as they were in earlier stages of visual cortex) (Desimone, Albright, Gross, & Bruce, 1984). So how is the information encoded at these later stages? Generally, there are two strategies for how the brain can encode information in visual cortex: **sparse coding** and population coding (review by Reddy & Kanwisher, 2006). Say you were displaying one of two visual objects, either Barack Obama's face or a Tesla sports car. In sparse coding, a small number of neurons would become active in response to a specific visual stimulus—say, a small cluster of cells for Obama and a completely different cluster for the Tesla. In population coding, *most* neurons in ventral visual cortex would provide some response when shown either stimulus, but they would fire to different degrees (FIGURE 5.21).

As it turns out, different parts of visual cortex use different coding schemes. Face recognition, for example, seems to be highly specific to a small number of neurons, at least for famous faces and for people you know well. This is tested by showing a great number of faces to a monkey while recording from a single, face-sensitive neuron—and the result is often that the neuron will fire to one face and one face only, not to any of the rest. The same sparse coding has been found with hands, bodies, and letter strings as well.

However, for many other stimulus types—say, houses, cityscapes, or the general shape of an object, population coding seems to be in effect: many neurons are involved at varying levels of response rather than a few at binary (**all-or-none**) responses (Pasupathy & Connor, 2002).

Why do some stimuli seem to be sparsely encoded whereas others are population coded? The answer seems to pivot on familiarity with the stimuli being represented: the more familiar the stimuli, the sharper the representation of individual neurons, the sparser the encoding, and the more clustered the neurons become that represent the object. Thus, expertise in a category begets sparse, clustered populations devoted to that kind of object (Op de Beeck, Baker, Rindler, & Kanwisher, 2005). Presumably, we all possess small neural populations in our ventral visual stream that are specialized to, say, cell phones—something our ancestors never had in their temporal lobes.

To summarize our tour of the ventral pathway, neurons in early visual areas faithfully encode simple properties of objects. As processing moves in a hierarchy toward the anterior part of the inferotemporal cortex, neurons have larger receptive fields and encode an increasingly abstract form of the stimulus—that is, local characteristics (including position and size) become less relevant. For example, when a neuron in the **fusiform face area** (an area of inferotemporal cortex specialized for faces) is presented with a face built of

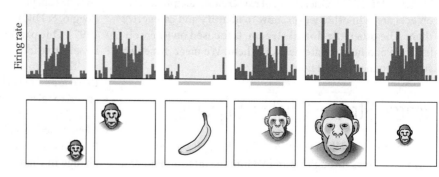

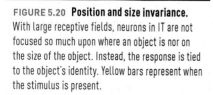

FIGURE 5.20 Position and size invariance. With large receptive fields, neurons in IT are not focused so much upon where an object is nor on the size of the object. Instead, the response is tied to the object's identity. Yellow bars represent when the stimulus is present.

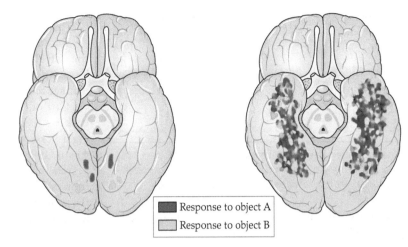

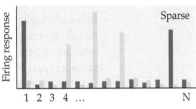 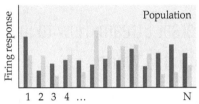

FIGURE 5.21 **An illustration of sparse versus population coding schemes.** (a) Where sparse coding is found in the brain, small numbers of responsive neurons usually lie in close proximity to one another. (b) In population coding, responsive neurons tend to be more spread out. The brain here is viewed from underneath to see the inferior temporal lobes. Figure from Reddy and Kanwisher (2006).

THE BIGGER PICTURE:
Reading the Movies in Our Minds

When you watch a changing visual scene, the patterns of activity are constantly shifting. So could you record the changing pattern across the cortex and predict what a person is seeing? It sounds like science fiction, but in September 2011 it became reality.

Researchers at Berkeley recorded from their own brains while watching hours and hours of Hollywood movie trailers on YouTube (Nishimoto et al., 2011). They then used a computer to find correlations between the properties of each video and the patterns of fMRI activity induced in the visual

cortex. From this, the computer "learned" to recognize what people were seeing, based on the patterns of activity in their brains. Next, new subjects watched a new set of videos. Without knowing what the subjects had watched, the researchers tried to reconstruct what those videos looked like, based only on the measured neural activity. After measuring the activity, their model chose the top 100 videos that best matched the activity patterns, and then it averaged those together for its best guess of what the new video must have looked like. The match was stunningly good.

These results support the story that we have been building so far: the visual stimulus is broken down and processed by the brain, resulting in certain types of brain activity. Working in reverse, researchers can look at the activity to make predictions about what the initial stimulus must have been. This technology for decoding and reconstructing people's dynamic visual experiences may be used, someday, to read out one's dreams or even the visual imaginings of a coma patient.

FIGURE 5.22 **Different representations of faces.** The details between these faces trigger different responses in early visual areas. However, all are recognized as faces by neurons in the fusiform face area; the details are abstracted away.

sketched lines, paint strokes, or pieces of fruit, it responds to the *faceness* of the object (FIGURE 5.22).

Dorsal Stream: How to Interact with the World

Let's now return to V1 and V2 to examine the other processing pathway, the dorsal stream. This path relates less to *what* an object is and instead processes *where* it is in space. It is typically referred to as the "where" pathway.

As you can probably guess, the source of the information in the dorsal stream begins with the rods in the retina and the magnocellular cells in the LGN: these are tuned to fast changes rather than sustained details. This information works its way through V1 and V2 into **area V5**, an area specialized for motion detection, and onward into the parietal lobe (FIGURE 5.23). As a result of the information in this stream, the posterior parietal cortex is necessary for understanding spatial relationships between objects as well as the coordination of one's own body in space (Goodale & Milner, 1992).

Because such a major part of the dorsal stream involves the detection of motion, we will begin there, then turn to issues of attention, and finally investigate the effects of damage to the dorsal stream.

One of the oldest visual illusions in neuroscience dates back to Aristotle, who noticed something after intently watching a horse stuck in a flowing river (Mather, Verstraten, & Anstis, 1998). When Aristotle looked at the riverbank, it appeared that everything was drifting the opposite direction from the river's flow. What Aristotle experienced is now called the motion aftereffect: following exposure to a visual field moving in one direction, other things appear to drift the other way (Tootell et al., 1995). This striking perception is also known colloquially as the waterfall illusion, so named because staring at a waterfall is an efficient way to induce the aftereffect: when you look away from the waterfall, the rocks and dirt and trees appear to be levitating upward. Perhaps the strangest part of the illusion is that things appear to move, but with no change in their position—a physical impossibility. The rocks don't end up any higher than where they started.

How can it seem as though motion occurs even though nothing in the outside world changes position? The answer is that the inside of the brain is not equivalent to a television screen (Dennett, 1992), and so it can easily handle motion with no change in position. In fact, there are many illusions of motion with no change in position. Recall the rotating snakes illusion from FIGURE 5.3 at the beginning of this chapter. Similarly, FIGURE 5.24 demonstrates that static images can

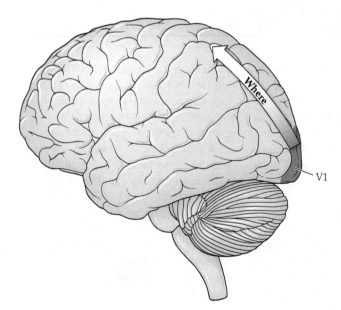

FIGURE 5.23 **The dorsal stream moves from V1 into the parietal lobe.**

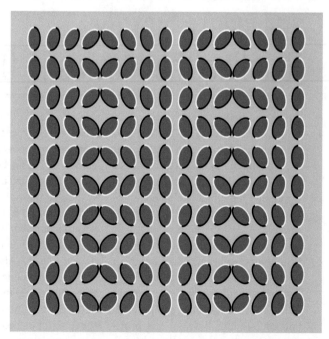

FIGURE 5.24 **Motion can be seen even when there is no change in position.** In the optical illusion shown here, leaves appear to wave.

CASE STUDY:
The World in Snapshots

In 1978, a woman we'll call Melissa was locked in her garage while her car was running. She sustained carbon monoxide poisoning. Fortunately, she lived, but unfortunately, the oxygen deprivation caused irreversible damage to a specific region of her visual cortex: area V5, which is necessary for the representation of motion. The remainder of her visual system escaped injury, so she could still see objects and their positions with no problems (Zihl, von Cramon, Mai, & Schmid, 1991).

However, Melissa could no longer see motion (Zihl, et al., 1991). Standing on a sidewalk, looking around to cross a street, she might see something like a blue truck on the road. A moment later she would see that truck closer to her. Then, she would see it right in front of her. But everything she perceived was in snapshots; the truck had no movement to it. As a result, she could no longer perform even the most basic tasks. Pouring water from a pitcher into a glass became a challenge. Rather than seeing the liquid move smoothly, it would seem to Melissa that she was catching glimpses of it through a strobe light.

appear to move if they happen to activate motion detectors in the right way.

Such motion illusions occur because the exact shading in the pictures happens to stimulate the visual system's mechanisms for detecting motion. When those are activated, you see motion—whether or not something is *actually* moving out there (Mather et al., 1998). When the right keys are turned, your perceptual system has an experience as genuine as any other motion you've seen. We'll turn to a remarkable illustration of this principle now.

This patient's condition, known as **motion blindness**, highlights the strange fact that motion and position are separable to the brain. To a physicist, motion is change in position; to the brain, motion is painted on—as we see with illusions like waving leaves and rotating snakes.

How, then, do we sense motion? To a physicist, motion *is* change in position through time, but not so for the brain. From the point of view of the brain, motion detection can be achieved with neural mechanisms that are directly sensitive to a target's velocity, without regard to position. The first example of this appeared in 1875, when the Austrian physiologist Sigmund Exner (1846—1926) demonstrated that the detection of motion does not depend on position change. He rigged two electric sparks to appear in rapid succession, one beside the other. At the right distance in space and time, observers perceived the motion of a single spark from the point occupied by the first to the point occupied by the second. Exner then moved the sparks closer together until the two sparks—when set off simultaneously—could not be distinguished from a single spark. So although the two positions were now indistinguishable, a sequential sparking still caused the perception of motion. The direction of motion was distinguishable with a gap as small as 15 milliseconds

(Exner, 1875). This demonstrated that the perception of motion does not depend on detecting positions and then comparing them.

But can the visual system work directly with motion signals and not care much about position? In many cases, yes. Just using direct motion signals, animals can intercept, capture, and avoid. But this seems strange, doesn't it? If position is not always represented, how could a baseball outfielder possibly know where to go to catch a ball? The answer is that the outfielder does not need to use position—or velocity or acceleration—to catch the ball. When he runs to catch a fly ball, his brain (unconsciously) converts the temporal problem (determining acceleration) into a spatial one by selecting a running path that keeps the optical trajectory of the ball going in a straight line (McBeath, Shaffer, & Kaiser, 1995). This way, spatial cues guide him toward the ball's destination point, and acceleration never needs to be computed. As a side note, this strategy does not tell a person precisely where the ball will land, but instead only how to keep running—as illustrated by baseball players who crash into walls when chasing pop fly balls. This model of catching was verified by aerial photography, which quantified outfielders' trajectories. Indeed, the paths they run in are not straight; they are curvy, as guided by the algorithm their brains employ (McBeath, et al., 1995). This strategy is also used by fighter pilots when pursuit tracking (O'Hare, 1999), fish (Lanchester & Mark, 1975), and hoverflies (Collett & Land, 1975).

The bottom line is this: to catch or intercept a moving object, the visual system does not need an explicit representation of position, or even velocity or acceleration. This counterintuitive finding merely reinforces that we have little intuitive access to the mechanisms of the visual cortex that underlie our abilities (Eagleman, 2011).

FIGURE 5.25 **How many horses are in the picture?**

Attention and the Dorsal Stream

Take a look at FIGURE 5.25 and see how quickly you can name the number of horses in the scene.

Difficult, isn't it? If the world were processed like a camera, you would have the answer instantly. But with our visual systems, it is impossible to process everything at once. Instead, to pull out the visual features of interest, you must select particular parts of the image for more detailed analysis. This process is known as focusing your **attention**.

The key to attention is that it is selective: it *improves* perception of stimuli that are attended to, and it *interferes* with the processing of those that are not. We will learn about attention in much greater detail in Chapter 8, but for now the key principle to appreciate is that attention can be *spatial*. At any moment, attention involves particular places in space. If you want to better understand what someone is saying, you can attend to her moving mouth. If you want to know whether she's happy or sad, you may watch the muscles around her eyes. If you hear her doorbell ring, you may shift your attention to the doorway. In all cases, attention must be focused on an area. Like a spotlight, attention can be adjusted to span a larger or smaller area, but it cannot be split up into multiple areas. You may attend to small eye muscles or a large doorway, but you cannot do both at the same time.

The dorsal stream is critical for guiding and adjusting the spotlight of attention. Although we do not usually think about the movements of our attention, its role becomes clear when there is damage to parietal lobe, a key component of the dorsal stream.

Consider **hemineglect**, a bizarre disorder in which a person will disregard one half of the world. This is typically caused by brain damage (usually a stroke) to the right parietal lobe, which causes total neglect of everything on the left side of the person (Vallar, 1993). There is nothing wrong with a person's visual system—instead, the problem is purely one of placing his attention anywhere in the left side of the world. Such patients behave as though one half of the world does not exist. They are completely unaware of the vanished half and do not usually miss it. For example, a typical hemineglect patient will only dress the right side of his body, shave the right side of his face, and eat the dinner on the right side of his plate (Tsirlin, Dupierrix, Chokron, Coquillart, & Ohlmann, 2009). These bizarre behaviors are not caused by a blindness to the neglected side; instead, the problem is one of attention (in fact, the disorder is often called "hemi-inattention"). This can be demonstrated by calling a patient's attention to his neglected side—say, by presenting a toy snake there or more simply by getting him to reach over into his neglected field with his opposite hand. Such tricks will help a subject notice the unattended side—demonstrating that he is not blind there—but this shift of attention does not last. Once the subject is distracted from the intervention, he will again neglect the left side (Tsirlin et al., 2009). We will return to hemineglect in detail in Chapter 8. For now, the important principle is that the dorsal stream steers the spotlight of attention.

This fact is made even more apparent in **Balint's syndrome**, a disorder caused by damage to the parietal lobes on *both* sides (FIGURE 5.26a).

Although patients with Balint's have a functioning ventral stream (and can therefore consciously recognize objects), their loss of attentional steering steals away their ability to comprehend the big picture of a visual scene. Consider a patient with Balint's, as he uses great effort to describe the scene in FIGURE 5.26b. He slowly reports what he sees: "... *a car, a police car, another police car, a bus, a gorilla, a building, a man (standing on a bus).*" Although his ability to see details is unimpaired, the patient is unable to see the larger picture of the scene (a giant ape running amok through a city) because his attentional systems are not functioning correctly.

Part of the patient's difficulty in understanding the scene stems from his **simultagnosia**, another symptom of Balint's syndrome. Simultagnosia is an inability to recognize multiple elements in a scene (FIGURE 5.27) (Bose, 2008) and therefore the visual field as a whole. Imagine you placed a cell phone and a bottle of water in front of one another on a table. You then ask a patient with Balint's syndrome to describe what he sees. He would tell you, "a cell phone." Anything else? "No." Then, a few moments later, he might say, "I see a bottle of water." Anything else? "No, just the bottle of water." He cannot see both at the same time. You can imagine the difficulty one would have, then, in describing a complex scene: it would be impossible to see the forest for the trees.

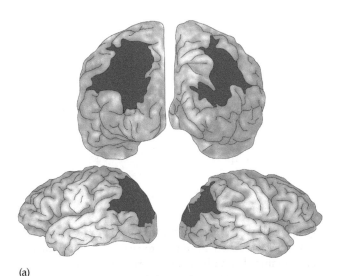

(a)

(b)

FIGURE 5.26 **Balint's syndrome.** Typical areas of damage leading to Balint's syndrome. (a) When the dorsal stream is damaged in both hemispheres, a person can no longer use attention to understand the visual world. (b) When trying to describe a complex visual scene, a patient with Balint's syndrome will see the details, but not understand the bigger picture.

Comparing the Ventral and Dorsal Processing Streams

A good way to understand the differences between the ventral and dorsal streams is to compare what happens with damage to them. Bilateral damage to the face areas in the ventral visual stream, for example, will lead to a disorder known as **prosopagnosia (face blindness)** (Damasio, Damasio, & Van Hoesen, 1982). In this condition, the visual system functions, but one cannot recognize faces. When looking at the face made of vegetables in FIGURE 5.22, a person with prosopagnosia merely sees the pieces of produce.

FIGURE 5.27 **A typical test for simultagnosia.** A person is asked to look at a picture like this one and describe what he or she sees. A person with simultagnosia will report seeing only one object at a time.

Lesions in the dorsal stream, on the other hand, result in problems with knowing *how* and *where* to interact with objects (Pisella et al., 2009). As we saw in the case study of the woman previously mentioned, damage to her motion-processing areas rendered her perception of the world as a series of snapshots. And patients who sustain damage to larger areas of their parietal lobes find themselves unable to move their attentional spotlight appropriately—as in the cases of hemineglect or Balint's syndrome (Egly, Driver, & Rafal, 1994).

Let's consolidate what we've just learned by thinking through two clinical cases. The first patient we'll consider is named D.F. (Milner, 1995). Because of damage to her cortex, she is blind. She cannot name objects, and she cannot distinguish among circles, triangles, and squares right in front of her. But strangely, she can grasp objects correctly. And if you ask her to put an envelope through a slot (one that can be tilted to any angle), she can do that perfectly well, although she claims to see neither the letter nor the slot (FIGURE 5.28).

Let's compare D.F.'s case to that of another patient named A.T. He can see objects just fine, but he cannot pick them up them correctly (Goodale & Milner, 1992). When asked to pick up a small block of wood, he bluntly lowers his palm down toward it and tries to pull all his fingers together at once. Although he can see, he simply cannot make use of the visual information in the scene.

These two patients have opposite problems: the first can interact with objects correctly, but cannot *see* them. The second can see and recognize objects with no trouble, but cannot *interact* with them correctly.

Where are the areas of brain damage in these patients?

At this point in the chapter, you should have no trouble identifying that D.F.'s lesion is located in the ventral visual stream, which involves the temporal lobe, whereas A.T.'s is in the dorsal visual stream, which involves the parietal lobe.

FIGURE 5.28 **Patient D.F.** (a) D.F. cannot correctly report the orientation of a slot. (b) If you ask D.F. to "mail" a letter through the slot at any orientation, she does so with no problem.

(a)

(b)

The Bigger Picture of the Visual Brain

As we have been seeing, layers of visual processing are organized in a hierarchy. As signals move from the eyes to the LGN and through the visual cortex, processing changes from specific, signal-oriented responses to more abstract, object-oriented responses. Neuronal populations become more specialized the higher in the hierarchy they live—from spots of light in retinal ganglion cells to face recognition in anterior temporal lobe neurons. At higher stages, neurons have larger receptive fields, and fewer neurons respond to any particular stimulus.

As a result of this hierarchical structure, damage to primary visual cortex leads to scotomas, areas of diminished vision or complete blindness in the visual field. Damage to secondary visual cortex leads to visual agnosias, loss of recognition or meaning of objects. Damage to tertiary areas (such as those in inferotemporal cortex or parietal cortex) leads to specific deficits, such as face blindness or the inability to see motion.

We also learned in this section about the dorsal and ventral processing streams—the where and what pathways. Damage to the former can make a patient unable to attend to or interact appropriately with objects in the world, whereas damage to the latter can leave a patient unable to see or recognize objects. Keep in mind that both systems work together under normal circumstances. As Goodale and Milner remind us, "Both systems have to work together in the production of purposive behavior—one system to select the goal object from the visual array, the other to carry out the required metrical computations for the goal-directed action" (Goodale et al., 1994).

Although we have learned about the concept of a visual hierarchy, we will see in the coming sections that this story is not, in itself, complete. The brain is characterized by feedback loops. As a result, although the ventral and dorsal streams are specialized, they interact with one another. As one example, we mentioned that patients with ventral stream lesions may have prosopagnosia, or face blindness. However, when shown a picture of a familiar face—compared to an unfamiliar face—a prosopagnosic will still have an increase in the galvanic skin response (a signature of the autonomic nervous system related to an emotionally significant event) (Fox, Iaria, & Barton, 2008). This suggests that face recognition is partially accomplished in areas other than the classic "face areas" in the ventral stream. More generally, other, rare agnosias that are beyond the scope of this chapter reveal a

CASE STUDY:
The Blind Woman Who Could See, Sort Of

A patient we'll call Amanda suffered a stroke that injured her primary visual cortex on one side. As a result, she now has blindness in one half of her visual field.

Imagine that you pick up a cardboard shape, hold it up on Amanda's blind side, and ask her to describe what she sees.

Not surprisingly, Amanda will report that she has no idea.

You encourage her to take a guess anyway. There's obviously no consequence if she's wrong.

But Amanda insists that she really is unable to tell you. She's blind in that hemifield.

You assure her that's fine, but that you still want her to guess.

Finally, eager to get you to quit asking, she floats a guess that the shape is a hexagon. To her surprise and yours, her rate of guessing correctly is well above chance (Weiskrantz, 1990a,b). Some part of her brain is seeing unconsciously. This phenomenon is called **blindsight**. A recent demonstration of blindsight shocked research professionals: a doctor blinded by two strokes in his primary visual cortex was able to navigate an obstacle course in a hallway (de Gelder et al., 2008).

complexity of relationships among seeing, naming, recognizing, interacting, gesturing toward an object, pantomiming what to do with an object, and so on. Therefore, we should consider the separation of the ventral and dorsal streams a useful model that is clinically relevant, but not complete.

Consider another example of complexities beyond a simple visual hierarchy. We learned earlier that visual information follows a pathway from the retina to the LGN to V1. But that's only true for 90% of the information leaving the eye via the retinal ganglion cells. The other 10% of information bypasses the LGN in favor of other destinations, including the superior colliculus, amygdala, and pulvinar nucleus of the thalamus. Do these subcortical pathways from the retina serve any purpose in vision? Indeed they do, as we can see from the following strange case.

These cases demonstrate that *something* in the brain is seeing—it's just not the part of the pathway that depends on the integrity of the visual cortex. For many patients with blindsight, the damage that makes them blind is within V1. However, as we have described so far, seeing involves many other parts of the brain. We do not know how blindsight works, but the best-described theory involves the different pathways from the retina to the brain. The pathway from the retina to the LGN to V1 accounts for about 90% of the output from the eyes to the brain. The other 10% projects from the retina to other areas, including the superior colliculus and the pulvinar nucleus of the thalamus. These areas are important for visual attention, and it may be that, even with V1 damage, the subcortical pathways like those of the superior colliculus and amygdala are still intact. These are sufficient to carry some degree of visual information, but, because of the damage to V1, that information does not rise to the level of visual awareness (Cowey, 2010).

Perception Is Active, Not Passive

Interrogating the Scene with Our Eyes

In the late 1960s, the psychologist Alfred Yarbus set out to understand how the brain actively seeks information from the world—sometimes in ways we're not aware of. To that end, he showed volunteers a copy of Ilya Repin's painting *An Unexpected Visitor* (FIGURE 5.29). Their task was simply to answer questions, such as: "How wealthy are the people in the painting?", "How old are they?", "What were they doing just before he walked in?", "How long had the visitor been away?" During the inquiries, Yarbus used an eye-tracker to measure where the participants' eyes were looking.

We might assume that gazing upon a painting involves simply aiming your eyes there. However, with each question, the subjects' eyes traversed the canvas in different patterns to ferret out the clues needed to answer the questions (Yarbus,

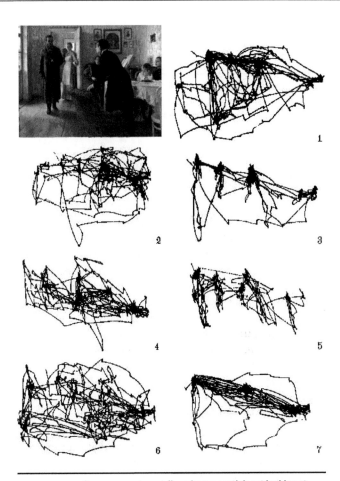

FIGURE 5.29 **Eye movement recordings from a participant looking at** *The Unexpected Visitor.* The different conditions were: (1) Free examination. Then, before the next recordings, participants were asked to (2) judge the wealth of the family, (3) estimate the ages of the people, (4) deduce what the family was doing just before the arrival of the unexpected visitor, (5) recall the clothes worn by the people, (6) remember the positions of the objects and people in the room, and (7) guess how long the unexpected visitor had been away. Each eye-recording lasted 3 minutes.

1967). When assessing the ages, they looked at the faces; when judging affluence, they focused on the possessions and clothes.

The brain directs the eyes to very specific locations to obtain the information it needs. It interrogates a scene to pick up details on a need-to-know basis. In other words, despite the impression that we see everything at once about a painting, we don't. And this is because the brain does not need to. It only requires a strategy that allows it to find where it needs to go when it comes time to answer a question.

Although you have lived with your pair of eyeballs from the beginning of your life, you have little direct knowledge about what they're up to. Your introspection is limited; you can gain much more insight from watching other people's eyes. To appreciate how little you know about your own eye movements, reflect on the rapid, precise saccades you're making right now, as you read this page. This is just one demonstration of the fact that vision is not a passive process, but an active one.

FIGURE 5.30 The blind spot. Close your left eye and keep your right eye on the plus sign. Then, position the page closer to and farther from your face until the black dot disappears. At that distance, the dot is hidden in your blind spot.

The Blind Spot

The brain does more than deduce what's happening in the outside world—it often fabricates things entirely. For this reason, one basic feature of the retina was not discovered until 1668, many centuries after people could have easily noticed it. While studying a retina laid out in his laboratory, the French philosopher and mathematician Edmund Mariotte had a striking insight: where the retinal ganglion cell axons passed through the retina to become the optic nerve, there were no photoreceptors: there's simply no room for them because of the axons. Why does this matter? Because if there are no photoreceptors in that region of the retina, it should be blind there. And it's not.

Or isn't it? Mariotte had to do some careful observation to determine something that no one had noticed before: in each eye, there is a spot in the visual field that captures no information—known commonly now as the "blind spot." Demonstrate it to yourself in FIGURE 5.30.

To experience the region where you have no vision, drag the page closer to and farther from your eyes. At some point, the dot seems to disappear. It's now hitting your retina at the spot where you have no photoreceptors.

You might assume that you've never noticed your blind spot because it's tiny, but in fact it's huge. You can fit an area equal to 17 moons in your blind spot.

With so large an area of missing vision, why did it take so long for someone to notice before 1668? How did brilliant and curious minds like Michelangelo, Galileo, Newton, Shakespeare, and Kepler miss this basic observation? The reason it is so easy to miss is that we have two eyes, and their regions of blindness do not overlap. That means when both of your eyes are open, together they fully cover the scene. There is another and more significant reason as well: no one had noticed the blind spot because of a phenomenon called

"filling in." Your brain completes the scene, using information from around the missing region to fill the gap. As a result, you do not experience a hole (Ramachandran, 1992). In the case of FIGURE 5.30, you don't see a chasm when the black dot disappears; you instead see a patch as though the page's background has poured in. When the brain doesn't have information from a region, it simply fills things in.

As with the earlier examples, the blind spot underscores the fact that you do not necessarily perceive what is out there. You perceive whatever your visual system tells you.

Seeing the Same Object Different Ways: Multistability

As another example of the illusory nature of vision, consider a **multistable percept**. This is an ambiguous stimulus that can be perceived in more than one way and that typically flips back and forth between the different options (FIGURE 5.31). You may have experienced the strange reversals of the Necker cube. A simple wireframe figure, it appears to you as a box oriented in a particular direction. However, if you continue to stare at it, it will reverse direction, appearing to come out of the page in a different way. The image remains exactly the same on the page, *so whatever is changing must be inside your head.* That is, your retina is receiving the same information on its photoreceptors, but your brain is not just a passive recorder: instead it actively processes input to "see." There is more than one way for the visual system to interpret the stimulus, and so it flips back and forth between the possibilities (Bradley & Petry, 1977).

Binocular Rivalry: Different Images in the Two Eyes

As we learned above, the brain exploits the slightly different information entering the two eyes to construct a perception of depth. But what happens when the information coming to the two eyes is not slightly different, but radically different? This situation leads to **binocular rivalry** (FIGURE 5.32). In binocular rivalry, you don't see both images simultaneously nor a fusion. Instead, you see one image, then the other, and then

FIGURE 5.31 Ambiguous figures. The Necker cube (a) can be perceived as coming out of the page in one of two ways, as can the cylinder (b). The staircase (c) can be viewed as going up and into the page or as the underside of a staircase coming out of the page. The perceived "switching" of the figure orientation takes place because "seeing" is an active process: nothing about the figure on the page has changed.

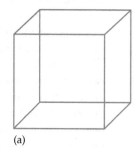 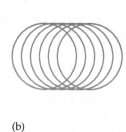 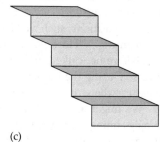

(a)   (b)   (c)

FIGURE 5.32 **Binocular rivalry.** When two different images are presented individually to the two eyes, the brain does not perceive a fusion of both images. Instead, it perceives one image alternating sporadically with the other.

the first again (Blake & Logothetis, 2002). The visual system is locked in a battle between conflicting interpretations. You don't see what's actually there (two incompatible images); instead, you see a transitory perception of the image that's winning at the moment. Nothing changes on the page, but your visual system is trapped in a dispute that tips back and forth. This parallels the multistable percepts in FIGURE 5.31, but here the rivaling interpretations are competing within the channels of the two eyes.

Binocular rivalry is not as simple as the information from the two eyes competing. Instead, the competition is between higher-level percepts. This can be demonstrated by swapping the two images presented to the eyes several times each second (such that each eye sees A, then B, then A…). This rapid alternation of the images does not alter the amount of time it takes for the percept to change—usually a few seconds. In other words, a single phase of perceptual dominance can span multiple alternations of the stimuli (Logothetis, Leopold, & Sheinberg, 1996). This indicates that the neural representations of the two stimuli contend for visual awareness regardless of the eye through which they reach the higher visual areas. It is not the eyes that are competing, but the higher-level representations.

The examples of monocular rivalry (e.g., the Necker cube) and binocular rivalry (different images in each eye) lead to a question: why doesn't a person perceive both options at once? The fact that he does *not* suggests that the visual system forces a single outcome between competing percepts (Tong, Meng, & Blake, 2006). That is, perception appears to be a winner-take-all process. The strongest neural population at any moment determines the perception.

But if the system is really winner take all, then why does the percept switch instead of sticking to one conclusion?

One possibility is that although different populations of neurons compete for control of the percept, extended amounts of activity in one population cause it to fatigue, giving competing populations a chance to win (Orbach, Ehrlich, & Heath, 1963). Although fatigue may result from low-level functions (say, depletion of neurotransmitter vesicles), it can serve a higher-level adaptive strategy: if the percept is ambiguous, do not stay on one interpretation too long in case the other one may be more useful (Orbach et al., 1963).

Multistable figures and binocular rivalry both illustrate the active nature of perception. Nothing in the visual scene has changed, but your perception actively projects an interpretation onto the input.

We Don't See Most of What Hits Our Eyes: Fetching Information on a Need-to-Know Basis

For many years, neuroscientists struggled to determine how the brain constructs a three-dimensional model of the outside world. Eventually, it became clear that there was an assumption built into this pursuit, and a new idea arose: that the brain's model is closer to a two and a half-dimensional *sketch* (Marr, 1982). This concept simply means that you don't need to store a high-resolution model of the world out there—instead, you simply need to know the gist of it so you can determine where to look next. For example, you don't need to actually store a complete representation of your bathroom counter. You have a general sense that there's a surface with several scattered items, and a mirror, and a wall. It's only when you need the toothpaste that it becomes time for your visual system to search for it. If you were to wonder how much toothpaste is left in the tube, or what color the tube is, you'd be able to place your attention on the details, incorporating the answer into your internal model. Even though the toothpaste tube was impinging upon your retinas the whole time you stood at the counter, you weren't attending to its details. You needed to fill in the finer points of the picture.

In the same vein, it's often the case that we know some features of an object while we're unaware of others. Imagine we asked you to look at these symbols and tell us what you saw: //////////////. You would easily describe that it is composed of diagonal lines. But if we now asked *how many* lines, you would find that difficult to answer. You can see there are a finite number, but you can't quantify them without some work. Thus, you can be aware of some aspects of a scene and not others; you become aware of further details (and realize what you're missing) only when you ask yourself further questions.

The secret to understanding this aspect of the visual system is that an organism does not require all of the data in the world around it. It simply figures out how to retrieve the data it needs. It gathers information on a *need-to-know basis*. And what it needs depends on its goal at the moment.

If this view of vision comes as something of a surprise, just consider that you're not aware of much at all until you ask yourself a question. What is the position of your tongue in your mouth? What does your right shoe feel like on your foot? What sound is the traffic outside making? Our typical state is to be unaware of most of the data hitting our sensory receptors. It's only by turning our attention to small questions that we add those bits to our model. (We will explore attention in depth in Chapter 8). Prior to asking questions of the scene, we are usually unaware that we're not seeing the whole picture: we're blind to our blindness. We typically walk around with a false confidence that we're engaged in a complete picture of the world. Despite the persuasive force of the illusion, however, we see mostly what our brains need to know.

There's a strange consequence to this. How could it be that we're missing so much information from a scene, but not at all aware that we're missing that information? We turn to this now.

Vision Relies on Expectations

We are not aware that we're missing information from the visual world because what we see is not the raw data from the outside, but instead our **internal model** of the world. Let's explore this concept with a few examples.

Change Blindness

Two images are shown in FIGURE 5.33. Can you see the difference between them? They look identical, but they're not—and it will require some work for you to figure out where. Even if you overlapped and alternated the images on a screen, it would still be difficult to spot the difference. We're surprisingly poor observers when it comes to discerning what's changed between two images, even if the changes are quite large. For example, there might be a crate in one image that's not in the other, or a car, or an airplane—and those differences go undetected. To discern the difference between the images, we have to trawl the scene carefully. We have to analyze landmarks one at a time, comparing each sequentially. Once we find a mismatch, the difference then seems obvious—but it wasn't at first. The lesson from **change blindness** is that we are not directly analyzing the visual input in front of us, but rather the rough sketch—or internal model—of what we believe is out there (Blackmore, Brelstaff, Nelson, & Troscianko, 1995; Rensink, O'Regan, & Clark, 1997; Simon, de Araujo, Gutierrez, & Nicolelis, 2006). It's only when our model becomes updated that we see the next level of detail. (If you haven't spotted it yet, the change in FIGURE 5.33 is the presence or absence of the

FIGURE 5.33 **Two slightly different pictures to demonstrate change blindness.**

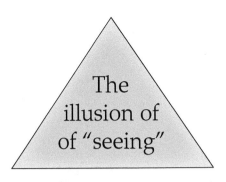

FIGURE 5.34 Visual illusion. The word "of" is repeated at the end of line 2 and the beginning of line 3.

black rectangle on the white cylinder at the left-hand side of the photo.)

As another example, imagine watching a short video of a person frying eggs. Now imagine the camera angle cuts to a different view. You would surely notice if the cook were suddenly being played by a different actor, right? Strangely, the majority of observers fail to notice the change (Levin, 1997).

Consider another surprising demonstration of change blindness. In an experiment in Boston, random pedestrians were asked for directions by an experimenter. As they were explaining a route, several rude workmen carrying a door wedged themselves between the two people. The conversation resumed seconds after the workmen passed . . . and most of the subjects did not notice that the person they were talking with (the experimenter) was a different person entirely, having been swapped out with a person who had been hiding behind the door (Simons & Levin, 1998). How did they miss it? Because they were only incorporating a small bit of the outside world into their internal models.

Looking directly at something is no guarantee of "seeing" it. However, neuroscientists weren't the ones to figure this out—magicians were. Their profession capitalizes on this knowledge (Macknik et al., 2008). Once a magician directs your attention, he or she can then execute sleights of hand in full view. Even though your retina is being struck by the photons that convey the trickery, the magician can act with confidence that your brain won't see it. You're only going to see your expectations.

Our poor ability to see what's really happening out there explains many events on our roadways, such as the number of traffic accidents that happen in plain view of pedestrians, other cars, or trains. In so many of these cases, a driver's eyes are aimed in the right direction, but the brain isn't seeing. Vision requires more than looking at the right place at the right time. In fact, we're guessing you didn't notice that the word "of" appears twice in the triangle (FIGURE 5.34).

Saving Resources by Embedding Prior Experience

Internal models of the outside world allow the brain to save time and resources and to come to rapid perceptual conclusions. Consider how the pattern of gradient-filled circles in FIGURE 5.35 produces a perception of three-dimensional bumps and dimples. Look at FIGURE 5.35a and note that the shading on the circles could be consistent with lighting from above or below—the information in the picture is ambiguous. However, if you are like most people, your brain assumes the light source comes from above—in keeping with the sun, moon, overhead lights, etc. (Ramachandran, 1988) This makes the middle circle in FIGURE 5.35a appear as a dimple while the surrounding ones appear as bumps. In FIGURE 5.35b we've simply turned the image upside-down. This change causes the bumps to become dimples and the dimple to become a bump, in keeping with a light source coming from its usual location: overhead. When the picture is rotated by 90 degrees (FIGURE 5.35c), the light source can be easily perceived as coming from either the right or the left; with a little practice one can switch the perception (bumps become dimples and vice versa), although that is much more difficult in FIGURE 5.35a and FIGURE 5.35b.

This assumption of overhead light sources allows the brain to save on computational resources, at least until further information demands it to reconsider. Since the lighting of a visual scene in our world is almost always from above, that provides a reasonable starting point for visual analysis.

Importantly, the visual system embeds its prior experience with the world into our present perceptions. In this way, the system can opt for the most likely interpretation, based on what it's seen before.

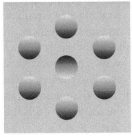
(a)

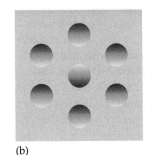
(b)

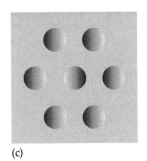
(c)

FIGURE 5.35 Light sources are preferentially seen as coming from the top. (a) Generally interpreted as bumps with a dimple in the middle. (b) Merely the same picture upside down—but it is now interpreted as dimples with a bump in the middle. (c) The same picture rotated 90 degrees; the depth information now appears ambiguous.

In another example of this point, the movement of a shadow is perceived as movement in depth (Mamassian & Kersten, 1996). Note that such "movement" is ambiguous: a shadow can move because of a change in the depth of an object or instead because the position of the light source has changed. In general, however, the visual system not only assumes the overhead source, but also a source *fixed in position*. In other words, the brain makes a reasonable assumption based on accumulated experience.

Unconscious Inference

As we have learned in the previous sections, data from the world are not simply analyzed with unbiased interpretations. Instead, the visual system capitalizes on prior expectations.

Although this idea might be a bit surprising, it is not new. The German physician and physicist Hermann von Helmholtz (1821–1894) was one of the first people to entertain this model of perception. He suspected that the small amounts of information dribbling in through the eyes were too slight to account for the rich experience of vision. He therefore deduced that the brain makes *assumptions* about the incoming data, based on previous experiences (von Helmholtz, 1867). By this method, the brain can use its best guesses to rapidly turn a little information into a much larger picture.

In this sense the brain is a hypothesis generator, building models of the world and striving to verify them based on input through the tiny windows of the senses. As a result, we often see what we are expecting to see and hear what we are expecting to hear.

Helmholtz thus proposed that vision arises from a process of "unconscious inference." The word *inference* means the brain infers, or deduces, what is likely to be out there, and *unconscious* simply reminds us that we're unaware of the deductions. We have no direct access to the neural machinery that analyzes the statistics of the world. We simply perceive the end result of the calculations.

As an example of this point, let's return to depth perception. Earlier we learned that the visual system can judge depth from the disparity between the two eyes. However, this is only useful out to 30 meters—past that distance, the line of sight to distant objects falls on nearly corresponding points of the retinas (Coltekin, 2009). As a result, the brain uses other cues to determine depth (Swan, Jones, Kolstad, Livingston, & Smallman, 2007). One of them comes down to mere experience with the world. The visual system builds up prior expectations about the relative sizes of objects (Swan et al., 2007). Even in the minimalist cartoon of FIGURE 5.36, you would probably guess that the cat is closer to you than the artist, who is closer than the Eiffel Tower he is painting in the distance. This doesn't have to be the case: it could be a giant feline eyeing the artist he is about to eat, who in turn is painting a small model of the Eiffel Tower. However, the latter interpretation doesn't seem the most

FIGURE 5.36 **Our prior knowledge about size is a cue for depth.** Because we know the size of cats, artists, and the Eiffel Tower, we assume that they exist in that order of nearness to us in the cartoon. An alien from a planet with giant cats and tiny towers would interpret the depth in the scene differently.

likely one. This exemplifies how the brain employs prior experience to settle on an interpretation of the highest likelihood from many possibilities.

Unconscious inference can be formalized through the mathematics of the English reverend Thomas Bayes (1702–1761). Although the details of "Bayesian inference" are beyond the scope of this chapter, the concept is simple enough: the probability that a stimulus in the world is, say, possibility A or possibility B depends on the probability of each of those options (given the input on the retina), as well as the overall likelihood of each of those possibilities happening in the world (Uka & DeAngelis, 2004). Let's take the example of the illusion of movement based on the position of a shadow, described above. Although the moving shadow gives equal probability to either (A) a change in depth or (B) a moving light source, the likelihood of B is low in the face of previous experience (light sources don't typically change position rapidly); thus interpretation A wins. If you lived on an alien planet on which the overhead light sources danced around frequently but objects rarely changed heights, you would interpret the stimulus in the opposite manner. Same input, different output based on prior experience.

To summarize where we are, we've seen that the visual system relies on internal models built from best guesses, given retinal input and prior experience. The important lesson is that the brain's perceptions are not constructed from scratch, with no prior information. That was a mistake made by some early pioneers of computer vision, who assumed that visual systems have to parse all of the input and build visual objects from scratch (Knutsson & Granlund, 1994). In fact, vision involves the comparison of incoming information with detailed internal models of the world.

But how does the concept of an internal model mesh with what we learned of the visual system in the first half of the chapter? Didn't it seem as though neural signals from the retina simply worked their way up the hierarchy until they were perceived? We'll now see why that process is only half the story.

Activity from Within

In the traditional model of perception, information from sensory receptors streams along pathways into the brain, eventually becoming sight, hearing, touch, taste, and so on when they reach an end point. However, that model covers only part of the story. In reality, much of the brain's activity comes from within (Llinás, 2002; Eagleman, 2011).

If that seems strange, consider other examples of internally generated activity: all the details of your breathing and digestion are controlled by internal activity in your brainstem. As it turns out, this happens not only in the brainstem, but throughout the rest of the brain as well. Most neural activity is produced on the inside, and it is merely altered by external sensory input. Consider what this means: the visual experiences you have when you're dreaming are really the same thing as the visual experiences you have while you're awake (Llinás, 2002). The only difference is that in your waking life, your eyes are open, allowing a bit of activity from the outside world to anchor your experience; during dreaming, on the other hand, the visual system is free to roam. Minds roam in other situations as well. For example, people in sensory deprivation chambers and prisoners in solitary confinement both experience hallucinations (Vernon, Marton, & Peterson, 1961; Vernon, McGill, & Schiffman, 1958). As the external input wanes, the internal activity picks up the slack (Allan, 1977; Eagleman, 2011).

As an example of the interplay of internal activity and external data, consider a disorder known as **Charles Bonnet syndrome**. Characterized by visual hallucinations, this syndrome affects ten percent of patients who have visual loss due to eye disease (Gillig & Sanders, 2009). As they lose their sight, they begin to see things—such as flowers, birds, people, buildings—that are not real. Bonnet, an eighteenth-century Swiss philosopher, first described this phenomenon after observing his grandfather (Berrios & Brook, 1982). He noticed that as his grandfather lost his vision to cataracts, he would attempt to interact with things and people who weren't there. As the input of external data slows down, the internal activity is enough to produce an outside world. The syndrome is essentially equivalent to an intrusion of dreaming into the waking state.

The surprising bottom line is that normal vision is hardly different from hallucinations; they differ only by the degree to which they're anchored by external data. Hallucinations are normal vision untethered.

Together, these observations present a more realistic model of the visual system. Let's now circle back to the anatomy to understand how the internal activity and external data interact.

Feedback Allows an Internal Model

It's a common mistake to think of the brain like a computer—or an assembly line—with signals coming in, getting processed in successive stages, and finally reaching some finish line. In fact, it is such an easy mistake that almost all early theories (and many unsophisticated modern theories) begin with this assumption. However, there is a critical clue that the assembly-line model does not account for. Along with brain wiring that proceeds in the forward direction (say, from hypothetical areas 1 to 2 to 3), there are **feedback loops** (from 3 to 2 to 1). In fact, there is just as much feedback in the brain as there is feedforward, a concept referred to as **recurrence** or loopiness (Bell 1999). Once theoreticians began to consider the feedback seriously, instead of sweeping it under the rug, this opened up brand-new models of brain function. For example, one model suggests that the visual system should not be understood as a succession of signals climbing a hierarchy; instead, it should be understood as a **reverse hierarchy**: a system that makes a best guess about the essence of a scene ("there is an animal moving my way") and then sends that guess down to successively lower areas to see if the incoming details are consistent (Ahissar & Hochstein, 2004).

Such a model is consistent with the fact that a sufficient amount of feedback allows a system to run "backward." Try closing your eyes and imagining a scene—rays of sun breaking through clouds over a snowy mountaintop, or a banana sundae festooned with chocolate sprinkles. When you imagine those scenes, your visual cortex becomes active. You're not actually gazing upon those items—but when you visualize them, the higher regions in your visual cortex send information down to lower areas. Obviously, under daily circumstances your eyes are involved in pushing signals up to your higher areas—but connections going the other way make it possible for the cortical areas to get by without any contributions from the eyes at all. When you visualize, you run the whole system in reverse.

As it turns out, recurrent networks have a few great advantages over a simple assembly line model. For one thing, a system that can generate internal events can build up representations of the world—enabling it to outperform anything a feedforward system could do. Consider the act of trying to hit a rapidly flying racquetball. If your visual system were only feedforward, you'd always be swinging for the ball at some distance behind its actual position. Why? Because signal processing takes time. But now consider a recurrent system that has a representation of Newtonian physics: it can make a guess about exactly where the ball is right now and where it is going (Lacquaniti & Carrozzo, 1993; Tresilian, 1999; Zago et al., 2004). A feedforward system is always playing catch-up, but a system that deals with an internal model can incorporate effects of gravity to estimate when and where the ball will make contact with the racquet (Wolpert & Flanagan, 2001; Wolpert & Miall, 1996). Using this trick, the brain can make predictions rather than being bound to only the latest sensory data that comes in.

This is a specific example of the broader concept of internal models of the world. Beyond predicting the physics of moving objects—so that you can intercept or dodge—internal models may also be the key to understanding our conscious awareness. Specifically, some frameworks suggest that your view of the world is not assembled from incoming data (the way a camera would "see" the world), but instead perception only arises when your expectations ("it's an animal") successfully match the incoming data (e.g., Grossberg, 1980).

As strange as this seems, consider it in light of something you already know: that your expectations influence what you see. Try to make sense of FIGURE 5.37. Difficult, right? Your brain doesn't have an expectation about this pattern, and so you see nothing but…blobs. Without a way to connect your predictions and the incoming photons, you "see" very little.

Given all of these considerations, let's take a fresh look at the visual system. In the model we've been building up to, the job of the visual cortex is to construct expectations of what the world "out there" will look like. In the 1950s, neuroscientist Donald MacKay proposed that the visual cortex builds an internal model—the purpose of which is to predict the information that comes up from the eyes to the cortex (MacKay, 1956). With this as the goal, the visual system uses feedback connections to tell the LGN what it anticipates. The LGN then uses feedforward connections to report on the *difference* between what actually came in and what was predicted. When the visual cortex receives the information about that difference—known as the prediction error—it then updates its internal model. The aim is to have less error next time—that is, to learn from its mistakes. This model is consistent with a strange fact about the anatomy: there are ten times more axons projecting from the visual cortex to the

LGN than axons going the other way. This is just what we'd expect from a system that sends detailed predictions "down" to the LGN, and only returns the difference signal back "up."

Once we begin to think about the brain as a heavily recurrent network that generates its own models about the world, other mysteries begin to resolve. Consider the disorder known as **Anton's syndrome**, in which a person becomes blind (usually from a stroke) but *denies* his blindness (Symonds & Mackenzie, 1957). An interaction with a patient with Anton's syndrome might go something like this: you hold up two fingers and ask the patient to report how many fingers. Without hesitation, the patient says, "five." You ask what color your shirt is, and the patient confidently gives an answer, even though the response has no relation to the color you're actually wearing.

It's not that the Anton's patient is lying (or embarrassed or roguish)—it's simply that he's not experiencing blindness. He's seeing, because his internal model is still cranking along—even though it's not meaningfully anchored to the outside world. It often turns out that patients with Anton's do not go to the doctor's for a while after they experience a stroke—because although they are blind, they don't *know* that they are blind. They begin to realize something strange is happening only after repeated collisions with furniture and people. To summarize, the Anton's patient makes strange claims about the number of your fingers or the color of your shirt because he is seeing his internal model—a model that's normally anchored by external data, but has now become unmoored from reality. If it seems difficult to imagine what this would be like, just consider that you have this experience every night when you dream.

And this leads us to highlight an important distinction between the words **sensation** and **perception**. Sensation is the detection of a signal. For example, when an electric motion detector turns on your garage lights, we say your car's movement has been *sensed*. But we have no reason to think that the motion detector, a simple circuit, *perceives*—it is perfectly adequate to assume that electrons move through the wires of the detector, pushing the current above a threshold voltage to activate the lights. The first sections of this chapter taught what's known about the sensation of photons at the retina and the passage of signals from there. But for the *perception* of the world, much more is required—specifically, an internal model against which the input is constantly compared for mismatches.

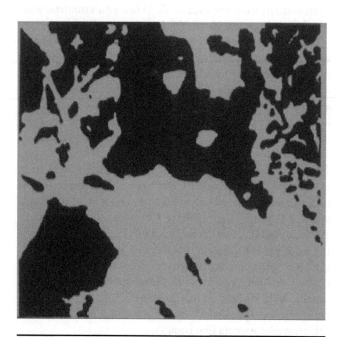

FIGURE 5.37 **The role of expectation in perception.** Perception requires a model of what is being seen. Although a figure is in these blobs, it is difficult to see. Only after receiving a hint (see Figure 5.38) does the figure appear as something interpretable. Figure from Ahissar and Hochstein (2004).

Conclusion

Attempts to build artificial computer vision used to assume that the human visual system produces a three-dimensional, high-resolution model of the world, distinguishing and representing all objects. That turned out to be a misdirected approach and an impossible feat to realize. Scientists now appreciate that they do not need to solve the complete-model-of-the-world problem:

not everything in the outside world *needs* to be represented. Instead, the information needed depends on the goal: it is task dependent. When you want to find the correct gate at the airport, you do not need to process and represent all the light signals hitting your retina. You do not need to represent the details of other passenger's faces, the titles of the books in the gift shop, the color of the carpet, the shape of the ceiling tiles, and the signs displayed at other gates. You simply need the information that will get you to your gate and allow you to recognize it. That information will differ if you are looking for a snack or a restroom. The selection of information happens via attention, which we will return to in Chapter 8.

We have also seen that perception is the result of inferences about what is probable, based on prior experiences. These unconscious inferences result in rapid perceptions of the most likely scenario given the data. Thus vision is determined by two streams: the ongoing input of external data and prior expectations. Note that expectations can be both genetic (nature) and experiential (nurture)—take as an example a horse bucking at the sight of a snake (genetic) and salivating at the shape of the metal feeding trough (experiential). The main challenge for a brain is to compute through many alternative interpretations of the input and to settle on the best one (or at least the best one for the moment). In this way, perception is an active process.

The first half of this chapter presented the anatomical framework of a hierarchy in the visual system—one in which signals move from the retina to the LGN to the sprawling regions of the visual cortex. By the end of the chapter, we appreciated that the concept of a hierarchy, although useful to understand the anatomy, is not complete. There is no "finish line" where signals reach perception. Instead, like all parts of the brain, the visual system is a massively recurrent (loopy) system. In the end, the most accurate way to understand the visual system is to recognize its confluence of forward and reverse directions—in other words, internal expectations meeting up with external data.

Let's now return to Mike May, the blind downhill skier whom we met at the beginning of the chapter. After the operation that cleared his corneas, it seemed as though his vision would be functional: after all, photons were now successfully impinging on his retinas, becoming transduced into signals that traveled to his LGN and on to his visual cortex.

But when the bandages were removed from his eyes and his children walked in the room, he couldn't *see* them. His brain didn't know how to interpret the torrent of action potentials coursing up the optic nerves. As you now know, this is because Mike's brain did not know how to make an internal model of the world to be compared to the new external data. The incoming signals were not sufficient by themselves—his visual system needed expectations against which to compare them. Without that, nothing could be perceived.

By practicing for several weeks—reaching for objects, touching them, knocking on them—Mike was able to align his expectations with the incoming signals. And then there was light.

P.S. If you are still struggling with FIGURE 5.37, see the hint in FIGURE 5.38.

FIGURE 5.38 **With a simple hint, the blobs in Figure 5.37 instantly take on meaning as a bearded man.** Now that you've established an expectation, you can't "un-see" the bearded man in Figure 5.37.

KEY PRINCIPLES

- Although seeing the world seems effortless, approximately 30% of the brain is devoted to constructing vision.

- Photoreceptors in the retina transduce photons into neural signals that move into higher parts of the visual system.

- The visual system is hierarchical, building from fine details to larger concepts.

- Damage to lower parts of the visual system leads to a lack of sensation (that is, blindness), whereas damage to successively higher areas leads to more specific deficits of perception (e.g., ability to see but inability to recognize).

- As visual information becomes more abstracted at higher levels of the visual system, the information moves in two distinct processing "streams": the ventral stream and the dorsal stream. The ventral stream deciphers *what* objects are—in other words, how to identify and categorize them. The dorsal stream is focused on *where* objects are and how to interact with them.

- Vision is active, not passive. Without being consciously aware of it, we actively interrogate the world with our eyes, pulling details into our internal models.

- The visual scene relies on internally generated activity as much as on data from the outside world.

- The visual system contains both feedforward and feedback projections, making it "loopy."

- Much of what we see comes from unconscious inference—that is, our expectations of what we believe is "out there."

KEY TERMS

Visual Perception
Mach bands (p. 132)
sensory transduction (p. 133)
hair cells (p. 134)

Anatomy of the Visual System
cornea (p. 134)
iris (p. 134)
pupil (p. 134)
lens (p. 134)
retina (p. 134)
retinal ganglion cells (p. 134)
amacrine cells (p. 134)
horizontal cells (p. 134)
phototransduction (p. 134)
rods (p. 135)
cones (p. 135)
fovea (p. 135)
receptive field (p. 136)
center-surround structure (p. 136)
contrast enhancement (p. 136)
optic nerve (p. 138)

blind spot (p. 138)
optic chiasm (p. 138)
parvocellular retinal ganglion cells (p. 139)
magnocellular retinal ganglion cells (p. 139)
optic radiations (p. 139)
striate cortex (p. 139)
simple cells (p. 139)
complex cells (p. 139)
blobs (p. 140)

Higher Visual Areas
secondary visual cortex (V2) (p. 142)
tertiary visual cortex (p. 142)
ventral stream (p. 143)
dorsal stream (p. 143)
inferotemporal cortex (p. 143)
position invariance/size invariance (p. 144)
sparse coding (p. 144)
all-or-none (p. 144)
fusiform face area (p. 144)

area V5 (p. 146)
motion blindness (p. 147)
attention (p. 148)
hemineglect (p. 148)
Balint's syndrome (p. 148)
simultagnosia (p. 148)
prosopagnosia (face blindness) (p. 148)
blindsight (p. 150)

Perception Is Active, Not Passive
multistable percept (p. 152)
binocular rivalry (p. 152)

Vision Relies on Expectations
internal model (p. 154)
change blindness (p. 154)
Charles Bonnet syndrome (p. 157)
feedback loops (p. 157)
recurrence (p.157)
reverse hierarchy (p. 157)
Anton's syndrome (p. 158)
sensation (p. 158)
perception (p. 158)

REVIEW QUESTIONS

1. Explain how the responses of a simple cell in V1 can be constructed from the input it receives from several LGN cells. How can a complex cell's responses be constructed from the input it receives from several simple cells?

2. Explain the difference between the dorsal and ventral visual processing streams.

3. What might be the expected result of damage to the eyes? To the primary visual cortex? To the dorsal stream? To the ventral stream?

4. Would we still have depth perception if our eyes were one above the other instead of side by side? Why or why not?

5. In binocular rivalry, why does the perception switch back and forth instead of sticking to only one interpretation?

6. Why do prisoners who have been put in pitch-black solitary confinement cells begin to hallucinate?

7. How are blindsight and Anton's syndrome like opposites of one another?

8. Scientists have discovered that there is as much feedback as feedforward circuitry in the brain. How does this challenge the assembly-line model of visual processing?

9. Give an example in which prior experience influences what is perceived.

10. Define sensation and perception. Why does there need to be a distinction drawn between these two terms? Can one exist without the other?

CRITICAL-THINKING QUESTIONS

1. From an evolutionary perspective, why do you think that the human brain has separate dorsal and ventral processing streams? Why would it not have just one processing stream that served the functions of both the dorsal stream and the ventral stream?

2. Do you think that some areas of the human brain that are devoted to vision in sighted individuals are devoted to other functions in blind individuals? What research methods would you use to test your hypothesis? Explain your reasoning.

3. Imagine that Mike May, the blind downhill skier whose case study you reviewed at the beginning of the chapter, had been 6 years old at the time of his successful corneal transplant (and restoration of sight) instead of 46 years old. Would you expect his visual perception to be different in that case? Explain. Would you expect to see a different time course, with therapy, for the improvement of his visual perception? Explain your reasoning.

- Explain how the principles of perception and transduction that we learned about in vision (Chapter 5) also apply to hearing, touch, smell, and taste.

- Describe how sound is transduced from pressure waves in the air to electrical signals in the nervous system.

- Characterize the importance of labeled lines for the transduction of sensory signals.

- Differentiate the five major types of information perceived by the somatosensory system.

- Compare and contrast the chemical senses and the other senses.

- Provide two examples of phenomena that support the idea that the brain integrates information from the different senses.

- Explain why time perception could be considered a sense and the difficulties involved in studying it.

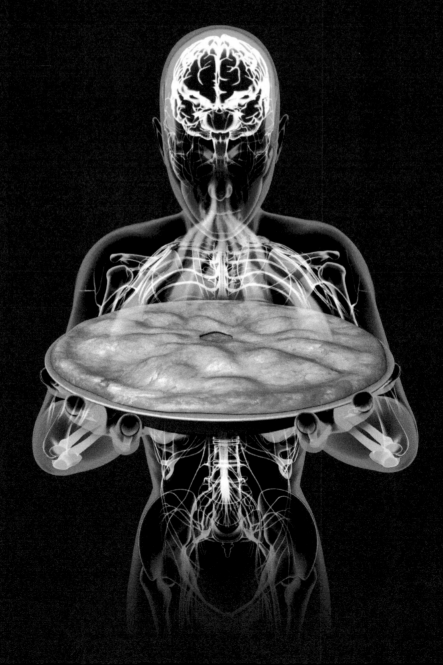

Other Senses

STARTING OUT
The Man with the Bionic Ear

FIGURE 6.1 Michael Chorost. Michael was born mostly deaf because of a case of rubella during his mother's pregnancy but regained his hearing after undergoing surgery for a cochlear implant.

Michael Chorost (FIGURE 6.1) was born mostly—but not entirely—deaf because of a case of rubella during his mother's pregnancy. Michael functioned just fine during his young adult life with the help of a hearing aid. But one day, while waiting to pick up a rental car, the battery to his hearing aid died. Or so he thought. He replaced the battery but found that all sound was still missing from his world. He drove himself to the nearest emergency room and discovered that the remainder of his hearing—his thin auditory lifeline to the rest of the world—was gone for good. For unknown reasons, his only functioning ear had suffered "sudden-onset deafness."

A hearing aid would do him no good now. Hearing aids work by blasting a partially functioning ear with increased volume. In other words, a hearing aid takes sounds from the world and rebroadcasts them more loudly into the ailing auditory system. But this strategy only works if everything beyond the eardrum is functioning. If the inner ear is defunct, no amount of volume amplification will solve the problem. Given the available technology, it seemed as though Michael's enjoyment of the world's soundscapes had come to a sudden end.

But then he found out about a single remaining possibility. In 2001, Michael underwent surgery for a *cochlear implant*. This tiny device circumvents the broken hardware of the inner ear to speak directly to the functioning nerve bundle just beyond it. It is essentially a minicomputer implanted directly into his inner ear, one that receives sounds from the outside world and passes them to the auditory nerve by means of 16 tiny electrodes (Wilson et al., 1991).

Although the damaged part of the inner ear is bypassed, the experience of hearing doesn't come for free. Michael had to learn to interpret the foreign language of the electrical signals being fed to his auditory system. Here is Michael's description of his experience:

When the device was turned on a month after surgery, the first sentence I heard sounded like "Zzzzzz szz szvizzz ur brfzzzzzz?"

My brain gradually learned how to interpret the alien signal. Before long, "Zzzzzz szz szvizzz ur brfzzzzzz?" became "What did you have for breakfast?" After months of practice, I could use the telephone again, even converse in loud bars and cafeterias. (Chorost, 2011)

Although a minicomputer implant sounds like science fiction, cochlear implants have been on the market since 1982. Tens of thousands of people are walking around with these bionics in their heads, according to the National Institute on Deafness and Other Communication Disorders (2011). The software on the cochlear implant is hackable and updateable, so Michael has spent years improving the quality of the implant without further surgeries. Almost a year after the implant was activated, he upgraded to a program that gave him twice the resolution. And it will only improve. As Michael puts it, "While my friends' ears will inevitably decline with age, mine will only get better" (Chorost, 2011).

How does the cochlear implant work? And what does it teach us about the brain and its thirst for information from the outside world—not just via hearing but by all the senses? And how do the other senses utilize the same principles we've already learned about in regard to vision in Chapter 5? In this chapter, we'll find out.

Detecting Data from the World

In the previous chapter we learned about vision as an inroad to several general principles of perception. Remember that transduction is the process of converting energy or information outside the body into the neural code used inside the body. In this chapter, we will extend the principles of perception and transduction to hearing, touch, smell, and taste. After all, you may have begun reading the previous chapter with the impression that vision was effortless and, with minor exceptions, accurate—in other words, that your eyes were essentially like a high-resolution video camera. If that's where you started, you learned an interesting set of lessons to the contrary. Now extend that reasoning. It may seem intuitive to think of your auditory system as two high-fidelity microphones. Likewise, it may seem reasonable to believe that your fingertips simply reach out and detect what is out there. As we've learned already, our intuition often suggests ideas that are incorrect.

The person on the street will usually tell you that there are five senses: vision, hearing, touch, taste, and smell. But as we will see, there are many other ways of detecting data from the outside world, including vibration, pain, temperature, acceleration, head position with respect to gravity, joint position and motion, pheromones, and the sense of time. There are also critical sensory signals that we detect from *inside* the body, such as stretching in our bladder or our gut. As we will see, not all senses are of equal importance to survival: although the visual system is highly represented in human brains, one can live without vision much more easily than one can live without, say, the sense of pain or the sense of body position.

What exactly is a sense? A sense is built from specialized cells that respond to particular physical phenomena, and the sense corresponds to brain networks that receive, interpret, and act on those signals.

All sensory systems fundamentally attempt to accomplish the same goal: detect useful information sources from the world. Whereas your eyes are sensitive to electromagnetic radiation in a particular wavelength (as we saw in the previous chapter), your ears pick up information contained in air compression waves. Your fingertips sense temperature and pressure data, and your nose and mouth detect chemicals in the air and in objects.

Our relatives in the animal kingdom have developed an endless variety of exotic ways of picking up information from the world. The ghost knifefish of South America has specialized sensors to detect disturbances in the electrical field that surrounds it. In some species of snake, specialized detectors called heat pits allow the snake to detect energy in the infrared range. Many insects, birds, and even cows have small particles in their heads that allow them to orient to—and navigate by—the earth's magnetic field. For our aquatic mammalian neighbors, whales and dolphins, the murkiness of water makes it an environment that is ill suited for vision—and so they have developed sonar as an imaging strategy.

Regardless of the sensory system considered, the information is sent to what is known as the primary sensory cortex. A common feature across the senses is the concept of a map: information is laid out in specific ways on the surface of the brain. As we saw in Chapter 5, in the primary cortex of the visual system (V1), the map is *retinotopic*: neighboring neurons represent neighboring parts of the visual field, as mediated by neighboring cells in the retina. In this chapter, we will see that in primary auditory cortex (A1), the layout of cells is *tonotopic*: neighboring frequencies are neighbors on the cortical map. In primary somatosensory cortex (S1), we will find a map of the body's surface—a layout called *somatotopic*. Taste and smell employ a different approach: their primary cortical areas function by recognizing subtly different patterns rather than specific layouts.

In all the main senses, primary sensory cortex is surrounded by neighboring regions of cortex (*secondary* and *tertiary*) in a hierarchical relationship that leads to more abstract processing. Thus, the primary visual cortex (V1) is sensitive to simple lines, whereas higher visual areas respond to cars, houses, or movie stars. In the auditory system, A1 is responsive to simple tones, whereas surrounding areas encode more complex sound textures. (In Chapter 11, we will see how these areas produce language.) In somatosensation, S1 responds to a stimulus on a particular spot on the skin, whereas higher cortical areas allow the deciphering of a larger sensation, such as a cat rubbing against one's leg. In taste, the primary taste cortex communicates with the secondary cortical taste area, which allows for the decoding of food type and flavor intensity. Finally, in olfaction, the primary olfactory cortex receives basic information from the olfactory bulb and feeds its outputs to a network of higher areas for more subtle processing. The same general principles are at work in all the systems.

Perceiving, combining, and using various information streams is the key to interacting in the world—that is, to constructing a rough picture of what's happening outside of the body. In the coming pages we'll learn how we detect the world "out there" (e.g., hearing, touch, pain, temperature, and chemicals) as well as the internal world (e.g., hunger, thirst, and fatigue).

Hearing

Detecting sounds from the outside world is critical to survival and reproductive success—whether it's the faint crack of a tree branch that announces the presence of a predator or the cry of an offspring separated from the pack. When we hear sounds we are detecting *vibrations* carried through a conductive medium (usually air or water). The precise characteristics of these vibrations—their size, shape, and frequency—determine how we perceive those sounds.

Specifically, sound travels through the air as pressure waves: increases and decreases in pressure occurring at regular intervals when small segments of air are either compressed (increase in pressure) or decompressed (decrease in pressure) (FIGURE 6.2). Every sound is composed of several different simultaneous pressure waves, each of which oscillates between high and low pressure at a particular rate. The number of high/low-pressure cycles that occur per second is referred to as the frequency of the sound wave, measured in hertz (Hz). The size of the pressure change (from the peak to the trough) is called the **amplitude**. Frequency and amplitude are terms that refer to the characteristics of the pressure waves themselves. **Pitch** is our perception of a sound's frequency (e.g., a high note or a low note), whereas **loudness** is our perception of its amplitude.

The sensitivity and fidelity of the auditory system are stunning. In 1935, the scientist Alvar Wilska discovered that the human eardrum could detect sounds that make it move

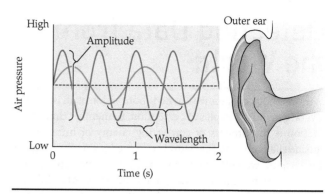

FIGURE 6.2 **Pressure changes in the air are interpreted as sound by the brain.** Amplitude is the size of the pressure change, and frequency (Hz) refers to the number of waves that occur per second.

as little as 10^{-9} centimeters, or the diameter of a single hydrogen atom (Hudspeth, 1983; Wilska, 1935). Amazingly, the sensitivity of the ear is limited by the properties of air: if the auditory system were any more sensitive, it would

RESEARCH METHODS
Psychophysics

In elementary school, you likely took a hearing test in which you responded to increasingly higher or lower pitch tones. What was that about? It was an example of *psychophysics*, a branch of research that systematically changes physical stimuli and assesses the accompanying changes to your personal experience, or *perception*, of what you just sensed (Gescheider, 1997). In other words, psychophysics (literally, measuring the physics of the psyche, or mind) characterizes the relationship between external stimuli and internal perception. By presenting high and low pitches and asking you to report when you detected something, the elementary school hearing test was using psychophysics to determine the physical range of your senses. Similarly, when you're judging whether a note is sharp or flat, psychophysics allows us to determine *how much*

the note needs to be off-key for you to detect it as such.

Over the centuries, psychophysics has described the relationship between stimuli and perception. As one example, imagine that you are looking at two identical spots of light. You now turn up the intensity of one of the spots until you can just notice a brightness difference between the two. The minimum threshold at which this occurs is known as the *difference threshold*, or more commonly the **just-noticeable difference**. The 19th-century psychologist Ernst Weber was the first to notice that the size of the just-noticeable difference was systematically related to how intense the lights were to begin with. For example, imagine the two lights began at 10 units of intensity. You may discover that one of them needs to be turned up to 11 to notice a brightness difference. But if they both

start off at 100 units of intensity, then you would need to crank it up to 110 units. A fixed fraction of increase is required. This is known as **Weber's law**, and the exact amount of increase required is known as the *Weber fraction*. Although the Weber fraction differs across the senses, what is remarkable about Weber's law is that it holds across the sensory systems—whether for noticing differences in how much two items weigh, the volume of two sounds, or the size of two items.

Many useful real-world techniques emerge from psychophysical studies. For example, quantifying the limits of people's senses allows for online audio and visual data to be compressed with new algorithms that throw away undetected information. This has allowed low-bandwidth compression schemes that are used widely in music and video streaming online.

register the random movement of molecules in the air, drowning out the more information-rich signals (Sivian, 1933). In other words, hearing in humans is as sensitive as it can usefully be. Despite its exquisite sensitivity, the ear can also gauge the loudness of sounds up to 1 million times louder than the quietest sounds it can detect.

The frequency range of the ear is equally impressive—roughly 20 to 20,000 Hz in humans (Zwicker, 1961). That is, we can perceive vibrations in the air occurring between 20 and 20,000 times per second as sounds. Despite this broad range, we can distinguish between two sounds differing in frequency by only 0.8 of 1%—which translates to a note that is just barely sharp or flat (Tervaniemi, Just, Koelsch, Widmann, & Schröger, 2005).

In our noisy world, the air is filled with pressure waves that bombard our auditory system. The first step to actually *hearing* those sounds is to capture the waves themselves. We turn to that now.

The Outer and Middle Ear

Capturing the sound waves is the job of the outer ear, made up of the convoluted, cartilaginous structures that feature prominently on the side of your head (FIGURE 6.3). The folds of your outer ear, the **pinna**, certainly look random—but they're not. The pinna selectively amplifies certain frequencies of sounds coming from in front or to the side of us and selectively diminishes certain frequencies of sounds coming from behind us. The exact shape of the pinna conditions the sound coming into your ears. If you change that shape—for example, by inserting a cardboard cone in your ear—you

will have a difficult time understanding the world around you until you adapt to the new sound textures.

Because of the contours of the pinna, the orientation of the ear in relation to the sound source is crucial to how easily we can perceive a sound, its location, or even whether we hear it at all. Many animals are able to take advantage of this feature of the auditory system—consider dogs and cats, which rotate their ears toward the sound to enhance their ability to hear it. Although humans can't rotate their ears independently from the rest of their head, note the way that people will unconsciously cock their heads in one direction or another to capture an elusive, unidentified sound.

The deepest part of the outer ear is known as the **tympanic membrane** (FIGURE 6.3). This membrane vibrates like the skin of a drum—hence this is also commonly known as the *eardrum*. All of the features of the outer ear are shaped to capture the pressure waves in the outside world—and the design culminates here, as the sound waves hit this membrane.

In the next step of the hearing process, the movement of the eardrum is mechanically transmitted to the next stage—and this job falls to the structures of the **middle ear**, just on the other side of the eardrum from the outer ear (FIGURE 6.3). The middle ear consists of three tiny bones, called **ossicles**, which are named for their suggestive shapes: **malleus** (hammer), **incus** (anvil), and **stapes** (stirrup). These tiny bones are connected to one another in a mechanical chain that transfers the energy from the larger window of the tympanic membrane to the much smaller **oval window**, the gateway to the inner ear. In this way, the job of the outer and middle ear is to shape sound in the environment and deliver it to the place where the real magic happens: the inner ear.

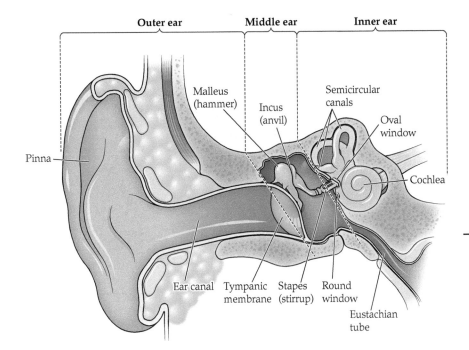

FIGURE 6.3 **Anatomy of the ear.** The pinna of the external ear captures sound and reflects it down the auditory canal. The pressure waves vibrate the tympanic membrane. These vibrations are passed by the bones of the middle ear (malleus, incus, stapes) to the cochlea, a part of the inner ear.

Converting Mechanical Information into Electrical Signals: The Inner Ear

The inner ear contains the **cochlea**. The cochlea, from the Greek word *cochlos*, meaning snail, is a spiral structure (resembling a snail's shell) made up of three fluid-filled tubes wound around a cone-shape bony core (FIGURE 6.4).

Running along the length of the cochlea is the **basilar membrane**, which is exposed to the fluid waves triggered by the vibrations of the oval window. This membrane goes from small and tight at one end (the base) to larger and floppier at the other end (the apex). This continuum means that fluid vibrations of different frequencies will cause different parts of the basilar membrane to vibrate, effectively creating a *tonotopic map* of the incoming frequencies—that is, neighboring frequencies laid out next to one another (FIGURE 6.4). Specifically, the small, tight (basal) end vibrates in response to higher-frequency vibrations, whereas the larger, floppier (apical) end vibrates in response to lower frequencies—and intermediate positions along the membrane vibrate to intermediate frequencies. Because the basal end moves more readily than the apical end, sound appears as a traveling wave down the basilar membrane.

Running along the edge of the basilar membrane is a single row of 16,000 specialized cells called **inner hair cells** (FIGURE 6.5). The inner hair cells are the key component of the inner ear because they transduce sound into electrical signals that will be interpreted by the central nervous system. In this way, inner hair cells are similar to the photoreceptors

we learned about in the previous chapter: both are sensory transducers.

The unique structure of the inner hair cells is fundamental to their function. Extending from one side of the cell body is the hair bundle (FIGURE 6.6a). When the basilar membrane vibrates as described above, the fluid motion creates mechanical force on particular hair bundles. Each hair in a bundle is connected to adjacent hairs by a thin tip link. Motion of the hair bundle causes the hairs to slide relative to each other, which results in tension on the tip links. This tension literally pulls open ion channels tethered at the ends of the tip links (FIGURE 6.6b), resulting in an ultrarapid depolarization of the cell—and this triggers the release of neurotransmitters at the other end of the cell (which signal the auditory nerve, which we'll return to momentarily). This *mechanoelectrical transduction* by the hair cells is how sound is turned into electrical signals—which then can participate in the brain's ongoing orchestration of actions.

As amazing as tip-link transduction is, this is only a part of the cochlea's mission: the mechanical amplification of sound. The passive mechanical resonance in the basilar membrane described above separates the sound frequencies,

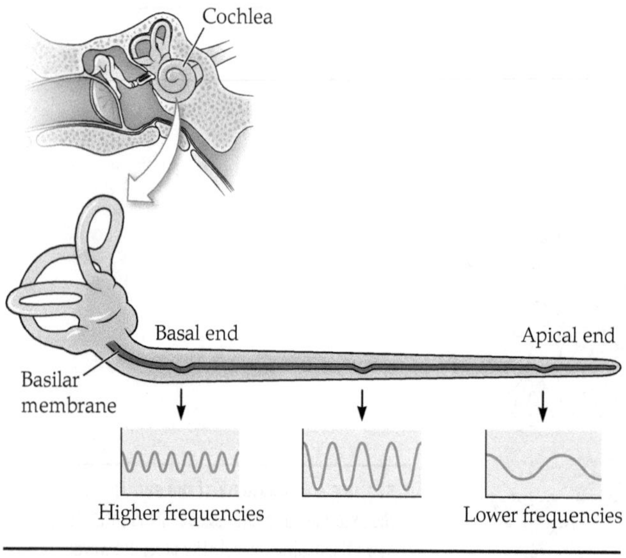

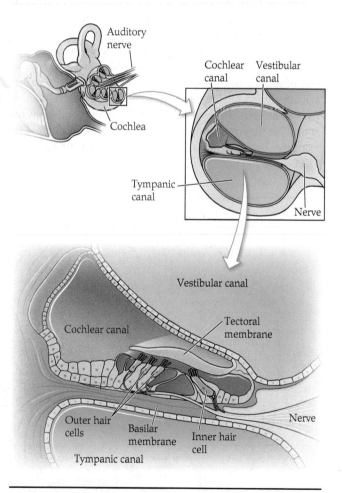

FIGURE 6.5 **The hair cells of the inner ear.** Here you see a transverse cut across all three canals of the cochlea, showing inner and outer hair cells and the overlying tectorial membrane.

FIGURE 6.4 **The cochlea.** In the inner ear, the cochlea is coiled up much like a snail's shell. If you could unroll it, the tube would be about 35 mm long for humans. As shown here, the basilar membrane of the cochlea maps frequencies, with higher tones near the oval window.

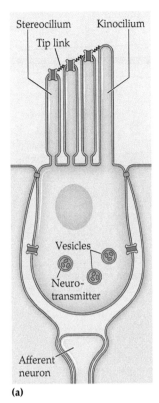

(a)

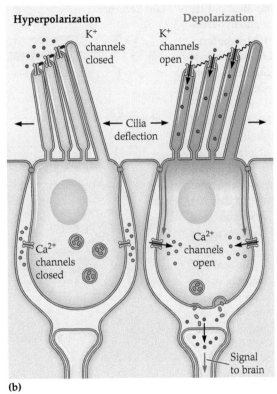

(b)

FIGURE 6.6 **Structure of an individual hair cell.** (a) The stereocilia and the kinocilium of the hair cell, connected by the tip links at the top of the stereocilia. (b) Movement of the hair cells can increase or decrease the force on the tip links, causing ion channels to open or close. Opening the channels depolarizes the cell, whereas closing the channels hyperpolarizes the cell.

but not sharply. **Further sharpening** is performed by the **organ of Corti**, which lies on top of the basilar membrane. It is packed with **three rows of outer hair cells,** which run parallel to the inner hair cells. These cells are positioned such that their bottoms are lodged in the basilar membrane and their hair bundles are connected to the overlying **tectorial membrane**. This position is key, as we will see in a moment.

NEUROSCIENCE OF EVERYDAY LIFE
The Undetectable Cell Phone

As people age, they lose the ability to hear in the high-frequency ranges (ranges near 20,000 Hz). The hair cells coding for that range have died with age and do not return. In light of this, some clever students realized that because they had high-frequency hair cells intact and their more elderly professors did not, the students would be able to hear a high-frequency cell phone ringtone that their professors could not. They could thereby receive text messages during class for which they would hear a ringtone on receipt,

but which flew under the "sonar" of the more aged cochlea of the professor at the front of the room. This application of neuroscience won the Ig Nobel Prize in 2006.

But don't think that the loss of hair cells happens only to aging people: when you go to a loud concert, hair cells die. Have you ever heard a high-pitched squealing sound in your ear that no one else hears? Sadly, that is the swan song sound of your hair cells dying from *excitotoxicity*: death caused by overstimulation (Pujol & Puel, 1999). However, new research

does provide some hope for the future treatment of hearing loss and deafness. A 2013 study demonstrated that hair cells can be regenerated in an adult mammalian ear and this resulted in partial recovery of hearing in mouse ears damaged by noise trauma (Mizutari et al., 2013). So, although hearing naturally diminishes with age and overuse, research may bring us ways to restore it. Enjoy those high-pitched cell phone ringtones while you can!

The outer hair cells have similar hair bundles and tip links as the inner hair cells, so they depolarize and hyperpolarize as the hair bundle is moved back and forth by the fluid. However, outer hair cells also have a special feature unique to the animal kingdom: in response to the oscillating voltage, they physically shorten and lengthen, cycle for cycle, as fast as the sound itself (tens of thousands of times per second!). This electromechanical transduction is mediated by special proteins in the outer hair cell membrane (Cimerman et al., 2013). It results in movements much larger than the amplitude of the sound that stimulated the hair bundles in the first place. The outer hair cells' location (strung across both membranes) allows them to mechanically amplify the incoming sound, making it much more detectable and sharply tuned, so that the inner hair cells then receive a much better signal.

All this fine-tuning means that for a given frequency of sound, only inner hair cells along distinct portions of the basilar membrane will be stimulated (this is the hair cells' *characteristic frequency*). As a result of the number of hair cells lining the basilar membrane and the tonotopic arrangement of the membrane itself, adjacent hair cells can have characteristic frequencies that differ by only 0.2% (Maoiléidigh & Hudspeth, 2013). Compare this to the 6% difference in frequencies between neighboring strings on a piano.

As a result of the fine-tuning for hair cells, only a small number will become active and send along signals when presented with a specific frequency—and all of a sudden we have a code for sound frequency in electrical signals understood by the rest of the nervous system. Neighboring frequencies are laid out along neighboring parts of the basilar membrane, and these frequencies cause electrical signals in neighboring axons.

This strategy accounts for the multiple frequencies that occur within most sound stimuli, including human speech. The spatial separation of vibration frequency along the basilar membrane breaks down complex sounds into their component frequencies (FIGURE 6.7). What the brain receives, then, is not the complex sound, but rather all of the individual frequency components of the sound.

The Auditory Nerve and Primary Auditory Cortex

The **auditory nerve**, also called the **cochlear nerve**, consists of the fibers connecting the cochlear inner hair cells to the cochlear nuclei in the brainstem. In humans, approximately 30,000 fibers make up the auditory nerve (Spoendlin & Schrott, 1989). Each *afferent fiber* (a neuron transmitting signals from the cochlea to the brainstem) innervates a single hair cell, although each hair cell may be contacted by 20 or more afferent fibers (Spoendlin, 1978). Given the tonotopic mapping of the basilar membrane, this organization means that each afferent fiber is activated only by signals of a

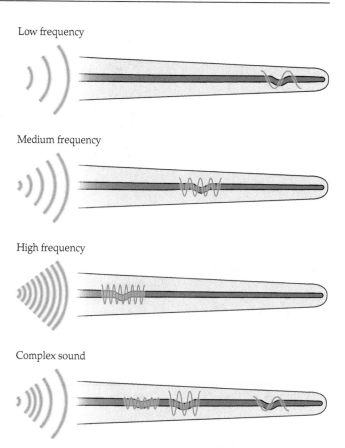

Low frequency

Medium frequency

High frequency

Complex sound

FIGURE 6.7 Sound encoding by the basilar membrane. The tonotopic map of the basilar membrane represents different frequencies at different locations. The map codes complex sounds by breaking them into simpler components.

particular frequency. In this way, the auditory system uses a **labeled line** coding approach to signal transduction. Labeled line coding refers to the strategy found in several different sensory modalities: different neurons carry different, specific information (Nieder & Merten, 2007; Reich, Mechler, & Victor, 2001). In the case of the auditory pathway, the frequency of a given stimulus is encoded by the set of afferent fibers that happen to innervate the hair cells stimulated by that frequency. These fibers carry information that is "labeled" with a given frequency, as dictated by their connectivity. Labeled lines are also important in other sensory systems, including the visual system (Chapter 5), the vestibular system, and the somatosensory system (Kevetter, Leonard, Newlands, & Perachio, 2004; Nieder & Merten, 2007; Reich et al., 2001).

We have followed the auditory pathway from the outer ear, through the middle ear and cochlea, to the auditory nerve, and into the cochlear nuclei in the brainstem. From there, the information is relayed to the olivary nuclei (olive) on both sides of the brainstem. These nuclei are important for localizing the source of the sound. From the olive, auditory information passes over the lateral lemnisci to the

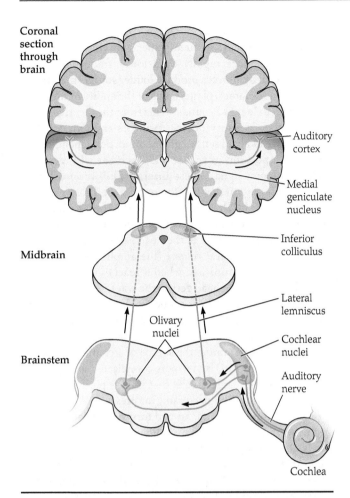

Coronal section through brain

Auditory cortex

Medial geniculate nucleus

Inferior colliculus

Midbrain

Lateral lemniscus

Olivary nuclei

Cochlear nuclei

Brainstem

Auditory nerve

Cochlea

FIGURE 6.8 Pathways from the ear to the primary auditory cortex.
From the auditory nerve, sound information travels to the cochlear nuclei in the brainstem, which relay information to the olivary nuclei (olive) on both sides of the brainstem. From the olive, auditory information passes over the lateral lemnisci to the inferior colliculi and on to the medial geniculate nucleus of the thalamus, which relays the information to the primary auditory cortex.

The Hierarchy of Sound Processing

Scientists have deduced the function of different parts of the brain's auditory pathway based on what happens when those regions are damaged or absent. The most obvious auditory sensory disorder is deafness. Deafness can result from damage to the outer or middle ear that prevents transmission of sound information to the cochlea (so-called *conduction deafness*) or from damage to the cochlea itself (*sensorineural deafness*), which usually involves the hair

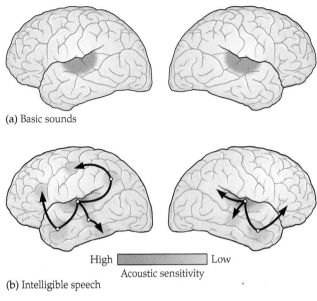

(a) Basic sounds

High ▭ Low
Acoustic sensitivity

(b) Intelligible speech

FIGURE 6.9 Hierarchical organization of the human auditory cortex.
Primary area A1 is responsive only to basic sounds and their modulation; surrounding areas become activated only by intelligible speech.

cells (Willott, Bross, & McFadden, 1994). Hearing aids can amplify sounds such that severely impaired auditory structures can perceive and transmit them. Alternate devices such as cochlear implants have allowed patients to completely bypass their own nonfunctioning cochleas and transmit sounds directly to the auditory nerve—as in the case of Michael Chorost, from the beginning of this chapter. When there is no damage to downstream auditory pathways, these patients can "hear" useful representations of sounds that they can then train their brains to interpret (Chorost, 2011).

Damage that affects the auditory system downstream of the inner ear generally does not result in deafness, but rather in deficits in the ability to process sounds. For example, damage to primary auditory cortex on one side of the brain (unilateral damage) leads to impaired sound localization. Higher areas of auditory cortex—referred to as secondary or tertiary auditory cortex (FIGURE 6.9)—are critically involved in the interpretation of sound (King & Schnupp, 2007). In monkeys, for example, damage to higher areas of auditory cortex leads to an inability to understand monkey calls (Rauschecker & Romanski, 2011). In humans, these higher areas make it possible to understand and produce speech, extract melodies from within complex musical compositions, and distinguish the intonations of praise from sarcasm (Obleser et al., 2006). The precise neuronal circuitry of these processes is less well understood, but involves interactions among several different sensory and motor pathways (Uchiyama et al., 2006). We will revisit the role of higher-order auditory processing as it pertains to language in Chapter 11.

inferior colliculi and on to the medial geniculate nucleus of the thalamus. After synapsing through all of these nuclei, the auditory information is transmitted to primary auditory cortex (A1), in the temporal lobes of the brain (FIGURE 6.8). The tonotopic map originating in the cochlea is preserved in primary auditory cortex.

(a)

FIGURE 6.10 Sound sources can be localized within the environment. The auditory system uses timing and volume cues to localize sounds in the environment, even if the eyes are closed.

Sound Localization

As important to the animal as being able to identify sounds is being able to determine the origin of those sounds. Knowing there is a predator in the vicinity is not as good as knowing that it is roughly 20 meters to your left and closing in fast. We depend on our ability to localize a sound based on its position in the medial plane (front, above, back, below), lateral plane (left, right, front), and distance from us (FIGURE 6.10).

At a general level, sound localization within the medial plane relies on the relative orientation of the sound source and the structures of the outer ear. Distance cues rely on evaluation of a sound's frequency spectrum (higher frequencies diminish more rapidly than lower frequencies) and loudness (nearby sources produce louder sounds than those far away). In the lateral plane, much of the ability of the auditory system to localize sounds stems from the fact that there are two sets of sensory organs: two ears and two cochlea. Both ears are likely to sense a given sound, but depending on the relative position of that sound, each ear will receive a slightly different signal. These **interaural differences** provide the information that the downstream auditory pathway can then use to localize the source of the sound. There are differences in interaural *timing* (the time it takes a signal to reach the ear on one side of the head versus the other) and differences in interaural *volume* (the amplitude of a sound from one side is diminished when it reaches the far ear because the intervening head gets in the way).

For a sharp, intermittent sound (such as a bark), the ears can compare the timing of the onset of the sound: whichever ear is reached first reveals which side the sound is coming from (FIGURE 6.11a). Determining the source of a continuous sound (such as a rolling growl) is a bit more complicated, although the general idea is the same. Recall that sounds produce cyclical waves of increasing and decreasing air pressure. When listening to a continuous sound, an auditory system localizes the origin by comparing the interaural difference in *phase* timing— that is, the time at which the peak of the sound wave reaches each ear (FIGURE 6.11b). This strategy works well for localizing low-wavelength sounds, whereas interaural volume differences are more useful for localizing higher-frequency sounds.

The importance of interaural timing and level differences is reflected in the downstream circuitry of the

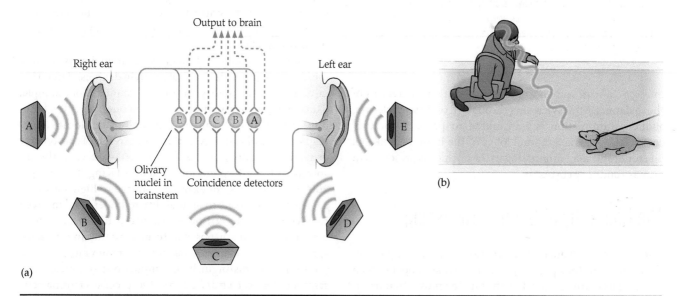

(a)

(b)

FIGURE 6.11 Interaural differences enable us to locate sounds. (a) Differences in the timing of when a sound reaches the two ears can be used to locate a sound source. Noise from a source at position A would strike the right ear first and, later, strike the left ear. The signal from the right ear would travel farther along the neurons, whereas the signal from the left ear would travel less far. These signals would combine by spatial summation at coincidence detector A in the olive, enabling you to locate the source of the sound. (b) Interaural differences in the phase of the sound wave are important for localizing the source of a continuous sound. For a lower-frequency sound, the sound is at a different phase of the wave when it strikes the left ear from when it strikes the right ear. This phase difference enables you to identify the location of the sound.

auditory pathway. Much like the tonotopic map created in the auditory nerve by frequency-selective hair cells, neurons located in the olivary nuclei of the brainstem that are sensitive to specific interaural timing or level differences form a two-dimensional map of sounds in space. Input from both cochlea converges on the same group of cells, and the net effect of the signals (for example, a 10-microsecond interaural timing difference) stimulates specific cells within this group, thereby allowing timing differences to map onto spatial differences. This feature of the auditory system has been extensively studied in the brains of barn owls, whose sound localization abilities allow them to hunt in complete darkness (von Campenhausen & Wagner, 2006).

Because we are such visual creatures, we often don't appreciate the precision with which sounds can be localized. But you need only watch a blind person navigate the busy streets of your city to appreciate the precision of the data coming in through the ears and getting processed by the auditory system.

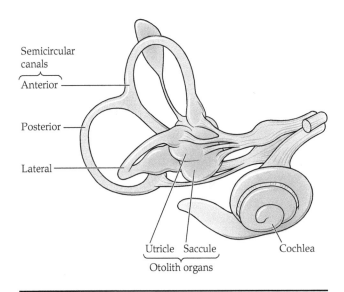

FIGURE 6.12 The vestibular system. Showing the relative locations of the otolith organs and the semicircular canals.

Balance

As anyone who has suffered through a bad ear infection can tell you, hearing is not the only sense dependent on the integrity of your inner ear. Right next to the cochlea are several more fluid-filled structures, each with their own complement of hair cells. These are responsible for your sense of balance. To prove this to yourself, try standing up and spinning your body around as quickly as possible for a few seconds. Even after you stop, the room will continue to feel as if it is still spinning. Why does this happen?

The **vestibular system** provides important information about head movements, acceleration, and head position relative to gravity. All of these are vital to keeping an animal upright even as the rest of the body moves and contorts. The core of the vestibular system is adjacent to (but distinct from) the cochlea in the inner ear: three **semicircular canals** (which sense head rotation and angular acceleration) and two otolith organs (which sense head tilt and linear acceleration) (FIGURE 6.12). They all use the common strategy of having hair cell bundles in fluid that shifts as the head moves. Directional information is elegantly provided by the specific orientation of each fluid-filled chamber. The three semicircular canals are positioned orthogonal to each other, meaning that there is roughly a 90-degree angle between any two. Stimulation of hair cells in each semicircular canal therefore conveys the component of the movement that occurred within its plane. Together, the three semicircular canals can encode the movement in three dimensions.

Detecting linear acceleration relies on the otolith organs, which take advantage of inertia to provide sensory information about changes in speed. An independently moving structure called the otolith (Greek for *ear + stone*) sits inside each fluid-filled otolith organ. As the head starts to accelerate, the otolith (not solidly attached to the head) moves relative to the hair cells (attached to the head) according to the inertia produced by the acceleration (FIGURE 6.13). At constant speed there is no acceleration and no relative movement, but as the head slows down (i.e., decelerates), the inertia of the otolith again stimulates the hair cells to signal that change. The two otolith organs function in the horizontal and vertical planes, sensing horizontal acceleration (think of a car gaining speed) and vertical acceleration (think of an elevator ride).

Along with keeping your balance, the vestibular system keeps your eyes pointing in the right place. Try looking at this sentence while you move your head back and forth as though you were shaking your head "no." Easy, isn't it? How do your eyes so rapidly adjust to all the head movement? The feat relies on the vestibular system providing rapid information about head movements to the oculomotor system, which makes instantaneous compensatory eye movements. **Vestibulo-ocular reflexes** drive eye movements in opposition to head movements such that vision can remain honed onto its target.

One way of testing your vestibular organs in a doctor's office is called caloric vestibular stimulation. The doctor tilts your head to a specific angle so that one of the semicircular canals is aligned vertically, then carefully irrigates the inner ear with either cold or hot water. The temperature difference between your body and the water creates a convective current in the fluid of semicircular canal. These currents stimulate the hair cells of the vestibular system, giving your brain a false sensation of head movement and inducing vertigo (dizziness). Damage or disease that impairs the vestibular system can be debilitating, as is the case in Meniere's disease. Sufferers of Meniere's disease experience bouts of prolonged vertigo, often without a known trigger or cause. More commonly,

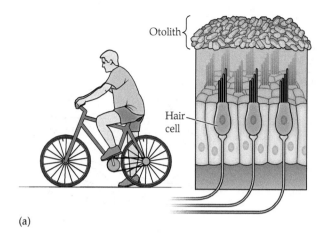

Otolith

Hair cell

(a)

(b)

FIGURE 6.13 Otolith organs detect acceleration by changes in the position of the otoliths. The otoliths are not connected to the vestibular system except by the hair cells. (a) You can see a person standing still, and the otolith is centered over the hair cells. (b) The person has just started moving. The otolith is left behind by inertia, causing the hair cells to bend. This opens ion channels, just like in the auditory system, causing the cells to depolarize or hyperpolarize.

people experience a decline in vestibular function with age that may contribute to falls among the elderly (Ganança, Gazzola, Aratani, Perracini, & Ganança, 2006).

The Somatosensory System

Although you may not always think about it this way, your entire body is covered by one giant sensory organ: the skin. Through our skin we sense touch, temperature, and pain. And on the inside of our bodies, a distributed system of sensation allows us to know where our limbs exist in space (body position) and what is happening with our internal

organs. All of these sensory modalities are grouped into what is known as the **somatosensory system**. It refers to the ability to detect sensory information throughout the body and transmit that information to the central nervous system, where it can inform behavior. Unlike vision or hearing, somatosensation does not take place in a discrete sensory organ. Instead, receptors are distributed throughout the skin, muscles, bones, joints, internal organs, and cardiovascular system. Calling it the somatosensory system is deceptively simple. Sensations of touch, temperature, pain, and body position are all aspects of somatosensation.

Touch

Your skin, a large, seamless sensory sheet, is packed with receptors that allow you to feel when something, or someone, makes contact with you, or when a nearby object is vibrating, or when something is hot or cold. Together, these feelings of pressure, vibration, and temperature create the sense of touch.

To detect pressure and vibration, the skin employs a specific class of sensory receptors called **mechanoreceptors**. Mechanoreceptors have specialized structures that give them acute sensitivity to physical distortions like stretching or bending. Different types of mechanoreceptors vary in their location, structure, and response profiles, creating the ability to sense and interpret a great diversity of touch stimuli. A closer look at four types of mechanoreceptors found in the skin reveals how their characteristics combine to create sensitivity to various stimuli. **Meissner's corpuscles** and **Merkel's disks** are found in the superficial layers of skin and have small receptive fields (areas of sensitivity)—only a few millimeters (**FIGURE 6.14**). A receptive field in this context refers to the area of the skin in which the corpuscle or disk responds to touch stimuli. In contrast, **Pacinian corpuscles** and **Ruffini's endings** are found in the deeper layers of skin and have much larger receptive fields, on the order of tens of centimeters. Already you can predict that Meissner's corpuscles and Merkel's disks might be more likely to respond to fine, light touch (because of their superficial location), whereas Pacinian corpuscles and Ruffini's endings might be more likely to respond to stronger and cruder pressure stimuli.

We can further distinguish among these receptor types by their ability to adapt to ongoing stimuli. *Rapidly adapting receptors* (Meissner's and Pacinian corpuscles) respond quickly at the onset of a stimulus but then stop firing as the stimulus continues. *Slowly adapting receptors* (Merkel's disks and Ruffini's endings) fire more consistently throughout a long-lasting stimulus. As you might expect, rapidly adapting receptors are better suited to respond to high-frequency stimuli (vibrations): they stop responding shortly after an initial stimulus and are therefore ready to respond to another stimulus occurring soon thereafter. Indeed, Pacinian corpuscles, with their deep location, large receptive field, and fast

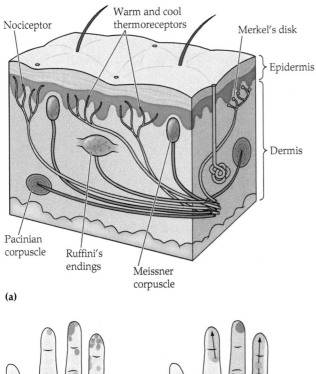

(a)

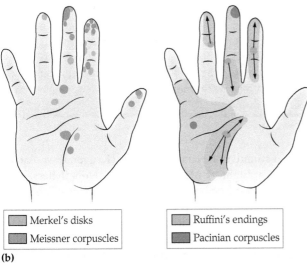

| Merkel's disks | Ruffini's endings |
| Meissner corpuscles | Pacinian corpuscles |

(b)

FIGURE 6.14 **Somatosensory receptors and their receptive fields.**
(a) There are a number of different somatosensory receptors within the skin. These include the Meissner's corpuscles and Merkel's disks near the surface and Ruffini's endings and Pacinian corpuscles further below the surface. There are also warm and cool thermoreceptors and nociceptors. (b) The receptive fields of somatosensory neurons vary in size. Those receptors close to the surface have a small receptive field, whereas those farther from the surface have a larger receptive field.

adaptation, are necessary for the sensation of high-frequency vibrations (like those you would experience from the rumbling in your chair at a loud concert). Meissner's corpuscles, located more superficially, with small receptive fields and slow adaptation, make it possible to feel rough textures (think of running your fingers over a burlap sack).

It is the interplay of these different receptor types that yields the rich, multilayered sensation of touch—fine and coarse, fast and slow.

Temperature

Mechanoreceptors that relay temperature information are called **thermoreceptors**. Similar to other modalities, different classes of receptors are sensitive to particular temperature ranges—in this case, there are "cold" and "warm" thermoreceptors. In both cases, these receptors detect changes in temperature on the surface of the skin relative to body temperature. So a cold thermoreceptor located in your finger will cause a neuron to change its firing rate only a little when you test the cool water for a bath, but it will trigger a strong signal if you dunk your hand into a bucket of ice water (Viana, de la Pena, & Belmonte, 2002). Speaking of ice water, did you ever notice that a cold lake *feels* warmer the second time you dip your toes in? Obviously, the temperature of the water has not changed, but the *relative* temperature of the water compared to your (now chilled) skin has decreased, changing your perception of the water temperature.

A separate set of fibers carries information about warmth. These warm receptors are also activated in proportion to the amount of temperature change from your hand in the air to your hand touching the warm object (Darian-Smith et al., 1979). But these receptors track change only to a point—after that, their firing rate drops off and information about *heat* (not merely warmth) is carried on pain fibers, which we will return to below. Similarly, cold receptors stop firing in response to cold surfaces (below about 10°C)—and then pain receptors take over.

At a constant temperature, thermoreceptors fire at a slow, steady rate. Thus, changes in temperature are signaled by changes in the rate of firing. These changes in firing rate are transient because thermal receptors adapt to long-lasting temperature stimuli, much like the mechanoreceptors described in the previous section.

Both warm and cold thermoreceptors can be activated by other stimuli. Capsaicin, the active ingredient in chili peppers, triggers warm thermoreceptors to create the illusion of heat. Capsaicin is therefore used in topical ointments, such as IcyHot. Menthol, obtained from peppermint or other mint oils, activates the cold receptors to give the impression of coolness. Because of this pleasant sensation, menthol is a popular addition in toothpastes and shaving creams.

Pain

Imagine never feeling physical pain, regardless of what happened to you. Then read the story of one young man for whom this idea was a lifelong reality.

Nature's gift of pain is not accidental: it is critical to survival. Feeling pain is how we sense damage to our cells and tissues.

Our perception of pain is mediated by specialized sensory receptors called **nociceptors**, the activity of which is

CASE STUDY
The Pain of a Painless Existence

As a child, Paul W. would push the swing on the swing set and then let it smash into his face. He enjoyed the reaction it stimulated in the other children. And he didn't mind the hospital visits for broken nose and teeth. Paul felt no pain.

Paul has the rare disorder of congenital analgesia, an inability to register painful sensations. He can feel a knife if it slices his finger, but only the touch is registered, not the pain of the injury. Because his thermoreceptors are intact, he can easily tell the difference between hot and cold water—but he does not feel the *pain* of either extreme.

Although one might think that feeling no pain would be a blessing, it is actually a curse. Pain is critical to avoiding bodily damage. When Paul interacts with extreme temperatures, he gets no immediate feedback signal telling him to withdraw his hand or avoid the situation. One of his most frequent injuries as a child was burning himself: he was interested in listening to the sizzling sound his skin made. Paul's parents were constantly forced to take creative and desperate measures to keep their son safe, such as putting adult socks over both his hands and goggles over his eyes. Often they resorted to a helmet to protect him

from his regular risk of head injury. They constantly checked him for swelling, bruising, or burns all over his body. Because of his lack of internal sensation, this sort of outside inspection was the only way they could reveal whether tissue had been damaged.

Much of Paul's childhood was spent in hospitals. Whether from jumping off extreme heights or banging his head against the wall until his forehead swelled up, Paul is lucky to be alive. Not everyone with congenital analgesia makes it through childhood. Pain is two-faced: it hurts, but it also protects (Zimmerman, 2010).

---

stimulated by tissue damage (Woolf & Ma, 2007). There are three main types of nociceptors, classified based on the types of noxious stimuli they respond to: mechanical, thermal, and chemical. Mechanical nociceptors are activated by physical damage to tissue caused by intense pressure, such as a needle stick or broken bone. Thermal nociceptors respond to stimuli that are either extremely hot (>45°C) or extremely cold (<5°C). Chemical nociceptors are activated by stimuli such as several cooking spices, some poisonous gases (used as chemical weapons in World War I), and spider toxins. Some nociceptors are sensitive to more than one category of stimulus—for example, extreme pressure or temperature as well as noxious chemical stimuli—and are therefore categorized as *polymodal*. Finally, some other receptors do not respond to any of the above noxious stimuli, but instead contribute indirectly to nociception by responding to the body's own chemicals released by damaged tissue. As a result of these *silent nociceptors*, some of the body's released chemicals may trigger *hyperalgesia*, or an increase in the sensitivity of the nociceptor to subsequent noxious stimuli. This is why even the gentlest touch can be torture on severely sunburned skin.

How nociceptors generate membrane depolarizations and action potentials in response to noxious stimuli is not completely understood. Unlike the specialized receptors relied on to transmit touch stimuli, most nociceptors are free nerve endings (FIGURE 6.14), meaning they lack obvious structural features that would allow for the translation of

external stimuli into electrical signals (Kruger, Kavookjian, Kumazawa, Light, & Mizumura, 2003). Nonetheless, specialized proteins embedded in the membranes of nociceptors confer sensitivity to certain chemicals or molecules. These proteins can depolarize the nociceptors in response to the presence of noxious stimuli such as capsaicin, the chemical that gives hot peppers their heat (Szolcsanyi, Anton, Reeh, & Handwerker, 1988). Further transmission of electrical signals depends on properly functioning sodium channels in the membranes of the downstream nerves. At least some families with congenital analgesia (as in the case of Paul W., described in the previous case study) have **mutations** in these sodium channels (Cox et al., 2006).

Different types of nociceptors transmit their signals at different speeds, depending on their diameter and degree of myelination. For example, the small-diameter unmyelinated C fibers conduct signals relatively slowly (about 1 meter per second) and are generally associated with polymodal nociceptors, whereas the myelinated Aδ fibers (pronounced A-delta) associated with mechanical or thermal nociceptors conduct more quickly (roughly 5–30 meters per second). The next time you stub your toe, pay attention to the way the pain is registered: first, thanks to the Aδ fibers, you'll register a fast, sharp pain. Once the C fibers catch up, you'll feel the more prolonged (but slightly less intense) pain.

Like touch receptors, nociceptors are distributed throughout the body and viscera: they are found just under the skin, in organs, and in joints. The one notable exception is the brain, which has no nociception. This is why patients can be kept conscious during brain surgery: they can provide useful feedback to the surgeon about their sensory perceptions without feeling any pain from the surgery itself.

Proprioception

When we think about losing a sense, most people dread the idea of losing vision. But blind people can still learn to climb mountains, play the piano, and become governors (Ravitch et al., 2008). Things do not usually turn out as well for those who lose their proprioceptive sense. **Proprioception**, or the sense of position and movement of one's own body, provides a constant information stream of where we are in space. Receptors primarily located in muscles and joints provide information about the stationary position of limbs (limb-position sense) and limb movement (kinesthesia).

Proprioceptors in the muscles monitor several properties. The **muscle spindles** report on the length of the muscle and the speed of any stretching (FIGURE 6.15a). Muscles involved in fine motor movements have a higher density of muscle spindles: the brain requires more feedback for finer changes. Another proprioceptor, the **Golgi tendon organ**, seats itself where the tendons meet the muscle (FIGURE 6.15b). Golgi

tendon organs transmit information about muscle tension, limiting the maximum amount of contraction to prevent overload and muscle damage. Other proprioceptors send signals from joints and ligaments.

Among other critical functions, proprioception allows us to manipulate objects and remain upright. Consider the case of Ian Waterman, a 19-year-old male who lost proprioceptive and tactile input below the neck after a viral infection. The sudden silence from his body's sensors left him unable to walk (Cole & Paillard, 1995). He required a year of hard work to improve his mobility, and even then the challenge of simultaneously speaking and walking eluded him. Similarly, the neurologist Oliver Sacks described a "disembodied lady" who could walk only if she stared at her feet and could keep her arms still only if she stared at her hands (Sacks, 1970). In both cases some recovery was possible because we can estimate where our limbs are by looking at them—but one cannot completely make up for a loss of proprioception by relying only on vision. When the lights are turned out, Ian falls to the floor. He cannot maintain posture, much less make any sort of fine movements, without visual feedback. As these examples illustrate, although we are rarely aware of proprioception's existence, its loss is debilitating (Gallagher, 2005; Gordon, Ghilardi, & Ghez, 1995).

Interoception

Beyond monitoring the positions of the limbs, the brain devotes a great deal of its resources to monitoring the internal environment. The term **interoception** refers to our ability to perceive the current state of our body. This includes visceral sensations (movements in the gut, muscle stretch, and such) as well as homeostatic information such as hunger, thirst, and mood state. It tells you "how you feel" at any given point in time.

Interoception signaling arises throughout the body and travels to the brain for interpretation and response. Sensory stimuli that contribute to interoception can trigger many different types of receptors. For example, *stretch receptors* in the lung help modulate breathing rate, whereas those in the gastrointestinal tract indicate fullness or distention. **Chemoreceptors** in the brain monitor carbon dioxide levels and give a sense of suffocation, those in the circulatory system monitor blood levels to trigger thirst, and others in the brainstem trigger vomiting in response to poisons. Other specialized receptors in the throat, close cousins of touch receptors in the skin, detect foreign objects to trigger gagging.

Research in this field is dedicated to identifying sensory pathways involved in interoception and to determining how they are distinct from other somatosensory information streams (Craig, 2002; Zaki, Davis, & Ochsner, 2012). Interoception also raises interesting philosophical questions as scientists ponder the physiological basis of self-awareness in humans and other primates.

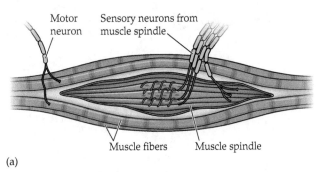

(a)

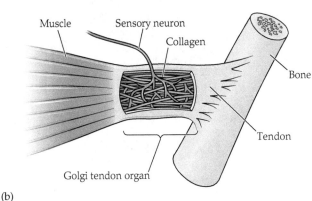

(b)

FIGURE 6.15 **The muscle spindle and Golgi tendon organ.** (a) The muscle spindle, embedded in the body of the muscle, reports on muscle length and stretch. (b) The Golgi tendon organ is interwoven with the fibers of the tendon and reports on the amount of tension in the muscle.

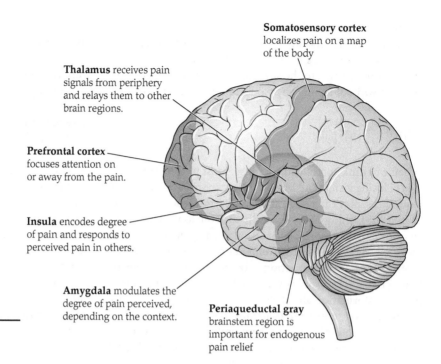

Somatosensory cortex localizes pain on a map of the body

Thalamus receives pain signals from periphery and relays them to other brain regions.

Prefrontal cortex focuses attention on or away from the pain.

Insula encodes degree of pain and responds to perceived pain in others.

Amygdala modulates the degree of pain perceived, depending on the context.

Periaqueductal gray brainstem region is important for endogenous pain relief

FIGURE 6.16 Brain areas involved in perceiving the emotional and cognitive components of pain.

Earlier we learned about nociceptors, which allow us to detect noxious stimuli from the environment. But the signals transmitted by nociceptors from the periphery are only part of our perception of pain: numerous regions throughout the cerebral cortex, the limbic system, and the brainstem are implicated in the emotional and cognitive components of pain (FIGURE 6.16). For example, imagine you are playing soccer and sprain your ankle. Many factors will converge to determine whether this particular noxious stimulus is perceived as painful enough to warrant leaving the playing field (FIGURE 6.17). In this case, contextual cues (the game's not over), attention (a person is falling on top of you), and endogenous analgesic agents (endorphins) all contribute to final perception of how much your ankle hurts. This illustrates the idea behind the **gate control theory**, which stipulates that pain results from the balance of activity in both nociceptive and nonnociceptive pathways (Crown, Grau, & Meagher, 2004; Melzack & Wall, 1965). Information from these pathways converges in the spinal cord. However, the convergent point has a limited capacity to receive incoming signals. Thus, when this site is overloaded, further pain is blocked—a sensory "gate" is closed (Basbaum & Fields, 1978). In contrast, nonnociceptive pathways can cause this area to become sensitized—for example, by negative emotions—thereby causing an increased sensitivity to pain. As a result, patients sometimes experience pain with no obvious cause at the level of the nociceptors—instead the problem is later down the central nervous system pathway (Woolf & Mannion, 1999). This kind of pain, known as **neuropathic pain**, is often much more difficult to treat than the kind that simply results from the activation of nociceptors.

FIGURE 6.17 Although nociceptors carry information about noxious stimuli to the brain, the final perception of pain depends on context, including your goals and your attentional focus.

The Somatosensory Pathway

With the exception of stimulation of the head and face, all somatic sensory signals travel to the cortex along the spinal cord. Because the head and face are above the level of the spinal cord, they have their own path to the brain via the cranial nerves that make up the *trigeminal pathway* (FIGURE 6.18a). Everywhere else, mechanoreceptors and nociceptors transmit their responses to physical stimuli via the *primary afferent fibers* of *dorsal root ganglion* neurons (FIGURE 6.18b). Generally speaking, neurons innervating a specific area of skin come together to form a single **dorsal root**, or bundle of fibers entering the spinal cord at the same place. The entire body is divided into dermatomes—areas of skin to which the dorsal root bundles respond (FIGURE 6.18c). Although we are not typically aware that our body is divided into regions this way, dermatomes become obvious in patients suffering from shingles, which is caused by the reactivation of dormant chickenpox virus. The reactivated virus usually attacks sensory fibers within a single dorsal root, thereby causing intense pain and other unpleasant sensory experiences that are limited to a specific segment of skin.

Once in the spinal cord, different types of somatosensory information segregate and follow their own distinct paths to the brain. Some information remains ipsilateral to the original stimulus for a time, but almost all somatosensory information eventually **decussates** (crosses the midline of the body) so that it is contralateral to the original stimulus. Just as in vision and hearing, somatosensory information decussates and travels first to the contralateral thalamus (in this case, to the **ventral posterior nucleus**) and then to contralateral primary sensory cortex. The primary somatosensory cortex (S1) is located in the parietal lobe adjacent and posterior to the central sulcus (FIGURE 6.19a). The origin of sensory information is laid out in S1 to create a *somatotopic* map of the body (FIGURE 6.19b). The representation of the body in S1 is often referred to as the *homunculus*, meaning "little man." Interestingly, rather than being scaled to the size and shape of the body itself, representation on the somatotopic map reveals differences in the density of somatosensory receptors and the relative importance of sensation among different body parts (Erzurumlu, Murakami, & Rijli, 2010). In humans, a disproportionately large area of the primary sensory cortex is devoted to information coming from the hands, fingers, mouth, and lips. Not surprisingly, you are able to discern much more subtle sensory stimuli on these parts of your body, than, say, your knee or back, which have smaller representations in the cortex. The relative size of sensory cortex devoted to different parts of the body varies across species because different animals rely on different sensations to survive in their niche environment. For example, an enormous portion of the rodent sensory cortex is devoted to the mechanoreceptors associated with whiskers, thus enabling rodents to navigate dark alleyways to find food and avoid obstacles (Erzurumlu et al., 2010).

Just as with vision and audition, the neighboring **secondary somatosensory cortex** and tertiary somatosensory cortex in the parietal lobes mediate more complex sensory

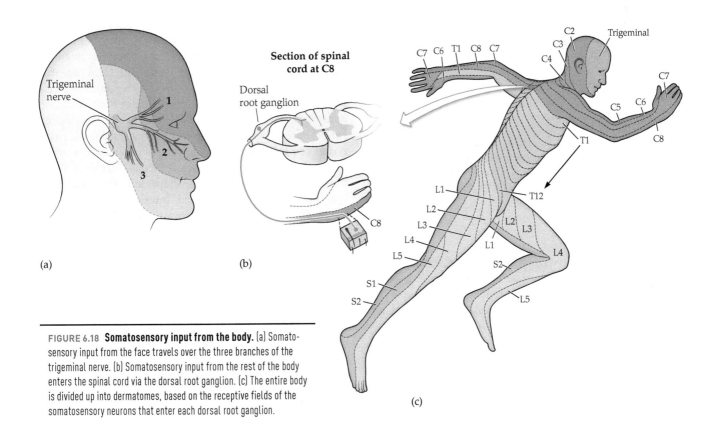

FIGURE 6.18 Somatosensory input from the body. (a) Somatosensory input from the face travels over the three branches of the trigeminal nerve. (b) Somatosensory input from the rest of the body enters the spinal cord via the dorsal root ganglion. (c) The entire body is divided up into dermatomes, based on the receptive fields of the somatosensory neurons that enter each dorsal root ganglion.

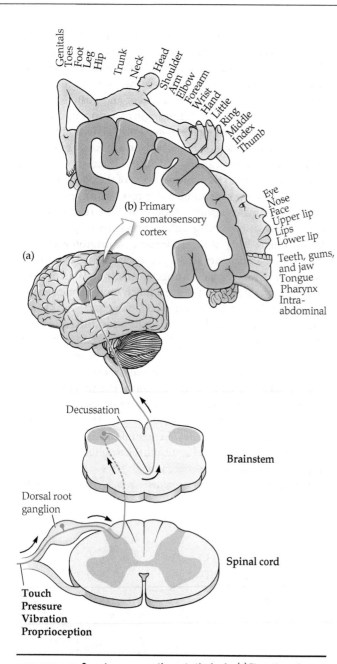

FIGURE 6.19 Somatosensory pathway to the brain. (a) The pathway from the periphery to the primary somatosensory cortex, on the contralateral side of the brain. (b) The somatosensory homunculus, or somatotopic map, of the body within the primary somatosensory cortex.

integration—such as that needed to recognize objects based on touch. This sort of higher-order sensory processing lets us translate "round and smooth" into the feel of an "apple" or perceive exhausted muscles as painful. Damage to these higher areas leads to disorders such as *tactile agnosia*. Patients with tactile agnosia cannot identify an object based on touch even if they can name the object when they see it visually.

Finally, consider the role of motor movements in somatosensation. Although some somatosensory stimuli arrive at touch receptors passively (e.g., someone's coat brushing

against your hand or cold rain hitting your face), much of the information is gathered actively (e.g., reaching out to feel the fabric of your friend's sweater). This process requires tight coordination between sensory information and motor commands. The cerebellum receives tactile information from mechanoreceptors involved in touch perception as well as proprioceptive signals. It is also the main brain area involved in motor coordination and timing. Thus, the cerebellum is well positioned to mediate the process of motor movement based on sensory feedback. However, it is not the only brain structure that contributes to this process. Although neuroscience tends to divide the functions of the brain into *sensation* on the one hand and *movement* on the other, the two processes are always intertwined: the brain is constantly reaching out to seek sensation.

Chemical Senses

Taste and smell differ from other senses in that they are chemically based: they rely on the binding of molecules to the taste buds of the tongue or to the mucous membranes of the nose and throat. In contrast, the other senses work via the transduction of photons (vision) or mechanical forces (touch and hearing). Thus, taste and smell have a different organization in the brain than vision, hearing, and touch.

Taste

The *gustatory pathway* allows us to discriminate among various forms of taste stimuli. In addition to on the tongue, taste receptors are also found on the palate, pharynx, epiglottis, and the upper half of the esophagus. The taste receptors themselves are located in *taste cells* (FIGURE 6.20). Taste cells cluster into **taste buds** (50–150 cells per bud), and taste buds cluster to form **papillae** (1–100 taste buds per papilla). Papillae are the bumps on your tongue visible to the naked eye. If you look closely at your tongue in a mirror, you will notice that not all papillae look the same. Papillae fall into three categories based on their shape: foliate (leaflike), vallate (pimplelike), and fungiform (mushroomlike). The initial contact between taste receptors and the chemical stimuli to which they are sensitive occurs on the microvilli of taste cells. Taste cells arrange themselves within a taste bud such that their microvilli line a central *taste pore*, thereby exposing membranes packed with receptors to catch chemical stimuli.

Pure taste stimuli, or *tastants*, are chemicals that can trigger depolarization of taste cell membranes. Tastants are classified into five basic categories. Four you're already familiar with: sweet, salty, bitter, and sour. A fifth taste category, **umami** (a Japanese word meaning "delicious taste"), was more recently added. Umami can be described as savory or meaty.

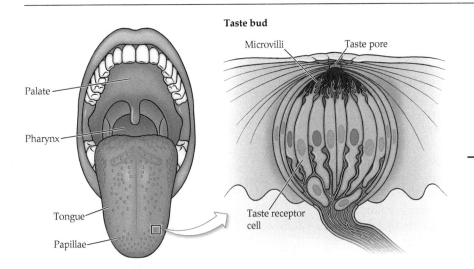

Taste bud

Microvilli

Taste pore

Palate

Pharynx

Tongue

Papillae

Taste receptor cell

FIGURE 6.20 **Taste receptor cells on the tongue and around the mouth.** Taste buds contain taste receptor cells and are found on the tongue, palate, pharanyx, epiglottis, and esophagus. The microvilli of the taste receptor cells contain receptors to detect chemical stimuli.

Taste categories are often talked about in terms of the prototypical stimuli that result in the perception of that taste. So the prototypical stimuli for the five taste categories are sucrose (sweet); sodium chloride (salty); citric acid (sour); quinine (bitter); and monosodium glutamate (umami) (FIGURE 6.21). Referring to the different taste categories by their prototypical stimuli can cause some confusion—for example, several other types of chemicals besides sucrose are perceived as sweet, including aldehydes and ketones. However, the prototypical stimuli are useful for understanding the transduction pathways for various taste stimuli, as we are about to see.

At the first point of contact in the gustatory pathway, taste cell membranes depolarize in response to the presence

(a)

(b)

(c)

(d)

(e)

FIGURE 6.21 **The prototypical stimuli for the five taste categories are (a) sucrose (sweet); (b) sodium chloride (salty); (c) citric acid (sour); (d) quinine (bitter, like baking chocolate); and (e) monosodium glutamate (umami—savory, like tomatoes).**

of various chemical compounds. There are currently thought to be about 50 different types of taste receptors and at least two major mechanisms by which salty, sweet, sour, bitter, or umami foods activate their various taste receptors: (1) direct activation or permeation of ion channels and (2) activation of G-protein-coupled receptors (GPCRs) to trigger downstream signaling cascades (see Chapter 3 for a review of ion channels and GPCRs) (Chandrashekar, Hoon, Ryba, & Zuker, 2006; Takeda, Kadowaki, Haga, Takaesu, & Mitaku, 2002). The activity of salty foods on taste receptors is a good example of the first type of mechanism. Sodium chloride, or table salt, depolarizes taste cell membranes via direct influx through ion channels selective for sodium. Interestingly, the type of anion (negatively charged ion) that associates with the sodium (positively charged) ion to form a salt can affect the degree of "saltiness" of a given compound. Anions can block the sodium ion channel, and larger anions block it more effectively than smaller ones (Beidler, 1954).

The key element in sour compounds, hydrogen ions, can also act directly on ion channels in the taste cell membranes. In this case, free hydrogen ions present in acids (most acids are perceived as sour) can block potassium channels. Because potassium channels flux potassium ions out of the cell at rest, blocking these channels leads to membrane depolarization. Hydrogen ions may also permeate certain types of sodium channels to cause depolarization (Hille, 1971).

Sweet and bitter compounds mainly trigger taste receptors through the activation of GPCRs. As you may remember from Chapter 3, GPRCs are embedded membrane proteins that undergo a conformational (shape) change when a specific ligand (e.g., sucrose) binds to them. The conformational change leads to the activation of a closely associated protein, thereby triggering a signaling cascade that can depolarize the taste cell. Many different compounds can bind to many different types of GPCRs, triggering many different types of signaling cascades. Some sweet and bitter compounds can also act directly on ion channels to activate taste receptors. Umami tastants activate both types of signaling mechanisms as well (Zhang et al., 2003). This variability underlies some of the nuanced taste perception we enjoy when we sit down to a well-balanced meal. (And even more nuance comes from the interplay of taste and smell, which we will discuss momentarily).

Because they develop from different (epithelial) tissue, taste cells are not technically neurons; however, like neurons, taste cells can fire an action potential (or a series of action potentials, depending on stimulus intensity) in response to membrane depolarization and subsequently release neurotransmitters (Huang et al., 2005, 2007; Nagahama & Kurihara, 1985). The recipients of chemical release from taste cells are *primary gustatory afferent* neurons that relay information about taste stimuli to the brainstem. From the brainstem, signals travel to the thalamus and finally to the gustatory cortex (FIGURE 6.22). The **frontal operculum**, located on the side of the head along the border of the parietal and temporal lobes, is the *primary gustatory*

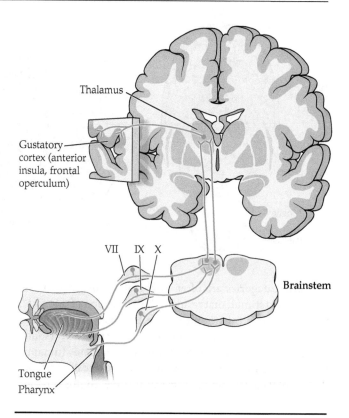

FIGURE 6.22 Gustatory pathway from tongue to primary gustatory cortex. Information travels over cranial nerves VII, IX, and X to the brainstem and then on to the thalamus and the gustatory cortex.

cortex. Damage to this area impairs taste. Remember what we've learned from our discussion of the other senses about the more abstract processing roles of higher-level, neighboring areas? The same applies in taste: deeper in the parietal lobe is the secondary cortical taste area located in the *limen insula.* Damage to this area spares basic taste while impairing accurate recognition of food type and flavor intensity (Pritchard, Macaluso, & Eslinger, 1999).

We have taste receptors that respond preferentially to sweet tastes and those that respond preferentially to salty ones, but how do we get from salty and sweet to "chocolate-covered peanut butter cup"? In our perception of taste we learn to recognize countless combinations of flavors. Part of this diversity stems from the early steps of taste sensation. Most taste receptors have a preferred stimulus, one they will respond to even at low concentrations. However, those same receptors may also activate in response to other types of stimuli if present in high enough concentrations. Adding another layer of complexity, each primary gustatory afferent fiber can innervate several taste buds and many different taste cells within each taste bud. In this way, a given stimulus triggers a pattern of taste receptor activation, which in turn stimulates a specific population of gustatory afferents (Simon, de Araujo, Gutierrez, & Nicolelis, 2006). Unlike the senses we have discussed so far, it seems that the sense of taste does not use a labeled line to convey the sensation, but instead relies on populations of neurons to encode the sensation. This *pattern encoding* makes it possible to perceive complex flavors and identify new tastes.

We rely on our sense of taste to motivate us to seek nourishment, explore new food sources, and avoid potentially hazardous ones. *Dysgeusia*, the distortion of the sense of taste, can result from many different conditions and often leads to severe weight loss. Fortunately, as epithelial-type cells, taste cells turn over quickly (approximately every couple of weeks). Therefore, damage to the taste cells themselves is often reversible. For example, the famous chef Grant Achatz made headlines after being diagnosed with tongue cancer and losing his sense of taste as a result of radiation treatment. He described how, with time, he regained taste sensation one category at a time (Landau, 2010).

Taste sensation begins with chemical compounds triggering responses in individual receptors, but taste perception involves many more sensory modalities. We usually first experience the food we are about to eat by smelling it, and our experience of each bite includes intensive somatosensory information about texture and temperature. Loss of any one component drastically alters the flavor of the food, as anyone who has ever suffered a bad head cold can attest. Even memories and mood can affect the sensory experience.

Smell

The other chemical sense—smell, or **olfaction**—allows people and other animals to perceive airborne chemicals. We humans do not rely on our sense of smell as much as we do other sensory modalities like vision. However, other species, such as dogs and rodents, capitalize on olfaction to read the environment around them. A dog can tell that the neighbor's dog wandered onto the lawn several minutes after the trespass occurred, and rats can locate morsels of food buried beneath layers of cage bedding. Despite the differences in reliance on smell, the olfactory systems of dogs, rats, and humans share many important structural and functional features.

The sensory organ and downstream neuronal circuitry involved in smell are collectively called the *olfactory system*. Chemical signals that are perceived by the animal as scents are also called *odorants*. They are inhaled through the nose or mouth to reach the main sensory organ, the **olfactory epithelium**, located at the back of the nasal cavity (FIGURE 6.23). The olfactory epithelium is the location of signal transduction. In humans this structure is less than 10 square centimeters; compare that to scent-driven canines whose epithelia are greater than 170 square centimeters (Quignon et al., 2003)! A layer of mucus covering the epithelium provides a substrate for cilia extending from the dendrites of primary olfactory neurons (also called *olfactory receptor cells*) to come into contact with inhaled odorants. Along with olfactory receptor cells, the epithelium contains *supporting cells* and *basal cells*. Supporting cells secrete the mucus, maintain ionic gradients, and perform other tasks that generally

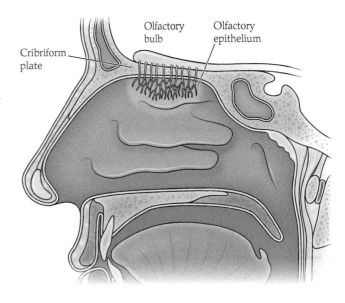

FIGURE 6.23 **The olfactory epithelium.** Olfactory sensory neurons detect odorant molecules in the olfactory epithelium.

support the health of receptor cells and the efficiency of odor detection. Unlike most other neurons, olfactory receptor cells undergo constant turnover, regenerating every 4 to 6 weeks (Graziadei, 1973). This turnover is made possible by the basal cells—stem cells capable of differentiating into new olfactory receptor cells or new supporting cells.

A number of unique structural and signaling features of the olfactory system enable us both to distinguish among closely related odorants and to recognize a wide array of different odorant types. Much of the groundbreaking work in this field was performed by Richard Axel and Linda Buck, who discovered a staggering number of olfactory receptor genes in rats (roughly 1,000 in all). Olfactory receptor genes constitute the largest known gene family in the rodent genome (Buck & Axel, 1991). Humans also possess this large gene family, but only about 400 of these genes remain functional in us (Malnic, Godfrey, & Buck, 2004). Axel and Buck also found that despite this diversity, olfactory receptors all fall into the same major category of GPCRs. Recall that these types of receptors are membrane proteins that undergo conformational change in response to ligand binding. They subsequently release activated proteins to trigger downstream signaling cascades that lead to the activation of the receptor neuron. Even more surprising was the subsequent discovery that each olfactory receptor neuron expresses one type of receptor exclusively (Ressler, Sullivan, & Buck, 1994). Axel and Buck were awarded the Nobel Prize in 2004 for their work on the olfactory system.

Since the discovery of olfactory receptors in 1991, researchers have found that these diverse receptor types recognize odorants based not on the actual odor itself, but rather on its individual molecular features (Buck, 1996). Thus, each olfactory receptor can respond to many different odorants

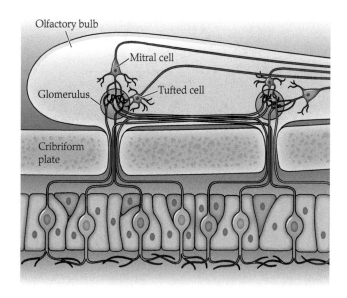

FIGURE 6.24 The olfactory bulb. The olfactory sensory neurons project through the cribriform plate to the glomeruli, located within the olfactory bulb. Tufted and mitral cells surround the glomeruli within the olfactory bulb.

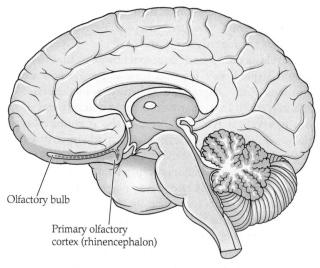

FIGURE 6.25 The rhinencephalon. The olfactory bulb projects to the primary olfactory cortex, or rhinencephalon.

that share a particular molecular feature. This mechanism forms the basis of the pattern encoding that allows for the recognition of and discrimination among many thousands of different stimuli. Like the sense of taste, then, it seems that the sense of smell does not use labeled lines to convey the sensation to the brain.

The remarkable features of the olfactory system continue downstream of the olfactory epithelium. The unmyelinated axons of the olfactory receptor cells travel from the epithelium to the olfactory bulb—a noncortical structure located inferior to the frontal lobe of the brain (FIGURE 6.24). The axons from each type of olfactory receptor cell converge onto a single point, called an **olfactory glomerulus**, in the olfactory bulb (Buck, 1996). In each glomerulus the axons of tens of thousands of receptor cells expressing the same receptor type synapse onto the dendrites of *mitral cells* and *tufted cells*. The structure of the olfactory bulb means that the information about odorant type is maintained as the signals leave the bulb and travel to olfactory cortex. Unlike other sensory pathways, the olfactory pathway travels directly from the peripheral sensory transducers to cortical areas first, without stopping at the thalamus. This is significant because, unlike all other senses, olfactory information can directly influence areas of the brain that are involved in memory and emotion without being filtered or processed by the thalamus. *Primary olfactory cortex* is known as *rhinencephalon* (literally, "nose brain"). This area, located at the bottom surface of the frontal lobe (FIGURE 6.25), receives input directly from the olfactory bulb.

From the rhinencephalon, olfactory information travels to a network of other areas of the brain, with different areas involved in detection, familiarity, and edibleness (Royet et al., 1999)—this should strike you by now as a familiar theme of the way in which higher-level cortical processing extends away from primary sensory areas.

Many animals smell to understand not only *what*, but also *where*: they navigate space by smelling their way around. Take the examples of a puppy finding its mother's nipple, lobsters locating their prey, moths finding their lovers, pigeons finding their way home, or salmon returning to their stream of origin (Arzi & Sobel, 2010). How do animals extract spatial information from smell? In our discussion of the auditory system, we saw that the *timing* between a signal hitting the two ears (the interaural timing difference) allowed for sound localization. Believe it or not, the same strategy can be used to localize the source of a smell. For example, sharks decide which way to turn while following a plume of smell by exploiting the internostril differences in odorant time of arrival, not (as one might have intuited) by the total odorant concentration difference (Gardiner & Atema, 2010). By exploiting a timing comparison across two spatially distributed channels (two ears or two nostrils), we find another principle of processing in common across the senses.

The Sense of Flavor

The reason foods lose their flavor when you have a cold is that a plugged nose affects your sense of smell—and without smell, there is little flavor. What we commonly experience as flavor is actually a compound sensation of basic tastes along with smell, temperature, and texture. For example, the sweetness of a sugar solution is enhanced by adding a sweet-smelling odor (a phenomenon exploited by commercial manufacturers). Similarly, the addition of the same sweet-smelling odor reduces the perceived sourness of an acidic solution. Given the dramatic effect of smell on taste perception, it is surprising that we have so few unique words to describe smells. Rather, we borrow nearly all of them from other senses—as revealed by terms such as sweet, sharp, bright, clean, fresh, soft, or spicy (Cytowic & Eagleman, 2009). Higher-level processing of olfactory information associates odor cues with other sensory perceptions occurring simultaneously and memories of other sensory perceptions that have occurred alongside those cues in the past. Thus, an old piece of fruit smells "moldy" and a bouquet of flowers smells "floral." Because of this seamless integration of olfactory processing with other sensory information, we are often unaware of the extent to which smell is influencing our perception of the world around us.

In terms of sensory perception, it might not be useful to think about taste and smell as independent senses, but rather to consider the composite "flavor" sense. For example, certain odors such as vanilla are consistently said to smell sweet, although sweetness belongs to the domain of taste (I. Stevenson & Cook, 1995). In fact, "sweet" is the most common description of odor. When one researcher asked 140 participants to describe a strawberry odor, 79% said it smelled sweet, whereas only 43% said it smelled like strawberry and 71% reported that it was fruity (Dravnieks, 1985). Other experiments (using chemicals such as amyl acetate, commonly used as banana flavoring) yield the same result. When smelling an odor, a majority of people perceive tastelike qualities such as sweetness rather than smell-specific ones such as "strawberrylikeness" or "bananalikeness" (R. J. Stevenson & Boakes, 2004).

Pheromones

Pheromones are chemicals broadcast by a member of an animal species to transmit information (such as identity and sexuality) and trigger behaviors within other members of the same species (Ferrero & Liberles, 2010). As one example, pheromones given off by queen bees will halt the sexual development of the other females and trigger them to become workers. Indeed, drifting molecules can carry a high density of information, including data about a prospective mate's gender, virility, genetics, emotions, age, and fitness.

The effect of pheromones has been studied extensively in the laboratory. Consider this experiment: female mice are presented with a choice of males. It turns out that a female's choice of mate is not random, nor based on visible attributes. Instead, it results from the relationship between her genetics and that of her suitors. The trick is how she accesses the data. Mammals possess a set of immune system genes summarized as the major histocompatibility complex (MHC). Following the strategy of keeping the gene pool well-stirred, the female mouse will choose those mates whose MHC genes are the most different from hers (Potts, Manning, & Wakeland, 1996). But here's the mystery: how do the female mice, almost-blind, figure out who's like them and unlike them? The answer: inside their noses, the

vomeronasal organ detects the pheromones carried by this genetic calling card.

The discovery of pheromones across mammals opens up the possibility that humans communicate (unconsciously) using pheromones. Indeed, some receptors in the human nose are identical to receptors that mice use for pheromonal signaling (Liberles & Buck, 2006; Pearson, 2006). It is not yet clear whether our pheromonal systems are actually operational. However, several groups have presented behavioral evidence that supports the possibility. In one study, males wore T-shirts for several days, allowing their sweat to soak into the cotton. Then, females were given these shirts to sniff. The females smelled the armpits and selected the body odor they preferred the most. Strikingly, and just as one would expect from the mice studies, the female students favored the males with MHCs that were different from their own (Wedekind et al., 1995). So although we're not consciously aware of our pheromonal signals, they may influence our attraction judgments.

Beyond mate selection, pheromones may convey other sorts of data in humans. One study demonstrated that newborns prefer pads that have been brushed against their mother's breast, as opposed to clean pads. The reason for this is hypothesized to be because of pheromones (Varendi & Porter, 2001). Moreover, after a female sniffs the armpit sweat of another woman, the length of her menstrual cycle can change (Stern & McClintock, 1998). (It is commonly stated that women who live together synchronize their menstrual cycles; however, this claim is unsupported. Large-scale studies demonstrate that synchronization does not happen, but that statistical fluctuations can give the illusion of synchrony (Yang & Schank, 2006).)

While pheromones may convey some information in humans, the amount they influence our behavior remains undetermined. Human cognition is profoundly more complex than that of mouse cognition. It is possible that pheromones have diminished to minor roles—similar to legacy software that is left over on a computer system that has been updated many times.

The Brain Is Multisensory

The job of the brain is to determine what's occurring in the outside world, and yet it must peer through only small portals sensing different energy sources: light, vibrations, pressures, and so forth. So why do events in the world seem so perceptually unified? Why doesn't the world seem to be made of separate visual events, disconnected sound events, independent touch events, and so on? The answer is that the brain is fundamentally multisensory, and it goes through a great deal of trouble to stitch independent senses together, as we are about to see.

Synesthesia

There is more than one way to combine sensory information. Imagine a world in which senses were blended—a world in which music was perceived in wavy green lines, food on the tongue tingled the fingertips, or flashing lights triggered an experience of sound. Does this sound like a flight of the imagination? In fact, about 1 person in 20 experiences the world in these unusual types of sensory blendings. **Synesthesia** (meaning "joined sensation") is a harmless perceptual condition in which one hears colors, tastes, or shapes or experiences other equally startling sensory blendings (Cytowic & Eagleman, 2009).

Synesthesia seems to reflect the system combining information in a slightly different way—specifically, neighboring brain areas communicate with each other more in synesthetes than in nonsynesthetes. That is, synesthesia results from an increased degree of crosstalk between normally separated brain areas, such that activity in one area kindles activity in another (FIGURE 6.26). For example, when a letter–color synesthete hears a spoken letter, there is measurably higher activity in regions specialized for color vision (for example, V4) when contrasted with nonsynesthetic controls (Tomson, Narayan, Allen, & Eagleman, 2013). Such findings demonstrate that the increased crosstalk in synesthetic brains is quantifiable and automatic and reflects genuine subjective experience. Because synesthesia runs in families, it is likely that a genetic difference causes increased

connectivity—by overgrowth between areas, defective neural pruning, or too little inhibition between adjacent brain areas (Tomson et al., 2011).

Synesthesia causes us to consider the amount of integration that is useful for brains. Too much integration between the senses means that signals cannot be differentiated. Nonetheless, the integration of senses may have an upside. One possibility is that integration across the senses engenders more *metaphor*—that is, the identification of underlying similarities between different domains (Ramachandran & Hubbard, 2001). In other words, it may be that synesthetes, because of their blended senses, end up being more creative. Indeed, many famous musicians and artists—from Franz Liszt to Itzhak Perlman to Tori Amos—are synesthetes.

Combining Sensory Information

Although the sensory systems are traditionally studied in isolation, the fact is that the brain is fundamentally multisensory—not just in synesthetes, but in everyone. The brain looks to many energy sources simultaneously to construct its best model of the world.

In fact, many neurons in the brain respond best if presented with not just one, but two senses simultaneously. For example, recordings from single neurons show that sensory cues from different modalities that appear at the same time and in the same location can increase the firing rate of multisensory cells in the superior colliculus and insula to a level exceeding that

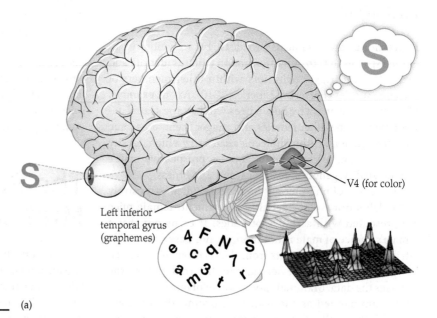

(a)

FIGURE 6.26 **Synesthesia.** In this model of synesthesia, neural populations coding for graphemes (right inferior temporal gyrus) interconnect on those coding for colors (area V4). As a result of these connections, activity triggered by a grapheme inappropriately triggers V4 activity and hence a color experience.

(b)

SYNESTHESIA

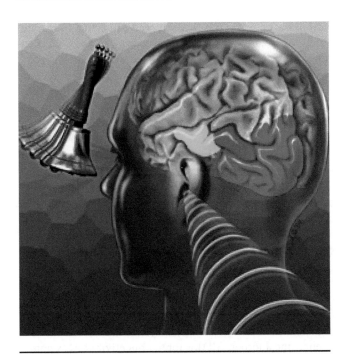

FIGURE 6.27 **Some brain areas show greater activity when stimulated by more than one sensory modality at a time.** When a person both hears and sees a bell, the researchers showed that some areas prefer auditory stimulation (blue), some areas prefer visual stimulation (pink), and some areas respond preferentially to both stimuli at the same time (green).

predicted by summing the responses to the unisensory inputs (Meredith, Nemitz, & Stein, 1987) (FIGURE 6.27).

When first learning the details of neuroscience, one might find oneself looking at a strange commune of different cortical and subcortical systems that care about vision, hearing, balance, touch, temperature, pain, limb position, hunger, taste, smell, and many other channels of information. How do they ever coordinate? For example, the auditory system deals with one-dimensional signals (e.g., air compression waves through time), whereas the neighboring visual system must analyze two-dimensional sheets (e.g., the retinas)—which have different statistics and data structure.

The key thing to appreciate about brain function is that all these disparate systems find ways to work seamlessly together and even to help one another. For example, when trying to understand a new object, you might look at it, turn it in your hands, heft it, shake it, smell it, and so on—combining your different modalities to land on an integrated picture of the object.

To be maximally useful, the information coming through the different sensory organs should be combined cleverly. Imagine trying to estimate a shape of a new object by tracing it with your fingers and looking at it with your eyes. Vision typically dominates in these cases because it typically provides better (and more reliable) spatial information (Kitagawa & Ichihara, 2002). But if the detail and reliability of the visual measurements are made worse than the somatosensory measurements (for example, by making the visual

signal blurry), then touch can suddenly come to dominate (Ernst & Banks, 2002). In other words, the nervous system combines cues in an optimal fashion, weighing the various cues based on their reliability for the given task—this is called the modality appropriateness hypothesis (Massaro, 1985; Welch & Warren, 1980). That is, the brain not only combines votes across the senses, but also weighs each vote by its *believability*. In a task involving timing judgments about audiovisual stimuli, the auditory system has more temporal precision. In these cases the auditory system's vote is more weighty, and it dominates perception (Welch, DuttonHurt, & Warren, 1986).

Sometimes the pressure on the systems to act in concert can lead to incorrect perceptions. We can learn more about the integrating machinery by examining cases in which the battles between the senses are stronger and the lopsided victories become more apparent. The mismatch between information from different modalities lies at the heart of a class of famous illusions that hint at the way sensory areas interconnect (Eagleman, 2001). In the illusion of ventriloquism, for example, the ears hear sound from one direction, and the eyes see a mouth moving from a slightly different location (FIGURE 6.28). The brain incorrectly concludes that the sound

FIGURE 6.28 **A ventriloquist and his dummy.** Although it is commonly thought that voices can be "thrown," the illusion relies entirely on the brain of the observer.

is emanating from the direction of the mouth—the sight of the speaker's lip movements influences the auditory localization of speech. This illustrates the pressure of the system to get different systems to collaborate—all with the goal of generating a single answer.

As another example of the pressure of different systems to arrive at a single answer, consider the **McGurk effect**. Imagine that an audio recording of someone's voice saying "ba" is synchronized with a video of his or her lips mouthing the syllable "ga." What you will experience is the illusion that a different syllable is being spoken (typically "da"). Why does this happen? The McGurk effect underscores the point that auditory (voice) and visual (lip-movement) signals are forced to come together for a single perception, even if both senses could have independently and differentially "decided" what is "out there" on their own (McGurk & MacDonald, 1976; Schwartz, Robert-Ribes, & Escudier, 1998). Listen to an example of the McGurk effect at CogNeuro.info. If you close your eyes, you will hear the actual syllable being spoken; as soon as you open them, the visual signals combine with (and change) the auditory percept.

In the above examples, vision influences hearing. A counterexample can be found in the illusory flash effect: when a single flash of light is accompanied by two beeps, it *appears* as though the light flashed twice (Shams, Kamitani, & Shimojo, 2000). Similarly, in the "auditory driving" effect, the apparent frequency of a flickering visual stimulus is driven faster or slower by an accompanying auditory stimulus presented at a different rate (Gebhard & Mowbray, 1959).

The Binding Problem

The above examples illustrate the most surprising property of multisensory experience: despite the extensive division of labor in the cortex (vision, hearing, balance, vibration, temperature, pain, proprioception, and so on), none of that division is apparent perceptually. Instead, we enjoy a unified picture of the world out there instead of having a separate visual world, auditory world, tactile world, and so on. When you watch a blue bird flying to the left and squawking, the blueness and the motion and the sound do not bleed off one another, but instead appear irrevocably bound. How does the brain produce a unified picture of the seen world given its specialized processing streams? This is known as the binding problem.

The binding problem remains unsolved. After all, there is no single anatomical location in the brain where information from all the different senses converges for a final perceptual answer. Instead, the solution must draw on the observation that the coordination of different sensory subsystems is underpinned by recurrent connections (Roelfsema, 2006). As we learned in Chapter 5, *recurrence* refers to the massive feedback found in neural circuitry: signals do not just pass forward in the brain; there is typically just as much (or more) signaling moving in the opposite direction (FIGURE 6.29). In this way, lower areas influence higher areas, higher areas influence lower areas, and different senses influence one another. All this interconnectivity forces populations of cortical neurons to "come to agreement" in their firing patterns.

The key lesson from this section is that specialized sensory areas all interconnect *with one another*. These connections are sometimes direct and sometimes indirect (passing through other areas)—but in any case, they all contribute to a vast, communicating network in which global patterns settle into place based on all the simultaneous push–pull activities (Cappe, Rouiller, & Barone, 2009; Sepulcre, 2014). The final global pattern, in which everyone is satisfied (or at least, minimally dissatisfied), is the resulting perception. In this way, activity in different subsystems can be coordinated without the need for a central supervisor, like a little man in the head that decides which sense to believe (Edelman, 1993; Zeki, 1994). Instead, an integrated perception of the world emerges naturally from the networking of activated cortical areas.

FIGURE 6.29 **The binding problem.** (a) Although it's easy to imagine signals climbing up an assembly line of processing, (b) the real anatomical fabric is characterized by interconnections between areas.

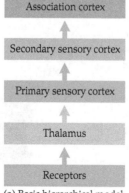

Association cortex

Secondary sensory cortex

Primary sensory cortex

Thalamus

Receptors

(a) Basic hierarchical model

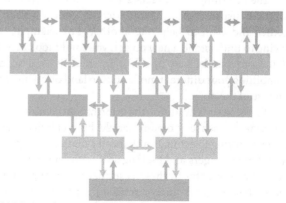

(b) More realistic model including crosstalk and feedback

Although studies of brain microcircuitry demonstrate recurrence, there has been surprisingly little direct research on large, recurrent networks. This is in part because it is easier for humans to think about assembly lines than about richly connected networks. But in the end, the plush tapestry of recurrent circuitry rules out the hopes of early neuroscience that brain areas would be understood as successive modules in a causal chain. Instead, brain areas are dependent for their normal functioning on the interwoven connections they exchange. One of the most promising future directions of neuroscience is a closer study of the weave of the anatomical fabric. In the absence of understanding interconnectivity, drawing conclusions about the function of a brain area from single-cell electrode recordings may be as doomed as studying one person's actions in the absence of any context of his family, friends, and culture. This is why biology can be more difficult than physics. In physics, isolating a part of the system allows you to understand it directly; this does not hold true with brain areas.

The Internal Model of the World

As a result of the brain's recurrent connections, the story of the senses gets stranger. One's final perception does not rely solely on the information coming in through the various channels. Instead, just as we saw with vision, much of what the brain believes it is experiencing depends on its *expectations*. One of the best ways to understand this concept is to see what happens when things go wrong.

Justice Douglas experienced a condition known as **anosognosia**: an absence of awareness about a physical impairment. Anosognosic patients do not purposefully lie. Nor are they driven by malice, humiliation, or pride. Instead, their neural networks manufacture narratives in an attempt at a coherent story. They need to be able to explain the lack of agreement between their motor expectations (my left arm should be moving) and their lack of sensory feedback (it neither looks nor feels as though it's moving). So their brains fabricate. If a partially paralyzed patient is asked to place his hands out to carry a tray, he may put out just one hand but assert that they are both up. If a tray is then handed to him, and falls, he will claim it was the experimenter's fault, not his. If the patient is asked to clap his hands, he will suggest that he has done so (even though he cannot), or will claim that he simply doesn't feel like doing it. Similarly, some patients who go blind will deny their deficit, asserting that their vision is fine, even as they collide with objects in a room. They may make excuses for the poor balance and rearranged furniture, even as they deny being blind.

Shouldn't the obvious signals—both social and sensory—indicate to an anosognosic patient that there is a problem? After all, if you want to clap your hands but you hear no sound, shouldn't that alert you to a problem or disconnect? The fact that this doesn't happen in anosognosic patients is a clue to the neurobiology. Specifically, humans have certain regions—such as the anterior cingulate cortex—that serve to alert the brain to contradictions (Etkin et al., 2006). Such regions monitor for conflict and ensure that one conflicting idea or the other wins out. However, when this region of the brain is damaged, the arbitration no longer occurs. In these situations, contradictory ideas pose little problem for the person affected (Eagleman, 2011). As a result, Justice Douglas's case illustrates that the sensory input to the body tells the brain a great deal of information—but one's final perception still depends on a collaboration of the system as a whole.

CASE STUDY
The Paralyzed Supreme Court Justice Who Claimed He Could Play Football

In 1974, William O. Douglas, a member of the U.S. Supreme Court, suffered a stroke. The damage to his brain tissue caused paralysis in the left side of his body, confining him in a wheelchair. However, then something very strange happened: Douglas insisted that he was fine. He demanded to be released from the hospital. He asserted that reports of his paralysis were mere "myths." Douglas's behavior baffled those around him, especially as his claims became more outrageous—for example that he was punting footballs and hiking. In light of his apparent delusions, Justice Douglas was encouraged to retire, which he did in 1975 (Eagleman, 2011).

Time Perception

We'll now turn to one last sense—one that has received less attention because it is more difficult to study: time perception. Time can be described as "metasensory" because it involves all the other senses. For example, you can compare the duration of a beep to the duration of a flash—and this means that temporal judgments function across other sensory areas. Although it is less well understood than the other senses, it is one of the most important perceptions that we have.

At some point, the Mongol military leader Kublai Khan (1215–1294) realized that his empire had grown so vast that he would never be able to see what it contained. To remedy this, he commissioned emissaries to travel to the empire's distant reaches and convey back news of what he owned. Since his messengers returned with information from different distances and traveled at different rates (depending on weather, conflicts, and their fitness), the messages arrived at different times. So the Great Khan was constantly forced to solve the same problem a human brain has to solve: what events in the empire occurred in which order (Eagleman, 2009)?

Your brain, after all, is encased in darkness and silence in the vault of the skull. Its only contact with the outside world is via the electrical signals exiting and entering along the superhighways of nerve bundles. Because different types of sensory information (hearing, seeing, touch, and so on) are processed at different speeds by different neural architectures, your brain faces an enormous challenge: what is the best story that can be constructed about the outside world?

The days of thinking of time as a river—evenly flowing, always advancing—are over. Time perception, just like vision, is a construction of the brain and can be experimentally manipulated. In the previous chapter we unmasked secrets of the visual system through optical illusions, in which things appear different from how they are physically presented; there is also a world of temporal illusions (Eagleman, 2008). In the movie theater, for example, we perceive a series of static images as a smoothly flowing scene. Or perhaps you've noticed when glancing at a clock that the second hand sometimes appears to take longer than normal to move to its next position—as though the clock were momentarily frozen.

Try this exercise: put this book down and go look in a mirror. Then move your eyes back and forth, so that you're looking at your left eye, then at your right eye, then at your left eye again. When your eyes shift from one position to the other, they take time to move and land on the other location. But here's the kicker: you never see your eyes move. What is happening to the time gaps during which your eyes are moving? Why do you feel as though there is no break in time while you're changing your eye position? (Remember that it's easy to detect someone else's eyes moving, so the answer cannot be that eye movements are too fast to see.)

All these illusions and distortions are consequences of the way the brain builds a representation of time. When we examine the problem closely, we find that "time" is not the unitary phenomenon we may have supposed it to be. For example, when a stream of images is shown over and over in succession, an oddball image thrown into the series appears to last for a longer period, although presented for the same physical duration (Pariyadath & Eagleman, 2007). In the neuroscientific literature, this effect was originally termed a subjective "expansion of time," but that description begs an important question of time representation: when durations expand or contract, does time *in general* slow down or speed up during that moment?

If our perception works like a movie camera, then when one aspect of a scene slows down, everything should slow down. In the movies, if a police car launching off a ramp is filmed in slow motion, not only will it stay in the air longer but also its siren will blare at a lower pitch and its lights will flash at a lower frequency. An alternative hypothesis suggests that different temporal judgments are generated by different neural mechanisms—and although they often agree, they are not required to. The police car may seem suspended longer, whereas the frequencies of its siren and its flashing lights remain unchanged.

Available data support the second hypothesis (Eagleman & Pariyadath, 2009). Duration distortions are not the same as a unified time slowing down, as it does in movies. Like vision, time perception is underpinned by a collaboration of separate neural mechanisms that usually work in concert but can be teased apart under the right circumstances.

This is what is found in the lab, but might something different happen during real-life events, as in the common anecdotal report that time "slows down" during brief, dangerous events such as car accidents and robberies? In 2007, Stetson and colleagues reasoned that if time as a single unified entity slows down during fear, then this slow motion should confer a higher temporal resolution—just as watching a hummingbird in slow-motion video allows finer temporal discrimination on replay at normal speed, because more snapshots are taken of the rapidly beating wings.

So the researchers designed an experiment in which participants could see a particular image only if they were experiencing such enhanced temporal resolution. They leveraged the fact that the visual brain integrates stimuli over a small window of time: if two or more images arrive within a single window of integration (usually less than 100 milliseconds), they are perceived as a single image. For example, the toy known as a thaumatrope may have a picture of a bird on one side of its disc and a picture of a tree branch on the other. When the toy is wound up and spins so that both sides of the disc are seen in rapid alternation, the bird appears to be resting on the branch. The researchers decided to use stimuli that rapidly alternated between images and their negatives. Participants had no trouble identifying the image when the rate of alternation was slow. However, at faster rates the images perceptually overlapped, just like the bird and the branch, with the result that they fused into an unidentifiable background (Stetson, Fiesta, & Eagleman, 2007).

To accomplish this, they engineered a device (the perceptual chronometer) that alternated randomized digital numbers and their negative images at adjustable rates. Using this, they measured participants' threshold frequencies under normal, relaxed circumstances. Next, they harnessed participants to a platform that was then winched 15 stories above the ground. The perceptual chronometer, strapped to the participant's forearm like a wristwatch, displayed random numbers and their negative images alternating just a bit faster than the participant's determined threshold. Participants were released and experienced free fall for three seconds before landing (safely!) in a net (FIGURE 6.30). During the fall, participants attempted to read the digits. If higher temporal resolution were experienced during the free fall, the alternation rate should appear slowed, allowing for the accurate reporting of numbers that would otherwise be unreadable.

The result? Participants weren't able to read the numbers in free fall any better than previously. They could not, after all, see time in slow motion (or in "bullet time," like Neo in *The Matrix*). Nonetheless, their perception of the elapsed duration itself was greatly affected. When asked to retrospectively reproduce the duration of their fall using a stopwatch, their duration estimates of their own fall were a third greater, on average, than their re-creations of the fall of others.

How can we make sense of the fact that participants in free fall reported a duration expansion yet gained no increased discrimination capacities in the time domain during the fall? The answer is that time and memory are tightly linked. In a critical situation, the amygdala becomes highly active, commandeering the resources of the rest of the brain and forcing everything to attend to the situation at hand. When the amygdala gets involved, memories are laid down by a secondary memory system, providing the later disturbing memories of post–traumatic stress disorder (Phelps, 2004). So in a dire situation, the brain may lay down memories in a way that makes them "stick" better. On replay, the

FIGURE 6.30 Participants fell 150 feet into a net below. Could they see in slow motion during the event?

higher density of data would make the event appear to last longer. In fact, this may be why time seems to speed up as you age: you develop more compressed representations of events, and the memories to be read out are correspondingly impoverished. When you are a child and everything is novel, the richness of the memory gives the impression of increased time passage—for example, when looking back at the end of a childhood summer (Eagleman, 2013).

To further appreciate how the brain builds its perception of time, we must understand where signals are in the brain and when. As we saw above, the nervous system faces the challenge of **feature binding**—that is, keeping an object's features perceptually united, so that, say, the redness and the squareness do not bleed off a moving red square. But there is even a deeper challenge the brain must tackle, without which feature binding would rarely be possible: the problem of temporal binding, or the assignment of the correct timing of events in the world. The challenge is that different stimulus features move through different processing streams and are *processed at different speeds*. The brain must account for speed disparities between and within its various sensory channels if it is to determine the timing relationships of features in the world (Eagleman et al., 2005; Schmolesky et al., 1998).

What is mysterious about the wide temporal spread of neural signals is the fact that humans have quite good precision when making temporal judgments. Two visual stimuli can be accurately deemed simultaneous down to 5 milliseconds, and their order can be assessed down to 20-millisecond precisions. How is that possible, given that the signals are so smeared out in space and time?

To answer this question, consider the tasks and resources of the visual system. As one of its tasks, the visual system must correctly judge the timing of outside events. But it must deal with the peculiarities of the equipment that supplies it: the eyes and parts of the thalamus. These structures feeding into the visual cortex have their own evolutionary histories and idiosyncratic circuitry. As a consequence, signals become spread out in time from the first stages of the visual system (for example, based on how bright or dim the object is).

So if the visual brain wants to get events correct time-wise, it may have only one choice: *wait for the slowest information to arrive*. To accomplish this, it must wait about a tenth of a second (Eagleman & Sejnowski, 2000). In the early days of television broadcasting, engineers worried about keeping audio and video signals synchronized. Then they accidentally discovered that they had about 100 milliseconds of leeway. As long as the signals arrived within this window, viewers' brains would automatically resynchronize the signals (Schlafly, 1951). Outside that tenth-of-a-second window, it suddenly looked like a badly dubbed movie.

This brief waiting period allows the visual system to discount the various delays imposed by the early stages. However, it has the disadvantage of pushing perception into the past. There is a distinct survival advantage to operating as close to the present as possible. Therefore, the tenth-of-a-second window may be the smallest delay that allows higher areas of the brain to account for the delays created in the first stages of the system while still operating near the border of the present. This window of delay means that awareness incorporates data from a window of time after an event and delivers a retrospective interpretation of what happened.

Among other things, this strategy of waiting for the slowest information has the great advantage of allowing object recognition to be independent of lighting conditions. Imagine a striped tiger coming toward you under the forest canopy, passing through successive patches of sunlight. Imagine how difficult recognition would be if the bright and dim parts of the tiger caused incoming signals to be perceived at different times. You would perceive the tiger breaking into different space–time fragments just before you became aware that you were the tiger's lunch. Somehow, the visual system has evolved to reconcile different speeds of incoming information.

This hypothesis—that the system waits to collect information over the window of time during which it streams in—applies to all the senses. We have measured a tenth-of-a-second window in vision, but the breadth of this window may be different for hearing or touch. If we touch your toe and your nose at the same time, you will feel those touches as simultaneous. This is surprising, because the signal from your nose reaches your brain well before the signal from your toe. Why didn't you feel the nose touch when it first arrived? Did your brain wait to see what else might be coming up in the pipeline of the spinal cord until it was sure it had waited long enough for the slower signal from the toe? Strange as that sounds, it appears to be the case.

It may be that a unified, multisensory perception of the world has to wait for the slowest overall information. Given conduction times along limbs, this leads to the bizarre but testable suggestion that tall people may live further in the past than short people. The consequence of waiting for temporally spread signals is that perception becomes something like the airing of a live television show. Such shows are not truly live but are delayed by a small window of time, in case editing becomes necessary.

A second problem is this: if the brain collects information from different senses in different areas and at different speeds, how does it determine how the signals are supposed to line up with one another? To illustrate the problem, snap your fingers in front of your face. The sound of the snap and the sight of your fingers seem synchronized. But your hearing and your vision process information at different speeds. A gun is used to start sprinters, instead of a flash, because you can react faster to a bang than to a flash. This behavioral fact has been known since the 1880s and in recent decades has been corroborated by physiology: the cells in your auditory cortex can change their firing rate more quickly in response to a bang than your visual cortex cells can in response to a flash (Breznitz & Meyler, 2003).

The physiological measurements are clear. Yet when we go outside the realm of motor reactions and into the realm of perception (what you report you saw and heard), the plot thickens. Your brain goes through a good deal of trouble to perceptually synchronize incoming signals that were synchronized in the outside world. So a firing gun will seem to you to have banged and flashed at the same time. (At least this will be true when the gun is within 30 meters of you; past that, the different speeds of light and sound cause the signals to arrive too far apart to be synchronized.)

It may seem strange that we live in the past, as dictated by our brains taking time to construct a story of "what just happened" in the world. But note that this parallels what we learned above in the context of multisensory processing (FIGURE 6.29): the interconnected sensory areas of the brain must all come to agreement before a perception is finalized. That coordination between areas takes time.

Everything we've been discussing here is in regard to conscious awareness. It seems clear from preconscious reactions that the motor system does not wait for all the information to arrive before making its decisions but instead acts as quickly as possible, *before* the participation of awareness, by way of fast subcortical routes. This raises a question: what if the use of perception, especially since it lags behind reality, is retrospectively attributed and is generally outstripped by automatic (unconscious) systems? The most likely answer is that perceptions are representations of information that cognitive systems can work with later. Thus, it is important for the brain to take sufficient time to settle on its best interpretation of what just happened rather than stick with its initial, rapid interpretation.

Neurologists can diagnose the variety of ways in which brains can be damaged, shattering the fragile mirror of perception into unexpected fragments. But one question has gone mostly unasked in modern neuroscience: what do disorders of *time* look like? We can roughly imagine what it is like to lose color vision, or hearing, or the ability to name things. But what would it feel like to sustain damage to your time-construction systems?

Recently, a few neuroscientists have begun to consider certain disorders—for example, in language production or reading—as potential problems of timing rather than disorders of language as such. For example, stroke patients with language disorders are worse at distinguishing different durations, and reading difficulties in dyslexia may be problems with getting the timing correct between the auditory and visual representations (Tallal, Miller, Jenkins, & Merzenich, 1997). It may also be that a deficit in temporal order judgments underlies some of the hallmark symptoms of schizophrenia, such as delusions of passivity ("My hand moved, but I didn't move it") and auditory hallucinations, which may be an order reversal of the generation and hearing of normal internal monologue (Eagleman & Pariyadath, 2009).

As the study of time in the brain moves forward, it will likely uncover many contact points with clinical neurology. At present, most imaginable disorders of time would be lumped into a classification of dementia or disorientation, catch-all diagnoses that miss the important clinical details we hope to discern in coming years. As we begin to understand time as a construction of the brain, as subject to illusion as color or shape, we may eventually be able to remove our perceptual biases from the way we see the world. Essentially all our physical theories are built on top of our filters for perceiving the world, and time may be the most stubborn filter of all to budge out of the way.

Conclusion

All senses start out with the same job: converting energy sources from the world into a single, common currency that the brain can use: action potentials. Thus, as we saw in Chapter 5, the mission of the peripheral visual system is to convert (or *transduce*) photons into electrical signals. In this chapter, we saw that the outer, middle, and inner ear collaborate to convert vibrations in the density of the air into electrical signals. Receptors on the skin and in the body allow the somatosensory system to convert pressure, temperature, and noxious chemicals into electrical signals. The nose converts drifting odor molecules and the gustatory system converts tastants. Just as in a country with visitors from all over the world, the foreign money must be translated into a common currency before meaningful transactions can take place.

From these sensory receptors, the signals project to the primary sensory cortex, where they are mapped in a way that is consistent with the layout of the receptors. For example, the visual system uses a retinotopic map, such that neighboring parts of the cortex respond to adjacent points on the retina. Hearing uses a tonotopic map to place the neural activity associated with one frequency close to the activity associated with a slightly different frequency. For the somatosensory system, we learned about the homunculus, which provides a somatotopic map of the body. The chemical senses of taste and smell seem to be an exception to this mapping, instead recognizing slightly different patterns of activity rather than activity at one particular location. Beyond these primary areas, we found that there are additional areas, known as secondary or tertiary cortices, which process more elaborate features of the sensory stimulus.

The brain is multisensory and is striking in its ability to integrate information across different sensory modalities. The binding problem refers to how the brain is able to produce a unified picture of the world, given its specialized processing streams from different senses. The massive interconnectivity of the brain's networks is at the heart of the solution to the binding problem. The final perception of a unified world depends on the coordination between sensory inputs and on the brain's expectations.

Time perception is a critically important sense that involves all of the other senses. Given that different types of sensory input are processed at different speeds by different neural architectures, the brain faces a significant challenge in synchronizing information and integrating input. We saw in this chapter that the sensory systems must "come to agreement" with one another. This process takes time, and as a result our final perceptions of the moment "now" lag behind reality. Future research will provide greater insights into the brain's ability to integrate input from multiple senses to construct a unified perception of the world in which we live.

KEY PRINCIPLES

- Different sensory systems share common principles of operation: receptors transduce data into electrical signals.

- Primary sensory areas are surrounded by neighboring regions of cortex (secondary and tertiary) that process information at successive levels of abstraction—that is, from specific details (e.g., tones) to general (your favorite song).

- What we perceive as sound are pressure fluctuations in the air that strike the eardrum and cause it to vibrate at the same frequency. These vibrations ultimately are passed to the basilar membrane, where they are transduced into a neural signal.

- Most sensory systems, other than the chemical senses, use labeled lines to convey information to the brain. In this system, each individual neuron carries information from just one aspect of one sense. For hearing, a neuron would carry only information about a particular frequency; for vision, a neuron would transmit information from just one part of the visual field.

- Somatosensation refers to the sensory feedback we receive from all over our body. Types of somatosensation include touch, temperature, pain, proprioception (body position in space), and sensory feedback from our internal organs.

- The chemical senses of taste and smell detect and respond to stimuli based on their chemical properties. They encode information not using labeled lines or as a map, but instead as patterns of cortical activation.

- The brain is multisensory and attempts to integrate information from the different senses in an optimal manner. This integration sometimes goes beyond the norm, as is the case for synesthesia. Researchers are studying the binding problem to try to understand how the brain integrates information about one object from the different sensory systems, such as when you hear and see something fly past your head and recognize that the shape, sound, color, and movement all are part of the same object.

- Our sense of time perception encompasses the other senses. Different types of sensory input are processed at different speeds by different neural networks. The brain faces the challenge of integrating this input and constructing a unified perception of time. Researchers are just starting to consider how best to study this temporal integration.

KEY TERMS

Detecting Data from the World
olfactory bulb (p. 165)

Hearing
amplitude (p. 166)
pitch (p. 166)
loudness (p. 166)
just-noticeable difference (p. 166)
Weber's law (p. 166)
pinna (p. 167)
tympanic membrane (p. 167)
middle ear (p. 167)
ossicles (p. 167)
malleus (p. 167)
incus (p. 167)
stapes (p. 167)
oval window (p. 167)
cochlea (p. 168)
basilar membrane (p. 168)
inner hair cells (p. 168)
organ of Corti (p. 169)
outer hair cells (p. 169)
tectorial membrane (p. 169)

auditory nerve (cochlear nerve) (p. 170)
labeled line (p. 170)
interaural differences (p. 172)
vestibular system (p. 173)
semicircular canals (p. 173)
vestibulo-ocular reflexes (p. 173)

The Somatosensory System
somatosensory system (p. 174)
mechanoreceptors (p. 174)
Meissner's corpuscles (p. 174)
Merkel's disks (p. 174)
Pacinian corpuscles (p. 174)
Ruffini's endings (p. 174)
thermoreceptors (p. 175)
nociceptors (p. 175)
mutations (p. 176)
proprioception (p. 177)
muscle spindles (p. 177)
Golgi tendon organ (p. 177)
interoception (p. 177)
chemoreceptors (p. 177)
gate control theory (p. 178)
neuropathic pain (p. 178)

dorsal root (p. 179)
decussates (p. 179)
ventral posterior nucleus (p. 179)
secondary somatosensory cortex (p. 179)

Chemical Senses
taste buds (p. 180)
papillae (p. 180)
umami (p. 180)
frontal operculum (p. 182)
olfaction (p. 183)
olfactory epithelium (p. 183)
olfactory glomerulus (p. 184)
pheromones (p. 185)
vomeronasal organ (p. 185)

The Brain Is Multisensory
synesthesia (p. 186)
McGurk effect (p. 188)
anosognosia (p. 189)

Time Perception
feature binding (p. 191)

REVIEW QUESTIONS

1. What is the function of the pinna? Why do people move around and cock their heads when they can't find the source of a sound?

2. Why is the cochlea of the inner ear small at one end and larger at the other? How is this critical to its function?

3. Name four types of sensation that fall under the umbrella term of touch and describe how their information is carried to the brain.

4. How does the gustatory system detect molecules in the food you eat?

5. For vision, hearing, touch, taste, and smell, give an example of a specific stimulus that is encoded in primary sensory cortex and a more abstract stimulus that is encoded in neighboring, higher-level cortical areas.

6. What is synesthesia, and what does its neural basis appear to be?

7. What is the modality appropriateness hypothesis?

8. Why might schizophrenia and dyslexia be considered disorders of time perception?

CRITICAL-THINKING QUESTIONS

1. What types of deficits would you expect to see in a patient whose process of labeled line coding is malfunctioning in the auditory system and the somatosensory system? Give examples. What does this reveal about the importance of the labeled line coding approach? Explain.

2. Why do you think that incoming information is not encoded as maps for the senses of taste and touch, as it is for the senses of vision and hearing? Explain.

3. In addition to the research focus on the properties of recurrent networks, what other approaches do you think should be used to gain insights into the binding problem? What are the critical questions that scientists should ask? What insights will the answers to such questions give us on the integration of functions in the human brain? Explain.

- Describe the structure of muscle tissue and the mechanism by which motor action potentials cause muscular contractions.

- Explain how spinal reflex arcs and central pattern generators produce simple movements.

- Identify the structure and functions of the cerebellum.

- Characterize the classically recognized organization of the motor cortex and how newer findings call this organization into question.

- Identify the functional organization of the prefrontal cortex in motor control.

- Clarify the role of sensory feedback in motor control at all levels of the nervous system.

- Distinguish the two types of circuitry in the basal ganglia.

- Explain the five commonly recognized functions performed by basal ganglia–cortical loops.

- Contrast the different contributions of medial and lateral prefrontal systems to motor control.

- Characterize what the study of neuroscience has revealed about the difference between voluntary and involuntary actions.

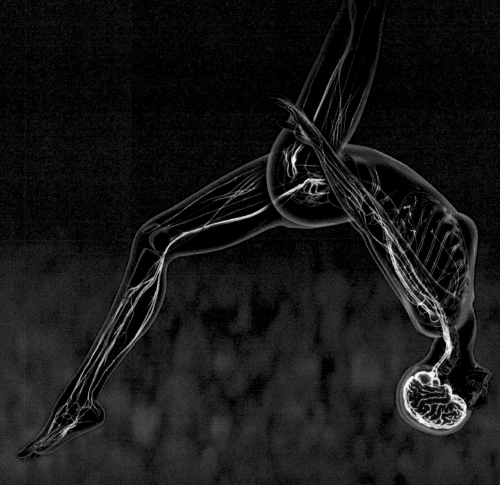

The Motor System

STARTING OUT
"Locked-In Syndrome"

In 1995, just a few days before New Year's Eve, a man awoke to find himself in the hospital. With his first attempts to raise himself from the bed, he realized that something was very wrong. Try as he might, he was almost completely unable to move. His arms and legs no longer responded to his brain's commands. He could not so much as raise a finger. Worse yet, when he tried to speak, his lips and tongue would not budge. He could not make a sound: not to cry out for help, not to ask what had happened, not even to let anyone know he was awake. Although his consciousness was intact, he was effectively "locked inside" an almost completely immobile body.

The man's name was Jean-Dominique Bauby. He was 43 years old. Before his hospitalization, he had been a successful and vivacious journalist who had risen to become the editor in chief of *Elle* magazine in France. Then, without warning, he had suffered a stroke affecting his brainstem. He had lain in a coma for 20 days, his recovery uncertain. Once he was restored to consciousness, no one could say for certain whether some motor functions might return or whether he was destined to remain trapped in an immobile body for the rest of his life. All these details he learned, over time, from the team of neurologists, nurses, and physiotherapists who attended his recovery. Since his senses remained intact, his medical team could

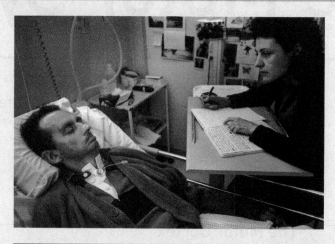

FIGURE 7.1 **Locked-in syndrome.** After suffering a stroke in the brainstem, the consciousness of the author Jean-Dominique Bauby remained intact, but his body was almost entirely immobile. He wrote *The Diving Bell and the Butterfly* by dictating it to his physiotherapist through eye blinks.

communicate with him without difficulty (Bauby, 2008).

But how did he communicate with them? How do we know what he experienced over the months and years that followed his accident? The bodily pains and itches he could still experience, but do nothing to address? The flights of imagination and reminiscence he used to keep his mind entertained? The private moments of joy, and amusement, and shame, and dejection? How did we learn that inside his deteriorating body remained the same lively and playful personality that had existed before his injury?

The answer is that he told us. Before he fell ill, he had signed a contract with a publisher to write a book about his remarkable life. After the stroke, and despite being

locked in, he resolved to complete the book anyway (FIGURE 7.1). He had found that one part of his body still responded to commands: his left eyelid. Blinking became his communication line to the outside world. His physiotherapist printed the alphabet on a large card. She, or his friends and family, could move a finger along the card from letter to letter. He would blink when the finger reached the appropriate letter. Using this code, he could slowly construct words and sentences (Bauby, 2008).

Each day he would mentally compose and review another few paragraphs of his memoirs before "dictating" them to his physiotherapist, blink by blink, at 2 minutes per word. Two hundred thousand blinks later, he succeeded in completing his book, which he titled *The*

Diving Bell and the Butterfly. The "diving bell" was his body, immobile as if crushed under tremendous pressures; the "butterfly" was his imagination, free to travel where it pleased. The book itself became a tremendous success worldwide and was later made into a successful film of the same name. Tragically, the author himself passed away a mere 2 days after the book's publication in 1997.

He had been locked in for nearly 15 months.

Despite being almost disconnected from the outside world, Jean-Dominique Bauby ultimately managed to communicate with an audience of millions of people. His story is compelling because it reminds us of how much we take our able bodies for granted. The intrinsic wonder of being able to walk, or speak, or even scratch an itch all too often escapes our notice. We fail to appreciate the true importance of our motor functions until they are lost. The memoirs of M. Bauby beautifully illustrate how motor functions are essential for even the simplest facets of everyday life. In this chapter, we will discover how the brain accomplishes the easily overlooked but all-important function of controlling our movements.

Muscles

Why don't plants have neurons? The simplest answer is that their daily survival does not require movement, and so they do not have muscles that require control signals. For a human being, or almost any other animal, the situation is different. Survival means locating, capturing, and/or consuming other organisms, and so movement is essential to life itself. Seen from this point of view, movements are the ultimate ends of most of the activities of the human brain: seeing, hearing, navigating, setting goals and strategies, learning, remembering. Speech is the controlled movement of the vocal apparatus to produce vibrations in the air. Even vision involves carefully adjusting the contractions of the six muscles that point each eye at the most relevant regions of the surrounding environment. Skeletal muscles are the means through which the brain manipulates the external environment. Hence, we'll begin our tour of the motor system with a look at the muscles themselves.

Skeletal Muscle: Structure and Function

The human body contains around 640 skeletal muscles, which collectively form the largest single organ in the body. Muscles attach to the skeleton at an origin (the structure that remains in position during contraction) and an insertion (the structure that moves during contraction). Each individual muscle contains a collection of **muscle fibers**, arranged into bundles known as fascicles (FIGURE 7.2). The strength of a muscle depends on the cross-sectional area of its fibers, whereas the contraction speed of the muscle depends on the length of the fibers. Each muscle fiber in turn is a fusion of many embryonic muscle precursors (called

myoblasts) into a single, multinucleated cell. The muscle fiber contains a bundle of smaller **myofibrils**, each of which contains a series of sarcomeres, the basic functional unit of a muscle fiber, attached end to end.

The muscle also has proprioceptive (or "position sense") organs to provide sensory feedback to the nervous system about its contraction and load. First, muscle spindles, or "stretch receptors," are tiny bundles of muscle fibers, buried deep within muscles, surrounded by coiled sensory axons sensitive to changes in length. As the muscle stretches or contracts, the sensory neurons detect these changes and convey this information to the central nervous system. Second, sensory receptors called Golgi tendon organs resemble spindles in some ways, except that their axons are located in the tendon and oriented perpendicular to the muscle body. Tendon stretch reflects muscle tension, so the Golgi tendon organs detect the amount of strain, or load, on the muscle.

Muscles that work in opposing pairs are called **antagonistic muscles**. For example, your biceps and triceps work in opposition: to extend your arm, your triceps contracts and your biceps relaxes. To produce the opposite effect, the biceps contracts and triceps relaxes. **Extensors**, such as the triceps, extend a joint, whereas **flexors**, such as the biceps, contract it.

There are different types of muscle fibers in the body, each specialized for a different type of activity. **Type I fibers** (also known as red or slow-twitch fibers) are specialized for endurance at the expense of power and speed, whereas **type II fibers** (also known as white or fast-twitch fibers) are specialized for speed and power, at the cost of being quickly fatigued. Type II fibers are sometimes divided into subcategories, some of which have intermediate properties balancing endurance with speed and power.

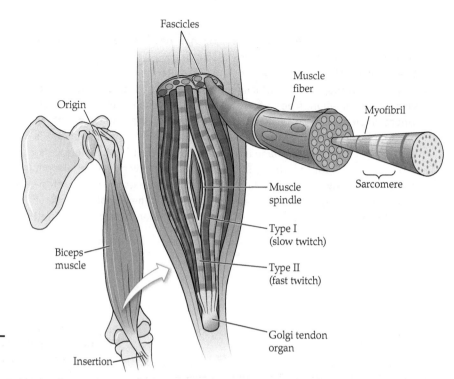

FIGURE 7.2 **The major structures of a skeletal muscle.**

The Neuromuscular Junction

Motor neurons make contact with muscle fibers at a specialized structure called the neuromuscular junction (FIGURE 7.3), which in many ways resembles a synapse between two neurons. The axon of a motor neuron ends in a flattened bulb or motor neuron terminal, which is analogous to the presynaptic axon terminal at a connection between two neurons. The so-called endplate on the muscle fiber is analogous to the postsynaptic cell membrane of a neuron. The terminal and endplate membranes are separated by a narrow space, much like a neuron-to-neuron synapse.

The key neurotransmitter of the neuromuscular junction is acetylcholine. Motor neuron terminals are filled with vesicles, each containing around 10,000 molecules of acetylcholine, awaiting release into the synapse. When an action potential is generated at the axon hillock of a lower motor neuron, which is found in the spinal cord, it propagates down the axon and reaches the motor neuron terminal. This causes voltage-gated calcium channels to open and calcium ions to flow into the presynaptic terminal. This activates a cascade of interacting proteins, which results in vesicles fusing with the presynaptic membrane and releasing their contents into the space between the terminal and the endplate. The newly released acetylcholine molecules bind to fast-responding ionotropic acetylcholine receptors on the endplate. This causes a depolarization called the miniature end-plate potential.

If enough miniature end-plate potentials sum together, they can activate voltage-gated ion channels on the muscle fiber membrane. The resulting depolarization prompts a release of calcium, which, in turn, activates the process by which myosin filaments ratchet their way up the actin filaments to produce a muscle fiber contraction (FIGURE 7.3a). Meanwhile, at the neuromuscular junction, the released acetylcholine is broken down by an enzyme in the synaptic cleft, called **acetylcholinesterase**, to clear the way for the next contraction.

Blocking acetylcholine neurotransmission can weaken or completely paralyze muscles. In surgical procedures, the anesthetist may administer a muscle-relaxing agent called rocuronium to keep the patient's muscles from contracting during intubation or the surgery itself. Rocuronium and other medications of its type block the binding of acetylcholine to its receptors on the muscle fiber endplate (FIGURE 7.3b), preventing muscle contraction even if the motor neurons fire (Hunter, 1996). They are actually derived from the active ingredient of **curare**, a toxin found in certain South American plants and traditionally used by local hunter-gatherers in poison arrows for hunting. When a curare-poisoned arrow strikes an animal, it paralyzes the skeletal muscles so that the animal cannot move. However, as long as respiration can be maintained, the paralysis eventually resolves with no lasting adverse effects (Griffith & Johnson, 1942). As these properties were discovered, curare-derived compounds began to be used in surgery in the 1940s.

Some diseases also produce weakness via effects at the neuromuscular junction. Myasthenia gravis is an autoimmune disease in which antibodies bind to the acetylcholine receptors, blocking neurotransmission and ultimately causing the receptors to be consumed faster than they can be produced. This leads to fluctuating and progressive weakness, particularly in the muscles of the eye. One treatment for this

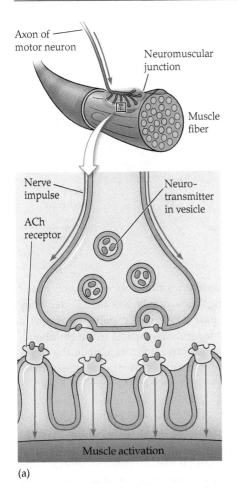

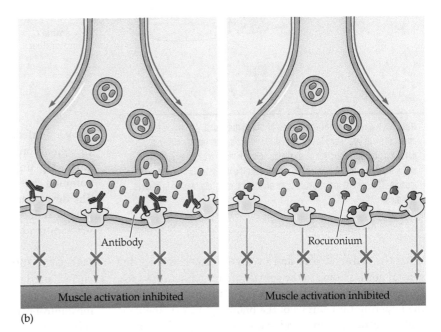

(a)

(b)

disease uses acetylcholinesterase inhibitors, which increase acetylcholine levels by blocking the enzyme that clears acetylcholine from the neuromuscular junction. This helps to increase signaling at the remaining receptors and restore muscle contraction strength.

Another neuromuscular blocker, botulinum toxin, is the most potent neurotoxin currently known. Produced by the anaerobic bacterium *Clostridium botulinum* (which may grow in poorly sterilized canned meat), it acts at the motor nerve terminal to prevent vesicles of acetylcholine from fusing with the presynaptic membrane. As a result, motor neurons cannot release acetylcholine and paralysis results, with death typically from asphyxiation. Therapeutic uses have been discovered for botulinum toxin as a cosmetic agent (known popularly by the brand name "Botox"). Minute doses of the toxin can reduce the appearance of skin wrinkles by paralyzing the underlying facial muscles.

Other medical uses of botulinum toxin lie in relieving muscle spasms in conditions such as strabismus (crossed eyes) and torticollis (a severe and chronic spasm of the neck muscles) or in muscle spasms resulting from other neurological disorders such as multiple sclerosis or cerebral palsy. These spasms are typically the result of overactive spinal reflexes in the spinal cord, whose circuitry can control some surprisingly complex forms of movement. In the next section, we will look at how this circuitry operates.

FIGURE 7.3 **The neuromuscular junction.** (a) The microscopic structure of the neuromuscular junction. (b) In myasthenia gravis, antibodies block the receptor for the neurotransmitter acetylcholine, weakening the muscular contractions. The neuromuscular-blocking medication rocuronium also blocks the acetylcholine receptor, and it is sometimes used to relax the body's musculature during surgery.

The Spinal Cord

Within the spinal cord, the neurons that project out to the periphery to control the muscles of the body are grouped together and organized. These lower motor neurons are important for simple, reflexive movement as well as more elaborate rhythmic movements generated by spinal motor circuits. Although these reflexes and rhythmic movements are themselves important behaviors, the activity of these lower motor neurons is influenced by descending motor control pathways from the brain, allowing simple movements to be grouped together into complex voluntary movements.

Lower Motor Neurons

You may recall from Chapter 2 that the spinal cord consists of an outer white matter and an inner gray matter. The gray

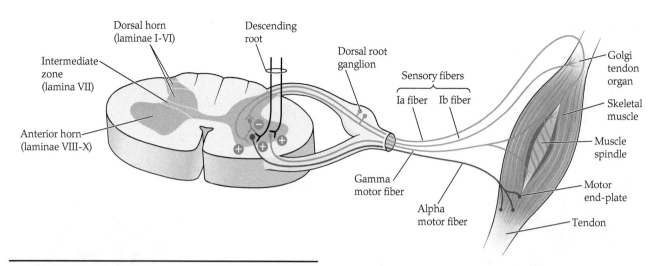

FIGURE 7.4 Lower motor neurons of the spinal cord. Alpha and gamma motor neurons are found in the ventral horns of the gray matter of the spinal cord. A motor unit consists of all the muscle fibers innervated by a single alpha motor neuron. A motor pool includes all the motor units of a single muscle. The gamma motor neurons innervate and maintain tension in muscle spindles.

matter has a **dorsal horn** and a ventral or anterior horn. The ventral horn is home to the spinal cord motor neurons (also known as **lower motor neurons** to distinguish them from the upper motor neurons of the brain, FIGURE 7.4). The large **alpha motor neurons** send axons out through the peripheral nervous system to the muscles. These terminate at the neuromuscular junction to stimulate contractions in the muscle fibers of skeletal muscle, which result in bodily movements. Smaller **gamma motor neurons** maintain tension in tiny muscle fibers inside the muscle spindles. These do not contribute to contracting the muscle mass, but maintain tension so that the muscle spindles can accurately detect the stretch or contraction in the muscle as a whole.

In vertebrates, each muscle fiber within a muscle receives input from one motor neuron. However, a single alpha motor neuron will innervate anywhere between 10 and 1,000 different muscle fibers within a specific muscle. A **motor unit** consists of an alpha motor neuron and all of the muscle fibers it innervates. The more fibers that it innervates, the stronger a contraction it produces when it fires. The motor units that work together within a single muscle are referred to as that muscle's motor unit pool (FIGURE 7.4). Since the number of muscle fibers per motor unit is variable, each motor unit pool can produce a wide range of muscle contraction forces by recruiting different motor units. Motor units are generally recruited from smallest to largest. For weak contractions, the motor pool draws on a small collection of small motor units; for stronger contractions, it can add in the activity of progressively larger motor units. Muscles that need precise control, such as the muscles that position the eye, may have many small motor units to enable fine adjustments of contraction strength.

Viral infections sometimes attack the motor neurons of the spinal cord, causing flaccid paralysis of the affected body parts. Up until the past century, the polio virus was a common cause of motor paralysis, particularly in childhood. The development of an effective polio vaccine in the 1950s greatly reduced the incidence of this disease. Since then, mass immunization programs around the world nearly eradicated the polio virus (Kew, Sutter, de Gourville, Dowdle, & Pallansch, 2005). However, renewed outbreaks have occurred, particularly in conflict-ridden areas of the developing world. Another pathogen, West Nile virus, is a mosquito-borne disease that can damage the ventral horn cells, and extreme cases (accounting for fewer than 1% of cases) cause severe and lasting muscle weakness (Drebot & Artsob, 2005). At present, no available vaccine or specific treatment for West Nile virus exists, and the disease continues to spread around the world.

Spinal Motor Circuits: Reflexes

Many basic forms of motor control rely on circuits through the gray matter of the spinal cord. The simplest example is a **spinal reflex**. For example, if a muscle is stretched suddenly and unexpectedly, it must contract to maintain position. Proprioceptors, such as those in the muscle spindles described above, detect sudden muscle stretch. They then send input along sensory nerves to the spinal cord, where they connect with spinal interneurons in the dorsal horns of the spinal gray matter. These interneurons in turn stimulate alpha motor neurons in the ventral horn. These motor neurons in turn send signals back out to the muscle to stimulate a contraction.

The classic example of this kind of spinal reflex is the **deep tendon reflex** (FIGURE 7.5). A doctor taps a patient below the kneecap with a reflex hammer, stretching the patellar tendon and quadriceps muscle suddenly and unexpectedly. In response, the quadriceps muscle contracts vigorously, producing an involuntary kick of the lower leg. Of course, one difficulty with spinal reflexes is that they would also

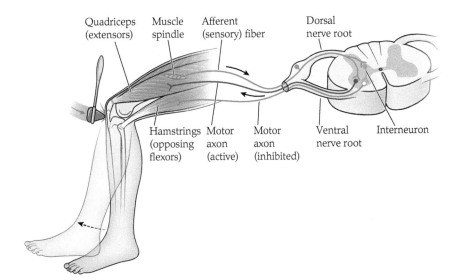

Quadriceps (extensors) Muscle spindle Afferent (sensory) fiber Dorsal nerve root

Hamstrings (opposing flexors) Motor axon (active) Motor axon (inhibited) Ventral nerve root Interneuron

FIGURE 7.5 The neural circuitry of a deep tendon reflex. Striking the tendon stretches the muscle spindle in the attached muscle, sending a sensory signal via the dorsal root ganglion to the spinal cord. After crossing an interneuron, the signal returns to the muscle to trigger a counterbalancing contraction. An inhibitory efferent signal also relaxes the opposing muscle to prevent another stretch reflex from occurring.

counteract any deliberate movements desired by the organism unless they can be turned off. As it turns out, motor neurons also have outgoing connections to inhibitory interneurons, so that as they contract one muscle, they can allow the opponent muscle to relax without triggering its own spinal stretch reflex.

What happens if the inhibitory feedback mechanism is lost? This is precisely what occurs in lethal conditions such as strychnine poisoning or tetanus. Strychnine is a potent neurotoxin that blocks the inhibitory neurotransmitter receptors on the motor neurons. The result of systemic strychnine is a severe spasm of every muscle in the body, including the muscles of respiration, resulting in death by asphyxiation (Sugimoto, Bennett, & Kajander, 1990). The anaerobic bacterium *Clostridium tetani* also produces a potent toxin, tetanospasmin, which prevents the release of inhibitory neurotransmitter, with similarly lethal effects (Cook, Protheroe, & Handel, 2001). The tetanus bacterium lives in soil and can enter the body through contaminated wounds. Before the 20th century, tetanus was a common cause of death in wounded individuals. Today, we prevent tetanus through regular immunizations every 10 years in adults. The immunizations contain tiny doses of inactivated tetanus toxin, enabling the immune system to recognize and inactivate the toxin before it can cause damage.

Spinal Motor Circuits: Central Pattern Generators

As we saw in Chapter 2, at the beginning of the 20th century, the British physiologist Sir Charles Sherrington speculated that spinal reflexes alone might be able to drive complex forms of movement such as walking or swallowing (Sherrington, 1900). Shortly afterward, his student T. Graham

Brown found that the spinal cord could still generate simple walking movements in a cat on a treadmill, even if the brainstem was cut to isolate the spinal cord from all descending input from the brain (Brown & Sherrington, 1912). He proposed that the spinal cord neurons formed central pattern generators for the rhythmic movements of walking (FIGURE 7.6) (Brown, 1911).

More recently, neuroscientists have begun to identify the spinal circuitry of the central pattern generators for locomotion (Goulding, 2009; Kiehn, 2006). The rhythmical activity necessary for walking can be found in excitatory spinal interneurons lying between the dorsal and ventral horns. These excite alpha motor neurons to produce muscular contractions. However, as they fire, they also gradually excite local, inhibitory interneurons. These inhibitory neurons project back to the originally excitatory interneurons, so that as they fire, they eventually turn themselves off. After a period of inactivity, they then begin to fire again, so that an oscillating rhythm of activity results. Multiple circuits of this type exist at different segments of the spinal cord. By working together, they can drive multiple groups of muscles for complete rhythmical movements. Interneurons travel across segments to connect these pattern generators, so that activity in one will then drive activity in the next, and the next, and so on. The result is a chain of repeating activation traveling down the spinal cord, like the flashing lights running along the border of a marquee sign in an old movie theater.

In most species, locomotion requires alternating rather than simultaneous movements of the left and right sides of the body. So there are also inhibitory interneurons that cross the midline of the spinal cord between one set of rhythm-generating neurons and the other. This ensures that the activity of each side alternates: when one is on, the other is off. Molecules in the developing spinal cord guide the axons of these inhibitory neurons across the midline

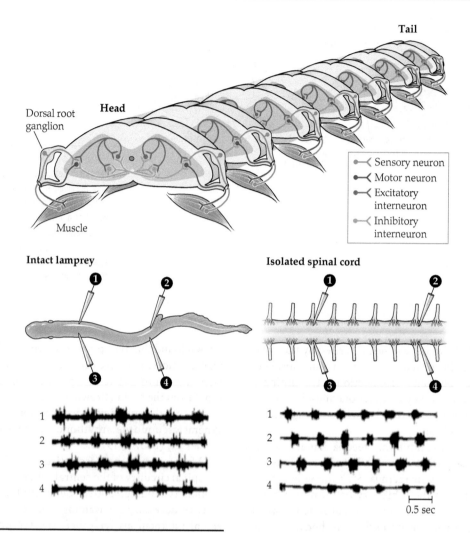

FIGURE 7.6 Spinal motor pattern generator circuits. Central pattern generator circuits in each segment of the spinal cord create naturally oscillating, alternating rhythms of activity that can be used to drive alternating movements of each side of the body. Each segment fires just a little after the one anterior to it, so that waves of alternating activity pass down along the body to drive locomotion.

(Kullander et al., 2003). Mice that have lost the genes for producing these molecules lose the alternating pattern of activity on each side of the spinal cord. These mice have abnormal locomotion: rather than walking with alternating steps, they actually hop like rabbits (Yokoyama et al., 2001)!

Descending Pathways of Motor Control

In some animal species, such as fish, local spinal cord circuits and central pattern generators are capable of performing many functions on their own, without much guidance from the brain. In humans, descending motor control pathways are much more important, and their loss in spinal cord injury causes motor paralysis. There are actually many different motor control pathways in the spinal cord, each with slightly different connections and functions.

The most important pathway in humans is the **cortico-spinal tract**, which contains axons that travel down from the **upper motor neurons** of the primary motor cortex and connect to the lower motor neurons of the spinal cord. This enormous white matter tract passes down through the internal capsule and cerebral peduncles and then along the anterior surface of the brainstem (**FIGURE 7.7**). This pathway is often injured in **cerebral palsy**, a crippling condition in which the brain is injured through bleeding or other processes occurring during pregnancy, birth, or infancy. As a result, inhibitory cortical input from the motor system cannot reach the spinal cord, and so spastic contractions of the muscles occur, interfering with normal movements.

At the level of the medulla, the descending axon bundles of the corticospinal tract are called the **pyramids** (because of their triangular appearance in cross-section). This is the point at which axons cross over to the contralateral (opposite) side of the body, so that the right hemisphere ends up controlling the left side of the body and vice versa. The region where the crossing takes place is called the pyramidal decussation. About 80% of the axons cross at this point and form

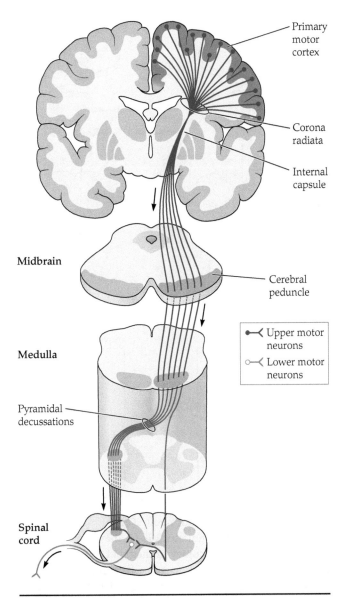

Primary
motor
cortex

Corona
radiata

Internal
capsule

Midbrain

Cerebral
peduncle

Medulla

● ◄ Upper motor
    neurons
○ ◄ Lower motor
    neurons

Pyramidal
decussations

Spinal
cord

FIGURE 7.7 **The corticospinal tract.** The corticospinal tract travels from the upper motor neurons of the primary motor cortex down through the corona radiata and the internal capsule, through the cerebral peduncles, crossing over the opposite side of the body at the pyramidal decussastions, and then continuing down the spinal cord to the lower motor neurons.

regions of the brain can have devastating effects. Locked-in patients, such as Jean-Dominique Bauby, typically have suffered an injury to the medulla at the level of the pyramids. Since virtually all motor output passes through the pyramidal decussation, a stroke here can produce near-total paralysis. In some cases the musculature of the eyes is spared, because the cranial nerves that control these muscles exit the brainstem above the pyramidal decussation (Hopper, Fisher, & Kleinman, 1979).

Although the corticospinal tract is the most important motor pathway for fine motor control in humans, we also retain many other motor pathways (FIGURE 7.8), whose role in other species is more important (Lemon, 2008). For example, the rubrospinal tract sends input from the **red nuclei** of the brainstem to control movements of the limbs, particularly of the muscles such as the biceps and quadriceps. This pathway may expand its role after stroke or other injury to the corticospinal tract to aid in recovery of limb motor functions (Takenobu et al., 2013). The **vestibular nuclei** of the brainstem send inputs to the spinal cord via the vestibulospinal tract. These inputs are important for coordinating balance movements of the head, neck, trunk, and proximal limbs. The tectospinal tract sends inputs from the spatial-localizing systems of the midbrain's **tectum** to the spinal cord to help coordinate movements for capturing or avoiding moving targets in the surrounding environment. The tectospinal circuitry is an important motor control system in some animals, such as in frogs who are attempting to catch insects in midair. In humans, its functions have been largely taken over by circuits in the cortex and corticospinal tract (Dicke, Roth, & Matsushima, 1999; Sklavos, Anastasopoulos, & Bronstein, 2010). Finally, the reticulospinal tract sends input from the brainstem reticular formation to the spinal cord. It is important in coordinating startle and escape reflexes.

Of course, in humans, the most elaborate forms of motor control rely on the extensive motor circuitry of the cerebrum, basal ganglia, and cerebellum. To understand how actions and behaviors arise, we will now need to look above the spinal cord to examine the workings of these large and complex structures. This is the subject of the following sections.

the **lateral corticospinal tract**. The remaining 20% do not cross at the pyramidal decussation; these axons form the ventral corticospinal tract. About half of these (10% of the total) cross lower down, at the point at which they exit the ventral horn of the spinal cord. The rest of the axons remain ipsilateral: on the same side of the body. If spared, these uncrossed connections can be important for recovering motor functions in paralyzed parts of the body after a brain injury such as a stroke or trauma (Gerloff et al., 1998; Small, Hlustik, Noll, Genovese, & Solodkin, 2002).

Note that because the entire motor output of the cortex passes through "bottlenecks" at the pyramids, injury to these

The Cerebellum

The cerebellum is an intriguing organ. Although it occupies less than a tenth of the total volume of the nervous system, it contains more neurons than all the other structures combined (Schlaug, 2001). Even in humans, its neurons outnumber those of the cortex. At the same time, it is an old organ in evolutionary terms. Much older than the cortex, it is present in most vertebrate species, including all mammals, reptiles, birds, and amphibians and all but a few species of fish. It packs an enormous surface area into a densely folded

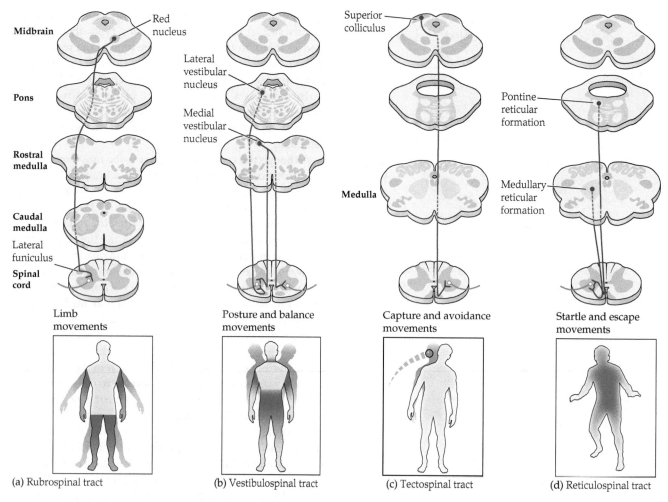

(a) Rubrospinal tract

(b) Vestibulospinal tract

(c) Tectospinal tract

(d) Reticulospinal tract

FIGURE 7.8 Noncorticospinal motor control pathways. (a) The rubro-spinal tract. (b) The vestibulospinal tract. (c) The tectospinal tract. (d) The reticulospinal tract.

structure of lobes, each made up of smaller lobules, which in turn fold into even smaller folia (Latin, "leaves") (FIGURE 7.9).

The cerebellum has long been known to have important functions in motor coordination. As early as 1824, the French physiologist Jean Pierre Flourens noted that destruction of the cerebellum interfered with the regularity and coordination of movement (Pearce, 2009). Today, commonly recognized symptoms of cerebellar injury include impairments in the coordination, rhythm, magnitude, accuracy, and timing of movements in various parts of the body. For example, if asked to reach out and touch a moving object, patients may overshoot or undershoot the target, point too far to the right or left, or point along a wobbly path. This is sometimes called an intention tremor: an overshooting to the left and right during movement, as patients attempt to compensate for previous errors.

Patients with cerebellar injury may also have difficulty performing rapid alternating movements of the hands or feet, such as tapping the front and then the back of the hand on a surface over and over, although they have no such problems in performing continuous (nonalternating) tapping movements (Schmahmann, 2004). They may have similar problems with the accuracy of the rapid eye movements (or **saccades**) needed to follow a visual target. In addition, they may have difficulty maintaining balance while they stand or walk, adopting a wide-based gait in compensation. If pulled off balance, they may make excessive or insufficient compensating movements and fall over. Their speech may be similarly uncoordinated, with slurring and irregular fluctuations in rate, rhythm, and volume (Schmahmann, 2004). Note that many of these features of cerebellar injury can also be seen in cases of alcohol intoxication. As it turns out, relatively small amounts of alcohol can impair the delicate computations of cerebellar function before having obvious effects in other areas of the brain.

The Circuitry of the Cerebellum

At the microscopic level, the folded sheet of **cerebellar cortex** has a remarkably uniform circuitry throughout. It has three layers: an inner granule cell layer, packed with tiny neurons that make up most of the cerebellar population; a middle Purkinje cell layer, composed of a single thin layer of the large Purkinje cells that integrate information from the

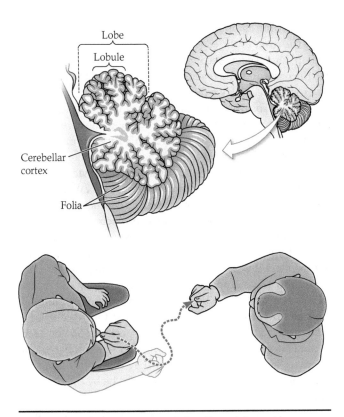

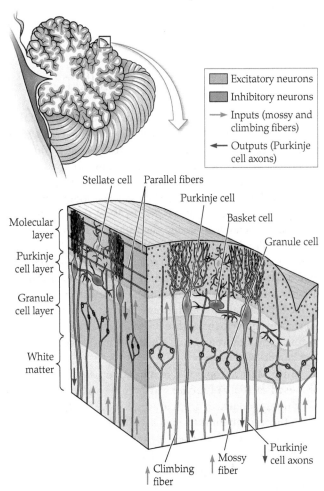

FIGURE 7.9 **Macroanatomy of the cerebellum.** The cerebellum contains as many neurons as the entire cortex. Its gray matter is densely packed into leaflike folia, which themselves are grouped into larger lobules and lobes. It is responsible for smoothness and accuracy of movements. Lesions of the cerebellum cause overshooting and overcorrection of movements, resulting in wobbly movement trajectories.

FIGURE 7.10 **The microscopic circuitry of the cerebellum.** The connection patterns of the neurons in this cerebellar circuit are repeated over and over again, like a motif, in a "crystalline" fashion throughout the cerebellar cortex.

other neurons and send output back to the rest of the nervous system, and an outer molecular cell layer: a communication zone filled with the axons of the granule cells, the dendrites of Purkinje cells, and various forms of small interneurons (FIGURE 7.10).

The Purkinje cells provide all of the output from the cerebellum. Their axons send inhibitory output to the deep cerebellar nuclei and vestibular nuclei in the brainstem. Neurons in these nuclei, in turn, send excitatory outputs caudally to the spinal cord and rostrally to the thalamus and from there to the widespread areas of cortex. These outputs allow the cerebellum to fine-tune the motor activity of both the lower motor neurons of the spinal cord and the upper motor neurons of the cortex. They also exert a similar influence on non-motor cortex, as we will see below.

There are two main sources of input to the cerebellum. The first comes from the **mossy fibers**. These arise from multiple sources throughout the nervous system, including the cortex and spinal cord, brainstem nuclei, and vestibular system. These provide excitatory input to the granule cells, which in turn send excitatory input upward to the molecular cell layer, forming parallel fibers. These parallel fibers pass through the enormous dendritic trees of multiple Purkinje cells, providing weak, continuous excitatory input. Golgi cells form connections from the parallel fibers back to the

granule cells. The Golgi cells are inhibitory, providing negative feedback signals to the local and neighboring granule cells. This feedback inhibition helps to sharpen the granule cells' responses both in terms of timing and in terms of spatial extent.

The second source of cerebellar input is from the **climbing fibers**. These arise from the inferior olivary nucleus, which is the cerebellum's main input nucleus (Sotelo, Llinas, & Baker, 1974). Climbing fibers wrap around the Purkinje cells near the cell body and axon rather than the dendrites, providing powerful excitatory input that varies in time to modulate Purkinje cell activity.

Several types of interneurons complete the circuitry of the cerebellum. **Basket cells** and **stellate cells** lie in the molecular layer. Like the parallel fibers, these cells also send connections across multiple Purkinje cells. However, these are **lateral inhibitory connections**, and they run perpendicular to the excitatory parallel fibers. Basket cells wrap around the Purkinje cell bodies, whereas stellate cells thread their more subtle connections through the Purkinje cell dendrites.

Motor Functions of the Cerebellum

The remarkably consistent and well-mapped circuitry of the cerebellum suggests that it performs a specific computational function on its inputs and outputs. What could this function be? For the past 40 years, various computational models have been proposed to account for the functions of the cerebellum in motor coordination and motor learning (Wolpert, Miall, & Kawato, 1998). In 1969, the British neuroscientist David Marr made the influential proposal that the cerebellum's Purkinje cells adjust their synaptic connections so as to associate particular actions with the context in which they are performed (Marr, 1969). Once this learning process is complete, the context alone can cause the Purkinje cell to fire. This allows one movement to provide the context for the next movement, and so on, so that the brain can learn to link simple movements into more complex, coordinated movement sequences.

Since Marr's proposal, a number of other theories have proposed cerebellar functions in learning and coordinating the timing, sequence, or accuracy of movements. Many of these theories attempt to match the microscopic architecture of the cerebellum itself to a specific mathematical or computational function, such as a particular kind of filter function or learning algorithm. At present, no consensus has emerged as to which of these theories best captures the role of the cerebellum in motor control.

One attractive proposal is that the cerebellum performs forward modeling to fine-tune motor control (Desmurget & Grafton, 2000). The concept of forward modeling arose in engineering, in situations in which a time delay prevents instantaneous travel of input and output signals from a controller to the device it controls (Desmurget & Grafton, 2000). Imagine, for example, that we are trying to pilot a moon rover by remote control from a station on the Earth. The difficulty is that, even at the speed of light, the video signal from the rover takes nearly 2 seconds to reach our viewscreen. Our outgoing radio control signals would take

as much time again to reach the rover. If we are trying to drive the rover to the edge of a crater, we would need to send a "stop" signal a few seconds in advance. If we wait until we see the rover actually reach the edge, it will be too late—the rover will already have fallen in by the time our stop signal reaches it. To avoid this catastrophe, we need a forward model that will predict ahead of time where the rover will be by the time our signal gets there. This forward model will apply to both the sensory inputs (showing us where the rover will be, as opposed to where it was when the video signals were generated) and the motor outputs (calibrated to what the rover will be doing when the signals get there).

In fact, the brain faces a similar problem in controlling movements (FIGURE 7.11). If you need to catch a fast-moving baseball, you need to steer your hand not to where the ball is, but to where it will be by the time your hand gets there. To complicate the picture, it takes time for sensory and motor signals to travel along the nerves between your brain and your hand. The delay is actually different for every muscle used to steer your arm into a catching position! So you need to send "stop" and "start" signals to your muscles based not on where your sensory nerves say they were a few milliseconds ago, but on where they are going to be by the time the signals get there!

Patients with cerebellar injury often have great difficulty following moving targets with any part of their body (Schmahmann, 2004). The cerebellum may be the brain's forward model for motor guidance. Building a forward model requires both sensory and motor connections. In keeping with this requirement, the cerebellum has massive input from both the sensory and the motor regions of the cortex. These connections provide the necessary information for guiding smooth, accurate movements in relation to the constantly changing outside world. Whether the cerebellum actually functions in this way remains to be determined.

Nonmotor Functions of the Cerebellum

Classically, the cerebellum was considered purely a motor control structure, and neurological tests of cerebellar function tend to focus on motor symptoms: balance, coordination, rhythmical movement, smooth pursuit movements. Yet in

FIGURE 7.11 Forward modeling. (a) When trying to touch a moving object, you will miss the object if you steer your hand toward its current location, which will be out of date by the time your hand arrives there. (b) If you can forward-model the expected location of the ball by the time your hand arrives, you will be closer. However, you may overshoot, since your information about your arm position is also slightly out of date. (c) If you forward-model the position of both your arm and the ball, then you can reach for it accurately.

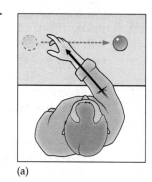
(a)

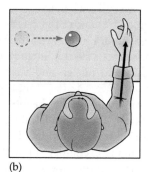
(b)

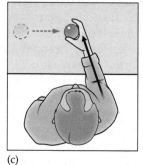
(c)

recent years it has become clear that the outgoing connections of the cerebellum project far beyond the motor cortex alone (Strick, Dum, & Fiez, 2009). In fact, some parts of the cerebellum send a large number of outputs to frontal lobe areas known to be involved in cognition, emotion, motivation, and judgment (Leiner, Leiner, & Dow, 1993). This observation has prompted neuroscientists to look more closely at the effects of cerebellar injury on nonmotor functions. They are beginning to find evidence that the cerebellum is important for a variety of nonmotor functions as well.

The cerebellar cognitive affective syndrome (Schmahmann & Sherman, 1997) describes a collection of nonmotor symptoms that are now proposed to result from cerebellar injuries. These include impairments in cognitive functions such as planning, abstract reasoning, working memory, and changing goals; impairments in spatial memory and visuo-spatial processing; and language processing impairments in speech fluency, speech prosody (tone), and even grammar. Also included are abnormal and unanticipated changes in emotional state and affect (the physical display of emotions, as in facial expressions, laughter, or crying).

The forward-modeling functions of the cerebellum may thus apply not only to motor coordination, but also to the recruitment of accurate and appropriate activity in areas of the cortex responsible for higher cognitive and emotional functions, including language processing and arousal (Poeppel & Monahan, 2011). Different regions of the cerebellum apply their computational powers to different regions of cortex. Thus, depending on its location, a cerebellar injury could cause motor symptoms alone, motor as well as cognitive or psychiatric symptoms, or, more rarely, cognitive or psychiatric symptoms alone.

The emerging picture of the cerebellum is that it is very much a "little brain" of its own, with a wide range of functions, much like the cerebrum itself. Yet the cerebral cortex remains central to the extremely complex forms of behavior found in all human beings. In the next section, we will look at how the cerebral cortex guides motor behavior, both simple and complex.

The Motor Cortex

Most of us have heard the mistaken assertion that "we only use 10% of our brain." By this point in your reading, you should have noted that this simply isn't true. We use every part of our brain, and very efficiently at that. So where did the "10%" notion arise? Although it is hard to be certain, here is one possibility: in the 1870s, neuroscientists began to stimulate different areas of the cortex with electrical currents. They found that stimulating most areas of the cortex produced no obvious effects. However, there was a narrow strip, covering about a tenth of the brain's surface, where stimulation produced specific kinds of body movements. Of course, this was not and was never intended to be a demonstration that we only use 10% of our brain! Instead, it was a milestone in neuroscience research: the discovery of the primary motor cortex (Penfield & Boldrey, 1937) (FIGURE 7.12).

The first map of the motor cortex was discovered by the German anatomist Gustav Fritsch and neurologist Eduard Hitzig in 1870 (Fritsch, 1886). They applied electrical stimulation to a strip of cortex in the frontal lobe of a dog, just in front of the central sulcus. They found that stimulating different areas within this strip produced movements in different parts of the dog's body, as if there were a tiny motor "map" of the body within the cortex itself. Soon afterward, in 1873, the Scottish neurologist Ferrier identified a similar map along the precentral gyrus of the monkey brain, in an area now known as the primary motor cortex (Ferrier, 1874) (FIGURE 7.12a).

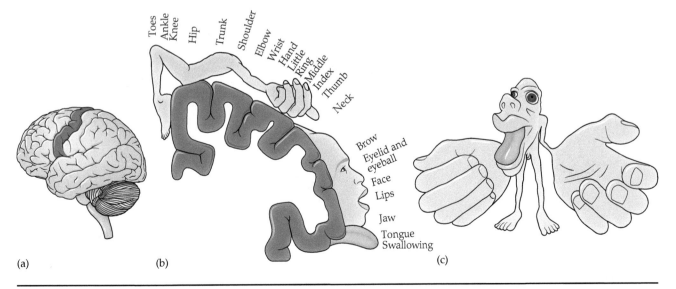

(a)   (b)   (c)

FIGURE 7.12 **The primary motor cortex.** (a) The primary motor cortex, located along the precentral gyrus, occupies less than 10% of the entire cortical surface.
(b) Stimulation at different points along the precentral gyrus elicits movements of different body parts, from the posterior to the anterior end of the organism.
(c) The "motor homunculus" illustrates that the size of each body part's representation in the cortex is proportional to its dexterity, not its physical size.

Incidentally, you may recall that the neuroanatomist Brodmann made a map of the areas of the cortex, based on their microscopic appearance, in 1911 (see Chapter 2). The primary motor cortex turns out to correspond almost exactly to Brodmann area 4 on this map (Geyer et al., 1996). Once again, function follows from form: it is the microcircuitry of inputs and outputs that gives each neuron or brain region its specific function.

In the 1950s, the neurosurgeons Wilder Penfield and Herbert Jasper published a map of the motor cortex in human patients (Penfield & Jasper, 1954). While performing surgery on patients with epilepsy, they would stimulate the cortex and observe the patient's movements. This would help them to avoid removing areas critical for motor control, to minimize the patients' disabilities after the surgery. During stimulation, the patients remained awake and under only local anesthesia, so that they could also report any sensations that occurred during stimulation. Using this technique, the surgeons were able to study many different brain functions, including motor control.

The surgeons found that the most reliable area for eliciting movements lay, once again, just anterior to the central sulcus, in the precentral gyrus (FIGURE 7.12b). Furthermore, the precise movement seemed to depend on which part was stimulated. Stimulation near the top of the gyrus produced lower leg or foot movements; as the stimulation moved further laterally, the movement shifted to the upper leg, then the torso, then the upper arm, then the lower arm, then the hand, then the face and lips, then the tongue, and finally the throat and vocal cords. It was as if this movement-related region of the brain contained a

map of a "little man"—the **motor homunculus**. Since each place (in Greek, *topos*) in the brain corresponds to a different part of the body (*soma*), the primary motor cortex is also described as a somatotopic map of motor function, just as the visual cortex is described as a retinotopic map of visual input (see Chapter 5).

What was interesting about the motor map was its proportions. The size of the motor representation of each body part was often substantially different from the size of the same part on the body itself (Penfield & Jasper, 1954). Areas with fine motor control, such as the feet, toes, hands, fingers, mouth, and tongue, occupied large sections of the map. Areas with less precise control, such as the arms, legs, and torso, had much smaller representations. A sculpture of the human body from the motor cortex's point of view (FIGURE 7.12c) would look very odd indeed!

Penfield and his colleagues also found other somatotopic maps in their patients (Penfield & Boldrey, 1937). All along the postcentral gyrus, just adjacent to the primary motor cortex, lay a primary somatosensory cortex (FIGURE 7.13). Stimulating this area caused human patients to report tactile sensations in particular parts of the body, in the absence of actual sensory stimuli. Like the motor cortex, the primary somatosensory cortex had a somatotopic organization, with more sensitive body parts assigned more space. The **somatosensory homunculus** was quite similar in proportion to its motor counterpart. In fact, the primary somatosensory and motor cortices proved to be densely interconnected, as one might expect: planning and executing a movement requires detailed feedback about each body part's current position and tactile sensation,

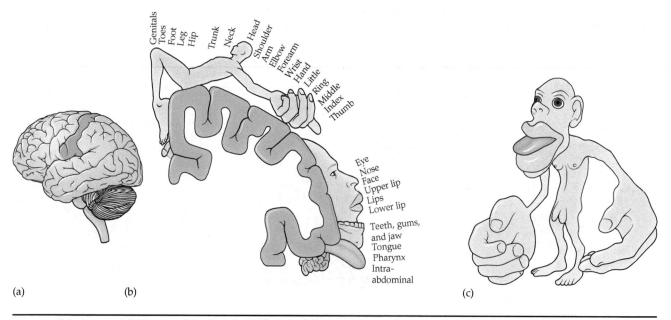

(a)   (b)   (c)

FIGURE 7.13 **The primary somatosensory cortex.** (a) The primary somatosensory cortex is located along the postcentral gyrus, in close physical proximity to its motor counterpart. (b) Stimulation at different points along the precentral gyrus elicits sensations in different body parts, from the posterior to the anterior end of the organism. (c) The "somatosensory homunculus" illustrates that the size of each body part's representation in the cortex is proportional to its sensitivity, not its physical size.

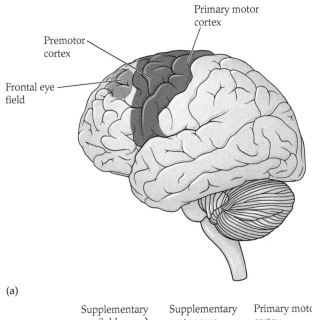

(a)

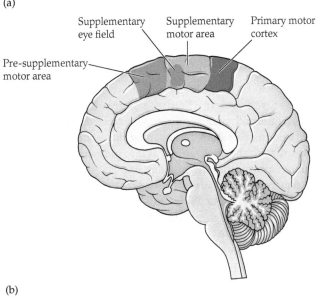

(b)

FIGURE 7.14 **Premotor regions.** (a) Lateral premotor regions include the premotor cortex, just anterior to the primary motor cortex, and the frontal eye field, just anterior and dorsal to the premotor cortex. (b) Just anterior to the medial primary motor cortex are several medial premotor regions including the supplementary motor area, supplementary eye field, and presupplementary motor area.

from start to finish. As we will see, this is a key principle of the motor system: *motor control requires sensory guidance of the appropriate level of complexity.*

There were also other motor areas to be found in the frontal lobes (FIGURE 7.14). Immediately in front of the precentral gyrus lay another motor region, which had been previously noted in the monkey and dog maps of the 19th century (Parsons, 1900). It seemed to require a stronger current to elicit a movement, but the movements elicited also appeared more complex than those of the primary

motor cortex (Gerardin et al., 2000). Today, this region is known as the **lateral premotor cortex**. A distinct area controlling eye movements, the **frontal eye field**, lies dorsal and anterior to this region. Another entirely separate motor area lies tucked in the central sulcus, along the midline of the hemisphere, again just in front of the primary motor cortex. This area has a separate somatotopic map, arranged with the head anterior and the lower body and legs posterior. It became known as the **supplementary motor area (SMA)**. Just anterior to this region lies a supplementary eye field and then a **pre-supplementary motor area (pre-SMA)**. We will look at the functions of these additional motor areas later in the chapter.

Motor Cortex: Neural Coding of Movements

In the second half of the 20th century, neuroscientists began to study how the neurons of the motor cortex controlled movement. As we described above (under the "Descending Pathways of Motor Control" heading), neuroanatomists had already traced the outgoing connections from the large pyramidal neurons of the motor cortex. These so-called upper motor neurons send signals directly to the lower motor neurons of the spinal cord via the descending lateral and ventral corticospinal tracts.

Upper motor neurons connect to the lower motor neurons of many spinal levels, allowing them to drive the muscles through a nearly direct pathway. They also connect to the interneurons of the spinal cord, allowing them to modulate ongoing activity of the built-in reflexes and central pattern generators of the spinal cord itself. So, the primary motor cortex is wired to drive muscles to produce simple movements directly or modulate spinal circuits to excite or inhibit more complex movements such as locomotion or scratching.

But how do the upper motor neurons themselves organize movements? In the 1980s, neuroscientists discovered evidence that the primary motor cortex uses population coding to control movements (Georgopoulos, Kettner, & Schwartz, 1988). That is, each neuron has a general direction preference in driving movement, but this preference is quite vague, spanning a range of around 90 degrees. So, no one neuron codes the direction of the overall movement. Instead, the final movement is a summing up of the activity of the whole population of neurons, each with a slightly different direction preference. So, if a monkey pushes a joystick from a central position to the 12-o'clock position, neurons with direction preferences toward 12 o'clock fire strongly, whereas those with a 1 o'clock or 11 o'clock preference fire somewhat less and those with a preference between 3 o'clock and 9 o'clock fire hardly at all (FIGURE 7.15).

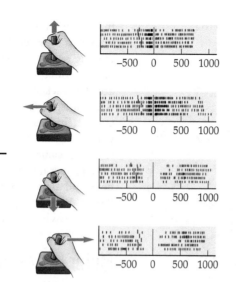

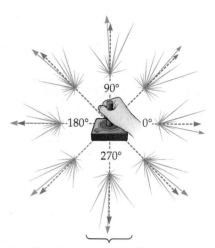

FIGURE 7.15 **Population coding.**
(a) An individual neuron in the primary motor cortex fires more rapidly during movements of a joystick in certain directions—in this case, forward and to the left. However, the preferred direction is "fuzzy" at the individual-neuron level. (b) During movements in a given direction, neurons fire at higher rates when the direction is closer to their preferred direction. Summing together the firing rates across the entire population gives a much less fuzzy, precise prediction to the movement direction. This finding has been used to suggest "population encoding" of movement directions in the primary motor cortex.

Firing pattern of neuron "5":
Increased for forward or for left movements
Suppressed for backward or right movements

Movement direction not encoded very precisely
(a)

Activity of neurons "1" to "12" for each direction of movement:
The length of each gray line shows the amount of firing for the neuron that prefers that direction. Activity across whole population of neurons encodes movement direction more precisely.
(b)

In fact, it was possible to work out the ultimate direction of movement by looking back at the firing rate of each neuron in the population. By multiplying the firing rates of each neuron by its preferred direction, the scientists created a "direction vector" for each cell for each movement. Adding together the direction vectors for each cell gave quite a close approximation of the original movement (Sanger, 1994). Population coding thus seemed a likely mechanism for explaining how the upper motor cortex regulated the control of movements. This idea had the added appeal of familiarity: population coding mechanisms were also thought to exist in sensory regions, such as the motion-detecting areas of visual cortex (Salinas & Abbott, 1994). However, in the past few years, new discoveries have led us to question some long-held ideas about how the motor cortex works.

Motor Cortex: Recent Controversies

The classic motor homunculus of Penfield's surgical maps suggested a motor cortex organized into the most basic units of movement: individual muscle contractions. Yet this map was based on brief periods of stimulation (only 10 or 20 milliseconds), often at the minimum threshold necessary for a movement (Penfield & Boldrey, 1937). More recent studies have begun to use stimulation that is sustained over a longer period of time, presumably more similar to the natural activity of the motor circuitry. Studies of longer-duration stimulation seem to reveal a different kind of map in the primary motor cortex (Graziano, 2006).

First, rather than eliciting a simple muscle twitch, a 500-millisecond stimulation evoked a complete action: moving the hand to the mouth and opening the mouth, or reaching outward with the hand shaped as if to grasp an object. These actions involved the use of many muscles, many joints, and often many separate parts of the body.

Second, different areas of the motor cortex seemed to code for different categories of action rather than different body parts. Moving anteriorly from the central sulcus, stimulation evoked hand manipulations in nearby space, then reaching movements into distant space, and then defensive warding-off movements in peripheral space. Other areas evoked climbing and leaping movements of the arm and leg.

Third, there was no obvious population coding of movement direction. Instead, stimulation seemed to drive the limb toward a final common posture (for example, in front of the chest with fist clenched), regardless of its original position. The population encoding thus appeared to change completely depending on the limb's starting position. Since the starting position in the earlier experiments had always been the same (a joystick in a central position), this feature might have been previously missed (FIGURE 7.16).

Finally, there was no obvious distinction between the motor cortex and the more anterior premotor cortex with more prolonged stimulation. Originally, the premotor cortex was thought to be involved in planning movements and in organizing more complex assemblies of the simpler movements coded in primary motor cortex. Yet with sustained stimulation, both regions coded for complex movements, with no obvious border separating them.

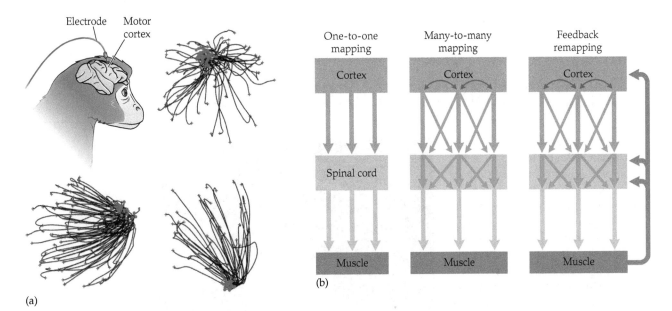

(a)

(b)

FIGURE 7.16 Feedback mapping. (a) Longer trains of stimulation in the primary motor cortex tend to drive the limb toward a specific final position (blue) and posture, regardless of initial position (red). (b) Classically, each neuron in the primary motor cortex relays signals through the spinal cord to drive a specific muscle in a one-to-one mapping. In the more complex view of many-to-many mapping, each neuron can drive many muscles and each muscle can be driven by many neurons. In the still more complex view of feedback mapping, incoming sensory feedback signals from the muscles and joints can resculpt the many-to-many mapping patterns between upper motor neurons and muscles.

These more recent findings suggest that, if there is a neural site for the control of individual muscle movements, it is not in the primary motor cortex. Stimulating the same site may lead to an arm flexion or an arm extension, depending on initial position. Hence, the same set of motor neurons might drive the biceps muscle to contract in one setting, but the triceps muscle to contract in another. In keeping with this finding, upper motor neurons typically project to multiple spinal levels, where they can stimulate different sets of muscles or spinal central pattern generators depending on the circumstances (Strong et al., 2009).

So, if individual muscle contractions are not the fundamental organizing principle of the primary motor neurons, then what is? Movements have many other possible parameters that might be useful to control: direction, velocity, force, joint angle, limb posture, muscle activity level. Examining each of these parameters alone and in combination is a laborious process. Instead, what if we were to look at individual primary motor neurons during carefully measured, free, natural movements (e.g., scratching, picking fruit, grooming)? We could then analyze the data and see which movement parameters most closely matched the activity of the neurons.

In fact, when these studies were performed, the results were even more confusing (Aflalo & Graziano, 2006). Direction tuning did not account for the neurons' activity in monkeys, except for limited sets of movements. The final location of the hand in space also accounted for almost none of the neurons' activity. The best match seemed to be with a complex feature: the final overall posture of the limb, taking into account eight different parameters specifying the degree of rotation and flexion at the shoulder, elbow, and wrist. Yet even this parameter explained only a portion of the activity of each neuron. Much of the activity remained left to as yet unexplained factors.

So, some somatotopy, some directionality, some end posture, and a lot of unexplained factors. How can we make sense of this bewildering organization in a region we thought we had mapped out more than a century ago? One proposal is that all of these "maps" are simply our best understanding of how the neurons organize a vast number of movement "dimensions" (force, direction, location, muscle group, body location, and all of the other factors above) onto a two-dimensional sheet of cortex (Martindale, 2001). Like trying to draw a three-dimensional scene on a two-dimensional sheet of paper, the final result will appear somewhat confusing to the uninitiated: objects at the top of the page will sometimes (but not always) be more distant than those at the bottom, and two lines that are supposed to be parallel may seem to converge. Likewise, the two-dimensional organization of the motor cortex may appear partly somatotopic, or partly postural, or partly category based, depending on circumstances.

If such complexity is the rule even for primary motor cortex, then mapping will only become more difficult for the even larger sets of dimensions that need to be captured by higher-order motor control areas in the prefrontal cortex. Keep this point in mind as we move into the next section, where we take a look at the organization of these complex areas in more detail.

THE BIGGER PICTURE
Neural Implants for Motor Control

Remember the tragic case of Jean-Dominique Bauby from the beginning of the chapter? He had suffered a stroke affecting the medulla and the nearby pyramidal decussations: the outgoing pathway for virtually all of the motor cortex. Locked-in syndrome is the usual result of this kind of stroke. Without any connections to the spinal cord or lower cranial nerves, the cortex is unable to send output to nearly any parts of the body. A few cranial nerves above the injury may be spared, allowing some movement of the eyes and eyelids only. Since these pathways do not easily regenerate, the hopes for recovery are slim.

Yet the motor cortex itself is still intact. What if there were some way to read the activity of the upper motor neurons directly? Could we use them to drive an artificial arm, or a wheelchair, or a computer cursor? Perhaps even a simple speech synthesizer? In fact, for more than a decade, neuroscientists have been using **brain–computer interface** technologies to help locked-in patients communicate with the outside world (Kennedy, Bakay, Moore, Adams, & Goldwaithe, 2000). One strategy involves implanting a set of electrodes directly in the motor cortex, in the part of the homunculus that controls the hand or the mouth. The electrodes may be coated with neural growth factors to encourage the neurons to grow connections to the implant itself.

As one example, in 2006, a research team from Massachusetts General Hospital and Brown University inserted a small electrode array (FIGURE 7.17) into the motor cortex of Matthew N., a 25-year-old who had

FIGURE 7.17 **A neuromotor prosthetic.** A tiny electrode array implanted in the motor cortex of Matthew N. enabled him to control his wheelchair and actions on a screen.

been quadriplegic since a knife attack five years earlier. A successful example of "neuromotor prosthetics" in humans, the sensor was able to read the signals that Matthew's brain was trying to send out to his body, and convert those signals into commands that could direct the movements of a prosthetic arm or a pointer on a computer screen (Hochberg et al., 2006).

Decoding the neural activity into meaningful signals can be difficult. Computer algorithms can learn to interpret the collective activity of a population of neurons as signaling a particular movement, or syllable. The patients themselves can learn to use the prostheses, rewiring the local connections to improve their ability to communicate over time. More

recently, a young man with locked-in syndrome has begun to use this system to produce simple syllables with reasonable accuracy after several years of training for both patient and computer (Guenther et al., 2009).

So far, the technology is still in its infancy. Interpreting the neural signals remains difficult. The signals themselves fade over time as glial cells gradually build up around the implanted electrodes, rendering the electrodes useless. At present, no implant has been able to match the efficacy of the simple blink-coding card used by M. Bauby to write his memoirs. Developing effective brain–computer interfaces will be one of the most important technological challenges of the 21st century.

The Prefrontal Cortex: Goals to Strategies to Tactics to Actions

Even as simple an action as raising your hand requires a complex hierarchy of control. All actions have an origin in the body's basic needs. These needs must be remapped into goals and these goals translated into a strategy, based on what is going on in the current environment. This strategy in turn must be mapped into a set of behavioral tactics in the immediate surroundings and these tactics broken down into a sequence of specific actions, each also guided by immediate sensory feedback. Hence, hunger in the classroom may prompt you to the goal of acquiring a meal, which may lead to the strategy of buying a sandwich at the local cafeteria, which might require tactics for extracting yourself from the ongoing lecture, which might lead you to the action of tiptoeing out the back door of the classroom.

Human behavior is perhaps the most complex of any living species on the planet. Human beings have the same needs as other primates, but pursue these needs through an enormous range of different possible behaviors. Sorting through this "possibility space" in search of a behavior plan is an immense task, and not surprisingly, the prefrontal cortex of the human brain has expanded dramatically to meet these requirements (Amodio & Frith, 2006). In this section, we'll look at how the prefrontal cortex builds the complex hierarchy of control by which human needs are mapped into human actions.

The Functional Organization of the Prefrontal Cortex in Motor Control

In the broadest terms, the lateral frontal lobe areas are divided into three zones (FIGURE 7.18). Primary motor and premotor cortex have direct connections to the spinal cord and therefore can provide the most direct and low-level control over actions and simple movements. They also have strong communication with the primary somatosensory cortex and nearby sensory association cortex, which provide detailed tactile feedback useful for guiding movements. These two motor areas have the most obvious and consistent body-centered organization of all frontal areas (Yousry et al., 1997), although as we saw earlier, they may also be organized according to categories of movement or final end postures (Hazy, Frank, & O'Reilly, 2007). For example, the most dorsal parts of premotor cortex (labeled F2 in monkeys) guide movements of the leg and the arm and a more ventral area known as F4 largely guides movements of the face (Raos, Franchi, Gallese, & Fogassi, 2003; Rizzolatti, Fogassi, & Gallese, 2002).

More anteriorly, the ventrolateral, dorsolateral, and dorsomedial prefrontal cortices have no direct connections to the spinal cord, but instead provide output to primary motor and premotor cortex. They also take extensive inputs from posterior areas in the superior and inferior parietal lobule. These inputs provide higher-level sensory input about the spatial location, shape, and potential action properties of objects in the sensory environment. This information is useful for more complex forms of action

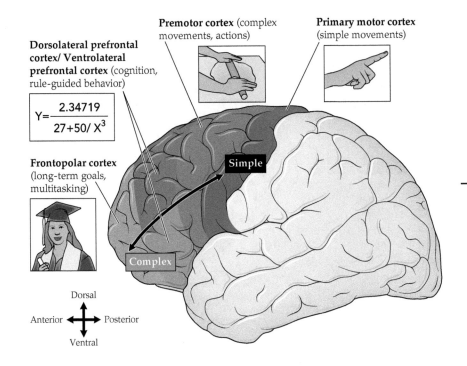

Dorsolateral prefrontal cortex/ Ventrolateral prefrontal cortex (cognition, rule-guided behavior)

$$Y = \frac{2.34719}{27 + 50/X^3}$$

Frontopolar cortex (long-term goals, multitasking)

Premotor cortex (complex movements, actions)

Primary motor cortex (simple movements)

Simple

Complex

Dorsal

Anterior ◀▶ Posterior

Ventral

FIGURE 7.18 **The hierarchy of behavioral control in the frontal lobes.** From posterior to anterior, the primary motor cortex directs simple movements, the premotor cortex directs more complex actions, the lateral prefrontal cortex directs complex cognition and planning, and the frontopolar cortex represents long-term goals. The detailed somatotopic organization of the primary motor cortex is gradually lost in the more anterior areas, higher in the hierarchy. The frontopolar cortex has no direct sensory input at all.

planning, such as cognition. These areas also have a loose somatotopic organization, with the most dorsal regions most active for tasks involving eye movements, more ventral regions most active for tasks involving hand and arm movements, and still more ventral regions most active for tasks involving movements of the lips and tongue, including speech (Buccino et al., 2001). However, the somatotopy is not as clear as in more posterior motor areas, and much overlap exists.

Still more anteriorly lies the **frontopolar cortex**, also known as Brodmann area 10. Dramatically expanded in humans, this area is unique in that it has no direct sensory inputs, but instead connects only to other areas of the frontal lobes. Why would this area have no direct connections to the outside world? This pattern of connectivity is useful for setting long-term goals that are independent of the current sensory environment or for holding one goal in mind while pursuing another more immediate goal (Koechlin, Corrado, Pietrini, & Grafman, 2000). Research suggests that this area is important in decision making (Lau, Rogers, Ramnani, & Passingham, 2004) and that damage to this area is associated with an impaired ability to multitask (Dreher, Koechlin, Tierney, & Grafman, 2008). By linking to other areas of the prefrontal cortex, the frontopolar cortex can then use these goals to select the most appropriate strategy for behavior in the current environment.

Sensory Feedback

No motor region can function effectively without sensory feedback. Recall from our discussion of the spinal cord and the patellar tendon reflex that a sensory signal from the muscle spindles causes the motor neuron to fire to prevent overstretching the muscle. Similarly, flexing a muscle causes its opponent to relax. Motor control in the cortex is no different. Somatosensory feedback from primary somatosensory cortex is essential for guiding the actions of primary motor cortex. Tactile feedback can help to calibrate grip strength when holding an object. Proprioceptive (position-sense) feedback helps to guide body parts to the desired postures. Nociceptive (pain-sense) feedback can help to guide a withdrawal response or an adjustment of position. As you may recall from Chapter 6, all of these forms of somatosensory input are represented in sensory cortex.

The more complex activity of anterior prefrontal areas requires higher-level sensory feedback. Here the parietal lobes provide the necessary information (FIGURE 7.19). The intraparietal sulcus, which separates the superior and inferior parietal lobules, contains multiple areas that represent the spatial locations of objects in the sensory environment. Each area computes spatial locations in a different frame of reference, centered on a specific body part. For example, the lateral intraparietal area represents stimuli in eye-centered coordinates, useful for guiding rapid eye movements. A ventral intraparietal area represents object locations in head-centered space, useful for guiding movements of the head or for guiding objects to the mouth (Andersen & Buneo, 2002). Other areas may also represent stimulus location in overall body-centered coordinates, useful for planning movements of the entire body via locomotion.

Why so many different spatial maps? The answer is probably that the location of an object depends on what one is planning to do with it (Van Hulle, 1997). A coffee cup on a table in front of you may be "up and left" with respect to the right hand, "down and centered" with respect to the mouth, and "down and right" with respect to the left eye, while being "straight ahead" with respect to the body (FIGURE 7.19). By

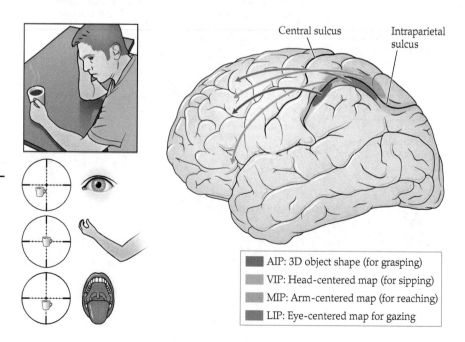

FIGURE 7.19 **Spatial maps of the parietal lobe.** Parietal lobe regions provide guidance to lateral prefrontal regions. To do this, they use input from the external senses: vision, hearing, and touch. The intraparietal sulcus contains multiple maps of the shapes and locations of objects in our surroundings. Each map is centered on a different body region and connects to the appropriate region of the prefrontal cortex to guide that body part.

Central sulcus   Intraparietal sulcus

AIP: 3D object shape (for grasping)
VIP: Head-centered map (for sipping)
MIP: Arm-centered map (for reaching)
LIP: Eye-centered map for gazing

computing different spatial maps for each body part, the parietal lobe can locate objects in frames of reference that are useful to different parts of the frontal lobes.

As it turns out, each parietal subregion does send its information to a slightly different part of the prefrontal cortex. In the white matter, long bundles of axons travel in bundles to connect each parietal region with its prefrontal partner. For example, the lateral intraparietal area connects largely to the frontal eye field and supplementary eye field. The head-centered maps of the ventral intraparietal area connect to slightly more ventral areas of premotor cortex, which guide movements of the face (Rizzolatti & Luppino, 2001). So each region of the premotor cortex works closely with a partner sensory region of the parietal cortex to plan its movements. This principle applies to the rest of the prefrontal cortex as well.

Mirror Neurons in Premotor Cortex

In the 1990s, a team of Italian neuroscientists discovered a new class of neurons in the premotor cortex of the monkey (Di Pellegrino, Fadiga, Fogassi, Gallese, & Rizzolatti, 1992;

Gallese, Fadiga, Fogassi, & Rizzolatti, 1996; Rizzolatti, Fadiga, Gallese, & Fogassi, 1996). These neurons had an interesting property: not only did they fire when the monkey performed a particular action, but also they fired when the monkey witnessed someone else (monkey or human) performing a similar action. They called these "monkey-see, monkey-do" neurons **mirror neurons**. Later, neuroimaging studies provided evidence for the presence of the same kind of "mirror" activity in the analogous brain areas in humans (Chong, Cunnington, Williams, Kanwisher, & Mattingley, 2008). These neurons are particularly common in the ventral premotor cortex, known in monkeys as F5. The sensory partner areas of this region lie in the **superior temporal sulcus** and anterior inferior parietal lobule. These areas have important functions in perceiving social stimuli (such as the body and eye movements of others) as well as in action-related perception (Calder et al., 2007).

What is the function of mirror neurons? One proposal is that these neurons form a basis for action imitation or even action understanding (Chong et al., 2008). The neurons do seem to code for actions even when the actions cannot be seen directly (FIGURE 7.20). For example, a mirror neuron that

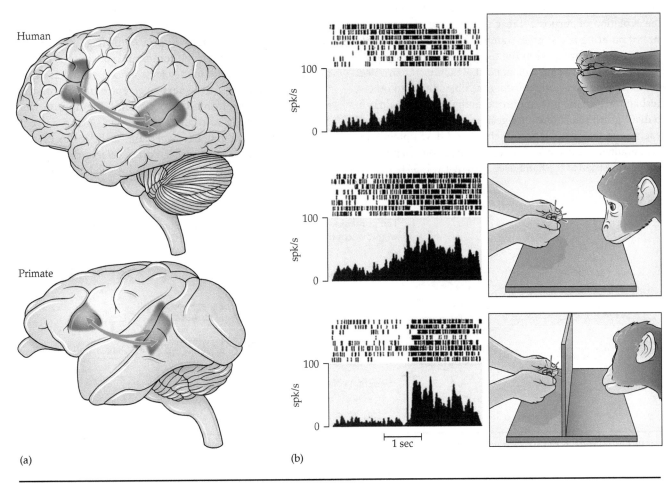

(a)

(b)

FIGURE 7.20 **Mirror neurons.** (a) In both humans and nonhuman primates, mirror neurons are found in the premotor cortex and anatomically connected regions of the superior temporal sulcus. (b) Mirror neurons are active both when individuals perform an action and when they observe another individual performing the same action.

responds to a grasping movement can also respond if the final part of the movement is hidden behind a screen (Rizzolatti & Craighero, 2004). A mirror neuron that responds during a paper-ripping movement can even respond to the sound of the paper being ripped outside the monkey's field of view! In general, the mirror neurons require an action to have a goal before they will fire. An undirected grasping movement, for example, tends to have little effect (Williams, Whiten, Suddendorf, & Perrett, 2001). However, a purposeful movement to grasp a specific object will activate the mirror neuron, even when the object itself is hidden. Hence, mirror neurons may provide a basis for representing the intention or goal of a movement as much as the movement itself.

What is the significance of mirror neurons, if any? Some have proposed that the mirror neuron system lies at the heart of **theory of mind** (Gallese & Goldman, 1998)—our ability to understand the thoughts and feelings of others, which is crucial for the complex social behavior of human beings. However, as we will see later in the book, other brain regions appear to be more important for this function. Others have proposed that these neurons provide a foundation for imitation of actions or for a shared understanding of purpose or meaning (Rizzolatti & Craighero, 2004). Imitation and shared meaning are a potential basis for the evolution of human communication—both by gestures and by language. The evolution of purposeful reaching into the symbolic gesture of pointing is a simple example. Mirror neurons could have started off by representing the goal of a reaching movement rather than the movement itself. Reaching for an object would thus be a way of indicating the object itself to others. Reshaping the hand into a pointing configuration would help to distinguish the "indicating-gesture" reach from an actual reaching movement. Hence, in childhood development, infants gradually learn to look along the direction of a pointing hand rather than at the hand itself (Vygotsky, 1934).

Control Stages of the Motor Hierarchy

Neuroimaging studies in humans have provided some of the clearest illustrations of the hierarchy of motor control in lateral prefrontal areas. In one experiment, subjects had to either make choices among stimuli based on their sensory properties (e.g., red squares but not white squares) or choose among tasks according to context (e.g., choose lowercase letters when green, but vowels when red) or the overall episode (e.g., choose task according to what tasks have previously been performed). The most posterior areas of lateral prefrontal cortex were active when selecting based on sensory properties. Immediately anterior areas were active when choosing which sensory rules to use based on the current context. The most anterior areas were active when choosing a task based on the current episode of the overall experiment (FIGURE 7.21). This required information about what tasks had previously been performed to succeed in the long-term goal of completing the entire experiment successfully (Koechlin, Ody, & Kouneiher, 2003).

The results of this and other related neuroimaging studies have led to a proposed functional hierarchy of motor control in the prefrontal cortex (Koechlin & Summerfield, 2007). At the lowest level, sensory control, the premotor cortex selects among responses based on a given sensory cue using a simple stimulus–response rule (e.g., green = go; red = stop). At the next level, contextual control, the posterior lateral prefrontal cortex selects among rules based on the current context. At the next level, episodic control, the anterior lateral prefrontal cortex selects the appropriate context for making rule selections, based on the current episode of the overall behavioral plan. At the highest level, branching control, frontopolar cortex selects the current episode of the overall behavioral plan while keeping track

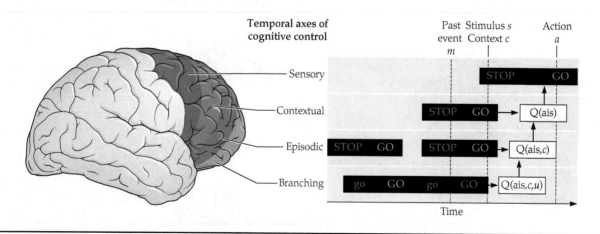

FIGURE 7.21 Control of complex behavior in the prefrontal cortex. More anterior areas of the prefrontal cortex guide progressively more complex forms of conditional behavior. The premotor cortex controls actions regulated by sensory cues using simple if–then rules (if go, then press button). More anterior areas can override these simple if–then rules based on context (if go, then press button unless uppercase). Still more anterior areas can switch contexts episodically (if lowercase is go last time, then uppercase is go this time). Still more anterior areas can switch contexts conditionally (if a green go appears, then its case becomes go from now on). With these capabilities, bewilderingly complex behaviors become possible.

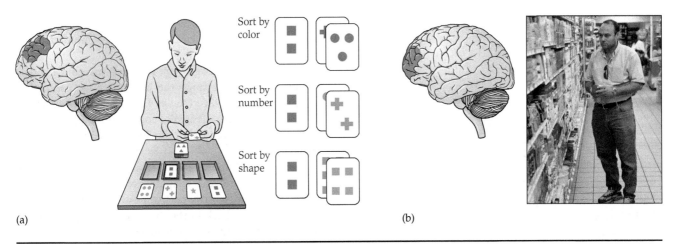

(a)

(b)

FIGURE 7.22 **Effects of prefrontal lesions on behavior.** (a) Lesions of the dorsolateral prefrontal cortex can impair rule shifting on tests such as the Wisconsin card-sorting task. As the rules change over time, patients "perseverate" on the old rules even when they know they are incorrect. (b) Patients with lesions of the frontopolar cortex can do well on the Wisconsin card-sorting task and other well-structured tests of general intelligence, yet flounder in real-world situations that require goal setting and multitasking (such as running simple errands in a shopping mall).

of the other episodes to eventually reach the ultimate behavioral goal.

Patients with injuries of the frontal lobe often have difficulties with various components of this hierarchy of motor control. For example, patients with lesions of the lateral prefrontal cortex often have difficulty shifting between different strategies (or contexts) in behavioral experiments (Tanji & Hoshi, 2008). A classic demonstration of these kinds of errors is patients' performance on the **Wisconsin card-sorting task** (FIGURE 7.22a). In this task, the subject is given a set of cards marked with various kinds of shapes, appearing in various numbers and colors. The subject must learn a hidden rule to sort the cards by shape, color, or number, using only "right" or "wrong" feedback. Once the subject has learned to sort by one rule, the rule is suddenly changed. The subject is told that the previously "correct" responses are now "incorrect" and must then learn the new rule. Patients with injury to the dorsolateral prefrontal cortex tend to stick with, or perseverate on, the old rules, being unable to use feedback to shift to the new rules.

Patients with injury to the frontopolar cortex often do surprisingly well on standard tests of cognitive function, despite a near total inability to function in unstructured, real-world situations such as shopping for groceries. The problem in this case is an inability to keep long-term goals in mind independent of the current task or to shift efficiently between tasks as needed. If asked to complete a "shopping task" involving a number of errands in a real street, they fail to complete most of the assigned tasks (FIGURE 7.22b) and instead may complete additional random errands that had nothing to do with the original plan (Burgess, Gilbert, & Dumontheil, 2007; Shallice & Burgess, 1991)! In fact, most of us have probably found ourselves in a similar predicament at one point or another; the frontopolar cortex is only recently enlarged in human beings, and even so, its capacity is somewhat limited (Koechlin et al., 2000).

Basal Ganglia

The basal ganglia work closely with the cortex in motor control. Like the cerebellum, they serve areas of the cortex well beyond primary motor areas, including areas critical to higher-level cognition, motivation, and judgment. Like the cerebellum, they contain a common circuitry that likely performs a common computation across all the areas they serve. The precise nature of this computation is still under debate, but diseases of the basal ganglia may provide clues. First, however, we'll review the large- and small-scale structure of the basal ganglia before delving into its more detailed circuitry and functions.

Components of the Basal Ganglia

The basal ganglia are gray matter structures that lie deep within the telencephalon, rather than on the surface as with the cortex. The largest and outermost component is the striatum, which in humans is split in half by the descending white matter tract of the internal capsule as it travels to the thalamus and onward to the spinal cord. The two halves are the comet-shaped caudate (tailed) nucleus and the disc-shaped putamen, connected only by a few residual stripes (also called striae) of gray matter, which give the striatum its name. Next to the putamen, closer to the center of the brain, lies the globus pallidus, with an outer external and an inner internal part.

Under this lies the posterior part of the internal capsule and under this, the thalamus. Although not considered part of the basal ganglia, it functions intimately with the striatum and globus pallidus. The same goes for the neighboring subthalamic nucleus and, just underneath it, the dopamine-rich substantia nigra (FIGURE 7.23).

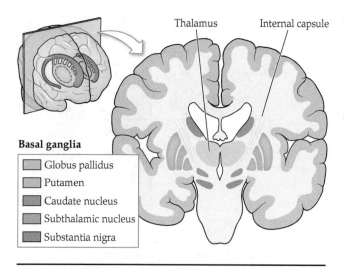

FIGURE 7.23 Major structures in the circuitry of the basal ganglia.
Included are the comet-shaped caudate nucleus, round putamen, the deeper
globus pallidus externa and interna, the subthalamic nucleus, and the
substantia nigra, pars compacta.

Basal ganglia circuits help to initiate and maintain activity in the cortex—particularly in the frontal lobes and especially in the medial frontal lobes. What these medial frontal areas have in common is that, unlike lateral prefrontal cortex, they have fewer external inputs to drive them. Instead, they rely on internally generated signals to initiate and maintain their activity as needed. We'll learn more about this distinction in the next section.

Circuitry of the Basal Ganglia

The basal ganglia interact with the cortex through a complex circuitry of loops. With the exception of low-order sensory areas, every region of the cortex is served by loop circuits through the basal ganglia. The cortex sends excitatory connections to the striatum, which in turn sends inhibitory inputs to the internal globus pallidus, which is itself a motor inhibitory structure. There are actually two pathways to the internal globus pallidus. The indirect pathway is inhibitory overall. It receives striatal input and travels via the external globus pallidus and subthalamic nucleus to reach its destination in the internal globus pallidus. The direct pathway is excitatory overall and travels directly to the internal globus pallidus. From here the circuit continues to the thalamus and then back once again to the cortex to complete the loop. The substantia nigra provides dopamine inputs to the striatum, and these inputs have essential roles in both the excitatory and the inhibitory functions of the basal ganglia (FIGURE 7.24).

Even for well-seasoned neuroscientists, keeping track of this complex circuit of inhibiting inhibitors of inhibition can be confusing. The key points to bear in mind are that the basal ganglia have both excitatory and inhibitory circuitry

for modulating cortical activity. As we will see, when these circuits go awry, either a lack or an excess of motor activity can result.

Neuroscientists recognize at least five anatomically distinct loops passing through the basal ganglia (Alexander, DeLong, & Strick, 1986) (FIGURE 7.24b). Each of these loops serves a slightly different area of cortex and so has a slightly different function (and slightly different consequences if damaged).

The most well-known of these basal ganglia loops is the motor loop, which gathers inputs from premotor, primary motor, and somatosensory cortex, passes through the putamen, and ends up back in the motor cortex, especially the premotor area and the supplementary motor area (a medial-wall motor area; see below).

There is also a separate oculomotor loop for eye movements; a dorsolateral prefrontal loop that is important in cognitive functions; and a lateral orbitofrontal loop that serves cortical areas important for judgment, emotional regulation, and assigning value to external stimuli.

Other similar loops could probably be added to this list, and these loops themselves could probably be further subdivided on closer study. In addition, the loops are not completely separate, but instead are "open" circuits that partially spill into one another, allowing communication across functions (Alexander et al., 1986). The key point is that the basal ganglia, although they are best known for their motor functions, serve a variety of other functions as well. This is apparent when we look at diseases in which the functions of the basal ganglia are impaired.

Diseases of the Basal Ganglia

Huntington's disease (HD) is a rare neurodegenerative disorder caused by an autosomal dominant genetic abnormality in a gene on chromosome 4 that produces huntingtin, a protein occurring normally in tissues throughout the body. For unclear reasons, the abnormal protein is toxic specifically to the caudate and putamen, causing them to degenerate markedly in adulthood (FIGURE 7.25a). Degeneration preferentially affects the inhibitory circuitry of the basal ganglia before it affects the excitatory circuitry, although ultimately both are severely damaged.

The most obvious symptom in HD is motor disinhibition. Patients begin to show chorea: involuntary, restless, "dancelike" movements of the head, trunk, and limbs. They may also find it difficult to maintain simple voluntary movements, such as sticking out the tongue for a sustained period of time. In advanced stages, motor rigidity and immobility may set in. Progressive **dementia** is another common feature: increasing difficulty in task switching, multitasking, problem solving, and decision making. Psychiatric symptoms of emotional dysregulation are also prominent. Irritability, angry outbursts, depressed mood, and difficulty with relationships are often evident even before other signs of the disease emerge. HD is ultimately

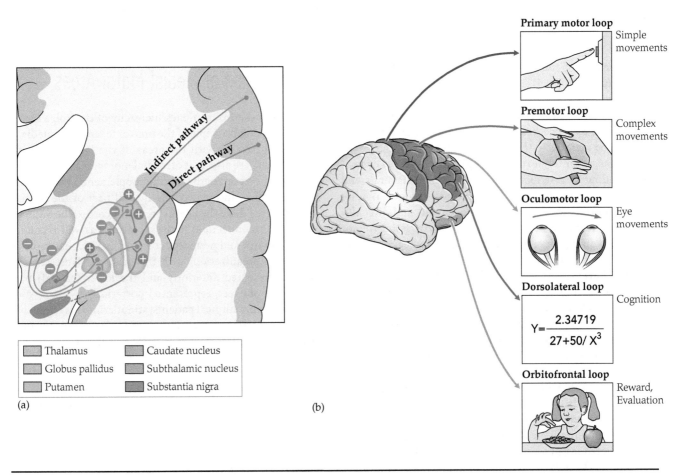

FIGURE 7.24 Cortical loops. (a) Loop circuits from the cortex through the basal ganglia, comprising the direct (excitatory) and indirect (inhibitory) pathways, allow the brain to initiate, maintain, and terminate various classes of thought and behavior. (b) At least five major cortical–striatal–thalamic–cortical loops are recognized, each serving different functions.

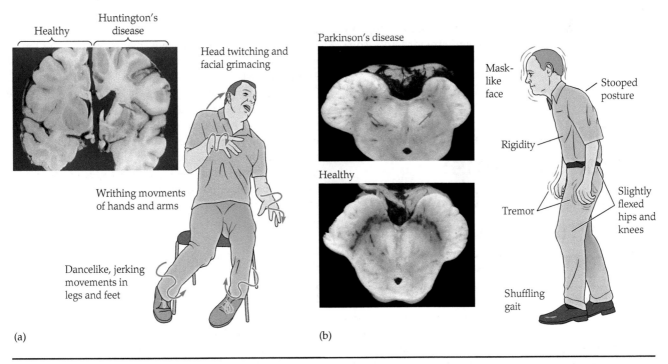

FIGURE 7.25 Diseases of the basal ganglia. (a) In Huntington's disease, the caudate nucleus shows dramatic atrophy. The inhibitory, indirect pathway is more affected early in the illness, leading to writhing movements known as "chorea" and difficulties with self-control of thoughts, emotions, and behavior. (b) In Parkinson's disease, the dopamine-containing neurons of the substantia nigra degenerate and are lost. The excitatory, direct pathway is more affected early in the illness, leading to resting tremor as well as difficulties initiating and maintaining movements and behaviors.

fatal because of the severity of motor and cognitive decline. Huntington's disease will be covered in more detail in Chapter 16.

Parkinson's disease is another classic movement disorder, caused by a progressive destruction of the dopamine-containing neurons in the substantia nigra. With the loss of dopamine, the inhibitory indirect pathway becomes overactive, leading to a reduced excitation of the thalamus and cortex. Effects on the motor loop are most obvious: rigidity of the limbs, bradykinesia (slow movements and difficulty initiating and maintaining movements), and a resting tremor that often disappears if the patient is able to begin a movement (Volkmann et al., 1996) (FIGURE 7.25b). Cognitive decline and eventually dementia also result from hyperactive inhibition in the dorsolateral prefrontal loop (Bosboom, Stoffers, & Wolters, 2004).

Medical treatment involves increasing dopamine activity, generally using dopamine agonist medications, which stimulate dopamine receptors, or using **levodopa**, a biochemical precursor that the brain can convert into dopamine itself, to replace the missing neurotransmitter (Lloyd, Davidson, & Hornykiewicz, 1975). Over time, these treatments become less effective. Ultimately, some patients undergo neurosurgery to have deep brain stimulator electrodes implanted in their subthalamic nucleus (Kumar et al., 1998). Despite their name, deep brain stimulators actually have inhibitory effects on local neural activity (Dostrovsky & Lozano, 2002). Treatments for brain disorders often work by inhibiting an inhibitory process, thereby exciting the ultimate target. By inhibiting the inhibitory subthalamic nucleus, the stimulation improves Parkinsonian symptoms. Unfortunately, despite ongoing research, there is still no permanent cure for Parkinson's disease.

Medial and Lateral Motor Systems: Internally and Externally Guided Movement Control

In addition to the lateral motor areas of the prefrontal cortex we discussed above, there are also a number of areas involved in motor control along the medial aspect of the frontal lobe. Roughly speaking, the medial motor system controls movements that are guided by internal states or motivations, whereas the lateral motor system controls movements that are guided by external stimuli.

Organization of Medial Motor Areas

Aside from the front-to-back hierarchy of control, a second key organizing principle of the prefrontal cortex is medial to lateral. In parallel with the areas of the lateral prefrontal cortex, there are also a set of medial motor areas (FIGURE 7.26). The most posterior of these is the supplementary motor area, which lies just in front of the medial part of the primary motor cortex. Like the lateral premotor cortex, the SMA has some direct connections to the spinal cord as well as connections to motor and premotor cortex. The SMA has some somatotopic organization, with the head-end (rostral) body parts represented anteriorly and the lower (caudal) body parts, like our feet, represented posteriorly (Mitz & Wise, 1987). In neurosurgical patients, stimulating this region produces a sensation that a movement is about to occur or an urge to move some part of the body. If the stimulation increases, the urge becomes irresistible and the movement occurs (Fried et al., 1991).

As we noted earlier, there is also a pre-supplementary motor area (pre-SMA) just anterior to the SMA, as well as a supplementary eye field lying between the two (FIGURE 7.26). Like the dorsolateral and ventrolateral prefrontal cortex, the pre-SMA lacks direct connections to the spinal cord and instead connects to the lateral prefrontal cortex. Somatotopy is less obvious in the pre-SMA. However, once again, stimulation of the pre-SMA produces an urge to move, and with stronger stimulation, actual movements (Fujii, Mushiake, & Tanji, 2002). Activity in this area also occurs in the seconds leading up to self-initiated (as opposed to externally cued) movements, as we will see below. This area is also important in preparing sequences of movements, even if the movements are not actually performed (Nachev, Kennard, & Husain, 2008).

In monkeys, neurons in the SMA and pre-SMA have complex properties (Nachev et al., 2008). Some neurons respond more to specific movement cues than other neurons do (for example, to visual cues more than to auditory or tactile cues). Some respond to cues to use a particular rule in a task; others respond to cues to perform a specific action or to inhibit a specific action. Overall, the functional organization of the medial motor areas is even less clear than that of the primary motor cortex.

Functions of Medial and Lateral Motor Systems

Why have more than one motor control system? You may recall from Chapter 2 that the brain draws input from two general sources: sensory input about the contents of external world and interoceptive input about the state of the "internal world" of the body. As we saw earlier, the lateral

Free eye movements versus
cued eye movements

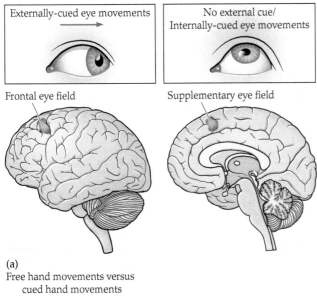

Externally-cued eye movements	No external cue/ Internally-cued eye movements

Frontal eye field   Supplementary eye field

(a)

Free hand movements versus
cued hand movements

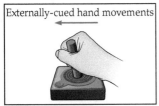 

Externally-cued hand movements	No external cue/ Internally-cued hand movements

Lateral prefrontal cortex   Pre-supplementary motor cortex

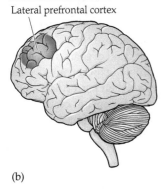 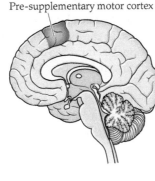

(b)

FIGURE 7.26 Lateral and medial motor areas. Lateral and medial regions of the prefrontal cortex guide behavior from external and internal cues, respectively. (a) The supplementary eye field is active during free exploratory eye movements, with no external cue. The frontal eye field, in the lateral prefrontal cortex, activates for eye movements guided by visual cues such as arrows. (b) Freely chosen movements of a joystick, with no external cue, activate the presupplementary motor area on the medial wall. When the movements are directed by an external visual cue, the lateral prefrontal cortex activates instead.

motor system draws heavily on sensory input from the external world for guidance. However, the entire purpose of the motor control system is to respond to the body's internal needs: hunger, thirst, cold, and so on. Hence, the motivational states that arise from the body's internal world are also essential in guiding what the motor system chooses to do: specifically, which features of the external

world it uses to guide behavior. This creates a need for a motor control system driven by internal states rather than external sensory input.

For an illustration, take a moment to look at your current surroundings. There are an enormous number of sensory stimuli that you could be using to guide your current behavior. However, you are only using a small proportion of these (hopefully, the words on this page) to guide your behavior at this moment. If you were to suddenly become hungry or thirsty, the words on this page might no longer be the main stimulus guiding your behavior; you might instead begin searching for a snack or a drink. Medial motor areas seem to become active when internal rather than external signals are required to select the most appropriate behavior (Picard & Strick, 1996).

Lesion studies in monkeys in the 1990s helped to illustrate the difference between the medial and lateral systems. Monkeys with lesions of the medial premotor cortex had difficulty raising their arm in a self-paced (internally cued) task. However, they could perform well if given an external auditory cue to guide their actions. Monkeys with lesions of the lateral premotor cortex showed the opposite effect: they had trouble raising their arm in response to an external cue, but could perform the same task well when raising their arm at their own pace (Goldman & Rosvold, 1970) (FIGURE 7.27).

Neuroimaging studies showed a similar effect in humans: medial areas in the pre-SMA were more active for self-paced than for externally paced actions (Cunnington, Windischberger, Deecke, & Moser, 2002). The pre-SMA also shows an increasing level of activity in the seconds leading up to a self-paced movement (Libet, Gleason, Wright, & Pearl, 1983). More anteriorly, medial areas of the frontopolar cortex also show more activity for self-selected goals rather than for externally cued goals during the performance of a task (Koechlin, Ody, & Kouneiher, 2003). Medial frontopolar areas show activity up to 8 seconds before a subject makes a randomly chosen, self-paced movement (Soon, Brass, Heinze, & Haynes, 2008). More posterior medial areas are also necessary for simple but internally driven acts, such as urination (or the inhibition of urination) (Kuhtz-Buschbeck et al., 2007). As these areas mature during brain development, children gain voluntary control over urination and bowel movements. If these pathways are injured or atrophy with age, voluntary control may be lost once again.

In fact, damage to the medial motor areas can cause two apparently paradoxical effects: a lack of spontaneous behavior and an excess of externally driven behavior (also called utilization behavior). For example, damage to medial motor areas such as the SMA and pre-SMA may result in a neurological condition called akinetic mutism (Watson, Fleet, Gonzalez-Rothi, & Heilman, 1986). In this state, the patient is awake and alert, but the motivation to behave is severely diminished. In one notable case, a patient repeated

(a)

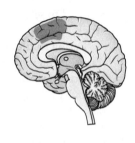

(b)

(c)

FIGURE 7.27 **Distinct effects of lateral and medial prefrontal lesions.** (a) Lesions of the lateral premotor cortex interfere with externally cued movements, such as raising the arm in response to a light signal. Conversely, lesions of medial motor areas, such as the supplementary motor area and the pre-supplementary motor area, interfere with internal control of movements. This can lead to either (b) automatisms, in which movements are triggered automatically by outside stimuli, or (c) akinetic mutism, in which no spontaneous behavior occurs.

phrases but made no spontaneous speech for a month after suffering a stroke in this area. After her recovery, she reported that she had understood all of the requests put to her but did not talk because she "felt no will to reply" and "had nothing to say"; she felt as if "nothing mattered"; her mind was "empty." In short, her internal motivation to respond to outside stimuli had been severely impaired (Devinsky, Morrell, & Vogt, 1995).

Another patient with a medial prefrontal lesion showed a lack of internal inhibitory motivation, leading to the utilization behavior described above (Biran, Giovannetti, Buxbaum, & Chatterjee, 2006). During an interview with this patient, the examiner left a knife and apple on the table. The patient spontaneously picked up the knife and the apple, peeled the apple, and began to eat it. Asked why he had done this, he answered that he knew the apple was not his and that he was not hungry; he was eating it "because it is here." In such patients, external stimuli may drive behavior with little guidance from internal motivations. Even those of us without neurological injury may find ourselves engaging in these kinds of simple motor automatisms if our attention is strongly focused elsewhere (for example, doodling or playing with small objects while engaged in conversation) (Penry & Dreifuss, 1969). Presumably, our medial motor areas are otherwise occupied at the time.

Once again, neuroimaging studies in humans have helped to clarify the role of the medial prefrontal areas in motivational aspects of motor control. Just as a hierarchy of control exists in the lateral prefrontal cortex, a similar hierarchy of control seems to exist in the medial prefrontal cortex. In the medial areas, this hierarchy reflects the motivational factors used during the selection of goals, strategies, actions, and tactics. In one example, experimenters offer subjects the chance to win money via their performance on a complex task where the correct answer depends on the stimulus, or the context, or the current episode of the overall experiment (as described at the beginning of the section above, *Control Stages of the Motor Hierarchy*). With the increased motivation of monetary gain, a medial hierarchy of prefrontal areas appeared alongside the lateral hierarchy seen when no money was at stake. Furthermore, each medial area's activity became more tightly correlated with its corresponding partner in the lateral prefrontal cortex (Koechlin & Summerfield, 2007).

Overall, then, there seem to be distinct medial and lateral motor control systems in the prefrontal cortex, each with a slightly different role. Through medial areas, motivational factors provide voluntary, or internally driven, control over motor functions in terms of selecting appropriate goals, strategies, tactics, and actions. Through lateral areas, external stimuli and contexts provide nonvoluntary, or externally driven, guidance of motor functions along the same hierarchy of levels. These two sets of areas work together to transform internal motivations into an appropriate set of motor responses, or behaviors.

NEUROSCIENCE OF EVERYDAY LIFE:
Why Can't I Multitask?

Why is it so hard to do more than one thing at once? Why should doing one task interfere with doing another? Our mouths and lips are not necessary to drive a car, so why is it dangerous to talk on a hands-free cell phone while driving? When we look at a face, we don't need to examine each part of the face one at a time to tell who we are looking at. We simply do it all at once. Why can't we perform many behaviors at once, in the same way that we perform many sensory tasks at once?

Neuroimaging studies have begun to search for the apparent "bottleneck" in information processing that limits our ability to multitask (FIGURE 7.28). One study (Dux, Ivanoff, Asplund, & Marois, 2006) had subjects perform two tasks almost simultaneously: pressing buttons according to an auditory cue and pronouncing syllables according to a visual cue. When these tasks occurred close together in time, the subjects' reaction times began to slow: the limits of their multitasking abilities had been reached.

Functional MRI revealed a possible basis for the slowing. Some brain regions were active for only one of these two tasks. However, other areas responded for both tasks; these areas could be potential sites of the multitasking bottleneck. Two of these regions showed responses that reflected the degree of reaction-time slowing (Dux et al., 2006). The posterior lateral prefrontal cortex and, to some extent, the SMA both showed this apparent slowing of response activity. For competition between these two simple cue–response tasks, the bottleneck appeared to be in areas low in the motor hierarchy. However,

multitasking at higher levels of cognitive control may have a different basis. For example, compared with healthy individuals, patients with damage to the frontopolar cortex have trouble multitasking among competing goals rather than competing responses (Dreher et al., 2008; Shallice & Burgess, 1991).

So why do we need to perform many motor tasks slowly, step by step (for example, performing long division to find the answer to 247 divided

by 13), although we can perform many kinds of much more complex sensory tasks simultaneously, quickly, and effortlessly (for example, recognizing a face as male or female)? The answer may lie in the differing architecture of motor control versus sensory perception systems. Sensory perception involves integrating multiple features of a stimulus into a final result—a set of computations that can be done simultaneously (in parallel), to arrive at an answer quickly (FIGURE 7.29a). Most

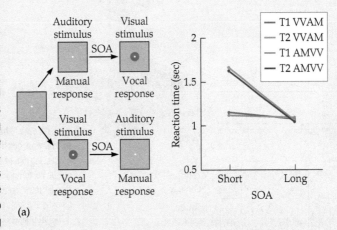

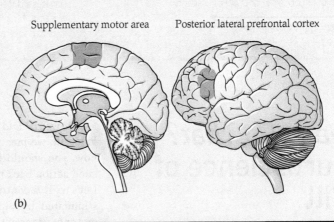

FIGURE 7.28 **An fMRI study of multitasking.** (a) Subjects had to press buttons according to an auditory cue and then, after a short interval (SOA), pronounce a syllable according to a visual cue (or vice versa). When the intervals were short, reaction times were delayed, suggesting a "bottleneck" in information processing. (b) fMRI localized this bottleneck to the medial and lateral prefrontal cortex, which were slower to activate as reaction times increased during multitasking (Dux et al., 2006).

of the computations can be done independently of one another; in face perception, there is no need to process the eyes before the nose before the mouth. The parallel architecture of sensory perception is "multitasking friendly."

Motor control is different. The motor hierarchy involves dividing a goal into a sequence of subgoals, then dividing each subgoal into further substeps, then each substep into a series of simple actions, and so on. The order of the sequence is critical: try rearranging the steps of a recipe for making an omelette, and you'll quickly see why. Also, many steps can be performed only one at a time: you cannot crack the egg for the omelette while chopping the mushrooms. Hence, the motor control system needs an architecture designed to break a task into steps, arrange them in a sequence, and allow the performance of only one step at a time while inhibiting all the others (FIGURE 7.29b). Any kind of behavior that borrows this system (like long division) will therefore run into a bottleneck arising from the intrinsic architecture of motor control (Kieras & Meyer, 1997). If one can find a way to shift the behavior onto a sensory system (like memorizing a division table), response time decreases dramatically. However, for many tasks, there is no easy way to do this: sequence matters, and so the architecture of motor control makes multitasking a difficult proposition.

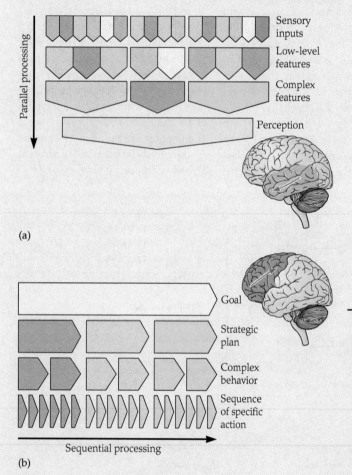

(a)

(b)

FIGURE 7.29 **The distinct computational architectures of sensory perception versus motor control.** (a) Sensory processing can be accomplished rapidly because all of the steps can be performed simultaneously, in parallel. Any kind of cognition that borrows the brain's sensory pathways can therefore be done quickly, and multitasking is possible. (b) Motor control is a different process that requires dividing a task into multiple substeps and then performing them one at a time, in the correct sequence. Any kind of cognition that borrows the brain's motor hierarchy is therefore slower, and multitasking is harder.

Did I Really Do That? The Neuroscience of Free Will

Neuroscience sometimes ends up having strange philosophical implications for how we think about ourselves as human beings. Let's end the chapter by looking at one of these strange implications. Start by trying this simple experiment: at the end of this sentence, lift either your left or your right hand.

Go on, try it—the choice is up to you!

Or was it? Did you really make a free, voluntary choice? What do we mean by a voluntary movement, anyway? By now, you should be able to trace your simple, internally cued action back through the nervous system to its origin. Let's try it: a contraction of the deltoid and tricep muscles is stimulated by alpha motor neurons, directed by upper motor neurons of the primary motor cortex, under the guidance of a hierarchy of medial frontal areas: SMA, pre-SMA, frontopolar cortex, and so on. But where does this process all begin? Doesn't each action begin with a free choice? After all, you could have raised either hand, correct? So where, if anywhere, does free will come into the neural picture?

One of the classic studies of voluntary movement was performed by the American physiologist Benjamin Libet in 1983 (Libet et al., 1983). He made EEG recordings on volunteers while asking them to raise their fingers periodically at a time of their own free choice (FIGURE 7.30). At the same time, the volunteers watched a clock with a rapidly spinning hand. They noted the position of the clock's hand at the exact moment that they became aware of their intention to raise their finger. By later reporting this position, they could indicate the exact timing of their intention, to an accuracy of within a few milliseconds. On average, the intention seemed to form about 200 milliseconds before the movement. The remarkable finding was that the EEG showed preparatory activity in the brain more than 1 full second before the movement! Somehow, brain activity was taking place not only before a movement occurred, but also before even the intention of a movement occurred!

Since then, other EEG, MEG, and neuroimaging experiments have mapped out the sources of the so-called "readiness potential" preceding voluntary movements. The SMA and pre-SMA seem to be the main sites of activity preceding conscious intentions to act (Haggard, 2008). More recently, it has become clear that choice-related brain activity takes place much more than 1 second before conscious awareness of the choice itself. One fMRI study found that activity in the frontopolar cortex could reliably predict whether a subject would raise his or her left or right hand, a full 8–10 seconds before the subject became conscious of his or her own so-called "free" choice (Soon et al., 2008)!

If the conscious intention to move comes after rather than before the readiness potential, then we need to ask another fundamental question: is our "intention" to move really a motor command, or is conscious intention actually more like a sensation of what is about to happen? As we saw earlier, sensory representations for action are formed in the inferior parietal cortex. In addition, the cerebellum may provide a forward model of one's own future actions. What happens to conscious intention if these areas are damaged?

As it turns out, patients with cerebellar injury performed similarly to normal subjects in Libet's free-movement task: they judged their intention to move as occurring around 200 milliseconds before the actual movement. However, patients with parietal injury did not become aware of their intention to move until much later—just 50 milliseconds before the movement itself. Damage to a sensory area, not a motor area, had interfered with the conscious intention to make a voluntary movement (Sirigu et al., 2004).

Another more recent experiment by the same researchers gave an even more powerful demonstration of the difference between conscious intention and motor action (Desmurget et al., 2009). Here, a neurosurgeon electrically stimulated either the lateral premotor cortex or the inferior parietal lobule of patients undergoing surgery (FIGURE 7.31). Stimulating the lateral premotor cortex produced movements such as raising the hand or the arm. Other observers could see these movements clearly, yet the patients strongly denied having made any movement at all!

On the other hand, stimulating the inferior parietal cortex caused the patients to report an "urge" or intention to move various body parts. Stronger currents made the patients feel as if they had actually performed a movement: "I moved my mouth; I talked; what did I say?" Yet in fact, the patients hadn't moved at all. Electrical recordings from the muscles confirmed that there had not been so much as a twitch in the body parts in question. Conscious intention in these patients was a sensory, not a motor phenomenon. Conversely, movement without sensory stimulation remained an unconscious act.

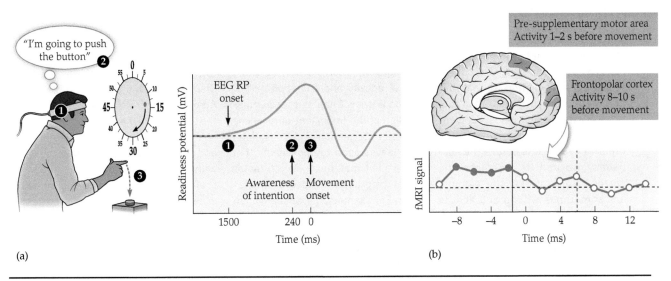

(a)   (b)

FIGURE 7.30 The neuroscience of free will. (a) In Libet's classic experiment, an EEG signal was detected in medial motor areas more than 1 second before the person became aware of deciding to press a button. (b) More recently, fMRI studies have found that patterns of activity in the frontopolar cortex can predict whether the person will decide to press a button with the left or right hand—8 to 10 seconds before they are aware of their own decision.

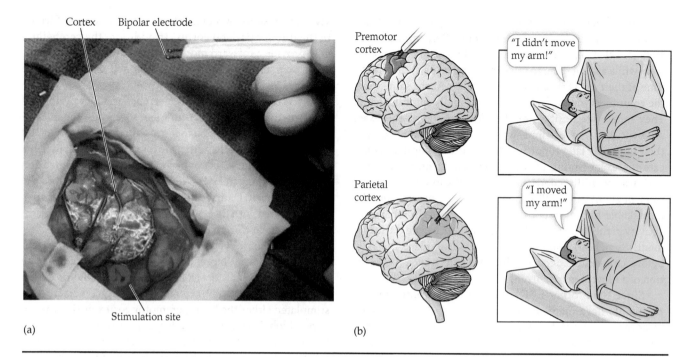

(a)

(b)

FIGURE 7.31 **Dissociating conscious intention from motor action.** (a) In patients undergoing surgery, a handheld electrode can be used to stimulate points on the surface of the cortex directly. (b) In one recent study, stimulating the premotor cortex elicited movement without intention or awareness. Stimulating the parietal cortex elicited a will to move, or even a sensation of movement, but no actual movement.

RESEARCH METHODS:
Neurosurgical Stimulation

Stimulation experiments have been a classic method for exploring brain function since the first motor cortex studies of Fritsch and Hitzig in 1870 (Fritsch & Hitzig, 1870). Neurosurgical patients must often remain awake during the initial phase of the operation, so that they can help the surgeons map out areas of the brain critical for sensation, movement, language, and other key functions before the surgeons proceed to cut into the cortex. While awake, the patients are sometimes willing and able to participate in experiments as well. They can often give detailed subjective reports of the effects of the stimulation, which can be valuable in understanding the function of the area.

Brain stimulation experiments can help to establish a causal role between activity in a given brain region and a given cognitive function. By contrast, neuroimaging and electrophysiological experiments ultimately measure only correlations between neural activity and cognition or behavior. (Review Chapter 1 for our discussion of the important differences between correlation and causation.) This leaves open the possibility that some additional, unsuspected factor might underlie the observed correlations. For example, a brain activation correlated with pain intensity might actually be involved in inhibiting the withdrawal response. Stimulation experiments would help to reveal the motor rather than the sensory role of such an area.

Of course, there are drawbacks to the technique of brain stimulation. Stimulation can spread to local and distant areas of the brain, so that the observed effects do not necessarily arise from the stimulated area alone (McIntyre, Mori, Sherman, Thakor, & Vitek, 2004). Also, many brain areas (such as those deep in the sulci or in deep structures such as the thalamus and basal ganglia) are hard to reach with exploratory electrodes. Deep brain stimulators may be implanted in such areas, however. As these devices enter more widespread use in treating specific neurological disorders like Parkinson's disease, they may also help us to better understand the function of the brain in general terms.

CASE STUDY:
Alien Hand Syndrome

A 56-year-old Italian woman once suffered a stroke leading to severe damage to the medial frontal lobes, including the supplementary motor area. Although she recovered, she was left with some unusual symptoms. One of her hands began acting as if it had a mind of its own. It would grab objects out of her other hand and try to use them in a different and unhelpful way. It would try to pick up a hot cup of tea, although she had intended to wait until the tea cooled. It would even scratch her genitalia in public, much to her embarrassment. She would sometimes sit on this hand, or even hit it, to stop it from acting against her intentions in these ways. Although she knew the hand was hers, she felt as if it had a will of its own (Della Sala, Marchetti, & Spinnler, 1991).

The woman in question had fallen victim to **alien hand syndrome**, a rare neurological disorder typically resulting from injury to the SMA or other regions of the medial prefrontal cortex (Biran et al., 2006). In a patient with this syndrome, the arm on the opposite side of her body to the injury will often perform automatic actions based on external stimuli. The patient may be powerless to inhibit these actions without physically restraining the "alien hand" with another part of the body. Without the internally generated motor control functions of the medial motor system, it can be difficult to get the hand to follow the patient's own internal set of plans, goals, and motivations.

Neuroimaging studies have revealed further details about the mechanism of alien hand movements. Normal voluntary movements involve the activation of not just primary motor cortex, but also the rest of the motor hierarchy: frontal pole, lateral prefrontal cortex, premotor areas, and the high-level action-oriented sensory regions in the inferior parietal cortex (Assal, Schwartz, & Vuilleumier, 2007). Alien hand movements, on the other hand, involved isolated "rogue" activation of the primary motor cortex in the absence of any of the other brain regions of the motor hierarchy (Assal et al., 2007). Motor activation alone, it seems, is not enough to create a sense of voluntary action. For a movement to be "voluntary," it must fit into the context of a complete motor control hierarchy and its sensory counterparts: the action must fit into the larger scheme of one's plans, motivations, goals, and sensory expectations (Assal et al., 2007).

Taken together, these findings have some startling implications for our own sense of being "free agents." At least in these studies, it seems as if our sense of conscious intention is just that: a sensation, not a cause of action. If we feel as if we control our actions, it may simply be because our parietal cortices have had a lifetime of practice at predicting what our frontal lobes are going to do next! When these predictions fail or when there is a break in the smooth flow of goals into plans into actions, we feel as if we are not responsible for the outcome. "It's not me doing this!," we say, even when it cannot be anyone else. For a clear illustration of this point, look at the case study of "alien hand syndrome."

Conclusion

The complexity of human behavior requires, if anything, even greater complexity in the brain circuitry to enable it. Although it is easy to get lost in the ongoing research controversies on how our motor functions work, some general principles of function do emerge. First, the brain shows a front-to-back hierarchy of successively lower-level motor control regions. This hierarchy allows our long-term goals to be broken down into a series of cognitive operations, each of which helps to plan a series of actions in premotor cortex, each of which can be further broken down into specific movements in motor cortex, finally guiding the lower motor neurons of the spinal cord to execute specific patterns of muscle contractions. This hierarchy is actually two parallel hierarchies of regions: a lateral hierarchy that uses guiding signals from our external senses and a medial hierarchy that applies prioritizing signals from our internal drives and motivations. The basal ganglia guide the delicate process of initiating, maintaining, and terminating activity in the proper sequence at every step along the way. The cerebellum helps to smooth the timing of each step, possibly by using forward models to anticipate when movements will need to stop and start. Together, this elaborate system provides us with a huge repertoire of abilities to meet our survival needs.

KEY PRINCIPLES

- Muscles are the brain's tools for manipulating the external environment.

- Motor action potentials cross the synapse-like neuromuscular junction to activate the electro-chemical mechanisms of muscle contraction.

- Spinal cord motor neurons operate within the simple circuitry of reflex arcs and central pattern generators. This circuitry coordinates muscle contractions, usually with guidance from local sensory input and descending modulation from the brain.

- The cerebellum provides further refinement and coordination of movements, possibly through a predictive mechanism known as forward modeling. In addition, it plays a role in nonmotor functions.

- The primary motor cortex provides motor output to the spinal cord and is organized by body part, type of action, and possibly other dimensions.

- The prefrontal cortex provides the circuitry for a hierarchy of motor control in which needs are broken down into more specific goals, strategies, tactics, and actions.

- The basal ganglia may help to initiate and maintain motor control processes via a circuitry of excitatory and inhibitory cortical–subcortical loops.

- Lateral motor areas perform under the guidance of external sensory input, whereas medial motor areas perform under the guidance of internal motivations and priorities.

- The field of neuroscience is beginning to explore the mechanisms of voluntary and involuntary behavior, with implications for understanding our sense of free will.

KEY TERMS

Muscles
muscle fibers (p. 199)
myofibrils (p. 199)
antagonistic muscles (p. 199)
extensors (p. 199)
flexors (p. 199)
type I fibers (p. 199)
type II fibers (p. 199)
acetylcholinesterase (p. 200)
curare (p. 200)

The Spinal Cord
dorsal horn (p. 202)
lower motor neurons (p. 202)
alpha motor neurons (p. 202)
gamma motor neurons (p. 202)
motor unit (p. 202)
spinal reflex (p. 202)
deep tendon reflex (p. 202)
corticospinal tract (p. 204)
upper motor neurons (p. 204)
cerebral palsy (p. 204)
pyramids (p. 204)

lateral corticospinal tract (p. 205)
red nuclei (p. 205)
vestibular nuclei (p. 205)
tectum (p. 205)

The Cerebellum
saccades (p. 206)
cerebellar cortex (p. 206)
mossy fibers (p. 207)
climbing fibers (p. 207)
basket cells (p. 207)
stellate cells (p. 207)
lateral inhibitory connections (p. 207)

The Motor Cortex
motor homunculus (p. 210)
somatosensory homunculus (p. 210)
lateral premotor cortex (p. 211)
frontal eye field (p. 211)
supplementary motor area (SMA) (p. 211)

pre-supplementary motor area (pre-SMA) (p. 211)
brain–computer interface (p. 214)

The Prefrontal Cortex: Goals to Strategies to Tactics to Actions
frontopolar cortex (p. 216)
mirror neurons (p. 217)
superior temporal sulcus (p. 217)
theory of mind (p. 218)
Wisconsin card-sorting task (p. 219)

Basal Ganglia
Huntington's disease (HD) (p. 220)
dementia (p. 220)
Parkinson's disease (p. 222)
levodopa (p. 222)

Did I Really Do That? The Neuroscience of Free Will
alien hand syndrome (p. 229)

REVIEW QUESTIONS

1. How do muscles respond to sudden loads or stretches? How does the nervous system contribute to this process?

2. Describe three ways in which paralysis can arise from a blockade of the neuromuscular junction. Why can botulinum toxin be lethal in such small quantities?

3. How does a neck-level spinal cord injury prevent walking in human beings? What circuits might remain intact, to offer a chance of recovery?

4. Why might cerebellar injuries make it difficult to catch a ball or write a sentence?

5. What evidence supports a somatotopic organization of the primary motor cortex? What evidence supports a behavior-category organization of the primary motor cortex?

6. Describe three different loop circuits between the cortex and basal ganglia. What functions do they serve? How do the symptoms of Parkinson's disease arise? How and why are these different from the symptoms of Huntington's disease?

7. What are the differences in function between medial and lateral motor areas of the prefrontal cortex? Why might we need these two separate motor control systems in the human brain? Why do injuries of the medial system sometimes lead to the spontaneous movements of "alien hand syndrome"? Why do they sometimes cause a lack of spontaneous movements in "akinetic mutism"?

8. What do experimental studies tell us about the origin of "voluntary" movements?

CRITICAL-THINKING QUESTIONS

1. Imagine you were a neurosurgeon, planning to implant a brain-interface electrode in a patient with locked-in syndrome. What might a patient be able to do with an electrode implanted in primary motor cortex? Supplementary motor area? Intraparietal cortex? Dorsolateral prefrontal cortex? Frontopolar cortex? Where do you think would be the most useful place to implant the device?

2. How might mirror neurons be important for the development of language and communication? Do human babies show any behaviors that might involve mirror neuron functions? What about adults?

3. What do you think the difference is between "voluntary" and "involuntary" actions? Do you think we freely choose what to do? If so, why? If not, why does it *feel* as if we are freely choosing what to do?

- Explain how the phenomena of change blindness and inattentional blindness demonstrate that awareness requires attention.

- Describe the orienting and oddball paradigms for studying attention as well as the use of perceptual rivalry to study awareness.

- Identify which brain regions are important for attention and awareness, what hemispatial neglect reveals about the basis of attention and awareness, and the evidence that multiple networks of brain regions exist for different kinds of attention and awareness.

- Assess effects of attention on the activity of single neurons and local ensembles of neurons.

- Examine how neural synchronization contributes to attention and awareness.

- Describe the underlying forms of brain injury in coma and vegetative state.

- Explain how anesthesia produces a state of unconsciousness while leaving brain anatomy intact.

- Assess current theories of how neural activity gives rise to conscious experiences.

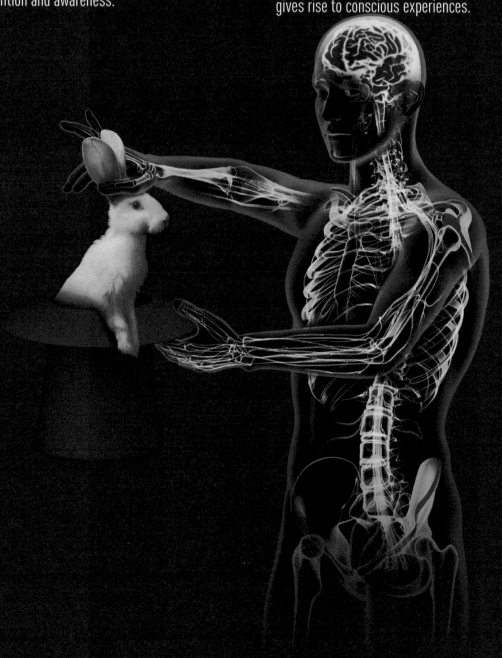

CHAPTER 8

Attention and Consciousness

STARTING OUT:
The Stream of Consciousness

Next time you're bored, try this simple exercise: see how much of the world you're missing. Try to turn your attention to all the sensory input that normally escapes your notice. Start with somatosensation. Is there an itch somewhere on your skin, just on the threshold of awareness? Does it dissipate, or grow, when you pay attention to it? Which of your fingers is closest to your chin right now? Are your teeth clenched or open? Did any of these things reach your awareness before you paid attention to them?

Now try auditory input. How many different sounds can you make out, going on around you, beneath your notice until this very moment? Can you hear your own breathing? Did you notice it until just now? You might even try olfactory and gustatory input. If you pay attention, is there any smell, or any taste, that has escaped your notice before this moment?

You could also look at the movements of your own body. What was the last movement you made? Did you do it on purpose? Were your feet fidgeting or your fingers tapping? Have you been absentmindedly doodling or playing with some nearby object? When was the last time you blinked? After reading this last sentence, how many times will you notice your own blinking before it falls once again out of your awareness?

Finally, turn to visual input. Keeping your eyes fixed on some nearby point, turn your attention slowly to the different parts of the visual field. Is there anything gray that you can see? If so, if it somehow changed color slowly, would you notice the difference? Pick some obvious object nearby: maybe a piece of furniture or even another person. If we suddenly replaced this object with another one, vaguely similar, would you be able to tell?

Once you are done, go back and read over this text again and see how many different kinds of sensation passed through your awareness in just a couple of minutes. Are you still monitoring your blinking? How do these things slip out of our consciousness so easily? Like momentary ripples on the surface of a stream, the sensations that pass through our conscious awareness are numerous, but fleeting. They are dwarfed by the vastly greater currents that travel underneath them, never reaching the surface at all. For every speck we see afloat on the stream of consciousness, there are thousands of others, buried deeper, that remain forever out of sight and out of mind (FIGURE 8.1).

FIGURE 8.1 A woodland stream, with eddies, ripples, and currents. Much like consciousness, some of these are seen and some remain unseen beneath the surface.

Why are we aware of so little of the world around us? Why are we aware of so little of what we do, even as we do it? Or we can turn the question on its head: why are we aware of anything at all? Couldn't we just roam about the earth like little robotic vacuum cleaners, charging ourselves up with energy and performing our daily functions, without ever having the rich internal life of subjective events that we call "experiences"? For some reason, this is not what happens. Instead, the activity of all the billions of neurons in our brains gives rise to consciousness, and this consciousness can contain an immense variety of different experiences over the course of even a single minute.

As we'll see in this chapter, conscious perception is an active process: one that requires attention. And although we can choose to attend to many different things, the choice itself is far from arbitrary. Our attention depends on what we are doing right now, which depends in turn on the larger context of our current behavior, which depends in turn on our short-term and long-term goals, which in turn depend on the basic needs we all must satisfy as living human beings.

Attention brings together sensation and action so that they can serve a common purpose. This process is delicate and easily disrupted by disease, drugs, or even the nightly cycle of sleep. Yet when it works properly, somehow it produces the mysterious phenomenon of consciousness.

Awareness Requires Attention

The link between attention and awareness has been appreciated for centuries. "My experience is what I agree I attend to," noted the pioneering psychologist William James in his classic textbook, *Principles of Psychology*, in 1890 (James, 1890). The 17th-century German philosopher Gottfried Wilhelm Leibniz described this notion more poetically: "At every moment there is in us an infinity of perceptions, unaccompanied by awareness or reflection . . . because these impressions are either too minute and too numerous, or too unvarying" (Leibniz, 1896).

Stage magicians have understood these principles for even longer. They have found that they can make a person unaware of an event that would normally be salient (such as having a watch taken from her wrist) simply through misdirection of the person's attention away from the event (Kuhn, Tatler, Findlay, & Cole, 2008). In the case of **covert misdirection**, the person misses the event even if her gaze remains right on the object in question: it is her attention, not her gaze, that is in the wrong place (Macknik et al., 2008). Using these techniques, a skilled performer can create the illusion that objects have appeared, disappeared, or undergone a dramatic change (FIGURE 8.2).

Change Blindness

The illusionist's disappearing act relies on a phenomenon that neuroscientists have labeled change blindness (Simons & Levin, 1997) (see Chapter 5). In one early example, experienced pilots in a flight simulator failed to notice if a large airplane was placed on the runway, directly in their path, during a simulated landing (Haines, 1991). Likewise, experimental subjects would fail to notice large changes in visual scenes, so long as there was a brief visual interruption before the change,

FIGURE 8.2 **A magician can misdirect your attention away from the trick, creating the illusion that something appeared or disappeared in front of your eyes.**

as in a slideshow. In many cases, they would fail to notice the change even when looking directly at its location, if they were attending to the wrong feature (Simons & Levin, 1997). You can experience this effect for yourself by comparing the photographs in FIGURE 8.3. Do you see the change?

FIGURE 8.3 **Change blindness.** Can you see the difference between the two images?

FIGURE 8.4 People are often blind to changes around them. In this experiment, (a) one experimenter asked people for directions and was then (b) "interrupted" by two movers. (c) Unbeknownst to the subject, a second experimenter replaced the first while the movers were in the way. Only about half of the subjects noticed the change. (d) The two experimenters side by side.

The implication of change blindness is that we are actually aware of much less of the world than we might think. Although it appears that we are conscious of everything before our eyes, in fact we are consciously perceiving only the tiny fraction of the world that is at the focus of our attention. If we distract attention with a flicker in the scene, or a page turn, or even an eye movement, major changes in the scene can completely escape our awareness (Hayhoe, Bensinger, & Ballard, 1998; O'Regan, 2000; Rensink, O'Regan, & Clark, 1997).

As it turns out, we don't even have to block out the entire image between changes to get the effect. In other versions of the change blindness experiment, the subjects are distracted by "mudsplashes" that pop up on the screen at the same time as the change, but do not actually cover up the changed area. Even this minor disruption is enough to hide the change from awareness (O'Regan, Rensink, & Clark, 1999). The mudsplashes seem to draw one's attention elsewhere. But if the mudsplash appears *right over* the location of the change, it seems to help rather than hinder

subjects' awareness of the change. With attention drawn to the right place, the change can finally reach awareness (O'Regan et al., 1999).

Change blindness operates outside the laboratory as well. In a real-life demonstration (FIGURE 8.4), experimenters pretended to be visitors to a university campus. They would stop randomly chosen individuals to ask them for directions. During the middle of the conversation, two other experimenters dressed as construction workers would rudely march between them carrying a large door. Behind the door, the pretend "visitor" would switch places with a different visitor, who would pick up the conversation exactly where it had been left off. Remarkably, only about 50% of subjects noticed that they were now speaking to an entirely different person. The rest carried on as if nothing had happened (Simons & Levin, 1998).

Inattentional Blindness

Another powerful demonstration of the link between attention and awareness is the phenomenon of **inattentional blindness**. Closely related to change blindness, this phenomenon is also exploited by stage magicians, when they use misdirection to distract the audience from the truth behind the trick. Psychologists began studying inattentional blindness experimentally in the 1990s. In one early experiment, subjects were asked to judge the length of two arms of a plus sign, called the fixation cross, on which they maintained their gaze during the experiment. After a few warm-up trials, the experimenters added an unexpected "stimulus"—such as a face—in one quadrant of the cross during the trial for 200 milliseconds. Immediately afterward, they asked the subjects whether they had seen anything out of the ordinary. Most subjects turned out to be completely unaware of the unexpected stimulus, although it appeared near the center of the fixation cross (Mack & Rock, 1999).

Inattentional blindness is just as powerful a phenomenon in real-world scenes (FIGURE 8.5). In one famous demonstration, experimenters asked subjects to count basketball passes between players in a short video. During the middle of the video, a man in a gorilla suit appeared unexpectedly and walked slowly across the screen. Halfway across, he stopped and beat his chest a few times before continuing to walk off the screen once again. All throughout, the players ran around the gorilla actor, continuing to pass the balls back and forth. Nearly half of all subjects completely failed to notice the gorilla. With the task difficulty increased, only 8% of subjects noticed anything unusual (Simons & Chabris, 1999).

But is it really true that subjects are completely unaware of these unexpected events at the time they occur? Might

FIGURE 8.5 Illustration of the "gorillas in our midst" experiment. Nearly half of all subjects completely failed to notice the gorilla.

they actually be aware of them on some level, but somehow forget about them by the time they are asked?

One way to tell the two apart is to look at subjects' brain activity while the unattended stimuli are present,

NEUROSCIENCE OF EVERYDAY LIFE:
Stage Magic

Inattentional blindness and change blindness are powerful laboratory demonstrations of the link between attention and awareness. Outside the laboratory, however, illusionists have exploited these same effects for centuries. Their performances

entertain us and at the same time baffle us. By drawing our attention to the wrong place at the wrong time, a skilled performer can perform the trick in plain sight, without us ever being aware of what really happened (FIGURE 8.6).

The effects of misdirection are not restricted to the visual system. There are professional pickpockets who make a living not as thieves, but as entertainers. Some are sufficiently skilled that they can even warn their "victims" ahead of time

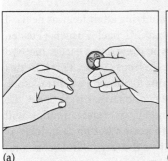
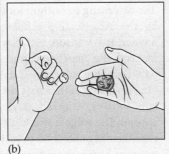
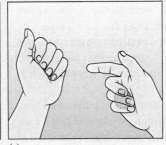
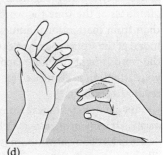

(a) (b) (c) (d)

FIGURE 8.6 **How to make a coin "disappear."** (a) Hold the coin between your thumb and forefinger. (b) Covertly hide the coin while directing the audience's attention somewhere else. (c) Misdirect the audience to the empty hand. (d) "Disappear" the coin by throwing your empty hand upward.

that they are going to pick their pockets. Even with the warning, the victims do not realize that anything is amiss until the performer hands them back their watch, their wallet, their phone, and in some cases even their glasses. One competition challenged a pickpocket to relieve an audience member of his wallet, watch, phone, and necktie in less than 60 seconds. The pickpocket succeeded with ease, much to the audience member's chagrin. In this case, misdirection draws attention away from both the visual and the somatosensory cues that would normally raise one's awareness of a theft in progress (BBC, 2006).

These types of stage performance are compelling demonstrations of the limited scope of our attention and awareness. Recognizing this, neuroscientists have now begun to collaborate with stage performers to develop new experimental methods for studying attention.

rather than ask about the unattended stimuli at a later time. In a neuroimaging experiment, subjects watched a rapid stream of pictures and letter strings, superimposed on one another in the center of their visual field. Some of the letter strings were real words; others were nonsense strings of letters. The subjects' task was to pay attention to one of the two streams and detect any repetitions of the same stimulus twice in a row. When they had been paying attention to the letters, subjects did well on surprise recognition **memory** tests of those words after the task was over. In these tests, subjects viewed a list of words that included some of the words they had just seen as well as some new words. They were more likely to correctly identify words they had just seen when they had been paying attention to the letter strings as opposed to when they had been paying attention to the pictures, so the unattended stimuli were not remembered (Rees, Russell, Frith, & Driver, 1999).

But was this inattentional blindness or amnesia? Here, the neuroimaging data provided further clues. When subjects were paying attention to the letter strings, their brains showed different activity for words than for nonsense strings in a widespread network of frontal, parietal, and temporal lobe areas. However, when they were paying attention to the pictures, these same brain areas made no distinction between real words and nonsense strings. This provided evidence that the poor recognition truly came from inattentional blindness at the time the words were on the screen, rather than from inattentional amnesia at a later time point. The moral of the story: your eyes can directly fixate on words, yet the words might still not reach your conscious awareness if your attention is elsewhere (as you may have noticed while reading a textbook!).

The point to take away from this section is that *there is no awareness without attention*. Although we may feel as if we are aware of all of our surroundings, in fact only a tiny fraction of all the sensory input to our retina is actually incorporated into conscious perception at any given time. Conscious perception is not a passive process of receiving information, but an active process of constructing a representation of some piece of the world around us.

Approaches to Studying Attention and Awareness

Inattentional blindness and change blindness serve as reminders of the close link between conscious perception and attention. But to study the brain mechanisms behind these two related functions, we'll need some ways of studying awareness and attention under carefully controlled conditions. We'll also need something specific to study. We cannot directly measure attention, as we can do for blood pressure or temperature. Instead, we'll need to use some kind of correlate of attention: either a behavioral measure, like reaction time, or a physiological signal, like an evoked potential on EEG or a signal change on fMRI. There are several commonly used methods for studying attention and awareness. Let's take a moment to review them before we turn to the brain's attentional mechanisms themselves.

Attentional Orienting Paradigms: Aiming the "Spotlight" of Attention

The **orienting paradigm** for studying attention was devised by the American psychologist Michael Posner (Posner, Snyder, & Davidson, 1980), who drew on an earlier method for studying visual perception in frogs (Ingle, 1975). In this paradigm, the subject maintains fixation on a central cross. On either side of the cross are two squares. Inside one of the two squares, selected at random, a target stimulus will appear. The subject's task is to press a button as quickly as possible once she or he perceives the target. The behavioral measure here is the subject's reaction time (FIGURE 8.7).

To study the effect of attention, on some trials, we present a brief **central cue** slightly before the stimulus appears. The cue is an arrow that points to one of the two squares, indicating where the target is going to appear, so that the

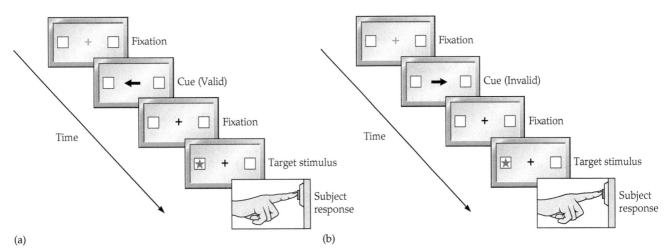

(a)   (b)

FIGURE 8.7 The Posner orienting paradigm. These figures show the sequence of events for this experiment. First, the subject fixates on a "+" sign in the middle of the screen. Then, a cue (an arrow) predicts where the stimulus will appear, followed by a return to the basic fixation condition. Finally, the stimulus appears in one of the two boxes and the subject responds. (a) A valid cue and (b) an invalid cue.

subject can pay attention to that square (while maintaining eye fixation on the cross). When the cue is added, the subjects respond more quickly: there is a **reaction time benefit** to having one's attention in the right place at the right time. However, the cue is not perfectly reliable: on some trials it points to the wrong square, so that the subject is paying attention to the wrong location when the target appears. The result is that there is a **reaction time cost** to having one's attention in the wrong place at the wrong time (Brown, Friston, & Bestmann, 2011). By comparing the subject's reaction times on the different kinds of trials, we now have a precise behavioral measure of visuospatial attention. This is sometimes called **voluntary** or **endogenous attention**, since the subjects themselves must direct their attention to the location suggested by the cue. The premise is that attention operates a little bit like a "spotlight" that can be directed to monitor a specific location in space, at the expense of monitoring other locations (Chong, Tadin, & Blake, 2005).

This paradigm can also probe **involuntary** or **exogenous attention**. In this case, an **involuntary cue** draws the subject's attention to one of the two target locations. For example, one of the squares might briefly blink just before the target appears (Jonides & Irwin, 1981). As before, this gives a reaction time benefit for a valid cue (that is, a brightening of the square where the target will actually appear) and a reaction time cost for an invalid cue (a blinking of the wrong square, opposite to where the target will actually appear).

The orienting paradigm thus allows us to study two different mechanisms of attention: the **top-down mechanism** by which we deliberately focus on a feature of the environment (such as a traffic light at an intersection) and the **bottom-up mechanism** by which our attention jumps to unexpected but salient features of the sensory environment

(such as a pedestrian suddenly running out in front of the car) (Brown et al., 2011). It can also be adapted to other sensory modalities: auditory, tactile, and cross-modal variants of orienting have all been investigated, showing similar effects of attention on reaction time (Butter, Buchtel, & Santucci, 1989; Farah, Wong, Monheit, & Morrow, 1989; Hugdahl & Nordby, 1994). There are even nonspatial variants, in which the cue indicates *what* rather than *where* to attend during the task. The orienting paradigm is thus quite a flexible approach for studying attention via behavioral measures.

The Oddball Paradigm: Monitoring a Physiological Measure of Attention

Another approach to studying attention is to measure neural rather than behavioral responses. A common method for doing this is called the **oddball paradigm**. Here, we present the subject with a long train of repetitive stimuli, interrupted occasionally by an attention-drawing deviant or "oddball" stimulus that differs from the standard stimuli in some quality such as shape, color, or brightness (or pitch or duration in the case of auditory stimuli). We then measure the brain's response to the oddball stimulus using EEG, MEG, or fMRI. Oddball paradigms can be applied in many different sensory domains: visual, auditory, somatosensory, and even olfactory modalities (Courchesne, Hillyard, & Galambos, 1975; Linden et al., 1999; Pause, Sojka, Krauel, & Ferstl, 1996; Yamaguchi & Knight, 1991).

Like the orienting task, the oddball paradigm allows us to study voluntary and involuntary (or "top-down" and "bottom-up") attentional mechanisms. For bottom-up mechanisms, we insert a third kind of stimulus into the train: a "novel oddball" that is entirely different from the usual oddballs in the train (Swick & Knight, 1998). The novel oddballs draw attention through involuntary mechanisms, something like the peripheral cues in the orienting task. We then compare the brain's responses to the novel oddball versus the standard oddballs to examine the neural mechanisms of involuntary attention.

To study top-down mechanisms, we present the train of stimuli in the context of a behavioral task. In the task, the subject must respond to some types of oddball stimuli (the "task-relevant" oddballs) but does not need to do anything with others (the "task-irrelevant" oddballs). We then compare the brain's responses during task-relevant versus task-irrelevant oddballs. The effect of task relevance on brain responses is analogous to the effect of the central cue on reaction times in the orienting paradigm: it enhances the behavioral salience of one sensory input over another.

The orienting and oddball paradigms offer two different ways of measuring the mechanisms of attention, each with its own sets of advantages and disadvantages. However, neither one directly addresses the phenomenon of awareness: the conscious perception arising from the attended stimulus. Studying awareness is trickier than it might seem. As you have seen, most of the available methods for studying brain function rely on comparisons. Ideally, we want to keep as many factors as constant as possible between the conditions we are comparing, aside from the function we are studying. For example, in a working memory study, we might present a random sequence of letters to the subject every time, but vary the memory load by changing the task so that the subject must think back one, two, or three letters to make a response. But how do we do this for conscious perception? Is there some way to keep all incoming sensory input constant, but still have the conscious percept change? As it turns out, there are several ways of doing this. Let's consider them briefly here.

Uncoupling Sensory Input from Perception: Sensory Rivalry

One method for studying conscious perception exploits **perceptual rivalry**, in which the same stimulus gives rise to more than one type of conscious percept. A powerful example is binocular rivalry, first studied nearly 200 years ago in a series of experiments by British scientist and inventor Sir Charles Wheatstone (Wheatstone, 1838). Wheatstone invented a device called a **stereoscope** that allowed viewers to see an apparently three-dimensional scene by presenting a slightly different two-dimensional perspective of the scene to each eye. These devices are still popular as children's toys, and the same principle is exploited by the glasses for 3D films.

However, Wheatstone noticed that binocular vision had a strange property. If he presented a completely different image to each eye, the viewer did not simply see a blend of the two images. Instead, the perception would alternate: the viewer would perceive only the left-side image for a few seconds, then only the right-side image, then the left again, and so on. The two images were rivals competing to dominate

perception in an all-or-nothing fashion. We have encountered this phenomenon previously, when we were describing the visual system. You can see this in Figure 5.32, pg. 153 (Chapter 5).

Binocular rivalry is just one example in which the conscious perception changes whereas sensory input remains the same. Ambiguous figures such as the old woman/young woman in FIGURE 8.8 also involve alternating perceptions in the face of constant sensory input (Marken, 2002; Orbach, Ehrlich, & Heath, 1963). The same is true of the rotating three-dimensional shapes perceived in patterns of moving dots: they will appear to rotate first one way and then the other (Murray, Olshausen, & Woods, 2003). Other examples include figure-ground illusions in which the perception shifts from a vase to a pair of faces looking at one another (Takashima, Fujii, & Shiina, 2012). Note that in many cases, you can reverse the figures deliberately through voluntary or top-down attentional mechanisms. At other times, the figure may seem to reverse spontaneously, via involuntary or bottom-up mechanisms (Orbach et al., 1963).

FIGURE 8.8 **Perceptual variance.** This image can look like a young woman or an old woman. *Hint: The young woman is looking away from you, toward the back of the left side of the picture, and you can see her left ear. The old woman is looking out of the picture, toward the bottom left of the image, and you can see her left eye and her nose and her mouth.*

Once again, the link between attention and conscious perception is apparent.

As we will see later, phenomena like binocular rivalry open inroads into the basis of conscious perception in the brain. The same is true for studies of change blindness, inattentional blindness, orienting tasks, and oddball tasks. By applying the techniques of fMRI, EEG, MEG, and single-unit recording in these kinds of settings, we can see how the processes of attention and awareness are represented in the brain.

Neural Mechanisms of Attention and Awareness

Seeking the Correlates of Consciousness

Over the past two decades, many neuroscientists have sought to identify the so-called **neural correlates of consciousness**—that is, specific neuroanatomical regions, or neurophysiological processes, that correlate with conscious perception. Attention and awareness seem to require the activation of a widespread network of areas, spanning both sensory and motor regions of the cortex.

Consider change blindness. Here it is possible to construct an elegant fMRI experiment: imagine presenting subjects with a subtle change in an image and comparing the brain activation when subjects are aware of the change to the brain activation when subjects are unaware of the same change. As a control condition, one can also include trials in which there really is no change in the image. Using images of faces and houses, one can also look at the activity of high-order visual regions like the fusiform face area, which is involved in recognizing faces (Chapter 5), and the **parahippocampal place area**, which is involved in recognizing places, during awareness versus unawareness of the changes.

When this experiment was conducted, it turned out that the fusiform face area and parahippocampal place area became active during changes in face and house images, even when the subjects themselves did not notice the change (Beck, Rees, Frith, & Lavie, 2001). However, the activation did not spread widely beyond visual cortex. On the other hand, in trials in which the subjects *did* notice the change, the activation spread dramatically. Not only was there stronger activity in the relevant visual area, but also there was widespread activation in large regions of lateral prefrontal cortex and parietal cortex. Activation of this widespread network took place only when subjects

consciously perceived the changes. So even if high-order visual areas of the brain register the change, this is still not enough for awareness to emerge. Conscious perception of changes seems to require the activation of frontal and parietal areas as well (Beck et al., 2001) (see FIGURE 8.9). In further support of this idea, disruption of the activity of the right parietal lobe by transcranial magnetic stimulation (Chapter 1) alters the rates of change blindness (Beck, Muggleton, Walsh, & Lavie, 2006).

Similar results have appeared in fMRI studies of inattentional blindness. Recall for a moment the experiment in which subjects had to attend to either a stream of letter stimuli or a stream of pictures. When subjects were attending to the letter stream, the widespread network of frontal, parietal, and temporal regions became active for real words, but not for nonsense strings. However, when they shifted their attention to the pictures instead of the letters, this widespread network no longer distinguished between real words and nonsense strings. In the absence of attention, these brain areas in effect became blind as to whether they were viewing real words or not (Rees et al., 1999).

The same link between widespread activity and awareness can be seen in another study of conscious perception using a different method called **masking**. In one experiment, subjects viewed words that flashed on the screen briefly before being "masked" by another visual stimulus. If the duration of the flashed word was brief, the subjects often reported that they did not know what word appeared. However, if asked to guess the word from a list, they tended to guess correctly far more often than would be predicted by chance (Dehaene et al., 2001). In other words, they still had unconscious perception of the word, although conscious perception was absent. In an fMRI study of masking, the masked words activated high-order visual areas even when subjects could not consciously report the words, but could

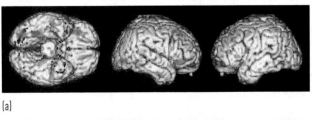

(a)

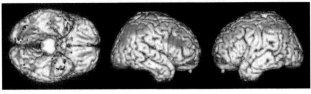

(b)

FIGURE 8.9 **Brain activity associated with (a) perceived changes or (b) changes that were not perceived.**

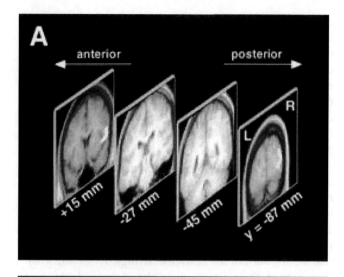

FIGURE 8.10 **Areas of the brain that change their activity as perception shifts between the two images during binocular rivalry.**

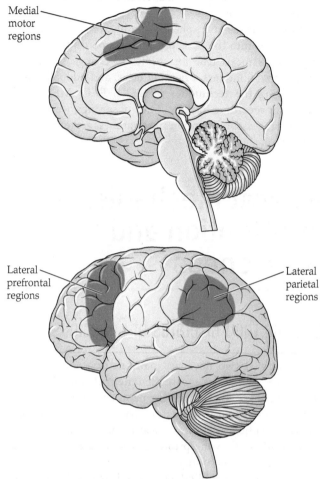

FIGURE 8.11 **Regions of the brain commonly damaged in patients who display hemineglect.** Most often, the damage is around the border between the parietal and temporal lobes of the right hemisphere. Less commonly, hemineglect results from damage to the medial motor areas.

only guess them. However, when the duration and mask timing were adjusted so that subjects were conscious of the words, the activity now became widespread, including parietal, lateral prefrontal, and medial prefrontal cortex as well as the insula (Dehaene et al., 2001). Once again, activation of visual cortex alone was not sufficient for conscious perception. What was needed was activation in a widespread network of brain regions in frontal, parietal, and temporal cortex.

The activity of these regions also tracks the perceived image in fMRI studies of binocular rivalry. Recall that in rivalry, the conscious percept switches back and forth between the left and right eye image, although the sensory input remains constant. Once again, in an fMRI study, a right-lateralized network of lateral prefrontal, medial prefrontal, parietal, and temporal areas showed activity that increased during changes in the *perceived* image, with sensory input held constant (FIGURE 8.10; Lumer, Friston, & Rees, 1998). In other words, these areas activate for the illusory image changes of binocular rivalry as well as the real image changes of the change blindness experiment. The implication is that the activity of these areas is important for conscious perception.

Hemineglect: A Disorder of Attention and Awareness

We have now seen what looks like a common network of areas that are important for conscious perception. But what happens if parts of this network are damaged? Injury to the lateral parietal, lateral prefrontal, or medial motor cortex is fairly common in stroke and in some other forms of neurological illness. Frequently, injury to these regions gives rise

to the curious syndrome of hemispatial neglect, or hemineglect (Buxbaum et al., 2004) (FIGURE 8.11).

As we will see with Timothy on the following page, patients with hemineglect fail to pay attention to stimuli on one side of space—usually the left. They also show a greatly reduced tendency to explore the "neglected" side of space with either eye movements or limb movements. Hemineglect patients tend to write on just the right side of a page, read only the right half of a word or a sentence, eat from only the right side of the plate, shave only the right side of the face, or dress only the right side of the body (Mesulam, 1999). Being made aware of these deficits doesn't seem to alter them. In one case, a patient wrote a detailed, coherent account of what it was like to experience hemineglect—yet wrote almost every line of this account on only the right side of the page (Halligan & Marshall, 1998)!

Hemineglect is distinct from the purely sensory deficits of patients who have damage to visual, auditory, or

CASE STUDY:
Unaware of Half of the World

Timothy, a truck driver in Canada, suffered a stroke at age 53. A small blood clot formed in his circulation and cut off the blood supply to part of his right frontal and parietal lobes. Alas, he did not immediately realize that anything was wrong. The very brain regions that might have noticed something amiss were the same regions that had been damaged by the stroke. By the time his family noticed his left facial droop and weakness, several hours had passed. They brought him to the hospital, but a CT scan showed that the damage had already been done. A small region of his right parietal lobe had been irreversibly injured (Heilman & Valenstein, 1979).

Following his injury, Timothy began to show some strange symptoms. He often acted unaware of the left side of the world. He ate food from only the right side of the plate. He would put on the right sleeve of his hospital gown, but forget about the left. If asked to read, he would generally skip over words on the left side of the page. He would tend to ignore people who came to speak to him on the left side of his bed, especially if there were other people present on the right. When these omissions were pointed out, he seemed surprised and compensated briefly, but after a few moments would return to ignoring the left half of the world once again.

Was there a problem with Timothy's vision? Apparently not—an ophthalmological exam showed that his visual fields were still intact.

FIGURE 8.12 **Drawings made by a patient with hemispatial neglect.** The left column shows the sample images and the right column shows the drawings made by the patient.

Besides, the problem affected other sensory modalities as well. He would ignore not only visual events on the left, but also taps on the left wrist or sounds coming from the left side. And no purely sensory problem could explain the bizarre drawings he would produce when asked to sketch a clock or an animal. They, too, were missing the features on the left side (FIGURE 8.12)! The problem was not with sensation, but with attention itself.

The medical team told Timothy's family that he was suffering from hemineglect, a common effect of strokes affecting the right parietal lobe. Unfortunately, because of this problem, he was unable to return to his previous occupation. When driving a truck, his failure to notice another vehicle on the left could have had fatal consequences. In some ways, his partial loss of attention turned out to be more disabling than a partial loss of vision itself.

somatosensory areas. The latter patients are generally aware of their deficits and make efforts to compensate for them. In contrast, hemineglect patients suffer from a kind of blindness of attention itself. This "blindness" often extends over multiple sensory modalities: vision, hearing, touch, and even smell (Heilman & Valenstein, 1979). It even extends to imaginary scenes, in which external sensory input is completely absent. In a classic study by the Italian neurologists Bisiach and Luzzatti, hemineglect patients were asked to describe the buildings visible from a particular point of view in the main town square of Milan (Bisiach & Luzzatti, 1978). They consistently neglected to mention the buildings that would have appeared on the left from the imagined perspective. The omitted buildings actually changed, depending on the imaginary perspective. This key finding helped to establish that neglect was more than just a sensory or intellectual deficit in the affected patients.

What about the subjective sense of awareness that goes along with attention? What happens to stimuli that make it as far as the eye, or the visual cortex, but then somehow fail to reach attention or awareness? Neuroimaging studies have begun to explore the fate of sensory stimuli that fall victim to neglect, or more specifically, a milder version known as **extinction** (Driver & Vuilleumier, 2001). In extinction, patients can detect a stimulus on the left side if it appears by itself. However, if it appears along with a competing stimulus on the right, then the patients will often fail to notice the stimulus on the left, as if its presence has been "extinguished" by the more salient right-side stimulus (Driver & Vuilleumier, 2001). Although neglect is a fairly common syndrome after stroke or other injury, it rarely persists beyond a few weeks or months. Instead, as the brain recovers, neglect retreats into the more subtle deficit of extinction (Karnath, 1988).

In an fMRI study, one group of researchers presented a patient with visual stimuli such as faces, which activate specific areas of the inferior visual pathway (Rees et al., 2000). The patient had suffered a right parietal stroke and had left-side extinction. When a face or a house appeared by itself on the left or right, he usually detected it without difficulty. However, when a stimulus appeared on *both* sides simultaneously, the patient often reported only the stimulus on the right side.

As it turns out, the "extinct" stimulus was not totally ignored by the brain: it actually did activate primary visual and inferior temporal visual cortex (FIGURE 8.13). Yet somehow, this activation was not enough to allow the patient to become conscious of the face. On other identical trials, she sometimes *was* aware of both the left and the right stimulus. In these cases, the left-side stimulus activated not only the right visual cortex, but also the parietal cortex in the still-intact left hemisphere. Furthermore, on trials in which the patient was aware of the left-side faces, the primary visual cortex became

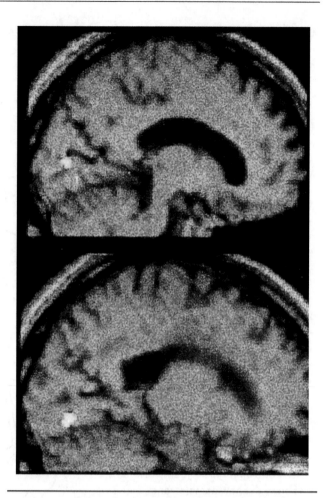

FIGURE 8.13 fMRI of patient with hemispatial neglect. The right visual cortex is active even when the patient reports there is nothing present in the left visual field. The patient was shown a picture in both the left and the right visual fields but only reported seeing the one in the right visual field. However, there was still activity in the (top) right primary visual cortex and (bottom) extrastriate visual areas for the unattended stimulus in the left visual field.

synchronized with the activity of a widespread network of left frontal, parietal, and anterior temporal areas. This widespread synchronization was seen specifically for the trials where the patient was aware, rather than unaware, of the left-side stimulus.

The syndrome of hemineglect therefore confirms three previous points about the neural basis of attention and awareness. First, attention and awareness are closely linked functions that do not clearly map onto purely sensory domains, but instead span the gap between sensation and action. Second, attention and awareness rely on a widespread network of high-level sensory and motor areas, specifically in the parietal and prefrontal cortices. When these areas are damaged, the result is a deficit of attention and awareness itself, not just a deficit of sensory or motor faculties, as occurs in cases of injuries to lower-level sensory and motor cortex. Finally, activation of sensory cortex in isolation does not seem to be sufficient for sensory awareness. However, even in a partly damaged brain, attention and awareness can still emerge via synchronized activity between early levels of sensory cortex and the more widespread network of sensory association areas.

Neural Correlates of Attention: A Single Network or Many?

As we have seen in the cases above, much overlap exists between the neural correlates of attention and conscious perception. Neuroimaging studies of the orienting and oddball paradigms partly confirm this overlap. In the orienting paradigm, for example, we see activation in a network of areas including the intraparietal sulcus, the frontal eye field within dorsolateral prefrontal cortex, the anterior cingulate cortex, and higher-order visual areas in the occipital and temporal cortex (Gitelman et al., 1999; Kastner & Ungerleider, 2000; Nobre, 2001). These areas are active both for exogenous and for endogenous shifts of attention, suggesting they are part of a general network for directing visuospatial attention (FIGURE 8.14).

The neural correlates of attention in the oddball paradigm are similar to that of the orienting paradigm, but with some subtle differences (again, see FIGURE 8.14). Once again, we see activation in higher-order sensory cortex. The area of cortex involved depends on which sensory modality is involved: visual areas for visual oddballs, auditory areas for auditory oddballs, and so on. There is also a common network of activation in parietal and frontal cortex, similar to the orienting paradigm. Yet in the oddball paradigm, the activations are at slightly more inferior locations: the inferior parietal lobule and the **temporoparietal junction** and inferior prefrontal cortex (Downar, Crawley, Mikulis, & Davis, 2002; Linden et al., 1999; Opitz, Mecklinger, Friederici, & von Cramon, 1999).

So are there different neural pathways for spatial and nonspatial attention? We can compare the two forms of attention separately with a version of the visual oddball task that has two kinds of deviant stimuli: spatial oddballs (in which the location, or "where," is unexpected) and object oddballs (in which the object itself, or "what," is unexpected) (Marois, Chun, & Gore, 2000). In this case, we see that spatial oddballs preferentially activate more superior parietal areas in the intraparietal sulcus (part of the dorsal or "where" visual pathway, described in Chapter 5). In contrast, object oddballs preferentially activate regions in the inferior temporal cortex (part of the ventral or "what" visual pathway). However, both types of oddballs activate the temporoparietal junction and lateral temporal cortex.

As with the oddball paradigm, we can compare spatial and nonspatial orienting. If we modify the orienting task so that the cue predicts the *timing* (early or late) rather than

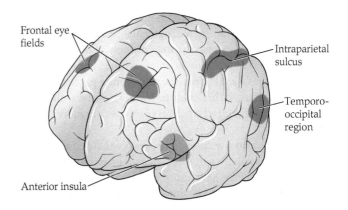

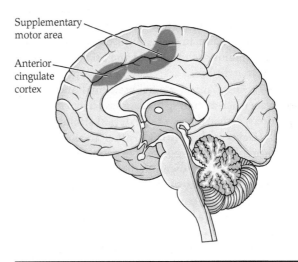

FIGURE 8.14 **Brain regions activated by exogenous and endogenous shifts of attention.** Research suggests that this network of areas is important for both types of attentional shifts.

the location (right or left) of the target stimulus, we find that the activation changes. Temporal orienting tends to activate more inferior areas in the frontal and parietal lobes and also tends to be more left lateralized (Coull, Frith, Buchel, & Nobre, 2000; Coull & Nobre, 1998). So the neural correlates of attention seem to shift slightly depending on whether the task involves spatial or nonspatial features of external stimuli.

The shift is even more dramatic when we look at tasks in which attention is shifted away from external sensory stimuli altogether. For example, in spatial navigation tasks, subjects must attend to the locations of destinations that lie beyond their immediate sensory range. In this case, activation shifts away from the lateral surface of the brain to a network of medial prefrontal and parietal areas, as well as regions closely connected to the hippocampus, such as the parahippocampal gyrus and retrosplenial cortex (FIGURE 8.15) (Burgess, Maguire, Spiers, & O'Keefe, 2001). These areas have little direct input from external sensory areas, but closer connections to the hippocampus and to areas of the fronto-polar cortex involved in setting goals, reconstructing episodic memories, and navigating through space. Here, the degree of overlap with the previous studies becomes much smaller. So for tasks that require attention to past events and distant locations, rather than to features of the immediate sensory environment, the neural correlates are more medial than lateral.

There are also a wide variety of tasks that require attention to things other than one's external surroundings, and these tasks likewise have quite different neural correlates. For example, shifting attention to the thoughts and feelings of other individuals activates the medial prefrontal cortex and precuneus (Amodio & Frith, 2006). The same is true if we ask subjects to attend to their own goals, hopes, dreams, and aspirations (Strauman et al., 2012). We can also present an external stimulus such as a word and ask subjects to reflect on how well this word describes them as a person (Farb et al., 2007). Once again, medial prefrontal and parietal areas activate when attending to these associated memories and emotions, rather than to the external stimulus of the word itself (Davis et al., 2010). Still other areas such as the anterior insula become prominent in tasks in which subjects must monitor their own internal sensations, such as their heart rate (Critchley et al., 2003). Each of these activated networks is different from the others and different from the activations we see in the orienting and oddball attention tasks.

So is there really a single overall network of cortical areas for attention, or are there actually multiple networks for multiple forms of attention? The notion of a general attention network arose in a time when studies of attention typically used a relatively small number of tasks: mostly variations on the orienting and oddball paradigms (Posner & Petersen, 1990). Over the past 10 years, the study of many other forms of attention has revealed that the neural correlates vary widely depending on the kinds of sensory information and the kinds of behavioral responses that are required (Mesulam, 1999).

That said, the areas involved in attention and awareness share some common features. These areas generally exclude primary sensory or motor cortex, as well as low-level sensory and motor areas. Instead, the association areas of the lateral and medial parietal cortex tend to bridge the gap between high-level perception and action. The ventrolateral, dorsolateral, and dorsomedial prefrontal cortex are good examples of these kinds of areas on the motor side (Mesulam, 1998). As we saw in Chapter 2, high-order association areas in parietal and frontal cortex are strongly connected to one another, as "partners" with closely related functions.

When these high-order areas are not involved, we can still get behavior, but it tends to be the kind of behavior that proceeds without conscious attention or awareness of exactly what is taking place. One example of this is musical improvisation. Unlike a set musical piece, an

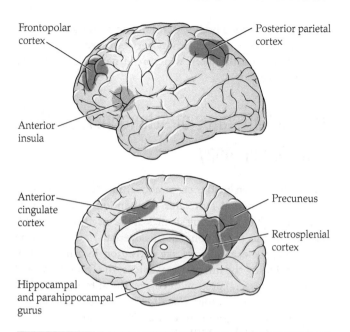

FIGURE 8.15 Brain regions active during spatial navigation or spatial memory tasks. Compared to spatial orienting or oddball tasks, tasks that require attention to locations outside of immediate sensory range tend to engage more medial parietal areas in the precuneus and retrosplenial cingulate cortex, as well as the hippocampus and parahippocampal gyrus.

improvised performance tends to take place without a clear awareness of what is about to happen next, and paying too close attention to the process seems to actually inhibit the performance. Brain activity in musical improvisation is almost like a negative image of activity during conscious perception and attention. In improvisation, most of the higher-order prefrontal and parietal regions show significantly less activity. On the other hand, the lower-level primary and unimodal auditory, somatosensory, and motor cortex show significantly more activity (Limb & Braun, 2008).

Overall, then, attention and conscious perception seem to converge in the brain, just as they converge in psychophysical phenomena like change blindness and inattentional blindness. Attention and awareness require activity in a widespread network of areas throughout the cortex. Although the precise network changes depending on the sensory and motor aspects of the task, it generally includes high-level sensory and motor areas rather than low-level sensory or motor areas. The **contents of consciousness**—the subjective experiences that take place when our attention focuses on a particular part of the sensory environment, such as a face or a name—seem to depend on the activity of these regions whose function spans sensation and action. Damage to these regions, as in hemineglect, causes profound deficits of attention and awareness.

CASE STUDY:
Whose Arm Is This, Anyway?

In 1990, an 84-year-old woman we'll call Sarina suffered a right hemisphere stroke. As often happens, she developed symptoms of left hemineglect after her injury. Sarina also suffered paralysis of the left side of her body—again, a fairly common symptom of right hemisphere stroke. However, she showed some rarer, and much stranger, symptoms as well (Bisiach & Geminiani, 1991).

First, she completely denied that she had any form of paralysis. She insisted that the left side of her body was working perfectly and would behave as if it were normal. This condition is called *anosognosia*, or denial of deficit (see Chapter 6). It is much more than a psychological coping mechanism. Patients with anosognosia will attempt to complete tasks like picking up a tray or tying their shoes as if they had two working hands—with predictably disastrous results! They are genuinely puzzled as to why their efforts are unsuccessful (Bisiach & Geminiani, 1991). This condition sometimes accompanies hemineglect.

More strangely, however, Sarina developed a stubborn belief that her left arm actually belonged to someone else—in this case, her mother. Her explanation was equally bizarre: "I found it in my bed . . . She forgot it when she was discharged from hospital." She seemed unaware of the implausibility of her belief. At times, she would change her mind about the owner of the arm, thinking it belonged to her son instead. However, she insisted at all times: "It's not mine." This condition is called *somatoparaphrenia*: the belief that part of one's body belongs to someone else (Vallar & Ronchi, 2009).

Somatoparaphrenia is not simply a case of dementia or a psychiatric delusional illness. Instead, it seems to be related to the attentional deficits of hemineglect (Vallar & Ronchi, 2009). We know this because certain medical procedures can temporarily relieve both hemineglect and somatoparaphrenia. For example, neurologists can stimulate the vestibular system

on the left side by injecting cold water into the ear canal. This changes the spatial-sensory information reaching the cortex and thereby relieves the symptoms of neglect: for a few minutes, patients become aware of the left side of the world once again (Rode et al., 1992). Oddly, patients with somatoparaphrenia also take ownership of their limbs once again for a few minutes. Immediately after a cold water injection, the patient in this case was asked where her left arm was. "Here it is," she said, pointing to her own left arm. Asked about her mother's left arm, she said, "It is somewhere about," and looked fruitlessly under the bedsheets. Two hours later, her symptoms had returned exactly as before, and she once again thought her arm belonged to her mother (Bisiach, Rusconi, & Vallar, 1991).

Findings like these challenge our intuitions and give us rare clues about how our brains build the apparent reality of our conscious experiences.

Sites of Attentional Modulation: Neurons and Neural Populations

The Biased-Competition Model of Attention

We have so far been looking at the neural correlates of attention at the macro scale: large regions of association cortex whose activity seems to be necessary for attention and

conscious perception. These high-level areas are sometimes described as the *sources* of attentional modulation because their activity modulates the activity of lower-level sensory cortex. Yet the effects of attention are much more fine grained than this crude regional neuroanatomy would suggest. Different stimuli are represented by large populations or **ensembles** of neurons within a given region. For example, within the neurons of the fusiform face area, different faces elicit different patterns of activity among the entire population as a whole: there is no "grandmother cell," but instead a different pattern for each member of the family, and indeed for every face one might encounter (Kanwisher, McDermott, & Chun, 1997).

Thus, attention must select among the many possible ensembles of neurons within a single anatomical region of the cortex. In the **biased-competition model** of attention,

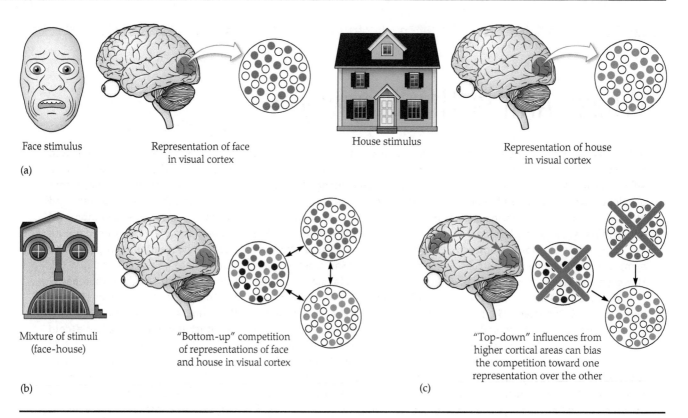

Face stimulus

Representation of face in visual cortex

(a)

House stimulus

Representation of house in visual cortex

Mixture of stimuli (face-house)

"Bottom-up" competition of representations of face and house in visual cortex

(b)

"Top-down" influences from higher cortical areas can bias the competition toward one representation over the other

(c)

FIGURE 8.16   **The biased-competition model of attention.** (a) When presented alone, a given type of sensory stimulus (such as a face or a house) will activate a specific representation, or pattern of activity, within the lower-level sensory cortex. (b) When a mixture of stimuli are presented, the representations will compete with one another in a "bottom-up" fashion, each attempting to dominate the activity of the lower-level sensory cortex. (c) Top-down influences from higher cortical areas, such as the prefrontal cortex, can bias the competition to enhance one representation and suppress the others. Top-down influences include cognitive factors, such as context.

the multitude of different sensory inputs compete with one another to control behavior (Treue & Martinez Trujillo, 1999). At the neural level, within each region, many different ensembles of neurons compete with one another to dominate the pattern of activity in the local population of neurons as a whole. For example, when listening to two people speaking at the same time, the ensembles of neurons representing one person's speech might compete with the different ensembles of neurons representing the other person's speech, in some site in the auditory association cortex.

Which ensemble emerges as the winner? The result depends partly on the intrinsic or bottom-up sensory features of the inputs: pitch, volume, clarity, and so on. Yet it is also possible to bias the competition toward one input or the other, in a top-down fashion, depending on the current behavioral context. For example, if one person were engaged in an in-person conversation with you and the other person were talking to you on the telephone, the brain could bias the competition toward the more relevant sensory inputs from the in-person conversational partner and away from the less relevant sensory inputs from your more distant conversational partner on the telephone. Descending inputs from higher-order brain regions (such as the prefrontal cortex)

would enhance the activity of one group of neurons at the expense of the other (FIGURE 8.16). Hence, the competition among the sensory inputs would be *biased* based on the current behavioral context.

Attention and Single Neurons: Enhancing the Signal

If attention is a mechanism for selecting the most relevant stimuli among competing sensory inputs, then how does this mechanism operate at the level of individual neurons? Neuroscientists have been studying this question for nearly three decades. One commonly used technique is to implant microelectrodes within the visual cortex of a primate, such as a macaque monkey, who can be trained to perform tasks involving visual attention (FIGURE 8.17). During these tasks, the monkey is often required to maintain eye fixation upon a central point, so as to avoid eliciting activity resulting from movements of the eyes or changes in the retinal position of the stimuli. Once the monkey is trained on the task, one can record the electrical activity from individual neurons in different regions of the

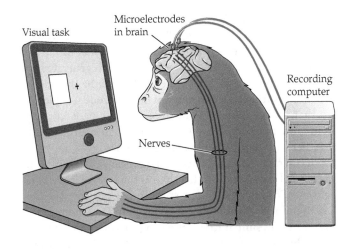

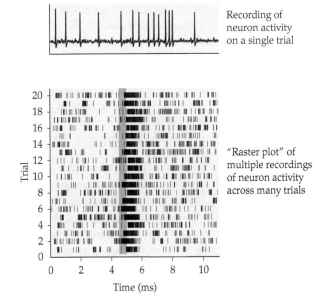

Recording of neuron activity on a single trial

"Raster plot" of multiple recordings of neuron activity across many trials

FIGURE 8.17 **Microelectrode recording from a monkey performing a visual task.**

visual cortex. One can then compare how visual attention affects various properties of the neuron's activity: its baseline firing rate, its responsiveness to a given stimulus, its degree of inhibition by nearby competing stimuli (Treue & Martinez Trujillo, 1999).

Using these kinds of methods, early studies of visual attention found that neurons in the V4 region of visual association cortex showed attentional modulation. As we saw in Chapter 5, individual V4 neurons have a receptive field: a certain region of the overall visual field where visual stimuli need to appear to elicit a response. They also tend to have a preference for visual stimuli of a particular color and orientation: for example, a horizontal blue bar might elicit high rates of firing, but a vertical red bar might not. But what if we were to place *both* stimuli in the receptive field and then have the monkey report the identity of just one of the stimuli by moving its eyes or pushing a button to obtain a juice reward? As it turns out, the neuron responds more strongly when the monkey needs to pay attention to the preferred stimulus compared to when it needs to pay attention to the nonpreferred stimulus (Moran & Desimone, 1985). Attention pushes the response of the neuron toward one stimulus or the other, even when both are present in the neuron's receptive field. In other words, the attended stimulus gets preferential control over the response of individual neurons (FIGURE 8.18). This principle of attentional modulation is seen increasingly throughout and beyond the visual cortex (Reynolds & Chelazzi, 2004).

Other studies have found a variety of different effects of attention on the activity of single neurons. For example, attention increases the **gain** of the response to a given stimulus, so that the neural response to an attended stimulus is

larger than the response to the same stimulus in the absence of attention (McAdams & Maunsell, 1999; Reynolds, Pasternak, & Desimone, 2000; Treue & Martinez Trujillo, 1999). At the same time, the **feature selectivity** of the neuron may be unchanged. For example, the preferred orientation of V4 neurons remains unchanged with attention, and the range

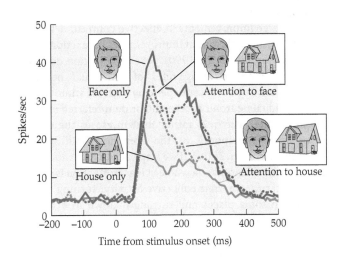

FIGURE 8.18 **Effects of attention on neural activity.** The neuronal response depends on which stimulus within the receptive field is attended to. This graph represents the level of activity of a cell within V4 to a preferred (face) and nonpreferred (house) stimulus. When both stimuli are presented at the same time and the subject is told to attend to just one of the two objects, the response after about 150 milliseconds resembles the response by the subject to the attended object, regardless of whether the attended object is preferred or nonpreferred.

of orientations that elicit a response does not become narrower or broader (McAdams & Maunsell, 1999). The same is true for other kinds of stimulus features, such as direction of motion (Treue & Martinez Trujillo, 1999).

Attention can also enhance the response to weak stimuli. Attention reduces the minimum threshold at which a stimulus will activate the neuron, so that weaker stimuli produce a stronger response, and stimuli that are normally too weak to activate the neuron now produce a response (Reynolds & Chelazzi, 2004).

What do these attentional effects mean in general terms? By enhancing the firing rates of individual neurons in response to a stimulus, attention may enhance the **signal-to-noise ratio** of the neuron's activity: that is, the magnitude of the firing rate elicited by the stimulus compared to the baseline firing rate. Enhancing the signal-to-noise ratio presumably allows for improved transmission of information to sites elsewhere in the brain. This gives attended stimuli a better chance of producing widespread networks of coordinated activity between distant cortical sites in high-order sensory and motor cortex (Servan-Schreiber, Printz, & Cohen, 1990). These widespread networks, as we have seen, are essential for linking together sensation and action and for producing conscious awareness of the stimulus.

Yet this model may not tell us the whole story, for several reasons. First, we know that sensory stimuli are represented by groups of neurons, rather than individual neurons. So, the effects of attention on single neuron activity may be only a tiny part of the bigger picture. For example, the effect of attention on individual neurons' signal-to-noise ratio is fairly small, but the effect on behavioral performance is much greater: large improvements in effective contrast, detection thresholds, and substantial improvements in reaction times (Servan-Schreiber et al., 1990). Second, attention does not uniformly increase firing rates of individual neurons; instead, the results seem to depend on both the stimulus and the individual neuron concerned. For nonpreferred stimuli, attention often *decreases* rather than increases the overall firing rate in response to the stimulus (Grill-Spector, Henson, & Martin, 2006). If we step back to think about the population of neurons as a whole, it is as if attention is sculpting a pattern from their collective activity: turning up the activity in some places and turning it down in others to emphasize one pattern over its many competitors. To understand how this happens, we must look beyond the activity of single neurons to consider the activity of larger populations as a whole.

Attention and Local Groups of Neurons

In recent years, new technologies have allowed recordings from multiple neurons simultaneously. One method is to insert several electrodes into a given region, in the hopes of recording from more than one neuron at the same time (Constantinidis, Franowicz, & Goldman-Rakic, 2001). Another simple method is to add an additional electrode that records the **local field potential**, which is generated by the summed electrical fields generated by all the thousands of neurons within a certain range of the electrode—typically less than half a millimeter (Murthy & Fetz, 1996). Recording from more than one neuron illuminates how neurons work together in groups, rather than in isolation.

The most important effects of attention often occur at the level of populations rather than at the level of individual neurons. For example, in one study, monkeys were cued to pay attention to one of two spatial locations and monitor for a target event, similar to the orienting paradigm we saw earlier in the chapter (Cohen & Maunsell, 2009). As in previous studies, attention increased the firing rates of individual V4 neurons in response to the target event—a slight change in the orientation of a visual stimulus. However, the increase was fairly small: typically only a few spikes per second in any given neuron. Yet the monkeys' performance improved dramatically: from around 40% of the unattended targets to nearly 100% of the attended targets correctly detected (FIGURE 8.19), when the target event was a change in orientation of 11 degrees.

What effects did attention have on the population as a whole? The biggest effect was on the neural noise rather than the signal itself. Noise in a population of neurons can be divided into two categories: *uncorrelated* noise, which is different in each neuron, can be filtered out by simply averaging the activity across many neurons; however, *correlated* noise occurs with the same pattern across different neurons and so continues to interfere with the signal even after averaging across the whole population (Alspector, Gannett, Haber, Parker, & Chu, 1991; Lee, Port, Kruse, & Georgopoulos, 1998). Picking out the signal from uncorrelated noise is a bit like listening to a lecture over the random hubbub of a crowd: difficult, but not impossible. However, picking out the signal from correlated noise is like trying to listen to the same lecture over a crowd that is chanting a slogan in unison: a much more challenging endeavor, unless you can get the crowd to stop chanting for a moment. Attention seems to eliminate the *correlations* in the noise of a neural population, thereby allowing the signal to come through more clearly.

Synchronization, Attention, and Awareness

We just described how attention makes it easier to detect a signal by decreasing the correlated noise within the nervous system. We'll now take a closer look at how attention affects

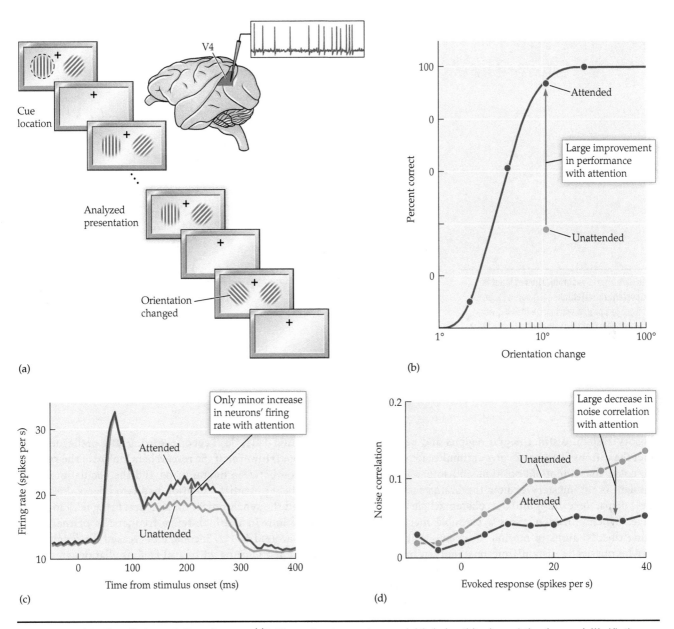

FIGURE 8.19 Attention affects populations of neurons. (a) In this experiment, researchers recorded the brain activity of a population of neurons in V4 while the monkeys attended to a spatial location to detect a change in the orientation of the presented lines. (b) Results showed that the monkeys' performance was significantly more accurate for stimuli presented to the attended region as opposed to stimuli presented in the unattended region, but that (c) this difference was not the result of significant changes in the response rate of individual neurons. (d) Rather, there was a significant decrease in the correlated noise within the population of neurons for the attended stimulus as opposed to the unattended stimulus.

the synchronization, frequency, and phase of neural activity on both the large scale and the small scale.

Synchronization refers to the simultaneous firing of neurons in two distinct areas, either near or far from one another. It is distinct from simple increases or decreases in firing rates. Two different areas could both show increases in firing rate without showing any increase in synchronization. They could also both show decreases in firing rate, yet become more synchronized with one another.

Synchronization is special in that it can link together the activity of distant neurons in different areas. If a neuron has

many sources of input, it is more likely to respond to those inputs if they are firing in a coordinated fashion than if they are firing out of step with one another (FIGURE 8.20) (Varela, Lachaux, Rodriguez, & Martinerie, 2001). Within a region, synchronization can link together populations of neurons into the ensembles that represent one particular sensory stimulus or motor plan (Varela et al., 2001). Between regions, synchronization can help with the transfer of information from one synaptic level to the next (Chawla, Lumer, & Friston, 1999).

Synchronization also provides a potential solution to the binding problem of sensory perception (Chapter 6). In every

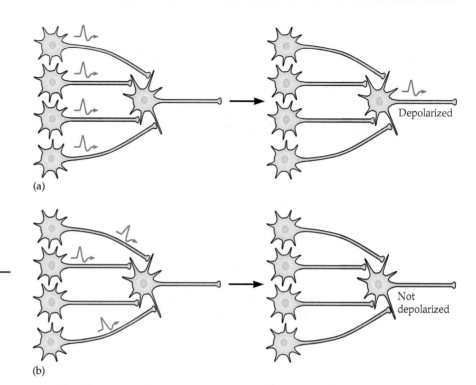

FIGURE 8.20 Synchronization of input is important for attention. (a) If several sources of input to a neuron synchronize their activity, it is more likely that they will be able to depolarize the target neuron. (b) If their activity is not synchronized, it is less likely that they will be able to depolarize the target.

sensory system, distinct neural regions and pathways extract the various features of a given stimulus: for visual stimuli, color, shape, motion, position, and so on. The binding problem is the mystery of how the brain reassembles all these disparate features into the coherent whole that we perceive. Synchronization offers a plausible mechanism for doing this. Neurons in motion- or color-sensitive regions may be physically distant from one another, but they can still synchronize their activity into a coherent pattern. This not only allows the pattern to remain distinct from other ongoing neural activity, but also allows a single, coordinated influence on other regions involved in planning motor behavior. In this way, the many different sensory features of an object can be bound together into a unified sensory whole (Varela et al., 2001).

Attention can increase the synchronization between individual neurons. For example, one experiment looked at the activity of pairs of neurons in the somatosensory cortex of monkeys (Steinmetz et al., 2000). These neurons showed more synchronized firing when the monkey was performing a tactile discrimination task: trying to determine the shape of letters on a finger pad. However, when the monkey switched to performing a visual discrimination task, the neural activity became much less synchronized.

Attention also increases synchronization of whole populations or neurons, beyond just pairs of neurons. Researchers looked at how neurons in visual area V4 responded to stimuli in the receptive field; on some trials the monkeys attended to the stimulus and on other trials they didn't.

Attention had little effect on the firing rates of the individual neurons. However, if the researchers looked at the synchronization between neural firing and the oscillations of the local field potential, attention had two effects. First, it increased the synchronization of neural firing with local field oscillations in the high-range frequencies of the gamma band, around 40 Hz. Second, it decreased the synchronization of neural firing with local field oscillations in the low-range frequencies of the alpha band, around 10 Hz. Thus, attention accomplished two things: enhancing synchronization at high frequencies while simultaneously dampening synchronization at lower frequencies (Womelsdorf, Fries, Mitra, & Desimone, 2005).

Attention also increases the long-range synchronization between distant regions of the cortex. For example, in one study of visual attention in cats, experimenters measured local field potentials in several areas of visual and motor cortex (Roelfsema, Engel, Konig, & Singer, 1997). The cats monitored a visual stimulus and pressed a lever when its orientation changed. When the cats were paying attention to the stimulus, synchronization increased along a chain of areas proceeding from primary visual cortex, through visual association cortex, through somatosensory association cortex, to primary motor cortex. The synchronization began to increase in anticipation of the task, increased further during task performance, and then dissipated once the task was completed.

As we saw earlier in the chapter, many fMRI studies show that widespread, synchronized activation through frontal and parietal regions correlates with attention and awareness. These findings therefore fit nicely with the widespread gamma-band synchronization that we see in similar studies performed using techniques with better temporal resolution, like MEG and EEG.

Coma and Vegetative State: Anatomy of the Conscious State

So far in this chapter, we have been looking at how attention relates to the contents of consciousness. Yet the contents of consciousness exist within a larger framework: the **state of consciousness** itself. To have subjective experiences, we first need to be in a conscious state. During deep stages of sleep, our brain is intact, but we do not respond to our surroundings. If woken, we do not report any subjective experiences as we might if woken from the dreams of **rapid-eye-movement (REM) sleep** (Llinas & Ribary, 1993). The same is true when we suppress consciousness using medications, as in surgical anesthesia. Again, so long as the anesthetic dose is strong enough, we do not respond to pain or other sensory inputs, and we do not register or remember the experiences of the surgery (Amzica & Steriade, 1998). We can also enter a reduced state of consciousness after certain forms of brain injury that produce the neurological syndromes of **coma**, **vegetative state**, or **minimally conscious state**.

These altered states of consciousness are useful windows into understanding how brain activity leads to conscious awareness. To look for clues to consciousness, we can compare brain activity before and during sleep, or during anesthesia, or in patients before and after they recover from a comatose state (**FIGURE 8.21**). Let's now take a look at what happens to the brain in these impaired states of consciousness.

Why Should Synchronization Matter?

The studies we have seen seem to tell us that the synchronization of neural activity is an important mechanism underlying attention and awareness. As we have seen earlier, the idea of synchronization is attractive because it helps to explain how the many different features of a stimulus can be bound together into a coherent whole. The same is true for the many components of the motor response and for the delicate process of tying together sensation and action. So when we say that conscious perception involves widespread synchronization of neural activity in sensory and motor association areas, it is tempting to jump to the simple

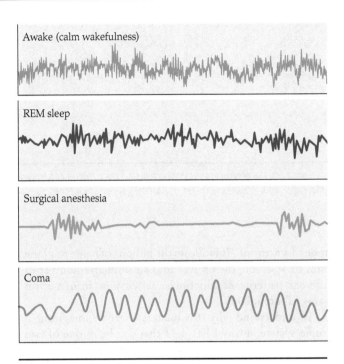

FIGURE 8.21 **EEG waves associated with different states of consciousness.**

conclusion that neural synchronization equals attention equals consciousness.

Yet this simple explanation quickly runs into problems. For one thing, synchronization of neural activity can take place at many different frequencies. Why should synchronization at high frequencies lead to attention and awareness, whereas synchronization at low frequencies has the opposite effect? Another problem is that widespread synchronization of neural activity doesn't always lead to conscious perception. For example, in deep, slow-wave sleep, widespread, low-frequency oscillations of electrical activity take place throughout the cortex. Yet there are few, if any, conscious perceptions that take place during this dreamless form of sleep (Llinas & Ribary, 1993). Or, what if we took the process to its logical extreme and synchronized neural activity throughout the entire cortex? The result is not attention or awareness, but an epileptic seizure. Patients who suffer from generalized tonic–clonic seizures suffer through episodes when all of the neurons of the cortex are firing together, in synchronized fashion, stimulating one another with regular bursts of activity. During these episodes, the patients completely lose consciousness. When activity does return to normal, they are severely disoriented and have no recollection of their experiences during the seizure.

So why should synchronization matter at all? One theory is that the synchronization itself is not the crucial ingredient. Rather, synchronization is simply a mechanism that allows the brain to communicate information more efficiently

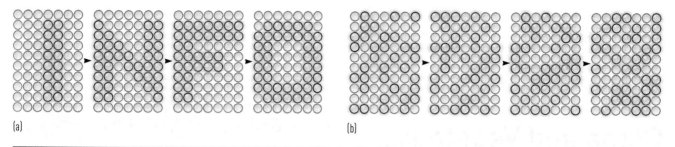

(a)

(b)

FIGURE 8.22 **The effects of synchronization.** (a) If the activity of different units in a network can be synchronized, the network can carry patterns of useful information, such as a sequence of letters. (b) If they are not synchronized, no information can be carried.

among its neurons. This allows the billions of neurons of the brain to assemble themselves into an immense number of different patterns of functional activity, or **information states** (Tononi, 2008).

To understand why this matters, start by imagining a simple system, a tiny LED light that can be in one of two information states: *on* or *off*. Now, instead of a brain full of neurons, imagine a square array of a hundred LEDs, each one of which can be *on* or *off* (FIGURE 8.22). In theory, even this small array could be used to represent an immense number of different states: 2 to the power of 100, or a hundred trillion trillion. Using just a fraction of these states, we could do many things: represent letters or numbers, point arrows in various directions, make a crude image of a face or an object, or show a simple two-handed clock. We can even do all of these things, one after the other, in whatever sequence we like.

But there is a catch: if each LED acts independently, we'll have trouble using the array at all. Instead, we'll just have uncoordinated noise, like static on a television screen. However, by synchronizing their activity, we can create temporary, useful patterns or information states on the array and maintain them so long as their functions are needed. It is these patterns and their functions that are important, not the synchronization itself. If we synchronize all the LEDs together, we are back where we started, with a large array of many units but only two possible states: *on* or *off*. With this limited repertoire, far fewer functions are possible.

Although this account is just one of many competing theories of consciousness, it does help us to understand why synchronization matters for attention and awareness: it is through synchronized activity that the brain's neurons coordinate their activity into useful patterns or information states. It also helps us understand why we do not see a direct relationship between widespread synchronization and attention or awareness. It is not the synchronization itself that matters, but the immense repertoire of information states that become possible via synchronized patterns of activity within the hundred billion neurons of the brain.

Of course, the implication of this is that there are not only an immense variety of different *contents* of consciousness (one for each possible pattern of activity), but also more than one *state* of consciousness. We'll now turn to the neural mechanisms behind the state of consciousness itself.

Unconsciousness: Coma and Vegetative State

The most unequivocal state of unconsciousness, of course, is death. After severe brain injury, many patients lapse into unconsciousness, never to return. Some of these patients still have beating hearts. So long as their lungs are supplied with oxygen by a mechanical ventilator, their other organs will continue to function, still burning glucose to generate the energy to keep their cells alive. We can see evidence of this metabolic activity with a PET scanner, using radioactive glucose to show that the cells are still performing their basic "housekeeping" functions. However, if we turn the PET scanner to the patient's head, we see the unarguable evidence of **brain death**: a "hollow skull" image, showing that metabolic activity in the tissues of the brain is totally absent (FIGURE 8.23) (Momose et al., 1992). Likewise, the

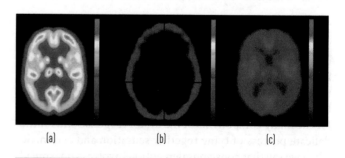

(a)   (b)   (c)

FIGURE 8.23 **PET scan images of a brain in the (a) normal resting state, (b) brain death, and (c) vegetative state.**

CASE STUDY:
Waking the Brain

A young man we'll call Daniel was once assaulted and beaten unconscious during a mugging. His brain was so severely injured in the attack that he remained in a minimally conscious state more than two years later. He made no sign of verbal communication, rarely responded to commands, and had severely spastic limbs. At this point, with little hope for further recovery, Daniel was transferred from the hospital to a long-term care facility. More than six years after the injury, his condition was not much improved. However, a new series of tests gave some cause for optimism. Brain imaging showed that the network of regions for language function was still intact; other networks might have been similarly spared (Nordqvist, 2007).

In brain injury, certain areas are sometimes damaged to the point of causing unconsciousness, although the rest of the brain's circuitry is not as badly affected. If the patient could only be "awakened," many functions might return. To reactivate consciousness, in 2007 a team of neurologists and neurosurgeons implanted electrodes of a deep brain stimulator, a sort of pacemaker for the brain, into Daniel's thalamus (Schiff et al., 2007).

The results of the stimulation were striking. After being virtually unresponsive for nearly seven years, Daniel began opening his eyes and turning his head to the sound of a voice. He became able to swallow food placed on his tongue and even began to speak some simple sentences. His condition continued to

improve over the following months. He began communicating reliably with his family and the medical staff, watching movies, and even laughing at appropriate times. Since then, other minimally conscious patients have undergone the procedure with similar improvements in their level of consciousness (Schiff, Giacino, & Fins, 2009). Although resuming a completely independent life is rarely possible after such severe injuries and deep brain stimulation is not always as successful as it was in Daniel's case, deep brain stimulation has the potential to return these patients to their families and to the world of waking life.

EEG shows a "flatline" tracing with neither high- nor low-frequency activity (Laureys, 2005). From this state, there is no recovery.

Brain activity in coma is different from brain death. Comatose patients are unconscious and cannot be roused to wakefulness. They do not open their eyes spontaneously, respond to their own name, or react normally to a painful stimulus such as a vigorous rubbing on the sternum. Nonetheless, their brain metabolism remains active, at around 50% of normal levels overall. Likewise, they continue to show low-frequency EEG activity (Boveroux et al., 2008). Unlike brain death, the state of coma is sometimes reversible, and the patient's level of consciousness may improve over time.

What happens in the brain if the patient is lucky enough to recover? Once again, using PET imaging, one can create maps that compare the brain activity before and after the patient's return to waking life. As it turns out, some brain regions are more important than others when it comes to being awake and alert. The activity of low-level sensory and motor parts of the cortex does not change dramatically with recovery from coma. Instead, it is the higher-level

association areas, in the lateral and medial prefrontal and parietal cortex, whose activity recovers as the patient regains consciousness (FIGURE 8.24) (Laureys, Owen, & Schiff, 2004). If this collection of areas sounds familiar, it should: these are many of the same areas that we see injured in patients with hemineglect. It is also the same set of areas whose activity is crucial for conscious perception in experimental studies of change blindness and inattentional blindness, as we saw in the first section.

The same brain areas are involved in recovery from a milder form of coma known as vegetative state. Patients in a vegetative state seem to have retained the capacity for wakefulness without regaining the capacity for awareness. Their sleep–wake cycle reemerges, and for part of the day, they open their eyes as if alert and awake. However, they still show no signs of being conscious. They do not communicate or make any regular purposeful movements, and they rarely respond to events in their surrounding environment, including painful stimuli. Again, some (but not all) patients continue to recover from the vegetative state and ultimately regain consciousness (Laureys et al., 2004). Those who do not regain consciousness within a month are said to be in a

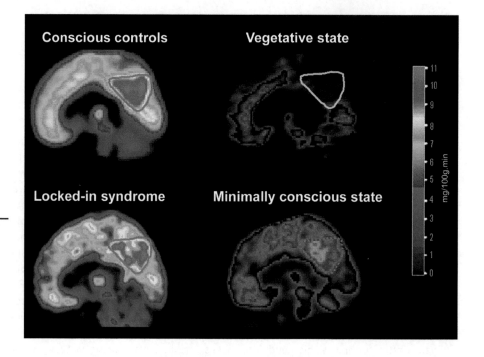

FIGURE 8.24 **Brain activity associated with varying levels of consciousness.** The activity in the medial parietal cortex (outlined as a red or blue triangle) is high for conscious subjects, but low for patients in a vegetative state. There is also increasing activity in the medial prefrontal cortex as subjects return to consciousness.

persistent vegetative state. The ones who recover show changes on their PET scans much like the changes seen in patients who recover from coma (Laureys et al., 2004). Medial and lateral parietal and prefrontal areas show an increase in activity (FIGURE 8.24). Lower-level sensory and motor areas remain relatively unchanged. Once again, the key to recovering consciousness seems to lie in reactivating the set of high-level association areas involved in conscious sensory perception and action.

In fact, early sensory areas can respond to outside stimuli although the patients themselves do not. For example, in the vegetative state, simple auditory stimuli like sounds or words will activate primary auditory cortex (FIGURE 8.25), but not the usual widespread network of higher-order association areas (Laureys et al., 2000). The same is true for painful stimuli: in patients who are in a vegetative state, these kinds

of stimuli activate only the brainstem, thalamus, and primary sensory cortex, but not the usual widespread network of areas including secondary somatosensory cortex, insula, parietal cortex, and anterior cingulate cortex (Laureys et al., 2002). The patients themselves show no signs of responding to the painful stimulus. The low-level primary sensory activity is effectively isolated, and the stimulus fails to rise to conscious awareness.

Midbrain and Thalamus: Key Players in the Conscious State

What kinds of brain lesions produce changes in the state of consciousness itself? The areas that are usually injured in coma or vegetative state are somewhat different from the network of high-level association cortex we have been discussing so far. As we saw earlier, damage to the high-level association cortex typically leads not to coma but to hemineglect: a disorder of the *contents* of consciousness rather than the state of consciousness itself. Patients with coma typically have injuries to areas outside the cortex itself: namely, the midbrain or the thalamus. The activity of these areas seems to be critical for maintaining the *state* of consciousness, as opposed to its contents.

The midbrain is an old region of the brain in evolutionary terms. As we saw in Chapter 2, the neurons of the midbrain tend to cluster into discrete nuclei, each with a specific sensory or motor function. Yet there is also a collection of other nuclei that send output much more widely throughout the nervous system and participate in a much broader range

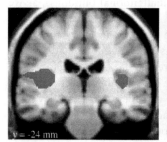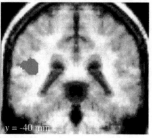

FIGURE 8.25 **Activity in the auditory cortex in (a) healthy control subjects and (b) areas showing less activity in patients in a persistent vegetative state.** In patients in the vegetative state, the primary auditory cortex continues to respond to auditory stimuli, but the association cortex shows significantly less activation (Laureys et al., 2000).

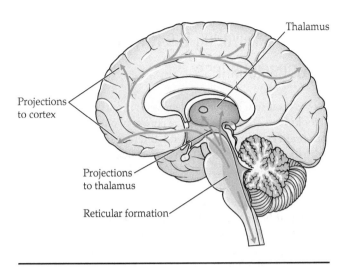

Thalamus

Projections to cortex

Projections to thalamus

Reticular formation

FIGURE 8.26 **The reticular formation.** The reticular formation is a collection of nuclei in the brainstem that project up to the thalamus and cortex and are important for attention and arousal.

of functions often lumped together into "arousal" or "wakefulness." The diffusely projecting neurons of these structures are woven intricately through all the other nuclei in the midbrain, like the many branches of a vine. These nuclei make up the midbrain's reticular (or "netlike") formation (FIGURE 8.26): an ancient structure that can be found in ancestors as distant as sharks or hagfish, but whose function remains essential for consciousness even in humans (Ronan, 1989).

Neurons of the reticular formation fire up arousal levels. Rather than sending outputs down the spinal cord, they send ascending, activating projections toward the telencephalon and the diencephalon (terms you may recall from Chapter 2). This circuitry is sometimes called the **ascending reticular activating system** (Magoun, 1952).

How do these connections contribute to the conscious state? Animal experiments as early as the 1930s showed that cutting the connections between the brainstem and spinal cord caused paralysis but did not impair consciousness; in contrast, cutting through the brainstem at the level of the midbrain or upper pons caused the profound unconsciousness of coma (Bremer, 1935; Parvizi & Damasio, 2003). Over the next few decades, studies of comatose patients gradually narrowed down the set of brainstem areas where damage produced unconsciousness. The key areas for maintaining consciousness lie in the midbrain reticular formation and the area just below it, in the upper pons (Parvizi & Damasio, 2003). Patients unlucky enough to suffer a stroke or other injury in this part of the brain usually fall into a comatose state (Parvizi & Damasio, 2003).

For an organism to remain conscious, these neurons must be not only intact, but also firing in a particular way. During normal wakefulness, the neurons fire continuously,

at a relatively high frequency. During deep sleep or unconsciousness, the neurons switch to a lower-frequency pattern (Saper, Chou, & Scammell, 2001). This switch has major effects on the activity of the entire cortex. When the reticular formation fires at high frequency, the cortical EEG enters a high-frequency, low-amplitude pattern of activity: the pattern normally seen during wakefulness (Kajimura et al., 1999). When the reticular formation neurons fire at lower frequencies, or if they are destroyed outright, then the cortical EEG switches to the low-frequency, high-amplitude pattern of activity that is characteristic of deep sleep or unconsciousness (Moruzzi, 1972). Keep in mind how a simple change in firing pattern dramatically alters the state of consciousness. We'll return to this point later in the chapter.

The thalamus also plays a critical role in maintaining the conscious state. The thalamus lies just above the midbrain, connecting different areas of the cortex to one another and relaying information to the cortex from elsewhere in the nervous system. Like the midbrain, the thalamus contains many discrete nuclei. Each of these discrete nuclei connects to a particular swath of cortex and therefore serves a particular sensory, motor, or associative function. Also, as in the midbrain, there are other thalamic nuclei that project diffusely throughout the cortex and are not restricted to any one particular sensory or motor function. These are the **intralaminar nuclei**.

The intralaminar nuclei are closely connected with the midbrain reticular formation, and like the reticular formation, they are critical for maintaining arousal and alertness. Damage to the intralaminar nuclei produces a comatose state, much like damage to the reticular formation. This happens more commonly than one might expect. The intralaminar nuclei are especially vulnerable to damage in situations in which the brain becomes starved of oxygen, as in asphyxiation. With the intralaminar nuclei damaged, the victim may remain in a minimally conscious state even if much of the surrounding brain tissue in the cortex and elsewhere is still relatively intact.

If the rest of the brain is still more or less in working order, is there some way to restore the patient to consciousness? Recently, neurologists and neurosurgeons have begun to explore this possibility (Schiff et al., 2007). The first step is to determine how much residual brain function remains within a patient who appears outwardly unconscious. Using functional MRI, physicians can identify patients who still show some evidence of widespread brain activity in response to sensory input (Schiff et al., 2005). This widespread activity offers some hope that the patient might be restored to a higher level of consciousness if the effects of the intrathalamic lesion could be somehow reversed.

The next step is to restore the activity of the damaged area. To do this, neurosurgeons implant deep brain stimulator electrodes within the intralaminar nuclei of the thalamus. Like a neural pacemaker, these electrodes stimulate the remaining neurons in the damaged area so that their activity recovers to the levels necessary to support consciousness (Schiff et al., 2007). The results can be quite dramatic. Patients who had been minimally conscious for years can begin to turn their heads toward a voice, swallow food placed in their mouths, respond to questions from other people, and even express meaningful sentences. When the rest of the brain is still functioning, thalamic stimulation may allow a patient to return to waking life.

The dramatic effects of deep brain stimulation give us a powerful illustration of just how crucial the intrathalamic nuclei are in maintaining the conscious state. Later in the chapter, we will consider exactly how the activity of the brainstem and thalamus enables consciousness and allows its contents to flourish. For now, the key point is that the processes of attention and awareness require the brain to be in a conscious state, and this conscious state cannot be supported by the cortex alone. The complete neural architecture of conscious perception involves the midbrain reticular formation and the intrathalamic nuclei, as well as the widespread network of frontal and parietal association areas we saw earlier in the chapter (FIGURE 8.26).

Now that we have an idea of what brain regions are involved in constructing the state and the contents of consciousness, we can turn to the more important question of how these many different regions work together.

Anesthesia and Sleep: Rhythms of Consciousness

As we have seen in the past two sections, a specific network of brain areas must be intact to support the conscious state.

Yet we have also seen that simply possessing the necessary neural wiring is not enough to maintain a state of consciousness. Unless these neurons are active in a particular way, the brain remains in an unconscious state, and no contents of consciousness can be generated. Every one of us has been in situations where our brain is anatomically intact, but consciousness is absent. The most common examples are deep sleep, which most of us experience every night, and anesthesia, which most of us will encounter at some point in our lives. What happens to the brain during these states? What patterns of normal activity are lost when the brain becomes unconscious, although its anatomical pathways remain undamaged? In this section, we'll look at what sleep and anesthesia teach us about the basis of the conscious state.

Sleep: Unraveling the Rhythm of Consciousness

As we'll see in Chapter 10, sleep is far more complicated than it looks from the outside. In the course of our nightly slumber, our brain cycles through several different stages of sleep, each with its own signature pattern of electrical activity observable on EEG. In one of these stages, REM sleep, dreams are prevalent and the EEG pattern looks in many ways similar to that of the waking brain (Crick & Mitchison, 1983). **Non-REM sleep** can be subdivided into three stages from the lightest (stage 1) to the deepest (stage 3) sleep (Brodbeck et al., 2012) (FIGURE 8.27), with each successive stage characterized by more synchronized patterns of EEG activity.

What about the *subjective* experience of each of these sleep stages? During sleep, although the person may seem unresponsive to the outside world, his inner world is sometimes very much alive. People awoken from REM sleep typically report vivid dreams in which they are intensely aware of sensations, emotions, events, narratives, goals, motivations, and social interactions (Pace-Schott, 2003). Those

Non-REM sleep

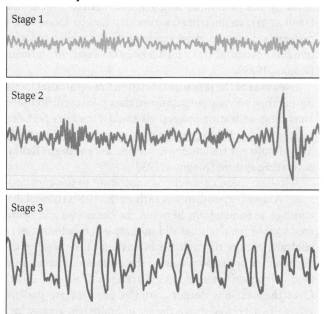

Stage 1

Stage 2

Stage 3

REM sleep

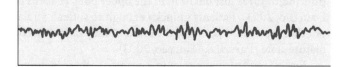

FIGURE 8.27 **Characteristic EEG recordings for different phases of sleep.**

woken from stage 1 or 2 sleep are much less likely to report any such experiences, whereas those woken from the deepest stage of sleep (stage 3) typically report either no subjective experiences at all or mostly rudimentary sensations without a coherent narrative (Hobson & Pace-Schott, 2002). In other words, different degrees of consciousness accompany the different levels of sleep, and these range from vivid and life-like to nearly nonexistent.

So what does the brain itself do during the unconsciousness of non-REM sleep? Intuitively, we might expect that sleep is simply a "powering down" of the brain: as the neurons reduce their activity level, we drift off into unconsciousness. However, the reality is more interesting. Certainly, in non-REM sleep, there is a widespread reduction in the metabolic activity of the brain. The decrease is especially pronounced across most of the lateral prefrontal and parietal cortex, as well as the medial prefrontal cortex and precuneus (Crick & Mitchison, 1983): areas that are especially active in our so-called "default state" of mind wandering during waking life: thinking about the future, or the past, or hypothetical situations, or events other than those going on in the here and now. A wide variety of subcortical structures are also less active, including the pons, caudate nucleus, hypothalamus, and thalamus (FIGURE 8.28) (Hobson & Pace-Schott, 2002; Maquet et al., 1996). Notice that many of the regions that power down in sleep are similar to the regions that we have seen involved in attention and awareness in the sections above.

Yet this reduction in overall metabolic activity is only part of the story. If we look at the individual cortical neurons themselves, we find that their individual firing rates are often close to or even above the levels that we see during wakefulness (Steriade, 2001). However, the rhythm of neural activity changes considerably (FIGURE 8.29). The

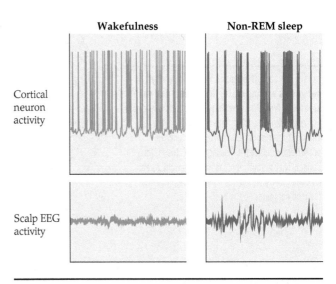

FIGURE 8.29 **Activity of cortical neurons during wakefulness and non-REM sleep.**

high-frequency, synchronized long-range cortical oscillations of waking life dissipate. Instead, they are replaced by slower oscillations of less than four cycles per second (Hobson & Pace-Schott, 2002). The sources of this modulation appear to lie in the brainstem and thalamus: during sleep, brainstem neurons of the reticular activating system switch from a continuous (**tonic**) pattern of firing to a bursting (**phasic**) pattern of firing (Hobson & Pace-Schott, 2002). A similar change occurs in the thalamus, where the inhibitory neurons of the nucleus reticularis of the thalamus switch into a bursting pattern of firing (Domich, Oakson, & Steriade, 1986).

One of the key effects of these changes is a shift in the patterns of neural communication between the thalamus and different regions of cortex. During the consciousness of waking life, distant areas of the cortex are able to communicate with one another and influence one another's activity through long-range corticocortical connections, as we saw earlier in the chapter. During sleep, however, the activity of the different cortical areas becomes decoupled. If we think of the brain as a social network of neurons, what has happened is not that the neurons have gone silent. Rather, they have drifted off into hundreds of separate conversations, rather than one large and coordinated discussion.

To support this point, an fMRI study provided evidence that deep sleep disrupts the coupling of activity between the medial prefrontal and parietal cortex that is seen in the default mode of waking consciousness (FIGURE 8.30) (Horovitz et al., 2009). Building on this finding, another fMRI study found that during the lighter stages of sleep (stage 1 and stage 2), there was a sharp drop in the usual coupling of activity between the thalamus and cortex, but surprisingly, there was a preservation and even an increase in

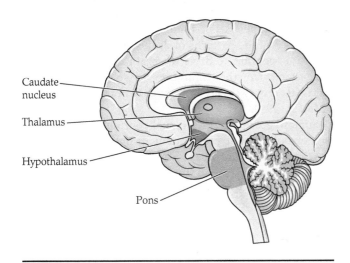

FIGURE 8.28 **Subcortical regions of the brain that are less active during non-REM sleep than during wakefulness.** These areas include the pons, caudate nucleus, hypothalamus, and thalamus.

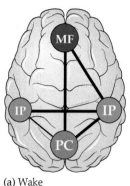 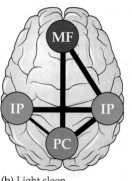 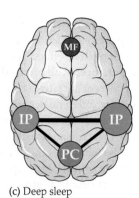

(a) Wake (b) Light sleep (c) Deep sleep

FIGURE 8.30 Differences in connectivity between a waking state, light sleep, and deep sleep. (a) Typical connectivity between the medial prefrontal/anterior cingulate cortex (MF), the left and right inferior parietal cortex (IP), and the posterior cingulate (PC) during wakefulness. (b) Connectivity actually increases during light sleep. (c) Connectivity during deep sleep is significantly reduced compared to the waking state.

the connectivity between cortical regions, particularly among the short-range rather than the long-range connections. With progression into the deeper sleep (stage 3), this corticocortical connectivity also dissipated (Spoormaker et al., 2010).

Of course, correlation does not equal causation, and so if we want to demonstrate a change in communication patterns between brain areas, it is much more convincing if we actually try to send signals through the brain's network during various states of consciousness. One way this can be done is using transcranial magnetic stimulation (TMS) to send a pulse of artificial stimulation into the neurons in some region of the brain and then looking at how this pulse "echoes" through the rest of the brain (Bestmann, Baudewig, Siebner, Rothwell, & Frahm, 2004). This approach reveals a clear difference in the connectivity of the network during wakefulness and sleep. During wakefulness, a single TMS pulse applied to the premotor cortex resounds back and forth through a widespread network of other prefrontal and parietal areas over the next few hundred milliseconds. However, during non-REM sleep, the same pulse causes a strong activation of the premotor cortex, but this activation fails to spread throughout the rest of the brain (Massimini et al., 2005). So deep sleep seems to look not so much like silence, but more like uncoordinated babble.

Anesthesia: Reversible, Artificial Unconsciousness

We just saw that sleep affects awareness by disrupting coordination among different brain areas. Let's now turn to the form of unconsciousness brought about by general anesthesia. The discovery of effective anesthesia represents one of the greatest advances in the history of medicine. It allows patients to undergo lengthy and complicated surgical procedures without having to suffer through pain, forced immobility, or the awareness that one was

undergoing a risky and potentially fatal medical intervention. Only recently have neuroscientists begun to understand the details of how anesthetics alter brain activity to produce a state of unconsciousness.

A wide variety of chemical substances can be used as anesthetics. However, they have a common effect of inhibiting neural activity, either by increasing inhibitory signaling or by decreasing excitatory signaling (Belelli, Pistis, Peters, & Lambert, 1999). Since anesthetics travel through the bloodstream to affect the entire brain, the major effect of increasing anesthetic dose is to reduce the overall level of metabolic activity in the brain. The pattern of electrical activity on EEG gradually changes from the low-amplitude, high-frequency oscillations of wakefulness to the high-amplitude, low-frequency oscillations seen in deep sleep (Worrell et al., 2004). Further increases in anesthetic dose produce still further decreases in overall brain metabolism: down to as little as 40% of normal levels, as opposed to 60% in deep sleep (Alkire et al., 1995; Zepelin & Rechtschaffen, 1974). At these higher doses, the EEG switches to a characteristic burst-suppression pattern, in which periods of intense electrical activity alternate with periods of almost no activity, that is quite different from the patterns of deep sleep. At even higher doses, it is possible to drive the brain into an isoelectric state, in which the inhibition is so profound that electrical activity ceases entirely, as in brain death (Doyle & Matta, 1999).

Somewhere along this gradual continuum of decreasing metabolic activity, the patient abruptly switches from consciousness to unconsciousness: a flip switch, rather than a dimmer switch, on the light bulb of consciousness (Alkire, Hudetz, & Tononi, 2008). Because the change in consciousness happens so abruptly, we can use neuroimaging to see whether there are any specific brain areas whose activity drops suddenly as the patient crosses into unconsciousness.

This experiment has now been performed for many different classes of anesthetics, with many different mechanisms of action. In almost all cases, there is a common set of

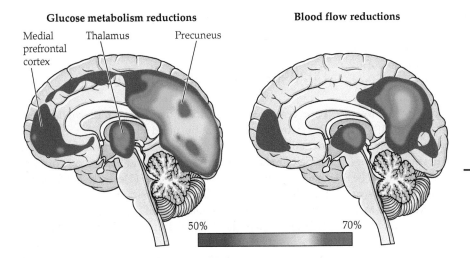

Glucose metabolism reductions

Medial prefrontal cortex   Thalamus   Precuneus

Blood flow reductions

50%   70%

FIGURE 8.31 **Brain areas that show decreased activity with anesthesia.** The most pronounced reductions are in the thalamus, medial prefrontal cortex, precuneus, and lateral parietal lobe.

findings (FIGURE 8.31). First, when anesthetics produce unconsciousness, they reduce the activity of higher-order sensory and motor association areas much like the set of areas we have been seeing again and again in this chapter: prefrontal and parietal cortex, on the medial and lateral surfaces of the hemisphere (Mashour, 2004). Second, the effects are especially pronounced on the medial areas: the precuneus and to some extent the medial prefrontal cortex (Bonhomme et al., 2011; Mashour, 2004). As we'll see in Chapter 9, the precuneus is especially important for memory formation and retrieval and orientation to time and place. Hence, some of the early effects of anesthesia include amnesia and disorientation. So the cortical areas affected by anesthesia match up with the cortical areas involved in the conscious state and its contents, as seen in studies of coma and neglect.

However, the most marked and most common effect of anesthesia occurs outside the cortex: a sudden downward shift in the neural activity of the thalamus as the patient crosses into unconsciousness (Bonhomme et al., 2011). There is some debate over whether this decrease is important on its own or whether it is simply a result of the more general decreases in cortical activity (Alkire et al., 2008). After all, the thalamus is strongly interconnected with the cortex, so decreasing the cortical activity should also reduce the metabolic demands on the thalamus. At the same time, we know from studies of coma that the thalamus is especially important in maintaining the conscious state (Bogen, 1997). Accordingly, it turns out that we do not need to infuse the entire brain with an anesthetic to produce unconsciousness: in animal studies, microinjections of an anesthetic directly into the intralaminar nuclei of the thalamus shift the animal into unconsciousness, just as if we had applied the anesthetic to the entire brain (Sukhotinsky et al., 2007). And the opposite is also true: animals rendered unconscious with anesthesia can be returned to a conscious state by applying electrical stimulation to the intralaminar nuclei of the thalamus (Kinomura, Larsson, Gulyás, & Roland, 1996).

Why is the thalamus so important for consciousness? One possibility is that the neurons in this area act something like the conductor of a symphony orchestra, ensuring that all the different players remain synchronized with one another, engaged in the same task, and acting in a coordinated fashion. Without the help of this thalamic "conductor," all the different cortical regions still have activity, but the activity cannot be assembled into a useful whole. The different cortical regions responsible for sensory perception, recognition, localization, action planning, goal-setting, task monitoring, and movement coordination no longer work as a team. The result is a loss of a key hallmark of the waking state: the capacity for attention, the purposeful linking of action planning to the sensory world in which the actions must be performed (Bovill, 2007).

Anesthetics disrupt the usual pattern of tightly coordinated activity between thalamic and cortical neurons. In the waking state, different regions of the cortex show coherence of activity: their high-frequency activity oscillates, rises, and falls in a coordinated fashion, and we can observe this synchronization using techniques like EEG or fMRI. With anesthesia, this synchronized, long-range communication among cortical regions is lost (Alkire et al., 2008). The thalamus becomes disconnected from the cortex—not because of lost anatomical connections (as in coma after brain injury) but this time because of lost *functional* synchronization (White & Alkire, 2003).

We can use TMS to send pulses of activation through the human brain in anesthesia, as we saw earlier for deep sleep. Once again, during wakefulness, a TMS pulse to the prefrontal cortex resounds widely through prefrontal and parietal cortex over a few hundred milliseconds. During anesthesia, the same pulse fails to spread beyond the premotor cortex (Ferrarelli et al., 2010).

In animal studies, we can investigate the mechanisms of anesthesia even more closely. Anesthetics like isoflurane alter the activity of thalamic neurons so that they become less excitable (**hyperpolarized**) and shift away from a high-frequency, tonic mode of firing to a lower-frequency, bursting mode of firing (Ries & Puil, 1999). This seems to prevent the thalamic neurons from responding to neurons from the cortex. Anesthetics interfere with information transfer through the thalamus. The result of this interference is, once again, a breakdown in the ability to coordinate activity across the brain as a whole. Subjectively, the result is a loss of consciousness (Jones, 2002).

As you may have noticed, a recurring theme over the past few sections has been the link among attention, consciousness, and the long-range synchronization of neural activity between a specific set of brain regions. Neurological injury to these brain regions certainly seems to interfere with attention and the conscious state, as we have seen in the cases of hemineglect, coma, and vegetative state. However, we do not need to physically damage these regions to disrupt consciousness: in the case of anesthesia, as with sleep, merely changing the pattern of electrical activity from one mode to another is enough to cause an abrupt switch from the conscious to the unconscious state.

Why should this be? Earlier in the chapter, we saw how synchronization of neural activity might allow the brain to operate in a variety of different information states. Some of these information states link together sensation and action into a coherent whole. These particular states emerge with attention and are associated with a sense of subjective, conscious experience.

Theories of Consciousness

Everything we've learned in this chapter still leaves unanswered one of the deepest mysteries of modern neuroscience: how does the activity of billions of neurons, synchronized or not, produce conscious *experience* itself? For centuries, the basis of human consciousness was considered the realm of philosophy alone. In the past 20 years, however, the neuroscience of conscious experience has begun to emerge as a field in its own right (Dehaene & Naccache, 2001). Today, theories of consciousness draw heavily on the findings of this neuroscience. In the final section, we'll look at some of the current ideas that have been proposed to explain how consciousness emerges from the functions of the brain.

Dualism: The Mind–Body Problem

Four centuries ago, in 1641, the French philosopher René Descartes proposed that the mind and the body were fundamentally distinct from one another, with the body being made of material "stuff" and the mind being made of spiritual (or at least, nonmaterial) stuff (Descartes, 1996). The idea that there is a fundamental separation between a material human body and a nonmaterial human consciousness is called Cartesian dualism, or simply **dualism** (MacKinnon, 1928). Similar ideas can be found not only in European philosophy, but also in the philosophical and spiritual traditions of most cultures around the world, both literate and nonliterate. In fact, even young children show an innate tendency toward dualism: insisting that the brain is needed for some activities, like doing math problems, but not for others, like loving your brother or pretending to be a kangaroo (Bloom, 2004).

In the 21st century, there are few philosophers and even fewer neuroscientists who argue in favor of Cartesian dualism. For one thing, it is extremely hard to see how a nonmaterial mind is supposed to interact with the material stuff of the brain to produce a movement, an emotion, a desire, an action, or a memory. Likewise, it is hard to see how a material brain is supposed to convey the sensory impressions of a word, a face, a smell, or a stomachache to a nonmaterial mind. If the stuff of the mind is truly nonmaterial, it is hard to explain how it can have any influence over the material universe at all.

In addition, it is hard to overlook the mounting evidence that the intuitively "nonmaterial" faculties of emotion, sensation, motivation, and consciousness are in fact tightly bound to complex, specific, and delicate material processes in the brain (Adcock, Thangavel, Whitfield-Gabrieli, Knutson, & Gabrieli, 2006; Frackowiak et al., 1997; Wager, Phan, Liberzon, & Taylor, 2003). Sever a few fibers of white matter leading to the primary visual cortex and subjective vision ceases to be. Cut off the supply of oxygenated blood to certain brain areas for more than a few seconds and the faculty of speech disappears, only to return if the blood flow is quickly restored. Stimulate a pathway near the subthalamic nucleus of the brain and a bout of overwhelming and inexplicable sadness drives the patient to tears within seconds. Stop the stimulation and the sadness resolves, again within seconds (Tommasi et al., 2008). Block a single type of calcium channel in a single population of neurons in the ventral tegmental area of the midbrain, and its firing pattern changes from tonic to phasic, collapsing the entire house of cards of consciousness itself (Waroux et al., 2005).

But if Cartesian dualism is increasingly discredited by our advancing knowledge in neuroscience, other controversies and puzzles remain. For one thing, our intuition still struggles to see *why* a tonic pattern of neural firing should be linked to conscious wakefulness, whereas a phasic pattern should not. For that matter, why should *any* pattern of firing in *any* kind of neural architecture give rise to a subjective experience at all?

Functionalist Theories of Consciousness

One theoretical approach to consciousness is called **functionalism**. Functionalist theories of mind specify that mental states depend on the functional role they perform, rather than on the specific kind of "hardware" in which they are implemented (Jackson & Pettit, 1988). So the mental state of pain, for example, could be generated not only by the specific set of neural pathways used in a mammal or an insect, but also by any kind of hardware that implemented the same basic functions of detecting damage-indicator stimuli and assigning them negative valence and high priority, marking a displacement from the homeostatic ideal, reshaping the motivational landscape to prioritize escape and defense behaviors, promoting avoidance learning, and generating preemptive motivational states to avoid similar stimuli in the future.

One type of functionalist theory is the **higher-order theory** of consciousness (Rosenthal, 2000). In this theory, simply building a representation of say, a face, is in itself insufficient for a subjective conscious perception of the face. What is needed is a second, higher-order representation *of* the representation of the face. In general, a conscious perception arises from three components: a lower-order representation, a higher-order representation, and a functional link that makes the higher-order representation "about" the lower-order representation.

A real-world example consistent with the higher-order theory would be the fMRI study of the patient with hemineglect from the third section of this chapter. When a face appeared on the left, the fusiform face area became activated. However, this lower-order representation was not in itself sufficient for conscious perception of the face. Instead, higher-order representations in a network of frontal and parietal areas were needed, and these areas had to synchronize their activity with the fusiform face area before the patient could subjectively "see" the face. The same was true for the fMRI studies of change blindness, inattentional blindness, and binocular rivalry (FIGURE 8.32): sensory activation alone was insufficient for conscious perception, and a subjective experience arose only when the lower-order sensory area became synchronized with the higher-order frontal and parietal network.

So the higher-order theories of consciousness are at least grossly consistent with some findings in neuroscience. Yet they do leave some questions unanswered. For example, the fusiform face area is itself a higher-order representation of lower-order visual representations in primary, secondary, and other regions of visual cortex. Yet for some reason this doesn't seem to be enough to generate a subjective sensation. There seems to be something different about the higher-order representations in frontal and parietal cortex compared to the higher-order representations within the visual cortex itself. So far, the higher-order theories cannot specify exactly what this difference might be.

One strange possibility is that fusiform activity actually *does* produce a subjective sensation, but that people cannot report their sensation without bringing in the frontal and parietal cortex (Baars, 2002). This raises the

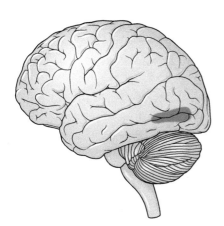

Unnoticed changes in visual scenes

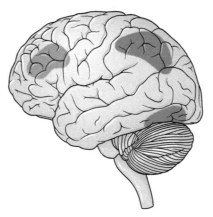

Consciously perceived changes in visual scenes

FIGURE 8.32 **Brain activation during consciously perceived versus unnoticed changes in visual scenes.** If a change in the visual environment activates only the visual cortex, the change does not reach conscious awareness. However, if the activation spreads to a larger network of frontal and parietal areas, then the visual change reaches conscious awareness.

confounding possibility that people can be aware of a stimulus at a perceptual level, but not aware that they are aware of it for the purposes of actually doing anything about it! Such a fragmented version of consciousness is highly counterintuitive, but not necessarily incorrect, given the many other forms of fragmented perception that we see in change blindness, in inattentional blindness, and in patients with blindsight or other neurological injuries. However, some clever experimental designs would be needed to demonstrate the existence of "awareness without awareness."

Another, less-fragmented functionalist theory is known as the **global workspace theory** of consciousness (Baars, 2005). In this framework, the brain is organized as a series of relatively specialized, parallel processors with distinct functions in visual perception, auditory perception, spatial localization, action planning, goal-setting, value determination, and so on (FIGURE 8.33). Functionally speaking, consciousness is a method for coordinating the actions of all these different functions into an integrated whole. It does so by creating a *global workspace* in which the contents of consciousness are available not just locally for a single brain function, but also globally for all of the brain's functions. It is by entering the global workspace that a stimulus such as a face moves from unconscious, background processing of the visual pathway to the conscious foreground of the

global workspace. The global workspace thus corresponds somewhat to the "spotlight" metaphor of attention, explaining why the scope of consciousness is not limitless, but instead tends to focus on just a handful of stimuli or actions at a time of the many millions of potentially available stimuli and actions represented across the diverse functions of the brain.

In terms of brain anatomy, the global workspace is hypothesized to map on to the highest-order neurons of the brain: those that lie at the greatest distance (say, number of synaptic hops) from the extremities of the nervous system in the retina, cochlea, peripheral nerves, and neuromuscular junction (Baars, 2002). It is these association areas of the cortex that would be best positioned to link together the many functions of the brain, and thus it is these association areas that would be most central to conscious perception. This prediction is in keeping with most of the findings that we have reviewed in this chapter, in which the synchronization of frontoparietal association areas to lower-level sensory and motor areas is essential for the emergence of subjective experiences (FIGURE 8.34).

Thus, the global workspace theory provides a more specific prediction about what kinds of functions are required for consciousness and why these map onto higher-order frontoparietal areas but not to higher-order visual, auditory, or somatosensory cortices alone. It also suggests an adaptive

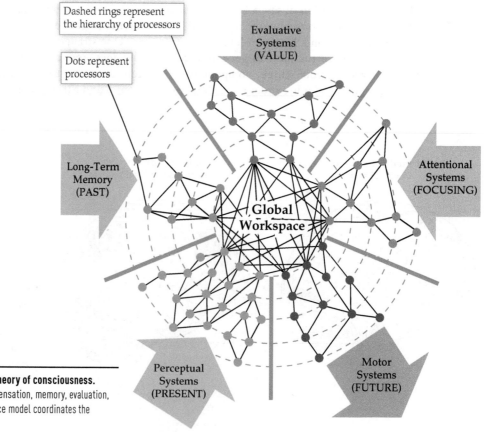

FIGURE 8.33 The global workspace theory of consciousness. The brain contains separate systems for sensation, memory, evaluation, attention, and action. The global workspace model coordinates the activity of all these systems.

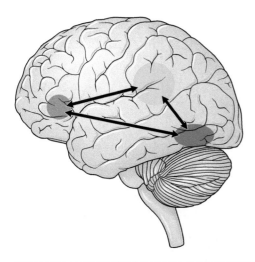

FIGURE 8.34 **Activity within the frontal and parietal lobes is important for consciousness and the emergence of subjective experience.**

role for consciousness itself, in enabling a wider range of responses to a given sensory stimulus and a wider range of sensory inputs to guide a given motor process. In addition, it hints at an explanation for some of the limitations of consciousness: why we can't pay attention to everything at once, why we can perform some simple or overlearned sensory-motor tasks without turning the full force of our attentional spotlight toward them, and why we describe automatic actions as "so easy that I could do it in my sleep."

Consciousness and the Integration of Information

Although we are still some way off from answering the question of why red feels different from green or tastes feel different from smells, there have been some recent attempts at explaining the qualitative features of consciousness. One example is the **integrated information theory** of consciousness (Boly, Massimini, & Tononi, 2009). This theory proposes that consciousness has two key properties. First, it is subjectively *informative*: to experience "red" is *not* to experience any of its many possible alternatives: green, blue, turquoise, and so on, not to mention the far vaster repertoire of noncolor experiences available to a conscious brain. Second, it is highly *integrated*, in that conscious experiences are subjectively unified: to experience a face is usually not to experience independent patches of light and dark on the retina, and to experience a word is usually not to experience its many component phonemes as sets of independent component frequencies and harmonics. So a useful measure of consciousness should capture both properties: the amount of information and the degree of integration of this information.

From these two premises, the theory proposes a method for calculating the amount of *integrated information* in any system, called "phi" and denoted by its Greek symbol, ϕ. Imagine a room with 100 people in it, speaking to one another. We could divide the group into 50 pairs that talk among themselves but not to any other pairs. This would give us lots of information (50 completely independent conversations), but little integration. Alternatively, we could combine all of the people into a single group (say, a crowd of football fans) and have them all chant their favorite team's cheer together. This would give us a lot of integration, but much less information than the 50 independent conversations. Both of these kinds of social networks have relatively low ϕ and are limited in their capacity: although a team of 100 people can accomplish many tasks, they are limited in what they can accomplish if they are all forced to work in independent small groups or if they are all forced to do exactly the same thing.

But what if we were to divide the 100 people into a few subgroups, each with a slightly different task, and then still allow higher-level communication between the "leaders" of each subgroup? Now our social network has both high information (since the activity of each member is a little different from all the others) and high integration (since each member has at least some influence over the activity of all of the other members, even if indirectly). This high-ϕ group has a much wider range of abilities. In the social world, we notice a big difference in collective capability among 100 people assembled shouting in a mob, 100 people paired on dates in a restaurant, or 100 people arranged into subcommittees in a national legislature. In the integrated information theory of consciousness, we expect the brain to show "higher" states of consciousness when its neurons are networked like a legislature in session and a lower state of consciousness when the same neurons are networked like a mob shouting a slogan or a few billion couples whispering to one another across the table (FIGURE 8.35).

What makes the theory interesting is that it does seem to explain why some brain states are associated with high levels of consciousness and a rich, informative, detailed subjective experience, whereas others are associated with low levels of consciousness and a coarse, murky degree of subjective experience. For example, during anesthesia, there is a disruption of the usual long-range synchronization of activity between distant functional subunits of the brain. The integration of the brain's information processing is lost, and unconsciousness results (Alkire et al., 2008). In contrast, during an epileptic seizure, the brain becomes excessively integrated: all the neurons fire in synchronization with all of the others, so that only two states (on or off) can be represented. Once again, unconsciousness results (Boly et al., 2008). During waking consciousness, there is a balance between partial integration and partial independence of different neurons, which allows them to distinguish many different alternative states but also allows these representations to be bound together as needed (Tononi, 2008). So the integrated information theory

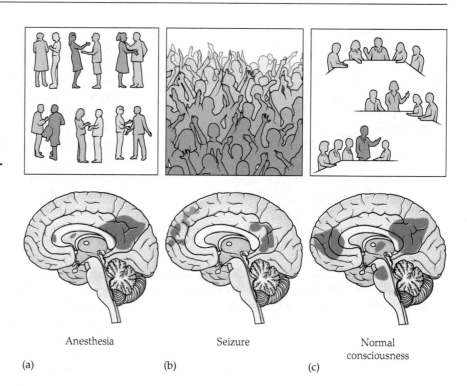

FIGURE 8.35 Examples of information content and integration. (a) A high-information, low-integration system, such as a large number of people who are each speaking to only one other person. (b) A low-information, high-integration system, such as a large number of people chanting in unison. (c) A moderate-information, moderate-integration system, such as committees of people reporting to leadership. The possible brain equivalents of these levels of information content and integration are shown here. From left to right: default-mode brain activity in an anesthetized brain, a brain having a seizure, and a working brain.

Anesthesia   Seizure   Normal consciousness

(a)   (b)   (c)

might help to explain why neither sheer synchronization nor sheer information capacity is a good predictor of the level of consciousness in the brain.

The theory can also be tested empirically by placing the brain into various altered states of consciousness and then determining the approximate ϕ from neuroimaging, EEG, MEG, or implanted electrode recordings. States with high ϕ should have a high level of consciousness, whereas states with low ϕ should not. For example, some hallucinogenics are known to disrupt the contents but not the overall level of consciousness (Tassi & Muzet, 2001). In contrast, other medications such as anesthetics and benzodiazepines tend to impair the level of consciousness (the *state* of consciousness) (John & Prichep, 2005). Similarly, REM sleep preserves a relatively rich sensory experience, whereas non-REM sleep is characterized by a relatively impoverished state of unconsciousness. By obtaining estimates of ϕ in each of these different states, it may be possible to test at least some of the basic predictions of the theory. As of this writing, such experiments are already underway.

Conclusion

Understanding the basis of human consciousness remains one of the great Holy Grails of 21st-century neuroscience.

Although we are still just beginning to come to grips with the problem, we are starting to get some sense of how it might be approached. From behavioral studies, we have learned that subjective experiences require attention. From neuroimaging studies, electrophysiological studies, and studies of neurological patients, we have begun to gather clues as to the underlying mechanisms of attention and awareness in the brain. Both attention and awareness rely on coordinated patterns of cortical activity that bridge the gap between sensation and action. These patterns emerge only in certain states of consciousness, and these states can be easily disrupted by interfering with subcortical structures—the midbrain and thalamus—which are ancient in evolutionary terms. It is still unclear why some patterns of activity give rise to subjective experiences whereas others do not: there are several theories but no consensus. There is not even a consensus on whether current neuroscience is capable of explaining consciousness at all or whether we will need to call upon some as yet undiscovered scientific principles to close an "explanatory gap" between neural activity and subjective experience. Nonetheless, over the past 20 years, attention and consciousness have made a decisive shift from the realm of philosophical speculation to the realm of empirical scientific investigation. Today, the science of conscious experience has developed into one of the great frontiers of modern neuroscience, ripe for exploration in the decades to come.

KEY PRINCIPLES

- Without attention, there is no conscious awareness of sensation or action.

- Attention links our sensations to our actions to serve a common purpose.

- Researchers have developed various means of studying attention and awareness in the laboratory. The orienting paradigm measures a subject's reaction time to the appearance of a visual stimulus in the presence and absence of reliable cues. In the oddball paradigm, researchers record the brain activity of a subject who views a series of similar items with an occasional markedly different item. Researchers studying perceptual rivalry monitor the brain activity of a subject who shifts between multiple possible interpretations of an ambiguous stimulus (like the old woman/young woman image).

- Attention and awareness require activity in a widespread network of cortical regions including high-order sensory and motor association areas.

- Attention improves one's ability to identify a stimulus by increasing the rate of firing within the neuron that is detecting the stimulus and also decreasing the unrelated background "noise" within the population of neurons responding to the stimulus.

- Neural synchronization helps to keep these widespread patterns of activity coordinated and distinct from competing patterns of activity.

- Distinct brain areas and mechanisms maintain the state of consciousness.

- These mechanisms can be disrupted by injury or drugs to produce a state of unconsciousness while most of the brain's architecture remains intact.

- Theories that attempt to explain how neural activity brings about conscious experience include dualism, now largely discarded by neuroscience, functionalism, which suggests that consciousness arises from the specific function of brain activity, and the integrated information theory, which suggests that consciousness gathers and integrates a great deal of information about the world.

KEY TERMS

Awareness Requires Attention
covert misdirection (p. 235)
inattentional blindness (p. 236)
memory (p. 238)

Approaches to Studying Attention and Awareness
orienting paradigm (p. 238)
central cue (p. 238)
reaction time benefit (p. 239)
reaction time cost (p. 239)
voluntary (endogenous) attention (p. 239)

involuntary (exogenous) attention (p. 239)
involuntary cue (p. 239)
top-down mechanism (p. 239)
bottom-up mechanism (p. 239)
oddball paradigm (p. 239)
perceptual rivalry (p. 240)
stereoscope (p. 240)

Neural Mechanisms of Attention and Awareness
neural correlates of consciousness (p. 241)

parahippocampal place area (p. 241)
masking (p. 241)
extinction (p. 244)
temporoparietal junction (p. 245)
contents of consciousness (p. 246)

Sites of Attentional Modulation: Neurons and Neural Populations
ensembles (p. 247)
biased-competition model (p. 247)
gain (p. 249)

feature selectivity (p. 249)

signal-to-noise ratio (p. 250)

local field potential (p. 250)

Synchronization, Attention, and Awareness

synchronization (p. 251)

Coma and Vegetative State: Anatomy of the Conscious State

state of consciousness (p. 253)

rapid-eye-movement (REM) sleep (p. 253)

coma (p. 253)

vegetative state (p. 253)

minimally conscious state (p. 253)

information states (p. 254)

brain death (p. 254)

ascending reticular activating system (p. 257)

intralaminar nuclei (p. 257)

Anesthesia and Sleep: Rhythms of Consciousness

non-REM sleep (p. 258)

tonic (p. 259)

phasic (p. 259)

hyperpolarized (p. 262)

Theories of Consciousness

dualism (p. 262)

functionalism (p. 263)

higher-order theory (p. 263)

global workspace theory (p. 264)

integrated information theory (p. 265)

REVIEW QUESTIONS

1. How might it be possible to remove someone's glasses from his or her own face without that person noticing what had happened? How could the intended "victim" of such a prank try to defend against it?

2. We cannot measure attention directly, as we measure heart rate or muscle contraction. What are some common ways of measuring attention indirectly? Are there any possible issues that might arise in using these approaches?

3. It has been suggested that a widespread network of frontal and parietal activity is important for subjective perception. What lines of evidence support this idea?

4. Patients with hemineglect, after parietal lobe injury, may fail to respond to stimuli located on the left side of space. Yet patients with right occipital lobe injury might also fail to respond to stimuli on the left side. How do we know that hemineglect is a deficit of attention and not just a case of simple cortical blindness?

5. Is there a single common network of brain regions for attention and awareness? What are the common features of brain areas involved in attention and awareness, anatomically and functionally?

6. What is meant by the "biased-competition model" of attention? What are the effects of attention at the level of single neurons? Local groups of neurons? Widespread networks of brain regions across the cortex?

7. How might neural synchronization help to support attention and conscious awareness? Why is "widespread neural synchronization" inadequate to explain the basis of attention and awareness in the brain?

8. What brain areas show a recovery of activity when a patient recovers from coma or vegetative state? What areas are common sites of injury in such patients? How do these areas help to maintain the conscious state?

9. How do anesthetics interfere with the conscious state? Why might the brain be able to generate conscious experiences during wakefulness, but fail to do so under anesthesia, although no neurological damage has occurred?

CRITICAL-THINKING QUESTIONS

1. In studies of perceptual rivalry, the subjects must report their subjective experiences to us using button presses or some other kind of behavioral response. What kind of problems could this create if we are trying to identify the neural correlates of the subjects' subjective experiences? Can you think of any ways around these problems?

2. Imagine that, as a scientist, you must design a brain imaging experiment to test the global workspace theory of consciousness. Describe the basics of a brain imaging experiment that you have designed to test this theory. What experimental results would support this theory? What experimental results would provide evidence against this theory? Explain.

3. To what extent do you think that current neuroscience is capable of explaining consciousness? What are its limitations in explaining consciousness? Explain, using what you have learned from this chapter as well as your own experiences from your everyday life.

- Distinguish among the different types of memory, including working, long-term, implicit, and explicit.

- Explain the role of the medial temporal lobe in the creation and re-creation of episodic memories, spatial memory, and navigation.

- Describe the components of the core network of memory and their role in the functions of prospection and recollection.

- Detail how the suppression of irrelevant information is critical to memory function and identify three common forms of memory error.

- Explain the basic mechanisms by which experiences rewire the brain at the molecular, cellular, synaptic, and network levels.

- Identify four mechanisms by which memories might be stored without altering neural connections.

- Summarize four unresolved issues in memory research and assess how a person might be able to recall events from almost every day of her life.

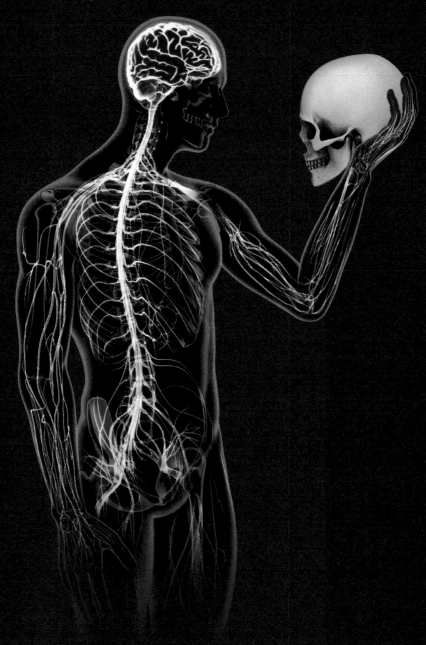

CHAPTER 9

Memory

STARTING OUT:
The Woman Who Cannot Forget

Imagine being able to remember every day of your life. Of course, some memories come easily to us all: the day we moved to a new home; the day we won a victory we once thought beyond our reach; the day the telephone rang with news of a life-changing tragedy. But imagine having a clear and immediate memory for all the events of day-to-day life: the dinner you had on March 30, 2007; the friend who dropped by to visit on June 20, 2004; the airliner that crashed on July 25, 2000. Imagine having a vivid, movielike recollection of what you were doing on today's date 1 year ago, 3 years ago, 10 years ago.

These recollections fill your mind and dominate your thoughts. They run in parallel with the events of your waking life as you travel to work or school, have conversations, go shopping, and spend time with your family. Other people marvel at your exceptional powers of memory and wish that they possessed the same ability. You, however, find the process uncontrollable, overwhelming. Many of the memories are painful or traumatic; you wish you could be rid of them. Exhausted by their presence, you finally contact a pair of neuroscientists, hoping they can help you understand what is happening.

This story is not a work of fiction, but is the reality of life for a woman named Jill Price (FIGURE 9.1), who has come to be known as "the woman who can't forget." On June 5, 2000 (a date she remembers as clearly as every other), she described her experiences for the first time to James McGaugh and Larry

FIGURE 9.1 **Jill Price, the woman who can't forget.**

Cahill, two memory researchers at the University of California at Irvine. Although initially skeptical, the researchers investigated her abilities through a series of careful tests and interviews over a period of five years.

The results showed that Jill Price did indeed have a rare and astonishingly powerful memory, at least for certain types of information. Given a date, within seconds she could recall the day of the week, the details of what she did on that day, and what newsworthy events took place on that day. Without any preparation, she easily recalled the dates of every Easter from 1980 to 2003, as well as her own activities on each date. Her recollections were detailed and consistent across interviews. Given a list of randomly selected news events, she gave correct dates and personal anecdotes for all of them: the start of the first Gulf War on January 16, 1991; the bombing of the Atlanta Olympic

Games on July 26, 1996; the death of Princess Diana on August 31, 1997. Strangely, her general intelligence and her memory for other types of information appeared average: she never excelled in school and had difficulty memorizing dates in history books rather than in her own personal life. Her abilities, although powerful, were at the same time oddly limited.

The researchers (along with their colleague, Elizabeth Parker) published their first report of the case of Jill Price in 2006 (Parker, Cahill, & McGaugh, 2006). She quickly became a news item in her own right. Her story drew headlines around the world. She appeared as a guest on Oprah's television show. Her memoirs appeared under the title *The Woman Who Can't Forget*. And while neuroscientists continue to search for the source of her remarkable abilities, the public fascination with her case has grown and continues to grow.

Why does the story of Jill Price capture our imagination so strongly? Perhaps, in part, because we recognize the value of a powerful memory in an age in which intellectual achievement and access to information are so often crucial to success in life. Or, perhaps, because we see how failing memory is so crippling in old age and we hope to find a way to escape the fate of our grandparents. Or, perhaps, simply because we recognize how little we truly retain from the vast, rich set of life experiences that, collectively, have made us into the people we are today.

To understand where Jill Price's remarkable abilities come from and what we ourselves might learn from her experience, we must understand how memory works. In this chapter, we will discover what memory is, how it functions, how it fails, and what purpose it serves in helping us to survive and thrive. Be prepared for some surprises along the way.

The Many Kinds of Memory

One of the first surprises about memory is that it comes in many forms. Although Jill Price has become famous as the woman who can't forget, she would point out that this is an exaggeration of the truth. Her memory for dates and for her personal experiences is indeed remarkable. Yet her memory in many other domains is remarkably unremarkable. Even her detailed memories are specific to events of high personal relevance: illnesses or dramatic news items. Asked to close her eyes and describe her interviewers' clothing, she draws a blank (Parker et al., 2006).

The highly specific nature of Jill Price's remarkable memory abilities illustrates that the brain contains multiple systems of memory that function independently in many ways. Researchers have therefore created a taxonomy of memory, consisting of multiple divisions and categories (Momose et al., 1992), including working, long term, implicit, and explicit.

Working and Long-Term Memory

The broadest division is between short- and long-term memory (FIGURE 9.2). The concept of "short-term memory" is more than 100 years old and refers to the information that decays in a short time (seconds to minutes) if you do not use it. The phrase "short-term memory" has largely been replaced in cognitive psychology and neuroscience by the phrase "**working memory**." Working memory works with or uses information to address a particular question or situation. This information can be drawn from either short-term or long-term storage. This is just one of many examples of how the field of cognitive neuroscience is changing as our understanding of the brain increases.

Although there is no absolute time limit, working memory typically lasts from a few seconds to around a minute or two: generally just for the duration of the task at hand. Working memory itself is not a single system. For example, you can keep in mind a series of words, or a sentence, or a phone number by repeating it over and over internally. This system is sometimes known as the *phonological loop*. You might also hold in mind a visual image of the words, or a simple drawing, or a sequence of colored shapes appearing in different locations. This system has been called the *visuospatial sketchpad*.

Regardless of subdivision, most working memory systems have a limited information-holding capacity. The maximum capacity is surprisingly similar in size across many kinds of

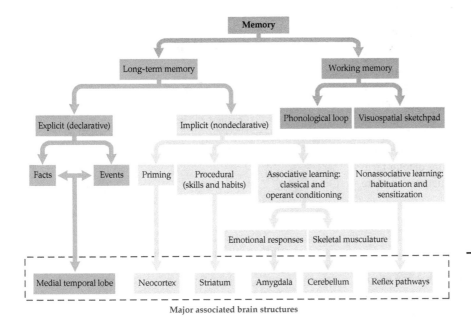

FIGURE 9.2 **The major subdivisions of memory.** Memory is divided between working memory and long-term memory, but each of those is further subdivided into different types and abilities.

Major associated brain structures

working memory. This was first recognized by the cognitive psychologist George Miller in 1956 in a landmark paper, "The Magical Number Seven, Plus or Minus Two: Some Limits on Our Capacity for Processing Information" (G. A. Miller, 1956). Working memory systems in most people seem capable of holding around seven items of information at a time: seven shapes, or seven locations, or seven numbers—which may explain why many different countries' telephone systems use around seven digits for each subscriber.

The "7 ± 2" finding has been surprisingly robust across working memory systems studied over the past 50 years, although the exact capacity of any given system varies in some circumstances. Whether this limit is pure coincidence—or whether it reflects some deeper truth about the nature of working memory—has been debated extensively (Cowan, N., Morey, C. C., & Chen, Z., 2007; G. A. Miller, 1956). We will return to this topic in more detail later in the chapter.

Long-term memory refers to systems that are capable of encoding, storing, and retrieving information over periods of time, anywhere from minutes to a lifetime. Their capacity is also much greater than that of the working memory systems, as dramatically illustrated in the case of Jill Price. Long-term memory systems are themselves typically grouped into two subdivisions. The first subdivision is known as **implicit memory** or nondeclarative memory. This system encodes information that, although held in the long term, does not lend itself to conscious recall or expression. Examples might include unconscious motor memories, such as knowledge of the movements required to operate a bicycle, or unconscious emotional memories, such as unease about riding a bicycle years after a childhood accident, even if the accident itself is long forgotten.

The second subdivision is known as **explicit memory** or declarative memory. This system encodes information that can be consciously recalled and expressed. Examples include memories of life episodes, such as your first day of college, or memories of facts, such as the knowledge that a bicycle has two wheels.

Implicit and explicit memory have both been studied extensively in humans and in animals. In the process, memory researchers have identified many different further subdivisions of long-term memory, each with its own distinct brain circuitry. They have also made progress in understanding how long-term memories might be stored at the cellular level: neurons, receptors, and synapses. We will take a close look at these intricate mechanisms later in the chapter. First, however, let us take a look at the major divisions of long-term memory and the large-scale anatomical structures that are important for each one.

Implicit Memory

Implicit memory involves skills and learning that can occur without conscious awareness. **Procedural memories** are memories for how to perform skills or habits: reading,

typing, swimming, juggling, playing piano, or riding a bicycle. These kinds of memory are acquired slowly, through repetition and practice, and can endure long after the sessions of practice. Many patients with brain injury have severe difficulty remembering experiences of even a few minutes earlier, yet nonetheless can learn and master new skills (Cohen, Eichenbaum, Deacedo, & Corkin, 1985). Studies in animals and humans suggest that the neural circuitry of the striatum is essential for forming procedural memories (FIGURE 9.3) (Doll, Shohamy, & Daw, 2014; Gasbarri, Pompili, Packard, & Tomaz, 2014). Interestingly, this includes the pathological habits of addiction to substance use or gambling.

Priming is another form of unconscious long-term memory, in which past experiences influence or increase the response to a given sensory stimulus. In a priming experiment, you might be asked to determine the content of an incomplete picture (for example, a partial sketch of an elephant) as it is gradually filled in with more and more detail (see FIGURE 9.4). After a few experiences, you will be able to identify the elephant much earlier in the filling-in process, based on much less perceptual information. This phenomenon is known as *perceptual priming*. Many other forms also exist. For example, in *semantic* or *conceptual priming*, seeing a word such as *car* can speed the response to a related word such as *truck*, shown at a later time. Once again, amnesia patients still show priming effects even when they have no conscious recollection of the past experiences that produced the effects in the first place. A widespread set of sensory and motor areas throughout the cerebral cortex is thought to be important for priming in its various forms (Dehaene et al., 2001).

Classical conditioning is another form of implicit memory (FIGURE 9.5), first described by the Russian physiologist Ivan Pavlov at the end of the 19th century (Pavlov,

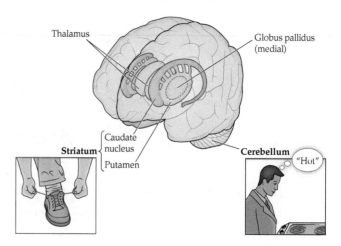

FIGURE 9.3 Brain regions involved in implicit memory. The striatum, made of the caudate nucleus and the putamen, and the cerebellum are important for different types of implicit memory. The striatum is essential for forming procedural memories, and the cerebellum is involved in classical and operant conditioning.

response to these learned consequences. Learning of emotional responses for both classical and operant conditioning (including autonomic responses, such as increased heart rate or salivation) appears to depend on the neural circuitry of the amygdala. Learning skeletal muscle responses (such as eye blinks to tones predicting a sudden puff of air to the face) relies on the cerebellum and other associated structures of the brainstem (Thompson, Thompson, Kim, Krupa, & Shinkman, 1998).

Nonassociative learning typically describes long-term changes in reflex pathways in the nervous system. An example is habituation, in which repeated exposure to the same stimulus causes a gradual decrease in the response. An everyday example would be gradually adapting to the water temperature in a hot shower. An opposing phenomenon is **sensitization,** where the response to a given stimulus increases following exposure to an especially strong or noxious "sensitizing" stimulus. An everyday example would be an increased sensitivity to heat following exposure to scalding hot water. Although classically described for simple reflex pathways, the effects of habituation and sensitization can be seen at all levels of the nervous system (Kaplan, Werner, & Rudy, 1990). In fact, studies of these nonassociative learning mechanisms in *Aplysia* earned the Nobel Prize in Physiology or Medicine for Eric Kandel, Arvid Carlsson, and Paul Greengard in the year 2000.

Explicit Memory

Although implicit memory involves skills and learning that can occur without conscious awareness, explicit memories are memories of facts that you are aware that you know. The two basic forms of explicit memory are episodic memory and semantic memory.

Episodic memories are memories for past autobiographical events, such as birthdays, meetings, discoveries, and travels. They are distinct from implicit memories in that they can be consciously recalled and described, written in a journal, and used in a flexible way to guide future behavior. It is worth noting that episodic memories often have a vivid, cinemalike quality to them. They have a particular context: a specific place and a specific time (for example, "in the living room on New Year's Eve"). It is often possible to pick out specific objects and features in the surroundings (a sofa, a television, a family member). Sequences of actions and occurrences are usually a key part of the memory (donning party hats, watching as drinks are served, clinking glasses).

Memory researchers sometimes distinguish between **familiarity** and **recollection**. Familiarity involves a more vague sense of emotional content, without any accompanying context. In contrast, a complete recollection involves a rich recreation of place, time, surroundings, actions, and events. The **medial temporal lobe** and in particular a region known as the hippocampus are key structures for the

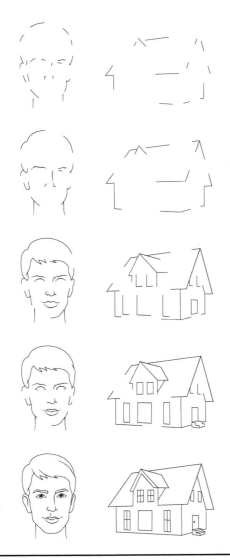

FIGURE 9.4 **Perceptual priming experiment.** Images can be recognized more rapidly and with less detail with repeated exposure.

1927). In his experiments, Pavlov built on the observation that dogs normally respond to food (called the **unconditioned stimulus**) by salivating (called the **unconditioned response**). Over time, dogs learned to associate the ringing of a bell or another signal (called the **conditioned stimulus**) with the impending delivery of food. With repeated experiences, they began to salivate in response to these conditioned stimuli alone (salivation is now called a **conditioned response**), even before the arrival of the unconditioned stimulus of the food itself.

Another form of implicit memory, known as **operant conditioning,** was studied extensively by the American psychologists Edward L. Thorndike and later B. F. Skinner, in the mid-20th century (Skinner, 1938; Thorndike, 1898). In this case, animals learned to associate their own behavior (for example, pressing a lever) with rewarding or aversive outcomes (such as the delivery of food or electric shocks). They then gradually increased or decreased the behavior in

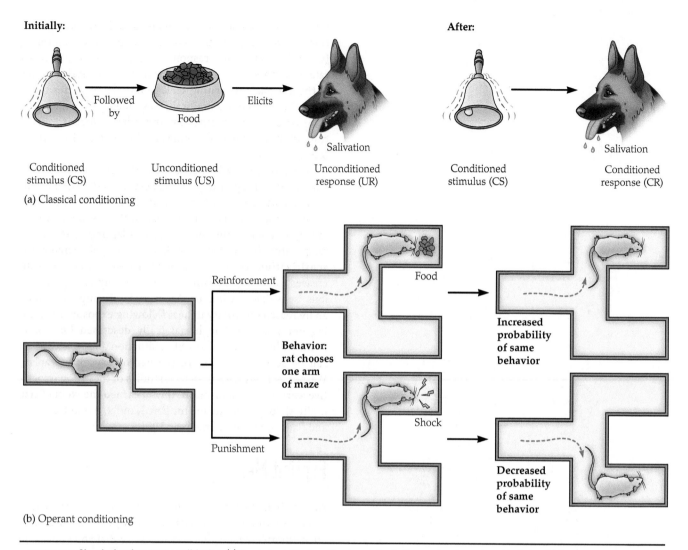

Initially:

Followed by

Food

Elicits

Salivation

Conditioned stimulus (CS)

Unconditioned stimulus (US)

Unconditioned response (UR)

After:

Salivation

Conditioned stimulus (CS)

Conditioned response (CR)

(a) Classical conditioning

Reinforcement

Food

Increased probability of same behavior

Behavior: rat chooses one arm of maze

Shock

Decreased probability of same behavior

Punishment

(b) Operant conditioning

FIGURE 9.5 **Classical and operant conditioning.** (a) Classical conditioning with a dog, similar to the experiments conducted by Pavlov. (b) Operant conditioning in a rat, similar to work done by Skinner.

recollection and recreation of episodic memories. The field of episodic memory research is vast. The hippocampus alone has been the subject of thousands of studies over the past half-century.

Semantic memories are memories for facts about the outside world. Often, these involve information about the properties of things: the fact that a sheep has four legs, makes a noise that sounds like "baa," grows wool that can be made into clothing, and so on. Semantic properties are more general than sensory or perceptual properties like color, size, and so forth. Since they are independent of any one particular kind of sensory input, they are useful for organizing the world into categories of semantically related stimuli: animals, tools, vehicles, professions.

What makes this type of memory tricky is that a semantic memory can sometimes masquerade as an episodic memory (FIGURE 9.6). For example, you may recall that you took an examination in chemistry many years ago without being able to say in which room you took it, who else was present around you, or what questions were asked. In a more

"Paris is the capital of France..."

(a) Semantic

(b) Episodic

FIGURE 9.6 **Semantic versus episodic memories.** Semantic and episodic memories are both forms of explicit memories. (a) Semantic memories are general knowledge; you have no personal recollection of when or where you learned it. (b) Episodic memories are of specific events for which you can re-create the time, place, and surroundings as a mental scene.

obvious example, you may know the date and time of your birth, the name of the hospital in which you were born, and the obstetrician who was present, although you have no actual recollection of the experience of birth itself! Memory researchers must conduct careful interviews to distinguish between the vivid recollections of episodic memory and the recall of autobiographical facts, which may be equally detailed in content, but are divorced from a mental re-creation of past experience.

Semantic memories are distinct from episodic memories, and even patients with severe amnesia for personal experiences can retain a good general knowledge for facts learned before their injury or illness. In some forms of dementia, such as early **Alzheimer's disease**, episodic memory often suffers dramatically, long before semantic knowledge begins to fail (Perry, Watson, & Hodges, 2000). Conversely, in a rarer illness known as **semantic dementia**, episodic memory is preserved although even basic forms of semantic knowledge (such as what a sheep is or what sound it makes) are lost (Hodges, Patterson, Oxbury, & Funnell, 1992). Semantic dementia involves degeneration of the anterior temporal lobes (Mummery et al., 2000), rather than the medial temporal lobes as in episodic memory loss (Guedj et al., 2009).

Travels in Space and Time: The Hippocampus and Temporal Lobe

In the early decades of the 20th century, many researchers believed that memories did not depend on any one particular region of the brain, but were stored diffusely across the nervous system as a whole (Herrick, 1930). However, in 1957, a stunning case report brought the hippocampus to center stage in the neuroscience of memory (Scoville & Milner, 1957).

The hippocampus is also known to have an important role in the recollection of space, as well as time. In 1971, neuroscientists John O'Keefe and Jonathan Dostrovsky reported that the hippocampus contains **place cells** (O'Keefe & Dostrovsky, 1971): neurons that fire only when the organism is located in a particular place in its local environment. Subsequent work suggested that the hippocampus might also play a key role in forming **spatial cognitive maps** useful for

CASE STUDY:
Gone but Not Forgotten: Henry Molaison, 1926–2008

In 1957, the neurosurgeon William Scoville and the neuropsychologist Brenda Milner published their first account of amnesia patient Henry Molaison, known during his lifetime by his initials, H. M. Henry's striking memory deficits eventually made him one of the most famous cases in the history of neuroscience.

Henry had suffered severe and frequent epileptic seizures after a head injury at the age of 9. When no other treatments could successfully control the seizures, he underwent surgery at the age of 27. Dr. Scoville removed parts of the medial temporal lobes including the hippocampus, parahippocampal gyrus, and amygdala.

Following surgery, the seizures abated. However, Henry was left with severe **anterograde amnesia** for the events following his surgery. He could not form new episodic memories. Nor could he recall events that had taken place even a few minutes before. His interviewers would have to re-introduce themselves at each meeting, even after leaving the room only briefly. He also suffered from a gradual **retrograde amnesia** for memories of events before the surgery. This retrograde amnesia was near total for the days before the surgery, but for events that took place months or years before the surgery, Henry was able to remember more details. However, some memories

even several years before the surgery were affected. Henry could recount the events of his childhood in general terms, although he was unable to organize them into a specific narrative (Scoville & Milner, 1957).

Interestingly, implicit memory remained intact. Over many trials, Henry learned to trace a five-point star viewed through a mirror, drawing on procedural memory. He had no recollection of his learning episodes, however, and would express surprise at how well he performed on a task that (from his point of view) he had never encountered before. Likewise, semantic memory for knowledge acquired long before the surgery remained intact. His working memory also remained well within the range of the magical 7 ± 2. Landmark findings such as these helped to define the taxonomy of memory systems as we know it today (Wickelgren, 1968).

Henry never regained the ability to form episodic memories. His dense amnesia left him unable to work or pursue a career. Nonetheless, he remained affable in manner and open to participating in researchers' studies of memory function. He continued to participate in these investigations up until the end of his life in 2008. Despite their tragic circumstances, Henry and thousands of other less well-known neurological patients have provided all of us with a valuable legacy: a better understanding of the functions of our own brains and minds.

navigating through the world around us (DiMattia & Kesner, 1988). Notably, Dr. O'Keefe shared the 2014 Nobel Prize for Medicine with husband-and-wife team Drs. Edvard and May-Britt Moser for their work on the spatial navigation functions of the hippocampus.

How can we reconcile these two apparently different roles for the same brain structure? Over the years, many theories of hippocampal function have been proposed in an attempt to explain its role in cognition. In this section, we will look at how the hippocampus contributes to episodic and spatial memory before turning to some of the major theories of hippocampal function overall.

A Map of the Medial Temporal Lobe

Let us begin by getting ourselves oriented within the landscape of the medial temporal lobe (FIGURE 9.7). The hippocampus proper lies on the underside of the cerebral cortex, on the medial edge of the temporal lobe. Through a microscope, we can see that it consists of four distinct regions or fields of neurons, which are designated CA1, CA2, CA3, and CA4. The larger region known as the **hippocampal formation** includes the adjacent **dentate gyrus**, named for the serrated, "toothed" appearance of its surface. Also included is the subiculum, which lies on the border between these structures and the rest of the cortex.

The parahippocampal region of cortex is the major source of input and output to the hippocampal formation. It has two parallel pathways for conveying spatial and nonspatial information to the hippocampus (Witter et al., 2000). The more anterior pathway projects from the perirhinal cortex to the lateral entorhinal cortex to the hippocampal formation. This pathway is important for object recognition memory (Murray & Mishkin, 1998). The more posterior pathway projects from the postrhinal cortex to the medial

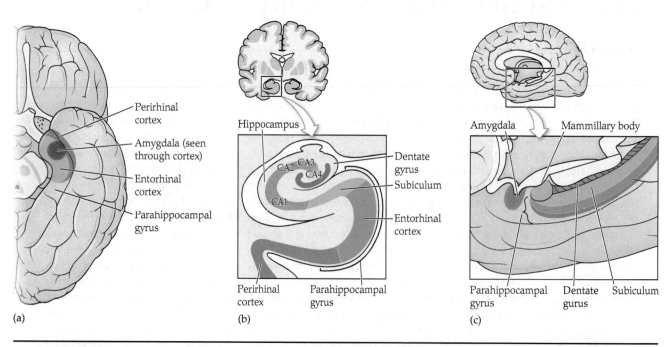

(a)   (b)   (c)

FIGURE 9.7 **Medial temporal lobe structures associated with explicit memory.** (a) A view of the inferior surface of the brain, showing the location of the parahippocampal gyrus, the perirhinal cortex, and the entorhinal cortex. (b) The hippocampus is located within the medial temporal lobes, and it is subdivided into regions CA1, CA2, CA3, and CA4; this is shown in the coronal cross-section of the medial temporal lobe. (c) A midsagittal view of the medial temporal lobe, showing the relative positions of the amygdala, parahippocampal gyrus, dentate gyrus, and subiculum.

entorhinal cortex to the hippocampal formation. This pathway is important for spatial memory and spatial cognitive mapping (Van Strien, Cappaert, & Witter, 2009). Together, the hippocampus and its surrounding areas of cortex are known as the hippocampal complex.

Another important player in the medial temporal lobe memory systems is the amygdala, an almond-size structure lying just anterior to the hippocampus. It plays an important role in emotional memory, assigning value (positive or negative) to visual, auditory, olfactory, and other stimuli based on past experiences (Paton, Belova, Morrison, & Salzman, 2006). It is capable of coordinating all three branches of the emotional response to a stimulus: the autonomic (e.g., increased heart rate), the endocrine (e.g., secretion of stress hormones such as corticotropin), and the behavioral (e.g., fear and avoidance responses) (Goldstein, Rasmusson, Bunney, & Roth, 1996). It has strong connections to the hippocampal formation, particularly its anterior portions (Richardson, Strange, & Dolan, 2004), which may help to explain why emotional events are more likely to be remembered.

If all of these anatomical structures and pathways seem confusing, do not be too concerned. Some recent maps of medial temporal anatomy describe more than 1,600 different connection pathways (Van Strien et al., 2009)—it would be futile to try to memorize them all! Just try to remember that there are distinct pathways and structures for spatial and episodic memories and additional contributions from the amygdala for emotional memories.

Episodic Memory

Since the initial description of Henry Molaison, the link between medial temporal lobe lesions and episodic memory impairment has been confirmed in many other patients (Nyberg, McIntosh, Houle, Nilsson, & Tulving, 1996). However, the precise contributions of the hippocampus to episodic memory remain a subject of vigorous debate to this day.

One area of dispute centers around the issue of whether Henry really did retain the same memories of his remote past as he had had prior to surgery. Initially, the observation that he could recount his remote but not his recent past led to the suggestion that the hippocampus might serve as a kind of temporary memory storage site. In this view, the hippocampus would hold fragile new episodic memories together until they became sufficiently consolidated in the cortex, at which point they could exist and be retrieved on their own (McGaugh, 2000). However, more recent theories have suggested that the hippocampus might remain essential for vivid, lifelike re-creation of past experiences throughout one's entire lifetime (Nadel, Samsonovich, Ryan, & Moscovitch, 2000; Söderlund, Moscovitch, Kumar, Mandic, & Levine, 2012).

Another area of debate centered around whether episodic memories really depended on the hippocampal complex at all

(Clark & Squire, 2010). Experiments that caused medial temporal lesions in rodents often failed to reproduce the anterograde amnesia of Henry Molaison (Clark & Squire, 2010). To add to the confusion, an MRI scan of Henry revealed that, on one hand, his surgery had actually spared some of the hippocampus, but on the other hand had removed parts of the amygdala and parahippocampal cortex (Corkin, Amaral, González, Johnson, & Hyman, 1997).

After the development of noninvasive human neuroimaging techniques such as PET and fMRI, one of the first areas of cognition to be studied was episodic memory function. These techniques (FIGURE 9.8) showed the hippocampus to be active during the retrieval of both recent and remote autobiographical episodes. However, these studies also showed widespread activity in regions of the cortex well beyond the temporal lobe (Ryan et al., 2001). We will consider the role of this extended circuitry later on.

Interestingly, activations for recent memories seemed to cluster in the anterior hippocampus, whereas activations for remote memories seemed to cluster in the posterior hippocampus (Gilboa, Winocur, Grady, Hevenor, & Moscovitch, 2004; Poppenk, McIntosh, Craik, & Moscovitch, 2010). Since neuroimaging studies reveal brain–behavior correlation rather than causation, there are many possible interpretations of this finding. For example, other neuroimaging studies suggest that the anterior hippocampus is active when recalling memories with high emotional content (as is more true of recent events), whereas the posterior hippocampus is more active when recalling emotionally neutral memories (Dolcos, LaBar, & Cabeza, 2004). This seems logical if one remembers that the anterior hippocampus is more tightly connected to the neighboring amygdala, a key structure for emotional learning and memory.

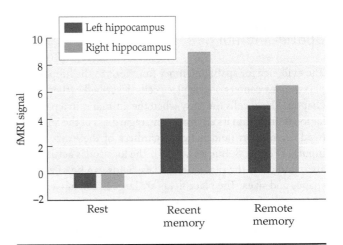

FIGURE 9.8 **The hippocampus is active during the recall of recent and remote autobiographical memories.** Researchers used fMRI to measure the level of activity in the left and right hippocampus of volunteers while they were at rest or while they recalled autobiographical memories from the past 4 years (recent) or autobiographical memories from more than 20 years ago (remote). The results show that the hippocampus is more active during both the recent and the remote memory tasks than during the rest condition.

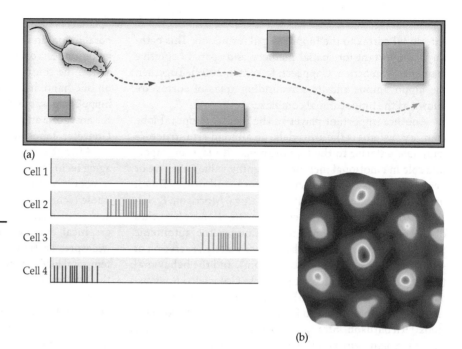

(a)

Cell 1

Cell 2

Cell 3

Cell 4

(b)

FIGURE 9.9 **Place cells and grid cells exist in the medial temporal lobe.** (a) Place cells are found in the hippocampus and fire only when the animal is in a particular location within a local environment such as a box or a cage. (b) Grid cells are found in the entorhinal cortex and form a regular grid to map the location of the animal in its environment.

Neurosurgical techniques have advanced substantially since the time of Henry Molaison. In patients undergoing epilepsy surgery, it is now possible to implant dozens of fine electrodes in the medial temporal lobes and other brain areas. These electrodes are sensitive enough to eavesdrop on the activity of individual neurons (Hoppe, 2006). Recently, studies using these techniques have found hippocampal neurons that are active during the recall of specific episodic memories, such as short clips of popular television shows (Quiroga, Kreiman, Koch, & Fried, 2008). Techniques such as these may help to resolve some of the longstanding debates on the mechanisms of episodic memory.

Spatial Memory

The evidence for spatial memory functions in the hippocampal complex centers on the place cells described earlier in the chapter. These cells fire only when the animal is in a particular location within its environment, regardless of the animal's head orientation (and hence, regardless of the exact visual input) (O'Keefe & Burgess, 1996). The location is actually an area, known as the **place field**. Place fields can be of various shapes and sizes. The place fields are large in the most posterior parts of the hippocampus and become progressively smaller toward the anterior end (Kjelstrup et al., 2008). Since each field alone is imprecise, the exact position of the animal is best represented not by any one place cell, but by an *ensemble*, or group of cells, whose collective activity provides sufficient information to pinpoint one's location precisely (Hollup, Molden, Donnett, Moser, & Moser, 2001) (FIGURE 9.9).

The posterior entorhinal cortex also contains place cells. In addition, it contains another type of neuron known as the **grid cell**. Unlike place cells, grid cells have multiple receptive fields that are arranged in a grid pattern covering the

local environment (N. Burgess, Barry, & O'Keefe, 2007). Once again, the spatial resolution of the grid is coarse at the posterior end and becomes finer at the anterior end (Kjelstrup et al., 2008). Grid cells of a given resolution also have different, nonoverlapping receptive fields (N. Burgess et al., 2007). As with place cells, the precise location of the organism is best represented by an ensemble of grid cells of different spatial resolutions and locations (Hafting, Fyhn, Molden, Moser, & Moser, 2005).

The hippocampal complex not only encodes current position, but also is crucial for spatial memory. Two behavioral tasks are commonly used to study spatial memory in rats. One of these is the **Morris water maze** task (Morris, 1984). In this task, rats are placed into a large tub of cloudy water. Just beneath the surface of the water, where it cannot be seen by the rat, is a platform where the rat can stand to rest from swimming. Initially, the rat is placed on the platform and allowed to look around. Then, it is placed in the tank and has to use the visual cues around the room to find its way back to the platform. The other commonly used task is the **radial arm maze**, in which rats explore the different arms that radiate from the center of the maze (Olton, Collison, & Werz, 1977). Each arm has a food reward at the far end, and rats receive this reward once they have explored the arm. Then they would need to explore a different arm to receive another reward. The key is to use the spatial cues in the environment to remember which arms they have explored and which still have rewards. Performance on both of these spatial memory tasks is impaired in rats with bilateral hippocampal lesions (P. B. Lavenex, Amaral, & Lavenex, 2006).

Hippocampal-like structures with similar spatial memory functions (complete with place cells) can be found throughout the animal kingdom, not only in mammals but also in birds and even in goldfish (Hodos, 1982). The size of the hippocampus is related to territory mapping and spatial memory demands (Brodin & Lundborg, 2003). Squirrels, for example, spend the autumn months hiding up to 10,000 seeds and nuts in different locations throughout their territory to ensure a steady food supply through the winter. During this period, the volume of their hippocampus may increase by up to 15% (P. Lavenex, Steele, & Jacobs, 2000). Likewise, food-caching species of birds have larger hippocampal volumes than non-caching species, and caching behavior itself appears to stimulate hippocampal growth (Jacobs & Schenk, 2003).

What is true of animals is also true of human beings. Taxi drivers in central London are required to master "The Knowledge": a detailed cognitive map of thousands of destinations in an urban territory encompassing some 25,000 streets. They must be able to determine the most efficient routes between any two points within this territory and recite points of interest along the way (such as the names of all the theaters, in sequential order, along a major avenue). Neuroimaging studies (FIGURE 9.10) have shown progressive growth in the posterior hippocampus of these taxi drivers with increasing navigational experience compared with novice taxi drivers (Maguire et al., 2000). Interestingly, the same is not true for physicians, who must master a similarly large but nonspatial body of knowledge (Woollett & Maguire, 2011).

Theories of Hippocampal Function

In the **declarative theory**, the hippocampus (and associated medial temporal regions) is crucial for all forms of memory that can be consciously recalled. These include both episodic and semantic memory and both vivid recollection and the general sense of familiarity (N. Burgess, Maguire, & O'Keefe, 2002). However, the hippocampus is involved for a limited time only, when the memories are relatively new. Over time,

the memories undergo consolidation (discussed later in this chapter) in circuits throughout the cortex. Once this is complete, they are no longer affected by hippocampal injury. Hence, patients such as Henry Molaison still have declarative memories for events that took place well before the loss of their hippocampal function.

In the **multiple-trace theory** (Nadel et al., 2000), the hippocampus is also critical for acquiring episodic and semantic memories. However, despite appearances, the hippocampus is actually always necessary for recalling episodic memories, no matter how old. Only semantic memories can actually become fully independent of the hippocampus, being gradually built into the cortex as sets of recalled facts extracted from repeated recollections and rehearsals. Hence, by repeatedly recalling the moment you won a valuable scholarship, you gradually learn the fact that you won the scholarship as a separate, semantic memory. This factual memory survives even if the rich, vivid imagery of the original episode is forgotten. In patients like Henry Molaison, old episodic memories might seem to be intact, but they are actually detailed semantic memories of childhood facts.

In the **dual-process theory**, the hippocampus (as well as related structures such as the mamillary bodies) is critical for detailed recollection of the context of an episode: place, time, surroundings, events, actions (Eichenbaum, Yonelinas, & Ranganath, 2007). The more vague sense of familiarity is actually the result of an entirely different process that relies on medial temporal lobe structures outside the hippocampus. This would explain how it is possible for us to have a general sense of recognition for previously encountered stimuli (such as faces, voices, books, or words) without quite being able to "place" them in their original context.

The **relational theory** (Eichenbaum & Cohen, 2001) proposes that the hippocampus plays a general role in storing the relations between elements of scenes or events. By storing the relations rather than the items of information themselves, the hippocampus allows for flexible use of old information in novel situations. The relations in question could be spatial relations between objects, or temporal relations between events, or potentially other forms of association between pieces of information. So, the relational theory offers one way to reconcile the spatial and episodic memory functions of the hippocampus.

The **cognitive map theory** (O'Keefe & Nadel, 1978) suggests that the original role of the hippocampus in nonhumans was to create and store territory maps for orientation, navigation, and resource finding. However, in humans, this system has been coopted to create and store episodic memories as well. Since events typically have a particular setting in space and since movement across locations also involves movement in time, the hippocampus would be naturally well suited to capture sequences of events in time (i.e., episodes) as well as sequences of locations in space. It does appear clear that the hippocampus functions in both spatial and episodic memories. However, it is much less clear whether episodic memory is unique to humans or primates alone (Clayton, Salwiczek, & Dickinson, 2007).

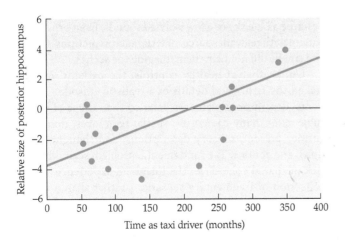

FIGURE 9.10 **The posterior hippocampus is larger in taxi drivers who have more months of experience.** In a study of London taxi cab drivers, MRI images were collected and used to measure the size of the posterior hippocampus. The relative volume of the posterior hippocampus was greater for subjects who had been driving for a longer time.

Unifying the Functions of the Hippocampus

The literature on hippocampal memory functions is already so vast that it now takes many years of study to master. As we have seen, many different theories strive to reduce this vast set of findings into a simpler set of basic principles for hippocampal function. However, there is at this point no consensus on a winner in the war of the theories. How do we make any sense of all these findings?

One perspective that may be helpful is the evolutionary one. The brain is fundamentally a predictive organ, designed to use sensory input and past experience to help the organism make good guesses about what future behavior will give the best chance of survival and eventual reproduction. Outside the laboratory setting, the means of meeting our needs (food, water, shelter, mates) are rarely close at hand. Instead, many organisms have a territory, and this territory is filled with potential resources that may be useful when the organism becomes hungry, thirsty, cold, or pursued. Getting to these resources requires a territory map, and this map must be constantly updated with new events to stay accurate. So spatial maps require episodic memories to be useful for survival. The unique circuitry of the hippocampus allows for the rapid learning and high information capacity needed to make the whole system work effectively (Amaral, 1993; Lynch, 2004).

One implication of this view is that what we call an episodic "memory" system actually serves not only to record the events of the past, but also to make predictions about possible events in the future. A thirsty animal in the desert must recall past watering holes, but also must predict which of these would be most likely to provide water in the near future. Interestingly, this is exactly the finding of recent studies: the hippocampus and related systems are as much involved in imagining the future as in remembering the past (Squire et al., 2010). In the next section, we will take a closer look at the role of these areas in future memory.

Remembering the Future: Prospection and Imagination

Are you hungry right now? What would you most like to eat? Perhaps a plate of hot, salty fries? Or a grilled sandwich with fresh sliced tomato, basil, and mozzarella? Do you plan to make this tasty meal on your own or go out and buy it? Let's say you decide to buy it. Where are you going to go? On the one hand, you'll need a map of all the nearby restaurants, snack bars, cafeterias, and other sources of ready-made food. Then, you'll need to decide which one would most likely

satisfy your current craving. To plan your excursion, you'll need to go through your past experiences of meals at the places on your map. One snack bar is nearby and inexpensive, but the food there was greasy and left you feeling ill in the past. Another makes your favorite sandwich, but always has a long line. Thinking ahead, you're not sure you want to wait that long. In fact, right now, you feel so hungry that the thought of eating a big plate of greasy fries seems quite appealing. Putting together the experiences of your recalled past and your imagined future, you decide on the cheap snack bar, consult your spatial map for directions, and head out the door.

If you play through this little scenario in your mind's eye, you will see immediately how our remembered past and imagined future are closely interwoven in helping us decide what to do to meet our needs. However, only recently have we discovered that the brain's episodic memory systems are just as important for imagining future experiences as they are for imagining past experiences. The term **prospection** has been coined to describe the process of "remembering the future" (Ingvar, 1985), just as the term **recollection** describes remembering the past. The influential memory researcher Endel Tulving once described the function of episodic memory as "mental time travel" (Tulving, 1985). In this section, we will see how episodic memory systems engage in time travel to the future as well as the past.

How We Imagine Future Experiences

In 2007, Demis Hassabis and other researchers at the Institute of Neurology in London made the striking observation that patients with hippocampal lesions not only had amnesia for past experiences, but also could not imagine new experiences (Hassabis, Kumaran, Vann, & Maguire, 2007). For example, when asked to imagine standing in a museum full of exhibits, one patient stated "there's not a lot coming… it's not very real… I'm not picturing anything… I'm not imagining it." In other scenarios, such as lying on a beach, patients might describe a blue sky or a few isolated sounds. Even providing a patient with relevant source material such as pictures, sounds, and smells did not help them imagine the scenes.

Unlike that of healthy controls, the patients' imagery lacked the rich, vivid details of a realistic episode. The patients' descriptions were less detailed than those of control subjects in many categories: spatial references, number of entities present, sensory descriptions, and thoughts, emotions, and actions. The fundamental problem seemed to be a lack of spatial coherence: the imagined experiences were a collection of fragmentary sensations rather than a unified episode in a particular setting (Hassabis et al., 2007).

Neuroimaging studies have provided strong evidence that the brain uses a core network of regions both for remembering past experiences and for imagining new or hypothetical experiences (FIGURE 9.11) (Schacter, Addis, & Buckner, 2008). Yet the hippocampus and parahippocampal cortex are merely one part of this network. Also involved are areas well outside

Medial prefrontal cortex

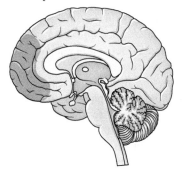

Inferior parietal lobule

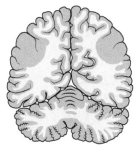

Posterior cingulate and precuneus

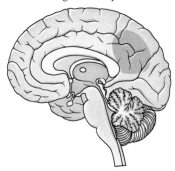

Medial temporal lobe

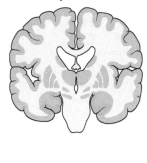

FIGURE 9.11 **Network of brain regions involved in remembering the past and imagining the future.** Areas highlighted in blue are important for simulating future events, and activity in these areas is correlated with activity in the hippocampus.

the medial temporal lobes: medial parietal and prefrontal areas are prominent, along with regions in the lateral temporal and lateral parietal lobes. These areas seem to be especially important for the elaboration of the details of imagined and remembered episodes. A common imagination circuitry seems to be emerging, linking hippocampus to cerebral cortex.

What to make of these additional areas? How does each one contribute to recollection and imagination? Many of the same brain areas had previously appeared in neuroimaging studies of episodic memory retrieval for simple stimuli, such as memorized lists of words or pictures (Schacter et al., 2008; C. E. Stern et al., 1996). Furthermore, a similar network of areas seemed to be active when subjects were simply "resting quietly" between tasks in a wide range of different neuroimaging experiments. These areas, sometimes described as the **default network**, had been connected to mind wandering, self-reflection, autobiographical memory, and the general state of wakeful, conscious awareness (Spreng & Grady, 2010).

The problem with these findings is that they still do not tell us exactly what contribution each area makes to recollection or prospection overall. This is actually a common problem encountered by researchers who use neuroimaging techniques like PET and fMRI. These techniques reveal correlations between cognitive states and brain activity, but these correlations do not definitively pin down a function to any given area or set of areas. Finding blobs of brain activity on any given task is relatively easy with current technology. Interpreting the significance of the blobs is a trickier problem.

RESEARCH METHODS:
Localizing Human Brain Function

The brain is a network, not an assembly line. Asking what a given part of the brain does is thus a little like asking where a particular highway is: the function comes from what endpoint it links and how, rather than where it is. That said, we can often assign distinct computational roles to the distinct parts of the active network for a given kind of cognition. This process of **functional localization** can draw on at least four different kinds of evidence:

1. **Correlation evidence** links particular forms of behavior or cognition to some specific measure of neural activity. Electrophysiological recordings from single neurons or groups of neurons are one form of this. Changes in metabolic markers such as glucose uptake, blood flow, or blood oxygenation are another, indirect, form of this. Neuroimaging studies using PET or fMRI fall into this category. However, mistaken impressions can arise from these types of studies. For example, in studies of pain sensation, one might see activations of motor cortex simply because of movement suppression. Without other evidence, one could mistakenly conclude that the motor cortex was important in pain perception.

2. **Lesion evidence** links particular deficits in behavior and cognition to damage affecting a particular part of the brain. The studies of Henry Molaison and other similar patients are examples of this. One can also cause brief, temporary focal inactivations in healthy subjects using transcranial magnetic stimulation (described in Chapter 1). However, naturally

occurring lesions are rare and rarely affect a single brain structure in isolation (as in Henry Molaison, whose "hippocampal resection" in fact spared some hippocampus but removed parts of surrounding structures). Hence, although these studies can suggest a general functional role for a region, precise conclusions about brain function are sometimes hard to determine.

3. **Stimulation evidence** examines the effects of directly stimulating the neurons in the area of interest. Neurosurgeons sometimes perform direct electrical stimulation of the brain during surgery to map the area to be removed, so as to limit the impairment of critical functions. The patients, who are awake during this part of the procedure, can report (or demonstrate) the effects of stimulation. The difficulty with this line of evidence is that many brain areas are not easy to access for stimulation (Roux et al., 2000). Microstimulation experiments in animals can circumvent this, but animals cannot report stimulation effects explicitly. Also, it is often difficult to tell whether the effects of the stimulation are from the local area being stimulated or from the unintended spread of the electrical stimuli to more distant areas.

4. *Connectivity evidence* relies on the principle that the function of a neuron in a network derives from its position in the network as a whole: in other words, its inputs and outputs. If the major connections of a given brain area are known and if the functions of the main input and output areas are also reasonably well known, it is sometimes possible to make good guesses about the function of the brain area. For example, if someone proposed that a particular brain structure was important for self-consciousness, but its neurons mostly took inputs from the retina and mostly had outputs to the musculature of the eyes, we would consider the proposed function unlikely and a function in eye movement control or tracking much more likely.

The Circuitry of Prospection and Recollection

With these principles of localizing brain function in mind, let us look once again at the core network of brain areas involved in recollection and prospection (FIGURE 9.12).

The **medial prefrontal cortex** connects to anterior and medial temporal lobes as well as emotional and internal-need tracking areas in the anterior insula and amygdala. It also connects to the medial parietal lobes. Neuroimaging studies show that this area is active when tracking the value of stimuli based on current needs or when viewing valuable stimuli such as desirable consumer goods (Knutson et al., 2008). It may also be important for generating longer-term goals based on internal needs (Knutson et al., 2008; Tsujimoto, Genovesio, & Wise, 2011). Lesions in this area often lead to an inability to distinguish relevant from irrelevant memories. Overall, activity here may involve specifying items and goals that are relevant to the current needs and goals of the organism. These can be used to guide the construction of relevant scenarios from the past or future.

The medial parietal lobe, or precuneus, connects medial temporal areas involved in spatial navigation and episodic memory to parietal areas capable of mapping the locations of stimuli in space—a function useful for guiding body movements. It also connects to medial prefrontal areas that specify goals or targets based on current needs, as we have seen. Neuroimaging studies show activity during spatial navigation and

FIGURE 9.12 **The brain areas important in recollection and prospective memory.** The medial prefrontal cortex is active when considering goals, which can be used to generate past and future scenarios. The medial parietal lobe/precuneus is involved in spatial imagination or memory, and the retrosplenial cortex, as a gateway to the posterior hippocampus, aids in navigation through space. On the lateral surface of the brain, the temporoparietal junction plays a role in multimodal sensory integration, and the lateral temporal cortex assists with object recognition.

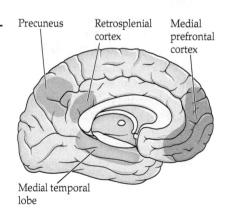
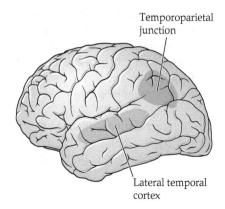

Precuneus

Retrosplenial cortex

Medial prefrontal cortex

Temporoparietal junction

Medial temporal lobe

Lateral temporal cortex

while locating items in nearby and distant space (Ghaem et al., 1997). The nearby **retrosplenial cortex**, also part of the core network, is wired as a sort of gateway to the posterior hippocampus and plays an important role in route mapping during navigation. Lesions of the precuneus are rare but tend to cause severe navigation deficits (Maguire, 2001); lesions of the retrosplenial cortex result in profound retrograde amnesia in addition to navigation deficits (Haijima & Ichitani, 2008). Overall, this area may help provide a spatial context for recalled or imagined scenarios and the features within them.

The lateral parietal lobe (more specifically, an area bordering the temporal and parietal lobes and known as the temporoparietal junction) is a multimodal sensory area taking input from visual, auditory, and tactile areas and connecting to the lateral prefrontal cortex. Neuroimaging studies show that it is active during the detection of target stimuli or simple events in the local sensory environment, particularly when these are relevant to the task at hand (Corbetta, Kincade, Ollinger, McAvoy, & Shulman, 2000; Downar, Crawley, Mikulis, & Davis, 2001). Lesions of this area may produce the syndrome of hemineglect (described in Chapters 5 and 8), in which the patient fails to notice relevant stimuli on the contralateral side of space. Overall, this area may help to specify events or target stimuli within recalled or imagined scenarios (Corbetta & Shulman, 2002).

The lateral temporal lobe, specifically an area known as the superior temporal sulcus, is another region with inputs from multiple visual and auditory sensory areas in the

NEUROSCIENCE OF EVERYDAY LIFE:
Simonides and the Champions of Memory

The World Memory Championships are an annual event in which competitors from around the globe strive to memorize as much information as possible in a limited time. There are 10 different events, all of astonishing difficulty. One event involves memorizing large numbers of fictional "historic dates" with associated fictional "historic events." The world record is 132 dates and events memorized accurately in 5 minutes (Orton, 2011).

In another example, would-be champions have 30 minutes to memorize up to 4,500 computer-generated binary digits: six sheets of paper, covered in ones and zeroes. The numbers are arranged in rows of 30 digits. They then have an hour to score points by writing down as many rows as they can remember—with the digits in perfect order. A single mistake on a row cuts the number of points won from 30 to 15. Two mistakes cut the number of points to zero. The world record? A remarkable 3,915 points—more than 2 per second of study time!

How do they do it? Memory researcher Eleanor Maguire and her colleagues used fMRI to map the

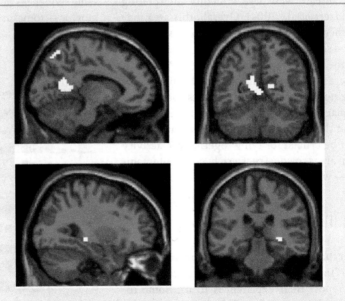

FIGURE 9.13 **Individuals with superior memory use parts of the brain typically associated with spatial navigation.** Maguire and colleagues used fMRI to study the brains of participants in the World Memory Championships. They found significantly more activity in areas typically associated with navigational skills in the participants with superior memory than in control subjects with normal memory. The upper panels show this increased activity in the retrosplenial cortex, and the lower panels show this increase in the posterior hippocampus.

brain activation in memory champions during challenging tasks of memorization (Maguire, Valentine, Wilding, & Kapur, 2003). The intriguing finding was that these champions were drawing on brain regions usually active during spatial navigation through landscapes and territories—as if finding their way around a familiar neighborhood (FIGURE 9.13). The memory champions confirmed that they used a special strategy to learn and recall information: they would imagine walking a familiar route and picture placing the items to be remembered at salient points along the way. During recall, they would imagine walking the same route again and simply recall the items as they saw them. Through extensive practice, they were able to use this system to rapidly acquire and recall prodigious amounts of information. This method may partially explain Jill Price's extraordinary memory abilities. She has spatial sequence synesthesia, meaning that she tends to think of years and dates as belonging to specific locations in space (Eagleman, 2009).

This memory strategy is not a recent innovation—it is almost two and a half thousand years old. The Greek poet Simonides is recorded to have used the same approach, known as the **method of loci** (places), to recall important information by imagining it as placed in a particular location within a familiar environment (Yates, 1966). Classical orators ever since have used similar imaginary journeys through "palaces of memory" to remember long and detailed speeches. Although they did not know it, they were essentially reframing the problem in terms the hippocampus could easily understand. The next time you have something complex but important to remember, try this method!

ventral, object-recognition pathways of the temporal lobe. In neuroimaging studies, it is particularly active during the observation of social cues and social stimuli such as biological movements, eye direction gaze, and even yawning (Allison, Puce, & McCarthy, 2000). Abnormalities of this area appear in patients with autism, who have difficulty interpreting social cues (Boddaert et al., 2004). Overall, this area may help to specify other individuals and their actions within recalled or imagined scenes.

What about the medial temporal lobe itself? As we saw earlier, lesions here seem to impair the spatial coherence of recalled or imagined scenes, so that patients cannot picture a specific place, or detailed surrounding events, or other entities and their actions. This suggests that the hippocampus might be crucial for tying together the activity of the other brain areas to construct a rich, coherent imaginary experience—whether past or future.

Prospection in Other Species

Can species other than human beings engage in prospection and imagination? This issue is a difficult one, since animals cannot verbally report their experiences to us. Some researchers have argued that they actually lack the capacity for episodic memory, or mental "time travel" (Tulving, 2005). Yet they do share much of the same circuitry we have explored earlier. Careful observations of their behavior also suggest that they share some of the features of human episodic memory and prospection.

For example, the scrub jay, a food-caching bird, can apparently recall not just where they cached a particular item, but also what that item was and even when it was cached (Clayton & Dickinson, 1998). Skeptics have suggested that this behavior might result from semantic or procedural memory systems, driven by current needs (Naqshbandi & Roberts, 2006). Yet the jays also appear to cache food in a way that reflects anticipated future needs, not just current motivational state (Correia, Dickinson, & Clayton, 2007).

In rats, direct recordings of hippocampal activity suggest that they, too, may be able to engage in prospection as well as recollection. During movement, hippocampal place cells fire in sequences as the rat moves through adjacent place fields (FIGURE 9.14). Interestingly, place cells sometimes replay these same sequences of activity later on, when the rat is no longer moving—sometimes even when the rat is sleeping after the

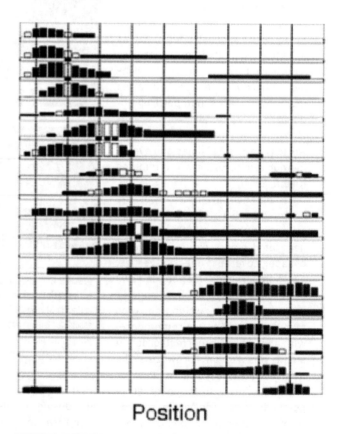

Position

FIGURE 9.14 **Place cells in the hippocampus fire in sequence as a rat moves along a path.** Researchers collected electrical recordings from 19 place cells in the hippocampus and showed a pattern of activity as a rat moved from left to right in the environment.

experiment is over (Foster & Wilson, 2006). Place cells can also "preplay" a sequence of activity before the rat has actually started to move along the route (Foster & Wilson, 2006). If the rat has to make a decision about which path to take in a T-maze, the place cells preplay first one route and then the other, as if in consideration of both possible movement scenarios (Johnson & Redish, 2007; Schacter et al., 2008).

These findings are recent, as is the field of prospection itself. We will likely have much more detailed information about animal prospection and memory in the near future. This information may help to at least settle the issue of their capabilities, if not the age-old question of their internal, subjective experiences.

Models of Prospection

Despite the novelty of this field of research, several models of how the brain constructs mental images in prospection or recollection have already arisen.

The **BBB model** (named after its authors' initials: Byrne, Becker, and Burgess) proposes that hippocampal place cells are central to mental imagery in general (Byrne, Becker, & Burgess, 2007) (FIGURE 9.15). The model proposes that hippocampal place cells reactivate representations of the spatial environment in the parahippocampal cortex and representations of the objects within the environment in the **perirhinal cortex**.

The medial parietal and retrosplenial cortex help to translate the locations of these objects into a body-centered or "egocentric" framework. This helps us to arrange the objects and their setting into a spatially coherent, vividly imagined scene. The prefrontal cortex contributes simulated movement signals that allow us to explore our imaginary environment as we search for target stimuli. As we (virtually) move, the place cells of the hippocampus keep the scene coherent and consistent. In a similar fashion, the researchers Hassabis and Maguire have proposed that this "core network" of regions is critical for scene construction in general rather than episodic memory alone (Hassabis & Maguire, 2009).

Other researchers have argued that the core network has an even broader role that encompasses prospection, spatial navigation, and even taking the perspectives of other people. Buckner and Carroll (2007) suggest that all of these functions actually share a common process of using past experiences adaptively to imagine events or perspectives beyond the immediate sensory environment—a crucial function for survival, as illustrated by the "hunger-satisfying" scenario we imagined at the beginning of this section.

The **constructive episodic simulation hypothesis** (Schacter et al., 2008) also focuses on the adaptive role of the core network. This hypothesis is designed to account for the remarkable fuzziness and malleability of episodic memory, as evident in the all-too-fallible reports of eyewitnesses to criminal acts. Why isn't memory a simple, literal recording

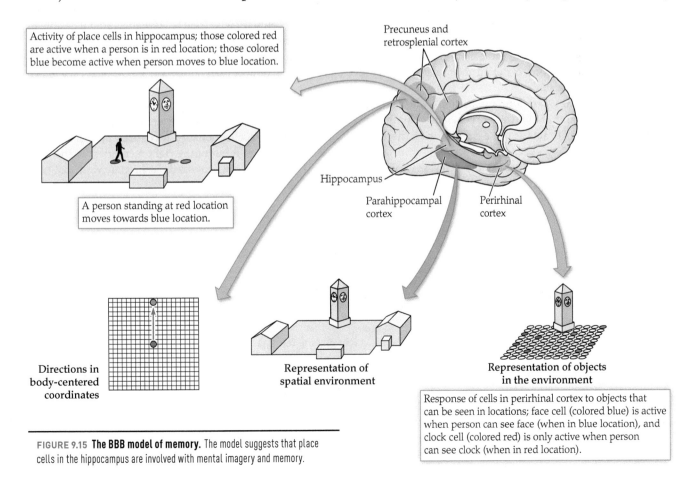

Activity of place cells in hippocampus; those colored red are active when a person is in red location; those colored blue become active when person moves to blue location.

Precuneus and retrosplenial cortex

Hippocampus

Parahippocampal cortex

Perirhinal cortex

A person standing at red location moves towards blue location.

Directions in body-centered coordinates

Representation of spatial environment

Representation of objects in the environment

Response of cells in perirhinal cortex to objects that can be seen in locations; face cell (colored blue) is active when person can see face (when in blue location), and clock cell (colored red) is only active when person can see clock (when in red location).

FIGURE 9.15 **The BBB model of memory.** The model suggests that place cells in the hippocampus are involved with mental imagery and memory.

of the past? Their answer is that such a system (aside from being quickly overloaded with information irrelevant to survival) would lack the flexibility to simulate future events. They propose that a key feature of the core network is its capacity to recombine the details of past events, in a flexible manner, to construct future or hypothetical scenarios.

The benefit of such a system is that it allows the organism to use past experiences to predict ways of meeting its current and future survival needs. The drawback to this flexibility is that past as well as future events are reconstructed rather than literally recalled—leaving room for errors to creep in. This weakness provides a reason for us to invent books, cameras, databases, and other devices, which are able to record information in a literal manner our own brains cannot. In other words, if our brain worked like a video recorder, we would have no need to record trips, parties, and family events so we could remember what happened or who was there.

The Confabulation of Reality

In the last section, we saw how the structures we have long associated with episodic memory might actually have a much more general function: to help us reconstruct past, future, and hypothetical experiences. Although this flexibility may be useful in predicting how to meet our current and future needs, it does have one major side effect: memory errors. In this section, we will see how these errors of memory can sometimes add up to a work of fiction and make us believe in a reality that never existed.

There are certain, rare amnesia patients who seem to live in a world of fantasy. A retired psychiatrist, admitted to hospital after a stroke, acts as if she is a physician there and insists on going through each night's previous admissions. A retired tax accountant repeatedly tries to leave the hospital, convinced that there is a taxi waiting outside to take him to an important meeting. Or, as in the case study, a woman hospitalized for a ruptured aneurysm believes she is at home and says she needs to feed her "baby," who in reality is more than 30 years old at the time of her admission. These patients are not just disoriented. They are spontaneously **confabulating**—creating a shifting version of reality that does not currently exist and acting as if they believe in this reality with utter conviction. Researchers such as the neuroscientist Armin Schnider have studied and written about these patients extensively over the past century (Schnider, 2003; Schnider, von Daniken, & Gutbrod, 1996). As it turns out, confabulation has a lot to teach us about the way that normal memory functions.

Confabulation in the Injured Brain

One of the first things to bear in mind about confabulations is that they come in two distinct kinds. **Provoked confabulations** can arise even in people with uninjured brains, when we are pressed for the details of a memory beyond our ability to recall them accurately. **Spontaneous confabulations**, however, arise only in patients with a particular kind of brain injury. Unlike the rest of us, these patients generate confabulations even with no external cues. They are also so convinced of the confabulated memories that they will sometimes act on them. In the process, they often put themselves at risk—like the accountant who tried to leave the hospital despite his profoundly disoriented state.

Another important point about spontaneous confabulations is that, despite their fantastical appearance, they tend to contain kernels of truth. The psychiatrist really did at one point work in a (different) hospital and review admissions; the accountant really did have important meetings with clients in the past. Their recollections are not entirely imaginary—they are simply not built out of the right memories for the situation at hand. Hence, when asked, "Where are you?" or "What

CASE STUDY:
The Woman with a Thirty-Year-Old Baby

She was in the hospital, but thought she was at home (Schnider, 2003). She needed to feed her baby, who would surely die without her. She did not know why she was being told she was in the hospital or why the doctors and nurses insisted on keeping her there. There must have been some mistake. After all, she felt fine. She clearly remembered that her baby was alone and hungry. Again and again, she told them that she needed to feed her baby. Why wouldn't they let her go? Why did they keep trying to tell her that she had suffered a stroke? Or that she was 58 years old, not in her 30s? Or that her baby had long since grown up and was now a healthy, 30-year-old adult? Wouldn't she remember these things if they were true? How could she possibly be so far out of touch with reality? Surely, no one's memories could lead them so far astray.

are you going to do now?", they confabulate an answer. But when asked questions about completely nonexistent semantic knowledge, such as "Who is Princess Lolita?", they will say they do not know, rather than create a fictional answer.

So how does a confabulated reality grow from the seeds of real episodic memories? It seems that one of the key problems in confabulating patients is a failure to inhibit currently irrelevant memories in favor of currently relevant ones (P. W. Burgess, 1996; Schnider, 2001). One way to measure this is by showing the patient a series of images (mouse, phone, flower, phone, lamp, watch, mouse) and asking them to point out the repeated items in the series as they appear. Both ordinary amnesia patients and confabulators can do this, although with more missed items than healthy control subjects (Moscovitch & Melo, 1997).

Next, we reshuffle the same set of images and ask subjects to do the same task all over again on the new series alone, putting aside their memories of the old series. The key to good performance on the second run is to avoid making "false-positive" responses to the first appearances of items in the new series just because they seem familiar from the old series. Ordinary amnesia patients seem to do fairly well on this second run, still missing some items but not making inappropriate, false-positive responses any more than controls. Confabulators, however, seem unable to inhibit the now-irrelevant memories of seeing the images in the first run. They make many false-positive responses, and if we add a third and a fourth run, the percentage of false positives keeps increasing every time (FIGURE 9.16) (Moscovitch & Melo, 1997).

It seems that, unlike the rest of us, confabulating patients have particular trouble suppressing memories that become activated by sensory cues, but that are irrelevant in the current behavioral context. This may help to explain why they have trouble suppressing memories of past events in the current circumstances of their hospitalization.

The Anatomy of Spontaneous Confabulation

The neuroanatomy of the lesions in patients with spontaneous confabulation is quite distinct from that of amnesia patients like Henry Molaison. Whereas amnesia patients tend to have injuries affecting the medial temporal lobes (as we have seen), spontaneous confabulation patients have injuries of a different part of the core network: the medial orbitofrontal and prefrontal cortex (Schnider, 2003; Turner, Cipolotti, Yousry, & Shallice, 2008). The ventral part of this area is a common site for aneurysms of a blood vessel known as the anterior cerebral artery. When these aneurysms rupture, the resulting bleeding damages the surrounding brain structures. The other areas sometimes damaged in spontaneous confabulation are the dorsomedial thalamic nucleus (which relays information to the medial prefrontal cortex) and the hypothalamus (through which connections pass between these other areas and the hippocampus) (Isaac et al., 1998; Ptak et al., 2001). There is also evidence that additional damage to the surrounding orbitofrontal cortex may be needed before

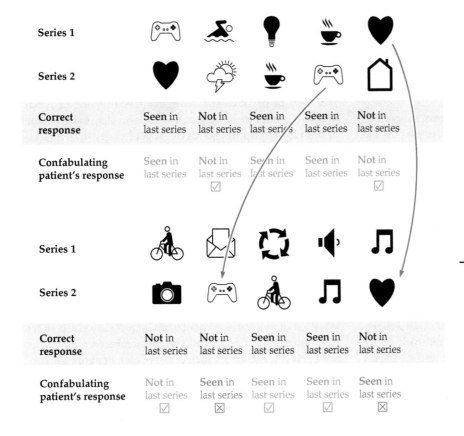

FIGURE 9.16 **Testing for the ability to inhibit irrelevant memories.** By showing sequences of images and asking the subject to find repetitions of the same image, we can distinguish confabulating from nonconfabulating patients. Confabulating patients have trouble telling which images they have seen recently rather than in the remote past—after many viewings, the images all start to seem familiar, and the irrelevant memories cannot be suppressed.

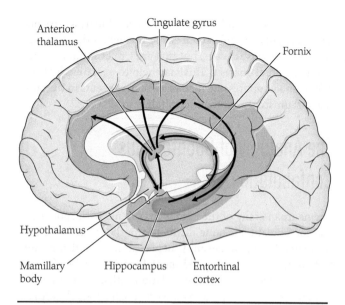

FIGURE 9.17 **Circuit of Papez.** This circuit of interconnected brain areas links retrospection and prospection with current needs. In the circuit, the hippocampus projects to the hypothalamus, thalamus, and cortex before these areas project back to the hippocampus.

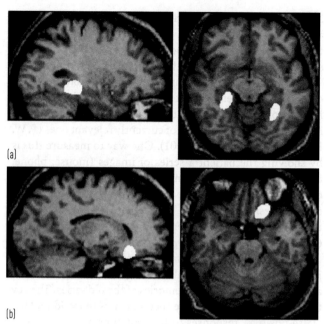

FIGURE 9.18 **The orbitofrontal cortex is more active during suppression of earlier memories.** (a) Brain activity associated with the first exposure to the task. (b) Increased activity in the orbitofrontal cortex associated with suppressing memories from the first exposure to focus on memories from the second exposure to the task.

errors of temporal context blossom into full-blown spontaneous confabulation (Gilboa et al., 2006).

These areas are all part of the circuit of Papez, a ringlike pathway linking the hippocampus to the hypothalamus, thalamus, and cortex before proceeding back to the hippocampus once again (FIGURE 9.17). When the neuroanatomist James Papez first described this pathway in 1937 (Papez, 1937), he speculated that it would be an important pathway for the generation of emotions. However, many of the areas it links are members of the core network, and at least part of this circuit seems to be necessary for selecting relevant versus irrelevant memories (Parmeggiani, Azzaroni, & Lenzi, 1971). Therefore, it might be more reasonable to suggest that this circuit is important for linking recollection and prospection to the current needs of the organism.

How does the ventral medial prefrontal cortex suppress irrelevant memories? The process appears to be a subtle one, and neuroimaging techniques like PET and fMRI generally do not have sufficient temporal resolution to reveal the millisecond-by-millisecond activity of the brain during recollection. However, EEG and MEG do have this capability, at the cost of some spatial resolution. They can also examine the synchronization of activity across brain regions, an important measure of the flow of information between the brain regions.

Armin Schnider and his colleagues have used these techniques to look at irrelevant-memory suppression in normal subjects performing the same image-series task we discussed. In the first image series, recognizing previously seen images seems to involve widespread, synchronized activity across regions similar to those of the core network, as we would expect. However, in the second image series, subjects must often suppress their currently irrelevant recollections of the previously seen images. When they do so successfully,

the ventral medial prefrontal cortex is active and inhibits the synchronized activity of the other areas (FIGURE 9.18). When this process fails to happen, the subjects tend to make false-positive responses (Schnider & Ptak, 1999).

So inhibiting the synchronization of the core network seems to be an important mechanism by which the ventral medial prefrontal cortex inhibits memories that are not relevant to the current circumstances. This seems to fit well with the other functions researchers have found for this area outside the field of memory altogether. For example, this area also helps track the changing reward value of food-predicting cues in hungry macaques and the reward value of desirable consumer goods in gadget-hungry undergraduates (Knutson et al., 2008; Rolls, 2004). It also inhibits the amygdala—a structure to which it is strongly connected, like the adjacent hippocampus. Altogether, this area seems to be in the right place, and active at the right time, to match up recollection and prospection to the organism's current needs by inhibiting irrelevant activity in the hippocampus and the rest of the core network (Schnider, 2013).

Confabulation in the Normal Brain

What about those of us without brain injury? Do we, too, suffer from intrusions of fiction into our remembered reality? The answer is yes, and in fact such errors of memory are common. Lapses of memory function have been studied for decades and come in several forms. Memory researcher Dan Schacter once classified these lapses into what he termed the seven sins of memory (Schacter, 1999). Three of these are forms of memory distortion, rather than forgetting or unwanted remembering. All of them occur in healthy individuals. Let's take a closer look at each of these three distorting "sins" in turn.

Misattribution describes our innate tendency to attribute an idea or a recollection to the wrong source: we recall a past experience, but ascribe it to the wrong time, the wrong place, or the wrong person. We may even confuse something we imagined with something that took place in real life. Getting the source wrong can have serious consequences. For example, eyewitnesses to a crime might recall seeing a particular suspect at the scene, when in fact they encountered that person in a completely different setting. In one unfortunate example, a victim of a rape recalled a respected psychologist as the perpetrator, in a vividly detailed memory (Schacter, 1996). However, she had in fact seen his face while watching him in a live television interview, shortly before the crime took place (fortunately, this interview provided an alibi for the incorrectly accused psychologist).

Suggestibility describes a related process by which false memories can be implanted by overt suggestions after the fact. In one such experiment, subjects could be induced to create detailed memories of childhood events that had never happened (such as becoming lost in a shopping mall or knocking over a punch bowl at a wedding). They would even add more and more detail to these memories over successive interviews (Loftus & Pickrell, 1995). The key was to persuade them that other people, such as family members, remembered such events taking place. In a large percentage of subjects, merely asking them to imagine events seems to produce false memories that the events took place in real life (Hyman & Pentland, 1996).

Suggestibility can not only distort eyewitness reports, but also even lead to false confessions. In one experiment, subjects performing a reaction-time task were falsely accused of crashing a computer by pressing the ALT key. When the accusations were corroborated by false "witnesses" to the event (actually confederates of the experimenter), nearly 100% of the subjects eventually signed a written confession that they had crashed the computer, and a third of these confabulated detailed memories of their nonexistent "error" (Klaver, Lee, & Rose, 2008).

Finally, the phenomenon of **bias** describes how semantic memory—one's current knowledge and beliefs—can create unconscious distortions in what we recall about the past. A classic example of this effect was noted by the British psychologist Sir F. C. Bartlett (Bartlett, 1932). He asked subjects to memorize an eerie Native American fable, called *The War of the Ghosts*, in which there were subtle inconsistencies of detail. He found that when subjects later recalled the story, they misremembered certain details so as to smooth out these inconsistencies. The ways in which they did so tended to reflect their own preexisting knowledge and belief systems. Other studies have demonstrated that people misremember their own past attitudes about social and political issues, so as to preserve the consistency of their beliefs over time (Levine,

Lench, & Safer, 2009). Bias even extends to how we remember our past feelings toward our romantic partners. If the relationship deteriorates, we tend to remember our past feelings as more negative than they really were. If it improves, we remember our feelings as better than they were—as if through rose-colored glasses (Karney & Coombs, 2000).

The Anatomy of a False Memory

How do false memories arise in the brain? We are now able to use neuroimaging techniques to study how mechanisms like misattribution and source monitoring errors lead us to remember things that never actually happened. Early studies of false memory asked subjects to memorize lists of words before scanning and then examined their brain activity while they were asked to pick out these words from a new list that also included distracter words they had never seen before.

As it turned out, the brain activity for both correctly recognized and falsely recognized words was surprisingly similar. Recognition, true or false, seems to activate both the hippocampus and other areas of the core network, in particular the lateral and medial parietal cortex. These areas are also active when perceiving or imagining actual events (Cabeza, Rao, Wagner, Mayer, & Schacter, 2001; Kahn, Davachi, & Wagner, 2004; Wheeler & Buckner, 2003). In other words, recollection seems to have some of the characteristics of actual sensory experience, whether or not the memory is a false one.

The difference between true and false memories is more obvious in studies that look at brain activity during the initial experience, or encoding, of the memory, rather than the activity during its subsequent recollection or **retrieval**. Other researchers have studied both of these processes by scanning subjects while they served as eyewitnesses to events such as a theft, using slide show vignettes. As in the car accident experiment we saw earlier, the experimenters then tried to distort subjects' memories by showing them the same stories again with subtle changes in them. After the scanning, they tested the subjects' recollection of the original stories to see which events had indeed been distorted by the subsequent misinformation (Okado & Stark, 2005).

The researchers found a number of brain areas whose activity at the time of learning distinguished true from false memories (FIGURE 9.19). False memories seemed to form when these areas showed strong activation for the original event, but a failure to activate during the second, misinforming version of the same event. The areas in question included the hippocampus and nearby parahippocampal cortex (whose role, as you may recall, is important in establishing the context rather than the details of a memory), as well as the medial and lateral prefrontal cortex (which, as we saw in confabulators, are important for inhibiting currently irrelevant memory activity). So, the false memories seemed to arise from a failure of inhibition during the irrelevant, misinforming events as well as a failure to place these events in their proper context: extraneous to the true, original story.

THE BIGGER PICTURE:
Scanning for the Truth

Given the importance of distinguishing true from falsely recalled memories during criminal and other legal proceedings, there is currently a great deal of interest in whether neuroimaging techniques can help differentiate recalled fiction from reality. Government and private organizations are all trying to find ways of creating a foolproof fMRI lie detector. So far, the technology is not sufficiently reliable to be used in this way even in cooperative subjects, let alone in the potentially unwilling suspects of criminal proceedings (Spence, 2008). Even if these obstacles are eventually overcome, the ethics of allowing authorities to use "mind-reading" technologies on willing or unwilling subjects are far from clear. Would these technologies really make our world a safer place? Such issues may become a potent source of controversy in the years to come.

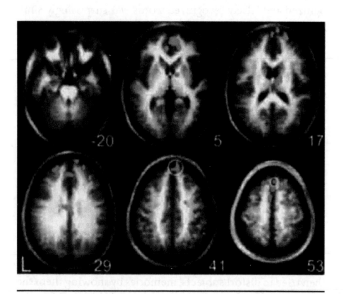

FIGURE 9.19 **True and false memories can be distinguished based on patterns of brain activity.** The panel highlights the parts of the brain that show different patterns of activity during the recollection of true versus false memories. These areas include the hippocampus, parahippocampal cortex, and prefrontal cortices.

The Mechanisms of Memory

How are memories written into the circuitry of the brain itself? So far, we have reviewed a few of the various kinds of memory systems thought to exist. We have also taken a more detailed look at the operations of one of the best studied of those systems, episodic memory. What we have learned is that this system does not rely on a single brain structure but, like all memory systems, involves activity spread widely across the nervous system.

But how does all this activity store information in the long term? If different forms of cognition rely on different pathways of the nervous system, then changes in cognition (in other words, learning and memory) require lasting changes in those pathways. How do these changes occur? Over the past century, we have discovered a variety of ways in which the brain can change its circuitry, not just in early childhood, but also throughout life. In this section, we'll take a look at what has been discovered so far about how these changes occur.

General Mechanisms of Learning and Memory

Although different types of memory depend on specialized structures, it is possible that general learning mechanisms underlie all these different types. It is notable that the different brain areas have many properties in common: short-term and long-term memory, one-trial learning and multiple-trial learning, similar cellular mechanisms and biochemical pathways, and activation of identified memory genes. The commonality of function across diverse regions suggests the possibility that general principles govern plasticity at the cellular and subcellular levels, regardless of the brain region. This possibility has inspired thousands of researchers to seek those principles.

Currently, almost all theories of plasticity presuppose some variant of the idea that efficacy of the connections between cells—the synapses—can be modified based on their previous activity. This simple idea has spurred a productive industry of biophysicists and mathematical modelers for several decades, all asking the same question: how does experience change a synapse?

Memory as Synaptic Change

Just over a century ago, microscopes lacked the power to visualize neurons or their interconnections in detail. In those days, scientists believed that neural tissue was a continuous network, like the blood vessels. This idea was overturned by the Spanish neuroscientist Ramón y Cajal. Based on careful microscopic observations, he theorized instead that the nervous system is a coalition of billions of discrete cells. His **neuron doctrine**, which turned out to be correct, ushered in an important new idea: separate cells influence each other primarily through the specialized connections between them, known as synapses (Ramón y Cajal, 1899/1995). Ramón y Cajal is credited as the first to suggest that learning and memory might occur by changes in the connections between neurons (Ramón y Cajal, 1894).

Some decades later, in 1949, a neuroscientist named Donald Hebb made a specific proposal for how synapses should adjust themselves to usefully underlie memory:

> *When an axon of cell A is near enough to excite cell B and repeatedly or persistently takes part in firing it, some growth process or metabolic change takes place in one or both cells such that A's efficiency, as one of the cells firing B, is increased.* (Hebb, 1949)

In other words, if a presynaptic cell (A) consistently participates in driving a postsynaptic cell (B), the connection between them is strengthened (potentiated) (**FIGURE 9.20**). Hebb's hypothesis goes on to prescribe that if A consistently

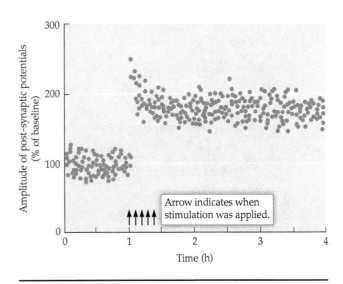

FIGURE 9.21 Long-term potentiation of a synapse in the hippocampus. The baseline rate (time = 0 hours) of synaptic activity was set at 100%. The resulting increase in firing rate (up to 300% of baseline) remained for up to 10 hours.

fails to drive B, the connection is weakened (depressed). Systems that display this fire-together wire-together behavior are said to follow a **Hebbian learning** rule. Most models of memory formation employ such a rule.

Long-Term Potentiation and Depression of Synaptic Connections

At the time Hebb proposed his hypothesis, there was no experimental evidence that could be marshalled in its support. Then, in 1973, two researchers discovered a neuron-to-neuron phenomenon that suggested a Hebbian mechanism for the long-term storage of changes. After stimulating input nerve fibers in the rabbit hippocampus, the neuroscientists Bliss and Lomo (1973) found an increased electrical response from the postsynaptic cell for up to 10 hours (**FIGURE 9.21**). Called **long-term potentiation (LTP)**, this was the first direct demonstration that synaptic connections could be modified as a result of the history of the activity of the cells involved.

The NMDA Receptor

How does LTP arise at the biophysical level? One mechanism that has taken the spotlight centers on a subtype of glutamate receptor called the **NMDA receptor** (NMDA-R) (**FIGURE 9.22**). As you may recall, glutamate is the major excitatory neurotransmitter of our central nervous system. Many postsynaptic membranes contain NMDA glutamate receptors as well as non-NMDA glutamate receptors, such as AMPA glutamate receptors. During normal low-frequency stimulation, only non-NMDA receptors will open, allowing neurotransmission without LTP or other lasting synaptic

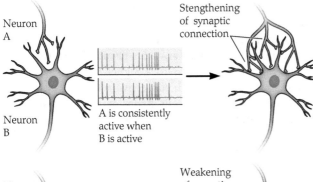

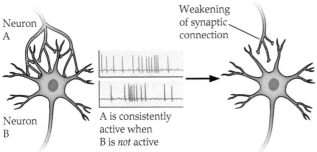

FIGURE 9.20 The Hebbian synapse. When one cell consistently activates another, the connection between them is strengthened. If it consistently fails to do so, the connection between them is unchanged or weakened.

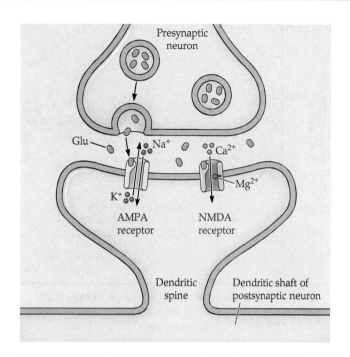

Presynaptic
neuron

Glu

Na⁺

Ca²⁺

K⁺

Mg²⁺

AMPA
receptor

NMDA
receptor

Dendritic
spine

Dendritic shaft of
postsynaptic neuron

FIGURE 9.22 The NMDA glutamate receptor and long-term potentiation.
Under normal conditions, the NMDA receptor is blocked by a magnesium (Mg²⁺)
ion. Repeated stimulation of the postsynaptic cell decreases the membrane
potential holding the magnesium in place and allows calcium and other ions
to flow through the channel of the NMDA receptor.

changes. NMDA receptors stay out of the process because magnesium ions block the NMDA receptors' ion channels from the outside, like tiny plugs.

In contrast, high-frequency presynaptic input depolarizes the postsynaptic membrane. This weakens the negative membrane potential that holds these magnesium ion "plugs" in place. With these plugs out of the way, calcium and other ions can now flow through the open channel when the NMDA-R is stimulated by glutamate. The calcium ions are particularly important for memory: once inside the postsynaptic neuron, they induce a second-messenger system that can change which genes are expressed and result in long-term structural changes.

The result of all this is that the NMDA-R can act as a "coincidence detector," activating only when presynaptic activity (i.e., glutamate release) coincides with postsynaptic activity (i.e., membrane depolarization). This means that NMDA-R synapses essentially follow the rules of the theoretical Hebbian synapses, which would make them useful for learning and remembering associations.

In most neuronal types, the NMDA-R is crucial for induction of LTP. An animal can be taught a behavioral task, but with the infusion of NMDA-R antagonists, the ability to remember the specifics of the task seems to disappear (van der Meulen, Bilbija, Joosten, de Bruin, & Feenstra, 2003). But note that the NMDA-R is only necessary for the initial stages of the process. Other mechanisms underlie the maintenance of the changes. For synaptic changes and memories

to last, in general, new protein synthesis is required at the nucleus of the cell. If protein synthesis is blocked, an animal can form short-term but not long-term memories. For example, protein synthesis inhibitors can prevent an animal from learning to associate two stimuli, such as shock paired with a light in classical conditioning (Lattal & Abel, 2004).

In most cases, LTP is induced only when the activity in the postsynaptic cell (depolarization) is associated with activity in the presynaptic cell. Depolarization alone or presynaptic activity alone is ineffective. Additionally, LTP is synapse specific, which means that each individual synapse on a cell could, in principle, strengthen or weaken according to its own personal history.

But if a connection has the ability to potentiate, it also needs the ability to depress, for the same reasons that a computer screen must be able to brighten or darken its pixels. A screen that could only ever grow brighter would quickly saturate, unable to carry or store new images. As it happened, researchers soon found a pixel-darkening counterpart of LTP, known as **long-term depression (LTD)**. After the right kind of stimulation (for example, presynaptic input with no postsynaptic response), the strength between two cells becomes weakened. LTP and LTD are in fact two halves of the same phenomenon. Both are found at the same synapses and depend on the same biochemical mechanisms.

As we saw at the beginning of the chapter, organisms display learning and memory at a variety of timescales, both short and long term. Suggestively, changes in synaptic efficacy, or strength, also occur at many different timescales. Aside from the long-term changes of LTP and LTD, sometimes the modification of synaptic efficacy is short term, lasting from seconds to minutes. The two most commonly studied examples of this are short-term potentiation and short-term depression (also known as fast synaptic depression). The former can be brought about by increased levels of intracellular calcium in an axon terminal resulting from recent activity. This leads to a higher probability of neurotransmitter release with successive activity, and thus the connection between the cells is considered potentiated.

Short-term depression can come about by a depletion of the readily releasable pool of neurotransmitter vesicles, which take time to be repackaged and docked. When high activity causes increased vesicle release, the terminal becomes depleted of neurotransmitter. It is then, temporarily, less able to respond to future activity and is thus considered depressed. These kinds of fast modifications in synaptic connection strength can cause rapid, dynamic changes in the behavior of neural networks, arising as a function of recent activity (Chung, Li, & Nelson, 2002).

Consolidation and Reconsolidation

As we have seen earlier in the chapter, short-term memories transition into long-term memories. This process is known as **consolidation**, and it can take days to weeks to years. You use this process all the time, such as when you are studying what you just learned, which is still in your working memory, for the upcoming test, when you will need long-term memory. Current research suggests that this process takes place in the hippocampus (Takashima et al., 2009), which may explain why Henry Molaison had severe retrograde amnesia for events that occurred immediately before his surgery, but less severe amnesia for events that occurred earlier in his life. Although actions at the NMDA receptor can start this process, there are many additional steps required to produce the lasting neural-circuitry changes of a new memory. Despite many years of investigation, we are still just beginning to understand this process in detail. One thing we have learned is that memories require continuous maintenance at the molecular and cellular level. In addition, they must be consolidated again after they have been recalled, a process known as **reconsolidation**. Hence, long-term memories require many iterations of activation, consolidation, reactivation, and reconsolidation to persist over time (R. R. Miller & Matzel, 2000).

As it turns out, interfering with the process of reconsolidation can actually eliminate an established memory. In 2000, the neuroscientists Nader, Schafe, and LeDoux found a way to effectively erase a fear response learned through classical conditioning (FIGURE 9.23). First, they trained rats to fear an auditory tone by pairing it with an electric shock. Rats learn this association quickly—in fact, in a single trial—and afterward freeze in response to the tone (Nader, Schafe, & LeDoux, 2000).

Twenty-four hours later the experimenters presented the tone again. At the same time, they injected a protein synthesis inhibitor called anisomycin into the rats' lateral basal amygdala—a key structure for fear conditioning. By this time, according to standard theory, the memory should have been well established and the injection should not have had an amnestic effect. But the result was unexpected: the rats injected with anisomycin no longer showed a fear of the tone. However, the more astonishing result was that the fear memory had to be reactivated by playing the tone for the injection to work. If rats heard no tone at the time of the injection, the anisomycin had no effect!

These findings rekindled widespread interest in the phenomenon of reconsolidation. Soon a variety of other studies had confirmed the fragility of memories at the time of their reactivation across a wide variety of species and memory systems. They also found that anisomycin was not the only treatment capable of disrupting a memory's reconsolidation. Other blockers of protein synthesis, RNA synthesis, NMDA receptors, and even interference by learning new material could all interfere with reconsolidation (Schiller et al., 2010).

The exact mechanisms of disrupted reconsolidation are still being debated. In addition, some researchers have questioned the validity of the findings themselves, suggesting that the treatments in fact produce mild lesions, retrieval deficits, extinction, or other nonspecific effects (Debiec, LeDoux, & Nader, 2002; R. R. Miller & Matzel, 2000). At the same time, the treatments hold out hope of relief to patients suffering from post-traumatic stress disorder—where forgetting a fearful memory could be a step toward recovery. In any case, reconsolidation is sure to be an active area of future research.

Associative Neural Networks

As you may recall, early studies of learning and memory focused on classical conditioning and operant conditioning. Classical conditioning involves the association of stimulus with stimulus (for example, the paired tone and shock in the anisomycin-injected rats or Ivan Pavlov's famous dogs, who salivated when they heard the bell that signaled meat powder). Operant conditioning involves the association of behavior and outcome (as in the rats who learned to press a lever to obtain food). An appealing idea in neuroscience has been that if an association is learned between two stimuli, or between an action and an outcome, then perhaps there is a neural substrate that directly reflects this learning.

Theoreticians have used artificial neural networks to simulate learning (FIGURE 9.24). In artificial networks, unlike real brain tissue, all of the parameters are ours to control and all the effects ours to observe. What we find is that small, subtle changes in the way cells communicate in a network can actually change the output behavior of the entire network. By tuning the parameters of the network just right (or, in practice, letting a network adjust its own interconnections

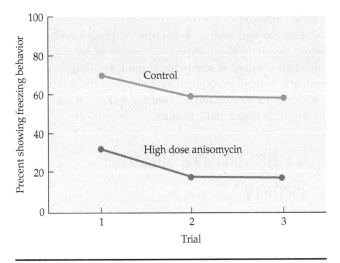

FIGURE 9.23 **A protein synthesis inhibitor can block reconsolidation of fear memories.** In an experiment using classical conditioning, researchers measured how well rats froze after learning to fear a tone. After the initial learning, rats were injected with either a high dose of the protein synthesis inhibitor anisomycin or a control solution. When they were injected with the control, their learning remained, and they froze in response to the tone. When they were injected with anisomycin, they failed to freeze at the sound of the tone. This suggested that blocking protein synthesis can prevent reconsolidation of memories.

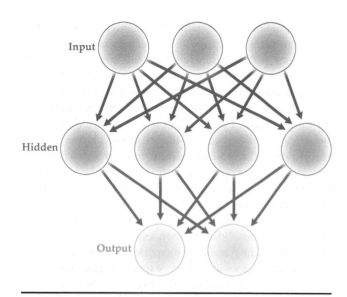

FIGURE 9.24 Artificial neural network. Artificial neural networks have been used to simulate learning. These networks contain an input layer, which represents the sensory neurons, an output layer, which represents behaviors, and a "hidden layer," which represents all of the cognitive processing that occurs in the nervous system.

according to an algorithm), a network can "learn" to associate inputs and remember what it has learned. In these kinds of networks, we find that one stimulus can readily trigger the remembrance of another. This is, in effect, artificial learning and memory.

In the early 1980s, the physicist John Hopfield tried to understand whether a simplified artificial neural network could be used to store memories (Hopfield, 1982). He exposed such a network to some patterns of input and reinforced the synapses between neurons that fired simultaneously in response to this input. The result was that the network "memorized" the pattern. Furthermore, the network was capable of pattern completion: when given a corrupted, noisy version of the pattern as input, the network activity would spontaneously converge on the pattern within the noise. This was a useful proof of **associative memory** effects in a simplified neural network, and it opened the door to a flurry of quantitative studies on Hopfield nets.

Associative neural networks display this sort of property: cue items can prime webs of association, in the same way that the smell of coffee can immediately conjure associations with the sight of the black liquid, the sensation of warmth on the hands, the bitter taste, and so on (Baars & Franklin, 2003). Moreover, associative nets are robust to noisy input, such that the word "cahfee" can kick off the same web of association. They are also robust to degradation: unlike the memory systems of your phone or computer, if you lose some of the circuitry, the distributed memories of the network will still be retrievable (Ernst & Bülthoff, 2004).

Understanding the properties of neural networks in the living brain, rather than in a computer simulation, will be critical for understanding how real memories work. In the

human brain, no neuron is an island. Every cognitive function requires information flow through a complex and recurrent circuitry that adjusts itself to new demands on the fly. Emerging techniques now allow us to record the activity of hundreds of neurons simultaneously. Interpreting the volumes of data that result is a tricky process, like trying to follow all of the conversations in a street market at the same time. However, methods for analyzing the structure of networks are developing rapidly as well. As they improve, we will be able to learn how memories write themselves into whole communities of neurons, rather than synapses in isolation.

Beyond Synaptic Plasticity: The Frontiers of Memory Mechanisms

In the ongoing search for the substrates of memory, changes at individual synapses have received the most attention, both theoretically and experimentally. However, there are many other possible substrates in which to store activity-dependent changes in brain activity. One example is intrinsic changes within the neurons themselves: in the excitability of the cell, in the distribution of ion channels, in the shape of dendritic trees, in the phosphorylation states of intracellular proteins, and so on. With so many degrees of freedom in biological systems, the number of possible ways to store memory in a brain is truly vast.

Here we will look at a handful of these possibilities. Recent research has unearthed a variety of ways to store long-term changes in the brain without invoking synaptic plasticity. We will proceed from the large to the small scale, looking at whole neurons, dendritic spines, mnemogenic chemicals, and epigenetic changes.

Whole Neurons as a Substrate for Memory?

The traditional story of memory for most of the 20th century was that mammals are born with a fixed number of neurons. This initial supply would gradually diminish with age, but could never increase (Eriksson et al., 1998). But researchers eventually found techniques for labeling newborn cells and spotting the labeled cells under a microscope (FIGURE 9.25). Using these techniques, researchers discovered that in a process termed **neurogenesis**, the hippocampus is churning out thousands of new neurons each day, in species from mice to humans, in the young and the old alike (Eriksson et al., 1998; Gould, Beylin, Tanapat, Reeves, & Shors, 1999).

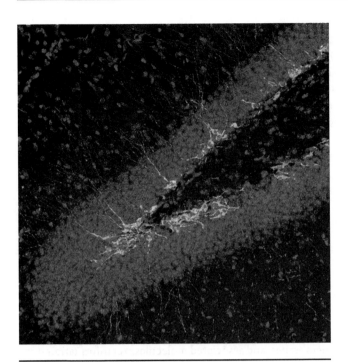

FIGURE 9.25 **Neurogenesis in an adult hippocampus.** The cells labeled in bright green are immature neurons in the hippocampus of an adult rat.

These cells are born near the ventricles and crawl outward into the cortex, looking for a place in the community and a function to perform. If new neurons insert themselves into the mix, why doesn't that scramble up the painstakingly constructed patterns already in place?

It is only through a historical mistake that this finding of neurogenesis came as such a surprise (more on that later). After all, new cell growth characterizes every other part of the body and the brains of other species. We have known for a long time that bird brains grow new neurons each mating season—when the brain needs to learn a new song. Mammalian neurogenesis was in fact suspected for a long time, but the supporting observations were overlooked or ignored.

Recent findings hint at involvement of neurogenesis in memory formation. For example, in the dentate gyrus of the adult rat, the number of newborn neurons doubles if the rats undergo training on learning tasks that depend on the medial temporal lobe. By way of experimental control, there is no such increase in the dentate gyrus during training on other learning tasks that are independent of the medial temporal lobe (Gould et al., 1999). These findings suggest that associative memory may involve newborn neurons and that these neurons take root specifically in the places where they are needed.

New Neurons for New Memories

What exactly would these new cells be doing? Newly grown neurons may be especially good at forming new connections with each other—as if they retain the plastic youthfulness of

the childhood brain, even in adults. Oddly, however, many of these new neurons also die young. One of the least understood aspects of adult neurogenesis is that the life of the new neurons is often counted in terms of a few months, or weeks, or perhaps even days. How could such an ephemeral existence contribute to building lasting memories in the brain? One hypothesis from bird studies is that the new cells form a rapid but temporary scaffolding of connections to help establish a new memory, and then they are eliminated (Alvarez-Buylla, 1990). The youthful characteristics of newborn neurons might make them uniquely qualified to grow new connections rapidly. This would be an especially useful property for the rapid memory formation we see in the hippocampus.

But there is another puzzling issue. If memory circuits must be preserved for a lifetime, wouldn't they be disrupted by the arrival of young, upstart neurons? Yet, apparently, the new neurons do not interfere with existing memories (Deng, Aimone, & Gage, 2010). If new cells can insinuate themselves into the fabric of the cortex without corrupting stored old memories, something about the old paradigm may need rethinking.

The classical synaptic-change paradigm should give brains all the plasticity they need to remember new memories and forget old ones. So why are cells constantly being dismissed and replaced? Perhaps neuronal replacement occurs because synapses, by themselves, and by virtue of the turnover of their constituent molecules, are not reliable repositories for learned, long-term information. Instead, to build the infrastructure of a robust, lasting memory, the brain requires entirely new neurons.

In this speculative framework, the storage of a memory involves the activation of a set of genes that leads to cell differentiation. Cell division is an irreversible process—just what one would want for long-term memory storage. The end result is that entire neurons, rather than synapses, would be the units of memory storage.

A variant of this hypothesis could be that each neuron contains several memory domains, each one determined by, for example, its number of primary dendrites. To test this theory, we will need to know more about which new neurons are replaced or die off during memory formation. Are the dying neurons of the brain merely a random sample? Or are they instead the failed efforts, the ones that do not encode new learning—the "ignoramuses," as Fernando Nottebohm calls them? As Nottebohm writes, "if the cells replaced turned out to be misfits that had failed to achieve a role in information processing or behavioral control, then their replacement should be eyed as the fine tuning of a complex network, rather than as the rejuvenation of existing circuits" (Nottebohm, 2002).

To explore this idea, we will need to determine which neurons get eliminated, what position they hold in the larger circuitry of a given memory, and what functions they serve within this circuitry. More generally, we will need to test whether learning makes certain neurons repositories for

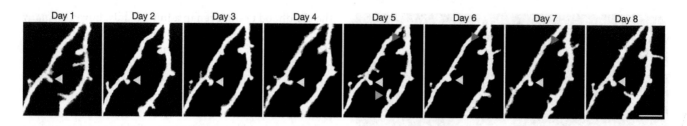

Day 1   Day 2   Day 3   Day 4   Day 5   Day 6   Day 7   Day 8

FIGURE 9.26 Dendritic spines in an adult mouse change as a result of sensory experience. Microscopy in the barrel cortex of an adult mouse showed that the dendritic spines form and disappear over the course of days to weeks.

long-term memories—and, in so doing, irreversibly inhibits their ability to acquire new information.

It may be important to do all these experiments in animals in rich, pseudo-natural environments. We now know that both stimulating environments and exercise are critical to neurogenesis. It has been speculated that the reason early primate studies did not spot neurogenesis is because the laboratory monkeys led predictable, stimulus-impoverished, caged lives: a poor environment for learning (Gould & Gross, 2002). This mistake in experimental design underscores once again the neglected predictive function of memory: not a simple tool for blindly recording the past, but a clever mechanism for predicting how to get what we need to survive.

Spines: Another Structural Basis for Memory?

Dendritic spines—tiny protrusions from dendrites—extend and retract over hours in young animals. However, such changes are absent in adults. The architecture of spines is another potential structural basis for long-term information storage in the nervous system. Recently, multiphoton-based imaging technologies have been used for time-lapse observation of spines in the cortex of live mice. Using these techniques, a group of researchers have confirmed that spines, initially plastic during development, eventually stabilize in the adult brain (Grutzendler, Kasthuri, & Gan, 2002).

However, another group, using the same techniques, found that spines could in fact be altered by sensory experience in adults (FIGURE 9.26) (Trachtenberg et al., 2002). Despite the stable architecture of axons and dendrites in adults, the second group concluded that adult plasticity could still involve structural change—at the finer level of spines. If the second group is right—that spines are constantly changing, even in the adult—then the classical views on memory storage may be too simple. In either case, the new technologies of imaging the living brain are bound to

reveal new levels of complexity in the way the brain adjusts itself to experience.

Looking inside the Cell: Memory in Chemical Reactions

One of the central questions about memory is how it is kept stable while all the pieces and parts renew themselves continuously over time. All biological systems are characterized by molecular degradation and replacement of proteins, lipid membranes, and associated molecules. Yet information storage requires preservation and consistency. So how do memories endure over the years?

Roberson and Sweatt (1999) have suggested that one basis of information storage could be a specific type of "mnemogenic," or memory-forming, chemical reaction (FIGURE 9.27). These reactions involve modifying some chemical substrate, such as an enzyme precursor, so as to switch it from an inactive to an active form. Such a reaction can be triggered using any one of a number of mechanisms: protein kinases, transcription factors, and others. However, once activated, the enzyme itself can activate other enzymes on its own, even without the use of the trigger. So even if the originally activated protein is lost,

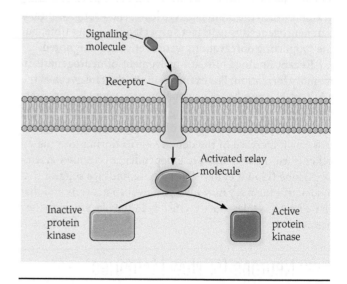

FIGURE 9.27 A possible mnemogenic chemical reaction. In these reactions, a chemical substrate is modified. This may be by phosphorylation, or activating a transcription factor, or by some other cellular mechanism.

other activated copies can take its place. As in a playground game of tag, someone is always "it," so the game can be sustained indefinitely even as individual players come and go. Hence, even in the face of constant turnover, the memory is retained.

Certain proteins are stable entities, typified by the long-lasting memory inherent in their chemical structure itself. This stability is theoretically useful for long-term information storage. The idea of activated proteins storing memories is novel in part because it puts the storage element of memory at a more microscopic level—not neurons, not synapses, but individual proteins. If proved correct, this idea will force us to consider that memory mechanisms may operate at widely different spatial scales, in parallel.

But is there evidence that mnemogenic reactions really serve as a substrate for long-term memories? The enzyme calmodulin-dependent protein kinase II (**CaMKII**) is important to the postsynaptic, intracellular mechanisms for forming long-term memories (Hudmon & Schulman, 2002). Excitement grew with the discovery that a CaMKII enzyme, once activated, could activate other CaMKII enzymes on its own, thus remaining autonomously active despite protein turnover (**FIGURE 9.28**) (Hudmon & Schulman, 2002).

Unfortunately, permanent activation of CaMKII has yet to be demonstrated in a living cell. However, another candidate protein is cytoplasmic polyadenylation element binding protein (CPEB). This protein is required for cementing cellular long-term memories in neurons of the sea slug Aplysia,

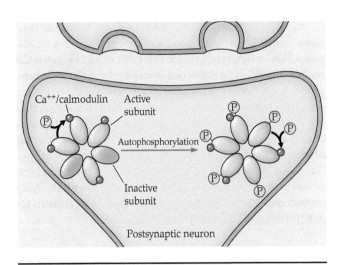

FIGURE 9.28 **The CaMKII enzyme can phosphorylate inactive subunits of itself, and even other CaMKII enzymes.** This autophosphorylation enables the enzyme to remain active, even when the original stimulus has ended.

a classic model organism in memory research (Heinrich & Lindquist, 2011). Typical proteins degrade within hours, but one end of CPEB carries a sequence that resembles one found on an extremely stable protein with known mnemogenic properties, called prion protein (Heinrich & Lindquist, 2011). In yeast, anyway, CPEB acts like prion protein, and its activated form appears to be involved in memory formation (Heinrich & Lindquist, 2011).

CASE STUDY:
The Flies with Photographic Memory

One of the hopes of memory research is to find ways of enhancing our ability to recall information. In 1994, Yin and colleagues created transgenic fruit flies who showed such rapid and long-lasting learning that their memory seemed almost "photographic" (Yin et al., 1994).

How can we tell what a fly remembers? In a form of classical conditioning, the researchers exposed the flies to two different odors, one of which was followed by an electric shock applied to the wires on which they were roosting. Like rats and other animals, the fruit flies

eventually learned to fly away from the shock-paired odor when given a choice of the two in a simple T-maze.

Whereas ordinary fruit flies take several trials to learn this odor-avoidance response, the transgenic flies got the message after a single session. Furthermore, unlike normal flies, they remembered to avoid the odor even if they did not encounter it again until near the end of their fruit-fly lives, several weeks later.

The source of their photographic memory? Their mutation produced excess amounts of cyclic AMP-responsive element-binding protein,

a protein in the postsynaptic cell that promotes the expression of genes crucial for plasticity, spatial memory, and long-term memory formation (Silva, Kogan, Frankland, & Kida, 1998; S. A. Stern & Alberini, 2013). Yet if this simple mutation really produced superior memory and this memory helped with survival, shouldn't every organism on the planet have evolved it long ago? Most likely, there are hidden downsides to this kind of memory and hidden upsides to forgetfulness—as the case of Jill Price may illustrate.

By the way, another way of looking at mnemogenic reactions is that the proteins become "infected" and are "contagious." Unfortunately, in some cases this model becomes the reality. The prion proteins just mentioned are a literal example of mnemogenic contagion. These misfolded versions of normal proteins are known as **prions**, and they can spread their misfolding to other proteins, and in so doing, cause deadly neurodegenerative diseases. A well-known example of prion disease is bovine spongiform encephalopathy—"mad cow" disease. The offending protein? A misfolded version of prion protein. So another major incentive for studying protein memory is that it may help us develop treatments for deadly illnesses that are currently incurable.

Epigenetics: Making a Single Genome Play Different Tunes

An exciting new area of research is in **epigenetics**, a term that describes self-perpetuating modifications of DNA and nuclear proteins (FIGURE 9.29). One mechanism is **DNA methylation**, which can inactivate a gene by preventing its transcription into RNA. Another mechanism is histone acetylation. Histones serve as tiny protein "spools," which DNA strands wrap themselves around to remain stable when not being expressed into proteins. Acetylating a histone can also alter the expression of the specific gene wrapped around it. In other words, there are "switches" on gene expression that are not coded in the DNA sequence itself, but can be passed from generation to generation. These switches can allow even genetically identical cells (all the cells in your body) to appear and behave differently (Simonsson & Gurdon, 2004).

One key feature of these processes is that patterns of methylation and acetylation can actually be inherited from the maternal and paternal lines. Crucially, these patterns can also be altered by changes in the environment, and the altered patterns are then also passed down along generations. Epigenetics is therefore a potential substrate for any biological process that involves an interaction between genes and the environment—which is to say, most biological processes, including memory.

Although epigenetics is still a new field, there are already strong indications that it will play a role in learning and memory. As an example, mouse offspring that are well nurtured by their mothers (for example, by frequent licking and grooming) show lifelong alterations in the patterns of DNA methylation when compared to mouse pups who did not receive so much attention from their mothers (Roth, Lubin, Funk, & Sweatt, 2009). These changes apparently lead to decreased anxiety and increased nurturing behaviors in the adult offspring. In another example, epigenetic tagging of the genome occurs during consolidation of long-term memories of contextual fear conditioning (Lubin, Roth, & Sweatt, 2008). Moreover, inhibiting the enzymes that deacetylate histones seems to enhance the formation of long-term memories. Different patterns of histone modification may also affect different memory systems. For example, latent inhibition (another form of long-term memory in which the animal learns that certain stimuli are unimportant) involves altered acetylation of a different histone from contextual fear conditioning (Korzus, Rosenfeld, & Mayford, 2004). The field of epigenetic memory mechanisms is ripe for future investigation.

The Mysteries of Memory

So far in this chapter, we have done our best to weave a century's worth of vigorous debates, competing hypotheses,

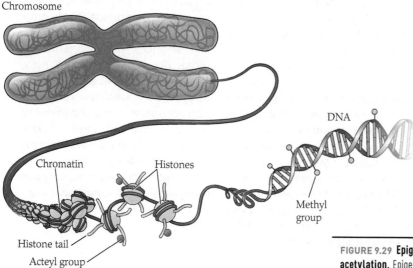

Chromosome

Chromatin

Histones

DNA

Histone tail

Acteyl group

Methyl group

FIGURE 9.29 **Epigenetic mechanisms of DNA methylation and histone acetylation.** Epigenetic information encoded in these patterns can endure for long periods of time and can even be passed on to future generations.

inspired experimentation, and bafflingly unexpected findings into a coherent story of how memories arise in the human brain. But is this story itself a kind of confabulation? The fact is that the field of memory research still faces a number of unsolved mysteries, nagging questions, and inconvenient truths. In this final section of the chapter, we will look at a couple of remaining questions in the study of memory and consider how these might be resolved.

Are the Roles of LTP and LTD Overstated?

LTP and LTD have long been considered key mechanisms for synaptic change. Initially, researchers hoped to find a simple relationship between stimulation parameters and synaptic change: a high firing rate will strengthen, and a low firing rate will weaken a synapse. But this relationship did not always bear out in practice. Why should this be? In some cases, investigators who found that a synaptic response did not depress as predicted would tend to reject the data, under the assumption that the neuron was somehow injured during experimentation. However, the truth may not be so simple. Not all synapses behave alike. There is evidence that the cellular processes going on inside the neuron at a particular time play a role in determining how synapses change in response to stimulation (Gazzaniga, 2004). Therefore, synaptic learning rules may well have intracellular determinants that remain to be identified.

Are LTP and LTD really central to memory? By now, hundreds of researchers have investigated the basis of experience-dependent changes in the brain. In thousands of studies, they have sought to map out the detailed parameters of the phenomenon and to discover the molecular mechanisms that make it possible. After more than 30 years of studying synaptic changes, data support the notion that synaptic plasticity is necessary for learning and memory, but little data currently support that it is sufficient. In fact, it is still unclear whether LTP and LTD will be the only, or even the most important, mechanisms involved in memory—or, perhaps, whether they will be involved at all.

If LTP and LTD do turn out to have only minor roles in memory, what other roles might they play? One possibility is this: a dense net of intertwined cells must orchestrate a careful balance between excitation and inhibition—otherwise the subtle signaling within a cortical sheet could swiftly kindle into the violent oscillations of epilepsy or subside into widespread depression. So the possibility remains that LTP and LTD are mechanisms to keep the system away from epileptic overload or synaptic shutdown, and memory either rides on top of these homeostatic functions or is stored in an entirely different manner (Kullmann, Asztely, & Walker, 2000).

It remains an open possibility that by concentrating so intently on LTP and LTD, the field is missing the main mechanisms of memory. After all, everywhere we look in the central nervous system we find adjustable parameters: change something here, and the brain behaves differently there. As we have seen, there are many other possibilities for plastic storage in the brain. One of them could easily prove to be memory's Rosetta Stone.

The Timing of Spikes

Aside from going beyond LTP and LTD, future models of synaptic change will, at a minimum, have to expand to encompass issues of spike timing. Although Hebb's rule is useful for forming associations, one of its theoretical shortcomings is that it is insensitive to the order of events. Experimenters have long observed that animal learning is strictly sensitive to the order of sensory inputs. For example, Pavlov's dogs did not show learning if the meat powder was presented before the bell, rather than after. The same is true for learned food aversion. Animals (and humans) will develop a strong aversion to a formerly preferred food if they experience a single experience of nausea after eating it. However, if the nausea precedes the food, no aversion develops.

Recently, an interesting parallel has been noted at the synaptic level: changes in synaptic strength depend on the order of pre- and postsynaptic activity (Wolters et al., 2003). If an input from A precedes the firing of neuron B, then the synapse is strengthened. If an input from A comes after cell B has fired, the synapse is weakened (FIGURE 9.30). This learning

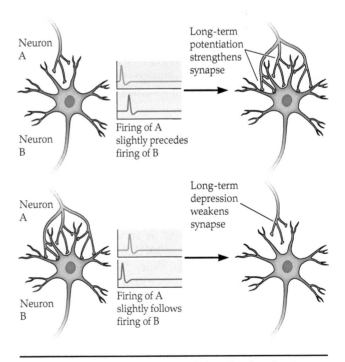

FIGURE 9.30 **Changes in synaptic strength depend on the order of pre- and postsynaptic activity.** If the activity in the presynaptic cell happens first, the result is LTP. If activity in the postsynaptic cell happens first, the result is LTD.

rule is commonly called a temporally asymmetric Hebbian rule, and it suggests that spike timing matters.

How might the asymmetric rule be more effective for learning and memory? It helps to identify relationships that are predictive. The mere correlation of two events A and B does not guarantee that one will accurately predict the other. However, if A consistently fires before B, but the reverse is not true, A is more likely to be a successful predictor of B. So, if neuron A consistently fires before and not after B, the connection of A to B can be considered predictive and strengthened accordingly.

The Limitations of Neural Networks

For the moment, let us leave aside the issues raised so far and assume that synaptic change is sufficient for storing memories. If we assume that associative networks—such as the Hopfield model we discussed earlier—are the mechanism for memory in the brain, what is left out of the story? Unfortunately, lots.

First, Hopfield's model made many simplifying assumptions. The artificial "neurons" in the model are nothing like real neurons, which we now know to have complex properties of integration, baseline activity, and many intracellular modifiable parameters. As a result, such networks have been described as a "clever step backwards" from biology (Toulouse, 1992). Its starting point was remote from the biological realities.

More important, an associative neural net has no easy way of telling apart relevant from irrelevant input during learning. Without such a filtering mechanism, any helpful pathways built from past experience are quickly washed away by a flood of irrelevant new input. During memory consolidation in real brains, spurious associations and details irrelevant to an animal's goals are weeded out or not encoded in the first place.

Relevance is often coded directly into the neural wiring. For example, many birds imprint, forming a strong emotional bond at birth to any nearby distinctive and animate object. Imprinting is a good example of one-trial learning. Simple neural network approaches fail at such learning, requiring instead many repeated trials to learn even simple tasks (Horn, 1981). Thus, more recent neural network models have begun to consider context as an important variable (Nishizawa, Izawa, & Watanabe, 2011).

The notion that particular types of learning are triggered to occur at certain times is called **schematic learning**. This is an expression of an important principle of neuroscience: the brain is not a blank slate on which the world scrawls its stories. Instead, the brain comes pre-equipped for certain types of learning in particular types of situations. Experience is more likely to result in learning when it has relevance to the survival of the organism—for example, when "tagged" by powerful emotional states

such as fear or pleasure (Nairne, VanArsdall, Pandeirada, & Blunt, 2012).

One way that context is likely to be expressed, biochemically, is through neuromodulatory systems: widely broadcast neural systems that signal reward, punishment, alertness, and so on. With neuromodulators, the plasticity of synapses can be gated, such that learning takes place only at the appropriate times, instead of each time activity passes through the cell (Hoke & Pitts, 2012). In the adult animal, reorganization of parts of the cortex can only occur when paired with the release of particular neuromodulators such as acetylcholine or dopamine (FIGURE 9.31) (Veena, Rao, & Srikumar, 2011).

Another mechanism for establishing context exists in specific regions of the brain that directly match needs to behavior at the level of strategy and long-term goals. These areas lie in the prefrontal and frontopolar cortex: parts of the core network we have seen earlier (Barbas, Zikopoulos, & Timbie, 2011). However, their anatomical positioning is less important than their functional positioning. Simply put, these areas translate the current needs of the organism into long-term goals and translate these goals into specific contexts or strategies within the current environment (for example, "I'm hungry" into "I'm going to eat out" into "I'm getting on the bus.") Artificial neural networks may need to incorporate needs, goals, and strategies into their architecture before they can establish a contextual filter for learning and remembering the right kinds of input. Otherwise, like

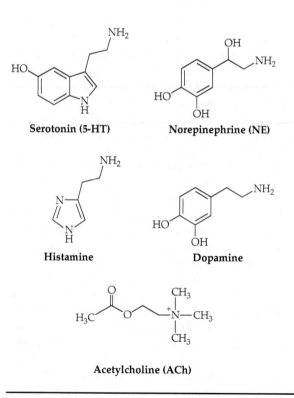

FIGURE 9.31 **Common neuromodulators and their chemical structures.**

the prefrontally injured patients with spontaneous confabulation, they become lost in a sea of irrelevant information.

Neural Networks: Solving the Wrong Problem?

One of the main difficulties with neural networks as we now understand them is that they seem to be trying to solve the wrong problem. After all, memory does not store a string of phonemes or a matrix of pixels, as an artificial network would. When someone tells you a joke, you do not encode a neural log file of each word and its inflection, but instead the gist of the joke. If you are bilingual, you may hear the joke in one language and turn around and tell it to someone else in a different language. This is a ready clue that human brains do not store memories like computers do.

Take neural network pattern completion as an example of addressing the wrong problem. One appealing thing about associative neural networks is that they do not need to see an entire pattern to recognize an object. For example, after training a network on digitized faces, you can show it half the face and it will recognize the other half. Although this is a seductive and impressive feat for a computer, brains do not memorize faces as a collection of pixels. Nor would they want to. If the lighting conditions change (that is, the face is lit from the other side), the pattern of pixels is rendered unrecognizable to the network.

Instead of encoding pictures as pixels, we encode new stimuli with respect to other things we have learned, including concepts both physical and social. It is intuitively clear that much of what we learn is represented in terms of what we already know. When you read this chapter, the points made here would be meaningless unless you already came to this chapter preequipped with an idea of how to operate a book, how to read this language, and what a brain is. Two people can look at a list of important dates in Mongolian history, but if one of them already commands a richly developed Mongolian timeline, new facts are more readily incorporated into that person's network of knowledge.

At the psychological level, the concepts of relational memory and the matching of recollection to existing knowledge are not entirely new. In fact, they have been central to memory theory at least since Bartlett's *War of the Ghosts* in the 1930s. What is unclear, however, is how to translate this (and many other psychological models of memory) into the architecture of a neural network. Such work requires both mathematical expertise and familiarity with the extensive body of literature on memory accumulated over the past century. By training across multiple disciplines, the neuroscientists of the 21st century will be better equipped to take on such challenges in the years to come.

Remembering Relationships, Not Features

Let's look at one example of multidisciplinary thinking in addressing the problem of object recognition. When it comes to how we recognize objects we've seen before, an important clue is that memory seems to encode the relationships between things as opposed to the details of the things themselves. When you memorize a musical melody, you encode the relationships between the notes rather than the notes themselves—this is why you can recognize or reproduce the musical sequence in any key.

The same applies to face recognition: the details of scruff, a tan, and a different haircut are less important than the relative distances between the nose, eyes, lips, and so on that define a face. Concentrating on relationships gives us insight into how brains can recognize a familiar face: even when it is close, far, to the right, or to the left, its internal relationships will not have changed at all.

These examples about phoneme strings and pixel patterns highlight the issue of invariance—one of the great unsolved engineering problems of recognition. Invariance means that the details of size, lighting, position, rotation, and so on do not change our ability to recognize a pineapple as a pineapple. Instead, brains retain and retrieve memory about animals without encoding them pixel by pixel or favorite stories without encoding them word for word. But how?

One possibility is that brains store what are known as basis functions: collections of exemplars about objects in the world (Kolcz & Allinson, 1999). Any new stimulus can be represented efficiently as a sort of mathematical combination of these various basis functions, appropriately weighted. For example, if you stored a set of exemplars derived from a wide-ranging set of different, canonical faces, any new face you see could be represented by a combination of those "basis faces." Storing only the coefficients, rather than the large amounts of mostly redundant information in the low-level image, makes for efficient encoding (FIGURE 9.32).

The challenge for a system is to learn the best basis set for representing the world while simultaneously learning the coefficients—a difficult task that many computational modelers are trying to optimize. Although we do not yet have a complete theory for how brains do this, the basis function hypothesis leads us away from the notion that brains are passive recorders and toward the idea that brains are dynamic synthesizers whose mnemonic operations are quite unlike information storage in computers.

The Future of Memory Research

Further progress in memory research will likely depend on at least two important steps. The first, already underway, is

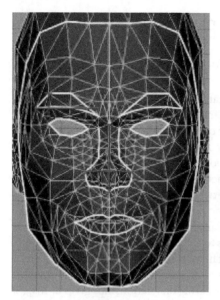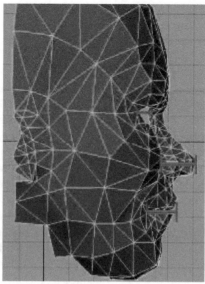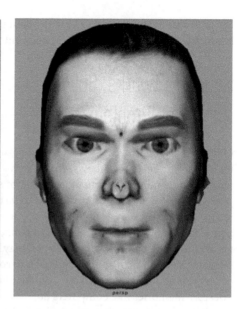

FIGURE 9.32 **Facial recognition programs map key points on a face and use just the distances and angles between those points to recognize faces.** It is possible that human memory works in a similar way.

to develop new technological ways to probe submicroscopic plastic changes in the nervous system. Although synapses have monopolized the spotlight for 100 years, the picture of memory will likely be incomplete without an understanding of plastic changes at the level of biochemical cascades and epigenetic alterations.

The second requirement to move forward is to take on a more realistic view of the phenomenon we are attempting to explain. Although artificial neural networks using LTP and LTD succeed in accomplishing certain functions, they do not capture the character of real memory. Computational modelers and theoreticians must be willing to take on a more realistic view of what is typically remembered—that is, only the few details that have relevance to the animal and only those that plug into previously available relationships with things already known. Expanding the architecture of neural net models to take into account needs, goals, and strategies may help in this regard.

Conclusion

Let's return once again to the case of Jill Price and her extraordinary episodic memory. Her case is particularly interesting because, as with the field of memory itself, there are still so many unanswered questions. How does she do it? We do not yet know the whole picture, but we do have some important clues. As an exercise, you may wish to try applying what you have learned here to the mystery of Jill Price's meticulous recollections.

First, think back to the set of memory systems from the first section. Which systems of memory are normal and which ones unusual in her case? Next, consider brain anatomy. From what you have learned in this chapter, what parts of her brain might you examine to see whether they are enlarged or if they are connected differently to other parts of her brain? Next, consider some features of the memories themselves. They are imagined episodes. They are accurate. They arise without effort or intent, but they are not relevant to the task at hand. Instead, they spring up in parallel to her ongoing life, unwanted and unbidden. What does this suggest about her retrieval process?

What about at the synaptic level? Is her memory the result of some genetic quirk, some abnormality of LTP, or NMDA receptors, or protein synthesis, or neurogenesis? Bear in mind that her abilities do not seem to extend to all forms of learning and memory in her brain. Also bear in mind that she, alone in her family, bears the trait of extraordinary and intrusive autobiographical memory. So far, we have not discovered any cases of extraordinary memory that runs in families. What does this imply?

Remember that having a strategy to organize your memories is important and the method of loci is one such organizational strategy. Jill Price tends to think of years and dates as being arranged in a spatial sequence. Competitors in the World Memory Championships are able to memorize large numbers of fictional historic dates with associated fictional historic events by imagining themselves walking along a familiar route. To memorize the information, they put these "facts" at specific places on the route, and to recall the information, they walk the route again.

With the right strategy and enough repetition, could a person learn 365 dates a year, even without planning to do so? Bear in mind what drove Jill Price to seek help in the first place: that her memories were deeply emotional, that they sprang up over and over again, throughout the waking day. Some observers have noted that she pores over her past in obsessive detail, hoarding mementos from childhood onward and becoming distressed by changes such as moving

to a new home. Some have even suggested to her that her memories are part of a rare sort of obsessive–compulsive hoarding of past experiences.

Could these features, in combination, explain her extraordinary ability? Once again, the answer remains to be seen. However, we hope that you have now learned enough about the powers of memory that, if you are interested, you can start to ask the right questions.

KEY PRINCIPLES

- There are many different memory systems, including working, long-term, implicit and explicit, each with its own distinct functions and neuroanatomy.

- The medial temporal lobe contains several structures that are important for creating and storing long-term semantic and episodic memories. These include the hippocampus, the parahippocampal region, and the amygdala.

- Prospective memory helps in predicting the future. This type of memory provides a survival advantage by enabling us to guess where we might find food or how another person might act.

- Memory systems do not record and store information like a video, but rather store the main points of an idea or experience. This can lead to memory errors, such as the Seven Sins of Memory. Failing to suppress information that is not relevant can lead to confabulation.

- Currently, the basic mechanisms for storing memory are believed to be long-term potentiation and long-term depression, which involve changing the strength of synaptic connections between neurons.

- Researchers are actively trying to understand other mechanisms for storing memories. These may include adding new neurons, changing the function of enzymes within the cell, and influencing the epigenetic modifications of the DNA.

- Despite more than a century of study, our understanding of memory is incomplete and many puzzling questions remain to be answered. One such question is whether all memory comes from LTP or whether there might be other cellular mechanisms. Another asks about the usefulness of neural network models to understanding human memory.

KEY TERMS

The Many Kinds of Memory
working memory (p. 273)
implicit memory (p. 274)
explicit memory (p. 274)
procedural memories (p. 274)
priming (p. 274)
classical conditioning (p. 274)
unconditioned stimulus (p. 275)
unconditioned response (p. 275)
conditioned stimulus (p. 275)

conditioned response (p. 275)
operant conditioning (p. 275)
nonassociative learning (p. 275)
sensitization (p. 275)
familiarity (p. 275)
recollection (p. 275)
medial temporal lobe (p. 275)
semantic memories (p. 276)
Alzheimer's disease (p. 277)
semantic dementia (p. 277)

Travels in Space and Time: The Hippocampus and Temporal Lobe
place cells (p. 277)
spatial cognitive maps (p. 277)
anterograde amnesia (p. 277)
retrograde amnesia (p. 277)
hippocampal formation (p. 278)
dentate gyrus (p. 278)
place field (p. 280)
grid cell (p. 280)

REVIEW QUESTIONS

1. What are the major categories of memory systems in the brain? Which of these systems are normal and abnormal in the case of "the woman who cannot forget"?

2. What are the major structures of the medial temporal lobe? How do we think each of these structures contributes to episodic memory?

3. What are the components of the core network of brain regions for episodic memory recall? What might each component contribute to episodic memory?

4. What are the common features of prospection and recollection? What are their differences? Why might the brain use the same circuitry for both functions?

5. Why do some amnesia patients confabulate? What has gone wrong with their memory function?

6. What are the common forms of memory error in the healthy brain? What are some examples of each? How are these different from spontaneous confabulation?

7. How do long-term potentiation (LTP) and long-term depression (LTD) work? What is a Hebbian synapse? How does adjusting synaptic strength result in learning and memory formation?

8. What is an artificial associative neural network? What functions of a real brain can it reproduce? What functions of a real brain does it fail to reproduce?

9. What are some mechanisms by which the brain could store memories without adjusting existing synapses? What special abilities might these mechanisms provide compared to simply adjusting synapses?

CRITICAL-THINKING QUESTIONS

1. Besides the possible reasons discussed in this chapter, why do you think that many of the new neurons that form in adult neurogenesis die young (within a few days, months, or weeks)? If your hypotheses turned out to be correct, what would be the implications for the role of the new neurons in human memory?

2. Imagine that you have been assigned to develop a drug to treat Jill Price ("the woman who cannot forget"). What else would you want to learn about Jill Price's brain and the characteristics of her memory before you started to develop the drug? What studies would you perform? How would this additional knowledge help you to determine potential target sites and mechanisms of action for the drug?

3. What do you think is a major unsolved mystery in memory research? If you could solve one question about how memory works, what would it be? Can you think of an experiment that might help to answer your question?

- Describe the use of electroencephalography (EEG) to study sleep, the stages of sleep, and the brain's electrical activity in each stage.

- Explain the neural basis and function of the circadian rhythm.

- Assess theories for the purpose of sleep, as well as sleep's potential role in learning and insight.

- Examine theories for the purpose of dreaming.

- Discuss the effects of sleep deprivation and common sleep disorders.

Sleep

STARTING OUT:
Caught between Sleeping and Waking

In 1987, Kenneth Parks (FIGURE 10.1) drove across Toronto, Canada in the middle of the night. He broke into the home of an elderly couple, stabbed the wife to death, and assaulted the husband. Then, he drove himself to the police station and turned himself in. Beyond the crime itself, the story includes several strange elements (Eagleman, 2011). The first is that the victims were his mother-in-law and father-in-law. The second is that Kenneth had no motive: he loved his in-laws, and he had a close relationship with them. The third is that Kenneth appears to have been asleep the whole time.

The final claim seems outrageous, especially as Kenneth had to drive 14 miles to reach his in-laws' home. But as the case was investigated, a more convincing sleepwalking story began to emerge. When Kenneth arrived at the police station, he looked down in confusion at his bloodied hands and said, "I think I may have killed some people" (Broughton et al., 1994). He claimed to have no memory of what had happened, and he appeared horrified when he learned the details. Essentially, Kenneth claimed that he was not awake and present during the crime—and his testimony did not change over the course of the next year, even as prosecutors tried to lead him off track. His legal team contended that the case represented homicidal somnambulism: killing while sleepwalking (Broughton et al. 1994). Electrode recordings in a sleep laboratory showed that the electrical activity in his brain was highly unusual, and consistent with sleepwalking.

FIGURE 10.1 Murder during sleepwalking, also known as homicidal somnambulism. Kenneth Parks was allegedly asleep when he got up, drove across town to his in-laws' house, and murdered his mother-in-law.

Do you think Kenneth was culpable? Or, was he just making an excuse? Consider the expert testimony given by psychiatrist R. Billings during the trial:

Q. Is there any evidence that a person could formulate a plan while they were awake and then in some way ensure that they carry it out in their sleep?

R. Billings. No, absolutely not. Probably the most striking feature of what we know of what goes on in the mind during sleep is that it's very independent of waking mentation in terms of its objectives and so forth. There is a lack of control of directing our minds in sleep compared to wakefulness. In the waking state, of course, we often voluntarily plan things, what we call volition—that is, we decide to do this as opposed to that—and there is no evidence that this occurs during the sleepwalking episode. . . .

Q. And assuming he was sleep-walking at the time, would he have the capacity to intend?

R. B. No.

Q. Would he have appreciated what he was doing?

R. B. No he would not.

Q. Would he have understood the consequences of what he was doing?

R. B. No, I do not believe that he would. I think it would all have been an unconscious activity, uncontrolled and unmeditated. (Ridgway, 1996)

What would your opinion be if you were a juror on this case? After all, doesn't sleepwalking sound like an excuse? Isn't one either asleep or awake—or can a brain be caught between two states?

In this chapter, we will explore the fundamental differences between the states of wakefulness and sleep, their purposes, and how transitions between them can go awry. Armed with our new knowledge, we will return to Kenneth's case at the end of the chapter to see what the jury concluded.

Sleep and the Brain

One of the most astonishing facts in neuroscience is that we, as adult humans, spend a third of our time in the strange world of sleep (FIGURE 10.2). Newborn babies spend about double that. It is inordinately difficult to remain awake for more than a full day–night cycle. Continuous wakefulness of the nervous system results in cognitive impairment in humans (Pilcher & Huffcutt, 1996), and forced sleep deprivation for days or weeks can kill a rat (Rechtschaffen & Bergmann, 1995). Sleep is conserved through evolution: all mammals sleep, reptiles and birds sleep, and voluntary breathers such as dolphins sleep one brain hemisphere at a time (Hunter, 2008; Zepelin & Rechtschaffen, 1974). Even the fruit fly *Drosophila* displays sleep–wake cycles, and three days of sleep deprivation result in the fly's death (Shaw, Cirelli, Greenspan, & Tononi, 2000). The fact that all animals sleep suggests that sleep is functional, not accidental. In the next few sections, we will learn about the biological basis of sleep, then turn to its purpose, and finally look at the ways in which sleep systems can go awry.

The Brain Is Active during Sleep

When you observe a sleeper, it looks as though everything has shut down: eyes are closed, muscles are relaxed, breathing is regular, and there is no response to sound or light. A century ago, people thought that wakefulness was the natural state of the brain and that sleep was a state in which activity decreased or shut down. But scientists discovered that injuries to the brainstem could cause the forebrain to fall into the sleeplike state of coma (Parvizi & Damasio, 2003). This eventually led to the understanding that the brain is not so much naturally awake as it is *kept* awake by a system of brainstem projections to the forebrain (Moruzzi & Magoun, 1949). On the flipside, injury to part of the hypothalamus produces long-lasting sleeping difficulties (Lu, Greco, Shiromani, & Saper, 2000), as we will see in more detail shortly. In other words, not only is waking an active state, but also sleeping requires activity of special nerve cells. The primary technology for eavesdropping on the brain's activity during sleep is the use of electro-encephalography (EEG). Before exploring what scientists have found, we'll turn to this technology now.

FIGURE 10.2 **Hypnos, god of sleep.** Sleep is such a large part of our lives that people make gods to it.

RESEARCH METHODS:
Electroencephalography

In Chapter 3, we learned about the electrical activity in the somas, dendrites, and axons of individual neurons. This activity is at far too low of a level to be detected from outside the skull—but when thousands or millions of neurons interact, the synchronized group activity can be picked up in what's known as a **field potential**. This larger, averaged signal can be detected by electrodes placed on the scalp, a technique known as electroencephalography (EEG) (FIGURE 10.3). Returning to the analogy we used in Chapter 3, if you were standing outside a baseball stadium, you would have little hope of distinguishing the conversation of any individual inside—but when most of the crowd shouts at once, it can be surmised that something interesting has just happened. Similarly, EEG therefore tells us something about the large-scale structure of the electrical activity in the brain at any moment, rather than about the details of the activity of individual neurons.

Researchers noted from the beginning that the EEG signals appeared to oscillate—that is, they were composed of several different wavelengths of activity (FIGURE 10.3). By convention, the different bands of wavelengths are denoted by a series of Greek letters, and the number of cycles per second is denoted by Hertz (Hz):

Delta waves	up to 4 Hz
Theta waves	4–7 Hz
Alpha waves	8–12 Hz
Beta waves	12–30 Hz
Gamma waves	30–100+ Hz

(a)

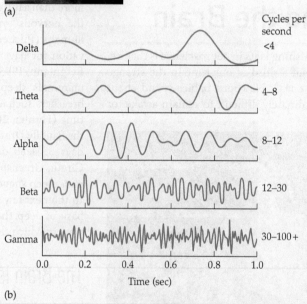
(b)

FIGURE 10.3 **Electroencephalography (EEG).** (a) An EEG recording cap on a participant in a brain wave study. (b) Different wavelengths of electrical activity recorded during EEG.

These rhythmic oscillations are popularly referred to as **brain waves**, and the different frequencies typically correlate with different functions. For example, the alpha wave rhythm indicates relaxation, whereas the high-frequency beta and gamma waves are associated with cognitive functions that require concentration (Difrancesco, Holland, & Szaflarski, 2008; Kopell, Ermentrout, Whittington, & Traub, 2000). As we will see in this chapter, delta waves characterize "slow-wave sleep".

EEG originally found its major clinical use from epilepsy studies and in the diagnosis of coma. By the mid-1950s, EEG revolutionized our understanding of sleep, as we will see in this chapter. Along with the EEG, these sleep researchers also monitored the movement of the eyes, using a technique known as **electrooculography**, and the activity of skeletal muscles, using a technique known as **electromyography**. Together with EEG, these two techniques were important for understanding and differentiating the different stages of sleep that we will see in this chapter. The use of EEG in the diagnosis of brain lesions—such as localizing a stroke or tumor—has fallen off with the arrival of neuroimaging techniques such as CT and MRI (see Chapter 1 and *Research Methods*, Chapter 4).

Sleep researchers have pointed out that the experience of dreams alone should have motivated scientists to look for evidence of brain activation during sleep (Hobson, 1988). But it wasn't until 1953 that researchers serendipitously discovered that sleep follows a regular cycle each night: the EEG pattern changes in a predictable way several times during a single period of sleep (Dement & Kleitman, 1957a). The sleeping brain follows cycles that last between 90 and 100 minutes each, repeating four or five times in a course of a night (FIGURE 10.4).

There are two basic forms of sleep: rapid eye movement (REM) and non-REM (or NREM). NREM comprises 80% of sleep and consists of three successive stages of depth. During NREM sleep, heart rate and breathing become slow and regular. The deepest stage of NREM sleep (stage 3) is known as **slow-wave sleep (SWS)**, so named because the brain's electrical activity oscillates at a low frequency with high amplitude.

REM sleep is quite different from NREM. During REM, the heart rate and breathing speed up, and small muscles (such as facial muscles) can twitch. However, the major muscle groups are paralyzed by an elaborate neural circuitry, which we will learn more about momentarily.

During REM, brain waves become high frequency and low amplitude, reflecting more complex cognitive function. REM sleep is sometimes called "paradoxical sleep" because it is the most neurally active of sleep states, and, as you can see in FIGURE 10.4b, its EEG signature resembles that of the waking state much more than that of deeper stages of sleep (Luppi et al., 2006). This is the stage that usually includes dreaming. Scientists discovered this fact very simply: by waking up sleepers during this stage and asking what they were experiencing. During REM sleep, people will report 80% of the time (Pagel, 2000) that they were having storylike dreams. (In contrast, during NREM sleep, dreaming is less common, and when it does occur it is usually less visual and more thoughtlike [Suzuki et al., 2004].) As a side note, everyone dreams (apart from a few rare cases of patients with specific brain injuries). Some people have more difficulty remembering their dreams and sometimes come to believe that they do not dream—but if you awaken them during REM, they will report having just been dreaming. Another characteristic of

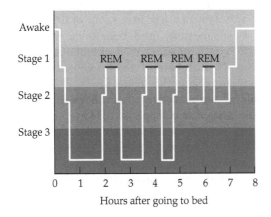

(a)

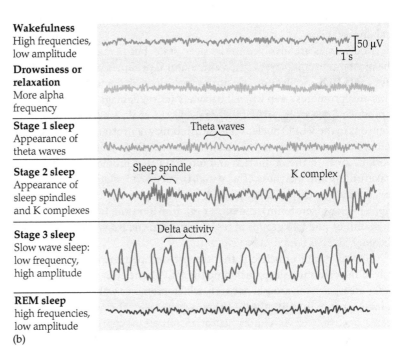

(b)

FIGURE 10.4 **Sleep cycles and typical patterns of brain waves during sleep.** (a) The sleeping brain cycles through the different stages during the night, repeating four or five approximately hour-and-a-half cycles. (b) EEG recordings from different sleep stages.

REM sleep is penile erection, which almost always occurs during REM sleep in males, but does not relate to erotic dream content: it is merely a side product of the neural circuits activated during this sleep stage. Although all animals seem to have NREM sleep, REM has been found only in mammals and in young birds (Hobson 1987).

As shown in **FIGURE 10.4a**, the nightly cycle of sleep follows a clear pattern. First, NREM sleep proceeds into successive stages of depth from stages 1 through 3, and then the stages reverse to reach REM sleep. As the cycles continue through the night, people tend to experience less deep sleep and more REM. People typically experience their first dreams of the night after the completion of the first cycle of deep sleep—REM sleep is also known as emergent stage 1 sleep because one is emerging from deep sleep into this lighter state of sleep.

The Neural Networks of Sleep

Although we use a single word ("sleep") for the phenomenon this chapter describes, the sleep state emerges from a collaboration of many areas in the brain interacting in a complex network. These areas involved in sleep normally work in concert to give us the state of sleep as we normally experience it. However, under special conditions (such as REM-sleep deprivation or the absence of light cues), the different areas can desynchronize and thereby reveal the richness of the underlying mechanisms. For our purposes, cataloging the numerous brain areas involved in sleep will not provide a big-picture understanding of the principles. It will therefore suffice to underscore the main functions that the circuitry implements and to highlight some anatomical areas of special importance.

Many areas are involved in the sleep state, but perhaps the most important player is the **ventrolateral preoptic nucleus (VLPO)**, a collection of neurons in the hypothalamus. This area promotes sleep when it becomes active; damage to it produces **insomnia** (an inability to sleep) (Lu et al., 2000). Neurons in the VLPO nucleus release inhibitory neurotransmitters to several areas in the brain and especially to a network of areas in the brainstem and forebrain that promote wakefulness and alertness. This **arousal network** includes several nuclei: the locus coeruleus (norepinephrine), the raphe nucleus (serotonin), the **tuberomammillary nucleus** (histamine), and two groups of acetylcholinergic neurons in the pons and basal forebrain (FIGURE 10.5).

The important principle is that the network of areas involved in promoting sleep, including the VLPO nucleus and other areas, and the arousal network, which promotes wakefulness, engage in **mutual inhibition**: when one of the networks is active, it uses inhibitory neurotransmitters to suppress the other. Mutual inhibition can give rise to a **bistable** system, one with two stable states—in this case, waking and sleeping. (Researchers sometimes refer to this type of bistable system as a flip-flop (FIGURE 10.6), named after an electronic device that

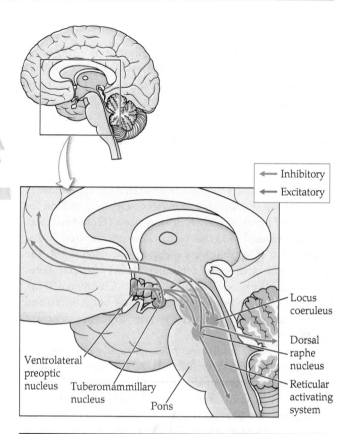

FIGURE 10.5 **Arousal network of the brain.** The brain structures involved in wakefulness and alertness include the locus coeruleus, raphe nucleus, tuberomammillary nucleus, and reticular activating system. The ventrolateral preoptic nucleus of the hypothalamus acts in opposition to the arousal network, promoting sleep.

toggles between two states.) Because of the dynamics of mutual inhibition, the system can be in one state or the other, but not in both at the same time. This is because the winning state (the state that is the most active) releases inhibitory neurotransmitters onto the other network and thereby prevents a takeover. In the absence of any other inputs, a mutually inhibitory system would fall into one active state and never leave that state (because the other state is suppressed). However, other brain areas can help stabilize or destabilize the balance, such that the network can tip into the other state (more on that below in the discussion of narcolepsy).

As FIGURE 10.5 indicates, the arousal systems in the brainstem and forebrain (the arousal network) inhibit the VLPO nucleus when it is active. The flip-flop of the network leads the brain into sleep—and, specifically, into SWS. As we will see in a moment, REM sleep has another principle that comes into play, which puts the brain in a state that shares some qualities of both the sleeping state and the waking state.

The Brain during REM Sleep

Electrical activity during REM sleep looks quite a bit like that during the waking state. During both REM sleep and

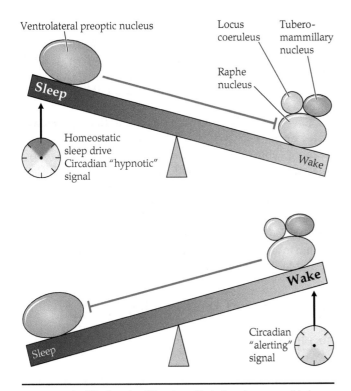

FIGURE 10.6 **Flip-flop circuit for sleep.** The brain regions responsible for the sleep and awake states are mutually inhibitory, resulting in either sleep or wakefulness, but not both at the same time.

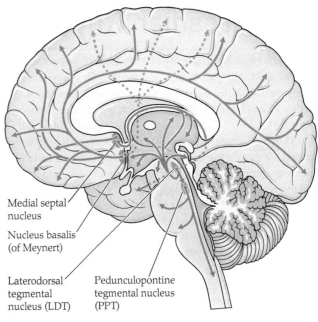

FIGURE 10.7 **Cholinergic neurons involved in both arousal and REM sleep.** The neurons projecting from the basal forebrain and the pons use the neurotransmitter acetylcholine.

waking, there is increased synchronization of neural activity in the gamma wave frequency (30–70 Hz) (Uchida, Maehara, Hirai, Okubo, & Shimizu, 2001). In the waking state, gamma wave activity reflects cognitive processing; we do not yet know whether it reflects the same thing during sleep (Kopell et al., 2000).

Just before the onset of REM, acetylcholinergic neurons in the pons become active, and these neurons trigger several consequences. The most important is **atonia** (paralysis) of the major muscle groups. Elaborate neural circuitry keeps the body paralyzed during dreaming, and its very elaborateness further emphasizes the biological importance of dream sleep. Presumably, dreaming would be unlikely to evolve and remain without an important function behind it. Note that muscular shutdown in atonia allows the possibility of the brain "practicing" motor programs without actually moving the body around. We will examine this idea further when we look at the purpose of sleep.

The second consequence of the increased activity in the acetylcholinergic neurons is that waves, known as **PGO waves (pontogeniculo-occipital waves)** because they originate in the pons, move to the lateral geniculate nucleus, and from there propagate to the occipital cortex, and they can be measured in all three (McCarley, Nelson, & Hobson, 1978). The appearance of PGO waves just precedes the appearance of REM sleep, and the density of the waves correlates with the amount of eye movement (Nelson, McCarley, & Hobson, 1983). As we will see below, some theories suggest

that PGO waves are the neural correlate of dreaming: supposedly the onset of the waves corresponds with recalling the day's memories, and then the visual areas (LGN and occipital cortex) become active for the visual aspect, allowing us to "see" our dreams.

Note the acetylcholinergic neurons that trigger the onset of REM are the same ones involved in the arousal network (FIGURE 10.7). It should not be surprising that acetylcholine is involved in both REM sleep and wakefulness: with the exception of the muscular atonia and lack of visual input, the states of REM sleep and wakefulness strongly resemble one another. Again, looking at the traces of electrical activity, the two states are almost indistinguishable.

Although REM sleep and wakefulness have many similarities, critical differences also exist. One major difference involves the role of the thalamus. The thalamus traditionally (and mistakenly) has been considered the gateway between the sensory organs and the neocortex: a relay station while the body is awake and a blockade during sleep. But we now know better: the thalamus plays a key role in organizing complex dynamical behaviors—including a variety of oscillations—during the different stages of sleep (Steriade, McCormick, & Sejnowski, 1993). The major cellular players in the sleep rhythms are **thalamocortical cells (excitatory)** and cells of the thalamic reticular nucleus (inhibitory). What remains to be understood are the origins of the different oscillations and the transitions between them and how a single, anatomically fixed structure can produce such different rhythms. These rich questions remain for the future, and their answers will have ramifications for neuroscience of the awake brain.

The Circadian Rhythm

There are two important aspects to the sleep–wake cycle: *how much* you sleep and *when* you sleep. As for *how much*, not everyone needs to sleep the same amount. In fact, most people sleep about 6.5–7 hours a night, with a range between 4 and 11 hours (National Sleep Foundation, 2005, 2011, 2013). How many hours you sleep correlates with what you have done during the day, and periods of intense stimulation (such as going to a museum, an amusement park, and so on) during the day tend to make people sleep longer that night (Shapiro, Bortz, Mitchell, Bartel, & Jooste, 1981). How much sleep you require in general appears to have at least some genetic basis, although this is poorly understood (Franken, Malafosse, & Tafti, 1999).

The rest of this section discusses the second half of the story: *when* you sleep. Why is sleep on such a regular cycle, and with what environmental factors is the sleep cycle synchronized? The answer to that question involves the **circadian rhythm**, a natural internal rhythm that runs on an approximately 24-hour cycle (*circa* meaning "about" and *dian* referring to a "day") and controls our sleep–wake cycles (Richardson, 2005). All animals appear to have some form of circadian cycle. This circadian rhythm influences not just sleep and wakefulness, but also coordination, blood pressure, alertness, and body temperature (FIGURE 10.8).

The circadian rhythm is **endogenously generated**, meaning that it comes from programmed mechanisms in our brain and persists even in the absence of external cues. Some animals, like the blind mole rat, maintain their endogenous

rhythms in the absence of light cues like the sun (Rado, Gev, Goldman, & Terkel, 1991). Incredibly, this complex network of biochemical cascades results in a clock whose natural period is 24 hours and 11 minutes. Across subjects, the variation is remarkably small: plus or minus only 16 minutes (Czeisler et al., 1999).

The primary clock in mammals lies in the **suprachiasmatic nucleus (SCN)** of the hypothalamus (from supra meaning "above" and chiasmatic referring to the optic chiasm, or crossing of the optic nerves; the two nuclei (left and right hemisphere) are located just above this crossing, see FIGURE 10.9) (Klein, Moore, & Reppert, 1991). Cells of the SCN maintain their own rhythm when cultured in a dish, and damage of the SCN obliterates a regular sleep–wake rhythm in animals (Ibuka & Kawamura, 1975; Welsh, Logothetis, Meister, & Reppert, 1995).

Entrainment of the Circadian Rhythm by Light Cues

Although the circadian rhythm is endogenously generated, it becomes **entrained** to various environmental stimuli, known as **zeitgebers** (Aschoff, Daan, & Honma, 1982). The most important of these is the light–dark cycle—that is, the phase of the circadian rhythm is set by the planet's rotation into and out of light from the sun. The SCN receives information about external light levels from the eyes, but not via the rods or cones that we learned about in Chapter 5. The retina contains a third type of light-sensitive cell: retinal

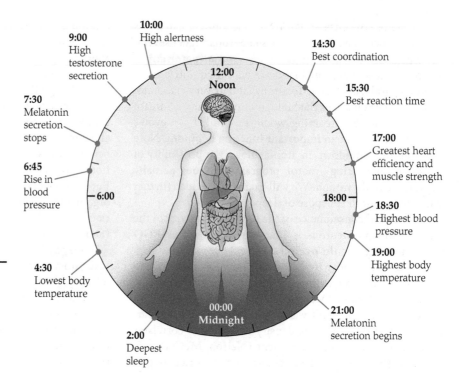

FIGURE 10.8 Physiological changes tied to the circadian rhythm. The circadian rhythm runs on an approximately 24-hour cycle and controls sleep-wake cycles. It also influences other physiological and cognitive processes, including temperature, alertness, blood pressure, and hormone levels.

9:00 High testosterone secretion

10:00 High alertness

14:30 Best coordination

12:00 Noon

15:30 Best reaction time

7:30 Melatonin secretion stops

17:00 Greatest heart efficiency and muscle strength

6:45 Rise in blood pressure

6:00

18:00

18:30 Highest blood pressure

19:00 Highest body temperature

4:30 Lowest body temperature

00:00 Midnight

21:00 Melatonin secretion begins

2:00 Deepest sleep

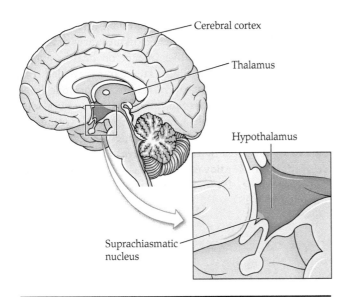

Cerebral cortex

Thalamus

Hypothalamus

Suprachiasmatic nucleus

FIGURE 10.9 The suprachiasmatic nucleus. The suprachiasmatic nucleus is part of the hypothalamus and is located just above the optic chiasm. It is important in maintaining the circadian rhythm.

ganglion cells that contain a pigment called **melanopsin**. Axons from these retinal ganglion cells, instead of traveling with the rest of the optic nerve to the visual thalamus, peel off and go directly to the anterior hypothalamus, thus earning the name **retinohypothalamic tract**. Within SCN neurons, a complex biochemical network of gene expression and feedback gives the cells their 24-hour periodicity (Kornhauser, Nelson, Mayo, & Takahashi, 1990).

Neurons in the SCN send signals to the **pineal gland** (pineal means "pinecone-shape"), a tiny structure in the brain's midline (FIGURE 10.10a). The pineal gland produces and releases the hormone **melatonin** into the cerebrospinal fluid. Under normal circumstances, the level of melatonin remains low throughout the day and gradually increases as the night sets in (FIGURE 10.10b). It reaches a plateau during nighttime sleep and then begins to decline as the morning comes. Melatonin is not directly a "sleep" hormone, as people sometimes think, but instead a "darkness" hormone. It gets its darkness information from the SCN, and, as we

shall see in a moment, these melatonin cycles influence wakefulness (Hardeland, 2008).

The Circadian Rhythm Is Not Fixed

In 1972, the French caver Michel Siffre descended a 100-foot vertical shaft into the Midnight cave near Del Rio, Texas. Inside he had stashed a campsite with food, water, and books—enough to last him the six months of the astounding time-isolation experiment he was about to undertake. The bowels of the cave contained no light cues to tell day from night. He forbade any incoming contact from the outside world, he had no timepieces of any sort, and he had only a telephone to make outgoing calls. In this self-imposed experimental condition, he kept careful track of his sleep and wake times by calling his support team when he woke up, when he ate, and when he went to sleep (Foer & Siffre, 2008). He quickly lost a conscious sense of what time it was in the outside world. Interestingly, his body continued to sleep on a roughly 24-hour cycle. His general finding: without the ability to see the light and dark cycles of the world, the period of his circadian rhythm drifted to around 25 hours (Colin, Timbal, Boutelier, Houdas, & Siffre, 1968). Subsequent experiments have verified that the circadian rhythm is not an exact 24-hour clock: it is an *approximate* cycle that is entrained by (nudged into rhythm with) the solar cycle (Tankersley, Irizarry, Flanders, & Rabold, 2002). Presumably, if we had evolved on a different planet with a different light–dark period, we would have a different approximate period length to our internal rhythms. Indeed, with false lighting cues, humans have entrained easily to a 23.5-hour cycle or a 24.65-hour cycle—researchers chose the latter because it is the period of day and night on Mars (Scheer et al., 2007).

Although the period is essentially the same for all of us earth-dwellers, the phase of the rhythm (the time of day when the oscillation peaks or sinks) can vary across the population (Horne & Ostberg, 1976). Some people are night owls, meaning that their natural rhythm keeps them up late at night and sleeping late into the morning, whereas others are morning larks, early to bed and early to rise. About 60%

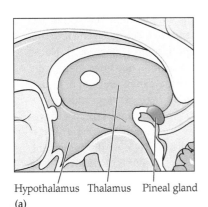

Hypothalamus Thalamus Pineal gland

(a)

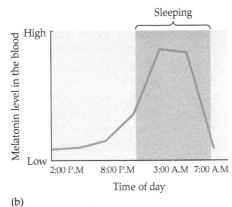

High

Melatonin level in the blood

Sleeping

Low

2:00 P.M   8:00 P.M   3:00 A.M 7:00 A.M

Time of day

(b)

FIGURE 10.10 Anatomy and circadian rhythm of sleep. (a) The location of the pineal gland along the midline of the brain. (b) Blood levels of melatonin change as a function of time.

of the population is intermediate between night owls and morning larks (Brown et al., 2008). Although normal variation exists in the population of night owls and morning larks, some people on the extremes must take drastic measures to adapt their lives to the societal norms. Let's look at the case of Melinda.

Disruption to the circadian rhythms can have negative effects on the brain. If you've ever traveled to a distant time zone, you've probably experienced the fatigue and disorientation of **jet lag**, a mismatch of your circadian time with the local day–night period. Symptoms typically include irregular sleep patterns, fatigue, irritability, and disorientation as

the rhythm struggles to regain alignment (Herxheimer & Petrie, 2002). Long-term, repeated disturbances of the synchronization have a negative impact on health: experiments in transoceanic flight attendants revealed that repeated exposure to jet lag raises stress hormone levels and physically diminishes the volume of the temporal lobe, leading to demonstrable effects on spatial learning and memory (Cho, 2001). In animal models, ongoing disturbances in the circadian rhythm have been linked to increased risk for cardiovascular disease and cancer (Muller, Tofler, & Stone, 1989; Shanmugam, Wafi, Al-Taweel, & Büsselberg, 2013).

CASE STUDY:
The Shifted Circadian Rhythm

Melinda S. is a mother of two children, ages 13 and 11. They all go to bed at 4 a.m. and typically wake up around noon. This is not just on weekends: this is every day. Although some of her neighbors think she's a bad mother, Melinda and her children suffer from **delayed sleep phase syndrome**, a disorder of the circadian rhythm in which a person has no trouble maintaining sleep, but cannot fall asleep and wake up at the same time as the rest of society (Dagan, 2002). Melinda essentially lives with a constant six hours of jet lag.

Delayed sleep phase syndrome is not the only disorder of the circadian rhythm. Another is **advanced sleep phase syndrome**, in which a person falls asleep much earlier than the rest of society and wakes up much earlier (Toh et al., 2001). Finally, in **non-24-hour sleep-wake syndrome**, the period of the circadian rhythm is warped to be much longer or shorter than the normal 24-hour cycle, rendering a person incapable of aligning their sleep patterns to the social norm (Okawa & Uchiyama, 2007).

Melinda has had a difficult time holding on to jobs that require her to

FIGURE 10.11 **Construction workers take a nap on a steel beam above Manhattan in 1932.**

be present early in the morning. This is not because of her lack of dedication to the job, she tries to explain, but instead because of her biological clock. Patients with these disorders of the circadian rhythm typically work to adapt their lives and careers around their own rhythms. "Instead of changing myself to keep other people's schedule," she says, "I have changed my life so I can function on my time." She operates a freight brokerage business that she runs from home. Melinda's children share the disorder, and she homeschools

them through the afternoon and evening (Pierce, 2008).

Some companies have recognized that circadian rhythms differ for different people and that it is not necessary to force everyone into the same time mold (FIGURE 10.11). Netflix, for example, does not keep track of their employees' work hours, just so long as their work produces results. Netflix spokesman Steve Swasey points out that rigid office hours are a "relic of the industrial age" (Pierce, 2008).

The Circadian Rhythm and Napping

Most of us sleep only once in the 24-hour cycle. But the single, long period of daytime wakefulness that follows is not necessarily the way our natural rhythms have evolved. You have certainly noticed that you experience a dip during the afternoon when you feel less alert. The basic circadian rhythm that makes you sleepy at nighttime contains a second rhythm that nudges you toward a nap in the early afternoon. The decrease in the circadian arousal occurs in part because of the effects of endogenous melatonin interacting with the melatonin receptors within the SCN (Broughton, 1998).

It turns out that sleeping only once at nighttime, as most of us do, is not the only way to get the optimal amount of sleep. Some people engage in **polyphasic sleep** (also known as segmented sleep), meaning that they sleep more than once in a 24-hour period (FIGURE 10.12). For example, one polyphasic sleep technique is to sleep twice, once for 6 hours during the night and again in the afternoon for 90 minutes. Other commonly used patterns include sleeping for a half hour every 6 hours (the sleep pattern of Buckminster Fuller) ("Dymaxion Sleep," 1943), or napping 15–30 minutes every 4 hours (the alleged sleep pattern of Leonardo da Vinci) (Stampi & Davis, 1991). The obvious advantage of polyphasic sleep is that the total number of hours can be greatly reduced from 8 hours, in some cases down to 2–4 hours of sleep per night without ill effects (Fuller, Brattinga, & de Jong, 1958). These different patterns of polyphasic sleep are shown in FIGURE 10.12d.

The pattern of polyphasic sleep is common in historically older cultures and in current nonindustrialized societies, especially during the winter months (Wehr 2001; Ekirch 2005). Even in industrialized countries, many cultures engage in a daily afternoon nap, or *siesta*, sleeping for an hour after lunch before returning to work. In general, infants and the elderly have natural polyphasic sleep patterns, as do many patients after head injury (Askenasy & Rahmani, 1987; Reynolds, Kupfer, & Sewitch, 1985). Polyphasic sleep is often adopted in the military, especially in missions that do not easily allow for long periods of unalertness (K. Opstad, 2000).

Polyphasic sleep forms the norm, not the exception, throughout the animal kingdom (Campbell & Tobler, 1984). Some researchers take our unusual **monophasic sleep** schedule not as evidence that we have evolved to be fundamentally different, but instead that we are merely *capable* of fighting off sleep when we don't want it (for example, with the help of caffeine) and forcing sleep when we feel we should be getting it (for example, with sleeping pills) (Campbell & Murphy, 2007).

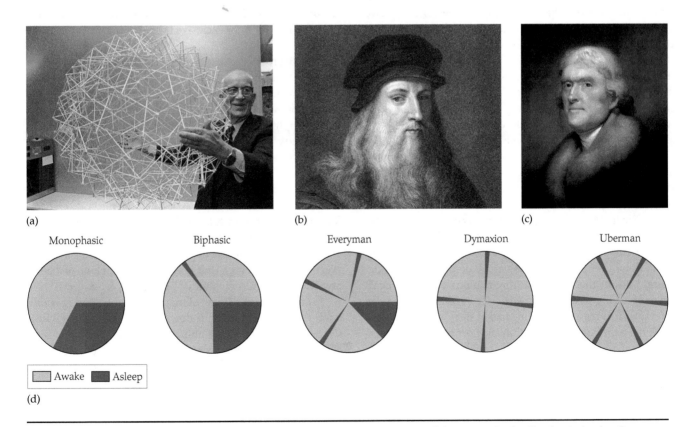

(a)

(b)

(c)

Monophasic   Biphasic   Everyman   Dymaxion   Uberman

☐ Awake ■ Asleep

(d)

FIGURE 10.12 **Polyphasic sleep.** Some people sleep more than once in a 24-hour period, claiming that this is more natural and enables them to sleep less time overall than they would if they slept just once. Some famous individuals thought to have used this polyphasic sleep schedule include (a) Buckminster Fuller, (b) Leonardo da Vinci, and (c) Thomas Jefferson. (d) Different patterns of polyphasic sleep are shown.

THE BIGGER PICTURE:
Schools and Circadian Rhythms

As children enter their adolescent years, the circadian rhythm naturally shifts later, causing them to have trouble falling asleep early and difficulty getting out of bed early (Duffy, Dijk, Hall, & Czeisler, 1999). Unfortunately, high schools have moved to a trend of beginning earlier and earlier, with many of them, at least in America, starting first classes at 7:30 a.m. Although this schedule is convenient for parents trying to get to work, it does not concord with the biological needs of the children. These early-morning classes may explain the excessive sleepiness and low retention of information from those classes (Kopasz et al., 2010), although that has not been decisively proven yet by neuroscience. In an attempt to address this possible cause, several legislators, inspired by new knowledge from the neuroscience community, have been campaigning to better align school time with circadian rhythms of teenagers (Born, Costantini, Naegeli, & Rolfes, 2007). In experiments in Massachusetts, several schools have moved their starting classes one hour later. In these studies, the students are more alert, grades have improved, and students and teachers are happier (Cline, 2011).

Why Do Brains Sleep?

Sleep entails lost time and reduced defenses, so it is striking that all species across the animal kingdom engage in it. In fact, animals in situations that do not easily allow for sleep have evolved elaborate mechanisms to obtain it. Take as an example the Indus river dolphin, which lives in river waters so muddy that it long ago became effectively blind, and instead expertly navigates by echolocation. Because strong currents and fast-moving debris are a constant feature of life in the river Indus, the dolphin cannot afford to sleep for long periods of time the way most creatures can. Therefore, it has evolved to sleep for short bursts, from 4 to 60 seconds, and it does this enough to add up to an amazing 7 hours per day (Tobler, 1995). This amazing adaptation underscores an important clue for us: sleep must serve a necessary function because otherwise it would be likely to go away completely, like the Indus dolphin's vision. But it appears that sleep, even with an elaborate adaptation, remains to serve some key biological function.

The importance of sleep is further supported by the Indus dolphin's cousins, the bottlenose dolphin and the porpoise. Both of these air-breathing mammals face the challenge of having to come to the surface to breathe at regular intervals. This regular surfacing makes sleep a difficult proposition. So the bottlenose dolphin and porpoise have evolved a different sort of solution to the problem: the two hemispheres of the brain take turns going to sleep (Mukhametov, 1987). Again, these complex adaptations suggest that sleep serves some important biological function.

Given the missed opportunities while asleep and the dangers of sleeping—as well as the convoluted evolutionary adaptations that come about to allow it—sleep clearly seems to perform some function for the nervous system. But what is it?

Four Theories of Sleeping: Restoration, Survival, Simulation, Learning

As for the purpose of sleep, the answers proposed over the years fall into four nonexclusive frameworks:

1. Sleep is restorative, saving energy and allowing metabolism to replenish.
2. Sleep provides a survival advantage by keeping animals out of trouble during the dark hours.
3. Sleep allows the simulation of rare situations to keep circuits "tuned up."
4. Sleep plays a role in information processing.

Theory 1: Sleep as Restoration

Sleep may be a metabolic necessity, helping the body recover from the work it did while awake. The amount of SWS correlates with the amount of exercise during the day (Shapiro et al., 1981). If people are deprived of SWS by being awoken every time they enter that stage, they complain of being physically tired (Lentz, Landis, Rothermel, & Shaver, 1999).

From the point of view of metabolism, serotonergic and noradrenergic neurons shut down completely during REM sleep (Fenik, Davies, & Kubin, 2005). One idea holds that REM sleep allows replenishment of stocks of neurotransmitters to be used during wakefulness (Ezenwanne, 2013). On the other hand, because of the high neural activity during REM, and even during NREM, sleep-as-restoration seems unlikely to be the entire answer (Backer, 1994).

Further, although sleep appears to be necessary to all species, there does not appear to be a fixed amount necessary (FIGURE 10.13). Horses sleep only about 3 hours per night,

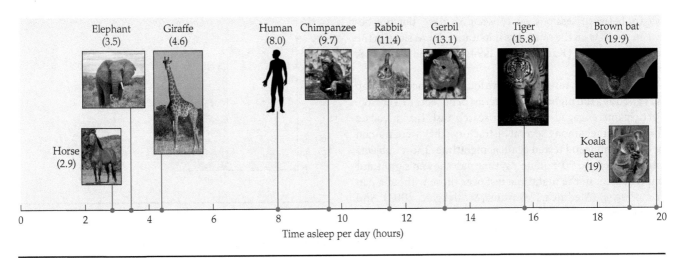

Elephant (3.5) Giraffe (4.6) Human (8.0) Chimpanzee (9.7) Rabbit (11.4) Gerbil (13.1) Tiger (15.8) Brown bat (19.9)

Horse (2.9) Koala bear (19)

Time asleep per day (hours)

FIGURE 10.13 **Different animals sleep for different amounts of time.** All animals require sleep, but how much they need varies across species.

whereas koala bears sleep 19 hours per day (Angellis, 2007; Campbell & Tobler, 1984). The high activity of horses and the low activity of koalas do not seem to accord with the sleep-as-restoration hypothesis.

Theory 2: Sleep as a Survival Advantage

Most animals find the search for food and water to be easier during the sunlight hours. At night, it is best for these animals to save energy, avoid getting eaten, and avoid falling off cliffs they cannot see. This framework proposes that sleep protects organisms who cannot see well in the dark and would run greater risks if active at night. In other words, sleeping confers a survival advantage (Meddis, 1975).

This framework seems to have little going for it: darkness as a survival threat can be addressed by the evolution of night vision. Relatedly, nocturnal animals sleep, but during the day. Finally, note that this theory sheds little light on the strange sleep habits of, for example, the dolphin species that we met at the beginning of this section.

Theory 3: Sleep to Simulate Rare Situations

Developing animals spend a much larger percentage of their sleep time in REM. This observation has invited speculations that nocturnal neural simulations may be a useful (or necessary) exercise before animals test out activities in the real world (Basner et al., 2008). Presumably, one would want to practice these programs with the musculature shut down. According to this theory, the periodic stimulation of the cortex in a semi-random and unspecific manner can maintain circuits vital for survival but rarely activated by external stimuli, such as emergency defense procedures (Gordon, 1992). No direct evidence supports this theory, but the neural data are at least consistent: during REM sleep, PGO waves stimulate the cortex in an apparently random way (Nelson et al., 1983). But some researchers have speculated that perhaps the PGO waves are not random after all and instead represent the signature of practicing neural programs.

A specific version of this framework, threat simulation theory, suggests that sleep exists to simulate threatening events and to rehearse threat perception and threat avoidance (Revonsuo, 2000). The theory suggests that people exposed to more survival threats in waking life should more commonly experience threat dreams at night. Researchers compared participants in a high-crime area in South Africa to those living in a low-crime area in Wales and obtained detailed dream reports over a long period of time. Contrary to the predictions of the threat simulation theory, those in the high-crime area actually reported a lower, not higher, number of threat dreams. Moreover, the overall incidence of realistic threats in dreams was lower than expected, about 20%, and escape from these threats only occurred in less than 2%, suggesting that it was not much of a simulation (Malcolm-Smith, Solms, Turnbull, & Tredoux, 2008). Such tests have therefore failed to support the threat simulation theory (Malcolm-Smith et al., 2008).

Theory 4: Sleep Plays a Role in Information Processing

Other theories propose that sleep plays an important role in learning and in consolidating memories, in forgetting potentially less important or incorrectly formed memories, and in comparing new memories with older memories or genetic instructions. In this view, sleep allows the brain to cement in important memories and to deprogram the miscellaneous events that are not to be stored (Siegel, 2001). The data most support the idea that sleep plays an informational role, and therefore we will concentrate on it for the remainder of this section, investigating examples of rehearsal, erasure (forgetting), and insight.

Rehearsal

REM sleep appears to play a critical role in learning. On visual discrimination tasks, for example, improved performance occurs between sessions on consecutive days, but not between sessions on the same day, implicating REM sleep in the learning process (Karni et al., 1994; Stickgold, James, & Hobson, 2000).

More recently, researchers have found evidence that a nap is as good as a full night's sleep in terms of benefits to learning. Participants engaged in a visual search task that involved finding a target among several distractors. They were trained in the morning and tested again at nighttime. Those subjects who had a 60- to 90-minute daytime nap showed significant improvement in the nighttime test over those without a nap (FIGURE 10.14) (Mednick, Nakayama, & Stickgold, 2003). And their improvement was comparable to that of other subjects who had a full night's sleep before testing. Interestingly, the nap was linked with improved performance only if it included both REM and SWS sleep stages. In the absence of one or the other, the learning improvements vanished.

But why does learning improve? Some evidence suggests that the **reactivation** of memories during sleep may underlie their long-term encoding (Wilson & McNaughton, 1994). Memories for events form in at least two stages, both of which involve the hippocampus: an initial process that occurs during the experience itself, followed by a consolidation period in which the experience becomes part of long-term memory. The consolidation stage requires sleep (Stickgold, 2005). In one study, researchers trained rats to scurry around a circular track for a food reward. Neurons known as place cells—which show distinct patterns of activity depending on the rat's location in the maze—were recorded from the rat's hippocampus. Subsequently, while the rats enjoyed REM sleep that night, the recordings continued. About half of the episodes of REM sleep repeated the exact pattern of hippocampal activity that was seen as the animal ran throughout the maze (Louie & Wilson, 2001; Wilson, 2002). In other words, the rat appeared to be *rehearsing* the trajectory it learned through the maze (FIGURE 10.15).

The correlation was so close that the researchers claimed that as the animal "dreamed," it could reconstruct where it

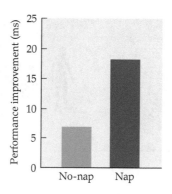

FIGURE 10.14 **Taking a nap improves learning.** Researchers found that taking a 60- to 90-minute nap significantly decreased the time needed to find a target among distractors. From Mednick, Nakayama & Stickgold (2003).

would be in the maze if it were awake. They could further determine, they suggested, whether the animal was dreaming of running or standing still. This same suggestion of "rehearsal" appears in songbirds, whose neural activity during sleep resembles their song production activity (Dave & Margoliash, 2000).

Previously, scientists thought that only a handful of species—among them chimps and dolphins—recalled and evaluated detailed sequences of events after they occurred (Smith, 1965). But these studies suggest that even rats' nocturnal visions may be constructed from the events of their daily lives and replayed in detail. This replay may be a part of consolidating events into long-term memory. It remains to be seen how teaching rats a variety of tasks will influence their dreams—that is, which waking patterns will create patterns when the animal is asleep. And perhaps technologies of the future may eventually be able to evaluate the content of dreams with higher resolution, but at the moment, this is science fiction.

The hypothesis emerging from these studies is that information replayed during sleep determines which events we

FIGURE 10.15 **Patterns of cellular activity during REM sleep resemble patterns in the same cells when learning the task.** Rats were trained to explore a circular maze to search for a food reward. While they were doing that, researchers recorded the pattern of activity of 10 place cells within the hippocampus (RUN). Later, the rats were allowed to sleep and the recordings continued (REM). The recordings closely resembled those made while the rats were awake, suggesting the rats were rehearsing what they learned while awake. From Louie and Wilson (2001).

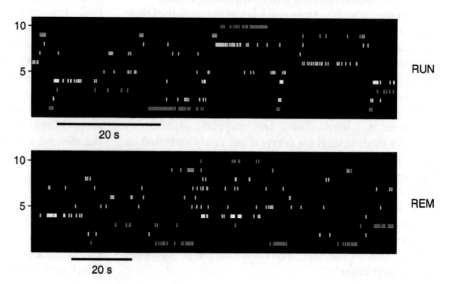

later remember. This is consistent with human studies in which the learning of repetitive tasks relies on REM sleep to enhance performance. In some cases, this "offline" practice session seems to be just as useful as practicing the experience when awake. Both rats and humans perform better at a recently learned task after a period of sleep (Walker & Stickgold, 2004). It has been speculated that dreams may represent an opportunity for us to continue to rehearse a problem while we're asleep (Walker & Stickgold, 2006).

The "dreaming" rat studies are consistent with a human study in which subjects who had never before played the video game Tetris learned to play the game. That night, the subjects dreamt of falling Tetris blocks. When subjects with amnesia were trained on the game, they reported the same dreams of the colorful falling blocks, but had no idea why they were dreaming about such things (Stickgold et al., 2000). Just as rats dream about repetitive tasks performed during the day, the Tetris players dreamed about their new video game experience.

Although much research has studied the effects of REM sleep on learning, SWS is also important in rehearsal and learning. The SWS activity involved in consolidation is not equally distributed across the brain. Instead, it is found most strongly in the areas involved in the task. For example, in one study human subjects performed a complex task requiring hand–eye coordination. Then they went to sleep. During posttraining sleep, SWS activity increased over normal levels *only* in the regions of the right parietal cortex that were involved in the task (Huber, Ghilardi, Massimini, & Tononi, 2004). This finding suggests that the slow-wave activity relates to synaptic potentiation triggered by the learning: the more synaptic strengthening, the more slow-wave activity. The size of the local increase in parietal slow-wave activity predicted performance enhancement in subsequent testing, supporting its role in learning. As a further test, the research team then wondered what would happen if they immobilized a participant's arm, leading to deteriorating motor performance and synaptic depression in the contralateral motor cortex. They found that during subsequent sleep, slow-wave activity over that cortical area lessened (Huber et al., 2006). Again, this slow-wave activity indicates not only that learning is taking place, but also the *location* in which it is taking place.

Forgetting

If dream sleep consolidates memories, this leaves open an important question: which experienced events are the important ones to cement in and which should be taken out with the neural trash? In 1749, the English philosopher David Hartley suggested that "the wilderness of our dreams seems to be of singular use to us, by interrupting and breaking the course of our associations. For, if we were always awake, some accidental associations would be so much cemented by continuance, as that nothing could afterwards disjoin them;

which would be madness" (Hartley, 1749). This idea was taken up again by Francis Crick and Graeme Mitchison, who in 1983 hypothesized that we dream to forget: that is, REM sleep erases spurious associations between neurons before they can inappropriately trigger synaptic plasticity and learning (Crick & Mitchison, 1983). In their model, a "reverse Hebbian" rule weakens (rather than strengthens) connections when a dream coactivates neighboring neurons. Note this theory posits forgetting as an *active* nightly practice—quite different from the traditional view of forgetting as a slow, global degradation of information.

Artificial associative neural networks turn into "memory mud" when they are exposed to too many associations. Crick and Mitchison were inspired to make their proposal not only by the fact that such networks fail, but also by the way in which they fail. When artificial networks become overloaded with associations, their output can mistakenly associate incorrect inputs, give the same output irrespective of the input, or respond to stimuli that would normally not evoke a response (Eppler & Mengis, 2004). These types of pathological output may loosely parallel fantasy, obsession, and hallucinations—all of which occur in humans following a lack of REM sleep (K. Opstad, 2000). Simulations in simple neural networks verify the benefits of actively downregulating weak associations caused by random input. In the absence of this active cleaning, the network will produce meaningless memories and have difficulty accessing real ones (Hopfield, Feinstein, & Palmer, 1983).

The view of dreams-to-forget parallels what we already know about development: new connections blossom richly and then are fine-tuned and thinned out by experience. In adults, according to this view, daily experience with the world leads to rich synaptic changes, and sleep then erases spurious associations ignited by random bursts of electrical activity that could otherwise become fantasies, obsessions, or hallucinations (Röschke & Aldenhoff, 1993). Crick and Mitchison later pointed out that some mammals—such as the spiny anteater (FIGURE 10.16)—do not have REM sleep

FIGURE 10.16 **Spiny anteaters have no REM sleep.**

and that these animals also have larger-than-normal brains. This suggests the possibility that animals without REM sleep require a larger brain (more storage volume) to prevent overloading (Crick & Mitchison, 1995).

Insight and the Restructuring of Information

The two ideas outlined above—rehearsal and forgetting—can operate hand in hand. But a deeper understanding of intelligent brains requires not simply consolidation and cleaning up, but also the *restructuring* of experience. This lies at the heart of what we call understanding and insight. And sleep appears to be involved in this process.

People often claim to have gained insight into a problem through sleep. Do you remember the story of Otto Loewi discovering neurotransmission with his Nobel Prize–winning experiment on the frog's heart (Chapter 3)? He had long believed that chemical transmission occurred in the nervous system, but he didn't know how to prove it—until one night when he woke up, having dreamed the outline of the frog heart experiment. He got up and jotted the experiment down, but the next morning discovered that he couldn't read his own handwriting. He went to sleep again that night and had the same dream again. In his biography, he relates of that second night: "I awoke again, at three o'clock, and I remembered what it [the experiment] was.... I got up immediately, went to the laboratory, made the experiment . . . and at five o'clock the chemical transmission of the nervous system was conclusively proved" (Baylor, 2001).

Recently, the connection between sleeping and insight has been supported by the results of experimental studies. In one report, subjects performed a cognitive task in which they learned to respond to particular cues with particular responses. Practice made them better at the task—but, unbeknownst to them, there was also a hidden rule underlying the order of the sequences (Wagner, Gais, Haider, Verleger, & Born, 2004). Figuring out this rule improved subjects' performance. After the initial training on the task, subjects experienced eight hours of sleep, nocturnal wakefulness, or daytime wakefulness. When subjects were retested, those who had slept were twice as likely to gain insight into the hidden rule, irrespective of the time of day (FIGURE 10.17). This suggests that sleep facilitates extraction of the hidden rule by restructuring memory.

The issue of insight and restructuring of information during sleep remains a wide-open field, in large part because we poorly understand these issues (even outside of the context of sleep). Clearly, insight and restructuring require rehearsal and forgetting, but they go beyond those concepts, involving a higher-level assessment of the results of the rehearsal as well. How insight comes about remains a challenge for a future generation of scientists.

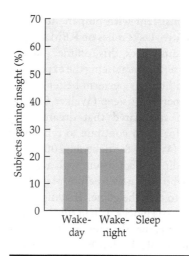

FIGURE 10.17 Effects of sleep and wakefulness on the probability of having an insight. Bars show the percentage of subjects gaining insight into a hidden rule of a game. Subjects either slept at night (right bar) or remained awake (during the day or night, left two bars) between the initial training and retesting. From Wagner et al. (2004).

Dreaming

As we saw at the beginning of this chapter, most dreaming occurs during REM sleep. During REM sleep, the brain remains isolated from its normal input, with only internal activation producing cortical stimulation. Infants spend half of their sleep time in REM, adults spend 10–20% of their sleep time in REM, and the elderly spend less than 15% of their sleep time in REM (Bes, Schulz, Navelet, & Salzarulo, 1991). Note that REM sleep is not equivalent to dreaming. Children have REM sleep, but experience little dreaming; the same was reported to be true of schizophrenia patients who underwent prefrontal lobotomies in the last century (Solms, 2000; Jus et al., 1973). Moreover, not all dreaming occurs during REM sleep: some forms of dreaming occur during NREM sleep (Kleitman, 1963). These NREM dreams are typically quite different from the more common REM dreams. On awakening from NREM sleep, subjects usually report no dream recollection whatsoever. If they do recollect mental activity, it usually relates to plans or elaborate thoughts and lacks the visual vividness and hallucinatory components of typical dreams (Suzuki et al., 2004).

Although dreams seem so ethereal, we do understand something of their neural underpinnings. Dreaming depends on the normal functioning of a relatively specific neural network located primarily in the limbic, paralimbic, and association areas (FIGURE 10.18). Defects in this network can produce temporary or permanent dream loss or impairment (such as loss of visual dream imagery) (Solms, 2000).

Further, note that the repetitive nightmares of post-traumatic stress disorder appear to be linked with the emotional hotbox of the limbic system. The repetition of the

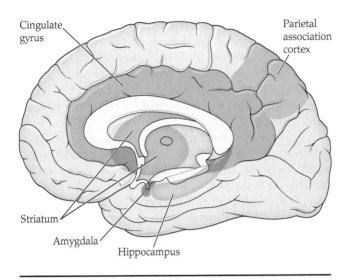

Cingulate gyrus

Parietal association cortex

Striatum

Amygdala

Hippocampus

FIGURE 10.18 The brain network involved in dreaming. Dreaming depends on the normal functioning of a relatively specific neural network located primarily in the parietal association cortex and the limbic and paralimbic systems.

nightmares parallels the persistence of negative emotional memories that get hardwired into the amygdala. The amygdala provides a record of fears and traumas; so do repetitive nightmares (De Bellis & Thomas, 2003).

Beyond these facts, much remains unknown about dreams. Does their content have meaning? Can dreaming shed any light on consciousness?

Dream Content

Dreaming is characterized by hallucination, strange beliefs, intense emotions, bizarreness, and a lack of memory. It appears that the onset of dreaming cannot be triggered by external stimuli, and dream content is largely impervious to the wide range of stimuli that have been used in an attempt to influence it (Dement & Kleitman, 1957a,b). One theory holds that dreams are the fortuitous derivative of two evolutionary adaptations: sleep and consciousness (Flanagan, 2000).

The meaning of dreams has always fascinated humans, spurring societies to invent cultural uses for dreams in religious ceremonies, medicinal practices, or doomed attempts to predict the future. Sigmund Freud (FIGURE 10.19), who lived decades before modern brain science, thought dreams provided an inroad into the underlying functions of the brain and especially the subconscious. He suggested, as had many before him, that dreams concealed hidden meanings that were just at the threshold of breaking through the barrier to consciousness. More specifically, he proposed that dreams constitute a disguised attempt at wish fulfillment (Freud, 1965). Similarly, Carl Jung suggested that dreams may offset features of character or personality that individuals may

FIGURE 10.19 Sigmund Freud proposed that dreams provided insight into the subconscious mind.

ignore while awake (Jung & von Franz, 1968). In general, both theories have been criticized because they cannot be proven wrong. Moreover, critics have pointed out that the wish-fulfillment interpretation seems improbable in view of the recurring nightmares that attend post-traumatic stress disorder (Notturno & McHugh, 1987).

Although people still disagree about the meaning of dream content, one modern theory suggests that dreams may have no meaning at all. The **activation-synthesis model** (Hobson & McCarley, 1977) proposes that random activity from the brainstem is sent to the cortex, which tries to turn it into motor output. But given paralysis of the major muscle groups, the brain must then explain the paradox between outgoing motor signals and a lack of expected sensory feedback. In this situation, the theory goes, the cortex "synthesizes" an explanation—essentially weaving a story from the random inputs. Note that in this theory, the dreams are "telling stories" to explain away random activity and thus have no consequential meaning at all. The proposers of the theory, Hobson and McCarley, faced criticism for this aspect of the theory because dreams do often have relationships to life experience (Revonsuo & Salmivalli, 1995).

Therefore, by 1988 they modified the idea to allow that dream content related to memories, fears, desires, hopes, and so on—but that these provide the background context (and not the exact content) of the cortex's interpretation of the random activity (Hobson, 1988).

Although the meaning of dreams remains uncertain, many researchers have studied the *content* of dreams. Those studies reveal a remarkable consistency of themes. Across cultures and across decades, the same kinds of dreams are reported—for example, being unable to find one's way or being late for an important event (Domhoff & Schneider, 2008). In their dreams, both men and women usually experience more aggression than friendliness (although men in almost all societies have greater physical aggression in their dreams than women do), more misfortune than good fortune, and more negative emotions than positive emotions (Domhoff, 2001). Cross-cultural research suggests that dreams are similar across a wide range of cultures in terms of subject matter, level of aggression, and familiarity with the people in the dreams (Domhoff, 1996). Other research suggests that the

dream content has not changed for college students over the second half of the 20th century despite major cultural changes (Hall, Domhoff, Blick, & Weesner, 1982).

Can dream content tell us anything about neural development? Let's look further into the clues. Dreaming develops gradually in children, with increased dream reporting in young children correlating with visuospatial skills. Preschool children's dreams are largely static, involving little movement (Foulkes, 1999). The same is true of adults with specific lesions in visual association cortex. Some adults with injuries to the parietal lobe on either side can lose the ability to dream altogether. Together, these data suggest that adult-like dreaming depends on the maturation of a neural network for dreaming centered in the parietal lobes, which are involved in spatial construction (Domhoff, 2001).

Beyond issues of movement, children's dream reports consist largely of boring, bland images: seeing an animal, thinking about eating and sleeping, and so on. Their dreams are remarkably bland in terms of level of aggression, misfortune, and negative emotion when compared to adult dreams

NEUROSCIENCE OF EVERYDAY LIFE:
Lucid Dreaming

One way in which people try to use dreams to understand consciousness is through **lucid dreaming**—a dream in which the sleeper realizes that he is dreaming (LaBerge, 2000). When lucid, a dreamer can often take control of the plot of the dream, choosing to fly, control other people's actions, or generally manipulate the physical world of the dream.

Lucid dreams can begin accidentally, when a sleeper recognizes that his experience is not actually representing the real world. But lucid-dream aficionados train themselves in a variety of ways to have lucid dreams more often. For example, one technique to induce lucid dreaming is to set an intention to look for signs of dreaming just before going to sleep. Such signs of dreaming can then be used to alert the dreamer to enter a lucid state in which he can take control (LaBerge, 2009).

FIGURE 10.20 **Dr. LaBerge presents research on Dream Time experiments at his *Dreaming and Awakening* workshop.**

The discovery and understanding of lucid dreaming has opened the door to probing several interesting questions about dreaming (FIGURE 10.20). As one example, consider the experience of time in dreams. Are 10 seconds in a dream the same as 10 seconds in the real world? To address this, researchers asked subjects to estimate 10 seconds in real life and then again in their lucid dream (LaBerge, 2000). While inside the dream, they indicated their time estimate by looking sharply to the left once at the beginning of the period and then again when they thought 10 seconds had passed. This was their way of communicating to the outside world: since their eye movements were being recorded in the sleep lab, the researchers could look at the time between the leftward events. In this way, researchers found evidence that real-time and dream-time (at least lucid-dream-time) were the same (LaBerge, 2000). So why does it often feel that dreams lasted such a long time? This is likely because we have false memories within dreams, such that the dream begins with a storyline already underway. When we wake up and attempt to describe the dream, the background storyline must be included in our description, and the whole event seems to have taken a longer time (Dement & Kleitman, 1957a,b).

If dreaming is the form that consciousness assumes during sleep, then lucid dreaming may be a product of a dream state in which the higher-order neural patterns that generate a representation of the *self* are more active than usual. This speculation is consistent with the higher levels of alpha wave activity during lucid dreaming than during normal REM (LaBerge, 2009).

(Foulkes, 1999). This has led to the speculation that dreaming may be a cognitive achievement that develops gradually, like language or walking (Domhoff, 2002).

Can Dreams Shed Light on Consciousness?

Let's take a moment to consider the bigger picture of why studying sleep can be important. One example is the quest to understand consciousness. Subjectively, it seems we are conscious during our dreams and unconscious during the rest of the sleep period—and that fact adds one more constraint in our search for the neural correlates of consciousness. As discussed in Chapter 8, scientists have speculated that a particular network of cells may be necessary for conscious experience, but we don't yet know what that network is. Could we possibly use dream sleep as a tool to separate out the parts of the brain responsible for conscious awareness (as during dreams) from those parts that seem to be unconscious during most of NREM?

As an example, one can compare the activation of visual areas during REM sleep and wakefulness, using NREM sleep as a control. The extrastriate visual areas are more activated during REM sleep than during NREM, with the activation higher in the ventral stream than in the dorsal stream (Braun et al., 1998) (recall that the ventral pathway is more correlated with our perceptions, whereas the dorsal pathway is more involved in visuospatial processing; see Chapter 5). Limbic and paralimbic regions—areas involved in emotions—are also more activated during REM than during NREM or even the awake state, corresponding with the high emotional content of dreams (Nofzinger, Mintun, Wiseman, Kupfer, & Moore, 1997). During REM high activity also occurs in several parts of the temporal lobe, which elicits vivid visual hallucinations in human epileptic patients (Epstein & Hill, 1966).

While dream sleep may become a useful tool to study consciousness, some caveats exist. Although dreams resemble conscious experience, there are important differences. First, the hippocampus and prefrontal cortex are less active during REM sleep than in the waking state, which could, in theory, explain why we have trouble remembering our dreams. Further, because not all of REM sleep includes dreaming, we could not look at brain activity during REM sleep and firmly conclude whether the subject was conscious at any given moment.

Dreams of the Future and How to Study Them

Future neuroscientists will face the challenge of tying different aspects of neuroscience firmly to the general nature of dreaming. Some promising leads have come from the way dream content changes with drugs and disease. Researchers hope to study the neural network for dreaming by determining how various drugs affect dream content. For example, dreams can be made more vivid and frightening by drugs affecting the dopaminergic system and by alkaloids (Solms, 1997). Antidepressants such as Prozac generally quicken sleep onset and suppress REM (FIGURE 10.21) (Mouret, Lemoine, Minuit, Benkelfat, & Renardet, 1988; Sharpley, Walsh, & Cowen, 1992). Systematic studies showing the effects of different drugs on dream content, in conjunction with neuroimaging studies, might pinpoint relationships between repetitive dream content and specific components of the dream-generation network. Patients suffering from epilepsy might be potential candidates for such content studies, because medications that eliminate epileptic seizures also reduce or eliminate the patients' nightmares (Berlin, 2007).

Another method of studying dream content includes examining the dream reports of patients in a wide variety of disease states. Specific neural defects can lead to the loss or impairment of dreaming. For example, adults can lose dreaming with injuries to the inferior parietal lobe on either side. Patients with certain forms of dementia have reported bland dreams involving less aggression, less narrative complexity,

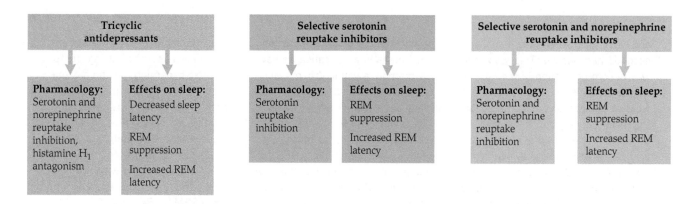

FIGURE 10.21 **Effects of antidepressant medications on sleep.** Different classes of antidepressant medication affect sleep in different ways.

and less emotional content, compared to people without these disorders (Kramer, Roth, & Trinder, 1975).

Remaining mysteries about sleeping and dreaming include the sense of rational organization that accompanies bizarre events and situations. Dream content has reasonable narrative flow. We seem to believe patently impossible situations in dreams, and we accept false memories during dreaming, even when they contradict events known to be true in waking life. Scientists seem to be some distance from directly tackling observations like these—hopefully, progress on other fronts will direct experiments forward into this fascinating territory.

Sleep Deprivation and Sleep Disorders

Sleep Deprivation

Whereas economists worry about the national debt, sleep scientists have become concerned about the national sleep debt. With the demands of modern life, many students and workers get less sleep than the demands of body and brain would call for. The effects of mild sleep deprivation (say, losing a few hours of sleep for one night) will be familiar to most readers: irritability, muscle aches, yawning, and difficulty maintaining attention. When young adults are deprived of 1–1.5 hours of sleep for a single night, their alertness decreases by up to 32% (Bonnet & Arand, 1996). Effects of sleep deprivation can be measured by how quickly a subject falls asleep in a dark, quiet situation. In general, across many studies, the main effects of mild sleep deprivation are increased sleepiness, reduced ability to stay concentrated, and disturbances of mood ("crabbiness") (Kahn-Greene, Killgore, Kamimori, Balkin, & Killgore, 2007).

With more severe sleep deprivation—say, lasting 2 or 3 days or longer—one also begins to experience **microsleeps**,

brief sleep periods in the second or even subsecond range. Common and dangerous for drivers on the road, microsleeps show up as a short moment of cognitive absence. Unfortunately, people experiencing microsleeps will often be unaware that they were just sleeping—they will instead believe themselves to have been awake or else to have temporarily "spaced out" (Durmer & Dinges, 2005). As you can imagine, for operators of heavy machinery or vehicles, these brief moments can have dire consequences.

Many studies show negative effects of chronic sleep deprivation on physical health, such as stress hormone levels, glucose metabolism, and heart disease (FIGURE 10.22). But the studies performed over the decades generally converge on a common theme: the effects of sleep deprivation are more detrimental to the mind than to the body. Subjects with sleep deprivation often perform fine on physical tasks the next day (although stamina tends to diminish a bit faster than it would if they were not sleep deprived)—but the most striking effects are on cognition and mood (Durmer & Dinges, 2005; P. Opstad, Ekanger, Nummestad, & Raabe, 1978).

Sleep deprivation is a real-world problem. Medical residents, pilots, soldiers, truck drivers, and others frequently work long shifts, which lead to sleep deprivation. Excessive sleep deprivation leads to poor decision making, which in turn may result in avoidable accidents (Rigaud & Flynn, 1995). For example, years of research make it clear that sleep deprivation causes doctors to make more errors reading charts, have lower performance because of disinclination to apply effort, and have decreased mood and poor attitudes (Eddy, 2005). A review of sleep deprivation studies on physicians from 1970 to 1990 showed that doctors could still respond without trouble to novel situations (for example, if asked to learn a new routine). But problems arise because they become more error prone on routine and repetitive tasks that characterize a night in the hospital: on these tasks, their decreased vigilance leads to mistakes (Cox, King, Hutchinson, & McAvoy, 2006).

Despite the adverse consequences of sleep deprivation, extraordinary cases exist in which someone can stay awake for a long time. We turn to one of the best documented of those cases on page 329.

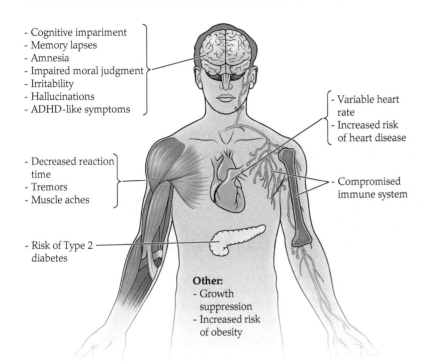

- Cognitive impariment
- Memory lapses
- Amnesia
- Impaired moral judgment
- Irritability
- Hallucinations
- ADHD-like symptoms

- Variable heart rate
- Increased risk of heart disease

- Decreased reaction time
- Tremors
- Muscle aches

- Compromised immune system

- Risk of Type 2 diabetes

Other:
- Growth suppression
- Increased risk of obesity

FIGURE 10.22 **Effects of sleep deprivation on cognitive function and the body.** Sleep deprivation affects many cognitive processes, as well as many other body processes.

In light of stories like Randy's below, one must be cautious in interpreting studies of long-term sleep deprivation. In a famous animal experiment on sleep deprivation, rats lived on a specialized platform in a cage, and every time they began to fall into slumber (as indicated by their EEG patterns), the platform would begin to rotate. If the rat didn't wake up immediately, it would be dunked into a shallow pool of water. Most of the sleep-deprived rats died within days to weeks (Rechtschaffen & Bergmann, 1995). However, later interpretations of this study have pointed out that the death of the rats may not have resulted from the sleep deprivation so much as the severe stress. After all, the rats also suffered from pathological thermoregulation (control of their body temperature), increased eating, imbalanced hormones, and lesions on their tail and feet (Rechtschaffen & Bergmann,

1995). In other words, it would be a stretch to attribute their untimely death to the sleep deprivation alone, especially in light of extraordinary demonstrations like Randy Gardner's week-and-a-half adventure of wakefulness.

Relatedly, people often report feeling unwell after a night of reduced sleep, but we must interpret these reports with caution: often the poor night of sleep comes from a stress inducer such as an important examination or deadline. The poor physical feelings that follow might be caused in large part by the effects of the stress from the event rather than the sleep deprivation itself (Minkel et al., 2012).

Finally, many people report a sensation that they have poor sleep and believe they are sleep deprived. However, measurements taken at home or in a sleep lab reveal that many people sleep better than they believe. Sometimes a

CASE STUDY:
Staying Awake

In 1964, a 17-year-old high school student named Randy Gardner decided he was going to shoot for the world's record for sleep deprivation (FIGURE 10.23). In collaboration with Stanford sleep researcher William Dement and physician John Ross, he was continuously monitored as he

kept himself awake for a stunning 264 hours (11 days) (Johnson, Slye, & Dement, 1965).

At the end of Gardner's extraordinary run of no sleep, he went to sleep and woke up feeling fine 14 hours and 40 minutes later. On subsequent nights, he slept a normal 8 hours. In

other words, he didn't require catching up on a "sleep debt"; he merely fell back into the normal rhythm.

Dr. Dement, the sleep researcher who monitored Randy, reported that the main effect of the sleep deprivation was on Randy's mood, involving all the changes that are typical of fatigue, such as irritability and mood swings. Dr. Dement wrote that the deprivation had had little effect on Randy's cognitive abilities, pointing out that on the 10th day Randy was able to win at a game of pinball, and by day 11 Randy gave a press conference in which he appeared healthy and his speech was unslurred (Moorcroft, 1993). However, Dr. Ross, the presiding physician, reported a somewhat different story (Ross, 1965). Beyond the mood swings, Ross reported extreme problems with Randy's ability to concentrate. For example, when asked to start at 100 and continuously subtract 7, Randy stopped about a third of the way through. When Ross asked him if he was stuck, Randy replied that he forgot what he was doing. Randy also appeared to have paranoia and hallucinations, as well as a delusion (by the 4th day) that he was a famous football player. At one point, he mistook a street sign for a person. So the

FIGURE 10.23 Sleep deprivation. Dr. William Dement (left) talks with American student Randy Gardner about the results of a polygraph test during a sleep deprivation experiment (San Diego, California, 1964). Gardner set the world record during the experiment, staying awake for more than 264 hours.

effects of staying awake that long may not have been as harmless as Dr. Dement wanted to portray. In any case, the fact that such an extraordinary stretch without sleep is even possible serves as an important data point for any theory of sleep.

Subsequent to Randy's extraordinary experience, other claims at the sleep deprivation record have been made, extending to 18 days, 17 hours, but these are less well documented and did not monitor for microsleeps (Butler, 2011). The Guinness World Records no longer maintains a sleep deprivation record for fear of encouraging people to try this at the risk of health consequences.

period of wakefulness in the middle of the night gives the lasting impression of a poor night's sleep, when in fact the period was only a few minutes (Pinto et al., 2009).

We have seen that acute sleep deprivation causes negative changes in both cognition and mood. But there is an interesting postscript to this issue, because the brain appears to display long-term adaptability to consistent sleep reduction over a period of time. For example, one study showed that when participants successively reduce their sleep by just a small amount each week, they can work their way down to about five and a half hours of sleep with no ill effects (Porter, Kershaw, & Ollerhead, 2000). As long as the amount of sleep is relatively steady from one night to the next, one can adjust the nervous system to get by on less sleep than usual. Subjects in one such study slowly reduced their sleep until they were functioning at up to 18 hours less sleep per week than before the study (Porter et al., 2000). One year into the study, their performances on cognitive tasks displayed no detectable deficits.

Although many people suffer sleep deprivation because of their circumstances, some people suffer chronic sleep disorders, the most common medical complaint second only to pain (Mahowald & Schenck, 2005). There are currently about 100 different types of wake–sleep disorders, but almost all can be encompassed in four categories: insomnia (difficulty falling to sleep or maintaining sleep), **hypersomnia** (extreme daytime sleepiness), **parasomnias** (complex behaviors performed during sleep), and circadian rhythm disorders. We discussed circadian rhythm disorders earlier; we now turn to the other three.

Insomnia

Insomnia, the most common sleep problem, involves not getting enough sleep to feel rested the following day (**FIGURE 10.24**). Scientists currently understand insomnia as a continuous state of **hyperarousal**: compared to people without insomnia, insomniacs are less sleepy during the day, have a higher metabolic rate, and show more activity in EEG (Bonnet & Arand, 2000; Mahowald & Schenck, 2005). A bidirectional link can also exist between insomnia and psychiatric disorders—that is, one can lead to the other (Breslau, Roth, Rosenthal, & Andreski, 1996). In contrast, although insomnia often grows from psychiatric conditions, it can also be part of one's biological makeup, unrelated to any other condition.

To confront insomnia, some people take **hypnotics** (sleep aids). Although people have used dozens of compounds as hypnotics over the millennia—such as opium and barbiturates—these often lead to addiction and respiratory

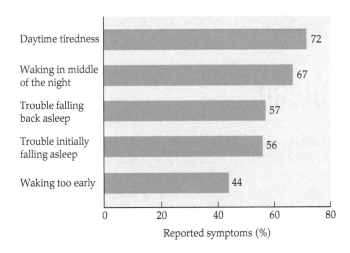

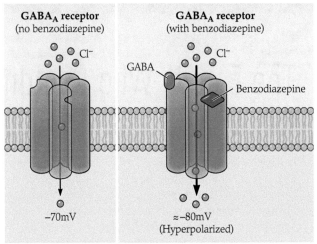

FIGURE 10.24 Symptoms of insomnia. The frequency of different symptoms of insomnia reported by patients. From Ancoli-Israel and Roth (1999).

FIGURE 10.25 Effect of benzodiazepine on GABA$_A$ receptor. Benzodiazepines are agonists to the GABA$_A$ receptor, allowing more chloride ions to enter the cell, resulting in hyperpolarization.

problems (Neubauer, 2007). Unregulated over-the-counter sleep aids (such as valerian, hops, lavender, and melatonin) generally appear to be of no benefit for insomnia (National Institutes of Health, 2005). The over-the-counter hypnotics that are approved by the Food and Drug Administration are all antihistamines. These may produce not only next-morning sleepiness, but also eventual tolerance to the sedating effects and the risk of several side effects (National Institutes of Health, 2005). Only a few approved classes of pharmaceutical treatments exist for insomnia: these include the **benzodiazepines**, as well as a class of nonbenzodiazepine medications (sometimes known as "Z-drugs") with similar effects to the benzodiazepines, and a selective melatonin receptor agonist.

The benzodiazepine medications and the Z-drugs modulate the effects of the neurotransmitter GABA, the most common inhibitory neurotransmitter in the central nervous system (FIGURE 10.25). Specifically, benzodiazepines interacting with the GABA$_A$ receptor complex change the conformation of the proteins so that more chloride ions enter the cell and cause greater polarization of the neuron. Generally, medications that promote GABA activity are used as sedatives, muscle relaxants, anxiolytics, and anticonvulsants, as well as hypnotics. Although a generalized cortical sedating effect may contribute to the hypnotic action of benzodiazepine receptor agonists, there likely is an important targeted action at the ventrolateral preoptic nucleus, a key structure involved in sleep promotion, as we saw earlier (Mendelson, 2002). In 2005, the Food and Drug Administration approved a new insomnia medication with a novel mechanism of action: an agonist for selected melatonin receptors, which are present in the suprachiasmatic nucleus (Sanfilippo, 2005).

Insomnia can take a heavy toll in terms of mood and productivity. In the most extreme and rare cases, it can be fatal, as seen in the following case.

Thankfully, cases of insomnia are typically much milder, and more treatable, than fatal familial insomnia. For example, one of the most common forms of insomnia is **restless legs syndrome (RLS)**, in which a person upon falling asleep feels unbearable discomfort in the legs that calls for relief by stomping, rubbing, walking around, or twitching the legs. RLS is experienced by 5–15% of the population. It appears to have a genetic component because it runs in families (Allen et al., 2005; Montplaisir et al., 1997; Watson, Dikmen, Machamer, Doherty, & Temkin, 2007). Fortunately, dopaminergic medications successfully address RLS in most cases (Ferini-Strambi, 2009).

Hypersomnia

People with hypersomnia suffer an excessive amount of sleepiness, typically in recurring episodes. This is different from being tired because of a late night out on the town, but instead exists at such a high level that one has no choice but to nap frequently during the day. This includes napping at inappropriate times, such as in the middle of a conversation, in a work meeting, or while eating lunch. The naps typically provide little relief from the excessive sleepiness. Hypersomnia often comes with anxiety, disorientation upon waking, diminished energy, and memory problems. As you can imagine, people with hypersomnia often cannot participate in the normal settings of family and work life.

Hypersomnia sometimes occurs as a result of taking medications for depression, as a result of excess body weight, or from brain damage (Bluthé, Dantzer, & Kelley, 1997; Detre, Himmelijoch, & Swartzburg, 1972). Treatment options for hypersomnia typically target the symptoms because the cause is often unknown.

Hypersomnia is the main symptom of **narcolepsy**. A narcoleptic experiences extreme fatigue that leads to falling into naps at inappropriate times. Some narcoleptics also suffer poor nighttime sleep. In addition, some people with narcolepsy experience **cataplexy**, in which their muscles suddenly

CASE STUDY:
The Family Who Couldn't Sleep

What would it be like to never sleep again? In 1978, an Italian woman in her forties went to the doctor with a terrible insomnia. Sleeping aids were useless—she simply couldn't fall asleep anymore. As the toll of insomnia grew over the course of a few months, she could no longer walk and could barely speak. Within one year of the onset of her insomnia, she passed away, her body exhausted. A year later, the woman's sister presented with exactly the same symptoms and soon died the same death. For both women, their minds remained sharp as their bodies disintegrated from beneath them.

Dr. Ignazio Roiter, a nephew (by marriage) to these two sisters, was drawn to this mystery and began to plumb his wife's family tree for clues. He discovered that this fatal insomnia had struck down other ancestors in the family tree, and he suspected he was on the trail of a rare genetic disorder. When his wife's uncle Silvano came to visit, Dr. Roiter spotted the early onset of the symptoms. He convinced Silvano to go to an Italian sleep clinic in 1984, where his worsening insomnia and progressive decline were documented on videotape. Eventually Silvano died with an exhausted body at the age of 52.

Silvano's brain was quickly removed and flown to a lab at Case Western Reserve University in Cleveland. Dr. Pierluigi Gambettito, a neuropathologist, examined the brain and noticed that it was shot through with tiny holes, like a sponge. This reminded him of something he'd seen before: the spongiform encephalopathy (spongelike brain disease) known as Creutzfeldt–Jacob disease, the human form of mad cow disease. Gambettito picked up the phone and called Dr. Stanley Prusiner in California, a scientist who had recently suggested that these encephalopathies were caused by abnormal proteins called prions.

Examination of Silvano's brain provided the key to the mystery: the insomniac family was indeed the victim of a prion disorder. Dr. Prusiner won the Nobel Prize in 1997 for his work on prions, in part for the work on this Italian family.

In the intervening years, more than 30 other families have been discovered who are carriers of this genetic disorder, now known as **fatal familial insomnia** (Lugaresi & Provini, 2007).

---

weaken (Nishino & Kanbayashi, 2005). This can manifest as a slight sagging to a complete shutdown of the muscles leading to total collapse (FIGURE 10.26). How can we understand this? Note that narcoleptics will fall abruptly into REM sleep directly from the waking state, whereas the normal progression passes through the stages of NREM first. Recall that in REM sleep, the major skeletal muscles are shut down by an inhibitory pathway that descends the spinal cord. The cataplexy seen in narcolepsy is a manifestation of this atonia: the body drops straight into REM sleep and causes the major muscle groups to stop functioning. Mistimed atonia also plays a role in another common symptom of narcolepsy: **sleep paralysis**. Here, the REM atonia commences before it should, leaving an awake person paralyzed; in other cases, it lasts longer than it is supposed to, such that the brain wakes up but the body is unable to move for a short period. Narcoleptics also experience **hypnagogic hallucinations**, in which illusory visions or sounds present themselves in the transition between wakefulness and sleep, and **automatic behaviors**, in which a person will spontaneously produce purposeless sounds or acts without conscious intervention or censorship.

Narcolepsy appears to be a genetic condition. In the late 1990s it was discovered that narcolepsy results from a lower level of a hormone called **orexin** or **hypocretin**. This

FIGURE 10.26 Narcolepsy. This dog is experiencing cataplexy, a symptom of narcolepsy in which all the muscles weaken suddenly, resulting in collapse.

hormone promotes wakefulness. Researchers soon discovered that narcoleptics have fewer orexin/hypocretin-producing neurons than those without narcolepsy (Mieda et al., 2004). Subsequently, other researchers identified narcolepsy as an **autoimmune disorder**, in which the immune system attacks these neurons (Hallmayer et al., 2009).

Remember the flip-flop system of sleep and wake (FIGURE 10.6)? Scientists now think that the orexin/hypocretin system works to stabilize the system in the waking state. Without the proper level of these molecules, the flip-flop is unstable and can switch states at inappropriate times (Mieda et al., 2004).

Parasomnias

We've been talking about the states of sleep and waking as a flip-flop system, but keep in mind that each state consists of a vast network of different areas. These areas typically work together in a smooth manner: when the flip-flop switches, all the appropriate systems come online while others go offline. But given the complexity and size of the networks, the brain sometimes gets caught between stages—that is, some neural areas have completed the "switchover" whereas others have not. In these cases, we find parasomnias: actions performed during sleep that are not under voluntary control—for example, sleepwalking, also known as **somnambulism**, as in the case of the sleepwalker who began this chapter (Plante & Winkelman, 2006).

Parasomnias used to be thought to be a single disorder, but they are now understood to represent a mixture of the waking state and NREM sleep (known as NREM parasomnias) or waking and REM (known as REM parasomnias). Both types come into being as the brain transitions from one state to the next.

NREM parasomnias are disorders of arousal that happen when a sleeper's brain tries to move directly from SWS to the waking state and becomes caught in between. Besides sleepwalking, this category of parasomnias includes talking in one's sleep (somniloquy), sleep eating, teeth grinding, and **night terrors**, in which a sleeper will bolt up in bed in fear, often accompanied by screaming or gasping, with a temporary inability to regain consciousness. Most of these NREM parasomnias exist more commonly in childhood and tend to diminish in frequency with age (FIGURE 10.27). For example, whereas up to 17% of children experience sleepwalking episodes, sleepwalking remains in only 4% of adults (Mahowald & Schenck, 2005).

The most common REM parasomnia is **REM sleep behavior disorder**, in which the muscle atonia that usually accompanies the REM stage is absent. Sleepers therefore will act out their dreams, which usually results in injury to themselves or others. Ninety percent of patients with this disorder are male, and they will sometimes try to deal with the problem by tying themselves directly to the bed and/or constructing fortresses of pillows (Boeve, 2010). We previously discussed another common REM parasomnia, sleep paralysis, in which the brain exits REM into the waking state but the atonia temporarily persists. Fortunately, many parasomnias can be managed successfully using behavioral and pharmacologic therapies.

In closing, we'll mention that as the neuroscience of sleep progresses, new parasomnias are being identified. For

	Night terrors	Sleepwalking
Time during sleep	Early	Early–mid
Sleep stage	Slow wave sleep	Slow wave sleep
Presence of screaming	Significant	No
CNS activation	Significant	Slight
Motor activity	Slight	Significant
Awakens	No	No
Duration/minutes	1–10	2–30
Post-event confusion	Slight	Slight
Genetic association	Slight	Slight

FIGURE 10.27 NREM parasomnias in children. Some of the characteristics of night terrors and sleepwalking in children.

example, a newly described NREM parasomnia is sleep sex, or sexomnia, in which a person engages in sexual acts while asleep (Schenck, Arnulf, & Mahowald, 2007). Several defendants in sexual assault trials have been found not guilty because of their sexomnia (Xu, 2008). The reaction of many people is to decry this plea as an excuse. Now that you have read this chapter, you might instead understand that there are detectable differences in the activity of the sleeping brain in people with parasomnias. Although we tend to assume the brain must be either awake or asleep, many well-studied phenomena, like the parasomnias considered here, present the brain truly caught in an intermediate state between the two. In a network of a hundred billion neurons, there is room for a tremendous diversity of different modes of activity—many of which we are only just beginning to understand.

Conclusion

We still do not know why we spend so much of our lives in the doppelganger brain state of sleep. Arguments from different angles suggest sleep promotes restoration, keeps us out of trouble in the dark, allows us to practice neural programs, and/or helps us consolidate memories. These suggestions are neither exclusive nor, perhaps, complete. It remains to be understood how sleep restructures memory and inspires insight. Dream content might tell us about the neural underpinnings, and someday we may even measure the neural underpinnings to read out dream content. Studying dreaming may help us comprehend consciousness. Understanding the effects on sleep and dreaming from a host of perturbations—including trauma, drugs, and disease—is a rich field for future progress. We need new research paradigms to generate data related to the organization of mental functions during dream sleep and the neural similarities between REM sleep and an awake state.

At the beginning of this chapter, we introduced Kenneth Parks, the man who killed his mother-in-law during an apparent sleepwalking episode. The idea of murdering in one's sleep tends to challenge public credulity, eliciting accusations of fraud and pretense. But whatever the merits of an individual case, we know that sleepwalking is a real phenomenon. We learned that transitions between waking and sleeping result from opposing networks (FIGURE 10.6), and we also learned that parasomnias can result when those networks don't hand off power smoothly.

As we saw in FIGURE 10.4, a normal sleep cycle moves from stage 3 to stage 2 to stage 1, and from there into wakefulness. But Kenneth's EEG revealed a NREM parasomnia: ten to twenty times each night, his brain networks attempted to transition from stage 3 directly to wakefulness. The jury understood that there was no way for Kenneth to intentionally fake EEG results, and so the measures proved critical to his defense.

In May of 1988, after hours of deliberation, the jury declared Kenneth Parks "not guilty"—neither of the murder of his mother-in-law nor of the assault on his father-in-law. However,

other cases have not fared similarly. In 1997, Scott Falater was accused of stabbing his wife 44 times and holding her head underwater. He pled homicidal somnambulism but was convicted to life in prison (Teacher, 2009). In total, there have been some 68 cases of homicidal somnambulism tried in North America, going back to the 1600s (Jonston as cited in Collin, 1818; Smith-Spark, 2005). More recently, parasomnia defenses have been mounted in cases of "sleep sex." Can the legal system assume that some of these defenses represent fakery? Perhaps. But presumably not all of them; in many cases, defendants have been acquitted via careful measurements of brain activity.

The vast majority of somnambulists are nonviolent. However, note that Kenneth had been suffering from insomnia, was depressed, was trying to overcome a gambling problem, and had financial and marital problems—and he had been massively sleep deprived from not having slept the night before the event. Although it is difficult to know exactly how these factors played a role, the physiology of his brain, as measured in an EEG laboratory, was the clinching piece of evidence in convincing the jury that he did, indeed, suffer from abnormal transitions from SWS to the waking state—transitions that made his actions involuntary. Cases like Kenneth's highlight the mysterious and poorly understood borderlands between wakefulness and sleep.

The three states of waking, REM sleep, and NREM sleep differ fundamentally: they represent the same machinery running different tasks. One of the amazing features of the brain is its ability to transition—usually without a problem—between these states. Although the parasomnias represent cases in which the brain has trouble getting a state fully into place, it is notable that these do not happen more often.

KEY PRINCIPLES

- All species sleep, indicating that sleep is an important biological function.

- The brain is active during sleep—essentially as active as it is during wakefulness.

- The brain operates in three distinct states, as can be seen via electroencephalography: wakefulness, REM sleep, and NREM sleep. These fundamentally different states represent the same machinery running different tasks.

- A natural internal rhythm known as the circadian clock keeps the sleep–wake cycle aligned with darkness and daylight.

- Although sleep may be involved in restoration and the practice of neural programs, its main function seems to be one of learning and restructuring of information.

- Dream content may result from a combination of memories, fears, desires, and hopes, all interpreted within the context of random cortical activity.

- Dreams happen predominantly during REM sleep and depend on the activity of a network of limbic, paralimbic, and associational areas.

- Short-term sleep deprivation has negative consequences on cognition and mood; however, long-term adjustments to shorter sleep periods are possible.

- Sleep is a function of the brain that is implemented by a complex network of neural areas; several sleep disorders exist as breakdowns in communication within this network.

KEY TERMS

Sleep and the Brain

field potential (p. 312)

delta waves (p. 312)

theta waves (p. 312)

alpha waves (p. 312)

beta waves (p. 312)

gamma waves (p. 312)

brain waves (p. 312)

electrooculography (p. 313)

electromyography (p. 313)

slow-wave sleep (SWS) (p. 313)

ventrolateral preoptic nucleus (VLPO) (p. 314)

insomnia (p. 314)

arousal network (p. 314)

tuberomammillary nucleus (p. 314)

mutual inhibition (p. 314)

bistable (p. 314)

atonia (p. 315)

PGO waves (pontogeniculo-occipital waves) (p. 315)

thalamocortical cells (p. 315)

The Circadian Rhythm

circadian rhythm (p. 316)

endogenously generated (p. 316)

suprachiasmatic nucleus (SCN) (p. 316)

entrained (p. 316)

zeitgebers (p. 316)

melanopsin (p. 317)

retinohypothalamic tract (p. 317)

pineal gland (p. 317)

melatonin (p. 317)

jet lag (p. 318)

delayed sleep phase syndrome (p. 318)

advanced sleep phase syndrome (p. 318)

non-24-hour sleep–wake syndrome (p. 318)

polyphasic sleep (p. 319)

monophasic sleep (p. 319)

Why Do Brains Sleep?

reactivation (p. 322)

Dreaming

activation-synthesis model (p. 325)

lucid dreaming (p. 326)

Sleep Deprivation and Sleep Disorders

microsleeps (p. 328)

hypersomnia (p. 330)

parasomnias (p. 330)

hyperarousal (p. 330)

hypnotics (p. 330)

benzodiazepines (p. 331)

restless legs syndrome (RLS) (p. 331)

narcolepsy (p. 331)

cataplexy (p. 331)

fatal familial insomnia (p. 332)

sleep paralysis (p. 332)

hypnagogic hallucinations (p. 332)

automatic behaviors (p. 332)

orexin (p. 332)

hypocretin (p. 332)

autoimmune disorder (p. 332)

somnambulism (p. 333)

night terrors (p. 333)

REM sleep behavior disorder (p. 333)

REVIEW QUESTIONS

1. Sleep has been suggested to achieve several purposes. List three.

2. How does the brain regulate its own state of sleep and wakefulness?

3. How does the same hardware run different programs (awake mode versus asleep mode)?

4. Orexin has been described as a "wakefulness-promoting" hormone. In one sentence, how does it do its job?

5. Is sleeping for remembering or for forgetting? Explain your answer.

CRITICAL-THINKING QUESTIONS

1. Does it make sense to think of sleep as a "default" state of the brain, whereas wakefulness requires special activity? Or is it the other way around? Or is neither state the default state? Argue for a position.

2. People often report feeling physically unwell after a night of reduced sleep. However, the poor night of sleep often results from a stress inducer such as an important examination or a deadline. How would you design an experiment to test whether the poor physical feelings are caused more by the stress inducers or by sleep deprivation itself? Explain.

3. Make an argument that conscious perception is just "awake dreaming."

LEARNING OBJECTIVES   By the end of this chapter, you should be able to:

- Define speech, language, and communication.

- Describe how the brain systems underlying language can go awry.

- Identify the network of brain areas implicated in speaking and understanding.

- Explain the functional differences between the brain's hemispheres.

- Assess the interaction of genetic and environmental influences on language acquisition.

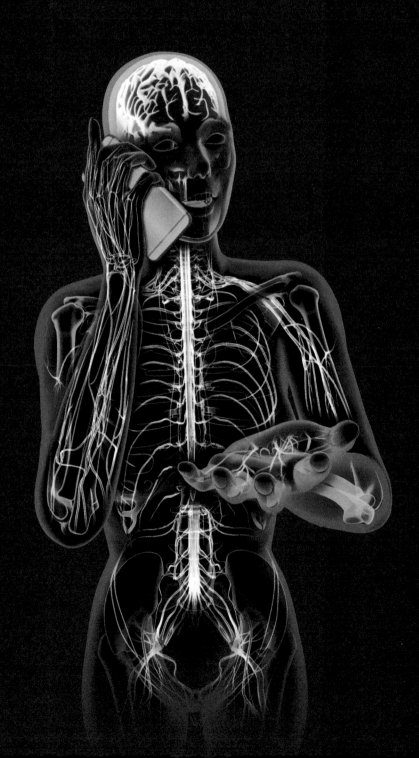

Language and Lateralization

STARTING OUT:
The Stuttering King

The brain has captivated filmmakers and actors in Hollywood. In 2010, Leonardo DiCaprio starred in two major hits, one about dreams (*Inception*) and the other about psychiatric illness and lobotomy (*Shutter Island*). In 2011, we were thrilled with the potential to take a drug to make us *Limitless* and the idea of salvaging the brain and running *Source Code* on it.

In line with this interest in neuroscience, the 2010 Academy Award for Best Picture went to a film about a man who cannot articulate a simple string of words. *The King's Speech* wasn't simply about a monarch who stutters (FIGURE 11.1); it related a true story of the way in which a friend, who was not a physician or a scientist, was able to rid England's king of a disability. How did making the king sing like a schoolchild and curse like a sailor allow the king to deliver a perfect speech?

In this chapter, we will see how stuttering and much more serious problems with expressing or understanding language originate in particular regions of the brain. We

FIGURE 11.1 **King George VI, King of the United Kingdom from 1936 to 1952 and the subject of *The King's Speech*.** Here, King George VI delivers a speech during the Royal Tour of South Africa in 1947.

will examine the anatomy of various brain areas to understand how language is both produced and comprehended. We will examine how specific functions lateralize to one side of the brain. Examples of lesions, animal models, and deficits will give us the keys to unpack the development of language in the brain. We will see that a particular area of King George VI's brain was not being sufficiently activated and how singing and cursing were able to close the loop for his speech. Although an understanding of language in the brain is complex, "we shall prevail" (as King George liked to say).

Speech, Language, and Communication

Our small planet contains more than 6,000 human languages (Morseley, 2010), each of which gives speakers the ability to combine finite symbols in arbitrary, essentially infinite complexity. Language—our capacity to translate our inner thoughts into packets of communication—is such a fundamental part of our existence that we typically appreciate the massive underlying language systems only when they stop functioning correctly.

First, note that speech is not the same thing as language. **Speech** is the output of sounds from one human intended for another. The output occurs when the vocal equipment of the tongue, larynx, and airway is used to direct sound waves outside of the body (FIGURE 11.2). The input to a listener consists of

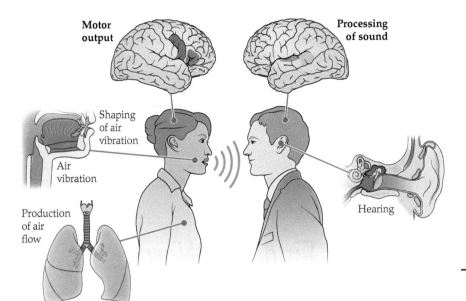

Motor output

Processing of sound

Shaping of air vibration

Air vibration

Production of air flow

Hearing

FIGURE 11.2 **Speech involves the production and transmission of sound waves.**

the fundamental elements of the physics carried by the sound waves: the frequency, the amplitude, and the machinery of the auditory system (Chapter 6). The study of speech stays in this domain of sound waves. It does not concern the elements of the brain that are used to think of the words to say or to understand them. That lies in the realm of language.

Language is the result of the ability to translate ideas into signals meant for another person. It consists of a set of learned codes that can be used to express our needs to others and understand their own needs. Significant cognitive skill is required to acquire and use the rules that relate symbols to meanings. Such rules involve creating meaning (words or signs) from smaller units (sounds, letters, or hand gestures) and combining words in particular ways (to form the **grammar** of the language).

It is sometimes helpful to define language by clarifying what it is not. First, language is not the same as ideas; instead, it is the medium by which we transmit ideas to one another. Second, language should not be assumed to involve only sound; sign language, for example, involves vision and movement. More generally, gestures, reading, and writing are all expressions of language.

We need one more concept: **communication** is the ability to convey ideas to one another, irrespective of the underlying media. To summarize with an example, the sound of my words, "I need water," is the *speech*. The *language* is English in this case, and I am *communicating* to you the concept of my thirst.

As an example of the differences among these three key concepts, consider **autism spectrum disorders**, a range of conditions in which individuals have difficulty with both language and communication. Autistic children suffer a reduced ability to use a medium to carry information. Although their speech is intact and they can produce sounds,

they are often limited to the utterances of meaningless repetitions and words.

As another example, consider **Williams syndrome**, a condition in which speech and language abilities are intact but communication is largely impaired. Patients with this condition have well-developed verbal skills and an extraordinary politeness to strangers. However, their cognition is highly impoverished, and they are unable to form and communicate ideas in a meaningful manner.

Aphasia: The Loss of Language

There are several reasons a person may suddenly have trouble speaking. **Dysphonia**, for example, results from an injury or overuse of the muscle fibers or sound-producing organs used to produce speech. As an example of dysphonia, you may have previously experienced laryngitis, an inflammation of the vocal folds. In more serious situations of damage to motor nerves, a person may suffer from **dysarthria**, a disorder that results from the paralysis or incoordination of the muscles needed to physically produce the sounds needed for language.

But there is a different, deeper reason someone may lose the ability to speak: damage to particular areas of the brain. The Ebers Papyrus, an ancient Egyptian medical paper, describes a man who suffered a head injury and lost the ability to speak. To the amazement of the Egyptian physicians 4,500 years ago, there was nothing wrong with the man's mouth or muscles, and he had no trouble moving his tongue normally (Minagar, Ragheb, & Kelley, 2003). Perhaps without realizing it, these early physicians were marking a distinction between the possible diagnosis of dysarthria and the disorder from which this man suffered: aphasia. Aphasia refers to the loss of the ability to produce or comprehend language for reasons based on damage to the brain. As we are about to see, there is more than one type of brain damage that can result in aphasia and more than one type of aphasia.

We will consider two of the better-described forms of aphasia: **Broca's aphasia** and **Wernicke's aphasia**. However, the American Speech–Language–Hearing Association recognizes more than 10 different types of aphasia (Davis, 2007). Once we see what can go wrong, we'll see how that knowledge leads to the current view of how the brain organizes and learns language.

CASE STUDY:
The Woman Who Couldn't Find Her Words

To gain insight into the type of language deficits that can occur, read this transcript of a conversation between an examiner and a patient with Broca's aphasia (Schwartz & Linebarger, 1985). The patient was asked to relate the tale of Disney's *Cinderella*. While you read, imagine her producing these words slowly, and with great effort.

Patient: Cinderella . . . poor . . . um 'dopted her . . . scrubbed floor, um, tidy . . . poor, um . . . 'dopted . . . Si-sisters and mother . . . ball. Ball, prince um, shoe . . .

Examiner: Keep going.

Patient: Scrubbed and uh washed and un . . . tidy, uh, sisters and mother, prince, no, prince, yes. Cinderella hooked prince. (Laughs.) Um, um, shoes, um, twelve o'clock ball, finished.

Examiner: So what happened in the end?

Patient: Married.

Examiner: How does he find her?

Patient: Um, Prince, um, happen to, um . . . Prince, and Cinderella meet, um met um met.

Examiner: What happened at the ball? They didn't get married at the ball.

Patient: No, um, no . . . I don't know. Shoe, um found shoe . . .

There are several aspects of her speech to note. First, the patient was indeed able to communicate something to the examiner about the story of Cinderella. In fact, almost the entire tale is told. This indicates that comprehension is intact in patients with Broca's aphasia.

Further analysis of the word usage shows that the patient was able to convey key content words, such as "Cinderella," "shoe," "sisters," and "married." However, she was not able to produce the linking words necessary for the proper grammar. Instead of saying, "Cinderella was poor and adopted," she dropped the "was" and the "and." This type of speech is referred to as **agrammatical** (lacking grammar). Also notice that she often says "um" and seems to stumble, reflecting her struggle to find the words to say. This word-finding difficulty is universal in patients with Broca's aphasia and is referred to as **anomia**. Listening to a patient with Broca's aphasia, you would also notice that the patient has difficulty with the pronunciation and the articulation of the speech, analogous to a person in severe pain. Imagine encountering a person stranded in the desert. He might say, "Water . . . please . . .

need . . . water." The speech contains only the bare bones of what is necessary, with the grammatical fillers removed. Likewise, the speech of a Broca's aphasic appears struggled and difficult to produce, although the message is often clear.

To further illustrate that comprehension is mostly intact in Broca's aphasia, follow along with this transcript of an examiner and another patient with Broca's aphasia.

Examiner: All right, I'm going to ask you to tell me some answers to these questions. What do you do with a hammer?

Patient: Found . . . flound . . . uh . . . sss . . . tuh found . . . oh . . . ssst. . . .

Examiner: You know, don't you?

Patient: Yes . . . sss . . . sss.

Examiner: Do you write with it?

Patient: No.

Examiner: Do you eat with it?

Patient: No.

Examiner: Do you pound with it?

Patient: Yes.

Examiner: Okay.

Broca's Aphasia

Unlike dysphonia or dysarthria, aphasia involves damage to brain areas that deal with language concepts. In 1836, a French doctor named Paul Broca cared for two end-of-life patients whose problem resembled that of the man in the Ebers Papyrus: they had both lost the ability to produce language. One patient, a 51-year-old named Leborgne, had been unable to speak for the past 30 years. The other, an 84-year-old named Lelong, had suffered a stroke a year before and since then could utter only five words, including a mispronunciation of his own name. When both patients died, Broca autopsied their brains. In both brains, Broca discovered a lesion in the same area of the lateral frontal lobe—and only in the left hemisphere. This apparent coincidence grabbed his attention. After examining eight more patients with the same language problems, Broca announced his famous maxim: "We speak with the left hemisphere." By identifying the areas of damage common to all the patients, he was able to refine his region of interest to the left inferior frontal gyrus, a region today called **Broca's area** (FIGURE 11.3) (Dronkers, Plaisant, Iba-Zizen, & Cabanis, 2007).

As it turns out, Paul Broca had the foresight to preserve the brains from his two original autopsies (FIGURE 11.3). A team of researchers in America and France performed detailed anatomical MRI scans of the original brains of Leborgne and Lelong and published the results in 2007. Because of Broca's foresight, Leborgne and Lelong are able to speak to the scientific community in a way they could not in Broca's day (Dronkers et al., 2007).

Patients with damage to Broca's area suffer from an **expressive aphasia**, meaning their language problem is not one of comprehension, but instead one of communicating ideas to others. And their incapacity is not limited simply to spoken language: they are no better at *writing* an intended message either. In fact, deaf people who suffer damage to Broca's area lose the capacity to communicate with sign language—their fingers, although physically functioning properly in tasks of everyday life, find themselves frozen, stuttering, and mute when trying to express an idea (Hickok, Bellugi, & Klima, 2001). Thus, Broca's aphasia reflects a problem *expressing* language rather than a particular motor problem with the mouth or hands.

As we can observe from these exchanges, the patient's problem is not one of understanding; instead it is a lack of ability to translate internal understanding into linguistic output.

Wernicke's Aphasia

A decade after Broca studied his aphasic patients in France, a German physician named Carl Wernicke studied a group of patients with a different kind of language problem. Instead of damage to the left frontal cortex, these patients had sustained damage to their left temporal cortex—specifically, the medial and posterior portion of the left superior temporal gyrus, now known as **Wernicke's area** (FIGURE 11.4).

Unlike Broca's findings, Wernicke's patients could generate speech fluently. The trouble was that they could not understand what others were saying to them, and the content of their own speech output made no sense. Thus, Wernicke's aphasia is also called a **receptive aphasia** because the problem lies in receiving and comprehending language. Let's take a look at another dialogue to get a better feel for the type of speech deficits Wernicke's patients have.

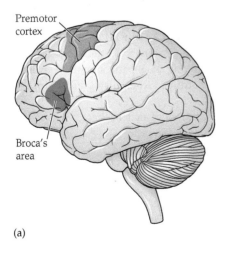

(a)

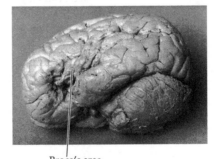

Broca's area

(b)

FIGURE 11.3 Broca's area. (a) Damage to this region leads to a diminished ability to express language. Such damage usually results from blockage or hemorrhage of the middle cerebral artery, tumors, or traumatic brain injury. Note the proximity of Broca's area to the premotor cortex. The preserved brains of Broca's patients, (b) Leborgne (upper) and Lelong (lower).

CASE STUDY:
The Woman Who Makes Up Words

Examiner: I'm going to ask you some question, and I just want you to answer "yes" or "no." Okay? "Yes" or "no." Is your name Smith?

Patient: Where would I be what they're eating averment I don't know.

Examiner: Is your name Brown?

Patient: Oh mistress triangland while listen you walking well things things this for for thee.

Examiner: Okay, just say "yes" or "no." Okay, is your name Brown?

Patient: What it is here, then let me see. I just don't know. No I'm not going to an eat sigh no.

Examiner: No? . . . Are the lights on in this room?

Patient: No [laughs] not. I just don't sorry what you're doing and you just saving walking and walking around here.

Examiner: You're doing fine. That's okay. I know it's kind of hard for you. You're doing fine.

Patient: I kind my own my eat my only for my and everything like that an cleanin' my dead me by is always clean me breveret eating and I can watch and everything in the morning.

(Dialogue from Carlson, 2011.)

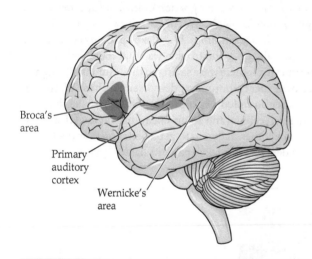

Broca's area

Primary auditory cortex

Wernicke's area

FIGURE 11.4 Wernicke's area. Damage to this region leads to receptive aphasias. Wernicke's aphasias result most commonly from damage to the posterior branches of the middle cerebral artery, whether by blockage of the artery or by hemorrhage, and sometimes from tumors or from traumatic brain injury to the region.

In contrast to the Broca's aphasic patient we encountered earlier, note that this Wernicke's aphasic patient has a fundamental problem with comprehension. The patient is unable to answer the examiner's question with anything meaningful at all. The patient's speech contains no relevant content words. Instead, the speech contains many filler words—such as prepositions and to-be verbs—and the overall grammar seems in place. If you were to hear a Wernicke's aphasic patient speaking from a far distance, you might mistakenly think he sounded perfectly normal and that you simply could not follow his stream of thought. In other words, the

grammar and the fluency are intact—hence the other name for Wernicke's aphasia, **fluent aphasia**.

Because Wernicke's aphasic patients lose the ability to understand the meanings of words, this translates to a reduced ability to produce intelligible speech because of an inability to self-monitor. Their speech sounds normal but has no meaning. This type of speech is often referred to as a **word salad**. Two more terms help to characterize the type of speech found in Wernicke's aphasia. A **neologism** refers to the invention of a new word, as in "triangland" or "breveret" in the previous dialogue. Neologisms have no meaning and are a product of a deficit in language comprehension. Similarly, Wernicke's patients will create a **paraphasia**, in which an incorrect word is substituted for a correct word. As a result of these problems, patients drift in a sea of expressions and utterances that have little meaning. Follow along as a patient with Wernicke's aphasia tries to identify ordinary items displayed to him.

Examiner: Tell me the names of each of these.
Patient: [cigarette] This is a cigarette
[comb] a wongt
[fork] a fillt
[key] a wote
[knife] a mergiss
[matches] a cigarette bakt
[pen] a lined
[pencil] a wiltee
[quarter] mully
[toothbrush] and a rockstreen
    (Dialogue from Carlson, 2011.)

Patients who recover from Wernicke's aphasia report that, while aphasic, they found the speech of others to be unintelligible. In addition, despite recognizing when they themselves were speaking, they could neither stop themselves nor understand their own words (Marshall, 2001). Generally, Wernicke's patients will not ask for clarification or attempt to convey their message through other methods.

There is an important psychological difference between Broca's and Wernicke's aphasias. In Broca's aphasia, the patient is in distress about his inability to express language. Like a person trapped inside a glass bottle, the patient has a good working comprehension of what's happening around him, but he cannot communicate to others. In Wernicke's aphasia, on the other hand, the patient typically remains cheerful and even mildly confused that people do not understand him.

Interestingly, patients with Wernicke's aphasia retain the **prosody** of their speech—that is, the intonations, stresses, and rhythms. This preserved "music of speech" suggests that ideas and communicative intent lie behind their utterances, despite the bizarreness of their speech production. Prosody is retained because it is typically lateralized to the opposite hemisphere (we discuss lateralization later in this chapter).

Patients with Wernicke's aphasia also retain the ability to recognize the prosody of speech in other people. This is illustrated by one of Dr. Oliver Sacks's observations. A group of his patients with Wernicke's aphasia watched a televised speech by Ronald Reagan, a former actor who later became president of the United States. The aphasic patients, of course, were not able to understand the words of the president's speech. However, to Sacks's surprise, the patients started to laugh as they listened to the speech.

> One cannot lie to an aphasic. He cannot grasp your words, and so cannot be deceived by them; but what he grasps, he grasps with infallible precision, namely the expression that goes with the words, that total spontaneous, involuntary expressiveness which can never be simulated or faked, as words alone can, all too easily.
>
> It was the grimaces, the histrionics, the false gestures and, above all, the false tones and cadences of the voice which rang false for these wordless but immensely sensitive patients. It was to these (for them) most glaring, even grotesque, incongruities and improprieties that my aphasic patients responded, undeceived and undeceivable by words.
>
> **This is why they laughed at the President's speech.**
>
> (Sacks, 1970)

You may be wondering: why don't Wernicke's aphasic patients simply *write down* their thoughts to communicate clearly? Unfortunately, just as with Broca's aphasics, this compensatory strategy does not work with Wernicke's aphasics. Since the patients' problem is fundamentally one of language comprehension, changing the method of expression is of no help. Take a look at FIGURE 11.5 to see how a Wernicke's aphasic writes his thoughts about a drawing of the Eiffel Tower. Similarly, deaf Wernicke's patients lose their ability

FIGURE 11.5 **The attempts of a patient with Wernicke's aphasia to write the name of the Eiffel Tower would result in nonsensical words or phrases.**

to produce normal sign language; they appear to be "babbling" with their fingers. In other words, aphasia applies to all language modalities—it is not simply restricted to spoken language (Damasio, Bellugi, Damasio, Poizner, & Van Gilder, 1986).

We are now ready to turn to an understanding of how Broca's area and Wernicke's area work together in the context of a larger language network.

A Language Network

At first glance it can appear that neural areas of interest are spread randomly around the map of the brain. But there is a logic to the organization of language.

Look at FIGURE 11.6 and note where Wernicke's area is located. It is wedged between the primary auditory cortex and the angular gyrus, two areas that bring in information from the *auditory* world and the *visual* world, respectively. Damage to the primary auditory cortex causes deafness, whereas damage to the angular gyrus causes **alexia (word blindness)**, in which a person can stare at a written word but have no interpretation of its meaning. Wernicke's area, sitting between these two cortical regions, is perfectly situated to process language input—irrespective of whether the input is obtained by ear or by eye.

The primary auditory cortex and the angular gyrus provide input to Wernicke's area—but where does the output from Wernicke's area go? Information travels through a group of axons called the **arcuate fasciculus** (Latin for *curved bundle*) to reach Broca's area. This bundle provides the link from language comprehension to production (or input to output). Once information has reached Broca's area, an output response is formulated prior to being physically produced. The compiled signals then travel to the premotor cortex and motor cortex, which is finally responsible for carrying the signals to the necessary muscles to produce speech. This description summarizes the theory of language called the **Wernicke–Geschwind model** (Geschwind, 1970).

Although the Wernicke–Geschwind model (FIGURE 11.6) has been a gold standard for clinical applications, the model is too simplified to capture everything. For example, the arcuate fasciculus is not the only route from Wernicke's to Broca's area: neuroimaging has revealed an alternative route through the left inferior parietal lobule, a region heavily connected to both Wernicke's and Broca's (Kim, Relkin, Lee, & Hirsch, 1997). It appears that the inferior parietal lobule serves as a parallel information path, one that is involved in classifying and labeling items. More generally, the Wernicke–Geschwind model is incomplete, because damage to brain areas outside the circuitry laid out in the model (for example, to the basal ganglia or thalamus) can cause aphasias (Sebastian, Schein, Davis et al., 2014). A related finding is that patients with isolated damage to Broca's area will often experience a temporary aphasia that resolves; however, if the damage involves Broca's area *and* the underlying white matter and neighboring structures, the effects of the aphasia are permanent (Bonilha &

Fridriksson, 2009; Fridriksson, Bonilha, & Rorden, 2007). For all these reasons, the Wernicke–Geschwind model should not be thought of as complete; nonetheless, it continues to serve an important function in roughly sketching the layout of language in the brain.

To appreciate the usefulness of the model, consider the bundle of axons that connects Wernicke's area to Broca's area, the arcuate fasciculus. Before we tell you what damage to this bundle causes, make a guess. You already know that Wernicke's area is involved in speech comprehension and that Broca's area is involved in speech output, so what would happen if the linking path between them were damaged? Take a moment to think about this.

The answer is that with damage to the arcuate fasciculus, language comprehension is normal and speech production is normal. But patients are unable to *repeat* words. This is known as **conduction aphasia** and is tested by simply asking a patient to repeat some simple sentences. Consider this dialogue of an examiner asking a patient with conduction aphasia to repeat some simple phrases:

Examiner: The pastry cook was elated.
Patient: The baker was . . . What was that last word?
Examiner: The pastry cook was elated.
Patient: The baker-er was vaskerin . . . uh . . .

The patient with conduction aphasia understands the command to repeat just fine, and he has no trouble speaking—it's simply that he cannot move linguistic information rapidly from input to output stages.

When all aspects of language are affected, this is called a **global aphasia.** This type of aphasia combines the disabilities of Broca's, Wernicke's, and conduction aphasias. Patients cannot speak, cannot comprehend, and cannot repeat language. Not surprisingly, global aphasia results from widespread damage to the lateral cortex of the left hemisphere, typically because of blockage or rupture of the left middle cerebral artery (FIGURE 11.7).

The Larger Picture of Language-Specific Regions

The concept of a word is more complex than it appears at first glance: humans have learned memories of what words sound like, what they mean, how to say them, what they reference, and how to use the object they reference. All of these memories involve different regions in the brain.

For example, sometimes brain damage leads to selective naming impairments for a specific object category. One patient will not be able to identify or name living things; another can't identify a flower; another, furry animals. Such lesions can be traced to one place: the temporal lobes. Damage to one part of the brain impairs the naming of familiar people, whereas damage to other parts impairs naming of

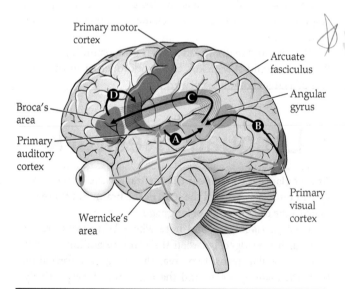

FIGURE 11.6 **Wernicke–Geschwind model.** This circuit diagrams the path of language in the brain. (A) Auditory inputs (spoken words) move from the auditory cortex to Wernicke's area. (B) Visual inputs (written words) move from the occipital cortex through the angular gyrus to Wernicke's area. (C) After an analysis of the input, language information moves to Broca's area via the arcuate fasciculus. (D) Broca's area is necessary to create the production of a response to the input. Finally, Broca's area outputs the articulation of a response through the motor cortex, which then passes the signal to the muscles needed to produce the response (e.g., speech sounds, writing, or sign language).

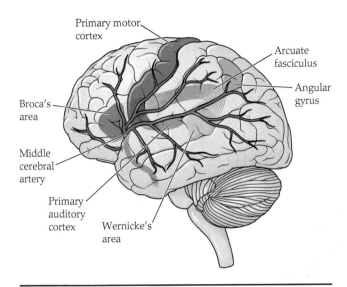

FIGURE 11.7 Areas supplied by the middle cerebral artery. When this artery is blocked or ruptured, the underlying brain tissue becomes damaged. Widespread damage includes damage to Broca's and Wernicke's areas, as well as the arcuate fasciculus, leading to a global aphasia.

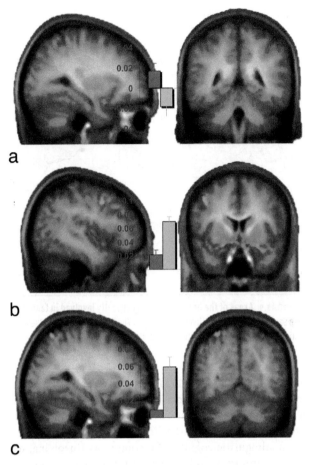

FIGURE 11.8 Different brain areas are activated when producing nouns (red areas) than when producing verbs (green areas).

animals or naming of tools (Martin & Chao, 2001). The different regions are thought to be involved in associating meanings with the phonological forms of words and consequently to be involved in the retrieval of names (Damasio, Grabowski, Tranel, Hichwa, & Damasio, 1996). These same areas become active in word naming in non–brain damaged people in imaging studies. As a side note, the naming of animals leads to some activation in early visual cortex, suggesting that people evoke the appearance of the animal in naming it (Martin, Wiggs, Ungerleider, & Haxby, 1996).

Nouns and verbs are basic word classes in all languages, and the distinction between them is a fundamental aspect of all grammars (Shapiro, Moo, & Caramazza, 2006). The processing of nouns and verbs can be selectively impaired as a result of brain damage; this is evidence that they are represented in different brain regions (FIGURE 11.8). As we just saw, lesions of the left anterior temporal lobe impair the processing of nouns. In contrast, damage to the left premotor cortex impairs verb retrieval—a condition known as **averbia** (Damasio & Tranel, 1993). This can be verified as a deficit in retrieval rather than general cognitive problems in describing actions and things because patients with averbia often create neologisms (new, made-up words) to describe actions—for example, saying I'm "going . . . scissoring" or "sailboating." They know what they want to describe; they simply cannot access the proper verb. Similarly, patients with noun troubles can still identify objects: when told to pick up the salt shaker, they have no problem doing so. This verifies that the damage is not a cognitive impairment; rather, the patients suffer from a decreased ability to retrieve the appropriate word.

We are seeing so far that language is composed of multiple components and that language functions are spread widely across different brain regions. This leads to the question of whether language areas are involved *only* in language functions.

Recently, Nancy Kanwisher and her colleagues were able to shed some light on this debate of language specificity. Dr. Kanwisher uses functional imaging to try to understand what structures are involved in language and other higher-level cognitive tasks. She noted that most functional imaging studies, however, do not allow us to make inferences about the selectivity of specific brain regions. Most such studies involve averaging data across multiple subjects to make generalizations about the relation of functions and brain structures. The problem is that each participant has a different brain with varying shapes of sulci, gyri, and ventricles. Although combining data across subjects increases statistical power, it blurs information together. Kanwisher describes this effect as similar to averaging the images of 10 faces: the resultant image would still have the overall shape of a face, but the individual details of structures would be blurred together (Finn, 2011).

To overcome these limitations, Kanwisher used individual subjects' data to find functional brain areas involved in language—and to see whether those same areas were activated in tasks that did not involve language (Fedorenko,

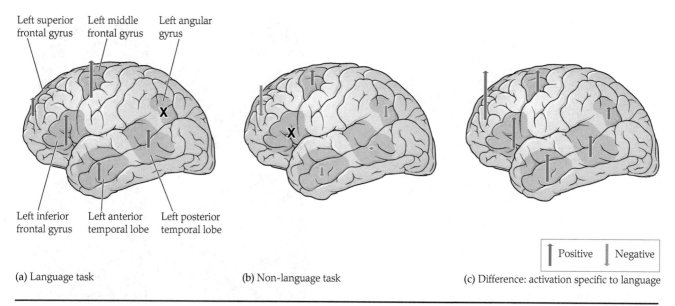

(a) Language task

(b) Non-language task

(c) Difference: activation specific to language

↑ Positive   ↓ Negative

FIGURE 11.9 Areas of the brain that are specifically involved in language functions. (a) The language-related activity in six regions of the brain. (b) Activity in these same areas during nonlinguistic tasks. (c) The difference between these two conditions (activity during linguistic tasks minus activity during nonlinguistic tasks), highlighting areas important for linguistic tasks.

Behr, & Kanwisher, 2011). Participants first performed language-specific tasks, including language production and comprehension, to determine what areas of the brain were activated in the language tasks. Then the subjects performed seven nonlinguistic cognitive function tasks (involving, for example, arithmetic, working memory, cognitive control, and music). The researchers discovered several areas that were activated *only* during the language tasks and not during the nonlinguistic tasks. As seen in FIGURE 11.9, these language areas are located in the left frontal lobe and in the left temporal–parietal area.

Although the previous study provides support for functional specificity for language, functional imaging results are limited to showing only *correlations* between brain activity and linguistic functions. This provides evidence that the regions are involved in language, but does not demonstrate that activity in these areas is necessary and critical for language. Is there a way to map out such causality?

Kuniyoshi Sakai and his group at the University of Tokyo have been working to identify which brain regions are critical for specific linguistic elements such as grammar, syntax, and sentence comprehension. To this end, they utilize a technique called transcranial magnetic stimulation (see Chapter 1 for a description) to excite areas in the left inferior frontal gyrus (Sakai, Noguchi, Takeuchi, & Watanabe, 2002). By exciting neurons directly, this research provides evidence for a more causal relation rather than a correlation. Native Japanese speakers were presented with sentences and asked whether each had a syntactic error or a semantic error. An example of a syntactic error occurs in the sentence "I ated cheese," whereas an example of a semantic error occurs in the sentence "The cheese ate me." They found evidence that transcranial magnetic stimulation to the inferior frontal gyrus (particularly Broca's area) 150 milliseconds after a verb was presented

reduced participants' reaction times on the syntactic task, but not on the semantic task. These findings imply that these brain areas are specialized for grammar processing, but not for the processing of meaning. Through studies like these, Sakai's lab provides support for functional maps like the one in FIGURE 11.10 (Sakai, 2005).

Finally, what about second languages? Are these represented in the same regions as native tongues or in different areas? We already saw in Chapter 4 that as a primary language (L1) is acquired, it becomes more difficult to acquire a secondary language (L2). This results from a closing window of plasticity. Learning a primary language requires fine-tuning of the musculature in the larynx, articulators, and even in the breathing apparatus—all of which require motor and sensory plasticity. Pronunciation and syntax are much more difficult to acquire later in life (in secondary-language learning) because of the plasticity constraints of age. However, aspects of language like vocabulary—which depend on higher-order cognitive functions rather than on motor and sensory skills—are easier to acquire than pronunciation and syntax in a second language.

Because primary and secondary languages have these different behavioral and learning aspects, it seems plausible that they might be coded differently in the brain. To address this possibility, neurosurgeon George Ojemann and neurolinguist Harry Whitaker applied the technique of **electrical stimulation mapping** to two bilingual patients in a seminal study (Ojemann & Whitaker, 1978). In this technique, patients in brain surgery have various parts of the cortex stimulated by a small electrode while they read a list of words. When the electric current causes a patient to stumble in her reading and speaking, that area of the brain is presumed to be implicated in language. One of the patients in the study was bilingual in Dutch and English, whereas the other was bilingual in Spanish and English. Within Broca's and

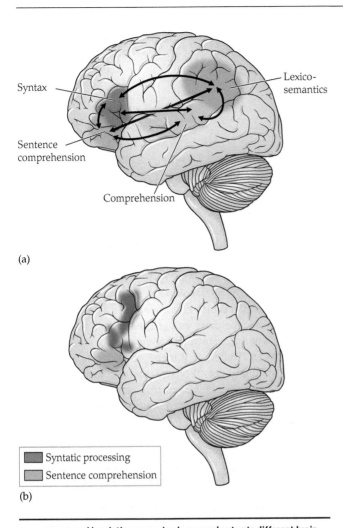

(a)

(b)

Syntatic processing

Sentence comprehension

FIGURE 11.10 Linguistic processing is mapped out onto different brain areas. (a) The parts of the brain specialized for grammar processing. (b) The areas involved in sentence comprehension (green) and areas involved in syntactic processing (purple). Adapted from Sakai et al. (2005).

Wernicke's areas, there were spots in which electrical stimulation caused disruption in the reading task in *both* languages. However, other spots of stimulation (still within Broca's and Wernicke's areas) caused selective deficits in only *one* language. The cortical areas that involved L2 for both patients encompassed a wider area than L1 did. This study suggested that foreign languages may indeed be encoded differently in the brain, a finding that shed light on an old mystery: why some bilingual patients have strokes and show deficits in only one language. Since this study in 1978, several imaging studies have provided evidence that L1 and L2 can be encoded in slightly different manners in the brain (Kim et al., 1997; Simos et al., 2001).

Dyslexia

In the world of the past 6,000 years, reading has become a critical linguistic skill (Mitchell, 1999). Like other linguistic skills, reading seems like a straightforward developmental step—until the complexity of the task is unmasked by a

reading disorder, or **dyslexia**. A dyslexia is a developmental reading disorder in which an individual fails to properly recognize and process alphabetical symbols and words.

Dyslexia is not exclusively a problem with the sensory systems, nor is it a problem with intelligence or capacity to think (in fact, many people with dyslexia have above-average intelligence). Rather, the problem is associated with the language networks. Individuals who suffer from dyslexia fail to read at a level commensurate with their intelligence and educational circumstances. Although most of the research on dyslexia has focused on its impact on language functions, other research has identified abnormalities in sensory systems, in balance, and in structural differences in the brain. Here, however, we will focus on the language difficulties observed in individuals with dyslexia.

It is popularly thought that dyslexia involves letter reversals during reading, such as *p* for *q* or *b* for *d*. But dyslexia typically entails more generalized problems with understanding words and sentences. Dyslexia is often detected when children have difficulty copying from written material or the classroom board or remembering content from something they've read. Often an individual with dyslexia has auditory problems as well: a child may have difficulty understanding or remembering parts of what she has just heard, or recalling sequences of commands, or sounding out the pronunciation of an unfamiliar word.

The act of reading—taking in symbols, converting them to imagined sounds, understanding their meaning—involves wide-ranging collaboration of many brain areas. As a result, many things can go wrong with such a network. Dyslexia has many different forms. (As an analogy, consider deafness. More than 200 genes have been associated with deafness because there are so many ways for the complex functioning of audition to go wrong.)

Dyslexic readers can have trouble picking up the patterns of a language at the **orthographic level** (how the word looks) and the **phonological level** (how the word sounds). These problems are sometimes divided into **surface dyslexia** (an orthographic problem) and **deep dyslexia** (a fundamental problem at the phonological level). In surface dyslexia, word reading is impaired. This is tested for by counting mistakes when pronouncing nonwords (such as *phronk* or *giller*). By contrast, deep dyslexia can be detected by problems in identifying individual sounds and identifying syllables in a word, poor rhyming skills, and trouble identifying the number of words in a sentence.

What are the neurobiological differences underlying these reading problems? As you will expect by this point in the chapter, imaging studies demonstrate that dyslexia is a disorder of language areas in the left hemisphere (Shaywitz & Shaywitz, 2005). Dyslexic readers have less activation in posterior regions critical to the development of fluent reading (e.g., Wernicke's area), and they have compensatory activity in more anterior areas and in the right hemisphere (FIGURE 11.11). They also show less-than-normal activation of visual cortex in response to written words (Demb, Boynton, & Heeger, 1997). Further, the left and right hemispheres of dyslexic readers are

Dyslexic   Normal

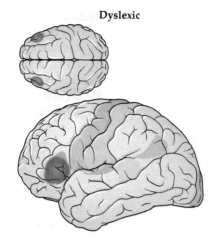
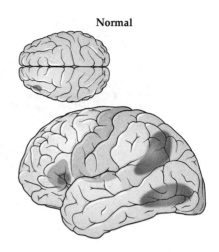

FIGURE 11.11 **Activity in the language-related areas in dyslexia.** During language tasks, individuals with dyslexia have less activity in the more posterior language-related areas and greater activity in the anterior areas.

more symmetrical than those of nondyslexic readers (more on hemispheric differences in the next section).

Fortunately, the neural systems involved in reading appear to be plastic, and they can be remediated with early, evidence-based reading intervention (Temple et al., 2003).

Stuttering

With our understanding that language involves many brain regions, let's return to the stuttering King George. Stuttering is a problem that affects 1% of the population, with men more than three times more likely to suffer than women (Dowling, 1994). Brain imaging using fMRI reveals that stutterers have higher-than-normal activation in several regions: Broca's area, the insula, the supplemental motor area, and parts of the cerebellum (Neumann et al., 2003). These areas play roles in the formation of words (Broca's area), articulation (the insula), and the motor output of sound (supplemental motor area and the cerebellum). Equally important, stutterers show decreased activity in the auditory regions of the temporal lobe (Beal, Gracco, Lafaille, & De Nil, 2007). This appears to be because of a lack of auditory feedback from the speaker's own voice. In fact, this might explain a strange fact: if a person's own voice is played back to him with a slight delay, this can reduce stuttering (Foundas et al., 2004). Consistent with this hypothesis, neuroimaging reveals more activation in the temporal lobe when playing back a speaker's own voice with a slight delay versus without a delay (Neumann et al., 2003). As we mentioned, fMRI is a correlational technique, and such correlations cannot establish causation. We would have a better sense of causation if there were also supporting evidence from studies of patients with strokes or other brain lesions who started stuttering as a result of the injury. These studies have started (Lundgren, Helm-Estabrooks, & Klein, 2010), but because relatively few patients have these conditions, there are no definitive results yet.

What about the stuttering king, George VI? Why did his friend Lionel make him sing? In 2010, scientists turned to neuroimaging to see whether they could find an answer.

Stutterers and control participants read a piece of narration normally and also sang a narrative using a metronome. The results showed that there was greater activation in the auditory areas when the stutterers were singing compared with reading (Wan, Ruber, Hohmann, & Schlaug, 2010). The king had to sing to get more sensory feedback. The trick his friend used wasn't crazy! Even without knowing the neural details, he was doing exactly what he needed to do: rebalancing the king's input–output networks.

Lateralization: The Two Hemispheres Are Not Identical

To a neurosurgeon, there is the left hemisphere, and then there is the hemisphere that is not the left hemisphere. Why do they care? Because as Broca discovered, language is typically localized to the left side. And if you cut off someone's language, you cut the communication channel to the outside world.

Imagine a scenario in which you damage your spinal cord and cannot move your body from your neck down. You cannot walk, you cannot move your arms, you cannot feed yourself. A horrible thing to imagine, no doubt, but at least you can communicate your thoughts to your loved ones; you can share your grief and hopes. In contrast, imagine a patient who sustains left hemisphere damage and can no longer speak. She is cut off in a fundamental way from the human realm. She is locked into a vault of silence from which her ideas, aspirations, and fears cannot be shared with anyone but herself.

To avoid this fate, neurosurgeons are careful to understand which hemisphere is the dominant one before operating on the brain with a scalpel (say, for tumors or epilepsy). The complication is that language is on the left for most people, but not for everyone. The left hemisphere is dominant for speech in 92% of right-handers and 69% of those who are left-handed or ambidextrous (Knecht et al., 2000; Milner, 1974). So before a surgeon cuts into neural tissue, it is important to know which hemisphere is dominant.

Tests for Dominance

In 1960, Wada and Rasmussen created a method now termed the **Wada test** to determine an individual's brain lateralization for language (Wada & Rasmussen, 1960). They injected sodium amobarbital, a member of a class of drug known as **barbiturates**, into the carotid artery on one side of the neck. The drug courses into the middle cerebral artery and circulates within only one hemisphere of the brain (FIGURE 11.12). The sodium amobarbital, acting as an anesthetic, temporarily inhibits the function of the entire hemisphere. If the language-dominant hemisphere is paralyzed, then speech production and comprehension are impaired—so one simply needs to ask the patient to speak and respond after the barbiturate has invaded one hemisphere or the other. With this technique, Wada and Rasmussen were able to determine which side was dominant for language in an individual in a minimally invasive fashion.

Although the Wada test is straightforward, it's not ideal for most people: injecting a barbiturate into a healthy person is invasive and can have side effects. Is there a way to determine hemispheric dominance in a normal, healthy human? In recent years, researchers have turned to functional brain imaging (typically fMRI) to measure which hemisphere of the brain is active during a language task. In one simple test, patients determine whether sentences in different sensory inputs (for example, written versus spoken) have the same meaning. As the patients analyze sentences, the hemisphere dominant for language is more active than the nondominant hemisphere (Jansen et al., 2004; Rihs, Sturzenegger, Gutbrod, Schroth, & Mattle, 1999). In this way, functional brain imaging can be used as a less invasive measure of hemispheric dominance than the Wada test.

Apraxia

The left hemisphere is dominant for more than language—it is also involved in fine motor control. Damage to parts of the left hemisphere often causes **apraxia**, difficulty performing movements when asked to do so out of context (from the Greek *praxis*: producing an action or movement). In apraxia, there is no muscular paralysis, incoordination, or sensory problem. Rather, just as we saw in aphasias, there is a more fundamental problem—in this case, with understanding how to perform fine motor acts (see FIGURE 11.13 for a sample of some of the tasks performed in a medical evaluation of apraxia). Apraxia can be diagnosed by asking a person to respond to the following sorts of commands:

- Blow out a match
- Stick out the tongue
- Wave goodbye
- Brush the teeth
- Flip a coin
- Hammer a nail into wood
- Cut paper with scissors
- Thread a needle
- Tie a necktie

A normal, healthy person will be able to adopt the positions and mime the requested actions. An apraxic patient will struggle to complete these tasks because the brain circuitry required for planning these motor outputs has been damaged.

Hemispheric Differences

We've seen that the left hemisphere is usually dominant for language and elements of fine motor control. What about the right hemisphere? Are there any specialized tasks for which it dominates? Indeed, there are several. The right hemisphere seems to have a greater spatial ability. For example, when subjects are given the task of matching a three-dimensional image with its two-dimensional counterpart, the right hemisphere plays a greater role. The right hemisphere is also superior at understanding emotion: it is better at perceiving facial expressions and mood.

When it comes to music, the right hemisphere seems to be involved in the perception of music and melodies.

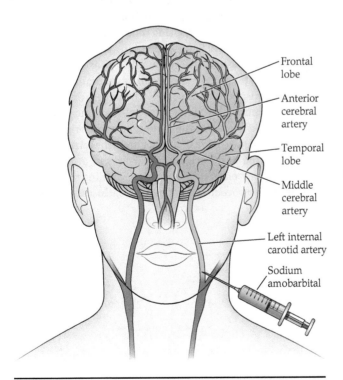

Frontal lobe

Anterior cerebral artery

Temporal lobe

Middle cerebral artery

Left internal carotid artery

Sodium amobarbital

FIGURE 11.12 The Wada test. In the Wada test, sodium amobarbital is injected into the carotid artery to anesthetize half of the brain. This helps clinicians find out whether language functions are on the right half or the left half of a person's brain.

"Pretend to..."

...blow out a match

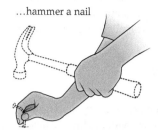

...hammer a nail

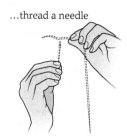

...thread a needle

FIGURE 11.13 A physical exam for apraxia.
A person with apraxia is unable to mime requested actions involving fine motor control out of context, such as blowing out a match, hammering a nail, or threading a needle.

(However, the left hemisphere plays an important role in musicians with perfect pitch.) Patients with damage to a right hemisphere analog of Wernicke's area can end up with **amusia,** an inability to understand music. Related to its musicality, the right is better suited to detecting the prosody of language (Wildgruber, Ackermann, Kreifelts, & Ethofer, 2006). Remember Dr. Sacks's aphasic patients who laughed at Reagan's speech? Although they had damage to the language areas of the left hemisphere, their intact right hemispheres may have allowed them to understand that his cadence and emphasis were left over from an acting career.

This brain lateralization can be detected early in life. In babies only two months old, sounds are already processed in a lateralized manner. Speech sounds are directed to the left posterior temporal lobe, whereas music sounds are more distributed to the right and left hemispheres. The sound of the mother's voice modulates the amygdala in addition to the left posterior temporal lobe, leading to the suggestion that the mother's voice may help the early shaping of the lateralization of language areas (Dehaene-Lambertz et al., 2010).

Although the left and right hemispheres look approximately the same to the naked eye, one can measure anatomical differences between the hemispheres. The **planum temporale** lies in the region of Wernicke's area in the temporal lobe (FIGURE 11.14). The planum temporale is typically larger on the left, leading some to propose that it has allowed language to evolve. Moreover, people with dyslexia often have planum temporale equal or greater in size on the right side. However, the association of this area to language is not fully

supported by all the evidence: although 92% of right-handers have language dominance in the left hemisphere, research has been unable to establish a clear relationship between planum temporale asymmetry and hemispheric dominance for language. That is, some 30% have larger planum temporale on the nondominant side, and the remaining few percent are equal on both sides (Dorsaint-Pierre et al., 2006; Eckert, Leonard, Possing, & Binder, 2006). Furthermore, the planum temporale is already enlarged by 29 weeks into gestation, before language acquisition (Bossy, Godlewski, & Maurel, 1976).

Two Brains in One? The Case of the Split-Brain Patients

In many cases, the differences between the hemispheres were discovered by studying cases of brain damage. But there has been another, more surprising route to discovery as well.

Although the two hemispheres are separate, they are heavily interconnected. Large bundles of axons cross the midline of the brain, communicating essential information from one hemisphere to the other. The largest of these bundles is the corpus callosum (FIGURE 11.15). In some patients, as we have seen a couple of times now, seizures originate at a particular epileptic center, or focus. Often, the seizure spreads from its starting point, triggering seizures in other parts of the brain. To prevent the seizures from reaching the opposite hemisphere, a procedure known as a **callosotomy** can be

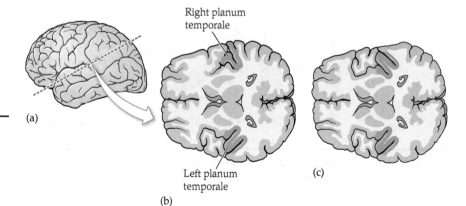

FIGURE 11.14 Hemispheric asymmetry in the planum temporale. (a) The planum temporale is located on the temporal lobe. (b) It is generally larger in the left hemisphere than in the right in fluent readers. (c) This asymmetry is absent or reversed in individuals with dyslexia.

Right planum temporale

Left planum temporale

(a)

(b)

(c)

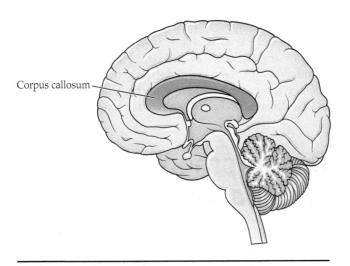

Corpus callosum

FIGURE 11.15 The corpus callosum.

performed: the corpus callosum is sliced down the middle, severing the connection between the two hemispheres. This procedure tends to be successful in limiting convulsive activity, and many patients never have another major convulsion once they undergo a corpus callosotomy. But this immediately leads to a mystery: the corpus callosum has 200 million axons, but when it is severed, the patient acts essentially normal! How could that be? Does it mean the corpus callosum has no important function?

The answer turns out to be that the corpus callosum *does* have an important function, but that function must be teased out carefully. Patients who have undergone this type of surgery are known as **split-brain patients**. To identify the

deficits these patients encountered, Roger Sperry and his colleagues developed some clever experiments (Gazzaniga, 2005; Sperry, 1961). Sperry's group reasoned that because of the severed connections, each hemisphere might act independent of the other. To test this, they had split-brain patients hold an object in one hand and describe it. When the patient held the object in his right hand, he had no trouble naming and describing the object. However, when the patient held the object in his left hand, he was unable to name the object (Gazzaniga, 2005). In fact, you could place an object in the patient's left hand and the patient would carry on a conversation without ever mentioning the object in his speech. This results from the fact that the left hemisphere is specialized for language; all of the sensory input from the patient's left hand travels to the patient's right hemisphere, and the information is never relayed to the (verbal) left hemisphere. Thus, the object could not be acknowledged verbally.

In another study, patients were shown items specific to only one visual field. When an item was shown to the right visual field (left hemisphere), the patient could name the object and could point to it with his right hand. When an item was shown to the left visual field (right hemisphere), the patient could no longer name the item. He could only point out the item with his left hand (and no longer with the right) (Gazzaniga, 2005).

Split-brain patients appear to have two brains: that is, each hemisphere can learn and perform independently and simultaneously when presented with different visual stimuli (FIGURE 11.16). In split-brain patients, one hemisphere must use external cues to signal something to the other hemisphere. For example, the right hemisphere can't explicitly

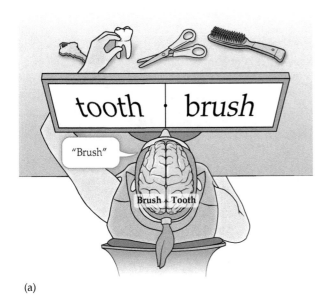

(a)

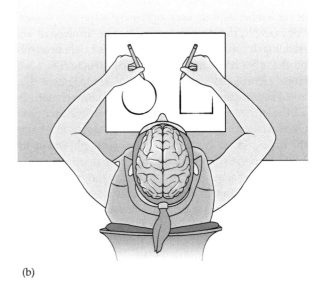

(b)

FIGURE 11.16 **Behavioral studies of split-brain patients.** (a) A compound word is presented briefly, so that what is presented on the left side of the screen only goes to the right side of the brain and what is presented on the right side of the screen only goes to the left side of the brain. The patient can say what was on the right side of the screen, but can identify the word on the left side of the screen only by touch with the left hand. (b) Because the two hemispheres of the brain have been disconnected from each other, split-brain patients can easily perform two separate actions with their left and right hands.

generate language, but it can precipitate a frown—which in turn cues the left hemisphere that something bad has happened. This phenomenon is known as **cross-cueing**. A related finding is the **helping-hand phenomenon**. In this case, one hemisphere may have access to the location of an item. The hand that "knows" may correct the positioning of the other hand to help perform the task.

Thinking about Cerebral Asymmetry

Why do the right and left hemispheres of the brain differ in their functions? Scientists have proposed several answers to this question, all of which share the general assumption that it is better to have brain areas that perform similar functions located in the same hemisphere.

The language theory suggests that functions related to language are most efficiently consolidated into one hemisphere (Allen, 1983). For example, when comparing hearing and deaf babies, the maturational time course, structure, and content of early signed and spoken language acquisition are similar. Functional imaging provides evidence that the brain regions used in deaf adults to process language are the same left-hemisphere regions that were previously thought to be exclusively for sound processing (Cardin et al., 2013; Corina, Lawyer, Hauser, & Hirshorn, 2013). That supports the notion that the left hemisphere is really about *language* more than something particular to listening to words or mouth movements.

But there are two other ways to look at the left–right hemisphere distinction. One is that the left hemisphere is more involved in analytic thinking, whereas the right hemisphere is more specialized for synthesizing concepts. This framework is called the **analytic–synthetic theory**. The analytic thinking of the left hemisphere uses logical and sequential reasoning. For example, the left hemisphere may be involved in understanding that a man asked how you are. The right hemisphere, on the other hand, is used for the construction of a whole, larger picture, perhaps making a holistic judgment that he asked because he is alone and would like conversation. Overall, the left hemisphere is thought to take in evidence piece by piece, whereas the right hemisphere is thought to synthesize the larger picture. In this view, language might end up in the left hemisphere simply because it is an analytic function.

An alternative way of looking at the left–right hemisphere distinction is the **motor theory**, which argues that the left hemisphere controls fine movements and that speech (or writing or sign language) is just a category of movement (Liberman & Mattingly, 1985). This framework is supported by the fact that left-side brain damage produces speech and motor deficits, as we saw in the case of apraxia. Note that these frameworks may not be exclusive, but instead represent different ways of trying to capture the differences between the two hemispheres.

Finally, although differences exist between the two hemispheres, one should be careful not to overinterpret the distinctions. Language is the most lateralized brain function, but even it is not absolute: aspects of language, such as prosody, are mediated by the right hemisphere (Ross & Mesulam, 1979). Keep in mind that the hemispheres do not differ in their contributions to many nonlanguage functions, and the differences that do exist tend to be minimal.

Development of Language

Having traveled the world, Charles Darwin noted with interest that human language is instinctively—and universally—learned by babies: "Man has an instinctive tendency to speak, as we see in the babble of our young children, while no child has an instinctive tendency to brew, bake, or write" (Darwin, 1891, p. 131). And humans seem to be the only species with the ability to communicate with true language, at least one as rich and complex as ours.

So how do we acquire language in the first place? Just consider the challenge of listening to a foreign language. It is often difficult to know where one word ends and the next begins—in other words, how to **parse** (or divide up) the incoming stream of information. Although you might guess that words are conveniently separated by small silences, they typically aren't (FIGURE 11.17)—and this makes the infant's challenge of learning language even harder. So how do they ever figure it out? Are we born with an innate ability to absorb language, or is it simply a motor task that

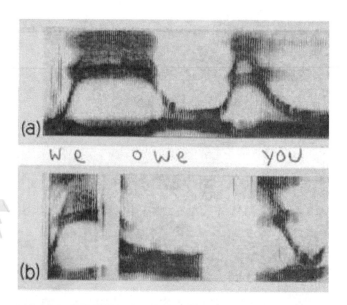

FIGURE 11.17 A spectrogram of spoken English. (a) A recording of the spoken phrase "We owe you." (b) The same phrase spoken with clear pauses between the words: "We," "owe," "you." Note in (a) that there are no pauses in the recording, although we hear them between the words.

is learned later in life? In this section we will see that language requires both experience with the world and innate predispositions.

Learning Language from Experience

Infant brains perform an enormous amount of statistical analysis on the inputs. For example, having heard "What a cute baby!" several times, they might also overhear "What a cute puppy!" The violation from their expectation for the last word helps them reveal the boundaries between separate words (Saffran, Aslin, & Newport, 1996). This is known as **statistical learning**.

The learning of language is greatly aided by an instinctive service from the parents: baby talk. Parents and caregivers typically speak in a different manner to their babies than to adults, using higher pitches and elongated words. This type of spoken language is often referred to as **parentese**. The next time you're around a new parent, pay attention to the difference between the pitch and pace of words when the parent is speaking to the infant versus another adult. This baby talk is neither accident nor inanity: the slowed articulation produces a clearer signal for the infant's brain to capture and interpret. A fascinating feedback loop between parent and infant brain allows this to happen: when babies are given a choice of whether to listen to parentese or normal language, they will always try to turn their head toward the person speaking parentese. This is true even if the voice speaking in parentese is not even that of a baby's own parent (Kuhl et al., 1997). Think about this: when parents express language in a way that is optimized for infant brains to analyze, the infants give feedback that the parents want (attention and smiles), thereby creating a feedback loop that results in the maximization of language learning. As you might guess, elements of parentese are helpful even to adults learning foreign languages. The high pitch doesn't add much, but the stretching of the sounds probably helps adults learn other tongues (Golinkoff & Alioto, 1995).

An example of experience influencing language development can be found in the learning of phonemes, which are the perceptually distinct units of sound that distinguish one word from another (for example, the *p*, *b*, and *m* sounds distinguish *pat*, *bat*, and *mat*). Prior to infants' first spoken words or word comprehension, they have already begun to recognize the phoneme characteristics of their native language (Baumann & Kuhl, 2002). By nine months of age, infants prefer the sound patterns of words in their native language over others (Jusczyk, Cutler, & Redanz, 1993).

But this learning of language goes beyond mere preference. Infants start life with the capacity to hear all possible sounds of human languages—but with progressive exposure to their mother tongue, they *lose* the ability to hear sound differences not utilized by their native tongue. Recall from Chapter 4 that at the age of 6 months, Japanese and American infants can both distinguish R and L sounds: if they hear a steady sound like *RRRRLLLLL*, they will notice the sudden change in the middle. At 10 months, American babies continue to notice the change, but the Japanese babies lose the capacity to detect the difference between R and L phonemes (and hence the change). The sound structure of the Japanese language causes these infants to not only ignore the difference between these phonemes, but also be *unable* to detect the difference (Kuhl, 2004).

Phoneme learning exemplifies the kind of statistical analysis that babies' brains perform on the input they hear. Their brains perform a frequency analysis to figure out where the "hotspots" are—that is, they learn which sounds carry meaning in their native language and they begin to develop categories that center on those spots in space (FIGURE 11.18). Once these categories are formed, babies no longer discriminate differences that aren't important to their language. As an example, Swedish speakers naturally divide phoneme space into 13 categories, English speakers into 8, and Japanese speakers into 5.

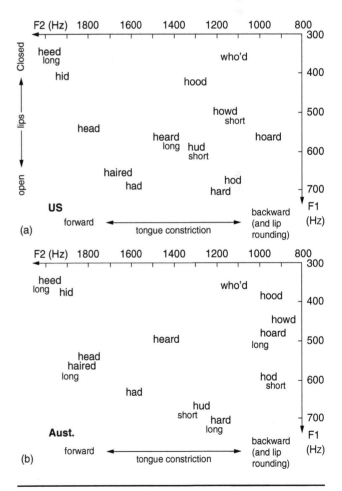

FIGURE 11.18 **Building boundaries in phoneme space.** Through exposure to spoken language, infant brains divide the space of possible phonemes into categories. This example shows the differences in vowel planes for (a) American and (b) Australian accents of English. The F1 frequency measurement (vertical axis) relates to how open the mouth is, and the F2 frequency measurement (horizontal axis) relates to whether the tongue is constricted toward the front or the back of the mouth.

Hand in hand with these perceptual changes, the kind of speech infants can *produce* also becomes language specific (Baumann & Kuhl, 2002). By nine months, infants begin to babble—and these babblings are specific to the phonemic structure of their native language: one can easily distinguish the babbling of American and Japanese babies.

Note that the critical window for phonemic learning results from the diminishing plasticity of the motor and sensory (mostly auditory) brain areas as the infant ages (Leung & Kao, 1999; Kuhl 2004). FIGURE 11.19 shows linguistic developmental milestones for both the perception and the production of speech (Leung & Kao, 1999; Kuhl 2004). As we've just seen, during the first year of life, an infant's perception of language becomes tuned to the particular phonemes of his or her native language, even without ever having spoken a word in any language. This is why it can be so challenging to learn a foreign language as an adult: the space of phonemes is often different in different languages, making the recognition of subtly different sounds grueling. Moreover, the babbling stage is absent later in life: an adult learner typically does not find himself babbling in his new language. Instead, his brain employs a more top-down approach to language learning, one that relies heavily on the frontal cortex. These are the major reasons why, as we saw in the previous section, primary and secondary languages become represented somewhat differently in the brain.

Interestingly, autistic infants prefer nonspeech analog signals produced by the computer over motherese (Kuhl, Coffey-Corina, Padden, & Dawson, 2005). The strength of the autistic symptoms positively correlates with a greater preference for the nonmotherese sounds. Because little data characterizes autism prior to age two, such findings have the potential to provide an early diagnostic test for autism.

To summarize where we are so far: by the time an infant is a year old—well before she has conquered vocabulary and grammar—her perceptual systems have already been altered by exposure to her native tongue. Likewise, the kind of speech she can produce has become language specific. These developmental stages are driven by her exposure to language. As we saw in Chapter 4 (on neuroplasticity), input from the world is required for these stages of language acquisition. For example, infants who are born deaf do not babble with their mouths, although their vocal cords would be perfectly capable of doing so. However, deaf infants exposed to sign language will "babble" with their hands (Petitto & Marentette, 1991). In other words, a baby's brain does not develop language in a vacuum—instead, it is "wired up" by the specifics of the input from the environment.

But this leads to a question. If babies simply absorb the statistics of language around them, why don't all animals do this? For that matter, why can't we easily hook a microphone to a computer and have *it* learn language as well? Is there something special about human brains? Are they predisposed to learn language?

Innate Language Tendencies

In the 1200s, Roger Bacon noted with fascination that grammars have many similarities across cultures and languages (Hackett, 2012). The deep structures found in one language are found in the others. By the 1960s, the linguist Noam Chomsky suggested that there was something deeply telling about this similarity: it implied the existence of an innate set of rules—often called a **universal grammar**—by which infants are born with the rules of grammar already in place (Chomsky, 1965). In other words, the human brain comes genetically equipped with a basic set of guidelines for organizing language.

The speculation of innate language skills is based on several simple observations. First, Chomsky noted that both kittens and children are capable of inductive reasoning. However, if you expose a kitten and a child to human language, only one of them will learn how to understand and produce it. This implies that something in the human brain is naturally capable of absorbing linguistic data, whereas the kitten brain is not.

Second, language *development* in children is fundamentally the same across languages. Infants in all cultures go through the same orderly transition, at approximately the

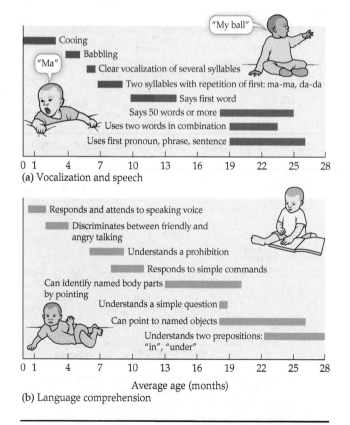

FIGURE 11.19 **Developmental milestones for language.** (a) The ages at which children typically are able to make sounds or speak. (b) A similar timeline for when children typically comprehend language.

same time, of linguistic developmental milestones (Baumann & Kuhl, 2002). No matter what language children are learning (English, Spanish, Dutch, French, Hebrew, Italian, or Korean), they learn vocabulary through the same sequential process, with nouns first, followed by verbs, and then adjectives. Even when deaf babies are compared to hearing babies, the maturational time course, structure, and content of early signed and spoken language acquisition are similar (Petitto et al., 2001). This suggests something fundamental and inborn about language acquisition (as opposed to the particulars of speaking or signing).

Finally, a fundamental argument for the existence of a universal grammar is the **poverty of the stimulus** argument: children simply do not hear *enough* examples of language construction during development to build a working model from scratch (Clark & Lappin, 2011). Put another way, the rules of language are too complex to be learned from the limited, patchy, untidy, incomplete word data to which children are exposed. Just think of how difficult it is to learn a second language; now consider that infants have the challenge of learning a first language with no guidance or rule book, from a restricted set of examples. Again, this indicates there may be innate structure in the brain that acts as the rule book.

The viewpoint that babies are not blank slates, but instead come wired for language, is known as **linguistic nativism**, sometimes referred to informally as the language instinct (Pinker, 1994). As an example, consider this sentence: *What did Susan meet a man who traveled?* Although the words are all reasonable, the sentence does not make sense; the construction is incorrect. Speakers of a language know what sorts of constructions are not acceptable—that is, the restrictions of their language. But the mystery is how one comes to learn these restrictions, given that such sentences are never part of the input to babies. How would a child learn whether it was acceptable unless she had heard it before? In other words, there is an absence of negative evidence for the child, and this issue is core to the poverty of the stimulus argument. A universal grammar solves the poverty of the stimulus problem by providing a rough framework of rules and restrictions. By restricting all languages into channels this way, the learner does not have to begin from scratch. Children are able to make correct decisions in language regarding the rules of grammar without ever formally being introduced to those rules or even to the concept of grammar (Berwick, Pietroski, Yankama, & Chomsky, 2011).

Note that a universal grammar does not imply that linguistic systems are *wholly* determined by genetic factors. Instead, languages vary based on cultural details. For example, English places verbs in a different part of the sentence than German does. The idea is that a universal grammar constrains the range of that variation, holding it within certain bounds. So the same verb placement in English is found in most other languages, and the verb placement in German is found in other, completely unrelated languages such as Kashmiri (Indian subcontinent), Vata (Ivory Coast), and Karitiana (Brazil). *No* known languages have verb placements in other positions that are feasible and equally imaginable; those are simply never used (Lidz et al., 2003). These observations support the proposition that genetic constraints allow languages to vary, but within limits.

How can one better understand the fundamental, innate structure? In 1981, linguist Derek Bickerton turned to **creoles**—new languages that arise among children exposed to simplified versions of other languages, as often happens when geographical displacement has broken ties with a people's original tongue (for example with slavery) (Bickerton, 1981). He suggested that creole languages give the best representation of what happens when the details of cultural history are stripped away, leaving the genetically constrained language structure to blossom on its own. For example, although different creole languages share no common history with each other, they share many grammatical features when referring to time, tense, and mood—or even how they turn a statement into a question simply by changing the sentence's intonation (rather than the words). Although Bickerton's interpretation has been influential, it has also been controversial (Mufwene, 1996).

Beyond creoles, one can look to the animal kingdom for evidence that innate, species-specific language constraints exist (**FIGURE 11.20**). Consider songbird learning. Songbirds learn their song structure from listening to other birds, but even songbirds raised in total isolation will nonetheless develop a rudimentary song that matches the parameters of their species' "grammar" (Marler, 1991). This exposes the existence of an innate, species-specific constraint on how their "language" expresses itself.

Despite the arguments for a universal grammar, there is lively controversy about the details of the proposal. Some argue that the poverty of the stimulus problem can be solved in other ways besides an assumption of innate language constraints. For example, children may make generalizations about new words based on what they already know ("similarity-based generalization") (Yarlett, 2008), and children may learn the distribution patterns of words in a probabilistic manner (McDonald & Ramscar, 2001). It is also possible that the orderly set of milestones in linguistic development may simply be explained by the observation that children acquire nouns first because nouns are concrete objects that can be seen and touched (Gentner, 1982). In early life, these physical elements of life may be the most novel and exciting. Later in life, the child constructs relations between the tangible items he or she possesses. As a result, the child learns verbs and adjectives, which are progressively more abstract (Bornstein et al., 2004).

Although the idea that genetic endowment constrains language remains controversial in its details, it is consistent with the emerging understanding that babies are not blank slates, but instead are primed for certain types of learning.

FIGURE 11.20 **Language can be found in other species.** (a) The eastern yellow robin. (b) Alex, the African gray parrot studied for more than 30 years by Dr. Irene Pepperberg. (c) Washoe, the first chimpanzee who learned to communicate using American Sign Language.

Socially and Emotionally Directed Learning

At the interface of statistical learning and innate predisposition for language is the issue of socially directed learning. Babies learn by experience, but appear to be hardwired to leverage social feedback from adults to *guide* their learning. In other words, a system that does pure statistical extraction of all inputs would try to learn everything in the environment. But human brains arrive in the crib with a more efficient strategy: only learn those things that are colored with social importance.

Consider the interaction between the infant and caregiver. As early as five months of age, infants appear to learn the social effects of their vocalization on caregivers' behavior. Caregivers respond to an average of 30% to 50% of infants' noncry vocalizations, and this responsiveness seems to facilitate the development of particular phonemes in the infants. This is supported by the fact that infants show an extinction burst in vocalizing when adults stop responding to them. That is, if the adults show a blank expression in response to the infant making sounds, the infant tries vigorously to get some response from them—and then stops producing that sound altogether. Thus, even at five months of age, infants are already using the feedback they receive to shape the sounds they are producing (Goldstein, Schwade, & Bornstein, 2009). In other words, infants use social direction to filter incoming information.

In another study that demonstrates the importance of social interaction, Dr. Patricia Kuhl and her colleagues took groups of 10- to 11-month-old babies—born into English-speaking monolingual homes in Seattle—and exposed them to several hours of Mandarin Chinese. One group of infants heard the Mandarin from live, native speakers, who spoke to them while they showed them books and toys. After a mere 12 sessions of 25 minutes each, these infants could pick up on subtle differences in two Chinese phonemes, whereas a control group, exposed to live English speakers, could not make this distinction (Kuhl, Tsao, & Liu, 2003).

But there was a second, critical part of the test. Another group of infants was exposed to the same number of Mandarin syllables over the same amount of time, but this time on a televised video of the same Mandarin speakers from the first group. Yet another group of infants simply listened to an audio recording of the speakers. Both these groups heard the same sounds, delivered in the same infant-directed naturalistic speech—but without the live interaction. When tested at the end, both groups had much less phonemic learning, performing about the same as the English-only control group (FIGURE 11.21).

These results provide strong evidence that social interaction (as opposed to merely watching a television or listening to an audio stream) is critical to language learning. In fact, the American Academy of Pediatrics issued a statement recommending that parents limit the amount of time their young children spend in front of a screen (American Academy of Pediatrics, 2013). As above, the babies seem to be using social direction to guide their learning. As is true of human development in infancy overall, language development occurs in the

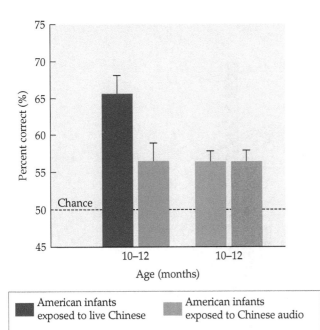

American infants
exposed to live Chinese

American infants
exposed to live English

American infants
exposed to Chinese audio

American infants exposed
to Chinese audio and video

FIGURE 11.21 **Effects of live interaction in language learning.** American infants were tested on Mandarin Chinese speech discrimination. When exposed to live interaction with actual speakers of Chinese, there was significantly more learning than from exposure to American English. In the absence of a live person (audiovisual or audio only), there was no learning.

context of relationships. Emotion and language development in the early years are linked. At the beginning of life, a good deal of communication between infants and caregivers pivots on relationships and emotions (Bloom & Capatides, 1987). In fact, that importance of relationships is evident from the first day: newborns prefer the sounds of their mothers' voices (DeCasper & Fifer, 1980) and prefer the language spoken by their mother during her pregnancy (Moon, Panneton-Cooper, & Fifer, 1993).

Language is not a solo act. Sensitivity to the timing of conversational exchanges can be studied through research on back-and-forth communication involving young infants (Rochat, Querido, & Striano, 1999). Infants use speech, gestures, facial expressions, and direction of attention to communicate with others. As they grow and gain an expanded vocabulary to express themselves, they increasingly decipher the rules and conventions of social communication. As they develop, infants benefit from communicating with both peers and adults, very different conversational partners. Peers offer less language skill and less cooperation than adults, and this can be valuable. It forces the development of more complex conversational dexterity, such as figuring out how and when to interject, how to manage conversational overlaps, what to do when interrupted by another, and how to keep a conversation on topic (Pan & Snow, 1999).

To put together everything we've learned so far, let's have a look at a powerful, and unusual, method for studying language development in children.

RESEARCH METHODS:
The Baby with No Privacy

What if you could remember the first word you ever uttered in this world? Your parents probably remember it and may have recorded it. But that is probably it. Your parents likely did not record the next day you spoke or the day after. Not unless you were one of Deb Roy's children. Deb Roy and his group at MIT's Media Lab set up 11 overhead cameras and 14 microphones around the house where Roy's newborn son would be (Roy et al., 2006). For the next five years, they captured every moment and every sound Roy's son would make on film, creating the Human Speechome Project.

For the first time, Deb Roy and his group were able to see and hear how an individual child acquires language. Given the vast amount of data collected, they developed novel algorithms to sort through the enormous amounts of data. With powerful analytics, they were able to perform interesting longitudinal studies on the "birth of words" in children. Roy and his team defined the "birth of a word"—the first utterance of a word to be detected. The analysis revealed an interesting pattern in the birth of words as the child ages (Roy, 2009). FIGURE 11.22 shows the number of word births per month as the child

ages from 9 months to 24 months. Note the peak of word births at age 20 months, giving a "shark's fin" curve: an increase in word births followed by a sudden decline after 20 months. It has long been assumed that a child's vocabulary exponentially increases in the early developmental period; however, Roy's recording of all of his son's speech unmasks a different distribution. Why the shark's fin? One reason may be that the child begins to shift his focus from saying new words to combining learned words into new sequences and words.

Could Roy examine the issue of social interaction? Indeed, his recordings shed light on the feedback loop between adult speakers and infants during the birth of words. Remember that the recordings capture not only the son's voice, but also the voice of his caregivers (father, mother, babysitters, friends, etc.). Roy's team analyzed the average length of a caregiver's word utterance over time, before and after the birth of the word. Earlier utterances of the word are much longer compared with later utterances. Presumably, caregivers are priming the child to learn the word, making it easier for the child to sound out the word. Once the child is more familiar with the word, the caregiver can say it more rapidly and increase the complexity of the utterance. Roy's experiments provide a telling snapshot of the utility of parentese in action.

His team also created new mapping techniques to track the position of the child *and* the caregivers as they interacted. With these tracings, Roy found that the child and caregiver interact in "social hotspots" in the home. For example, he could track all the locations in the house where the word "water" was uttered; in **FIGURE 11.23** the height of the

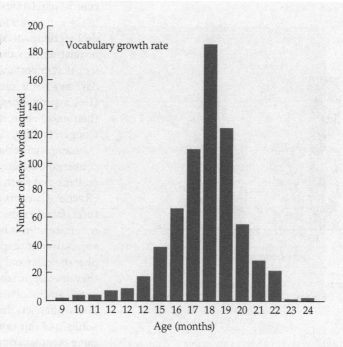

FIGURE 11.22 Number of new words acquired per month, age 9–24 months.

landscape shows the number of times in each location. On the right, the final wordscape demonstrates a few key hotspots where the word was spoken: the kitchen (left), living room (right), and a sharp peak near the bathroom sink (rear right).

Similarly, the word "bye" was unwittingly taught (and learned) near

the front door of the house. Although this sort of approach is in its early stages, such real-world, data-rich visualization has the potential to reveal the relationships between language learning and social structures.

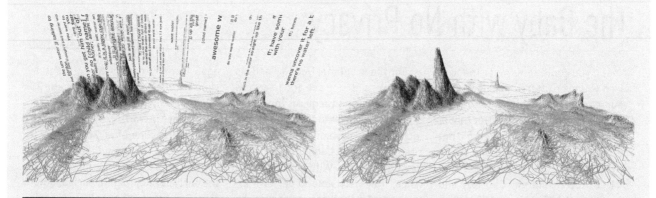

FIGURE 11.23 Wordscapes of every utterance of the word "water," by child or caregiver, mapped to the location where it happened. (a) The height of the landscape shows the number of times in each location. (b) The final wordscape demonstrates a few key hotspots where the word was spoken: the kitchen (left), living room (right), and a sharp peak near the bathroom sink (rear right).

Before we end our discussion of language, one question remains: is language unique to humans? This continues to be hotly debated. For some time, scientists wanted to train apes to talk. However, they soon realized that the physics of the ape larynx would not allow a sufficient range of vocalization (Lieberman, 1968; Simonyan & Horwitz, 2011). So they began to train chimpanzees to use sign language; there was more success with that approach, most notably with the ape Koko (Patterson, 1981). But some scientists took a different tack. A type of chimpanzee known as the bonobo (*Pan paniscus*) is quite humanlike. Bonobos can stand on their hind legs easily, can understand the concept of a mirror, and are less aggressive than their other chimpanzee counterparts. Dr. Sue Savage-Rumbaugh and her team taught one particular bonobo, Matata, how to associate symbols with particular meanings. These symbols were visuographic representation of words, or **lexigrams**. Matata made some progress and learned several symbols. But more amazing was the fact that Matata had an infant son, Kanzi, who was watching his mother learn. Kanzi learned the symbols by simple observation, soon mastering 150 symbols on the keyboard. What's more, Kanzi began to understand many words of spoken human language, reaching the comprehension of a two or two-and-a-half-year-old human child. Kanzi also learned a pattern of language that the common chimpanzee could not learn: the agent–verb–recipient form of language ("Bob gives to Amy"), in which the recipient did not have to be Kanzi and the agent did not have to be the person Kanzi was addressing. Having mastered these feats, Kanzi was then able to teach his younger sister Mulika the concept of the symbols. Whether these represent true language is still debated; however, the bonobos are a clear link to our evolutionary history of language development (Lyn & Savage-Rumbaugh, 2000; Savage-Rumbaugh, McDonald, Sevcik, Hopkins, & Rubert, 1986). Such studies of language in other species help us to understand better our own human language.

Conclusion

We have learned that infants will absorb whatever language they are born into—and with the opening of that door comes the closing of other doors. That is, as the space of phonemes becomes carved up to represent the sound space of one's native language, it becomes less useful for discriminating differences in other tongues.

If you are studying a foreign language, you are likely familiar with these challenges. In part the learning is difficult because second languages are typically learned after phonemic categorization has taken place, making recognition and production of subtly different foreign sounds challenging. More generally, the early developmental stages of primary language acquisition (including babbling) are typically absent when acquiring a second language. Given this, it is hardly surprising that primary and secondary languages become represented somewhat differently in the brain.

Language is learned from experience (nurture), but we also saw that genetic endowment sets the stage for that learning in the first place. A newborn infant innately holds the ability to acquire whatever language she is exposed to. This is no small feat. The child must learn to recognize, understand, and reproduce sounds that are important for the language needed—and she must learn to discriminate native language–related sounds from all other sounds, including sounds from other languages.

Returning to the beginning of the chapter, King George VI had no idea why he stuttered. But during an age in which live radio broadcasts had just been introduced, he had no choice but to succeed in delivering speeches. Fortunately, his friend had some insight on how to treat him with methods science did not yet understand. King George's problem quite likely lay in his inability to hear his own voice properly: he lacked the auditory feedback needed to complete the loop of his language circuit.

From conditions like stuttering in King George, we have learned much about language. And we know that sometimes we have to dig under the surface of the problems to find the answers. King George didn't have any problems with his muscles in his throat. Aphasia is not a result of aberrant motor cortex function; recall that patients can move their tongues. Cases of brain damage—in conjunction with electrical stimulation and neuroimaging—have enabled us to get a rough picture of the network underlying our unique ability for language.

KEY PRINCIPLES

- Speech describes the sounds we make when talking to another person. Language is translating ideas into some form of signal, such as speech or written communication, that can be shared with another person. Communication is transmitting information from one person to another.

- Human communication is unique in its almost infinite complexity of possible methods for expressing intention, signifying identity, and broadcasting social signals.

- Although the brain as a whole gives rise to language, key regions play crucial roles in the comprehension and production of language. Each of these regions, when damaged, gives rise to unique communication problems.

- Broca's area is found in the frontal lobe of the left hemisphere and is involved in the production of language. Wernicke's area is found in the temporal lobe of the left hemisphere and is involved in the comprehension of language.

- Damage to Broca's or Wernicke's area results in problems with producing or comprehending language. These problems are known as Broca's aphasia and Wernicke's aphasia, respectively.

- A simplified circuit of language in the brain (the Wernicke–Geschwind model) is incomplete, but nonetheless provides a useful clinical categorization of language deficits.

- The left and right hemispheres appear symmetrical, but there are functional differences between the two hemispheres, with language typically found in the left hemisphere and spatial ability in the right hemisphere.

- Elements of language are acquired during development from a combination of genetic predispositions and environmental inputs. This developmental process interacts with an innate human capacity for language.

KEY TERMS

Speech, Language, and Communication

speech (p. 338)
language (p. 339)
grammar (p. 339)
communication (p. 339)
autism spectrum disorders (p. 339)
Williams syndrome (p. 339)

Aphasia: The Loss of Language

dysphonia (p. 339)
dysarthria (p. 339)
Broca's aphasia (p. 340)
Wernicke's aphasia (p. 340)
agrammatical (p. 340)
anomia (p. 340)
Broca's area (p. 341)
expressive aphasia (p. 341)
Wernicke's area (p. 341)
receptive aphasia (p. 341)
fluent aphasia (p. 342)
word salad (p. 342)

neologism (p. 342)
paraphasia (p. 342)
prosody (p. 343)

A Language Network

alexia (word blindness) (p. 343)
arcuate fasciculus (p. 344)
Wernicke–Geschwind model (p. 344)
conduction aphasia (p. 344)
global aphasia (p. 344)
averbia (p. 345)
electrical stimulation mapping (p. 346)
dyslexia (p. 347)
orthographic level (p. 347)
phonological level (p. 347)
surface dyslexia (p. 347)
deep dyslexia (p. 347)

Lateralization: The Two Hemispheres Are Not Identical

Wada test (p. 349)
barbiturates (p. 349)

apraxia (p. 349)
amusia (p. 350)
planum temporale (p. 350)
callosotomy (p. 350)
split-brain patients (p. 351)
cross-cueing (p. 352)
helping-hand phenomenon (p. 352)
analytic–synthetic theory (p. 352)
motor theory (p. 352)

Development of Language

parse (p. 352)
statistical learning (p. 353)
parentese (p. 353)
universal grammar (p. 354)
poverty of the stimulus (p. 355)
linguistic nativism (p. 355)
creoles (p. 355)
lexigrams (p. 359)

REVIEW QUESTIONS

1. If a person were to lose her tongue to cancer and therefore be unable to speak, would this be considered an aphasia? Why or why not?

2. What kind of aphasia is associated with neologisms and paraphasias?

3. Compare and contrast language deficits in Broca's and Wernicke's aphasias.

4. Draw the Wernicke–Geschwind model of the language circuit in the brain. Label each region and describe its function. Trace the path of a visual word (a word that is seen) and an auditory word (a word that is heard) through the circuit.

5. Which functions are more dominant in the left hemisphere? In the right hemisphere?

6. Describe how Roger Sperry and his team were able to uncover the deficits involved in split-brain patients.

7. What sorts of questions can Dr. Deb Roy begin to address by recording every moment of the first 5 years of his son's life at home?

8. What was unique about the bonobo chimpanzees and their acquisition of language characteristics that other chimpanzees and animals were not able to produce?

CRITICAL-THINKING QUESTIONS

1. If you had to choose between having Broca's aphasia and Wernicke's aphasia, which would you choose and why? With which type of aphasia would it be most difficult for you to cope in your daily life? How would your friends and family be impacted in their interactions with you? Explain.

2. From a biological standpoint, why do you think that one's native language (L1) and a second language learned later in life (L2) are represented differently in the brain? Explain.

3. Is language innate, or learned, or a combination of both? Give examples and reasons for your argument.

LEARNING OBJECTIVES By the end of this chapter, you should be able to:

- Define the concepts of expected utility theory and *Homo economicus*.

- Explain when and how *Homo sapiens* typically reaches different decisions than *Homo economicus*.

- Describe known differences between humans and other species in delay discounting and risk taking as well as two explanations for irrational human behavior.

- Explain dual-systems models of human decision making and the neural basis of delay discounting, impulsivity, risk aversion, framing effects, and endowment effects.

- Describe the neural basis of subjective value, the role of the orbitofrontal cortex, and the brain regions controlling internally guided decision making.

- Characterize the mechanisms behind strategic control of competing decision-making systems and the modulatory effects of neurotransmitters.

Decision Making

STARTING OUT:
A Fatal Mistake, at the Highest Place on Earth

Mount Everest, the tallest mountain on earth, rises to a height of more than 29,035 feet (FIGURE 12.1). It is also one of the least hospitable places on the planet. At its peak, temperatures reach –20°F on a warm day and can plummet as low as –100°F. A climber at the summit can face winds of more than 100 miles per hour. The air itself has oxygen levels only a third of those found at sea level. In this "death zone," without supplemental oxygen tanks, climbers' blood oxygen saturation drops to 50% of normal: a level at which body tissue functions begin to cease and neurons die by the thousand every hour. This lack of oxygen is one of several physiological factors that can impair our ability to make good decisions.

Despite these adverse conditions, many thousands of people have attempted to reach the summit of Everest over the past hundred years. Although around 3,000 have succeeded, more than 200 have died in the attempt. Many of these fatalities came not on the way up, but during the even trickier descent. For best chances of survival, climbers attempt the summit only when the weather conditions are perfect. They will also turn around and descend by early afternoon, whether or not they have reached the top, even if they are only a few hundred vertical feet from their goal. Yet even experienced climbers have been known to attempt the summit at times when the winds

FIGURE 12.1 **Mount Everest.** The tallest mountain in the world.

are too high, or the weather too unstable, or even at an hour when it is too late to reach the summit and still make it back to camp before the end of the day.

These kinds of miscalculations have sometimes led to disasters. In 1996, during a major storm, eight climbers perished in a single day. The events leading to the disaster were chronicled in a bestselling book, *Into Thin Air*, by Jon Krakauer (Krakauer, 1997), a mountaineer and journalist who was present. Although the causes of the catastrophe are still debated, many people agree that if the climbers had decided to turn around at the usual early afternoon deadline (2 p.m.) rather than push for the top, many deaths could have been avoided.

So why do experienced climbers sometimes heed the risks and play safe, but at other times drive onward, even at the cost of their own lives? If they have had the intelligence, judgment, and reserve to survive many other ascents, why would this judgment desert them here? Partially, it is because the lack of oxygen at that altitude impairs judgment and decision making. However, human beings often make decisions that are irrational or foolhardy, even when they know better. These decisions can carry heavy consequences, from death and dismemberment to poor health, conflict, warfare, poverty, or even just a bulging waistline. If we hope to avoid these kinds of mistakes in future generations, we will first need to understand where they come from. In this chapter, we explore the neural mechanisms that drive human decision making, at its best and worst.

How Do We Decide What to Do?

To be human is to live with a strange conundrum. We have the ability to imagine the future with unprecedented detail and accuracy. We can envision the consequences of our actions in ways that no other living species can match. Not only that, but we can also benefit from the hard-earned wisdom of other human beings around us, so that we need not repeat their mistakes. Armed with the collective wisdom of billions of other lifetimes and the foresight to apply this experience to our own lives, we ought to be shining examples of wisdom and good judgment.

With such powerful faculties at our disposal, we should be living lives that are free of repeated and foreseeable mistakes. There should be no broken New Year's resolutions, no abandoned diets or training schedules, no exams failed through insufficient studying or assignments late because of excessive procrastination. Dysfunctional families should be raising children who learn from the experience and emerge well equipped to avoid the errors of their parents. Workers should never fall into debt, knowing they are living beyond their means but somehow unable to rein in the spending.

Yet all too often, our judgment falls short of our intelligence. We make bad decisions, knowing full well that they are bad decisions, even knowing that we will certainly regret them later. Perplexingly, we are even aware of our own irrationality in this regard, and yet this insight fails to help us. Somehow, the architecture of our motivations and decisions is made of more than simple rationality and enlightened self-interest.

The Scorpion and the Frog

Before we explore these factors that affect decision making, let us first define a decision as a choice one makes after considering different alternatives. This is a process that you do many times per day. Think back to yesterday. How many decisions did you make about food? Participants in a study in 2006 estimated that they made about 14 decisions about food per day. The actual number of food-related decisions was much higher; the average subject made more than 220 such decisions per day (Wansink & Sobal, 2006). Such a lack of awareness of decisions may contribute to the irrationality of some of the decisions we make.

Why should decisions be made for something other than rational reasons? As a species, we have puzzled over this conundrum since before the dawn of recorded history. The folklore of many cultures makes reference to our pervasively irrational behavior. The tale of *The Scorpion and the Frog*, attributed to Aesop, tells of a scorpion who asks a frog to carry him across a river. The frog refuses, fearing that the scorpion

FIGURE 12.2 *The Scorpion and the Frog.* The tale of *The Scorpion and the Frog*, attributed to Aesop, carries a message about the behavior of human beings. It asks us to consider why we make irrational decisions, even when we know better.

will sting him and kill him. However, the scorpion points out that it would not be in the scorpion's own interest to do so, since he would then drown, being unable to swim on his own. The frog accepts this point as reasonable and allows the scorpion to climb on his back before setting out across the river (FIGURE 12.2). Suddenly, halfway across, the frog feels a terrible pain in his back and realizes the scorpion has stung him. "Why did you do that?" the frog demands to know. "Now we will both die." But the scorpion can only answer, "I couldn't help myself. It's in my nature to sting."

Of course, *The Scorpion and the Frog* is about the behavior of human beings, rather than frogs and scorpions. And although the story is thousands of years old, the questions it raises are just as important today. Why do we make irrational decisions, even when we know better? Why is it hard to do what we know is right? How do we decide what to do in the first place? For centuries, such questions lay firmly in the domain of philosophy and, sometimes, of religion. Over the past 50 years, however, we have studied human decision-making behavior closely in experimental settings. This work has helped us to start mapping out the previously uncharted landscape of human decision making: reliable, reproducible patterns in how human beings choose one alternative course of action over another, whether rationally or irrationally. In the past 10 years, we have begun to study the actual brain mechanisms that guide human decision making and how these mechanisms operate during rational and irrational decisions. In this chapter, we'll look at a few classic examples of rational and irrational human decision making before delving into what neuroscience has taught us about why our decisions operate as they do. Finally, we'll look at how this new knowledge could help us make better decisions by maneuvering around the roughest parts of our motivational landscape, even if the landscape itself is not likely to change any time soon.

The Search for a "Physics" of Human Decisions

Some of the first efforts to build a formal model of human decision making began during the historical period of the Enlightenment, in 18th-century Europe. This period sought to build on the remarkable successes of mathematical models in advancing astronomy, physics, and chemistry during the preceding century. Kepler had described the previously inscrutable movements of the planetary bodies in mathematical terms. Newton and Galileo had likewise helped to create a physics of natural laws expressed mathematically. Boyle had helped to turn the mystical art of alchemy into the modern science of chemistry, again governed by laws that could be summarized in mathematical formulas and used to predict the behavior of the natural world. If the mysteries of alchemy and astrology could be untangled through natural laws and mathematical models, could it not be possible to untangle the mysteries of human behavior in the same way?

One of the first to attempt such a feat was the English philosopher Jeremy Bentham, who devised the moral precepts of **utilitarianism**. The central idea was that any given action could be assigned a value known as its "utility": the amount of happiness or pleasure that the action would bring to all human beings. Choosing the best action at any given time could then be considered a mathematical process of maximizing utility: in other words, choosing whatever action would bring the greatest good to the greatest number of people. But how could anyone actually calculate the utility of a given action (for example, eating eggs versus bacon for breakfast) in a mathematically precise way?

Bentham, like Newton, was a child prodigy. He had already obtained a bachelor's degree, master's degree, and law degree by the age of 21. Like Newton, he devised a complex mathematical algorithm to describe the idealized behavior of his subjects—in this case, human beings rather than planetary bodies (FIGURE 12.3). Bentham's "**felicific calculus**" involved measuring pleasure or pain in terms of intensity, duration, probability, time until occurrence, likelihood of being followed by more of the same, likelihood of being followed by more of the opposite, and number of people affected. Of course, this method quickly proved to be impractical for most real-life decisions. The values were too difficult to estimate, too subjective, and too numerous. If we were to use the felicific calculus for a real-life decision, like figuring out what to eat for breakfast, we could easily starve to death before reaching a solution! Since human beings solve such problems easily in real life (as do mice, goldfish, and fruit flies), the brain certainly seems to have a better system.

Homo economicus and Rational Choice Theory

Despite its impracticality, Bentham's approach left its mark on the future study of human decision making. Today, economists continue to use the concept of **utility** to describe the desirability, or value, of a given course of action (such as acquiring a consumer good). Modern economic models of human behavior even incorporate some elements of Bentham's felicific calculus. For example, they describe how the value or **expected utility** of a given course of action, such as buying a lottery ticket, can depend on factors like the size of the prize, the probability of winning, the length of time until the prize becomes available, and so on. Such models typically describe the behavior that would be expected of an idealized human being who makes perfectly rational choices to obtain the maximum utility in any given situation (Schoemaker, 1982).

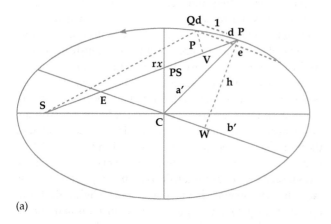

(a)

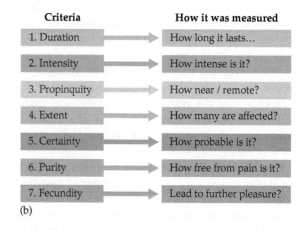

Criteria	How it was measured
1. Duration	How long it lasts…
2. Intensity	How intense is it?
3. Propinquity	How near / remote?
4. Extent	How many are affected?
5. Certainty	How probable is it?
6. Purity	How free from pain is it?
7. Fecundity	Lead to further pleasure?

(b)

FIGURE 12.3 Newton's laws of motion and Bentham's felicific calculus. Both Newton and Bentham adopted a quantitative, scientific approach to better understand the properties of their subject. (a) For Newton, that subject was the movement of planets. (b) For Bentham, it was pleasure.

This theoretical rational economic agent is sometimes called **Homo economicus**, or "economic man." As a creature of the Enlightenment period, he embodies many of the ideals of his time. *Homo economicus* makes decisions by a process that is perfectly rational (in the mathematical sense, if not in a broader social sense). He seeks to obtain the greatest happiness, or utility, for himself based on the information he has about the options available. He desires to maximize gains and minimize losses. He is neither averse to taking calculated risks nor lured into gambling for large but unlikely rewards. He accurately assesses short-term gains and long-term pains, deciding in a consistent way which is more important. He is not swayed by emotional considerations. If he is willing to buy a good for a given price, he is willing to sell the good for the same price. Faced with two given options, his choice will always be the same regardless of how the options are described (R. H. Thaler, 2000).

Now, if we imagine a group of these idealized, theoretical beings, we can then devise theories about how they might interact in an "efficient marketplace" where everyone has accurate information about the supply of goods available, their relative costs and benefits, the demand for the goods in question, and the other agents in the market. We can even formulate a series of principles of human behavior in such a marketplace, each one backed by a logical mathematical proof. Akin to the Newtonian laws of motion in physics, these principles form the basis of **rational choice theory** (Coleman & Fararo, 1992).

Economics is an entire field in itself. The key question for our purposes is whether these theories can help us to understand how human beings make decisions. And although they describe certain forms of human behavior quite well, there are also many situations in which the very assumptions of rational choice theory seem to be violated. So if we want to understand why the scorpion stings the frog, we will need to look at the behavior of actual human beings in real-life situations, with all the uncertainty and risk that real life entails.

The Predictably Irrational *Homo sapiens*

Homo sapiens versus *Homo economicus*

Decisions and interactions under rational choice theory are a sort of human equivalent of idealized "billiard-ball physics." The mass, position, and velocity of all of the objects are known in perfect detail ahead of time, and their interactions can be predicted with perfect detail afterward using precise mathematical formulas. Using these approaches, in theory, it would be possible to model a game of billiards and predict exactly where every billiard ball will end up after a player takes a shot with a given force and direction. Of course, real billiard balls do not operate exactly like their flawless, frictionless theoretical equivalents.

In the same way, the behavior of actual *Homo sapiens* has proven to be somewhat different from that of his theoretical counterpart, *Homo economicus*, in many situations. Behavioral studies of human choice gradually evolved over several decades into the field of **behavioral economics** (Camerer, Loewenstein, & Rabin, 2011). Essentially, this field examines human decision making using empirical rather than theoretical methods. This involves placing real human subjects in various situations and recording their actual choices under different kinds of controlled conditions. When we look at decision making in this way, we find a wide variety of startling, yet reliable, forms of irrationality and inconsistency in how we decide.

One example is the observation that real humans have **relative preferences**, rather than the **absolute preferences** predicted for *Homo economicus*. Under the assumptions of rational choice theory, a person's preference for A versus B should remain constant regardless of whether we introduce a new option, C. Yet in real-world studies, we find that you can shift a person's preference from A to B by introducing a third option, B', that is more similar to B than to A but clearly inferior to B (Ariely, 2008) (FIGURE 12.4.) For example, imagine someone who is having trouble deciding whether to buy a high-quality large sedan or a high-quality small SUV. It is actually possible to push them toward buying the SUV by offering the option of another, low-quality SUV. By comparison, the high-quality version looks better and so becomes more attractive. The *mere presence* of the inferior option affects a person's perceived value of the two superior options. So it seems that we judge value in relative terms, rather than in absolute terms (Tremblay & Schultz, 1999). This violates the assumptions of rational choice theory, that a person will always make the same logical decisions.

Relative valuation explains why restaurants will sometimes include absurdly overpriced dishes or wines on their menu. They don't expect customers to order those items, but the mere presence of the options leads customers to choose a more expensive dish than they otherwise would have. The price of the slightly more expensive dish seems more reasonable compared with that of the overpriced item. We also seem to get overwhelmed if there are *too many* options available (Schwartz, 2009), in which case we may abandon or postpone the decision to buy. For this reason, retailers sometimes find that they can boost sales by offering *less* selection and more obvious differences between each of the options: 2 or 3 models, rather than 10 in any given category of good. These widespread phenomena are well known to those who specialize in marketing and advertising, but once again, are inexplicable under rational choice theory alone.

(a)

(b)

(c)

FIGURE 12.4 **Relative versus absolute preference for an option.** When trying to decide between (a) option A (a sedan) and (b) option B (an SUV), your preference for B can be increased by introducing a third option, (c) B′, which is a lower-quality version of option B.

Confused by Uncertainty

One of the classic examples of inconsistency in human choice involves decisions under risk and uncertainty. In many real-life situations, the consequences of choosing a given action are far from certain: there may be a payoff or there may not, and we simply do not know the outcome ahead of time. For example, someone could offer you a 50% chance of winning $100 on a coin toss. Guess correctly and you win the money; guess incorrectly and you win nothing. Now let's say that you were offered the chance to take a smaller, but certain, amount

of money rather than take the gamble. How much would this amount have to be for you to give up the gamble? *Homo economicus* would simply determine the overall utility of the options mathematically. He would multiply out the odds and the prize to get $50: the so-called **point of indifference** where either option would be equally acceptable. But what about *Homo sapiens*? As it turns out, most people would rather take $35 or $40 as a sure thing than take a gamble for $100, but with only a 50% chance of winning. In other words, they are willing to pay a substantial penalty to avoid risk. Behavioral economists would describe people as **risk averse** for gambles with a moderate chance of winning (Rabin, 2000).

What if we change the odds? Now let's say that you are entered in a lottery in which you have a 1 in 100 chance of winning a large prize of $1,000 dollars. Alternatively, you can take a smaller but certain amount. Once again, *Homo economicus* would happily take $10 and give up the chance at $1,000 (Rabin, 2000). Would you do the same? In this case, it turns out that most people would not give up their ticket for only $10. Instead they would be willing to do so only for a larger sum: $15, $20, or even more (Weber, 2005). Strangely, they have become **risk seeking** for gambles with a small chance of success.

Now let's turn the situation around. Let's say that you are told that your name is on a list of 100 people and that one of these people is about to be fined a sum of $1,000. However, you are offered the chance to take your name off the list by paying a small fee of $10. Would you do so? Most *Homo sapiens* would—in fact, many would pay $20, $30, or even more. But note that this is simply the mirror image of the previous example: the only thing that has changed is the sign of the prize, from positive to negative. Yet somehow, the certain option has become preferable to the gamble. *Homo sapiens* has switched from being a risk-seeking creature to being a risk-averse creature, simply because we are dealing with losses rather than gains. *Homo economicus* would never show such inconsistent behavior!

In the real world, this explains why people like to play the lottery, but also tend to buy insurance. Lotteries and insurance companies are immensely profitable because people are willing to pay over the odds to seek large but unlikely gains and also to avoid large but unlikely losses. So inconsistency reigns, under conditions of uncertainty.

The inconsistent decisions of human beings under uncertainty cannot be explained by rational choice theory. However, they are described by a model known as **prospect theory**, developed in 1979 by the behavioral economists Amos Tversky and Daniel Kahneman (Kahneman & Tversky, 1979). Kahneman and Tversky created an empirically based "utility curve" to describe how people assign value to options with the prospect of a loss or a gain (**FIGURE 12.5**). The curve has two major features that are worth noting. First, it has a different shape on the "losses" side than it does on the "gains" side. Second, because of these two different shapes, it has a "kink," or discontinuity, at the zero mark. In other words, the curve is not continuous but is more like two different curves, with different properties, glued together at the middle. The findings of two curves suggest that we may use different processes for

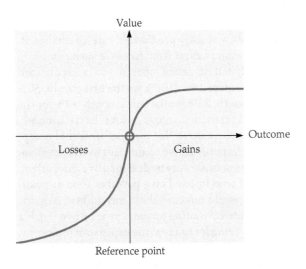

FIGURE 12.5 **The utility curve under "prospect theory."** This function was developed by Kahneman and Tversky using behavioral data from experimental studies in which people choose among different options. Note the shape of the function, which looks like two different curves stuck together at the Y-axis. The different shapes of the curves suggest that we may use different mechanisms for evaluating gains versus losses.

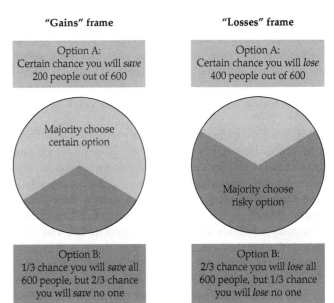

FIGURE 12.6 **Framing effects in medical decision making.** In the first scenario, the emphasis is on the number of lives saved. With this frame, the majority of subjects selected the first treatment option, which was to save 200 people. In the second scenario, the emphasis is on the lives lost. With this frame, the majority of subjects selected the second treatment option, which was to take a two-thirds chance that all the patients would die.

evaluating losses and gains (Kahneman & Tversky, 1979). Keep this hypothesis in mind—it will be important later in the chapter, when we look at the mechanisms of decision making in the human brain.

The Framing Effect and the Endowment Effect

One of the strange consequences of these inconsistencies is that *Homo sapiens* can be manipulated into choosing either the certain option or the risky option, simply by describing the options in terms of potential gains or potential losses. In one classic example (Tversky & Kahneman, 1981), people are asked to choose a treatment plan in a hypothetical scenario where 600 people have been infected by a deadly virus. In the scenario, all will die without treatment. Treatment plan A will save 200 people. Treatment plan B has a one-third chance of saving all 600 people and a two-thirds chance of saving no one. Most respondents choose the safe bet of plan A over the gamble of plan B.

Now, let's change the wording of the scenario slightly and ask another group of people to choose a treatment plan. This time we present the options as follows. Under treatment plan A, 400 people will die. Treatment plan B has a one-third chance that no one will die and a two-thirds chance that everyone will die. Faced with the prospect of losing 400 lives under plan A, most people now choose to gamble on plan B. So even in a situation where the decision has major consequences, inconsistency reigns once again. The most popular choice may depend on whether the decision makers are focusing on the number of lives being *saved* or on the number of lives being *lost*, even if the overall rates of survival are identical in both

cases. So the response can depend on whether the outcomes are *framed* as a gain or a loss. Hence, this particular form of inconsistency is known as the **framing effect** (Malenka, Baron, Johansen, Wahrenberger, & Ross, 1993) (FIGURE 12.6).

Framing effects are common in many real-life scenarios, especially in medical decision making (Almashat, Ayotte, Edelstein, & Margrett, 2008; Moxey, O'Connell, McGettigan, & Henry, 2003). With regard to decisions about immunization, patients make different decisions depending on whether the benefits or the adverse effects are emphasized. The same can apply to more invasive treatments such as surgery versus radiation for lung cancer. Framing effects also apply to preventative measures, like choosing to exercise to improve cardiovascular function or deciding to quit smoking (Moxey et al., 2003). Given the importance of such decisions, some important questions arise here. Exactly why do people switch their decision depending on whether they are considering losses or gains? Which of the two mutually exclusive decisions should we be counting as a patient's "real" decision? Can we reduce or eliminate the framing effects to reveal a more consistent form of preference? Finally, and most importantly for our purposes, how can neuroscience help us understand how decision making occurs in the brain, and what can neuroscience tell us about the basis of the framing effect? We'll look at answers to all of these questions later in the chapter.

In addition to the framing effect, another manipulation that can produce inconsistent decisions is the **endowment effect** (R. Thaler, 1980). *Homo economicus* should assign a consistent value to any given item, regardless of whether he is planning to buy it or sell it. However, in behavioral studies, people often demand a much higher price to *give up* something they own compared to the price they would be willing to pay to acquire such an object (R. Thaler, 1980). In other words, being "endowed" with the object ahead of time increases its subjective value (Kahneman, Knetsch, & Thaler, 1990).

This difference in value can cause people to reverse their preferences between two items, depending on which one they already own. For example, a classroom of students was offered a choice between a coffee mug and a chocolate bar. The students showed a roughly even split in their preferences: 59% chose the coffee mug over the bar. In a second classroom, students were given a chocolate bar and then asked whether they wished to trade it for the mug. This time, only 10% chose the coffee mug—90% held on to the chocolate bar. For comparison, in a third classroom, students were given a mug and then asked whether they wished to trade it for the bar. Now, only 11% chose the chocolate bar—89% held on to the coffee mug. So, this provided evidence that the endowment effect was able to create a nearly perfect reversal of preferences among these two common items (Knetsch, 1989).

Why do people reverse their preferences in this way? One popular suggestion is that the endowment effect is a side effect of **loss aversion** (Kahneman, Knetsch, & Thaler, 1991). For those already endowed with an object, the decision ends up being "framed" in terms of losing something one already has. For those without the object, there is no loss, and hence no loss aversion. Is this explanation plausible? As we'll see later in the chapter, brain imaging studies have examined the neural basis of both loss aversion and the endowment effect.

The Illusory Value of Procrastination

How does value change over time? What is the worth of a dollar today, compared with the worth of a dollar tomorrow, or in a week, or in a month? *Homo economicus* has a straightforward answer to this question. A reward that comes tomorrow carries some "opportunity cost" from the delay, as well as some risk of an unforeseen event happening between now and then to prevent the delivery of the goods. So the value of a reward should decline at a steady rate with later and later delivery. This concept, known as **delay discounting**, was originally formalized in the 18th century, in Jeremy Bentham's felicific calculus (Read, 2007). However, it almost certainly emerged thousands of years earlier, along with the origins of commerce, loans, and the interest paid on them. It exists in the same form today. For example, if you owe $100 on your credit card and you elect to repay the debt in one year rather than today, then the repayment will have to be a certain percentage larger to compensate for the delay: the repaid amount gets *discounted* over time. Note that the rate of interest is a constant, so that the obligation grows

exponentially over time. Exponential discounting of value over time implies a steady, predictable rate of change in value, just as we would expect from *Homo economicus.*

However, what if someone offered you a credit card where the rate of interest was 100% for the first month, 50% for the second month, 25% for the third month, 12% for the fourth month, 6% for the fifth month, 3% for the sixth month, and little interest thereafter? Not many of us would accept such a card, and certainly *Homo economicus* would never approve. Such a system could only be designed by an impatient, impulsive banker who insisted on a payoff as soon as possible. This banker would not care about any additional gains that could be made by waiting an extra year or two. Such a banker would be living for today at the expense of tomorrow. Why would anyone value the future in such a way? This question turns out to be more than just theoretical, because as you have probably guessed, the banker is *Homo sapiens.*

In experimental studies, human beings do not show exponential discounting of value, with its steady rate of change over time. Instead, they assign a disproportionately high value to immediate rewards and a disproportionately low value to delayed rewards (Laibson, 1997). The apparent discounting rate is steep initially but flat at remote points in time. This is sometimes described as **quasi-hyperbolic discounting**, since the curve looks more like a hyperbolic function than an exponential function (FIGURE 12.7) (Laibson, 1997). What this means in practical terms is that human beings are once again inconsistent in their preferences. Offered a choice between $200 in 52 weeks and $250 in 53 weeks, most respondents will take the larger, later sum. However, if we reduce the delays by a year and offer $200 right now versus $250 in 1 week, many people will take the smaller, sooner sum instead (Ainslie & Haslam, 1992). For a real-life demonstration, you can try the scenario yourself or ask a couple of friends in an informal survey. How many people switch their preference?

We can think of hyperbolic discounting as an optical illusion, but applied to value rather than vision. A "small but soon" reward can appear to be bigger than a "large but late" reward, depending on the perspective. You can experience this effect using an object's apparent size (or *angular diameter*) to represent its value and its distance from the eye to represent time. As in FIGURE 12.8, try holding a quarter about 2 inches behind a dime to represent two rewards, one small but "sooner," and the other large but "later." Now move this entire arrangement to an arm's-length distance, to represent a remote point in time. Close one eye. When held at a distance, there is no "illusion": the quarter seems larger than the dime, as it really is. But now, keeping the same gap between the coins, slowly bring them toward your open eye. When you get close enough, you will gradually be able to completely eclipse the quarter with the dime. The dime thus appears larger than the quarter. And no matter how well we know better, we cannot translate this knowledge into making the quarter *appear* bigger than the dime. The "illusion of bigness" is robust, and the same principle applies to value.

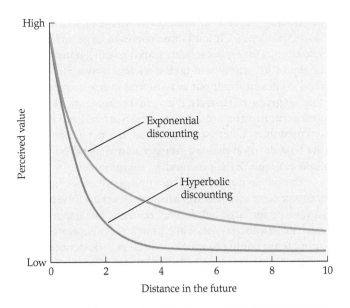

FIGURE 12.7 **Hyperbolic and exponential discount curves.** These graphs show the standard hyperbolic (orange line) and exponential (green line) discount curves. Both show that something that has high value in the near future rapidly drops off in value. Experimental results identify a curve that is similar to the hyperbolic curve shown here.

These illusions of value have been used to explain many forms of commonplace but perplexingly irrational human behavior. Drug addiction exemplifies extremely impulsive, steep discounting. In the remote future, the benefits of *not* smoking a cigarette vastly exceed the brief rush of pleasure derived from choosing to smoke the cigarette. As such, most smokers agree that *not* smoking cigarettes would be preferable to smoking cigarettes 10 years from now. But *right now,* thanks to hyperbolic discounting, the small-but-soon reward of smoking the cigarette seems bigger than the larger-but-later reward of not smoking the cigarette (Ainslie & Haslam, 1992). The same applies to other *right now* decisions: the Friday night binge-drinking session versus the desire not to have a Saturday morning hangover, the tasty plate of fries versus the long-term goal of weight loss, the decision to spend a paycheck now versus saving for retirement, and so forth. Immediate rewards are tempting, and procrastination often wins over prudence, even when part of us is aware of the illusion that holds us under its sway.

Where Do Our Irrational Decisions Come From?

Irrational or not, our decisions ultimately result from processes within our nervous system. That system is the end result of evolutionary fine-tuning over more than a hundred

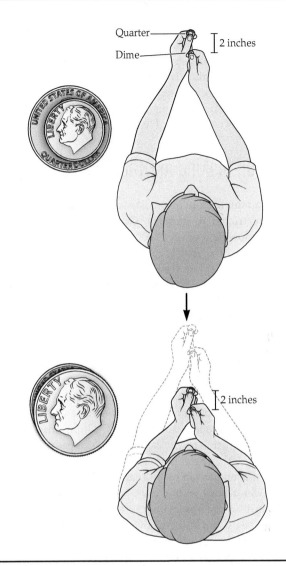

FIGURE 12.8 **The relative size of a dime and quarter vary, depending on how far you hold them from your eye.** If you hold a quarter 2 inches behind a dime, the size difference is clear when they are held at arm's length. But, as you bring them closer to your eye, the dime appears bigger than the quarter.

million generations since the first vertebrates swam through the oceans. Over that time, evolutionary processes have produced all sorts of supremely powerful survival-enhancement tools in the brain. Visual and motor systems allow archerfish to knock a spider off its perch by spitting water from their mouths. Cerebellar feed-forward models allow birds to zip through dense forest at high speed without crashing (Barmack, 2003). We ourselves have motor circuits that allow us to execute a perfect sequence of more than a thousand delicate movements of the mouth and larynx, all with flawless timing, if we decide to read this paragraph aloud. So why can't we stick to a diet? Why are our decisions so inconsistent and, at times, so counterproductive to survival? Has evolution brought us this far, only to let us down on the things that matter most?

To address these questions, it would be useful to know whether other animals also show the same kind of inconsistent decisions that behavioral economists see in humans. Over the past decade or so, researchers have started to team up across the various disciplines of zoology and economics to study decision making in animals under conditions similar to the ones we examined in the previous section.

Decision Making in Other Species

One common form of inconsistency, the endowment effect, is not restricted to humans. Capuchin monkeys show a strong endowment effect (FIGURE 12.9). They have equal preference for cereal or fruit at baseline, but show a strong preference for cereal when already endowed with cereal and a strong preference for fruit when endowed with fruit (Lakshminaryanan, Chen, & Santos, 2008). Since capuchin monkeys and humans have not shared a common ancestor in 30 million years, this suggests that the mechanisms behind the endowment effect are old indeed.

Recall that humans may be either risk averse or risk seeking, depending on the prospects of gain or loss, and its probability. For a 50–50 chance of a gain, humans are risk averse and prefer a certain option of lesser overall value (Rabin, 2000). But what about our nearest relatives? Chimpanzees and a closely related primate species, bonobos, diverged from human ancestors less than 8 million years ago. As it turns out, bonobos also act like humans in such situations. They seem to universally prefer a bowl with a 100% chance of containing four grapes instead of a bowl with a 50–50 chance of one grape or seven grapes. Chimpanzees, however, do the opposite. Unlike us, most of them prefer to gamble on the chance of getting the seven grapes rather than take the smaller, certain option (Heilbronner, Rosati, Stevens, Hare, & Hauser, 2008).

Why should this be? For most animals, the most important risky decisions involve foraging for food. The best risk profile may depend on what the animal eats and where it lives (FIGURE 12.10). If food often comes in large but hard-to-find chunks (as for polar bears stalking seals), it may be necessary to be patient and take risks to survive. However, if food comes in small but easy-to-find morsels, as for birds that eat grubs and insects, it may make more sense to be impatient, moving on quickly if no food is around and avoiding risky gambles. Likewise, for primates, human or nonhuman, the best decision-making strategy may depend on the options available in the surrounding environment.

So how do humans measure up against other species in terms of delay discounting? Most species show little patience in waiting for large but delayed rewards. For triple the immediate reward, studies have shown that the average time animals are willing to wait is as little as 3–5 seconds for pigeons or starlings (Ainslie, 1974; Bateson & Kacelnik, 1996), 8 to 14 seconds for tamarins and marmosets (Stevens, Hallinan, & Hauser, 2005), just over a minute for bonobos, and only about 2 minutes for chimpanzees (Rosati, Stevens, Hare, & Hauser, 2007). In comparison, human beings are often patient enough to wait days or even years for monetary

FIGURE 12.10 **Food-gathering behaviors for polar bears and grackles.**
(a) Polar bears engage in more risk-taking behavior when foraging for food than do (b) grackles.

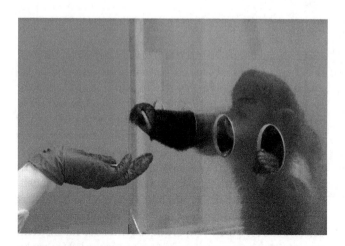

FIGURE 12.9 **A capuchin monkey participating in an experiment on the endowment effect.**

rewards (Frederick, Loewenstein, & O'Donoghue, 2002). But money emerged only recently as a reward and has no natural equivalent in other species. What if we offered similar food rewards to both the chimps and the humans, in a direct comparison? In such a study, the humans were actually *more* impulsive than the chimps (Rosati et al., 2007). Both preferred a large reward of six food pieces over a small reward of two food pieces if the rewards were available immediately. But if the large reward was delayed 2 minutes, the humans switched to choosing the smaller, immediate reward more than 80% of the time. The chimps were much more patient than the humans, opting to wait for the larger reward about 70% of the time. So again, the notion of greater human patience may apply more to our abstract rewards, like money, for which there is no immediate evolutionary value, than to **primary rewards** such as food, which do have immediate value (Rosati et al., 2007). This may have something to do with the mechanisms human brains have developed to represent abstract rewards, as we'll see later in the chapter.

Do Irrational Decisions Come from Irrational People?

Let's return now to the question of why human beings make decisions that are sometimes inconsistent with rational choice theory. We'll examine two proposed explanations for irrational behavior before moving on to the neuroscience of decision making.

The most conventional explanation for irrational or self-destructive human decision making is a sort of "defective brain" hypothesis. This proposal is not a scientific theory, but rather a sort of folk wisdom. Our intuitions tend to tell us that stupid decisions come from stupid people. Failed diets, broken New Year's resolutions, spending today rather than saving for tomorrow: all of these decisions are made by people who ought to know better. They are perfectly aware that their behavior is counterproductive, so if they choose to make bad decisions anyway, they are clearly lacking in some fundamental faculty of judgment or "moral fiber." Their character must be weak; their brains must be defective. And who are these people with defective brains, according to our intuitions? Usually people other than ourselves or people with whom we fail to identify.

The defective brain hypothesis may not be empirically based, but it permeates everything from our informal social life to our formal legal framework. Unfortunately, this hypothesis itself reflects human inconsistency in social cognition (as we'll see in Chapter 15). The **attribution effect**, sometimes called *correspondence bias*, describes a pervasive tendency in human thinking: we tend to explain our own behavior in terms of situational factors, but we tend to explain other people's behavior in terms of their essential character or disposition (Gilbert & Malone, 1995; Jones & Harris, 1967). We're happy to say "I skipped going to the gym because I had

a long day," while at the same time saying "You skipped going to the gym because you are lazy."

As you will hopefully have seen by this point in the chapter, irrational or inconsistent decision making is not just something we see in a few "bad apples." It is a universal feature of *Homo sapiens*, and, although some studies have found that higher IQ is associated with less risk aversion (Dohmen, Falk, Huffman, & Sunde, 2010), neither intelligence nor advanced education nor careful upbringing can eradicate it. Situational factors profoundly influence decision making, as does the framing of the decision and the relative prospects of gain or loss. Rather than blame bad decisions on bad brains, a more productive approach would be to understand *how* certain situations lead to irrational or counterproductive decisions and what brain mechanisms cause this to be so. This is where the neuroscience of decision making enters the picture.

One Brain, Two Systems

A more nuanced alternative to the defective brains hypothesis is the "obsolete brains" hypothesis. In this view, irrational decisions arise because we have inherited the brains of our hunting-and-gathering ancestors and, before them, our foraging mammalian forebears. The brains we have may be well adapted for survival in the wild, but they have not had time to adapt to the different challenges of modern civilization. As a result, our decisions are the result of a clumsy tug-of-war between two different systems: an ancient, intuitive, emotional, rapid, unconscious decision-making system that thinks like our animal ancestors and a more recently evolved rational, deliberative, slow, and conscious decision-making system that thinks like *Homo economicus*.

This dual-processing account of decision-making processes has been proposed by various authors in social and cognitive psychology and behavioral economics (FIGURE 12.11) (Evans, 2008). The evidence comes from behavioral experiments that show people acting like *Homo economicus* under some circumstances, but switching to a less rational and more intuitive system at other times. The **intuitive system (system 1)** and the **rational system (system 2)** each have several distinctive characteristics (Evans, 2008). We will be able to use these characteristics to help understand their underlying brain mechanisms, as we'll see in the next few sections.

The intuitive decision-making system operates unconsciously and implicitly: people can use it to identify a preference, but cannot say precisely why they made that choice over the others or what steps they took to arrive at their choice. In contrast, the rational system operates consciously and explicitly: people deliberate their way to a logical conclusion. Afterward they can explain the reasons for their choice as well as the steps they took to reach this conclusion. The rational system tends to focus on one aspect of a decision at a time and then uses this input to work through a series of logical steps by **sequential processing**, something like the motor system that breaks down a behavior into its

FIGURE 12.11 **Dan Ariely, who has written extensively about behavioral economics and** *Homo economicus.*

component actions and runs through them one at a time (as we saw in Chapter 7). For this reason, it can be slow to arrive at a conclusion and may even remain undecided after days of deliberation. In contrast, the intuitive system seems to have a higher capacity to consider all of the features of each option at the same time, by **parallel processing**. This is something like a sensory system that puts together all of the sensory features of an object to decide, for example, whether a face is male or female. Although the conclusion is rapid, it can be hard to explain its basis, just as it is sometimes hard to explain precisely why one face looks male and another looks female. In contrast, the rational system is linked to language and can operate in explicit verbal terms. The intuitive system seems to operate independent of functions like general intelligence, working memory, rule-based cognition, or sustained attention. The rational system is closely linked to all of these.

Why does the rational system have these features? The typical explanation is that this system is recent in evolutionary terms: so recent that it is nearly unique to humans (Evans, 2008). Although powerful in some ways, it has not yet had time to evolve the efficiencies of the much older, intuitive system. So its capacity remains low, its speed remains slow, and its conclusions are all too often trumped by the more deeply rooted intuitive system. In the next few sections, we'll see whether these explanations are consistent with the mechanisms of the brain itself.

How the Brain Decides

The Neural Mechanisms of Delay Discounting

In delay discounting, why is it that we make choices like a rational *Homo economicus* for remote points in time, but switch to being an impulsive *Homo sapiens* when it comes to the present or the near future? The dual-systems model suggests that evolutionarily recent brain structures should be active for decisions on future rewards, but more ancient brain structures should be active for decisions on present or near-future rewards (Bechara, Damasio, Damasio, & Lee, 1999; Hayashi, Ko, Strafella, & Dagher, 2013).

Neuroimaging studies of delay discounting have found that there are indeed separate neural systems active during decisions for immediate versus delayed monetary rewards (McClure, Laibson, Loewenstein, & Cohen, 2004). In one of the first studies in this area, researchers offered subjects choices between different amounts of money at different delays from zero to 6 weeks: say, $20 in 2 weeks versus $40 in 4 weeks. The choices were real, not hypothetical: after the experiment, subjects were paid actual money according to one of their decisions. This study found a set of areas active for *all* choices, regardless of the delay time (FIGURE 12.12). These included mostly lateral cortical areas: the dorsolateral prefrontal cortex, the intraparietal cortex, and supplementary and premotor areas. These areas, as you may recall, had been previously linked to "rational" functions like cognition, working memory, problem solving, and calculation. There were also some active areas in the ventrolateral and lateral orbitofrontal cortex, whose significance we'll consider in the next section. So these "rational-decision" areas, making calculations of monetary value and time, were active for both immediate and late time points.

However, a second set of areas was active only for choices in which money was available immediately as one of the options. These included mostly medial cortical areas: the medial prefrontal cortex, the **medial orbitofrontal cortex**, and the ventral striatum and the left posterior hippocampus. Several of these areas fall within the domain of the limbic system, long known for its role in emotion and motivated behavior, as you may recall. The limbic system is also considered a more ancient system in evolutionary terms when compared to the lateral prefrontal areas, which are dramatically expanded in humans compared to most other species (MacLean, 1990). The prospect of an immediate reward seemed to bring these additional areas into the decision-making process.

How did these two systems work to guide decisions? As it turned out, the relative activity of each of these systems changed from trial to trial during the experiment. Sometimes the medial areas were more active, and sometimes the lateral areas were more active. When the lateral areas were more active, subjects seemed to act like *Homo economicus* and chose the larger, later rewards. When the medial areas were more active, subjects made the more impulsive choice for the smaller, immediate reward. Research suggests that these areas do not work in isolation from each other, but are interconnected as part of a decision-making circuit (Hare, Camerer, & Rangel, 2009; Sanfey & Chang, 2008; Xu et al., 2013). For example, studies of emotional decision making describe increased activity within the amygdala and ventromedial prefrontal cortex when decisions were made that were consistent with the framing effect, but an increase in activity within

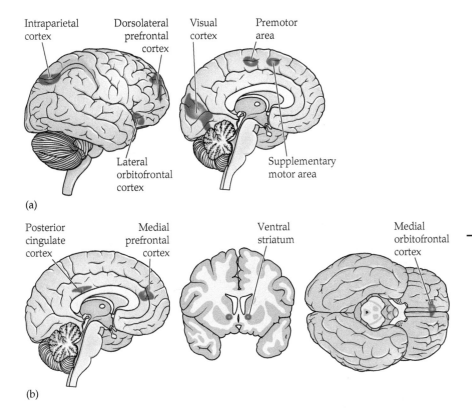

(a)

(b)

FIGURE 12.12 **Brain regions activated during choices among immediate and delayed rewards, from the study of McClure, Laibson, Loewenstein, & Cohen, 2004.** (a) More lateral regions, including the dorsolateral prefrontal cortex and intraparietal cortex, were active for all choices, regardless of the delay. (b) More medial regions, including the medial prefrontal cortex, medial orbitofrontal cortex, and ventral striatum, were more active when there was no delay between the choice and the reward.

the more analytic system and the prefrontal cortex when the decisions were inconsistent with the framing effect (Xu et al., 2013). Another study considered how the value placed on a reward by the ventromedial prefrontal cortex is modulated by input from the dorsolateral prefrontal cortex, which is associated with exercising self-control in pursuit of long-term goals (Hare et al., 2009). Understanding this circuitry connecting the two decision-making systems remains an active area of research in cognitive neuroscience (Laureiro-Martinez et al., 2013; Roy, Buschman, & Miller, 2014).

As we discussed earlier, money is an unusual reward in that it did not exist until recently and has abstract rather than direct value to survival. So would the same processes still hold sway for decisions about primary rewards like water or juice? The researchers decided to repeat the experiment, delivering squirts of water or juice to the thirsty subjects in the scanners, at various delay times from 0 to 25 minutes (McClure, Ericson, Laibson, Loewenstein, & Cohen, 2007). The results were similar to that of their 2004 study, which used money as a reward. The regions active for *all* decisions were nearly identical, lying within lateral prefrontal and parietal cortex. The regions active for immediate decisions were slightly different in terms of exact location, but still fell within the general regions of the medial prefrontal and medial orbitofrontal cortex and ventral striatum. Once again, the subjects' actual decisions seemed to depend on which of these two systems was more active for any given choice.

Correlation does not equal causation, however. If the lateral prefrontal cortex is truly important in suppressing impulsive decisions, then disrupting the function of this area should increase impulsive decision making. This is precisely the

finding of a study that used transcranial magnetic stimulation (TMS) to temporarily inhibit the activity of the left lateral prefrontal cortex. After this treatment, subjects became more likely to choose the smaller, sooner reward over the larger, later reward in a choice task. As the effects of the TMS wore off, their degree of impatience returned to baseline once again. The effects were specific to left lateral prefrontal cortex; inhibition of right prefrontal cortex or sham TMS had no such effect (Figner et al., 2010). This **loss-of-function** evidence gives stronger backing to the idea that the lateral prefrontal cortex is important for impulse control in delay discounting. Another study suggests that the neurotransmitter dopamine is important for decision making and delay discounting (Pine, Shiner, Seymour, & Dolan, 2010).

Neural Mechanisms of Decisions under Risk

What about the kinds of inconsistencies we see for decision under risk? Recall the unusual-looking utility curve of value from prospect theory, with two differently shaped curves for losses and for gains. The discontinuity or kink between losses and gains suggests that two separate mechanisms might be at work for evaluating risky losses and gains (FIGURE 12.13). What are the neural correlates of these two mechanisms?

Many studies have looked at brain activation during risky decisions for financial rewards and losses (Knutson & Bossaerts, 2007). The results point toward distinct brain

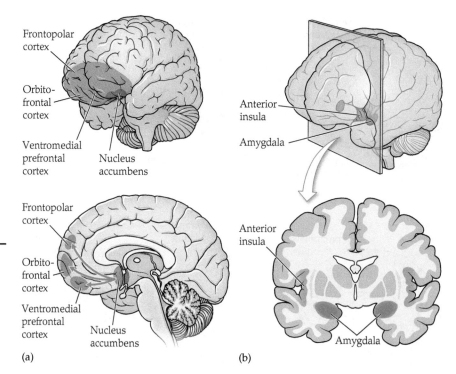

FIGURE 12.13 Neural mechanisms for evaluating uncertain risks and uncertain rewards. (a) The cortico-striatal loop through the nucleus accumbens and ventromedial prefrontal cortex represents the reward value of a stimulus and is more active for higher-value rewards. (b) The amygdala and the anterior insula are more active for more aversive stimuli.

regions behind risk seeking and risk aversion. The ventral striatum and its targets in ventromedial prefrontal cortex seem to be more active in decisions to pursue a reward, despite potential risks (Knutson, Taylor, Kaufman, Peterson, & Glover, 2005; Yacubian et al., 2006). The ventromedial prefrontal cortex also seems to show increasing activity with increasing probability of a gain. These regions are generally considered important for representing reward value, as we'll see in Chapter 14. However, their activity also predicts decisions to pursue nonrisky rewards, such as purchasing consumer goods (Knutson & Bossaerts, 2007) or opting for immediate financial or primary rewards, as we saw in the previous section (McClure et al., 2007; McClure, Li, et al., 2004). It may be that these areas are active in risk seeking because as the potential reward value increases, the temptation to ignore risk also increases—a question of impulsivity, just like choosing the smaller but immediate reward in delay discounting (Knutson & Bossaerts, 2007).

As for risk aversion, one of the key players seems to be the insula, in particular the **anterior insula** (Knutson & Bossaerts, 2007). As this area becomes more active, subjects become increasingly loss averse and risk averse in their decision making. This is an interesting finding because the insula is generally considered a key area for interoception: the perception of internal bodily states (Craig, 2002). As we will see in Chapter 13 on emotion, insular activity is seen for "gut feelings" of hunger, thirst, pain, fatigue, sexual arousal, and other internal states. Risky decisions may therefore create an immediate internal feeling of aversion, and the magnitude of this feeling may factor into the decision itself (Paulus & Stein, 2006). So if we see differently shaped curves on the positive and the negative side of the utility function in prospect theory,

it may be because of different dynamics in the separate systems of the ventral striatum and anterior insula. Consistent with this, neuroimaging studies have shown that it is possible to predict whether a subject will choose to purchase a given good for a given price (such as streaming a movie for $8.99) by comparing the relative activation in the medial prefrontal cortex versus the anterior insula (Knutson & Bossaerts, 2007).

Of course, it is always helpful to compare the results of correlation studies against loss-of-function or lesion studies. And if we look at the effects of brain lesions on decision making under risk, we see a similar set of results (Clark et al., 2008). In one study, patients with three different kinds of brain lesions saw a row of 10 boxes, some red and some blue. A hidden token lay under one of the boxes, randomly chosen on each round of the task. The goal was to guess whether the token lay under a red box or a blue one. The number of red boxes varied from 1 to 9, so that the amount of risk on any given bet varied from round to round. All subjects, including patients with lesions and healthy control subjects, tended to pick the majority color, suggesting that they were all capable of understanding the basic premises of the task (FIGURE 12.14) (Clark et al., 2008).

But this is where the similarity ended. Compared with healthy controls, patients with damage to either the ventromedial prefrontal cortex or the insula were willing to gamble higher amounts of money for any given level of risk. However, there were differences between the two groups. Patients who had ventromedial damage (i.e., those who still have an intact insula) still adjusted the size of their bets downward as the risk went up. In other words, they still had some loss aversion and took into account the odds of winning in deciding how much to bet. In contrast, patients who had lesions of the insula seemed to almost completely ignore

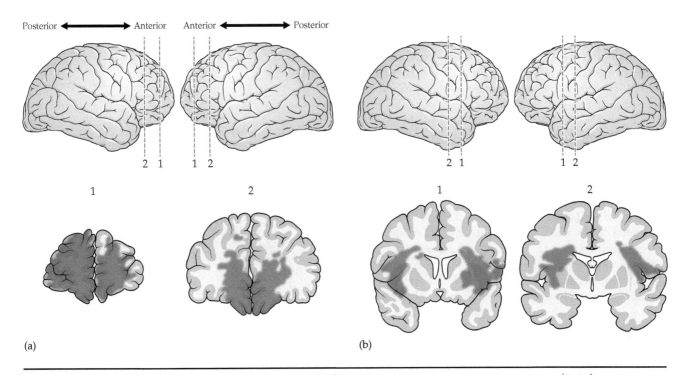

(a)   (b)

FIGURE 12.14 Focal brain lesions can impair decision making under risk. (a) Patients with lesions of the ventromedial prefrontal cortex (shaded) but an intact insula, gamble higher amounts than controls; however, they are still sensitive to the level of risk when placing a bet. (b) Patients who have lesions of the insula (shaded) but an intact ventromedial prefrontal cortex, ignore the level of risk when placing a bet; they do not show "loss aversion" in risky decision making.

the degree of risk involved when deciding how much to bet. Their aversion to the prospect of a loss seemed to have vanished. So once again, the insula seems to be an important structure for generating the aversive gut feelings that lead to loss aversion under uncertainty.

The Neural Basis of the Endowment Effect

As we saw earlier, the endowment effect may be a sort of side effect of loss aversion: people are more concerned about parting with a thing they already own than about acquiring the same thing if they do not yet own it. Why should this be? As we saw just now, the brain seems to have two separate mechanisms within the domain of emotional decision making. Gain seeking seems to depend on the reward-value calculations of the ventral striatum and ventromedial prefrontal cortex, whereas loss aversion seems to depend more on the interoceptive functions of the anterior insula. If so, then perhaps the "value gap" we see in the endowment effect is a byproduct of these two systems coming to different conclusions about the value of an item.

It is possible to re-create the endowment effect during an fMRI experiment by giving subjects a few consumer goods prior to the scan, then offering them chances to sell these items, buy other items, or choose between an item versus a certain sum of money, over many trials (Knutson et al., 2008). It is then possible to determine the point of indifference for each item: the price at which the person would be equally

happy to have the item or the cash (FIGURE 12.15). If subjects insist on a higher price for selling decisions than for buying decisions, then an endowment effect is present. The neural substrates of each type of decision can then be compared.

As it turns out, the size of the endowment effect varies from person to person. Individuals with a stronger endowment effect (that is, a supposedly greater degree of loss aversion when selling) showed stronger activation in

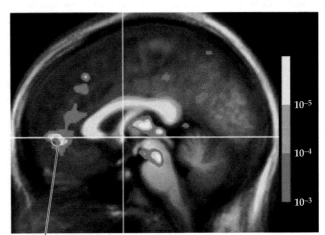

Medial prefrontal cortex

FIGURE 12.15 Activity in medial areas, including the medial prefrontal cortex, is associated with choosing whether to buy or sell an item for a particular price.

the right insula during selling decisions. The strength of the insular activation during selling decisions could be used to predict the strength of the endowment effect. So, as we suspected, loss aversion (and the insular activity behind it) seem to be an important factor in explaining the endowment effect.

Conversely, the ventral striatum and medial prefrontal cortex had important, but not identical, roles to play during the decision to buy. The ventral striatum activity depended on product preference regardless of price and regardless of whether the decision was about buying or selling. In other words, this area seemed to be about the overall desirability of the item, with all other considerations put aside. The medial prefrontal cortex added an additional layer of subtlety. For buying decisions, it became more and more active as the price became lower for any given item. However, for selling decisions, it became more and more active as the price became *higher* on a given item. In other words, this area seemed to be assessing the desirability of the *deal*, rather than the item itself. This suggests the medial prefrontal cortex has a representation of the item's overall **subjective value** to the individual—a theme we'll revisit in detail in the next section of the chapter.

The Neural Basis of the Framing Effect

As we saw earlier, the framing effect describes how option preference can reverse itself depending on whether the losses or the gains are emphasized. Under prospect theory, losses are evaluated differently from gains. So does the framing effect result in a flip between two distinct systems for evaluating losses versus gains?

Neuroimaging studies of the framing effect can help us answer this question (De Martino, Kumaran, Seymour, & Dolan, 2006). As in the other studies we have seen, participants had to choose among real monetary rewards while undergoing fMRI scanning. For each decision, they were first given a sum of money: say, $50. In the gains condition, they were then asked whether they wanted to gamble the money on an all-or-nothing bet or, instead, choose to "keep" $20. In the losses condition, they were again asked whether they wanted to gamble the money or, instead, choose to "lose" $30. Note that in both of these choices the overall outcome is the same—only the framing of the options is different.

As predicted under prospect theory, the subjects preferred the sure option when the outcomes were framed as a gain, but preferred the gamble when the same outcomes were framed as a loss. Along with this behavioral preference reversal, the amygdala was more active for risky options and less active for sure options in the "gains" frame, but had the opposite activity for decisions in the "loss" frame (FIGURE 12.16). As we will see in Chapter 13 (on emotion), the amygdala has an important role in assessing the emotional valence of external stimuli and in driving a behavioral

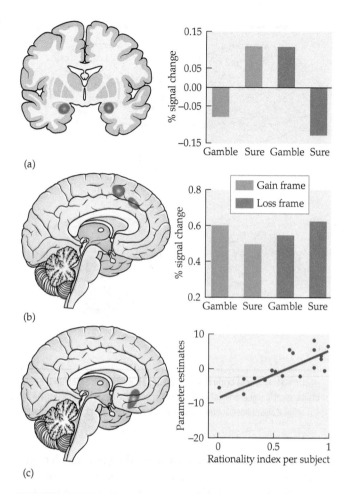

FIGURE 12.16 **The neural basis of the framing effect in risky decision making.** (a) Subjects chose the certain option when the decision was framed in terms of gains; in this frame, the amygdala was more active for risky options. Subjects usually switched to become risk seeking when the decision was framed in terms of losses; in this frame, the amygdala was more active for certain options. (b) In some cases, subjects overrode their usual tendencies, choosing the risky option for gains or the certain option for losses; in these instances, activation appeared in the dorsomedial prefrontal cortex. (c) Some individuals were less susceptible to framing effects and assigned value to the options fairly similarly, regardless of whether they were presented as gains or losses; activation appeared in the ventromedial prefrontal cortex for these individuals exhibiting higher "rationality."

response, particularly for aversive stimuli or potential threats. Its activity in this task suggests that framing effects are at least partly about inconsistent patterns of loss aversion, as we discussed earlier.

Although the subjects' preference reversals in this experiment suggested a framing effect, the effect was not absolute. There were trials in which subjects chose to gamble even for gains or chose the sure option even for losses. These atypical choices went against the subjects' usual behavioral tendencies. The areas active in this case lay in the medial prefrontal areas near the presupplementary motor area and a slightly more anterior region in the dorsomedial prefrontal cortex (FIGURE 12.16). As we'll see later in the chapter, these same areas seem to be active in pathological gamblers who go against their usual tendencies and walk away from big losses rather than trying to win them back (Campbell-Meiklejohn, Woolrich, Passingham, & Rogers, 2008).

Not all people are equally susceptible to framing effects. Some show little tendency toward preference reversals, whereas some show extremely reliable reversals of preference across conditions. In this study, those with the highest "rationality" (that is, those with the least susceptibility to framing effects) showed the strongest activation in **ventromedial prefrontal cortex** and orbitofrontal cortex during decision making. As we'll see in a moment, these areas have strong regulatory outputs to the amygdala and are able to adjust its reactivity to outside stimuli. Furthermore, as we saw earlier, the ventromedial prefrontal cortex tends to assign value based on the immediate value of the reward. Since framing effects are in part about context, it may be that ignoring these contextual clues helps to mute the amygdala response, thereby reducing the switch from gain seeking to loss aversion.

Orbitofrontal areas have an important role in emotion regulation, as we'll see in Chapter 13. By involving the orbitofrontal cortex, subjects may be able to override their initial emotional reactions to the options and thereby minimize the framing effect. In any case, these areas are important for a critical function that is the foundation of all decisions, rational, consistent, or otherwise: establishing a "common currency" of value.

The Common Currency of Subjective Value

In many life situations, we have trouble making an objective comparison between two options. For example, most of us would choose a four-day vacation over a two-day one. But how would you rather spend your time? Enjoying the nightlife in a thriving metropolis or camping under the stars, hundreds of miles from civilization?

Comparing Apples to Oranges

When the options are sufficiently different from one another, we sometimes say that there is no point in arguing that one is objectively better than the other—"it's like comparing apples to oranges." This familiar saying implies that we cannot compare options in such situations.

Yet in reality, our brains compare apples to oranges all the time. What's more, most of the time, we make these kinds of comparisons quickly and easily. But how is this possible? One possibility is that the brain uses a sort of "common currency" to compare options that are intrinsically dissimilar. For example, if we asked you whether you would rather have 100 Mexican pesos or 100 Turkish lira, you would probably have to consult a table of exchange rates. You might even convert each sum into a more familiar currency, such as the dollar or the euro, to compare them. Using this common currency, you could determine which sum would be preferable.

But what if we offered you a choice between three tomatoes or two grapefruits? This time, no currency converter will help you. Assuming you are planning to eat the items rather than sell them on the open market, the value of the two options is subjective. Your friend may choose the tomatoes, but you might happily opt for the grapefruits instead. To make up your mind, you'll need to read your own internal state (hunger, thirst, and so forth), know your preferences for eating tomatoes versus grapefruit, and also predict whether your overall state will improve more after eating the tomatoes versus the grapefruits. And to calculate this improvement, you'll presumably need to convert the two options into a common currency of subjective value.

For many decades, economists have studied subjective value according to an **axiom of revealed preferences** (Chiappori & Rochet, 1987). The idea is that we can learn how people assign subjective value to different options by offering them a choice between the two options and seeing which one they select. For example, you could offer an employee a choice between taking a coffee break or being paid a sum of money to forego the break and keep working (FIGURE 12.17). Above a certain sum, the employee would indicate a preference for the money over the break. This preference would then "reveal" the subjective value of the coffee break overall.

FIGURE 12.17 **The axiom of revealed preferences.** To learn how people assign subjective value to different options, we can offer a choice between two options, and the choice will "reveal" a person's preference. For example, we could reveal the subjective value of a coffee break by offering a choice to forego the break in order to receive a sum of money. At what point would you prefer the sum of money over the coffee break?

RESEARCH METHODS:
Charting the Landscape of Subjective Value

Within the study of decision making, there is an emerging field of **neuroeconomics**. In this new field, subjects participate in neuroimaging studies while they perform various behavioral tasks, such as mapping their **delay discounting curve** or their **risk discounting curve**. This can be important because each person has a slightly different sense of subjective value. Some of us are highly impulsive: small-but-soon rewards are attractive, and large-but-late rewards hardly matter at all. Some of us are highly risk averse: small-but-certain rewards are valuable, whereas large-but-long-shot rewards count for little.

Others of us have the opposite pattern. So we can plot a curve with the time delay of the reward on the horizontal axis and the reward's subjective value on the vertical axis as the delay discounting curve. Alternatively, we can plot a curve with the riskiness of the reward (often expressed as the *odds against* winning the reward) on the horizontal axis and the reward's subjective value on the vertical axis. Together, these curves can be used to illustrate an individual's "landscape of subjective value": a sort of hill with its peak in the middle for the certain rewards of the present moment, dropping away downslope as the

rewards become more distant in time or more uncertain.

Methods like these can be useful for studying the brain's own mechanisms of assigning subjective value to different options during a decision. By combining these behavioral approaches with neuroimaging, we can ask what brain areas track the subjective value of rewards in different parts of the landscape or whether the landscape itself can change under different conditions (for example, states of desperation such as hunger, thirst, or poverty) and, if so, what brain mechanisms might create and undo these changes.

Of course, as we have seen already, many factors can introduce distortions into the "revealed preferences" of *Homo sapiens*: framing effects, loss aversion, delay discounting, risk aversion, and so on. So the search for a common currency of subjective value must go beyond behavioral measures and into the neural mechanisms of decision making itself. So how does the brain determine subjective value? Are there neural circuits that calculate the subjective value of dissimilar options to compare them? If so, what are those mechanisms, and how do they contribute to decision making? Thanks to functional MRI and other noninvasive brain imaging techniques, we are finding some answers to such questions (Montague & Berns, 2002).

A Consistent Neural Basis for Subjective Value

One way to study the neural basis of subjective value is by looking, once again, at brain activity during **intertemporal choice**, in which subjects can assign different values to a reward that occurs soon versus a reward that occurs in the more distant future (Kable & Glimcher, 2007). As we already saw, distinct medial areas are more active when

choosing smaller-sooner rewards and other, more lateral regions are more active when choosing larger-later rewards (McClure, Laibson et al., 2004). But are there areas that actually track the overall subjective value of each option, whether immediate or late?

To find out, we can place each subject in the scanner, then offer her or him various amounts of money at various times in the future, and look for brain regions whose activity reflects the subjective value of each offer, according to that specific person's tendency to discount future events. As it turns out, there is a specific network of regions whose activity seems to reflect the subjective value of monetary rewards: more activity for earlier rewards and less activity for later rewards, along a quasi-hyperbolic curve (FIGURE 12.18). This network involves the medial prefrontal cortex, posterior cingulate cortex, and nucleus accumbens (Kable & Glimcher, 2007).

Specific areas in the brain do seem to track the subjective value of a certain type of reward: sums of money delivered at specific points in time. What's more, these areas also seem to be important for tracking the subjective value of other kinds of rewards. For example, another study found that activity in a similar medial prefrontal region tracked the subjective value of not only monetary rewards, but also other secondary reinforcers, such as snack foods and small consumer items (Chib, Rangel, Shimojo, & O'Doherty, 2009).

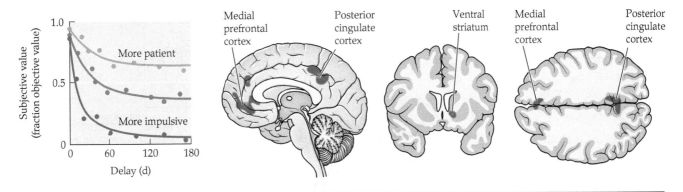

FIGURE 12.18 Brain regions representing the subjective value of a delayed monetary reward. (a) The subjective value of delayed rewards falls over time according to a hyperbolic function; more impulsive individuals have steeper curves, while more patient individuals have more shallow curves. (b) A specific network of regions, including the medial prefrontal cortex, posterior cingulate cortex, and ventral striatum, show activity that reflects the subjective value of delayed monetary rewards.

But the neural correlates of subjective value also seem to change in other situations. For example, we can compare the brain regions whose activity tracks the delay discounting curve with the brain regions whose activity tracks the risk discounting curve for each subject. As it turns out, the brain regions that track subjective value for risky rewards are not identical to those for delayed rewards (Peters & Buchel, 2009). On the one hand, there are some overlapping regions in the ventral striatum and orbitofrontal cortex. On the other hand, there are also widespread areas in the lateral parietal, frontal, and occipital lobes that seem to track subjective value only for risky rewards and not for delayed rewards. Conversely, there are regions in the medial prefrontal cortex, posterior cingulate cortex, and lateral parietal cortex that seem to track subjective value only for delayed rewards and not risky rewards. So the neural bases of subjective value have some parts that overlap and some parts that are distinct. To understand how these different substrates might work together, let's begin with the common pathway for subjective valuation in the orbitofrontal cortex and ventral striatum before turning to the roles of other pathways.

Evaluation and the Orbitofrontal Cortex

Studies of monetary decision making give us a convenient way of studying the mechanisms of subjective valuation in human beings. But the brain's valuation mechanisms are far older than money and far older than the human species itself. If we look at studies of other species ranging from mice to macaques, one of the key brain areas for subjective valuation of punishments and rewards is the orbitofrontal cortex (Rolls & Grabenhorst, 2008).

The remarkable orbitofrontal cortex takes input from essentially every sensory modality. Visual, auditory, somatosensory, olfactory, and gustatory areas of the brain all send connections to the orbitofrontal cortex, as do the visceral sensory (or interoceptive) areas of the brain, such as the insula. The amygdala, another region that rapidly evaluates external stimuli, also sends strong connections to the orbitofrontal cortex (FIGURE 12.19). The orbitofrontal cortex itself also sends outputs back to most of these areas, as well as to the homeostatic circuits of the hypothalamus, and the reward circuits in the **corticostriatal loops** through the ventral striatum. It also has cortical links to limbic regions like the anterior cingulate cortex and to prefrontal regions like the frontopolar cortex and lateral prefrontal cortex. So we can think of the orbitofrontal cortex as a sort of convergence zone that assembles information about the identity and properties of outside stimuli, the current internal state of the organism, and homeostatic drives and examines this information in the context of current goals and behavior (Morecraft, Geula, & Mesulam, 1992).

This complex interplay of circuitry allows the brain to assign different subjective values to the same stimulus depending on a wide variety of factors, both internal and external. For example, imagine providing a hungry subject with a tasty piece of chocolate and then performing brain imaging as the rewarding chocolate piece is consumed. Then imagine repeating this process over and over again, until the subject becomes overwhelmed by satiation and nausea and refuses to eat any more chocolate, no matter what incentives are offered. With each piece of chocolate consumed, the subjective tastiness and reward value of the next piece goes down a little more, although the stimulus itself remains the same. In neuroimaging studies of chocolate lovers, areas of the medial orbitofrontal cortex show less and less activity with each successive piece of chocolate, tracking the decreasing *intrinsic* reward (Small, Zatorre, Dagher, Evans, & Jones-Gotman, 2001).

But this doesn't necessarily mean that the *overall* reward value of the chocolate has vanished. On the contrary, subjects will continue eating the chocolate even when they no longer feel hungry, for a variety of reasons: to keep the experimenters happy, to hold to a prior commitment to complete the experiment, and possibly to obtain the delayed cash reward for participating. As these external or contextual

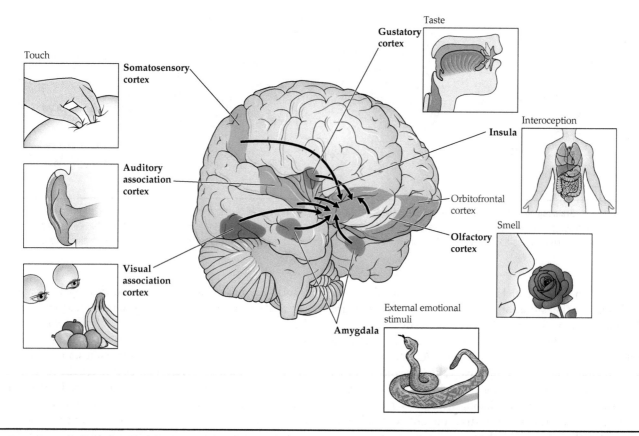

FIGURE 12.19 Inputs to the orbitofrontal cortex. The orbitofrontal cortex receives input from the external senses (vision, hearing, touch, smell, and taste) as well as the internal state of the body, via the insula. By obtaining information about the properties of an external stimulus (watery, sugary, chilly, friendly, hostile) and comparing this information to the body's current internal state, the orbitofrontal cortex decides how valuable the stimulus is to the organism at any given moment.

factors kick in, areas of the **lateral orbitofrontal cortex** show more and more activity with each successive piece of chocolate. The shift in activation from medial to lateral seems to track a shift in the basis of the subjective value. Initially, the subjects eat the chocolate because it's tasty: the reward is in the eating. By the end, they're eating the chocolate although it's *not* tasty: the reward is in keeping a prior commitment.

One Currency, but Many Markets

So far, we have seen that the orbitofrontal cortex is an important "marketplace" for determining the subjective value of stimuli in the outside environment: chocolate, brussels sprouts, consumer goods, and monetary rewards, among other things. As for the subjective "common currency" within this market, an important clue comes from the dopaminergic **loop circuits** that connect this region to the ventral striatum. The orbitofrontal loop seems to be critical for determining the reward value of specific stimuli like the ones we have seen in studies throughout this chapter (Zald et al., 2004). One of the key neurotransmitters for computing

reward value is dopamine. In fact, dopamine itself has been suggested as the brain's common currency for evaluating and deciding among different kinds of rewards (Montague & Berns, 2002). We'll explore the complex topic of dopamine and reward value in Chapter 14.

But if, for the moment, we consider dopamine the brain's common currency, then is the orbitofrontal cortex the only marketplace in which this currency is spent? As you may recall, the orbitofrontal loop is just one of many different loops serving various parts of the prefrontal cortex; there are also motor loops, premotor loops, oculomotor loops, dorsolateral loops, ventrolateral loops, and cingulate loops, to name some that have been proposed. And every one of these loops involves a common circuitry passing through a swath of cortex, basal ganglia, thalamus, subthalamic nucleus, and substantia nigra. Each loop has a different function, however, because it has a different pattern of connections to all of the other motor, sensory, and association areas of the brain. (Chapter 7 describes the function of some of these loops.)

As it turns out, each of these functions may require its own "marketplace" for comparing the values of different

NEUROSCIENCE OF EVERYDAY LIFE:
Snack Food or Brussels Sprouts?

Why is it sometimes so hard to eat healthfully? When on a diet, some of us manage to ignore the temptation of the candy bar, whereas others succumb. Even when we can muster up the self-control to take prior commitments into account, our resolve doesn't always last: diets fail, lost pounds return, and active lifestyles lapse back into laziness. The effects of these lapses are substantial: the prevalence of obesity in both developed and developing countries has increased massively in the past three decades (Flegal, Carroll, Ogden, & Johnson, 2002; Prentice, 2006). As a result, rates of insulin resistance and diabetes are skyrocketing, even among young adults and adolescents (Wiedman, 1989). Over the next 20 years, excess weight is set to replace malnutrition among the leading causes of disease and death in developing nations (World Health Organization, 2006).

The neuroscience of decision making may help us to unravel the brain mechanisms that make it so hard to resist the lure of tasty but unhealthful foods. In neuroimaging studies of dieters, ventromedial regions of the prefrontal cortex track the subjective value of a food stimulus, be it brussels sprouts or sugarloaf. However, the activity of this region is in turn subject to influence from ventrolateral prefrontal areas (FIGURE 12.20). In those with

high impulse control, a study provided evidence that the lateral areas increase the medial areas' response to untempting but nutritious foods, while at the same time decreasing their response to tempting, tasty, but unhealthful foods (Hare et al., 2009). In those with low impulse control, contextual factors do not appear to have this sort of influence.

Of course, the larger question is how to improve impulse control in those who find themselves lacking. This is a centuries-old problem that neuroscience is only just beginning to address. Certainly, changing the

external environment itself will be crucial. Our brains are little different today than they were 50 years ago, before the rates of obesity began to soar worldwide. The widespread availability of cheap, tasty, high-calorie foods in large portions must certainly account for much of the change. Yet many individuals have remained "immune" to obesity despite the changing environment. By looking inside the brains of such individuals, neuroscience may offer clues as to how the rest of the population can match their success.

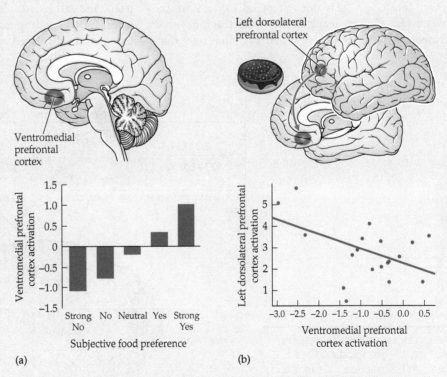

(a)

(b)

FIGURE 12.20 **Brain activation during self-control of food preference.** (a) The ventromedial prefrontal cortex is more active for more enjoyed foods. (b) In individuals with high impulse control, a region in the dorsolateral prefrontal cortex can decrease the ventromedial prefrontal activation for enjoyable but unhealthy foods, or increase its activation for unenjoyable but healthy foods.

options. Comparing two options means assigning a value to each one in a common currency and then choosing the one with higher value. Yet the options themselves can take many forms: resources like apples versus oranges, actions like sitting versus standing, behaviors like greeting someone versus saying nothing, plans like attending class versus socializing with friends, and goals like becoming an artist versus becoming an athlete. To choose among each of these kinds of options, we must weigh not only external factors, but also internal values. So there is a hierarchy of internal valuation: a whole *set* of marketplaces, ranging from simple movements to complex behaviors; from short-term plans to long-term goals. As for the neural substrates of these marketplaces, they extend far beyond the orbitofrontal cortex and into much of the frontal lobe, as we'll see in the next section.

A Hierarchy of Internally Guided Decision Making

When we considered the motor system in Chapter 7, we explored the idea of two separate divisions, one that influences movements guided by external factors and one that influences movements based on internal factors. As we examine the neural substrates of decision making, might we find the same division between internally guided and externally guided decisions?

Internally and Externally Guided Decision Making

As we saw in Chapter 7, one division of the motor system has extensive inputs from **exteroceptive areas**: regions of the brain that process sensory information from the external-world senses like vision, hearing, and touch. These external-guidance systems have circuitry that lies along the lateral areas of the prefrontal cortex (FIGURE 12.21): the primary motor cortex, premotor cortex, "cognitive" areas of the dorsolateral and ventrolateral prefrontal cortex, and so on. These areas are good at using external sensory information to predict the outcomes of specific kinds of movements, behaviors, and strategies. For this reason, they are helpful in figuring out problems with an objectively "correct" answer determined by outside-world factors: the best way to shape your hand's fingers to pick up a mug on the table, or what sequence of button presses will result in a telephone call to a specific friend, or how many coins to insert into a vending machine to obtain a specific drink, based on the displayed price.

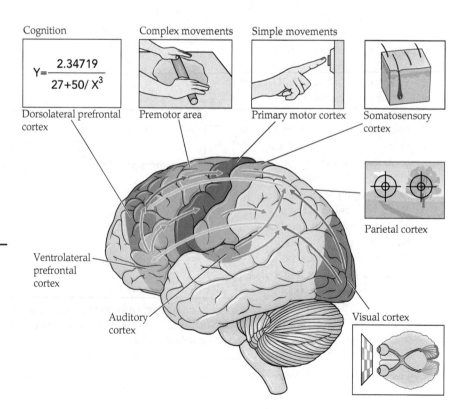

FIGURE 12.21 Lateral motor hierarchy. The lateral frontal lobe guides decision making and behavior using information about the external world obtained from sensory association areas in the parietal and temporal lobes. More anterior areas of the frontal lobe send signals back down the hierarchy to the lateral premotor areas—to direct complex movements or actions—and finally to the primary motor cortex to break these down into simple movements.

All of these externally guided behaviors count as "decisions" in the sense that they involve making a choice among various mutually exclusive alternatives. However, when external factors rather than internal factors guide the decision, we tend to refer to the process as cognition, or problem solving, or general intelligence, or motor control. The neuroscience of decision making tends to explore a different class of decisions: those that cannot be made solely on the basis of features of the external sensory environment, but must take into account one's internal priorities, needs, drives, and past experience. These kinds of decisions are complementary to cognition. For example, external sensory features can help you decide how to pick up a hot cup of coffee by the handle or by the round cup itself. However, they cannot decide *which* of these two is most appropriate: that depends on subjective factors like whether you're afraid of burning your hands or trying to warm them on a cold day in the snow. There is an objectively correct and incorrect sequence of button presses or taps on a touch screen to contact your friend or your parent. However, only internal factors can guide your decision as to *which* of these is the best person to contact if you get locked out of your home one day. Likewise, these externally guided, cognitive processes can be used to determine how many coins would be needed to pay for drink A versus drink B at a vending machine, but they cannot decide *which* of the two drinks you would prefer.

Only subjective factors like internal sensations, emotional states, and basic drives can guide decisions like which side of the cup will be more comfortable to grasp, which person will be most helpful in a crisis, or which soft drink will be more enjoyable to consume. The classical psychology of the 19th century had a separate term for this kind of internally driven decision making: **conation**, a function distinct and complementary to cognition. Conation referred to the processes by which internal impulses, drives, and motivations served to guide voluntary behavior (Hilgard, 1980). And just as cognition draws on the refined external sensory inputs we call *perception*, conation draws instead on the refined interoceptive sensory inputs we usually call *emotion*. (*Conation*, however, is a term that has changed its meaning over time, and now it is not used as widely as it was in the 19th century. When used today, it refers to a combination of cognitive and emotional factors that interact to bring about purposeful actions.)

The four general categories of perception, emotion, cognition, and conation may still be useful to us today because they correspond roughly to the highest levels of the four quarters of the "four-sided brain" in Chapter 2. Almost all of the kinds of decision making we have seen in this chapter so far fall into the category of conation: internally guided rather than externally guided decisions. So far we have considered these kinds of decisions mostly in terms of known forms of inconsistency or irrationality in human behavior. As we have seen, these inconsistencies probably arise from switches in the underlying decision-making pathways. One kind of switch may involve shifting from lateral prefrontal, externally guided to medial prefrontal, internally guided decision making (Koechlin & Hyafil, 2007). An example would be the preference reversal from the larger, later rewards of *Homo economicus* to the sooner, smaller rewards of impulsive *Homo sapiens* during delay discounting choices.

A more subtle kind of switch might arise when internally guided decision making shifts from one source of emotional inputs to another, as in switches from loss aversion to gain seeking in the endowment effect. The cognitive equivalent of this would be shifting which sensory input you use to guide your behavior. Imagine trying to find a fast-moving airplane in the sky. You might first hear the plane and try looking where the sound seems to be coming from, but you can switch to searching the sky with your eyes if the plane is not where sound localization suggests it ought to be.

Having covered these points, we're now ready to focus in on the mechanisms of internally guided decision making itself. What are the pathways by which the brain uses internal rather than external sensations and motivations to guide behavior? In the rest of this section, we'll look at the hierarchy of medial rather than lateral areas of the prefrontal cortex and how these regions use internal factors to assign priorities to goals, plans, and actions.

Values into Goals

Before you can decide what to do, you must know what you want to get. An essential drive like hunger or thirst lets us assign value or priority to the resources in our environment. As we saw in the previous section, the orbitofrontal cortex plays a key role in assigning subjective value or "utility" to resources by drawing on information about the resource's properties and then matching these up against current needs. This process of valuation can draw on external (contextual) factors, as when we assign high value to spinach because "it's good for you" rather than because we like the taste. However, we can also assign value based solely on internal factors, like how the resource makes us feel at the moment that we obtain it (FIGURE 12.22). Values based on internal motivations and drives, bereft of external influence, seem to be represented in the most ventral parts of the medial prefrontal cortex (van den Bos, McClure, Harris, Fiske, & Cohen, 2007).

A nice demonstration of this function came from a neuroimaging experiment in which the researchers gave subjects small tastes of two popular soft drinks, Coke and Pepsi. Most of the subjects had previously reported preferring Coke to Pepsi (FIGURE 12.23). However, when the squirts of drink were delivered in a "blind taste test" in the scanner, about half of the subjects described the Pepsi as tastier. The

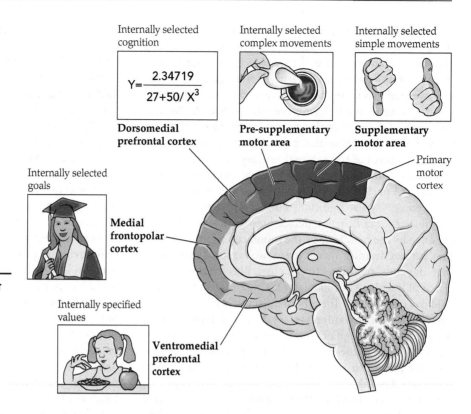

FIGURE 12.22 **Our goals are influenced by our values.** These values can be internal or external. Suppose our goal is to consume some nutrients. If you consider candy, your internal values might indicate that it will taste good, but your external values might indicate that it represents empty calories. Both of these values influence the ultimate goal.

brain area whose activity most closely tracked the subjective ratings of tastiness lay in the ventromedial prefrontal cortex (McClure, Li et al., 2004). However, once the subjects were informed what they were drinking, their preferences reverted back once again to their stated preferences.

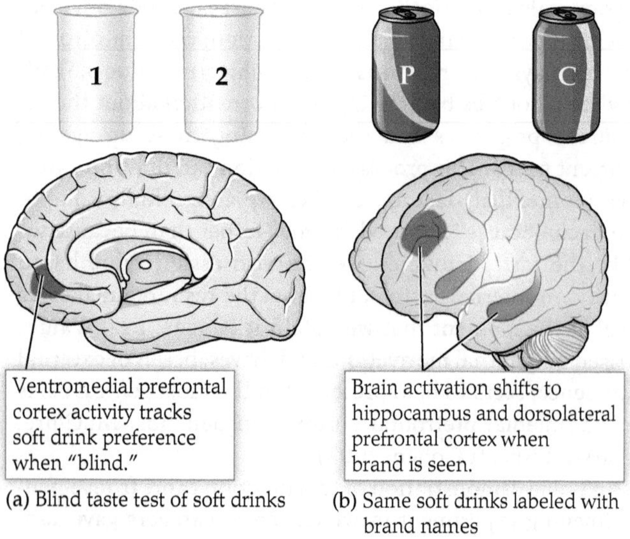

Ventromedial prefrontal cortex activity tracks soft drink preference when "blind."

Brain activation shifts to hippocampus and dorsolateral prefrontal cortex when brand is seen.

(a) Blind taste test of soft drinks

(b) Same soft drinks labeled with brand names

FIGURE 12.23 **Brain activation during taste tests of familiar soft drinks.** (a) In the absence of any external cues, such as brand names, the ventromedial prefrontal cortex tracked the person's subjective preference. (b) With the brand names added as external cues, activation shifted away from the medial wall onto the hippocampus and dorsolateral prefrontal cortex.

Once the subjects knew what they were drinking, the greatest brain activity was no longer associated with the more medial regions, but switched to the more lateral dorsolateral prefrontal cortex.

What if the decision became a little more abstract: not "which drink do you want?" but "which deal do you want?" In consumer purchases, the internal decision to buy depends not only on the subjective attractiveness of the item, but also on the subjective attractiveness of the price: both subjective features that must be combined to reach a decision. In one study, the desirability of a given good *at the given price* correlated closely with activity in ventromedial prefrontal region, just slightly more dorsal than the region seen in the blind taste test of soft drinks (Knutson & Bossaerts, 2007). This was approximately the same medial prefrontal region that we saw earlier in the neuroimaging study of the endowment effect (Knutson et al., 2008).

Just slightly dorsal to this region lies the area known as the medial frontopolar cortex, which is thought to represent a different type of goal from those we have just been describing. As you may recall from Chapters 2 and 8, the frontopolar cortex in general is a unique area of prefrontal cortex that lacks direct sensory input. Its input comes from higher association areas and regions of the prefrontal cortex that represent internal states and goals (Burman, Reser, Yu, & Rosa, 2011). Because of this, it is well suited to represent long-term goals that are independent of the immediate sensory surroundings or emotional states. The medial part of the frontopolar cortex activates in studies in which we ask subjects to reflect on their own long-term goals, hopes, dreams, and aspirations (Johnson et al., 2006). Along the same lines, the medial frontopolar cortex is also active in studies in which subjects need to use their own internal cues to keep track of the goal of the task they are trying to perform. When the goal is specified by an external cue, the lateral parts of this region are active instead (Koechlin, Corrado, Pietrini, & Grafman, 2000). Patients with lesions of the frontopolar cortex struggle when they need to juggle multiple subtasks while trying to keep in mind a larger overall goal (Dreher, Koechlin, Tierney, & Grafman, 2008).

Goals into Plans

Once a goal is established, the next step is to translate it into a plan or strategy: a general approach that specifies what steps need to be taken, without necessarily spelling out exactly what actions will be needed to accomplish each step. The choice of strategy is itself a decision, and this decision often must be based on internal factors or experience. For example, if one establishes the goal of contacting a friend to help move some furniture, either a telephone call or an email could potentially accomplish the goal. If both options are available, then external factors might not settle the decision. Instead, the choice will depend on which one seems like it will take less effort, result in a faster reply, be more persuasive, and so on.

Decisions that delineate strategies serve an important function that is hard to capture in experimental studies of decision making: they help subjects decide whether to participate in the experiment in the first place! However, once subjects are in the scanner, we do have some studies on how they decide whether to participate in individual trials of the task. For example, in a task called the **Ultimatum Game** (FIGURE 12.24), subjects must decide whether to accept a series of offers to split some money with another person (Sanfey, Rilling, Aronson, Nystrom, & Cohen, 2003). The other person proposes how the money should be split, and sometimes the proposals are quite unfair: "$15 for me, and $5 for you." However, if the proposal is rejected, both parties get nothing on that trial. So the decision is difficult.

As subjects decide whether to participate, they must use internal factors to decide not on a goal but on a strategy: take all offers to avoid missing out on any chances to win money or reject unfair offers and hope that this "punishment" leads to better offers down the road. Again, no external cues can provide the right or wrong answer—only internal feelings and motivations. The prefrontal area active during these strategic decisions lies just dorsal to the medial frontopolar cortex, in an area neighboring the region we see for deciding on long-term goals (Rilling, Sanfey, Aronson, Nystrom, & Cohen, 2004). Stronger activity in this area predicts a decision to reject the offer despite the monetary loss. (This activity stems from emotional

(a)

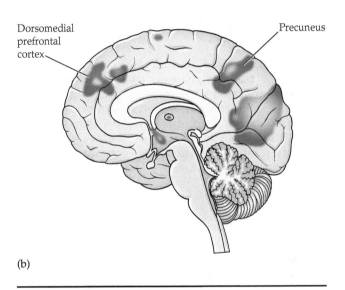

(b)

FIGURE 12.24 **The Ultimatum Game.** (a) The first player offers to split the money with the second player. If the second player accepts, the second player gets to keep the money offered by the first player. If the second player does not accept, both players receive no money. (b) The brain activity associated with the second player deciding whether to accept or reject the offer from the first player.

considerations such as a sense of unfairness or internal expectations about the effects of punishment.) Conversely, stronger activity in the lateral counterparts of this area in dorsolateral prefrontal cortex predicts the emotionless decision of *Homo economicus*, who accepts all offers because even $1 is a gain in utility.

Just dorsal to these areas lie still other dorsal medial prefrontal areas that are involved in selecting slightly more specific strategies, based on internal rather than external factors. For example, these areas are active when subjects decide for themselves, without external cues, whether to perform a syllable-counting or a word-meaning task on verbal stimuli (Forstmann, Brass, Koch, & von Cramon, 2006) (FIGURE 12.25). Likewise, when subjects decide on their own whether to perform either addition or subtraction on pairs of numbers, the pattern of activity within this area

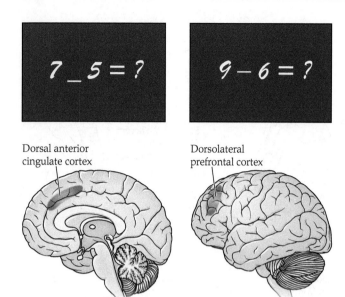

Dorsal anterior
cingulate cortex

Dorsolateral
prefrontal cortex

FIGURE 12.25 **Brain activity associated with freely choosing between different types of cognition.** The dorsal anterior cingulate cortex and the dorsomedial prefrontal cortex are active when a person freely chooses whether to perform addition or subtraction, or whether to perform a syllable-counting or word-meaning task. If the choice is not free, but is instead specified by an external cue, then activity shifts from the medial to the lateral prefrontal cortex.

displays subtle differences depending on the task selected (Haynes et al., 2007).

As you may have noticed, these particular dorsal medial areas are the same regions we see involved in the preference reversals of the framing effect. Just as the outcome of the adding/subtracting task depends on the internal choice of whether to focus on the difference or the sum of the two numbers, so the outcome of a decision under uncertainty depends on whether the focus is on the prospect of losses or gains. Since internal strategic considerations guide this decision, it makes sense that we should see the dorsomedial prefrontal cortex involved in strategic preference switching, as in the framing effect.

One interesting role of this area is in gambling. Pathological gamblers tend to get into trouble because they "chase losses": they place bigger and bigger bets to try to make up for their mounting debts. This dorsal medial prefrontal area shows increased activity at the point when they finally accept that the cause is hopeless and walk away from the gambling table (Campbell-Meiklejohn et al., 2008). In effect, they have reframed the gambling option as a loss rather than a gain and altered their plans in response.

Plans into Behavior and Action

Once a strategy or a plan is chosen, the final steps are to select the specific sequence of behaviors required to execute it and the specific sequence of actions and movements that make up each behavior. These behaviors may be partly constrained by the external environment, but they also require internal guidance and prioritizing. For example, if you've decided to make a sandwich, your plan may include a knife, a cutting board, a bun, and some tomatoes.

But as you stand before the kitchen counter, which of these items will you reach for first? Will you open the drawer to get the knife or first reach into the refrigerator for the tomatoes? Internal factors will assign priority to each behavior so they can be sequenced accordingly. As you go to open the refrigerator, what specific movements will you make? Will you swing the door open freely or hold it to make sure it doesn't smack against the wall? Again, internal factors guide even these simple actions.

Just posterior to the dorsomedial prefrontal cortex lies another area known as the presupplementary motor area, or pre-SMA (see Chapter 7 for more detail). This area activates not for externally cued movements, but for internally guided movements of the hand, as in pushing on a joystick in a sequence of freely chosen directions rather than according to a series of visually presented direction cues (Lau, Rogers, Ramnani, & Passingham, 2004). We see the same area active when subjects must choose to raise their hands at their own, self-directed pace, rather than in time with an external cue (Haggard, 2008). As for the SMA itself, this area shows a precise somatotopy for decisions about movements of individual body parts (Mitz & Wise, 1987), something like the somatotopy of the primary motor cortex (see Chapter 7). SMA activity appears in internally generated simple movements and also in internally generated suppression of simple movements. For example, the SMA activates during internally generated pelvic floor contractions (Kuhtz-Buschbeck et al., 2007). It also activates in subjects with full bladders, as they suppress involuntary contractions of the bladder's detrusor muscle to avoid urination during scanning (Kuhtz-Buschbeck et al., 2005).

What about the evidence from nonimaging experiments? Lesion studies show similar roles for medial areas in internally guided decisions to make simple movements. In primate experiments, lesions of these medial motor areas disrupt the animals' ability to make internally guided, self-paced movements (FIGURE 12.26). Lesions of lateral premotor areas leave these internally guided movements intact, but disrupt the ability to make movements according to a cue (Thaler, Chen, Nixon, Stern, & Passingham, 1995). Along the same lines, stimulation of lateral premotor cortex in human subjects produces movements without an internal sense of a decision to move or even an awareness of the movement (Desmurget & Sirigu, 2009). However, stimulation of medial motor areas results in an increasing sense of a desire to make a bodily movement, which eventually culminates in an irresistible urge or internal drive to move (Fried et al., 1991).

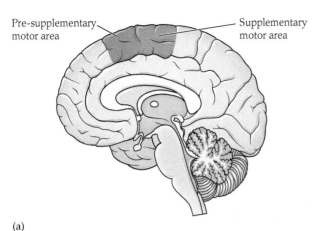

Pre-supplementary motor area

Supplementary motor area

(a)

Before lesion: self-paced movements intact

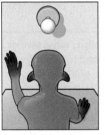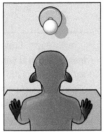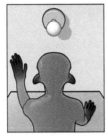

After lesion: self-paced movements impaired

After lesion: externally cued movements still intact

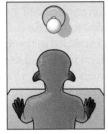

(b)

FIGURE 12.26 Motor planning areas along the midline of the brain.
(a) The supplementary motor area and presupplementary motor area are important for internally guided movements. (b) If these areas are lesioned in a primate, the animal loses the ability to make self-paced movements, such as raising the arm at regular intervals. However, the animal can still make these arm movements if given an external cue, like a flashing light.

Modulators of Decision Making

Looking back over what we have learned so far, we see that there are many forms of inconsistency, and at times irrationality, in the ways that human beings make decisions. When we examine the brain to see why this might be, we find that many different neural systems can be brought to bear on any given decision. Each system uses a slightly different set of inputs, and so each one arrives at a different conclusion.

Strategic Use of Decision-Making Systems

The advantage of having multiple decision-making systems is that it allows more behavioral flexibility for survival. When clear-cut external signals are available and outcomes are predictable, the simple if–then rules of the dorsal striatum and lateral prefrontal cortex can do the job. When inputs or outcomes are ambiguous, the past emotional experiences of orbitofrontal cortex and ventral striatum may serve as a better guide. For obvious threats, the amygdala can assemble a rapid and decisive response.

Yet having all of these decision-making systems available raises a bigger question: how do we decide which system is the best one to use in any given setting? With this question in mind, the neuroscience of decision making is now beginning to explore the mechanisms by which the brain decides on how it is going to decide.

One type of strategic decision making involves the use of different approaches to solving moral dilemmas, as we'll see in Chapter 15. These dilemmas involve difficult moral decisions, like whether to kill one person to save five others. There are different approaches to solving these dilemmas: for example, the loss-averse strategy of "do no harm" or the utilitarian strategy of "the greatest good for the greatest number." A couple of studies by Greene and colleagues have looked at these different approaches and found that in decisions that opt for the former approach of not harming others, medial prefrontal activity dominates the deliberations (FIGURE 12.27). In decisions that opt for the utilitarian approach, which is essentially a mathematical calculation, dorsolateral prefrontal activity predominates. Arbitrating between the two is a region of the lateral frontopolar cortex, where activity increases as subjects spend more time agonizing over which strategy to pursue (Greene, Nystrom, Engell, Darley, & Cohen, 2004; Greene, Sommerville, Nystrom, Darley, & Cohen, 2001). So this region, which keeps track of long-term goals, also has a key role in strategic decision making by serving as a referee between various competing mechanisms in different areas of the prefrontal cortex.

Another study examined how different subjects employ different strategies for decision making under risk (Venkatraman, Payne, Bettman, Luce, & Huettel, 2009). In this case, subjects made choices among gambles for monetary gains and

(a)

Internally-cued moral decision-making

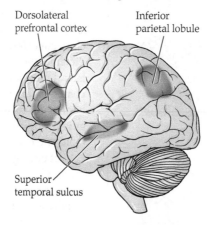

Rule-based or externally-cued moral decision making

(b)

FIGURE 12.27 **Brain activity during decision making in moral dilemmas.** (a) The "trolley problem" is a classic example of a moral dilemma: if a trolley is out of control and about to kill five people, would you flip a switch to send it to another track where it will kill only one person? (b) Different brain regions are involved in different types of moral decisions. When the decision is based on internal emotional cues, activity is stronger in medial wall areas, and in the amygdala and striatum. When the decision is based on external cues or mathematical rules ("do the greatest good for the greatest number"), activity is stronger in lateral areas of the cortex.

losses of various sizes and probabilities. The gamble options were designed so that subjects could pursue one of three different strategies: maximizing the potential gains in the gamble, minimizing the potential losses in the gamble, or maximizing the probability of winning at least some money in the gamble.

Subjects mostly tended to use this latter, "simplifying" strategy of just maximizing the overall chances of winning rather than losing, regardless of the amounts of money involved. In the simplifying strategy, the decision is simply a matter of ignoring the amounts, tallying up the overall probabilities of winning or losing, and then choosing the gamble with the best chance of winning. The areas most active for these kinds of choices lay in lateral areas known to be involved in arithmetical calculation: the dorsolateral prefrontal and posterior parietal cortex (FIGURE 12.28), as we tend to see for other *Homo economicus*–type decisions.

However, in many instances, the subjects deviated from this simplifying strategy and considered how much money they stood to gain or lose in the gamble. In these instances, the neural correlates also shifted. In the anterior insula, increasing activity appeared on trials in which subjects decided to minimize potential losses. In the ventromedial prefrontal cortex, increasing activity appeared on trials in which subjects decided to maximize potential gains. This dissociation is similar to the one we saw earlier in the chapter, for the neural predictors of choosing to reject versus accept a given consumer good at a given price (Knutson et al., 2008).

But what brain areas decided on the strategy itself? When subjects decided to deviate from the usual, simplifying strategy, activity increased in the dorsomedial prefrontal cortex and ventrolateral prefrontal cortex. Furthermore, as subjects shifted from one strategy to another, the dorsomedial prefrontal cortex shifted its functional connectivity from one brain region to another: increased connectivity to insula and amygdala when minimizing potential losses, but increased activity to the dorsolateral prefrontal cortex when maximizing the probability of winning.

The "referee" area in the dorsomedial prefrontal cortex also seems to be more or less the same area involved in the framing effect, which we saw earlier in the chapter. The preference reversals of the framing effect have to do with whether the subject chooses to focus on the prospect of losses or gains. As we saw, this strategic focus leads to differential activation of the amygdala for the certain versus the risky option, as we saw earlier (De Martino et al., 2006). In other words, the amygdala is usually more active during decisions made in accordance with the framing effect. However, subjects are sometimes able to suppress the framing effect and make

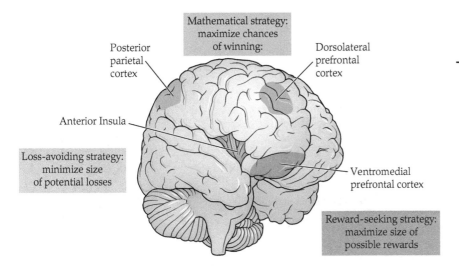

Posterior parietal cortex

Mathematical strategy: maximize chances of winning:

Dorsolateral prefrontal cortex

Anterior Insula

Loss-avoiding strategy: minimize size of potential losses

Ventromedial prefrontal cortex

Reward-seeking strategy: maximize size of possible rewards

FIGURE 12.28 Brain activation for different strategies of decision making. In individuals who seek to minimize the size of potential losses, the anterior insula is more active during decision making. In individuals whose strategy is to maximize the size of potential rewards, the ventromedial prefrontal cortex is more active. However, most people simply choose the option that has the best chance of resulting in a reward, regardless of size. This strategy, of maximizing the probability of winning, uses areas involved in mathematical calculations: the lateral parietal and prefrontal cortex.

decisions against their usual tendencies. Once again, this shift in strategy involves activation of the dorsal striatum, dorsomedial prefrontal cortex, and nearby anterior cingulate cortex (De Martino et al., 2006; Fehr, Fischbacher, & Kosfeld, 2005). Some subjects are also less prone to the framing effect in general, suggesting a strategic shift away from the use of the amygdala in these decisions. Such subjects show greater activation in areas that modulate the activity of the amygdala: namely, the lateral orbitofrontal cortex and ventromedial prefrontal cortex (Roiser et al., 2009).

So overall, if we look at the brain regions involved in deciding how to decide, we find regions relatively near the top of the hierarchy of decision making from the previous section. The emotion-modulating functions of the orbitofrontal cortex, the goal-tracking functions of the frontopolar cortex, and the plan-selecting functions of the dorsomedial prefrontal cortex can all help determine which decision-making rules will apply in any given scenario (FIGURE 12.29).

One final issue that arises here is what makes different people lean toward different strategies by default? For example, if some people are less susceptible to the framing effect in general, then do they have some inborn trait that leads them to act more strategically? As it turns out, subjects who carry the "long allele" of the serotonin transporter gene 5HTTLPR (which leads to increased serotonin levels and lower anxiety traits) are generally less susceptible to framing effects (FIGURE 12.30). They show more activation of the dorsomedial and ventromedial prefrontal cortex during decisions under risk (Roiser et al., 2009). Those with the "short allele," who are known to have greater amygdala activation to emotional stimuli (Hariri et al., 2002), have greater framing effects and less activation in these cortical areas.

Genetic studies like these suggest that, quite aside from neuroanatomical effects, neurotransmitters may affect overall strategic tendencies. Neurotransmitters sculpt and fine-tune the electrical activity of neural circuits, and this may be an important modulatory influence on decision making. So let's now take a look at what has been discovered about how neurotransmitters influence our decision-making tendencies.

Neurotransmitter Effects on Decision Making

Essential physiological parameters like heart rate, blood pressure, respiration, alertness, sleep, wakefulness, and reproduction all require modulation and regulation to adapt to changing circumstances. The body uses signaling mechanisms involving hormones, peptides, and other chemical transmitters to modulate each of these functions according to survival needs. The heart, lungs, and digestive organs must operate in a different way when fleeing a threat than when relaxing and digesting a meal. Of course, the same is true for the brain and its decision-making mechanisms: we need different modes for different circumstances.

As we have seen, decision making can slide along a scale from risk seeking to risk averse, or from impulsive to patient, or from internally to externally guided. These shifts involve changes in the neural pathways used to select among alternatives. As we have seen, preference reversals occur when the neural emphasis shifts from lateral to medial prefrontal pathways, from aversive interoception to reward prediction, or from intrinsic to contextual factors in stimulus evaluation. To accomplish these shifts, neurons must somehow be persuaded to change the patterns of their activity, increasing their activity in some places and decreasing it in others. Through these changes in activity and responsiveness, the landscape of evaluation and motivation can be reshaped.

The agents of this reshaping process are the brain's neurotransmitters: dopamine, serotonin, norepinephrine, and so on. At this point, research suggests that many of these neurotransmitters are involved in the decision-making process. This is why psychoactive chemicals, such as medications or substances of abuse, affect the processes of decision making along with those of cognition, perception, and interoception. We now have reasonable evidence about the effects of many common categories of medication on judgment and decision making, as measured using the standard intertemporal

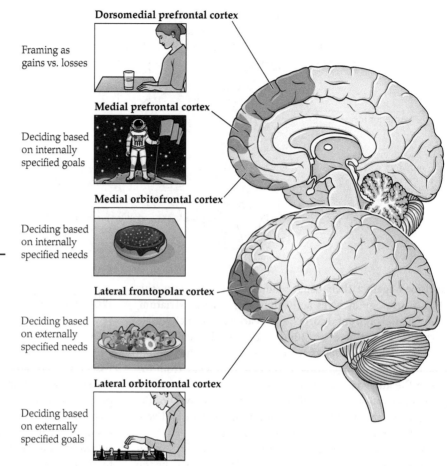

Dorsomedial prefrontal cortex

Framing as gains vs. losses

Medial prefrontal cortex

Deciding based on internally specified goals

Medial orbitofrontal cortex

Deciding based on internally specified needs

Lateral frontopolar cortex

Deciding based on externally specified needs

Lateral orbitofrontal cortex

Deciding based on externally specified goals

FIGURE 12.29 **Brain regions involved in decision making.** Different strategies, goals, and values help guide our decision making. The dorsomedial prefrontal cortex can frame options in terms of associated losses or gains ("is the glass half-empty, or half-full?"). The frontopolar cortex can help determine how well different options map onto our long-term goals or plans, whether specified by ourselves (medial) or by external circumstances (lateral). The medial orbitofrontal cortex can assign values to options based on internal needs, such as hunger or thirst; the lateral orbitofrontal cortex can assign values to options based on external context or circumstances.

choice and risky-decision tasks that we've been discussing throughout this chapter. However, the research is incomplete, and we do not yet know the details of how the neurotransmitters are involved or the different roles played by the different transmitters. In this section, we will focus on a

couple of the better-understood agents that influence decision making, but, remember, there remains much to learn!

As one might expect, alcohol increases the degree of impulsivity at lower levels of the decision-making hierarchy, for example, in the inhibition of simple actions (de Wit, Crean, & Richards, 2000). Alcohol affects a number of neurotransmitter systems but acts especially on the receptors of the inhibitory neurotransmitter GABA. Another class of drugs that stimulate the GABA receptor is the benzodiazepines—sedative and antianxiety medications such as diazepam (Valium) and lorazepam (Ativan). Diazepam also impairs performance on tasks requiring the inhibition or suppression of behavioral responses, like the go/no-go task, in which subjects must decide to respond or not respond based on some characteristic of the stimulus (Deakin, Aitken, Dowson, Robbins, & Sahakian, 2004). Surprisingly, however, neither alcohol nor diazepam seems to affect the discounting curves for choices among delayed monetary rewards (de Wit, 2009). However, this may be because choices among only delayed rewards fail to generate conflict between internal and external valuation processes, as we saw earlier in the chapter (McClure, Laibson et al., 2004). When the choices involve delays on the order of less than a minute, alcohol does increase delay discounting and impulsive decision making (Reynolds & Schiffbauer, 2004).

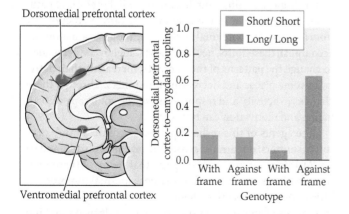

FIGURE 12.30 **Genetic influences on brain activity underlying the framing effect.** Individuals with the long allele for the serotonin transporter gene are better able to engage the dorsomedial and ventromedial prefrontal cortex to suppress the amygdala during decision making. This helps to control excessive anxiety over losses, and overcome the framing effect.

The neurotransmitter serotonin also seems to have important effects on impulse control and decision making. To make serotonin, the brain requires a precursor molecule known as **tryptophan**, which is normally found in the diet. However, if human subjects eat a low-tryptophan diet for a few days, their brains become partially depleted of serotonin, and various emotional and behavioral effects ensue (Bhatti et al., 1998). Among these effects are increased impulsivity in animals (Bizot, Le Bihan, Puech, Hamon, & Thiebot, 1999; Wogar, Bradshaw, & Szabadi, 1993) and humans (Schweighofer et al., 2008). Subjects are more likely to choose sooner, smaller rewards over larger, later rewards when low on serotonin. As we saw in the previous section, low serotonin may also lead to stronger loss aversion, with resulting changes in decision making under risk (Roiser et al., 2009).

Other medications seem actually to *reduce* impulsivity at certain doses. The stimulant medication dextroamphetamine stimulates the release of dopamine from synaptic terminals. This medication has long been known to be effective for improving attention span and reducing hyperactivity and impulsivity in people with **attention deficit hyperactivity disorder (ADHD)** (Weiss & Hechtman, 2006). Acute doses also seem to reduce impulsivity during a task that measures the relative value of immediate versus delayed rewards in subjects without ADHD (FIGURE 12.31) (de Wit, Enggasser, & Richards, 2002), as well as causing acute improvements in mood, sociability, and arousal level. However, other studies come to a different conclusion. In a study of 14 healthy control subjects, Pine et al. (2010) found that increasing the amount of dopamine in the brain made the subjects more impulsive and more likely to value immediate rewards. Similarly, individuals who *chronically* abuse similar stimulants, such as methamphetamine, have markedly *increased* impulsivity and steeper delay discounting (Hoffman et al., 2006), possibly because of increased activity of the amygdala when faced with the prospect of a delayed reward (Hoffman et al., 2008). So for dopamine, the effects on decision making may be different for acute versus chronic manipulations and it may be different for subjects with ADHD as opposed to healthy control subjects. Clearly, more research is needed to understand the role of dopamine on decision making.

The brain's **cannabinoid** neurotransmitter system may also have some effects on decision making. **Tetrahydrocannabinol**, one of the active ingredients in cannabis, stimulates the brain's cannabinoid receptors. When given capsules of tetrahydrocannabinol compared with a placebo, subjects show higher impulsivity on some simple measures, such as impulsive responding on a "stop task" that involved inhibiting simple motor actions. They also reported a slowing of subjective time over short intervals. However, measures of delay and risk discounting showed no changes, at least for the single doses administered in this study (McDonald, Schleifer, Richards, & de Wit, 2003). Likewise, **opioid** medications, such as the powerful analgesic oxycodone, do not seem to have any major effects on impulsivity in acute doses (Zacny & de Wit, 2009), although they have powerful effects on mood. Opioid neurotransmitters may be more important

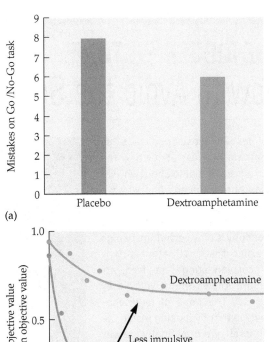

(a)

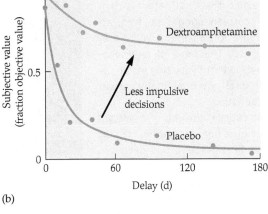

(b)

FIGURE 12.31 Effects of 20 mg of dextroamphetamine on impulsivity in healthy control subjects. (a) After dextroamphetamine, subjects made fewer mistakes on the "Go/No-Go task," in which they must press a button as quickly as possible for "Go" signals but avoid responding to "No-Go" signals. (b) After dextroamphetamine, subjects also made less impulsive choices on the delay discounting task: the hyperbolic discounting function became less steep, indicating that subjects needed less incentive to accept a later reward.

for the degree of "liking" options already taken rather than the "wanting" of options under consideration, as we'll see in Chapter 14 on motivation.

What about hormonal modulators? As we saw earlier, strong emotional states (such as fear or desperation) can have marked effects on decision making. These states induce **stress**, which results in a triad of physiological responses: the autonomic response (e.g., increasing heart rate and respiration to prepare for action), the endocrine response (e.g., stimulating the release of stress hormones like **cortisol** to trigger changes in function across many bodily organs), and the behavioral response coordinated by the brain. Part of this response involves a restructuring of decision making. For example, chemical analogues of the stress hormone cortisol can be placed in capsules and administered to healthy volunteers. When under the influence of cortisol, subjects then become more likely to choose the riskier of two gambles for monetary rewards, especially when the riskier choice offered the prospect of a larger reward (Putman, Antypa, Crysovergi, & van der Does, 2010).

THE BIGGER PICTURE:
How to Avoid the Scorpion's Sting

The best neuroscience tells us something not just about how the brain works, but also about who we are as human beings and why we do the things we do. One of the oldest puzzles in literature and philosophy is why we human beings can act so irrationally at times: why the scorpion stings the frog, although it knows that it will die by doing so. The hope of neuroeconomics is that by looking inside the brain itself, we may finally answer this question.

Of course, the more important question is how *not* to sting the frog in the first place. If bad decisions are simply in our nature, then the cause is hopeless. At times, every one of us is a scorpion, knowingly acting against our own interests: the failed diet, the skipped class, the doomed relationship. The gambler, the smoker, the rationalizer, and the procrastinator cannot be banished from our world without leaving it empty altogether.

But there may be better ways to avoid the scorpion's sting. For example, consider impulsivity: a temporary triumph of immediate over long-term interests, driven by medial over lateral prefrontal areas. Our dorsolateral prefrontal cortex cannot always be counted on to drive the decision, nor should it. But if we have already decided that we want to go to the gym and are having trouble sticking by our commitments, then there is a second option: borrow *someone else's* dorsolateral prefrontal cortex to keep you to your prior decision.

This method is sometimes called a self-binding contract, or a **Ulysses contract**. The name comes from

FIGURE 12.32 Ulysses. In the *Odyssey*, Ulysses relies on his sailors to keep him honest when sailing past the Sirens.

Homer's classical Greek epic, the *Odyssey*. Ulysses (**FIGURE 12.32**), the sea captain, wishes to hear the irresistible song of the beautiful Sirens as he sails past their island. The problem is that anyone who hears their song becomes overpowered by its beauty, jumps overboard to swim to the Sirens, and drowns in the process. So, he has his sailors plug their ears to block out the song. Then, he orders them to tie him to the mast and to ignore his orders to untie him. As they approach the Sirens, he is overcome by the song and begins to beg, cajole, and finally rage at the sailors to untie him. However, they ignore him until the Sirens are safely behind them.

Although most of us lack a crew of Greek sailors to keep us honest, we can still make use of our own personal Ulysses contracts. Bringing a workout partner to the gym, quitting smoking with a friend, or forming a study group are all ways

of using another person's dorsolateral prefrontal cortex to reinforce our own. Similar methods are now working their ways into law, finance, and international development. "Casino blacklist" laws allow people to ban themselves from gambling institutions under penalty of arrest. Automatic debits allow people to commit themselves to saving for retirement. Harvest timing initiatives encourage farmers in developing nations to plant their crops so that they will be ready just when the school year begins, so there will be money to pay their children's school fees.

Behavioral economists are now searching for ways to use prospect theory, framing effects, delay discounting, and endowment effects to encourage *better* decision making when it comes to our health, our education, our financial decisions, and our involvement in risky behavior. In one example of this, Penn

State University imposed a fee of $100 per month if their employees did not participate in a wellness plan (Jensen, 2013). The aim of this, like all such attempts to encourage better decision making, was to treat the brain's sometimes irrational decision-making mechanisms as "features" rather than "bugs." To do this properly, we will need to have a solid understanding of exactly how those mechanisms work: how internal and external inputs drive decision making, how emotion and desperation play into the process, and what tips the balance from immediate, internal to long-term, external factors in driving the choices we make. Unfortunately, in the case of Penn State, the fee was dropped because of many objections to the plan (Powers, 2013). Whether or not we can change our "nature" as scorpions, the neuroscience of decision making may help us find ways to make that nature work for us, rather than against us.

This finding makes intuitive sense: desperate times call for desperate measures, and when survival is under threat, the organism may have little to lose in "going for broke." We know that stress, anxiety, depression, poverty, abuse, physical conflict, and many other deprivation states will increase stress hormone release in all primates, including humans (Sapolsky, 2005). These hormones, in turn, have effects on the neural substrates of emotion and motivation and thus on decision making itself (Rodrigues, LeDoux, & Sapolsky, 2009). So in the end, one of the most important sculptors of our decision-making circuitry may be distress and deprivation—a point that has broader social implications, as we'll discuss in the conclusion below.

Conclusion

Just as in *The Scorpion and the Frog*, human beings have a persistent and peculiar tendency to make irrational decisions, even when these decisions lead to their own demise. We are often raised to think that poor decisions reflect poor judgment, or at least poor upbringing. Yet every one of us knows how it feels to be "of two minds" about a decision, and every one of us has at times succumbed to impulsivity, procrastination, excessive caution or recklessness, overattachment to our belongings, or the subtle effects of framing.

Why should this be? In the quest for a "physics of human decisions," many different authors have proposed that our brain really does contain two systems: rational versus emotional, conscious versus unconscious, modern versus primitive, and so on. The implication is often that our poor decisions simply reflect the "quick and dirty" output of a primitive system that may have served our ancestors well, but is ill-suited to the challenges of modern life. The centuries-old search for a felicific calculus continues under many different names today: a search for rational, objective algorithms to guide us through all perplexing decisions, a search for external cues to which we may anchor ourselves, so that we no longer need to entrust our decisions to the uncertain and irrational output of our partially outdated brains.

But can the "primitive" system really be jettisoned so easily? Is the "modern" system really modern at all? Are they even in competition? When we look at the neural substrates of decision making, what we see is more of a collaboration between two completely different approaches to guiding decisions. The first, guided by medial prefrontal areas, relies mostly on internal-world inputs to choose among options. Far from being primitive, many of these areas are greatly expanded in humans over other species. They are also indispensable: damage to these areas causes, at best, major problems in judgment and motivation, and at worst, a state of complete apathy.

As for the second system, it seems to use lateral prefrontal areas whose inputs draw on the outside rather than the inside world. This system may be useful for learning how to operate a mobile phone, but is often stumped when it comes to choosing *which* mobile phone to buy in the first place. It is also far from modern: analogues of the same areas can be found in other species whose ancestry diverged from ours tens of millions of years ago: apes, monkeys, and even rodents. So the real differences between the objective, rational system and the subjective, intuitive system may lie in their inputs. Some decisions can be made using objective, outside world cues and rational calculations. Other decisions *require* information about internal states, motivations, and past experiences. The fittest of our ancestors had brains that drew upon *both* approaches to decision making.

At the end of the day, the quest to "rationalize" our decisions is a quest to find objective guides through all situations—to eliminate the role of subjective judgments. But subjective decisions are rooted in our basic needs, values, and drives: the very keys to survival. When these mechanisms are removed from the picture, as in neurological patients with medial wall damage, the results are disastrous.

If we want to improve human decision making, the real trick may be not so much to eliminate our subjective influences as refine them. Specifically, we may need to find ways to build a longer-term valuation into our drives, goals, plans, and actions. It may be the long view, more than rationality, which distinguishes us from our ancestors, animal or otherwise.

As for the role of emotion in human decisions, a better plan may be to find ways of reshaping the emotional and motivational landscape to fit our modern environment, rather than eliminating it altogether. This doesn't have to mean physically modifying our brains—modifying our social environment and its incentive structures may be enough to do the trick. The problem is that our technologies for doing so are still in their infancy. The new field of neuroeconomics has only just emerged and is only just beginning to produce hints on how to change our behavior for the better.

Reducing human desperation may help: when basic needs call out for satisfaction, we tend to become blinded to the long view. With basic needs addressed, the frontopolar cortex can begin once again to weigh long-term goals and aspirations over short-term gains. In the neuroeconomic version of the fable, the scorpion did not sting the frog because it was his nature, or because his brain was defective, or even because his brain was obsolete. The scorpion stung the frog because, despite his best efforts, he was stressed.

We started this chapter at the summit of Mt. Everest, 29,035 feet above sea level. In 1996, eight climbers died near the summit. Partially, that was because of unpredictable weather conditions, but partially it was because of poor decision making. It was widely known by the climbers and their guides that it was important to reach the summit by early afternoon. If they did not, even if they were just a few hundred feet away, they had to turn around. It was also known that being physically healthy was crucial to the ability to summit the mountain and get down safely, yet one of the guides exhausted himself climbing up and down to cater to his clients. For many of the reasons we have talked about in this chapter, the clients and the guides both allowed themselves to focus on the short-term goal of reaching the summit of Everest, not on the long-term goal of surviving the adventure. Physiology and lack of oxygen certainly played a role in making these decisions, but so did the delay discounting described in this chapter. The emerging field of neuroeconomics has much to offer, whether you are a scorpion, a mountain climber, or a college student trying to convince yourself to study for the upcoming test.

KEY PRINCIPLES

- *Homo economicus* is a hypothetical cousin of *Homo sapiens* who always makes rational choices by weighing all the relevant factors. *Homo economicus* calculates the expected utility, or value, of choices and always choses the option with the greatest value.

- *Homo sapiens* does not always make rational choices. We do not factor uncertainty into our decision making, are swayed by a problem's framing, and consider an object we possess to be endowed with greater value than if we wanted to purchase the same object.

- Delay discounting means that we tend to value near-term rewards more than rewards farther in the future. One study found that humans are even more impulsive in this manner than chimpanzees.

- The brain contains multiple decision-making systems, and these systems do not always concur in their output.

- Neuroimaging studies are revealing how these competing systems produce common forms of inconsistent or irrational human decisions.

- A common currency of subjective value allows the brain to compare options when making a decision.

- This common currency operates in distinct neural "markets" depending on whether the options under consideration are resources, goals, plans, or actions.

- A hierarchy of medial prefrontal areas uses internal factors to assign priority to competing resources, goals, plans, actions, and movements.

- The brain can use different strategies to deploy different decision-making mechanisms under different circumstances, allowing more flexible behavior.

- The emerging science of neuroeconomics may help us find ways to improve human decision making and avoid its more destructive forms of irrationality.

KEY TERMS

REVIEW QUESTIONS

1. What are some examples of human behavior that cannot be easily explained in terms of rational economic agents?

2. What are some real-world examples of the framing effect and the endowment effect? Why do people play lotteries, but also buy insurance?

3. How do humans differ from other related species in terms of their decision making? What changes in the brain might account for these differences?

4. What are the "defective brain" and "obsolete brain" explanations for irrational decisions? What are some weaknesses of each model in explaining human behavior?

5. What happens in the brain when people choose smaller, sooner rewards over larger, later rewards? What happens when people make the opposite choice?

6. By what brain mechanisms do emotional states and "gut feelings" affect decision making under risk? How do these mechanisms lead to the endowment effect and the framing effect?

7. Is there a "common currency" of subjective value and, if so, what form might it take in the brain?

8. What brain mechanisms are likely involved in choosing an apple versus an orange? Art school versus medical school? Chasing your losses versus cutting your losses? Shaking hands versus giving a high-five?

9. How might the brain decide what kind of decision-making strategy to use in a given situation? Based on the brain areas involved, how likely is it that external, rather than internal, factors will guide a person's choice of decision-making strategy?

CRITICAL-THINKING QUESTIONS

1. Give three different ways in which neuroscience could help to discover ways to improve our decision-making abilities.

2. Imagine that you work for the Centers for Disease Control and that you are in charge of a public campaign to encourage parents to have their infants receive standard immunizations at the ages of two, four, and six months. How would you use your knowledge of the framing effect to encourage parents to have their infants immunized? Explain your reasoning.

3. Why do you think that scientists have so little knowledge of the role of specific neurotransmitters in decision making? What major challenges do you think that scientists who investigate the role of neurotransmitters in decision making face? Explain.

- Differentiate among the major theories of emotion, including bottom-up, top-down, and two-factor.

- Describe the three major classes of survival behaviors regulated by the hypothalamus, the contributions of the amygdala to emotion and behavior, the contributions of the hippocampus to emotion and memory, and the contributions of the ventral striatum to pleasure and reward.

- Detail the roles of the insula, cingulate cortex, and ventromedial prefrontal cortex in emotion and emotion regulation.

- Summarize the brain mechanisms of emotion regulation and reappraisal.

- Explain how serotonin, norepinephrine, and GABA exert their effects on emotion.

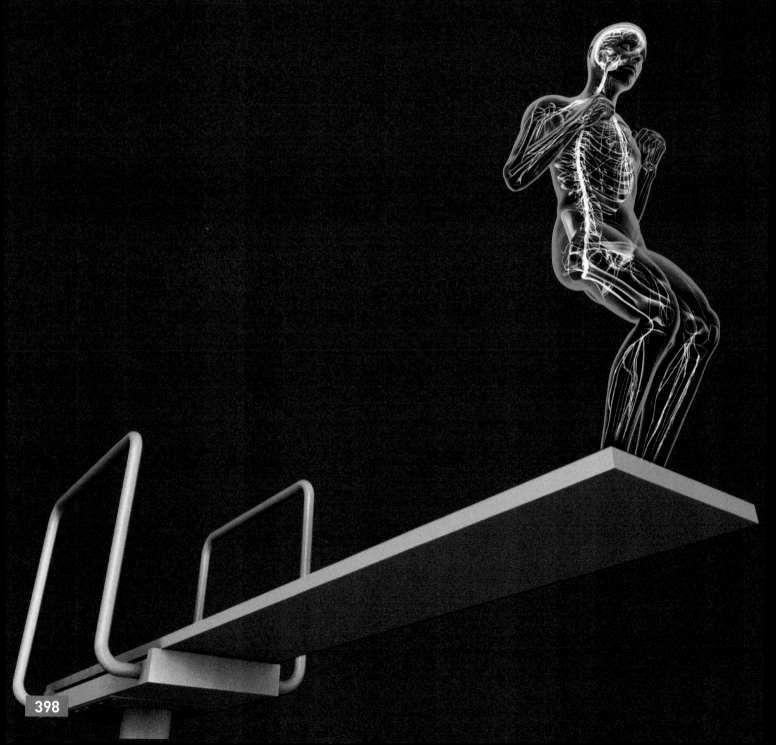

Emotions

STARTING OUT:
Sadness, at the Flip of a Switch

She was desperate for a cure. At the age of just 26, a woman we'll call Susanna had begun to notice a strange tremor in her hands. After a visit to a neurologist and a thorough medical evaluation, she was diagnosed with Parkinson's disease—an illness usually not seen until much later in life. Over the next 10 years, she tried various regimens of medication, but her tremor and stiffness continued to worsen. In addition, as is often the case, the medications gradually became less and less helpful. Where they once granted her long windows of time with normal movement, these windows of time became narrower. Instead, with each dose of medication, she began experiencing "on–off" fluctuations between excessive, involuntary writhing movements called dyskinesias, followed by a swift descent into rigidity, immobility, and slowness. Susanna had struggled with depression from an early age, even before her diagnosis.

Because her symptoms had become so disabling and because the medications were no longer working, her doctors offered her a more drastic intervention: deep brain stimulation. A neurosurgeon would carefully lower a pair of electrodes into her left and right subthalamic nucleus: a tiny region just a few millimeters wide and deep in the brain. The electrodes would then be connected to a small, pacemakerlike device implanted under her left collarbone (**FIGURE 13.1**). When activated, this neural pacemaker would interfere with the inhibitory motor pathways coursing

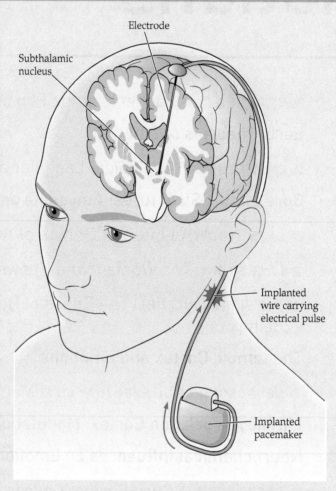

FIGURE 13.1 Deep brain stimulation to treat Parkinson's disease. A pacemaker-like device delivers pulses of electrical stimulation to the subthalamic nucleus, via electrodes implanted directly in the brain.

through this tiny brain region and thus restore her movements to something closer to normal. Susanna opted to undergo the surgery, and her neurosurgeon implanted the electrodes as precisely as possible.

Once the surgery was over, the next step was to fine-tune the stimulation parameters. To offer the best chances of success, the tip of each electrode came equipped with not one but four electrical contacts, each a couple of millimeters apart. Susanna's team of physicians would try stimulating each of the eight possible contacts with different voltages and frequencies of electrical current to see which ones were most effective. In her left subthalamic nucleus, after a few trials, they soon found a combination of stimulus parameters that improved her tremor and stiffness considerably.

But when they began testing the right side, something unexpected happened. As soon as they activated the lowermost two contacts, Susanna became overwhelmed by intense sadness and began to cry uncontrollably. When they turned off the stimulation, her mood improved again, but each time they turned it back on, the crushing sadness returned almost instantly. Later, she described the experience as the most abhorrent of her life: "A deep down bad feeling in the pit of my stomach . . . similar in

some respects to my depression but a thousand times worse . . . I did not care about myself or anything . . . someone could have come in to shoot me and I could not have cared less" (Stefurak et al., 2003).

Susanna's experience, although startling, was not unique. Over the past two decades, several other neurosurgical teams have also reported patients who developed intense and instantaneous sadness at the flip of a switch with stimulation of part of the subthalamic nucleus. So far, it remains a mystery as to why a small number of patients have such catastrophic reac-

tions to stimulation, whereas the vast majority do not.

As for Susanna? A few months later, her surgical team repositioned the right-side electrode slightly, and it finally began to exert its intended effect. Two years later, the stimulator continued to help to improve her motor symptoms, without any side effects on her mood. Yet she continued to recall her initial experience as so distressing that she would never have been able to tolerate it in the long term, no matter how much her motor symptoms might have improved (Stefurak et al., 2003).

To be human, for better or worse, is to ride a lifelong roller-coaster of feelings: sadness, joy, pride, anger, fear, disgust, boredom, and curiosity. Our emotions lie at the very core of our identity. They seem ineffable, sublime, immaterial: the very things that distinguish us from cold, inanimate matter. We reserve the epithet "inhuman" for those members of our species who lack the feelings of empathy or kindness and commit atrocities without any sense of wrongdoing. We may be prepared to accept the idea that a robot could work more quickly than we do or a that a computer could solve a problem faster than we do, yet we comfort ourselves with the notion that, unlike computers, human beings can enjoy the radiance of the summer sun on our cheeks or the warmth of a loved one nestled in our arms.

So what does it mean if our feelings can be turned on and off at the flip of a switch? If our emotions have circuit diagrams and are subject to material manipulations just like any other process in the universe? How can there be "happy" or "sad" areas in the brain? How can there be "mood-altering" substances, and how exactly do they exert their effects? Can emotions be lost to disease, as vision or memory can be? Could a computer be built to have emotions, and if so, how?

Traditionally, the scientific understanding of the neuroscience of emotion has lagged far behind the scientific understanding of the more mature neurosciences of vision, language, memory, movement, and cognition. Yet over the past decade or two, we have begun to devise better techniques for studying this cherished, yet mysterious, function of the brain. With the new techniques have come new discoveries and at least the beginnings of a sketch of where our emotions come from and how they work.

Early Theories of Emotion

As we will see later in this chapter, modern neuroscience techniques have allowed us to study the neural basis of emotion. Before these recent discoveries, however, psychologists still sought to understand emotion. Three main psychological theories to explain emotion remain today. All three have strengths and weaknesses, and none is clearly superior to the others. Let's start our discussion of emotion by considering these psychological explanations.

Emotional Expressions: Signposts on a Landscape of Inner States

One of the pioneers in the scientific study of emotional expression was none other than Charles Darwin. In 1872, some 13 years after his seminal work *On the Origin of Species*, he published another book, *The Expression of the Emotions in Man and Animals*. Using sketches and photographs, he surveyed the characteristic behaviors of a wide variety of species in different emotional states.

Emotional expressions act as a sort of "prosthetic telepathy," sending out clear and unambiguous signals about our otherwise-invisible internal states. The male blue-footed booby signals its desire to mate by spreading its wings, raising its head, and displaying its wide blue feet: an attention-getting maneuver, not likely to appear by accident. Dogs wag their tails to indicate a friendly disposition to other dogs or

(a)

(b)

(c)

FIGURE 13.2 **Emotional expressions send out clear and unambiguous signals about internal states.** (a) A blue-footed booby signals its desire to mate. (b) A dog wags its tail to indicate a friendly disposition. (c) A shark kinks its body when on the verge of attack.

humans. When on the verge of an attack, sharks kink their bodies into a characteristic "threat posture" easily recognized by other sharks (and wary human scuba divers) (Johnson & Nelson, 1973; Vas, Topal, Gacsi, Miklosi, & Csanya, 2005; Velando, Beamonte-Barrientos, & Torres, 2006). These kinds of overt displays (FIGURE 13.2) are a gateway into the inner world of emotions, and we can use them as a starting point for understanding the emotional repertoires of human beings.

One of Darwin's major insights was that animal emotional expressions were effectively homologues of human emotions (Griffiths, 2003). In comparative anatomy, homologous structures share a common ancestry even if their outward form and function have changed: for example, the hand of an orangutan, the hoof of a horse, and the flipper of a seal are all homologues. Human emotions, as homologues of animal emotions, share a common evolutionary origin in the representation of an organism's internal state.

Darwin also provided illustrations of human beings in a variety of different emotional states, and he made a key suggestion: that a common set of emotions could be identified in the facial expressions of human beings, of all ages and both genders, in all cultures across the world. His survey of

human emotions included fear, anger, surprise, joy, sadness, and disgust, among others (Griffiths, 2003). A more basic set of emotions could be found across many species as well: anger, fear, surprise, and sadness (FIGURE 13.3).

The identification of a common palette of human emotions was not in itself a new idea. In fact, more than 2,000 years ago, an ancient Indian work called the *Natyashastra* described in detail eight basic *rasas*, or emotional expressions, for use in drama and dance. The *rasas* specified not only the facial expression, but also the bodily posture and style of movement associated with each emotion. What is noteworthy is that even today, in a much different time and culture, we can easily recognize and label the *rasas* with analogous emotion words: love, mirth, fury, compassion, disgust, horror, amazement, and steely determination. Later additions included expressions of tranquility, parental love, and devotion. Each of these emotions is recognizable across most if not all cultures, suggesting universal neural underpinnings (Griffiths, 2003).

The James–Lange Theory of Emotion: A Bottom-Up Theory

So where do our basic emotional states originate? Intuitively, we tend to feel as if our emotions arise in response to some outer stimulus and that the inner physiological responses come afterward. In other words, we see an oncoming car rushing toward us, then we feel a sudden rush of fear, and then comes the shiver running down the spine, the sudden tightness in the chest, the flash of heat in the face, the racing, pounding heart, and so on. Yet in the late 19th century, the American psychologist William James and the

FIGURE 13.3 Basic emotions, such as (a) fear, (b) anger, (c) surprise, (d) joy, (e) sadness, and (F) disgust, can be identified across cultures.

Danish physiologist Carl Lange independently proposed a new theory of emotion that turned this intuitive sequence upside down.

According to the **James–Lange theory** of emotion, it is not the feeling of fear that causes the bodily reactions; instead, it is the feeling of the body's reactions that causes the fear (Cannon, 1927). When the car rushes toward us, the visceral reactions occur rapidly, involuntarily, and unconsciously: increases in respiration and heart rate, tensing of the muscles, slowing of digestion, diversion of circulation to the musculature, stimulation of the adrenal glands, perspiration, piloerection (that is, raising of the body hair away from the skin). As we'll see in the next section, we have an entire division of the peripheral nervous system dedicated to organizing these and other **fight-or-flight** functions, and this system can be deployed within less than 100 milliseconds in response to a threat (Gonon, Msghina, & Stjarne, 1993).

In the James–Lange theory, the actual emotion of fear arises when the brain senses these kinds of changes going on in the body itself and interprets them as an emotional response. In James's words, "we feel sorry because we cry, angry because we strike, afraid because we tremble," and so on (James, 1890). In its strongest form, the James–Lange theory argues that if the bodily response is blocked or the brain somehow cannot sense the body's response, then no emotional response should occur.

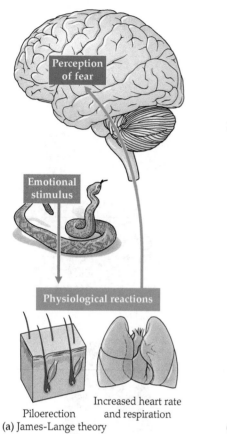

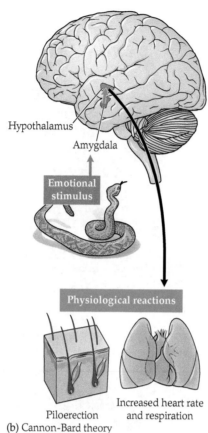

FIGURE 13.4 **The James–Lange (bottom-up) and Cannon–Bard (top-down) theories of emotion.** (a) In the James–Lange theory, physiological signals travel up from the visceral organs of the body to produce emotional states in the brain. (b) In the Cannon–Bard theory, emotional states arise in the brain, which then sends signals down to produce physiological reactions in the visceral organs of the body.

We can think of the James–Lange theory as an example of a **bottom-up theory**: emotions originate from the visceral signals in the periphery of the nervous system, which are then interpreted by so-called "higher" areas in the central nervous system. As you may recall from Chapter 8, this is somewhat analogous to the bottom-up theories of attention, in which a stimulus grabs our attention based on its own intrinsic sensory properties, such as its color or motion or loudness. The major difference is that in bottom-up theories of emotion, the inputs are coming from the inner-world, visceral sensory neurons of the internal organs, rather than the outer-world sensory neurons of the retina, cochlea, and other external sensory organs as in bottom-up theories of attention (FIGURE 13.4).

The Cannon–Bard Theory: A Top-Down Theory

Although influential, James and Lange's bottom-up theory of emotion ran into some major difficulties early on. In the 1920s, the American physiologist Walter Cannon cited a wide variety of physiological evidence to challenge the James–Lange theory on several grounds (Cannon, 1927).

First, in animal studies, total surgical separation of the visceral organs from the brain did not abolish emotional behavior (Bard, 1934). In cats lacking visceral innervation, the

sudden appearance of a dog would still lead to hissing, growling, ear retraction, teeth baring, lifting of the paw to strike, and other typical threat responses. Second, visceral changes were too nonspecific to signal a single emotional state. For example, the bodily effects of activity in the sympathetic nervous system (increases in heart rate, respiration rate, and so on) occur in fear but also in rage, as well as in fever or exposure to cold temperatures or even with excessively low blood sugar (Maickel, Matussek, Stern, & Brodie, 1967; Rainville, Bechara, Naqvi, & Damasio, 2006; Rowe et al., 1981). Third, many bodily responses were too slow to generate emotions, on the order of minutes rather than seconds (Stewart, Hake, & Peterson, 1974). Thus, the flushed face or dry mouth of embarrassment might occur well after the onset of the emotion itself. Finally, artificially inducing bodily responses using hormonal injections or other experimental manipulations was insufficient to generate the subjective emotional state (Marañon, 1924).

On the basis of these findings, Cannon suggested that bottom-up processes alone would not be sufficient to explain how emotions arose in the nervous system (Dalgleish, 2004). To emphasize this point, Cannon and his colleague, the physiologist Philip Bard, performed a series of animal experiments to show that stereotypical emotional responses could occur even after the separation of the entire cortex from the rest of the nervous system. For example, "decorticated" cats became liable to display spontaneous activation

CASE STUDY:
Pathological Laughter and Crying

A 55-year-old woman with multiple sclerosis had suffered for years from the on-and-off symptoms of her disease. During flare-ups of her illness, patches of demyelination would appear in the white matter tracts of her brain (FIGURE 13.5), cutting off the connections between distant brain regions. Depending on the location of the patches, any number of unpleasant and disabling symptoms could appear during an attack of the illness: weakness in the limbs, difficulty walking, slurring of speech, impairment of vision, or impairments of memory and concentration. However, one day she came to the clinic with a symptom that was stranger, and in many ways more disabling, than any she had experienced before: uncontrollable bursts of laughter and crying, known in medical terminology as pseudobulbar affect.

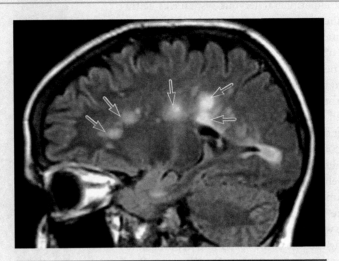

FIGURE 13.5 **MRI of a patient with multiple sclerosis.** Note the plaques in the white matter, where the axons have suffered demyelination.

She reported that she would often begin to smile and then laugh loudly and uncontrollably, for no apparent reason, and often in inappropriate circumstances, such as when shopping for groceries. At other times, she would become tearful and begin to sob and cry, as if being confronted with terrible news. This could happen at any time, often to the bewilderment of those around her, and so she had begun staying at home and avoiding public places out of embarrassment.

The oddest thing about these attacks is that they were completely unaccompanied by the usual emotions. This was laughter without inner mirth and sobbing without inner sadness. This feature of the illness was particularly hard for her to convey to her friends and family and even her physicians. At one medical appointment, when asked about her symptoms, she simply began sobbing and contin-

ued to do so as she attempted to answer the doctor's questions. Her tearfully recounted history aroused the empathy of all the medical staff in the room. But, when asked whether she was feeling sad, she paused, then shook her head and said, "No . . ." while at the same time crying out, covering her face, and launching into another bout of intense and uncontrollable weeping. The scene was a confusing one, to say the least. Although her inner emotional state was neutral, an outside observer might have guessed that she had just been given the worst news of her life.

An MRI showed the probable cause of her symptoms: new patches of demyelination had formed among the descending tracts of white matter connecting the cortex to the brainstem. These higher connections tend to be inhibitory, so that when they are lost, the reflex actions of lower neural circuits often emerge. For example, knee-jerk reflexes can become more intense after a stroke, even if the affected limb is no longer under voluntary control. In her case, the severed

connections were probably linked to the periaqueductal gray columns for the species-specific vocalizations of human beings. With these connections lost, the neural circuits of laughter and crying could become active on their own, without being driven by the usual inner emotion. As with the "sham rage" of Cannon's decorticate cats, the pathways of inner emotion and its outer expression turn out to be separable.

Fortunately, in her case, the outcome was good. The bouts of inappropriate emotion responded well to a serotonin-boosting medication called citalopram, more commonly used to treat depression. Serotonin levels have a critical function in modulating the reflexes of the brainstem, and with the reflex intensity reduced, the bouts subsided quickly. Over the next few months, the culprit plaques healed, and in time the pseudobulbar affect resolved. With her emotional expressions returned to normal, she at last had a reason for a genuine smile.

of the fight-or-flight system, called **sham rage**, with hissing, teeth baring, and so on, despite the interruption of the sensory and motor pathways through the cortex itself.

So if the visceral peripheral nervous system was neither necessary nor sufficient for emotional responses, then what other brain regions might be involved? After experimenting with various sites of disconnection at different points up and down the central nervous system from cortex to spinal cord, Cannon and Bard suggested that the sensory information relayed through the thalamus split into two separate pathways, one destined for the cortex, which triggered the emotion, and the other destined for the hypothalamus, which is a key structure in coordinating emotional responses to stimuli within the body. Further, the cortex could play a role in inhibiting these behaviors and restricting their display to the appropriate circumstances (Dalgleish, 2004). Hence, with the removal of the cortex, uncontrolled emotional displays such as sham rage would arise spontaneously.

In emphasizing the role of the cortex and hypothalamus over the peripheral nervous system, the **Cannon–Bard theory** can be considered more of a **top-down theory** of emotion. In this framework, the wiring of our basic emotional and physiological responses lies in evolutionarily "primitive" brain regions, such as the brainstem and hypothalamus. However, the actual expression of these responses lies under the top-down control of our so-called higher brain regions, such as the cerebral cortex.

Let's leave aside for the moment whether the distinction between primitive versus more recently evolved brain structures is truly accurate. For now, let's just note three key features of the Cannon–Bard theory. First, it emphasizes top-down rather than bottom-up processes in the nervous system as critical for emotions. Second, it describes the neuroanatomy of emotions in terms of a single, integrated system for "emotion," centered with the hypothalamus, rather than a family of separate systems for separate emotions, located in the periphery of the body. Third, it represents one of the first attempts to link the mechanisms of emotion to a specific set of neuroanatomical structures. In the next few sections, we'll see how the successors to the Cannon–Bard theory have approached each of these three issues.

Two-Factor Theories: Reconciling Central and Peripheral Influences on Emotion

As it turns out, problems exist with both the top-down and the bottom-up theories of emotion. On the one hand, the human capacity for emotions clearly does survive even if visceral sensory and motor connections are lost. Every year, thousands of patients undergo life-saving heart and lung transplants. When we see the smiling faces of these recovered patients, it is easy to forget that the transplant operation does not involve reconnecting the brain's visceral inputs and outputs to the newly transplanted organs. Despite their

FIGURE 13.6 **Emotional states remain intact after organ transplants.** Kelly Perkins is an avid mountain climber despite having had a heart transplant in 1995. This type of operation severs the autonomic connections from the brain to the heart. However, patients do not lose the ability to feel emotional states.

disconnected hearts and lungs, transplant patients certainly retain the capacity for love, fear, sadness, joy, excitement, and the rest of the panoply of human emotions (FIGURE 13.6).

On the other hand, in the decades since Cannon's work, we have learned that visceral sensory inputs *do* have some effect on emotions. For example, in a rare disorder called **pure autonomic failure**, the autonomic nervous system degenerates in middle age, whereas the rest of the brain and peripheral nervous system remain intact (Mathias & Bannister, 1999). Consequently, patients with this disorder lack either input or output connections between their brain and their visceral organs. These patients have some obvious physiological symptoms: for example, if they stand up too quickly, they can lose consciousness because their brains cannot stimulate their blood vessels to contract and maintain their blood pressure against the force of gravity (as most of us do automatically). However, patients with pure autonomic failure also undergo some subtle emotional changes. Despite being quite disabled in many cases, they tend to report lower anxiety levels following the degeneration of their autonomic nervous systems and are more likely to endorse statements such as "I can no longer feel sad" or "I have lost my ability to feel emotions" (Critchley, Mathias, & Dolan, 2001).

Given the general principle that connections between different parts of the nervous system tend to be bidirectional, top-down and bottom-up accounts of emotion may not need to be mutually exclusive. As an analogy, attention can be drawn by bottom-up, peripheral sensory input and can also be directed by the context of the organism's current behavior, represented centrally. Similarly, an emotion could be brought about by a combination of visceral sensations from the periphery and cortical representations of the *context* of those inputs.

This kind of **two-factor theory** of emotion gained support from a widely cited experiment in the 1960s, conducted by the American psychologists Stanley Schachter and Jerome Singer (Schachter & Singer, 1962). The aim of the study was to determine how a physiological stimulus and a cognitive context might interact to produce the emotional state. To manipulate the physiological factor, a series of healthy human subjects received injections of either **epinephrine** (also known as adrenaline) or a saline placebo.

To create a cognitive context, some subjects were informed about the likely bodily effects of the injections, whereas others were actively misinformed about the effects, and a third group was left uninformed. Subjects were then led to a room to interact with another individual for 20 minutes. This individual was secretly part of the experiment and had been trained to act in either a pleasant, "euphoric" manner or a hostile, "angry" manner around the subject. The investigators then made observations of the subjects' emotional states and associated behavior during the social interaction (FIGURE 13.7).

As it turned out, both the physiological stimulus and the cognitive context made contributions to the subject's emotional state. Subjects receiving the real epinephrine injection showed stronger emotional responses during the social interaction, but the direction, or valence, of the response depended on the context itself. Subjects in the euphoric context showed a more positive emotional response, especially if they were misinformed or ignorant about the effects of the injection so that they did not attribute their visceral sensations of excitement to the injection itself. Subjects in the angry context showed more negative, angry responses. Again, the effect was strongest for those who were uninformed or misinformed about the injection. So the physiological stimulation did lead to an emotional response, but the resulting emotion depended on the behavioral context. Thus, the investigators theorized that the two factors of bottom-up visceral stimulation and top-down cognitive context interacted to produce the emotional state.

The two-factor model received additional support from a second widely cited study in the 1970s (Dutton & Aron, 1974). Here the physiological arousal was provided not by an injection, but by exposure to another adrenaline-inducing stimulus: a precarious, wobbly, 450-foot-long wood-and-wire suspension bridge passing more than 20 stories above the rocks and rapids of the Capilano Canyon, a popular tourist site in Vancouver, Canada, that is crossed voluntarily by people every day (FIGURE 13.8). For comparison, investigators

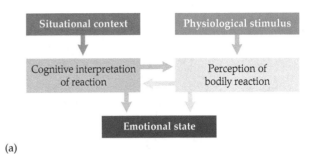

(a)

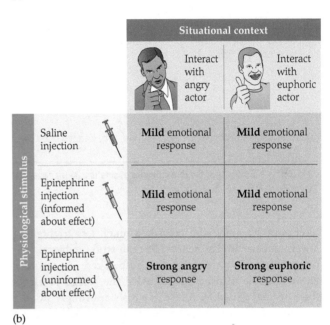

(b)

FIGURE 13.7 **The Schachter–Singer theory of emotion.** (a) According to this two-factor theory, both the visceral response to the stimulus and the cognitive evaluation of this stimulus contribute to the emotional response. (b) Summary of Schachter and Singer's 1962 experiment. Subjects' emotional responses to an injection of epinephrine depended on whether they interacted with an angry or euphoric person. If they were told ahead of time about the bodily effects of the injection, the emotional response was weaker.

FIGURE 13.8 **The Capilano Canyon suspension bridge in Vancouver.**

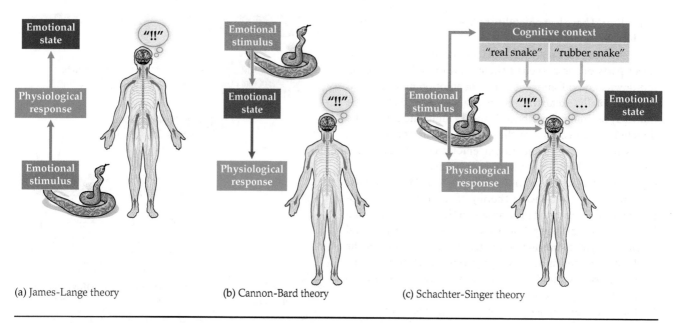

(a) James-Lange theory   (b) Cannon-Bard theory   (c) Schachter-Singer theory

FIGURE 13.9 Summary of the three theories of emotion. (a) The James–Lange theory, a bottom-up theory; (b) the Cannon–Bard theory, a top-down theory; and (c) the Schachter–Singer theory, a two-factor theory.

interviewed people who crossed a much less frightening, lower, sturdier bridge nearby. For the study, subjects were not recruited to participate, but, rather, researchers interviewed people who had just crossed the bridge as part of their normal daily life. A research assistant simply stood at one end of the bridge and asked young men who had just crossed the bridge whether they would mind filling out a survey, in which they had to write a brief story. The assistants then tore off a corner of the survey and wrote down a fictitious personal name and an actual telephone number at which they could be reached, handed the piece of paper back to the participants, and invited the participants to call if they wanted to talk further.

After crossing the lower, sturdier bridge, only a small minority of the (all male) participants actually called the number of the female assistant. However, after crossing the high suspension bridge, the majority of the subjects called the female assistant. Their stories also showed stronger ratings for sexual imagery than the stories of those who had crossed the lower bridge. Neither of these effects turned up when the assistant had been male. The male assistant received calls from fewer than 10% of subjects who crossed either type of bridge. These findings were taken as further evidence for both the two-factor model of emotion and the misattribution of physiological arousal to emotional state: in this case, sexual attraction rather than fear. (See FIGURE 13.9 for a comparison of the three theories of emotion discussed so far.)

How far have our theories of emotion come since the two-factor models of the 1970s? Over the past four decades, three major trends have taken place among theories of emotion. First, most of the modern accounts of emotion incorporate both bottom-up visceral factors and top-down contextual factors, although the degree of emphasis varies

between these two poles. Second, many modern accounts have moved away from single-system explanations of emotion and toward multiple, partly dissociable systems to supply the rich array of colors in our emotional palette, often drawing on studies of aberrant emotion in people with neurological illnesses, as we'll see in some examples later in this chapter. Third, the accounts themselves have become more and more anatomically specific in their descriptions of the underlying neural circuitry of emotions.

Core Limbic Structures: Amygdala and Hypothalamus

To connect the emotional responses to the appropriate inner states, we must add another layer to the neural hierarchy of emotion. This layer will draw on a much more sophisticated set of inner-world and outer-world sensory inputs than the brainstem: visceral sensations, hormone levels, and serum concentrations of key electrolytes and biochemical compounds, as well as visual input, auditory input, somatosensory input, olfactory input, and input from all the other external-world senses. Thanks to these rich and diverse inputs, the neurons in this next layer will be in a much better position to determine the organism's basic survival needs and to promote the appropriate behaviors to address them. This layer encompasses the core structures of the limbic system, and two of its most important centers are the hypothalamus and the amygdala.

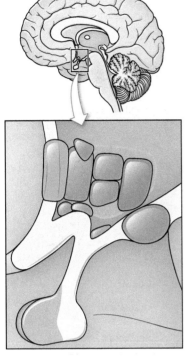

Homeostatic functions
Appetite and thirst
Heat dissipation
Heat conservation
Satiety

Agonistic functions
Predation
Anti-predation
Offensive aggresion
Defensive aggresion

Reproductive functions
Mate seeking
Nesting
Reproduction
Parenting

FIGURE 13.10 **The hypothalamus and survival drives.** The nuclei of the hypothalamus coordinate core survival functions, including homeostatic drives, agonistic drives, and reproductive drives.

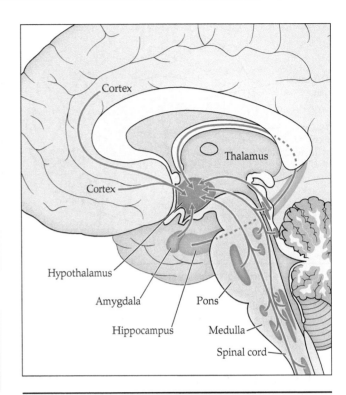

FIGURE 13.11 **Major input pathways to the hypothalamus.** Inputs come from the visceral sensory neurons of the spinal cord, visceral sensory nuclei within the brainstem, limbic regions of the cortex, and from the hippocampus and amygdala.

Hypothalamus: Internal States, Homeostatic Drives

The hypothalamus lies just below the thalamus (FIGURE 13.10) and is highly conserved in structure across a wide variety of animal species, from hagfish to human beings (Sower, Freamat, & Kavanaugh, 2009). This commonality of structure stems from a commonality of purpose: all living animals must take care of reproductive, appetitive, and agonistic functions to survive. Reproductive behaviors are essential to every animal that wants to keep its genes in circulation. Appetitive behaviors, like feeding and drinking, are essential to every animal that wants to survive long enough to reproduce. Finally, so-called agonistic behaviors (attack and defense) are essential to every animal that wants to avoid being eaten or killed by its competitors. Whether you swim, fly, or ride the bus, your brain must be able to perform these three classes of motivated behavior.

Appetitive behaviors help the body meet its basic needs for energy, water, electrolytes, temperature maintenance, and so on. The process of keeping these critical internal-world parameters in balance is called homeostasis, and the maintenance of homeostasis is one of the key functions of the hypothalamus. To keep track of the body's internal state, the hypothalamus draws on the same visceral sensory input pathways that we have been tracing up from the internal organs through the spinal cord and brainstem (FIGURE 13.11).

Yet the hypothalamus also has a second major source of input that is unavailable to most of the brainstem nuclei: sensors that monitor the composition of the bloodstream itself. This is a highly unusual feature. The vast majority of the brain's neurons hide behind a sort of cellular insulation known as the **blood–brain barrier**, which keeps them in an optimized chemical environment free from noxious substances. Yet there are a handful of regions where the blood–brain barrier is porous, allowing neurons to peek out and monitor the composition of the bloodstream. Some can sense the bloodstream's concentration of electrolytes, to monitor water balance. Others can sense the levels of glucose, insulin, or other markers of energy balance. Still others can identify circulating levels of various hormones: stress hormones like cortisol, female sex hormones (**estrogens**) like **estradiol**, male sex hormones (**androgens**) like **testosterone**, metabolic hormones like **thyroid-stimulating hormone** and **growth hormone**, and so on. Others even monitor the blood for markers of infection and immune system activity like **cytokines**, interleukins, or complement proteins. So the hypothalamus can sense when you are overfed, underfed, dehydrated, lacking in glucose, coming down with the flu, or ovulating—to name just a few of its interoceptive abilities (FIGURE 13.12).

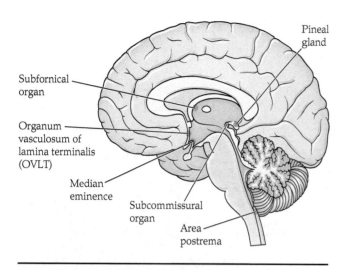

FIGURE 13.12 Regions of the brain where the blood–brain barrier is more permeable. These regions act as "windows" through which the hypothalamus and other brain regions can sense the chemical and hormonal composition of the blood, to monitor the internal environment.

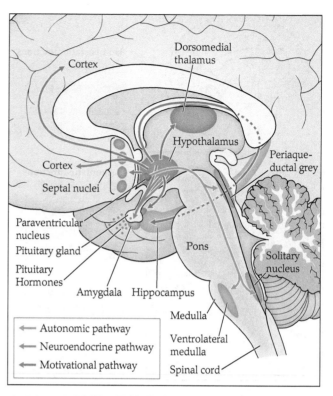

FIGURE 13.13 Three output pathways from the hypothalamus. An autonomic pathway regulates the sympathetic and parasympathetic nervous system; a neuroendocrine pathway regulates hormone secretion in the pituitary gland; a motivational pathway up through to the cerebral cortex sets behavioral priorities.

These kinds of internal sensory inputs are critical for guiding the appetitive categories of behavior: foraging, feeding, drinking, staying warm, and so on. Some of the dozens of nuclei in the hypothalamus serve appetitive functions. For example, the **lateral hypothalamus** regulates hunger and is counterbalanced by a **ventromedial hypothalamus** that regulates satiety. An anterior nucleus of the hypothalamus regulates heat dissipation, whereas a posterior nucleus regulates heat conservation. Activity in a tuberomammillary nucleus promotes wakefulness, whereas activity in a ventrolateral preoptic area promotes sleep.

The hypothalamus also plays a key role in regulating reproductive functions, including sexual behavior and parenting behavior. The size and structure of the ventromedial hypothalamus are different in males and females. Neurons in this region direct a variety of sexual behaviors, such as copulating, vocalizing, and scent marking (Harding & McGinnis, 2004). They also drive some sex-specific behaviors, such as the female-specific sexual posture of **lordosis** in rats (Pfaff & Sakuma, 1979). Another region, called the **medial preoptic area**, is involved in male copulatory behaviors: erection, intercourse, and ejaculation. In females, however, this same nucleus is several times smaller and instead regulates maternal-specific behaviors: keeping the infant close by, nursing the infant, grooming and cleaning the infant, and so forth.

Agonistic functions also fall under the purview of the hypothalamus. Both aggressive and defensive behaviors can be elicited by stimulation of various hypothalamic nuclei, including the anterior hypothalamic nucleus (Adams, 2006; Adams et al., 1993), the dorsal premammillary nucleus (Canteras, Chiavegatto, Ribeiro do Valle, & Swanson, 1997), and the ventromedial nucleus (Lin et al., 2011; Martinez, Carvalho-Netto, Amaral, Nunes-de-Souza, & Canteras,

2008). We will explore the role of the ventromedial nucleus further in a case study later in the chapter.

To effect changes in one's internal state, the hypothalamus has three output pathways available (**FIGURE 13.13**). First, an autonomic output pathway via the **paraventricular nucleus** serves to stimulate the sympathetic and parasympathetic nervous system. For example, low glucose can prioritize feeding activities like salivation, biting, chewing, and swallowing (Cai et al., 1999; Tolle et al., 2002). So the hypothalamus has pathways capable of deploying simple brainstem action plans when internal conditions require them.

Another output pathway, the neuroendocrine pathway, regulates hormone levels. The hypothalamus is often called the master control gland or master endocrine gland because it controls the activity of every other **endocrine gland** in the body. For example, in response to various kinds of stress, the hypothalamus secretes **corticotropin-releasing hormone**, which passes into the pituitary, causing it to release **adrenocorticotropic hormone (ACTH)**, which in turn passes to the body's adrenal glands to stimulate the production of the so-called stress hormone, cortisol. Cortisol itself has a wide variety of bodily effects: suppressing the immune system, increasing blood sugar, and altering metabolism to promote fat storage and weight gain. Many varieties of stress can

CASE STUDY:
An Internal Growth of Rage

In 1962, a 20-year-old bookkeeper in New York was admitted to the hospital with some unusual changes in her behavior (Reeves & Plum, 1969). For the past year, she had begun eating ever-increasing amounts of food and drinking increasing amounts of fluid, far beyond her usual intake. Her menses had stopped altogether, and she complained of frequent headaches.

Her doctors suspected that she had a brain tumor, but in those days, before the invention of CT or MRI scans, brain imaging techniques were relatively crude. To outline the structures of the brain, they performed a pneumoencephalogram. This involved literally filling the brain's ventricles with air rather than cerebrospinal fluid and then taking an X-ray to examine the ventricles' appearance, as the doctors would with a pair of air-filled lungs. On the X-ray, they saw evidence of a growth near the hypothalamus and performed a surgical "exploration" of the patient's brain in an attempt to find and remove the suspected tumor. Unfortunately, the surgeons saw no obvious abnormality, and the patient soon recovered and went home untreated.

However, nearly two years later, the patient returned, this time with symptoms much more severe (Reeves & Plum, 1969). She was socially withdrawn, but would explode into fits of laughing, crying, and rage without obvious reasons. However, unlike in pseudobulbar affect, this was more than a mere reflex reaction. In her irritable state, the patient would refuse to cooperate with simple requests or

would scratch and even attempt to bite her examining physician. She was admitted to the hospital, where she persisted in hitting, biting, scratching, or throwing objects at people around her. This behavior was not entirely automatic, but internally driven: she had taken to eating 8,000–10,000 food calories a day and would invariably attack her attendants when they refused to give her any further food. Only when given food nearly continuously would she desist from her aggressive behavior.

Once again, surgical exploration was performed. This time, the surgeons found a tumor in the expected area, near the ventromedial hypothalamus. However, because of its location, they were unable to remove it without endangering her life. With the growth in her hypothalamus, other key functions became impaired: her blood sugar rose into the diabetic range, her thyroid hormone levels dropped, she began spiking fevers without external cause, and her electrolytes fell rapidly out of balance. Three weeks after the operation, she developed a critically high level of sodium in her blood and died.

A postmortem examination found a rare kind of tumor in the ventromedial hypothalamus. The effects of a hypothalamic tumor are quite unusual: changes in eating behavior, precocious puberty and other hormonal changes, fits of laughter, and,

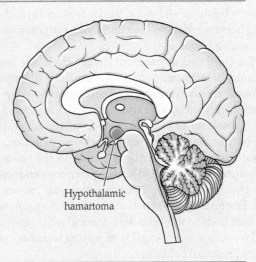

Hypothalamic
hamartoma

FIGURE 13.14 Hypothalamic hamartoma. This very rare tumor can cause fits of laughter, crying, or aggressive behavior by triggering abnormal bursts of activity in the nuclei of the hypothalamus.

often, fits of inappropriate rage (FIGURE 13.14) (Veendrick-Meekes, Verhoeven, van Erp, van Blarikom, & Tuinier, 2007). Some patients develop symptoms of depressed mood, or anxiety, or rapid mood swings (Veendrick-Meekes et al., 2007). As with the woman in this case, the disturbances typically have reportable, internal emotional content. Unlike in pseudobulbar affect, the manner of emotional expression can be quite variable (Lieberman & Benson, 1977; Veendrick-Meekes et al., 2007). Rage may be expressed verbally, physically, or through passive resistance and withdrawal. The symptoms of these patients are not empty automatism, but real subjective emotional states, driven by damage to a specific pathway in the circuitry of the brain.

produce increased cortisol: illness, fever, injury, pain, and physical exertion, as well as the emotions of anxiety or depression (Maglione-Garves, Kravitz, & Schneider, 2005). Conversely, cortisol itself can affect mood, often producing a sense of euphoria when administered as a medication (Ling et al., 1981). So the hypothalamus provides a key pathway that links hormonal activity to emotional state. Similar links between hormone and mood can be seen for thyroid-stimulating hormone and some sex hormones, including the estrogens and androgens.

The third pathway is motivational. If glucose levels are dropping, all of the autonomic and hormonal adjustments in the world are no substitute for finding and ingesting a good square meal. Getting a meal, or a drink, or a mate is no simple feat. A whole series of problems must be solved: evaluation, goal-setting, strategy formation, behavior selection, action planning, and the matching of actions to the surrounding environment. Each one of these steps requires far more complex circuitry than the hypothalamus can muster on its own. Fortunately, the hypothalamus has a third output pathway that leads to forebrain structures like the striatum and cerebral cortex: areas capable of putting together complex, flexible, nuanced behaviors.

Do Hypothalamic Circuits Generate Inner Emotional Experiences?

Up until now in the hierarchy, we have seen circuits that generate the building blocks of outward emotional expression, but not the actual inner experience of emotion. The brainstem can produce sham rage or mirthless laughter, but not the real thing. Can the hypothalamus do any better? Does activity here also generate a subjectively empty behavior or a complete emotion with both subjective experience and outward manifestations?

Case reports of patients undergoing therapeutic deep brain stimulation (DBS) can offer us some clues. In one case, inadvertent stimulation of the posterior medial hypothalamus caused the patient to develop an instantaneous attack of emotional rage, agitation, and shouting. In the middle of the surgery, the patient attempted to forcibly remove the stereotactic frame from his own skull, which might have been a lethal act if he had succeeded. Fortunately, he was physically restrained and briefly sedated. After the sedation cleared, the patient recalled that he had felt angry and acted aggressively, but could not explain why (Bejjani et al., 2002).

In another case, a 50-year-old woman underwent DBS implantation for obesity. Here, stimulation of the ventromedial hypothalamus produced all the features of a panic attack, complete with physiological effects (hyperventilation, increased blood pressure, and increased heart rate), interoceptive features (nausea and a sensation of shortness of breath), and subjective emotional experiences of overwhelming anxiety (Wilent et al., 2010).

Why should subjective emotional experiences emerge at this level of the hierarchy and not in others? Although no one is sure so far, we can make note that the hypothalamus is one of the first levels of the hierarchy that ties together three functions: the perception of inputs relevant to survival drives, the representation of internal drive states engendered by these inputs, and a process for modifying those internal states through changes in physiology and motivation. These three processes seem to be common to most of the core circuitry of subjective emotion throughout the brain.

Amygdala: Externally Generated States and Drives

The amygdala is another core limbic structure, like the nearby hypothalamus. But where the hypothalamus looks inward to the body, the amygdala looks outward to the world. Its sensory sources come from visual inputs, auditory inputs, and olfactory inputs via the thalamus and cortex. Some interoceptive information is also available via the ascending pathways through the brainstem (FIGURE 13.15a). The amygdala's output pathways lead in three main directions: down to the somatic and autonomic nuclei in the brainstem, over to the hypothalamic nuclei responsible for hormone secretion and for the three main classes of motivated behaviors, and up via the striatum and other ascending pathways to large swaths of the cortex involved in evaluation, motivation, and behavioral control.

Like the hypothalamus, the amygdala is organized into a collection of more than a dozen different nuclei (FIGURE 13.15b), all richly interconnected, most of whose functions are still being worked out. Some of these nuclei fall into a subdivision known as the **basolateral amygdala**, whereas others fall into a subdivision known as the central amygdala (Cardinal, Parkinson, Hall, & Everitt, 2002).

The basolateral amygdala has its strongest connections with higher sensory regions in the cortex, and its microscopic structure is also more akin to that seen in the cortex. Its role is sometimes summarized as a tracker of value because its neurons are capable of learning and tracking the emotional significance of stimuli from the outside world, drawing on every sensory modality: visual, auditory, somatosensory, gustatory, and olfactory (Pickens et al., 2003; Zald, 2003).

The **centromedial amygdala**, in contrast, has its strongest connections with regions further down the hypothalamus and brainstem. Its role is sometimes summarized as a controller of these regions (Phillips & LeDoux, 1992). As the output rather than the input side of the amygdala, it draws on external-world sensory information to modulate the internal drives and hormonal functions of the hypothalamus (Pessoa, 2010).

These two regions are closely interlinked and serve complementary functions. Where the basolateral amygdala is

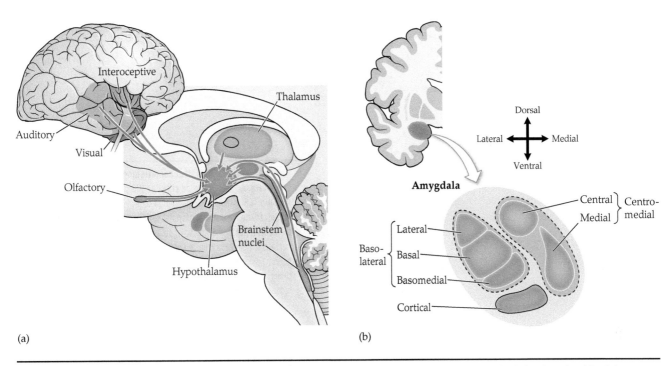

FIGURE 13.15 The amygdala. (a) Input pathways to the amygdala. (b) Some of the major subdivisions of the amygdala, including the basolateral nuclei and the centromedial and cortical nuclei.

wired to interpreting the emotional value of a stimulus, the centromedial amygdala is wired to implementing an appropriate emotional response, with autonomic, hormonal, and behavioral components. To paraphrase one author, the amygdala proceeds from the question of "what is it worth?" to the question of "what is to be done?" (Pessoa, 2010).

One of the key emotional roles for the amygdala lies in the detection of threats and the implementation of fear responses (LeDoux, 2007). For example, in the classical **fear conditioning** paradigms of behaviorists, animals are exposed to an auditory tone, which is soon followed by a painful electrical shock. Over time, the animals learn the association between the unconditioned stimulus of the shock and the conditioned stimulus of the auditory tone. Eventually, they begin to exhibit fear responses to the tone itself: freezing, increases in heart rate, and so on.

The amygdala is critical for conditioned fear learning. Through a circuit that is now quite well studied, the unconditioned stimulus of the shock activates pain receptors in the skin, which send signals via the thalamus and somatosensory cortex to the **lateral nucleus** of the amygdala (Phillips & LeDoux, 1992). Signals then pass to the centromedial amygdala to coordinate the appropriate fear response: freezing, stress hormone secretion, increased heart rate, and so forth. As for the conditioned stimulus of the auditory tone, this produces activity in auditory regions of the thalamus and cortex, which stimulates neurons within the lateral nucleus of the amygdala (Phillips & LeDoux, 1992). Through the learning mechanisms of synaptic plasticity and long-term potentiation (Chapter 9), the connections between these neurons and the output neurons in the central nucleus

are gradually strengthened. In time, the auditory stimulus alone becomes capable of driving the fear responses of the central nucleus, through the newly strengthened pathways (**FIGURE 13.16**) (Rogan & LeDoux, 1995).

Some other amygdala neurons track positive value, or reward, rather than negative value, or aversiveness. In another type of conditioning experiment, animals learn to associate a conditioned stimulus (such as a colored box) with a rewarding unconditioned stimulus (such as a tasty piece of food inside the box). Just as some networks of neurons in the amygdala can learn and unlearn the "threat value" of a stimulus, so other networks can learn and unlearn the "reward value" of a stimulus. They can even adjust the reward value based on the organism's internal state. For example, if we offer an animal a choice between two different boxes with two different foods, A and B, the neuron may respond equally to either box. But if we first feed the animal to satiety on one food, the neuron may cease to respond to the box containing that food, while continuing to respond to the box with the other food inside. So amygdala neurons can take into account the organism's needs when calculating the value of a stimulus in the outside environment (Pessoa & Engelmann, 2010).

The Amygdala and Emotional Experience

Like hypothalamic lesions, amygdala lesions have profound impacts on behavior and emotion. In the 1930s, the psychologist Heinrich Kluver and neurosurgeon Paul Bucy studied the effects of removing the anterior temporal lobes (including the amygdala) in rhesus monkeys (Kluver &

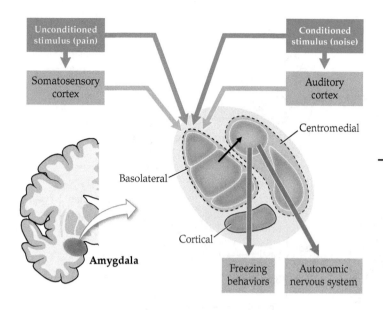

FIGURE 13.16 The classical conditioning pathways in the amygdala. An unconditioned stimulus (US), pain, and a conditioned stimulus (CS), a noise, are presented together. Both the US and the CS stimulate the basolateral amygdala and are paired together, stimulating the central nucleus of the amygdala. The output from the central nucleus triggers the freezing behaviors and activation of the autonomic nervous system. Over a few trials of learning, the connections between these nuclei are strengthened, so that the noise comes to trigger the response on its own.

CASE STUDY:
The Woman Who Knows No Fear

Of the more than 7 billion people in the world, fewer than 300 are known to have the rare illness known as **Urbach–Wiethe disease** (Feinstein, Adolphs, Damasio, & Tranel, 2011). In addition to developing lesions throughout their skin and mucous membranes, these patients sometimes suffer destructive lesions through their medial temporal lobes: a region containing the hippocampus and amygdala. In even rarer cases, the amygdala alone is destroyed, whereas the rest of the brain remains intact (Sainani, Muralidhar, Parthiban, & Vijayalakshmi, 2011).

The most famous of all such cases is a woman known by the initials S. M., the so-called "woman without fear" (Young, 2010). She lacks an amygdala on either side, but her brain MRI shows no other lesions (FIGURE 13.17). Although her general intelligence, memory, language, and perceptual functions all fall within the normal range, she

has one major difficulty: a severe impairment in the ability to either experience or recognize the emotion of fear. When viewing emotional film clips, she experiences all the rest of the usual palette of human emotions: happiness, sadness, disgust, anger, and surprise, all expressed in the usual human ways. With frightening films, however, her experience is one not of fear, but of excitement and exhilaration.

A recent study of her real-life experiences makes for astonishing reading (Young, 2010). Despite an avowed fear of snakes, when brought to a pet store she rushed over to the snakes, overcome by a feeling that she described as excitement and curiosity rather than fear. She held nonpoisonous snakes, stroked them, and touched their tongues. She reported feeling compelled to poke and touch even the large, dangerous snakes in the store and asked over and over again for permission to do so.

The next visit was to a famous "haunted house," the Waverly Hills Sanatorium. S. M. spontaneously led a group of visitors through its darkened hallways, filled with hidden actors in monster costumes. As the actors sprang out from their hiding places, the other group members screamed loudly. In contrast, S. M. smiled or laughed, approached the monsters, or tried to start conversations with them. At one point she even frightened one of the monsters by giving the actor a firm poke in the head "to see what it would feel like."

S. M.'s altered emotional repertoire has had a significant impact on her life. Her inability to detect or respond to environmental threats or to learn from past experience has placed her in grave danger many times. Living in a poor urban area, she has been held at knifepoint and gunpoint, physically attacked by a much larger woman, explicitly threatened with death,

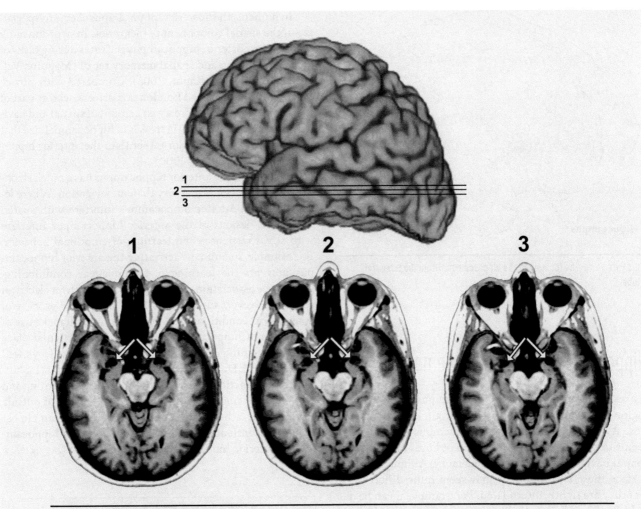

FIGURE 13.17 **MRI scans of Patient S.M.'s brain.** The arrows point to the amygdala, the region of the brain that S.M. is missing, as shown by the vacant black holes underneath the arrows.

and nearly killed in an act of domestic violence. In one case, after being physically attacked in a park, she returned to the same park the very next day!

S. M.'s rare case sheds new light on the contentiously debated role of the amygdala in human emotion. The loss of the amygdala has not removed her capacity for all emotions, but has had specific effects on her ability to evaluate threats and to deploy the sense of fear as appropriate. In the absence of fear, excitement and curiosity combine to produce approach rather than retreat, with consequences that have proved nearly lethal on more than one occasion. As the authors conclude in their report, "it appears that without the amygdala, the evolutionary value of fear is lost" (Young, 2010).

Bucy, 1939/1997). The monkeys developed a sort of fearless curiosity in exploring their surroundings. This was accompanied by **visual agnosia** (an inability to interpret what they saw before them), which has been explained by damage to the ventral visual stream (Chapter 5). Also, the monkeys displayed inappropriate forms of motivated behavior: they showed hyperorality (an indiscriminate tendency to place objects in their mouths, whether edible or not). In addition, they showed hypersexuality, masturbating constantly and attempting to copulate indiscriminately, even with objects or members of other species. This constellation of symptoms was termed **Kluver–Bucy syndrome**.

In human beings, similar symptoms were later reported in cases of widespread lesions of the anterior temporal lobes and amygdala (Terzian & Ore, 1955). However, the most recent studies of humans with isolated amygdala lesions suggest that the full Kluver–Bucy syndrome does not arise in humans (Hayman, Rexer, Pavol, Strite, & Meyers, 1998). Instead, such patients have mostly normal emotional functioning, with the exception of severe impairments in the learning and expression of fear.

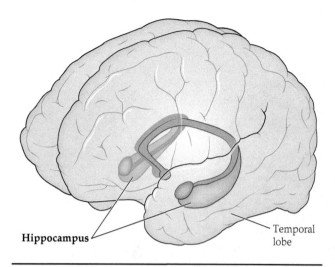

FIGURE 13.18 The location of the hippocampus within the temporal lobe.

Hippocampus: Emotional Memories

As we saw in Chapter 9, the hippocampus is a key brain region for encoding and retrieving certain kinds of memories. As you may recall, the hippocampus (FIGURE 13.18) seems to perform at least two different kinds of functions: spatial navigation and episodic memory. Although on the surface these two functions may seem quite different, in fact they are tightly interrelated. For example, it can be delightful to recall spending an afternoon in a beautiful, atmospheric café in a tiny square in a foreign city, but it can also be frustrating if you return to that city a year later and cannot find your way there again. Conversely, it can be helpful to remember the location of a secret shortcut to your place of work, but if a new construction project blocks your shortcut, you must update your map of the territory using episodic memory or else risk a long detour. If you have ever used a Web-based map service to find a store or restaurant, only to arrive there and find that it closed six months ago, you can appreciate the need for episodic memories to keep your maps up to date.

So, emotional, episodic memories and spatial navigation are interrelated functions. How does a single brain region look after both of these functions at once? As it turns out, the anatomical structure we call the hippocampus may actually consist of at least two (and possibly more) distinct subregions (Moser & Moser, 1998). Although invisible to the naked eye, these subregions are distinguished by completely different patterns of connectivity to the cortex and elsewhere in the brain. They also have different patterns of gene expression within their neurons (Fanselow & Dong, 2010). Furthermore, they seem to have distinct functional roles, as revealed by lesion and neuroimaging studies.

In humans, the posterior hippocampus seems to specialize in the spatial component of memories. In neuroimaging studies, the posterior hippocampus activates during tasks of spatial navigation and spatial memory recall (Maguire, Valentine, Wilding, & Kapur, 2003). Compared with novice taxi drivers, experienced London taxi drivers, who as part of their profession must store a vast amount of spatial and navigational knowledge, show increases in hippocampal size that are specific to the posterior rather than the anterior hippocampus (Maguire et al., 2000).

In contrast, the anterior hippocampus has a much stronger role in emotional memory than in navigation. Where lesions of the posterior hippocampus interfere with spatial navigation, lesions of the anterior hippocampus interfere with stress responses and learning of emotional behavior. For example, in animals, activating the anterior hippocampus prevents the learning of stimulus-fear conditioning, such as the association of an auditory tone with an electrical shock. However, such lesions leave intact the process of context-fear conditioning: the animals can still make use of the posterior hippocampus to learn that a particular place (like the training cage) is associated with shocks (reviewed in Fanselow & Dong, 2010). In this respect, the anterior hippocampus functions more like the amygdala in learning and recalling the emotional value of a specific kind of outside world event, rather than a specific place. So we can almost imagine a continuum of function from posterior hippocampus to anterior hippocampus to amygdala (FIGURE 13.19): a

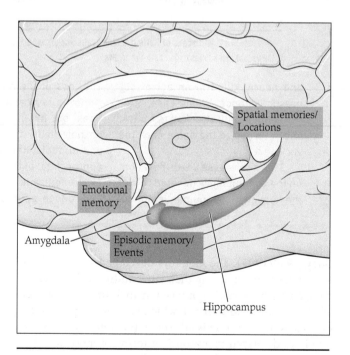

FIGURE 13.19 The amygdala and hippocampus and their contributions to memory. The amygdala and anterior hippocampus are important for emotional episodic memories, and the posterior hippocampus is important for spatial memories and navigation.

steady progression from remembering *where* an emotional event happened, to remembering *what* event happened, to tracking the emotional *value* of a specific stimulus in the current environment.

The anterior hippocampus also has a neuroendocrine function in regulating the release of stress hormones. For example, hippocampal lesions can impair the usual hypothalamic regulation of the stress hormones corticotropin-releasing hormone, adrenocorticotropic hormone, and cortisol (Cullinan, Herman, & Watson, 1993). Conversely, elevated levels of these stress hormones can lead to hippocampal dysfunction, suppress the growth of new hippocampal neurons, and reduce the volume of the hippocampus itself (McEwen, 1999). Reductions of hippocampal volume are often seen in mood and anxiety disorders such as major depression, post–traumatic stress disorder, and bipolar disorder (Bonne et al., 2008; Frey et al., 2007). However, it is still unclear whether the smaller hippocampi are actually *causal* in emotional disorders or more of a side effect of the hormonal stress response. For example, patients who suffer lesions of the anterior hippocampus (for example, the famous case of Henry Molaison from Chapter 9) show profound memory deficits, but do not show higher rates of depression or posttraumatic stress (Scoville & Milner, 1957, 2000). However, there are several brain regions where lesions *do* cause these kinds of effects, as we'll see later in the chapter.

Ventral Striatum: Pleasure and Reward

In 1954, at McGill University in Montreal, Canada, the psychologists James Olds and Peter Milner implanted a pair of electrodes in the brain of a rat, hoping to study the effects of stimulation on its movements. However, the results were unexpected: the rat began returning again and again to the place in the cage where it received stimulation, as if strongly rewarded for doing so (Olds & Milner, 1954). Surprised to see this effect, Olds and Milner then tried providing the rat with a lever that would trigger stimulation. The rat soon began pressing this lever repeatedly, hundreds of times an hour, often to the exclusion of all other activities. The effects of the stimulation bore all the behavioral hallmarks of intense reward.

X-rays and postmortem examinations eventually revealed that the electrode had missed its intended target and instead had reached a region known as the septal area, near the ventral striatum. In a series of experiments and later in televised demonstrations, Olds and Milner showed rats braving severe electric shocks to obtain stimulation and engaging in self-stimulation so fervently as to reach the point of starvation. As a result, this region, and its nearby connections through the **medial forebrain bundle**, soon became popularized as the so-called "pleasure center of the brain" (FIGURE 13.20) (Olds & Milner, 1954).

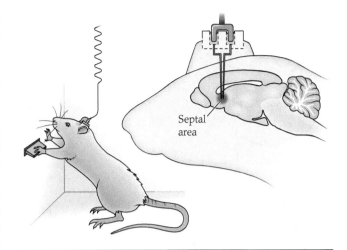

FIGURE 13.20 **Electrodes implanted into the septal area of a rat, near the medial forebrain bundle.** The rat repeatedly presses a lever to receive stimulation, as if the stimulation itself is rewarding. This region became popularized as a "pleasure center" within the brain.

Over the next two decades, studies provided evidence that these same regions have a similar function in human beings who underwent neurosurgical implantation of DBS electrodes for the treatment of psychiatric and neurological illnesses.

A wide variety of recent studies have confirmed that the ventral striatum plays a crucial role in pleasure and reward. It is one of a handful of "hedonic hot spots" in which electrical or chemical stimulation increases the magnitude of pleasure for enjoyable stimuli such as tasty, sugary water (Pecina, Smith, & Berridge, 2006). In human neuroimaging studies, the ventral striatum shows activation for a wide variety of rewarding stimuli including juice, pleasant images, monetary rewards, social praise, or positive outcomes in games (Kringelbach & Berridge, 2009). Likewise, in those rare and unfortunate cases where a patient suffers bilateral lesions of the ventral globus pallidus (which lies adjacent to the ventral striatum), the result is severe depression with **anhedonia**: a complete loss of the capacity for pleasure or enjoyment (Miller et al., 2006).

Neurosurgeons are also beginning once again to exploit the role of the ventral striatum in pleasure and reward, with the goal of treating patients with severe depression (Bewernick et al., 2010). By implanting DBS electrodes in this region (FIGURE 13.21), the surgeons are sometimes able to alleviate the depression and, more specifically, to restore the capacity for pleasure and enjoyment that is so often lost in depressed patients. One interesting effect of this stimulation is that it appears to *decrease*, rather than increase, activity in some of the cortical regions that connect to the ventral striatum: for example, the ventromedial frontopolar cortex (Benazzouz et al., 2000). Keep this point in mind when you read the case study *A Cure Born of Desperation*, later in this chapter.

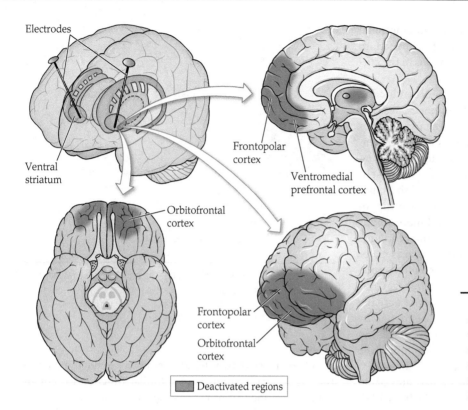

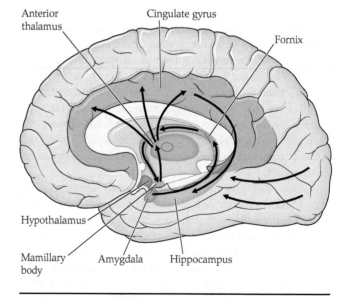

FIGURE 13.21 **Effects of deep brain stimulation (DBS) in the ventral striatum.** In patients with treatment-resistant depression, DBS of the nucleus accumbens results in decreased activation in frontal regions of the brain and decreased symptoms of depression for some patients.

Bringing It All Together: The Circuit of Papez and the Ring of Limbic Cortex

We have now looked at several core limbic structures that lie as intermediaries between the cortex and the brainstem. The hypothalamus monitors the internal environment, represents internal states and drives, and coordinates appropriate autonomic and neuroendocrine responses. The amygdala performs similar functions, but concentrates on the external rather than internal environment, with an emphasis on the emotion of fear. The anterior hippocampus performs similar functions as well, but draws on past experiences and memories to generate the appropriate emotional states. Finally, the ventral striatum has a particularly important role in representing reward value and may also have a role in generating pleasurable emotional states.

These structures do not function in isolation; instead, the structures are densely interconnected with one another and act in concert. Each of them also draws heavily on the massive computational powers of the cortex to determine the significance of complex, ambiguous sensory inputs and to implement the complex, flexible behavioral plans engendered by our basic emotional states. All of these areas are tied together by a circuit first identified in 1937 (Papez, 1937) and bearing its discoverer's name: the **circuit of Papez** (**FIGURE 13.22**).

One of the key nodes in this circuit is the hypothalamus. Connections from the many nuclei of the hypothalamus project in one direction toward the cortex, leaving via a

white matter tract known as the mammilothalamic tract and connecting to the anterior nucleus of the thalamus, which in turn services the cingulate gyrus: a sort of motor cortex for limbic structures like the hippocampus, amygdala, hypothalamus, endocrine, and autonomic nervous system, as we'll see below. From the other direction, projections pass

FIGURE 13.22 **Circuit of Papez.** These interconnected brain areas are important for controlling emotional expression and were first described by Papez in 1937. The areas involved include the thalamus, hippocampus, amygdala, and hypothalamus/mammillary bodies. The arrows represent the flow of information through the circuit.

THE BIGGER PICTURE:
The Ethics of Brain Stimulation in Human Beings

When it comes to treating disorders of the brain, medications alone do not always provide relief. Although effective drugs exist for treating Parkinson's disease, major depression, obsessive–compulsive disorder, and pain syndromes, in many cases the usual medications have insufficient effects or no effects. For these cases, DBS is becoming increasingly used. Some neurosurgical teams have begun to apply the technique to cases of excessive aggression or of substance addiction.

As the range of applications for DBS continues to widen, concerns over the ethics of human brain stimulation have arisen (Synofzik & Schlaepfer, 2011). Under what circumstances should a surgeon offer DBS treatment? In a patient with severe depression who does not want to try cognitive-behavioral therapy or medications? What about in a 16-year-old whose parents are worried about his suicidal thinking? A middle-age, severely mentally retarded woman with uncontrolled bouts of aggression and self-injury (Synofzik & Schlaepfer, 2011)? These examples are not purely hypothetical: neurosurgeons are now regularly faced with requests for DBS implantation in precisely these kinds of situations. Given that DBS carries a 1–4% risk of severe complications like bleeding, seizures, or other injury to the brain (Beric et al., 2002; Binder, Rau, & Starr, 2005), how do we decide when the benefits outweigh the risks?

To muddy the ethical waters, the long-term outcomes of DBS are mixed. For example, patients with Parkinson's disease may undergo DBS and find that their motor functions improve dramatically. However, in many cases, their overall quality of life does not always improve. Some patients develop apathy, cognitive dysfunction, or depressed mood after the procedure (Kenney et al., 2007). Others find that their limb movements improve, whereas their speech becomes slurred (Kenney et al., 2007). Detailed follow-up interviews find that many Parkinsonian patients are actually *not* happier after surgery (Okun et al., 2009): despite improvement in motor symptoms, they may still be unable to return to work; they may lose the sense of purpose that had previously been provided by their fight against a chronic disease; their marriages may fail as the spouse loses the role of caregiver or is forced to continue in this role despite prior expectations of a miraculous improvement. So if patients have unrealistically high expectations of DBS treatment, are they truly making an informed choice about undergoing surgery?

There is an emerging consensus among biomedical ethicists on the principles that ought to guide DBS or any other medical treatment. The principles include beneficence (the obligation to promote the well-being of others), nonmaleficence (the obligation to do no harm), justice (equal distribution of the burdens and the benefits of medical treatments among all members of society), and respecting patient autonomy (the individual's right to self-determination through informed decisions) (Cassell, 2000). The tricky part is deciding which principles ought to take precedence in any given case. If a patient demands DBS for, say, memory enhancement and is prepared to take the risk of death or brain injury, does autonomy prevail over nonmaleficence?

One thing that would definitely help to clarify these issues would be a better supply of hard data on the long-term outcomes and adverse effects of DBS. However, with so many different stimulation sites being tried and so many disorders currently under treatment, it will likely be some time before such information is available. In the meantime, one proposed approach is to take into account a patient's preferences, but not necessarily leave these as the sole arbiter of whether to proceed with implantation. A committee including the physicians directly caring for the patient, the neurosurgical team, and an independent psychiatrist could then evaluate the patient's expectations and motivations. Where benefits roughly equal risks, DBS could ethically be offered. Where benefits exceed risks, DBS could be explicitly recommended (Synofzik & Schlaepfer, 2011).

Of course, no physician can ensure good outcomes for everyone undergoing treatment. However, this kind of approach would help to avoid cases in which the decision to implant electrodes in the brain is driven by patients' unrealistic expectations, families' desperation, or the overzealous enthusiasm of the physicians themselves. And as the data on long-term outcomes accumulate, the final decision regarding whether brain stimulation is justified should gradually become less of an educated guess and more of an informed choice.

from the hypothalamus's mammillary bodies via a pair of curved white matter tracts known as the fornix ("arch," in Latin) to reach the anterior and posterior hippocampus, thus tying basic drives like thirst or hunger to the memories of places and events that might be useful for satisfying them. From the hippocampus, connections continue via a white matter tract known as the subiculum to the nearby **entorhinal cortex**—an input and output region for the hippocampus. Connections proceed to the nearby parahippocampal gyrus and then along through the cingulum bundle of white matter back to the cingulate gyrus, thus completing the circuit. Thus, within the span of a few connections, this double-looped pathway brings together homeostatic drives, relevant memories, endocrine and autonomic control, and the cortical pathways that modulate emotional responses.

Whereas the circuit of Papez brings together cortical and subcortical areas relevant to emotion, there is also a second ringlike circuit that lies within the limbic cortex alone (Mesulam, 1998). This ring includes the limbic motor cortex of the cingulate gyrus, continues to the adjacent parahippocampal cortex in the medial temporal lobe, takes in the nearby anterior insula deep within the lateral fissure, and also includes the posterior and medial parts of the orbitofrontal cortex, which in turn lie adjacent to the anterior and inferior parts of the cingulate gyrus, thus completing the limbic ring.

The Limbic Cortex and Emotions

As with the regions in the circuit of Papez, the regions of this limbic ring of cortex tie together diverse functions: visceral sensation in the insula, visceral motor control in the orbitofrontal cortex, control of subcortical limbic structures in the anterior cingulate cortex, and control of the hippocampus in the posterior cingulate cortex. These regions and their functions have a major role in human emotions, and this role is complex enough that we will now spend some time to explore each region in more detail.

The Interoceptive Insula: The "Feeling" Side of Emotions

Limbic regions of the cortex play crucial roles in generating and modulating emotional states. As with all the lower levels of the emotional hierarchy, we can divide the limbic cortex into a visceral-sensory side and a visceral-motor side. The core region of the limbic sensory cortex is the insula (FIGURE 13.23). This region plays a critical role in the

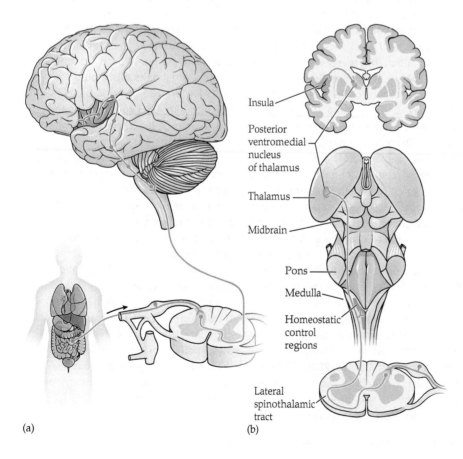

Insula

Posterior ventromedial nucleus of thalamus

Thalamus

Midbrain

Pons

Medulla

Homeostatic control regions

Lateral spinothalamic tract

(a)

(b)

FIGURE 13.23 **The core region of the limbic sensory cortex is the insula.** (a) The insula represents the body's internal state. (b) Internal sensory neurons (interoceptors) from the visceral organs send signals through the spinal cord and brainstem to the ventromedial nucleus of the thalamus, which serves the posterior insula.

subjective, sensory experience of emotions: the part we think of as the bodily "feeling" of an emotional state.

As we saw in Chapter 2, the brain has sensory pathways that lead to a strip of primary somatosensory cortex for representing the tactile inputs to the body surface: light touch, vibration, proprioception, and so on. In the same way, it also has a parallel pathway dedicated to representing the physiological conditions of the body itself, or interoception (A. D. Craig, 2002; M. C. Craig et al., 2009). The body's diverse array of interoceptive inputs run in a pathway from the visceral organs, via the spinal cord, up through the nucleus solitarius and parabrachial nucleus of the spinal cord via a dedicated thalamic nucleus to the posterior insula.

The posterior insula represents visceral sensations. Neuroimaging studies reveal the activation of this region for a wide variety of inner-world sensations including pain, muscle fatigue, itch, cold, the internal pressure sensation produced by the Valsalva maneuver (attempted, forceful exhalation when the mouth is closed and the nostrils are pinched shut), deep breathing, changes in blood pressure, and hunger for food or for air (A. D. Craig, 2002). Like the primary somatosensory cortex, the visceral sensory cortex of the insula is organized somatotopically (Mazzola, Isnard, Peyron, Guenot, & Mauguiere, 2009). In epilepsy patients undergoing surgery, stimulation of the posterior insula produces both painful and nonpainful visceral sensations such as warming, cooling, buzzing, burning, or stinging in specific regions of the body (Ostrowsky et al., 2002). The seizures themselves can produce experiences that feel much like the subjective "building blocks" of the sensations associated with many strong emotional states (FIGURE 13.24): constriction of the larynx, buzzing or numbness in various parts of the body, heaviness in the abdomen, pleasant warmth in the body, constriction of the ribcage, pain in the upper throat, or unpleasant butterflylike feelings in the stomach or chest (Isnard, Guenot, Sindou, & Mauguiere, 2004).

As we move toward the anterior insula, these basic interoceptive building blocks coalesce into integrated, whole-body sensations that no longer seem to lie in any one specific body part but do seem to be associated with specific emotional states: in other words, the "feel" part of "feelings." Seizures coming from the anterior insula tend to produce sudden-onset emotional states with a strong sensory component, often pleasant. In a famous case, the 19th-century Russian author, Fyodor Dostoyevsky, experienced and wrote about having seizures with an "ecstatic" aura (Morgan, 1990). In a more recent scientific paper, a patient with anterior insular seizures described their effects as "a well-being inside, a sensation of velvet . . . my inner body rises from an unalterable bliss." Another described the experience as "a feeling of pleasure. I felt intensely well in my body . . . a physical state, an overload. The sensation is certainly more intense than could be achieved with any drug" (Picard & Craig, 2009). Insular seizures can also produce other emotional states such as mirth or anxiety (Isnard et al., 2004). In the

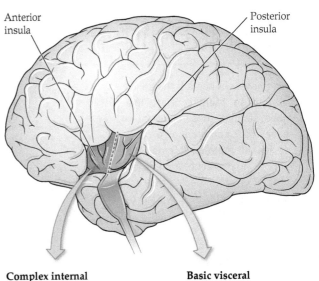

Complex internal sensations or feelings	Basic visceral sensations
Anger	Pain
Sadness	Temperature
Elation	Fatigue
Disgust	Itch
Sexual arousal	Pressure
Anxiety	Tension

FIGURE 13.24 Distinct roles of the anterior and posterior insula. The posterior insula represents basic visceral sensations like pain, temperature, fatigue, or itch. The anterior insula represents the more complex whole-body sensations associated with emotional states: feelings of sadness, happiness, anger, disgust, or elation.

healthy brain, neuroimaging studies show a wide variety of feelings associated with activation of the anterior insula. These include sadness, anger, elation, disgust, sexual arousal, and panic (A. D. Craig, 2002).

Cingulate Cortex: A Motor Cortex for the Limbic System

As you may recall from Chapter 7, the brain has a strip of primary motor cortex whose neurons provide controlling output to the skeletal muscle system for voluntary movements. Like the sensory system, the motor system has a parallel visceral motor system that can modulate the activity of lower limbic structures including the autonomic nervous system, brainstem, amygdala, hypothalamus, and hippocampus. The limbic motor cortex has its own home among the many subregions of the **cingulate cortex**.

As we saw earlier, the circuit of Papez runs from the hypothalamus via the thalamus to a bundle of fibers running around and over the corpus callosum, feeding the cingulate

NEUROSCIENCE OF EVERYDAY LIFE:
Mental Effort

Every student has felt the sense of intense mental effort that goes along with composing an essay or completing a long series of math problems. But why is there such a thing as mental effort? Muscles may accumulate lactic acid with prolonged exertion, and insular circuits can draw on muscle interoceptors to register this work as subjective fatigue (A. D. Craig, 2002). But what accounts for the same effect in the interoceptor-free environment of brain tissue itself? Neural activity alone does not seem to do it: we effortlessly crunch through the complex calculations required to recognize a face or a famous painting, but become mentally exhausted by some tasks that are much simpler by comparison.

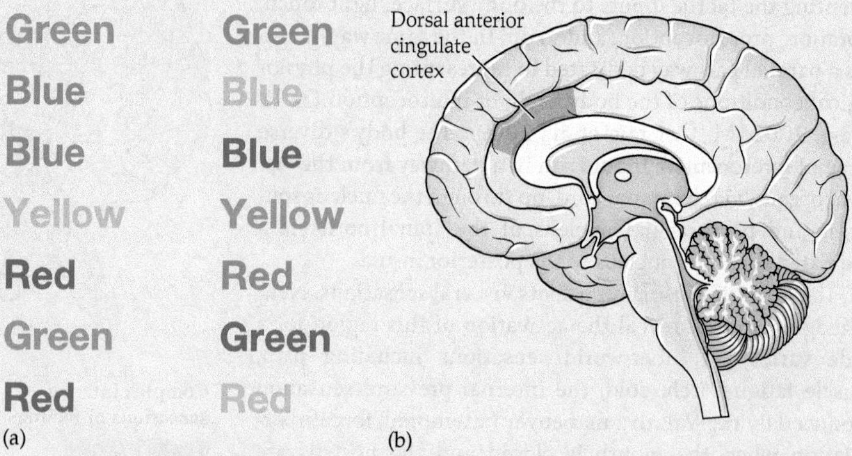

As an example, try this short version of the Stroop color-naming task (FIGURE 13.25a). Go through the first list of words and try to say aloud the printed *color* of each word as quickly as possible, doing your best not to make any errors. Easy? Now try the second column, again making sure to name the printed color rather than simply reading the word. When the word and its color do not match, the task becomes harder, in a psychophysical phenomenon known as the **Stroop effect**. Objectively, reaction times and error rates increase. In neuroimaging studies by Pardo and colleagues (Pardo, Pardo, Janer, & Raichle, 1990), the incongruent version of the task produces increased activation in a limbic motor region: the anterior cingulate cortex (ACC) (FIGURE 13.25b). Subjectively, the task seems harder. There is a sense of emotional stress, or mental effort, involved.

What is the role of the ACC in the Stroop task? A number of different hypotheses have been proposed, including attention, error detection, error correction, conflict detection, and performance monitoring, all on the basis of cleverly designed psychophysical and fMRI experiments (Carter & van Veen, 2007). Yet perhaps the most intriguing findings come from studies of rare patients who have suffered damage to the ACC from strokes or other diseases. Despite the loss of the ACC, such patients can perform normally on the Stroop task: the error rate does not increase, and the magnitude of the Stroop interference effect is no larger than in healthy controls (Pacherie, 2008; Stuss, Floden, Alexander, Levine, & Katz, 2001). What does change is the sense of mental effort: in the words of one patient, "Yes, this one was a tricky trial, with ink opposite to the word, thus it should be more difficult to me, however I do not feel any sensation of difficulty here." These patients also lose the usual ability to tell apart "easy" from "difficult" cognitive tasks based on their subjective feeling of mental effort (Pacherie, 2008). In addition, they stop showing galvanic skin responses (GSRs) during difficult tasks. The GSR is an increase in perspiration, measurable as increased conduction of electrical currents across the skin, and an indicator of sympathetic nervous system activity. In normal subjects, tricky tasks result in an increased GSR (Horvath, 1978). Patients with ACC damage, however, not only lose the sense of effort, but also quite literally lose the feeling of mental effort that goes along with performing cognitively stressful tasks (Naccache et al., 2005).

Cases like these help to illustrate the role of limbic motor cortex in providing a pathway by which cognitive activity can modulate the autonomic, endocrine, and motivational responses that are coordinated by subcortical limbic regions. We often speak of the mind–body connection: the power of positive thinking, the benefits of mental relaxation, and the dangers of emotional stress for bodily health. The ACC and other regions of limbic motor cortex provide a pathway by which these kinds of effects can take place.

Green	Green
Blue	Blue
Blue	Blue
Yellow	Yellow
Red	Red
Green	Green
Red	Red
(a)	(b)

Dorsal anterior cingulate cortex

FIGURE 13.25 **The Stroop effect.** (a) Try to name the color of each word in both lists. Most people will find this much easier to do for the list on the left, where the word matches the name of the color. For the list on the right, where the word is different from the name of the color, it usually takes longer to name each color, and subjects make more errors in naming the color. (b) Activity increases in the anterior cingulate cortex when subjects perform the task where the colors do not match the text.

gyrus. Although this gyrus looks smooth and featureless to the naked eye, it is in fact divided up into at least a dozen distinct subregions, each providing output to a different set of regions elsewhere in the brain (Beckmann, Johansen-Berg, & Rushworth, 2009). Among other functions, research has suggested that these areas connect to the posterior hippocampus in support of navigation (Addis, Wong, & Schacter, 2007) and may provide an emotional context to motor behaviors (Ikemoto, Witkin, & Morales, 2003). More anterior aspects of the cingulate cortex connect to the dorsolateral prefrontal cortex to influence emotional feelings of effort during some kinds of mental activities, but not others.

Ventromedial Prefrontal Cortex: A Generator of Gut Feelings

In 1848, Phineas Gage, a young construction foreman in Vermont, suffered a tragic accident. While working on a railway construction gang, he was placing a dynamite charge in a borehole with a long, iron rod. The charge exploded prematurely, blasting the rod instantly up through the underside of his left cheek, through his ventromedial prefrontal cortex (VMPFC), and out through the top of his skull (Damasio, Grabowski, Frank, Galaburda, & Damasio, 1994). Gage survived, and although his perception, movement, intelligence, and language function remained intact, his personality seemed to change dramatically. He became impulsive, "intemperate," prone to social gaffes and inappropriate behavior, disorganized, and irresponsible. In the words of his physician, "Gage was no longer Gage" (Harlow, 1868).

In modern times, neuroscientific investigations have begun to define the role of the VMPFC more precisely. Like Gage, patients with VMPFC lesions often have great difficulty functioning in day-to-day life. However, standard neuropsychological tests often show these patients to have normal intelligence, language, and motor control. So where does the problem lie?

In the 1990s, a group of researchers at the University of Iowa devised a new test in which performance depended on "gut feelings" and the ability to foresee the emotional consequences of one's behavior (Bechara, Damasio, Damasio, & Anderson, 1994). In the **Iowa gambling task (IGT)**, subjects try to win money by drawing cards from four different decks (FIGURE 13.26). Decks A and B offer automatic gains of $100, but some cards offer much larger losses, up to $1,250. By the end of the game, a subject lured to just decks A and B will end up losing money overall. In contrast, decks C and D offer smaller immediate gains of $50, but also smaller losses, so that the overall outcome ends up being positive by the end of the game.

On the IGT, subjects with healthy intact brains may initially draw cards from decks A and B, but after encountering a large initial loss, their behavior changes. They soon switch to decks C and D and accept the smaller losses, leaving the

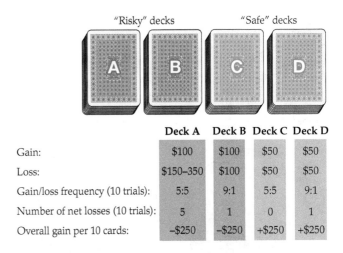

	Deck A	Deck B	Deck C	Deck D
Gain:	$100	$100	$50	$50
Loss:	$150–350	$100	$50	$50
Gain/loss frequency (10 trials):	5:5	9:1	5:5	9:1
Number of net losses (10 trials):	5	1	0	1
Overall gain per 10 cards:	–$250	–$250	+$250	+$250

FIGURE 13.26 **The Iowa gambling task.** Players can pick from the risky deck, where the gains are greater, but so are the losses; or they can pick from the safer deck, where the gains are smaller, but so are the losses.

game with somewhat more money than when they started. In contrast, patients with VMPFC lesions continue to draw from decks A and B and typically leave the game with less money than when they started. Some are even aware that their decisions are disadvantageous, but find themselves lured to the short-term-gain, long-term-pain choice of decks A and B nonetheless (Bechara, Tranel, & Damasio, 2000).

Why would VMPFC patients show this kind of "myopia for future consequences"? As it turns out, the autonomic functions of VMPFC patients are also abnormal during the IGT. In control subjects, good and bad outcomes produce GSRs. In addition, as the subjects become more experienced at the task, they also begin to generate GSRs when they merely contemplate drawing from the risky decks A or B, as if in anticipation of the emotional outcome to follow. In contrast, VMPFC patients seem to have difficulty generating GSRs in anticipation of a risky choice, although they remain capable of generating after-the-fact GSRs following good or bad outcomes (Bechara, Tranel, Damasio, & Damasio, 1996).

Why should this matter? To illustrate, let's look at what happens in the brain when a subject needs to know what lies on the back side of a card. When subjects get to see the card beforehand, an external cue can drive the behavior, and the dorsolateral prefrontal cortex (DLPFC) is the key area involved in declaring the suit of the card. However, if the subjects actually have to guess the suit of a card before seeing it, only gut feelings are available, and the VMPFC is active in generating these kinds of internal signals to help guide the decision (FIGURE 13.27; Elliott, Rees, & Dolan, 1999).

In the IGT, when no external signals are available to guide behavior, internal signals must suffice. And for these internal signals to be helpful, they must be able to accurately reflect the emotional outcome of a choice before the choice is actually made. In other words, to avoid the danger of a risky deck, you must be able to feel the pain of a punishing loss

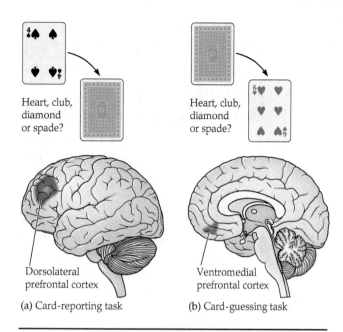

Heart, club, diamond or spade?

Heart, club, diamond or spade?

Dorsolateral prefrontal cortex

Ventromedial prefrontal cortex

(a) Card-reporting task

(b) Card-guessing task

FIGURE 13.27 **Brain activation for decision making using external versus internal cues.** (a) Subjects who have to report the suit of a nonhidden card can use external cues: the visual appearance of the card. The dorsolateral prefrontal cortex, which guides behavior using external cues, is active during this "card-reporting task." (b) Subjects who have to guess the suit of a hidden card can only use "gut feelings," or internal cues. The ventromedial prefrontal cortex is active for card-guessing rather than card-reporting.

before you even make the choice. This "don't-go-there" gut feeling can serve as a useful guide to behavior if no external signals are present and if the gut feeling accurately reflects the most likely final outcome. These guiding gut feelings are sometimes called somatic markers: visceral rather than external signals that act as emotional guides to behaviors. In the **somatic marker hypothesis** (Damasio, 1994), emotional decision making relies on the brain generating these visceral signals ahead of time. According to this hypothesis, the deficits of VMPFC patients in decision making arise not from a failure of intellect, but from a failure to generate the bodily signals of trepidation that would normally help a person to steer clear of bad decisions.

Although the somatic marker hypothesis has been criticized on several grounds (Dunn, Dalgleish, & Lawrence, 2006), there is a general consensus that the VMPFC plays a key role in driving autonomic, neuroendocrine, and other visceral signals. In this respect it somewhat resembles the centromedial parts of the amygdala, to which it is closely connected. The VMPFC also has strong modulatory outputs to other core limbic regions like the hypothalamus, anterior hippocampus, and brainstem. So, like much of the anterior cingulate cortex, the VMPFC acts as a sort of limbic motor cortex. The difference is that the VMPFC also has extensive inputs from all sensory modalities, much like the amygdala: olfactory, gustatory, visual, auditory, somatosensory, and visceral. By linking these inputs to visceromotor outputs, the VMPFC is ideally placed to learn and generate

the most appropriate visceral responses when presented with a given sensory stimulus. As in the amygdala, this turns out to be a useful function for evaluating the emotional valence and relevance of outside-world sensory stimuli.

The VMPFC, like the centromedial amygdala, is involved in generating fear responses such as increased heart rate during stressful events like being told that one will have to prepare a public speech (Wager et al., 2009). Unlike the amygdala, however, the responses of the VMPFC seem to go beyond fear alone. For example, some patients with schizophrenia experience anhedonia. In these patients, the degree of underactivity in the VMPFC correlates with the degree of anhedonia (Park et al., 2009). The VMPFC also has a more direct role in representing reward value. For example, the VMPFC is active in chocolate-lover subjects who are given successive pieces of chocolate to eat. However, this activity gradually decreases with the decreasing reward value of the chocolate as the subjects eat more and more pieces (FIGURE 13.28), eventually becoming satiated (Small, Zatorre, Dagher, Evans, & Jones-Gotman, 2001).

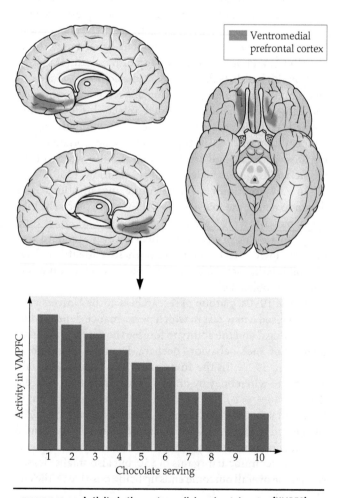

Ventromedial prefrontal cortex

Activity in VMPFC

Chocolate serving

FIGURE 13.28 **Activity in the ventromedial prefrontal cortex (VMPFC) and other brain areas decreases as the perceived reward value decreases.** When subjects were overfed chocolate, they went from liking it to disliking it. At the same time as their subjective rating of the desirability of chocolate decreased, activity in the VMPFC also decreased.

So the VMPFC is critical for evaluating stimuli in the sensory environment and generating a preemptive gut feeling about those stimuli, which can serve as a useful guide to behavior. But the value of a stimulus is not always apparent from its superficial appearance. If you come home to find your front door ajar, this could be good, bad, or neutral, depending on your expectations. So the VMPFC, insula, and cingulate cortex also need guidance themselves to ensure that the emotional response is appropriate to the larger environmental and behavioral context. This final layer of guidance comes from the last layer of the emotional hierarchy: the emotional association cortex.

Limbic Association Cortex: Modulation of Emotion

What is the emotional significance of an empty parking spot? If you are a pedestrian passing by, perhaps there will be none at all. But imagine the emotional reaction you might have if you are in a car, running late for an appointment in the building nearby, and happen to encounter the same scene. The previously neutral stimulus of the parking spot might now engender a great sense of pleasure: you will make it to your appointment on time after all! But now imagine another scenario: you *had* parked there an hour ago, had gone to your appointment, and have now returned, only to encounter an empty parking spot where you were expecting to find your car waiting for you! This time, the scene signals disaster: a case of grand theft or at least the unwelcome attentions of a tow truck.

In these three examples, the same stimulus (or rather, *lack* of a stimulus) can have an emotional valence that switches from neutral to strongly positive to strongly negative, entirely depending on the context in which it arises. Likewise, the set of motivations, goals, and behaviors engendered by the stimulus might vary from "none whatsoever" to "approach quickly and park the car, before someone else gets there first" to "call the police for help," depending on the circumstances.

The contextual modulation of emotion is the trickiest and the most complicated of all the brain's emotional tasks. To decide whether an empty parking spot is a good thing or a bad thing, the brain needs access to entirely new categories of information: representations of current behavior, future goals, expectations, interpretations of environment, episodic memories, and more. On their own, none of the brain structures we have discussed so far in this chapter has the right kinds of inputs and outputs to represent this kind of complex and continuously changing information. To find neurons that are capable of working together to perform these tasks, we must move to the highest levels of the brain's

emotion-regulating circuitry: the limbic and paralimbic regions of the cortex.

The Mechanisms of Emotional Reappraisal

One of the key emotional functions of the cortex lies in **reappraisal**: the adjustment of emotional responses to outside stimuli, based on their context. For example, if we show a person a picture of a man being bitten by a snake (FIGURE 13.29), the usual reaction would be one of shock and fear. However, if we then tell the person that the picture is a fake, the snake is a prop, and the apparent "victim" is an actor, the emotional response may be one of relief. On the other hand, if we tell the person that the picture is real and that the victim later died in the hospital, the emotional reaction will probably become even more severe.

FIGURE 13.29 **Cognitive reappraisal of emotional stimuli.** When confronted with an emotional stimulus, we can use context and cognition to adjust our emotional response. In this example, you could adjust your reaction to the snake by imagining that the photograph was faked, or that the snake was not poisonous and had no sharp teeth.

So what is the basis of emotional reappraisal in the brain? Neuroimaging studies have now begun to explore the role of the cortex in using context to regulate emotions. In one example, subjects were asked to view a series of emotional pictures (such as the one with the man being bitten by the snake) and either simply attend to the stimulus or engage in reappraisal strategies to either increase or decrease the emotional response. For example, to decrease the emotional intensity, the subject would be instructed to imagine that the victim recovered from the apparently dire situation or that the picture itself was a fake (Johnstone, van Reekum, Urry, Kalin, & Davidson, 2007). To see whether the reappraisal was working to regulate emotions, the researchers used an objective measure, pupil dilation, as a marker of autonomic arousal in response to each picture.

When the subjects tried to use reappraisal to decrease their emotional reactions, several brain regions became active. These included both dorsal and ventral regions of the lateral prefrontal cortex, as well as activity in the anterior insula (FIGURE 13.30). There were also some changes in functional connectivity among regions. As we saw earlier, the VMPFC provides visceromotor output to the amygdala, hypothalamus, and brainstem. During emotion regulation, this region appears to act to suppress amygdala and autonomic activity: higher VMPFC activation seems to lead to lower activation in the amygdala and reduced pupil dilation. The VMPFC in turn seems to be driven by activity in the nearby ventrolateral prefrontal cortex (VLPFC). So the overall picture is that emotional reappraisal activates the VLPFC, which in turn activates the visceromotor cortex of the VMPFC, which in turn acts to reduce the autonomic and amygdala activity elicited by an emotional stimulus.

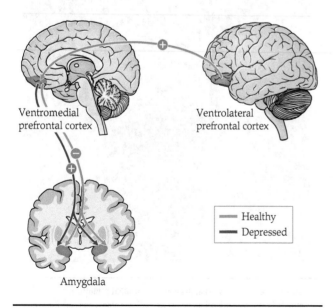

Ventromedial prefrontal cortex

Ventrolateral prefrontal cortex

Healthy
Depressed

Amygdala

FIGURE 13.30 **The ventromedial and ventrolateral prefrontal cortex can decrease amygdala activity during emotion-regulation. But in depressed patients, the opposite effect occurs.**

The same study also looked at how this process works in patients with depression. In these patients, during reappraisal, the VLPFC once again seemed to drive activity in the VMPFC. However, the VMPFC activity had a counterproductive effect: rather than suppressing amygdala and autonomic activity, higher VMPFC activity was linked with an actual *increase* in the activity in these areas. There are two possible ways to interpret this result: either the VMPFC is paradoxically *amplifying* rather than suppressing emotional responses in patients with depression or the VMPFC is attempting to suppress the emotional response, but somehow failing to do so. To distinguish between the two, we would need a study using methods of causation (for example, reversible lesion (TMS) or stimulation studies) rather than correlation (as with the neuroimaging-behavior correlations in this study).

Another similar study used functional MRI to identify the network of regions involved in reappraisal while viewing unpleasant emotional images. This study again found a widespread "reappraisal network" including widespread dorsal, ventral, medial, and lateral areas of prefrontal cortex as well as parietal and superior temporal cortex (Wager, Davidson, Hughes, Lindquist, & Ochsner, 2008). But which of these areas were truly critical to effective reappraisal and which were simply active because of associated functions like eye movement, working memory, stimulus identification, and so forth? To find out, the authors performed a more sophisticated analysis to identify regions mediating successful emotion regulation via a circuit including the amygdala and nucleus accumbens. In this analysis, mediators would be regions where, when their activity increased, amygdala activity was suppressed and nucleus accumbens activity was enhanced, and the size of these effects would accurately predict how successful the subject was in reducing his or her negative emotional responses.

In this study, only a few regions stood out as true mediators in emotion regulation (FIGURE 13.31). These were the VLPFC, the VMPFC, the medial frontopolar cortex, and the dorsomedial prefrontal cortex (DMPFC). This and other neuroimaging studies point to these regions as the core areas of emotional association cortex: lying nearby the visceromotor and viscerosensory cortex of the cingulate gyrus and anterior insula and standing at the interface among emotion, cognition, and behavioral control (Pochon et al., 2002; Wager et al., 2008).

Brain Injury, Brain Stimulation, and Emotion Regulation

Neuroimaging studies can reveal brain areas where activity correlates with a behavior like emotion regulation. However, the "acid test" is to examine the effects of either reversible TMS lesions or stimulation of these brain areas to see whether their activity has a causative rather than merely a correlational role in regulating emotions.

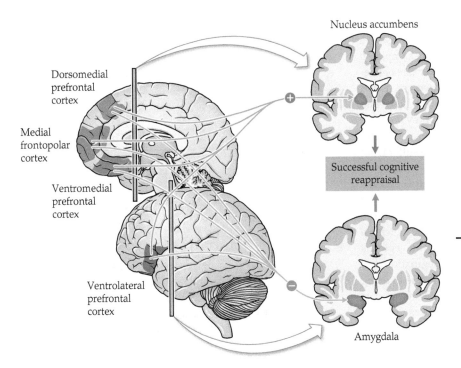

FIGURE 13.31 **Mechanisms of successful cognitive reappraisal.** A set of areas in the prefrontal cortex are active during successful regulation of emotional responses. They exert their effects by influencing the response of the nucleus accumbens and amygdala to an emotional stimulus. When they succeed in altering the activity of these structures, cognitive reappraisal is successful.

Studies of patients with brain injuries have begun to identify the key areas where lesions can affect emotion regulation. We have already seen how lesions of the VMPFC appear to interfere with the ability to generate somatic markers, or gut feelings. More recent studies have examined the effects of prefrontal lesions on mood itself.

One such study looked at symptoms of depression in veterans who had suffered focal brain injuries during combat (FIGURE 13.32) (Koenigs & Grafman, 2009). As a baseline, the study first looked at a group of veterans who had not suffered any brain injury. As it turned out, depression was common in this group: more than half of the veterans with intact brains

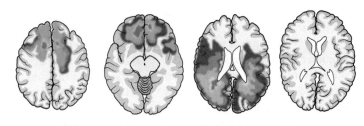

	Dorsomedial prefrontal cortex lesions	Ventromedial prefrontal cortex lesions	Non-prefrontal cortex lesions	No lesions
Low BDI No depression	20%	100%	65%	44%
Intermediate BDI Mild depression	0%	0%	25%	32%
High BDI Moderate/severe depression	80%	0%	10%	24%

FIGURE 13.32 **Effects of brain lesions on depression severity in combat veterans.** Veterans with lesions in DMPFC have a high incidence of severe depression compared to veterans with no lesions or those with lesions outside the frontal lobes. Lesions to VMPFC have the opposite effect and actually appear protective against severe depression.

had either moderate or high levels of depression. How did brain injury change the picture? Surprisingly, veterans with brain injuries outside the prefrontal cortex (for example, in and around the parietal lobes) actually had *lower* rates of depression than those with intact brains: nearly two-thirds had no significant depression symptoms, and only 1 in 10 had high levels of depression. So, despite the high prevalence of sensory and motor deficits resulting from injuries in these areas, the patients themselves were less likely to suffer from depressed mood.

Alas, the same was not true of another group: patients with lesions of the DMPFC. Fully 80% of these patients had depression scores that were not merely elevated, but in the "high" range. Why might DMPFC lesions confer such an enormous risk of depression? As we saw earlier, this region is one of the core areas involved in emotional regulation and reappraisal. It also seems to play an important role in using cognition to override emotional impulses. For example, this same region is activated in pathological gamblers during a losing streak, at the moment when they finally quit chasing their losses and force themselves to abandon the game (Campbell-Meiklejohn, Woolrich, Passingham, & Rogers, 2008). In non–brain injured patients with depression, this area also seems to have a protective role. Depressed patients with higher baseline DMPFC activity are more likely to respond to treatment with repetitive transcranial magnetic stimulation (rTMS) (Downar & Daskalakis, 2013).

What about lesions in the VMPFC? Here the results were astonishing. Not a single one of the VMPFC-injured patients in the study had depression: every one of them scored in the range considered normal. So again, despite the quite disabling changes in social function and decision making that are seen in this population of modern-day Phineas Gages, the patients themselves did not feel depressed.

As for the VLPFC, this area is now known to be abnormal in many disorders of mood stability. Compared to control subjects without bipolar disorder, patients with bipolar disorder (who suffer from episodes of both abnormally low and abnormally high mood) show reductions of gray matter in the VLPFC in neuroimaging studies using voxel-based morphometry (Ellison-Wright & Bullmore, 2010).

What about other prefrontal regions outside the emotion-reappraisal network? Doctors once thought that left lateral prefrontal lesions were more likely to cause depression than right prefrontal lesions were. For example, patients suffering a left-hemisphere stroke would be expected to show not only an impairment of language (aphasia), but also depressed mood. However, larger, more recent studies eventually found that the side of the lesion made no difference to the risk of depression (Carson et al., 2000). Still more recent studies, again in veterans with focal combat injuries, showed no significant differences in depression rates for left versus right DLPFC injuries (FIGURE 13.33). In fact, neither left nor right DLPFC injuries conferred *any* significant increase in the rates of depression when compared to lesions outside the prefrontal cortex altogether or even

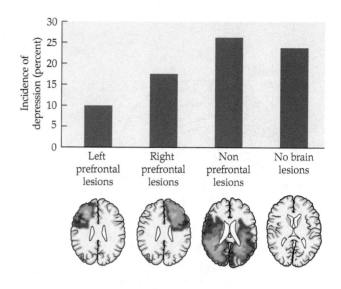

FIGURE 13.33 **Effects of left and right DLPFC brain lesions on depression incidence in combat veterans.** Neither left nor right DLPFC lesions cause a higher risk of depression in veterans. The incidence of depression is actually slightly lower in these groups compared to veterans without lesions.

compared to veterans with no brain injury at all (Koenigs & Grafman, 2009).

So the lesion studies concur with the neuroimaging studies that the VLPFC, DMPFC, and VMPFC are important for emotion regulation, whereas the DLPFC is at best a minor player. They also agree that both the right and the left hemispheres play important roles in emotion regulation and reappraisal. When it comes to deciding whether an empty parking spot is a good thing or a bad thing, a bilateral network of cortical areas helps to determine which emotional responses are the right ones to deploy. This emotion-regulation network bridges both the functional and the anatomical gap among internal sensation, visceral motor control, environmental context, and behavioral control. By bringing together all of these diverse sources of information, the neural circuits of the cortex are able to achieve a subtlety of emotion regulation that surpasses all other levels of the hierarchy.

Neurochemical Influences on Emotion

Throughout this chapter, we have been exploring the neural architecture of emotions solely in terms of its wiring: inputs and outputs, pathways and circuits, the flow of information from one domain into another. The reason for putting so much emphasis on emotion as circuitry in this chapter is that our popular culture sees emotions differently. We talk of emotions as "chemistry," describe anger in terms of

CASE STUDY:
A Cure Born of Desperation

The University of Iowa maintains a registry of hundreds of patients who have suffered localized brain lesions of one form or another, along with their case histories and the results of neuroimaging and neuropsychological testing. Among all the cases in the Iowa registry, one stands out as both disturbing and illuminating. A woman had suffered for years from severe depression. Having lost hope of recovery, she attempted suicide in 1997 by means of a gunshot to the head. Remarkably, she survived. However, the gunshot destroyed most of her frontopolar cortex and VMPFC, although leaving intact her DMPFC and the rest of her brain (FIGURE 13.34) (Koenigs et al., 2008).

On recovery, her emotional state was changed dramatically and forever. Sixteen months after the injury, her boyfriend reported that she had exhibited "no signs of depression whatsoever since the accident." Her neurosurgeon and neuropsychologist both concurred with this assessment. In a standard questionnaire of depressive symptoms, the patient herself reported a complete absence of sadness, self-dislike, guilt, or thoughts of suicide. She did continue to show some of the common neurovegetative, or homeostatic, signs of depression: loss of libido, weight loss, and low energy levels. However, the subjective emotions and thoughts that normally accompany depression were all abolished after the injury (Koenigs et al., 2008).

Similar effects sometimes appear in other dramatic cases. For example, one case of a modern-day "reverse Phineas Gage" involves a man who, prior to his injury, had a history of pathological aggression and violent behavior. At the age of 33, he attempted suicide by the grisly method of shooting himself in the head with a crossbow. The bolt

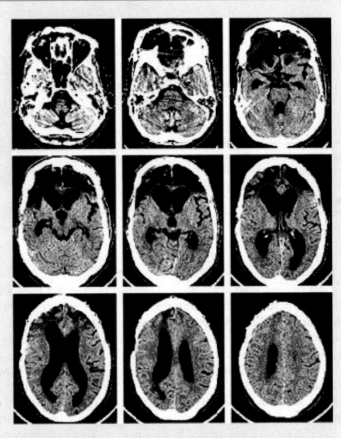

FIGURE 13.34 **Damage to the prefrontal cortex following a suicide attempt.** The suicide attempt damaged the ventral prefrontal cortex extensively (top two rows), but left the dorsal prefrontal cortex largely intact (bottom row).

passed upward through his VMPFC and was stopped by the inside of his skull. Remarkably, he survived, and thereafter became "docile, indifferent to his situation, and inappropriately cheerful" (Ellenbogen, Hurford, Liebeskind, Neimark, & Weiss, 2005).

Is there any way to make use of these findings to help people with mood disorders? As it turns out, neuroimaging studies show that in patients who undergo **electroconvulsive therapy** for the treatment of severe depression, the ones who improve show decreases in metabolic activity in the ventromedial and frontopolar cortex: a "functional lesion" rather than the anatomical one in the cases above (Fosse & Read, 2013). But can this

effect also be replicated without resorting to electroconvulsive therapy? As you may recall, some patients have undergone DBS of the nucleus accumbens for treatment of severe depression. In these patients, too, the effect is a reduction in the activity of ventromedial and frontopolar cortex. There may also be even less invasive ways to produce this effect. For example, low-frequency TMS can reduce the activity of cortical regions safely and noninvasively, using focused pulses of powerful magnetic fields. Scientists are currently investigating the use of TMS for depression. In the future, TMS might allow patients with severe depression to recover from illness without resorting to extreme methods.

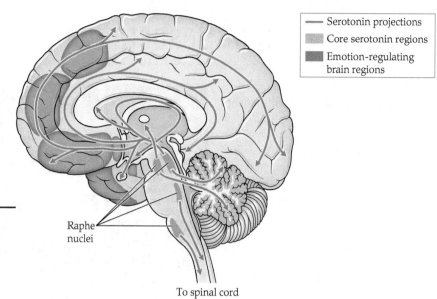

FIGURE 13.35 **The serotonin pathways in the brain.** Note that serotonin-containing neurons project to many different areas of the cortex, brainstem, and spinal cord, and thus perform a wide variety of functions. The mood-altering effects of serotonin are just one of these many functions.

"hormones," and speak of depression as a "chemical imbalance." Our medications for psychiatric illnesses are described in terms of their pharmacological effects. Serotonin-boosting medications end up being called "antidepressants," as if serotonin equates to happy mood. Medications that activate GABA receptors end up being called "anxiolytics," as if GABA equates to tranquility.

It is all too easy to forget that emotions, like all other brain functions, arise from the coordinated activity of neurons in specific pathways (FIGURE 13.35), defined by their patterns of connection, and allowing specific patterns of information flow to take place. What this means is that unless a molecule of serotonin can somehow persuade a neuron to alter its patterns of firing, it cannot affect the emotional state or anything the mind does at all. So what determines whether that molecule of serotonin acts to dampen your sad sensation of a lump in the throat, or to generate an unpleasant sensation of nausea in the stomach, or to cause you to hallucinate vivid patterns of color and light in a darkened room? The answer lies in *which* neurons pick up the signal it represents and how they alter their activity as a consequence.

All that said, there are myriad important ways in which neurotransmitters influence emotion. Many of our most widely used medical treatments exploit these effects to alleviate the symptoms of psychiatric disease. In this section, we will take a look at the effects of three "mood-altering substances": serotonin, norepinephrine, and GABA.

Serotonin and Mood

The monoamine neurotransmitter serotonin is central to mood regulation. Even short-lived increases or decreases in serotonin levels can have measurable effects on emotional regulation in human beings. For example, it is possible to reduce a person's serotonin levels by feeding them a diet low in the amino acid precursor of serotonin, tryptophan. After a few days on a tryptophan-depletion diet, subjects begin to show signs of a negative mood bias (van der Veen, Evers, Deutz, & Schmitt, 2007). They show increased amygdala responses to fearful faces, slower responses to positive words, and reduced memory for positive emotional information. They become worse at discriminating among rewards during decision making, yet better at predicting punishments and less cooperative in social interaction games (van der Veen et al., 2007). Alongside the bias toward negative information and away from positive information, subjects develop changes in ventral striatal and VMPFC activity reminiscent of patients with depression (van der Veen et al., 2007). In patients who have actually suffered depression in the past, evidence suggests that a short period of tryptophan depletion causes them to develop a bias toward negative emotional stimuli (Harmer, 2008).

Medications that boost serotonin levels (**selective serotonin reuptake inhibitors [SSRIs]**) are commonly used as treatments for depression. These medications boost serotonin levels within hours, yet for some reason, they typically require several weeks to relieve the symptoms of depression (Blier & de Montigny, 1994). However, their immediate effects tend to look like the opposite of tryptophan depletion. Even a single dose of an SSRI can increase the recognition of happy facial expressions and increase attention to positive social cues (FIGURE 13.36; Harmer et al., 2003). In neuroimaging studies, the amygdala shows reduced responses to aversive facial expressions (Harmer et al., 2003). Slightly longer regimens of SSRIs are associated with increases in social confidence and cooperative behavior in social situations,

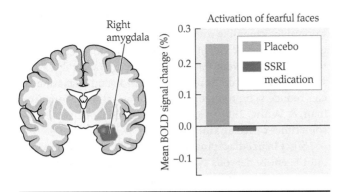

FIGURE 13.36 Effects of serotonin on the amygdala response to emotional faces. A single dose of a selective serotonin reuptake inhibitor (SSRI) can abolish the amygdala's response to faces with fearful emotional expressions.

increases in the tendency to see ambiguous faces as happy, improved ability to recall positive personality adjectives in a word recall task, and reduced perceptions of fearful, angry, or disgusted facial expressions (Del-Ben, Ferreira, Alves-Neto, & Graeff, 2008; Hadreas, 2010; Harmer, Mackay, Reid, Cowen, & Goodwin, 2006; Harmer, Shelley, Cowen, & Goodwin, 2004). So, with ongoing exposure to SSRIs, the initial biases in emotional information processing seem to translate into improvements in social interaction.

What are the brain mechanisms by which these changes take place? The neuroanatomy of the serotonin system is complex, with clusters of serotonergic neurons all through the raphe nuclei of the brainstem and projecting throughout all levels of the emotional hierarchy: the spinal cord, pons and medulla, midbrain, amygdala, hypothalamus, and hippocampus, as well as to many different regions of the cortex (Azmitia & Segal, 1978). What's more, there are more than a dozen different varieties of serotonin receptor in the nervous system, each with its own effects on neural activity and its own distribution across the circuitry of emotional control (Hoyer et al., 1994). Although the details of these systems will take decades to work out, one important subsystem involves the serotonin 1A (5HT1A) **autoreceptors**, which are found in the presynaptic membrane of the serotonin-releasing neuron and regulate the amount of serotonin released via **negative feedback** mechanisms. SSRIs over time desensitize the 5HT1A autoreceptors, thus allowing the serotonin neurons' activity to gradually creep up (Hjorth, 1993).

In terms of brain activity, SSRI use is associated with an attenuation of activity in the medial prefrontal cortex and amygdala, which may be responsible for the shift in bias away from negative and toward positive social cues in the environment (Hajos, Hajos-Korcsok, & Sharp, 1999; Harmer et al., 2006). So increased serotonin may help to shift mood by affecting the cortical mechanisms of reappraisal. Rather than simply erasing sad mood, high serotonin promotes a tendency to see the glass as half-full—or at least, not half-empty.

Over time, this positive bias may allow the person's mood to climb back into a positive range.

Norepinephrine and Mood

Many antidepressant medications act on a different monoamine neurotransmitter, norepinephrine. For example, the antidepressant reboxetine selectively inhibits the reuptake of norepinephrine rather than serotonin. The effects of boosting norepinephrine levels can be seen immediately and are in many ways similar to those of boosting serotonin levels (Di Simplicio, Massey-Chase, Cowen, & Harmer, 2009; Simons, 2004). In people without a history of depression, a short course of reboxetine was still associated with a reduction in the identification of negative facial expressions such as fear and anger and an increase in the relative recall of positive over negative emotions (Harmer et al., 2004). Over time, such changes in emotional bias may be responsible for the antidepressant effects of norepinephrine reuptake, as with serotonin reuptake.

The neuroanatomy of the norepinephrine system is distinct from that of the serotonin system. The brainstem contains a variety of nuclei with neurons that use norepinephrine as their primary neurotransmitter. However, chief among these is the locus coeruleus (or blue spot, after its pigmented appearance in fresh neuroanatomical specimens). The locus coeruleus is a critical structure for the functions of alerting and arousal, and it sends projections widely throughout the entire brain (FIGURE 13.37). Norepinephrine receptors exist on neurons throughout the sensory pathways of the brain, where they modulate sensory

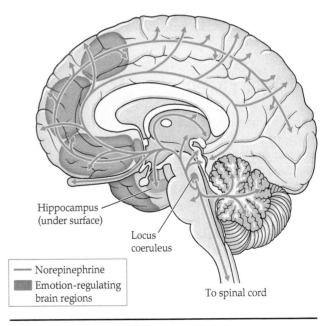

FIGURE 13.37 **The norepinephrine pathways in the brain.**

thresholds to promote vigilance. Norepinephrine receptors also exist in the prefrontal cortex, where they modulate the activity of regions that regulate attention, evaluation, and self-reflection.

Neuroimaging studies have now begun to compare the effects of acute increases in norepinephrine versus serotonin in terms of brain activation (Bruhl, Kaffenberger, & Herwig, 2010). For example, a single dose of citalopram (an SSRI) increases activation of a variety of brain regions during the anticipation of an emotional picture. This network looks much like the set of association areas involved in emotional reappraisal: DLPFC, VLPFC, and medial prefrontal cortex, as well as a region of midbrain near the periaqueductal gray (Bruhl et al., 2010). A dose of reboxetine has similar effects, enhancing activation of the DMPFC and DLPFC, as well as that of areas in the posterior cingulate cortex and temporoparietal junction, both important for prospection or the imagination of future scenarios (Bruhl et al., 2010).

The networks that show increased activation in response to norepinephrine versus serotonin differ somewhat. For example, increased serotonin seems to uniquely enhance the VLPFC, a key area in the suppression of emotional responses, as we saw in the last section (Bruhl et al., 2010). In contrast, a boost in norepinephrine seems to have stronger effects on the DLPFC and on sensory-processing areas in the occipital and parietal lobes (Bruhl, Jancke, & Herwig, 2011). This is consistent with the known effects of norepinephrine in arousal and in enhancing alertness to the outside sensory environment. The differences in neural effects might also help to explain why a given class of antidepressant, either one that increases serotonin levels or one that increases norepinephrine levels, helps some depressed patients greatly, although it has little effect in others. With further study, it may become possible to predict ahead of time which kinds of antidepressant are most likely to work in any given patient, thus sparing them the trial-and-error approach that currently prevails.

GABA and Anxiety

The neurotransmitter gamma-aminobutyric acid (GABA) (Chapter 3) is the main inhibitory neurotransmitter of the entire mammalian nervous system and consequently has an enormous variety of roles in almost every kind of brain function. That said, the GABA system is also the primary target of a wide variety of medications that relieve anxiety, agitation, and aggression.

Chief among these are the benzodiazepines: a class of medications that includes household-name sedatives like diazepam (also known by the brand name Valium), lorazepam (known by the brand name Ativan), and alprazolam (known by the brand name Xanax). Although they all differ slightly in their strength and duration of effect, what these medications have in common is that they all act as agonists to stimulate GABA receptors throughout the body. At high doses,

this can cause such profound inhibition of neural activity as to produce comalike unconsciousness and anesthesia (Mogensen, Muller, & Valentin, 1986). Lower doses can be used to abort and prevent epileptic seizures (Booker & Celesia, 1973). Still lower doses produce sedation and relaxation and can reduce symptoms of anxiety or agitation (Mora, Torjman, & White, 1989). For this reason, benzodiazepines are sometimes called **anxiolytics**.

Since benzodiazepines exert an inhibitory effect throughout the entire nervous system, a key question is where these effects actually translate into reductions in the experience of fear. Neuroimaging studies have now begun to address this question in detail. For example, single, mild doses of lorazepam are associated with reduced brain activity during the assessment of emotional faces. The reductions in brain activity do not occur throughout the entire nervous system, but are restricted to a specific set of structures: the amygdala, the anterior insula, and the visual cortex of the inferior temporal lobe (Paulus, Feinstein, Castillo, Simmons, & Stein, 2005).

Similar studies have examined the effects of benzodiazepines on brain activity during anticipatory anxiety, before any stimulus appears. For example, the short-acting benzodiazepine midazolam reduces the anxiety that precedes a painfully hot stimulus, without actually reducing the pain itself. The reduction in anticipatory anxiety correlates with a reduction in the activity of a specific set of brain regions: in this case, the anterior insula and the anterior cingulate cortex (FIGURE 13.38) (Wise et al., 2007). As we saw earlier, these areas form the sensory and motor components of the limbic cortex, respectively. So the generic neuron-inhibiting activities of a GABA agonist seem to translate into reductions in anxiety specifically when the neurons being inhibited are the ones that lie in limbic sensory and motor cortex (Wise et al., 2007).

If we zoom in to the cellular and molecular level, we find that there is actually a special subspecies of GABA receptor that lives in the circuitry of the limbic system and acts to regulate anxiety levels. The alpha-2 $GABA_A$ receptor is expressed widely in neurons of limbic regions of the cortex and striatum, in contrast to a closely related receptor, the alpha-3 $GABA_A$ receptor, which is expressed more in the brainstem and thalamus (FIGURE 13.39) (Low et al., 2000). In mice, it is possible to create a point mutation in either of these two kinds of receptors, so that they no longer function (Low et al., 2000). A point mutation of the alpha-2 $GABA_A$ receptor renders the mice completely insensitive to the antianxiety effects of benzodiazepines. However, a point mutation of the alpha-3 $GABA_A$ receptor has no such effect. So once again, the effects of GABA neurotransmission depend entirely on which neurons are being affected (Low et al., 2000).

One important corollary to this is that you can sometimes elicit the antianxiety effect by inactivating the appropriate neurons, even without the GABA agonist. In one study, researchers gave subjects either midazolam or a saline **placebo** and then looked at subjects' anxiety in response to

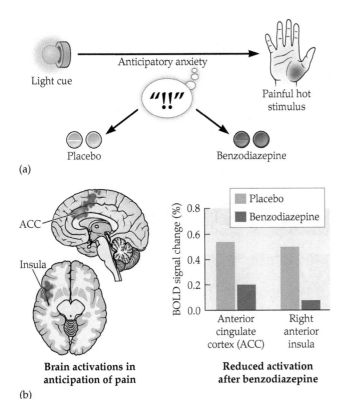

(a)

(b)

Brain activations in anticipation of pain

Reduced activation after benzodiazepine

FIGURE 13.38 **Effects of benzodiazepine medication on brain activity during anticipatory anxiety.** (a) During scanning, subjects saw a light predicting the delivery of a painful hot stimulus to the hand. Their anticipatory anxiety was then treated with either placebo or a benzodiazepine. (b) The anterior cingulate and anterior insula were activated during anticipatory anxiety, before the painful stimulus was delivered. However, if given a benzodiazepine, this activity was reduced, and anxiety diminished.

---

frightening visual images. As it turned out, when the subjects believed they were receiving midazolam, their anxiety levels dropped, although the injection actually contained nothing but saline solution (Petrovic et al., 2005)!

Once again, neuroimaging revealed the neural basis of this antianxiety effect (Petrovic et al., 2005). In addition to

reductions in the activity of visual cortex, the placebo was associated with a reduction in the activity of the amygdala in response to the emotional pictures. In contrast, the placebo seemed to increase the activity of a set of limbic motor and emotional-reappraisal regions including the anterior cingulate cortex, VLPFC, DLPFC, and orbitofrontal cortex. These activations did not appear in all subjects, but were specific to the subjects who showed a placebo antianxiety effect.

The take-home point here is that what makes a substance "mood altering" is not its molecular structure alone. Instead, what matters is whether that molecular structure is capable of producing alterations in the activity of the neural pathways that generate and modulate emotional states. In the case of benzodiazepines, the antianxiety effect comes from the drug interacting with a specific set of receptors that lie on a specific set of neural circuits relevant to fear. If we change the receptors, then the drug stops being "antianxiety." On the other hand, if we change the neural circuit's activity, the emotional effects can appear even if the "drug" is nothing but a weak saline solution.

Conclusion

At the beginning of this chapter we saw the case of Susanna, a woman who developed intense, crushing sadness mere seconds after the activation of a DBS in the subthalamic nucleus. Let's return now to this case and ask ourselves why this might have happened. What circuits might have been activated? Deactivated? What brain regions might have been involved? How might this have been avoided?

As it turns out, these questions actually have some concrete answers. In this woman's case, the neurosurgical team performed brain imaging with fMRI to identify the changes in neural activity that accompanied her sudden descents into sadness with the activation of the DBS electrode (FIGURE 13.40). The findings are published, and we can review them here. What might you expect to see?

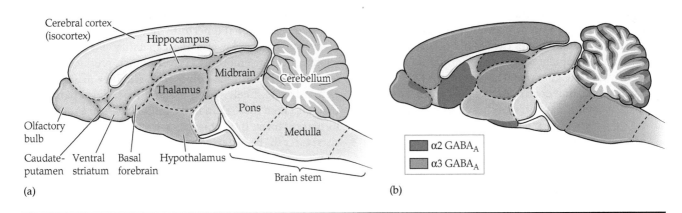

(a)

(b)

FIGURE 13.39 **GABA receptor distribution in the mouse brain.** (a) The mid-sagittal anatomy of the mouse brain, showing major brain regions and structures. (b) Regions where the alpha-2 GABA$_A$ and alpha-3 GABA$_A$ receptors are found. Note the high concentration of alpha-2 receptors in limbic areas: hippocampus, hypothalamus, basal forebrain, and ventral striatum. Benzodiazepine medications act via this receptor subtype to inhibit activity in these areas, which reduces anxiety.

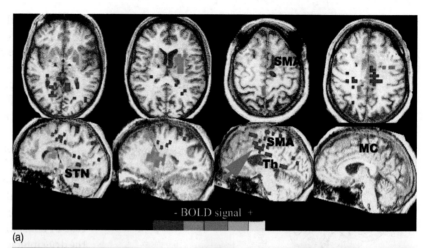

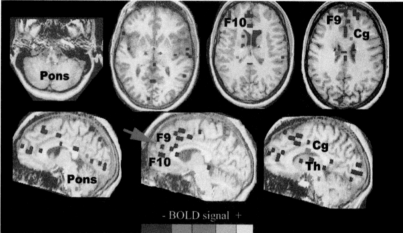

FIGURE 13.40 fMRI images show brain activity with stimulation of correctly and incorrectly placed deep brain stimulation electrodes in a patient with Parkinson's disease. (a) Stimulation of the correctly placed electrode deactivated the thalamus (Th) and supplementary motor area (SMA), improving the patient's tremor. (b) Stimulation of the incorrectly placed electrode deactivated more anterior regions in the dorsomedial prefrontal cortex (F9, F10), producing intense sadness during stimulation.

First, have a look at the effects of the correctly implanted electrode, which improved her motor functioning. We see an activation of the striatum, in a corticostriatal loop feeding motor regions like the primary motor cortex and SMA. Note that the overall effect is *inhibitory* in some places: the SMA is actually turned *off*, releasing the excessive inhibition and allowing movement to take place.

Now look at the images for the misplaced electrode. The inhibitory effects are similar, but shifted further forward, to the wrong swath of prefrontal cortex. The areas that are deactivated lie not in the SMA, but instead in the DMPFC and frontopolar cortex. In effect, the stimulation temporarily created "functional" lesions of the DMPFC, in emotional association cortex. As you may recall from earlier in the chapter, patients with structural lesions here showed extremely high rates of severe depression. If you look carefully, you may also see a side effect of this loss of cortical inhibition: increased activity in brainstem limbic regions where we would expect to find the periaqueductal gray and the serotonin-containing raphe nuclei of the pons. Without cortical modulation, these regions were free to activate.

Of course, not all DBS patients encounter such effects. Susanna had had a long-standing history of depression prior to the implantation of the electrodes. It may well have been that she relied more heavily than most people on the medial prefrontal cortex to suppress her depressive symptoms when in the presence of other people. With these emotion-modulating circuits out of the way, however, the lower levels of the emotional hierarchy were instantly freed to assert themselves once again.

As for the rest of us, there is a moral to this clinical tale. Sadness, happiness, fear, surprise, curiosity, and all the rest of our emotional repertoire may seem ineffable facets of human nature, beyond the capability of mere neural chatter. Yet our emotions are very much products of our brains, just like sound, color, or smell. They arise from a rich, intricate, finely tuned hierarchy of neural pathways that has taken more than half a billion years to evolve into its present form. If this hierarchy should fail, the effects on survival can be catastrophic. However, when in good working order, this hierarchy performs some of the brain's most indispensable functions. Through visceral feelings, it gently sculpts our priorities and goals, steering us through the opportunities and challenges of the world and ensuring that we are able to survive and thrive and, with luck, pass on the accumulated wisdom of our experience to the next generation.

KEY PRINCIPLES

- There are three common theories of emotional responses. The James–Lange theory suggests that emotions result from detecting the body's physical response to a stimulus ("bottom-up"). The Cannon–Bard theory proposes that emotions and the emotional response to a stimulus are coordinated at the level of the cortex and hypothalamus ("top-down"). The two-factor theory of Singer and Schacter suggests that both bottom-up and top-down processes are important in determining the emotional response.

- The hypothalamus coordinates three types of survival behaviors: reproductive, appetitive, and agonistic. Together, these are referred to as motivated behaviors.

- The amygdala receives sensory input from the outside world. It interprets the emotional value of the stimulus and initiates an appropriate emotional response.

- Another important limbic structure for determining the emotional response is the hippocampus. The anterior hippocampus plays an important role in remembering the emotional significance of events.

- Activity in the ventral striatum is associated with rewarding behavior and the sensation of pleasure.

- Circuits through these core limbic regions seem to generate subjective feelings and motivations, in addition to allied hormonal and autonomic responses.

- Studies have demonstrated that the limbic cortex, including the insula, cingulate cortex, and ventromedial prefrontal cortex, influences the hippocampus and amygdala and is important for generating and modulating emotions and emotional responses.

- In emotional reappraisal, the response to a stimulus is evaluated and altered based on the context. This involves activity in a range of prefrontal areas, including the ventromedial prefrontal cortex, ventrolateral prefrontal cortex, and dorsomedial prefrontal cortex.

- Emotions can be regulated by these same areas, but recent studies have shown that the dorsolateral prefrontal cortex is not directly involved in reappraising or regulating emotions.

- Brain stimulation or injury can alter emotional states if core limbic areas are affected or emotion regulation if the limbic association cortex is affected.

- Serotonin, norepinephrine, and GABA are the three neurotransmitters most commonly associated with the neuronal circuits involved in emotion. They can influence emotion by altering the activity of neurons within the hierarchy of emotional perception, evaluation, and control. Drugs that affect the levels of these neurotransmitters have been developed as treatments for depression and bipolar disorder.

KEY TERMS

Early Theories of Emotion
James–Lange theory (p. 403)
fight-or-flight (p. 403)
bottom-up theory (p. 404)
sham rage (p. 406)
Cannon–Bard theory (p. 406)
top-down theory (p. 406)
pure autonomic failure (p. 406)

two-factor theory (p. 407)
epinephrine (p. 407)

Core Limbic Structures: Amygdala and Hypothalamus
blood–brain barrier (p. 409)
estrogens (p. 409)
estradiol (p. 409)
androgens (p. 409)

testosterone (p. 409)
thyroid-stimulating hormone (p. 409)
growth hormone (p. 409)
cytokines (p. 409)
lateral hypothalamus (p. 410)
ventromedial hypothalamus (p. 410)
lordosis (p. 410)

medial preoptic area (p. 410)

paraventricular nucleus (p. 410)

endocrine gland (p. 410)

corticotropin-releasing hormone (p. 410)

adrenocorticotropic hormone (p. 410)

basolateral amygdala (p. 412)

centromedial amygdala (p. 412)

fear conditioning (p. 413)

lateral nucleus (p. 413)

Urbach–Wiethe disease (p. 414)

visual agnosia (p. 415)

Kluver–Bucy syndrome (p. 415)

medial forebrain bundle (p. 417)

anhedonia (p. 417)

circuit of Papez (p. 418)

entorhinal cortex (p. 420)

The Limbic Cortex and Emotions

cingulate cortex (p. 421)

Stroop effect (p. 422)

Iowa gambling task (IGT) (p. 423)

somatic marker hypothesis (p. 424)

Limbic Association Cortex: Modulation of Emotion

reappraisal (p. 425)

Neurochemical Influences on Emotion

electroconvulsive therapy (p. 429)

selective serotonin reuptake inhibitors (SSRIs) (p. 430)

autoreceptors (p. 431)

negative feedback (p. 431)

anxiolytics (p. 432)

placebo (p. 432)

REVIEW QUESTIONS

1. What are the differences between top-down and bottom-up theories of emotion? What evidence argues against each of these two types of theory? How might bottom-up and top-down theories of emotion be reconciled?

2. List three different kinds of physiological responses that might occur during the emotion of fear.

3. How does pathological laughter arise? In what ways does pathological laughter differ from normal laughter? Why do patients rarely experience pathological laughter as "funny"?

4. In single-unit recordings from the amygdala, some neurons fire in response to threats in the external sensory environment, whereas others respond to rewards. However, in the few rare cases of bilateral amygdala lesions, only the emotion of fear is lost; the capacity for pleasure and reward remains intact. How might we explain this discrepancy?

5. What are the similarities between the somatosensory cortex and the insula? What are the differences? What are the similarities between the primary motor cortex and the cingulate cortex? What are the differences?

6. Patients with damage to the ventromedial prefrontal cortex often show apparent changes in personality, making impulsive decisions and engaging in inappropriate acts. Why do ventromedial prefrontal lesions often have such dramatic effects on behavior? How might you explain such a patient's altered behavior to a concerned family member?

7. Repetitive transcranial magnetic stimulation (rTMS) is a method for increasing or decreasing the activity of local regions of the cortex using powerful, focused magnetic field pulses. If you wanted to use rTMS to help treat a person with a fear of flying in airplanes, what area of the brain might you target? Would you want to increase or decrease its overall activity? Why?

8. What effects does an SSRI antidepressant have on brain activity? Why might these effects help a person to overcome the negative thinking patterns of depression?

CRITICAL-THINKING QUESTIONS

1. In patients with major depression, the anterior hippocampus often decreases in size. How could we determine whether this shrinkage is a cause or an effect of the persistently depressed mood? Why might the answer to this question have important implications?

2. Given what you have learned about the risks, benefits, and long-term outcomes of deep brain stimulation (DBS), to what extent do you think that the decision to treat a patient with this method should be the patient's decision or the physician's decision? Does your answer differ depending on which disorder DBS would be targeted to treat in the patient? Explain.

3. How do you think that future neuroscience research might ultimately be applied to help regulate the emotions of individuals who have difficulty controlling their anger? What are the major research questions that would be most important to ask? What would the key research methods be to address these questions? Explain your answer.

- Describe the role of natural motivations in ensuring an organism's survival.

- Distinguish the roles of the hypothalamus and amygdala in anchoring motivations to the basic needs of the organism, as well as the role of dopamine in weighing competing sources of motivation.

- Explain how a reward gains its value from its ability to meet the basic needs of the organism, how the brain can learn to predict where it will find rewards, and how "liking" and "wanting" differ in terms of both what they represent and the underlying mechanisms.

- Explain the functions of the opioid system in pleasure and reward.

- Examine the functions of dopamine in learning, reward, and motivation.

- Identify how the same neurotransmitter system can perform many different functions.

- Describe how addictive substances produce addiction and its hallmark features of tolerance, withdrawal, neglect of other needs, and frequent episodes of relapse.

- Describe current and possible future approaches to the treatment of substance addiction.

Motivation and Reward

STARTING OUT:
"More Important Than Survival Itself"

"Frank" was a drug addict, and because of the consequences of his addiction, he was dying. No doubt, you can imagine the scene from some film or television show. You might imagine him to have a long record of arrest and imprisonment for drug possession, theft, perhaps even crimes of violence. You might imagine him to be poor or homeless, having lost all of his friends and family. You might imagine him huddling in some darkened alleyway, clutching a syringe full of heroin and tightening a belt around his arm. However, in all of this, you would be wrong.

In fact, Frank was a respected and distinguished physician. He had a long record, not of arrests, but of successfully treated patients. He was lying, not in an alley, but in a hospital bed, having barely survived a heart attack. He was well aware that the heart attack was a consequence of his lifelong addiction to cigarettes. As a physician, he was also well aware that even having survived this far, his risk of dying in the next 30 days was significant. Yet his addiction still gnawed at him. To his own dismay, he found himself sneaking outside for a quick smoke every few hours and then climbing back into bed. He saw this as a shameful loss of control, and the knowledge made him feel guilty, but his craving for tobacco always seemed to grow larger than the guilt.

His friends and family were baffled by his behavior. Surely, a doctor ought to know better. Surely, *anyone* ought to know better! How could someone not quit smoking even after a heart attack? For that matter, how could a doctor have seen so many patients with lung cancer and heart disease over the years, but continue to smoke himself into an early grave? How could the hunger for a cigarette become more important than survival itself (FIGURE 14.1)?

FIGURE 14.1 Motivation and survival. Why would a doctor who suffered a heart attack and had seen so many patients with lung cancer and heart disease over the years continue to smoke himself?

Motivation and Survival

We cannot understand addiction without first understanding motivation, which is essential to survival.

Addiction: An Illness of Motivation

Unlike many of the illnesses we have learned about in this book, addiction is commonplace, and its tragic effects are closer to the people in your life than you may realize. Many of us do not need to open a textbook to find a case of addiction. In fact, most people reading this page will have an acquaintance, a close friend, or a family member who has struggled with some form of substance dependence. The behavior of those who suffer through addiction is often incomprehensible to those around them. Why can't Mom quit smoking? Why did my friend start drinking again after six months of being sober? Why would a successful person lose his friends, his marriage, his career rather than stop using alcohol? A reasonable person would "just say no," wouldn't he? What is so hard about just saying no? Isn't it just a question of motivation? Shouldn't the person just try harder?

Addiction perplexes us because the normal rules of motivation and behavior seem not to apply. At its core, addiction is an illness that reshapes the circuitry of motivation itself and over time distorts it into a form different from the normal state. Hence, the behavior of those with addiction often challenges our patience and strains our capacity for empathy. When someone's motivations are so different from our own, it is hard to relate and much easier to relegate them to the ranks of the unsalvageable. Yet the truth is that every one of us struggles with motivational problems on some scale: eating healthier food, staying physically active, finishing work on time, or even just flossing our teeth in the morning. Whether or not we suffer from addiction, we all have a common interest in learning better ways to motivate ourselves toward our goals.

But how do we set and reach our goals in the first place? To answer this question, we must understand the architecture of motivation in the brain. As it turns out, this architecture is both ancient and essential to survival. In this chapter, we'll start by looking at the basic motivational circuitry needed by every animal to keep itself alive. By the end of the chapter, we will see how these same motivational mechanisms become disrupted, leading to the self-destructive behaviors of addiction. Finally, we'll look at how physicians and scientists are trying to teach the brain to "unlearn" addiction and return the motivational circuitry to its original purpose: ensuring survival.

Why Motivation Matters

Staying alive is a balancing act. From the moment an animal opens its eyes in the morning, it is faced with a series of dilemmas (FIGURE 14.2). Should I spend my time foraging for food and building my energy supplies? Or is it more important to find a source of water? Is it too cold to go outside today, even if I am hungry? Am I safe from predators here, or do I need to find a better shelter? Are there too many rivals in this territory? Should I drive them away and defend my food supply, even if it means going hungry and risking injury? And what about the all-important goal of reproduction? How important is it to find a mate if going outside to find one involves a risk of getting eaten?

With so many needs to meet, the brain needs to have some way of setting its priorities. Get the balance right, and the prize is survival and many offspring, who will probably have brains as crafty as your own. Get the balance wrong, and your kind of brain will in time go extinct. As one might imagine, the brain's current architecture for priority setting developed early on (at least half a billion years ago, as you may recall from Chapter 2) and has remained remarkably stable ever since. Many of the basic needs of a living creature have changed little, even as animals have moved from water to the land and diversified into thousands of species, one of which now has the intelligence to study its own brain's motivational mechanisms.

FIGURE 14.2 **Animals face survival dilemmas every day.** These range from what and where to eat, to whether water is safe to drink, to whether the need for food and water outweighs the need to stay where it is warm and safe.

It is worth mentioning here that the circuitry of what we usually mean by "intelligence" is a relatively new addition to an ancient basic brain plan. So-called "general intelligence" is also a different function from priority-setting. Intelligence is about being able to predict the outside-world consequences of your actions: for example, what sequence of button presses on your computer will result in your email being sent to the intended recipient. High intelligence typically refers to the ability to make accurate predictions about outside-world events based on one's actions: for example, reliably predicting which answers on a multiple-choice test will result in a response of "correct."

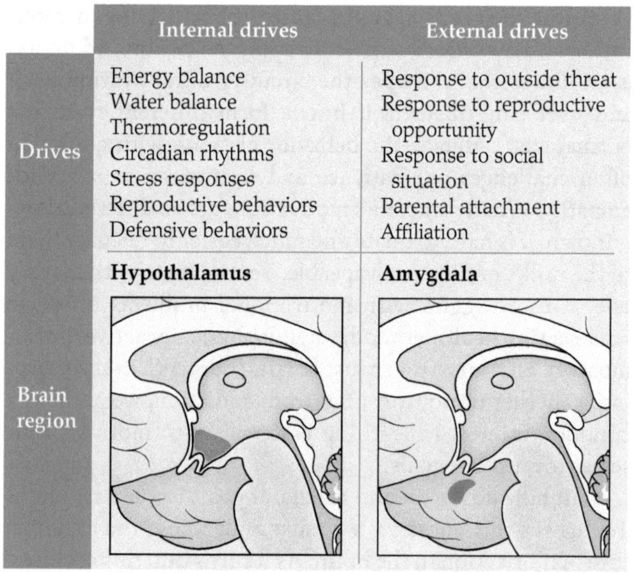

Motivation is more akin to judgment: the ability to make accurate predictions about what is most important in any given scenario. Of course, intelligence and judgment do not always go together. A person may have a high ability to memorize textbook content and predict the most appropriate answers on a test. However, this same person may have difficulty assigning the most appropriate priority level to reading the textbook over sending emails in the nights leading up to the examination and perform poorly on the examination as a result.

Human beings meet their survival needs with behaviors that are more complex than those of any other species on the planet. We make long-term plans for careers, relationships, social alliances, personal health, and survival in old age. Much of human day-to-day activity seems to have little immediate connection to survival needs as basic as maintaining our energy balance or avoiding threats. With such elaborate behavioral repertoires, it is easy for us to forget that our basic needs have remained the same as those of other living things. Yet ultimately, every behavior of every animal (humans included) has its origins in one of a fairly small set of basic survival needs.

What are these basic needs or drives? We can divide them into the drives arising from internal states or bodily functions and the drives arising from external sources or incentives (FIGURE 14.3). The internal drives include homeostatic drives such as energy balance, water balance, thermoregulation, circadian rhythms including sleep and wakefulness, and stress responses, as well as internal drives toward reproductive and defensive behavior. These drives are closely associated with the circuitry of the hypothalamus, as we'll see further below. External drives arise from sources outside the body itself. These include drives in response to threats, sexual or reproductive opportunities, parental attachment drives, social dominance, and affiliation. These types of drives are more closely associated with the circuitry of the amygdala, as we'll see in a moment. At this point in the progress of neuroscience, our list of drives is almost certainly incomplete. However, the ones listed above are the most well studied so far.

Feelings: The Sensory Side of Motivation

Before we turn to the circuitry of motivation in the hypothalamus and amygdala, let's consider one final point about

Internal drives	External drives
Drives Energy balance Water balance Thermoregulation Circadian rhythms Stress responses Reproductive behaviors Defensive behaviors	Response to outside threat Response to reproductive opportunity Response to social situation Parental attachment Affiliation
Hypothalamus	**Amygdala**

FIGURE 14.3 Internal and external survival drives. Internal drives tend to be coordinated by the hypothalamus from internal sensory inputs, while external drives tend to be coordinated by the amygdala from external sensory inputs.

motivations in general. Many basic drives are about keeping the body's internal parameters in balance: energy, temperature, chemical composition, and so on. Hence, many motivations become active only when these bodily parameters depart from the ideal points. This means that the brain needs a mechanism for sensing the body's internal state to set its motivational priorities in the first place.

As you may recall from Chapters 6 and 13, interoception refers to the brain function of internal sensory perception. Interoceptors in every body organ detect parameters like glucose concentration, sodium and potassium balance, temperature, hormone concentrations, heart rate, blood pressure, and metabolic signals from muscle and adipose (fat-storing) tissue. These signals tell the body which parameters are in balance and which ones have deviated to levels that may affect survival. This allows the brain to respond to deviations using the three mechanisms at its disposal: autonomic responses, neuroendocrine (hormonal) responses, and behavioral responses. For example, a dehydrated organism may need to increase its heart rate and blood pressure (autonomic responses), decrease urine output from the kidneys (via neuroendocrine responses), and, most importantly, drop whatever it's currently doing and locate a source of water.

Exactly how and where to find water are problems for other parts of the brain. However, these regions need to know what problem most urgently needs their attention. A motivational signal like thirst is thus a prioritizing signal that specifies the relative importance of a given drive without specifying exactly what needs to be done about it. Competing motivations are the brain's strategy for solving the difficult balancing act of survival. The challenge is to assign the right priority to each of the basic drives, so as to ensure the best chances of survival. To meet this challenge, the body needs accurate information about internal states via interoception and accurate information about external threats and opportunities via the external sensory organs. As we saw in Chapter 13, the bodily sensations or "feelings" generated by this information can be considered the "sensory side" of emotions. In this framework, we can think of motivation as the "motor side" of emotions, setting priorities to guide our behavior so that it meets our basic needs for survival.

The Circuitry of Motivation: Basic Drives

Let's now turn to the key brain structures involved in motivation.

Hypothalamus and Homeostatic Drives

The hypothalamus, as you may recall from Chapter 2, is a key structure in homeostasis: the maintenance of the internal environment at, or near, a balance optimal for survival. Maintaining homeostasis requires collecting information about the internal state of the body and then coordinating a response to any perturbations from the ideal set points. Hypothalamic neurons receive rich sensory input from the body's many kinds of interoceptors. In addition, certain parts of the hypothalamus have tiny "windows" in the otherwise nearly impermeable blood–brain barrier. Through these windows of permeability, hypothalamic neurons can sample the bloodstream itself to determine circulating levels of electrolytes, metabolic markers such as glucose or lactate, and various hormones and peptide signals secreted by organs throughout the body. Hypothalamic neurons can then use this information to coordinate the three-prong autonomic, hormonal, and motivational outputs needed to correct the imbalances.

The hypothalamus contains more than two dozen different nuclei (see FIGURE 14.4) (Iversen, Iversen, & Saper, 2000). It

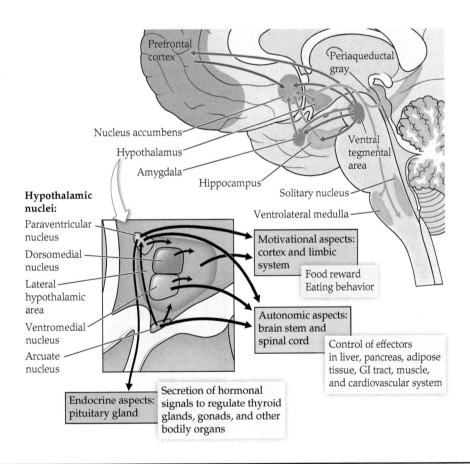

FIGURE 14.4 **The hypothalamus is involved in a wide range of behaviors.** The hypothalamus is connected directly with the nucleus accumbens, and indirectly with the prefrontal cortex, hippocampus, and amygdala, all of which are part of the brain's motivational architecture. These connections direct the autonomic, endocrine, and motivational aspects of homeostasis.

was once thought that each nucleus had a specific role in controlling one of the particular drive states. For example, one nucleus was considered a "hunger center," whereas another was considered a "**satiety** [i.e., fullness] center." Similarly opposed pairs of nuclei were thought to control thirst versus water satiety and heat-gaining versus heat-shedding drives.

We now know that this view of the hypothalamus was overly simplistic. As in almost every biological system, there is not a precise one-to-one mapping of a single specific function onto a single specific structure. For example, the ventromedial nucleus, once considered a satiety center, also plays a role in female sexual behavior (Griffin & Flanagan-Cato, 2011). The medial preoptic area is another example of differential function. In males, this area is greatly enlarged and coordinates sexual responses: hormone release, erection, sexual approach, and copulation. In females, however, this same nucleus is important not for sexual approach but for maternal behavior toward young offspring (Paredes, 2009). Neurons of the suprachiasmatic nucleus control circadian rhythms, a function important for the timing of drives as diverse as sleep, growth, feeding, reproduction, and more (Iversen et al., 2000).

Some structures also seem to have a more generic "input" or interoceptive function across many different drives. The bloodstream-sampling areas known as the organum vasculosum of the lateral terminalis and **subfornical organ** are examples of these kinds of input nuclei (McAdams & Maunsell, 1999; McKinley, Allen, Burns, Colvill, & Oldfield, 1998). Other structures have an "output" function across many kinds of drives; the **arcuate nucleus**, for example, coordinates many different forms of hormonal outputs from the pituitary gland (Zac-Varghese, Tan, & Bloom, 2010).

How do all these nuclei work together to generate a basic drive? Let's take the example of energy balance, which is probably the most well studied of all hypothalamic functions. Energy balance turns out to be much more complicated than simply monitoring glucose levels and driving a feeding behavior whenever the levels get too low. In fact, the body provides the brain with a vast and rich array of interoceptive inputs to guide feeding behavior and metabolism. During food consumption, the stomach produces a peptide called **ghrelin** that circulates to the hypothalamus and actually increases hunger to drive further eating. The pancreas not only secretes digestive enzymes into the gut, but also secretes a pancreatic polypeptide that alters the activity of hypothalamic neurons. Pancreatic **insulin** also serves as a feedback signal for energy regulation in the hypothalamus, quite aside from its well-known function in regulating blood glucose levels. The small intestine secretes a peptide called **cholecystokinin**, which acts throughout the digestive system to stimulate the secretion of digestive enzymes, while also acting on the hypothalamus and other areas of the central nervous system to suppress hunger and induce satiety.

Some of the most dramatic feedback effects, however, come from a protein called **leptin**. The source of leptin is the body's adipose tissue. As this tissue fills with stored fat, it releases more and more leptin into the bloodstream. Leptin acts in the hypothalamus to inhibit food consumption and energy storage. In effect, adipose tissue actually tells the brain when it is "full" and stimulates a reduction in energy intake. So-called **ob/ob mice**, which lack the genes for leptin (or its receptors in the brain), become strikingly obese (see FIGURE 14.5) (Friedman & Halaas, 1998). Humans with this rare mutation show similar effects, although the vast majority of people with obesity do not have any such mutation (Clement et al., 1998; Mantzoros, 1999). The discovery of leptin raised hopes of finding a "cure" for obesity in the form of a medication that would stimulate leptin receptors. Unfortunately, so far, such treatments have not shown much effectiveness (Jequier, 2002).

Inside the hypothalamus, the lateral hypothalamic area, ventromedial nucleus, and paraventricular nucleus are important regions for regulating energy balance (FIGURE 14.6). Here the signaling pathways become yet more complicated, and the details are still under study. We know that leptin acts on neurons in the arcuate nucleus and that these neurons stimulate energy intake using another neurotransmitter, **neuropeptide Y (NPY)**. NPY acts on the lateral hypothalamus, and in particular the paraventricular nucleus, to stimulate energy intake and feeding behavior. Blocking the function of NPY actually reduces the obesity of leptin-deficient mice, highlighting the importance of this system (Chugh & Sharma, 2012). Working in the opposite direction, a different collection of neurons in the arcuate nucleus uses a different set of neurotransmitters, called pro-opiomelanocortin (POMC), to reduce food intake and energy storage (Biebermann, Kuhnen, Kleinau, & Krude, 2012). So, inside the hypothalamus itself, the opposed neurotransmitter systems of NPY and POMC may work together to stimulate or inhibit energy intake as necessary to maintain an appropriate balance.

If all of this detail seems confusing, consider that the complete mechanisms of energy regulation in the hypothalamus are even more complex and not yet fully understood.

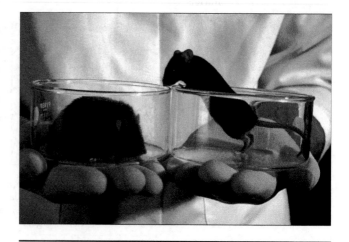

FIGURE 14.5 Obesity is influenced by the presence of hormones. The mouse on the left has a mutation in the ob gene and is unable to produce leptin. The mouse on the right is a wild-type mouse with normal leptin production.

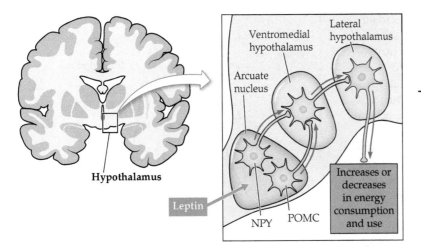

FIGURE 14.6 Regulation of eating behavior by the hypothalamus. Leptin stimulates receptors in the arcuate nucleus of the hypothalamus to release neuropeptide Y (NPY). An alternate pathway uses the neurotransmitter pro-opiomelanocortin (POMC). Although these pathways are not yet fully understood, the output from the arcuate nucleus stimulates the ventromedial hypothalamus and the lateral hypothalamus to change energy intake and use. The pathway that uses NPY generally increases energy intake, whereas the pathway that uses POMC generally reduces food intake.

However, we must remember two key points. First, the body itself is far from a passive recipient of neural output; it plays an active role in generating motivational signals through the hypothalamus and does so through sensory feedback mechanisms at least as rich and complex as those of vision, hearing, or touch. Much of our motivational signaling comes from our bodily needs, and the body uses a finely nuanced language of signals to tell the brain about those needs. Second, the complexity of even a so-called "basic" drive, such as maintaining energy balance, is far from fully understood, even after decades of investigation. Other survival drives almost certainly have an architecture of equal or greater complexity. Much of this complexity is devoted to the internal regulatory mechanisms: autonomic and hormonal responses. Motivation is only the third, behavioral, arm of the general homeostatic response.

Amygdala and External-World Drives

An organism whose motivations came only from internal needs would not survive for long. In the outside world lie both threats and opportunities: predators and rivals, sources of food, potential mates, and in social species, friends and allies. The sensory systems that tell us about the outside world are different from the interoceptive systems that tell us about the body. Instead of lactate levels, leptin proteins, and thermoreceptors, we have the photoreceptors of the retina, the auditory receptors of the cochlea, and the scent receptors of the olfactory bulbs. All of these systems provide input to the nuclei of the amygdala (FIGURE 14.7). However, many of the output channels of the amygdala are broadly similar to those of the hypothalamus: autonomic, endocrine, and motivational/behavioral. Through

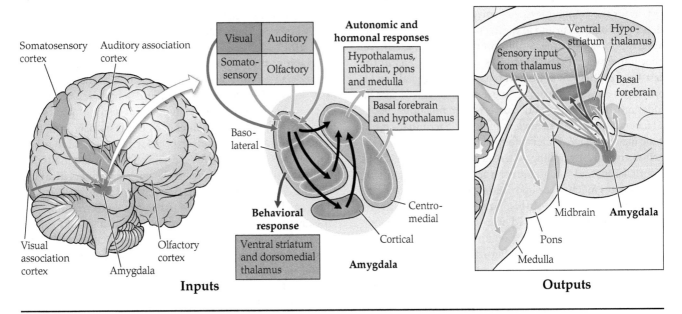

Inputs

Outputs

FIGURE 14.7 **The amygdala.** Like the hypothalamus, the amygdala contains several nuclei. This coronal section through the brain depicts the location of the amygdala and some nuclei within the medial temporal lobe. The basolateral nuclei take sensory input from the thalamus and cortex, while the central and medial nuclei send behavior-regulating output to the brainstem, the hypothalamus, and indirectly to the prefrontal cortex.

these pathways, the amygdala can coordinate responses to survival and reproductive needs that arise from external sources, much as the hypothalamus coordinates responses to survival and reproductive needs that arise from internal sources. The functional role of the amygdala is to determine the significance of outside stimuli to personal survival and reproduction and to initiate autonomic, endocrine, and behavioral responses accordingly.

The amygdala contains fewer nuclei than the hypothalamus, possibly because it manages a smaller set of inputs and drive states. Once again, there is no perfect one-to-one mapping of a single drive onto a single nucleus. However, some nuclei are more closely associated with particular functions. For example, electrical stimulation of the **basal nucleus** produces defensive behavior (Shaikh & Siegel, 1994), whereas stimulation of the **accessory basal nucleus** may produce fear or attack behaviors (Nader, Majidishad, Amorapanth, & LeDoux, 2001).

Some structures, often grouped together and known as the basolateral nuclei of the amygdala (or basolateral amygdala), collect input from multiple sensory areas in the cortex and brainstem (Turner & Herkenham, 1991). They are extraordinarily fast in their response to outside stimuli. Amygdala neurons can respond to threatening stimuli in as little as 25 milliseconds. This is much faster than in other complex sensory areas such as the cortex, where coordinated responses may not appear for 100–300 milliseconds (Quirk, Repa, & LeDoux, 1995). The rapid response time of the amygdala probably reflects its importance in escaping threats from predators or other hostile organisms.

Other amygdala structures, often grouped together and known as the centromedial nuclei (or centromedial amygdala), serve mostly as output nuclei for coordinating the responses of other areas. For example, the **central nucleus** is especially important for the autonomic side of amygdala responses: it connects to the brainstem and to the hypothalamus to coordinate these responses (Veening, Swanson, & Sawchenko, 1984). Another important output structure is the **bed nucleus of the stria terminalis**, which lies just outside the amygdala and is sometimes considered part of an extended amygdala that includes nearby structures with closely related functions (Fudge & Haber, 2001). The bed nucleus of the stria terminalis is one of the major endocrine and autonomic output pathways of the entire amygdala. By linking with neuroendocrine nuclei in the hypothalamus and autonomic control nuclei in the brainstem, it coordinates much of the body's stress response. Many of the autonomic components of this "fight-or-flight" response are familiar to everyone: increased heart rate and respiration, increased muscle tension to the point of tremor, sweating, and inhibition of digestive activity. Furthermore, important hormonal effects include a cascade of hypothalamic, pituitary, and adrenal gland activity that leads to the release of so-called stress hormones or **glucocorticoid hormones**. These hormones affect every cell in the entire body, promoting the release of glucose and other energy sources into the blood as well as suppressing inflammation and immune responses.

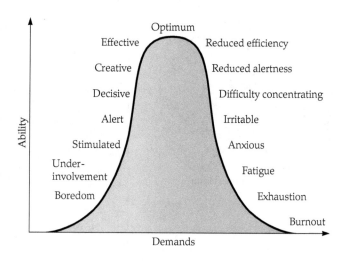

FIGURE 14.8 **The stress response curve.** Up to a point, increased stress enhances performance because it increases cognitive and immune function. Beyond that point, however, the body becomes exhausted and the same cognitive and immune functions that were previously improved are now impaired.

The stress response is sometimes called **allostasis**: achieving stability through physiological or behavioral change in the face of an external challenge, rather than by keeping internal parameters constant as in homeostasis. In the short term, allostatic responses prepare the body for challenge or injury (FIGURE 14.8). However, if activated chronically, harmful effects on the body may ensue. Immune suppression, metabolic changes, high blood pressure, and alterations in mood and brain function may all appear after prolonged allostatic challenges. The effects of chronic allostatic challenge have been proposed as a basis for many of the chronic illnesses that are prevalent in industrialized societies, such as heart disease and autoimmune disorders (McAdams & Maunsell, 1999; McEwen, 1999; Vitaliano et al., 2002).

Having prepared the body's physiology for action through autonomic and hormonal signals, the amygdala must also prioritize an appropriate behavioral response. Once again, the amygdala itself does not need to specify the precise strategy and movements as the response; it merely needs to provide a motivating or prioritizing signal to other brain areas so that they focus their efforts on the matter at hand. The basolateral nuclei of the amygdala are critical for this third arm of the allostatic response (Gardner, 2011). These nuclei send outputs to the thalamus and striatum, specifically to the parts of these structures that connect to areas in the frontal lobes that are critical for evaluation and decision making. We consider these cortical areas in more detail in later sections and in other chapters. For now, just remember that the amygdala coordinates motivational as well as autonomic and hormonal responses to outside stimuli and that the output pathway involves the striatum. We'll look at precisely *how* the striatum contributes to motivation later in the chapter.

Midbrain Dopamine Neurons and the Common Currency of Motivation

As we've seen, the hypothalamus and amygdala have just the right sorts of inputs and outputs to keep track of internal needs and external threats/opportunities. They also have just the right sorts of outputs to coordinate the body's responses to these kinds of disturbances. Yet when it comes to the motivational response, there is still one step missing: the assignment of priority, or importance. Without this step, it is impossible to sustain the delicate balancing act between all of the competing drives of survival and reproduction. Two drives often come into conflict, and satisfying one often means denying the other.

For example, imagine you are a thirsty antelope approaching a watering hole in the desert. From previous experience, you have seen that the watering hole can be dangerous: alligators often snatch unwary prey as they bend down to drink. Which should take precedence: the motivation to drink from the watering hole or the motivation to stay away from the predatory alligators lurking beneath the surface? To decide, you will need some sort of motivational common currency for predicting the relative value of different actions, behaviors, goals, or resources. This is where the activity of midbrain dopaminergic neurons becomes important.

Dopamine is a neurotransmitter that is critical to motivation, reward, and learning, as we will see later in the chapter. You may also recall its importance in motor functions and in internally generated actions from Chapter 7. This one neurotransmitter has an immensely important role in nearly every aspect of behavioral control, from reward to decision making, cognition, and movement. Yet there are fewer than 500,000 dopamine-containing neurons in the entire human brain (Brundin et al., 1987), of a total population of about 80 billion neurons (Geake & Cooper, 2003). To put these numbers in perspective, imagine a tiny village of 12,000 people setting most of the motivational priorities for an entire world population of 7 billion. Dopaminergic neurons are influential to a degree far beyond what their tiny numbers might suggest.

Most dopaminergic neurons live in one of two places in the midbrain: the substantia nigra and the **ventral tegmental area (VTA)** (FIGURE 14.9). The substantia nigra, or "black substance," is named for the dark appearance of its neurons, which contain the pigment melanin in addition to the neurotransmitter dopamine. Dopamine-containing neurons comprise around 90% of the neurons in the **substantia nigra pars compacta** (the subregion of the substantia nigra that is home to dopamine-containing neurons) (Lacey, Mercuri, & North, 1989). They are the origin of a dopamine pathway known as the **nigrostriatal pathway**, which leads (as one might expect) to widespread areas of the striatum (Guyenet & Aghajanian, 1978). Here they are essential to the proper

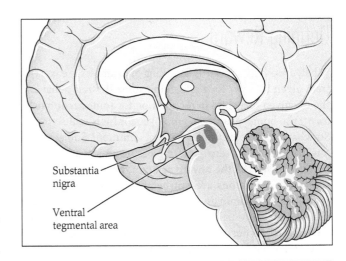

FIGURE 14.9 **The ventral tegmental area and the substantia nigra.** Both of these areas are important parts of the midbrain dopamine network.

functioning of the corticostriatal–thalamic loops that initiate and sustain activity in motor, premotor, prefrontal, orbitofrontal, and cingulate areas of the cortex. As you may recall from Chapter 7, substantia nigra neurons are progressively lost in Parkinson's disease. The results are progressive impairments in motor function as well as in cognition and mood regulation.

The VTA also contains many dopaminergic neurons, although here they are less densely packed and more intermixed with nondopaminergic neurons. These neurons send projections to the striatum and also to the cortex. The connections from the VTA to the cortex are sometimes divided into separate pathways depending on their precise destination. For example, a **mesocortical pathway** projects to areas of the prefrontal cortex involved in planning and cognition, whereas a **mesolimbic pathway** projects to more ventral and medial areas in the anterior cingulate cortex and orbitofrontal cortex. These areas are important in stimulus evaluation and emotion regulation. We'll consider these pathways in more detail later in the chapter.

Reward, Learning, and the Brain

How, exactly, do dopaminergic neurons contribute to reward, motivation, and learning? To understand this, we'll first need to understand exactly what a reward is supposed to be, how the brain might decide on the value of a reward, and how these functions are intimately intertwined with the functions of learning and motivation. So, before we delve any deeper into the functions of dopamine, let's spend this section examining these issues.

Defining Reward

What, exactly, is a reward? Thinking of examples is easy: the treat given to a pet for performing some desired behavior; the toy given to a child in recognition for some accomplishment; the bonus paid to an employee for high achievement. So what do these examples have in common? Subjectively, rewards bring us a sensation of pleasure or joy, as well as a motivation to seek the reward again in the future. However, subjective definitions are not helpful for studying reward processes in the brain under carefully controlled conditions. This is especially true for studies in animals, who cannot give us verbal reports of their subjective experiences. So how do we tell what is rewarding to a rat or a monkey?

Objectively, we find that rewards tend to promote the behavior that led to the reward. In the early 20th century, the **behaviorist** school of psychology (FIGURE 14.10) defined reward in such objective, operational terms: a reward, or **reinforcer,** was considered any stimulus that increases the frequency or the intensity of behavior that led to the reward in the first place. Alternatively, a reward could be considered any stimulus that an animal would work to obtain. Conversely, a punishment would be considered any stimulus that an animal would work to avoid. Since behavior is much more straightforward to measure than subjective experience, this definition allowed us to begin to tackle the problems of learning and motivation. Objective, behavioral measures of stimulus value (reward or punishment) are still used widely today.

Yet this operational definition leaves aside the bigger question of *why* a given stimulus should produce the behavioral effects of a reward. This question becomes all the more important

FIGURE 14.10 **John Watson was an early supporter of the behaviorist school of psychology.**

given that the value of a reward can be quite variable depending on the internal state of the organism. The subjective pleasure of eating that first handful of popcorn at a movie theater may be high, but the subjective experience of eating the 21st handful may actually switch to being negative (**aversive**). In behavioral terms, we might find that you would be willing to pay money to eat the first handful, but would also be willing to pay money to *avoid* being forced to eat the 21st handful.

How can we unify the objective and the subjective accounts of reward? Here we will probably find it useful to go back to the concepts of interoception, homeostasis, and allostasis from the previous section. Remember that the brain's job is to ensure that the body is able to survive and reproduce. The value of a stimulus like a piece of popcorn or a mouthful of water is not built into the stimulus itself. Instead, the value depends completely on whether the stimulus is helpful or unhelpful in satisfying the body's basic homeostatic and allostatic drives. We cannot predict anything about the reward value of a mouthful of water without knowing something about how it maps onto the internal state of the organism in question.

If we consider reward in these terms, we can go one step further than the operational definition of the behaviorists and define reward in more general terms: a **reward** is any stimulus that moves the homeostatic or allostatic balance of the organism closer to its ideal set points. In practical terms, researchers studying the effects of reward will usually deprive the subjects of food or water before the experiment to ensure that the rewarding stimuli have the desired homeostatic effect. Also, as we'll see later on, addictive substances can hijack the neural signaling mechanisms of reward, creating false signals of improvement in the homeostatic balance even when no actual improvement is occurring. Conversely, a **punishment** is any stimulus that moves the homeostatic or allostatic balance of the organism farther away from its ideal set points.

It is important to note the difference between primary rewards, which directly address homeostatic or allostatic needs, and **secondary rewards** (also called abstract rewards), whose value comes from indirect association with some set of primary rewards (FIGURE 14.11). Examples of primary rewards might include food, water, sexual opportunities, and, in social species, companionship. Examples of secondary rewards in humans might include money or consumer goods. In an animal such as a dog, a secondary reward might be the familiar sound of a box of treats being shaken. If that sound had previously been a reliable predictor of being given a treat, the sound itself can acquire a reward value through learning over repeated exposures.

Learning from Reward Using Prediction Error

The previous example brings us back to an essential feature of rewards: they produce learning. Why should this be so? Keeping the body alive is not an easy task for an animal. The

FIGURE 14.11 **Primary and secondary rewards.** (a) Primary rewards provide an inherent survival advantage, such as food or drink. (b) Secondary rewards have no direct survival advantage, but we have learned that they enable us to get the primary rewards.

necessary ingredients for survival are rarely close at hand. For example, in many environments, sources of food are widely scattered, undependable in availability, uncertain in quality and quantity, and all too often scooped up by some other organism a little quicker to arrive on the scene. To stay alive, animals must do more than just wander randomly, living in the present, spotting resources as they go and hoping for the best. They must not only spot the resources they need, but also spot the stimuli that *predict* how to find the resources they need.

Learning how to predict rewards is an essential cognitive function that is found in human beings, but is also far from specific to our species. All of our vertebrate relatives, from hagfish to hedgehogs, show some form of reinforcement learning (Stephenson-Jones, Floros, Robertson, & Grillner, 2012). The neural circuitry of reinforcement learning is also highly consistent across species, involving many of the same midbrain dopamine neurons and their targets in the striatum and the rest of the telencephalon (Stephenson-Jones et al., 2012). As we saw in Chapter 2, even the drive-building circuitry of the hypothalamus and amygdala is found in most vertebrate species in some form or another. Brains seem to have discovered the basic principles of effective valuation

and reward learning long ago and held to these principles ever since. So how does the brain learn to predict rewards?

The key to effective association learning seems to lie in **prediction error**: the discrepancy between the expected outcome of an action and the outcome that actually occurred. Let's take a simple example from an experimental setting (FIGURE 14.12). A monkey is placed in a room with a

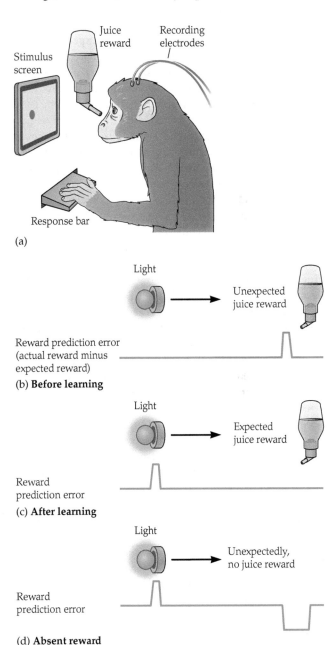

FIGURE 14.12 **The role of prediction error during associative learning.** (a) The monkey is seated and will receive a juice reward when the response bar moves. (b) Before learning, the juice reward is unexpected, so its arrival has positive prediction error (better than expected). (c) After learning, the juice is expected after the light, so it no longer has positive prediction error. The positive prediction error then shifts to the light, which signals that a reward will soon arrive. (d) If for some reason the juice does not arrive as expected, its absence has negative prediction error (worse than expected). These prediction error signals can be used to guide associative learning.

machine with a lever on the side. It pulls the lever, with no clear expectation of outcome. However, the machine suddenly dispenses a tasty treat to the hungry monkey. This produces a large, positive prediction error signal: the outcome was much better than expected. This signal increases the probability of the behavior that led to the unexpectedly rewarding outcome. Soon, the monkey pulls the lever again, and another tasty treat appears. Again, a positive prediction error signal arises, although the magnitude is slightly smaller this time because the monkey had some expectation of a reward. Over a few trials, the monkey's lever pressing gradually increases to a steady level and, at the same time, the reward prediction error gradually diminishes to zero. Now, when the monkey sees a treat appear after pulling the lever, the outcome is "just as expected." The treats no longer provide any "better than expected" signal, although they remain tasty. At this point, learning is complete. The reward prediction error signal has allowed the monkey to learn by increasing the frequency of the rewarded behavior.

Now let us imagine that the machine runs out of treats. Suddenly, when the monkey pulls the lever, no treat appears. This produces a large negative prediction error signal: the outcome was much worse than expected. This signal now *decreases* the probability of the behavior that produced the unexpectedly bad outcome. Frustrated, the monkey pulls the lever again, but once again, no tasty treat appears. Once again, a negative prediction error signal reduces the likelihood of future lever pulling. Over time, the monkey gradually gives up on pulling the lever; again, the negative prediction error gradually diminishes to zero. Just as it was in the beginning, the nonappearance of a treat after a lever press is now just as expected. Once again, learning is complete, and the reward prediction error signal has allowed the monkey to learn, this time by decreasing the frequency of the unrewarded behavior.

The usefulness of prediction error signals for reinforcement learning was first described mathematically by the psychologists Rescorla and Wagner in 1972, and such models of learning are therefore often called **Rescorla–Wagner models** of learning (Rescorla, 1972; Rescorla & Wagner, 1972; Wasserman, 1994). The model has become popular because it explains learning better than the previous models did. In addition, as we shall see in the next section, reward prediction error signals seem to have an actual biological substrate in the firing rates of midbrain dopamine neurons.

A more elaborate version of the prediction error model is known as the **temporal difference learning model** (O'Doherty, Dayan, Friston, Critchley, & Dolan, 2003; Seymour et al., 2004). This model incorporates not only the magnitude but also the timing of the expected reward, so that a reward of the expected size that comes *earlier* than expected will also have a positive prediction error, whereas a reward that comes *later* than expected will have a negative prediction error. Once again, the error signals in the temporal difference model seem to fit the firing rates of midbrain dopamine neurons quite well. Other, still more elaborate models have also been proposed to accommodate the degree of risk or

uncertainty of a reward and even the uncertainty *about* the degree of uncertainty of the reward (i.e., knowledge about whether something usually works or usually does not work in obtaining a reward) (Dreher, Kohn, & Berman, 2006; Schultz, 2006; Tobler, O'Doherty, Dolan, & Schultz, 2007). This field has lately become one of the more active fields of neuroscience, likely because of the exciting possibility of bringing together mathematical and neurobiological accounts of brain function. In the past, this kind of unification has been a prelude to major scientific advances, as in the physics of the 18th century and the chemistry of the 19th century.

"Liking" Is Different from "Wanting"

One last point to consider before we return to the world of neurotransmitters is the difference between **liking** and **wanting**. Intuitively, most of us would assume that the two go together: if we like something, we typically have a desire to obtain it, and if we want something, we typically enjoy getting it. In fact, the two are more separate than they may appear. Both the subjective sensations and the underlying neural mechanisms of liking and wanting are quite different, as we will see in the next section.

The difference between liking and wanting is especially relevant in the setting of addiction. For many addictive substances, the first few exposures produce a strong pleasant or rewarding sensation known colloquially as a *rush*. However, with subsequent exposures, the rush diminishes. At the same time, paradoxically, the amount of effort one is willing to expend to obtain the drug gradually increases. Ultimately, in full-blown addiction, this motivation supersedes almost all others, although the actual rush of pleasure from using the drug is small or nonexistent. For example, cigarette smokers sometimes report little actual enjoyment from smoking despite a ferocious compulsion to continue doing so (FIGURE 14.13).

FIGURE 14.13 Cigarette smokers sometimes report that they do not especially enjoy smoking, although they feel strongly compelled to smoke.

It is helpful to remember that liking is a present-moment, interoceptive sensation of well-being or homeostatic satisfaction. Wanting, on the other hand, is a future prediction of the outcome of liking. Although these two systems interact, their underlying circuitry is quite distinct, as are the relevant neurotransmitter systems. To understand how addiction develops, we must understand the separate basis of immediate liking versus learned wanting. Let's now turn to two neurotransmitter systems, the opioid system and the dopamine system, and see what roles they play in the subjective sensations of liking versus wanting.

Opioids and the Sensation of Pleasure

The opioid system has diverse functions, including some related to the experience of reward. Let's take a closer look.

Opioids, Opioid Receptors, and Opioid Functions

Two of the major functions of the opioid system have been known since antiquity. The first of these functions is in relieving the sensation of pain. The ancient Sumerian and Egyptian civilizations cultivated and made use of the opium poppy for pain relief, including analgesia during medical procedures. They also noted the powerful effect of opium in producing euphoria: a sensation of intense pleasure. Recreational use of opium is almost certainly as ancient. Widespread use of opium was well documented in the Middle

East, Europe, and China by the 14th and 15th centuries. The addictive potential of opium was also recognized early on, and official attempts to limit or prohibit its use go back nearly 300 years in some parts of the world, such as China.

Extracts of poppy seeds remained in widespread use through the 19th and early 20th centuries for the relief of pain, as well as for a bevy of other uses including sleep promotion and sedation and as a treatment for diverse forms of illness.

In the 19th century chemists isolated the active ingredient of the opium poppy seed and named it **morphine**, after Morpheus, the Greek god of dreams. Later in the century, they were able to alter this substance's chemical structure to give it even more powerful analgesic effects. For example, adding two acetyl groups to morphine produced a substance whose pleasure-inducing and analgesic effects were so powerful that its inventors described them as "heroic" and named the substance "heroin" in recognition of its potency. Its 19th-century inventors at the German pharmaceutical company Bayer intended heroin as a nonaddictive alternative to morphine—only later did its extremely high addictive potential become apparent. More than a century later, we are still in search of a substance that can replicate the analgesic and euphoric qualities of opioids without producing dependence.

One important question was not addressed until comparatively recently: why should the seeds of a flowering plant (FIGURE 14.14) contain a substance with such powerful effects on the nervous system of a completely different species? Being unable to flee from predators, plants have evolved the ability to synthesize these substances as a way of discouraging animals from eating them. An especially effective strategy is to evolve substances that act directly on "soft targets": the biological receptors of animals' cells. Neurons are particularly soft targets since even minor changes in their

FIGURE 14.14 Some species of poppies produce opium, which contains substances that are chemically similar to endogenous opioids used as neurotransmitters in the human brain. Compare the chemical structures of the pharmacologically active component of opium, morphine (and its chemically modified relative, heroin), versus endomorphin-1, one of the brain's endogenous opioids.

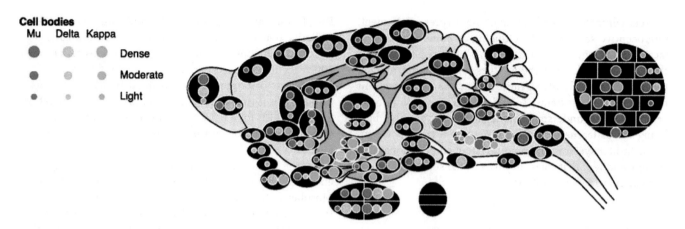

Cell bodies
Mu   Delta   Kappa

● ● ●   Dense

● ● ●   Moderate

● ● ●   Light

(See FIGURE 14.15

activity can have major effects on vital functions such as breathing and heart rate. By effectively hijacking the animals' built-in biological control systems, plants can make sure that any animal unwise enough to eat them will leave behind few offspring. Incidentally, this is a reason why so many medications (substances with disproportionately powerful effects on biological activities) have their origins in plant extracts.

If opium poppies have such powerful effects on the brain, then the brain itself should contain its own opiumlike substances, as well as receptors for those substances. As it turns out, this is precisely the case. Opioid receptors were identified in the brain in 1973. Today we recognize four different major subtypes, each with slightly different distributions in the central nervous system and, thus, slightly different functions (Dietis, Rowbotham, & Lambert, 2011).

The **mu-opioid receptors** are especially important in analgesia and in the euphoric and rewarding effects of opioids in the brain. As we will see, they are also important players in the addictive effects of opioids. Some of the side effects of morphine and its relatives, such as respiratory depression and constipation, also act through this receptor system. The mu-opioid system is also an important component of the brain's natural reward system, as we will see.

In contrast, the **kappa-opioid receptors** seem to mediate antirewarding effects of opioids in the brain. Substances that stimulate this receptor system, far from producing euphoria and addiction, actually produce dysphoric (unpleasant) reactions in humans and act as negative reinforcers in animals (Wee & Koob, 2010).

The mu- and the kappa-opioid receptors tend to be present in the same brain structures, suggesting that they may have opposite effects on the same systems. Although it is tempting to consider the mu- and kappa-opioid systems opposite players in reward and addiction, their actual roles do not complement one another exactly. For example, the kappa-opioid system seems to induce aversion while at the same time still relieving pain (although its pain-relieving effects take place more in the spinal cord than the brain). At this point, we are still attempting to tease apart the roles of these two systems in reward, addiction, analgesia, and other functions.

The two other subtypes of opioid receptors are known as the **delta-opioid receptors** and the **nociceptin receptors.**

FIGURE 14.15 **The distribution of the mu-, delta-, and kappa-opioid receptors in the rat brain.** The different type of receptor is indicated by the color. The density of receptors within a particular region is indicated by the size of the circle. The three black ovals outside the brain are blowups showing the receptors in (clockwise, from the top) the thalamus, the pituitary, and the amygdala.

These systems are less well understood. The delta-opioid receptors have a different brain distribution than that of the mu- and kappa-opioid receptors, although some of the functions of these different opioid receptor subtypes appear similar. For example, stimulating delta receptors also seems to produce some analgesia, and the delta-opioid system also appears to be important in opioid dependence. Recent studies have suggested that substances that stimulate the delta-opioid system may also have some antidepressant effects (Pradhan, Befort, Nozaki, Gaveriaux-Ruff, & Kieffer, 2011). However, it remains to be seen whether delta-opioid agonists will turn out to be useful antidepressant medications. (See FIGURE 14.15 for a depiction of where in the brain these different opioid receptors can be found.)

To make matters more complicated, the brain also contains an entire family of neurotransmitters that act on the opioid receptors. The opium poppy attempts to disrupt the functions of these transmitters by making its own "pirate versions" of these transmitters, such as morphine. The opioid neurotransmitter family is large and includes small proteins known as **enkephalins, dynorphins,** and **beta-endorphin.** All of the transmitters act on all of the receptors to some degree. In addition, both the transmitters and the receptors can be found widely throughout the brain and spinal cord.

Overall, the opioid system does not seem to segregate itself so neatly into a small set of neural structures and pathways (unlike the dopamine system, as we saw earlier in this chapter). Instead, a whole family of opioid neurotransmitters and receptors is distributed widely throughout the central nervous system. The various members of this opioid family also seem to have partly overlapping roles and do not map neatly onto separate functions. This is in part because each transmitter acts on many receptors and in part because each set of transmitters and receptors operates on many neurons all over the nervous system. Thus, stimulating any one neurotransmitter or receptor produces many different effects at many different sites in the brain. In broad terms, however, there is some distinction between the mu- and delta-opioid receptor system on the one hand and the kappa-opioid receptor system on the other. The mu- and delta-opioid system seems to be important for the euphoric, rewarding, and dependence-forming properties of opioids. By contrast, the kappa-opioid system has a role in aversion and antireward.

Opioids and Reward

How do we know what role opioids play in reward? Subjectively, humans have reported the intensely euphoric effects of opioid substances for thousands of years. However, opioids also seem to enhance the reward value of other kinds of naturally occurring rewards. For example, in China, centuries of historical reports describe human beings using opioids to enhance sexual pleasure. More recently, neuroscientists have been able to study the role of opioids in reward experimentally.

A key finding is that mu- or delta-opioid agonists enhance the pleasantness of natural rewards and decrease the unpleasantness of naturally aversive stimuli. For example, if we inject these substances into the VTA or nucleus accumbens of a rat, we find that this stimulates feeding behavior. More specifically, however, we find that the increase is especially pronounced for more rewarding foods such as a high-sucrose solution. When we inject the opioid agonists into the nucleus accumbens, the rats show more "food-enjoying" behaviors such as lip-licking. Conversely, blocking these mu receptors causes the rats to consume less of a high-sucrose solution, although they continue to eat the same amount of less tasty, standard rat chow (see FIGURE 14.16) (Giuliano, Robbins, Nathan, Bullmore, & Everitt, 2012; Katsuura, Heckmann, & Taha, 2011).

We see similar effects of such agonists on food preference. For example, we can offer a rat a choice between two foods with identical nutritional content but different flavors. Injecting a mu-receptor agonist into the nucleus accumbens leads the rat to consume more of its favorite-flavored food over its less-preferred food. Injecting a kappa-receptor agonist into the same area has the opposite effect: the rat now eats more of its less-preferred food and less of its favorite food. Similarly, blocking the mu receptor agonist causes the rat to eat less of its favorite food, reaching satiety earlier (Bodnar, Glass, Ragnauth, & Cooper, 1995; Kelley, Bless, & Swanson, 1996; Zhang & Kelley, 1997, 2000).

Overall, the mu-opioid system seems to play a key role in the current reward value or the liking of a given stimulus: a function that has to do with a state of euphoria, pleasantness, or well-being in the present moment. Let's note again that the present-moment liking of a stimulus is quite separate from the wanting of a stimulus in future: the former is about how pleasant a stimulus is *right now*, whereas the latter is about how pleasant a stimulus is *going to be*, so far as your brain can predict, based on past experience. Let's also note that you don't need any past experience to determine current liking or pleasantness: this is just a matter of reading your body's internal state and determining whether it is close to or far away from the ideal parameters. However, you do need past experience with a stimulus to decide whether you want it or not: only from past experiences of liking or disliking can you learn to determine whether a stimulus is worth wanting. Hence, although the mu-opioid system seems to be important for determining the current liking of a reward, a different mechanism is needed to actually learn what stimuli will bring these rewards and to motivate the organism to pursue them. This is where the dopamine system comes into the picture, as we'll see in the next section.

Dopamine, Learning, Motivation, and Reward

Dopamine is a key neurotransmitter for motivation and reward. Dopamine is also critical for reward learning, since predicting future rewards requires learning from the past. The dopamine-containing neurons of the substantia nigra

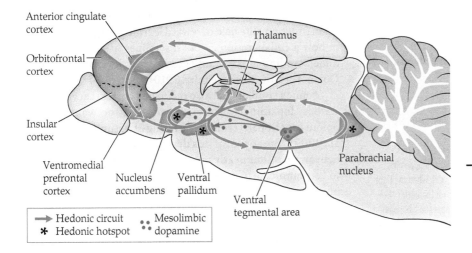

Anterior cingulate cortex

Orbitofrontal cortex

Insular cortex

Ventromedial prefrontal cortex

Nucleus accumbens

Ventral pallidum

Ventral tegmental area

Thalamus

Parabrachial nucleus

→ Hedonic circuit   •• Mesolimbic
✱ Hedonic hotspot   •• dopamine

FIGURE 14.16 Hedonic "hotspots" within the brain. In the rat brain, injections of opioids into the nucleus accumbens, ventral pallidum, or parabrachial nucleus in the brainstem increase food-enjoying behaviors such as lip-licking.

and VTA have been the most thoroughly studied with regard to these functions. Let's examine how these neurons contribute to reward learning.

Dopamine Functions in Motivation and Reward

In a typical reward learning experiment, we might provide an animal with an unexpected reward, such as a squirt of juice in the mouth (see FIGURE 14.17). The squirt of juice would be preceded by a **predictive cue** such as a flash of a light, which would reliably occur before each squirt of juice. If we

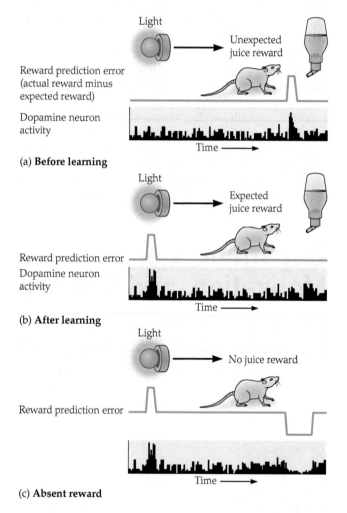

(a) **Before learning**

(b) **After learning**

(c) **Absent reward**

FIGURE 14.17 **Dopamine activity during reward learning.** (a) In this experiment, a light signals that a juice reward will soon appear. Before learning, the juice is unexpected. Its arrival has positive prediction error (better than expected), which is reflected in a burst of activity in dopamine neurons. (b) After learning, the dopamine neurons shift to firing when the light flashes, since the juice no longer has positive prediction error (no better than expected). (c) If the light flashes but no juice appears, its absence has negative prediction error (worse than expected), and the dopamine neurons temporarily reduce their activity.

now record from a dopamine neuron in the VTA or substantia nigra, we see an interesting pattern. The neuron has a "baseline" rate of firing at a low frequency, in the absence of any stimulation. However, if we suddenly provide the animal with a squirt of juice, the activity increases in a sudden burst.

Initially, the neuron shows this burst of firing only after the unexpected delivery of the juice and does not show any response to the light. However, over time, the firing pattern changes. As the animal learns that the light predicts the delivery of juice, the dopamine neuron gradually begins to fire more and more in response to the light and less and less in response to the juice itself. Once the animal has completed its learning, the dopamine neuron fires entirely in response to the light and no longer responds to the fully predicted arrival of the juice. Hence, fully predicted rewards have no effect on the activity of the dopamine neurons.

When predictions fail, we see the opposite effect. If we withhold the juice delivery, the dopamine neuron actually pauses, suspending its usual pattern of a low level of baseline activity. This is, in effect, a kind of "negative burst" relative to the baseline rate of activity. Likewise, if the juice arrives later than expected, there is a pause, followed by a burst of activity when the juice actually arrives. In either case, the amount of firing elicited by the cue (the flashing light) will decrease slightly on future trials.

As you may recall, this pattern of activity is reminiscent of the prediction error learning we discussed earlier in the chapter. According to prediction error learning models, the brain can learn how to predict future outcomes by comparing the expected outcome to the actual outcome of a given cue. If the outcome is better than expected, the prediction error signal is positive. If the outcome is worse than expected, the prediction error signal is negative. If the outcome is just as expected, then the prediction error signal is zero. We can also adjust these signals to take into account temporal errors such as "earlier than expected" or "later than expected." The dopamine neurons of the VTA and substantia nigra fire in a way that closely matches up with the prediction error signals used in models of associative learning. In fact, the role of these dopamine neurons in learning and predicting reward is one of the most prominent areas of agreement between purely mathematical and purely neurobiological accounts of brain function. The field of reward learning is a good example of how a collaboration across disciplines has improved our understanding of the brain (Pessiglione, Seymour, Flandin, Dolan, & Frith, 2006; Schultz, 2010).

A much simpler (but also much less correct) account describes dopamine function in terms of the wanting and opioid function in terms of the liking of a stimulus (Davis et al., 2009). The appeal of this description is that it maps each neurotransmitter neatly onto a specific function that is easy to communicate to patients or laypersons. It also helps us to understand a strange feature of substance dependence: how the wanting of the substance could increase over time (and be hard to unlearn) whereas at the same time the enjoyment or liking of the substance use could actually decrease.

The disadvantage of just mapping opioids onto liking and dopamine onto wanting is that it simply isn't true. As we have already seen, the opioid "system" is actually a complicated family of neurotransmitters, receptors, and neural circuits that participates in many different functions aside from reward. Likewise, the dopamine neurons of the midbrain project to different regions of the striatum and cortex in an organized fashion, via multiple different pathways, only some of which are involved in reward learning. We have already looked at some of these functions earlier in this book. So how should we think about the function of dopamine, or any other neurotransmitter for that matter? Let's take a look at this question before we move on to the specific roles of opioids and dopamine in addiction.

Unifying the Functions of Dopamine

If you think back to Chapter 7 and the role of dopamine in motor functions, you may find yourself a little bit confused at this point. Isn't dopamine the missing neurotransmitter in Parkinson's disease? And in Parkinson's disease, aren't motor symptoms the most obvious symptoms? Doesn't that mean that dopamine is important for motor functions? And if so, how does that fit with dopamine's role in learning and reward?

If you have trouble understanding how dopamine can be involved in both reward and simple movements, you're not alone. Even today, the neuroscientists who study these two separate functions struggle to find a common language for describing the functions of dopamine. And yet the architecture of the dopamine circuitry is surprisingly uniform through the nervous system: it's a highly organized system of multiple, parallel loops. Semidistinct loops of neural circuitry connect the cortex to the striatum to the globus pallidus to the thalamus, and these loops extend down into the substantia nigra (FIGURE 14.18). Some of these loops happen to serve the dorsal striatum and its cortical partners in low-level areas of motor and premotor cortex. Other loops happen to serve the ventral striatum, including the nucleus accumbens, and the orbitofrontal parts of the cortex that are crucial for assessing reward value. Common circuitry suggests a common computation, but what could this computation be? So far, we have some guesses about the general role of dopamine in the brain, but no consensus on a definitive answer.

Neuroscientists have tried to explain the different functions of dopamine in the brain in two main ways. One proposes that the different functions arise from "spatial" differences: the effects of dopamine vary depending on *where* it acts in the brain (Bergson et al., 1995; Hall et al., 1994). For example, some dopamine pathways affect basal ganglia loops through motor cortex; others affect premotor or oculomotor cortex; still others affect dorsolateral prefrontal or orbitofrontal cortex. In this view, dopamine performs essentially a similar computational function across all of these different parts of the brain, and the different behavioral functions simply depend on which neural targets are affected. For example, we might propose that dopamine is a sort of generalized neural "contrast enhancer" that increases neural firing in areas of high activity and dampens firing in areas of low activity. The observable effects of this contrast enhancement would be different depending on whether they were applied to neurons competing to control movement, neurons competing to control a cognitive strategy, or neurons competing to determine the value of a reward. Again, however, so far we have no consensus on a generalized function of any kind for dopamine neurons.

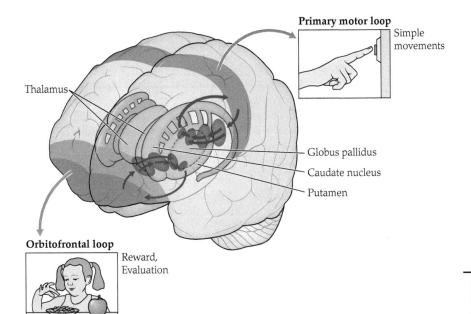

Primary motor loop

Simple movements

Thalamus

Globus pallidus

Caudate nucleus

Putamen

Orbitofrontal loop

Reward, Evaluation

FIGURE 14.18 Corticostriatal–thalamic loop circuits are important for both motor control and reward behaviors.

RESEARCH METHODS:
Measuring Neurotransmitter Levels in the Brain

Although we can measure the electrical activity of neurons, this doesn't tell us directly about how they release dopamine, serotonin, or any other neurotransmitter. To understand how neurotransmitters work in the living brain, we need methods for recording their levels directly.

One such method is microdialysis. This involves using a tiny probe to measure the neurochemical components of the extracellular fluid in some brain area, such as the nucleus accumbens (FIGURE 14.19). The probe is a tube with a semipermeable membrane that allows small molecules, such as neurotransmitters, to pass by osmosis from the extracellular fluid into the fluid (or "dialysate") within the tube itself. By collecting the dialysate, we can then determine the approximate concentration of neurotransmitters released over time. Unfortunately, the temporal resolution is low: typically, we must collect dialysate for several minutes to obtain a measurable quantity of neurotransmitter. Since many neural processes occur on the order of seconds or milliseconds, this limitation prevents us from studying many potentially important processes by microdialysis.

A more rapid method is called **fast-scan cyclic voltammetry**. Here we insert an electrode into the brain structure of interest. We then apply a voltage to the electrode and rapidly "sweep" this voltage up and down across a fixed range of values. The changes in voltage cause molecules near the electrode (such as neurotransmitters) to gain or lose

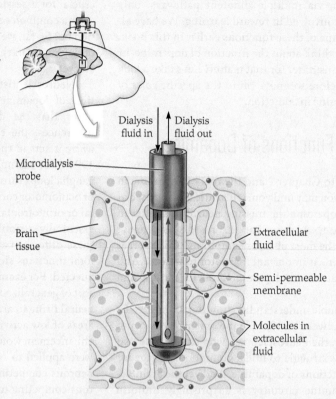

Dialysis fluid in   Dialysis fluid out

Microdialysis probe

Brain tissue

Extracellular fluid

Semi-permeable membrane

Molecules in extracellular fluid

FIGURE 14.19 Microdialysis enables researchers to sample the extracellular fluid in certain brain areas. A fluid that is chemically similar to the extracellular fluid flows into the probe. Once in the probe, it can absorb molecules from the surrounding extracellular fluid, and then it flows out again. The fluid is then analyzed to determine the chemical characteristics of the extracellular fluid.

an electron, thereby changing their charge. Since these electrochemical reactions occur at different voltages for different molecules, we can determine the precise concentration and identity of a given neurotransmitter by measuring tiny electrochemical fluctuations in the background current, using a second "working" electrode. Fast-scan cyclic voltammetry allows us to measure levels of neurotransmitters like serotonin or dopamine with high precision and with a temporal resolution of less than 100 milliseconds (Stamford, 1990). This technique is used primarily in experiments with animals, but can also be used in human beings undergoing neurosurgery for conditions such as Parkinson's disease.

Another proposal is that the different functions of dopamine arise from "temporal" differences in the timescales of dopamine release (Dreyer, Herrik, Berg, & Hounsgaard, 2010; Phillips, Stuber, Heien, Wightman, & Carelli, 2003; Wanat, Willuhn, Clark, & Phillips, 2009). In this view, the components of any given behavior operate at different timescales, and so the functions of dopamine also operate at different timescales. For example, simple sequences of movements (like pronouncing words) may take place over a few hundreds of milliseconds, whereas more complex behaviors (like planning an entire sentence or a speech) can take place over seconds or minutes. Learning skills or associations can take minutes to hours or longer. Moods can also shift over hours to days. Dopamine activity is also known to vary over different timescales, with fast phasic responses in some functions (such as movement or reward learning, as above) and much slower responses in others (such as changes in underlying mood or drive states, as seen with longer-timescale techniques like microdialysis). Even steady-state dopamine stimulation may have important functions, given that dopamine-restoring medications improve motor function and cognition (and may also have adverse behavioral side effects, as we'll see in a moment) in patients with Parkinson's disease.

Neurotransmitters Are Messengers, Not Functions

One thing to keep in mind is that these two interpretations are not exclusive. In many biological systems, a single protein or hormone or neurotransmitter can have many different effects depending on the timescale of its release and depending on the target of its release. This illustrates a key principle in neuroscience: a neurotransmitter is a messenger, not a function. We are sometimes tempted to generalize specific neurotransmitter roles, so that serotonin becomes a "mood" substance, dopamine becomes a "reward" substance, and opioids become a "pleasure" substance. This is a flawed way of looking at neurotransmitters.

Ultimately, a neurotransmitter can affect cognition and behavior only if it can persuade some neuron to change its activity in some way. And the effect will depend completely on which neurons are persuaded. Serotonin acting on receptors in visual cortex can produce the vivid hallucinations of psychotomimetic drugs. The same substance, acting in the brainstem, can produce nausea and vomiting. The same substance, acting in the spinal cord, can inhibit erection and orgasm. Dopamine is no different than serotonin in this regard. As a messenger between neurons, it can perform many different roles depending on how, when, and where its message is deployed.

Addiction: Pathological Learning and Motivation

We are now ready to go back to the case of addiction that started this chapter. We have seen how motivations begin with the basic survival drives of the organism and how the organism needs common currencies of reward and motivation to balance these drives against one another. Staying alive also means learning to predict what will be rewarding in the future and working toward obtaining predicted rewards. Yet this entire process can become subverted by substances that directly affect the brain's reward and motivation mechanisms. In addiction, a learning process designed to guide the organism to useful resources instead teaches it to pursue the substances themselves, ultimately at the expense of actual survival needs. Let's examine this vicious circle in detail before we turn to some promising new treatments for addiction in the final section.

Addictive Substances Have Distorted Reward Value

In a natural environment, stimuli have reward value when they help the organism improve its homeostatic or allostatic balance. For example, when in negative energy balance, an organism should attach positive reward value to energy-containing stimuli (such as a squirt of fruit juice in the mouth). After ingesting such a resource, the mu- and delta-opioid systems may play a role in signaling the associated improvement in the internal state. Subjectively, a sensation of pleasure or well-being results.

Likewise, any sensory cues that predict an energy-containing stimulus should elicit activity from the dopamine neurons of the VTA and substantia nigra. These neurons respond to a wide variety of cues from any external sensory modality: the sight of a food item, the smell of a food item, or even a sound that predicts the delivery of food (as any pet owner will attest!). Whether a given stimulus counts as a reward item will depend on the organism's current needs, as we saw earlier. Hence, the release of dopamine provides the animal with the signal that a reward is expected, and if the reward turns out to be bigger than expected, then the predictive signal will be even larger the next time around.

But what would happen if, instead of providing the animal with a natural reward, we provided it with a source of the reward-signaling neurotransmitter itself? This would shortcut the entire system. For example, flooding the brain

NEUROSCIENCE OF EVERYDAY LIFE:
The Pursuit of Happiness

Imagine how great you would feel if you got tickets to see your favorite band at a sold-out show. Or bought that fancy new e-gadget everyone's been raving about. Or went on holiday in a sunny and exotic locale (FIGURE 14.20). Wouldn't you just be the happiest person on earth?

Not necessarily. As most of us have experienced at one time or another, reality can sometimes leave us underwhelmed: the sold-out show is nowhere near as fun as we'd hoped, the novelty of the new gadget wears off in a few days, and the holiday cheer vanishes the moment we return home to our busy lives. Even winning a fortune may do little for us: a classic study (Brickman, Coates, & Janoff-Bulman, 1978) found that million-dollar lottery winners ended up no happier than controls in the long run and actually took less pleasure from everyday events.

So why do we work so hard to obtain rewards that, in many cases, do so little to improve our actual happiness? Why does our motivational circuitry have us running in circles after overhyped rewards, with all the furious purpose of a greyhound chasing its own tail? Time and time again, our brains overestimate how much we will enjoy our rewards, leaving us back at our starting point, disappointed.

The tendency of our brains to remain at the same overall level of happiness in the long run, despite the transient joys of life's rewards, has been called the **hedonic treadmill**. No matter how fast we run in pursuit of happiness, our expectations gather speed as well, so that we end up back in the same place once again. Although this pattern has been recognized since antiquity,

FIGURE 14.20 **Does winning tickets to your favorite concert or favorite vacation destination make you feel great?** Unfortunately, the research evidence suggests it does not—at least, not always, and not for long.

only now are we beginning to understand how the hedonic treadmill arises from the neurochemistry of our reward systems.

The point to keep in mind is that tomorrow's rewards, like tomorrow's sunny weather, cannot be directly enjoyed today—instead, our brains must rely on forecasts, and the forecasts can be wrong. The dopaminergic circuits that arise in the VTA and proceed through the nucleus accumbens to the orbitofrontal cortex are essential to this forecasting function: they allow us to want, value, or even crave rewards we have not yet attained. Yet, as we saw earlier, the spikes of dopaminergic activity in this circuit do not code for reward itself but for prediction error: the gap between expectation and reality. As expectations rise with each learning trial, the prediction error drops swiftly down to zero, and with it drops the hedonic response to the new concert, new gadget, new vacation spot, and all the other trappings of a lottery winner's newly affluent lifestyle.

So how do we get off the hedonic treadmill? An entire field of research, known as **positive psychology**, has devoted itself to answering this question. Although no definitive "secret of happiness" has been discovered so far, some helpful hints have emerged. Although single major events like winning lotteries have less long-term impact than we expect, repeated engagement in minor positive events like regular exercise, time with friends and family, or collective activities like religious worship (FIGURE 14.21) really do seem to enhance well-being over time (Mochon, Norton, & Ariely, 2008). Likewise, an intensely pleasurable state of **flow** can result when a person engages in a challenging task, yet has mastered the skills to meet the challenge (Csikszentmihalyi, 1997). In this state, a person can become immersed in his or her work and freed from the gnawing irritations and ruminations of day-to-day mental life. A similar shift in attention, away from self-reflection and judgment and toward the simple sensory experiences of the present moment, is central to the positive effects of mindfulness meditation on well-being (Kabat-Zinn, 1994).

Stepping off the hedonic treadmill is easier said than done, of

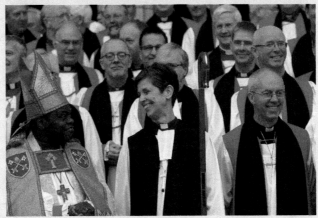

FIGURE 14.21 **Regular exercise or participation in collective social activities is more likely to result in feelings of happiness.**

course. Our motivational wiring will always tend to lure us back into the pursuit of our goals by promising a happy reward at the end. Although the neuroscience of motivation can help us understand why this happens, this insight alone is rarely sufficient to change our behavior. For the moment, perhaps the best we can manage is to try to be mindful of the gap between our mental forecasts of future happiness and their actual consummation. At the very least, this may help to grant us a little more contentment in our day-to-day lives.

with mu-opioid agonists could create a signal of increased well-being without any actual improvement in the internal state. In fact, with a large enough dose, we could create a signal of improved well-being more intense than we could ever achieve with a natural reward: better than the best glass of water on the hottest day or the tastiest morsel of food to a starving person (FIGURE 14.22).

The downside of this is that the mu-opioid reward system is plastic. Faced with strong stimulation, neurons turn down the opioid volume: they build fewer mu-opioid receptors, withdraw the ones that are present on their membranes, and also increase the expression of the kappa-opioid receptors (Le Merrer, Becker, Befort, & Kieffer, 2009).

One result of this is **tolerance**: the requirement for more and more opioid stimulation just to achieve the same effect as in the past. This can lead the organism to consume more and more of the "artificial reward" of the addictive substance, in amounts that might have been lethal earlier in the cycle of addiction. Another result of this is the decreasing value of all other rewards, including the "natural rewards" of eating and drinking that are necessary to survival, as well as other rewards natural to humans: social interaction, mate-seeking behavior,

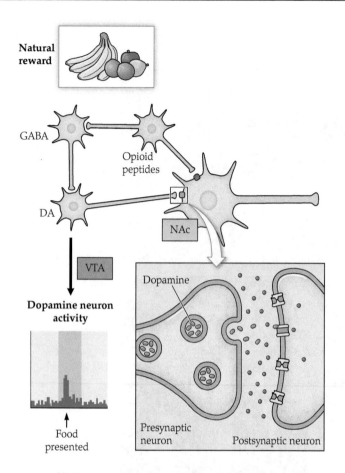

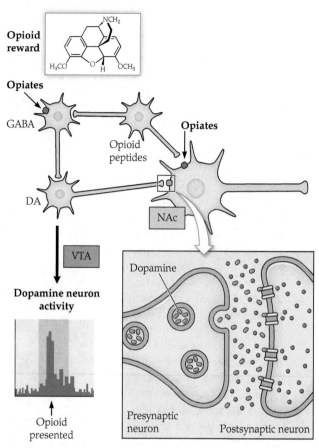

FIGURE 14.22 **Effects of natural and artificial rewards on dopamine activity in the reward circuitry of the brain.** Natural rewards, when they are better than expected, elicit a burst of activity from dopamine neurons. Drugs of abuse, such as opioids, produce artificially large reward signals in this system, even though the organism's internal state has not actually improved. Over many exposures, these artificially large signals can lead to addiction: "pathological learning" to prefer the substance over natural rewards.

parental behavior, and the pursuit of social status. In contrast, cues associated with the artificial reward gain more and more value, via a process of "pathological learning" sometimes called **incentive sensitization** (Robinson & Berridge, 1993).

A complementary result is **withdrawal**: the aversive effects that ensue if the organism ceases to consume the addictive substance. Withdrawal effects are sometimes divided into the "physical effects" on basic functions like digestion, temperature regulation, sweat production, and respiration and the "psychological effects" on functions such as mood, motivation, and the ability to experience pleasure. However, underlying this distinction is a common mechanism: the chronic downregulation of the affected neurotransmitter system (for example, the mu-opioid system) and the compensatory upregulation of opposing neurotransmitter systems (for example, the kappa-opioid system). As we saw earlier, these neurotransmitter systems operate in neurons throughout the brain and spinal cord, and so changing their relative activity levels therefore has consequences for many different kinds of functions performed at all levels of the central nervous system.

Addiction Is a Result of Pathological Learning

The second aspect of addiction is pathological learning. To understand how this works, let's imagine once again that we

flood an organism's brain with an artificial substance that increases the level of dopamine. This would produce a large better-than-expected prediction error signal. Again, depending on the dose, the positive prediction error could be much larger than that possible with any natural rewards, although the actual improvement in internal state would be zero or even negative.

However, there would also be a more insidious secondary effect: all of the sensory cues associated with the substance (including its sight, smell, and local environmental cues) would start to develop a positive predictive value. In other words, the mere appearance of the substance, or other cues associated with it, would start to signal an illusory opportunity to improve one's internal state. With each new exposure to the substance, these cues would develop a stronger positive predictive value. The problem is that, unlike with natural rewards, there would be no end to this process of illusory "reward learning." For a squirt of juice, the amount of dopamine release would gradually diminish to zero, so the cues would gradually stop gaining value in predicting a reward, until the learning process was complete. But if the substance always floods the brain with dopamine, then the learning process is never complete! On the contrary, every exposure increases the positive predictive value of the cues, so that the motivational value of pursuing the substance increases far beyond that of any natural reward (FIGURE 14.23). This leads to a third hallmark of addiction: increasing efforts to obtain the substance, even at the expense of other survival priorities and even in the face of substantial risks and consequences. With sufficient pathological "learning," these efforts may come to eclipse all of the usual sources of motivation, whether positive or negative. Previously enjoyed activities lose all motivational value, whereas previously feared consequences (for example, the risks of disease, job loss, social isolation, and imprisonment) no longer have enough motivational force to serve as deterrents. In severe cases, no natural deterrent can generate sufficient motivation to interfere with the pathologically large reward prediction signal. Having crossed this neurochemical event horizon, the usual physics of motivation no longer apply.

Escape from the motivational black hole is also more difficult than it seems. Brains learn far more effectively than they unlearn, and so a fourth hallmark of addiction is **relapse**. Even if an organism can avoid further exposures to the addictive substance, the changes in motivational circuitry are long-lasting. Exposure to previously "rewarded" sensory cues (be they the sight of a dimly lit bar or the smell of cigarette smoke) can reactivate the positive prediction signal, once again generating the illusion that consuming the substance will result in improved well-being (Roiser, Stephan, den Ouden, Friston, & Joyce, 2010; Schultz, 2000). The illusion can become particularly powerful if the organism is already in a state of distress. Hence, social threats, crises, challenges, or losses can enhance the vulnerability to relapse. The wanting aspect of addiction is persistent and is one of the major reasons why addiction remains so stubbornly resistant to treatment.

The Circuitry and Chemistry of Addiction

Although treatment remains challenging, neuroscientists have begun to learn about the neural circuitry and chemistry of addiction in an effort to discover treatments. The best-studied circuit in addiction is centered, once again, on the dopamine neurons projecting from the VTA to the nucleus accumbens.

The activity of neurons in the nucleus accumbens is an important basis of addiction. In a classic study in 1954, the psychologists Olds and Milner found that rats with electrodes in the nucleus accumbens quickly learned to "self-stimulate" these electrodes if given access to a lever controlling the current (Olds & Milner, 1954). They would press the lever hundreds of times per hour, to the exclusion of other activities including eating and drinking, even to the

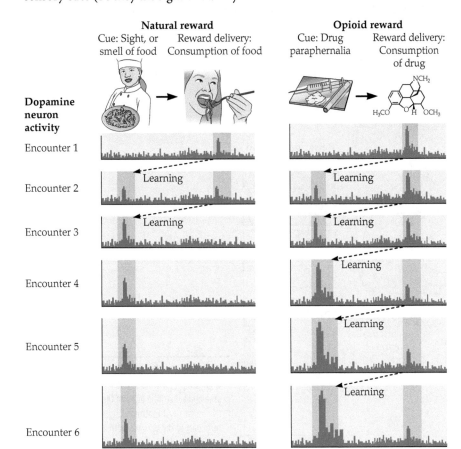

FIGURE 14.23 **Pathological learning mechanisms in addiction.** (a) Natural rewards produce a small "better than expected" signal on the first few encounters, but this signal diminishes, so the reward value of the cue eventually stabilizes. (b) Drugs of abuse, like opioids, can generate much larger "better than expected" signals, and these do not diminish as quickly over successive encounters. Therefore, the reward value of the cues keeps increasing and can eventually exceed the value of all natural rewards—even those required for survival.

point of exhaustion. Thanks to this famous finding, the nucleus accumbens became known somewhat inaccurately as the "pleasure center" of the brain. In fact, as we have seen, other areas of the brain are now known to have a larger role in emotion and in monitoring the internal state; likewise, other areas aside from the nucleus accumbens are important in the pathological learning processes of addiction.

Nonetheless, a common feature of addictive substances, whether in humans or in experimental animals, is that they cause dopamine release in the nucleus accumbens. The sources of dopamine projections to the nucleus accumbens are the midbrain dopaminergic neurons of the substantia nigra and VTA (FIGURE 14.24). Animal studies show that these neurons play a critical role in the development of addiction via the opioid as well as the dopamine neurotransmitter systems. For example, rats will also spontaneously learn to self-administer doses of mu- and delta-opioid agonists into the VTA when implanted with a microinjection device. The mu receptor agonists seem to directly activate VTA neurons via a process of disinhibition (Margolis, Toy, Himmels, Morales, & Fields, 2012). In contrast, kappa receptor agonists inhibit VTA neurons (Margolis, Hjelmstad, Bonci, & Fields, 2003; Margolis, Lock, Hjelmstad, & Fields, 2004). However, the key circuitry for addiction also involves other neurotransmitters and extends beyond the VTA neurons to their targets throughout the brain. Injecting dopamine antagonists into the nucleus accumbens, for example, blocks the self-stimulation learning effect (Fenu, Spina, Rivas, Longoni, & Di Chiara, 2006; Laviolette, Nader, & van der Kooy, 2002).

Activating the circuitry connecting the VTA to the nucleus accumbens seems to be enough to produce positive reinforcement, both in the case of natural rewards such as fruit juice and in the case of the "illusory rewards" of addictive substances. However, projections from the VTA to other brain regions are also important for reward learning and addiction. The VTA sends widespread projections to the prefrontal cortex, and the nucleus accumbens itself lies within a cortical–striatal loop circuit serving the orbitofrontal cortex. These regions play important roles in valuation and in decision making. They also seem to play important roles in addiction, supporting reward learning and self-stimulation even when the circuit through the nucleus accumbens has been blocked (Fields, Hjelmstad, Margolis, & Nicola, 2007). The role of the prefrontal cortex in addiction should not be too surprising to us, given its importance in turning motivations into specific sets of goals, behaviors, and actions and in predictive learning.

Unlearning Addiction

Can addiction be unlearned? Let's examine some of the difficulties and treatment approaches.

The Challenge of Treatment

At this point, you should now have a general idea about how the brain turns its basic survival needs into motivations and how it learns from past experience to predict what sorts of stimuli will best satisfy the organism's future needs. From the previous section, it should also be clear that addictive substances hijack these basic mechanisms in several different ways. First, they create the illusion of strong improvements in well-being, although no such improvements are actually taking place. Second, they create the illusion of always being better than expected, so that the motivational

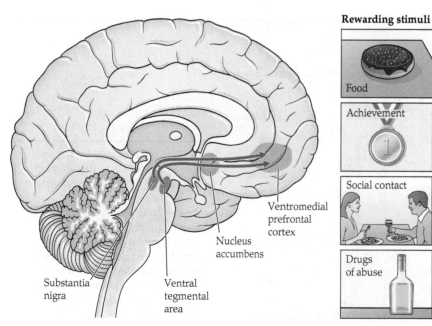

FIGURE 14.24 Dopamine pathways for reward signaling. Projections from the ventral tegmental area and substantia nigra to the nucleus accumbens and ventromedial prefrontal cortex form part of the pathway activated by natural rewards or addictive substances.

CASE STUDY:
Pathological Gambling in a Patient with Parkinson's Disease

Kathy, a British citizen and mother of two, was diagnosed with Parkinson's disease at the relatively young age of 44. Her doctors prescribed dopamine-enhancing medications to relieve her symptoms. However, she soon began to experience strange side effects.

At first, she started to buy lottery tickets—something she had never done before. She then found herself starting to play poker on the Web, despite not even knowing the rules of the game. She lost considerable sums of money. She began shopping impulsively, purchasing large numbers of items she did not need. Previously conservative in outlook, she developed a strong and uncontrollable libido. She began buying latex and leather fetish clothing and arranging to meet strangers for sexual liaisons in hotel rooms.

She experienced a strong sense of reward from these impulsive activities and a strong sense of remorse thereafter. Yet despite her guilty feelings, the motivation to pursue these activities would soon become overwhelming once again. Ultimately, her marriage deteriorated. Only later did she link these changes in her behavior to the dopamine-enhancing medications. On a lower dose, her behavior returned to normal.

Kathy's case is not unique. Pathological gambling, hypersexuality, compulsive shopping, and other impulse-control disorders are now known to be fairly common side effects of the dopamine-enhancing medications used in Parkinsonism

and other illnesses. Between 10 and 15% of patients taking these medications will experience these kinds of behavior to some degree.

The large numbers of people experiencing impulse-control problems on certain dopamine agonist medications has led to class-action lawsuits against their manufacturers. Physicians are now starting to routinely warn their patients to be on the lookout for pathological gambling and other impulse-control problems and to come in for reassessment if they emerge. As for those suffering from Parkinson's disease, they now face a troubling dilemma: the very medications that relieve one set of symptoms can produce a set of equally or more destructive side effects (Kendall, 2009).

---

value of the substance and its surrounding cues continues to increase with repeated exposures. The end result is a cycle in which basic survival needs are pushed aside and the normal motivational effects of natural rewards and punishments are greatly diminished. The further this pathological learning progresses, the harder it is to undo. Relapses are common, even after months or years of remission.

It is worth emphasizing that addiction is one of the most devastating of all illnesses, not just on an individual, but also on a global scale (FIGURE 14.25). Alcohol, tobacco, and illicit substances led to 9% of the entire global burden of disease in 2000 (Rehm, Taylor, & Room, 2006). Collectively, this exceeded the burden of nearly every other major cause of illness, with the exception of malnutrition. Importantly, the use of illicit substances represented less than a tenth of this total burden. Although the term "addiction" often brings to mind substances like **cocaine**, heroin, and marijuana, the damage caused by pathological use of alcohol and tobacco is much, much greater.

Unfortunately, the available treatments for addiction are much less potent than those for bacterial infection, heart

disease, cancer, or depression. A patient suffering from HIV has a much better life expectancy and many more treatment options available than was the case 25 years ago. We cannot say the same for a patient with addiction. Psychological approaches, group counseling, and pharmaceutical treatments all suffer from a common pitfall: limited long-term effectiveness and stubbornly high rates of relapse (Malivert, Fatseas, Denis, Langlois, & Auriacombe, 2012; Rodriguez-Arias, Aguilar, Manzanedo, & Minarro, 2010; Stead & Lancaster, 2012a, 2012b).

Drug addiction is a major problem not only for individuals, but also for the larger society. One-third of convicted inmates are found to be under the influence of drugs at the time of their criminal offense, and two-thirds of prisoners meet the criteria for substance abuse or dependence (Eagleman, Correro, & Singh, 2010). The global burden of drug-related crime is estimated at $108 billion per year (Fletcher & Chandler, 2012). Because we now know that drug addiction is rooted in the biology of the brain, our best hope for breaking addiction may lie in new ideas for rehabilitation, not in repeated rounds of incarceration.

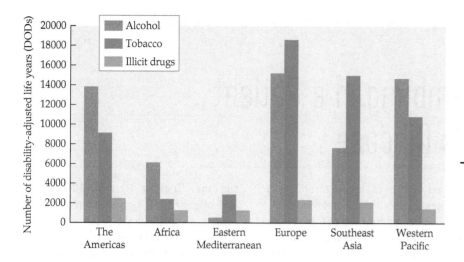

FIGURE 14.25 **The global burden of addiction, as measured by disability-adjusted life years.** The disability-adjusted life year is a way of measuring the health impact of a disease and calculating how many years of normal, healthy life are lost to the disease.

Existing Approaches to Treatment

Today, the treatment recommendations for most forms of addiction rely on a combination of counseling and medications that can interfere with either the acute effects of the drug or the cravings that lead to relapse. Here, we'll take a look at the existing treatment strategies for some common drugs of abuse.

In the case of alcohol, early stages of treatment often focus on managing the symptoms of withdrawal. It is often forgotten that alcohol is one of the few substances whose withdrawal symptoms can be fatal rather than merely unpleasant. Alcohol has effects on the inhibitory GABA receptors of the nervous system (FIGURE 14.26). With this inhibition suddenly removed, the results can include fever, intense anxiety and irritability, nausea, vomiting, instability of the heart rate and blood pressure, a state of delirium, and generalized seizures. A regimen of gradually decreasing doses of GABA-stimulating medications (such as benzodiazepines) can prevent or lessen these symptoms of withdrawal during the detoxification period, which may involve a stay of days to weeks in a specialized clinic (Edwards, Kenna, Swift, & Leggio, 2011; Tyacke, Lingford-Hughes, Reed, & Nutt, 2010). Thereafter, individual or group counseling may help to prevent relapse.

In addition, medications exist that reduce the risk of relapse. These include **naltrexone**, an opioid antagonist that helps to blunt the pleasurable effects of alcohol and reduce cravings. Unfortunately, long-term improvement in relapse rates is hard to demonstrate on this medication (Adi et al., 2007). Another drug, **acamprosate**, is also used to reduce the risk of relapse; although its mechanism is unclear, it is thought to reestablish a balance between GABA and glutamate activity (Kalk & Lingford-Hughes, 2014). The drug **disulfiram** inhibits the enzyme acetaldehyde dehydrogenase. A patient who drinks alcohol while on this medication experiences severe nausea and vomiting within 15 minutes of

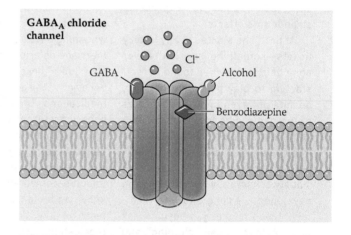

FIGURE 14.26 **Alcohol is an agonist for the GABA$_A$ ionotropic receptor.** Alcohol binding to the receptor makes the GABA more potent, resulting in greater inhibition of the neuron. Benzodiazepine medications have a similar effect on this receptor, and can be used to prevent withdrawal symptoms in patients with alcohol addiction.

ingestion. Although this sounds like a potent disincentive to relapse, patients often stop taking this medication, leaving them vulnerable once again. As a result, once again, long-term relapse rates show little improvement (Mutschler et al., 2010). A common problem limiting the effectiveness of all such antirelapse medications is **adherence**: for a variety of reasons, patients often do not adhere to the prescription and stop taking the medication. Once adherence is lost, relapse becomes all the more likely. For many, the battle against alcohol addiction is lifelong.

Nicotine is also famously and fiercely addictive. In any given year, more than 70% of smokers wish to quit, and 45% attempt to do so. Fewer than 5% succeed (D'Souza & Markou, 2011). Many smokers find themselves continuing to smoke even after personally experiencing a major negative outcome, such as a heart attack or a diagnosis of lung cancer. Although counseling can help, medications can improve quit rates two- to threefold (Hatsukami, Stead, & Gupta, 2008). Tapering doses of nonsmoked nicotine (via a patch, gum, or inhaler) reduce relapse by avoiding withdrawal and cravings. A medication called **bupropion** (also used as an antidepressant) seems to enhance quit rates by reducing both cravings and the pleasure of smoking (King et al., 2012). How it accomplishes this is not clear, although it seems to enhance dopamine levels mildly by blocking neurons' dopamine reuptake mechanisms. Another medication called **varenicline** also enhances quit rates by acting directly on nicotine receptors as a *partial agonist*: a substance that binds to the receptor but activates it only to a mild degree, providing enough stimulation to avoid withdrawal but not enough to perpetuate addiction (King et al., 2012). Partial agonists generally avoid the problem of overdose, because even a dose high enough to bind to 99% of the receptors might still provide a tolerable maximum of only, say, 30% stimulation.

Opioid addiction includes addiction to not only illicit substances such as heroin, but also prescription medications containing morphine, codeine, oxycodone, hydromorphone, and other kinds of opioids used for pain management. Addiction to prescription opioids is common and difficult to overcome: a study presented in 2014 reported that although the average age of an individual addicted to heroin is about 23, the fastest-growing segment of the American population addicted to opioids is individuals age 50–69 (Higgins, Zampogna, Pergolizzi, & LeQuang, 2014).

At present, the mainstay of treatment for opioid addiction is opioid replacement therapy (FIGURE 14.27). Supervised daily doses of a long-acting opioid, **methadone**, can alleviate withdrawal while allowing the patient to resume a productive lifestyle. Another treatment is buprenorphine: a partial opioid agonist that weakly stimulates mu-opioid receptors. The effect is enough to avoid withdrawal while at the same time blocking the action of other opioids on the bound receptors. Since buprenorphine does not overstimulate the receptors even in large doses, the problems of tolerance and overdose do not emerge. Over time, opioid replacement

doses can be tapered down. However, many patients remain on lifelong treatment. Patient outcome is also quite variable, even with treatment. Overall, about one-third of patients recover, another one-third show partial or fluctuating recovery, and another one-third show no improvement (Stephen et al., 2012).

Treatment for dopaminergic substance dependence is currently limited. For example, one of the most widely abused stimulants, **methamphetamine** (known colloquially as *crystal meth*) enhances synaptic dopamine levels by reversing the action of the dopamine transporter. There is currently no known medication with proven efficacy for methamphetamine withdrawal. Nor is there any currently approved treatment for addiction to cocaine, another stimulant that enhances dopamine levels by powerfully blocking dopamine reuptake transporters at neural synapses. Many medications have been tested as a potential treatment for cocaine addiction on theoretical grounds: disulfiram, bupropion, the antidepressant citalopram, the mild stimulant modafinil, and the antiseizure medication topiramate. None have shown dramatic efficacy against cocaine addiction in the long term. As with most addictive substances, no "magic bullet" for dependence exists. We are still searching for powerful, reliable, and above all, *long-lasting* treatments for addiction.

Future Approaches to Treatment

What might our treatments for addiction look like in a few decades? As we learn more about the mechanisms of addiction in the brain, our resulting knowledge will point the way toward new targets for treatment. However, it is worth pointing out that many effective treatments in every field of medicine have been discovered not by deliberate search, but by serendipity. Many theoretically promising treatments for addiction (and other medical conditions) have failed in real life for unforeseen reasons. Conversely, many important treatments have emerged from chance observations followed by aggressive investigation and development. Here we'll look at

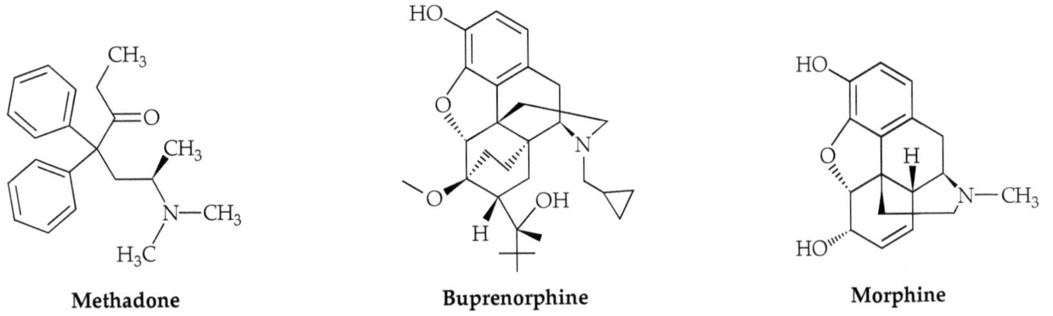

Methadone **Buprenorphine** **Morphine**

FIGURE 14.27 Chemical structures of medications for treating opioid dependence. Methadone is a long-acting opioid that helps individuals avoid withdrawal symptoms. Buprenorphine weakly stimulates opioid receptors, while also blocking them, preventing tolerance or overdose. Both have a similar chemical structure to morphine.

three possible future treatments that illustrate the serendipity of treatment discovery.

Immunization against addictive substances is a theoretically attractive idea that has been pursued with limited success since the 1970s. The idea is simple, in theory: stimulate the immune system to recognize cocaine (or some other substance) as a foreign invader, and the body itself will generate anticocaine antibodies to mop up any ingested cocaine, thus preventing future relapses into addiction (Shen, Orson, & Kosten, 2012). Since the immune system is a fast and efficient learner with a long memory, the premise is an attractive one. Yet in practice there have been many stumbling blocks. Cocaine and other addictive substances are small molecules—usually too small for antibodies to recognize directly. However, attaching a cocaine molecule to larger, more recognizable antigens can prime the immune response, so that afterwards, even the tiny cocaine molecule alone can trigger a response. Unfortunately, the response varies considerably across individuals. Some generate high levels of antibodies; others generate low levels. In many cases, simply ingesting a larger amount of cocaine can swamp the immune response.

An alternative is to use passive immunization: create large doses of specialized monoclonal antibody against cocaine using laboratory cell cultures and then give this antibody to the patient. The problem here is that passive immunization only lasts for the days to weeks before the antibody degrades. Also, the patient's own immune system learns nothing from this approach: all the work is done by the injected antibodies. Finally, monoclonal antibodies are expensive to manufacture—much too expensive for routine use in the huge number of people suffering from substance dependence. Researchers and physicians are continuing to collaborate to get around these obstacles. Yet so far, the clever idea of immunization as a treatment for addiction has failed to mature into an effective mainstream option (Moreno & Janda, 2009).

Ibogaine is another potential treatment for addiction that has struggled for decades to establish itself in the mainstream. In this case, its potential emerged serendipitously rather than from a strong theoretical basis. Ibogaine is a substance found naturally in the bark of the iboga tree of sub-Saharan West Africa (FIGURE 14.28). It has psychoactive (hallucinogenic) properties in high doses and is used spiritually and ceremonially by traditional cultures in this area of the world. In the 1960s, some Western subcultures became interested in ibogaine for its hallucinogenic and psychoactive properties. At the time, some users began reporting that even single doses of ibogaine had long-lasting antiaddictive properties, allowing them to easily stop using a wide range of substances including heroin, cocaine, amphetamine, alcohol, and nicotine without undergoing withdrawal or relapse. The effects reportedly lasted for months. Subsequently, animal studies have shown that ibogaine reduces the self-administration of morphine, cocaine, heroin, alcohol, and

FIGURE 14.28 **The iboga tree is native to western Africa.** The tree produces ibogaine naturally in its bark. Some people believe that ibogaine has antiaddictive properties.

nicotine and that these effects are long-lasting (Maciulaitis, Kontrimaviciute, Bressolle, & Briedis, 2008).

Unfortunately, confirming these reports with controlled studies in humans proved difficult. Many early studies were conducted informally, under poorly controlled conditions, or with inadequate numbers of patients. However, other early studies in animals suggested that ibogaine could have toxic effects at high doses, particularly on the cerebellum and the heart (Kovar et al., 2011). Safety trials in humans began in the United States in the 1990s, but were stopped prematurely after the death of a young female patient in the Netherlands, possibly but not conclusively attributable to ibogaine (Hoelen, Spiering, & Valk, 2009). To complicate matters, ibogaine has been classified as an illegal substance in the United States since 1970 because of its hallucinogenic properties. Since many other Western countries subsequently banned ibogaine, human studies of its safety and efficacy have been few and far between. This cost/benefit ratio of this decision is highly questionable, given the widespread prevalence of addiction and the urgent need for better treatment options.

What is most interesting about ibogaine is its rather "messy" mechanism of action. Although one might expect a potential magic bullet for addiction to have a precisely targeted effect on neural receptors, the opposite is true for ibogaine. It acts on many kinds of receptor families: NMDA receptors, serotonin receptors, nicotinic receptors, muscarinic receptors, kappa- and mu-opioid receptors, and neurotransmitter reuptake mechanisms. How these activities relate to its antiaddictive properties remains unclear. The broad mechanism of action could explain its efficacy against many forms of substance dependence in animal studies. Or, some other yet-undiscovered property of ibogaine could be the key to its efficacy. Or instead, its efficacy could turn out to be vastly exaggerated in humans. On the whole, we have far more questions than answers about the safety and efficacy of ibogaine and other naturally occurring psychoactive substances. However, when we consider the importance of serendipity in treatment discovery and the magnitude of the problem of addiction, it is unfortunate to see any potential treatment go so long without proper investigation.

Let's look at one final serendipitous discovery that may point the way to future addiction treatments. The effective agent in this case is actually not a treatment but a disease: lesions of the anterior insula. As we saw at the beginning of this chapter, patients often find it difficult to quit smoking even after they suffer a heart attack or a stroke. Yet there is a recently discovered exception to this rule. If the stroke damages the anterior insular cortex, the patients often report that they are able to quit smoking quickly, easily, and without cravings or relapse (FIGURE 14.29). In the words of one patient, it was as if his "body forgot the urge to smoke" (Naqvi & Bechara, 2009).

This strange finding makes sense if we think back to the function of the insula in *interoception*, or the perception of internal states and needs (see Chapter 3). Just as the somatosensory cortex keeps track of the body's external sensations, the posterior insula keeps track of its internal sensations: temperature, itch, fullness, nausea, and so on. The anterior insula integrates this information to reflect the organism's current internal states and needs. Pain, hunger, thirst, sexual arousal, fear, fatigue, and other complex internal states all activate the anterior insula. Now recall that natural motivations have their roots in these internal states and needs: before the brain can determine what will be rewarding in the near future, it has to know what it is lacking right now. Without the neurons of the anterior insula, tracking internal states becomes more difficult. Evidently, this includes tracking the internal state of a tobacco craving. Without a literal "sense of need," the motivation for tobacco use never emerges.

Patients with anterior insular lesions are more than 100 times more likely to quit smoking than patients with lesions in other parts of the brain (Naqvi, Rudrauf, Damasio, & Bechara, 2007). This number is astonishing when compared to the efficacy of all known treatments for substance dependence. But how do we turn this remarkable, serendipitous discovery into a practical treatment for addiction? Removing this brain area surgically could easily be as disastrous as a frontal lobotomy: as we have seen, the anterior insula performs many essential functions in interoception, emotion, judgment, and decision making. Implanting deep brain stimulators in this area is another possibility: these devices have been used successfully to inhibit neural activity in depression and in Parkinson's disease (Mayberg et al., 2005). Yet this option is also invasive, expensive, and limited in availability. In addition, it carries a small but significant risk of potentially fatal complications, such as hemorrhage or infection. To gain widespread use, any treatment acting on the anterior insula will need to be relatively noninvasive and spare this brain region's other essential functions. Noninvasive brain stimulation techniques such as transcranial magnetic stimulation or transcranial direct current stimulation could potentially provide a way of doing this. Forthcoming studies may help to reveal whether these techniques can serve as novel, effective treatments for addiction.

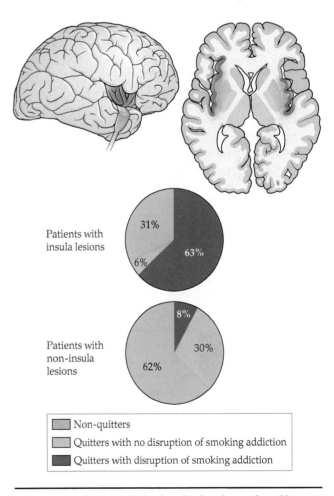

FIGURE 14.29 **Damage to the insula makes it easier to quit smoking.** Patients who had stroke damage to their insula (highlighted in red) were significantly more likely to successfully quit smoking than individuals without stroke damage or with stroke damage to other brain regions.

THE BIGGER PICTURE:
Finding the Motivation to Change

Finding the motivation to change is an elusive but essential step in overcoming a habit that endangers our health. This holds true not just for those with substance abuse, but also for the much larger number of people who suffer from common health problems: patients with high blood pressure who struggle to overcome cravings for high-sodium foods; patients with obesity who struggle to cut back their calories and ramp up their exercise; patients with diabetes who struggle to adhere to the strict daily regimens of insulin injections they need to keep their blood sugar under control. A person may have some motivation to change, yet find that the motivation is insufficient to overcome long-entrenched patterns of behavior.

To the frustration of doctors and nurses the world over, stern warnings and lectures typically have little effect in bolstering a person's motivation to change: patients are usually quite aware that they need to stop smoking, exercise more, and take their medications as prescribed. Yet change is challenging. Aggressive nagging from the doctor may do little to strengthen the patients' motivation and instead may simply drive the patients away. Likewise, when people develop substance addictions, their families and friends often find that begging, cajoling, demanding, or threatening all seem to be ineffective strategies. Even the threat of criminal sanctions has had little impact on the prevalence of substance misuse, despite decades of escalating penalties (Eagleman, 2013). Even when we have good reasons to change our behavior, our old habits die hard—

and this is all the more true for the pathologically strong "habits" of addiction.

So what do we do if we want to help bolster a person's motivation to change? This is a tricky issue: unlike blood, motivations cannot be transfused from one person into another. Yet a series of techniques, known as **Motivational Interviewing (MI)**, have been devised to help people find the motivation to change—within themselves (TABLE 14.1).

MI exploits the fact that most people are really of two minds about changing their habits: a part of them does have motivation to quit smoking, but another part, overstrengthened by the pathologically powerful motivations of addiction, finds reasons to put off the change until another day. The trick is to get the person thinking and talking about the former, rather than the latter.

TABLE 14.1

Core Techniques of Motivational Interviewing

TECHNIQUE	KEY ELEMENTS	EXAMPLE OF USE
"Rolling with resistance"	- Acknowledging the person's resistance rather than opposing it - Seeking out a more balanced perspective from the person	"OK—so you don't think using a patch would help you quit smoking. What other options do you know about?"
"Expressing empathy"	- Identifying and understanding reasons for resistance, without judgment - Creating trust and a sense of shared goals	"You are frustrated because of all the times you've tried to quit smoking before." "You feel it's pointless because it seems like nothing will work."
"Avoiding argument"	- Avoiding reinforcing resistance by arguing with the person - Avoiding challenging the person's feelings - Confronting and examining rather than arguing	"OK—so as of today, you are not interested in trying to quit smoking. Have you ever thought about quitting in the future?"
"Developing discrepancy"	- Motivating change by highlighting the discrepancy between the person's *own* goals and values, and his or her present behavior	"You want to live to see your grandchildren grow up, but you also know that smoking can harm your health."
"Supporting self-efficacy"	- Praising the person for what he or she is doing to make a change in behavior - Highlighting positive efforts the person has made	"So you have tried to quit before— that's great!"

Paradoxically, this often requires that the doctor take the part of discussing the reasons *not* to change. The patient then has no option but to take up the other side of the argument. For example, a physician might begin by asking the patient, "On a scale of 1 to 10, how much do you want to quit smoking?" The patient might reply, "Not much, maybe a 2." Although the physician's natural reaction might be to splutter, " Don't you realize the damage that smoking does to your health?", such an approach only makes the patient defensive, encouraging him to generate self-convincing reasons why it's too hard or too stressful to quit right now. A doctor trained in MI might instead say, "A 2 out of 10 ... OK, so why not a 1? Why not a zero?" This gets the person thinking and talking about the reasons they actually do want to change: setting a good example for their children, not wanting to leave their spouse alone and bereft in old age. By eliciting the other side of the argument, the physician gets the patient to think a little harder about his or her own motivations for overcoming the habit of smoking. With time and discussion, these motivations move to the forefront, increasing the chances that the person will make a break from prior habits (Rollnick, Miller, & Butler, 2007).

MI is not a cure-all, but it seems to work better than berating people for their bad habits in the hopes this will persuade them to change. Its take-home point: the motivation to change is hard to implant in someone from the outside. Instead, it must be found within the person's own set of values, goals, hopes, and ideals and then carefully coaxed out into the forefront. So next time you find yourself "wanting someone to want" something, give this approach a try.

Conclusion

The architecture of motivation and reward is ancient and essential to survival. Motivations arise out of basic survival needs, and resources become rewards when they help us meet those needs. The brain has an elaborate and ancient mechanism for learning to predict the value of rewards in meeting future needs. This mechanism relies on accurate measurements of the internal state and accurate measurements of prediction error: the difference between the expected and the actual outcomes. When these mechanisms operate normally, they are effective at keeping us alive.

Unfortunately, these mechanisms can be hijacked, with devastating consequences. By altering neurotransmitter signals, some substances can create powerful illusions of well-being and illusions of always being better than expected. When this happens, a vicious circle of pathological learning begins. This pathological learning creates an unnaturally strong motivation to obtain and consume the addictive substance. The strength of this motivation increases over subsequent exposures, in time eclipsing other survival needs.

Undoing this process is as difficult as unlearning a skill. Current treatments for addiction rely on a combination of counseling and, in some cases, medications to alleviate withdrawal and reduce the high risk of relapse. Unfortunately, effective treatments for addiction have been hard to find, and substance abuse ranks among the most devastating causes of disability and death worldwide. Finding a safe and effective treatment for substance dependence is one of the major goals in the neuroscience of the 21st century.

KEY PRINCIPLES

- Natural motivations, such as eating, drinking, and reproductive behaviors, help inform the brain what is needed and how to value those needs at the current time.

- The hypothalamus is important for homeostasis and for evaluating internally driven motivation, whereas the amygdala receives input from the external world and evaluates the importance of these outside factors. Dopamine is the neurotransmitter that most commonly conveys these reward and motivation signals.

- The brain learns to predict rewards by comparing the expected outcome of an action to the actual outcome. "Better-than-expected" outcomes increase the motivation toward that action in the future.

- "Liking" and "wanting" are two different things in the brain. Liking refers to the sensation of well-being that is being experienced at that time, whereas wanting refers to a future expectation of well-being.

- Opioids are naturally occurring chemicals in the brain that reduce pain and increase pleasure. These effects can be mimicked by synthetic opioids, such as morphine, heroin, and codeine. Recent research has identified several types of opioid receptors. Stimulation of some of these reduces pain, but stimulation of others produces unpleasant sensations.

- The neurotransmitter dopamine is important for motivation and in learning to predict rewards. It is especially important for assigning value to those rewards, based on how expected or unexpected the reward was.

• Although opioids and dopamine are commonly discussed in the context of motivation, reward, and addiction, these neurotransmitters, like all neurotransmitters, have many different functions, depending on where in the brain they stimulate their receptors.

• Addiction is an illness of pathological motivation, learning, and reward.

• Addictive substances artificially stimulate the opioid and dopamine neurotransmitter systems to create illusory signals of reward and false predictions of future reward. This kindles an abnormally strong learning process in which the motivation to pursue the substance gradually starts to outweigh all others, even at the expense of basic survival needs. Undoing this process can be difficult because it requires the brain to unlearn its addiction.

• Current treatments for most forms of substance dependence are not effective. Discovering better treatments will probably require a combination of serendipity and a better understanding of the basic mechanisms of motivation and reward in the brain.

KEY TERMS

The Circuitry of Motivation: Basic Drives

satiety (p. 444)
subfornical organ (p. 444)
arcuate nucleus (p. 444)
ghrelin (p. 444)
insulin (p. 444)
cholecystokinin (p. 444)
leptin (p. 444)
ob/ob mice (p. 444)
neuropeptide Y (NPY) (p. 444)
basal nucleus (p. 446)
accessory basal nucleus (p. 446)
central nucleus (p. 446)
bed nucleus of the stria terminalis (p. 446)
glucocorticoid hormones (p. 446)
allostasis (p. 446)
ventral tegmental area (VTA) (p. 447)
substantia nigra pars compacta (p. 447)
nigrostriatal pathway (p. 447)
mesocortical pathway (p. 447)
mesolimbic pathway (p. 447)

Reward, Learning, and the Brain

behaviorist (p. 448)
reinforce (p. 448)
aversive (p. 448)
reward (p. 448)
punishment (p. 448)
secondary rewards (p. 448)
prediction error (p. 449)
Rescorla–Wagner models (p. 450)
temporal difference learning model (p. 450)
liking (p. 450)
wanting (p. 450)

Opioids and the Sensation of Pleasure

morphine (p. 451)
mu-opioid receptors (p. 452)
kappa-opioid receptors (p. 452)
delta-opioid receptors (p. 452)
nociceptin receptors (p. 452)
enkephalins (p. 452)
dynorphins (p. 452)
beta-endorphin (p. 452)

Dopamine, Learning, Motivation, and Reward

predictive cue (p. 454)
fast-scan cyclic voltammetry (p. 456)

Addiction: Pathological Learning and Motivation

hedonic treadmill (p. 458)
positive psychology (p. 459)
flow (p. 459)
tolerance (p. 459)
incentive sensitization (p. 460)
withdrawal (p. 460)
relapse (p. 461)

Unlearning Addiction

cocaine (p. 463)
naltrexone (p. 464)
acamprosate (p. 464)
disulfiram (p. 464)
adherence (p. 464)
nicotine (p. 464)
bupropion (p. 465)
varenicline (p. 465)
methadone (p. 465)
methamphetamine (p. 465)
ibogaine (p. 466)
Motivational Interviewing (MI) (p. 468)

REVIEW QUESTIONS

1. Why might a smoker continue to smoke after a heart attack, even when hospitalized? Why does substance use persist despite the knowledge of the risks?

2. What is the difference between homeostasis and allostasis? How do the hypothalamus and amygdala contribute to these two processes?

3. Why might the brain need a "common currency of motivation"? What brain structures and neurotransmitters are important in this function?

4. What makes a reward a reward? How does the brain learn to obtain rewards?

5. How might it be possible for someone to want a cigarette or a drink of alcohol intensely, but enjoy it only mildly?

6. How does the opioid system contribute to reward and pleasure? Why is it overly simplistic to talk of a "pleasure center" or a "reward center" in the brain?

7. How does dopamine contribute to reward prediction, learning, and motivation? How do we reconcile this function with its other role in simple movements?

8. Why might a Parkinson's disease patient become a pathological gambler after taking high doses of dopamine-enhancing medications?

9. Should "pathological gambling," "shopping addiction," and "sex addiction" be considered "addictions" in the same sense as alcohol or nicotine addiction? Why or why not?

10. If a friend were performing poorly at work or school because of alcohol addiction, what would you recommend? Would you give different recommendations if the problem were cocaine or opioid addiction? Why or why not?

CRITICAL-THINKING QUESTIONS

1. Suppose that you sustained brain damage, such that you could no longer use the prediction error model to learn from reward. What would be some of the consequences in your everyday life? Give examples of situations in which your life would be negatively impacted by your lack of ability to use prediction error to learn from reward.

2. As you have learned in this chapter, scientists are searching for substances that can replicate the analgesic and euphoric properties of opioids without producing dependence. What factors in such substances' mechanisms of action do you think would be important to consider in evaluating them as potential candidates for this use?

3. Imagine that scientists developed a safe, effective vaccination against cocaine addiction. How significant of a development do you think this would be for the field of medicine? What problems would this solve? What problems might this create, and what could scientists and physicians do to prevent or address such problems?

- Explain how humans judge personality characteristics based on facial appearance alone, how experience can alter these judgments, and how the brain perceives visual and auditory social cues.

- Describe the concept of theory of mind, associated neural mechanisms including the potential relevance of mirror neurons, and disorders that disrupt theory of mind.

- Explain emotional mimicry, emotional contagion, and empathy, as well as neural mechanisms of empathy and disorders that disrupt empathy.

- Detail examples of social emotions and neural mechanisms of social emotions, social reward, social aversion, and deception.

- Assess the roles of oxytocin and vasopressin in the social behavior of males and females.

- Summarize self-awareness, its neural mechanisms, disorders that disrupt it, and its relationship to social cognition.

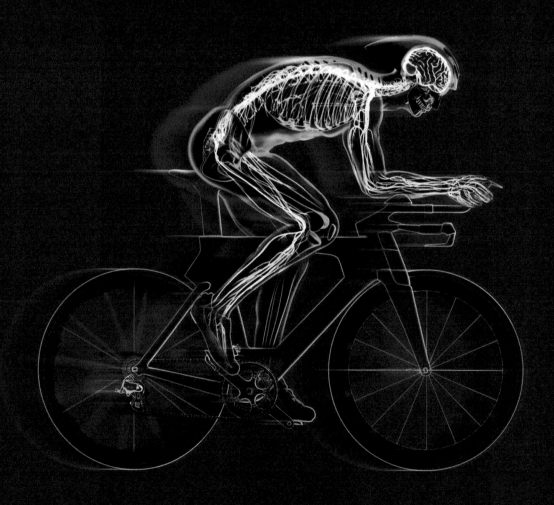

STARTING OUT:
Why Risk Your Life for a Yellow T-shirt?

The Tour de France cycling race is one of the most challenging athletic competitions in the world. The race lasts for around 21 days and stretches over a route 3,000 kilometers in length. Some stages of the course require riders to cover more than 200 kilometers in a single day, whereas others require grueling climbs up steep mountain roads to elevations of nearly 2,400 meters, repeated several times per day. Of the roughly 200 elite cyclists invited to the Tour de France each year, dozens do not even finish.

Tour de France competitors face real dangers—many of their own making. Four competitors have lost their lives while trying to complete the course. One died of heart failure after taking large doses of amphetamines to improve his performance. Many others have suffered disgrace and disqualification after similar attempts at chemical performance enhancement. Some have used the hormone erythropoietin to increase the body's production of red blood cells, in the process thickening the blood and creating a risk of stroke or heart attack. Others have even resorted to transfusing themselves with other people's blood, thereby potentially exposing themselves to blood-borne illnesses like HIV or hepatitis.

What kind of species would put itself through such desperate exertions and for what possible payoff? Pacific salmon may die by the millions while thrashing their way up mountain streams each autumn, but at least the survivors earn a chance to spawn thousands of offspring. Arctic Terns may fly a perilous migration route of 70,000 kilometers a year, but at least their journey keeps them in a perpetual summer, from rich Antarctic feeding grounds to sunny Arctic breeding grounds. So what lofty prize awaits the winner of the Tour de France? The answer is the *maillot jaune*—an unremarkable yellow bicycling jersey, replicas of which can be purchased by anyone with $80 to spend (FIGURE 15.1).

No survival-minded salmon or Arctic Tern would see much appeal in the *maillot jaune*, which cannot be converted into a clutch of fertilized eggs or a bellyful of fish. Yet among human beings who are elite cyclists, the coveted *maillot jaune* somehow becomes a prize worth the risk of death or dishonor. How can a near-worthless item gain so much value? Why risk your life for a yellow T-shirt?

FIGURE 15.1   **A cyclist wearing the *maillot jaune*—the leader's jersey—at the Tour de France.**

As you have probably guessed, it is social context that turns a scrap of cloth into a coveted prize for a human being. By the same mechanism, social context can turn a harmless conical hat into the clichéd marker of shame known as a dunce cap. It is these social forces that become the primary drivers of emotion, motivation, and behavior among the otherwise comfortable human beings of the developed world, who are generally well fed, well sheltered, free of predators, and provisioned with a ready supply of potential friends and mates.

Social emotions and motivations are the source of much of our exceptionalism as a species. Without them, the gallery of human achievement would likely appear quite bare: the mere chance of prize or praise has produced many a symphony, launched many an expedition, and driven many a scientific discovery. At the same time, social emotions have also helped to fill the human hall of shame: our long history of intolerance, atrocity, warfare, religious persecution, destructive personal rivalry, or fruitless political deadlock.

Why are we like this? Why does the *maillot jaune* bring out the best, and the worst, in human nature? These questions have been the subject of philosophical speculation for thousands of years. Since the turn of the millennium, however, they have also become the subject of neuroscientific investigations. In this chapter, we'll look at the neural mechanisms by which social factors feed into every aspect of human emotion, motivation, and behavior.

Social Perception

Although we often communicate verbally, many important social signals are sent via nonverbal communication. For humans, much of this nonverbal communication is conveyed by the face. In this section, we'll consider this communication and the brain regions that are attuned to these social signals.

What's in a Face?

The human social world is a world of faces. Moths may spread pheromones, and birds flash arrays of brightly colored plumage, but humans send nonverbal signals to one another via the forms and expressions of the face. Faces draw the attention of babies who are merely hours old and remain equally fascinating to us in our later years. Yet simply telling apart one face from another is no easy feat. Although our brains are well trained at telling apart our colleagues and people we know well, we struggle to do the same with a collection of baboon faces (FIGURE 15.2) (Ng & Lindsay, 1994).

Simply distinguishing male from female faces is a complex feat—one that eluded computer algorithms for decades, even as they played chess masters to a draw and landed space probes on distant planets. Yet infants' brains master this ability by the age of eight months (Yamaguchi, 2000). A dedicated region of the ventral visual pathway, the fusiform face area, is critical for recognizing and identifying human faces (Kanwisher, McDermott, & Chun, 1997). Damage to this area can produce prosopagnosia: the inability to recognize faces, with intact recognition of other classes of visual stimuli (Barton, Press, Keenan, & O'Connor, 2002; Damasio, Damasio, & Van Hoesen, 1982). Yet the fusiform face area is just one node in a large network of face-processing regions, including lower levels of the ventral visual hierarchy in the temporal lobe, as well as the frontal eye fields and supplementary eye fields, the ventrolateral prefrontal cortex, the anterior insula, and the amygdala (Fusar-Poli et al., 2009).

(a)

(b)

FIGURE 15.2 **It is easier to notice and remember differences between members of a familiar group than it is for members of a different or unfamiliar group.** (a) How different do the human faces appear to you? (b) How different do the baboon faces appear? Most people find it easy to identify differences between the human faces, but they fail to notice any significant differences between baboon faces.

This network of regions is especially important for recognizing the **social emotional cues** that we signal to one another through our facial expressions (FIGURE 15.3). As we saw in Chapter 13, the set of culturally universal facial expressions includes happiness, sadness, anger, fear, disgust, and surprise. The brain does not have a separate neural circuit for the recognition of each of these emotions. However, within the face-processing network, certain regions do respond more to certain types of emotional states. For example, the amygdala is especially responsive to fearful faces (Morris et al., 1996). In contrast, the insula is especially responsive to disgusted faces and somewhat less responsive to angry faces (Phillips et al., 1997).

Thanks to a shortcut in the visual pathways from the thalamus, the amygdala can identify emotional expressions like anger or happiness in less than 100 milliseconds (Willis & Todorov, 2006). In fact, 100 milliseconds is enough time for the brain to form fairly stable judgments of even more abstract qualities, such as a face's attractiveness, likeability,

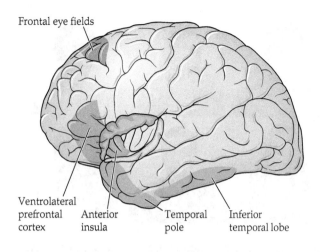

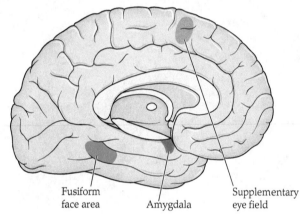

FIGURE 15.3 **Some of the areas in the face-processing network.** Areas involved in face processing include the fusiform face area, frontal eye fields, ventrolateral prefrontal cortex, anterior insula, temporal lobe, supplementary eye field, and amygdala.

trustworthiness, competence, and aggressiveness (Willis & Todorov, 2006). However, these "snap judgments" are not always advantageous.

Do I Look Like a Liar to You?

As we saw earlier, the amygdala is wired to pick up on the social cues inherent in facial expressions, even if they last less than a tenth of a second. But how influential are these first impressions? Enough to swing the outcome of political elections (Todorov, Mandisodza, Goren, & Hall, 2005). One recent study showed the participants brief images of the faces of candidates for U.S. Congress. Even with just 100 milliseconds of viewing time, the participants' first impressions of the quality of "competence" can predict the outcome of the election itself with an accuracy of around 70%. In fact, an extra period of unlimited viewing time did not improve the accuracy of participants' predictions (Ballew & Todorov, 2007).

Of course, the bone structure of a person's face is actually a poor predictor of trustworthiness, competence, or any other complex behavioral trait. Nonetheless, snap judgments of this kind influence life-or-death decisions. In one study in the United States, participants viewed the faces of defendants in murder trials and heard descriptions of their supposed crimes. They were then asked to decide whether the defendants deserved the death penalty. The sobering finding was that facial appearance had a marked effect on the likelihood of a death sentence. Specifically, defendants rated by another group of participants as having "stereotypically black" features were sentenced to death in nearly 60% of cases versus only 24% for those who were not rated that way (Eberhardt, Davies, Purdie-Vaughns, & Johnson, 2006).

NEUROSCIENCE OF EVERYDAY LIFE:
A Poker Face

Every week, millions of people around the world test their social-perception mechanisms against one another for high stakes. In the game of poker, each player's cards are hidden from the others, so winning requires a bit of luck and a lot of skill in reading opponents' emotional states. Professional poker players become expert at reading tells: the subtle changes in expression or behavior that can give away a player's intentions and emotional states. Tremulous fingers, furtive glances at a pile of winnings, or a hand held protectively over a strong card can all provide useful clues to the opponent who is able to read them. For this reason, many players attempt to fake their tells: adopting a meek silence when holding strong cards or blustering loudly through the round when stuck with a weak hand. Yet the expert player can often spot these basic forms of misdirection. Hence, many players attempt to cultivate an expressionless "poker face," devoid of any useful information.

Poker is a zero-sum game, in which one person's gain is the other's loss. Since zero-sum games are commonplace in human interaction, the game of poker is starting to be adopted as a convenient model system for studying competitive human social behavior. One study looked at how an opponent's facial trustworthiness might affect the player's decision about whether to wager money or withdraw from the round. Participants played poker against a virtual opponent, represented by a computer-generated face image that appeared as neutral, trustworthy, or untrustworthy based on previously obtained ratings (FIGURE 15.4) (Schlicht, Shimojo, Camerer, Battaglia, & Nakayama, 2010).

As it turned out, the best poker face was not a neutral one, but a trustworthy one. When playing against a trustworthy-appearing opponent, players took significantly longer to decide whether to bet, made significantly more "mistakes" (suboptimal choices about whether to accept the bet or withdraw), and were more likely to fold rather than bet against their opponent. Players displayed much closer to optimal behavior when faced with either neutral or untrustworthy-looking opponents.

Why should a nonthreatening opponent lead to more cautious, erroneous play? As we saw earlier, poker players expect their opponents to send false signals and may adjust their play accordingly. So one possibility is that the novice players in this study were overcorrecting for the honest appearance of their opponents. Either way, this finding may also have real-life implications in social interactions outside of poker because every one of us must at times enter into a zero-sum game of one kind or another.

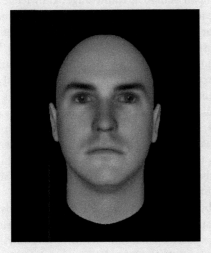 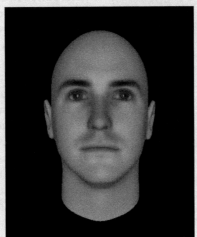 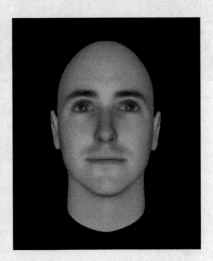

FIGURE 15.4 Computer-generated untrustworthy, neutral, and trustworthy faces that were used in a computerized poker game. The best poker face turned out to be a trustworthy one.

What evolutionary force would drive our brains to rely on the crude and faulty snap judgments of the amygdala to take the measure of a person's soul?

To find out, one group of researchers used a computer program to generate hundreds of random, realistic human faces with neutral expressions. Next, they asked participants to describe their impressions of the faces, in their own words. Sifting through the responses, they found some 12 general traits: confident, dominant, sociable, attractive, responsible, stable, caring, trustworthy, aggressive, unhappy, mean, and weird. Most of these 12 traits mapped onto just two main factors: trustworthiness and dominance (FIGURE 15.5). Next, by returning to the computerized faces, they found the precise sets of facial structure parameters (chin size, eye separation, brow shape, nostril size, and so on) that corresponded to ratings of either trustworthiness or dominance. Finally, they used the software to warp emotionally neutral faces to different points along the spectra of trustworthiness and dominance (Oosterhof & Todorov, 2008).

By exaggerating the changes, they uncovered the functional basis of these snap judgments of personality (Oosterhof & Todorov, 2008). Trustworthiness, in extreme form, begins to resemble the human expression of friendly recognition: raised eyebrows and a closed smile. Extreme untrustworthiness comes to resemble the expression of aggressive intent: a frown, flared nostrils, and a furrowed brow. Extreme submissiveness looks much like the big eyes, small chin, and upward gaze of a child. Extreme dominance looks uncannily like the jutting chin, wide nose, and enlarged lips of an adult male with acromegaly: the typical facial appearance of a person whose body has been steeped in prolonged, high levels of growth hormone. In addition, the combination of facial dominance and untrustworthiness seems to map onto ratings of facial threat.

The amygdala and its cortical allies are wired to be good at spotting facially expressed social signals like threat, friendliness, dominance, and submission. These kinds of facial expressions are intended to serve as accurate markers of our emotional state, for use in social interaction. Unfortunately,

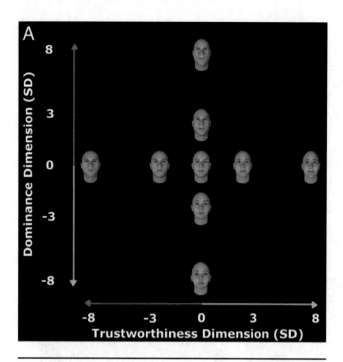

FIGURE 15.5 Personality judgments from facial shape. People can make quick judgments about a person's personality from the shape of the person's face, even when wearing a neutral expression. These personality judgments can be summarized by two main factors: trustworthiness and dominance.

the skeletal geometries of some faces happen to resemble watered-down versions of our most basic emotional expressions, generating false but influential signals of social intent. So the broad-chinned but clueless politician wins high office, the baby-faced criminal escapes the notice of police, and the honest but pinched-faced salesperson struggles to make a deal.

Social Knowledge and the Temporal Pole

Of course, there is much more to a person than meets the eye in the first hundred milliseconds. As we gain social experience with a person, we come to understand him or her in greater detail: simple semantic features like name, job, and marital status; episodic features like a history of friendly acts or broken promises; personality features like true levels of aggressiveness, confidence, subservience, and so on—appearances notwithstanding. Learning the "social properties" of the people with whom we live is an essential skill for survival and success when navigating the complex world of human relationships.

One of the first hints at the neural basis of **social semantic knowledge** came from the pioneering primate lesion studies of Kluver and Bucy in the 1930s. As we saw in Chapter 13, a variety of major social-cognition deficits arise in monkeys

with lesions of the anterior temporal lobe and the amygdala. The monkeys become docile, showing little fear, and they attempt to copulate indiscriminately, even with members of other species or inanimate objects. Mothers with these types of lesions may abandon or even attack their own infants. Notably, monkeys with these lesions quickly fall to the fringes of their social group. In many cases, formerly dominant individuals swiftly become outcasts. In the absence of appropriate social cognition, monkeys lose allies, gain enemies, and in many cases are eventually killed by members of their own species (Olson, Plotzker, & Ezzyat, 2007).

Although Kluver–Bucy syndrome can also arise in human beings, such cases are fairly rare. More commonly, lesions of the anterior temporal lobes in humans tend to cause more limited deficits. For example, injury to the temporal poles can impair **semantic knowledge**: knowledge of the meanings of concepts and the properties of objects, such as their edibility or dangerousness. Neuroimaging studies in healthy subjects show the anterior temporal lobes to be active in identifying unique entities, like famous landmarks (Simmons & Martin, 2009) or individual celebrities. Lesions of the left temporal pole are associated with deficits in the ability to recall the names of famous people (FIGURE 15.6). At the same time, the ability to name other items such as tools, animals, or landmarks sometimes remains. Right temporal pole lesions tend to impair the recall of nonverbal information about the famous people in question, such as their profession or country of origin (Tranel, 2009).

In healthy subjects, neuroimaging studies show activations in the left and right anterior temporal poles during celebrity-naming tasks (Damasio, Tranel, Grabowski, Adolphs, & Damasio, 2004). Other kinds of social knowledge may be represented nearby. For example, a small region in the lateral anterior temporal lobe shows activation during the learning and recall of social facts about a person: their age, occupation, marital status, and so on (Tsukiura, Suzuki, Shigemune, & Mochizuki-Kawai, 2008).

Other studies have found a specific subregion in the right superior anterior temporal lobe that seems to track abstract human-specific social-knowledge concepts such as "tactless," "ambitious," "polite," "honorable," or "stingy" (Zahn et al., 2007). As we will see in Chapter 16, patients with temporal lobe degeneration resulting from **frontotemporal dementia** sometimes lose these forms of knowledge and develop inappropriate social behavior (Zahn, Moll, Iyengar, et al., 2009).

The temporal poles' close functional and anatomical links to the basolateral amygdala allow the nuanced social and conceptual knowledge of the temporal cortex to influence the snap judgments of the amygdala regarding social cues (Willis & Todorov, 2006). Healthy subjects can overcome initial impressions of, for example, untrustworthiness—if they are given new, positive information about the person they are seeing (Kuzmanovic et al., 2012). So are patients with lesions of the posterior hippocampus, despite their difficulties with some forms of memory (Croft et al., 2010). However, patients with lesions of the temporal pole have

President Barack Obama

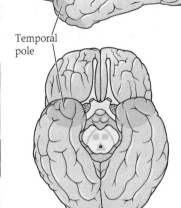

Temporal pole

Scientist Albert Einstein

Singer/Songwriter Katy Perry

British Royal Family Member Catherine, Duchess of Cambridge

FIGURE 15.6 **The temporal pole.** The temporal pole is located at the anterior end of the temporal lobe, and lesions to this area are associated with forgetting information about famous people, such as those pictured here.

great difficulty using new social knowledge to overcome first impressions. Despite hearing good things about a shifty-looking person, they still judge the person untrustworthy (Todorov & Olson, 2008).

It can be argued that the anterior temporal lobe–amygdala connection is, from a social and cultural point of view, one of the most profoundly important pathways in the entire brain. It is thanks to these pathways that we human beings are not left entirely at the mercy of first impressions, but can show our most admirable qualities of tolerance and understanding. Through these circuits, the ugly stereotype can be overcome, the scary-looking foreigner can become a trusted friend, and the physically unappealing can be recognized for their inner beauty.

Social Signals and the Superior Temporal Sulcus

There is a limit to how much can be learned from a face alone, regardless of how much social context is available. In human beings, as with most primates, our moment-to-moment social communication relies on a highly nuanced mixture of visual and verbal cues. Gaze direction, head and neck position, body posture, and vocalizations all combine to signal our social intentions to one another. But to be of any use, these sequences of visual and auditory stimuli must be picked out of their sensory surroundings and parsed into social signals. Once again, a widespread network of cortical

and subcortical regions participates in this essential function. However, one of the most important nodes of this network is the region around the superior temporal sulcus (STS). Lying at the interface between visual and auditory sensory areas, it is ideally positioned to pick up on social cues from both sensory modalities (FIGURE 15.7).

Gaze direction is a major form of social signal. In most primates, a direct gaze signals dominance or threat, whereas a lowered gaze signals submission or nonthreat. Many primate neurons in the STS respond to images of faces with particular gaze or head directions, and many of these respond specifically to direct gaze (Perrett et al., 1990). fMRI studies show activation of the STS when human participants view a virtual-reality stranger walking past them, pupils fixed unnervingly on them the whole time. Move just a half-dozen

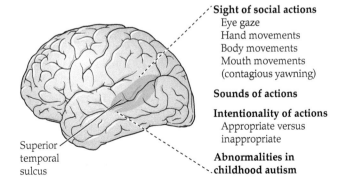

Sight of social actions
Eye gaze
Hand movements
Body movements
Mouth movements
(contagious yawning)

Sounds of actions

Intentionality of actions
Appropriate versus inappropriate

Abnormalities in childhood autism

Superior temporal sulcus

FIGURE 15.7 **The superior temporal sulcus is important for detecting and interpreting social cues.**

pixels so that the stranger's eyes are averted, and this activation disappears (Pelphrey, Viola, & McCarthy, 2004).

Plenty of other classes of visual social cues also activate the STS region. These include stimuli such as moving lips, gestures of the hands, bodily movements and postures, facial gestures or complex expressions, and contagious yawning. Purposeful movements seem to elicit stronger activation than purposeless or physically impossible movements (Shultz & McCarthy, 2012). The STS also activates strongly when we attempt to understand muted speech via lip-reading and in readers of manually based communication systems such as American Sign Language (Allison, Puce, & McCarthy, 2000).

Auditory social cues also figure prominently among the repertoire of the STS (Zilbovicius et al., 2006). The STS contains voice-sensitive regions with neurons that respond specifically to vocalizations rather than other sounds. A posterior STS area is especially active in recognizing individuals by voice, much as the fusiform face area is active in recognizing individuals by face (Zilbovicius et al., 2006). However, the STS also plays a role in parsing *sequences* of sounds, which are the building blocks of verbal communication in human beings. This function is consistent with the location of the STS near the border of Wernicke's area, a left temporoparietal region important in language comprehension.

Regions in the STS respond to words more than to auditory stimuli that sound similar but do not have linguistic content. Other STS regions respond to meaningful sentences more than to unconnected words or to meaningful narratives rather than to unconnected sentences (Belin, Fecteau, & Bédard, 2004; Kriegstein & Giraud, 2004) (FIGURE 15.8).

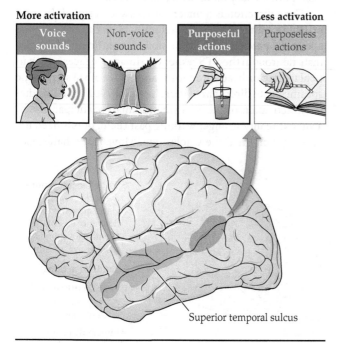

FIGURE 15.8 **Intentionality is represented in the superior temporal sulcus.** Areas in the superior temporal sulcus activate more for voice than for nonvoice sounds, and more for witnessing purposeful rather than purposeless actions.

However, many STS regions will also respond to socially meaningful nonlinguistic sounds, such as animal noises, human nonspeech sounds like laughter or crying, and even the sounds of tool use (Belin, Zatorre, Lafaille, Ahad, & Pike, 2000).

Social Thinking: Theory of Mind

The true meaning of a social cue like eye gaze may not be clear from appearance alone. Often, social cognition requires having some sense of what the other person is thinking as well as what he or she is saying or doing. If you are standing at the front of a line, and the cashier says, "Next!", it really means, "Right now I want you to step forward and tell me what you would like to eat." To understand the meaning of the word in this context, in effect, you must read the person's mind.

What Is Theory of Mind?

Theory of mind refers to our ability to attribute inner mental states like thoughts, beliefs, desires, and intentions to others and to appreciate how these may differ from our own. Since one brain cannot directly access the mental contents of another, a theory of mind is a sort of model, or educated guess, about what those contents might be. This overall theory of mind can be subdivided into at least two parts. **First-order theory of mind** refers to being able to predict the thoughts of a second person, whereas **second-order theory of mind** refers to being able to understand what a third person would think about the second person's thoughts (Liddle & Nettle, 2006).

Understanding the thoughts and intentions of other people turns out to be critical for interpreting even some of the most basic social cues. By the age of nine months, a human infant can look at a pointing finger and understand that the signal means "look at where I am pointing" rather than simply "look at my finger" (Stern, 2000). So social cue perception and a rudimentary theory of mind are closely linked.

Theory of mind also allows the brain to model the intentions, desires, and beliefs of other brains, even when these differ from our own. In a competitive social world, this can be a definite advantage. For example, if you are looking for a hidden cache of food and you know who hid it, you may be able to follow your competitor's gaze to work out the location of the hidden food. Conversely, if you know that your competitor has figured out where you have hidden a cache of food, you might move the cache before your competitor can get to it. Theory of mind is generally helpful for anticipating the actions of competitors, predators, or prey so that you can stay one move ahead of them.

Theory of mind may be even more useful for cooperative ventures than for competitive interactions. If your friend sees you shivering and looking around for a coat and he knows where a coat is to be found, he may bring it to you. Coordinating your actions and goals with those of your allies is critical for the success of any cooperative venture, from major projects like hunting or collective defense right down to mundane tasks like moving a sofa down a flight of stairs.

Researchers have assessed theory of mind in humans by examining their subjects' capacity to understand others'

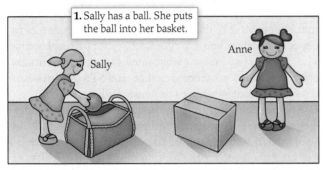

1. Sally has a ball. She puts the ball into her basket.

Anne

Sally

2. Sally goes out for a walk.

3. Anne takes the ball out of the basket and puts it into the box.

4. Now Sally comes back. She wants to play with her ball. Where will Sally look for her ball?

FIGURE 15.9 **The Sally–Anne task.** After viewing the picture story of Sally and Anne, subjects are asked where Sally should look for the hidden toy. Those who lack a theory of mind think that Sally will look in the box, where Anne hid it. They do not understand that Sally holds the false belief that the toy is still in the basket.

false beliefs. A common false-belief test is the **Sally–Anne task** (Bloom & German, 2000) (FIGURE 15.9). Here the child is presented with a cartoon or puppet show with two characters, Sally and Anne. Sally has a ball, which she places in a basket before leaving the room for a short walk. In her absence, Anne takes the ball from Sally's basket and places it in a box instead. Sally then returns and goes to look for her ball. The test question asks *where* Sally will look for her ball. Again, young children tend to say that Sally will look in the box, thus demonstrating a failure to represent her false belief that the ball is in the basket. Only after the age of five do children reliably come up with the correct answer about Sally's false belief.

Although human beings are the undisputed champions of theory of mind, some similar abilities can be observed in many social species. Not all researchers agree that these abilities should be described as theory of mind, largely because we cannot know what or if the animal is thinking (Povinelli & Vonk, 2003), but several researchers have observed behavior that seems similar to what is observed in theory of mind experiments in humans. Chimpanzees can infer the intentions and beliefs of other chimpanzees and also of humans (Premack & Woodruff, 1978). They may even use their understanding to guide altruistic acts: for example, handing down bananas to a human who struggles to reach them or helping a fellow chimpanzee retrieve food from outside its cage, even when the first chimpanzee is not feeling hungry (Cohen, 2011). Dolphins are also regularly reported to help ailing members of other species, such as whales or humans (Lilley, 2008; Servais, 2005).

Many rudimentary ingredients of theory of mind appear widely in the animal kingdom. The most widespread is **perceptual theory of mind**: picking up on social cues that may indicate intentions. Starlings can use a predator's head orientation and eye gaze direction to determine the risk of being attacked (Carter, Lyons, Cole, & Goldsmith, 2008). Many species can use humans' finger-pointing or head-turning cues to correctly identify which of several containers holds a hidden cache of food. These include orangutans, macaques, jackdaws, dolphins, some seals, wolves, domestic horses, and dogs (Emery & Clayton, 2009).

Tamarin monkeys, macaques, and chimpanzees have some signs of a more sophisticated motivational theory of mind: the ability to pick up on desires and intentions. For example, they can distinguish between accidental hand-flopping and deliberate pointing in deciding which container is being indicated (Wood, Glynn, Phillips, & Hauser, 2007). However, based on our current experimental tests of theory of mind in animals, all animal species lack informational theory of mind (Emery & Clayton, 2009). This is the level of understanding needed to perform false-belief tasks, such as the Sally–Anne task.

Neural Mechanisms of Theory of Mind

Of all species, human beings seem to have a special knack for representing the thoughts, beliefs, and desires of others. But if this is such a valuable skill to have, then why do so few species possess it? What unique neural mechanisms have human beings developed that allow them to excel in theory of mind?

Neuroimaging studies have revealed a set of brain structures that appear to be essential for theory-of-mind tasks in human beings. One common approach involves showing subjects cartoons or stories, the comprehension of which relies on theory of mind. For example, one cartoon would show a man fishing, with another man behind him surreptitiously fishing from the first fisherman's pile of caught fish. Getting the joke requires understanding that the first fisherman does not know what you know: that while he works diligently away on his fishing, someone is pilfering his catch. A control cartoon would involve humor that does not require mental state attribution: for example, showing a man fishing with cobwebs attached to his line. A comparison between subjects' brain activation in response to processing the two types of cartoons would reveal brain areas specifically associated with the representation of false beliefs.

Another approach involves looking at subjects' brain activations during competitive social interactions, which require trying to guess your opponent's move in advance: the children's game Rock–Paper–Scissors is a good example. Yet another method involves imaging subjects' brains as they give responses to moral dilemmas—problems that arise when one takes into account the thoughts, desires, and feelings of other people. Another approach involves looking at subjects' brain activations during the comprehension of irony or sarcasm—both of which require an understanding that someone's actual thoughts and feelings are the opposite of what they are literally saying.

In all of these diverse kinds of tasks, representing the beliefs, thoughts, and intentions of other people recruits a common network of regions (FIGURE 15.10) (Carrington & Bailey, 2009;

Van Overwalle, 2009; Van Overwalle & Baetens, 2009). This so-called "**theory-of-mind network**" includes the medial prefrontal cortex, associated parts of the precuneus and nearby posterior cingulate cortex, and, on the lateral wall, large activations in the temporoparietal junction and nearby STS.

One task that activates this network is the Prisoner's Dilemma. This is a two-player game in which both players pretend to be prisoners trying to decide whether to cooperate with the authorities. If both partners refuse to betray each other, they both win some points. However, if one prisoner stays faithful whereas the other defects, the defector wins a larger number of points, whereas the faithful partner gets nothing. At the same time, if both partners defect, they both get a much smaller number of points. To make the best choice about whether to cooperate or defect, you must guess what your partner is going to do. In one study, this task activated the medial prefrontal cortex, precuneus, posterior cingulate, and STS regions when subjects were contemplating a response (Rilling et al., 2002).

Another neuroimaging study asked participants to judge whether people were speaking literally or sarcastically in social scenarios: for example, sarcastically saying "nice job" after seeing someone make a clumsy mistake. Regardless of whether the statements were literal or sarcastic, the temporal pole activated when the subjects used social context to determine the appropriateness of the statement. However, when the statements were determined to be sarcastic (meaning that the person's actual mental state was the opposite of what they were saying), only the dorsal and ventral medial prefrontal cortex showed activation (Wakusawa et al., 2007).

As you may have noticed, most if not all of these areas in the so-called theory-of-mind network are also active in plenty of other nonsocial situations. For example, the temporoparietal junction is active in orienting attention to

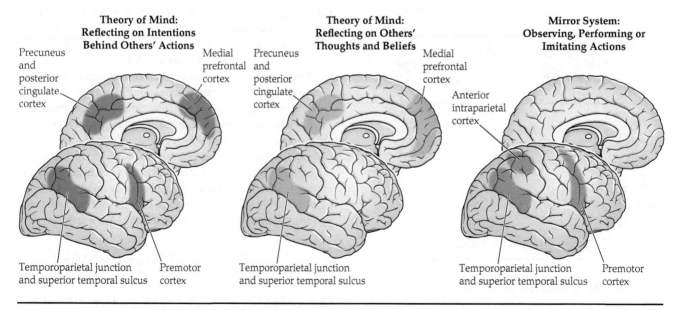

FIGURE. 15.10 **A common network of regions is involved in theory of mind functions.** These functions require the brain to represent the beliefs, thoughts, and intentions of others. The theory of mind network has some overlap with the mirror system, which is active when observing, performing, or imitating actions.

nonsocial visual, auditory, and tactile stimuli (as we saw in Chapter 8). The precuneus and posterior cingulate gyrus are both involved in scenario recollection and prospection (as we saw in Chapter 9). Much of the medial prefrontal cortex is also active in nonsocial decision making, emotion regulation, visceromotor control, and guessing (as we saw in Chapters 12 and 13). So we can legitimately ask which of these areas are truly critical for understanding false beliefs.

As always, in research studies, correlation does not imply causation. However, scientists can see whether lesion studies and stimulation studies provide further evidence that the brain regions that have been implicated as part of the theory-of-mind network are indeed involved in theory of mind. Are there patients in whom focal brain lesions disrupt theory of mind? The answer is yes, and we'll turn to them in a moment. First, however, let's look at another set of brain areas whose functions may provide a basic foundation for theory of mind in humans and some other primate species.

Mirror Neurons and Theory of Mind

One other form of cognition that may be relevant to theory of mind involves the brain's mirror neurons. As we saw in Chapter 7, mirror neurons were first discovered in macaques in the 1990s. These neurons fired not only when the monkey performed a specific kind of movement, but also when the monkey saw someone else performing the same action (Rizzolatti, Fadiga, Gallese, & Fogassi, 1996). These neurons are most commonly found in a region of lateral premotor cortex (FIGURE 15.11), designated F5 in the macaque (Rizzolatti & Craighero, 2004). Of all possible partner regions in the parietal or temporal cortex, it turns out that F5 connects most strongly with the neurons of the STS. So these neurons not only control complex movements, but also take input from regions that are especially good at parsing complex movements.

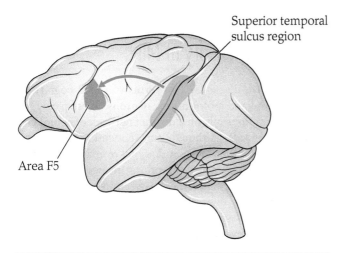

Superior temporal sulcus region

Area F5

FIGURE 15.11 Mirror neurons are found in area F5 of the monkey brain. This area is roughly equivalent to the lateral premotor cortex in the human brain. It takes input from the superior temporal sulcus region.

Mirror neurons have many interesting properties. They can fire during observed actions, even during periods when part of the action is obscured by a screen or out of the animal's view altogether. They can respond to the sounds that may be associated with a particular action, such as the sound of a paper bag ripping. Mirror neurons seem to fire the most for actions that are purposeful, such as reaching to grasp a particular object, rather than reaching aimlessly for thin air (Rizzolatti & Craighero, 2004). Hence, they could potentially provide a substrate for the brain to understand intentions—an important component of theory of mind.

In human beings, neuroimaging studies have found a similar **mirror system** that centers on the ventral premotor cortex but also includes partner nodes in the STS and intraparietal sulcus, which contains regions that work out the shape and location of external stimuli with respect to various body parts (Van Overwalle & Baetens, 2009). This system is active in a variety of tasks that involve observing, executing, or imitating body movements (Iacoboni et al., 1999).

Yet the mirror system has an influential sensory side. It is also active to some degree when representing the context in which actions occur, even if no actual action is seen (Rizzolatti & Craighero, 2004). This may help to explain why the mirror system is also active in representing the intention of a particular action, which may depend on its environmental context. For example, if we see a hand raising a half-empty cup near an untouched meal, we may infer that the intention is to take a sip of the drink. However, if the same hand raises the same half-empty cup on a background of a messy, finished meal, we may infer that the intention is not to drink but to clean up. Although the mirror system is active when viewing hands raising cups, it is also active when viewing table settings, and it is still more active when trying to infer the intention of the cup-raising action based on the appearance of the table setting (Iacoboni et al., 2005). Representing the intention behind an observed action is potentially an important building block toward representing the inner mental state of another.

So does the mirror system provide a concrete foundation for theory of mind? As we'll see shortly, there are some points of overlap between the anatomical regions that support the mirror neuron system and the theory-of-mind network. The area encompassing the inferior parietal lobule, superior temporal gyrus, and temporoparietal junction (FIGURE 15.12) is active to some degree both during tasks that require representing the actions and intentions of others, which uses the mirror neuron system, and during tasks that require representing the inner beliefs, desires, and long-term goals of others even before they have actually performed any specific actions, which uses the theory-of-mind network (Van Overwalle & Baetens, 2009).

In contrast, some clear distinctions exist between the brain areas that seem to support the execution of these two types of tasks. The biggest difference between the two is the presence of activations in the medial prefrontal cortex rather than the lateral prefrontal cortex during inferences about others' mental states, in the absence of any outer actions

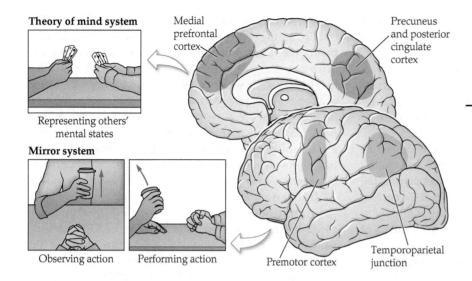

Theory of mind system

Representing others' mental states

Mirror system

Observing action   Performing action

Medial prefrontal cortex

Precuneus and posterior cingulate cortex

Premotor cortex

Temporoparietal junction

FIGURE 15.12 **The mirror system versus the theory of mind system.** Both systems draw upon the area around the temporoparietal junction, at the border of the inferior parietal cortex and superior temporal cortex. However, the mirror system relies more on the lateral premotor cortex, and activates for observing or performing specific external actions or movements. The theory of mind system relies more on the medial prefrontal cortex, and activates during reflection on mental states (in the absence of any observable actions).

(Gusnard, Akbudak, Shulman, & Raichle, 2001). As we saw in Chapter 7, the prefrontal cortex seems to have a functional divide between its medial and lateral walls. A front-to-back hierarchy of lateral prefrontal areas guides goals, plans, behaviors, and simple actions based on external sensory cues. A similar front-to-back hierarchy of medial prefrontal areas represents *internally driven* goals, plans, behaviors, and simple actions, guided by the organism's emotional and motivational states. When we reason about the inner states of another person rather than the person's outward actions, we seem to draw on the medial hierarchy more than the lateral hierarchy.

One intriguing possibility is that there are actually *two* mirror systems in the brain: the well-known lateral one we have just seen and a second system of medial mirror neurons. Just as lateral mirror neurons can represent a movement regardless of whether you do it yourself or observe it in someone else, so the medial mirror neurons would represent an inner motivation (like a goal, belief, thought, desire, or urge) regardless of whether you have the motivation yourself or infer it in someone else. These neurons would provide a specific substrate for representing the inner mental states of other people.

Do medial mirror neurons exist in human beings? To find out, we would need to record directly from medial prefrontal areas in humans, just as has been done for lateral areas in monkeys. Such recordings are rare, but can sometimes be obtained in patients who are having their brain functions mapped prior to undergoing neurosurgery. One report identified "pain mirror neurons" in the **cingulate motor area**, a medial analogue of the lateral motor cortex (Hutchison, Davis, Lozano, Tasker, & Dostrovsky, 1999). These neurons activated when the patient received a sharp poke in the finger from a pointy electrode tip, yet also activated when the patient observed one of the experimenters poking himself in the finger instead. The cingulate motor area is important for regulating internally guided urges to move body parts, as in the tics of **Tourette syndrome** (Devinsky, Morrell, & Vogt, 1995).

A more recent study has provided evidence for the existence of mirror neurons in human beings in a variety of different medial motor areas (Mukamel, Ekstrom, Kaplan, Iacoboni, & Fried, 2010). These mirror neurons appeared not only in two different cingulate motor areas, but also in the nearby supplementary motor area and presupplementary motor area. Some of these neurons showed increases in firing rate when patients with epilepsy either performed a movement or watched someone else performing the same movement. However, they did not fire when the patient simply read a card describing the movement. Intriguingly, the authors also found that these areas contained roughly equal numbers of antimirror neurons. These neurons increased their firing rate during the execution of an action, but *decreased* the firing rate during the observation of someone else performing the same action. Antimirror neurons would provide a possible solution to the problem of how we are able to represent someone else's thoughts and intentions, while still keeping them separate from our own thoughts and actions.

Disorders of Theory of Mind

So far, we have discussed two forms of social cognition: theory of mind and motor mirror neurons. These partly interrelated functions rely on a distinct network of neural circuits (**FIGURE 15.13**). Although this network spans many different parts of the cortex, it does *not* overlap much with the networks that are active in working memory, mathematics, logic problems, and other tests of so-called "general intelligence."

The lack of overlap implies that it may be possible, in theory, to have severe deficits in theory of mind but not in general intelligence or vice versa. So are there any disorders that affect one system while leaving the other more or less intact?

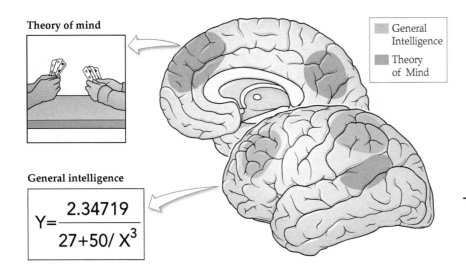

Theory of mind

General intelligence

$$Y = \frac{2.34719}{27 + 50/X^3}$$

General Intelligence

Theory of Mind

FIGURE 15.13 The brain regions associated with general intelligence (green) and the theory of mind (red) do not share a high degree of overlap.

People diagnosed with autism spectrum disorder have social and communication impairments as well as repetitive behaviors and restricted interests. Autism can vary in severity, but some people with autism have normal or higher-than-normal levels of general intelligence, as measured on traditional IQ tests (Charman et al., 2011). These individuals often have intense but restricted interests in features of the external world: memorizing an entire city's bus routes and schedules perfectly or learning sports statistics in extreme detail (FIGURE 15.14).

Yet despite their general intelligence being normal, they struggle with social intelligence and theory of mind (Baron-Cohen, 2004). They have difficulty picking up on basic social cues, such as eye gaze or gestures. They have trouble inferring a person's mental state from the appearance of their gaze in a given context. They take spoken language literally and have trouble following irony, humor, or sarcasm. They have difficulty understanding other people's beliefs, desires, and intentions. When the cashier calls out, "Next!", they cannot fill in the implicit gaps to understand that this person actually desires them to step forward and make a purchase.

People with autism also struggle with false beliefs like "You falsely believe that the cookie jar is full, even though I know it is empty." Children usually master false beliefs by around five years old, but those with autism may perform poorly on them even as adults (Ozonoff, Pennington, & Rogers, 1991). Because of the profound deficits in social cognition, people with autism are sometimes said to be "mind-blind" (Frith, 2001). Although people on the autistic spectrum often do have other cognitive difficulties, the social-cognitive impairments stand out.

Neuroimaging studies of people with autism also find differences in brain anatomy and activation in theory-of-mind regions compared to people without autism The STS shows decreased gray matter concentration, lower activity levels at rest, and abnormal activations during various forms of social cognition (Zilbovicius et al., 2006). Furthermore, people with autism show abnormalities of network connectivity: weaker functional connections between the posterior cingulate and medial prefrontal cortex compared to people without autism (Monk et al., 2009). In one study, when trying to attribute mental states to animated shapes, those with autism struggled with the task and showed much weaker activation than did control subjects (without autism) across the usual network of regions: STS, temporoparietal junction, temporal poles, and medial prefrontal cortex (Castelli, Frith, Happe, & Frith, 2002). This latter finding has led to some experimental therapies: a woman with autism showed improvements in social function and interpersonal understanding after a nine-day course of repetitive transcranial magnetic stimulation (rTMS) aimed at the medial prefrontal cortex (Enticott, Kennedy, Zangen, & Fitzgerald, 2011).

FIGURE 15.14 **Stephen Wiltshire draws a panorama of Singapore.** Stephen has been diagnosed with an autism spectrum disorder. He produces drawings of great complexity and accuracy from memory, after only a short time viewing the original scene.

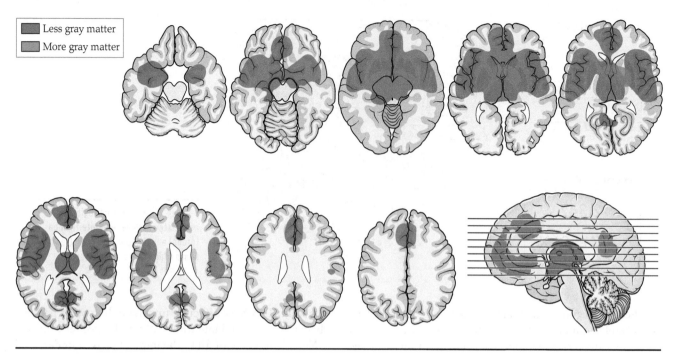

FIGURE 15.15 Brain regions with gray matter loss in schizophrenia. Compared to healthy controls, patients with schizophrenia have a reduction in gray matter in certain areas, including the medial prefrontal cortex, temporal poles, anterior insula, and some regions of the lateral prefrontal and premotor cortex. This network overlaps with the networks for social cue perception and theory of mind. (Lines at lower right indicate the positions of these axial slices within the brain.)

Multiple disorders in theory of mind also appear in **schizophrenia**—an illness we'll examine in more detail in Chapter 16. The bizarre symptoms of schizophrenia include social cue abnormalities like hearing voices talking to, or about, the patient. Many patients also have paranoid thoughts, which can include a false perception that people are looking at them or listening to them by invisible means. Many also have a strong sense that their actions are under the control of other people. Perplexed, they may devise bizarre beliefs in implanted microchips or mind-control rays to explain these weird experiences. Their social perceptions are badly distorted.

The ability to reason about intentions, beliefs, and desires can also be affected in schizophrenia. Schizophrenia patients often lose the distinction between their own thoughts and those of others. Hence, they may have a strange sense that their thoughts are being broadcast out of their heads for the world to hear. They may feel that they can literally hear the private thoughts of other people. They may even feel as if other people are controlling their minds, inserting and removing thoughts that do not belong there. Most of these symptoms can be described in terms of distortions of theory-of-mind functions.

The precise causes of schizophrenia are still being worked out. So far, the damage seems to involve subtle alterations in the microstructure of circuits linking the cortex and striatum (Cohen & Servan-Schreiber, 1992). However, some cortical areas are more affected than others, and voxel-based

morphometry (an imaging technique discussed in Chapter 16) can spot subtle, localized reductions in gray matter thickness in patients with schizophrenia. Across thousands of patients, the most common areas of reduced gray matter lie in the medial prefrontal cortex, posterior cingulate cortex, and superior temporal lobes, as well as the insula, thalamus, and striatum (FIGURE 15.15; Ellison-Wright & Bullmore, 2010).

As you can see, this network overlaps considerably with the areas that are most commonly active for social cue perception and theory of mind. It is not hard to imagine how disruptions of the microcircuitry in these areas might give rise to abnormal social perceptions and abnormal theory-of-mind functions. For example, only slight changes in the STS would be needed to create confusion between "he's looking away" and "he's looking at me." In fact, schizophrenia patients do tend to misinterpret averted gaze as directed at them (Hooker & Park, 2005).

Likewise, only slight changes in other STS areas might give rise to confusion between "my inner voice" and "someone else's voice": in other words, hallucinated voices talking. In the prefrontal cortex, changes to the wiring of medial mirror neurons and antimirror neurons could give rise to confusion between "I'm doing this" and "he's doing this" or "I'm thinking this" and "he's thinking this" or vice versa. So when patients with schizophrenia describe bizarre symptoms like hearing voices, being followed and stared at, or being subject to mind control, they may actually be faithfully describing their own perceptual experiences.

Social Feelings: Empathy and Its Many Components

Why does it hurt when someone else hurts? If a frail elderly woman should fall in the street, we may feel concern or a pang of pain, even if we are entirely uninjured. The death of a character in a film may bring tears to our own eyes, even if we know that the scene is pure fiction. But why and by what mechanisms do social cues compel us to tears in the first place? And how widely are these mechanisms shared outside the human species? In this next section, we will turn to the neural substrates of **empathy**.

An Emotional Theory of Mind

So far we have seen several subforms of theory of mind. A rudimentary perceptual theory of mind involves inferring mental states from specific social cues like eye gaze or posture. A slightly more complex motivational theory of mind involves inferring desires and goals based on observed behavior and context. The trickier informational theory of mind, at which only human beings seem to excel, involves inferring another mind's knowledge and belief, particularly if the belief is false or contradicts one's own. The last major subform that we will consider here is **emotional theory of mind**: the ability to infer another mind's inner emotional states, such as happiness, sadness, anger, fear, and so forth, even when these contradict one's own emotional state.

A short scenario may help to illustrate the different roles for emotional and informational theory of mind. Imagine the thief who has just stolen a purse from her unsuspecting victim in the painting of *The Fortune Teller* (FIGURE 15.16). Using informational theory of mind, she can determine that her victim will leave the scene under the false belief that he still has a purse full of money. Using emotional theory of mind, she can also determine that he should leave the scene feeling calm rather than angry because he has not yet learned of the theft. Should he suddenly discover that his purse is missing, she can again use her emotional theory of mind to infer that he will feel angry, although she herself feels happy about her successful liberation of the purse from its original owner.

Note here that emotional theory of mind is not necessarily equivalent to empathy. Empathy requires generating an appropriate emotional response to the other person's inferred emotion: guilt for causing hurtful feelings or concern for someone who is suffering. In this case, although the thief probably has a good *sense* of the other person's negative emotional state, this may not actually translate into any negative, compassionate emotional reactions on her own part. So we can think of empathy in terms of both a sensory side (being able to infer another

FIGURE 15.16 *The Fortune Teller* **by Georges de La Tour**. A good pickpocket (left) uses informational theory of mind to presume what a victim does and does not know about the location of his purse.

person's emotional state) and a motor side (actually generating your own appropriate inner emotional state, in response to the other person's inferred emotional state).

Alongside empathy are some lower-level processes by which emotional states can be communicated from one mind to another. The most basic example of this is mimicry. When two people interact with one another, they tend to gradually synchronize the expressions of their emotional state. Expressions on the emotional axis of **affiliation** tend to draw the same in return: a laugh draws a laugh, and an angry frown draws the same. Next time someone spies you in a crowd and gives you a friendly eyebrow-raise, try to suppress your own automatic response. It may take some effort!

Complementarity is a form of reverse mimicry that is important for other types of emotional communication. For example, emotional expressions on the axis of dominance tend to draw their opposite: dominant vocal tones draw submissive tones and vice versa. Likewise, dominant postures tend to draw submissive postures and vice versa. This countermimicry is important for building social connections. In experimental studies, human beings feel more comfortable when interacting with a partner who assumes a complementary posture and rate these partners as more likeable. Conversely, they feel less comfortable around those who stubbornly match their own posture and rate them as less likeable (Tiedens & Fragale, 2003).

This leads us to a second precursor of empathy: **emotional contagion** (Singer & Lamm, 2009). This refers to the tendency of emotional states to engender similar states in others, even in the absence of mental inference. As most parents know, babies reliably start crying when they hear other babies crying. Spending long periods of time with a sad person can become a saddening experience itself. Even brief exposure to a person in a panic can induce panic in others: hence the clichéd warning "Please remain calm..." during a crisis. Psychiatrists refer to the similar phenomenon of countertransference: the tendency for a therapist to develop an emotional state in reaction to the emotional state of the patient.

Empathy, Sympathy, and Compassion

Neither mimicry nor emotional contagion seems to add up to the full-blown phenomenon of empathy, although both may be contributing factors. What is missing? Mimicry and emotional contagion are both lower-level reflexive functions that lack the extra cognitive layer provided by an emotional theory of mind. Mimicry may be akin to the oculomotor reflexes by which the eyes track a simple visual stimulus: useful, but entirely automatic. Emotional contagion may be akin to the unconscious recognition processes of priming or blindsight: involving slightly more complex perceptual and motor activity, but still lacking in reflective awareness and inflexible in their outcome.

In contrast, empathy is a subjective experience that includes both the other person's emotional state and our own. For example, when we see a television commercial with a crying, disheveled child and are told that she is a hungry orphan (FIGURE 15.17), we may become conscious of her sadness and suffering. This can produce a powerful empathetic feeling of sadness and suffering in ourselves, which may lead to a telephone call and a pledge of monetary aid.

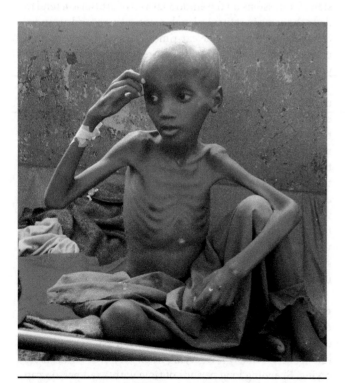

FIGURE 15.17 **Images of a starving or malnourished child can spark empathy, even in complete strangers.**

Here's one way that emotional theory of mind could work. Simple mimicry and complementarity is primarily a matching of expressions, which might be able to rely on social cue perception and premotor mirror neurons alone. In contrast, emotional contagion requires using social cues to drive the limbic circuitry of emotion and motivation. If emotional mirror neurons were to exist in the limbic motor regions of the brain, and there is not currently any evidence that they do, they would provide one obvious mechanism for emotional contagion. **Sympathy**, consciously sharing someone's emotional state, would resemble emotional contagion, but with additional mechanisms to allow for conscious reflection on the inner emotional state of each party. Empathy might be similar to sympathy, but drawing on emotional antimirror neurons that would generate an inner emotional state different from the one being perceived in the other person.

The simplest levels of this emotional theory of mind might also provide a foundation for the more complex levels. For example, when human beings watch short videos of people showing angry, happy, sad, or disgusted facial expressions, they tend to mimic the same expressions unconsciously (Hess & Blairy, 2001). However, the response doesn't end there. This unconscious mimicry also leads to emotional contagion: subjects develop subjective feelings of cheerfulness after viewing happy faces, sadness and irritation after viewing sad faces, and repulsion after viewing angry faces (Hess & Blairy, 2001).

Note that the contagious emotions do not always match the source emotions: anger did not give rise to anger, but to repulsion, and sadness engendered irritation as well as sadness. So emotion contagion can potentially lead to either sympathy or an opposite emotional response, depending on the circumstances. This can create an issue for some new mothers, who respond to the cries of their infants with distress and irritation rather than with compassion (Rapson, Hatfield, & Cacioppo, 1994). Such an inappropriate empathetic response may be a particular problem in mothers who are overwhelmed by their new responsibilities, have limited social supports, or suffer from **postpartum depression** (Murray & Cooper, 1997).

Empathy can also break down at many other points. There could be failure to interpret the social cues that predict others' emotional states: "Why is water coming out of your eyes?" There could be a failure of informational theory of mind mechanisms: "Why is it that you are feeling so sad?" Deficient limbic motor mechanisms could lead to a breakdown in sympathy: "I don't get why you're so broken up about this—you don't see *me* crying." A deficient emotional antimirror system could turn empathy into sympathy: "When I see you sad enough to cry, it makes me feel sad enough to cry!" Only with all of these components in place would there be a capacity for compassion: "I am moved by your sadness and care about your well-being."

The neural mechanisms behind emotional theory of mind and its various subcomponents have only recently come under study. Although much remains mysterious, we already have learned a surprisingly large amount about the basis of empathy, sympathy, compassion, and related social–emotional capacities of the human brain. Let's now turn to the neural basis of these processes in more detail.

Neural Mechanisms of Emotional Mimicry and Contagion

What neural mechanisms underlie the mimicry of emotional expressions? One neuroimaging study asked subjects to view a series of faces and rate them for sadness, intensity, and attractiveness. Unbeknownst to the subjects, the experimenters had digitally manipulated the faces to make the pupils of the eyes larger or smaller than they originally had been (FIGURE 15.18). Keep in mind that the parasympathetic nervous system decreases pupil size, whereas the sympathetic nervous system increases pupil size, via autonomic reflexes in the brainstem, under the control of limbic brain regions. So, pupil size provides a rough correlate of a person's emotional state.

When rating the faces, subjects did not consciously note any differences in pupil size. Nor did pupil size make any difference to ratings of intensity or attractiveness. However, for any given face, subjects gave higher ratings of sadness when the pupils were smaller. What's more, the raters' pupils tended to mirror the pupil size of the faces

they were viewing. When viewing smaller pupils, they themselves developed smaller pupils, in a form of completely unconscious emotional mimicry (Harrison, Singer, Rotshtein, Dolan, & Critchley, 2006). This reflexive mimicry appeared only for sad expressions and not for happy, angry, or neutral expressions.

On neuroimaging, even subtle changes in the pupil size of the faces (less than 0.1%) drove a widespread network of limbic regions including the amygdala, STS, insula, ventrolateral prefrontal cortex, and anterior cingulate cortex. Individual subjects varied in their susceptibility to the emotional contagion effect. The stronger the emotional contagion, the more tightly their pupil size correlated with the activity of the amygdala, STS, and frontal operculum. These higher limbic regions could be seen modulating the activity of a tiny pair of brainstem parasympathetic nuclei, called the **Edinger-Westphal nuclei**. These regions have long been known to regulate reflexive contractions of the pupils (FIGURE 15.18b).

So a distinct neural circuitry exists for emotional mimicry, and this circuitry involves limbic modulation of reflexes controlled at the brainstem level. Similar descending limbic mechanisms might explain how dominant postures elicit submissive ones and vice versa.

Of course, emotional mimicry is unconscious and does not necessarily lead to the subjective and behavioral effects of emotional contagion. So what extra ingredients are required for the spread of emotional states from one person to another? One obvious candidate would be the mirror

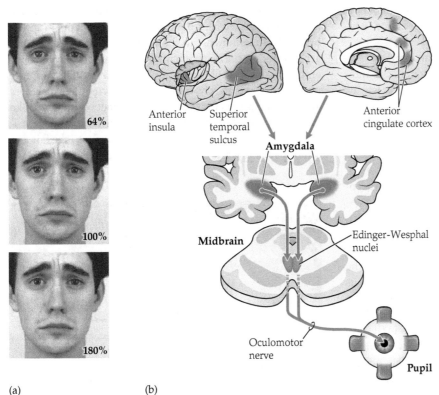

(a)　　　　　(b)

FIGURE 15.18 **Neural mechanisms of emotional contagion.** (a) Researchers manipulated the apparent pupil size of a person in a photograph, and they found that the subject appeared to be sadder when the pupils were larger. The numbers underneath each face describe how large the pupils were compared with the original image. (b) When subjects viewed sad faces with larger pupils, their own pupils also became larger. The neural pathways driving this emotional contagion included the superior temporal sulcus and anterior cingulate cortex, which can influence the amygdala. The amygdala in turn can drive activity in a midbrain nucleus—the Edinger-Westphal nucleus—which controls pupil size.

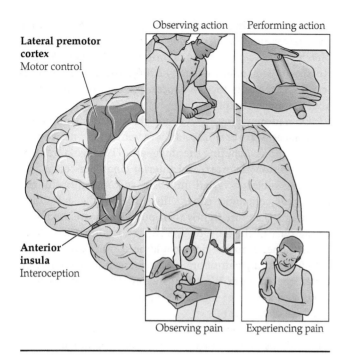

Observing action   Performing action

Lateral premotor cortex
Motor control

Anterior insula
Interoception

Observing pain   Experiencing pain

FIGURE 15.19 The lateral premotor cortex is active when performing or observing an action. Likewise, the anterior insula is active when experiencing pain or observing a person in pain.

neuron system, which can translate an observed action into a performance of the same action (FIGURE 15.19). The difficulty is that at least the lateral parts of this system seem to work primarily on motor actions themselves, rather than on the emotional states that might motivate them (Shamay-Tsoory, 2011). In other words, they may be good for "you-do–I-do," but not for "you-scared–me-scared."

In contrast, if the brain were to grow some mirror neurons just a little farther down the cortical sheet, in the anterior insula, these neurons might well do the trick. As we saw in Chapter 13, the insula is important for interoception: the sensation of internal states of the body, which represent the "feeling" part of emotional states like fear, anger, pleasure, or disgust. Theoretically, a population of mirror interoceptors would do a good job of representing either one's own emotional state or that of others. So are there mirror interoceptors anywhere in the brain?

So far, the answer is *maybe*. Either observing or experiencing disgust activates the anterior insula (Wicker et al., 2003). Likewise, either observing or experiencing pain activates the anterior insula (Singer et al., 2004). However, the spatial resolution of fMRI is not high enough to tell us whether these common activations are coming from the *same* common population of neurons or from two distinct but interwoven populations of neurons. As we saw in the previous section, there do seem to be some neurons with mirror properties in limbic motor areas like the cingulate cortex. However, so far we do not know whether this is also true of the limbic sensory cortex in the insula.

Neural Mechanisms of Empathy, Sympathy, and Antipathy

Empathy has become a hot topic in neuroimaging research. One of the first such studies looked at empathy for pain in romantically involved couples. The study compared brain activity in the female member of the couple during painful electrical stimulation of her hand versus when she was viewing the same stimulation applied to her partner's hand (Singer et al., 2004). Typically, painful stimulation activates a well-studied network of regions that includes somatosensory and primary motor areas, as well as limbic sensory and motor areas such as the insula and cingulate cortex (Peyron et al., 1999; Singer et al., 2004). Would any of these areas respond to a pain that was somebody else's?

The answer was yes. Primary and secondary somatosensory cortex activated only when the subject herself received painful stimulation. However, the anterior insula and anterior cingulate cortex activated during stimulation of either the subject *or* her partner (FIGURE 15.20). The same was true of subcortical pain-responsive areas in the brainstem and cerebellum. Typically, these areas are considered to represent the affective component of pain: in other words, its emotional unpleasantness, rather than its specific sensory features like location or quality. Subjects with higher scores on empathy questionnaires showed stronger empathetic pain activation in these regions.

Social context can also modulate these empathetic pain responses into either sympathy or antipathy. In another neuroimaging study, subjects began by playing a cooperative investment game with a possibility for either cooperation or betrayal. Unbeknownst to the subjects, their partners were actors hired by the experimenters. Some actors played cooperatively, and the subjects came to like them. Other actors played uncooperatively, frequently betraying their partners and keeping points for themselves. Subjects came to dislike these partners. The experimenters then reran the experiment on empathetic pain by delivering shocks to the fair and unfair partners while performing fMRI on the subjects.

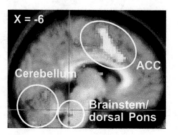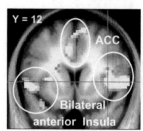

FIGURE 15.20 Pain networks. Brain regions including the anterior cingulate cortex, the anterior insula, and the cerebellum become more active both when a subject is experiencing pain and when the subject's loved one experiences pain.

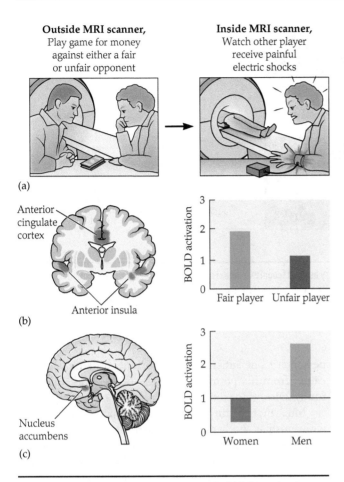

Outside MRI scanner,
Play game for money
against either a fair
or unfair opponent

Inside MRI scanner,
Watch other player
receive painful
electric shocks

(a)

Anterior
cingulate
cortex

Anterior insula

(b)

Nucleus
accumbens

(c)

FIGURE 15.21 **Mechanisms of empathy for pain.** (a) Subjects played a cooperation game against an opponent who played either fairly or unfairly. They then underwent fMRI while watching the opponent receive painful shocks. (b) The anterior insula and anterior cingulate cortex showed empathetic activation when watching the other player receive shocks. However, there was less activation when watching unfair players receive shocks. (c) Among male subjects, watching the unfair player receive shocks actually activated the nucleus accumbens—a key region in the reward pathway.

For shocks to the fair players, the results looked familiar: subjects activated anterior insula, anterior cingulate cortex, and brainstem, in sympathy for the partner's pain. However, these areas activated much less during shocks to the unfair players (FIGURE 15.21). In fact, male subjects did not activate these areas at all for shocks to players who were unfair. In postscan questionnaires, the subjects admitted a desire for revenge against the unfair players, and this desire was much stronger in men than in women. In keeping with this, the male subjects actually showed activation in the nucleus accumbens, an area usually associated with reward and positive emotion, during shocks to the unfair players. Female players, on average, showed a less vengeful deactivation of this area (Singer et al., 2006).

So the end result of empathy—a positive or negative emotional response to another's emotion—seems to play itself out among the usual neural substrates that we see activated in nonsocial emotions. Sympathetic negative emotions

involve activation of aversion-related areas in the insular and cingulate, whereas antipathetic positive emotions involve activation of reward areas in the ventral striatum. However, this result still leaves us with the question of which neural circuits are the *sources* of personal emotional activations, not in response to the direct input of visceral sensations or internal drives, but in response to the indirectly inferred mental states of other people.

To answer this last question, we'll turn to lesion studies rather than neuroimaging studies. We need a population of people who may be able to pick up on the emotional states of others, but cannot turn these inferences into emotional responses of their own. In other words, we must look for people who are lacking in empathy. Once we have found such a population, we can search for the specific neural abnormalities that might lead to such a breakdown in the normal mechanisms of social emotion.

Disorders of Empathy

Lesion studies have been teaching us valuable lessons about brain function ever since the famous discoveries of Broca's and Wernicke's areas for language expression and comprehension in the mid-19th century. More than 150 years later, lesions studies are beginning to explore the neural basis of empathy.

One recent study sought to uncover the neural basis of **emotional empathy** and **cognitive empathy**. Emotional empathy refers to the ability to generate emotional responses to those of others: "I feel what you feel." Cognitive empathy refers to the capacity to understand the feelings of others, without necessarily having an emotional reaction yourself: "I understand how you feel."

This particular study reported one of the Holy Grails of lesion research: a **double dissociation** (FIGURE 15.22). A double dissociation provides strong evidence that two types of cognition have distinct and nonoverlapping neural underpinnings, suggesting that they can be truly considered two different brain functions. In this case, the authors found that lesions of the ventromedial prefrontal cortex disrupted cognitive empathy, whereas lesions of the ventrolateral prefrontal cortex disrupted emotional empathy (Shamay-Tsoory, Aharon-Peretz, & Perry, 2009).

More specifically, the patients with ventromedial lesions had difficulty with theory-of-mind tasks, such as understanding false beliefs: "Anne falsely believes that Sally falsely believes that Anne has not stolen her ball, when in fact Sally knows exactly who took it." They were also rated as being more impaired at seeing things from other people's perspectives. In contrast, they had preserved abilities in recognizing the emotional states of others from photographs and were rated as still being able to have emotional contagion: feelings of compassion or anxiety in the appropriate social settings.

The ventrolateral lesion patients had the opposite pattern: preserved theory of mind, with impaired emotion recognition,

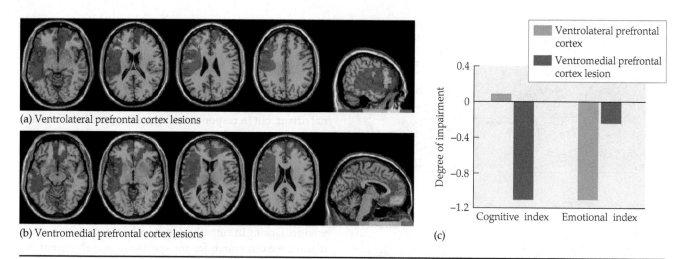

(a) Ventrolateral prefrontal cortex lesions

(b) Ventromedial prefrontal cortex lesions

(c)

FIGURE 15.22 Double dissociation between patients with impairments in theory of mind (cognitive index) and emotional recognition (emotional index). The MRI images show overlapping lesions for (a) patients who were impaired on the emotional recognition task and (b) on the theory of mind task. (c) The graph shows the double dissociation: the group with ventromedial prefrontal cortex lesions is impaired on the cognitive index, but not the emotional index, while the group with the inferior frontal gyrus lesions displayed the opposite pattern of impairments.

and preserved abilities to see things from others' perspectives, but impaired emotional contagion.

Patients with autism spectrum disorder often struggle with both kinds of cognition. As we saw earlier, patients with autism have widespread abnormalities in social perception and cognition brain areas including the STS, medial prefrontal cortex, and the frontal and parietal components of the lateral mirror system (FIGURE 15.23). On the one hand, they lack the cognitive empathy required for theory-of-mind tasks. On the other hand, they also tend to lack emotional empathy or emotion contagion. They may stare with incomprehension at a frightened person, rather than succumbing to contagious fear (Hadjikhani et al., 2009). On hearing a

person cry, one autistic child reportedly began to laugh because, from his point of view, the person was "making a funny noise" (Hobson, 1985).

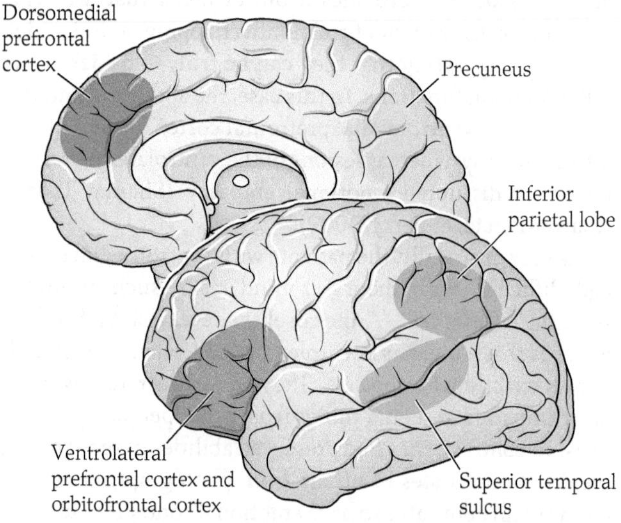

Much more disturbing than these social lapses of children with autism is another type of empathy deficit: **psychopathy**. Psychopaths typically show no deficits on theory-of-mind tasks: they are able to understand the beliefs, desires, intentions, and goals of others at a cognitive level. They are also able to recognize the emotional states of others (Dolan & Fullam, 2004). In these respects, they have a superficial appearance of social normality. The difference is that they simply don't care. The knowledge of another's suffering or sadness does not engender either emotional contagion or emotional empathy, although they are perfectly aware that the person is suffering and wants the suffering to stop.

Some people are born with psychopathic features, whereas others have acquired psychopathy (sometimes referred to as sociopathy) following a brain injury or disease. Acquired psychopathy sometimes appears in frontotemporal dementia, discussed earlier in this chapter. Some frontotemporal dementia patients start exhibiting psychopathic behaviors: unsolicited sexual acts, physical assaults, hit-and-run accidents, breaking and entering, and stealing food or simply eating food from grocery store shelves. These patients typically show widespread degeneration of the orbitofrontal and temporoparietal cortex (Ernst, Chang, Melchor, & Mehringer, 1997). Patients with traumatic injuries to the nearby ventromedial prefrontal cortex may also develop similar patterns of behavior (Barrash, Tranel, & Anderson, 2000).

Acquired psychopathy patients are perfectly able to describe the consequences of their actions, both for their victims and for themselves. They are able to understand that their behavior is unacceptable and know that it is wrong, even at the time they commit the acts. However, from an emotional point of view, they feel no particular sense of guilt

Dorsomedial prefrontal cortex

Precuneus

Inferior parietal lobe

Ventrolateral prefrontal cortex and orbitofrontal cortex

Superior temporal sulcus

FIGURE 15.23 Individuals with autism spectrum disorder often show abnormalities in the brain areas involved with social cognition.

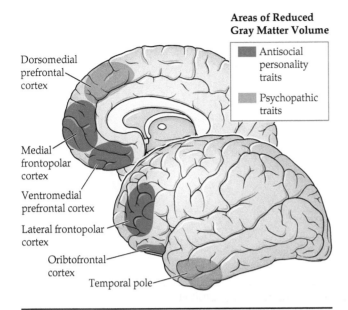

Areas of Reduced Gray Matter Volume

■ Antisocial personality traits

■ Psychopathic traits

Dorsomedial prefrontal cortex

Medial frontopolar cortex

Ventromedial prefrontal cortex

Lateral frontopolar cortex

Oribtofrontal cortex

Temporal pole

FIGURE 15.24 Individuals diagnosed as having antisocial personality traits often have reduced gray matter volume in the ventromedial and orbitofrontal regions of the prefrontal cortex. Those who also have psychopathic traits have additional reductions in gray matter in the dorsomedial prefrontal cortex and temporal pole.

or shame. Although they may express remorse verbally, they rarely engage in any remorseful behavior such as apologizing or making amends to their victims (Mendez, Chen, Shapira, & Miller, 2005).

Not all psychopathy is acquired. Some cases are **congenital**: appearing from birth. Such individuals tend toward a life-long history of aggressive or antisocial behavior toward others and frequently run afoul of the law. Neuroimaging studies show that such individuals tend to have reductions in gray matter volume in the ventromedial, orbitofrontal, and fronto-polar cortex (FIGURE 15.24). On the other hand, those who have the additional feature of psychopathy have additional gray matter loss in the temporal poles and dorsal medial prefrontal

cortex (Tiihonen et al., 2008). These individuals tend to have more difficulty assigning importance to social norms, and a lesser ability to register the emotional states of other people. In particular, without an intact ventromedial prefrontal cortex, they may have trouble in translating this knowledge so that they hurt when others hurt and thus guide them away from causing suffering to others (R. J. R. Blair, 2001).

Social Emotions, Motivations, and Behavior

Social interactions and knowledge of previous social experiences can influence our emotions, motivations, and behaviors. In part, theory of mind lets us understand how others might view our actions. Beyond that, socially derived ideas, such as "honor" and "virtue," can motivate us to act one way or another. In this section, we will explore these ideas to better understand the source of our social emotions and see how these same social factors can lead us to be deceptive.

Social Emotions from Theory of Mind

As we saw earlier, the emotion of guilt is an essential mechanism for adapting behavior to social and moral norms and for avoiding antisocial activities. This mechanism can go awry in disease states like acquired psychopathy, in which affected patients begin to show gross violations of socially acceptable behavior and an absence of the usual emotional responses of remorse or guilt. It can also go awry in mental illnesses like **major depressive disorder** (discussed in Chapter 16), in which one of the most common symptoms is a pathologically *high* level of guilt.

CASE STUDY:
Acquired Sociopathy

At the age of 56, an electrical engineer with the initials J. S. fell unconscious after suffering an injury to the front of his head (R. J. Blair & Cipolotti, 2000). When he awoke in the hospital, his temperament had changed dramatically. Before the injury, he had been a

quiet, somewhat withdrawn man with no history of psychiatric illness or aggression. Afterward, his behavior became bizarre. He became irritable and aggressive. He frequently threw objects or pieces of furniture at other people and, at one point, assaulted

and wounded a member of the medical staff.

Most disturbingly, he showed no remorse for his behavior and little empathy for his victims. At one point he began pushing a wheelchair-bound patient around the ward, ignoring her screams of terror. He took no responsibility for his violent actions toward the staff, justifying his behavior on the grounds that the staff were too slow in responding to his demands.

A CT scan of his head revealed damage to the orbitofrontal cortex on both sides, as well as to the left anterior temporal lobe (FIGURE 15.25). Neuropsychological assessments showed his general intelligence to be intact, with memory in the average to high-average range. He also showed no deficits in abstract knowledge of social norms and rules. By contrast, he was profoundly impaired in identifying examples of violations of these social norms. He also showed profound impairments in empathy, with difficulty attributing the emotions of fear, anger, or embarrassment to others. However, his performance on theory-of-mind tasks was unimpaired.

J. S. had developed the syndrome of sociopathy—a not-uncommon result of injury to the orbitofrontal or anterior temporal cortex. His behavior showed many of the features seen in antisocial personalities: irritability, aggression, poor impulse control, a reckless disregard for the rights of others, and persistent violation of social norms. The difference

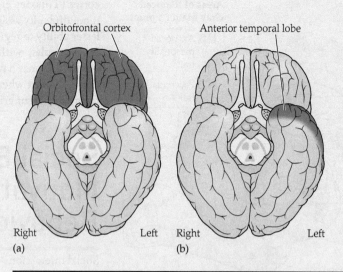

FIGURE 15.25 **Lesions causing acquired sociopathy in Patient J. S.** (a) Bilateral damage to the orbitofrontal cortex. (b) Damage to the left anterior temporal lobe.

was that these behaviors had not been lifelong, but had emerged only after traumatic brain injury. Unfortunately, the damage was permanent, and J. S. was never again able to work because of his severe difficulties in interacting appropriately with other people.

The case of J. S. raises the question of whether those with lifelong antisocial behavior have dysfunction in the same brain regions as J. S., but acquired at a much earlier age or even before birth. Neuroimaging and postmortem studies suggest that this may indeed be the case, at least for

some individuals with antisocial personality and criminal behavior (Craig et al., 2009; Weder, Aziz, Wilkins, & Tampi, 2007). Unfortunately, even in such cases, we are currently no better able to repair the damage than we would be in the case of J. S. or any other victim of traumatic brain injury. Containment and risk management may be the only workable strategy at present. Still, in the meantime, the case of J. S. may prompt us to generate some empathy for those unfortunate human beings who have none themselves.

So what is the difference, neurally speaking, between guilt and sadness? One important difference may be that guilt requires theory of mind in a way that simple sadness does not. A sense of guilt requires not only personal sadness or regret, but also a sense of having had a negative impact on the emotional states of other people.

In fMRI studies, robust guilty feelings can be elicited by having subjects recall episodes from their own lives during scanning (Wagner, N'Diaye, Ethofer, & Vuilleumier, 2011). For episodes evoking the emotions of guilt, shame, and sadness, there was a common network of activation that included recall-related regions such as the posterior and retrosplenial cingulate cortex, as well as social knowledge–related areas in the temporal poles, social-perceptual areas in the STS, and interoceptive areas in the anterior insula. Visceromotor regions in the ventromedial prefrontal cortex also

activated under all three conditions. However, there were also some activations appearing only for guilt and absent in sadness or shame: in the right lateral orbitofrontal cortex and dorsomedial prefrontal cortex (DMPFC) (FIGURE 15.26).

As you may recall from Chapter 13, lateral orbitofrontal areas help modulate emotional states based on context. Consistent with this, subjects with stronger feelings of guilt showed stronger activations in this region. This area also activates during nonguilty states such as **social rejection** (Eisenberger, Lieberman, & Williams, 2003). So this area may have a common role in translating conceptual knowledge (for example, the knowledge that one is being left out or has caused suffering to others) into the associated negative emotional responses.

As for the DMPFC, this area appears in a wide variety of studies of theory of mind tasks, as we saw earlier in

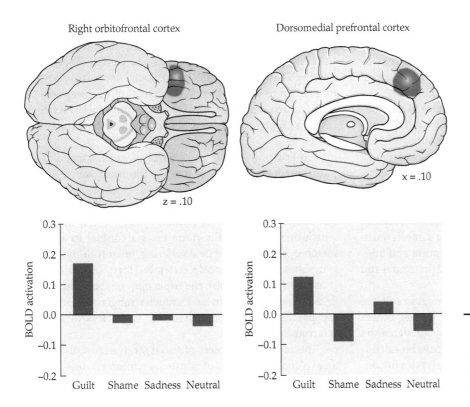

Right orbitofrontal cortex

Dorsomedial prefrontal cortex

z = .10

x = .10

FIGURE 15.26 The orbitofrontal cortex and dorsomedial prefrontal cortex are activated during guilty emotional states. These areas are less active during induction of other emotional states such as sadness or shame.

this chapter. Notably, whereas the DMPFC was activated during guilt, it showed a *deactivation* during shame. More than one interpretation is possible here. It is possible that guilt, more than shame or sadness, requires a representation of the thoughts of other people, thus evoking more DMPFC activation. It is also possible that guilt involves more **self-reflection** than shame or sadness, so that the DMPFC activation is a byproduct of greater rumination on one's own mental states.

Social Emotions from Social Values

Aside from theory of mind, **social valuation** is another important way by which social knowledge can feed into our emotions and motivations, guilty or otherwise. Social concepts like "kindness," "honor," and "stinginess" can be used as benchmarks against which to interpret the value of a given action. This value can then be translated into an inner emotional reaction: guilt may be one example, but other social emotions are also possible: pride, indignation, or gratitude are all forms of social emotional reaction.

The precise emotional reaction may depend not only on how the action measures up against one's inner social knowledge, but also on whether it is *you* or *I* who is the agent of the action. For example, if I present you with a birthday gift that exceeds my expected social norm of generosity, I may feel a sense of pride directed at myself; if you do the same to me, I may feel gratitude directed at you instead. If I present you with a stingy gift, I may feel guilt directed at

myself; if you do the same to me, I may feel indignation directed at you.

How do the mechanisms of social valuation play out within the brain? As we saw earlier, the anterior temporal lobes contain specific regions that seem to play a key role in representing social concepts. In fMRI studies, these areas are active when subjects use their knowledge of social concepts as benchmarks to evaluate their own actions or those of others (Zahn, Moll, Paiva et al., 2009). The activation in the temporal poles is of similar intensity regardless of who performs the action or whether the final emotional reaction is positive or negative: a profile consistent with an area that represents the social benchmark, rather than the final measurement of social value itself.

How does the agent factor in? In one study, emotional judgments of one's own actions (for example, actions leading to pride or guilt) involved activation of the ventromedial prefrontal cortex, although the precise region differed depending on whether the final emotional state was positive or negative. Conversely, emotional judgments of the actions of *others* (gratitude, or indignation) tended to involve activation of the lateral orbitofrontal cortex and anterior insula, rather than the medial wall (Zahn, Moll, Paiva et al., 2009).

What about the final emotional states? Positive emotional states, such as pride and gratitude, involved activation of a network of reward-related regions at multiple levels of the nervous system: the dopaminergic circuitry of the midbrain's ventral tegmental area, medial areas of the hypothalamus involved in affiliation and bonding, and reward-related areas in the **septum** and regions of the subgenual cingulate gyrus. Negative emotional states like indignation tended to activate anterior insula and orbitofrontal cortex—regions that are also involved in nonsocial aversive states like disgust, as we saw in the previous chapter.

Putting it all together, we can start to see how social emotions like gratitude or guilt might have some output features in common with nonsocial emotions like pleasure and aversion, while at the same time drawing on a wider set of inputs. An aversive social state like indignation has the insular activation of disgust, but this is also accompanied by the medial prefrontal and anterior temporal activations needed to represent theory of mind and social knowledge. A pleasant social emotional state like gratitude has the same reward-related activations we typically see in the septum and midbrain, but accompanied once again by medial prefrontal and anterior temporal activation as well.

Taking out sections of this network may remove some of the usual features of social emotions while leaving others intact (FIGURE 15.27). For example, frontotemporal dementia patients with damage to the temporal poles may show disinhibited or antisocial behavior, their emotional states unconstrained by the usual social checks (Miller, Darby, Benson, Cummings, & Miller, 1997). Patients with autism may laugh at the "funny noise" of a child crying, their pleasure untempered by an understanding of the other person's sad emotional state (Damasio, Maurer, Damasio, & Chui, 1980; Perlman, 2000). Psychopathic patients may be perfectly aware of social norms and of the suffering of the other person, yet be unable to translate this into a negative emotional state of their own, thus losing the capacity for empathy (Glannon, 1997).

Social Reward and Social Aversion

Social rewards are often the strongest rewards of all. For female rats, access to their pups is a more powerful reinforcing stimulus than any other, including cocaine (Insel, 2003). In human beings, the striatal circuitry of reward responds not only to juice, food, cocaine, or money, but also to positive

facial expressions, increases in **social reputation**, positive social feedback (Izuma, Saito, & Sadato, 2008), or even the suffering of a disliked person (Krach, Paulus, Bodden, & Kircher, 2010; Singer et al., 2006). Social rewards are powerful enough to drive athletes to exhaustion, or deception, or both in pursuit of the *maillot jaune*. They may fuel a dictator's ruthless climb to power or a teacher's selfless devotion to her students.

No less powerful is the impact of social aversion and punishment. Ostracism is among the most severe of all sanctions in many traditional cultures. Criticism, more than corporal punishment, is a primary form of negative reinforcement in nearly every human society. Social defeat, in which one member of a group loses a conflict to another member, more than physical suffering, reliably brings on the symptoms of depression (Keeney & Hogg, 1999). Among those who lose their jobs, the triple blow of social exclusion, criticism, and defeat can have a much stronger and more lasting psychological impact than the actual loss of income (Garrett-Peters, 2009).

The astonishing power of social motivation calls out for an explanation. Studies of nonsocial reinforcers, like food or electric shocks, have been underway ever since the classic experiments of Pavlov, Skinner, and other behaviorists in the early 20th century. However, so far, human studies of the mechanisms of social reinforcers are still in their infancy.

What do we know about the basis of social rewards? Both monetary rewards and social rewards share common neural substrates in the ventral striatum (FIGURE 15.28). Ventral regions of the caudate and putamen show strong responses to positive social feedback. The strength of these responses is similar to that seen for monetary rewards (Izuma et al., 2008). Striatal activation has therefore been proposed as the neural substrate for a "common currency" of value, whether social or nonsocial (Montague & Berns, 2002).

Social factors are particularly powerful in driving striatal activation. For example, in the absence of observers, subjects show little or no activation of the left striatum when they donate money to charity and substantially more activation when they keep the money for themselves. However, in the presence of observers, this pattern reverses: subjects show

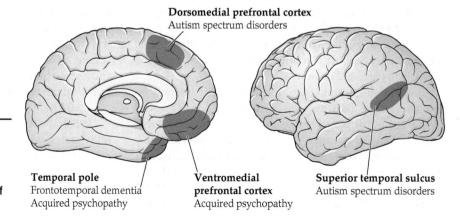

FIGURE 15.27 Disorders that affect social functioning (e.g., frontotemporal dementia, autism spectrum disorders, and psychopathy) often involve abnormalities of key brain regions involved in social perception, theory of mind, and empathy.

Dorsomedial prefrontal cortex
Autism spectrum disorders

Temporal pole
Frontotemporal dementia
Acquired psychopathy

Ventromedial prefrontal cortex
Acquired psychopathy

Superior temporal sulcus
Autism spectrum disorders

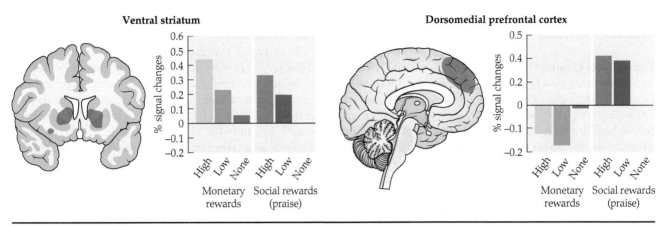

FIGURE 15.28 **Brain activation for social and monetary rewards.** Both monetary rewards and social rewards (such as praise) activate the ventral striatum bilaterally. However, the dorsomedial prefrontal cortex activates only for social rewards, and it is less active for monetary rewards.

less activation when they keep money for themselves and more activation when they donate the money to charity. The right striatum shows similar activation for either donated or kept money in the absence of observers, but once again, in the presence of observers, there is greater activation for donated money and less activation for kept money. So the mere presence of social observation seems to have powerful effects on striatal reward activity (Izuma, Saito, & Sadato, 2010a).

If the striatum serves as the site for social modulation of reward, then what regions serve as the source? This question is still under investigation, but some evidence comes from fMRI studies of the neural basis of social reputation. Unlike many personal qualities, one's reputation exists entirely in other minds. To gauge one's own reputation, one should therefore need to tap into theory of mind: "what do other people think of me?" Consistent with this prediction, both the medial prefrontal cortex and the associated dorsal striatum showed strong activation in one study when subjects reflected on how they were viewed by others (King-Casas, Tomlin, Anen, Camerer, Quartz, & Montague, 2005) (FIGURE 15.29).

How do the substrates of social reward compare to those of social aversion? One recent fMRI study looked at both types of reinforcer by presenting subjects with either verbal praise ("You're a genius"), verbal criticism ("You're an idiot"), or neutral statements ("You're a human"). As one might expect, social criticism activated the amygdala bilaterally in patients with **social anxiety disorder**, who show a disabling fear of social interactions. As we saw in Chapter 13, research has provided evidence that the amygdala is essential for many kinds of nonsocial fear responses as well. However, in this case, it was the medial prefrontal cortex whose activation appeared during the anxiety of social criticism specifically. In addition, the functional connectivity between the dorsomedial prefrontal cortex and the amygdala was increased during social criticism in patients with social anxiety compared with healthy control subjects (K. Blair et al., 2008).

As we will see later in the chapter, these particular regions of medial prefrontal cortex show strong activation during reflection on one's own personal qualities, dreams, hopes, and aspirations. These same representations may provide a source for modulating the reward-related activity of the striatum, thus creating a mechanism by which self-image and reputation can exert powerful effects on the landscape of reward and motivation (Izuma, Saito, & Sadato, 2010b). These regions also happen to be rich in von Economo neurons (see Chapter 3), whose connectivity and anatomical structure may help insert remote considerations into current calculations of value (Allman, Watson, Tetreault, & Hakeem, 2005).

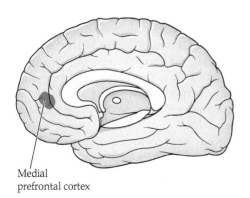

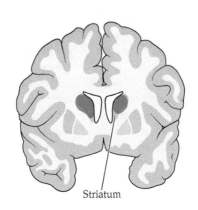

Medial prefrontal cortex

Striatum

FIGURE 15.29 **Neural mechanisms of social reputation.** When considering your own reputation (how others might think of you), activity increases in the striatum and also in the medial prefrontal cortex—an area that is important for theory of mind.

The Anatomy of a Lie

Deception is common in many competitive social species, and humans are no exception. Tour de France riders make headlines when they lie about their use of performance-enhancing drugs, but they are hardly alone in deceiving their fellow human beings when the stakes are high. Virtually everyone on the planet engages in some form of deception every day, and the motives are sometimes benign: telling Santa Claus stories to children, reassuring our friends about their physical appearance, or denying our sense of irritation if a friend asks us for a large and inconvenient favor. Opportunities to lie are commonplace, and if we stand to gain from deception, the temptation can be strong.

So what drives honesty in the human brain? Does telling the truth require us to actively resist the temptation to lie? Or is honesty a matter of not feeling the temptation in the first place? Neuroimaging studies are now beginning to address questions like these.

In one study, participants were asked to make guesses about whether a coin would come up heads or tails while undergoing fMRI (Greene & Paxton, 2009). To raise the stakes, participants won bonus money for correct answers and lost bonus money for incorrect answers. They were led to believe that the study was about the ability to predict the future. However, the study was actually about participants' behavior when given the opportunity to lie. On some of the trials, participants had to declare their prediction of heads or tails in advance. On others, they were told the outcome of the coin toss and *then* asked whether they had correctly predicted it, so that there was an opportunity to lie (FIGURE 15.30a).

When accurate reporting depended on the "honor system," some participants showed more honor than others. Statistically, the average performance in guessing coin tosses should be around 50%. Some subjects performed around this level on the honor system, whereas others claimed to have success rates that were improbably high. Even for lucky guessers, after 70 trials, the odds of getting more than 70% correct drop to less than one in a thousand. Nonetheless, of 35 participants, 14 claimed to have made the right prediction on more than 70% of the trials. Several reported better than 90% accuracy—a statistically improbable performance, with odds of roughly 1 in a trillion! Alas, these would-be psychics had nowhere near this level of accuracy when forced to declare their predictions ahead of time, rather than after the fact.

What differences appeared between the two groups? First, when offered the opportunity to lie, dishonest subjects showed longer reaction times to report their predictions—just as in other studies in which participants face a difficult moral dilemma. Honest subjects showed no difference in reaction time across all trials, whether or not there was a chance to lie. Likewise, in the fMRI results, honest subjects showed no differences in brain activation for any region in trials with an opportunity to lie versus trials without an opportunity to lie.

In sharp contrast, dishonest subjects showed evidence of additional brain activation when given the opportunity to lie. When deciding to lie to win money, these subjects showed greater activity in anterior regions of the dorsolateral prefrontal cortex (FIGURE 15.30b)—an area also known to be active in moral dilemmas, during utilitarian decisions that favor long-term gain over emotional pain (Greene, Nystrom, Engell, Darley, & Cohen, 2004). When deciding to be honest and accept a loss, these same subjects showed widespread activation bilaterally in the dorsolateral prefrontal cortex and dorsomedial prefrontal cortex (FIGURE 15.30c).

So it seems that honesty operates as both a state and a trait. Among honest individuals, researchers found no evidence of a cognitive battle against temptation, even when an opportunity arose to lie for personal benefit. Yet among dishonest individuals, both the decision to lie and the decision to be honest involved additional cognitive conflict and deliberation. Among liars, the decision to be honest engaged brain regions quite similar to the ones seen in studies of moral dilemmas.

If there really is a neuroanatomy of lying, then this opens up the strange possibility of stimulating or inhibiting these brain areas to either enhance or interfere with the tendency to lie. For example, brain stimulation with rTMS could be directed at the dorsomedial prefrontal cortex or dorsolateral prefrontal cortex in an attempt to either inhibit or suppress the baseline activity of these regions. Such techniques have already been shown to cause shifts in decision making during moral judgments (Young, Camprodon, Hauser, Pascual-Leone, & Saxe, 2010). If rTMS could be shown to produce a similar shift toward less deceptive behavior, this would constitute a worrisome technique for "truth compulsion" rather than "lie detection."

In fact, some mild, antideceptive forms of neurostimulation have already arrived. Transcranial direct current stimulation (tDCS) is being used more and more commonly as an alternative to rTMS for producing temporary alterations in neural activity in human beings, noninvasively. Recent studies have shown that applying tDCS to the dorsolateral prefrontal cortex can influence deceptive behaviors (Priori et al., 2008). As we saw earlier, deceptive responses tend to be associated with longer reaction times than truthful responses, probably because of the increased cognitive conflict between the dorsolateral prefrontal cortex and other prefrontal regions involved in behavioral control during decision making. The reaction time penalty for deceptive responses increases substantially after tDCS over the dorsolateral prefrontal cortex. So, at least in an experimental setting, neurostimulation could potentially make it easier to detect deceptive responses (Priori et al., 2008).

A more recent study has provided evidence that tDCS can also *enhance* deceptive abilities (Karim et al., 2010). In this case, the tDCS was applied over the frontopolar cortex rather than the dorsolateral prefrontal cortex. The subjects

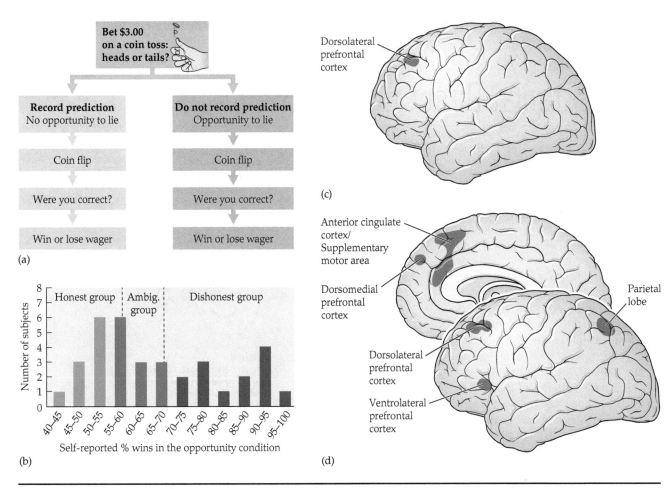

FIGURE 15.30 **Measuring lies.** (a) Subjects were told the amount of the wager and then asked to predict whether the coin toss would be heads or tails. In the condition in which they had no opportunity to lie, they recorded their prediction. When they had the opportunity to lie, they did not record their prediction. After the coin toss, subjects recorded whether their prediction had been correct or incorrect. If it was correct, they won the amount of the wagers; if it was incorrect, they lost that amount. (b) Some individuals showed honest behavior, guessing correctly around 50% of the time. Others were dishonest, reporting correct guesses more than 75% of the time. (c) Neural activity associated with the decision to lie. (d) Neural activity associated with the decision to tell the truth.

in this study were asked to play the role of a "thief" and were given instructions to steal some money from a room in the laboratory. After the theft, they underwent a mock interrogation by a researcher playing the role of a "police investigator." After tDCS of the frontopolar cortex, the "thieves" showed *faster* reaction times when lying about their behavior, generated smaller galvanic skin responses, and even reported lower feelings of guilt during deception. They also showed a more skillful pattern of lying: not simply increasing the number of false responses across the board, but also answering some questions truthfully and lying only in their answers to the questions that were critical to determining their innocence or guilt.

Findings like these raise a whole chorus of moral, ethical, social, and philosophical concerns. If this technology matures, will there be pressure to use it during real-world interrogations? Will prospective job applicants or wayward spouses be pressured to answer questions about their past behavior under tDCS? If the findings prove reliable, will they be used to determine criminal guilt or innocence? To address these kinds of concerns in a meaningful way, we'll first need to learn much more about the neuroscience of deception, including just how much influence techniques like tDCS and rTMS really do have on deceptive behavior in real-life circumstances. Nonetheless, this area is certainly bound to generate a flurry of research, and an even wider flurry of social commentary, in the years to come.

Neurotransmitters and Social Behavior

As is true for almost every topic within neuroscience, social behaviors can be explained, at least in part, by the interaction of neurotransmitters with their receptors. This section will focus on two peptide transmitters. At the risk of overgeneralizing, one is involved in forming attachments, whether between parent and child or between romantic partners, and

RESEARCH METHODS:
Transcranial Direct Current Stimulation

Transcranial direct current stimulation (tDCS) is a neurostimulation technique that involves applying low-intensity direct current to the brain using external electrodes for sessions of around 10–30 minutes (Priori et al., 2008). A tDCS device looks roughly like a small portable oscilloscope and is capable of delivering constant-current stimulation between two electrodes attached to the scalp (FIGURE 15.31). The technique is painless, and there is usually little or no sensation during stimulation. The energies involved are much smaller than those used in other neurostimulation techniques such as rTMS or electroconvulsive therapy (ECT). Whereas a typical ECT session involves applying pulsed currents of around 800 milliamps, tDCS employs continuous currents of just 1–2 milliamps.

Although it may seem counterintuitive that such a weak electrical stimulus could have much influence on the brain, the effects of tDCS on neural activity are substantial and well documented (Stagg & Nitsche, 2011). tDCS does not actually depolarize neurons, but instead modulates their ongoing activity. During tDCS, cortical neurons show increases in spontaneous neural activity under the negatively charged electrode, or anode. Under the positively charged cathode, the opposite occurs, and neurons show reduced spontaneous activity. The effects of tDCS can endure beyond the period of the stimulation itself. A 10-minute session of tDCS can produce neural

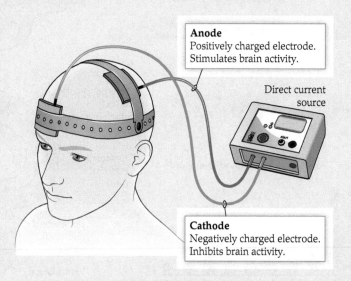

Anode
Positively charged electrode. Stimulates brain activity.

Direct current source

Cathode
Negatively charged electrode. Inhibits brain activity.

FIGURE 15.31 Transcranial direct current stimulation.

and behavioral effects lasting for hours.

So far, tDCS has remained relatively obscure when compared to much better studied counterparts such as rTMS or ECT. Despite this, it is actually the oldest of all neurostimulation techniques in clinical use. As far back as 1804, the Italian physicist Giovanni Aldini (nephew of electricity pioneer, Luigi Galvani) reported success in treating patients with depression by applying direct current to the scalp (Priori, 2003). Although studies continued over the next century, the technique eventually fell out of favor in the 1930s, with the discovery of ECT. Some studies of the effects of tDCS on neural activity and on mental illness continued through the 1960s and 1970s, but it was only in the late

1990s that tDCS emerged once again into its modern era of study (Priori, 2003).

To date, tDCS has been shown to exert behavioral effects on a wide variety of motor, sensory, and cognitive functions including working memory, visuomotor learning, risk aversion, language learning, and deception (Nitsche et al., 2008). Clinical studies have begun to investigate the effects of tDCS in major depression, chronic pain, alcohol and food cravings, Alzheimer dementia, and recovery of language and motor functions after stroke. Given that tDCS is relatively safe, inexpensive, noninvasive, and simple to perform, the clinical and research applications of this technique will almost certainly expand tremendously in the years to come.

the other is involved in social dominance and aggression. By this point, you surely know that nothing in neuroscience is that simple, so let's explore the history and function of these two peptides.

An Ancient and Fundamental System

The peptide neurotransmitters oxytocin and **vasopressin** are central to many forms of social behavior. Both the neurotransmitters themselves and the neural pathways that use them have been tightly conserved throughout the entire course of evolution of animal life. Vasopressin- and oxytocinlike peptides can be found in organisms that have not shared a common ancestor for more than 700 million years: humans, hamsters, salmon, snails, fruit flies, and earthworms. Over this vast timeline, they have changed so little that the blowfish isotocin gene can be transferred into the genome of a rat, and the peptide will still turn up in the appropriate neural structures and perform many of the same biological functions (Venkatesh, Si-Hoe, Murphy, & Brenner, 1997). To put this finding in perspective, not even the peptides that carry our *oxygen* have remained so unchanged for so long: flies and snails use copper-containing hemocyanin instead of the iron-containing hemoglobin of mammals. In evolutionary terms, social behaviors are more fundamental than our modes of respiration.

In terms of neuroanatomy, the receptors for both the oxytocin and the vasopressin peptides are densely concentrated in the (also highly conserved) core structures of the limbic system. Various regions of the hypothalamus, amygdala, septum, and hippocampus all have high levels of oxytocin and vasopressin receptors (FIGURE 15.32). This allows the two peptides to regulate an organism's mission-critical classes of motivated behaviors: in particular, the agonistic and reproductive classes of behaviors that are so essential to long-term survival. It also allows them to regulate the complex mixture of endocrine, autonomic, and motor responses that bring about basic drives.

One important point about the oxytocin and vasopressin systems is that, although they are ancient and universal, their distributions in the nervous system vary greatly from species to species. For example, monogamous mammal species have a much different distribution of vasopressin receptors than do nonmonogamous species, and it is these differences that are thought to drive their different approaches to mating, bonding, and parenting (Lim & Young, 2004).

Distributions of the oxytocin and vasopressin systems also vary widely between the sexes. For example, within a given species, females have much higher levels of oxytocin receptors in some hypothalamic nuclei regulating reproductive and parenting behaviors (Campbell, 2008). Conversely, males have much higher levels of vasopressin receptors in nuclei regulating aggression and social dominance behaviors (Bester-Meredith, Young, & Marler, 1999; Wersinger,

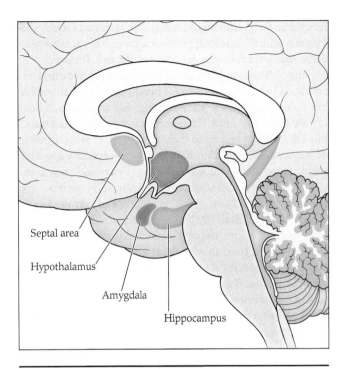

FIGURE 15.32 Oxytocin and vasopressin receptors are found in the hypothalamus, hippocampus, septal area, and amygdala.

Ginns, O'carroll, Lolait, & Young Iii, 2002). Sex hormones such as estrogen and testosterone help to drive these differential patterns of expression during the course of brain development (de Vries, 2008).

Finally, there is also considerable variation in these systems even between individuals of the same sex and species (de Vries, 2008). These differences help to account for the wide variation in most social drives and behaviors that exists from individual to individual, across the animal kingdom. When it comes to social behavior, no single solution seems to be best under all circumstances. An aggressive hawk may rise swiftly to dominance in a world of peaceful doves, but in a world filled with bloodied and battered hawks, a nonconfrontational dove may quietly thrive. For this reason, it pays to have an adjustable set of social neurotransmitters whose effects can be turned on and off as the situation requires. Let's now look at the specific effects of oxytocin and vasopressin in guiding social behavior.

Oxytocin

Oxytocin promotes affiliation, pair bonding, and parenting behaviors. It controls egg laying in female snails and reproduction-related behaviors in most other female animals, including humans: female sexual receptiveness, contractions of the uterus during birth, lactation, maternal–infant attachment, and pair bonding (Donaldson & Young, 2008). Why have a single dedicated neurotransmitter for all these different functions? Successful reproduction and parenting requires affiliation, which means suppressing a more basic tendency to drive away intruders who get close enough to harm you.

Oxytocin is crucial for inhibiting the more basic intruder-repulsion behaviors to allow for bonding and affiliation. For example, female rats show strong maternal attachment toward their own pups, but ignore or even attack unattended pups that do not belong to them. However, after an infusion of oxytocin, female rats happily adopt orphan pups, lick them, nurse them, and raise them as they would their own. Conversely, after an infusion of oxytocin receptor blockers, female rats fail to bond with their young and may neglect or abandon them (Insel, 1992).

Oxytocin is also important for female bonding to a reproductive partner, in the relatively small percentage of mammalian species that are monogamous (less than 5%) (Homer-Dixon, Boutwell, & Rathjens, 1993). For example, unlike rats or mice, female prairie voles form a monogamous pair bond after mating and show a strong preference for their partner over other potential mates (FIGURE 15.33). They will also bond with a partner even without mating if given oxytocin while in the presence of the male (Insel, 1992).

(a)

(b)

FIGURE 15.33 **(a) Prairie voles are monogamous and form social bonds, whereas the (b) montane voles are polygamous.**

Conversely, if oxytocin blockers are given around the time of mating, the female voles fail to bond with the partner as they normally would (Carter, DeVries, & Getz, 1995). However, in male prairie voles, pair bonding relies on a different neurotransmitter, as we'll see shortly.

In humans, oxytocin plays some similar roles in maternal attachment to infant and mate, although it is unclear whether the effect of oxytocin is as strong as the influences of cognition and cultural context (Heinrichs & Domes, 2008). Research studies have provided evidence that oxytocin also has more general effects on social perception. For example, doses of oxytocin seem to improve the ability to infer the mental state of a person from their facial expression, possibly because oxytocin also increases the duration and number of gazes toward the eye region of the face (Guastella, Mitchell, & Dadds, 2008). Studies provide evidence that oxytocin also enhances social memory for faces, improves male recognition of facial sexual cues, and increases perceived trustworthiness and attractiveness of faces in both sexes (Guastella et al., 2008).

Oxytocin affects social behavior as well as social perception. It has significant, **prosocial** influences on social affiliation, approach, and trust between human individuals (Kosfeld, Heinrichs, Zak, Fischbacher, & Fehr, 2005). But how can we measure trust? One method involves a two-player **trust game**, in which one partner plays the role of an investor, who chooses how much money to entrust to the other partner, or trustee (Kosfeld et al., 2005). After each loan, the trustee gains three times the entrusted sum and can then choose to return all, some, or none of this money to the investor before a new round begins (FIGURE 15.34). If the trustee breaks faith and keeps too much of the winnings, the investor can retaliate by lending much smaller sums on subsequent rounds. However, the trustee can try to regain the

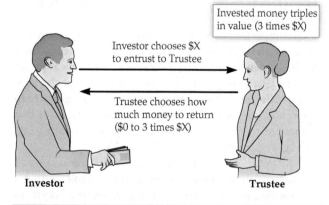

Invested money triples in value (3 times $X)

Investor chooses $X to entrust to Trustee

Trustee chooses how much money to return ($0 to 3 times $X)

Investor

Trustee

FIGURE 15.34 **The trust game.** The investor loans a certain amount of money to the trustee, and the invested money then triples in value. The trustee then decides how much money, if any, to return to the investor. If too little is returned, the investor may choose to loan out less money in future rounds of the game, as a punishment for breaking trust. However, unless the trustee sends some money to the investor, neither party can make any money.

investor's trust by offering large returns. To earn money, the trustee must win and keep the investor's trust.

Oxytocin can be administered to humans via an intranasal spray before they play the trust game. In male players, after a dose of oxytocin, investors entrust larger sums of money to the players. They also become willing to accept smaller returns without retaliating by cutting back their investments on later rounds (Kosfeld et al., 2005). Furthermore, they become willing to tolerate repeated breaches of trust (in which the trustees keep the winnings for themselves) without reducing the amount that they entrust to the trustees (Baumgartner, Heinrichs, Vonlanthen, Fischbacher, & Fehr, 2008). These effects appear only with human partners; when playing against a randomly acting computer, the oxytocin-dosed players show no changes in behavior (Kosfeld et al., 2005). Oxytocin also seems to attenuate the usual negative emotional response to social ostracism in a cooperative ball-tossing game and to increase the desire to continue playing the game despite being left out by other players (Alvares, Hickie, & Guastella, 2010).

We can see the neural basis of these effects in studies that combine neuroimaging and pharmacology. fMRI studies in humans have provided evidence that oxytocin reduces amygdala activation during the viewing of fearful faces and weakens the functional coupling of the amygdala to autonomic and motor regions of the brainstem (Kirsch et al., 2005). Similar reductions in the activity of the amygdala, midbrain, and striatum appear to underlie the increased levels of trust seen after oxytocin administration (Baumgartner et al., 2008).

High-resolution fMRI is now beginning to tease apart the neuroanatomy of different oxytocin effects. For example, in the lateral and dorsal amygdala, oxytocin is associated with increases in activation for happy expressions, but with decreases in activation for fearful expressions. In the posterior amygdala, oxytocin is associated with increases in activation for *all* expressions and also with increases in the functional coupling of this region to the gaze-controlling superior colliculus. Behaviorally, this translates into an across-the-board increase in gaze toward the eyes for all facial expressions (Gamer, Zurowski, & Buchel, 2010). Studies like these will in time help us to understand the mechanisms of oxytocin's diverse effects on the brain and how these translate into complex aspects of human social behavior, like friendship and cooperation.

Vasopressin

Vasopressin promotes social dominance, aggression, and other forms of agonistic behavior. These functions are essential in an environment where other members of the same species are competing with you for food, territory, mates, and the other necessities of life. A successful organism needs a mechanism for determining when to fight, when to run, when to take charge, and when to submit. The vasopressin system looks after many of these essential functions.

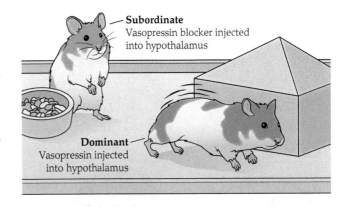

FIGURE 15.35 **Male golden hamsters asserting dominance.** Injecting vasopressin into the hypothalamus causes the hamster to become dominant, marking the habitat with his pheromones by rubbing objects with scent glands on his flank. Conversely, blocking vasopressin in the hypothalamus suppresses these dominance behaviors.

A popular model species for studying dominance is the golden hamster. When kept in pairs, male hamsters tussle and quickly sort out which one is the boss. The dominant male asserts his ownership of the cage by rubbing scent from his flanks onto objects in the environment, in a behavior called flank-marking. The subordinate male meekly refrains from such behavior. However, after an injection of vasopressin into the anterior hypothalamus, the subordinate male becomes dominant, flank-marking vigorously despite the presence of the dominant male (FIGURE 15.35). Conversely, after an injection of a vasopressin receptor blocker into the anterior hypothalamus, the dominant male becomes submissive, refraining from flank-marking when in the presence of his former subordinate. Once the injections wear off, the hamsters revert to their original dominance hierarchy (Ferris, Meenan, Axelson, & Albers, 1986).

Vasopressin is also important for partner bonding in males. Among montane voles, males are typically polygamous, having many different female partners. However, in the monogamous prairie vole, males bond to a particular female partner after mating. The bonded males prefer their mates over other females and groom and cuddle them affectionately. They remain with their mates, help to raise and care for the offspring, and repel intruders from the happy couple's nest (Thomas & Birney, 1979). However, the formation of this bond depends on vasopressin. If we inject a vasopressin receptor blocker into the male around the time of mating, the male will fail to bond with his female partner and will revert to the polygamous behavior of a montane vole (Lim & Young, 2004).

As it turns out, the brains of montane and prairie voles are quite different when it comes to vasopressin. Compared with the meadow vole, the monogamous prairie vole has a much higher concentration of the vasopressin receptor AVPR1a in the ventral pallidum (FIGURE 15.36): a limbic region of the basal ganglia, near the amygdala and hypothalamus (Young & Wang, 2004). What happens if we artificially

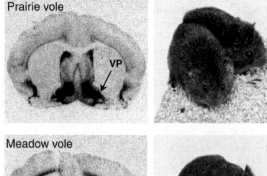

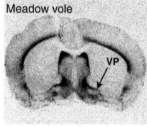

FIGURE 15.36 Vasopressin 1a receptor in the ventral pallidum (VP) of monogamous and polygamous voles. The greater extent of dark coloration for the monogamous prairie voles indicates a much higher concentration of the AVPR1a receptor than in the polygamous meadow vole.

increase the concentration of AVPR1a receptors in this region in a montane vole, using viral gene transfer? The male meadow voles now begin to show a strong partner preference after mating, just like the monogamous prairie vole (Young, Nilsen, Waymire, MacGregor, & Insel, 1999).

Even among individual prairie voles, levels of the AVPR1a in each brain region can vary up to 50% (Hammock & Young, 2005). The receptor density is under genetic control: carriers of a "long" allele of the AVPR1a gene show different receptor distribution patterns than carriers of a "short" allele. Male voles with the long allele have lower AVPR1a numbers in the amygdala and hypothalamus. They also show stronger bonding behaviors: stronger preferences for their female partner over a stranger and more time grooming and licking their pups (Hammock & Young, 2005).

Intranasal vasopressin also has direct behavioral effects in human beings. Whereas normal human males show an angry crinkling of the forehead when viewing another male's angry face, recipients of intranasal vasopressin begin to show this facial expression even for neutral faces (Thompson, Gupta, Miller, Mills, & Orr, 2004). They also begin to rate

THE BIGGER PICTURE:
The Brave New World of the "Cuddle Hormone"?

With the discovery of oxytocin's prosocial functions over the past 10 years, this once-obscure neuropeptide has developed a pop-science persona as "the cuddle hormone," capable of washing away our aggressive tendencies. Likewise, vasopressin is gaining a popular reputation as a neuropharmacological villain, fueling aggression and dominance: a "power trip" in a peptide. However, these depictions are probably too simplistic. The most recent research suggests that oxytocin and vasopressin have much more nuanced roles in directing social behavior.

For example, when it comes to promoting affiliative behavior, oxytocin may be choosy about who's in and who's out (Campbell, 2008). In sheep, we now know that oxytocin not only

promotes the pair bond between a mother and its offspring, but also promotes the mother's tendency to drive off other offspring that do not belong to her, sometimes quite aggressively (Keverne & Kendrick, 1994). In rats, oxytocin inhibits the mother from attacking her own pups, but also enhances her tendency to attack intruders (Insel, 1992). In humans playing cooperation games, oxytocin appeared to increase players' tendencies to contribute more of their money to an in-group, but also to increase their tendency to protect their in-group against a competing out-group of players, via "defensive aggression" plays (De Dreu et al., 2010). Oxytocin also seems to cause transient increases in-group favoritism as well as ethnocentrism in male

human volunteers (De Dreu, Greer, Van Kleef, Shalvi, & Handgraaf, 2011). So the supposedly prosocial cuddle hormone might be better described as a socially exclusive "huddle hormone" aimed at defense of one's kin against outsiders—not exactly a recipe for a chemical utopia.

Vasopressin might also be less universally antisocial than originally suspected. For example, women receiving intranasal vasopressin actually perceive faces as being *more* friendly and respond with affiliative rather than aggressive facial expressions—exactly the opposite of vasopressin's effects in men (Thompson, George, Walton, Orr, & Benson, 2006). Likewise, in male prairie voles, vasopressin seems to be important not just for aggression toward intruders but also for affiliation toward the partner and parenting toward the young, as we saw earlier. So the role of vasopressin in the male brain may well turn out to be quite similar to the role of oxytocin in the female brain: promoting affiliation within a group, while enhancing the defense of the group from outsiders.

Discoveries like these might help to cool some speculations about the impact of neuropeptides on society.

Pundits have already begun to warn against a world of love notes and sales contracts perfumed with oxytocin, dating services that demand genotyping for AVPR1a, or military forces steeped in vasopressin as they head for the front lines. At the same time, physicians have already begun exploring the use of neuropeptides to treat paranoid thinking in schizophrenia or theory-of-mind deficits in autism. Yet all of these

hopes and worries may be moot if oxytocin and vasopressin have both prosocial and antisocial effects that vary across genders, as now seems to be the case. Evidently, we still have some way to go before we understand the real personalities of our social neurotransmitters. Until then, there is little point in declaring them as either our allies or enemies.

---

faces as less friendly in general and show increased anxiety and stronger autonomic responses (Heinrichs, von Dawans, & Domes, 2009). These findings suggest that vasopressin can bias the brain toward perceiving social threat and thereby increase anxious or angry behaviors. These effects appear widely across vertebrate species, from rodents to chickens to humans. From these findings alone, it is tempting to see oxytocin as a "prosocial" peptide, with vasopressin as its "antisocial" evil twin. However, we are just beginning to explore the complexities of these peptides' functions. The most recent findings already suggest that the roles of oxytocin and vasopressin may not be quite so clear-cut after all.

The Social Self

What does it mean to be self-aware? This section tries to answer that question, describing different types of self-awareness and considering how we might test for self-awareness. We will also consider the neural basis for such awareness and how different disorders might affect it.

The Wondrous Self-Awareness of the Human Brain

Of all the capabilities of the human brain, self-awareness has always been considered one of the most profound and wondrous. Western philosophical traditions cite the Cartesian dictum: *I think, therefore I am.* Eastern philosophical traditions refer to a soul, or *atman*, whose fundamental property is the capacity for self-awareness. Arguably, the capacity for self-awareness really does make the human brain one of the most remarkable objects in the known universe. The earth-size storm that is Jupiter's Great Red Spot may spin century after century, crackling with lightning bolts the size of small continents, yet still be unaware of what it is. A supernova

may briefly outshine the entire galaxy of stars in which it orbits and still never know of its own life or death. Yet take a three-pound smattering of carbonaceous compounds and water, arrange them just so, and you get something unprecedented: a piece of universe that *knows* it is a piece of universe and knows that it exists *within* a universe.

Computer scientists have struggled since the 1950s to replicate self-awareness in transistorized form. Science fiction writers often assumed that by the turn of the millennium, computers with a humanlike capacity for self-awareness would be a common feature of our daily lives. So far, this has yet to happen. As of this writing, the world's largest computers come close to matching the raw computational horsepower of the human brain: some 20 quadrillion calculations per second, by some estimates (Kloeppel, 2005). Yet sheer calculating power alone doesn't seem to be enough to produce self-awareness.

Even among human beings, self-awareness is not universal. Young human children lack self-awareness until they reach a certain stage of development (FIGURE 15.37). Patients with certain neurological conditions show many forms of diminished or absent self-awareness. Conversely, a handful of nonhuman species show behavior that suggests they may have at least some forms of self-awareness similar to our own (Parker, Mitchell, & Boccia, 1994).

So what are the neural mechanisms of this most remarkable human capacity? Is self-awareness a unitary function, or does it consist of several different subforms? What is the link, if any, between social cognition and self-cognition? Can self-awareness emerge in nonhuman minds, and if so, what processes might be required? We will address these questions in this final section of the chapter.

Forms of Self-Awareness

Self-reflection can take on a variety of forms, most of which have counterparts in social cognition. For example, reflection on one's own thoughts can be considered a self-directed

FIGURE 15.37 **Humans start to show signs of self-awareness between 6 and 12 months of age.**

FIGURE 15.38 **In addition to humans, other animal species demonstrate self-awareness, as assessed by their behavior in front of a mirror.** Zippy, a chimp made famous by numerous TV appearances in the 1950s and 1960s, looks himself over in a three-way mirror as he tries on a jacket.

counterpart to theory of mind. Reflecting on one's own goals or future plans may be another form of self-directed theory of mind. Reflection on one's own feelings is a kind of self-directed version of empathy. Self-perception can also be considered a counterpart of the social perception abilities we saw earlier in the chapter. Perception of self-generated actions is a counterpart to action perception in others. As we will see, distinct neural mechanisms underlie each of these functions.

One simple proxy for self-awareness is the ability to recognize one's own image in a mirror. The **mirror test**, devised by the psychologist Gordon Gallup (Gallup, 1970), assesses self-recognition by placing a colored mark in a location on the individual's face or body that the individual can see only in a mirror. Individuals who react to seeing the strange mark in their own reflection pass the test and are considered capable of self-recognition.

Human babies begin to pass the mirror test around the age of 18 months (Keenan, Wheeler, Gallup, & Pascual-Leone, 2000). Remarkably, of all the millions of species alive on the planet, fewer than a dozen are capable of matching this feat. These include bonobos, chimpanzees, orangutans, elephants, bottlenose dolphins, orcas, and, perhaps surprisingly, magpies (Heschl & Fuchsbichler, 2009). Many of these species, when

exposed to mirrors, will also use them eagerly to explore hard-to-see parts of their bodies (FIGURE 15.38). Bonobos open their mouths and stick out their tongues. Chimps inspect their own backsides. Orangutans adorn themselves with pieces of vegetation, as if trying on a hat (Gallup, 1997).

Among other species, even those with high intelligence in other domains clearly fail the mirror test (Heschl & Fuchsbichler, 2009). When first exposed to a mirror, they respond to their own image as if it is another member of their species. Over time, most animals learn to ignore the strange image, yet never treat it as if it represents their own body. Gibbons will pick hungrily at a dab of sugary icing on their arms, yet ignore the same tasty treat if they see it on their face using a mirror (Suddendorf & Collier-Baker, 2009). Macaques show threat displays toward their own reflections (de Waal, Dindo, Freeman, & Hall, 2005). Even gorillas are, for the most part, oblivious when it comes to self-recognition (Gallup, 1997).

Why Bother with Self-Awareness?

Why do so many successful, intelligent species fail the mirror test? Why is self-reflection such a rare feature of animal cognition? Rather than asking the question this way, let's turn it around: why does a species *pass* the mirror test? Here we have some clues: the handful of species that *do* pass come from quite divergent branches of the evolutionary tree. So we can begin by asking: what do magpies and orcas have in common that gibbons and macaques do not? If so many species seem to get by without it, why bother with self-awareness at all?

Although such questions are still under debate, it might be worth considering the adaptive value of self-reflective cognition. Earlier, we considered the adaptive value of theory of mind. Some authors have proposed that theory of mind is an offshoot of self-consciousness: that the ability to infer mental states to others arises from the capacity to represent those same states in one's own self (Gallup, Anderson, & Shillito, 2002).

However, this view still leaves us with an open question: why should your brain bother to reflect on your own thoughts and emotions in the first place? After all, you're already having them. What more is to be gained by looking at them as if from the perspective of an outsider? Perhaps nothing—unless you are surrounded by outsiders and your survival depends on being able to see things from their perspective. You can gain an edge over your rivals, and more help from your friends, if you can guess what they are thinking.

But what happens if everyone else has evolved the same trick, so that inside each of their heads is a tiny little model of what's inside your head? Now, to guess what they think, you also have to guess what they think about what you think. Like in the game of Rock–Paper–Scissors, your next move depends on what you think your opponent thinks that you are thinking. For the first time, this means that you need to think about what your own thoughts might be, and in particular, think about them as they might appear through the eyes of others. This is precisely what happens when say we are feeling "self-conscious": what we are saying is that we feel a keen awareness of how we appear to others.

Note that this view is precisely the opposite view to the one presented above. Theory of mind is not built on a foundation of self-awareness. Instead, self-awareness builds on

the foundation of theory of mind, as the next step in a social-cognitive arms race between competitive social creatures who have *all* developed the theory-of-mind trick long ago.

If this view turns out to be correct, it does make some specific predictions about the basis of self-awareness, in any organism. First, self-awareness should be particularly useful in organisms that are both highly social and highly competitive with the other members of their society. So we would expect to see the rudiments of self-awareness in troops of primates, pods of dolphins, or flocks of birds, but not in hives of bees or nests of ants. Second, it should be possible to have first-order theory of mind without much capacity for self-awareness, but not vice versa. Third, self-awareness should be a special case of what we earlier described as second-order theory of mind: "he thinks that she thinks that he thinks . . ." So the neural correlates of self-reflection and second-order theory of mind should be similar, and disorders that affect one should also affect the other. Let's now turn to the neuroscience literature to see how these predictions stand up.

Neural Correlates of Self-Awareness

Neuroimaging studies have identified a consistent network of brain regions that become active during tasks of self-reflection. In a common self-reflection task, subjects view a word like "friendly" and are asked to decide whether this word describes them. In separate trials, they are asked whether the word describes a close friend or family member or a well-known person such as a celebrity or a political figure. Self-reflection on personal qualities reliably activates a network of areas that we have seen many times in this chapter: the temporal poles, temporoparietal junction, precuneus, and medial prefrontal cortex (FIGURE 15.39; Heatherton, 2011).

The precise regions of activation in the medial prefrontal cortex tend to shift slightly depending on the type of self-reflection (Amodio & Frith, 2006). For example, during **cognitive self-reflection**, or reflection on one's own current

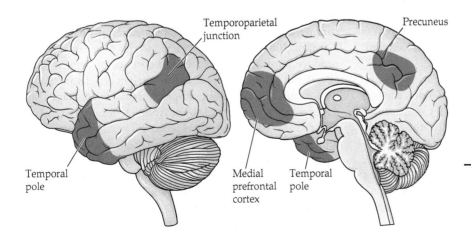

FIGURE 15.39 **Self-reflection on personal qualities activates the temporal poles, temporoparietal junction, precuneus, and medial prefrontal cortex.**

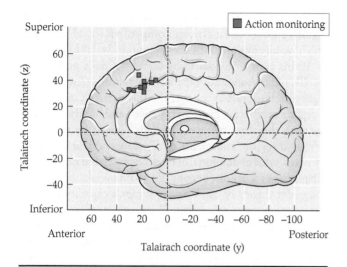

FIGURE 15.40 Monitoring one's own actions activates the medial prefrontal cortex and anterior cingulate. Each point represents the peak of the activated region in a different neuroimaging study of self-monitoring of one's actions.

thoughts, the activation is mostly in a more anterior region in the medial frontopolar cortex (Johnson et al., 2006). Conversely, during **emotional self-reflection**, activity is seen in more posterior regions of medial prefrontal cortex and cingulate cortex, but also in the ventrolateral prefrontal cortex (Herwig, Kaffenberger, Jancke, & Bruhl, 2010). As you may recall, a similar dissociation appeared in lesion studies of cognitive versus emotional theory of mind, so there are some parallels between the regions used to reflect on the self versus other people.

Neuroimaging studies have also investigated other forms of self-awareness. Monitoring or reflecting on one's own current actions tends to activate a slightly more posterior part of the medial prefrontal cortex (FIGURE 15.40), encompassing the rostral part of the anterior cingulate cortex (Amodio & Frith, 2006). As we saw in Chapter 13, this region is active during the monitoring of one's performance on cognitively challenging tasks such as the Stroop color-naming task and also shows increased activity with erroneous responses on the task (Carter et al., 1998). This region tends to be active during internally guided or "freely willed" actions, which tend to be associated with higher levels of self-awareness while they are performed (Nachev, Rees, Parton, Kennard, & Husain, 2005).

Facial self-recognition also seems to engage a specific network of brain regions (Platek et al., 2006; Uddin, Kaplan, Molnar-Szakacs, Zaidel, & Iacoboni, 2005). Compared to familiar faces, recognizing one's own face activates a largely right-lateralized network of regions that includes the temporal pole, lateral prefrontal cortex, and inferior parietal lobule. Recognizing one's own *voice* rather than face activates a slightly different set of regions, but with a common area of overlap in the right inferior frontal gyrus (Kaplan, Aziz-Zadeh, Uddin, & Iacoboni, 2008).

In interpreting all these findings, we must keep in mind that the neuroimaging studies of self-awareness show correlations, not causal links, between a cognitive function and its accompanying neural activity. For a more direct linkage, it helps to look for forms of disease or brain damage that actually disrupt the function of self-awareness itself. We'll now examine a few of these disorders.

Disorders of Self-Awareness

Because self-awareness comes in several different forms, there are several different ways in which it can go awry. Self-perception breaks down in the neurological condition of somatoparaphrenia. In this bizarre syndrome, patients fail to recognize their arm or leg as part of their own body and insist that it belongs to someone else (Vallar & Ronchi, 2009). A similar condition is anosognosia, which we discussed in Chapter 6: unawareness of paralysis, or even outright denial of paralysis despite an obvious inability to move, in part of one's body (Vallar, 1993).

Somatoparaphrenia and anosognosia are both closely associated with the syndrome of hemineglect (see Chapter 5), in which patients fail to pay attention to one side of space. Yet somatoparaphrenia and anosognosia can be fully dissociated from deficits in sensory input: patients without visual or somatosensory loss can still disown body parts. In one case, the patient could see clearly that the "foreign" left arm and leg were attached to her body, "but my eyes and my feelings don't agree, and I must believe my feelings. I know they look like mine, but I can feel they are not, and I can't believe my eyes" (Vallar & Ronchi, 2009).

A tight link exists between awareness of body ownership and awareness of one's own actions. In one case series of 79 stroke patients with anosognosia, 92% also had somatoparaphrenia or some other disturbance of body ownership (Baier & Karnath, 2008). Anosognosia, somatoparaphrenia, and hemineglect tend to arise from strokes or other lesions affecting the right parietal lobe, and in particular the right temporoparietal junction (FIGURE 15.41) (Starkstein, Fedoroff, Price, Leiguarda, & Robinson, 1992). Damage to this area tends to produce hemineglect in general, but for disturbed body ownership, the lesion also seems to need to encompass the interoceptive cortex of the right posterior insula (Baier & Karnath, 2008). A stroke restricted to this area can actually produce anosognosia even in the absence of hemineglect (Berti et al., 2005). To produce the outright denials and body ownership delusions of somatoparaphrenia, the damage also appears to need to extend to the frontal lobes: in particular, the right medial prefrontal cortex (Feinberg, Venneri, Simone, Fan, & Northoff, 2010).

What about a failure to recognize one's own body as a whole? In some forms of neurological disease, patients lose the ability to recognize their own reflection in a mirror (Breen, Caine, & Coltheart, 2001). Like the gibbon or the macaque, they begin treating their reflection as another

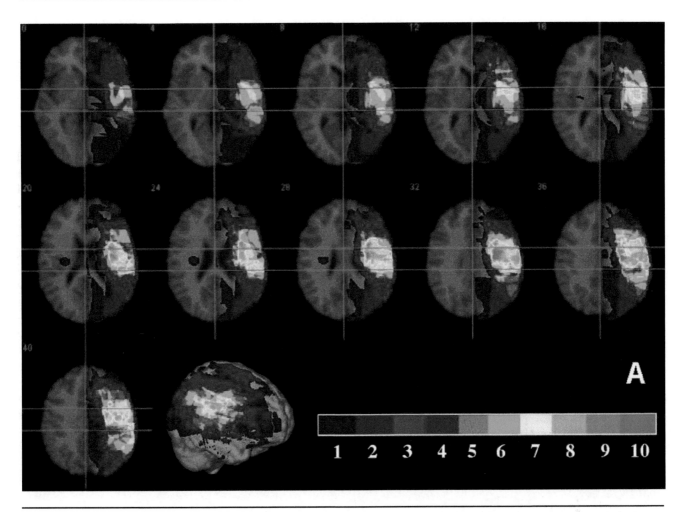

FIGURE 15.41 Lesion sites of patients diagnosed with anosognosia, somatoparaphrenia, and hemineglect tend to be found in the right hemisphere. The number of patients with damage at a particular location is indicated by the color scale at the bottom of the image.

person and will try to speak to it or interact with it. Usually, this deficit arises in severe dementia, but in rare cases, a relatively small brain lesion can produce the effect even in the absence of dementia. The lesion is typically in the right lateral prefrontal cortex (Villarejo et al., 2011). This location agrees with the results of neuroimaging studies in which the right lateral prefrontal cortex activates during self-image recognition (Sugiura et al., 2005).

Self-reflection can also be disrupted in some neurological disorders. For example, individuals with autism spectrum disorder not only have impairments in many forms of social cognition, but also show atypical self-representation at both the behavioral and the neural levels (Lombardo, Chakrabarti, Bullmore, Sadek et al., 2010). Such patients not only have trouble distinguishing their own mental states from those of others, but also have marked difficulties with self-referential cognitive processing. For example, they have difficulty reflecting on their own false beliefs, intentions, emotions, and personal experiences, and they also do not demonstrate the improved memory performance that is typically associated with self-referential thinking (Lombardo, Chakrabarti, Bullmore, Wheelwright et al., 2010).

Individuals with autism spectrum disorder are often quite capable when it comes to *first-order* theory-of-mind tasks, despite their problems with self-awareness. It is only when it comes to second-order theory-of-mind tasks that they become truly stumped (Tager-Flusberg & Sullivan, 1994). So deficits of self-awareness tend to go along with deficits of second-order, rather than first-order, theory of mind.

At the neural level, typical individuals tend to show greater activity in the ventromedial prefrontal cortex and middle cingulate cortex when reflecting on their own thoughts and personal characteristics, as opposed to the same traits in others. In contrast, those with autism show similar levels of activity in the ventromedial prefrontal cortex, regardless of whether they are reflecting on themselves or others. They also show a reversed pattern of greater activity in the middle cingulate cortex when reflecting on others, rather than greater activity during self-reflection as in control subjects without autism. Neurologically typical individuals also show greater connectivity to ventromedial prefrontal cortex during self-reflection in a widespread network of cortical regions including premotor, somatosensory, and middle cingulate cortex as well as the temporal pole and STS region. No such patterns appear in those with autism, suggesting that these individuals do not activate the usual set of social-perceptual, social-knowledge, and mirror-neuron regions when reflecting on themselves (Kennedy & Courchesne, 2008). This would leave them with a rather featureless representation of the self.

The evidence from autism suggests an intimate link between the neural mechanisms of self-reflection and social cognition. Our ability to reflect on our own thoughts, emotions, personal qualities, beliefs, and actions seems to tap into the same circuitry that we use to represent these mental states in others. So to a large extent, it appears that self-cognition really is a sort of special case of social cognition, at least at the neural level.

Self-Awareness and Social Cognition

If we look at all of these findings in overview, three general patterns emerge. The first is that there does not appear to be any one single "self area" or even "self circuit" in the brain. Instead, the neural correlates of self-awareness seem to depend upon what *aspect* of the self is being considered. They may help to explain why neurologists rarely see patients who are completely lacking in all forms of self-awareness—although isolated deficits in certain *kinds* of self-awareness certainly do exist.

The second point is that many of the areas that are active in tasks of self-awareness also show activity in tasks *without* any explicit link to self-awareness. For example, the precuneus is also active during tasks of spatial navigation, episodic memory, and prospection, as well as self-reflection (Spreng, Mar, & Kim, 2009). So not all of the activity in the so-called "self-awareness network" is truly specific to the representation of the self.

The third and final point is that self-cognition and social cognition are at least cousins, if not twins, in terms of their neural substrates. The neural correlates of many kinds of self-awareness and other-awareness show a substantial overlap. Disorders that are characterized by deficits in specific aspects of social cognition also tend to be characterized by similar deficits in self-cognition. Species with the strongest signs of self-awareness also seem to be the ones with complex yet competitive social lives. Where friend and foe may change from moment to moment, accurate mind-reading can make the difference between life or death. When everyone else is trying to guess what you are thinking, being able to take an outside perspective on yourself is essential for outsmarting your enemies and keeping your friends. Although much further research still remains to be done, self-awareness is starting to look like a nifty trick that the brain has developed to help navigate the labyrinthine complexity of human social life.

CASE STUDY:
The Man in the Mirror

Patient M. M. was a 90-year-old farmer in rural Spain and a veteran of the Spanish Civil War in the 1930s. Despite his advanced age, he was healthy and free of neurological illness or dementia. One day, he suffered a small stroke that produced numbness and clumsiness in his left hand. These symptoms were mild and resolved in less than a week, but his family soon noticed other symptoms that were much stranger. After the stroke, he began to believe that his own reflection in the mirror was actually his father-in-law, who had died more than 60 years earlier (Villarejo et al., 2011)!

He believed that his father-in-law was following him everywhere because he could see him in any reflecting surface. He tried to talk to him, and when he received no answer, concluded that "he is mute." When M. M.'s family brought him in for medical assessment, he wanted to introduce the doctors to his father-in-law and became angry that "he did not come." Although his family tried to reason with him, he remained convinced that his own reflection was really his father-in-law, until his family members were finally obliged to cover every reflective surface in M. M.'s house (Villarejo et al., 2011).

Cognitive testing showed that M. M.'s memory, attention, and most other functions were intact, with scores in the normal range aside from those on some visuospatial tasks. He had no difficulty understanding what a mirror was or using it for tasks such as shaving. When objects were placed behind his head so that he could see them only in a mirror, he reached behind his head rather than into the mirror to pick them up. Yet his ability to recognize his own self remained absent.

Neuroimaging (FIGURE 15.42) showed that the stroke had damaged his right lateral prefrontal cortex: a region close to the one seen in fMRI studies of self-recognition in healthy volunteers. Strokes in this area are common and usually do not produce such bizarre effects. However, the MRI also showed evidence of a much older, diffuse injury to the frontal lobes from a head trauma he had suffered decades earlier, during the war. Similar patterns of widespread frontal degeneration often occur in severe dementia, in which mirror misidentification can sometimes arise (Breen et al., 2001). So the loss of self-recognition seems to require more than just a single injury to a single region. The strange case of M. M. underscores the point that there is probably not any one single "self area" in the human brain, but rather a network of regions whose functions include self-perception and self-recognition.

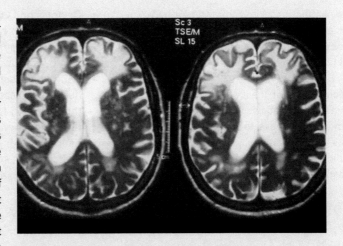

FIGURE 15.42 **The white regions in front of the lateral ventricles are signs of the bilateral frontal lobe damage suffered by Subject M. M.**

Conclusion

We began this chapter by trying to understand the mechanisms that can drive human beings to risk their lives in pursuit of superficially worthless prizes, such as the yellow T-shirt so coveted by the indomitable riders of the Tour de France. As we have seen, the value of the *maillot jaune* is not intrinsic, but social. It is in the complexity of our social behavior that we human beings stand out from every other species on the planet.

At its core, the mission of neuroscience is not merely to unravel the hidden mechanisms of the nervous system, but to help us better understand ourselves as human beings. What is it that empowers us to meld our garrulous selves together into tribes, nations, empires, and civilizations? To muster armies against collective threats or make peace with our mortal enemies? To build hospitals for the sick and the dying, even if they are strangers to us? To buy ourselves a little respite from the never-ending search for food, water, shelter, and safety

that consumes the waking hours of almost every living thing? To use those free hours to better understand the world we live in and to share that knowledge with each other, so that each generation sees a little farther than the one before? In every case, it is the uniquely powerful social faculties of the human brain that are responsible for the world we live in today.

Only recently has neuroscience had much to say about the social factors that shape our emotions, thoughts, beliefs, drives, behaviors, and daily interactions with one another. Although embryonic, the new neuroscience of social behavior has the potential to eclipse all its predecessors in terms of its relevance to everyday life. Rather than simply throw up our hands at the uglier features of human nature, we may now have the potential to understand their sources, and perhaps in time to remake them. Rather than simply marvel at the human capacity for altruism and compassion, we may be able to find their seeds and encourage them to grow. If the first step in human progress is to *know thyself*, then we may at last be poised for real progress indeed.

KEY PRINCIPLES

- The brain uses a widespread network of brain areas and specific pathways to interpret social cues from facial appearance, vocalization, bodily expressions, and other forms of visual and auditory input.

- The brain contains mechanisms for representing the thoughts, beliefs, and goals of other brains—a function known as "theory of mind." This may depend, in

part, on the function of "mirror neurons" that respond during either the observation or the execution of intentional actions. Disorders, such as autism spectrum disorder, can provide insight into what happens when this theory of mind is disrupted.

- Emotional mimicry and emotional contagion create a foundation for representing the emotional states of other brains—a function often called "empathy." Psychopathy is an example of a condition in which the patient does not show normal empathy for those around him or her.

- The neural mechanisms for theory of mind, empathy, social knowledge, and social perception all feed into visceral motor pathways to produce socially driven emotions and motivational states. Deception involves a cognitive conflict between internally and externally guided behavioral control pathways.

- Oxytocin and vasopressin are modulators of social behavior that can promote either affiliation or aggression, depending on gender and context.

- Self-awareness has many subforms. Of these, the humanlike capacity to reflect on one's own thoughts and feelings has arisen rarely in evolutionary history. Such self-reflection has a distinct neural circuitry that closely overlaps with certain subforms of social cognition, such as theory of mind and empathy.

KEY TERMS

Social Perception

social emotional cues (p. 475)

social semantic knowledge (p. 478)

semantic knowledge (p. 478)

frontotemporal dementia (p. 478)

Social Thinking: Theory of Mind

first-order theory of mind (p. 480)

second-order theory of mind (p. 480)

Sally–Anne task (p. 481)

perceptual theory of mind (p. 481)

theory-of-mind network (p. 482)

mirror system (p. 483)

cingulate motor area (p. 484)

Tourette syndrome (p. 484)

schizophrenia (p. 486)

Social Feelings: Empathy and Its Many Components

empathy (p. 487)

emotional theory of mind (p. 487)

affiliation (p. 487)

complementarity (p. 487)

emotional contagion (p. 487)

sympathy (p. 488)

postpartum depression (p. 488)

Edinger–Westphal nuclei (p. 489)

emotional empathy (p. 491)

cognitive empathy (p. 491)

double dissociation (p. 491)

psychopathy (p. 492)

congenital (p. 493)

Social Emotions, Motivations, and Behavior

major depressive disorder (p. 493)

social rejection (p. 494)

self-reflection (p. 495)

social valuation (p. 495)

septum (p. 496)

social reputation (p. 496)

social anxiety disorder (p. 497)

Neurotransmitters and Social Behavior

vasopressin (p. 501)

prosocial (p. 502)

trust game (p. 502)

The Social Self

mirror test (p. 506)

cognitive self-reflection (p. 507)

emotional self-reflection (p. 508)

REVIEW QUESTIONS

1. Why do we make rapid judgments about a person's trustworthiness based on facial structure alone?

2. By what mechanisms do we overcome our initial impressions of a person based on facial appearance alone?

3. What are mirror neurons? Where in the brain are they found? How might they be related to theory

of mind? What are antimirror neurons, and how might they contribute to social cognition?

4. What are emotional mimicry, emotional contagion, and empathy? How do these functions differ in terms of the underlying brain mechanisms?

5. Give two examples each of social and nonsocial emotions. How do social emotions differ from nonsocial emotions at the neural level?

6. How do social reinforcers, like praise and criticism, differ from primary reinforcers, like food or pain, at the neural level?

7. How do brain stimulation techniques like rTMS and tDCS cause increases or decreases in deceptive behavior?

8. Describe three different varieties of self-awareness, along with their underlying brain mechanisms. To what extent do social cognition and self-awareness overlap?

9. What brain mechanisms allow us to be aware of our own thoughts and beliefs?

CRITICAL-THINKING QUESTIONS

1. Imagine that a police investigator proposes to spray oxytocin into an interview room to make suspected criminals more trusting of their interrogators. Do you think that this strategy would be ethical? Do you think that this strategy would be effective? Why or why not?

2. Name some potentially practical applications for rTMS and tDCS, beyond the ones described in this chapter. Do you think that these applications are ethical? Explain.

3. What do you see as some of the major unanswered questions with regard to whether some animals have theory of mind? What types of experiments (beyond those described in this chapter) would provide further insights into whether some animals have theory of mind? Explain.

- Describe the major symptoms and the underlying brain abnormalities of Alzheimer's disease, as well as the currently available treatments.

- Compare Alzheimer's disease and frontotemporal dementia regarding each disorder's major symptoms, underlying brain abnormalities, and available treatments.

- Assess the causes, inheritance pattern, major symptoms, and treatment approaches in Huntington's disease, as well as why the genetic contribution is better understood in this disorder than in Alzheimer's disease.

- Examine the symptoms, underlying brain abnormalities, and available treatments for Tourette syndrome as well as its potential links with obsessive–compulsive disorder.

- Describe the factors that distinguish traditionally "neurological" diseases from traditionally "psychiatric" diseases and the ways that obsessive–compulsive disorder straddles these categories.

- Identify the key symptoms and main treatments for schizophrenia, as well as what is known about the underlying brain abnormalities and their causes.

- Explain the key symptoms of bipolar disorder, the main treatments for it, and the ways in which this disease both resembles and differs from schizophrenia.

- Describe the major symptoms of depression, the changes in brain function that occur in depression, and the three main types of available treatment.

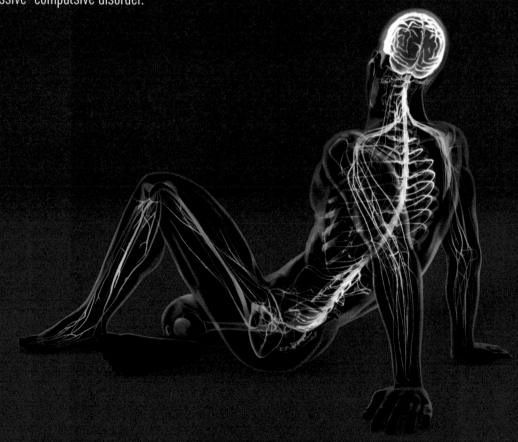

Neurological and Psychiatric Disorders

STARTING OUT: EPILEPSY:
"The Sacred Disease"

The ancient writings of many cultures around the world describe patients afflicted with a strange condition: they would suffer sudden attacks in which they would lose the power of speech, fall to the ground, thrash uncontrollably, foam at the mouth, and become unresponsive to the outside world for a period of time, before slowly awakening once again, as if from a malignant sleep. What could be the cause of such bizarre symptoms? For thousands of years, the most common explanation seemed to involve possession of the body by spirits—a sign of witchcraft in some cultures and cause for persecution and torture in medieval Europe. Later, patients with the illness were consigned to early mental hospitals or asylums. Only in the 19th century did physicians come to recognize the disorder as epilepsy: a neurological condition resulting from abnormal electrical activity within the brain.

In fact, this recent "discovery" was really a rediscovery of ancient knowledge. As early as 2,400 years ago, the renowned classical Greek physician Hippocrates wrote a treatise on epilepsy (FIGURE 16.1). "The Sacred Disease," as he called it, was neither "more divine nor more sacred than other diseases, but has a natural cause" that went unrecognized by the "conjurors, purificators, mountebanks, and charlatans" who professed to cure patients by casting out the evil spirits within them. Hippocrates declared instead that "the brain is the cause of this affectation":

> From nothing else but the brain come joys, delights, laughter and sports, and sorrows, griefs, despondency, and lamentations. And by this, in an especial manner, we acquire wisdom and knowledge, and see and hear, and know what are foul and what are fair, what are bad and what are good, what are sweet, and what unsavory . . . and by the same organ we become mad and delirious, and fears and terrors assail us, some by night, and some by day, and dreams and untimely wanderings, and cares that are not suitable, and ignorance of present circumstances, desuetude, and unskilfulness. All these things we endure from the brain, when it is not healthy . . . all the most acute, most powerful, and most deadly diseases, and those which are most difficult to be understood by the inexperienced, fall upon the brain.
>
> Hippocrates, *On the Sacred Disease*, circa 400 BCE

FIGURE 16.1 **The Greek physician Hippocrates.**

Hippocrates had already grasped that the brain was responsible not only for movement and sensation, but also for emotion, judgment, and the qualities of personality. Nonetheless, the human intuition of a fundamental split between the spirit or "psyche" and the brain's "wires" or "neurons" persists to this day. The medical specialties of neurology and psychiatry remain separate entities, each focusing on a distinct set of illnesses and treatments. In the public sphere, "mental illnesses" like bipolar disorder and schizophrenia continue to carry a special stigma, whereas other diseases of the brain like multiple sclerosis (Chapter 3) and Parkinson's disease (Chapter 7) do not. In the end, however, all of these illnesses arise from "nothing else but the brain," just as Hippocrates wrote many centuries ago.

In this final chapter, we'll survey a broad spectrum of brain disorders, beginning with the traditionally "neurological" and ending with the traditionally "psychiatric," including in the middle some disorders that seem to blur the artificial boundary between the two disciplines. Our survey will serve four purposes. First, it will help us to review everything that we have learned about the functions of the brain in previous chapters. Second, it will help us to understand how these functions disintegrate when the appropriate neural circuitry becomes disrupted by disease. Third, it will illustrate how neurological and psychiatric conditions can offer us important insights into how the brain works when it is healthy. Finally, it will follow the long and difficult process of discovering treatments for these debilitating illnesses: a process driven as much by happy accident as by rational investigation, even today.

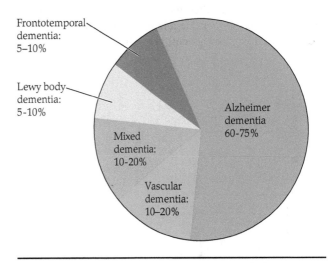

FIGURE 16.2 **Subtypes of dementia.** Alzheimer's disease is the most common form of dementia worldwide.

Alzheimer's Disease: Burning Out with Age?

The dementias are a category of neurological diseases in which there is a gradual deterioration of the so-called higher cognitive functions: memory, language, planning, judgment, social interaction, emotion regulation, and so on. There are many different forms of dementia and many different causes of progressive cognitive decline. Some kinds of dementia are reversible, but unfortunately, most are steadily progressive and (so far) incurable.

The most common form of dementia in the world today is Alzheimer's disease, also called Alzheimer's dementia (FIGURE 16.2). Some 24 million people worldwide suffer from this disorder (Ballard et al., 2011). It often begins with an early or "prodromal" form known as mild cognitive impairment, in which there are some minor and nondisabling problems with memory, spatial navigation, and language. However, with each passing year, the disease progresses steadily. The core deficit in Alzheimer's is now considered progressive impairment of episodic memory. **Executive functions** such as planning, reasoning, problem solving,

and judgment also deteriorate steadily. Spatial navigation difficulties may leave the patient prone to getting lost or wandering. Language difficulties such as anomia (word-finding difficulty) or aphasia (a more severe impairment in language production or comprehension) may also ensue. Unfortunately, most patients with Alzheimer's also lose insight into their own cognitive deficits, so they continue to attempt tasks beyond their declining abilities, such as driving a car or living independently. This brings them into conflict with family members and caregivers, who see the patients becoming a danger to themselves and others. Late in the illness, patients require help even with basic activities such as feeding, showering, and using the bathroom. Patients with Alzheimer's will typically survive 7–10 years from the time of initial diagnosis (Todd, Barr, Roberts, & Passmore, 2013).

Alzheimer's is a disease of the aging brain. Although uncommon before age 60, the rate of illness increases exponentially thereafter (FIGURE 16.3). At age 65, about 1% of people have the disease. By age 75, the rate increases to 10–15%. By age 85, the rate reaches nearly 40% (Launer et al., 1999). However, Alzheimer's disease is not an inevitable part of aging. There are well-documented cases of individuals up to 115 years old with no sign of the illness (den Dunnen et al., 2008). What enables some people to escape this debilitating illness whereas others fade slowly into their "second childhood"? Only in the past few years have we begun to understand the answer to this question. Today, with more and more people living into their 80s, 90s, and beyond, the race is on to discover ways of preventing and treating the disease.

What is the cause of the dementia we see in Alzheimer's disease? When trying to diagnose a patient, neurologists often start by asking themselves two key questions: "*Where* is the brain abnormality?" and "*What* is the brain abnormality?" In the case of Alzheimer's disease, the first answers to these questions came more than a century ago, when the German neuropsychiatrist Alois Alzheimer studied the brain of a patient who died with senile dementia (Maurer, Volk, & Gerbaldo, 1997). Alzheimer discovered that the patient's cerebral cortex was cluttered with abnormal debris

now known as **amyloid plaques** and **neurofibrillary tangles**. A century later, these microscopic accumulations of protein are still considered the definitive hallmarks of Alzheimer's disease. These abnormalities do not appear throughout the entire cortex, but are more densely concentrated in some of the association areas of the brain: the inferior parietal lobe, medial parietal lobe, medial frontal lobe, medial temporal lobe, and, in particular, the frontal lobes and posterior cingulate cortex (FIGURE 16.4). As we have seen in earlier chapters, these areas have important roles in memory, spatial orientation, language, attention, and the planning of complex actions. Hence, the classic symptoms of dementia in Alzheimer's seem to arise from the tendency of these abnormal protein deposits to form in some brain areas more than in others. Later in the chapter, we will see that the brain abnormalities of other dementias are found in slightly different areas, producing different deficits.

Both the plaques and the tangles of Alzheimer's disease are composed of certain kinds of proteins that are also found in normal, healthy neurons. The amyloid plaques are made of **beta-amyloid peptide**, which is generated during normal metabolic activity in many kinds of cells, not only neurons. Although we are still unsure of its function, in low quantities beta-amyloid peptide may act as an antioxidant, helping to protect cells from the toxic by-products of their own metabolism (Zou et al., 2003). When excessive quantities of the protein accumulate, however, they bind together and gradually form large, insoluble fibrils and plaques outside the neurons (FIGURE 16.5a). These plaques are harmful to neurons, although researchers are still debating whether the plaques themselves are truly the cause of the neural damage in Alzheimer's or whether other mechanisms are ultimately responsible (Huang & Mucke, 2012). This is an important issue because, as we will see, some of the proposed treatments for Alzheimer's disease involve removing accumulated plaques from the brain to restore lost functions.

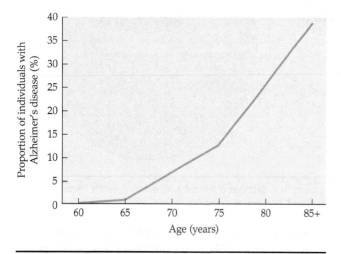

FIGURE 16.3 The prevalence of Alzheimer's disease increases dramatically with age, doubling every five years of life from age 60 on.

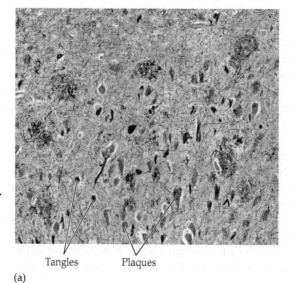

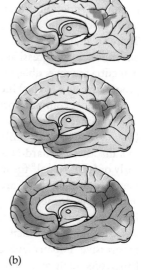

FIGURE 16.4 The plaques and tangles associated with Alzheimer's disease.
(a) A microscopic view of both the plaques and the tangles in the brain of a patient with Alzheimer's disease. (b) Plaques and tangles spread over the brain as the disease worsens.

Tangles   Plaques
(a)   (b)

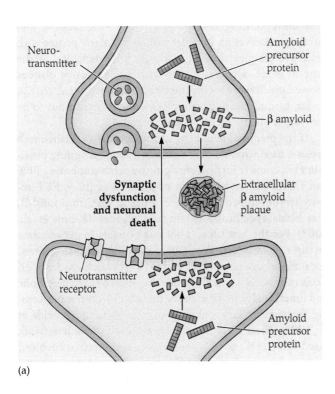

(a)

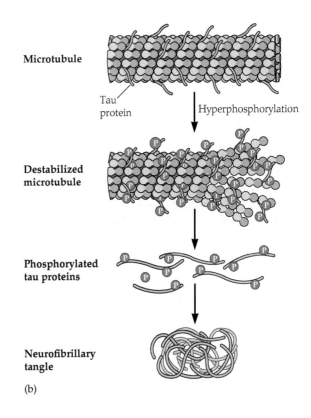

(b)

FIGURE 16.5 **The formation of beta-amyloid plaques and tau tangles in Alzheimer's disease.** (a) Beta-amyloid plaques form from extracellular accumulations of beta-amyloid peptides, which are generated during the normal metabolic activity of neurons. (b) Hyperphosphorylation of the tau proteins leads them to detach from microtubules and clump into neurofibrillary tangles.

The neurofibrillary tangles are made of **tau protein**, which normally binds to the **microtubules** within neurons, helping them to assemble and remain stable so that the neuron can retain its elaborate structure. To function properly, tau proteins must undergo a chemical modification known as *phosphorylation*. However, under some conditions, the tau proteins undergo excessive levels of phosphorylation. This causes them to detach from the microtubules and clump together inside the neuron, forming the nonfunctional or even toxic neurofibrillary tangles of Alzheimer's disease (**FIGURE 16.5b**).

But what makes these normal proteins go wrong in the first place? The answer seems to lie in a combination of genetic and environmental effects. We know that genetic factors can increase the risk of Alzheimer's disease or cause it to appear at an early age. For example, people with **Down syndrome** carry an extra copy of a specific **chromosome**, chromosome 21. This well-known, relatively common genetic quirk causes mental retardation and a host of brain abnormalities. Less commonly known is that people with Down syndrome also begin to suffer the additional neurological deficits of Alzheimer's disease at an early age—often in their 30s and 40s. As it turns out, the gene for amyloid precursor protein lies on chromosome 21. Having an extra copy of this gene could make it more likely that amyloid will accumulate to excessive levels and start to form the plaques of Alzheimer's disease.

Some rare forms of Alzheimer's disease run in families, causing dementia to emerge in middle age rather than the 70s and 80s (Lopera et al., 1997). However, more than 95% of Alzheimer's cases are "sporadic," or nonfamilial. No single gene causes Alzheimer's in most people, although many genes can contribute by increasing the risk. The risk for

Alzheimer's disease is therefore something like the risk of obesity: many genes affect weight and energy storage, all interacting with one another and with the environment to increase or decrease the chances of illness.

One such gene is **apolipoprotein E** (**ApoE**), which was originally discovered as a gene affecting cholesterol levels in the blood (Huang, 2006). The epsilon 4 variant of this gene, often abbreviated ApoE4, leads to higher cholesterol levels and greater risks of heart disease and stroke. Yet it is also the most powerful known genetic risk factor for Alzheimer's disease. Those who inherit the E4 version of the gene from both parents have a 14–18 times higher risk of developing Alzheimer's compared to those with other versions of the gene such as E3 or E2 (Breitner, Jarvik, Plassman, Saunders, & Welsh, 1998). However, researchers still do not agree on exactly how ApoE4 leads to the disease. Although higher cholesterol levels in general are associated with a greater risk of Alzheimer's, ApoE4 also increases the risk independent of cholesterol levels (Wolozin et al., 2006). Also, having ApoE4 does not automatically lead to Alzheimer's, and more than 40% of patients do not carry ApoE4 at all (Myers et al., 1996).

Despite many decades of research, we still have not discovered how to cure, reverse, or even slow down the progressive neural damage of Alzheimer's disease. So far, our treatments work by altering brain chemistry to partially compensate for the damage, thereby giving the patients a few extra months of preserved function. One class of medications is known as the acetylcholinesterase inhibitors. The neurotransmitter acetylcholine is important for many cognitive functions, including memory and attention. Alzheimer's disease damages acetylcholine-containing (acetylcholinergic) neurons, resulting in impaired memory and attention, confusion, and disorientation. By blocking the enzyme that breaks down acetylcholine, the acetylcholinesterase inhibitors increase the levels of this neurotransmitter somewhat. Although this treatment does help improve patients' cognitive function, the effect is mild and short lived. Another class of drugs used to treat the symptoms of Alzheimer's disease is NMDA glutamate receptor antagonists. Unfortunately, the few clinical research studies that have been conducted failed to identify any significant benefit of these drugs for patients with mild to moderate Alzheimer's disease (Schneider, Dagerman, Higgins, & McShane, 2011).

In the early 21st century, researchers began to try a novel approach to treating Alzheimer's disease: use the immune system to remove the plaques from the brain. It is possible to immunize people against the abnormal beta-amyloid protein. Once people begin forming antibodies against the protein, the immune system actually does start to clear plaques from the brain (FIGURE 16.6). In those with a strong immune response, the effects were sometimes dramatic: an almost total clearance of amyloid plaques from the cortex.

However, even when the treatment succeeded in clearing the amyloid plaques, the patients' cognition did not improve, nor did the progression of the disease slow down. The patients died just as quickly, and just as severely impaired,

despite their nearly plaque-free brains (Holmes et al., 2008). This disappointing result confirmed a longstanding and puzzling observation in neuropathology: many people with extensive plaques showed relatively little dementia at the time of death, whereas others with less extensive plaques showed much more severe impairment (Nelson et al., 2012). So far, plaque-clearing therapies have not turned out to be the "magic bullet" we had hoped to find.

If the plaques are not the ultimate cause of Alzheimer's disease, then what do they represent? One intriguing possibility has come from neuroimaging research combining PET and fMRI. Around the turn of the 21st century, PET researchers developed a radiotracer, **Pittsburgh Compound-B**, that binds specifically to amyloid plaques (Klunk et al., 2004). For the first time, it became possible to get accurate pictures of amyloid deposition in living human beings. Around the same time, PET and fMRI researchers identified a common set of cortical regions that showed high metabolic and functional activity in the brains of subjects not performing any specific task, but simply resting quietly (Raichle et al., 2001). These areas became known as the default network (see Chapters 8 and 9). These regions proved to be involved in spatial navigation, episodic memory recall, goal-setting, and planning—some of the first functions to be affected in Alzheimer's disease (Spreng, Mar, & Kim, 2009).

One recent study made a direct comparison of Pittsburgh Compound-B maps and fMRI maps of connectivity. First, the researchers created "hub maps" of the brain: effectively treating each point in the cortex like a person in a social network and asking how many significant connections (neural "friends") that person had among all the other points in the cortex. Across all cognitive tasks, a few key regions emerged as the winners in this neural popularity contest. The map of these hubs looked similar to the default network and likewise similar to the map of areas most strongly afflicted with amyloid plaques in the elderly brain (FIGURE 16.7; Buckner et al., 2009).

In other words, the brain areas that are most in demand over our lifetimes seem to be the most likely to "burn out" and accumulate plaques in our later years. The plaques themselves may actually be a consequence of the neurons' efforts to protect themselves from oxidative stress (the damaging effects of excessive levels of reactive oxygen–containing molecules on cell structures) via the antioxidant properties of beta-amyloid "monomers," or single proteins (Giuffrida et al., 2009). This might explain why many risk factors for Alzheimer's disease are similar to the risk factors for heart disease: **atherosclerosis** (the gradual deterioration in the local blood supply because of so-called "hardening of the arteries"), which in turn arises from high cholesterol, lack of exercise, high blood pressure, smoking, and so on. Recall that the cortex is one of the most metabolically demanding tissues in the entire body: the human brain weighs only 2% of the total body weight, but uses 20% of the body's energy (Raichle, 2006). A deterioration in the blood supply to the cortex would push neurons closer to their metabolic limits, and the hardest-working neurons would be the first to start burning out and accumulating

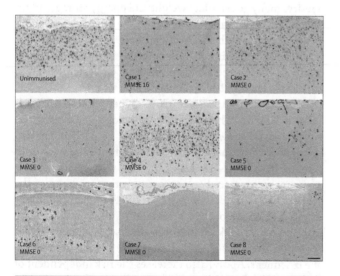

FIGURE 16.6 Beta-amyloid plaques in patients treated with antibodies. These images are from the temporal lobes of patients treated with antibodies. The beta-amyloid plaques are shown as brown dots. A nonimmunized control subject is shown in the upper left, and the other patients all received the antibody therapy. Although the number of plaques declined in almost all cases, the dementia symptoms remained, with the Mini Mental State Examination score declining to 0 at the time of their death.

**Hubs of functional connectivity
(from functional MRI scanning)**

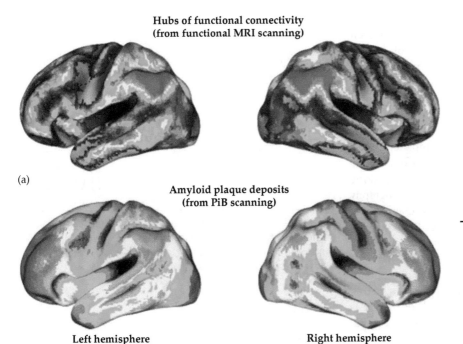

(a)

**Amyloid plaque deposits
(from PiB scanning)**

Left hemisphere   Right hemisphere

(b)

FIGURE 16.7 Comparison of maps of functional connectivity and amyloid plaque deposits in patients with Alzheimer's Disease. (a) A map showing areas of the brain that serve as the busiest "hubs" of brain activity. (b) The density of beta-amyloid plaques in patients with Alzheimer's disease. Note the overlap in brain regions apparent when comparing these two maps.

plaques of beta-amyloid and tau protein (Honjo, Black, & Verhoeff, 2012). So therapies that target plaques may be sweeping up the ashes without putting out the fire.

Does this mean that avoiding excessive brain use is a good way to avoid Alzheimer's disease? Fortunately not. There are many proven ways to reduce the risk of Alzheimer's, and none of them involves acting like a vegetable. Social, mental, and physical activity all reduce the risk and severity of the disease, both directly and indirectly. The direct effects likely involve brain plasticity and synaptogenesis, which help to build a "cognitive reserve" against the future encroachment of dementia and help to compensate for any declining abilities (Stern, 2012). Indirect effects come from the benefits of an active lifestyle: better cardiovascular condition, lower blood pressure and cholesterol levels, lower rates of stress and associated inflammation, and better health in the lungs, liver, kidneys, and other bodily organs whose activities help keep the brain's neurons well supplied with nutrients and out of metabolic overload (Erickson, Weinstein, & Lopez, 2012). Until effective treatments are found, the best way to prevent Alzheimer's disease is to keep the brain and the body in reasonable shape.

Frontotemporal Dementia: Like a Cancer of the Soul

The frontotemporal dementias affect a different set of brain areas than Alzheimer's disease, at an earlier age, and for

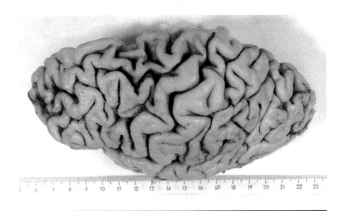

FIGURE 16.8 In patients with frontotemporal dementia, the frontal lobes and temporal pole degenerate, leaving smaller gyri and larger sulci.

slightly different underlying reasons. As the name suggests, this class of diseases spares many of the brain regions affected in Alzheimer's and instead causes progressive atrophy of the frontal and temporal lobes. Typically, the most atrophied areas are in the inferior frontal lobes (such as the orbitofrontal cortex) and the anterior temporal lobes (such as the temporal pole) (FIGURE 16.8). However, there is a great deal of variation from person to person in terms of which areas are most affected. In some cases, damage occurs almost entirely in the temporal poles and not in the frontal lobes. In others, the temporal lobes are spared and the frontal lobes are more badly affected. Often, the effects are asymmetrical: the left hemisphere is affected more than the right or vice versa (Boxer & Miller, 2005). With so much anatomical variation, the symptoms of frontotemporal dementia can vary widely from person to person.

Frontotemporal dementia patients begin to show symptoms much earlier than Alzheimer's patients—often in their 40s or 50s. They also typically retain the kinds of abilities lost in Alzheimer's disease. Because their hippocampus, medial temporal lobes, and precuneus remain intact, they may have no significant problems with their episodic memory and spatial navigation. However, their personality and social behavior can change so dramatically that family members feel as if they are dealing with a completely different person. A previously popular and high-functioning lawyer may become socially inappropriate at work, making off-color jokes to colleagues and downloading pornography at the office. Interests may change, and patients may become obsessed with a single activity such as reading romance novels or hoard belongings in a compulsive manner. Food preferences may change, and patients may begin eating large amounts of junk food and gaining substantial amounts of weight. Patients may abandon personal hygiene, urinating and defecating in inappropriate places. Lack of insight is often one of the most distressing features of the illness: patients themselves often show no awareness of the effect of their behavior on other people. Even when their inappropriate behavior is pointed out to them, they often show little concern and say that they themselves feel fine. Their families and friends often feel differently: they see everything they once loved about a person being slowly eaten away by an illness that has been called "the cancer of the soul."

Behavioral variant frontotemporal dementia (marked by early and progressive personality changes, emotional blunting, and/or loss of empathy) is the most common form of frontotemporal dementia, but others exist as well. When the disease affects the temporal poles rather than the frontal lobes, social functioning and behavior may be spared. Instead, the patients may develop semantic dementia: a loss of abstract conceptual knowledge. Semantic dementia is a deficit more fundamental than the language problems seen in other forms of dementia such as Alzheimer's. Patients with semantic dementia do not so much lose the word for "giraffe" as the very concept of a giraffe itself. However, their episodic memory, spatial navigation, and executive functions might remain surprisingly intact. In one case, a patient with semantic dementia was able to provide his wife with driving directions to a house in the countryside, although he had not visited the place for many years. However, when his wife pointed out some sheep on a hillside, he was baffled by their appearance and asked her, "What are those things?" (Patterson, Nestor, & Rogers, 2007).

Neuropsychological testing can reveal the deficits of semantic dementia in more detail. Patients seem to struggle with the atypical or unusual features of concepts more than their general features. For example, when asked to draw a duck, patients may draw an animal with four legs rather than two. They might also have trouble telling which drawing is abnormal: an elephant with its large ears or a monkey with similarly large ears (Jefferies & Lambon Ralph, 2006) (FIGURE 16.9). Again, the deficits are at a higher level than

FIGURE 16.9 **Patients with semantic dementia lose the ability to recall the concepts of things, not just their names.** Here, a patient with semantic dementia was asked to draw a swan from memory. The patient drew the swan as an animal with four legs, rather than the two legs of a bird.

sensory perception per se. Instead, it is the unique, characteristic, abstract properties of the stimuli that are lost.

In normal brain function, these properties may ultimately help in identifying how a given stimulus maps onto our basic set of homeostatic and allostatic drives: *What is this good for? Can I eat it? Can I drink it? Will it attack me?* Temporal pole neurons lie at the apex of the ventral sensory pathways, where high-level visual, auditory, and olfactory sensory pathways converge. They also have close connections with the insula, amygdala, hypothalamus, and orbitofrontal cortex. In losing the temporal poles, semantic dementia patients may be losing a key pathway for relating sensory stimuli to internal needs. Although they may still perceive the outside form of a stimulus, they have lost their usual sense of its semantic value: in essence, what it "means" to them.

There is also another rare but remarkable consolation for a small number of frontotemporal dementia patients: a blossoming of creativity. Neuroimaging studies have revealed that shutting down the inhibitory functions of the prefrontal cortex is a hallmark of many forms of artistic creativity, such as musical improvisation in jazz keyboardists. With the goal-oriented and task-directed functions of the prefrontal cortex out of the way, actions seem to be guided by lower-level sensory and motor cortices on their own (Limb & Braun, 2008).

Unfortunately for those with frontotemporal dementia, artistic gain-of-function symptoms are much, much rarer than debilitating loss-of-function symptoms. The vast majority of frontotemporal dementia patients become severely disabled within a matter of a few years, when their peers are still in late middle age. Those with the behavioral variant typically require institutional care for much of the remainder of their lives. No treatments have been proven capable of halting, slowing, or reversing the underlying illness. Antidepressant and antipsychotic medications are sometimes helpful in reducing aggressive, impulsive, inappropriate, or compulsive symptoms. However, the cognitive-enhancer drugs used for Alzheimer's disease seem to have little effect on patients with frontotemporal dementia (Mendez, 2009).

So far, researchers are continuing to unravel the genetic, cellular, and molecular mechanisms that cause the cortical neurons to degenerate in the first place. The emerging picture seems to be that what we call "frontotemporal dementia" is probably a diverse collection of different illnesses with different mechanisms affecting different cellular and meta-bolic functions, all of which lead to the final common result of neural degeneration in frontal and/or temporal areas of the cortex (Neumann, Tolnay, & Mackenzie, 2009). Reversing these mechanisms may therefore be quite challenging, since many different kinds of treatment will need to be developed to target different kinds of abnormal metabolic pathways. At this stage, the search for a cure for frontotemporal dementia is still in its infancy.

CASE STUDY:
Ravel and "Bolero"

Maurice Ravel was a French impressionist composer who produced many famous compositions for piano and for orchestra in the early decades of the 20th century. The most famous of his works was *Bolero*, a single-movement piece composed for full orchestra. *Bolero* was structurally very different from Ravel's previous work. It consisted almost entirely of a single, repetitive rhythm and two simple, alternating themes, repeated over and over with increasing volume and intensity (FIGURE 16.10), by a steadily expanding coterie of instruments, over 340 bars before reaching a sudden, dramatic climax and finale.

Bolero has been described as an exercise in **perseveration** (a pathological tendency to repeat an action persistently, even when it no longer serves a useful purpose), and some have suggested that the piece itself was partly a product of neurological illness (Seeley et al., 2008). A few years after composing it, Ravel began to show deteriorating handwriting, spelling errors, increasing difficulties in producing (but not comprehending) speech, increasing apraxia, and right-side motor deficits. After several years of declining function, in 1937 Ravel underwent an experimental neurosurgical procedure in an attempt to restore his health. However, he fell into a coma and died shortly after

FIGURE 16.10 **The score for Maurice Ravel's *Bolero* has a repetitive rhythm.**

the operation (Kanat, Kayaci, Yazar, & Yilmaz, 2010).

Ravel's long illness was initially attributed to a minor head injury suffered during an automobile accident in 1932, four years after he wrote *Bolero*. More recently, however, a number of researchers have concluded that the most likely diagnosis was actually frontotemporal dementia, on the basis of the symptoms described in his medical records, the characteristic patterns of errors seen in his writings (both verbal and musical), and the progressive nature of his decline (Amaducci, Grassi, & Boller, 2002). If so, then the repetitive, stereotyped structure of *Bolero* could represent an early, positive manifestation of what later developed into debilitating illness. Did this great composer labor under the shadow of a brain disease? And if so, was *Bolero* merely the swan song of his dying neurons?

Ravel's brain was not examined after his death, so we do not have a definitive answer to the first of these questions. As for the second, however, we can be fairly certain that his remarkable composition was more than just a side effect of neurological disease. The vast majority of frontotemporal dementia patients do not generate any significant works of art whatsoever. However, Ravel had a lifelong talent for music, studied at the Paris Conservatory, and spent many decades refining his skills as a musician and a composer before the onset of his neurological decline. If neurological illness did contribute to his creative powers, it was nonetheless his *educated* imagination that allowed him to produce such an enduring work of artistic genius.

Huntington's Disease: A Genetic Rarity, in Two Senses

In 1872, the American physician George Huntington described a strange, hereditary neurological condition affecting several generations of an extended family living on Long Island (Lanska, 2000). The disease that bears his name typically arises in the late 30s or early 40s, in people whose parents themselves suffered from the same illness. The most visible symptoms of Huntington's disease affect the motor system: restless, sinuous, writhing involuntary movements of the face, trunk, and limbs that become increasingly disabling over several years. Huntington referred to these movements as **chorea**, after the Greek word for "dance." The patients themselves would often be unaware of the movements or incorporate them somehow into purposeful actions. Another prominent feature is dementia. Unlike in cortical dementias such as Alzheimer's and frontotemporal dementia, the memory problems in Huntington's disease usually improve somewhat with cueing or reminding. This feature is considered more common in subcortical dementias, of which Huntington's is one example (as we'll see in a moment).

Also common in Huntington's disease are psychiatric symptoms: depressed mood, irritability, apathy, anxiety, and in some cases delusions and hallucinations. Impulsivity and aggression are also common, and perhaps as a result, up to 6% of patients die by suicide (Farrer, 1986). Significant personality changes may occur, along with changes in social behavior, with limited insight into inappropriate activities, as in the behavioral variant of frontotemporal dementia (as we have seen). These socially inappropriate behaviors were actually noted in Huntington's original description of the illness: "They are suffering from chorea to such an extent that they can hardly walk . . . but never let an opportunity to flirt with a girl go past unimproved . . . [their] wives are living, and [they] are constantly making love to some young lady, not seeming to be aware that there is any impropriety in it" (Huntington, 1872).

As with frontotemporal dementia, Huntington's disease often strikes individuals who are otherwise healthy and high functioning, with devastating effects on their families and friends. Unfortunately, the course of Huntington's is progressive and invariably fatal, somewhere between 10 and 30 years after the onset of the first symptoms. In the terminal stages of illness, patients lose the ability to control their swallowing and breathing, so that choking and lung infection resulting from aspirated food are common. In some cases, patients will take their own lives before reaching the terminal phase of illness. Either way, the families must not only cope with the patient's personality changes, behavioral aberrations, dementia, and death, but also realize that the patient's children might themselves go through the same ordeal in later life.

As mentioned earlier, Huntington's disease is considered a subcortical dementia, because the degeneration is most pronounced not in the cortex but in a subcortical structure—in this case, the striatum, and in particular, the anterior caudate nucleus (FIGURE 16.11). There are several different types of neurons within the gray matter of the striatum, with various inhibitory and excitatory roles in motor control. In Huntington's, the most affected neurons are called the medium spiny neurons (MSNs), which make up more than 90% of all the neurons in the striatum (Kreitzer, 2009). The MSNs are all inhibitory, using the neurotransmitter GABA to help dampen and control the activity of other neurons in control pathways passing through the striatum. As the disease progresses, these neurons are gradually lost, and the loss of their inhibitory functions leads to the motor, cognitive, and psychiatric symptoms of Huntington's.

To understand how this works, we must do a quick review of the role of the striatum in movement, cognition, and planning. Performing any given behavior involves solving a set of problems, two of which are selection and sequencing. For example, brushing your teeth requires selecting the

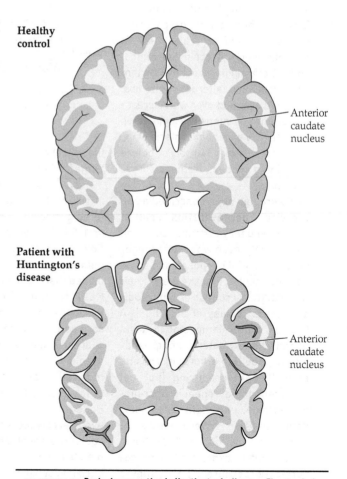

Healthy control

Anterior caudate nucleus

Patient with Huntington's disease

Anterior caudate nucleus

FIGURE 16.11 Brain degeneration in Huntington's disease. The atrophy is especially pronounced in the anterior caudate nucleus, as can be seen in these two coronal slices through the brain.

set of appropriate movements and then performing them in the proper sequence: getting the brush, opening the toothpaste tube, squeezing the tube, aiming toothpaste onto the brush, opening the mouth, bringing the toothbrush to the mouth, and so on. Perform these movements in the wrong sequence, and you'll end up with a mess instead of a clean set of teeth. So all of these steps must be inhibited aside from the one that comes next in the sequence: it must be released from inhibition, initiated, maintained to completion, and then terminated once again with a resumption of inhibition. So even for simple behaviors, motor control involves a delicate, sequenced balance of inhibitory and excitatory activity. The same is true for the sequences of steps required in cognition (think of long division or solving a maze) and also for longer-term planning (think of traveling to another city or applying to a university).

As you may recall from Chapter 7, inhibition and excitation in motor control depend on circuits connecting different parts of the frontal cortex to the striatum, globus pallidus, subthalamic nucleus, substantia nigra, thalamus, and cortex once again (Lenz & Lobo, 2013). Within these corticostriatal loops are two distinct, parallel pathways: an indirect inhibitory pathway that turns off cortical activity and a shorter direct excitatory pathway that turns on cortical activity

(FIGURE 16.12). These two functions must be in balance, and they must turn on and off at the right times and in the right sequence. The MSNs act as inhibitory controllers within both the direct and the indirect pathways. In the excitatory pathway, the MSNs get their input from the cortex and send output directly to the substantia nigra and internal globus pallidus. In the inhibitory pathway, they also get input from the cortex, but instead send output to inhibit neurons in the external globus pallidus, which then sends outputs onward through the rest of the loop. This extra inhibition step reverses the "sign" of the control signal from positive to negative.

Huntington's disease causes degeneration of the MSNs, but for reasons that are still unclear, the degeneration seems to affect the MSNs of the inhibitory pathway earlier than it affects the MSNs of the excitatory pathway (Cepeda, Wu, Andre, Cummings, & Levine, 2007). This explains why disinhibition is a key feature of the motor, cognitive, and psychiatric symptoms of early Huntington's: patients show the spontaneous, purposeless movements of chorea and difficulty multitasking and switching from one task to another, and they have trouble inhibiting their behavior and emotions. These symptoms are transient, however: they tend to occur more in the early than in the late phase of illness. As the disease progresses, the MSNs of the excitatory pathway

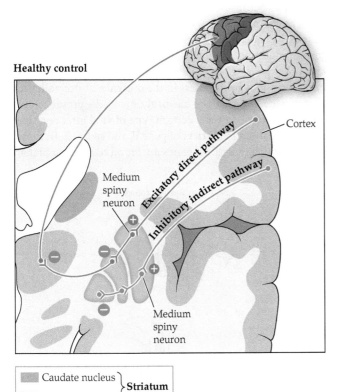

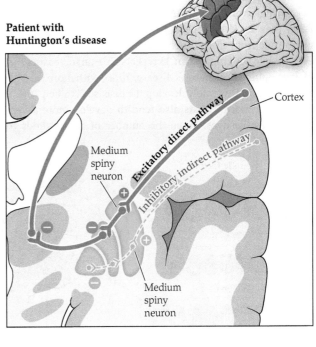

FIGURE 16.12 **A simplified view of the corticostriatal loop that is important for motor control and is affected in Huntington's disease.** In healthy control subjects, the excitatory direct pathway and the inhibitory indirect pathway are balanced, allowing for control of voluntary movement. In Huntington's disease, the medium spiny neurons of the indirect pathway degenerate, leaving the excitatory direct pathway as the main driver of behavior.

also become affected, and the symptoms shift to overinhibition rather than overexcitation. In the terminal stages, patients show increasing apathy, severe dementia, rigidity and immobility.

Why do the MSNs degenerate in the first place? When we look at the brains of Huntington's patients under a microscope, we see accumulations of abnormal protein in the striatum. In this case, the abnormal protein is a mutant form of **huntingtin**: a large protein found not just in neurons but also throughout the entire body (Cattaneo et al., 2001). The normal, nonmutant protein turns out to be essential for normal embryonic development. Normal huntingtin also seems to prolong the life of neurons that are degenerating because of mutant huntingtin in animal models of Huntington's disease (Cattaneo, Zuccato, & Tartari, 2005). The question of precisely how mutant huntingtin kills neurons remains unanswered, although much research is underway.

We do know that the mutations that cause Huntington's disease are passed down in an autosomal-dominant pattern of inheritance, meaning that someone with the illness has a 50% chance of passing it on to each offspring. DNA sequencing reveals a specific kind of mutation known as a trinucleotide repeat expansion. In some genes, there is a section of DNA where the same trio of nucleotides repeats itself over and over several times: in this case, . . . -CAG-CAG-CAG-CAG- . . . and so on. The exact number of repetitions varies from person and person and can actually increase over the generations because of copying errors during DNA replication. Most people have fewer than 28 CAG repeats in each of their two huntingtin genes (one from the mother and one from the father). However, people with more than 35 repeats have an increasing risk of developing Huntington's disease. Those with more than 40 repeats almost invariably develop the disease (Walker, 2007). Those with more repeats also tend to develop more severe forms at earlier ages. Since the number of copies tends to increase across generations, the disease is sometimes said to show anticipation: striking earlier and earlier in the children, grandchildren, and great-grandchildren of patients.

Huntington's disease is a genetic rarity in the human population. The overall number of people with the disease is fewer than 1 in 10,000 (Walker, 2007). Yet Huntington's disease is also a genetic rarity in that we can identify a single "Huntington's gene" behind Huntington's disease. For most common diseases, this is not the case. In the 1980s and 1990s, as the technology of DNA sequencing first started to become widely used, many believed that the "genomic revolution" would uncover the key genes behind widespread illnesses: a "schizophrenia gene," an "Alzheimer's gene," a "diabetes gene," a "breast cancer gene," and so on. It would then simply be a matter of identifying how the abnormal gene affects protein expression and developing a treatment to target the abnormal proteins and correct the resulting brain abnormality.

Unfortunately, the reality has not turned out to be so simple. It is true that for each of these illnesses we have discovered certain genes in which certain mutations cause a significant increase in disease risk (Joseph, Pare, & Anand, 2013; Sleegers et al., 2010). Yet, for most diseases, it turns out to be extremely difficult to predict an individual's risk of developing the disease just by looking at any one gene or even a handful of genes (Jostins & Barrett, 2011). This is most likely because of the importance of gene–gene interactions, as well as gene–environment interactions (FIGURE 16.13; Clarke, Kelleher, Clancy, & Cannon, 2012). For example, a certain mutation in gene X may be harmful only when certain other genes A, B, C, and D are also abnormal in some minor way, may be harmless in the presence of a certain version of gene E, or may be harmful only in the presence of a high-cholesterol diet or a certain type of viral infection that is more common in carriers of gene F, and so forth. In those cases in which individual genes *are* found to confer a higher

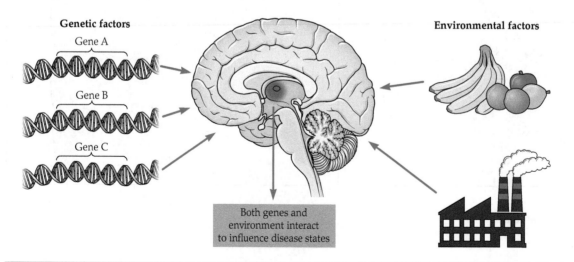

Genetic factors

Gene A

Gene B

Gene C

Both genes and environment interact to influence disease states

Environmental factors

FIGURE 16.13 Gene–environment interactions play a role in many diseases. Most disorders are not caused by a single gene. Instead, many different genes may interact with one another, with some combinations having protective and others having harmful effects. These effects also interact with environmental factors, which may also be protective or harmful in different combinations. This complex interaction of genetic and environmental effects determines the presence and severity of many diseases.

risk of disease, the effect size for each gene is usually fairly small—often much smaller than known environmental variables such as weight, diet, exercise, alcohol consumption, and so on. These issues may help to explain why in many diseases (such as autism or Tourette syndrome) twin studies show a strong genetic contribution overall, but more detailed linkage studies have trouble pinning this contribution onto any one gene or set of genes (Chaste & Leboyer, 2012).

Even when a single gene does turn out to be the culprit, translating this knowledge into a cure is no small feat. More than 20 years after the discovery of the huntingtin gene, we still have no disease-modifying treatments for Huntington's disease. What we do have, as with Alzheimer's disease, are medications that offer some symptomatic relief without changing the underlying course of illness. Tetrabenazine is a medication that depletes dopamine from synaptic vesicles, reducing dopamine neurotransmission. This can be helpful in controlling the milder forms of chorea in Huntington's disease. However, a significant proportion of patients develop unpleasant side effects such as depression, Parkinson-like rigidity or tremor, and sedation (Poon, Kang, & Lee, 2010). **Neuroleptic** medications, also called **antipsychotics**, are dopamine antagonists that can also help with chorea as well as some of the psychiatric symptoms of Huntington's disease, such as delusions, hallucinations, agitation, and impulsivity (Venuto, McGarry, Ma, & Kieburtz, 2012). (We'll learn more about this type of medication in this chapter's section on schizophrenia.) Medications that reverse the underlying neurodegeneration of the MSNs in the striatum are still under investigation, as are the basic mechanisms of the neurodegeneration itself. For the time being, a cure for Huntington's disease remains distant.

Tourette Syndrome: A Case of Involuntary Volition?

So far, we have been looking at a set of neurological disorders whose onset is in later life and whose symptoms affect cognition: the dementias. Among these dementias, we have considered two in which the cortex is the main structure affected (Alzheimer's disease and frontotemporal dementia) and one in which the striatum is the main structure affected (Huntington's disease). Now we'll turn to another syndrome in which the striatum is affected, but in childhood.

Tourette syndrome is considered primarily a movement disorder rather than a dementia (FIGURE 16.14): the most obvious symptoms involve lower-level simple or complex movements rather than higher-level cognitive, executive, or emotional processes. The classic features of Tourette syndrome are motor tics and vocal tics. Motor tics are urges to perform repetitive, purposeless movements such as head

FIGURE 16.14 **Georges de la Tourette, the physician who described the symptoms of Tourette syndrome.**

jerks, facial grimaces, eye blinks, or shoulder shrugs. More complex forms of motor tics might include jumping, scratching, kicking, or odd movements during walking. Vocal tics can likewise range from simple throat clearing, snorting, or noise making to urges to repeat certain words or phrases, which are often nonsensical. Verbal and motor tics sometimes have a "forbidden" flavor to them: the tics often involve urges to blurt out obscene or inappropriate words ("fat, fat lady"), to make obscene gestures, or to touch things that are inappropriate to touch (Faridi & Suchowersky, 2003).

Tics are distinct in character from other kinds of involuntary movements in other disorders, such as the tremor of Parkinson's disease (described in Chapter 7). Chorea and Parkinsonian tremor are truly involuntary and cannot be easily suppressed, sometimes persisting during sleep. In contrast, tics actually can be suppressed for a period of time if the circumstances demand it. For example, if the person is concentrating on a task or is in a social setting where the tics would be particularly inappropriate (for example, during a speech or a performance), he or she is often able to hold back from making the movements. However, an ongoing urge to perform the tic will continue to build up, and once the period of suppression is over, the tics will tend to be performed more often than usual, as if to make up for the suppression (Singer, 2005). Most of us can experience something similar if we try to suppress the urge to blink, or to scratch an itch, for a period of time.

Tourette syndrome usually arises in childhood and affects roughly 0.8% of children worldwide. A milder form, called transient tics of childhood, affects up to 3% of children at some point during their lives (Knight et al., 2012). In Tourette syndrome, although the syndrome sometimes persists into adulthood, the tics usually become less severe over time. By age 18, fewer than 0.05% of people still meet criteria for the disorder (Apter et al., 1993).

Many people with Tourette syndrome also have difficulty suppressing involuntary shifts of attention and, as a result, around 50% show symptoms of attention deficit hyperactivity disorder (Peterson & Cohen, 1998). Many individuals with Tourette syndrome also have urges to perform not only complex actions, but also yet more complex behaviors known as **compulsions**: for example, needing to arrange objects symmetrically or count the number of vowels on each line of a page. They may also have unwanted, intrusive thoughts known as **obsessions**: for example, irrational preoccupations with contamination, distressing sexual thoughts, or irrational fears that they have harmed someone. As a result, around one-third of Tourette syndrome patients meet the diagnostic criteria for **obsessive–compulsive disorder (OCD)** (Abi-Jaoude & Gorman, 2013) (which we'll discuss later in this chapter).

So far, the underlying causes of Tourette syndrome are mostly unknown. The syndrome does tend to run in families, but as with Alzheimer's disease, frontotemporal dementia, and many other neurological illnesses, it has been difficult to tie Tourette syndrome to the function of any specific gene. For example, the gene SLITRK1 has been linked to Tourette syndrome in some families, and this gene is known to be involved in dendritic growth in regions of the brain relevant to motor control: the cortex, striatum, globus pallidus, thalamus, and so on. Yet the vast majority of Tourette syndrome patients do not have any mutation in SLITRK1 (Paschou, 2013).

Another possible cause, surprisingly, is bacterial infection. Some studies have suggested a higher rate of Tourette syndrome in children who have recently suffered a throat infection with a specific kind of bacterium known as group A streptococcus (Swedo et al., 2010). It has long been recognized that this bacterium can provoke a strong autoimmune response, generating antibodies that cause inflammation of bodily organs such as the joints (arthritis) and the heart (endocarditis). Researchers suspect that the bacterium may cause the immune system to generate antibodies that attack the neurons of the basal ganglia, producing a temporary, Huntington-like state of disinhibition. In most people, the symptoms usually resolve in a matter of weeks to months. However, some patients go on to develop longer-lasting neuropsychiatric symptoms: either the tics of Tourette syndrome or the intrusive thoughts and behaviors of OCD. Such patients are said to suffer from PANDAS: a Pediatric Autoimmune Neuropsychiatric Disorder Associated with group A Streptococcal infection (Swedo et al., 1998). It would certainly be interesting if Tourette syndrome and OCD could all be explained in terms of the immune response to a common (and treatable) bacterial infection. However, it seems that PANDAS account for only a proportion of cases of these illnesses.

Although the underlying causes may be many, there does seem to be a final common pathway of neuroanatomical changes seen in Tourette syndrome. Neuroimaging studies have now begun to assess the volumes of structures such as the striatum and cortex in patients with Tourette syndrome as opposed to control subjects. These studies have found some reduced gray matter volumes in the caudate nucleus and to some degree in the lateral motor and premotor cortex, as one might expect (FIGURE 16.15) (Muller-Vahl et al., 2009).

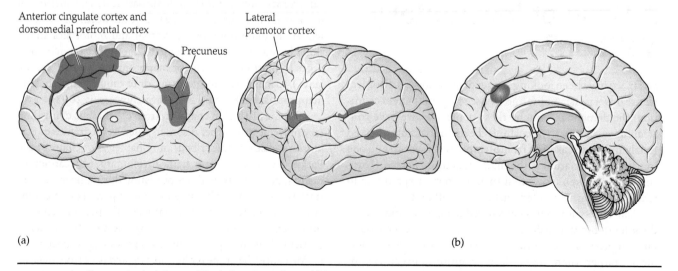

Anterior cingulate cortex and dorsomedial prefrontal cortex

Precuneus

Lateral premotor cortex

(a)   (b)

FIGURE 16.15 **Neuroanatomical abnormalities in Tourette syndrome.** (a) Areas of shared cortical thinning in siblings who both have Tourette Syndrome. The affected areas include the anterior cingulate cortex and dorsomedial prefrontal cortex, as well as the lateral premotor cortex. (b) Areas activated during motor tics of the fingers. Note the activation in the anterior cingulate cortex, within the area affected by the disorder.

As we saw in the case of Huntington's disease, alterations in the loop circuits connecting the cortex to the basal ganglia can disrupt the delicate balance between motor excitation and motor inhibition. Depending on which circuit is affected, the disinhibition can affect motor, premotor, oculomotor, cognitive, or affective-regulation mechanisms. This may help to explain why simple tics, complex tics, intrusive compulsive behaviors, and intrusive obsessional thoughts can all be found in patients with Tourette syndrome. The exact collection of symptoms may depend on which loop circuits are most strongly affected (Leckman, Bloch, Smith, Larabi, & Hampson, 2010).

A related finding in Tourette syndrome seems to be a thinning of the *medial* motor areas of the cortex, such as the supplementary motor area (SMA), presupplementary motor area (pre-SMA), and cingulate motor areas (Fahim, Yoon, Sandor, Frey, & Evans, 2009). This finding fits well with other studies linking these structures to the control and inhibition of voluntary (that is, internally generated) movements and behaviors (Haggard, 2008). For example, fMRI studies have shown that the cingulate motor area activates during motor tics and that this activity dampens when the tics are actively suppressed (Kawohl, Bruhl, Krowatschek, Ketteler, & Herwig, 2009). Likewise, primate studies show that stimulating this same area with an electrode produces involuntary, species-specific vocalizations or simple movements (Picard & Strick, 1996). The same is true in human studies of patients undergoing direct electrical brain stimulation for neurosurgical mapping. Stimulating the SMA or pre-SMA produces a growing urge to perform specific types of purposeless movement (Fried et al., 1991). If the electrical current is increased, the urge becomes irresistible, and the patient actually performs the movement. The same is true of the cingulate motor areas (Chassagnon, Minotti, Kremer, Hoffmann, & Kahane, 2008). If these areas of cortex are thinner in Tourette syndrome, this may reflect a decreased capacity for inhibitory control and a greater tendency for movements or behaviors to go unchecked even if they conflict with one's current goal, purpose, plans, or circumstances (Leckman et al., 2010). Once again, whether the disinhibition takes the form of motor tics, verbal tics, compulsions, or obsessions may depend on which loops are most strongly affected.

How do we treat Tourette syndrome? Fortunately, in many cases, the symptoms are not so much disabling as merely strange in appearance. Aside from their unusual movements, those with Tourette syndrome often do well academically, socially, and otherwise. So one of the major components of treatment in Tourette syndrome is education: of the patient, the patient's family and friends, the teachers, and the school community (FIGURE 16.16). With the education comes acceptance that a patient with Tourette syndrome is a normal, healthy person who simply has some unusual movements from time to time. In severe cases, the tics can be disruptive or distracting, and it may be difficult for the patient to participate normally in the classroom and other activities.

FIGURE 16.16 **Tim Howard, the goalkeeper for the 2014 U.S. Men's World Cup soccer team, receives the Tourette Syndrome Association Champion of Hope Award.** Howard has Tourette syndrome and has written a book about his experiences with the disorder to raise awareness and understanding.

In these cases, dopamine-blocking drugs known as neuroleptics can be useful in reducing the severity and intensity of the tics.

Obsessive–Compulsive Disorder: Neurological or Psychiatric?

So far, we have considered one form of dementia with relatively few psychiatric or motor symptoms (Alzheimer's disease), one form of dementia that sometimes has accompanying psychiatric symptoms (frontotemporal dementia), one form of dementia with prominent psychiatric and motor symptoms (Huntington's disease), and one form of movement disorder without dementia but with some psychiatric symptoms (Tourette syndrome). Traditionally, all of these illnesses tend to fall under the purview of neurology and are treated by neurologists rather than psychiatrists. Yet it is worth noting that three of these four illnesses have some symptoms involving affect regulation, judgment, decision making, or social behavior: symptoms that usually fall under the purview of psychiatry. This raises the question of why some illnesses are considered psychiatric whereas others are considered neurological.

In one school of thinking, an illness is considered psychiatric so long as it cannot be tied to any observable brain abnormality. Once a brain abnormality can be identified, the illness is considered neurological. Yet there are obvious problems with this way of thinking. In many cases, the

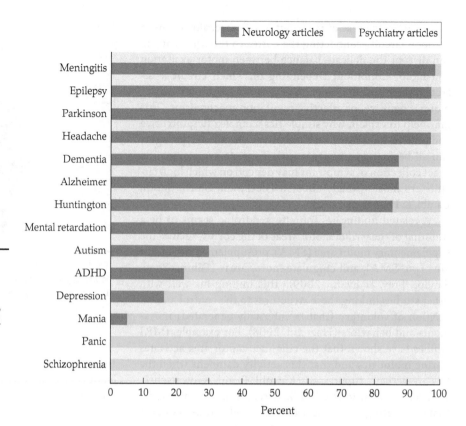

FIGURE 16.17 Some brain disorders are traditionally considered neurological, while others are traditionally considered psychiatric. The distinction is somewhat arbitrary, since both categories of disorders involve abnormal functioning of the neural pathways of the brain. This survey of scientific articles published in the peer reviewed journals *Neurology* and *American Journal of Psychiatry* from 1990 to 2011 shows whether the conditions named were more commonly considered neurological or psychiatric.

ability to observe a brain abnormality is simply dependent on the technology that is currently available. For example, epilepsy was once considered a psychiatric disease until advances in neuroscience made it clear that seizures were the result of abnormal electrical oscillations within the brain and that these oscillations typically arose from some type of abnormality in the cortex (FIGURE 16.17).

Another line of thought suggests that certain types of disorders will always be considered to fall within the realm of psychiatry, regardless of their underlying cause. Specifically, illnesses that have an impact on emotion, affect regulation, addiction, impulse control, motivations, basic drives, judgment, social behavior, personality, or reality testing tend to feel like disorders of the brain's "psyche," or spirit. In contrast, illnesses that have an impact on strength, movement, coordination, simple sensory input, sensory perception, pain sensation, attention, memory, spatial navigation, calculation, reasoning, or level of consciousness tend to feel like disorders of the brain's "wires," or neurons. According to this view, the division between neurology and psychiatry is not really about the actual presence, absence, or location of brain abnormalities. Instead, it reflects our own ancient, intuitive, dualistic sense that some of our faculties can arise only from the ineffable qualities of the soul, whereas others can be performed by the lowly mechanical functions of the body (i.e., the neurons of the brain). This intuition is powerful and deep rooted: even young children tend to believe that you need your brain to do math or move your body, but not to feel happy or sad (Johnson & Wellman, 1982).

Of course, one of the principles of neuroscience is that, regardless of our intuitions, both the "spiritual" and the "nonspiritual" faculties really do arise from the operations of our nervous system trying to reconcile the body's basic internal needs against the constraints of the outside environment. This principle has two implications: first, that there will be observable neural abnormalities behind both neurological and psychiatric disorders, and second, that some disorders will vary in their presentation: they may look more neurological or more psychiatric in different patients simply depending on whether the brain abnormality happens to fall in a motor/cognitive circuit or whether it happens to fall in a neighboring circuit more concerned with emotion regulation, valuation, and goal-setting. Tourette syndrome is a good example of a "crossover" condition in which there are some symptoms (for example, the motor tics) that seem neurological but also others (for example, obsessions and compulsions) that seem more psychiatric. Let's now look at another example that traditionally lies within the realm of psychiatry: OCD itself.

OCD is a severely disabling condition affecting around 2–3% of the population (Karno, Golding, Sorenson, & Burnam, 1988). The characteristic symptoms include intrusive, distressing thoughts known as obsessions as well as stereotyped, ritualistic behaviors known as compulsions. In general, obsessions tend to revolve around an irrational fear that some minor act or omission could lead to a catastrophic outcome. The compulsions tend to be superficially aimed at averting the catastrophe or neutralizing the fear, although they usually cannot actually do so in any realistic way. For example, patients may develop intense and persistent fears of becoming contaminated by "germs," and as a result, they may avoid touching potentially "unclean" objects even if this means foregoing important activities such as work or socializing. They may also wash their hands repeatedly, to the point of causing damage to their skin.

The actual content of the obsessions and the compulsions differs from person to person. However, the major categories are remarkably similar across all the cultures of the world. There are four main types. The first includes obsessions with contamination and compulsive washing. The second includes fears of committing inappropriate aggressive, sexual, or harmful acts and compulsive checking to make sure that one has not inadvertently caused harm. For example, some patients might drive to work, but have to return home again to make sure that they had not accidentally struck a pedestrian on the way there, without noticing. They might have to repeat the drive several times to address their irrational anxiety, thus arriving hours late for work. The third type involves obsessions with symmetry or number and compulsive counting and ordering. For example, a person might have to perform all acts an even number of times, count all instances of the letter "e" in a paragraph while reading, or arrange objects such as pencils or papers in a perfectly symmetrical position on the desk. The fourth type involves obsessions with hoarding items, which are often useless, garbage, or even noxious (such as old food). Severely affected patients may hoard so many items that they can barely open the door of their home or move around inside. In all cases, patients tend to recognize that these thoughts and behaviors are irrational and excessive, yet this knowledge does not help them to suppress the symptoms (Stein, 2002).

As you can imagine, OCD patients suffer a severe decline in their quality of life. The symptoms lead to shame, marked distress, hours of each day lost in performing compulsive behaviors, loss of friendships, and often an inability to work or attend school. More than 10% of OCD patients will attempt suicide (Torres et al., 2011). However, despite their suffering, patients often avoid seeking treatment for years or even decades.

There are two main peaks in the age of onset of OCD symptoms: one in childhood, around age 11, and one in early adulthood, around age 23 (Taylor, 2011). This suggests that the illness we call "OCD" may in fact be an amalgam of more than one different disease process, any of which will have a final common result of purposeless, intrusive, distressing thoughts and behaviors. In most cases, the underlying cause of the OCD symptoms is unclear. However, we have already seen how diseases of the basal ganglia, like Huntington's disease, Tourette syndrome, and PANDAS, can all produce OCD symptoms alongside their more immediately obvious effects on motor function. These kinds of cases, in addition to those described below, have been helpful in identifying the key brain regions involved in OCD.

Two main pathways consistently turn up in neuroimaging studies of OCD patients. These are the basal ganglia

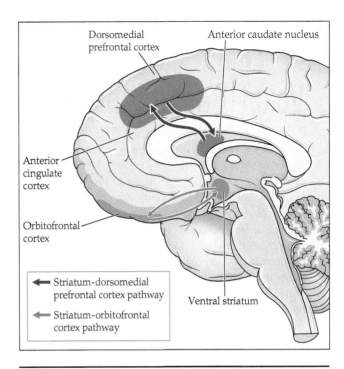

FIGURE 16.18 Two corticostriatal loops are consistently identified as important in studies of patients with OCD. One of the loops goes from the anterior caudate nucleus to the dorsomedial prefrontal cortex and nearby anterior cingulate cortex. The other loop goes from the ventral striatum to the lateral orbitofrontal cortex. These loop circuits tend to show excessive activity in OCD compared to healthy controls.

loops from the striatum through the orbitofrontal cortex and the anterior cingulate/dorsomedial prefrontal cortex (FIGURE 16.18; Radua & Mataix-Cols, 2009). Neuroimaging studies show that these areas are hyperactive in OCD patients at rest and that their activity increases if we "provoke" the symptoms experimentally (for example, by showing a compulsive-washing patient images of dirty clothes or rotten food) (Rotge et al., 2008).

But is the excess activity really the *cause* of the symptoms or simply a sign of the brain's losing battle to *inhibit* the obsessions and compulsions and the anxiety they create? It is hard to answer this question using purely correlational methods (see Chapter 1) such as fMRI and PET. However, we can also draw on the evidence of lesion studies (Chapter 1), which look at what happens when the brain areas are lost or damaged. "Acquired" OCD can result from strokes that damage the head of the caudate or other parts of the basal ganglia (Carmin, Wiegartz, Yunus, & Gillock, 2002; Chacko, Corbin, & Harper, 2000) or from lesions of the orbitofrontal cortex (Kim & Lee, 2002; Ogai, Iyo, Mori, & Takei, 2005).

In rare cases, patients with long-standing OCD have actually *improved* after suffering a stroke in the basal ganglia (Fujii, Otsuba, Suzuki, Endo, & Yamadori, 2005; Yaryura-Tobias & Neziroglu, 2003). So lesion studies confirm that the basal ganglia and orbitofrontal cortex are important areas in OCD, but unfortunately the studies give conflicting

RESEARCH METHODS:
Voxel-Based Morphometry

For some diseases such as stroke, tumor, or spinal cord injury, the brain abnormalities can be seen clearly via brain imaging or by a postmortem inspection of the neuroanatomical specimen. However, until quite recently, for illnesses like Tourette syndrome, OCD, bipolar disorder, or major depressive disorder, the question of "where is the brain abnormality?" had no clear answer.

Since the end of the 20th century, this has begun to change, in part thanks to a sophisticated neuroimaging technique known as voxel-based morphometry (VBM). VBM studies make use of the clear, high-resolution images of the brain that can now be acquired using high-field MRI scans. Modern MRI devices can, within a few minutes, make an image of the entire volume of the head and brain. The image consists of hundreds of slices, each one with a thickness of a millimeter or less. Each slice consists of a grid of hundreds-by-hundreds of voxels ("volume lements," the 3-dimensional equivalent of pixels), typically no larger than 1 × 1 × 1 mm in size. These voxels can be used to reconstruct the three-dimensional structure of the brain's gray matter, white matter, cerebrospinal fluid, and other tissues.

Mathematical techniques can be used to trace the upper and lower boundaries of the gray matter, measuring its intensity, thickness, and curvature. Then, these measurements can be compared across different groups of brains: for example, comparing patients with obsessive–compulsive disorder to healthy control subjects or patients with Tourette syndrome to unaffected siblings. If we scan the same person repeatedly over the lifespan, we can examine how the brain's gray matter grows and changes over time or how this "developmental trajectory" goes awry in children with autism or young adults with schizophrenia.

Over the past 15 years, so many VBM studies have been conducted that researchers are now publishing meta-analyses that combine the data from many different studies to allow comparisons of hundreds of patients versus healthy control subjects (FIGURE 16.19). With numbers this large, it becomes possible to identify and locate subtle patterns of abnormal thinning or thickening in the gray matter of patients with major depression, schizophrenia, or bipolar disorder. These maps, combined with other lines of evidence like functional neuroimaging, or lesion or stimulation studies, are helping to answer the question of "where is the brain abnormality" for psychiatric as well as neurological disorders. In the process, VBM is also helping to bridge the ever-narrowing conceptual division between these two categories of illness.

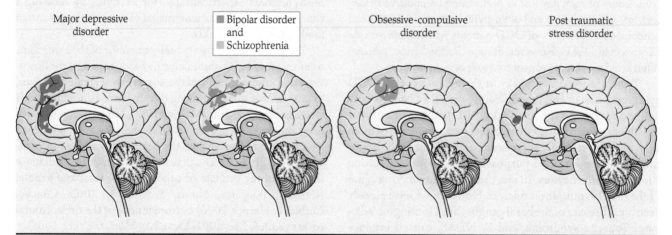

Major depressive disorder

■ Bipolar disorder and ■ Schizophrenia

Obsessive-compulsive disorder

Post traumatic stress disorder

FIGURE 16.19 Voxel-based morphometry can be used to identify brain regions where there is a significant difference in gray matter between patients and healthy control subjects. These images show areas with a loss of gray matter density in patients with various psychiatric disorders. Note that there are some zones of overlap across disorders—especially near the dorsomedial prefrontal cortex and neighboring anterior cingulate cortex.

evidence on whether these are causing, or merely responding to, symptoms. Why might this be? Recall that there are parallel inhibitory and excitatory basal ganglia circuits at work in the control of movement and behavior and that these circuits are woven into one another from the macroscopic viewpoint of MRI. So the effects of a large lesion (such as a stroke) could potentially influence both pathways, and the result may depend on whether the balance is shifted toward inhibition or excitation: something we cannot predict from looking at the MRI alone.

Another approach is to look at voxel-based morphometry studies (see "Research Methods" on previous page), which find areas of significantly increased or decreased gray matter density in high-resolution anatomical MRI scans. In general such studies tend to agree that the most affected areas lie in the orbitofrontal cortex, dorsomedial prefrontal cortex/anterior cingulate cortex, and the connected regions of ventral striatum (Radua & Mataix-Cols, 2009; Rotge et al., 2008). In the striatum, the gray matter volume tends to be increased rather than decreased in OCD.

Yet another difficulty with these kinds of studies is that, as we saw earlier, the illness we call OCD actually represents a diverse collection of several possible symptom clusters, any of which may be the end result of many different kinds of underlying disease. For example, the underlying causes and neural effects of childhood-onset OCD could be different from the causes and effects of adult-onset OCD. Within childhood-onset OCD, there may be important differences in those who also have Tourette syndrome versus those who do not (Eichstedt & Arnold, 2001). Within adults with OCD, there may be differences between those whose brains have been adapting to the disorder since childhood versus those whose brains did not become affected until early adulthood—a different world in terms of brain maturity and plasticity. We also must consider the different symptom clusters. Are "hoarders" the same as "checkers"? Are "symmetry" and "contamination fear" neurally distinct forms of OCD? Does each group have an abnormality in a slightly different basal ganglia loop circuit?

It is difficult to assemble large numbers of each type of OCD patient, which would be needed to answer these questions meaningfully. However, there are some early indications that the different manifestations of OCD may have different neural correlates. For example, one study sorted OCD patients into washers, checkers, and hoarders and then showed each group a set of emotional pictures tailor-made to provoke their particular OCD symptoms (Mataix-Cols et al., 2004). Each group turned out to activate a slightly different set of cortical and striatal areas (**FIGURE 16.20**). Washers showed more activity in a basal ganglia loop involving the medial orbitofrontal cortex and the head of the caudate. They also showed activity in the amygdala and **subgenual cingulate cortex** (an anterior region of the cingulate gyrus that is structurally similar to the primary motor cortex, with the exception that its connections go to the amygdala rather than to the lower motor neurons of the spinal cord), possibly related to the sense of disgust. Checkers, in contrast, showed

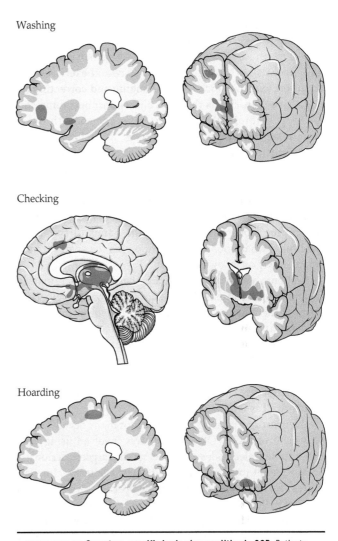

Washing

Checking

Hoarding

FIGURE 16.20 Symptom-specific brain abnormalities in OCD. Patients diagnosed with different types of OCD viewed images designed to provoke their specific symptoms, such as compulsive hand-washing, mistake-checking, or hoarding. The patients displayed different patterns of brain activity, depending on which type of symptoms they had.

more activity in a different loop, encompassing the dorsolateral prefrontal cortex, superior parietal lobule, putamen, and globus pallidus. Also, their subcortical activity lay not in the amygdala, but in the brainstem and subthalamic nucleus. Hoarders activated lateral orbitofrontal cortex, visual areas in the inferior temporal lobe, and premotor areas in the lateral prefrontal cortex (Mataix-Cols et al., 2004). The suggestion from these results is not only that OCD has different subcategories of symptoms, but also that the exact type of symptoms that arise in any given patient depends on which loop circuits are most affected by the disease.

These kinds of individual differences may turn out to be important when it comes to the treatment of OCD. Only about 10–15% of patients recover naturally (Mataix-Cols et al., 2004), and in most cases the symptoms persist for decades—a poor prognosis that is improved only partially in those who seek treatment. There are several options available. **Cognitive behavioral therapy** is the treatment of choice for those who tolerate it. Cognitive behavioral therapy involves both cognitive and behavioral exercises. The cognitive exercises focus on challenging and correcting the **cognitive distortions** that feed obsessions: becoming contaminated, unrealistic fears of harming someone, throwing away something important, and so on. The behavioral exercises focus on habituation to the anxiety provoked by the feared stimuli. A method called exposure and response prevention involves having the patient expose themselves to more and more intense stimuli (such as more and more "contaminated" objects) and then preventing themselves from responding (for example, getting the hands dirty but not washing them immediately) and allowing the anxiety to dissipate slowly on its own.

Patients who cannot tolerate these exercises may be helped by medications that enhance serotonin levels. High doses of these medications seem to reduce obsessions, compulsions, and anxiety. However, most patients do not achieve remission on medication alone, and the effects wear off when the medication is stopped. Medications that block dopamine D_2 receptors, also known as neuroleptics, can sometimes be helpful in severe cases, especially cases where tics are prominent as well as OCD symptoms.

Neurosurgery has also been tried for many decades in the treatment of OCD. Older procedures involved using carefully guided electrodes to make small, targeted lesions in areas thought to be relevant to OCD: the anterior cingulate cortex, for example. In one follow-up case series, about a third of patients showed at least a modest 35% improvement in symptoms. However, the rest showed only partial, temporary, or no response, and the lesions themselves were permanent (Dougherty et al., 2002). More recent approaches use deep brain stimulation electrodes rather than lesions to reduce hypothesized overactivity in specific brain regions. Several different brain regions are being targeted, including the subthalamic nucleus and the anterior internal capsule, which contains white matter tracts to the orbitofrontal cortex (Blomstedt, Sjoberg, Hansson, Bodlund, & Hariz, 2013). Although the remission rates seem to be improving, so far no one anatomical target has emerged as a magic bullet for OCD.

To sum up, we see that although OCD is traditionally considered a psychiatric illness, its symptoms also appear in many illnesses traditionally considered neurological. The difference among motor tics, obsessive checking, and compulsive washing may lie more in the subtleties of which basal ganglia loops are most strongly affected, rather than in any fundamental divide between what is neurological and what is psychiatric.

We would have the same trouble if we were to create a broad symptom cluster like "difficulty communicating through spoken language," then said that all such patients had an illness called "speech production disorder," and then tried to treat it with various medications without knowing whether the symptoms had come from a stroke, a brain tumor, a frontotemporal dementia, or just a bad sore throat!

In the case of some psychiatric disorders, this is roughly the dilemma we face: to understand the disease, we must be able to sort the patients into better categories, but to come up with better categories, we first must understand the disease. Despite this circular impasse, some progress is being made, as we'll see in the next three sections.

Schizophrenia: A Dementia of the Young

Schizophrenia is perhaps the best-known psychotic illness (FIGURE 16.21). **Psychosis** denotes a loss of contact with reality, characterized by perceptual disturbances called **hallucinations** and fixed, false beliefs called **delusions**, as well as more subtle impairments of cognition and motivation. Schizophrenia is found in every human culture and generally affects just

FIGURE 16.21 **John Nash was a mathematician who was also diagnosed with schizophrenia.** In 1994, he won the Nobel Prize in Economics, and he was the subject of the 2001 movie *A Beautiful Mind*. Nash died in an automobile accident in 2015.

under 1% of individuals worldwide (van Os & Kapur, 2009). It typically strikes in early adulthood and continues throughout life. Because its symptoms can be severe and incapacitating, it is one of the leading causes of disability worldwide, with a significant burden not only on those with the disease, but also on their families and other caregivers.

Descriptions of the illness date back to the early 1800s, and the historical writings of many cultures around the world also make informal reference to individuals with similar symptoms. In 1893, the pioneering German psychiatrist Emil Kraepelin gave a formal description of the illness, which he called dementia praecox, or early-onset dementia. Later, in 1908, the Swiss psychiatrist Eugen Bleuler coined the term "schizophrenia" to describe the same disease, and this term has been used ever since (Hoff, 2012).

The most striking features of schizophrenia are its so-called **positive symptoms**—abnormalities of perception and cognition that appear in those with the disease. Positive symptoms in schizophrenia include the fixed, false, and usually bizarre beliefs known as delusions. These may be paranoid delusions that the person is being followed, spied on, poisoned, or otherwise threatened by some sinister outside force: a person, a group of people, an organization, or even supernatural beings. There may be delusions of reference: a sense that ordinary events in the world have some hidden meaning that is only apparent to the patient. For example, if watching a movie, the patient may have a sense that the actors' lines are actually comments about the patient's behavior or secret instructions. There may also be delusions of passivity: a sense that one's actions or thoughts are being controlled by an outside force. Patients will say that their thoughts are being "taken out" of their heads, that other people's thoughts are being placed in their heads, or that others can actually hear their thoughts as if they were being broadcast by a radio. They may feel a loss of agency in their actions: they will explain that their movements or spoken words are being controlled. There may also be somatic delusions: a conviction that one's own bodily organs are somehow abnormal or have been tampered with in some way.

Hallucinations are also a common and prominent feature of schizophrenia. Most commonly, patients will say that they hear voices speaking to them, sometimes commenting on their actions or commanding them to do things and sometimes simply speaking nonsense words or phrases. Aside from these auditory hallucinations, there may also be somatic hallucinations of bizarre visceral sensations: a dripping sensation inside the brain, a sense that the lungs are being turned inside-out, or a feeling that the eyes are being pulled through the back of the head. Olfactory hallucinations of strange or offensive smells sometimes occur. Surprisingly, visual hallucinations are less common than other kinds of hallucinations in schizophrenia.

Other prominent positive symptoms include disorganization of behavior and speech. The person may engage in activities that seem bizarre to other people, often in response to their delusional beliefs or their hallucinations. They may

adopt strange forms of dress or take bizarre countermeasures to prevent themselves from being "spied on." Their speech may show evidence of **thought disorder**: loose associations between ideas, so that the path of conversation appears nonsensical to outsiders, or the linking together of unrelated ideas, or strange lapses in logic, or rambling speech with no clear meaning or purpose, or invented nonsense words known as neologisms. Collectively, hallucinations, delusions, and disorganized speech and behavior are considered different possible features of psychosis (TABLE 16.1).

Although it is the loss of contact with reality that usually brings schizophrenia to the notice of other people, it is actually the **negative symptoms** that are the most disabling. These are features of normal cognition and behavior that become *lost* in schizophrenia, as opposed to the positive symptoms, which are added. Negative symptoms can include apathy and a lack of volition, social withdrawal, a "poverty" of speech and of thoughts, anhedonia, and a loss of emotional reactivity known as flat affect. These are the symptoms that tend to prevent patients from pursuing the activities they previously enjoyed, interacting with friends and family, or pursuing an education or a career. Unfortunately these symptoms also tend to be the most resistant to treatment.

As with many of the other illnesses we have considered in this chapter, the treatment of schizophrenia involves medications that relieve some of the symptoms of the disease rather than treating the underlying pathology (which remains unknown). Antipsychotic medications, also known as neuroleptics, are the mainstay of treatment for schizophrenia and most other forms of psychotic illness. The first antipsychotics were developed entirely accidentally more than half a century ago. At the time, no one had considered that the diverse, bizarre, elaborate symptoms of schizophrenia

---

TABLE 16.1.

The Positive and Negative Symptoms of Schizophrenia

POSITIVE SYMPTOMS	NEGATIVE SYMPTOMS
Hallucinations—false perceptions: hearing voices or feeling strange bodily sensations are common examples	Poverty of speech or thought—a lack of spontaneous speech or thought or limited responses to cues to speak or think
Delusions—fixed, false, bizarre beliefs: paranoid delusions of being pursued or monitored are common examples	Apathy—a lack of motivation or initiative Social withdrawal—a tendency to self-isolate Depression—persistent low mood
Disorganized speech and/or behavior—nonsensical words or phrases or bizarre acts that are often motivated by delusions	Flat affect—a lack of emotional expression, apparent in speech or facial expressions during social interaction

might respond to a targeted pharmaceutical treatment. However, in the early 1950s, the French surgeon Laborit noted that a certain experimental sedative seemed to produce a unique state of "indifference" to surroundings in the patients who received it after surgery—in particular, a series of patients with schizophrenia who happened to be undergoing surgery for other ailments. Psychiatric colleagues Hamon and Delay then began using the treatment in other patients with schizophrenia and noted a dramatic improvement in symptoms within days. The first antipsychotic, **chlorpromazine**, was born (Kapur & Mamo, 2003).

In the ensuing years, dozens of other related "first-generation" medications have been developed, followed a couple of decades later by a series of "second-generation" antipsychotics. The goal for the second-generation antipsychotics has been twofold. First, they have tried to avoid some of the first-generation antipsychotics' unpleasant side effects, such as rigidity, **Parkinsonism**, and a disfiguring long-term motor side effect known as **tardive dyskinesia**, which involves permanent, abnormal movements or postures of body parts. The second goal for the newer antipsychotics is to achieve greater efficacy—in particular, to address the disabling negative symptoms as well as the more obvious positive symptoms. Unfortunately, despite initial optimism, the newer generation of antipsychotic drugs ultimately has not shown greater efficacy for either positive or negative symptoms (Leucht et al., 2009). Furthermore, with a couple of exceptions, most of the second-generation antipsychotics proved to have their own troublesome side effects: weight gain, increased cholesterol, diabetes, and the associated greater risks of heart disease and stroke (De Hert, Dobbelaere, Sheridan, Cohen, & Correll, 2011). They also do not reverse or modify the underlying causes of schizophrenia any more than do the older antipsychotics.

As it stands, the ultimate causes of schizophrenia remain mysterious, even after more than a century of research.

Genetics play an important role, and the overall heritability of schizophrenia is around 80% (Kapur & Mamo, 2003). Yet even in identical twins, when one twin has schizophrenia, the chances of the other one also having the illness are only around 40–50% (Onstad, Skre, Torgersen, & Kringlen, 1991). As with many of the other illnesses we have seen, it has been difficult to pin schizophrenia onto any single gene or mutation. Nonetheless, linkage studies have identified about a dozen genes in which mutations can cause a slight increase in the risk of schizophrenia. For example, the **DISC1** (or disrupted-in-schizophrenia) gene has mutations that run in certain families (FIGURE 16.22) and increase the risk of illness (Millar et al., 2000). Yet these strongly familial forms of schizophrenia are the exception rather than the rule. Many schizophrenia patients have no known relatives with the illness, probably because of the importance of gene–gene and gene–environmental interactions, as we saw earlier in the chapter.

Many of the most important risk factors for schizophrenia are environmental, and in fact many of these occur during pregnancy or delivery: decades before the onset of obvious symptoms in early adulthood. Maternal infections with rubella, influenza, polio, or other illnesses will increase the risk of a child developing schizophrenia (Brown & Patterson, 2011). Maternal stressors, such as famine, flood, unwanted gestation, depression, and bereavement, also have this effect (Khashan et al., 2008). Obstetrical complications such as brain injury or low blood oxygen during delivery, low birth weight, or blood type incompatibility can also increase schizophrenia risk (Cannon, Jones, & Murray, 2002). After birth, known risk factors include residing in a city, belonging to a minority ethnic group, childhood trauma, and social isolation (van Os & Kapur, 2009).

How might these early events light the fuse for schizophrenia in adulthood? **Neurodevelopmental theories** of schizophrenia describe a process of abnormal brain

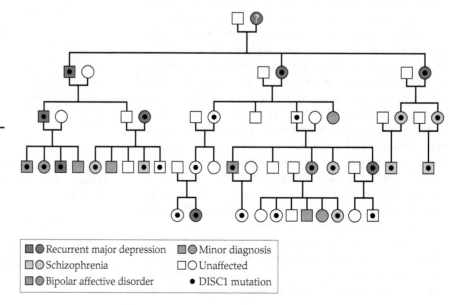

FIGURE 16.22 A family pedigree of the DISC1 gene. This pedigree shows five generations of a family known to carry the DISC1 mutation. Individuals with the mutation are marked with a dot, and individuals with a known diagnosis are indicated by a color code. Note that the same genetic mutation leads to different types of mental illness in different individuals, and that not everyone who carries the mutation has an illness; this illustrates the importance of gene–gene and gene–environment interactions.

■● Recurrent major depression ■● Minor diagnosis
□○ Schizophrenia □○ Unaffected
■● Bipolar affective disorder • DISC1 mutation

development, both at the macro and at the micro scale (Rapoport, Addington, Frangou, & Psych, 2005). For decades, neuroimaging studies have found neuroanatomical abnormalities in adult patients with schizophrenia. Enlarged lateral ventricles, reduced hippocampal volumes, smaller whole-brain volume, and thinning of the frontal lobes have all been seen in comparisons of patients with schizophrenia to healthy controls (Vita, De Peri, Silenzi, & Dieci, 2006).

More recently, studies using high-resolution anatomical MRI have begun to follow the brain volumes of high-risk individuals over several years, comparing those who develop schizophrenia to those who do not. The results of these studies show a picture of abnormal development: specifically, an excess of the normal pruning of cortical connections that takes place during adolescence (van Haren et al., 2008). All adolescent brains show a thinning of the gray matter over time as they mature because of this pruning and also because of increasing myelination of the underlying white matter. However, patients with schizophrenia show much more dramatic thinning of the cortex in a widespread set of areas (FIGURE 16.23), especially in the anterior temporal lobes and dorsal medial frontal lobes (van Haren et al., 2007). The ones with the most dramatic thinning are the ones who go on to develop the earliest symptoms of psychosis. Unfortunately, the thinning of the cortex continues after the onset of positive symptoms: an ongoing process of cortical atrophy beginning in adolescence instead of old age. In some ways, Kraepelin was ahead of his time in describing schizophrenia as a "precocious dementia" (Hoff, 2012).

Other accounts of schizophrenia have focused on microscale abnormalities of cortical neural circuits, rather than macro-scale changes in overall thickness. There are mild cytoarchitectural abnormalities in the neural circuitry of the cortex in patients with schizophrenia (Harrison, 1999). These include a smaller soma or cell body and decreased density of the dendritic spines in the pyramidal (output) neurons of microcircuits in the prefrontal cortex (Glantz & Lewis, 2000; Selemon & Goldman-Rakic, 1999). There is also reduced functioning of the GABA interneurons of the cortex, which provide inhibitory feedback to the pyramidal neurons. This reduced function may lead to a disinhibition of the pyramidal neurons, so that they become overly active or active at inappropriate times (Benes & Berretta, 2001). The pyramidal neurons themselves use the excitatory neurotransmitter glutamate, providing output to both the dopamine neurons of the ventral tegmental area and striatum and the GABA interneurons themselves, in a negative feedback loop.

As you can see, this circuitry is complicated even when presented in a simplified form. Researchers are still debating how abnormalities in these circuits might give rise to abnormal oscillations of neural activity or other abnormal patterns of activity, which might in turn give rise to the symptoms of schizophrenia (Lisman et al., 2008). Until these issues are resolved, perhaps the best general principles to keep in mind are as follows: abnormal genetics or abnormal developmental events can disrupt the delicate circuitry of pyramidal neurons and interneurons connecting the cortex and its subcortical partners in the striatum and midbrain. Within such circuitry, slight changes in neurotransmitter function can cause significant changes in the patterns of neural activity within these circuits.

In some cases, these changes can be remedied using medications that alter neurotransmission, such as the antipsychotics, which block D_2 dopamine receptors. Yet the underlying circuitry remains disordered, so that discontinuing the drug usually leads to a relapse. A permanent fix would

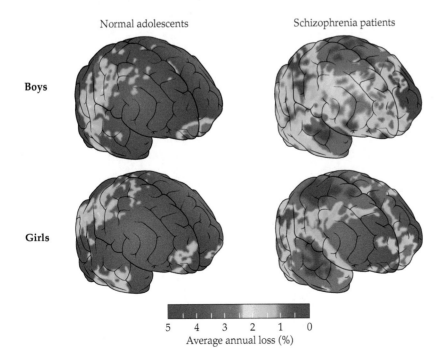

Normal adolescents   Schizophrenia patients

Boys

Girls

5   4   3   2   1   0
Average annual loss (%)

FIGURE 16.23 **Compared with healthy control subjects, individuals with schizophrenia show a decrease in gray matter over time.** The abnormal loss of gray matter usually begins in adolescence, well before the symptoms of psychosis become prominent in early adulthood.

involve changing the abnormalities in the underlying neural circuitry—a feat we are likely still decades away from achieving.

Yet how do these subtle brain abnormalities arise in the first place? In the developing brain, cortical neurons begin their lives near the ventricles and must "crawl" outward through the white matter to the outer regions of the neural tube, where they eventually form the cortex. Later-born neurons must "crawl through" the layers of existing cortical neurons to reach their final positions near the surface. As you might imagine, this many-layered neural migration is a complex and delicate process. Cortical neurons must make stops along the way, form temporary connections, dissolve those connections, migrate to the appropriate layer, and send out connections to the appropriate neurons in other layers. If there are abnormalities in the genes that sustain neuronal migration, or the genes that help neurons grow and form connections, or the activity of the neurotransmitters that help to guide migration and synapse formation, or if there are stressors (such as infection) that interfere with this process, then the neurons may end up in the wrong places or form connections to the wrong neighbors (FIGURE 16.24).

Why don't these brain abnormalities show their effects until much later in life? As you may recall from Chapter 4, the newborn brain starts out with many redundant or "reserve" neurons and neural connections. It does not immediately decide which ones are worth keeping and which ones are better off removed, but waits until many years later to refine its circuitry by pruning. The effects of any subtle miswiring may not become apparent until adolescence, when pruning starts to exceed new growth. At this point, the

reserve connections may get stripped away (Boksa, 2012). In any case, the effects are more subtle than one sees in Alzheimer's or frontotemporal dementia: just slightly altered circuits that do not function quite as they should.

Although the neurodevelopmental theories are still being refined, older and simpler theories of schizophrenia focus on abnormalities in certain neurotransmitter systems, while leaving aside the exact roles of these neurotransmitters in neural circuitry. For example, the long-standing **dopamine hypothesis** of schizophrenia suggests that abnormally high or dysregulated dopamine neurotransmission causes the symptoms of schizophrenia (Kapur, Mizrahi, & Li, 2005). The link between dopamine and schizophrenia came from two separate observations. First, the use of drugs that increase dopamine levels (such as amphetamines or cocaine) can produce some of the positive symptoms of schizophrenia, such as paranoid delusions. Second, every one of the dozens of known typical antipsychotic medications blocks dopamine from binding to the D_2 dopamine receptor, and the more strongly it binds to this receptor, the more potent its antipsychotic effect (FIGURE 16.25; Seeman & Lee, 1975). Specifically, the drugs must achieve around 65–80% blockade of the D_2 receptors in the ventral striatum (Howes et al., 2009). Below this level, the symptoms of psychosis tend to persist. Above this level, the adverse effects of low dopamine transmission begin to appear: Parkinsonian rigidity and tremor, dystonias, and a restlessness known as akathisia.

So is schizophrenia simply a matter of excessively high dopamine? The reality appears to be more complex and to involve other neurotransmitter systems as well. For example, cannabis use, especially in adolescence, is associated

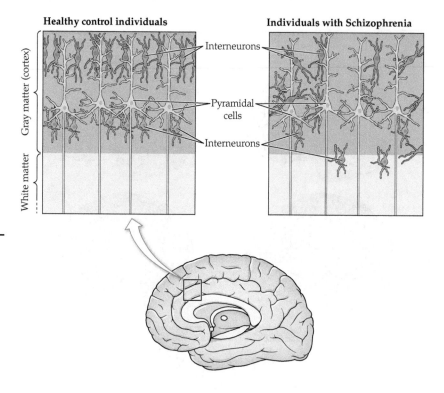

FIGURE 16.24 The hypothesis of abnormal neuron migration in schizophrenia. If neurons fail to migrate to the correct layers of the cortex during development, they may not connect or communicate properly. In some studies of the layers of cortex in individuals with schizophrenia, the GABAergic interneurons fail to migrate to the correct location. This disrupts the circuitry of the cortex at a microscopic level.

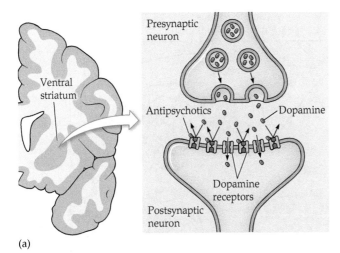

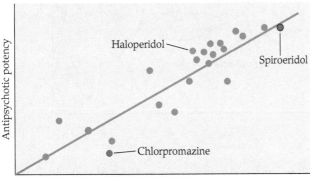

FIGURE 16.25 **Antipsychotic medications are D₂ receptor antagonists.**
(a) All known antipsychotic medications act by blocking the D₂ dopamine receptor. The medication must block about 65–80% of the receptors in the ventral striatum in order to achieve its desired effect. (b) The effective dose of antipsychotic medications correlates closely with how tightly they bind to D₂ receptors. Medications with higher affinity for D₂ receptors are effective at lower daily doses.

with a significantly higher risk of schizophrenia (D'Souza, 2007). Although the vast majority of those who use cannabis do not develop schizophrenia, there is nonetheless a small subpopulation of individuals who seem to be vulnerable. When these individuals use cannabis, they seem to develop symptoms of psychosis. Cannabis also worsens symptoms substantially in those who already have a diagnosis of schizophrenia.

It remains controversial as to whether cannabis can cause schizophrenia in those who would otherwise never have developed the disease or whether it simply "unmasks" schizophrenia in those with a genetic and environmental predisposition toward the disease (D'Souza, 2007). However, we do know that cannabis acts on a distinct neurotransmitter system involving cannabinoid receptors and that this system interacts with many other neurotransmitters in the brain aside from dopamine. Likewise, in recent years, researchers have turned to other neurotransmitter theories

beyond the dopamine theory in an effort to explain the symptoms of schizophrenia. Chief among these is the excitatory neurotransmitter, glutamate.

The **glutamate hypothesis** suggests that too little glutamate neurotransmission, rather than too much dopamine, could account for both the positive and the negative symptoms of schizophrenia (Olney & Farber, 1995). One factor in support of this idea is that drugs that block the NMDA glutamate receptors, such as **ketamine** or **PCP**, can produce a dissociative state with hallucinations, delusions of passivity, a sense of unreality, paranoia, and a sense of being in the presence of other entities, as well as negative symptoms such as motor unresponsiveness, flat affect, a lack of motivation, and even a catatonic-like state (Javitt, 2007). Schizophrenia patients tend to show low glutamate levels and changes in the expression of NMDA receptors (Corlett, Honey, & Fletcher, 2007). Many of the genes linked to schizophrenia seem to interact with the NMDA receptors in some way. Also, recent trials have shown that some drugs enhancing glutamate neurotransmission may function as effective antipsychotics, although they do not affect the dopamine D₂ receptor at all (Lesage & Steckler, 2010).

The latest models of neurotransmitter function in the cortex suggest that the glutamate and dopamine hypotheses may not be mutually exclusive (Corlett et al., 2007). The loop circuits among the cortex, striatum, thalamus, and substantia nigra involve many different kinds of neurotransmitters (FIGURE 16.26). Some experimental evidence suggests that decreased glutamate release by the prefrontal cortex could indirectly lead to increased dopamine release in the subcortical areas (Carr & Sesack, 2000). Therefore, low glutamate, high dopamine, or even low GABA neurotransmission could all lead to excessive, hyperresponsive activity in cortical circuits. Unified models such as these might help to bring the various neuroanatomical, neurodevelopmental, and neurochemical theories of schizophrenia onto common ground.

Such a unification is urgently needed. At the moment, the prognosis for a young person diagnosed with schizophrenia is not favorable. Under current treatments, about one-third of patients seem to improve significantly, whereas another one-third remain more or less unchanged and another one-third continue to decline in their overall level of function (Harvey, Jeffreys, McNaught, Blizard, & King, 2007; Menezes, Arenovich, & Zipursky, 2006). Even with treatment, only about 1 in 10 patients recover sufficiently to return to work (Marwaha et al., 2007). The challenge of schizophrenia may be harder than simply finding a new drug to treat the adult manifestations of the disease. If the roots of schizophrenia begin with abnormal brain development in childhood or even in pregnancy, then entirely new approaches may be needed. It may be necessary to identify and repair the neurodegenerative changes long before they show up in terms of obvious symptoms. This would mean providing some kind of neuroprotective treatment to at-risk patients without even being able to say for sure that they are

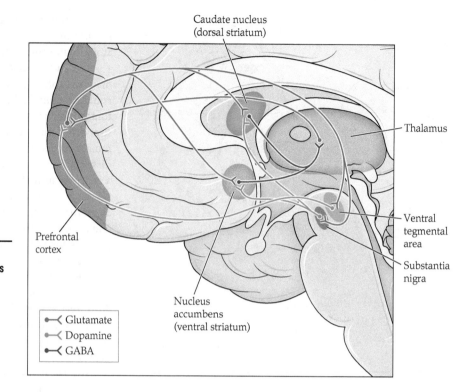

FIGURE 16.26 **The loops connecting the prefrontal cortex to the striatum and thalamus use a variety of neurotransmitters, including dopamine, glutamate, and GABA.** The interaction of dopamine and glutamate in these loops means that the glutamate and dopamine hypotheses of schizophrenia are not mutually exclusive—both neurotransmitters likely play a role in the illness, as does GABA.

destined to develop the disease: a tough sell even in adults, let alone in newborn or fetal children. Alternatively, future treatments may be able to stimulate new neural growth in the adult cortex, using neuroplasticity to reconstruct circuits that somehow went awry years ago. In either case, such treatments are still far away. It remains to be seen whether antipsychotic medications will still be the mainstay of schizophrenia treatment another 60 years from now or whether new avenues will at last be opened.

Bipolar Disorder

Bipolar disorder, formerly known as "manic–depressive illness," affects about 1% of the population; milder forms of the illness may exist in as many as 4–5% of individuals (Merikangas et al., 2007). The illness has been known since antiquity. Clear descriptions of the symptoms can be found in the medical texts of Hippocrates and Artaeus in classical Greece (Angst & Marneros, 2001). When their symptoms are under control, patients with bipolar disorder are often able to function at normal or even superior levels in terms of their work, studies, and social relationships. However, their periods of stable mood are interrupted periodically by episodes of low mood and other features of **depression**, alternating with other episodes of elevated mood, or **mania** (FIGURE 16.27).

In broad terms, mania looks something like the opposite of depression. During a manic episode, patients tend to develop an elevated or even euphoric mood, although some become angry and irritable instead. They have increased levels of confidence and may concoct elaborate plans to

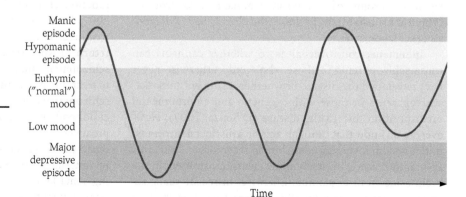

FIGURE 16.27 **Individuals with bipolar disorder cycle from a depressed state to a manic state and back again.** These cycles can vary in length, with a single phase of the cycle lasting from days to months, depending on the individual.

achieve fame and fortune. They pursue more activities, more vigorously than usual, with markedly increased energy. Their libido may increase markedly. They may have a decreased need for sleep and may go without sleep for days at a time. Their thoughts may race from one to the next in an uncontrolled fashion, and they may become much more talkative. They may also have trouble concentrating on any one thing and tend to be distracted easily. They also tend to become much more impulsive, taking on risky activities, spending far beyond their means, launching themselves into ill-advised business ventures, and pursuing inappropriate sexual relationships. Although the changes in behavior are obvious to others, patients with mania themselves typically have poor insight into their symptoms. If anything, they will tend to say that they feel wonderful and will minimize any problems that they might encounter—at least until the episode is over and they must deal with its aftermath.

Although some of these features of bipolar disorder may sound benign or even enjoyable on paper, in reality the illness has devastating effects. The episodes of mania tend to be even more damaging than the episodes of depression: careers are lost, marriages are broken, and finances are ruined. Thanks to the high impulsivity seen in bipolar disorder, around 15–20% of patients die by suicide, and nearly half of patients attempt to end their own lives at some point in the course of illness (Yatham et al., 2005). The disorder tends to be lifelong: although the typical age of onset is between 17 and 21 years of age, episodes often occur with increasing frequency over the lifespan, and even elderly patients with bipolar disorder can slip into dramatic episodes of mania or depression (Chengappa et al., 2003). Thanks to its typical age of onset, it is responsible for more years of life lost to disability than all forms of cancer combined (Merikangas et al., 2011).

Patients with bipolar disorder are also more likely to develop psychotic features during episodes of mania or depression. For example, a manic patient may develop delusions that she is the secret star of a reality television show in which all the rest of the world are extras; she may even have hallucinations of hearing stage directions telling her what to do or of seeing bright stage lights directed at her surroundings. A depressed patient may develop delusions that a global war or other catastrophe is coming because of something he has done or some conversation that he has had. This loss of touch with reality is reminiscent of schizophrenia, although the treatments and the course of illness for the two diseases, as well as their most common symptoms, are somewhat different.

The causes of bipolar disorder are still mysterious, although genetic factors seem to play a strong role, as in schizophrenia. If you have a parent or a sibling with bipolar disorder, your odds of developing the illness increase seven- to ninefold (Lichtenstein et al., 2009). If you have an identical twin with bipolar disorder, your chances of having the same illness are more than 40% (Kieseppa, Partonen, Haukka, Kaprio, & Lonnqvist, 2004).

At the same time, as with schizophrenia, it has been hard to map the illness onto any specific gene, although several types of mutations can increase the risk of illness. For example, the DISC1 gene is actually linked to both schizophrenia and bipolar disorder, despite its name (Hennah et al., 2009). Within a given family, some individuals with the mutation may develop schizophrenia, whereas others develop bipolar disorder or recurrent depression (Blackwood & Muir, 2004). The DISC1 gene itself codes for a protein that is involved in the growth, migration, and plasticity of neurons and their axonal connections. Hence, bipolar disorder and schizophrenia may share some common neurodevelopmental basis in a miswiring or mispositioning of the neurons of the cortex. The differences between the diseases would then be a matter of which parts of the brain were most severely affected by the abnormal developmental process.

In keeping with this idea, we can see a partial overlap between schizophrenia and bipolar disorder when we look at neuroimaging studies of the illness. One way of trying to locate the neuronal abnormalities of bipolar disorder is to identify regions of unusual thinning in the cortex, using voxel-based morphometry. A large meta-analysis of hundreds of patients with bipolar disorder found a few consistent regions of cortical thinning: the left and right ventrolateral frontal cortex, left and right anterior insula, part of the dorsomedial prefrontal cortex, and a small region in the subgenual cingulate cortex (FIGURE 16.28; Ellison-Wright & Bullmore, 2010). The dorsomedial and subgenual cingulate thinning is particularly interesting because these regions have also been linked to **unipolar depression**, a much more common form of mood disorder seen in up to a fifth of the population (Bora, Fornito, Pantelis, & Yucel, 2012; Hamani et al., 2011). The thinning of insular and ventrolateral prefrontal cortex is also interesting, given the roles of these areas in interoception and emotion regulation (see Chapter 13). In schizophrenia, all of these areas may also be affected, but there is also consistent thinning in a much more widespread swath of cortex extending through much of the medial prefrontal and inferior prefrontal cortex (Bora, Fornito, Yucel, & Pantelis, 2012; Ellison-Wright & Bullmore, 2010). This partial anatomical overlap may explain why *some* of the symptoms of schizophrenia, as well as its patterns of inheritance, can overlap with those of bipolar disorder. It also might help to explain why a single gene mutation can give rise to bipolar disorder in some family members, schizophrenia in others, and no obvious illness in the rest. The exact effects of the mutation may vary from individual to individual, depending on how much of the brain is affected and which areas are affected most.

Although we know relatively little about the underlying causes of bipolar disorder, we still have a number of fairly effective treatments. One of the most potent medications for bipolar disorder is not a synthetic chemical compound or a tailored protein, but a simple element: **lithium**. As with many treatments in medicine, the usefulness of lithium in bipolar disorder was discovered accidentally.

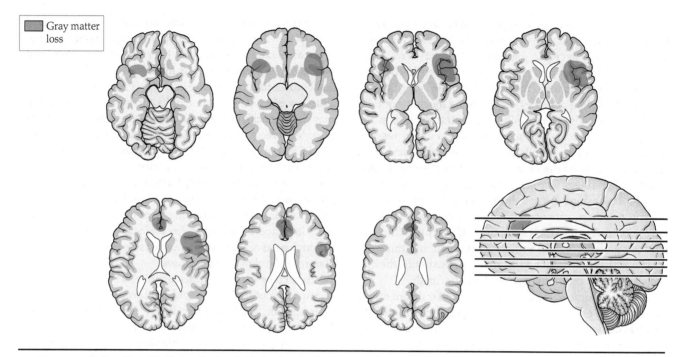

Gray matter loss

FIGURE 16.28 Brain regions with gray matter loss in bipolar disorder. Compared to healthy controls, patients with bipolar disorder have a reduction in gray matter in certain areas, including the anterior insula, ventrolateral prefrontal cortex, ventromedial prefrontal cortex, dorsomedial prefrontal cortex, and subgenual cingulate cortex. (Lines at lower right indicate the positions of these axial slices within the brain.

In 1949, the Australian psychiatrist John Cade accidentally found that lithium worked as a tranquilizing agent in laboratory animals. He then began using lithium salts to treat some of his patients and found that patients with bipolar disorder often returned to a normal mood state following such treatment. Lithium acted, in effect, as a **mood stabilizer** (Cade, 1949).

Unfortunately, the treatment worked only within a narrow dosage range: too little lithium was ineffective, whereas too much lithium produced severe toxicity and sometimes death. However, with careful monitoring of blood lithium levels, the medication could be maintained in its therapeutic range and the patients could reap the benefits of its mood-stabilizing effects without experiencing toxicity. Despite the effectiveness of lithium as a treatment for bipolar disorder, the rest of the world was slow to accept it. Its discoverer was obscure; the treatment was unconventional and with no well-understood therapeutic mechanism; the potential for toxicity was high and the consequences were severe. Nonetheless, the treatment was eventually adopted around the world. In the United States, lithium was finally approved by the Food and Drug Administration in 1970—more than 20 years after the treatment was first discovered.

To this day, lithium remains one of the most effective and widely used treatments for bipolar disorder (**FIGURE 16.29**). At the same time, its precise mechanism of action remains unknown. Some researchers have linked its effects to dopamine or glutamate neurotransmission, others to a neural signaling system involving the membrane phospholipid inositol

triphosphate, and still others to nitric oxide neurotransmission (Malhi, Tanious, Das, Coulston, & Berk, 2013). However, it is still unclear which of these effects, if any, is crucial for the mood-stabilizing effects of lithium. Nor is it clear what underlying abnormality of neural function is corrected by introducing lithium ions into the brain. As with many psychiatric illnesses, we have a well-established treatment that acts by mysterious means on the mysterious processes of a mysterious disease.

A second class of mood stabilizer medications includes certain antiepileptic drugs. Again, the usefulness of these drugs was discovered accidentally. Physicians had noted that the mood episodes of bipolar disorder seemed to become more frequent and more severe over time, just as epileptic seizures tend to kindle more and more severe seizures over time. They therefore tried using valproic acid, an antiseizure treatment, and found it to be effective in many patients (Henry, 2003). Two other antiseizure medications, carbamazepine and lamotrigine, also proved effective. The dopamine-blocking neuroleptic medications originally used in schizophrenia also proved to be helpful for bipolar disorder in many cases, especially during the acute phases of illness (Yatham et al., 2005).

Unfortunately, antidepressant medications often prove to be unhelpful and in some cases even harmful in treating episodes of depression in bipolar disorder. Many types of antidepressants can actually make the situation worse by switching the patient's mood episode from depression into full-blown mania (Sidor & MacQueen, 2012). Again, the

Lithium

Anti-epilepsy
medications

Valproic acid

Antipsychotic medications

Haloperidol

Carbamazepine

Risperidone

Lamotrigine

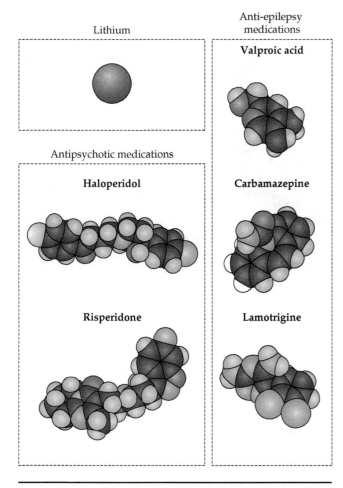

FIGURE 16.29 **Mood stabilizers for bipolar disorder.** Several different classes of medications are used as mood stabilizers in bipolar disorder. These include the element lithium, antipsychotic medications (of which haloperidol or risperidone are two examples among dozens available), and certain antiepilepsy medications such as valproic acid, carbamazepine, and lamotrigine.

underlying mechanisms behind all of these effects, both positive and negative, are still poorly understood despite these medications' many decades of success as treatments.

Mood stabilizers have changed the prognosis of bipolar disorder dramatically. Finding the right combination of treatments often takes time, and in some patients, mood episodes continue despite treatment. Many patients with bipolar disorder require more than one mood stabilizer to remain in a normal mood state that is neither manic nor depressed. Nonetheless, many patients with bipolar disorder do remain stable for years or decades, so long as they continue treatment. During these healthy periods, they tend to do much better than patients with schizophrenia. They maintain a social or a family life, return to work, form relationships, and pursue their ambitions. Many individuals with bipolar disorder have been able not only to survive but also to thrive and excel in their personal lives, perhaps benefitting from the energy and spontaneity of the milder manic episodes known as hypomania.

One final note about this illness: if you have been reading carefully, you may have noted that many of the brain areas affected in bipolar disorder are similar to the areas that atrophy in frontotemporal dementia: the orbitofrontal cortex, ventrolateral prefrontal cortex, and anterior temporal lobes. Although the symptoms of the two illnesses differ, they do share a common thread of disinhibition in the social, behavioral, and impulse-control domains. You may recall that one side effect of this disinhibition is increased creativity in some patients with frontotemporal dementia. This seems to be true of bipolar disorder as well. It turns out that a surprisingly high proportion of well-known artists, performers, composers, writers, and other creative individuals have some form of bipolar disorder (FIGURE 16.30; Andreasen & Glick, 1988; Richards & Kinney, 1989). In 1993, the clinical psychologist Kay Redfield Jamison wrote a book, *Touched with Fire*, arguing that many of history's most successful artists suffered from the illness: Picasso, Hemingway, van Gogh, and Lord Byron, among others (Jamison, 1993).

The stereotype of the "mad genius" artist, blessed with creative talent but cursed with mental instability, has long existed. Over the past 30 years, however, researchers have begun to confirm a specific link between bipolar disorder and high creativity. For example, in large community mental health surveys, individuals with bipolar disorder are more likely to work in jobs requiring high creativity and less likely to work in jobs requiring little creativity (Tremblay, Grosskopf, & Yang, 2010). They also score higher on the Barron–Welsh Art Scale (Tremblay et al., 2010), an objective measure of creativity that involves rating one's preference for a series of drawings of increasing asymmetry and complexity. Artists tend to prefer the more asymmetrical, complex figures. On this scale, bipolar patients have scores nearly 50% above those of healthy control subjects: essentially as high as the scores of students in university-level fine arts programs (Santosa et al., 2007). This finding was striking because the subjects came from a general sample of bipolar patients of no particular artistic ability.

Older research has also suggested higher creativity in the mentally healthy *relatives* of those with bipolar illness (Kinney & Richards, 1986). If so, this could explain why a disorder with such high mortality (recall the suicide rate of up to 15%) has not been removed from the gene pool by natural selection. Certain genetic diseases persist in the human population because they offer advantages to those who carry them in a mild, nonmalignant form. Sickle-cell anemia is a good example. One in four offspring of carrier parents will have two copies of the mutant gene and suffer childhood strokes, multiple organ failure, and an early death. However, one in two offspring will have just one copy and, as carriers, will enjoy resistance to malaria just like their parents. Likewise, if only one parent is a carrier, half of the offspring will also inherit a single copy of the mutant gene and enjoy the advantages of being carriers. In effect,

(a)   (b)   (c)

FIGURE 16.30 **(a) Hemingway, (b) Picasso, and (c) van Gogh are three famous artists thought to have had bipolar disorder.**

those with the full-blown illness shoulder the genetic burden of the disease, allowing close relatives to reap the benefits of its milder forms. Whether this is true of bipolar disorder remains to be seen.

Depression: A Global Burden

Major depressive disorder is one of the most widespread and disabling illnesses in the world (FIGURE 16.31). Going far beyond mere sadness, the persistent low mood of depression makes it difficult to perform the basic functions of everyday life. Yet persistent low mood is only one of the features of major depression. Anhedonia, the inability to enjoy one's usual pleasures, is another common symptom. Lack of motivation and energy are also common. Those who do remain active often have difficulty concentrating on their work or on other tasks. They tend to ruminate on the past or worry about the future. They may be mired in hopelessness or overwhelmed by feelings of guilt and inadequacy. There are also changes in basic hypothalamic drives, sometimes called neurovegetative symptoms. Sleep patterns are affected: some sleep restlessly and for fewer hours, whereas others sleep for hours longer than usual. Appetite may also change dramatically, and over time, sufferers may notice themselves gaining or losing weight. As the illness becomes increasingly severe, depressed individuals may no longer care whether they live or die. They may even harbor thoughts of suicide, make plans to end their lives, and, in some cases, carry out these plans. Overall, around 2% of patients with depression will ultimately take their own lives, and many

more will attempt to do so (Bostwick & Pankratz, 2000). This alone emphasizes the seriousness of depression as an illness: it is among the few conditions in which patients will routinely say they would rather be dead than go on living with the disease.

Impact of Depression

When we think of the major causes of human illness around the world, many culprits come easily to mind: heart disease, cancer, diabetes, malaria, HIV, malnutrition. However, you might be surprised to also see major depressive disorder near the top of the list. Depression is already ranked as the second highest cause of disability, worldwide, and its impact is growing every year (Grigoryev, 2012; World Health Organization, 2004). By 2030, depression will be the number one contributor to the global burden of disease worldwide, surpassing heart disease, road accidents, stroke, and infections when it comes to the number of years of health lost (Lepine & Briley, 2011).

Why should depression have such an impact on worldwide health? It strikes large numbers of people at a relatively young age compared with heart disease or cancer. It is widely underrecognized and undertreated. Its effects are chronic, and relapse is common even after recovery. Its victims become socially withdrawn, unable to find or hold a job, unable to properly care for their children or participate in the life of their community, and far more likely to neglect their own physical health as well. They become more vulnerable to other chronic illnesses: heart disease, diabetes, arthritis, asthma, and more (Moussavi et al., 2007). They may become drawn into addiction. The burden of their care falls on family members and friends and on local health organizations.

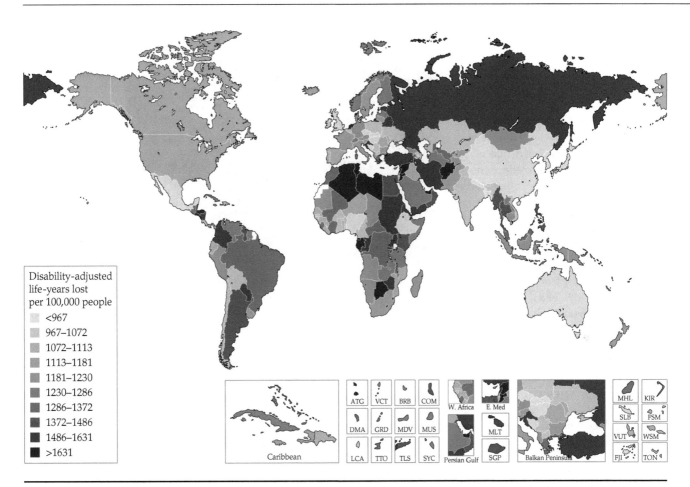

Disability-adjusted
life-years lost
per 100,000 people
- <967
- 967–1072
- 1072–1113
- 1113–1181
- 1181–1230
- 1230–1286
- 1286–1372
- 1372–1486
- 1486–1631
- >1631

FIGURE 16.31 Depression is one of the leading causes of years of life lost to disability, worldwide. Darker colors indicate countries with a higher burden of years lost to disability from depression.

CASE STUDY:
A Lifetime Studying, and Living with, Bipolar Disorder

Dr. Kay Redfield Jamison is an internationally renowned expert on bipolar disorder. Over the course of her career as a clinical psychologist, she has published dozens of scientific articles on the illness. She has also written popular books on bipolar disorder, creativity, and the artistic temperament. Her descriptions of the illness are particularly compelling, in part because she herself has lived with bipolar disorder for all of her adult life. She has had firsthand experiences with both mania and depression and writes of these experiences extensively in her memoir, *An Unquiet Mind* (Jamison, 1995).

Dr. Jamison (FIGURE 16.32) had her first episode of mania while still a senior in high school—a fairly typical age of onset for the illness. Her writing describes the racing ideas, the fascination with the beauty of the universe, the heightened creativity and energy that propelled her into a faculty position as a professor of psychiatry at UCLA before the age of 30. However, it also describes the destructive side: unrestrained spending sprees, tumultuous relationships with others around her, impulsive decisions, irritability, and anger during mania, as well as long periods of severe depression and a suicide attempt by lithium overdose.

Unfortunately, as is often the case in bipolar disorder, she delayed seeking treatment for many years. Patients with bipolar illness tend to have difficulty seeing the true severity of their illness—the very parts of the brain that would engage in such self-reflection are offline. Although she could see the destructive effects of her mood episodes, she also had a sense that she ought to be able to control her mood on her own.

Yet the most significant factor that held her back from seeking treatment was the enduring stigma of mental illness. For many people, bipolar disorder is still perceived as a sort of character defect or a sign of personal weakness, rather than a disease of the brain like epilepsy or multiple sclerosis. Dr. Jamison feared that if her illness were discovered, she could lose her faculty position and her clinical practice, as well as the esteem of her family and friends. Unfortunately, such fears are not always unfounded, even today. The high rate of suicide in mental illness stems, in part, from the unnecessary stigma that leads to shame, social withdrawal, and the abandonment of one's hopes for the future.

Fortunately, Dr. Jamison managed to survive the worst of her illness, began taking lithium regularly, and maintained her remarkable career. She also lifted the veil of secrecy around her own illness by writing a candid memoir of her experiences. In doing so, she has helped to raise awareness of bipolar disorder as a brain disease that has the potential to be devastating, but does not have to be debilitating. She has also shown the world, by example, that the illness need not be a barrier to a successful career, social life, or romantic life. She and others like her are helping to replace the stigma of mental illness with a sense of understanding, compassion, and hope: qualities that are surely deserved by those who suffer from any disease, of any organ.

FIGURE 16.32 Dr. Kay Jamison is a clinical psychologist and author of *An Unquiet Mind*, which describes her own experiences with bipolar disorder.

Ultimately, society at large suffers from the loss of human potential: the talent and energy and labor that might have been put to good use, but instead are eclipsed by a pervasive sense of hopelessness and despair.

How common is depression? Worldwide, at any given time, more than 350 million people (5% of the population) are estimated to meet the diagnostic criteria for major depressive disorder (Murray et al., 2012). In the United States, the point prevalence of depression (that is, the number of people with depression at any given time) is up to 5% in men and 10% in women (FIGURE 16.33). The lifetime prevalence (the number of people who will suffer depression at some point in their lives) is nearly twice as high (Kessler, Chiu, Demler, Merikangas, & Walters, 2005). In 2003, the economic burden of depression in the United States exceeded $80 billion per year, including medical costs, workplace costs, and the impact of mortality by suicide (Greenberg et al., 2003). These costs put depression in the same league as cancer, heart disease, and diabetes in terms of overall economic impact.

Causes of Depression

Most common chronic illnesses, like diabetes or heart disease, have causes that are multifactorial: genetic factors, environmental factors, individual behavior, and even social surroundings. Depression is similar in this regard. Depressed mood does tend to run in families, and genetic factors can create a *predisposition* to illness without completely determining whether a given individual will suffer from depression.

As we saw earlier in this chapter, twin studies are useful in revealing the relative genetic and environmental influences on disease. For depression, the monozygotic twin concordance is only around 40% overall. In other words, if one twin suffers from depression, it is only moderately likely that the other twin also will, despite having the same genetics and upbringing. For dizygotic twins, the concordance rate is even lower: around 11%. The overall heritability of depression is a little less than 40% (Sullivan, Neale, & Kendler, 2000).

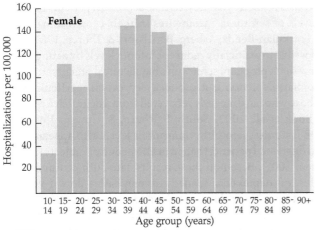

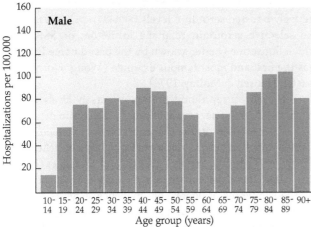

FIGURE 16.33 Depression over the adult lifespan. Hospitalizations for major depression peak at ages from the late 30s to early 50s, and again in late life. The rates of illness and hospitalization are nearly twice as high in women as in men.

However, there is a notable sex difference: heritability is stronger for women, at 40%, than for men, at around 30%. So the higher rates of depression in women go along with a stronger genetic influence on whether depression will emerge.

So far, the search for unambiguous "depression genes" has not turned up as many leads as expected. One gene that has been identified is 5HTTLPR, which lies in the promoter region near the DNA sequence for the serotonin transporter protein. This protein is a "reuptake pump," responsible for clearing serotonin out of the synapse and bringing it back into the axon terminal for reuse. The promoter region controls the level of expression of the protein: in theory, the higher its expression, the more quickly serotonin is cleared up after neural activity. This promoter region comes in different variants, including a "long" allele and a "short" allele, which cause different levels of transporter expression. In some studies, the short allele has been linked to depression. Depressed individuals with the short allele may also be less likely to respond to the class of antidepressant medications called selective serotonin reuptake inhibitors (SSRIs), which affect serotonin reuptake (Serretti, Kato, De Ronchi, & Kinoshita, 2007). However, these links are controversial:

some studies have found them, whereas others have not (Kraft et al., 2007; Murphy, Hollander, Rodrigues, Kremer, & Schatzberg, 2004). Again, it can be difficult to make a direct link from a single gene to a multifactorial illness like depression, and there is likely no single gene responsible for the symptoms of depression.

But what if we were to look at the interaction of this gene with environmental factors, such as stressful life events? These studies are more difficult to perform, but have also been more successful in finding consistent results. One large study of more than a thousand children in New Zealand looked at both genetics and the number of childhood stressful events. For individuals in which both copies of the 5HTTLPR gene were the long version, stressful childhood events did not predict depression in adulthood. However, in those who had one copy of the short version, stressful events in childhood did lead to a higher risk of depression. In those where both copies were the short version, the effect of stressful events was even stronger (**FIGURE 16.34**; Caspi et al., 2003). Some other similar studies have had similar findings (Kaufman et al., 2004; Wilhelm et al., 2006). However, other more recent studies have failed to replicate these results, and it remains controversial whether the link among 5HTTLPR, stress, and depression is as robust as it first appeared (Risch et al., 2009).

Nonetheless, studies of gene–environment interactions may help us to understand the mystery of resilience. Why do some individuals remain mentally healthy despite severe abuse and maltreatment, whereas others succumb to depression? The answer may lie in the interaction of genetic and environmental factors on brain function. And before we jump to the conclusion that the short alleles are defects in the genetic code, we should bear in mind that both kinds of alleles have roughly the same frequency in the population overall.

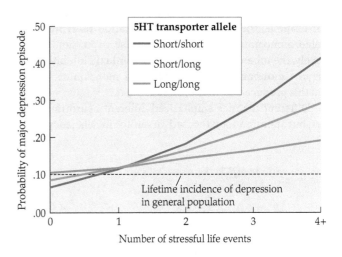

FIGURE 16.34 Interacting effects of genetic background and environmental events in depression. In one influential study (Caspi et al., 2003), having two copies of the short form of the 5HTTLPR serotonin transporter gene, as well as a more stressful life, significantly increased the individual's chance of developing depression.

About 45% of all the alleles in the gene pool are short versus 55% long (Caspi et al., 2003). Alleles that interfere with survival, even slightly, will drop to low frequencies in just a few generations through the effects of natural selection. When we see both kinds of alleles in a population, it tells us that neither one has a major survival advantage over the other.

But how could depression not be a disadvantage? Among humans, the biggest threats to survival often come not from predators or diseases, but from other human beings. In such a world, the best plan after a severe trauma or defeat may be to withdraw, lay low, and wait for better times to come. And after multiple defeats, it may be safer to stay out of the way of most of one's potential rivals (Sloman, Gilbert, & Hasey, 2003). In that way, the behaviors associated with depression may be a survival strategy, not just a form of pathology.

Neurochemical Effects of Depression on the Brain

What is the basis of depression in the brain? We often hear depression described as a "chemical imbalance," and certainly neurotransmitters have important effects on mood regulation, sleep, appetite, and so forth. Yet at the same time, before they can affect behavior, neurotransmitters must somehow persuade neurons to alter their activities in some way. So changes in neural activity also underlie depression.

Neurochemical theories of depression first emerged in the 1950s, around the time that the first effective antidepressant medications were discovered. An influential early proposal was the **monoamine hypothesis**, in which major depression was said to be caused by a deficiency of the monoamine neurotransmitters dopamine, norepinephrine, and/or serotonin in the brain (Hirschfeld, 2000). This hypothesis emerged from early observations of the effects of medications on mood. For example, the blood pressure medication **reserpine** depleted monoamines and tended to cause depression. Conversely, the tuberculosis medication **iproniazid** inhibited the enzyme **monoamine oxidase** to boost monoamine levels, and this produced an antidepressant effect.

Different theories emphasized different neurotransmitters, but attention soon focused on serotonin deficiency after studies in the 1970s showed that depressed patients had low levels of serotonin metabolites in their cerebrospinal fluid (Traskman-Bendz, Asberg, Bertilsson, & Thoren, 1984). It is possible to artificially reduce serotonin levels by eating a diet low in tryptophan, serotonin's biochemical precursor. Tryptophan depletion can produce depression, particularly in those who have recently recovered from a depressive episode (Booij et al., 2002; Smith, Fairburn, & Cowen, 1997). In PET studies, serotonin transporter levels also appear lower in depressed patients than in healthy control subjects (Dhaenen, 2001). Based on these results, late-20th-century theories of depression tended to emphasize low levels of serotonin. These theories helped to shape research on treatments as well. In the 1980s, a new class of antidepressant medications emerged that, unlike previous medications, selectively boosted serotonin levels (FIGURE 16.35). These were the selective serotonin reuptake inhibitors or SSRIs, of which fluoxetine (better known by the brand name Prozac) was the first and most famous example (Wong, Horng, Bymaster, Hauser, & Molloy, 1974).

Yet, just because an antidepressant boosts the levels of serotonin, this does not necessarily mean that serotonin deficiency is the basis of depression. As one psychiatrist memorably pointed out, headache is not a result of "aspirin deficiency" (Healy, 1997). In fact, a study by Kirsch and colleagues (Kirsch et al., 2008) found placebos to be as effective as SSRIs in relieving the symptoms of depression. Evidence suggests that the other monoamines also play a role. For example, depleting patients of norepinephrine and/or dopamine also seemed to precipitate depression in those who had suffered depressive episodes in the past (Berman et al., 1999; Charney, 1998). Also, some medications with little effect on serotonin, such as desipramine (a norepinephrine agonist) or bupropion (a norepinephrine and dopamine agonist), are equally effective to SSRIs as antidepressants (Bowden et al., 1993; Clayton et al., 2006). So the story of depression is certainly more complicated than "low serotonin equals low mood."

More recent research has focused on other neurotransmitters, many of them not monoamines. Medications that affect glutamate signaling, such as ketamine or riluzole, seem to have potent and rapid-onset antidepressant effects in experimental studies (Mathews & Zarate, 2013). Other studies have turned to a protein known as **brain-derived**

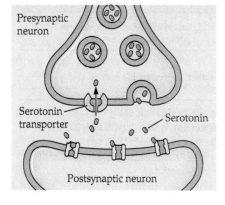

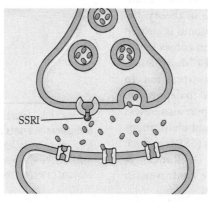

FIGURE 16.35 Selective serotonin reuptake inhibitors (SSRIs) work by blocking the reuptake of serotonin into the presynaptic terminal, thus increasing the concentration of serotonin in the synaptic cleft.

Presynaptic neuron

Serotonin transporter

Serotonin

Postsynaptic neuron

SSRI

neurotrophic factor (BDNF). This protein is a neuronal growth factor that regulates the growth, survival, and plasticity of neurons. Stress decreases the activity of BDNF, and studies of depressed suicide victims have found lower levels of BDNF in especially plastic regions of the brain, such as the hippocampus (Dwivedi et al., 2003). Conversely, many different treatments for depression (including sleep deprivation and seizures, as well as antidepressants) stimulate BDNF expression in the brain, which may explain why they alleviate the symptoms of depression (Fujihara, Sei, Morita, Ueta, & Morita, 2003; Nibuya, Morinobu, & Duman, 1995).

Functional Effects of Depression on the Brain

How do all of these neurochemical changes affect brain activity itself? Over the past 20 years, neuroimaging studies have given us a new window on how brain activity changes in depression and how it changes again with successful treatment. PET studies have shown patterns of under- and overactivity in a widespread network of brain areas (Seminowicz et al., 2004). A key node of this network is the subgenual cingulate cortex, which, you will recall, connects to the amygdala (FIGURE 16.36).

Why is this important in depression? As we saw in Chapter 13, the amygdala is a key area for assigning emotional valence to stimuli in the external environment: threats, mates, rivals, allies, offspring, and so forth. Although the circuits of the amygdala are excellent at assembling rapid emotional and visceral responses, they do not have the sophistication of cortical circuits in identifying and assessing outside stimuli. For example, they could easily overreact to a rubber snake or fail to react to an eviction notice. To deal with these subtleties, the cortex must be able to communicate with the amygdala: increasing the response to the nonobvious threat of a letter in the mail and decreasing the response to the apparent threat of a villain in a horror film. The subgenual cingulate provides an output channel from the cortex to the amygdala, so that these two structures can collaborate in emotion regulation.

In depression, this circuitry goes awry. The subgenual cingulate is consistently hyperactive in patients with depression (as well as in briefer periods of self-induced sadness in healthy volunteers). In patients who recover from depression, this region consistently returns to normal levels of activity. This is true regardless of whether the patients improve by taking medication, completing a course of psychotherapy, or even receiving electroconvulsive treatment. In those patients who fail to recover, the subgenual cingulate remains hyperactive (Drevets, Savitz, & Trimble, 2008; Mayberg, 2003). In patients with treatment-resistant depression, artificially turning down the activity of this area with deep brain stimulation often produces remission (Mayberg et al., 2005). So the emotion-regulation functions of this region are central to depression and its treatment.

At the same time, many other cortical areas modulate the activity of the subgenual cingulate itself. For example, the

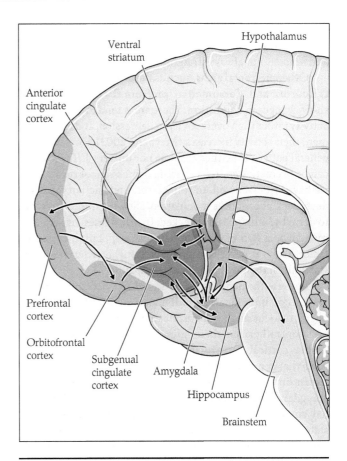

FIGURE 16.36 The subgenual cingulate cortex plays a key role in regulating the amygdala and other core limbic structures, and it is overactive in major depression. It is part of a larger network of cortical and subcortical regions involved in emotion regulation. In patients who recover from depression, the activity of the subgenual cingulate cortex returns to normal—a consistent finding across many different types of treatment for depression, including medications, therapy, and brain stimulation.

orbitofrontal and ventrolateral prefrontal cortex have strong inputs to this area and can modulate its responses to outside stimuli using cognitive strategies and context (Johnstone, van Reekum, Urry, Kalin, & Davidson, 2007). Human beings often use context to regulate their own emotions. For example, they may try to reduce negative emotional experiences by reappraisal: seeing the glass as half full rather than half empty or seeing a loss as an opportunity for change and growth. Unfortunately, we also tend to use cognitive strategies to make stimuli *worse* than they would otherwise be: a bad grade somehow seems like a career-ending disaster; a minor dispute somehow seems like the end of a friendship. For better or worse, cognitive factors and context influence our emotional states.

Either way, contextual and cognitive influences on mood exert themselves via the ventrolateral cortex. For example, the ventrolateral cortex activates during reappraisal of a distressing stimulus (such as a picture of a man being bitten by a snake). In healthy control subjects, this activation correlates with a deactivation of the amygdala and a reduction of sympathetic nervous system activity (as measured by pupil size). However, in depressed patients, the same activation actually leads to an *increased* activation of the amygdala (Johnstone et al., 2007). So the relationship between brain activation and mood is not always straightforward and predictable.

Other prefrontal areas, such as the **dorsolateral prefrontal cortex** and **dorsomedial prefrontal cortex**, can also show changes in depression. These areas tend to show underactivity rather than overactivity in depression, and after treatment their activity increases (Mayberg, 2003). However, this general pattern is neither absolute nor universal. These areas can be overactive *or* underactive in depression for the reasons we have just discussed. In some cases, underactivity may reflect a lack of cognitive modulation, allowing minor stressors to drive the amygdala unchecked. In other cases, hyperactivity may be a sign of ongoing negative reappraisal: cognitive factors (such as negative thought patterns) driving emotional states all on their own (Ochsner et al., 2004).

Because the neuroimaging "signature" of depression can vary from individual to individual, recent theories have begun to focus on the *interactions* among brain regions in depression, rather than their individual levels of activation. The limbic–cortical dysregulation model (Mayberg, 1997) suggests that depression results from abnormal interactions between limbic areas linked to emotional states (such as the amygdala, hypothalamus, hippocampus, insula, and subgenual cingulate) and the cortical areas that modulate these states (such as the dorsolateral and dorsomedial prefrontal cortex, ventrolateral cortex, and dorsal anterior cingulate). Restoring the functioning of these areas to what is typically observed in nondepressed individuals, by increasing activity in the cortical areas and decreasing activity in the limbic areas, seems to be mediated by the rostral anterior cingulate cortex and is associated with successful treatment of depression (FIGURE 16.37; Mayberg, 1997).

If depression arises from maladaptive interaction among these brain regions, then different treatment could work at different targets. For example, medications could reduce the overactivity of limbic regions such as the amygdala, whereas psychotherapy could improve the effectiveness of cortical regions in modulating limbic activity (Seminowicz et al., 2004). Other treatments could target the overactive subgenual cingulate directly. Let's now turn to the wide range of treatments that have been developed for depression.

Treatment of Depression

There are three major categories of treatment for depression: **psychotherapy**, which involves a combination of counseling and behavioral training, **pharmacotherapy**, which involves treatment with one of the many classes of antidepressant medications, and **somatic therapy**, which involves direct stimulation of the brain. Let's look at each of these treatments in turn, from the least invasive to the most invasive.

Psychotherapy is one of the oldest treatments for major depression. Many different approaches to psychotherapy have been developed over the past century. Some of these have been standardized into so-called manualized therapies with a defined duration, usually between 8 and 20 weeks, and with a specific curriculum and exercises. In cognitive behavioral therapy, patients might keep a "thought record," noting situations that trigger a collapse in their mood and discovering the chain of maladaptive automatic thoughts that led them there: "I missed the bus," "I'm disorganized," "I'm a failure." They would then practice making a more realistic assessment of the situation, often ending up with a different thought pattern (Disner, Beevers, Haigh, & Beck, 2011).

Cognitive behavioral therapy tends to be about as effective as medication (FIGURE 16.38), for those who have the time and motivation to complete their course. The effects of therapy also tend to be longer lasting than the effects of

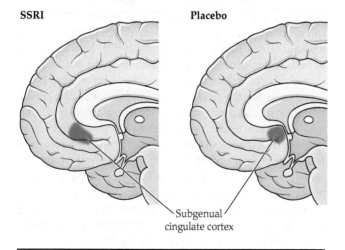

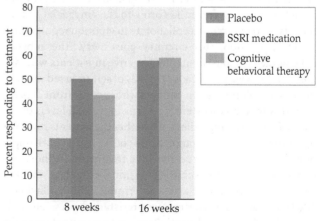

FIGURE 16.37 **Successfully alleviating the symptoms of depression is associated with a decrease in activity in the subgenual cingulate cortex.** This proved to be true not just for patients treated with an SSRI medication, but even for patients who improved while taking a placebo.

FIGURE 16.38 **Response to antidepressant medication versus cognitive behavioral therapy in depression.** After 16 weeks of treatment, the percent of subjects responding to treatment is similar for both antidepressant medication and for cognitive behavioral therapy.

medication, which often wear off once the treatment ends (DeRubeis, Siegle, & Hollon, 2008). The difficulty is that not all patients have the inclination, time, money, or motivation to complete therapy successfully. Further, psychotherapy is not widely covered by insurance and can be prohibitively expensive. In addition, many patients are so depressed that they have trouble keeping appointments, let alone pursuing a rigorous, structured course of therapy. Furthermore, the supply of depressed patients always tends to exceed the supply of trained therapists, so that accessing treatment can be a problem. As a result, many patients with depression pursue treatment with medication instead.

The oldest class of antidepressant medications are the **monoamine oxidase inhibitors (MAOIs)**. These drugs block the action of the enzyme monoamine oxidase, which normally breaks down serotonin and other monoamines in the synaptic cleft (Stahl, 1998). MAOIs were discovered accidentally in the 1950s, after observations that some patients who were undergoing treatment for tuberculosis with iproniazid also experienced relief of their depressed mood. This medication turned out to be an MAOI, and soon many others were developed (Lopez-Munoz & Alamo, 2009). Although as effective as modern antidepressants, MAOIs had a problematic side effect. Certain types of foods, such as cheese or smoked meat, are loaded with monoamines. Normally, MAO enzymes in the intestine destroy these compounds before they enter circulation. With MAOIs, however, the monoamines would enter circulation in large quantities, causing potentially life-threatening spikes in blood pressure (Feighner, 1999). Today, MAOIs are rarely used for treating depression.

Another old class of antidepressant medications is the **tricyclic antidepressants (TCAs)**, named after a common feature of their molecular structure. They work by blocking the reuptake of serotonin and norepinephrine from the synaptic cleft (Stahl, 1998). The first TCA, imipramine, was developed as an antipsychotic medication in the 1950s, but proved to have antidepressant effects instead. TCAs are as effective as MAOIs in treating depression, and they are somewhat safer in terms of side effects. However, they too can be toxic or even lethal in high doses—a significant consideration in patients who may be harboring thoughts of suicide. As a result, TCAs are now used much less often than newer, safer antidepressants.

The most recent major classes of antidepressants are targeted toward specific neurotransmitter systems. First developed in the 1980s, well-known medications such as fluoxetine (Prozac), sertraline (Zoloft), and paroxetine (Paxil) are examples of SSRIs. They have relatively selective effects in boosting serotonin rather than norepinephrine or dopamine. They also tend to be safer and to have fewer side effects than the older TCAs and MAOIs. Other antidepressants such as duloxetine (Cymbalta) inhibit the reuptake of norepinephrine as well as serotonin; still others do not affect serotonin, but do inhibit the reuptake of dopamine

(bupropion, also known by the brand name Wellbutrin). It is unfortunate to note that these newer medications are *not* significantly more effective than the ones developed in the 1950s, although they tend to be safer and have less severe side effects (Lam et al., 2009).

For patients who do not respond adequately to medication or therapy, somatic treatments (that is, treatments affecting the brain directly) are an option. The mildest of these in clinical use is repetitive transcranial magnetic stimulation (FIGURE 16.39). Patients undergo a series of sessions of brain stimulation, using a transcranial magnetic stimulation coil that is usually applied to the left dorsolateral prefrontal cortex, usually for a little less than 30 minutes per session. Repetitive transcranial magnetic stimulation is now proven as an effective treatment for depression, particularly when medications have failed (Berlim, Van den Eynde, & Daskalakis, 2013). The response rate seems to depend partly on what brain area is stimulated, and targets other than the dorsolateral prefrontal cortex will probably also be used in the near future (Downar & Daskalakis, 2013).

A more invasive option to treat severe depression is electroconvulsive therapy (ECT). This treatment was pioneered in the 1930s, following observations that mentally ill patients who also had epilepsy would often show significant, temporary improvement after having a seizure (Fink, 1984). Artificially induced seizures eventually proved to be effective in treating severe depression, mania, and some kinds of psychosis (Berrios, 1997). Unfortunately, in the early days, the side effects were significant: pain from the applied electrical current, dramatic bodily convulsions during the seizures, the need for physical restraint to reduce the rate of injury, vertebral fractures from the intense muscular contractions after the seizures, and significant cognitive and memory impairment after the treatment was over, especially with the older electrical current waveforms used. ECT became a highly controversial procedure for many decades, portrayed as barbaric in the media and banned outright in

FIGURE 16.39 **Transcranial magnetic stimulation is a noninvasive treatment for depression in patients who do not respond to medication.**

many jurisdictions. In some circles, it remains controversial even today.

Yet ECT has persisted as a valued medical procedure because of its unparalleled effectiveness, although we do not fully understand *why* it works. In patients so depressed that they were suicidal or even psychotic, ECT could restore normal mood in cases that would not respond to other treatments and could do so rapidly—often within just a few sessions (Sackeim et al., 2008). Over time, the techniques were improved: many decades ago, ECT became a procedure performed under brief general anesthesia, with pain control and muscle relaxation to avoid injurious movements or bone fractures. The stimulation parameters were refined to cause much less impairment of cognition and memory. The safety of the procedure is high: the mortality rate has dropped to an estimated rate of less than 1 per 73,000 treatments—essentially the same risk as having general anesthesia for any other reason (Watts, Groft, Bagian, & Mills, 2011). Today, tens of thousands of patients in North America undergo the procedure every year and experience relief from forms of depression severe enough to be life-threatening (Case et al., 2013).

Yet there are also many patients who do not respond to *any* treatment for depression. After multiple trials of medication, therapy, and even ECT, their depression remains unremitted. Until recently, such patients had essentially run out of options. Recently, however, a new kind of somatic treatment emerged for these otherwise untreatable cases of depression: deep brain stimulation (Mayberg et al., 2005).

Deep brain stimulation can either increase or decrease neural activity, depending on the placement of the electrodes and the frequency of electrical stimulation applied. In the case of depression, the electrodes are placed so that they *reduce* rather than increase neural activity in a small region around the electrode. As we saw earlier, neuroimaging studies in the 1990s and early 2000s showed an area of consistent overactivity in depression: the subgenual cingulate cortex. Drawing on this finding, a team of psychiatrists, neurologists, and neurosurgeons placed deep brain stimulation electrodes in the white matter surrounding this brain area and then turned on the current. The results were dramatic and nearly immediate: patients who had been depressed for decades reported marked improvements in their mood within a few seconds of the activation of the stimulators, and the effects were still present months later. PET imaging confirmed that the stimulation reduced overactivity in the subgenual cingulate and orbitofrontal cortex, while restoring activity in previously underactive areas such as the dorsolateral prefrontal cortex (Mayberg et al., 2005). These chronically depressed, dysregulated brains had been guided back into a normal pattern of activity by direct, targeted electrical stimulation.

Since the initial reports, several dozen severely depressed patients have undergone this invasive but effective procedure. Although deep brain stimulation has not worked in all of them, on the whole, roughly 60% have shown a significant improvement—a remarkable percentage, considering that

their depression had failed to respond to every other treatment available (Kennedy et al., 2011). Since the technique is still new, further improvements will probably come in the years ahead. The case of deep brain stimulation and depression gives us a dramatic illustration of how discoveries in basic neuroscience—the neuroimaging studies that identified the subgenual cingulate cortex as a linchpin area in depression—can be translated into treatments for crippling illnesses: from brain image to bedside.

Conclusion

Despite the traditional divide between neurological and psychiatric diseases, both kinds of illness come "from nothing else but the brain," just as Hippocrates said. The disorders we think of as psychiatric tend to have two qualities about them. First, the underlying brain abnormalities are subtle and difficult to spot with the naked eye. Second, the underlying brain abnormalities affect the neural wiring that guides emotion regulation, social behavior, judgment, and decision making: functions that our intuitions would have us assign to the soul rather than the circuitry. Yet, as we have seen in this chapter, these intuitions are misleading: neurological and psychiatric illnesses are both brain disorders—the latter simply involve slightly different networks of neurons and more subtle forms of injury.

Despite our modern understanding of diseases like schizophrenia and bipolar disorder, an enduring stigma attaches to psychiatric illnesses much more than to neurological illnesses. This undeserved stigma makes an already bad situation intolerable for many patients, just when their powers of resilience are weakest. Overcoming stigma is partly a matter of public education, but also a matter of developing better treatments, so that psychiatric illnesses no longer have such a debilitating impact on work, home, and social life. Already, some fairly effective treatments do exist for some neurological and psychiatric disorders. For others, there is currently no treatment available and none foreseen in the immediate future.

One of the obstacles to developing new treatments is that the underlying causes of many disorders are still poorly understood—in some cases, the diagnostic categories themselves are probably unhelpful for research purposes. Many, if not most, of our best treatments were discovered by accident or by investigators who were essentially doing the wrong thing for the wrong reasons on the wrong kind of patient, yet somehow stumbled upon the right answer. When dealing with a system as complex as the brain, it has been difficult to forge an unbroken, hypothesis-driven chain from our basic knowledge of disease, to an engineered solution to the problem, to a proven and effective clinical treatment. It may be that as our knowledge of basic neuroscience increases, we will get better at creating new treatments by design rather than by accident. Or instead, it may be that the nervous system is simply too complex and too nonlinear for such an approach to be practical: predicting the ultimate effects of a treatment will be like trying to forecast the weather 10 years in advance. Instead, wide searches, without preconceptions about underlying causes, and careful observation may help us to create "happy accidents" more frequently. Either way, clinical neuroscience is currently one of the richest scientific frontiers and is likely to remain so for our lifetimes and beyond.

KEY PRINCIPLES

- Alzheimer's disease is characterized by progressive impairments of episodic memory, navigational abilities, and executive functions. Current hypotheses suggest these impairments result from the buildup of beta-amyloid plaques and tau tangles in the brain. Different biomedical approaches to treating Alzheimer's disease have provided a short-term benefit, but none has yet been effective in the long term.

- Frontotemporal dementia is another form of dementia, which affects the frontal and temporal lobes, as opposed to Alzheimer's disease, which affects the medial temporal lobes. The age of onset is much younger for frontotemporal dementia, and this condition tends to affect personality more than episodic memory and executive functions. There are currently no effective treatments.

- Huntington's disease is a progressive, ultimately fatal neurodegenerative disorder that is the result of a mutation in a single gene. It is characterized by involuntary movements of the head and body, as well as impulsive behaviors and depression. No cure exists at this time.

- Tourette syndrome is a disorder in which the patient feels compelled to make unnecessary, repetitive movements. This compulsion leads researchers to suggest an overlap between Tourette syndrome and obsessive–compulsive disorder. The causes of Tourette syndrome are not clear, but some research suggests that there may be an autoimmune explanation for at least some cases.

- Traditionally, disorders discussed in psychology and neuroscience are divided into neurological disorders, which have a clear basis in the anatomy of the brain, and psychiatric disorders, which do not have a clear anatomical basis and which affect emotions, impulse control, or addiction. This division seems less warranted the more we learn about the structure and function of the brain.

- Obsessive–compulsive disorder involves a chronic cycle in which patients experience distressing, intrusive thoughts that they can only banish by performing ritualized actions, often repeatedly. Although the condition is traditionally considered a psychiatric disorder, many symptoms and emerging therapies are more commonly associated with neurological disorders.

- Schizophrenia is characterized by both negative and positive symptoms. Although they are not always effective, neuroleptic or antipsychotic drugs can reduce the positive symptoms, but they do not control the negative symptoms. Several theories have been proposed to explain schizophrenia, including a neurodevelopmental theory, a dopamine theory, and a glutamate theory.

- Bipolar disorder is characterized by an alternation between mania and depression. There seems to be a genetic influence on schizophrenia, and a thinning of specific cortical regions has been observed in patients with bipolar disorder. Treatment for bipolar disorder involves administering lithium or antiepileptic medications to stabilize the mood swings that are characteristic of the disorder.

- Depression is characterized by a lack of pleasure, motivation, and energy. Research has identified genetic and neurochemical factors. Treatment options include psychotherapy; medications, most commonly SSRIs; and invasive options, such as electroconvulsive shock therapy and deep brain stimulation, for treatment-resistant depression.

KEY TERMS

REVIEW QUESTIONS

1. In what parts of the brain do we tend to see the plaques and tangles of Alzheimer's disease? Why do you think that removing these plaques and tangles turned out to be a failure as a strategy for treating Alzheimer's disease?

2. Is it a reasonable metaphor to call frontotemporal dementia a "cancer of the soul?" What does this name tell us about our own intuitions on which faculties are proper to the "spirit," as opposed to the neural circuits of the brain?

3. Why does increased creativity emerge as a symptom of some neurological and psychiatric disorders? What do these disorders have in common?

4. In Huntington's disease, a disruption of a single gene gives rise to a diverse set of neurological and psychiatric symptoms. What are these symptoms, what common disease process creates them, and how does this common process disrupt such a wide variety of brain functions?

5. What different kinds of symptoms can arise in Tourette syndrome? What common neuroanatomical changes might give rise to these symptoms?

6. Should we describe symptoms of Tourette syndrome as "voluntary" or "involuntary"? Why so? Should ordinary blinking be considered a kind of motor tic? Why or why not?

7. Obsessive–compulsive disorder is traditionally considered a psychiatric rather than a neurological disorder. How would you classify the illness? Why? Do you think it should still be considered a single category of disease? Why or why not?

8. What are the positive and the negative symptoms of schizophrenia? Which symptoms can be relieved with currently available treatments and which cannot? Why don't these treatments provide a permanent cure?

9. What are three kinds of similarities between bipolar disorder and schizophrenia? What are some of the key differences between these disorders? Should we think of them as two forms of the same illness? Why or why not?

10. What kinds of factors can lead to depression? Is depression really a chemical imbalance in the brain, as it is sometimes described? What and where are the brain abnormalities of depression? How has this knowledge led to new treatments?

CRITICAL-THINKING QUESTIONS

1. Imagine that you are the head of a pharmaceutical research group that is dedicated to developing new, effective drug treatments for Alzheimer's disease. Given what you have learned in this chapter about the physiological basis and progression of Alzheimer's, what processes would you design the drugs to target? At what stage of the disease do you think that such drugs would be most effective? Explain.

2. How do patients with Alzheimer's disease, frontotemporal dementia, Tourette syndrome, obsessive–compulsive disorder, and bipolar disorder differ from one another in terms of their self-awareness of their symptoms? How could such differences be used to guide the development of new, specialized treatments for each disease?

3. Scientists are continuing to learn more about the influence of genetics on the likelihood of developing diseases such as schizophrenia. However, we are unable to know for certain whether individuals are destined to develop such diseases. If an effective neuroprotective treatment were discovered for schizophrenia, do you think it would be ethical to administer it to individuals who are at risk for developing the disease? What factors would influence your viewpoint? Explain your reasoning.

GLOSSARY

absolute preferences   The idea that a person's preference for option A or B will always remain the same, regardless of the context. [12]

acamprosate   A drug that is used to decrease the chance of a relapse into alcohol-seeking behavior. [14]

accessory basal nucleus   A nucleus within the amygdala, stimulation of which results in fear or attack behaviors. [14]

acetylcholine   A neurotransmitter used in both the central and the peripheral nervous system. [3]

acetylcholinesterase   An enzyme found in the synaptic cleft that breaks down the neurotransmitter acetylcholine. [7]

action potential (nerve impulse or spike)   A rapid change in the neuron's membrane potential that is used to transmit information from the cell body to the presynaptic terminal. [3]

activation-synthesis model   A hypothesis that explains dreams as the cortex's attempt to turn random activity from the brainstem into motor output. [10]

adaptations   Changes in biology or behavior that increase the probability that the organism will survive and reproduce. [1]

adaptive coding   The idea that the brain will have a larger or smaller physical representation of a particular function or sensation, depending on the needs and experiences of the individual. [4]

adherence   Continuing to take a medication according to the prescribed schedule; this is often a problem for patients taking antirelapse medication during treatment for substance addiction. [14]

adrenocorticotropic hormone (ACTH)   A hormone released by the pituitary gland in response to corticotropin-releasing hormone. [13]

advanced sleep phase syndrome   A disorder of the circadian rhythm in which an individual both falls asleep and wakes up much earlier than the rest of society. [10]

affect heuristic   The mental shortcut of addressing a question based on "How do I feel about this?" instead of "What do I think about this?" [1]

afferent neuron   A neuron that conveys sensory information into the nervous system. [3]

affiliation   Sense of belonging to a group or participating in social interactions. [15]

agonistic behavior   Behavior that defends one's own survival interests against other organisms; may include aggressive or defensive behaviors. [1]

agonists   Molecules that mimic or extend the activity of a neurotransmitter. [3]

agrammatical   Communication that does not follow the grammar conventions of the language. [11]

alexia (word blindness)   A language disorder in which the patient cannot understand written words. [11]

alien hand syndrome   A condition in which damage to the supplementary motor cortex or prefrontal region leaves the patient unable to control the actions of the contralateral arm. [7]

all-or-none   A property of neural activity via action potentials; a neuron either fires an action potential or does not, with no in-between states or levels of activity. [5]

allostasis   The process of achieving stability by varying the physiological or behavioral response to an external stimulus. [14]

alpha motor neurons   The neurons that control the contraction of the voluntary muscles of the body. [7]

alpha waves   Brain waves with a frequency of 8–12 Hz; associated with relaxation. [10]

Alzheimer's disease   A form of dementia marked by neurofibrillary (tau) tangles and beta-amyloid plaques in the brain, it causes loss of episodic memory, spatial navigation skills, language skills, and executive functions, ultimately ending in death. [9]

amacrine cells   Cells within the retina that facilitate communication between different parts of the retina. [5]

amino acids   Molecules that are the building blocks of proteins. [3]

amplitude   The size of the oscillations in a waveform, from peak to trough. [6]

amusia   The inability to understand music. [11]

amygdala   Part of the limbic system found within the medial temporal lobe, the amygdala influences the internal states of the body based on rapidly processed input from the outside world. [2]

amyloid plaques   Clusters of beta-amyloid peptides commonly found in the brains of patients with Alzheimer's disease. [16]

analytic–synthetic theory   A theory that suggests that language is in the left hemisphere because that hemisphere is specialized for analytic thinking, whereas the right hemisphere is specialized for synthesizing ideas. [11]

anchoring bias   The tendency to be influenced more than is appropriate by a single observation, usually the first. [1]

androgens   A class of male sex hormones. [13]

anhedonia   An inability to experience pleasure or enjoyment. [13]

anode   On an electrical brain stimulation device, the positively charged electrode applied to a conductor. In tDCS, neurons near the anode tend to be excited. [1]

anomia   The inability to recall or use the correct name for an object. [11]

anosognosia   A condition in which patients are unaware of their physical impairment. [6]

antagonistic muscles   Pairs of muscles that perform opposite functions. [7]

antagonists   Molecules that decrease the activity of a neurotransmitter. [3]

anterior   Anatomical term meaning toward the front; opposite of posterior. [2]

anterior cingulate cortex   The anterior portion of the cingulate gyrus, near the midline of the brain close to the corpus callosum; often found to be involved in functions such as motor control and decision making. [2]

anterior insula   The anterior region of the insular cortex, hidden within the lateral sulcus; linked to the perception of internal bodily states or feelings. [12]

anterograde amnesia   Inability to form new memories for a period of time following a brain injury. [9]

antipsychotics   A class of drugs that are dopamine antagonists, often used to treat the symptoms of schizophrenia and certain other psychiatric illnesses, such as bipolar disorder.

Anton's syndrome   A condition in which a blind patient denies being blind. [5]

anxiolytics   Pharmaceuticals used to reduce anxiety. [13]

aphasia   An impairment or loss of language skills, usually following brain damage. [4]

apolipoprotein E (ApoE)   A gene that encodes a protein that regulates cholesterol within the blood. The epsilon 4 variant of this gene is associated with higher risk of developing Alzheimer's disease. [16]

apoptosis   Cell death that occurs in a deliberate, internally controlled manner. [4]

apraxia   Difficulty performing skilled movements. [11]

arcuate fasciculus   The fiber tract connecting Wernicke's area to Broca's area. [11]

arcuate nucleus   A nucleus of the hypothalamus that coordinates the hormones released by the pituitary gland. [14]

area V5   Part of the visual processing pathway that is specialized for detecting motion in the visual field. [5]

arousal network   A network of brain areas that is important for maintaining alertness and wakefulness. [10]

ascending reticular activating system   Cells within the brainstem that project up to the more anterior regions of the brain to increase arousal. [8]

association areas   Regions of the cerebral cortex that integrate sensory and motor information. [2]

associative memory   A type of memory for which retrieval is stimulated by exposure to the original stimulus or something associated with the original stimulus. [9]

astrocyte   A star-shaped glial cell that regulates the chemical concentration gradient around the neurons. [3]

atherosclerosis   The hardening of the arteries that leads to decreased blood flow to an area. [16]

atonia   Loss of control of voluntary muscles, resulting in paralysis; typically occurs during REM sleep. [10]

attention   The process of selecting some parts of the scene for more detailed analysis. [5]

attention deficit hyperactivity disorder (ADHD)   A clinical condition in which individuals display increased activity and impulsivity, as well as a decreased capacity for sustained attention or concentration. [12]

attribution effect   The tendency to explain our own behavior in terms of the situation while explaining the behavior of others in terms of their character. [12]

auditory nerve (cochlear nerve)   The branch of the eighth cranial nerve that conducts auditory information from the organ of Corti to the cochlear nucleus in the brainstem. [6]

autism spectrum disorders   A set of developmental disorders that are characterized by impairments in communication and social interaction, as well as the presence of restricted interests and repetitive behaviors. [11]

autoimmune disorder   A condition in which the immune system attacks the cells of its own body; narcolepsy and multiple sclerosis are thought to result from autoimmune processes. [10]

automatic behaviors   Spontaneously produced, purposeless behaviors that occur without conscious intention or censorship; a characteristic of conditions including narcolepsy. [10]

autonomic nervous system   The branch of the peripheral nervous system that directs the activity of internal, or visceral, organs, as opposed to skeletal muscles. [2]

autoradiography   A technique in which a radioactive substance is taken up by some specific cells, allowing the location of those cells to be identified when a photographic emulsion is placed over the tissue. [3]

autoreceptors   Receptors on the presynaptic cell itself that provide feedback to regulate the amount of neurotransmitter released by that cell. [13]

availability heuristic   The idea that our thinking is more influenced by examples that we have recently encountered and that come to mind easily. [1]

averbia   A condition in which damage to the left premotor cortex impairs the ability to recall and use verbs. [11]

aversive   Something that is unpleasant or causes learned avoidance. [14]

axiom of revealed preferences   An experimental procedure for determining the subjective value of an item by having a subject choose between two options. [12]

axon   The long projection from the cell body of the neuron that is specialized for conveying information away from the neuron. [3]

axon hillock   The portion of the axon that connects to the cell body. [3]

axon terminals   Branches at the end of the axon, from which neurotransmitters are released. [3]

Balint's syndrome   A disorder resulting from damage to both the left and the right parietal lobes, preventing the affected person from understanding the big picture of a scene. [5]

barbiturates   A class of drugs that depress activity within the central nervous system; one example is sodium amobarbital, the anesthetic used in the Wada test. [11]

basal forebrain   Subcortical structures within the brain, including the nucleus accumbens. Some neurons in this region send acetylcholine projections throughout much of the cortex. [4]

basal ganglia   A collection of subcortical gray matter structures that are involved in initiating, maintaining, and terminating activity in the frontal lobes and other regions of the cortex; among other functions, they facilitate motor control. [2]

basal nucleus A nucleus within the amygdala, stimulation of which results in defensive behaviors. [14]

basilar membrane A flexible tissue within the cochlea that vibrates in time with incoming sound waves; it is stretched tight at one end, which is therefore sensitive to high-frequency stimuli, and it is less tight at the other end, which is therefore sensitive to low-frequency stimuli. [6]

basket cells Inhibitory interneurons of the cerebellum that influence the cell bodies of Purkinje cells. [7]

basolateral amygdala An "input region" of the amygdala that is strongly interconnected with the sensory regions of the cortex. [13]

BBB model A model of cognitive function that predicts that the hippocampus constructs spatial maps of any remembered scene. [9]

bed nucleus of the stria terminalis A nucleus adjacent to the amygdala that helps coordinate the body's stress response. [14]

behavioral economics A field that studies human decision making using empirical data from the observed behavior of individuals, rather than theoretical models. [12]

behaviorist A school of psychology that focuses strictly on studying observable behaviors and responses, such as classical or operant conditioning. [14]

belief bias The idea that we are more likely to accept conclusions that are easy to believe than we are to accept conclusions that are hard to believe. [1]

benzodiazepine Pharmaceutical compound that acts as an agonist to the $GABA_A$ receptor and therefore decreases brain activity; can be used to treat insomnia. [10]

beta waves Brain waves with a frequency of 12–30 Hz; associated with cognitive functions and concentration. [10]

beta-amyloid peptide The chain of amino acids generated by neurons and other cells as part of normal metabolic activity; these peptides can cluster together to form amyloid plaques. [16]

beta-endorphin A peptide neurotransmitter that binds to all types of the opioid receptors. [14]

bias Current knowledge or beliefs that can influence what one perceives or remembers from a situation. [9]

biased-competition model A proposal that bottom-up input from the various sensory systems competes to influence or control behavior, with the competition biased by top-down influences from frontal lobe structures representing context and current behavior. [8]

binding problem A currently unsolved problem within neuroscience, concerning how the brain joins together all the different aspects of sensory input from a single stimulus (such as shape, color, and motion) to make a unified percept (object that is perceived). [1]

binocular Visual input that comes from both eyes, allowing depth perception. [4]

binocular rivalry A situation in which different images are presented to the left and right eyes, and the perception shifts back and forth between the two stimuli. [5]

bionic retinal implant A patch of light-sensitive electrodes that can be implanted onto the retina to restore sight to individuals who have damage affecting the photoreceptors. [4]

bipolar disorder A mood disorder characterized by alternations between periods of euphoric or irritable mood (mania) and periods of low or despondent mood (depression). [16]

bipolar neurons Neurons with just one dendrite and one axon connected to the cell body. [3]

bistable Referring to a two-component system, like sleep and waking, that can exist stably in one state or the other, but not in both at the same time. [10]

blind spot The region of the retina where there are no photoreceptors because the optic nerve is exiting the eye through that point. [5]

blindsight The ability to detect and respond to visual stimuli in certain situations, despite a subjective sense of blindness. [5]

blobs Clusters of cells within the primary visual cortex that process color-related information. [5]

blood–brain barrier A barrier formed by the cells lining the circulatory system that regulates the movement of molecules between the blood and the brain. [13]

bottom-up mechanism Having one's attention drawn to a particular feature within the environment because something about the stimulus stands out. [8]

bottom-up theory In regard to emotion, a theory in which the emotional state is determined by the physiological reactions of the body, which are then interpreted by the brain; may be summarized as "we are afraid because we tremble." [13]

brain death The absence of metabolic activity within the brain. [8]

brain waves Rhythmic oscillations of electrical activity recorded during an electroencephalogram; examples include alpha, beta, delta, gamma, and theta waves, each with a characteristic frequency. [10]

brain–computer interface A device, often implanted directly into the brain, that enables the individual to communicate with a computer without the use of bodily movements or speech. [7]

brain-derived neurotrophic factor (BDNF) A protein that promotes growth and survival of neurons; many treatments for depression increase the levels of BDNF in the brain. [16]

brainstem The most caudal structures of the brain, below the diencephalon; composed of the midbrain, pons, and medulla oblongata. [2]

Broca's aphasia A loss of the ability to produce language because of damage in or near Broca's area in the left inferior frontal gyrus. [11]

Broca's area An area in the left inferior frontal gyrus that is important for language production. [11]

bupropion A drug that is used to help individuals quit smoking by reducing the cravings and pleasurable aspects of smoking. [14]

CaMKII Calmodulin-dependent protein kinase II; important in forming long-term memories. [9]

cannabinoid A neurotransmitter system in the brain; thought to be involved in a variety of functions including appetite, pain, and mood. [12]

Cannon–Bard theory A theory of emotion that states that the physiological reactions of the body during an emotional experience are separable from the subjective emotional experience itself; opposed to the James-Lange theory of emotion, in which emotional experiences arise from perceived bodily reactions. [13]

cataplexy Sudden weakening of the muscles, often leading to collapse; a common symptom of narcolepsy. [10]

catecholamines A subtype of monoamine neurotransmitters, including dopamine, epinephrine, and norepinephrine. [3]

cathode On an electrical brain stimulation device, the negatively charged electrode. In tDCS, neurons near the cathode tend to be inhibited. [1]

caudal Anatomical term meaning "toward the tail"; opposite of rostral. [2]

caudate nucleus Part of the basal ganglia, forming a large "C"-shaped structure. [2]

cell body See *soma*. [3]

center-surround structure A way of describing the receptive field of the retinal ganglion cells, which highlights the fact that stimulating the center of the receptive field will either excite or inhibit the cell, whereas stimulating the ring surrounding the center will have the opposite effect. [5]

central cue A stimulus used in a study of visual attention, presented at the center of the field of vision, alerting the subject to pay attention to one particular part of the visual field. [8]

central nervous system The portion of the nervous system that is made up of the brain and spinal cord. [2]

central nucleus A nucleus within the amygdala that coordinates the autonomic activity of the hypothalamus and brainstem. [14]

central pattern generator A collection of neurons within the central nervous system that is able to spontaneously generate and maintain rhythmic movements such as walking or swallowing. [2]

central sulcus The large sulcus along the lateral surface of the cerebral cortex, between the precentral and postcentral gyrus, dividing the frontal lobe from the parietal lobe. [2]

centromedial amygdala A region of the amygdala that influences the hypothalamus and brainstem. [13]

cerebellar cortex The gray matter on the surface of the cerebellum. [7]

cerebellum A large brain structure attached to the back of the pons in the brainstem, important for coordinating smooth, accurate movements. [2]

cerebral cortex The outermost structure of the brain, consisting of cells, dendrites, and synapses; also known as gray matter. [2]

cerebral palsy A movement disorder in which the motor control structures of the cortex or the descending corticospinal tract cannot reach the spinal cord because of injury around the time of birth. [7]

cerebrospinal fluid The fluid, chemically similar to blood plasma, that fills the ventricles and flows around the outside of the brain. [2]

cerebrum The most superior portion of the central nervous system; this includes the left and right hemispheres of the cerebral cortex, as well as subcortical structures such as the thalamus and basal ganglia. [2]

change blindness An inability to detect differences between two similar visual scenes when presented sequentially, with a brief interruption or distraction at the time of the change. [5]

Charles Bonnet syndrome A disorder in which patients in the process of losing their sight begin to perceive visual stimuli that are not actually present. [5]

chemoaffinity hypothesis The idea that migrating axons make a connection with their target based on specific chemical signals released by the target. [4]

chemoreceptors Somatosensory receptors that are sensitive to the concentration of specific chemical substances, such as carbon dioxide, within the body. [6]

chlorpromazine A dopamine antagonist that was the first antipsychotic drug used to treat psychosis (a failure of reality-testing) in schizophrenia. [16]

cholecystokinin (CCK) A peptide produced by the small intestine that stimulates the secretion of digestive enzymes and signals the hypothalamus to suppress hunger. [14]

cholinergic Neurons that release the neurotransmitter acetylcholine. [4]

chorea A term for restless, writhing involuntary movements of the face, trunk, and limbs; commonly used to describe the characteristic abnormal movements of Huntington's disease. [16]

chromosome A compact structure found in the nucleus of the cell that contains strands of DNA encoding many genes. Humans have 23 pairs of chromosomes. [16]

cingulate cortex The cortex that forms the surface of the cingulate gyrus; sometimes described as the limbic motor cortex. [13]

cingulate gyrus Gray matter structure near the midline of the brain, adjacent to the corpus callosum. [2]

cingulate motor area A motor planning area located along the midline of the brain. [15]

circadian rhythm A naturally occurring internal rhythm of about 24 hours that influences sleep–wake cycles, cognition, and body temperature. [10]

circuit of Papez An interconnected set of brain areas within the limbic system, considered important for controlling emotional expression. [13]

classical conditioning A form of implicit memory in which a previously neutral stimulus gains the ability to elicit a behavioral response, after becoming associated with another stimulus that naturally elicits the response. [9]

climbing fibers Neural pathways that carry excitatory input to the cerebellum from the inferior olivary nucleus and modulate the activity of the Purkinje cells. [7]

coalition   A group of neurons working together to encode a particular stimulus. [3]

cocaine   A stimulant that enhances dopamine activity by blocking the dopamine reuptake transporter at the synapse. [14]

cochlea   A spiral-shaped, fluid-filled structure within the inner ear that is important for transducing acoustic vibrations into the electrochemical signals of the nervous system. [6]

cochlear nerve   See *auditory nerve*. [6]

cognitive behavioral therapy   A therapeutic method that involves changing both the thoughts (cognitions) and the behaviors associated with depression, anxiety, and other forms of psychiatric illness. [16]

cognitive distortions   Excessive or emotionally overvalued thoughts and beliefs occurring in individuals with mental illnesses such as obsessive–compulsive disorder and major depressive disorder. [16]

cognitive empathy   The ability to understand the emotional state of another person, without necessarily sharing that emotional state. [15]

cognitive map theory   A model that proposes that the original function of the hippocampus was to form and store maps of spatial locations. [9]

cognitive neuroscience   A branch of neuroscience that seeks to understand the brain mechanisms underlying cognitive processes such as attention, memory, language, perception, and decision-making, among other topics. [1]

cognitive self-reflection   Thinking about one's own thoughts. [15]

coma   A state of unconsciousness in which an individual cannot be roused, lacks a normal sleep–wake cycle, does not respond to outside stimuli, and does not engage in voluntary actions. [8]

communication   The ability to convey information from one individual to another via a shared system of signals, regardless of form of transmission. [11]

complementarity   A form of reverse mimicry in which one form of emotional communication elicits the opposite form, such as responding to a dominant voice with submissive tones. [15]

complex cells   Cells within the primary visual cortex that respond best to lines of light at a particular angle, but at any location within the receptive field. [5]

compulsions   Repetitive or excessive behaviors, usually accompanied by powerful urges that are difficult to resist despite effort, often seen in obsessive-compulsive disorder or Tourette's syndrome. [16]

conation   The process by which internal factors, such as drives and motivations, guide voluntary behavior; sometimes considered complementary to cognition, in which external factors guide behavior. [12]

concentration gradient   The difference in concentration between ions outside versus inside the cell; ions move down the gradient, from an area of higher concentration to an area of lower concentration. [3]

conditioned response   A response to an originally neutral stimulus (the conditioned stimulus) that has been learned through classical conditioning. [9]

conditioned stimulus   In classical conditioning, the stimulus that was originally neutral but has come to evoke the conditioned response after repeated pairing with the unconditioned stimulus. [9]

conduction aphasia   A language disorder in which language comprehension and production are preserved, but the patient is unable to repeat words; often occurs following damage to the arcuate fasciculus. [11]

cones   Photoreceptors within the eye that are sensitive to different colors, but which require relatively high levels of illumination to function. [5]

confabulating   Unintentionally producing false or distorted recollections or narratives, often in the face of contradictory evidence. [9]

confirmation bias   The tendency to preferentially seek out evidence that supports a preexisting belief, while ignoring evidence that contradicts the belief. [1]

congenital   A disease or condition that has been present since birth. [15]

consolidation   The process of moving information from short-term memory into long-term memory. [9]

constraint therapy   A form of therapy in which the more functional limb is restrained to force the patient to get better at using the injured or less functional limb. [4]

constructive episodic simulation hypothesis   A model of memory that proposes that one function of memory is to recombine events from the past to imagine future situations. [9]

contents of consciousness   The information that is present within one's conscious experience at any given moment; often dependent upon the focus of one's attention. [8]

contralateral   Anatomical term meaning on the opposite side. [2]

contrast enhancement   A process of emphasizing the differences in brightness between two surfaces. [5]

cornea   The clear region at the front of the eye through which light passes to enter the eye. [5]

callosotomy   A surgical procedure in which the corpus callosum is cut to prevent the spread of seizure activity from one hemisphere to the other. [11]

corpus callosum   A large white matter structure connecting the two hemispheres of the brain. [2]

correlation evidence   Information that helps researchers understand the function of a brain region by identifying a relationship between a particular behavior and activity of that area; fMRI, PET, and EEG all provide such evidence. [9]

corticospinal tract   The descending motor control pathway from the primary motor cortex to the lower motor neurons in the ventral horn of the spinal cord. [7]

corticostriatal loops   Reciprocal neuronal connections between the cortex and the striatum and thalamus, involved in controlling the initiation, maintenance, and termination of many aspects of cognition and behavior. [12]

corticotropin-releasing hormone A hormone released by the hypothalamus in response to stress. [13]

cortisol A hormone released from the adrenal glands that is involved in the stress response. [12]

covert misdirection A technique used by stage magicians to direct the observer's attention toward something else, instead of what the performer is doing. [8]

cranial nerves Twelve pairs of sensory and motor neurons that originate from the brain and brainstem to innervate the sensory and motor structures in the region of the head and neck. [2]

creoles New natural languages that arise among children raised with exposure to "pidgin" or simplified versions of other languages. [11]

cross-cueing In split-brain patients, a signal generated by the hemisphere that perceived the stimulus to the hemisphere that did not perceive the stimulus. [11]

curare A toxin found in plants that inhibits acetylcholine from binding to the receptor, thereby preventing muscle contractions and causing paralysis. [7]

cytokines A family of cell-signaling molecules used by the immune system to stimulate an immune response to infection, inflammation, or injury. [13]

DBS See *deep brain stimulation (DBS)*. [2]

deafferentation The process of removing or interrupting the incoming sensory information to a neuron; may occur in a deliberate experiment or during an accidental injury. [4]

declarative memories Memories of facts or events that can be consciously recalled or verbally described by the individual. [1]

declarative theory A model that proposes that the hippocampus is necessary for any memory that can be consciously recalled. [9]

decussates Crosses the midline of the body from one side to the other. [6]

deep brain stimulation (DBS) A procedure that uses surgically implanted electrodes to electrically stimulate specific regions or pathways within the brain. [2]

deep dyslexia A subtype of dyslexia in which patients have trouble understanding words at the phonological level, i.e., the level of the sounds from which speech is made. [11]

deep tendon reflex The spinal reflex that occurs when the tendon of a muscle is suddenly struck or stretched, in which the muscle contracts forcefully to compensate for the additional load. [7]

default network A network of brain regions that is active while the brain is at rest, or engaged in self-reflection or rumination (as opposed to a specific external or cognitive task); it is the most active network of regions in the brain overall. [9]

degradation In the context of neurotransmission at the synapse, the process through which neurotransmitters are inactivated by being broken down by enzymes or other molecules. [3]

delay discounting The reduction in the subjective value of rewards that are offered after a delayed period of time, compared to an immediate reward. [12]

delay discounting curve The curve describing how the value of a reward declines as the delivery of that reward occurs further into the future. [12]

delayed sleep phase syndrome A disorder of the circadian rhythm in which an individual both falls asleep and wakes up much later than is typical of other people. [10]

delta-opioid receptors Opioid receptors of a type that produces some of the pain-relieving effects of opioids and may also produce antidepressant effects. [14]

delta waves Brain waves with a frequency of less than 4 Hz, associated with stage 3 NREM sleep. [10]

delusions Persistent fixed, false beliefs, commonly seen as symptoms in certain psychiatric disorders, including schizophrenia and bipolar disorder. [16]

dementia A syndrome of multiple cognitive deficits, in domains that can include memory, language, decision making, planning, or the execution of behaviors. [7]

dendrites Branching projections from the cell body of the neuron that are specialized for conveying information into the neuron. [3]

dendritic spines Small growths along dendrites that serve as points of input from incoming synapses; they can grow and change in response to stimulation, and are associated with forming and storing memories. [9]

dentate gyrus A brain structure adjacent to the hippocampus, involved in the functions of episodic memory and spatial navigation. [9]

depolarized A state in which the electrical charge across the cell membrane is reduced, during the course of an action potential or during communication across a synapse. [3]

depression Episodes of sustained low mood and loss of pleasure from normally rewarding activities, often occurring with changes in sleep, appetite, concentration, and with negative thoughts such as guilt or suicidal ideas. [16]

dermatome A region of the skin that receives input from a single spinal nerve. [2]

diencephalon A division of the central nervous system encompassing the brain structures immediately rostral to the brainstem, but below the telencephalon; primarily includes the thalamus and hypothalamus. [2]

diffusion tensor imaging A type of magnetic resonance imaging that is sensitive to the direction of water diffusion through tissue; enables researchers to trace the white matter tracts or connections between different brain areas, by following the patterns of water diffusion through the tracts. [1]

DISC1 The disrupted-in-schizophrenia gene, whose protein plays a role in neural development; those with mutations in this gene can have a high risk of developing schizophrenia or mood disorders [16]

distal Anatomical term meaning farther away from the center (for example, as in the digits on a limb). [2]

disulfiram A medication used to prevent relapse into alcohol addiction, by blocking the action of the enzyme acetaldehyde dehydrogenase; individuals who take this medication will develop severe nausea if they consume alcohol. [14]

DNA Deoxyribonucleic acid; a molecule found in the nucleus that encodes genetic information in living organisms. [3]

DNA methylation A form of epigenetic modification of the DNA in which a methyl group is added to DNA nucleotides to reduce the expression of nearby genes. [9]

dopamine A monoamine neurotransmitter that plays an important role in initiating, maintaining, and terminating neural activity for a variety of brain functions, ranging from reward to cognition to motor control. [2]

dopamine hypothesis A theory proposing that the symptoms of schizophrenia arise from excessive or poorly regulated levels of dopamine. [16]

dorsal Anatomical term meaning toward the top or back; generally contrasted with ventral. [2]

dorsal horn A region of gray matter in the spinal cord where incoming sensory information from the body makes synaptic connections with spinal cord neurons. [7]

dorsal root The branch of a spinal nerve that enters the spinal cord posteriorly, carrying sensory information from the body into the neurons of the spinal cord. [6]

dorsal root ganglion Located just outside the spinal cord, the collection of cell bodies of the sensory neurons of the peripheral nervous system. [2]

dorsal stream Pathway within the visual system from the visual cortex to the parietal lobe that focuses on determining an object's location, as opposed to its identity. [5]

dorsolateral prefrontal cortex A region of the prefrontal cortex that is involved in complex cognitive functions such as working memory, mathematical calculations, and rule-based decision making. [16]

dorsomedial prefrontal cortex A region of the prefrontal cortex that is involved in self-regulation of thoughts, emotions, and behaviors. It is also often active in tasks involving social cognition or theory of mind. [16]

double dissociation An experimental demonstration that two brain functions are distinct and rely on two different brain structures; disruption of one of the brain areas will disrupt one function but not the other, and vice versa. [15]

Down syndrome A genetic condition in which the person has an extra copy of chromosome 21; causes abnormalities in the development of multiple body organs, including the brain; mental retardation is a common result. [16]

DTI See *diffusion tensor imaging*. [1]

dualism (Cartesian) The proposition, first suggested by the philosopher René Descartes, that the mind and body are distinct from one another, and that the mind is nonmaterial and can exist independently of the material body. [8]

dual-process theory (hippocampus) A model that suggests that recognition memory can involve two distinct processes: general familiarity or specific recollection. These processes are thought to involve slightly different neural structures. [9]

dynorphin A peptide neurotransmitter that binds to opioid receptors. [14]

dysarthria A difficulty speaking caused by paralysis or lack of coordination of the muscles used to produce speech. [11]

dyslexia A disorder impairing reading abilities, in which the individual is unable to process and use letter sounds and words at an age-appropriate level. [11]

dysphonia A disorder of the voice; specifically, impairment in ability to produce the sounds of speech using the vocal cords and larynx, as opposed to the muscles of the mouth used for pronunciation. [11]

Edinger–Westphal nuclei Parasympathetic nuclei found in the brainstem that regulate the constriction of the pupils. [15]

EEG See *electroencephalography*. [1]

efferent neuron A neuron that conveys information out of the nervous system. [3]

electrical gradient The difference in electrical charge between two regions, such as the inside and outside of the cell; ions will move down the gradient toward the area with the opposite charge. [3]

electrical stimulation mapping A technique in which patients have parts of their cortex stimulated directly, via an electrode, to determine the function of the stimulated area. [11]

electrical synapses (gap junctions) Structures that connect neurons and allow direct transmission of the electrical signal from one neuron to the next, without requiring chemical neurotransmission across a physical gap between the cells as in a chemical synapse. [3]

electroconvulsive therapy (ECT) A treatment for severe depression that involves passing an electrical current through the brain under anesthesia, to induce a brief generalized seizure. [13]

electroencephalography (EEG) A noninvasive technique for recording the electrical activity of the brain using external electrodes applied to the scalp. Offers high time resolution to distinguish between rapidly occurring events in the brain, but poorer spatial resolution to distinguish where these events are taking place within the brain. [1]

electromyography (EMG) A technique for recording the electrical activity of muscles. [10]

electrooculography (EOG) A technique for recording the electrical activity of the muscles controlling eye movements. [10]

emergent properties Properties of a complex system that are not part of any one of the simpler component elements, but that emerge from the interactions of these elements with one another, and are thus a property of the system as a whole. [1]

emotional contagion The tendency for the emotional state of one member of a group to evoke the same emotional state in other group members. [15]

emotional empathy The ability to share the emotional state of another individual; related to emotional contagion. [15]

emotional self-reflection Thinking about one's own emotions. [15]

emotional theory of mind The ability to understand and predict the emotional state of another person, without necessarily sharing that emotional state. [15]

empathy The capacity to understand the experience of another individual – in particular, that person's emotional state or perspective. [15]

endocrine gland A gland that releases hormonal signals into the bloodstream in order to affect the activity of other organs in the body. Examples include the thyroid gland and the adrenal glands. [13]

endogenously generated Produced internally, even without external cues or inputs; for example, circadian rhythms. [10]

endowment effect An effect observed in behavioral economics, in which people assign more value to a given item if they own that item, and a lower value to the same item if they do not own it. [12]

enkephalins A class of peptide neurotransmitter that binds to opioid receptors; believed to function in the brain's endogenous pain-control mechanisms. [14]

ensembles Groups of cells whose collective activity serves a common function. [8]

entorhinal cortex A region of the medial temporal lobe, anterior to the parahippocampal gyrus; serves as part of the input and output pathway for the anterior hippocampus. [13]

entrained The state in which an internal rhythm is synchronized to an external rhythm; for example, the circadian rhythm is entrained to daily light–dark cycles. [10]

epigenetics Control of gene function by factors other than the DNA sequence itself; for example, methylation of DNA nucleotides or acetylation of histones can alter gene expression. [9]

epinephrine A molecule that acts as both a neurotransmitter and a hormone, stimulating fight-or-flight functions within the body; also sometimes known as adrenaline. [13]

episodic memory Memory for personal experiences that occur at a particular time and place. [2]

EPSP See *excitatory postsynaptic potential (EPSP).* [3]

estradiol A specific female sex hormone, belonging to the estrogen family of hormones. [13]

estrogens A class of female sex hormones. [13]

excitatory postsynaptic potential (EPSP) A change in the membrane potential of the postsynaptic membrane such that the inside of the cell becomes less negative, normally because of positively charged ions entering the cell; usually results from the release of excitatory neurotransmitters at the synapse. [3]

executive functions Higher cognitive functions, including planning, reasoning, problem solving, goal-setting, judgment, and decision making. [16]

expected utility The predicted reward value of a given option, calculated as the magnitude of the possible reward, multiplied by the probability that the reward will be delivered. [12]

explicit memory A type of memory that involves information that can be consciously or explicitly recalled, as opposed to unconsciously or implicitly recalled. [9]

expressive aphasia A disorder of language function that involves the loss of the ability to produce language, as opposed to the loss of the ability to comprehend language; applies to both spoken and written language. [11]

extensors Muscles around a joint that extend the joint or increase the angle between the bones that make up the joint. [7]

exteroceptive areas Brain regions that process information from the external world. [12]

extinction A disorder of attention in which the person fails to notice a stimulus (usually on the left) when it is presented simultaneously with a second competing stimulus (usually on the right). Often considered as a milder form of the syndrome of hemineglect. [8]

familiarity A form of memory in which the individual has an impression or a feeling of having previously encountered a given stimulus (often along with an emotional impression of its nature), but without being able to recall the specific setting, time, or circumstances of the encounter. [9]

fast-scan cyclic voltammetry A technique for determining the identity and concentration of neurotransmitters in a particular part of the brain by inserting an electrode and rapidly changing the voltage applied to the electrode. [14]

fatal familial insomnia An inherited sleep disorder in which the patient initially loses the ability to fall asleep, then develops progressive anxiety, hallucinations, and dementia; usually fatal within 1–3 years. [10]

fear conditioning A form of classical conditioning in which an animal learns to fear a sensory stimulus that has been paired with an aversive stimulus, such as an electric shock. [13]

feature binding The act of integrating all of the various perceptual features of a sensory stimulus (for example, size, shape, and color) so that they are perceived as all belonging to that stimulus. [6]

feature selectivity A characteristic of neurons in sensory areas of the brain, in which the neuron fires only when the sensory stimulus possesses certain specific features; for example, motion in a particular direction. [8]

feedback loops Neuronal connections that project back to the areas from which those neurons received input. [5]

felicific calculus A method proposed by the philosopher Jeremy Bentham (1748–1832) for mathematically representing the pleasure associated with an action. [12]

field potential Electrical field generated by the summed, synchronized activity of a large number of neurons, detectable using scalp electrodes or implanted electrodes. [10]

fight-or-flight A term used to describe a coordinated mode of activities in the body and brain that prepare the organism to either fight for survival or flee from danger; coordinated in part by the sympathetic nervous system. [13]

first-order theory of mind The ability to model or predict the thoughts, beliefs, intentions, desires or goals of another individual ("what are you thinking?"); second-order theory of mind involves the additional complexity of modeling another person's model of one's own thoughts, beliefs, and desires ("what do you think that I am thinking?"). [15]

flexors Muscles around a joint that contract the joint or decrease the angle between the bones that make up the joint. [7]

flow A pleasant internal state that occurs when one is fully immersed in performing a task that is both challenging and yet within one's capabilities. [14]

fluent aphasia A language problem characterized by impairment of the ability to comprehend language, but continued ability to use grammar and to produce a flow of speech; also called *Wernicke's aphasia*. [11]

fMRI See *functional magnetic resonance imaging*. [1]

forebrain The most anterior of three zones in the developing nervous system of vertebrates; develops into structures of the telencephalon (such as the cortex and basal ganglia) and the diencephalon (such as the thalamus). Also called *prosencephalon*. [2]

fornix A tract of white matter fibers connecting the hippocampus to the hypothalamus. [2]

forward model A model of motor control by the cerebellum in which the cerebellum takes into account the time delays that are involved in receiving input from sensory organs and sending motor output to the muscles, and calculates a model of the future positions of the body and external objects for more accurate movement guidance. [2]

fovea The region at the center of the retina where the cones are concentrated, making it important for detailed color vision. [5]

framing effect An observation in behavioral economics, in which individuals may choose inconsistently among two options, depending on whether the options are "framed" in terms of possible losses versus possible gains.

frontal eye field A region on the lateral surface of the frontal lobes that controls the movements of the eyes. [7]

frontal lobe The region of the cerebral cortex at the front of the brain, anterior to the central sulcus, whose functions include motor control as well as higher cognitive functions such as planning, decision making, goal selection, and assigning value to options. [2]

frontal operculum The part of the frontal lobes that lies within the "lip" of the lateral sulcus, next to the insula; the primary gustatory (taste) cortex is located here. [6]

frontopolar cortex The region of the prefrontal cortex located at the most anterior part of the frontal lobes; unique in receiving no direct sensory input, and considered important for representing goals, multitasking, and imagining the past and future. [7]

frontotemporal dementia A neurological disorder involving degeneration of the frontal and temporal lobes, leading to symptoms that can include dementia, aphasia, the loss of abstract conceptual knowledge, and inappropriate social behavior. [15]

functional localization The process of determining which brain regions or circuits are important for performing a given cognitive function. [9]

functional magnetic resonance imaging (fMRI) A brain-imaging technique that uses magnetic resonance imaging to measure changes in blood flow and blood oxygenation associated with neural activity over time; widely used to map areas of the brain that are involved in particular tasks or functions. [1]

functionalism A theory of consciousness that suggests that a mental state is determined by its functional role in relation to other mental states, rather than by the specific physical mechanisms or processes by which it is implemented. [8]

fusiform face area A region of visual association cortex in the inferior temporal lobe, playing a specific role in identifying faces. [5]

fusiform gyrus A gyrus on the inferior surface of the temporal lobe, adjacent to the parahippocampal gyrus; neurons in this area are part of the ventral pathway for identifying visual stimuli. [2]

GABA (gamma-aminobutyric acid) The major inhibitory neurotransmitter of the central nervous system in vertebrate organisms. [3]

gain The degree to which a neuron's activity multiplies or enhances the signal from a particular input. [8]

gamma motor neurons The neurons that control the contraction of the muscle spindle fibers inside the body of each muscle, enabling the nervous system to monitor the contraction of each muscle. [7]

gamma waves Brain waves with a frequency of 30–100 or more Hz, associated with cognitive functions and concentration. [10]

gap junctions See *electrical synapses (gap junctions)*. [3]

gate control theory A theory of pain perception that suggests that the amount of pain perceived depends upon the relative activity of both the nociceptive and the non-nociceptive pathways, with the non-nociceptive pathways able to "close the gate" of pain perception and suppress the input from nociceptive pathways. [6]

gating (sensory) A process of filtering out redundant information from sensory input, so as to prevent large volumes of irrelevant information from overloading cognitive processes and reducing their efficiency. [4]

G-coupled protein receptor A common type of metabotropic receptor that acts through a G-protein on the inner surface of the postsynaptic cell; some types of receptor for dopamine, serotonin, and norepinephrine fall into this class. [3]

genes Segments of DNA that contain the information necessary to produce a biologically active protein. [1]

ghrelin A peptide hormone released by the stomach that stimulates hunger and eating. [14]

glia See *glial cells*. [3]

glial cells (or glia)   A class of non-neuron cells within the nervous system that perform a range of supporting functions to ensure an optimal environment for the neurons themselves. [3]

global aphasia   A language disorder in which all aspects of language use are affected, including both language production and comprehension. [11]

global workspace theory   A theory that suggests that conscious experience arises from coordinating the activity of functionally specialized brain areas into an integrated whole, or global, workspace; includes components such as inner speech and visual imagery. [8]

globus pallidus   One of the structures of the basal ganglia, located underneath the putamen; contains an external part and an internal part, which respectively play excitatory and inhibitory roles in controlling movement and behavior. [2]

glucocorticoid hormones   Stress hormones produced by the hypothalamus, pituitary gland, and adrenal gland. [14]

glucose   A sugar molecule, widely used as an energy source by the cells in the brain and body. [1]

glutamate   A molecule that is both an amino acid and the most common excitatory neurotransmitter in the nervous system. [3]

glutamate hypothesis   A theory for the cause of schizophrenia that suggests the core deficit is too little glutamate neurotransmission. [16]

Golgi staining   A tissue-staining method developed by the neuroanatomist Golgi in the late nineteenth century; turns the entire membrane of a neuron dark, allowing the entire structure of the neuron to be seen under a microscope. [3]

Golgi tendon organ   Somatosensory receptor embedded in the tendons that connect the muscle to the bone, sensing changes in muscle tension; important for preventing too much tension or force from damaging the muscle. [6]

G-proteins   Molecules located on the inner surface of the cell membrane that carry the signal from the G-protein-coupled receptor to the metabolic cellular machinery that is the ultimate target of the signaling pathway. [3]

grammar   The set of rules for how words and ideas may be combined in a language. [11]

gray matter   A type of neural tissue consisting of the unmyelinated cell bodies and dendrites of neurons, as opposed to white matter, which consists of axons that carry signals between neurons in different regions of the nervous system. [2]

grid cell   A type of neuron involved in spatial navigation, whose receptive field consists of a triangular "grid" of spatial locations; found in the entorhinal cortex. [9]

growth hormone   A hormone released by the anterior pituitary gland that stimulates growth and maturation. [13]

gyri (singular, gyrus)   The rounded convolutions on the surface of the cortex; each is bordered by a groove on each side, known as a sulcus. [2]

hair cells   The cells of the inner ear that are important for perceiving sound and monitoring balance. [5]

hallucinations   Perception of stimuli that are not actually present; auditory hallucinations are common in patients with schizophrenia. [16]

Hebbian learning   A mechanism for learning proposed by the psychologist D. O. Hebb in the twentieth century, which states that the connection between two cells will be strengthened only if the presynaptic cell consistently fires at the same time as the postsynaptic cell; sometimes summarized by the phrase, "cells that fire together, wire together." [9]

hedonic treadmill   The tendency for human beings to return to a stable, baseline level of happiness over time, regardless of positive or negative life events that might occur. [14]

helping-hand phenomenon   In split-brain patients, a phenomenon in which the hand controlled by the hemisphere that perceived the stimulus will position the hand controlled by the other hemisphere (which did not perceive the stimulus) to help it perform the correct response. [11]

hemineglect   A syndrome in which the patient loses the ability to pay attention to or interact with stimuli in one half of the sensory environment, usually the left half; commonly seen in patients with strokes affecting the right temporoparietal cortex. [5]

hemispherectomy   A surgical procedure to remove one hemisphere of the brain, occasionally performed for severe and intractable epilepsy. [4]

higher-order theory   A theory of consciousness that suggests that conscious perception requires a higher-order representation of a lower-level sensory or perceptual representation [8]

hindbrain   The most posterior of three zones in the developing nervous system of vertebrates; develops into the structures of the brainstem: the midbrain, pons, cerebellum, and medulla oblongata. [2]

hippocampal formation   A set of structures of the medial temporal lobe, including the hippocampus itself as well as the dentate gyrus, subiculum, and entorhinal cortex; these structures are important for certain forms of explicit memory, including episodic memory. [9]

hippocampus   A key brain structure for episodic memory and spatial navigation, with neural circuitry capable of rapid learning and plasticity. Located along the medial edge of the temporal lobe, at the edge of the cerebral cortex. [2]

homeostasis   The process by which an organism maintains a stable internal environment in terms of temperature, energy, pH, oxygen, and other key parameters necessary to sustain life. [1]

Homo economicus   A theoretical model of human behavior that considers humans as idealized "rational economic agents," making consistent decisions to maximize gain and minimize loss. [12]

homunculus   A term meaning "little man," often used to refer to the representation of the body within the brain, such as within the primary somatosensory or motor cortex. [4]

horizontal cells   Cells within the retina that enable nearby regions of the retina to exchange information. [5]

hormone   A chemical that is released by one cell and is intended to affect the functioning of a large number of targets throughout the body. [2]

huntingtin   The protein that is encoded incorrectly in patients with Huntington's disease. [16]

Huntington's disease (HD)   An inherited neurological disorder in which the striatum undergoes degeneration; patients lose the ability to control or inhibit their movements, and develop problems with impulse control and emotion regulation; ultimately, the illness progresses to dementia and death. [7]

hyperarousal   A state of increased or excessive alertness and vigilance, often accompanied by anxiety and overactivity in the sympathetic nervous system. [10]

hyperpolarized   A state in which the membrane potential of the neuron is driven to be more negative than its usual resting potential, so that it becomes less likely to generate an action potential. [8]

hypersomnia   Excessive and recurring episodes of sleepiness. [10]

hypnagogic hallucinations   Dreamlike illusory visions or sounds that occur during the transition from sleep to wakefulness; a typical symptom of narcolepsy. [10]

hypnotics   A class of medications that act as sleep aids. [10]

hypocretin   A hormone, also known as orexin, that promotes wakefulness; a deficit of hypocretin is thought to cause narcolepsy. [10]

hypothalamus   Part of the diencephalon that is important for homeostasis and basic survival drives, including sleep, hunger, and thirst. [2]

hypothesis   A proposed explanation for an observation, used as the basis for experimental investigation. A good hypothesis should be testable (i.e., capable of being proven false) and based on the available facts and observations. [1]

ibogaine   A substance derived from the bark of the iboga tree in Africa that may be useful for treating addiction. [14]

illusory correlation   Our tendency to perceive a relationship between two phenomena, even when no relationship between them actually exists. [1]

immunocytochemistry   A technique in which antibodies are used to bind to specific proteins on a cell's surface, allowing researchers to identify where in the cell or the brain those proteins are found. [3]

implicit memory   A type of memory that learns and stores information that influences behavior, but is not typically consciously recalled; examples include acquired motor skills or unconscious emotional memories. Also called *nondeclarative memory*. [9]

***in situ* hybridization**   A technique that uses radioactive or fluorescent compounds to label a "probe" sequence of DNA or RNA; the probe can then bind to a complementary sequence of DNA or RNA in a sample of tissue, to identify cells where a gene of interest is expressed. [3]

inattentional blindness   A phenomenon in which subjects fail to notice a stimulus when their attention is focused elsewhere, even though the stimulus might normally be easy to detect when it is the focus of attention. [8]

incentive sensitization   A theory of addiction in which repeated exposures to an addictive substance cause the substance, and any associated cues, to become associated with pathologically high levels of incentive or "wanting." The high level of incentive can persist for long periods of time and can override the incentive value of natural rewards necessary for survival. [14]

incus   One of the three bones of the middle ear; its name means "anvil," after its approximate shape. [6]

inferior   Anatomical term meaning toward the bottom; opposite of superior. [2]

inferior colliculus   A paired structure located on the posterior aspect of the midbrain, below the superior colliculus; important for processing of auditory inputs. [2]

inferotemporal cortex   The inferior portion of the temporal lobe. [5]

information states   The patterns of functional activity exhibited by neurons communicating with other neurons; they carry information to the extent that they specify one possible state of activity, out of a larger repertoire of many possible states of activity. [8]

inhibitory postsynaptic potential (IPSP)   A change in the membrane potential of the postsynaptic membrane such that the inside of the cell becomes more negative, because of positively charged ions exiting the cell or negatively charged ions entering the cell; usually results from the release of inhibitory neurotransmitters at the synapse. [3]

inner hair cells   Cells located along the organ of Corti within the cochlea of the inner ear, that transduce sound waves into electrochemical signals. [6]

insomnia   The inability to fall asleep or remain asleep. [10]

insula   A cortical region within the lateral sulcus that plays an important role in interoception, or sensory perception of the internal state of the body. [2]

insulin   A hormone released by the pancreas to regulate glucose metabolism and energy storage within the tissues of the body. [14]

integrated information theory   A theory of consciousness that suggests that higher levels of consciousness require a system to represent a large amount of information, and for this information to be integrated, so that the system as a whole carries much more information than the sum of its parts. [8]

interaural differences   The differences in the sound signal perceived by the two ears, which can be used to help locate the source of the sound. Interaural time differences refer to differences in the timing of sound arriving at one ear versus the other, while interaural intensity differences refer to differences in the volume of sound arriving at one ear versus the other. [6]

internal model   A representation of the external world that is generated internally, rather than from incoming sensory information; may be innate or based on past experience. [5]

interneuron As opposed to a sensory or motor neuron, a neuron that connects two other neurons. Sometimes used specifically to describe small neurons that provide local connections between larger neurons in a given structure, such as the microscopic circuitry of the cortex. [2]

interoception Perception of the internal state of the organs and tissues of the body, as opposed to the external world. Interoceptive sensory modalities include temperature, pain, itch, stretch, fatigue, and chemical senses. [6]

intertemporal choice An experimental paradigm that assesses the subjective value of a delayed reward by having subjects choose between a smaller reward delivered sooner and a larger reward delivered later. [12]

intralaminar nuclei Thalamic nuclei that interact diffusely with many cortical regions and whose activity is not restricted to a single sensory or motor function. [8]

intuitive system (system 1) A proposed system of cognition that provides rapid, intuitive, unconscious assessments of options during decision making, often based on criteria that cannot be easily articulated explicitly; for example, deciding which of two paintings is more attractive. [12]

involuntary (exogenous) attention A form of "bottom-up" attention that is drawn to a particular stimulus automatically based on its own sensory features, such as differences in color or movement; stands in contrast to voluntary or endogenous attention, which is directed in a "top-down" fashion by current context and behavior. [8]

involuntary cue A cue stimulus that draws attention involuntarily based on its own intrinsic features; for example, a flash of light in a particular location. [8]

ion channels Proteins embedded in the cell membrane that allow ions to cross between the inside and outside of the cell. [3]

ionotropic receptors Receptors that, when activated by a neurotransmitter, open a channel through the cell membrane to allow ions to enter or leave the cell. [3]

ions Electrically charged atoms or molecules. [3]

Iowa gambling task (IGT) A behavioral task in which subjects try to win money by drawing cards from one of four decks, each of which has a different mixture of rewards and penalties of various sizes; optimal performance requires learning which decks are to be avoided, based on accumulated experience. [13]

iproniazid A medicine that blocks the activity of the monoamine oxidase enzyme, thereby increasing the concentration of monoamines; one of the earliest antidepressant medications to enter use, in the 1950s. [16]

ipsilateral Anatomical term meaning on the same side. [2]

IPSP See *inhibitory postsynaptic potential (IPSP)*. [3]

iris The colored ring of muscle that can expand or contract to control how much light enters the eye. [5]

James–Lange theory A theory of emotion that proposes that our emotions arise from our brain's interpretation of our body's physical reactions; "we feel angry because we strike, afraid because we tremble." [13]

jet lag A mismatch of the internal circadian time and the external day–night time, typically occurring after a flight across several time zones. [10]

just-noticeable difference The smallest subjectively detectable difference between the properties of two stimuli, such as loudness or brightness. [6]

kappa-opioid receptors Opioid receptors of a type that produces unpleasant reactions and acts as a negative reinforcer; sometimes described as part of an "anti-reward" system. [14]

ketamine A medication that is an antagonist of the NMDA glutamate receptors, and whose effects can mimic both the positive and the negative symptoms of schizophrenia. [16]

Kluver–Bucy syndrome A syndrome associated with bilateral damage to the anterior temporal lobes and amygdala, first described in primate studies in the 1930s; symptoms include visual agnosia, hyperorality (indiscriminately placing objects in the mouth), and hypersexuality. [13]

labeled line A form of information coding in which a given neuron carries only one specific type of sensory information. [6]

language A system for communicating complex ideas from one individual to another, by encoding them in a series of sounds, gestures, or other arbitrary symbols according to a system shared by both individuals. [11]

lateral Anatomical term meaning toward the side; opposite of medial. [2]

lateral corticospinal tract A bundle of white matter fibers leading from the upper motor neurons of the primary motor cortex, premotor cortex, and supplementary motor area to the lower motor neurons of the spinal cord; functions to deliver motor commands from each hemisphere to the muscles on the opposite side of the body. [7]

lateral geniculate nucleus A specialized part of the thalamus that is part of the visual pathway relaying information from the retina to the primary visual cortex. [2]

lateral hypothalamus A region of the hypothalamus that is involved with regulating hunger; stimulation of neurons in this area can cause increased appetite. [13]

lateral inhibitory connections (cerebellum) Inhibitory connections within the cerebellar cortex that decrease the activity of the Purkinje cells. [7]

lateral nucleus A nucleus of the amygdala that receives inputs from visual, auditory, somatosensory, olfactory, and other external senses, and plays an important role in fear conditioning. [13]

lateral orbitofrontal cortex A part of the prefrontal cortex that is involved in subjective valuation, emotion regulation, and decision making, and is thought to be particularly active when re-evaluating stimuli based on context or external factors. [12]

lateral premotor cortex A region on the lateral surface of the brain, anterior to the primary motor cortex, that is involved in planning and coordinating actions (sets of coordinated movements, such as hair-combing or tooth-brushing) based on external cues or stimuli. [7]

lateralization The specialization of the left or right hemisphere to perform certain tasks, such as the specialized ability of the left hemisphere to process the content of spoken language. [1]

lens The structure behind the pupil that changes shape to focus the incoming light on the retina. [5]

leptin A hormone released by adipose tissue (fatty tissue) to signal satiety and inhibit food consumption. [14]

lesion evidence Evidence that relates changes in behaviors or cognitive function to damage to a particular part of the brain. [9]

lesions Focal injuries to the brain, which can be produced accidentally, such as by a stroke, or deliberately, as in an experiment. [1]

levodopa A chemical precursor to the neurotransmitter dopamine that is able to cross the blood–brain barrier and is converted to dopamine within the brain; used as a treatment for Parkinson's disease. [7]

lexigrams Visual, symbolic representations of words used in studies of language in bonobos (a type of chimpanzee). [11]

liking In some theories of reward, "liking" refers informally to a current and internal feeling of well-being or satisfaction associated with a reward, as opposed to "wanting," which refers to a desire to obtain a reward. [14]

limbic system A collection of evolutionarily conserved structures surrounding the brainstem, considered important for motivation and emotion. [2]

linguistic nativism The idea that human infants are innately predisposed to learn language. [11]

lithium A chemical element that is commonly used as a medication to treat bipolar disorder. [16]

local coding A term describing a system of neural representation in which each feature of the outside world is encoded by a different neuron specialized to detect that particular feature, with no overlap in representation among neurons. [3]

local field potential The combined electrical fields generated by all of the neurons within about 0.5 mm of an implanted electrode; primarily reflects electrical fluctuations at the synapses, rather than action potentials, and thus is more reflective of input rather than output for the neurons in the local volume. [8]

locus coeruleus A nucleus in the pons that includes the largest collection of neurons containing norepinephrine; these neurons project throughout the brain and serve an important role in alertness and in arousal level. [2]

long-term depression (LTD) Long-lasting decreases in synaptic strength that are induced when the presynaptic cell consistently fails to activate along with the postsynaptic cell. [9]

long-term memory A form of memory that lasts substantially longer than the span of attention, capable of storing and recalling information for a span of hours to years. [1]

long-term potentiation (LTP) Long-lasting increases in synaptic strength that are induced when the activity of the presynaptic cell consistently activates along with the postsynaptic cell. [9]

loop circuits Neuronal connections from one brain region to another that are connected back to the initial area, forming a loop. A loop circuit may pass through multiple structures before returning to its origin, as is the case for cortical-striatal-thalamic-cortical loop circuits. [12]

lordosis A reflexive mating posture in female rats, used to signal that they are in a sexually receptive state; characterized by a downward flexion of the spine and upward flexion of the hips. [13]

loss aversion A phenomenon in which an individual assigns more value to the prospect of avoiding a loss than to the prospect of achieving a gain of the same magnitude. [12]

loss-of-function An experimental paradigm in which the loss of particular abilities following a lesion informs researchers about the function of the region that was lesioned. [12]

loudness The perception of a sound's amplitude. [6]

lower motor neurons The motor neurons that project from the spinal cord to the muscles of the body. [7]

lucid dreaming The phenomenon of a dreamer becoming consciously aware that he or she is dreaming, and being able to exert some voluntary control over the content of the dream. [10]

Mach bands An optical illusion in which stripes of slightly different shades of gray appear to have bands of brightness or darkness along the edges where they border one another, even though they are actually the same shade across their entire width. [5]

magnetic resonance imaging (MRI) A medical-imaging technology that can produce high-contrast, high-resolution images of biological tissues, based on subtle differences in the magnetic resonance properties of the hydrogen nuclei in the tissues. The technique does not require ionizing radiation, but instead places the tissue in a powerful magnetic field and uses radio waves to map its magnetic resonance properties. Widely used for structural, functional, and spectroscopic imaging of the living human brain. [1]

magnetoencephalography (MEG) A noninvasive technique that enables researchers to monitor electrical activity within the brain by placing an array of sensitive magnetic detectors on the scalp to detect the magnetic fields generated by coordinated neural activity; since the magnetic fields are not distorted as they pass through the head, source localization can be more accurate with MEG than with EEG, although MEG is substantially more expensive. [1]

magnocellular retinal ganglion cells Retinal ganglion cells that get their input primarily from rods, and are therefore not color sensitive; although they have relatively low spatial resolution, they are good at detecting moving stimuli. [5]

major depressive disorder   A common form of mental illness in which the person experiences periods of severe and sustained low mood and difficulty experiencing pleasure or interest in formerly enjoyed activities, along with changes in sleep and appetite; feelings of guilt and suicidal thoughts are common during these periods. [15]

malleus   One of the three bones of the middle ear; its name means "hammer," after its approximate shape. [6]

mamillary bodies   Part of the hypothalamus that plays a role in linking current needs to memories of past events. [2]

mania   A state of sustained high or irritable mood, accompanied by hyperactivity, a decreased need for sleep, feelings of grandiosity, poor impulse control, and disinhibited behavior; episodes of mania and depression occur in bipolar disorder. [16]

masking   A method for manipulating conscious perception in which the target stimulus is presented only briefly before being replaced or "masked" by another, so that the first stimulus is not consciously perceived. [8]

McGurk effect   An experimentally induced situation in which the person listens to a recording of one phoneme while watching a speaker say a similar but distinct phoneme; the subject perceives a third, related phoneme. [6]

mechanoreceptors   Sensory receptors that are triggered in response to movement, stretch, pressure or vibration; found in the skin, muscles, tendons, and some visceral organs. [6]

medial   Anatomical term meaning toward the middle; opposite of lateral. [2]

medial forebrain bundle   A collection of nerve fibers that connects the ventral tegmental area to the nucleus accumbens and plays a central role in the reward pathway. [13]

medial geniculate nucleus   A specialized part of the thalamus that is part of the auditory pathway relaying information from the cochlea to the primary auditory cortex. [4]

medial orbitofrontal cortex   A part of the prefrontal cortex that is more active in decision making when there is the prospect of an immediate reward. [12]

medial prefrontal cortex   A large region of the frontal lobes located on the medial wall of each hemisphere, containing a hierarchy of regions for selecting among values, goals, cognitive strategies, behaviors, and actions based on internal motivations and needs rather than external sensory cues (which guide an analogous hierarchy along the lateral wall of the prefrontal cortex). [9]

medial preoptic area   A region of the hypothalamus that is larger in males than in females, and is associated with sexual behavior in males and with parental behavior in females. [13]

medial temporal lobe   The portion of the temporal lobe closer to the midline; contains the hippocampus, parahippocampal gyrus, entorhinal cortex, subiculum, and amygdala; these structures are important for encoding and retrieving episodic memories, and for emotional memories. [9]

medulla oblongata   The most caudal part of the brainstem, immediately superior to the spinal cord; also known as the myelencephalon. [2]

MEG   See *magnetoencephalography*. [1]

Meissner's corpuscles   A type of rapidly adapting mechanoreceptor located close to the skin's surface and having a small receptive field. [6]

melanopsin   A light-sensitive pigment found in some retinal ganglion cells that helps entrain the circadian rhythm to light–dark cues. [10]

melatonin   A hormone produced and released by the pineal gland, influencing sleep and wakefulness. [10]

membrane   The double layer of phospholipids and proteins that isolates the inside of the cell from the outside. [3]

membrane potential   The difference in electrical potential between the inside and outside of the cell. [3]

memory   The process of encoding, storing, or retrieving information. Multiple systems for memory operate within the brain, serving a variety of functions. [8]

Merkel's disks   A type of slowly adapting mechanoreceptor located close to the skin's surface and having a small receptive field. [6]

mesocortical pathway   A dopaminergic pathway projecting to the cortex from the ventral tegmental area of the midbrain, thought to be involved in planning and cognition. [14]

mesolimbic pathway   A dopaminergic pathway projecting to the limbic regions of the telencephalon from the ventral tegmental area of the midbrain, and thought to be involved in emotion regulation; suppression of abnormal activity in this pathway is thought to be important to the mechanism of action for antipsychotic medications in treating schizophrenia. [14]

metabotropic receptors   Receptors that, when activated by a neurotransmitter, exert their effects on neural activity via cell-signaling pathways such as G-proteins or tyrosine kinases; in contrast, ionotropic receptors contain ion channels and exert their effects directly by altering the membrane potential of the neuron. [3]

metencephalon   The region of the central nervous system that lies between the midbrain (mesencephalon) and medulla (myelencephalon); part of the brainstem, it includes the pons and the cerebellum. [2]

methadone   A long-acting opioid that is sometimes used to prevent withdrawal symptoms and maintain abstinence from street drugs in individuals addicted to opioids such as morphine or heroin. [14]

methamphetamine   A stimulant that increases dopamine levels in the synapse by blocking dopamine reuptake; considered to have high potential for abuse and addiction. [14]

method of loci   A method for achieving rapid memorization of large amounts of information, by associating each item to be remembered with a particular spatial location. [9]

microdialysis   A technique for sampling the chemical properties of the extracellular fluid surrounding neurons via a miniaturized probe implanted in the brain. [1]

microelectrodes   Small electrodes surgically implanted into the brain that allow researchers to measure the electrical activity of neurons or to stimulate target brain regions. [1]

microglia   A subtype of glial cells that provide immune system functions for the central nervous system. [3]

microsleeps   Brief periods of sleep, ranging from less than a second to a few seconds. [10]

microtubules   Thin, tubular structures that are a component of the "skeleton" of a cell. In neurons, they support the shape of the neuron and provide a system to transport proteins or vesicles from the cell body to the synapses and back again. [16]

midbrain (mesencephalon)   The middle of three zones in the developing nervous system of vertebrates; develops into the midbrain in the adult brain, below the thalamus and above the pons. [2]

midbrain raphe nuclei   A set of nuclei within the brainstem that contain serotonin neurons, sending projections forward to the telencephalon and diencephalon to regulate a variety of functions, including sleep, appetite, and mood. [2]

middle ear   The portion of the ear between the eardrum and the oval window of the inner ear; contains three bones that transmit acoustic vibrations between these two structures. [6]

minimally conscious state   A disorder of consciousness in which patients have a sleep–wake cycle and show some limited signs of awareness of their surroundings when awake, unlike in coma or persistent vegetative state, where there is no sleep–wake cycle and no signs of awareness are present; typically a result of severe neurological injury, such as asphyxiation or head trauma. [8]

mirror neurons   Neurons that fire both when the subject performs an action and when the subject observes that same action being performed by another individual. [7]

mirror system   A network of cortical regions that are active during both the observation and the execution of actions; includes premotor cortex and the region of the superior temporal sulcus. [15]

mirror test   A test to determine whether an animal can recognize its own reflection in a mirror, by marking the animal with a spot of dye while it is asleep or unconscious, on a part of the body that it can only see with the aid of the mirror; if it later uses the mirror to inspect or react to the dye spot, this is taken as evidence of self-recognition. [15]

misattribution   Our innate tendency to attribute an idea or a recollection to the wrong source. [9]

monoamine hypothesis   A theoretical explanation for depression that proposes the disorder is caused by deficient levels of the monoamine neurotransmitters serotonin, norepinephrine, and dopamine. [16]

monoamine oxidase   An enzyme that breaks down monoamine neurotransmitters. [16]

monoamine oxidase inhibitors (MAOIs)   A class of early antidepressant medications, now rarely used; they boost monoamine levels by irreversibly inhibiting the activity of the monoamine oxidase enzyme, which normally breaks down serotonin and other monoamine neurotransmitters in the synaptic cleft. [16]

monoamines   A class of neurotransmitters playing an important role in sleep, appetite, mood, anxiety, and other homeostatic, motivational, and emotional functions; includes dopamine, epinephrine, serotonin, and melatonin. [3]

monophasic sleep   A pattern of sleep in which there is only one period of sleep during each 24-hour period. [10]

monopolar neurons   Neurons with just one connection to the cell body; this connection branches to form both the axon and the dendrite. [3]

mood stabilizer   A type of medication that is used to treat both mania and depression in bipolar disorder; several different classes of medications are used as mood stabilizers, including antipsychotics, anti-seizure medications, and lithium. [16]

morphine   The psychoactive ingredient of the opium poppy that relieves pain, suppresses respiratory drive, and causes sedation. [14]

Morris water maze   A behavioral test of spatial memory ability in rats in which the rat must use spatial cues to swim onto a platform submerged in cloudy water. [9]

mossy fibers   Neural pathways that carry excitatory input to the cerebellum from throughout the central nervous system. [7]

motion blindness   The inability to detect motion in visual stimuli although the stimuli themselves can still be seen; usually occurs following damage to the motion-detecting areas of the visual pathway, such as area V5. [5]

Motivational Interviewing (MI)   A type of therapy designed to help people find the internal motivation necessary to change their behavior; best known for its use in the treatment of addiction, although the techniques can be used in other areas of medicine in which patients are having difficulty adhering to the treatment plan. [14]

motor homunculus   A representation of the musculature of the body within the brain. [7]

motor neurons   Neurons that are specialized to convey motor commands from the brain and spinal cord to the muscles of the body. [2]

motor theory   A theory that suggests that language functions rely on the left hemisphere because that hemisphere is specialized for controlling rapid, intricate movements, such as those required for speech. [11]

motor unit   A functional unit for motor control, consisting of a single alpha motor neuron and all of the muscle fibers that it innervates. [7]

MRI   See *magnetic resonance imaging*. [1]

multiple-trace theory   A theory of memory consolidation that suggests the hippocampus is important for the storage and retrieval of episodic memories, but the cortex is capable of sustaining semantic memories once they are formed, even if the hippocampus is lost. [9]

multipolar neurons   Neurons with a single large axon and multiple branches of dendrites providing input to the cell body. [3]

multistable percept A phenomenon in which an ambiguous stimulus can be perceived in more than one way; the perception of the object often flips back and forth between the alternative views. [5]

mu-opioid receptors Opioid receptors of a type that is important for the pain-relieving and euphoric effects of opioids. [14]

muscle fibers Strands of muscle, capable of contracting in length to generate mechanical force and movement. Muscle fibers are made up of individual myocytes; these are bundled into fascicles, which in turn are bundled into a muscle itself. [7]

muscle spindles Somatosensory receptors embedded in the body of the muscle that sense the length of the muscle and prevent the muscle from being overstretched. [6]

mutations Heritable changes to the DNA sequence that can result in changes in the sequence of amino acids of a protein encoded by a gene, or differences in the activity of a gene. [6]

mutual inhibition A form of interaction between two networks of neurons in which the activity of one network suppresses the activity of the other network, and vice versa. [10]

myelencephalon The region of the developing nervous system immediately rostral to the spinal cord; the myelencephalon develops into the medulla oblongata. [2]

myelin A fatty material wrapped around the axons of neurons that provides electrical insulation of the membrane and thereby increases the speed of conduction of action potentials along the axon. [3]

myelin sheaths Collections of myelin, each of which is wrapped around the length of the axon to speed up neuronal conduction. [3]

myofibrils The components of the muscle fibers that consist of sarcomeres (the most basic functional units of muscle fibers) arranged end to end. [7]

naltrexone An opioid antagonist that can be used as a medication to block the pleasurable effects of alcohol, thereby reducing the risk of relapse in alcohol addiction. [14]

narcolepsy A sleep disorder characterized by recurring bouts of excessive daytime sleepiness and cataplexy (transient muscle weakness). [10]

necrosis Death of cells or tissues in an uncontrolled process that may be toxic to surrounding tissues, in contrast to apoptosis, programmed cell death, which avoids such toxicity. [4]

negative feedback A control mechanism in which greater output provides an inhibitory signal back to the source of the output, thereby preventing excessive output from occurring. [13]

negative symptoms Symptoms of schizophrenia that involve deficits in normal functioning; these include apathy, lack of pleasure and motivation, lack of emotional expression, and poverty of speech. [16]

neocortex The most recently evolved regions of cortex, containing six layers of neurons, as opposed to

evolutionarily older regions of cortex in the limbic system, which contain fewer layers. [4]

neologism A "new word," usually meaningless, that is produced by a patient with a brain disorder affecting language function. [11]

nerve growth factor A chemical signal secreted by cells to promote the growth and survival of adjacent axons and neurons. [4]

nerve impulse See *action potential (nerve impulse or spike)*. [3]

neural correlates of consciousness The brain regions or processes that are associated with conscious perception, or with the conscious awake state. [8]

neurodevelopmental theories Theories regarding the cause of schizophrenia that suggest the disorder results from abnormally developing neural circuitry within the brain, on both a microscopic and a macroscopic scale. [16]

neuroeconomics A field in cognitive neuroscience that seeks to understand the brain mechanisms underlying human decision making. [12]

neurofibrillary tangles Clusters of tau proteins commonly found in the brains of patients with Alzheimer's disease. [16]

neurogenesis The production of new neurons. [9]

neuroleptic See *antipsychotics*. [16]

neuromodulators Chemical substances used by neurons to affect the activity of many neurons, rather than just a single neuron as in standard synaptic neurotransmission. [4]

neuromuscular junction The point of interaction between a motor neuron and a muscle cell, akin to a chemical synapse between two neurons. [2]

neuron A cell in the nervous system specialized for quickly transmitting electrical signals to other neurons via connections known as synapses; networks of neurons can coordinate their activity to process information and to serve specific functions in guiding the behavior of the organism. [3]

neuron doctrine The idea that the nervous system comprises a network of many discrete, individual neuronal cells separated by synapses, rather than a continuous collection of fused cells; first proposed by the nineteenth-century neuroanatomist Ramón y Cajal based on his observations of the microscopic anatomy of the nervous system. [9]

neuropathic pain Pain caused by injury to the pain pathways of the nervous system, rather than by an external stimulus. [6]

neuropeptide Y (NPY) A neurotransmitter that acts on neurons within the hypothalamus to stimulate appetite and feeding behavior. [14]

neurotransmitters Chemical substances, released when a neuron is active, that transmit signals to another neuron, changing that second neuron's activity. [2]

neurotrophins A family of chemicals that promote neuronal growth and survival. [4]

nicotine A chemical compound found in tobacco, acting as an acetylcholine receptor agonist, indirectly enhancing the effects of dopamine in the reward pathway, and thus carrying a high propensity for addiction. [14]

night terrors A non-REM sleep disorder in which the sleeper suddenly experiences an outburst of what appears to be intense fear, sitting up in bed with an expression of panic, often accompanied by screaming or gasping, with a temporary inability to regain consciousness; more common in childhood. [10]

nigrostriatal pathway A projection of dopamine-carrying neurons from the substantia nigra to the striatum. [14]

Nissl staining A method of tissue staining that binds to the RNA in the cell bodies of neurons. [3]

NMDA receptor N-Methyl-D-aspartate receptor, a type of ionotropic glutamate receptor that is important for learning and memory. [9]

nociceptin receptors A type of opioid receptor that is similar to the kappa-opioid receptor. [14]

nociceptors Somatosensory receptors that convey information about pain in response to tissue damage. [6]

nodes of Ranvier Gaps in the myelin sheath that enable ions to cross the neuronal membrane in order to propagate the action potential along the axon. [3]

non-24-hour sleep–wake syndrome A sleep disorder characterized by a circadian rhythm significantly longer or shorter than 24 hours, making it difficult for the person to align her or his sleep–wake cycle to social norms. [10]

nonassociative learning Long-term strengthening or weakening of reflex pathways resulting from repeated exposure to a stimulus; examples include habituation and sensitization. [9]

nondeclarative memories Retained abilities to perform previously learned motor skills or tasks, such as tying a knot or riding a bicycle. Also called *procedural memories.* [1]

non-REM (NREM) sleep A term describing three stages of sleep distinct from REM sleep, each of which has characteristic patterns of EEG activity. [8]

norepinephrine A monoamine neurotransmitter, used throughout the brain to regulate levels of arousal, alertness, and attention. [2]

nucleus (plural, nuclei) Regarding neurons, a collection of neuron cell bodies within the central nervous system, with multiple nuclei typically gathered together to perform similar functions, such as control of a specific motor function or processing of a specific type of sensory information. [2] Regarding cells, a specialized part of the cell that contains the DNA. [3]

nucleus accumbens A region in the ventral part of the basal ganglia, playing an important role in reward, prediction error, and addiction. [2]

ob/ob mice Mice that have a mutation disrupting the gene for the production of leptin, preventing their adipose (fat-storing) tissue from signaling when they are in energy surplus; this results in high appetite, high blood sugar, high insulin, and obesity. [14]

obsessions The unwanted and intrusive thoughts experienced by patients with obsessive–compulsive disorder and some individuals with Tourette syndrome. [16]

obsessive–compulsive disorder (OCD) An anxiety disorder characterized by excessive, intrusive, obsessive thoughts and excessive, repetitive, compulsive behaviors often related to the obsessions. [16]

occipital lobe The posterior lobe of the cerebral cortex, largely devoted to processing visual information. [2]

ocular dominance columns Regions or stripes within the primary visual cortex that receive input from just one eye, alternating with regions that receive input from just the other eye. [4]

oddball paradigm An experimental procedure in which the subject is shown a long sequence of the same repeated stimulus, occasionally interrupted with a novel "oddball" stimulus; used to study mechanisms of "bottom-up," involuntary (exogenous) attention. [8]

olfaction The sense of smell. [6]

olfactory bulb The part of the brain that first receives and processes information about smell. [6]

olfactory epithelium A layer of tissue specialized for the sense of smell, located at the back of the nasal cavity. [6]

olfactory glomerulus The location within the olfactory bulb where all of the axons from olfactory receptor neurons expressing a particular receptor converge. [6]

oligodendrocytes Glial cells that wrap myelin around the axons of neurons in the central nervous system. [3]

operant conditioning A type of learning in which a behavior is made more likely by providing a "reinforcer" (reward) after it occurs, or less likely by administering an aversive stimulus (punishment) after it occurs. [9]

opioid A class of psychoactive molecules that are structurally similar to morphine and related compounds derived from opium poppies; often used to alleviate pain although tolerance, withdrawal, and addiction can result from regular use. [12]

optic chiasm The point at which the left and right optic nerves converge, allowing the information from both the left and the right eye to be recombined so that information from the right visual field reaches the left hemisphere, and vice-versa. [5]

optic nerve The second cranial nerve, containing the axons of the retinal ganglion cells, which converge to leave the eye and convey visual information into the brain. [5]

optic radiations The axons that carry the visual information from the lateral geniculate nucleus of the thalamus to the primary visual cortex. [5]

optic tectum A part of the midbrain that processes visual information, particularly for guiding eye movements; also known as the superior colliculus. [4]

orbitofrontal cortex The underside of the prefrontal cortex, just above the eye sockets (orbits); this region is important for assigning value to stimuli based on comparing their properties to internally and externally specified needs of the organism, and for modulating emotional states. [2]

orexin   A hormone, also known as hypocretin, that promotes wakefulness; a deficit of orexin is thought to cause narcolepsy. [10]

organ of Corti   An organ of the inner ear, important for transducing sound waves into neural signals; includes the tectorial membrane, the basilar membrane, and the inner and outer hair cells. [6]

orienting paradigm   An experimental procedure commonly used to study attention, in which the subject must respond to the appearance of a target stimulus as quickly as possible. Cue stimuli may appear in order to direct the subject's attention toward or away from the target prior to its appearance, thereby affecting the reaction time and providing a behavioral measure of the effects of attention. [8]

orthographic level   The level of representation that captures the physical appearance, spelling, or structure of a word, as opposed to the phonological level, which captures the sounds with which it is spoken. [11]

ossicles   The three bones of the middle ear. [6]

outer hair cells   Hair cells in the cochlea that run parallel to the inner hair cells and can shorten and lengthen to improve the signal received by the inner hair cells, thus acting as "pre-amplifiers" for acoustic sensory input transduced by the inner hair cells. [6]

oval window   The flexible membrane that is part of the inner ear and connected to the eardrum via the ossicles; it vibrates at the same frequency as the auditory stimulus reaching the eardrum. [6]

oxytocin   A hormone released by the pituitary gland that facilitates parental and partner bonding, and promotes some forms of social interaction. [2]

Pacinian corpuscles   A type of rapidly adapting mechanoreceptor located in the deeper layers of the skin and having a relatively large receptive field. [6]

papillae   Clusters of 1–100 taste buds that form the visible bumps on the tongue. [6]

parahippocampal place area   A region within the parahippocampal gyrus that is important for recognizing places, or landmarks, from their visual appearance. [8]

parallel processing   The simultaneous processing of multiple computations at the same time, rather than one after the other; allows for rapid information processing. Commonly used in the perceptual pathways of the brain to identify, locate, or assign value to a stimulus. Parallel processing is harder to apply to cognitive or motor control pathways since the steps of a behavior must often be performed in a particular sequence rather than in parallel with one another. [12]

paraphasia   A symptom of aphasia in which the patient uses an incorrect but related word in place of the intended word. [11]

parasomnias   A class of sleep disorders in which the patient performs complex behaviors while asleep. [10]

parasympathetic nervous system   The branch of the autonomic nervous system that coordinates behaviors and physiological processes associated with rest and regeneration; as opposed to the sympathetic nervous system, which coordinates behaviors and processes for fight-or-flight activities. [2]

paraventricular nucleus   A nucleus within the hypothalamus that provides output to regulate the autonomic nervous system. [13]

parentese   A term describing a particular type of speech used by parents when talking to infants, in which the pace of language is slowed and the transitions between words are exaggerated. [11]

parietal lobe   The region of the cerebral cortex at the upper and posterior side of the brain, whose functions include processing somatosensory information and mapping the locations of visual, auditory, and somatosensory stimuli into coordinates centered on various parts of the body to help guide movements of those body parts. [2]

Parkinsonism   Abnormal movements involving resting tremor, rigidity, difficulty initiating and maintaining movements, and slowing of movements; characteristic of Parkinson's disease. [16]

Parkinson's disease (PD)   A neurological disorder whose symptoms include rigidity and slowing of movements, and in many cases dementia and depression; caused by degeneration of the dopamine-producing cells of the substantia nigra. [7]

parse   To analyze a string of linguistic information by dividing it up into its component parts according to the rules specified by the grammar for that language. [11]

parvocellular retinal ganglion cells   Retinal ganglion cells that get their input primarily from cones and are therefore color sensitive, with high spatial resolution. [5]

PCP   An antagonist of the NMDA glutamate receptors, its effects can mimic both the positive and negative symptoms of schizophrenia in a manner similar to ketamine. [16]

peptide neurotransmitters   Neurotransmitters that are built from short chains of amino acids. [3]

perception   The identification and interpretation of a sensory stimulus by the nervous system. [5]

perceptual rivalry   A phenomenon in which an ambiguous stimulus is presented and can be perceived in more than one possible way (for example, a 2-dimensional drawing of a cube that can be perceived as if viewed from either above or below); the perception does not remain stable, but instead alternates between one possibility and the other. [8]

perceptual theory of mind   A rudimentary form of theory of mind found in some animals; involves interpreting the intentions of others by picking up social cues, such as gaze direction. [15]

periaqueductal gray matter   A gray matter structure in the midbrain, surrounding the cerebral aqueduct; consists of columns of neurons that organize stereotyped forms of basic survival behaviors such as defense, aggression, and reproduction. [2]

peripheral nervous system   The receptors and nerves that are found throughout the body, outside the brain and spinal cord; includes the somatic nervous system and the autonomic nervous system. [2]

perirhinal cortex   A region of the medial temporal lobe that is important for episodic memory and for recognizing objects in the environment. [9]

perseveration   The tendency to repeat an action again and again although it has no benefit or does not achieve its intended purpose; associated with some forms of dementia or frontal lobe injury. [16]

PET   See *positron emission tomography.* [1]

PGO waves (pontogeniculo-occipital waves)   Waves of coordinated neural electrical activity, detectable on EEG, that are generated in the pons and spread to the lateral geniculate nucleus and the occipital lobe; characteristic of REM sleep and dreaming. [10]

phantom limb   A limb that has been amputated or lost, but seems to still convey physical sensations; the perceived sensations may include touch, position, temperature, or pain. [4]

pharmacotherapy   Treatment of an illness with medications; in psychiatric illness, the term may refer to the use of medications such as antidepressants, as opposed to psychotherapy. [16]

phasic   In regard to neural activity, a pattern characterized by bursts of high activity, followed by low activity; tonic activity, in contrast, refers to continuous activity at a stable rate. [8]

pheromones   Chemical messengers emitted by one member of a species to send signals to another member of the species, and to influence the behavior of the other individual; may play a role in sexual or dominance behaviors. [6]

phonemes   Perceptually distinct units of sound that make up spoken words. [4]

phonological level   The level of representation that captures the sounds making up a word, as opposed to the orthographic level, which captures the word's appearance or spelling. [11]

photoreceptors   Light-sensitive cells of the retina. [2]

phototransduction   The process by which light is converted into the electrochemical signals used by the nervous system. [5]

pineal gland   A small structure along the midline of the brain near the thalamus; produces and releases the hormone melatonin. [10]

pinna   The external, folded portion of the ear. [6]

pitch   The perception of a sound's frequency. [6]

Pittsburgh Compound-B   A radioactive tracer molecule that binds specifically to amyloid plaques, enabling them to be seen using PET. [16]

pituitary gland   A projection from the inferior surface of the hypothalamus that is involved in releasing a variety of hormones to regulate the function of the thyroid gland, adrenal glands, kidneys, gonads, and various other organs of the body. [2]

place cells   Neurons in the hippocampus and entorhinal cortex that increase their firing rate when an animal is in a particular location. [9]

place field   The region of the external environment that elicits the activity of a particular place cell when the animal enters the region. [9]

placebo   A compound or procedure with no therapeutic benefits that may be used as a sham or control in order to establish whether the active treatment itself is more effective. [13]

planum temporale   Part of the superior temporal gyrus that is involved in language comprehension; it is typically larger in the left hemisphere than in the right hemisphere. [11]

plasticity   The ability of the brain to change its neural pathways and connections over time because of behavior changes, learning, or memory, or in response to injury or degeneration; allows the brain to develop new functions or to regain functions lost due to injury or illness. [1]

point of indifference   The point at which two alternatives are equally attractive, making an individual equally likely to choose either option. [12]

polyphasic sleep   A pattern of sleep that includes more than one period of sleep during 24 hours. [10]

pons   The part of the brainstem immediately superior to the medulla oblongata and inferior to the midbrain. [2]

pontogeniculo-occipital waves   See *PGO waves.* [10]

population coding   A property of neural representation in which a given stimulus or motor action is represented not by the activity of any single neuron, but by the collective activity of a group of neurons. [3]

position invariance/size invariance   A property of representations in the ventral visual pathway in which the neurons will respond to a particular type of stimulus, regardless of its size or position in the visual field. This property is useful for pathways that must identify an object reliably, regardless of its position or orientation in space. [5]

positive psychology   A branch of psychology that studies how to increase overall happiness and life satisfaction, to complement other branches that focus on the causes and treatment of mental illness. [14]

positive symptoms   Symptoms that are present in patients with schizophrenia that are not usually present in people without the disorder, such as delusions, hallucinations, and disorganized (nonsensical) speech. [16]

positron emission tomography (PET)   A research technique that involves injecting small amounts of radioactive tracer compounds into the body, then mapping where they bind within the brain. A wide variety of tracers can be used to map glucose consumption, the distribution of neurotransmitter receptors, or the presence of proteins or enzymes within the brain. [1]

postcentral gyrus   The region of the cortex immediately posterior to the central sulcus, containing the primary somatosensory cortex. [2]

posterior Anatomical term meaning toward the back; opposite of anterior. [2]

postpartum depression Symptoms resembling those of major depressive disorder that are experienced by some new mothers after giving birth. [15]

poverty of the stimulus The argument that children do not hear a broad enough sample of language to learn grammar purely from experience; often taken as support for an innate universal grammar within the brain. [11]

precentral gyrus The region of cortex immediately in front of the central sulcus, containing the primary motor cortex. [2]

precuneus The medial part of the parietal lobe along the midline of the brain; active during spatial navigation, recollection of the past and future, and mental imagery of scenes or scenarios. [2]

prediction error The difference between the expected and the actual result of a particular behavior. For example, failure to receive an expected sip of juice, after pressing a button that had previously delivered this reward, would carry negative prediction error. [14]

predictive cue A sensory stimulus that accurately predicts a subsequent event; for example, the sound of a bell that reliably predicts the delivery of a sip of juice. [14]

prefrontal cortex The portion of the frontal lobe anterior to the motor cortex of the precentral gyrus; involved in the coordination of complex behavior via stimulus evaluation, goal-setting, cognition, decision making, and motor coordination. [2]

presupplementary motor area A region along the midline of the brain that is anterior to the supplementary motor cortex and is important for the selection of courses of action according to internal cues or motivations, as opposed to external sensory signals. [7]

primary auditory cortex (A1) Located along the transverse temporal gyrus, this region is specialized for receiving and processing auditory information, analogous to the primary visual cortex of the occipital lobe. [2]

primary motor cortex Located in the precentral gyrus; the cells of the primary motor cortex send motor commands to the muscles of the body to direct simple movements. [2]

primary rewards Rewards that have direct survival value, such as food or drink, as opposed to secondary rewards such as money, game points, or praise. [12]

primary somatosensory cortex (S1) Located in the postcentral gyrus; the neurons of the primary somatosensory cortex represent tactile sensations from different parts of the external surface of the body, and are closely connected with corresponding regions of the primary motor cortex in the adjacent precentral gyrus. [2]

primary visual cortex (V1) The region of the occipital lobe of the brain where visual information is first processed to extract low-level visual features such as position, color, orientation, or spatial frequency. [2]

priming A form of implicit memory in which the presentation of a stimulus can exert an unconscious influence on the way the brain processes a subsequently presented stimulus. [9]

prions Incorrectly folded versions of normal proteins that can cause other proteins to misfold and thereby act as infectious agents to spread a disease. Creutzfeldt-Jakob disease and mad cow disease are examples of prion diseases. [9]

procedural memories Implicit memories for how to perform a habit or motor skill. [9]

proprioception The aspect of somatosensation that monitors the position and movement of the parts of one's own body. [6]

prosocial Intended to benefit another individual or a group. [15]

prosody The intonations, stresses, and rhythms of speech, as opposed to its content. [11]

prosopagnosia (face blindness) An inability to recognize faces, which may result from damage to the inferior temporal lobe encompassing the fusiform face area. [5]

prospect theory A model for the inconsistency of human decision making under conditions of uncertainty about the outcome of the decisions; features different-shaped curves for assigning value to gains versus losses, suggesting different systems at play for these two types of valuation. [12]

prospection The faculty of imagining future events or hypothetical scenarios, as opposed to recollection of past events; draws upon similar neural pathways to those involved in recollection. [9]

provoked confabulations Unintentionally distorted or fabricated memories that can arise in people with uninjured brains who are asked to recall details of past events beyond their capacity for accurate recollection. [9]

proximal Anatomical term meaning near a particular structure or closer to the center. [2]

pruning A process in which the brain modifies or optimizes its neural circuitry by removing or withdrawing nonessential axonal connections, dendrites, or entire neurons. [4]

psychopathy A clinical condition characterized by superficial social normality, but in which the individual does not experience emotional empathy; manipulative or callous antisocial behavior may result. [15]

psychosis Symptoms reflecting a deficit in reality-testing, such as hallucinations or delusions; associated with various severe mental illnesses, including schizophrenia and bipolar disorder. [16]

psychotherapy A form of treatment for mental illness that involves empathetic listening, counseling, training in self-regulation of cognition and emotion, behavioral modification, or all of the above. [16]

punishment An aversive stimulus that moves the homeostatic balance further from the set point, can be effective in suppressing occurrences of the behavior that led to the delivery of the punishment. [14]

pupil The opening at the center of the eye that is surrounded by the iris; it allows light to enter the eye and, ultimately, be focused on the retina. [5]

pure autonomic failure A disorder in which the autonomic nervous system degenerates, although the rest of the nervous system remains intact. [13]

Purkinje cells Neurons that form the major output connections from the cerebellum. [2]

putamen Part of the basal ganglia, overlying the globus pallidus and functioning with the caudate nucleus in the regulation of movement, behavior, and cognition. [2]

pyramids The structure in the medulla where the majority of the corticospinal tract crosses to the other side of the body, across the midline of the body. Damage to this region can produce the whole-body paralysis of locked-in syndrome. [7]

quasi-hyperbolic discounting A model of the subjective value of delayed rewards in which the perceived value can be best described using a hyperbolic function, which drops quickly at the beginning, but then flattens out. [12]

radial arm maze A behavioral test of spatial memory ability in rats, in which the rat explores a maze with several straight arms radiating out from a central hub. [9]

rapid-eye-movement (REM) sleep A stage of sleep in which dreams occur and the body is paralyzed, but the eyes exhibit rapid movements; has a characteristic appearance on EEG recordings. [8]

rate coding A system in which neurons encode information about the stimulus by changing the number of action potentials they generate within a short window of time. For example, a mechanoreceptor may use higher firing rates to encode stronger tactile stimuli. [3]

rational choice theory A theory of decision making based on the assumption that people make rational decisions to maximize their own happiness. [12]

rational system (system 2) A postulated system of cognition that provides slow, deliberative, reasoned assessments of options during decision making, usually based on criteria and decision rules that can be described explicitly (for example, deciding which food to eat based on its calorie content); stands in contrast to the intuitive system (system 1). [12]

reaction time benefit Regarding cued attention, the improved (shortened) reaction time displayed by a subject when the visual cue accurately predicts the location of the stimulus in a study of attention. [8]

reaction time cost Regarding cued attention, the worsened (lengthened) reaction time displayed by a subject when the visual cue inaccurately predicts the location of the stimulus in a study of attention. [8]

reactivation A process of revisiting memories while sleeping, thought to be important for long-term encoding and storage. [10]

reappraisal The use of context or other cognitive factors to change the emotional response to a given stimulus;

a well-known example would be thinking of a glass as half-full rather than half-empty. [13]

receptive aphasia A language problem characterized by impairment of the ability to receive and comprehend language. [11]

receptive field The region of the external world to which a sensory neuron is able to respond. Examples might include a spatial location, a part of the body, or a portion of the visual field, depending on the sensory modality. [5]

receptors Proteins embedded in the cell membrane that are specialized to interact with neurotransmitters and exert signaling effects on the cell, via mechanisms such as ion channels or metabolic signaling pathways. [3]

recollection In episodic memories, the ability to represent a specific past event, as well as its surrounding context; contrasts with familiarity, in which the emotional gist may be recalled but not the specific event or its context. [9]

reconsolidation A process by which a previously established, consolidated memory can be made unstable once again, and vulnerable to modification or rewriting, while it is being retrieved or recollected. [9]

recurrence A property of a neural network in which there are feedback connections backwards along stages of the hierarchy of processing as well as feedforward connections going forward along the hierarchy. It is theorized that feedback connections are as common as feedforward connections within the brain. [5]

red nuclei A region within the brainstem that is influential in motor control for locomotion. Its functions are mostly assumed by the corticospinal tract in primates. [7]

reflex An involuntary and automatic motor response to a sensory stimulation. [2]

refractory period The time following the action potential when the voltage-gated ion channels are inactivated and unable to generate another action potential. [3]

reinforcer In operant conditioning, a rewarding stimulus that makes the rewarded behavior more likely to occur in the future. [14]

relapse A re-emergence of the pursuit and use of an addictive substance, after the user had previously stopped using the substance. [14]

relational theory A theory of episodic memory that suggests that the function of the hippocampus is to store the relationships between objects or events. [9]

relative preferences The idea that a person's preference for option A or B is not fixed and unchanging, but can depend on context and even on what other options are available. [12]

REM sleep behavior disorder A sleep disorder in which the muscle paralysis typical of REM sleep is absent and the person is able to act out her or his dream, or to perform other behaviors while asleep. [10]

repetitive transcranial magnetic stimulation (rTMS) A technique for inducing lasting changes in neural activity and synaptic connections by applying a series of powerful, focused magnetic field pulses to a target brain region with a magnetic stimulator applied to the scalp. Used both as a research technique and as a treatment for psychiatric and neurological disorders that are resistant to medications. [1]

replication Reproducing an experiment and obtaining the same results as previously reported; provides confirmatory evidence to support a given hypothesis. [1]

reproduction The biological process of producing new offspring, which carry the genes of their parent organisms; considered an essential function for living organisms in order to avoid extinction. [1]

Rescorla–Wagner model A mathematical model of associative learning that uses prediction error to update representations of the links or associations between observed events. [14]

reserpine A medication once used to treat high blood pressure, acting by depleting monoamines from the synapses; sometimes caused depression as a side effect, and is rarely used today. [16]

restless leg syndrome (RLS) A neurological disorder involving intense, uncomfortable restless feelings in the lower limbs; relieved by stomping, rubbing, walking around, or twitching; often interferes with sleep due to the powerful urges to perform movements. [10]

reticular formation A network of neurons within the midbrain that project to the forebrain and are important for regulating consciousness. [2]

reticular nucleus A thin sheet of inhibitory neurons wrapped around the thalamus; regulates and coordinates the activity of the other nuclei of the thalamus. [2]

retina The region at the back of the eye, containing the light-sensitive cells of the visual system, such as rods and cones. [5]

retinal ganglion cells Retinal neurons that carry information to the lateral geniculate nucleus of the thalamus, on the way to the primary visual cortex. [5]

retinohypothalamic tract A pathway from the retina directly to the hypothalamus that helps the circadian rhythm become entrained to the environmental light–dark cycle. [10]

retinotopic The pattern of organization of the neurons of the visual cortex, in which adjacent parts of the retina are mapped to adjacent parts of the visual cortex. [4]

retrieval The process of recalling information stored in memory. [9]

retrograde amnesia An inability to retrieve episodic memories of events that occurred for a certain period of time immediately preceding a brain injury. [9]

retrograde transmitters Neurotransmitters that transmit signals in the opposite direction of most neurotransmission, i.e., backwards from the postsynaptic cell to the presynaptic cell. [3]

retrosplenial cortex A part of the posterior cingulate cortex that is closely connected to the hippocampus and is important for episodic memory and spatial navigation. Lesions to this area result in retrograde amnesia. [9]

reuptake The process through which neurotransmitters are inactivated by being transported back into the presynaptic neuron, where they can be reused. [3]

reverse hierarchy A system that inverts the typical hierarchy of information filtering upward to ever fewer regions during processing. Instead, the information spreads out to a wider number of areas as it is processed. [5]

reward A motivating stimulus that moves the homeostatic balance closer to the set point, and can be effective in promoting occurrences of the behavior that led to the delivery of the reward. [14]

risk averse A type of decision making in which greater value is assigned to options with more certain outcomes, compared to options with the same overall expected value but less certain outcomes; for example, choosing a $50 reward over a 50% chance of a $100 reward. [12]

risk discounting curve The curve describing how the subjective value of a reward declines as it becomes less probable that the reward will be received. [12]

risk seeking A type of decision making in which greater value is assigned to options with less certain outcomes, compared to options with the same overall expected value but more certain outcome; for example, choosing a 1% chance of a $1000 reward over a $10 reward. [12]

rods Photoreceptors within the eye that are insensitive to color, but are highly responsive to even low levels of light. [5]

rostral Anatomical term meaning toward the mouth; opposite of caudal. [2]

rTMS See *repetitive transcranial magnetic stimulation.* [1]

Ruffini's endings A type of slowly adapting mechanoreceptor located in the deeper layers of the skin and having a relatively large receptive field. [6]

saccades Rapid, directed movements of the eyes from one visual target to another. [7]

Sally–Anne task A behavioral task used to assess theory of mind; determines whether the subject can understand that another individual holds a false belief, when the subject does not share this belief. [15]

saltatory conduction The propagation of an action potential along a myelinated axon, in which the action potential "jumps" along the axon from one node of Ranvier to the next. [3]

satiety A sense of fullness, or the opposite of hunger; regulated in part by cholecystokinin acting on receptors in the hypothalamus. [14]

schematic learning The idea that the brain is predisposed to learn certain types of material in certain environments or under certain conditions; the relationships between the concepts are described as a schema. [9]

schizophrenia A psychiatric disorder characterized by disorganized thought, behavior, and speech, and by the emergence of hallucinations and delusional beliefs; onset is typically in early adulthood, and some symptoms may be relieved with antipsychotic medications, although no cure currently exists. [15]

Schwann cells Glial cells that wrap myelin around the axons of neurons in the peripheral nervous system. [3]

scientific method A set of techniques for systematic empirical investigation of phenomena in the world; involves systematic observation, the formulation of hypotheses to explain observed phenomena, the devising of experiments to test hypotheses, and progressive refinement of knowledge by the disconfirmation of false hypotheses. [1]

second messengers Molecules used by metabotropic receptors as part of the signaling cascade to trigger physiological changes in target processes in the cell; examples of second messengers include intracellular calcium, cyclic AMP, and nitric oxide. [3]

secondary rewards Rewards that do not directly alter homeostatic balance, but that are associated with primary rewards, which directly alter homeostatic balance. Examples include money, game points, or praise, as opposed to primary rewards like food or water. [14]

secondary somatosensory cortex A region within the parietal lobe that integrates somatosensory information and provides more complex processing of that somatosensory information; located within the parietal operculum inside the lateral sulcus. [6]

secondary visual cortex (V2) The second stage of the visual processing hierarchy; cells in this region have slightly larger receptive fields than those in the primary visual cortex. [5]

second-order theory of mind The ability to represent another person's thoughts about the thoughts of a third person, or another person's thoughts about one's own thoughts; "what do you think that I am thinking?" [15]

selective serotonin reuptake inhibitors (SSRIs) A class of medications that prevent serotonin from being transported back into the presynaptic neurons, thus boosting serotonin levels in the synapse; widely used to treat major depression and anxiety disorders. [13]

self-reflection Thinking about one's own thoughts, beliefs, goals, or personal traits. [15]

semantic dementia A form of brain damage in which semantic memory is lost but episodic memory is preserved; often results from lesions of the anterior temporal lobes. [9]

semantic knowledge Knowledge about the meanings of concepts, often represented in terms of their homeostatic properties, such as whether they are edible, drinkable, healthy, poisonous, hostile, friendly, and so on. [15]

semantic memories Memories of facts about the world, as opposed to personal experiences or events; for example, knowing that Paris is the capital of France, without necessarily being able to recall exactly where or when one learned this fact. [9]

semicircular canals The three fluid-filled tubes in the vestibular organ of the inner ear that encode information about head rotation and angular acceleration. [6]

sensation The detection of a sensory stimulus by the nervous system. [5]

sensitive period A period of time during which the brain is better able to learn a skill or ability. [4]

sensitization A form of nonassociative learning in which the response to a particular stimulus is greater following previous exposure to a strong or noxious stimulus. [9]

sensory addition A form of sensory augmentation using an artificial sensory transducer device, which enables the organism to detect and process sensory modalities beyond what is possible with its natural repertoire of sensory systems. [4]

sensory neurons Neurons that are specialized to convey sensory information from the periphery of the body to the central nervous system. [2]

sensory substitution A process by which information from a damaged sensory channel is replaced by information entering via other sensory channels. [4]

sensory transduction The process of transforming a sensory stimulus outside the body into the electrochemical signals used by the neurons of the nervous system. [5]

septum A brain region near the ventral anterior cingulate cortex that is interconnected with the limbic system and involved in reward; stimulation of this region can exert effects similar to natural rewards or addictive substances. [15]

sequential processing A mode of information processing in which one step is completed before the next is begun; sequential processing is required for some types of tasks, such as behavioral control, in which the sequence of operations is important, However, it is slow in comparison to parallel processing. [12]

serotonin A monoamine neurotransmitter, produced by neurons in the raphe nuclei of the brainstem and involved in a variety of functions including the regulation of appetite, sleep, and mood. [2]

set points The target physiological values for bodily systems, such as temperature or energy balance. Homeostasis seeks to maintain the organism's internal environment at these values in order to sustain life. [2]

sham rage A condition in which the stereotyped behaviors of aggression (biting, hissing, hair-raising) are activated either spontaneously or by innocuous stimuli; occurs experimentally in animals when the inhibitory inputs from the cortex are disconnected from the brainstem. [13]

short-term memory A form of temporary memory, storing a limited amount of information for seconds to minutes. Also called *working memory*. [1]

signal-to-noise ratio The ratio of the average magnitude of a signal to the standard deviation of the background noise. In neurons, either an increase in activity during stimulation or a decrease in background activity in the absence of stimulation can improve the signal-to-noise ratio. [8]

simple cells Cells within the primary visual cortex that respond best to lines of light at a particular angle and at a particular location within the receptive field. [5]

simultagnosia An inability to recognize and identify multiple objects in a visual scene; occurs following neurological injury to the region near the junction of the occipital and temporal lobes. [5]

sleep paralysis A sleep disorder involving temporary paralysis of the body while a person is falling asleep or waking up; may result from inappropriately timed activation of the muscle atonia that naturally occurs during REM sleep. [10]

slow-wave sleep (SWS) The deepest stage of NREM sleep; also known as stage 3 or N3 sleep. [10]

social anxiety disorder An anxiety disorder in which patients have severe and disabling fear of social interactions; also known as social phobia. [15]

social emotional cues Nonverbal signals for communication of an individual's emotional state to another person (e.g., facial expressions, gestures, or tone of voice). [15]

social rejection Deliberate exclusion of an individual from a group. [15]

social reputation An idea of the typical behavior or personal characteristics of an individual, held by other individuals in that person's social group. [15]

social semantic knowledge Knowledge of social concepts, such as the accepted conventions or rules of behavior in a society, the obligations and privileges associated with a given social role, or the social behavioral characteristics of a given individual. Regions of the anterior temporal lobes represent social semantic knowledge. [15]

social valuation The evaluation of a given option or action in terms of how it maps onto concepts of social behavior, such as kindness, honor, or selfishness; can be used as a signal to generate social emotions such as gratitude or guilt. [15]

soma (or cell body) The largest part of the neuron, the soma contains the nucleus and most of the specialized organelles of the cell. [3]

somatic marker hypothesis The proposal that emotional states can direct behavior by generating internal bodily reactions, or somatic markers. These can be used as an alternative to external cues to guide decision making, especially under conditions of uncertainty. [13]

somatic markers Internal bodily states, akin to the bodily "feel" of emotional states, that can be generated by the limbic system based on sensory input and behavioral context, and that can be used to guide behavior under conditions of uncertainty. [2]

somatic nervous system The branch of the peripheral nervous system that detects information about the external world and uses it to guide the body's movements via the body's musculature; complements the autonomic nervous system, which guides the activity of the visceral organs in response to signals from the internal environment. [2]

somatic therapy A class of treatments for psychiatric illness that involve stimulating the brain directly, via electrical or magnetic pulses. Examples include electroconvulsive therapy, repetitive transcranial magnetic stimulation, and deep brain stimulation. [16]

somatosensory homunculus A map-like representation of the somatosensory input of the body within the brain; localized to the primary somatosensory cortex along the postcentral gyrus. [7]

somatosensory system A sensory system that processes tactile stimuli such as touch, vibration, pressure, temperature, and pain from all over the body. [6]

somatotopic The organizational structure of the sensory and motor cortices, in which adjacent body parts are mapped to adjacent parts of the cortex; analogous to retinotopic organization of the visual cortex or tonotopic organization of the auditory cortex. [4]

somnambulism Sleepwalking; a sleep disorder typically occurring during NREM sleep. [10]

sparse coding A proposed method for encoding visual information in which only a few neurons out of the local population are involved in representing any particular stimulus. [5]

spatial cognitive maps Representations of the surrounding environment or territory that are indexed in the hippocampus and are useful for spatial navigation. [9]

spatial summation The idea that EPSPs and IPSPs that occur at different locations along the cell's membrane at approximately the same time can combine to change the cell's membrane potential. [3]

speech The vocal form of human communication through language, involving the production and comprehension of sequences of phonemes comprising words and sentences to convey concepts and ideas. [11]

spike See *action potential (nerve impulse or spike)*. [3]

spinal cord The portion of the central nervous system that extends from below the medulla through the spine, protected by the bones of the vertebral column. [2]

spinal reflex A simple, automatic movement in response to a particular stimulus that is controlled at the level of the spinal cord and can proceed without intervention from the brain. [7]

split-brain patients Patients who have undergone surgery to sever the connections across the corpus callosum so that the two hemispheres of the brain cannot communicate through this major pathway. [11]

spontaneous confabulations Unintentionally distorted, fabricated, or inappropriate recollections that arise without external cues in individuals with injury to certain limbic structures regulating the hippocampus. [9]

stapes One of the three bones of the middle ear; also known as the stirrup. [6]

state of consciousness Degree of awareness of and responsiveness to external stimuli. Examples include wakefulness, sleep, and coma. [8]

statistical learning The way infants are thought to learn language by attending to the relative frequency of different combinations of sounds. [11]

stellate cells Inhibitory interneurons of the cerebellum that influence the dendrites of Purkinje cells. [7]

stem cells Cells that have not yet differentiated into a specific cell type, and that are capable of giving rise to daughter cells that will differentiate into various types of cells; may be restricted to producing certain classes of cells (i.e., neural stem cells), or may be pluripotent, capable of giving rise to any kind of cell. [2]

stereoscope A device that enables the viewer to perceive a three-dimensional scene when viewing two images differing slightly in perspective. [8]

stimulation evidence Information about the function of a brain region or pathway that is gained from directly stimulating the neurons in that region and observing the resulting behaviors. [9]

stress A physiological state in response to perceived external challenges to survival; the response involves increased activity in the sympathetic branch of the autonomic nervous system, an endocrine response, and behavioral responses coordinated by the brain. [12]

stretch reflex The automatic contraction of a muscle that has been stretched, to help maintain a constant length and avoid injury. [2]

striate cortex Another name for the primary visual cortex. [5]

stroke An injury to the blood supply of the brain, which interrupts circulation and results in damage to the brain tissue from inadequate supplies of oxygen. Subtypes include ischemic stroke (from a blocked blood supply to an area of the brain) and hemorrhagic stroke (from a broken vessel that results in bleeding in the brain). [1]

Stroop effect The observation that individuals are able to name colors more rapidly if the printed color name matches the color of ink than if color name is printed using a color of ink that does not match the printed name. [13]

subfornical organ A part of the hypothalamus that detects the chemical composition of the blood, via a "window" of permeability in the blood-brain barrier. [14]

subgenual cingulate cortex A part of the ventral anterior cingulate cortex; observed to be overactive in major depression and to revert to normal levels of activity with successful treatment of depression. [16]

subjective value The value of an option to a given individual in a particular context; may be measured by examining the individual's choices when offered various competing options. [12]

substantia nigra A collection of cells within the midbrain that is important for movement, cognition, and rewarded behaviors. [2]

substantia nigra pars compacta The portion of the substantia nigra containing dopamine-rich cells that project to the striatum. These cells are lost in Parkinson's disease. [14]

subthalamic nucleus A small nucleus located inferior to the thalamus, connecting to the indirect pathway in the basal ganglia, and playing an inhibitory role in controlling voluntary movement and behavior. [2]

suggestibility The idea that false memories can be created in people's brains by providing a fictitious suggestion about a past experience and then encouraging the person to elaborate upon the false memory by trying to imagine or recall it in detail. [9]

sulci (singular, sulcus) Grooves between the convolutions (or gyri) of the cortex. [2]

superior Anatomical term meaning toward the top; opposite of inferior. [2]

superior colliculus A paired structure located on the posterior side of the midbrain, above the inferior colliculus; important for processing visual inputs and directing automatic eye movements. [2]

superior temporal gyrus The most superior gyrus of the temporal lobe, adjacent to the lateral sulcus. [2]

superior temporal sulcus (STS) A region of the temporal lobe, containing neurons that are important for perceiving social cues in visual and auditory stimuli. [7]

supplementary motor area A region along the midline of the brain, anterior to the primary motor cortex, that is involved in planning and coordinating internally guided movements. [7]

suprachiasmatic nucleus (SCN) A region of the hypothalamus in which cells maintain their own 24-hour rhythm of activity, and serve as a master clock for the body's circadian rhythms. [10]

surface dyslexia A subtype of dyslexia in which patients have trouble understanding words at the orthographic level (the level of spelling). [11]

sympathetic nervous system The branch of the autonomic nervous system that is involved in coordinating the activities of the body's organs for fight-or-flight responses. [2]

sympathy Consciously sharing the emotional state of another person. [15]

synapse A structure that serves as a point of connection and communication between one neuron and another; includes the presynaptic cell membrane, the synaptic cleft between the two neurons, and the postsynaptic cell membrane. [2]

synaptic cleft The space between the pre- and postsynaptic neurons across which the neurotransmitters diffuse. [3]

synaptic vesicles Membrane-bound sacs of neurotransmitters stored in the presynaptic terminal of the axon. [3]

synchronization The simultaneous activity of neurons in two different regions of the brain. [8]

synesthesia A perceptual condition of mixed sensations, in which a stimulus in one sensory modality (e.g., vision) involuntarily elicits a sensation or experience in another sensory modality (e.g., hearing). [6]

tardive dyskinesia A side effect of long-term use of antipsychotic medications, condition characterized by repetitive and involuntary movements of the tongue, face, and body. [16]

taste buds Sensory structures containing receptors for taste, usually located on or near papillae within the oral cavity; each bud contains a cluster of 50–150 taste cells. [6]

tau protein A protein that stabilizes the microtubules to support the structure of neurons. When disrupted, it can form the neurofibrillary tangles seen in Alzheimer's dementia. [16]

tDCS See *transcranial direct current stimulation.* [1]

tectorial membrane The flexible membrane above the basilar membrane of the inner ear, into which the tops of the inner and outer hair cells connect. [6]

tectum The more posterior portion of the midbrain, containing the superior and inferior colliculi. [7]

telencephalon The anteriormost section of the vertebrate nervous system, rostral to the diencephalon; includes the gray and white matter of the cortex as well as the basal ganglia, hippocampus, and amygdala. [2]

temporal difference learning model A model of learning that takes into consideration not only the size, but also the timing of the prediction error signal, so that it can respond to rewards that are earlier or later than expected, as well as rewards that are larger or smaller than expected. [14]

temporal lobe The inferiormost lobe of the cerebral cortex, below the lateral sulcus; functions include identification of visual and auditory stimuli, some aspects of language processing, social cue perception, and functions related to the hippocampus such as episodic memory recall and spatial navigation. [2]

temporal summation The process by which EPSPs and IPSPs that occur at slightly different times can combine to change the cell's membrane potential. [3]

temporoparietal junction The region on the lateral surface of the brain where the temporal and parietal lobes connect; a common site of damage in the neurological syndrome of hemineglect. [8]

tertiary visual cortex Regions, including V3, V4, and V5, that are involved in processing more complex aspects of visual stimuli. [5]

testosterone A specific male sex hormone; an androgen. [13]

tetrahydrocannabinol One of the psychoactive compounds in cannabis; this molecule stimulates the cannabinoid receptors in the brain. [12]

thalamocortical cells Cells that connect the thalamus to the cortex and play an important role in relaying and synchronizing information flow among regions of the cortex; thought to be important for maintaining the conscious, waking state. [10]

thalamus Part of the diencephalon containing numerous nuclei, each serving a different region of the cortex. Some nuclei act as relays for incoming sensory information, while others synchronize activity within and among different cortical areas so that they can work in a coordinated fashion. [2]

theory of mind The capacity to attribute mental states to other individuals; to understand that they have beliefs, intentions, thoughts, and desires that may differ from one's own. [7]

theory-of-mind network A network of brain areas involved in representing the beliefs and intentions of others. [15]

thermoreceptors Somatosensory receptors that convey information about temperature. [6]

theta waves Brain waves with a frequency of 4–7 Hz, sometimes associated with meditation and drowsiness, and also associated with changes in synaptic plasticity in the hippocampus. [10]

thought disorder A pattern of disorganized thought that is a feature of some psychiatric disorders such as schizophrenia or bipolar disorder. Abnormalities may include loose associations between ideas, a loss of the logical flow of one idea to the next, tangential veering away from the initial topic of thought, perseveration on a particular theme, or blocking of thoughts. [16]

threshold (action potential) The membrane potential at which a neuron will generate an action potential, typically, this is about -60 mV. [3]

thyroid-stimulating hormone A hormone released by the anterior pituitary gland that regulates the release of thyroid hormones, which in turn control metabolic rates throughout the body. [13]

tinnitus A persistent auditory ringing noise that is perceived even in the absence of an actual auditory stimulus; this "ringing in the ears" may result from damage to auditory sensory structures or nerves, or from distressed emotional states. [4]

TMS See *transcranial magnetic stimulation*. [1]

tolerance The necessity for ever-larger doses of a drug to achieve the same effects; commonly observed with drugs of addiction, such as opiates or stimulants. [14]

tonic A continuous, unchanging pattern of neuronal firing. [8]

tonotopic The organizational structure of the auditory cortex, in which neurons are arranged according to the frequency they represent. Low frequencies are mapped to one part of the auditory cortex and progressively higher frequencies are mapped to adjacent regions of the auditory cortex. [4]

top-down mechanism Regarding attention, a mechanism by which the focus of attention is directed voluntarily to a particular feature of the environment, selected based on the current context and behavior of the individual; contrasts with bottom-up mechanisms, in which the focus of attention is drawn involuntarily by an externally occurring stimulus. [8]

top-down theory A theory of emotion in which the emotional state is determined by the brain depending on the context and situation. The brain then drives the physiological state of the body that produces the physical reactions accompanying the emotion; as opposed to bottom-up theories of emotion. [13]

Tourette syndrome A disorder in which the patient experiences involuntary urges to perform purposeless movements or vocalizations, known as tics. [15]

tracer A chemical substance that is injected into a neuron and can move to adjacent neurons, enabling neuroscientists to map the circuits and connection pathways of the nervous system. [1]

tracts Discrete collections or bundles of axons that connect specific structures or regions of the nervous system to one another. [1]

transcranial direct current stimulation (tDCS) A method of noninvasive brain stimulation that applies very mild electrical currents to the brain using scalp electrodes; these currents can induce lasting changes in the activity of the neurons near the electrodes; used widely as a research technique, and beginning to enter use as an experimental treatment for some psychiatric and neurological disorders. [1]

transcranial magnetic stimulation (TMS) A method of noninvasive brain stimulation that applies brief, powerful, focused magnetic field pulses to a target region of the brain using an external magnetic coil placed against the scalp. Can be used to generate action potentials and is powerful enough to elicit muscle contractions; when repeated series of pulses are applied for research or therapeutic purposes, known as repetitive transcranial magnetic stimulation. [1]

transporters Proteins that move neurotransmitter molecules from the synapse across the cell membrane and back into the axon terminal as part of the reuptake process. [3]

traumatic brain injuries Brain injuries resulting from physical force to the head or brain tissue, such as those sustained during a violent altercation or a motor vehicle accident. [1]

tricyclic antidepressants (TCAs) A type of antidepressant medication that works by preventing the reuptake (inactivation) of serotonin and norepinephrine; used widely in the mid-to-late twentieth century but less commonly today in favor of newer antidepressants such as selective serotonin reuptake inhibitors (SSRIs). [16]

trust game A behavioral task that allows two individuals (playing the roles of an investor and a trustee) to cooperate to earn monetary rewards, yet also allows one to betray the other for personal financial gain. The amount of money entrusted to the trustee by the investor in each round of the game serves as a way of measuring trust and reputation during social interaction. [15]

tryptophan An amino acid obtained from the diet that is converted into serotonin in the body. [12]

tuberomammillary nucleus A region of the hypothalamus that is the major site of histamine-containing neurons in the brain. These neurons project widely throughout the central nervous system and play a key role in arousal and wakefulness. [10]

tumor An abnormal growth or swelling within a tissue of the body. Cancerous growths are often referred to simply as tumors, although a tumor may have causes other than cancer. [1]

two-factor theory A theory of emotion that combines both bottom-up and top-down factors, so that emotional states arise from a synthesis of the bodily physiological reactions or "feelings" detected by the brain, and the cognitive context under which the brain interprets those sensations. [13]

tympanic membrane The innermost portion of the outer ear, which vibrates at the same frequency as the sound wave; also known as the eardrum. [6]

type I fibers Muscle fibers that are adapted for endurance rather than speed. [7]

type II fibers Muscle fibers that are adapted for speed rather than endurance. [7]

Ultimatum Game A two-player cooperation game in which one subject must propose how to divide a sum of money with another player, who then decides either to accept or to reject the offer, in which case both players receive nothing. [12]

Ulysses contract A method for overcoming impulsive or counterproductive decision making, in which a person makes prior arrangements for someone else to prevent them from reneging on a previously declared decision. [12]

umami A taste category corresponding to "savory" or "meaty," sometimes described as a "fifth taste." [6]

unconditioned response In classical conditioning, the normal biological response to an unconditioned stimulus, occurring even without training. [9]

unconditioned stimulus In classical conditioning, the stimulus that naturally elicits an unconditioned response, even without training. [9]

unipolar depression Another term for major depressive disorder, to distinguish it from the episodes of depression that are seen in bipolar disorder. [16]

universal grammar The idea that humans are born with an innate set of grammatical rules for language. [11]

upper motor neurons The neurons that project from the primary motor cortex to the lower motor neurons in the spinal cord to control simple movements or muscle contractions. [7]

Urbach–Wiethe disease A rare recessive genetic disorder that can cause degeneration of the amygdala. Patients with this disorder may lose the ability to experience fear. [13]

utilitarianism A moral philosophy in which one should choose one's actions based on what would bring the greatest happiness to the greatest number of people; may therefore condone an action that causes harm to someone, if the harm is outweighed by the benefits to other people. [12]

utility The desirability or value of a particular action; may incorporate the probability of a gain as well as the magnitude of the gain associated with a given action. [12]

varenicline A medication that is used to help individuals quit smoking tobacco, by acting as a partial agonist at nicotinic receptors and thereby preventing nicotine withdrawal. [14]

vasopressin A peptide neurotransmitter that plays an important role in social interactions, among several other physiological functions. [15]

vegetative state A state of reduced consciousness following neurological injury. Patients lose responsiveness and awareness of their surroundings, but they continue to exhibit a sleep–wake cycle. [8]

ventral Anatomical term meaning toward the bottom or underside; generally contrasted with dorsal. [2]

ventral horns   Regions of gray matter in the ventral part of the central spinal cord, containing mostly motor neurons. [2]

ventral posterior nucleus (VPN)   The nucleus within the thalamus that receives and processes the ascending somatosensory information, relaying this information to the primary somatosensory cortex. [6]

ventral stream   A pathway within the visual system from the visual cortex to the inferior temporal area that specializes in determining the identity of an object, as opposed to its location in space. [5]

ventral tegmental area (VTA)   One of two midbrain structures that has a large concentration of dopamine-containing neurons. These neurons project to the telencephalon and are involved in the brain's reward pathway. [14]

ventricles   Fluid-filled cavities within the brain, containing cerebrospinal fluid. [2]

ventrolateral preoptic nucleus (VLPO)   A region of the hypothalamus that promotes sleep by inhibiting the arousal network of the brain. [10]

ventromedial hypothalamus   A region of the hypothalamus that is involved with regulating satiety. Lesions here lead to excessive food consumption. [13]

ventromedial prefrontal cortex (VMPFC)   A region of the prefrontal cortex that regulates the function of the amygdala and other limbic structures; considered to be important for generating somatic markers, and is active during emotion regulation, evaluation, and decision making under conditions of uncertainty. [12]

vestibular nuclei   Cells within the brainstem that use inputs from the vestibular system to guide the balance of the head, neck, and trunk. [7]

vestibular system   The system of semicircular canals and otolith organs in the inner ear that provides information about head movements, acceleration, and balance. [6]

vestibulo-ocular reflexes   Reflexes that use input from the vestibular system to drive eye movement in the opposite direction of head movement, allowing the eyes to maintain a steady viewpoint, regardless of head motion or vibration. [6]

visual agnosia   A neurological syndrome in which a person is unable to recognize or identify visual stimuli despite having intact visual acuity; may result from injury to the occipital or temporal lobes. [13]

voltage-gated ion channels   Ion channels that change from a closed to an open state when the membrane potential reaches a certain value. These types of channels play an important role in triggering and propagating action potentials along the axon. [3]

voltammetry   A method for measuring the concentration of neurotransmitters in a given structure of the brain, by implanting an electrode in the structure, applying a varying electrical potential to the electrode, and then measuring small fluctuations in the current as the potential is varied. The fluctuations can be used to calculate neurotransmitter concentrations. [1]

voluntary (endogenous) attention   A form of top-down attention in which the individual voluntarily directs attention toward a particular feature of the environment, based on the current behavioral context and goals. [8]

vomeronasal organ   A structure within the nasal passages that is specialized for detecting pheromones rather than odors. [6]

voxel-based morphometry   A method for measuring the volume, thickness, or shape of gray matter structures in the brain by computerized analysis of high-resolution structural MRI scans. This method can locate brain regions showing statistically significant differences in gray matter structure between different groups of individuals, such as patients with a brain disorder versus healthy controls. [1]

Wada test   A diagnostic test to determine which hemisphere is dominant for language by injecting a short-acting anesthetic into one hemisphere at a time, while having the patient try to perform language tasks such as object-naming. [11]

wanting   In some theories of reward, "wanting" refers informally to a desire to obtain a reward, based on a prediction that it will achieve a feeling of well-being or satisfaction, described informally as "liking." The prediction of "liking" may or may not prove to be accurate when the reward is actually delivered. [14]

Weber's law   An experimental observation that the just-noticeable difference between two stimuli consistently occurs in relative terms, as a percentage of the initial stimulus, rather than in absolute terms, as a fixed difference in intensity between the two stimuli. [6]

Wernicke–Geschwind model   A model of language comprehension and production that involves Wernicke's area, the arcuate fasciculus, and Broca's area. [11]

Wernicke's aphasia   A loss of language comprehension, with the preserved ability to produce fluent but nonmeaningful speech; often occurs following neurological injury in or near Wernicke's area in the left superior temporal gyrus. [11]

Wernicke's area   An area in the medial and posterior portion of the left superior temporal gyrus that is important for language comprehension. [11]

white matter   Tissue in the central nervous system consisting of the myelinated axons of neurons, which carry information over long distances; contrasted with gray matter, which consists of the cell bodies and dendrites of neurons. [2]

Williams syndrome   A genetic disorder that can cause learning disabilities or mental retardation, but with relative preservation of social functioning and language abilities. [11]

Wisconsin card-sorting task   A test of cognition in which subjects must learn rules for sorting cards based on shape, color, or number. The rules change periodically, and the subjects must learn the new rules by experience, based solely on feedback about whether each response is correct or incorrect. [7]

withdrawal   A symptom of addiction, in which the individual experiences unpleasant physiological and emotional effects when attempting to reduce intake of the addictive substance. [14]

word blindness   See *alexia (word blindness)*. [11]

word salad   A symptom in which the patient produces a nonsensical string of words or language sounds; may be seen in Wernicke's aphasia, as well as in some severe psychiatric disorders, such as schizophrenia. [11]

working memory   A form of short-term memory that maintains information in mind while it is being used to perform a task. This system is limited in capacity, and the contents are rapidly lost when attention shifts elsewhere. [9]

zeitgebers   External environmental cues that help align the circadian rhythm with the 24-hour cycle of light and dark; German for "time givers." [10]

Chapter 1

Adam, K. (1980). Sleep as a restorative process and a theory to explain why. *Progress in Brain Research, 53,* 289–305.

Ariely, D. (2009). *Predictably irrational: The hidden forces that shape our decisions* (revised and expanded ed.). New York, NY: HarperCollins.

Ariely, D., Loewenstein, G., & Prelec, D. (2006). Tom Sawyer and the construction of value. *Journal of Economic Behavior & Organization, 60*(1), 1–10.

Barnes, J. H. (1984). Cognitive biases and their impact on strategic planning. *Strategic Management Journal, 5*(2), 129–137.

Barrett, D. (1993). The "committee of sleep": A study of dream incubation for problem solving. *Dreaming, 3*(2), 115.

Becchio, C., Manera, V., Sartori, L., Cavallo, A., & Castiello, U. (2012). Grasping intentions: From thought experiments to empirical evidence. *Frontiers in Human Neuroscience, 6,* 117.

Birmingham, L., Mason, D., & Grubin, D. (1996). Prevalence of mental disorder in remand prisoners: Consecutive case study. *BMJ: British Medical Journal, 313*(7071), 1521.

Bliss, T. V., & Collingridge, G. L. (1993). A synaptic model of memory: Long-term potentiation in the hippocampus. *Nature, 361*(6407), 31–39.

Broca, P. (1861). New observations of aphemia produced by a lesion of the posterior half of the second and third frontal convolutions. *Bulletins de la Société Anatomique de Paris, 6,* 398–407.

Brown, B. B. (1970). Recognition of aspects of consciousness through association with EEG alpha activity represented by a light signal. *Psychophysiology, 6*(4), 442–452.

Buxhoeveden, D., Lefkowitz, W., Loats, P., & Armstrong, E. (1996). The linear organization of cell columns in human and nonhuman anthropoid Tpt cortex. *Anatomy and Embryology, 194*(1), 23–36.

Chance, J. E., & Goldstein, A. G. (1996). The other-race effect and eyewitness identification. In S. L. Sporer, R. Malpass, & G. Koehnken (Eds.), *Psychological issues in eyewitness identification* (pp. 153–176). Mahwah, NJ: Erlbaum.

De Haën, C. (2001). Conception of the first magnetic resonance imaging contrast agents: A brief history. *Topics in Magnetic Resonance Imaging, 12*(4), 221–230.

Dony, R. D., & Haykin, S. (1995). Neural network approaches to image compression. *Proceedings of the IEEE, 83*(2), 288–303.

Dowling, J. (2008). Current and future prospects for optoelectronic retinal prostheses. *Eye, 23*(10), 1999–2005.

Downar, J., Bhatt, M., & Montague, P. R. (2011). Neural correlates of effective learning in experienced medical decision-makers. *PloS One, 6*(11), e27768.

Eagleman, D. M. (2011). *Incognito: The secret lives of the brain.* New York, NY: Pantheon.

Eagleman, D. M., Correro, M. A., & Singh, J. (2010). Why neuroscience matters for a rational drug policy. *Minnesota Journal of Law, Science and Technology, 11*(1), 7–26.

Eakin, D. K., Schreiber, T. A., & Sergent-Marshall, S. (2003). Misinformation effects in eyewitness memory: The presence and absence of memory impairment as a function of warning and misinformation accessibility. *Journal of Experimental Psychology: Learning, Memory, and Cognition, 29*(5), 813.

Ekman, P., & Friesen, W. V. (1971). Constants across cultures in the face and emotion. *Journal of Personality and Social Psychology, 17*(2), 124.

Elliott, R., Agnew, Z., & Deakin, J. (2008). Medial orbitofrontal cortex codes relative rather than absolute value of financial rewards in humans. *European Journal of Neuroscience, 27*(9), 2213–2218.

Eriksson, P. S., Perfilieva, E., Björk-Eriksson, T., Alborn, A.-M., Nordborg, C., Peterson, D. A., & Gage, F. H. (1998). Neurogenesis in the adult human hippocampus. *Nature Medicine, 4*(11), 1313–1317.

Fellows, L. K., & Farah, M. J. (2007). The role of ventromedial prefrontal cortex in decision making: Judgment under uncertainty or judgment per se? *Cerebral Cortex, 17*(11), 2669–2674.

Fregni, F., Boggio, P., Nitsche, M., & Pascual-Leone, A. (2005). Transcranial direct current stimulation. *The British Journal of Psychiatry, 186*(5), 446–447.

Golden, R. M. (1996). *Mathematical methods for neural network analysis and design.* Cambridge, MA: MIT Press.

Goley, P. D. (1999). Behavioral aspects of sleep in Pacific white-sided dolphins (*Lagenorhynchus obliquidens*, Gill 1865) 1. *Marine Mammal Science, 15*(4), 1054–1064.

Gonzalez, O., Berry, J., McKnight-Eily, L., Strine, T., Edwards, V., Lu, H., & Croft, J. (2010). Current depression among adults: United States, 2006 and 2008. *Morbidity and Mortality Weekly Review, 59,* 1229–1235.

Gosling, S. D., & John, O. P. (1999). Personality dimensions in nonhuman animals: A cross-species review. *Current Directions in Psychological Science, 8*(3), 69–75.

Greenberg, B. D., Malone, D. A., Friehs, G. M., Rezai, A. R., Kubu, C. S., Malloy, P. F., ... Rasmussen, S. A. (2006). Three-year outcomes in deep brain stimulation for highly resistant obsessive–compulsive disorder. *Neuropsychopharmacology, 31*(11), 2384–2393.

Haselton, M. G., & Nettle, D. (2006). The paranoid optimist: An integrative evolutionary model of cognitive biases. *Personality and Social Psychology Review, 10*(1), 47–66.

Herrmann, C. S. (2001). Human EEG responses to 1–100 Hz flicker: Resonance phenomena in visual cortex and their potential correlation to cognitive phenomena. *Experimental Brain Research, 137*(3–4), 346–353.

Hitzig, E. (1900). Hughlings Jackson and the cortical motor centres in the light of physiological research: Being the second Hughlings Jackson lecture delivered before the Neurological Society of London. *British Medical Journal, 2*(2083), 1564.

Iáñez, E., Azorín, J. M., Úbeda, A., Ferrández, J. M., & Fernández, E. (2010). Mental tasks-based brain–robot interface. *Robotics and Autonomous Systems, 58*(12), 1238–1245.

Johnson, S., Morgan, D., & Finch, C. (1986). Extensive postmortem stability of RNA from rat and human brain. *Journal of Neuroscience Research, 16*(1), 267–280.

Kepler, J. (1604/2004). *Harmonies of the world.* Philadelphia, PA: Running Press.

Kovács, I., Papathomas, T. V., Yang, M., & Fehér, Á. (1996). When the brain changes its mind: Interocular grouping during binocular rivalry. *Proceedings of the National Academy of Sciences, 93*(26), 15508–15511.

Kramer, T. H., Buckhout, R., & Eugenio, P. (1990). Weapon focus, arousal, and eyewitness memory. *Law and Human Behavior, 14*(2), 167–184.

Lakoff, G. (2012). Explaining embodied cognition results. *Topics in Cognitive Science, 4*(4), 773–785.

Lassen, N. A. (1974). Control of cerebral circulation in health and disease. *Circulation Research, 34*(6), 749–760.

Laxton, A. W., Tang-Wai, D. F., McAndrews, M. P., Zumsteg, D., Wennberg, R., Keren, R., . . . Smith, G. S. (2010). A phase I trial of deep brain stimulation of memory circuits in Alzheimer's disease. *Annals of Neurology, 68*(4), 521–534.

Lehéricy, S., Duffau, H., Cornu, P., Capelle, L., Pidoux, B., Carpentier, A., . . . Bitar, A. (2000). Correspondence between functional magnetic resonance imaging somatotopy and individual brain anatomy of the central region: Comparison with intraoperative stimulation in patients with brain tumors. *Journal of Neurosurgery, 92*(4), 589–598.

Letcher, F. S., & Goldring, S. (1968). The effect of radiofrequency current and heat on peripheral nerve action potential in the cat. *Journal of Neurosurgery, 29*(1), 42–47.

Levy, J., & Trevarthen, C. (1976). Metacontrol of hemispheric function in human split-brain patients. *Journal of Experimental Psychology: Human Perception and Performance, 2*(3), 299.

Levy, J., & Trevarthen, C. (1977). Perceptual, semantic and phonetic aspects of elementary language processes in split-brain patients. *Brain: A Journal of Neurology, 100*, 105.

Mayberg, H. S., Lozano, A. M., Voon, V., McNeely, H. E., Seminowicz, D., Hamani, C., . . . Kennedy, S. H. (2005). Deep brain stimulation for treatment-resistant depression. *Neuron, 45*(5), 651–660.

Mineka, S., & Sutton, S. K. (1992). Cognitive biases and the emotional disorders. *Psychological Science, 3*(1), 65–69.

Mira, J., & Paredes, Á. (2005). Interlinguistic similarity and language death dynamics. *EPL (Europhysics Letters), 69*(6), 1031.

Murray, C. J., & Lopez, A. D. (1997). Alternative projections of mortality and disability by cause 1990–2020: Global Burden of Disease Study. *The Lancet, 349*(9064), 1498–1504.

Narayanan, S. (2003). The role of cortico–basal–thalamic loops in cognition: A computational model and preliminary results. *Neurocomputing, 52*, 605–614.

Naselaris, T., Kay, K. N., Nishimoto, S., & Gallant, J. L. (2011). Encoding and decoding in fMRI. *Neuroimage, 56*(2), 400–410.

Nash, J. M. (1997). Fertile minds. *Time, 149*(5), 49–56.

Neff, J. A. (1987). Major initiatives for optical computing. *Optical Engineering, 26*(1), 260102–260109.

Nitsche, M. A., & Paulus, W. (2000). Excitability changes induced in the human motor cortex by weak transcranial direct current stimulation. *The Journal of Physiology, 527*(3), 633–639.

Nitsche, M. A., Cohen, L. G., Wassermann, E. M., Priori, A., Lang, N., Antal, A., . . . Fregni, F. (2008). Transcranial direct current stimulation: State of the art 2008. *Brain Stimulation, 1*(3), 206–223.

Penfield, W., & Erickson, T. C. (1941). *Epilepsy and cerebral localization*. Oxford, UK: Charles C. Thomas.

Pérez-Cañellas, M., & García-Verdugo, J. (1996). Adult neurogenesis in the telencephalon of a lizard: A [³H]thymidine autoradiographic and bromodeoxyuridine immunocytochemical study. *Developmental Brain Research, 93*(1), 49–61.

Ragnehed, M. (2009). *Functional magnetic resonance imaging for clinical diagnosis: Exploring and improving the examination chain* (Doctoral dissertation). Umeå University, Umeå, Sweden.

Rechtschaffen, A., & Bergmann, B. M. (1995). Sleep deprivation in the rat by the disk-over-water method. *Behavioural Brain Research, 69*(1), 55–63.

Sara, S. J. (2000). Retrieval and reconsolidation: Toward a neurobiology of remembering. *Learning & Memory, 7*(2), 73–84.

Schmitt, F. O. (1966). Molecular and ultrastructural correlates of function in neurons, neuronal nets, and the brain. *Naturwissenschaften, 53*(3), 71–79.

Singer, W., & Gray, C. M. (1995). Visual feature integration and the temporal correlation hypothesis. *Annual Review of Neuroscience, 18*(1), 555–586.

Stein, N. L., & Trabasso, T. (1992). The organisation of emotional experience: Creating links among emotion, thinking, language, and intentional action. *Cognition & Emotion, 6*(3–4), 225–244.

Suner, S., Fellows, M. R., Vargas-Irwin, C., Nakata, G. K., & Donoghue, J. P. (2005). Reliability of signals from a chronically implanted, silicon-based electrode array in non-human primate primary motor cortex. *IEEE Transactions on Neural Systems and Rehabilitation Engineering, 13*(4), 524–541.

Treisman, A. (1996). The binding problem. *Current Opinion in Neurobiology, 6*(2), 171–178.

Walker, M. P., & Stickgold, R. (2004). Sleep-dependent learning and memory consolidation. *Neuron, 44*(1), 121–133.

Wang, J. Y., & Zhang, H. (2001). *Apparatus and a method for automatically detecting and reducing red-eye in a digital image: Google Patents*. Retrieved from http://www.google.sc/patents/US6278491

Wang, P. S., Lane, M., Olfson, M., Pincus, H. A., Wells, K. B., & Kessler, R. C. (2005). Twelve-month use of mental health services in the United States: Results from the National Comorbidity Survey Replication. *Archives of General Psychiatry, 62*(6), 629.

Wells, G. L., Malpass, R. S., Lindsay, R., Fisher, R. P., Turtle, J. W., & Fulero, S. M. (2000). From the lab to the police station: A successful application of eyewitness research. *American Psychologist, 55*(6), 581.

Wells, G. L., Small, M., Penrod, S., Malpass, R. S., Fulero, S. M., & Brimacombe, C. E. (1998). Eyewitness identification procedures: Recommendations for lineups and photospreads. *Law and Human Behavior, 22*(6), 603.

Whitlock, J. R., Heynen, A. J., Shuler, M. G., & Bear, M. F. (2006). Learning induces long-term potentiation in the hippocampus. *Science, 313*(5790), 1093–1097.

Winkielman, P., & Berridge, K. C. (2004). Unconscious emotion. *Current Directions in Psychological Science, 13*(3), 120–123.

Woolf, C. J., & Salter, M. W. (2000). Neuronal plasticity: Increasing the gain in pain. *Science, 288*(5472), 1765–1768.

Young, R. L. (1981). Supreme Court Report. *ABAJ, 67*, 340.

Chapter 2

Barlow, S. M. (2009). Central pattern generation involved in oral and respiratory control for feeding in the term infant. *Current Opinion in Otolaryngology & Head and Neck Surgery, 17*(3), 187–193.

Bartlett, E. L., & Wang, X. (2011). Correlation of neural response properties with auditory thalamus subdivisions in the awake marmoset. *Journal of Neurophysiology, 105*(6), 2647–2667.

Benarroch, E. E. (2008). The midline and intralaminar thalamic nuclei: Anatomic and functional specificity and implications in neurologic disease. *Neurology, 71*(12), 944–949.

Bhatt, S., & Siegel, A. (2006). Potentiating role of interleukin 2 (IL-2) receptors in the midbrain periaqueductal gray (PAG) upon defensive rage behavior in the cat: Role of neurokinin NK(1) receptors. *Behavioral Brain Research, 167*(2), 251–260.

Brown, T. G., & Sherrington, C. S. (1911). Observations on the localisation in the motor cortex of the baboon ("Papio anubis"). *The Journal of Physiology, 43*(2), 209–218.

Burke, R. E. (2007). Sir Charles Sherrington's *The integrative action of the nervous system*: A centenary appreciation. *Brain, 130*(Pt. 4), 887–894.

Damasio, A. R. (1996). The somatic marker hypothesis and the possible functions of the prefrontal cortex. *Philosophical Transactions of the Royal Society of London B: Biological Sciences, 351*(1346), 1413–1420.

Drake, M. J., Fowler, C. J., Griffiths, D., Mayer, E., Paton, J. F., & Birder, L. (2010). Neural control of the lower urinary and gastrointestinal tracts: Supraspinal CNS mechanisms. *Neurourology and Urodynamics, 29*(1), 119–127.

Edelstyn, N. M., Mayes, A. R., & Ellis, S. J. (2014). Damage to the dorsomedial thalamic nucleus, central lateral intralaminar thalamic nucleus, and midline thalamic nuclei on the right-side impair executive function and attention under conditions of high demand but not low demand. *Neurocase, 20*(2), 121–132.

Frigon, A. (2012). Central pattern generators of the mammalian spinal cord. *Neuroscientist, 18*(1), 56–69.

Gerhart, J. (2000). Inversion of the chordate body axis: Are there alternatives? *Proceedings of the National Academy of Sciences in the United States of America, 97*(9), 4445–4448.

Giacino, J., Fins, J. J., Machado, A., & Schiff, N. D. (2012). Central thalamic deep brain stimulation to promote recovery from chronic posttraumatic minimally conscious state: Challenges and opportunities. *Neuromodulation: Technology at the Neural Interface, 15*(4), 339–349.

Guldenmund, P., Demertzi, A., Boveroux, P., Boly, M., Vanhaudenhuyse, A., Bruno, M. A., . . . Soddu, A. (2013). Thalamus, brainstem and salience network connectivity changes during mild propofol sedation and unconsciousness. *Brain Connect, 3*(3), 273–285.

Hassabis, D., & Maguire, E. A. (2009). The construction system of the brain. *Philosophical Transactions of the Royal Society of London B: Biological Sciences, 364*(1521), 1263–1271.

Konishi, M. (2010). From central pattern generator to sensory template in the evolution of birdsong. *Brain and Language, 115*(1), 18–20.

Kow, L. M., Brown, H. E., & Pfaff, D. W. (1994). Activation of protein kinase C in the hypothalamic ventromedial nucleus or the midbrain central gray facilitates lordosis. *Brain Research, 660*(2), 241–248.

Kuroda, T., Yasuda, S., & Sato, Y. (2013). Tumorigenicity studies for human pluripotent stem cell-derived products. *Biological & Pharmaceutical Bulletin, 36*(2), 189–192.

Li, J., & Lepski, G. (2013). Cell transplantation for spinal cord injury: A systematic review. *Biomed Research International, 2013*, 786475.

Liu, J., Chen, J., Liu, B., Yang, C., Xie, D., Zheng, X., . . . Jin, D. (2013). Acellular spinal cord scaffold seeded with mesenchymal stem cells promotes long-distance axon regeneration and functional recovery in spinal cord injured rats. *Journal of the Neurological Sciences, 325*(1–2), 127–136.

Macias, M. Y., Syring, M. B., Pizzi, M. A., Crowe, M. J., Alexanian, A. R., & Kurpad, S. N. (2006). Pain with no gain: Allodynia following neural stem cell transplantation in spinal cord injury. *Experimental Neurology, 201*(2), 335–348.

Mahon, B. Z., Milleville, S. C., Negri, G. A., Rumiati, R. I., Caramazza, A., & Martin, A. (2007). Action-related properties shape object representations in the ventral stream. *Neuron, 55*(3), 507–520.

McLachlan, R. S. (2009). A brief review of the anatomy and physiology of the limbic system. *Canadian Journal of Neurological Sciences, 36*(Suppl. 2), S84–S87.

Mothe, A. J., Tam, R. Y., Zahir, T., Tator, C. H., & Shoichet, M. S. (2013). Repair of the injured spinal cord by transplantation of neural stem cells in a hyaluronan-based hydrogel. *Biomaterials, 34*(15), 3775–3783.

Nauta, W. J. H. (1979). Expanding borders of the limbic cortex. In L. V. Laitinen & K. E. Livingston (Eds.), *Surgical Approaches in Psychiatry* (pp. 303–314). Lancaster, UK: Medical and Technical Publishing.

Niewenhuys, R., Voogd, J., & van Huijzen, C. (2008). *The Human Central Nervous System*. Heidelberg: Springer, Steinkopff-Verlag.

Noonan, M. P., Kolling, N., Walton, M. E., & Rushworth, M. F. (2012). Re-evaluating the role of the orbitofrontal cortex in reward and reinforcement. *European Journal of Neuroscience, 35*(7), 997–1010.

Ohmura, Y., Izumi, T., Yamaguchi, T., Tsutsui-Kimura, I., Yoshida, T., & Yoshioka, M. (2010). The serotonergic projection from the median raphe nucleus to the ventral hippocampus is involved in the retrieval of fear memory through the corticotropin-releasing factor type 2 receptor. *Neuropsychopharmacology, 35*(6), 1271–1278.

Richter-Levin, G., & Akirav, I. (2000). Amygdala–hippocampus dynamic interaction in relation to memory. *Molecular Neurobiology, 22*(1–3), 11–20.

Saadai, P., Wang, A., Nout, Y. S., Downing, T. L., Lofberg, K., Beattie, M. S., . . . Farmer, D. L. (2013). Human induced pluripotent stem cell–derived neural crest stem cells integrate into the injured spinal cord in the fetal lamb model of myelomeningocele. *Journal of Pediatric Surgery, 48*(1), 158–163.

Schacter, D. L., Addis, D. R., Hassabis, D., Martin, V. C., Spreng, R. N., & Szpunar, K. K. (2012). The future of memory: Remembering, imagining, and the brain. *Neuron, 76*(4), 677–694.

Schiff, N. D., Giacino, J. T., Kalmar, K., Victor, J. D., Baker, K., Gerber, M., . . . Rezai, A. R. (2007). Behavioural improvements with thalamic stimulation after severe traumatic brain injury. *Nature, 448*(7153), 600–603.

Schiff, N. D., & Posner, J. B. (2007). Another "Awakenings." *Annals of Neurology, 62*(1), 5–7.

Schimitel, F. G., de Almeida, G. M., Pitol, D. N., Armini, R. S., Tufik, S., & Schenberg, L. C. (2012). Evidence of a suffocation alarm system within the periaqueductal gray matter of the rat. *Neuroscience, 200*, 59–73.

Schmahmann, J. D. (2010). The role of the cerebellum in cognition and emotion: personal reflections since 1982 on the dysmetria of thought hypothesis, and its historical evolution from theory to therapy. *Neuropsychology Review, 20*(3), 236–260.

Schmidt, M. F. (2003). Pattern of interhemispheric synchronization in HVc during singing correlates with key transitions in the song pattern. *Journal of Neurophysiology, 90*(6), 3931–3949.

Seidler, R. D., Noll, D. C., & Thiers, G. (2004). Feedforward and feedback processes in motor control. *NeuroImage, 22*(4), 1775–1783.

Stoodley, C. J., Valera, E. M., & Schmahmann, J. D. (2012). Functional topography of the cerebellum for motor and cognitive tasks: An fMRI study. *NeuroImage, 59*(2), 1560–1570.

Straus, C., Vasilakos, K., Wilson, R. J., Oshima, T., Zelter, M., Derenne, J. P., . . . Whitelaw, W. A. (2003). A phylogenetic hypothesis for the origin of hiccough. *BioEssays, 25*(2), 182–188.

Strick, P. L., Dum, R. P., & Fiez, J. A. (2009). Cerebellum and nonmotor function. *Annual Review of Neuroscience, 32*, 413–434.

Stuart, D. G., & Hultborn, H. (2008). Thomas Graham Brown (1882–1965), Anders Lundberg (1920–), and the neural control of stepping. *Brain Research Reviews, 59*(1), 74–95.

Sutherland, R. J., & Rodriguez, A. J. (1989). The role of the fornix/fimbria and some related subcortical structures in place learning and memory. *Behavioral Brain Research, 32*(3), 265–277.

Van der Werf, Y. D., Witter, M. P., & Groenewegen, H. J. (2002). The intralaminar and midline nuclei of the thalamus. Anatomical and functional evidence for participation in processes of arousal and awareness. *Brain Research Reviews, 39*(2–3), 107–140.

Wang, Q., Sporns, O., & Burkhalter, A. (2012). Network analysis of corticocortical connections reveals ventral and dorsal processing streams in mouse visual cortex. *The Journal of Neuroscience, 32*(13), 4386–4399.

Wang, X. J., & Rinzel, J. (1993). Spindle rhythmicity in the reticularis thalami nucleus: Synchronization among mutually inhibitory neurons. *Neuroscience, 53*(4), 899–904.

Wells, A. M., Lasseter, H. C., Xie, X., Cowhey, K. E., Reittinger, A. M., & Fuchs, R. A. (2011). Interaction between the basolateral amygdala and dorsal hippocampus is critical for cocaine memory reconsolidation and subsequent drug context-induced cocaine-seeking behavior in rats. *Learning & Memory, 18*(11), 693–702.

Xu, L., Xu, C. J., Lu, H. Z., Wang, Y. X., Li, Y., & Lu, P. H. (2010). Long-term fate of allogeneic neural stem cells following transplantation into injured spinal cord. *Stem Cell Reviews and Reports, 6*(1), 121–136.

Zhang, D. X., & Bertram, E. H. (2002). Midline thalamic region: Widespread excitatory input to the entorhinal cortex and amygdala. *The Journal of Neuroscience, 22*(8), 3277–3284.

Zilles, K., & Amunts, K. (2010). Centenary of Brodmann's map—Conception and fate. *Nature Reviews Neuroscience, 11*(2), 139–145.

Chapter 3

Abeles, M. (1982). Role of the cortical neuron: Integrator or coincidence detector? *Israel Journal of Medical Sciences, 18*(1), 83–92.

Adrian, E. D. (1928). *The basis of sensation: The action of the sense organs.* New York, NY: Norton.

Alkire, M. T., Hudetz, A. G., & Tononi, G. (2008). Consciousness and anesthesia. *Science, 322*(5903), 876–880.

Allen, N. J., & Barres, B. A. (2009). Neuroscience: Glia—More than just brain glue. *Nature, 457*(7230), 675–677.

Almor, A., Aronoff, J. M., MacDonald, M. C., Gonnerman, L. M., Kempler, D., Hintiryan, H., … Andersen, E. S. (2009). A common mechanism in verb and noun naming deficits in Alzheimer's patients. *Brain and Language 111*(1):8–19.

Alonso-Nanclares, L., Gonzalez-Soriano, J., Rodriguez, J. R., & DeFelipe, J. (2008). Gender differences in human cortical synaptic density. *Proceedings of the National Academy of Sciences of the United States of America, 105*(38), 14615–14619.

Amari, S., Nakahara, H., Wu, S., & Sakai, Y. (2003). Synchronous firing and higher-order interactions in neuron pool. *Neural Computation, 15*(1), 127–142.

Ames, A., III. (2000). CNS energy metabolism as related to function. *Brain Research Reviews, 34*(1–2), 42–68.

Andrada, J., Livingston, P., Lee, B. J., & Antognini, J. (2012). Propofol and etomidate depress cortical, thalamic, and reticular formation neurons during anesthetic-induced unconsciousness. *Anesthesia & Analgesia, 114*(3), 661–669.

Araque, A. (2008). Astrocytes process synaptic information. *Neuron Glia Biology, 4*(1), 3–10.

Bhatheja, K., & Field, J. (2006). Schwann cells: Origins and role in axonal maintenance and regeneration. *The International Journal of Biochemistry & Cell Biology, 38*(12), 1995–1999.

Bramao, I., Reis, A., Petersson, K. M., & Faisca, L. (2011). The role of color information on object recognition: A review and meta-analysis. *Acta Psychologica (Amsterdam), 138*(1), 244–253.

Bullock, T. H., Bennett, M. V., Johnston, D., Josephson, R., Marder, E., & Fields, R. D. (2005). Neuroscience. The neuron doctrine, redux. *Science, 310*(5749), 791–793.

Burks, J. S., Bigley, G. K., & Hill, H. H. (2009). Rehabilitation challenges in multiple sclerosis. *Annals of Indian Academy of Neurology, 12*(4), 296–306.

Butts, D. A., Desbordes, G., Weng, C., Jin, J., Alonso, J. M., & Stanley, G. B. (2010). The episodic nature of spike trains in the early visual pathway. *Journal of Neurophysiology, 104*(6), 3371–3387.

Churchland, P. S., & Sejnowski, T. J. (1992). *The Computational Brain.* Cambridge, MA: MIT Press.

Cimino, G. (1999). Reticular theory versus neuron theory in the work of Camillo Golgi. *Physis: Rivista Internazionale di Storia della Scienza, 36*(2), 431–472.

Connors, B. W., & Long, M. A. (2004). Electrical synapses in the mammalian brain. *Annual Review of Neuroscience, 27,* 393–418.

Cosgrove, K. P., Mazure, C. M., & Staley, J. K. (2007). Evolving knowledge of sex differences in brain structure, function, and chemistry. *Biological Psychiatry, 62*(8), 847–855.

deCharms, R. C. (1998). Information coding in the cortex by independent or coordinated populations. *Proceedings of the National Academy of Sciences of the United States of America, 95*(26), 15166–15168.

deCharms, R. C., & Merzenich, M. M. (1996). Primary cortical representation of sounds by the coordination of action-potential timing. *Nature, 381*(6583), 610–613.

deCharms, R. C., & Zador, A. (2000). Neural representation and the cortical code. *Annual Review of Neuroscience, 23,* 613–647.

Deneve, S., Latham, P. E., & Pouget, A. (2001). Efficient computation and cue integration with noisy population codes. *Nature Neuroscience, 4*(8), 826–831.

DeWeese, M. R., & Zador, A. M. (2006). Non-Gaussian membrane potential dynamics imply sparse, synchronous activity in auditory cortex. *The Journal of Neuroscience, 26*(47), 12206–12218.

Disanto, G., Morahan, J. M., & Ramagopalan, S. V. (2012). Multiple sclerosis: Risk factors and their interactions. *CNS Neurological Disorders—Drug Targets, 11*(5), 545–555.

Drachman, D. A. (2005). Do we have brain to spare? *Neurology, 64*(12), 2004–2005.

Eggermont, J. J., & Ponton, C. W. (2002). The neurophysiology of auditory perception: From single units to evoked potentials. *Audiology and Neurotology, 7*(2), 71–99.

Engel, A. K., Fries, P., & Singer, W. (2001). Dynamic predictions: Oscillations and synchrony in top-down processing. *Nature Reviews Neuroscience, 2*(10), 704–716.

Engel, A. K., & Singer, W. (2001). Temporal binding and the neural correlates of sensory awareness. *Trends in Cognitive Sciences, 5*(1), 16–25.

Ermentrout, G. B., Galan, R. F., & Urban, N. N. (2008). Reliability, synchrony and noise. *Trends in Neurosciences, 31*(8), 428–434.

Fellin, T. (2009). Communication between neurons and astrocytes: Relevance to the modulation of synaptic and network activity. *Journal of Neurochemistry, 108*(3), 533–544.

Gelbard-Sagiv, H., Mukamel, R., Harel, M., Malach, R., & Fried, I. (2008). Internally generated reactivation of single neurons in human hippocampus during free recall. *Science, 322*(5898), 96–101.

Gillespie, P. G., & Walker, R. G. (2001). Molecular basis of mechanosensory transduction. *Nature, 413*(6852), 194–202.

Gray, C. M., & Singer, W. (1989). Stimulus-specific neuronal oscillations in orientation columns of cat visual cortex. *Proceedings of the National Academy of Sciences of the United States of America, 86,* 1698–1702.

Haslinger, R., Pipa, G., Lima, B., Singer, W., Brown, E. N., & Neuenschwander, S. (2012). Context matters: The illusive simplicity of macaque V1 receptive fields. *PLoS One, 7*(7), e39699.

Herculano-Houzel, S. (2012). The remarkable, yet not extraordinary, human brain as a scaled-up primate brain and its associated cost. *Proceedings of the National Academy of Sciences of the United States of America, 109*(Suppl. 1), 10661–10668.

Hubel, D. H., & Wiesel, T. N. (1962). Receptive fields, binocular interaction and functional architecture in the cat's visual cortex. *The Journal of Physiology, 160,* 106–154.

Kang, J., Huguenard, J. R., & Prince, D. A. (2000). Voltage-gated potassium channels activated during action potentials in layer V neocortical pyramidal neurons. *Journal of Neurophysiology, 83*(1), 70–80.

Kettenmann, H., & Verkhratsky, A. (2008). Neuroglia: The 150 years after. *Trends in Neurosciences, 31*(12), 653–659.

Knoblauch, A., & Palm, G. (2005). What is signal and what is noise in the brain? *Biosystems, 79*(1–3), 83–90.

Koch, C., & Crick, F. (2001). Neural basis of consciousness. In N. J. Smelser, J. Wright, & P. B. Baltes (Eds.), *International Encyclopedia of the Social and Behavioral Sciences* (pp. 2600–2604). Cambridge, MA: Elsevier.

Koch-Henriksen, N., & Sorensen, P. S. (2010). The changing demographic pattern of multiple sclerosis epidemiology. *The Lancet Neurology, 9*(5), 520–532.

Konig, P., Engel, A. K., & Singer, W. (1996). Integrator or coincidence detector? The role of the cortical neuron revisited. *Trends in Neurosciences, 19*(4), 130–137.

Korenbrot, J. I. (1995). Ca²⁺ flux in retinal rod and cone outer segments: Differences in Ca²⁺ selectivity of the cGMP-gated ion channels and Ca²⁺ clearance rates. *Cell Calcium, 18*(4), 285–300.

Kourtzi, Z., & Connor, C. E. (2011). Neural representations for object perception: Structure, category, and adaptive coding. *Annual Review of Neuroscience, 34,* 45–67.

Kreutzberg, G. W. (1995). Microglia, the first line of defence in brain pathologies. *Arzneimittelforschung, 45*(3A), 357–360.

Lee, C. H., & Ruben, P. C. (2008). Interaction between voltage-gated sodium channels and the neurotoxin, tetrodotoxin. *Channels (Austin), 2*(6), 407–412.

Lehky, S. R., & Sereno, A. B. (2011). Population coding of visual space: Modeling. *Frontiers in Computational Neuroscience, 4,* 155.

Lin, R., Charlesworth, J., van der Mei, I., & Taylor, B. V. (2012). The genetics of multiple sclerosis. *Practical Neurology, 12*(5), 279–288.

Lopez-Munoz, F., Boya, J., & Alamo, C. (2006). Neuron theory, the cornerstone of neuroscience, on the centenary of the Nobel Prize award to Santiago Ramón y Cajal. *Brain Research Bulletin, 70*(4–6), 391–405.

Miller, G. (2009). Origins. On the origin of the nervous system. *Science, 325*(5936), 24–26.

Mormann, F., Dubois, J., Kornblith, S., Milosavljevic, M., Cerf, M., Ison, M., . . . Koch, C (2011). A category-specific response to animals in the right human amygdala. *Nature Neuroscience, 14*(10), 1247–1249.

Murphy, G. J., & Rieke, F. (2006). Network variability limits stimulus-evoked spike timing precision in retinal ganglion cells. *Neuron, 52*(3), 511–524.

O'Connor, D. H., Peron, S. P., Huber, D., & Svoboda, K. (2010). Neural activity in barrel cortex underlying vibrissa-based object localization in mice. *Neuron, 67*(6):1048–1061.

Pasupathy, A., & Connor, C. E. (2002). Population coding of shape in area V4. *Nature Neuroscience, 5*(12), 1332–1338.

Picones, A., & Korenbrot, J. I. (1995). Spontaneous, ligand-independent activity of the cGMP-gated ion channels in cone photoreceptors of fish. *The Journal of Physiology, 485*(Pt. 3), 699–714.

Pierrot-Deseilligny, C., & Souberbielle, J. C. (2013). Contribution of vitamin D insufficiency to the pathogenesis of multiple sclerosis. *Therapeutic Advances in Neurological Disorders, 6*(2), 81–116.

Puet, T. (2002, 2 January). *Multiple sclerosis won't keep speed skater from aiding team.* Retrieved from http://www.mult-sclerosis.org/news/Jan2002/MoreOnSpeedSkaterwMS.html

Quiroga, R. Q., Kreiman, G., Koch, C., & Fried, I. (2008). Sparse but not "grandmother-cell" coding in the medial temporal lobe. *Trends in Cognitive Sciences, 2*(3):87–91.

Ramón y Cajal, S. (1937). *Recollections of my life* (E. Horne-Craigie, Trans.). Philadelphia, PA: American Philosophical Society.

Reddy, L., & Kanwisher, N. (2006). Coding of visual objects in the ventral stream. *Current Opinion in Neurobiology, 16*(4), 408–414.

Rieke, F., Warland, D., & Bialek, W. (1999). *Spikes: Exploring the neural code.* Boston, MA: MIT Press.

Roy, S., & Wang, X. (2012). Wireless multi-channel single unit recording in freely moving and vocalizing primates. *Journal of Neuroscience Methods, 203*(1), 28–40.

Samengo, I., & Montemurro, M. A. (2010). Conversion of phase information into a spike-count code by bursting neurons. *PLoS One, 5*(3), e9669.

Super, H., & Roelfsema, P. R. (2005). Chronic multiunit recordings in behaving animals: Advantages and limitations. *Progress in Brain Research, 147,* 263–282.

Ungerleider, L. G., & Bell, A. H. (2011). Uncovering the visual "alphabet": Advances in our understanding of object perception. *Vision Research, 51*(7), 782–799.

Victor, J. D. (1999). Temporal aspects of neural coding in the retina and lateral geniculate. *Network, 10*(4), R1–R66.

Waydo S., Kraskov, A., Quian Quiroga, R., Fried, I., & Koch, C. (2006). Sparse representation in the human medial temporal lobe. *The Journal of Neuroscience, 26*(40):10232–10234.

Weiner, K. S., & Grill-Spector, K. (2012). The improbable simplicity of the fusiform face area. *Trends in Cognitive Science, 16*(5), 251–254.

Whitson, J., Kubota, D., Shimono, K., Jia, Y., & Taketani, M. (2006). Multi-electrode arrays: Enhancing traditional methods and enabling network physiology. In M. Baudry & M. Taketani (Eds.), *Advances in network electrophysiology using multi-electrode arrays* (pp. 38–68). New York, NY: Spring Press.

Zigmond, M. J. (1999). Otto Loewi and the demonstration of chemical neurotransmission. *Brain Research Bulletin, 50*(5–6), 347–348.

Chapter 4

Attardi, D. G., & Sperry, R. W. (1963). Preferential selection of central pathways by regenerating optic fibers. *Experimental Neurology, 7,* 46–64.

Bach-y-Rita, P. (2004). Tactile sensory substitution studies. *Annals of the New York Academy of Sciences, 1013,* 83–91.

Bach-y-Rita, P., Collins, C. C., Saunders, F. A., White, B., & Scadden, L. (1969). Vision substitution by tactile image projection. *Nature, 221*(5184), 963–964.

Bakin, J. S., & Weinberger, N. M. (1996). Induction of a physiological memory in the cerebral cortex by stimulation of the nucleus basalis. *Proceedings of the National Academy of Sciences of the United States of America, 93*(20), 11219–11224.

Bangert, M., & Schlaug, G. (2006). Specialization of the specialized in features of external human brain morphology. *European Journal of Neuroscience, 24*(6), 1832–1834.

Barinaga, M. (1992). The brain remaps its own contours. *Science, 258*, 216–218.

Basso, A., Gardelli, M., Grassi, M. P., & Mariotti, M. (1989). The role of the right hemisphere in recovery from aphasia. Two case studies. *Cortex, 25*(4), 555–566.

Bear, M. F., & Singer, W. (1986). Modulation of visual cortical plasticity by acetylcholine and noradrenaline. *Nature, 320*(6058), 172–176.

Bennett, E. L., Diamond, M. C., Krech, D., & Rosenzweig, M. R. (1964). Chemical and anatomical plasticity of brain. *Science, 164*, 610–619.

Benson, H. H. (1990). "Meno," the slave boy and the Elenchos. *Phronesis, 35*(2), 128–158.

Berman, N., & Murphy, E. H. (1981). The critical period for alteration in cortical binocularity resulting from divergent and convergent strabismus. *Developmental Brain Research, 2*(2), 181–202.

Borgstein, J., & Grootendorst, C. (2002). Half a brain. *The Lancet, 359*(9305), 473.

Borsook, D., Becerra, L., Fishman, S., Edwards, A., Jennings, C. L., Stojanovic, M., . . . Breiter, H. (1998). Acute plasticity in the human somatosensory cortex following amputation. *NeuroReport, 9*(6), 1013–1017.

Broide, R. S., & Leslie, F. M. (1999). The α7 nicotinic acetylcholine receptor in neuronal plasticity. *Molecular Neurobiology, 20*(1), 1–16.

Buonomano, D. V., & Merzenich, M. M. (1998). Cortical plasticity: From synapses to maps. *Annual Review of Neuroscience, 21*, 149–186.

Burton, H., & Sinclair, R. J. (2000). Tactile-spatial and cross-modal attention effects in the primary somatosensory cortical areas 3b and 1-2 of rhesus monkeys. *Somatosensory & Motor Research, 17*(3), 213–228.

Clark, S. A., Allard, T., Jenkins, W. M., & Merzenich, M. M. (1988). Receptive-fields in the body-surface map in adult cortex defined by temporally correlated inputs. *Nature, 332*(6163), 444–445.

Cohen, L. G., Bandinelli, S., Findley, T. W., & Hallett, M. (1991). Motor reorganization after upper limb amputation in man. A study with focal magnetic stimulation. *Brain, 114*, 615–627.

Conner, J. M., Culberson, A., Packowski, C., Chiba, A. A., & Tuszynski, M. H. (2003). Lesions of the basal forebrain cholinergic system impair task acquisition and abolish cortical plasticity associated with motor skill learning. *Neuron, 38*(5), 819–829.

Constantine-Paton, M., & Law, M. I. (1978). Eye-specific termination bands in tecta of three-eyed frogs. *Science, 202*(4368), 639–641.

Cronholm, B. (1951). Phantom limbs in amputees; a study of changes in the integration of centripetal impulses with special reference to referred sensations. *Acta Psychiatrica et Neurologica Scandinavica, Supplementum 72*, 1–310.

Darian-Smith, C., & Gilbert, C. D. (1994). Axonal sprouting accompanies functional reorganization in adult cat striate cortex. *Nature, 368*(6473), 737–740.

Darwin, C. (1871). *The descent of man.* London: John Murray.

DeGregory, L. (2008, July 31). The girl in the window. *Tampa Bay Times.* Retrieved from http://www.tampabay.com/features/humaninterest/the-girl-in-the-window/750838

Diamond, M. (1988). *Enriching heredity.* New York, NY: Free Press.

Diamond, M. (2001). Response of the brain to enrichment. *Anais da Academia Brasileira de Ciências, 73*(2), 211–220.

Djebali, S., Davis, C. A., Merkel, A., Dobin, A., Lassmann, T., Mortazavi, A., . . . Schlesinger, F. (2012). Landscape of transcription in human cells. *Nature, 489*(7414), 101–108.

Dowling, J. (2008). Current and future prospects for optoelectronic retinal prostheses. *Eye, 23*(10), 1999–2005.

Draganski, B., Gaser, C., Busch, V., Schuierer, G., Bogdahn, U., & May, A. (2004). Neuroplasticity: Changes in grey matter induced by training. *Nature, 427*(6972), 311–312.

Elbert, T., Pantev, C., Wienbruch, C., Rockstroh, B., & Taub, E. (1995). Increased cortical representation of the fingers of the left hand in string players. *Science, 270*(5234), 305–307.

Elbert, T., & Rockstroh, B. (2004). Reorganization of human cerebral cortex: The range of changes following use and injury. *Neuroscientist, 10*(2), 129–141.

Feuillet, L., Dufour, H., & Pelletier, J. (2007). Brain of a white-collar worker. *Lancet, 370*(9583), 262.

Flor, H., Elbert, T., Knecht, S., Wienbruch, C., Pantev, C., Birbaumer, N., . . . Taub, E. (1995). Phantom-limb pain as a perceptual correlate of cortical reorganization following arm amputation. *Nature, 375*(6531), 482–484.

Florence, S. L., Taub, H. B., & Kaas, J. H. (1998). Large-scale sprouting of cortical connections after peripheral injury in adult macaque monkeys. *Science, 282*(5391), 1117–1121.

Gopnik, A., & Schulz, L. (2004). Mechanisms of theory formation in young children. *Trends in Cognitive Sciences, 8*(8), 371–377.

Gu, Q. (2003). Contribution of acetylcholine to visual cortex plasticity. *Neurobiology of Learning and Memory, 80*(3), 291–301.

Halligan, P. W., Marshall, J. C., & Wade, D. T. (1994). Sensory disorganization and perceptual plasticity after limb amputation: A follow-up study. *NeuroReport, 5*(11), 1341–1345.

Hart, H. (2005). Can constraint therapy be developmentally appropriate and child-friendly? *Developmental Medicine & Child Neurology, 47*(6), 363–363.

Hasselmo, M. E. (1995). Neuromodulation and cortical function: Modeling the physiological basis of behavior. *Behavioural Brain Research, 67*(1), 1–27.

Hawkins, J., & Blakeslee, S. (2004). *On intelligence.* New York, NY: Times Books.

Held, R., & Hein, A. (1963). Movement-produced stimulation in the development of visually guided behavior. *Journal of Comparative and Physiological Psychology, 56*, 872–876.

Henderson, W. R., & Smyth, J. (1948). Phantom limbs. *Journal of Neurology, Neurosurgery, Psychiatry, 11*, 88–112.

Hertz-Pannier, L., Chiron, C., Jambaqué, I., Renaux-Kieffer, V., Van de Moortele, P. F., Delalande, O., . . . Le Bihan, D. (2002). Late plasticity for language in a child's non-dominant hemisphere A pre-and post-surgery fMRI study. *Brain, 125*(2), 361–372.

Hubel, D. H., & Wiesel, T. N. (1962). Receptive fields, binocular interaction and functional architecture in the cat's visual cortex. *Journal of Physiology (London), 160*, 106–154.

Ijichi, S., & Ijichi, N. (2004). The prenatal autistic imprinting hypothesis: Developmental maladaptation to the environmental changes between womb and the social world. *Medical Hypotheses, 62*(2), 188–194.

Issa, N. P., Trachtenberg, J. T., Chapman, B., Zahs, K. R., & Stryker, M. P. (1999). The critical period for ocular dominance plasticity in the ferret's visual cortex. *The Journal of Neuroscience, 19*(16), 6965–6978.

Jacobs, B., Schall, M., & Scheibel, A. B. (1993). A quantitative dendritic analysis of Wernicke's area in humans. II. Gender, hemispheric, and environmental factors. *The Journal of Comparative Neurology, 327*(1), 97–111.

Jacobs, G. H., Williams, G. A., Cahill, H., & Nathans, J. (2007). Emergence of novel color vision in mice engineered to express a human cone photopigment. *Science, 315*(5819), 1723–1725.

Johnson, J. S., & Newport, E. L. (1989). Critical period effects in second language learning: The influence of maturational state on the acquisition of English as a second language. *Cognitive Psychology, 21*(1), 60–99.

Karl, A., Birbaumer, N., Lutzenberger, W., Cohen, L. G., & Flor, H. (2001). Reorganization of motor and somatosensory cortex in upper extremity amputees with phantom limb pain. *The Journal of Neuroscience, 21*(10), 3609–3618.

Karni, A., Meyer, G., Jezzard, P., Adams, M. M., Turner, R., & Ungerleider, L. G. (1995). Functional MRI evidence for adult motor cortex plasticity during motor skill learning. *Nature, 377*(6545), 155–158.

Khoo, W. L., Seidel, E. L., & Zhu, Z. (2012). Designing a virtual environment to evaluate multimodal sensors for assisting the visually impaired. *Computers Helping People with Special Needs. Lecture Notes in Computer Science, 738*, 573–580.

Kilgard, M. P. (2003). Cholinergic modulation of skill learning and plasticity. *Neuron, 38*(5), 678–680.

Kilgard, M. P., & Merzenich, M. M. (1998). Cortical map reorganization enabled by nucleus basalis activity. *Science, 279*(5357), 1714–1718.

Klein, W. L. (2013). Synaptotoxic amyloid-β oligomers: A molecular basis for the cause, diagnosis, and treatment of Alzheimer's disease? *Journal of Alzheimer's Disease, 33*, S49–S65.

Kuhl, P. K. (2004). Early language acquisition: Cracking the speech code. *Nature Reviews Neuroscience, 5*(11), 831–843.

Kuhl, P. K., Conboy, B. T., Padden, D., Nelson, T., & Pruitt, J. (2005). Early speech perception and later language development: Implications for the "Critical Period." *Language Learning and Development, 1*(3–4), 237–264.

Kuida, K., Haydar, T. F., Kuan, C.-Y., Gu, Y., Taya, C., Karasuyama, H., . . . Flavell, R. A. (1998). Reduced apoptosis and cytochrome c–mediated caspase activation in mice lacking caspase 9. *Cell, 94*(3), 325–337.

Law, M. I., & Constantine-Paton, M. (1981). Anatomy and physiology of experimentally produced striped tecta. *The Journal of Neuroscience, 1*(7), 741–759.

Lenay, C. G. O., Hanneton, S., Marque, C., & Genouel, C. (2003). Sensory substitution: Limits and perspectives. *Touching for Knowing, Cognitive Psychology of Haptic Manual Perception, 275–292.*

Levi-Montalcini, R., & Angeletti, P. U. (1968). Nerve growth factor. *Physiological Reviews, 48*(3), 534–569.

Levy, B. (2008, June 23). The blind climber who "sees" with his tongue. *Discover Magazine.* Retrieved from http://discovermagazine.com/2008/jul/23-the-blind-climber-who-sees-through-his-tongue#.Uup84z1dVyI

Lockwood, A. H., Salvi, R. J., & Burkard, R. F. (2002). Tinnitus. *New England Journal of Medicine, 347*(12), 904–910.

Low, L. K., & Cheng, H.-J. (2006). Axon pruning: An essential step underlying the developmental plasticity of neuronal connections.

Philosophical Transactions of the Royal Society B: Biological Sciences, 361(1473), 1531–1544.

Lowel, S., & Singer, W. (1992). Selection of intrinsic horizontal connections in the visual cortex by correlated neuronal activity. *Science, 255*(5041), 209–212.

Maidenbaum, S., Abboud, S., & Amedi, A. (2013). Sensory substitution: Closing the gap between basic research and widespread practical visual rehabilitation. *Neuroscience & Biobehavioral Reviews, 41*, 3–15.

Maguire, E. A., Gadian, D. G., Johnsrude, I. S., Good, C. D., Ashburner, J., Frackowiak, R. S., & Frith, C. D. (2000). Navigation-related structural change in the hippocampi of taxi drivers. *Proceedings of the National Academy of Sciences of the United States of America, 97*(8), 4398–4403.

Mancuso, K., Hauswirth, W. W., Li, Q., Connor, T. B., Kuchenbecker, J. A., Mauck, M. C., . . . Neitz, M. (2009). Gene therapy for red–green colour blindness in adult primates. *Nature, 461*(7265), 784–787.

Marcus, G. (2004). *The birth of the mind: How a tiny number of genes creates the complexities of human thought.* New York, NY: Basic Books.

McKay, B. E., Placzek, A. N., & Dani, J. A. (2007). Regulation of synaptic transmission and plasticity by neuronal nicotinic acetylcholine receptors. *Biochemical Pharmacology, 74*(8), 1120.

Merzenich, M. (1998). Long-term change of mind. *Science, 282*(5391), 1062–1063.

Merzenich, M. M., Nelson, R. J., Stryker, M. P., Cynader, M. S., Schoppmann, A., & Zook, J. M. (1984). Somatosensory cortical map changes following digit amputation in adult monkeys. *The Journal of Comparative Neurology, 224*(4), 591–605.

Miah A., & Rich, E. (2008). *The medicalization of cyberspace.* New York, NY: Routledge.

Miller, T. C., & Crosby, T. W. (1979). Musical hallucinations in a deaf elderly patient. *Annals of Neurology, 5*(3), 301–302.

Muhlau, M., Rauschecker, J. P., Oestreicher, E., Gaser, C., Rottinger, M., Wohlschlager, A. M., . . . Sander, D. (2006). Structural brain changes in tinnitus. *Cerebral Cortex, 16*(9), 1283–1288.

Nakamura, A., Yamada, T., Goto, A., Kato, T., Ito, K., Abe, Y., . . . Kakigi, R. (1998). Somatosensory homunculus as drawn by MEG. *Neuroimage, 7*(4), 377–386.

Nathanson, M. (1988). Phantom limbs as reported by S. Weir Mitchell. *Neurology, 38*(3), 504–504.

Novich, S. D., & Eagleman, D. M. (under review). How many bits per second can be passed through the skin using vibration?: Toward full audio-tactile sensory substitution.

Nudo, R. J., Milliken, G. W., Jenkins, W. M., & Merzenich, M. M. (1996). Use-dependent alterations of movement representations in primary motor cortex of adult squirrel monkeys. *The Journal of Neuroscience, 16*(2), 785–807.

Oller, D. K., & Eilers, R. E. (1988). The role of audition in infant babbling. *Child Development, 59*(2), 441–449.

Orsetti, M., Casamenti, F., & Pepeu, G. (1996). Enhanced acetylcholine release in the hippocampus and cortex during acquisition of an operant behavior. *Brain Research, 724*(1), 89–96.

Pascual-Leone, A., Amedi, A., Fregni, F., & Merabet, L. B. (2005). The plastic human brain cortex. *Annual Review of Neuroscience 28*, 377–401.

Pascual-Leone, A., & Hamilton, R. (2001). The metamodal organization of the brain. *Progress in Brain Research, 134*, 427–445.

Pascual-Leone, A., Peris, M., Tormos, J. M., Pascual, A. P., & Catala, M. D. (1996). Reorganization of human cortical motor output maps following traumatic forearm amputation. *Neuroreport, 7*(13), 2068–2070.

Petitto, L. A., & Marentette, P. F. (1991). Babbling in the manual mode: Evidence for the ontogeny of language. *Science, 251*(5000), 1493–1496.

Poirier, C., De Volder, A. G., & Scheiber, C. (2007). What neuroimaging tells us about sensory substitution. *Neuroscience & Biobehavioral Reviews, 31*(7), 1064–1070.

Pons, T. P., Garraghty, P. E., Ommaya, A. K., Kaas, J. H., Taub, E., & Mishkin, M. (1991). Massive cortical reorganization after sensory deafferentation in adult macaques. *Science, 252*(5014), 1857–1860.

Ramachandran, V. S., & Blakeslee, S. (1998). *Phantoms in the brain: Probing the mysteries of the human mind.* New York, NY: Morrow.

Ramachandran, V. S., & Hirstein, W. (1998). The perception of phantom limbs. The D. O. Hebb lecture. *Brain, 121,* 1603–1630.

Ramachandran, V. S., Rogers-Ramachandran, D., & Stewart, M. (1992). Perceptual correlates of massive cortical reorganization. *Science, 258*(5085), 1159–1160.

Recio, J., Miguez, J., Buxton, O., & Challet, E. (1997). Synchronizing circadian rhythms in early infancy. *Medical Hypotheses, 49*(3), 229–234.

Richardson, R. T., & DeLong, M. R. (1991). Electrophysiological studies of the functions of the nucleus basalis in primates. *Advances in Experimental Medicine and Biology, 295,* 233–252.

Renier, L. A., Anurova, I., De Volder, A. G., Carlson, S., VanMeter, J., & Rauschecker, J. P. (2010). Preserved functional specialization for spatial processing in the middle occipital gyrus of the early blind. *Neuron, 68*(1), 138–148.

Rosenzweig, M. R., & Bennett, E. L. (1996). Psychobiology of plasticity: Effects of training and experience on brain and behavior. *Behavioural Brain Research, 78*(1), 57–65.

Sachdev, R. N. S., Lu, S. M., Wiley, R. G., & Ebner, F. F. (1998). Role of the basal forebrain cholinergic projection in somatosensory cortical plasticity. *Journal of Neurophysiology, 79*(6), 3216–3228.

Sanes, J. R., & Lichtman, J. W. (1999). Development of the vertebrate neuromuscular junction. *Annual Review of Neuroscience, 22*(1), 389–442.

Sarter, M., Bruno, J. P., & Turchi, J. (1999). Basal forebrain afferent projections modulating cortical acetylcholine, attention, and implications for neuropsychiatric disorders. *Annals of the New York Academy of Sciences, 877*(1), 368–382.

Schulz, L. E., & Gopnik, A. (2004). Causal learning across domains. *Developmental Psychology, 40*(2), 162–176.

Schweighofer, N., & Arbib, M. A. (1998). A model of cerebellar metaplasticity. *Learning & Memory, 4*(5), 421–428.

Sharma, J., Angelucci, A., & Sur, M. (2000). Induction of visual orientation modules in auditory cortex. *Nature, 404*(6780), 841–847.

Spedding, M., & Gressens, P. (2008). Neurotrophins and cytokines in neuronal plasticity. In D. J. Chadwick (Organizer) & J. Goode, *Growth Factors and Psychiatric Disorders: Novartis Foundation Symposium, 289* (pp. 222–233; discussion pp. 233–240). Chichester, England: Wiley.

Sperry, R. W. (1963). Chemoaffinity in the orderly growth of nerve fiber patterns and connections. *Proceedings of the National Academy of Sciences of the United States of America, 50,* 703–710.

Spurzheim, J. (1815). *The physiognomical system of Drs Gall and Spurzheim* (2nd ed.). London: Baldwin Cradock and Joy.

Thiel, C. M., Friston, K. J., & Dolan, R. J. (2002). Cholinergic modulation of experience-dependent plasticity in human auditory cortex. *Neuron, 35*(3), 567–574.

Torrão, A. S., & Britto, L. R. (2002). Neurotransmitter regulation of neural development: Acetylcholine and nicotinic receptors. *Anais da Academia Brasileira de Ciências, 74*(3), 453–461.

Udin, S. H. (1977). Rearrangements of the retinotectal projection in *Rana pipiens* after unilateral caudal half-tectum ablation. *Journal of Comparative Neurology, 173*(3), 561–582.

von Melchner, L., Pallas, S. L., & Sur, M. (2000). Visual behaviour mediated by retinal projections directed to the auditory pathway. *Nature, 404*(6780), 871–876.

Weiss, T., Miltner, W. H., Liepert, J., Meissner, W., & Taub, E. (2004). Rapid functional plasticity in the primary somatomotor cortex and perceptual changes after nerve block. *The European Journal of Neuroscience, 20*(12), 3413–3423.

Wiesel, T. N., & Hubel, D. H. (1963a). Effects of visual deprivation on morphology and physiology of cells in the cat's lateral geniculate body. *Journal of Neurophysiology, 26*(978), 6.

Wiesel, T. N., & Hubel, D. H. (1963b). Single-cell responses in striate cortex of kittens deprived of vision in one eye. *Journal of Neurophysiology, 26,* 1003–1017.

Wilson, J. A., Walton, L. M., Tyler, M., Williams, J. (2012). Lingual electrotactile stimulation as an alternative sensory feedback pathway for brain-computer interface applications. *Journal of Neural Engineering, 9*(4):045007.

Yang, T. T., Gallen, C. C., Ramachandran, V. S., Cobb, S., Schwartz, B. J., & Bloom, F. E. (1994). Noninvasive detection of cerebral plasticity in adult human somatosensory cortex. *NeuroReport, 5*(6), 701–704.

Zoubine, M. N., Ma, J. Y., Smirnova, I. V., Citron, B. A., & Festoff, B. W. (1996). A molecular mechanism for synapse elimination: Novel inhibition of locally generated thrombin delays synapse loss in neonatal mouse muscle. *Developmental Biology, 179*(2), 447–457.

Chapter 5

Ahissar, M., & Hochstein, S. (2004). The reverse hierarchy theory of visual perceptual learning. *Trends in Cognitive Sciences, 8*(10), 457–464.

Allan, J. (1977). The brain as a dream state generator: An activation-synthesis hypothesis of the dream process. *American Journal of Psychiatry, 134*(12), 1335–48.

Bell, A. J. (1999). Levels and loops: the future of artificial intelligence and neuroscience. *Philosophical Transactions of the Royal Society of London B: Biological Sciences, 354*(1392), 2013–20.

Berrios, G. E., & Brook, P. (1982). The Charles Bonnet syndrome and the problem of visual perceptual disorders in the elderly. *Age and Ageing, 11*(1), 17–23.

Blackmore, S. J., Brelstaff, G., Nelson, K., & Troscianko, T. (1995). Is the richness of our visual world an illusion? Transsaccadic memory for complex scenes. *Perception, 24*(9), 1075–1081.

Blake, R., & Logothetis, N. (2002). Visual competition. *Nature Reviews: Neuroscience, 3*(1), 13–21.

Bose, S. (2008). What are visual processing defects and how can I recognize them? In A. G. Lee (ed.), *Curbside consultation in neuroophthalmology: 49 clinical questions* (pp. 107–110). Thorofare, NJ: Slack.

Bradley, D. R., & Petry, H. M. (1977). Organizational determinants of subjective contour: The subjective Necker cube. *The American Journal of Psychology, 90*(2), 253–262.

Calkins, D. J., Schein, S. J., Tsukamoto, Y., & Sterling, P. (1994). M and L cones in macaque fovea connect to midget ganglion cells by different numbers of excitatory synapses. *Nature, 371*(6492), 70–72.

Collett, T. S., & Land, M. F. (1975). Visual spatial memory in a hoverfly. *Journal of Comparative Physiology, 100*, 59–84.

Coltekin, A. (2009). Space–variant image coding for stereoscopic media. Paper presented at the Picture Coding Symposium, 2009. PCS 2009.

Cowey, A. (2010). The blindsight saga. *Experimental Brain Research, 200*(1), 3–24.

Damasio, A. R., Damasio, H., & Van Hoesen, G. W. (1982). Prosopagnosia anatomic basis and behavioral mechanisms. *Neurology, 32*(4), 331–331.

de Gelder, B., Tamietto, M., van Boxtel, G., Goebel, R., Sahraie, A., van den Stock, J., . . . Pegna, A. (2008). Intact navigation skills after bilateral loss of striate cortex. *Current Biology: CB, 18*(24), R1128–1129.

Dennett, D. C. (1992). *Consciousness explained.* New York, NY: Little, Brown.

Desimone, R., Albright, T. D., Gross, C. G., & Bruce, C. (1984). Stimulus-selective properties of inferior temporal neurons in the macaque. *The Journal of Neuroscience, 4*(8), 2051–2062.

Dougherty, R. F., Koch, V. M., Brewer, A. A., Fischer, B., Modersitzki, J., & Wandell, B. A. (2003). Visual field representations and locations of visual areas V1/2/3 in human visual cortex. *Journal of Vision, 3*(10), 586–598.

Dowling, J. (2009). Current and future prospects for optoelectronic retinal prostheses. *Eye, 23*(10), 1999–2005.

Eagleman, D. M. (2001). Visual illusions and neurobiology. *Nature Reviews: Neuroscience, 2*(12), 920–926.

Eagleman, D. M. (2011). *Incognito: The secret lives of the brain.* New York, NY: Pantheon.

Eagleman, D. M. (2012). *LiveWired: How the brain rewires itself on the fly.* New York, NY: Oxford University Press.

Egly, R., Driver, J., & Rafal, R. D. (1994). Shifting visual attention between objects and locations: Evidence from normal and parietal lesion subjects. *Journal of Experimental Psychology: General, 123*(2), 161–177.

Exner, S. (1875). Experimentelle Untersuchung der einfachsten psychischen Processe. Pflügers Archiv: *European Journal of Physiology, 7*, 403–432.

Fildes, J. (2007, February 16). *Trials for "bionic" eye implants.* Retrieved from http://news.bbc.co.uk/2/hi/6368089.stm

Fleming, N. (2007, February 16). I could see my son for the first time in 13 years. *The Telegraph.* Retrieved from http://www.telegraph.co.uk/news/uknews/1542816/I-could-see-my-son-for-the-first-time-in-13-years.html

Foster, K., Gaska, J. P., Nagler, M., & Pollen, D. (1985). Spatial and temporal frequency selectivity of neurones in visual cortical areas V1 and V2 of the macaque monkey. *The Journal of Physiology, 365*(1), 331–363.

Fox, C. J., Iaria, G., & Barton, J. J. (2008). Disconnection in prosopagnosia and face processing. *Cortex, 44*(8), 996–1009.

Gattass, R., Gross, C., & Sandell, J. (1981). Visual topography of V2 in the macaque. *Journal of Comparative Neurology, 201*(4), 519–539.

Gattass, R., Sousa, A., & Gross, C. (1988). Visuotopic organization and extent of V3 and V4 of the macaque. *The Journal of Neuroscience, 8*(6), 1831–1845.

Gillig, P. M., & Sanders, R. D. (2009). Cranial nerve II: Vision. *Psychiatry (Edgmont), 6*(9), 32–37.

Goodale, M. A., Jakobson, L. S., Milner, A. D., Perrett, D. I., Benson, P. J., & Hietanen, J. K. (1994). The nature and limits of orientation and pattern processing supporting visuomotor control in a visual form agnosic. *Journal of Cognitive Neuroscience, 6*(1), 46–56.

Goodale, M. A., & Milner, A. D. (1992). Separate visual pathways for perception and action. *Trends in Neurosciences, 15*(1), 20–25.

Grady, D. (1993). The vision thing: Mainly in the brain. *Discover, 14*(6), 56–66.

Grossberg, S. (1980). How does a brain build a cognitive code? *Psychological Review, 87*(1), 1–51.

Hubel, D. H. (1995). *Eye, brain, and vision.* New York, NY: Holt.

Hubel, D. H., & Wiesel, T. N. (1968). Receptive fields and functional architecture of monkey striate cortex. *Journal of Physiology, 195*(1), 215–243.

Hung, C. P., Kreiman, G., Poggio, T., & DiCarlo, J. J. (2005). Fast readout of object identity from macaque inferior temporal cortex. *Science, 310*(5749), 863–866.

Julesz, B. (1986). Stereoscopic vision. *Vision Research, 26*(9), 1601–1612.

Kanwisher, N., McDermott, J., & Chun, M. M. (1997). The fusiform face area: A module in human extrastriate cortex specialized for face perception. *The Journal of Neuroscience, 17*(11), 4302–4311.

Knutsson, H., & Granlund, G. H. (1994). *Signal processing for computer vision.* Norwell, MA: Kluwer Academic.

Kobatake, E., & Tanaka, K. (1994). Neuronal selectivities to complex object features in the ventral visual pathway of the macaque cerebral cortex. *Journal of Neurophysiology, 71*(3), 856–867.

Kurson, R. (2008). *Crashing through: The extraordinary true story of the man who dared to see.* New York, NY: Random House.

Lacquaniti, F., & Carrozzo, M. (1993). Planning and control of limb impedance. In A. Berthoz (Ed.), *Multisensory control of movement.* New York, NY: Oxford University Press.

Lanchester, B. S., & Mark, R. F. (1975). Pursuit and prediction in the tracking of moving food by a teleost fish (*Acanthaluteres spilomelanurus*). *The Journal of Experimental Biology, 63*(3), 627–645.

Lee, T. S., & Nguyen, M. (2001). Dynamics of subjective contour formation in the early visual cortex. *Proceedings of the National Academy of Sciences of the United States of America, 98*(4), 1907–1911.

Levin, D. T. (1997). Failure to detect changes to attended objects in motion pictures. *Psychonomic Bulletin & Review, 4*(4), 501–506.

Llinás, R. R. (2002). *I of the vortex: From neurons to self.* Cambridge, MA: MIT Press.

Logothetis, N. K., Leopold, D. A., & Sheinberg, D. L. (1996). What is rivalling during binocular rivalry? *Nature, 380*(6575), 621–624.

MacKay, D. M. (1956). The epistemological problem for automata. In C. E. Shannon & J. McCarthy (Eds.), *Automata studies* (pp. 235–250). Princeton, NJ: Princeton University Press.

Macknik, S. L., King, M., Randi, J., Robbins, A., Teller, Thompson, J., & Martinez-Conde, S. (2008). Attention and awareness in stage magic: Turning tricks into research. *Nature Reviews: Neuroscience, 9*(11), 871–879.

Mainster, M. A. (2005). Intraocular lenses should block UV radiation and violet but not blue light. *Archives of Ophthalmology, 123*(4), 550–555.

Mamassian, P., & Kersten, D. (1996). Illumination, shading and the perception of local orientation. *Vision Research, 36*(15), 2351–2367.

Marr, D. (1982). *Vision: A computational investigation into the human representation and processing of visual information.* New York, NY: Freeman.

Martin, A., Wiggs, C. L., Ungerleider, L. G., & Haxby, J. V. (1996). Neural correlates of category-specific knowledge. *Nature, 379*(6566), 649–652.

Martin, A., Wiggs, C. L., & Weisberg, J. (1997). Modulation of human medial temporal lobe activity by form, meaning, and experience. *Hippocampus, 7*(6), 587–593.

Mather, G., Verstraten, F., & Anstis, S. (1998). *The motion aftereffect: A modern perspective.* Cambridge, MA: MIT Press.

McBeath, M. K., Shaffer, D. M., & Kaiser, M. K. (1995). How baseball outfielders determine where to run to catch fly balls. *Science, 268*(5210), 569–573.

Milner, A. D. (1995). Cerebral correlates of visual awareness. *Neuropsychologia, 33*(9), 1117–1130.

Mishkin, M., & Ungerleider, L. G. (1982). Contribution of striate inputs to the visuospatial functions of parieto-preoccipital cortex in monkeys. *Behavioural Brain Research, 6*(1), 57–77.

Nishimoto, S., Vu, A. T., Naselaris, T., Benjamini, Y., Yu, B., & Gallant, J. L. (2011). Reconstructing visual experiences from brain activity evoked by natural movies. *Current Biology, 21*(19), 1641–1646.

O'Hare, D. (1999). *Human performance in general aviation.* Aldershot, U.K.: Gower Technical.

O'Regan, J. K. (1992). Solving the "real" mysteries of visual perception: The world as an outside memory. *Canadian Journal of Psychology, 46*(3), 461–488.

Op de Beeck, H. P., Baker, C. I., Rindler, S., & Kanwisher, N. (2005). An increased bold response for trained objects in object-selective regions of human visual cortex. *Journal of Vision, 5*(8), 1056.

Orbach, J., Ehrlich, D., & Heath, H. A. (1963). Reversibility of the Necker cube: I. An examination of the concept of "satiation of orientation." *Perceptual and Motor Skills, 17*(2), 439–458.

Pasupathy, A., & Connor, C. E. (2002). Population coding of shape in area V4. *Nature Neuroscience, 5*(12), 1332–1338.

Pisella, L., Sergio, L., Blangero, A., Torchin, H., Vighetto, A., & Rossetti, Y. (2009). Optic ataxia and the function of the dorsal stream: Contributions to perception and action. *Neuropsychologia, 47*(14), 3033–3044.

Qiu, F. T., & von der Heydt, R. (2005). Figure and ground in the visual cortex: V2 combines stereoscopic cues with gestalt rules. *Neuron, 47*(1), 155–166.

Ramachandran, V. S. (1988). Perceiving shape from shading. *Scientific American, 259*(2), 76–83.

Ramachandran, V. S. (1992). Blind spots. *Scientific American, 266*(5), 86–91.

Rauschecker, J. P., & Tian, B. (2000). Mechanisms and streams for processing of "what" and "where" in auditory cortex. *Proceedings of the National Academy of Sciences of the United States of America, 97*(22), 11800–11806.

Reddy, L., & Kanwisher, N. (2006). Coding of visual objects in the ventral stream. *Current Opinion in Neurobiology, 16*(4), 408–414.

Rensink, R. A., O'Regan, J. K., & Clark, J. J. (1997). To see or not to see: The need for attention to perceive changes in scenes. *Psychological Science, 8*(5), 368–373.

Sary, G., Vogels, R., & Orban, G. A. (1993). Cue-invariant shape selectivity of macaque inferior temporal neurons. *Science, 260*(5110), 995–997.

Simon, S. A., de Araujo, I. E., Gutierrez, R., & Nicolelis, M. A. (2006). The neural mechanisms of gustation: A distributed processing code. *Nature Reviews: Neuroscience, 7*(11), 890–901.

Simons, D. J., & Levin, D. T. (1998). Failure to detect changes to people during a real-world interaction. *Psychonomic Bulletin & Review, 4*, 501–506.

Smith, A. T., Singh, K. D., & Greenlee, M. W. (2000). Attentional suppression of activity in the human visual cortex. *Neuroreport, 11*(2), 271–278.

Sterman, J. D. (1994). Learning in and about complex systems. *System Dynamics Review, 10*(2–3), 291–330.

Swan, J. E., Jones, A., Kolstad, E., Livingston, M. A., & Smallman, H. S. (2007). Egocentric depth judgments in optical, see-through augmented reality. *IEEE Transactions on Visualization and Computer Graphics, 13*(3), 429–442.

Swartz, B. E., & Brust, J. C. (1984). Anton's syndrome accompanying withdrawal hallucinosis in a blind alcoholic. *Neurology, 34*(7), 969–969.

Symonds, C., & Mackenzie, I. (1957). Bilateral loss of vision from cerebral infarction. *Brain, 80*(4), 415–455.

Tong, F., Meng, M., & Blake, R. (2006). Neural bases of binocular rivalry. *Trends in Cognitive Sciences, 10*(11), 502–511.

Tootell, R. B., Reppas, J. B., Dale, A. M., Look, R. B., Sereno, M. I., Malach, R., . . . Rosen, B. R. (1995). Visual motion aftereffect in human cortical area MT revealed by functional magnetic resonance imaging. *Nature, 375*(6527), 139–141.

Tresilian, J. R. (1999). Visually timed action: Time-out for "tau"? *Trends in Cognitive Sciences, 3*(8), 301–310.

Tsirlin, I., Dupierrix, E., Chokron, S., Coquillart, S., & Ohlmann, T. (2009). Uses of virtual reality for diagnosis, rehabilitation and study of unilateral spatial neglect: Review and analysis. *CyberPsychology & Behavior, 12*(2), 175–181.

Uka, T., & DeAngelis, G. C. (2004). Contribution of area MT to stereoscopic depth perception: Choice-related response modulations reflect task strategy. *Neuron, 42*(2), 297–310.

Vallar, G. (1993). The anatomical basis of spatial hemineglect in humans. In I. H. Robertson & J. C. Marshall (Eds.), *Unilateral neglect: Clinical and experimental studies* (pp. 27–59). Hove, UK: Erlbaum.

Vernon, J., Marton, T., & Peterson, E. (1961). Sensory deprivation and hallucinations. *Science, 133*(3467), 1808–1812.

Vernon, J., McGill, T. E., & Schiffman, H. (1958). Visual hallucinations during perceptual isolation. *Canadian Journal of Psychology/Revue canadienne de psychologie, 12*(1), 31–34.

von Helmholtz, H. (1867). *Handbuch der physiologischen Optik.* Hamburg, Germany: Voss.

Weiskrantz, L. (1990a). Blindsight: A case study and implications. New York, NY: Oxford University Press.

Weiskrantz, L. (1990b). The Ferrier lecture, 1989. Outlooks for blindsight: Explicit methodologies for implicit processes. *Proceedings of the Royal Society of London. Series B, Containing Papers of a Biological Character, 239*(1296), 247–278.

Wolpert, D. M., & Flanagan, J. R. (2001). Motor prediction. *Current Biology, 11*(18), R729–R732.

Wolpert, D. M., & Miall, R. C. (1996). Forward models for physiological motor control. *Neural Networks, 9*(8), 1265–1279.

Yarbus, A. L. (1967). *Eye movements and vision.* New York, NY: Plenum Press.

Zago, M., Bosco, G., Maffei, V., Iosa, M., Ivanenko, Y. P., & Lacquaniti, F. (2004). Internal models of target motion: Expected dynamics overrides measured kinematics in timing manual interceptions. *Journal of Neurophysiology, 91*(4), 1620–1634.

Zeki, S. (1996). Brain activity related to the perception of illusory contours. *Neuroimage, 3*(2), 104–108.

Zihl, J., von Cramon, D., Mai, N., & Schmid, C. (1991). Disturbance of movement vision after bilateral posterior brain damage. Further evidence and follow up observations. *Brain, 114* (Pt. 5), 2235–2252.

Chapter 6

Arzi, A., & Sobel, N. (2010). Spatial perception: Time tells where a smell comes from. *Current Biology, 20*(13), R563–R564.

Basbaum, A. I., & Fields, H. L. (1978). Endogenous pain control mechanisms: Review and hypothesis. *Annals of Neurology, 4*(5), 451–462.

Beidler, L. M. (1954). A theory of taste stimulation. *The Journal of General Physiology, 38*(2), 133–139.

Breznitz, Z., & Meyler, A. (2003). Speed of lower-level auditory and visual processing as a basic factor in dyslexia: Electrophysiological evidence. *Brain and Language, 85*(2), 166–184.

Buck, L. B. (1996). Information coding in the vertebrate olfactory system. *Annual Review of Neuroscience, 19*(1), 517–544.

Buck, L. B., & Axel, R. (1991). A novel multigene family may encode odorant receptors: A molecular basis for odor recognition. *Cell, 65*(1), 175–187.

Cappe, C., Rouiller, E. M., & Barone, P. (2009). Multisensory anatomical pathways. *Hearing Research, 258*(1–2), 28–36.

Chandrashekar, J., Hoon, M. A., Ryba, N. J., & Zuker, C. S. (2006). The receptors and cells for mammalian taste. *Nature, 444*(7117), 288–294.

Chorost, M. (2011). *World wide mind: The coming integration of humanity, machines, and the Internet.* New York, NY: Free Press.

Cimerman, J., Waldhaus, J., Harasztosi, C., Duncker, S. V., Dettling, J., Heidrych, P., . . . Zimmermann, U. (2013). Generation of somatic electromechanical force by outer hair cells may be influenced by prestin–CASK interaction at the basal junction with the Deiter's cell. *Histochemistry and Cell Biology, 140*(2), 119–135.

Cole, J., & Paillard, J. (1995). Living without touch and peripheral information about body position and movement: Studies with deafferented subjects. In J. L. Bermudez (Ed.), *The Body and the Self* (pp. 245–266). Cambridge, MA: MIT Press.

Cox, J. J., Reimann, F., Nicholas, A. K., Thornton, G., Roberts, E., Springell, K., . . . Woods, C. G. (2006). An SCN9A channelopathy causes congenital inability to experience pain. *Nature, 444*(7121), 894–898.

Craig, A. D. (2002). How do you feel? Interoception: The sense of the physiological condition of the body. *Nature Reviews: Neuroscience, 3*(8), 655–666.

Crown, E. D., Grau, J. W., & Meagher, M. W. (2004). Pain in a balance: Noxious events engage opposing processes that concurrently modulate nociceptive reactivity. *Behavioral Neuroscience, 118*(6), 1418–1426.

Cytowic, R. E., & Eagleman, D. M. (2009). *Wednesday is indigo blue: Discovering the brain of synesthesia.* Cambridge, MA: MIT Press.

Darian-Smith, I., Johnson, K. O., LaMotte, C., Shigenaga, Y., Kenins, P., & Champness, P. (1979). Warm fibers innervating palmar and digital skin of the monkey: Responses to thermal stimuli. *Journal of Neurophysiology, 42*(5), 1297–1315.

Dravnieks, A. (1985). *Atlas of odor character profiles.* Philadelphia, PA: ASTM International.

Eagleman, D. M. (2001). Visual illusions and neurobiology. *Nature Reviews: Neuroscience, 2*(12), 920–926.

Eagleman, D. M. (2008). Human time perception and its illusions. *Current Opinion in Neurobiology, 18*(2), 131–136.

Eagleman, D. M. (2009). Brain Time. In M. Brockman (Ed.), *What's Next? Dispatches on the Future of Science.* New York, NY: Vintage.

Eagleman, D. M. (2011). Your brain knows a lot more than you realize. *Discover.* Retrieved from http://discovermagazine.com/2011/sep/18-your-brain-knows-lot-more-than-you-realize#.Uaku_0CIN8s

Eagleman, D. M. (2013). *Brain food.* New York, NY: Pantheon.

Eagleman, D. M., & Pariyadath, V. (2009). Is subjective duration a signature of coding efficiency? *Philosophical Transactions of the Royal Society of London. Series B, Biological Sciences, 364*(1525), 1841–1851.

Eagleman, D. M., & Sejnowski, T. J. (2000). Motion integration and postdiction in visual awareness. *Science, 287*(5460), 2036–2038.

Eagleman, D. M., Tse, P. U., Buonomano, D., Janssen, P., Nobre, A. C., & Holcombe, A. O. (2005). Time and the brain: How subjective time relates to neural time. *Journal of Neuroscience, 25*(45), 10369–10371.

Edelman, G. (1993). *Bright air, brilliant fire: On the matter of the mind.* New York, NY: Basic Books.

Ernst, M. O., & Banks, M. S. (2002). Humans integrate visual and haptic information in a statistically optimal fashion. *Nature, 415*(6870), 429–433.

Erzurumlu, R. S., Murakami, Y., & Rijli, F. M. (2010). Mapping the face in the somatosensory brainstem. *Nature Reviews: Neuroscience, 11*(4), 252–263.

Etkin, A., Egner, T., Peraza, D. M., Kandel, E. R., & Hirsch, J. (2006). Resolving emotional conflict: A role for the rostral anterior cingulate cortex in modulating activity in the amygdala. *Neuron, 51*(6), 871–882.

Ferrero, D. M., & Liberles, S. D. (2010). The secret codes of mammalian scents. *Wiley Interdisciplinary Reviews. Systems Biology and Medicine, 2*(1), 23–33.

Gallagher, S. (2005). *How the body shapes the mind.* New York, NY: Oxford University Press.

Ganança, F. F., Gazzola, J. M., Aratani, M. C., Perracini, M. R., & Ganança, M. M. (2006). Circumstances and consequences of falls in elderly people with vestibular disorder. *Revista Brasileira de Otorrinolaringologia, 72*(3), 388–393.

Gardiner, J. M., & Atema, J. (2010). The function of bilateral odor arrival time differences in olfactory orientation of sharks. *Current Biology, 20*(13), 1187–1191.

Gebhard, J. W., & Mowbray, G. H. (1959). On discriminating the rate of visual flicker and auditory flutter. *American Journal of Psychology, 72*, 521–529.

Gescheider, G. (1997). *Psychophysics: The fundamentals* (3rd ed.). Mahwah, NJ: Erlbaum.

Gordon, J., Ghilardi, M. F., & Ghez, C. (1995). Impairments of reaching movements in patients without proprioception. I. Spatial errors. *Journal of Neurophysiology, 73*(1), 347–360.

Graziadei, P. (1973). Cell dynamics in the olfactory mucosa. *Tissue and Cell, 5*(1), 113–131.

Hille, B. (1971). The permeability of the sodium channel to organic cations in myelinated nerve. *The Journal of General Physiology, 58*(6), 599–619.

Huang, Y. J., Maruyama, Y., Dvoryanchikov, G., Pereira, E., Chaudhari, N., & Roper, S. D. (2007). The role of pannexin 1 hemichannels in ATP release and cell–cell communication in mouse taste buds. *Proceedings of the National Academy of Sciences of the United States of America, 104*(15), 6436–6441.

Huang, Y. J., Maruyama, Y., Lu, K. S., Pereira, E., Plonsky, I., Baur, J. E., . . . & Roper, S. D. (2005). Using biosensors to detect the release of serotonin from taste buds during taste stimulation. *Archives Italiennes de Biologie, 143*(2), 87–96.

Hudspeth, A. J. (1983). Transduction and tuning by vertebrate hair cells. *Trends in Neuroscience, 6*, 366–369.

Kevetter, G. A., Leonard, R. B., Newlands, S. D., & Perachio, A. A. (2004). Central distribution of vestibular afferents that innervate the anterior or lateral semicircular canal in the mongolian gerbil. *Journal of Vestibular Research, 14*(1), 1–15.

King, A. J., & Schnupp, J. W. (2007). The auditory cortex. *Current Biology, 17*(7), R236–R239.

Kitagawa, N., & Ichihara, S. (2002). Hearing visual motion in depth. *Nature, 416*(6877), 172–174.

Kruger, L., Kavookjian, A. M., Kumazawa, T., Light, A. R., & Mizumura, K. (2003). Nociceptor structural specialization in canine and rodent testicular "free" nerve endings. *Journal of Comparative Neurology, 463*(2), 197–211.

Landau, E. (2010). *How a top chef lost, regained his taste*. Retrieved from http://www.cnn.com/2010/HEALTH/05/03/alinea.chef .tongue.cancer/index.html/

Liberles, S. D., & Buck, L. B. (2006). A second class of chemosensory receptors in the olfactory epithelium. *Nature, 442*(7103), 645–650.

Malnic, B., Godfrey, P. A., & Buck, L. B. (2004). The human olfactory receptor gene family. *Proceedings of the National Academy of Sciences of the United States of America, 101*(8), 2584–2589.

Maoiléidigh, D. Ó., & Hudspeth, A. (2013). Effects of cochlear loading on the motility of active outer hair cells. *Proceedings of the National Academy of Sciences of the United States of America, 110*(14), 5474–5479.

Massaro, D. W. (1985). Attention and perception: An information-integration perspective. *Acta Psychologica, 60*(2–3), 211–243.

McGurk, H., & MacDonald, J. (1976). Hearing lips and seeing voices. *Nature, 264*(5588), 746–748.

Melzack, R., & Wall, P. D. (1965). Pain mechanisms: A new theory. *Science, 150*(3699), 971–979.

Meredith, M. A., Nemitz, J. W., & Stein, B. E. (1987). Determinants of multisensory integration in superior colliculus neurons. I. Temporal factors. *Journal of Neuroscience, 7*(10), 3215–3229.

Mizutari, K., Fujioka, M., Hosoya, M., Bramhall, N., Okano, H. J., Okano, H., & Edge, A. S. (2013). Notch inhibition induces cochlear hair cell regeneration and recovery of hearing after acoustic trauma. *Neuron, 77*(1), 58–69.

Nagahama, S., & Kurihara, K. (1985). Norepinephrine as a possible transmitter involved in synaptic transmission in frog taste organs and Ca dependence of its release. *The Journal of General Physiology, 85*(3), 431–442.

Nieder, A., & Merten, K. (2007). A labeled-line code for small and large numerosities in the monkey prefrontal cortex. *The Journal of Neuroscience, 27*(22), 5986–5993.

Obleser, J., Boecker, H., Drzezga, A., Haslinger, B., Hennenlotter, A., Roettinger, M., . . . Rauschecker, J. P. (2006). Vowel sound extraction in anterior superior temporal cortex. *Human Brain Mapping, 27*(7), 562–571.

Pariyadath, V., & Eagleman, D. M. (2007). The effect of predictability on subjective duration. *PloS One, 2*(11), e1264.

Pearson, H. (2006). Mouse data hint at human pheromones. *Nature, 442*(7102), 495.

Phelps, E. A. (2004). Human emotion and memory: Interactions of the amygdala and hippocampal complex. *Current Opinion in Neurobiology, 14*(2), 198–202.

Potts, W. K., Manning, C. J., & Wakeland, E. K. (1996). The role of infectious disease, inbreeding and mating preferences in maintaining MHC genetic diversity: An experimental test. In W. D. Hamilton & J. C. Howard (Eds.), *Infection, polymorphism and evolution* (pp. 99–108). New York, NY: Springer.

Pritchard, T. C., Macaluso, D. A., & Eslinger, P. J. (1999). Taste perception in patients with insular cortex lesions. *Behavioral Neuroscience, 113*(4), 663–671.

Pujol, R., & Puel, J. L. (1999). Excitotoxicity, synaptic repair, and functional recovery in the mammalian cochlea: A review of recent findings. *Annals of the New York Academy of Sciences, 884*, 249–254.

Quignon, P., Kirkness, E., Cadieu, E., Touleimat, N., Guyon, R., Renier, C., . . . Galibert, F. (2003). Comparison of the canine and human olfactory receptor gene repertoires. *Genome Biology, 4*(12), R80.

Ramachandran, V. S., & Hubbard, E. M. (2001). Psychophysical investigations into the neural basis of synaesthesia. *Proceedings of the Royal Society B: Biological Sciences, 268*(1470), 979–983.

Rauschecker, J. P., & Romanski, L. M. (2011). Auditory cortical organization: Evidence for functional streams. In J. A. Winer & C. E. Schreiner (Eds.), *The auditory cortex* (pp. 99–116). New York, NY: Springer.

Ravitch, R., Anglin, L. L., Beal, B., Burke, K., Catell, R., . . . & Vaccari, K. (2008). *Report to Governor David A. Paterson*. New York State Commission on Metropolitan Transportation Authority Financing.

Reich, D. S., Mechler, F., & Victor, J. D. (2001). Independent and redundant information in nearby cortical neurons. *Science, 294*(5551), 2566–2568.

Ressler, K. J., Sullivan, S. L., & Buck, L. B. (1994). Information coding in the olfactory system: Evidence for a stereotyped and highly organized epitope map in the olfactory bulb. *Cell, 79*(7), 1245–1255.

Roelfsema, P. R. (2006). Cortical algorithms for perceptual grouping. *Annual Review of Neuroscience, 29*, 203–227.

Royet, J. P., Koenig, O., Gregoire, M. C., Cinotti, L., Lavenne, F., Le Bars, D., . . . Froment, J. C. (1999). Functional anatomy of perceptual and semantic processing for odors. *Journal of Cognitive Neuroscience, 11*(1), 94–109.

Sacks, O. (1970). *The man who mistook his wife for a hat*. New York, NY: Simon & Schuster.

Schlafly, H. J. (1951). Some comparative factors of picture resolution in television and film industries. *Proceedings of the IRE, 39*(1), 6–10.

Schmolesky, M. T., Wang, Y., Hanes, D. P., Thompson, K. G., Leutgeb, S., Schall, J. D., & Leventhal, A. G. (1998). Signal timing across the macaque visual system. *Journal of Neurophysiology, 79*(6), 3272–3278.

Schwartz, J.-L., Robert-Ribes, J., & Escudier, P. (1998). Ten years after Summerfield: A taxonomy of models for audio-visual fusion in speech perception. In R. Campbell, B. Dodd, & D. Burnham (Eds.), *Hearing by eye II: Advances in the psychology of speechreading and auditory–visual speech* (pp. 85–108). East Sussex, UK: Psychology Press.

Sepulcre, J. (2014). Functional streams and cortical integration in the human brain. *The Neuroscientist : A Review Journal Bringing Neurobiology, Neurology and Psychiatry, 20*(5), 499–508.

Shams, L., Kamitani, Y., & Shimojo, S. (2000). Illusions. What you see is what you hear. *Nature, 408*(6814), 788.

Simon, S. A., de Araujo, I. E., Gutierrez, R., & Nicolelis, M. A. (2006). The neural mechanisms of gustation: A distributed processing code. *Nature Reviews: Neuroscience, 7*(11), 890–901.

Sivian, L. J. (1933). On minimum audible sound fields. *Journal of the Acoustical Society of America, 4*, 288–321.

Spoendlin, H. (1978). [Report of the conference for inner ear biology, Bordeaux 1977 (author's transl.)]. *HNO, 26*(11), 361–365.

Spoendlin, H., & Schrott, A. (1989). Analysis of the human auditory nerve. *Hearing Research, 43*(1), 25–38.

Stern, K., & McClintock, M. K. (1998). Regulation of ovulation by human pheromones. *Nature, 392*(6672), 177–179.

Stetson, C., Fiesta, M. P., & Eagleman, D. M. (2007). Does time really slow down during a frightening event? *PloS One, 2*(12), e1295.

Stevenson, I., & Cook, E. W. (1995). Involuntary memories during severe physical illness or injury. *Journal of Nervous and Mental Disease, 183*(7), 452–458.

Stevenson, R. J., & Boakes, R. A. (2004). Sweet and sour smells: Learned synesthesia between the senses of taste and smell. In G. A. Calvert, C. Spence, & B. E. Stein (Eds.), *The Handbook of Multisensory Processes* (pp. 69–83). Cambridge, MA: MIT Press.

Szolcsanyi, J., Anton, F., Reeh, P. W., & Handwerker, H. O. (1988). Selective excitation by capsaicin of mechano-heat sensitive nociceptors in rat skin. *Brain Research, 446*(2), 262–268.

Takeda, S., Kadowaki, S., Haga, T., Takaesu, H., & Mitaku, S. (2002). Identification of G protein-coupled receptor genes from the human genome sequence. *FEBS Letters, 520*(1), 97–101.

Tallal, P., Miller, S., Jenkins, B., & Merzenich, M. M. (1997). The role of temporal processing in developmental language-based learning disorders: Research and clinical implications. In B. Blachman (Ed.), *Foundations of Reading Acquisition* (pp. 49–66). Mahwah, NJ: Erlbaum.

Tervaniemi, M., Just, V., Koelsch, S., Widmann, A., & Schröger, E. (2005). Pitch discrimination accuracy in musicians vs nonmusicians: An event-related potential and behavioral study. *Experimental Brain Research, 161*(1), 1–10.

Tomson, S. N., Avidan, N., Lee, K., Sarma, A. K., Tushe, R., Milewicz, D. M., . . . Eagleman, D. M. (2011). The genetics of colored sequence synesthesia: Suggestive evidence of linkage to 16q and genetic heterogeneity for the condition. *Behavioural Brain Research, 223*(1), 48–52.

Tomson, S. N., Narayan, M., Allen, G. I., & Eagleman, D. M. (2013). Neural networks of colored sequence synesthesia. *The Journal of Neuroscience: The Official Journal of the Society for Neuroscience, 33*(35), 14098–14106.

Uchiyama, H., Seki, A., Kageyama, H., Saito, D. N., Koeda, T., Ohno, K., & Sadato, N. (2006). Neural substrates of sarcasm: A functional magnetic-resonance imaging study. *Brain Research, 1124*(1), 100–110.

Varendi, H., & Porter, R. H. (2001). Breast odour as the only maternal stimulus elicits crawling towards the odour source. *Acta Paediatrica, 90*(4), 372–375.

Viana, F., de la Pena, E., & Belmonte, C. (2002). Specificity of cold thermotransduction is determined by differential ionic channel expression. *Nature Neuroscience, 5*(3), 254–260.

von Campenhausen, M., & Wagner, H. (2006). Influence of the facial ruff on the sound-receiving characteristics of the barn owl's ears. *Journal of Comparative Physiology A, 192*(10), 1073–1082.

Wedekind, C., Seebeck, T., Bettens, F., & Paepke, A. J. (1995). MHC-dependent mate preferences in humans. *Proceedings of the Royal Society of London. Series B, Biological Sciences, 260*(1359), 245–249.

Welch, R. B., DuttonHurt, L. D., & Warren, D. H. (1986). Contributions of audition and vision to temporal rate perception. *Perception and Psychophysics, 39*(4), 294–300.

Welch, R. B., & Warren, D. H. (1980). Immediate perceptual response to intersensory discrepancy. *Psychological Bulletin, 88*(3), 638–667.

Willott, J. F., Bross, L. S., & McFadden, S. L. (1994). Morphology of the cochlear nucleus in CBA/J mice with chronic, severe sensorineural cochlear pathology induced during adulthood. *Hearing Research, 74*(1), 1–21.

Wilska, A. (1935). Eine Methode zur Bestimmung der Hörschwellenamplituden des Trommelfells bei verschiedenen Frequenzen. *Acta Physiologica Scandinavica, 72*, 161.

Wilson, B. S., Finley, C. C., Lawson, D. T., Wolford, R. D., Eddington, D. K., & Rabinowitz, W. M. (1991). Better speech recognition with cochlear implants. *Nature, 352*(6332), 236–238.

Woolf, C. J., & Ma, Q. (2007). Nociceptors—Noxious stimulus detectors. *Neuron, 55*(3), 353–364.

Woolf, C. J., & Mannion, R. J. (1999). Neuropathic pain: Aetiology, symptoms, mechanisms, and management. *The Lancet, 353*(9168), 1959–1964.

Yang, Z., & Schank, J. C. (2006). Women do not synchronize their menstrual cycles. *Human Nature, 17*(4), 434–437.

Zaki, J., Davis, J. I., & Ochsner, K. N. (2012). Overlapping activity in anterior insula during interoception and emotional experience. *Neuroimage, 62*(1), 493–499.

Zeki, S. (1994). *A Vision of the brain.* Hoboken, NJ: Wiley.

Zhang, Y., Hoon, M. A., Chandrashekar, J., Mueller, K. L., Cook, B., Wu, D., . . . Ryba, N. J. (2003). Coding of sweet, bitter, and umami tastes: Different receptor cells sharing similar signaling pathways. *Cell, 112*(3), 293–301.

Zimmerman, C. (2010). Life without pain unites friends from afar. *The Daily News.* Retrieved from http://tdn.com/lifestyles/life-without-pain-unites-friends-from-afar/article_e230b156-b22e-11df-93d9-001cc4c002e0.html

Zwicker, E. (1961). Subdivision of the audible frequency range into critical bands (Frequenzgruppen). *The Journal of the Acoustical Society of America, 33*(2), 248.

Chapter 7

Aflalo, T. N., & Graziano, M. S. (2006). Partial tuning of motor cortex neurons to final posture in a free-moving paradigm. *Proceedings of the National Academy of Sciences of the United States of America, 103*(8), 2909–2914.

Alexander, G. E., DeLong, M. R., & Strick, P. L. (1986). Parallel organization of functionally segregated circuits linking basal ganglia and cortex. *Annual Review of Neuroscience, 9*, 357–381.

Amodio, D. M., & Frith, C. D. (2006). Meeting of minds: The medial frontal cortex and social cognition. *Nature Reviews Neuroscience, 7*(4), 268 277.

Andersen, R. A., & Buneo, C. A. (2002). Intentional maps in posterior parietal cortex. *Annual Review of Neuroscience, 25*, 189–220.

Assal, F., Schwartz, S., & Vuilleumier, P. (2007). Moving with or without will: Functional neural correlates of alien hand syndrome. *Annals of Neurology, 62*(3), 301–306.

Bauby, J.-D. (2008). *The diving bell and the butterfly.* New York, NY: Random House Digital.

Biran, I., Giovannetti, T., Buxbaum, L., & Chatterjee, A. (2006). The alien hand syndrome: What makes the alien hand alien? *Cognitive Neuropsychology, 23*(4), 563–582.

Bosboom, J., Stoffers, D., & Wolters, E. C. (2004). Cognitive dysfunction and dementia in Parkinson's disease. *Journal of Neural Transmission, 111*(10–11), 1303–1315.

Brown, T. G. (1911). The intrinsic factors in the act of progression in the mammal. *Proceedings of the Royal Society of London. Series B, Containing Papers of a Biological Character, 84*(572), 308–319.

Brown, T. G., & Sherrington, C. (1912). The rule of reflex response in the limb reflexes of the mammal and its exceptions. *The Journal of Physiology, 44*(3), 125–130.

Buccino, G., Binkofski, F., Fink, G. R., Fadiga, L., Fogassi, L., Gallese, V., . . . Freund, H. J. (2001). Action observation activates premotor and parietal areas in a somatotopic manner: An fMRI study. *European Journal of Neuroscience, 13*(2), 400–404.

Burgess, P. W., Gilbert, S. J., & Dumontheil, I. (2007). Function and localization within rostral prefrontal cortex (area 10). *Philosophical Transactions of the Royal Society B: Biological Sciences, 362*(1481), 887–899.

Calder, A. J., Beaver, J. D., Winston, J. S., Dolan, R. J., Jenkins, R., Eger, E., & Henson, R. N. (2007). Separate coding of different gaze directions in the superior temporal sulcus and inferior parietal lobule. *Current Biology, 17*(1), 20–25.

Chong, T. T.-J., Cunnington, R., Williams, M. A., Kanwisher, N., & Mattingley, J. B. (2008). fMRI adaptation reveals mirror neurons in human inferior parietal cortex. *Current Biology, 18*(20), 1576–1580.

Cook, T., Protheroe, R., & Handel, J. (2001). Tetanus: A review of the literature. *British Journal of Anaesthesia, 87*(3), 477–487.

Cunnington, R., Windischberger, C., Deecke, L., & Moser, E. (2002). The preparation and execution of self-initiated and externally-triggered movement: A study of event-related fMRI. *Neuroimage, 15*(2), 373–385.

Della Sala, S., Marchetti, C., & Spinnler, H. (1991). Right-sided anarchic (alien) hand: A longitudinal study. *Neuropsychologia, 29*(11), 1113–1127.

Desmurget, M., & Grafton, S. (2000). Forward modeling allows feedback control for fast reaching movements. *Trends in Cognitive Sciences, 4*(11), 423–431.

Desmurget M., Reilly, K.T., Richard, N., Szathmari, A., Mottolese, C., Sirigu, A. Movement intention after parietal cortex stimulation in humans. *Science 324*(5928), 811-3.

Devinsky, O., Morrell, M. J., & Vogt, B. A. (1995). Review article: Contributions of anterior cingulate cortex to behaviour. *Brain, 118*(1), 279–306.

Di Pellegrino, G., Fadiga, L., Fogassi, L., Gallese, V., & Rizzolatti, G. (1992). Understanding motor events: A neurophysiological study. *Experimental Brain Research, 91*(1), 176–180.

Dicke, U., Roth, G., & Matsushima, T. (1999). Neural substrate for motor control of feeding in amphibians. *Cells Tissues Organs, 163*(3), 127–143.

Dostrovsky, J. O., & Lozano, A. M. (2002). Mechanisms of deep brain stimulation. *Movement Disorders, 17*(S3), S63–S68.

Drebot, M. A., & Artsob, H. (2005). West Nile virus. Update for family physicians. *Canadian Family Physician, 51*(8), 1094–1099.

Dreher, J. C., Koechlin, E., Tierney, M., & Grafman, J. (2008). Damage to the fronto-polar cortex is associated with impaired multitasking. *PLoS One, 3*(9), e3227.

Dux, P. E., Ivanoff, J., Asplund, C. L., & Marois, R. (2006). Isolation of a central bottleneck of information processing with time-resolved fMRI. *Neuron, 52*(6), 1109–1120.

Ferrier, D. (1874). Experiments on the brain of monkeys.—No. I. *Proceedings of the Royal Society of London, 23*(156–163), 409–430.

Fried, I., Katz, A., McCarthy, G., Sass, K., Williamson, P., Spencer, S., & Spencer, D. (1991). Functional organization of human supplementary motor cortex studied by electrical stimulation. *The Journal of Neuroscience, 11*(11), 3656–3666.

Fritsch, G. T., & Hitzig, E. (1870). Uber die elektrische Erregbarkeit des Grosshirns. *Arch. Anat. Physiol. Med. Wiss.* 300–32. Translation in Von Bonin, G., *Some Papers on the Cerebral Cortex.* Springfield, IL: Charles C. Thomas.

Fritsch, G. (1886). Open innovation challenges. *Nature, 33,* 559–559.

Fujii, N., Mushiake, H., & Tanji, J. (2002). Distribution of eye-and arm-movement-related neuronal activity in the SEF and in the SMA and pre-SMA of monkeys. *Journal of Neurophysiology, 87*(4), 2158–2166.

Gallese, V., Fadiga, L., Fogassi, L., & Rizzolatti, G. (1996). Action recognition in the premotor cortex. *Brain, 119*(2), 593–609.

Gallese, V., & Goldman, A. (1998). Mirror neurons and the simulation theory of mind-reading. *Trends in Cognitive Sciences, 2*(12), 493–501.

Georgopoulos, A. P., Kettner, R. E., & Schwartz, A. B. (1988). Primate motor cortex and free arm movements to visual targets in three-dimensional space. II. Coding of the direction of movement by a neuronal population. *The Journal of Neuroscience, 8*(8), 2928–2937.

Gerardin, E., Sirigu, A., Lehéricy, S., Poline, J.-B., Gaymard, B., Marsault, C., ... Le Bihan, D. (2000). Partially overlapping neural networks for real and imagined hand movements. *Cerebral Cortex, 10*(11), 1093–1104.

Gerloff, C., Cohen, L. G., Floeter, M. K., Chen, R., Corwell, B., & Hallett, M. (1998). Inhibitory influence of the ipsilateral motor cortex on responses to stimulation of the human cortex and pyramidal tract. *The Journal of Physiology, 510*(1), 249–259.

Geyer, S., Ledberg, A., Schleicher, A., Kinomura, S., Schormann, T., Bürgel, U., ... Roland, P. E. (1996). Two different areas within the primary motor cortex of man. *Nature, 38*(6594), 805–807.

Goldman, P. S., & Rosvold, H. E. (1970). Localization of function within the dorsolateral prefrontal cortex of the rhesus monkey. *Experimental Neurology, 27*(2), 291–304.

Goulding, M. (2009). Circuits controlling vertebrate locomotion: Moving in a new direction. *Nature Reviews Neuroscience, 10*(7), 507–518.

Graziano, M. (2006). The organization of behavioral repertoire in motor cortex. *Annual Review of Neuroscience, 29,* 105–134.

Griffith, H. R., & Johnson, G. E. (1942). The use of curare in general anesthesia. *Anesthesiology, 3*(4), 418–420.

Guenther, F. H., Brumberg, J. S., Wright, E. J., Nieto-Castanon, A., Tourville, J. A., Panko, M., ... Andreasen, D. S. (2009). A wireless brain-machine interface for real-time speech synthesis. *PloS One, 4*(12), e8218.

Haggard, P. (2008). Human volition: Towards a neuroscience of will. *Nature Reviews Neuroscience, 9*(12), 934–946.

Hazy, T. E., Frank, M. J., & O'Reilly, R. C. (2007). Towards an executive without a homunculus: Computational models of the prefrontal cortex/basal ganglia system. *Philosophical Transactions of the Royal Society B: Biological Sciences, 362*(1485), 1601–1613.

Hochberg, L. R., Serruya, M. D., Friehs, G. M., Mukand, J. A., Saleh, M., Caplan, A. H., ... Donoghue, J. P. (2006). Neuronal ensemble control of prosthetic devices by a human with tetraplegia. *Nature, 442*(7099), 164–171.

Hopper, A. H., Fisher, C. M., & Kleinman, G. M. (1979). Pyramidal infarction in the medulla: A cause of pure motor hemiplegia sparing the face. *Neurology, 29*(1), 91–95.

Hunter, J. (1996). Rocuronium: The newest aminosteroid neuromuscular blocking drug. *British Journal of Anaesthesia, 76*(4), 481–483.

Kennedy, P. R., Bakay, R. A., Moore, M. M., Adams, K., & Goldwaithe, J. (2000). Direct control of a computer from the human central nervous system. *Rehabilitation Engineering, IEEE Transactions on, 8*(2), 198–202.

Kew, O. M., Sutter, R. W., de Gourville, E. M., Dowdle, W. R., & Pallansch, M. A. (2005). Vaccine-derived polioviruses and the endgame strategy for global polio eradication. *Annual Review of Microbiology, 59,* 587–635.

Kiehn, O. (2006). Locomotor circuits in the mammalian spinal cord. *Annual Review of Neuroscience, 29,* 279–306.

Kieras, D. E., & Meyer, D. E. (1997). An overview of the EPIC architecture for cognition and performance with application to human–computer interaction. *Human–Computer Interaction, 12*(4), 391–438.

Koechlin, E., Corrado, G., Pietrini, P., & Grafman, J. (2000). Dissociating the role of the medial and lateral anterior prefrontal cortex in human planning. *Proceedings of the National Academy of Sciences, 97*(13), 7651–7656.

Koechlin, E., Ody, C., & Kouneiher, F. (2003). The architecture of cognitive control in the human prefrontal cortex. *Science, 302*(5648), 1181–1185.

Koechlin, E., & Summerfield, C. (2007). An information theoretical approach to prefrontal executive function. *Trends in Cognitive Science, 11*(6), 229–235.

Kuhtz-Buschbeck, J. P., van der Horst, C., Wolff, S., Filippow, N., Nabavi, A., Jansen, O., & Braun, P. M. (2007). Activation of the supplementary motor area (SMA) during voluntary pelvic floor muscle contractions—An fMRI study. *NeuroImage, 35*(2), 449–457.

Kullander, K., Butt, S. J., Lebret, J. M., Lundfald, L., Restrepo, C. E., Rydström, A., . . . Kiehn, O. (2003). Role of EphA4 and EphrinB3 in local neuronal circuits that control walking. *Science, 299*(5614), 1889–1892.

Kumar, R., Lozano, A., Kim, Y., Hutchison, W., Sime, E., Halket, E., & Lang, A. (1998). Double-blind evaluation of subthalamic nucleus deep brain stimulation in advanced Parkinson's disease. *Neurology, 51*(3), 850–855.

Lau, H., Rogers, R., Ramnani, N., & Passingham, R. (2004). Willed action and attention to the selection of action. *Neuroimage, 21*(4), 1407–1415.

Leiner, H. C., Leiner, A. L., & Dow, R. S. (1993). Cognitive and language functions of the human cerebellum. *Trends in Neurosciences, 16*(11), 444–447.

Lemon, R. N. (2008). Descending pathways in motor control. *Annual Review of Neuroscience, 31*, 195–218.

Libet, B., Gleason, C. A., Wright, E. W., & Pearl, D. K. (1983). Time of conscious intention to act in relation to onset of cerebral activity (readiness-potential) the unconscious initiation of a freely voluntary act. *Brain, 106*(3), 623–642.

Lloyd, K., Davidson, L., & Hornykiewicz, O. (1975). The neurochemistry of Parkinson's disease: Effect of l-DOPA therapy. *Journal of Pharmacology and Experimental Therapeutics, 195*(3), 453–464.

Marr, D. (1969). A theory of cerebellar cortex. *The Journal of Physiology, 202*(2), 437–470.

Martindale, D. (2001). Road map for the mind. *Scientific American, 285*(2), 13–14.

McIntyre, C. C., Mori, S., Sherman, D. L., Thakor, N. V., & Vitek, J. L. (2004). Electric field and stimulating influence generated by deep brain stimulation of the subthalamic nucleus. *Clinical Neurophysiology, 115*(3), 589–595.

Mitz, A. R., & Wise, S. P. (1987). The somatotopic organization of the supplementary motor area: Intracortical microstimulation mapping. *The Journal of Neuroscience, 7*(4), 1010–1021.

Nachev, P., Kennard, C., & Husain, M. (2008). Functional role of the supplementary and pre-supplementary motor areas. *Nature Reviews Neuroscience, 9*(11), 856–869.

Parsons, J. H. (1900). On dilatation of the pupil from stimulation of the cortex cerebri. *The British Medical Journal, 2*(2072), 738–740.

Pearce, J. (2009). Marie-Jean-Pierre Flourens (1794–1867) and cortical localization. *European Neurology, 61*(5), 311–314.

Penfield, W., & Boldrey, E. (1937). Somatic motor and sensory representation in the cerebral cortex of man as studied by electrical stimulation. *Brain: A Journal of Neurology, 60*(4), 389–443.

Penfield, W., & Jasper, H. (1954). Epilepsy and the functional anatomy of the human brain. *Brain: A Journal of Neurology, 77*(4), 639–641.

Penry, J. K., & Dreifuss, F. E. (1969). Automatisms associated with the absence of petit mal epilepsy. *Archives of Neurology, 21*(2), 142.

Picard, N., & Strick, P. L. (1996). Motor areas of the medial wall: A review of their location and functional activation. *Cerebral Cortex, 6*(3), 342–353.

Poeppel, D., & Monahan, P. J. (2011). Feedforward and feedback in speech perception: Revisiting analysis by synthesis. *Language and Cognitive Processes, 26*(7), 935–951.

Raos, V., Franchi, G., Gallese, V., & Fogassi, L. (2003). Somatotopic organization of the lateral part of area F2 (dorsal premotor cortex) of the macaque monkey. *Journal of Neurophysiology, 89*(3), 1503–1518.

Rizzolatti, G., & Craighero, L. (2004). The mirror-neuron system. *Annual Review of Neuroscience, 27*, 169–192.

Rizzolatti, G., Fadiga, L., Gallese, V., & Fogassi, L. (1996). Premotor cortex and the recognition of motor actions. *Cognitive Brain Research, 3*(2), 131–141.

Rizzolatti, G., Fogassi, L., & Gallese, V. (2002). Motor and cognitive functions of the ventral premotor cortex. *Current Opinion in Neurobiology, 12*(2), 149–154.

Rizzolatti G., & Luppino, G. (2001). The cortical motor system. *Neuron, 31*(6), 889–901.

Salinas, E., & Abbott, L. (1994). Vector reconstruction from firing rates. *Journal of Computational Neuroscience, 1*(1–2), 89–107.

Sanger, T. D. (1994). Theoretical considerations for the analysis of population coding in motor cortex. *Neural Computation, 6*(1), 29–37.

Schlaug, G. (2001). The brain of musicians. *Annals of the New York Academy of Sciences, 930*(1), 281–299.

Schmahmann, J. D. (2004). Disorders of the cerebellum: Ataxia, dysmetria of thought, and the cerebellar cognitive affective syndrome. *The Journal of Neuropsychiatry and Clinical Neurosciences, 16*(3), 367–378.

Schmahmann, J. D., & Sherman, J. C. (1997). Cerebellar cognitive affective syndrome. *International Review of Neurobiology, 41*, 433–440.

Shallice, T., & Burgess, P. W. (1991). Deficits in strategy application following frontal lobe damage in man. *Brain, 114*(2), 727–741.

Sherrington, C. S. (1900). The spinal cord. In *Textbook of Physiology*. Edinburgh, UK: Pentland.

Sirigu, A., Daprati, E., Ciancia, S., Giraux, P., Nighoghossian, N., Posada, A., & Haggard, P. (2004). Altered awareness of voluntary action after damage to the parietal cortex. *Nature Neuroscience, 7*(1), 80–84.

Sklavos, S., Anastasopoulos, D., & Bronstein, A. (2010). Kinematic redundancy and variance of eye, head and trunk displacements during large horizontal gaze reorientations in standing humans. *Experimental Brain Research, 202*(4), 879–890.

Small, S., Hlustik, P., Noll, D., Genovese, C., & Solodkin, A. (2002). Cerebellar hemispheric activation ipsilateral to the paretic hand correlates with functional recovery after stroke. *Brain, 125*(7), 1544–1557.

Soon, C. S., Brass, M., Heinze, H. J., & Haynes, J. D. (2008). Unconscious determinants of free decisions in the human brain. *Nature Neuroscience, 11*(5), 543–545.

Sotelo, C., Llinas, R., & Baker, R. (1974). Structural study of inferior olivary nucleus of the cat: Morphological correlates of electrotonic coupling. *Journal of Neurophysiology, 37*(3), 541–559.

Strick, P. L., Dum, R. P., & Fiez, J. A. (2009). Cerebellum and nonmotor function. *Annual Review of Neuroscience, 32*, 413–434.

Strong, M. J., Grace, G. M., Freedman, M., Lomen-Hoerth, C., Woolley, S., Goldstein, L. H., . . . Leigh, P. N. (2009). Consensus criteria for the diagnosis of frontotemporal cognitive and behavioural syndromes in amyotrophic lateral sclerosis. *Amyotrophic Lateral Sclerosis, 10*(3), 131–146.

Sugimoto, T., Bennett, G. J., & Kajander, K. C. (1990). Transsynaptic degeneration in the superficial dorsal horn after sciatic nerve injury: Effects of a chronic constriction injury, transection, and strychnine. *Pain, 42*(2), 205–213.

Takenobu, Y., Hayashi, T., Moriwaki, H., Nagatsuka, K., Naritomi, H., and Fukuyama, H. (2013). Motor recovery and microstructural change in rubro-spinal tract in subcortical stroke. *NeuroImage Clinical, 4*, 201–208.

Tanji, J., & Hoshi, E. (2008). Role of the lateral prefrontal cortex in executive behavioral control. *Physiological Reviews, 88*(1), 37–57.

Van Hulle, M. M. (1997). The formation of topographic maps that maximize the average mutual information of the output responses to noiseless input signals. *Neural Computation, 9*(3), 595–606.

Volkmann, J., Joliot, M., Mogilner, A., Ioannides, A., Lado, F., Fazzini, E., . . . Llinas, R. (1996). Central motor loop oscillations in parkinsonian resting tremor revealed magnetoencephalography. *Neurology, 46*(5), 1359–1359.

Vygotsky LS. 1934. *Thought and Language.* Cambridge, MA: MIT Press

Watson, R. T., Fleet, W. S., Gonzalez-Rothi, L., & Heilman, K. M. (1986). Apraxia and the supplementary motor area. *Archives of Neurology, 43*(8), 787.

Williams, J. H., Whiten, A., Suddendorf, T., & Perrett, D. I. (2001). Imitation, mirror neurons and autism. *Neuroscience & Biobehavioral Reviews, 25*(4), 287–295.

Wolpert, D. M., Miall, R. C., & Kawato, M. (1998). Internal models in the cerebellum. *Trends in Cognitive Sciences, 2*(9), 338–347.

Yokoyama, N., Romero, M. I., Cowan, C. A., Galvan, P., Helmbacher, F., Charnay, P., . . . Henkemeyer, M. (2001). Forward signaling mediated by ephrin-B3 prevents contralateral corticospinal axons from recrossing the spinal cord midline. *Neuron, 29*(1), 85–97.

Yousry, T., Schmid, U., Alkadhi, H., Schmidt, D., Peraud, A., Buettner, A., & Winkler, P. (1997). Localization of the motor hand area to a knob on the precentral gyrus. A new landmark. *Brain, 120*(1), 141–157.

Chapter 8

Adcock, R. A., Thangavel, A., Whitfield-Gabrieli, S., Knutson, B., & Gabrieli, J. D. (2006). Reward-motivated learning: Mesolimbic activation precedes memory formation. *Neuron, 50*(3), 507–517.

Alkire, M. T., Haier, R. J., Barker, S. J., Shah, N. K., Wu, J. C., & Kao, J. Y. (1995). Cerebral metabolism during propofol anesthesia in humans studied with positron emission tomography. *Anesthesiology, 82*(2), 393–403.

Alkire, M. T., Hudetz, A. G., & Tononi, G. (2008). Consciousness and anesthesia. *Science, 322*(5903), 876–880.

Alspector, J., Gannett, J. W., Haber, S., Parker, M. B., & Chu, R. (1991). A VLSI-efficient technique for generating multiple uncorrelated noise sources and its application to stochastic neural networks. *Circuits and Systems, IEEE Transactions on, 38*(1), 109–123.

Amodio, D. M., & Frith, C. D. (2006). Meeting of minds: The medial frontal cortex and social cognition. *Nature Reviews: Neuroscience, 7*(4), 268–277.

Amzica, F., & Steriade, M. (1998). Electrophysiological correlates of sleep delta waves. *Electroencephalography and Clinical Neurophysiology, 107*(2), 69–83.

Baars, B. J. (2002). The conscious access hypothesis: Origins and recent evidence. *Trends in Cognitive Sciences, 6*(1), 47–52.

Baars, B. J. (2005). Global workspace theory of consciousness: Toward a cognitive neuroscience of human experience. *Progress in Brain Research, 150*, 45–53.

BBC. (2006). *Pickpocket challenge.* Broadcast February 3, 2006, BBC1. Retrieved clip 4 May, 2014, https://www.youtube.com/watch?v=cZcyxq20N8U.

Beck, D. M., Muggleton, N., Walsh, V., & Lavie, N. (2006). Right parietal cortex plays a critical role in change blindness. *Cerebral Cortex, 16*(5), 712–717.

Beck, D. M., Rees, G., Frith, C. D., & Lavie, N. (2001). Neural correlates of change detection and change blindness. *Nature Neuroscience, 4*(6), 645–650.

Belelli, D., Pistis, M., Peters, J. A., & Lambert, J. J. (1999). General anaesthetic action at transmitter-gated inhibitory amino acid receptors. *Trends in Pharmacological Sciences, 20*(12), 496–502.

Bestmann, S., Baudewig, J., Siebner, H. R., Rothwell, J. C., & Frahm, J. (2004). Functional MRI of the immediate impact of transcranial magnetic stimulation on cortical and subcortical motor circuits. *European Journal of Neuroscience, 19*(7), 1950–1962.

Bisiach, E., & Geminiani, G. (1991). Anosognosia related to hemiplegia and hemianopia. In G. P. Prigatano & D. L. Schacter (Eds.), *Awareness of deficit after brain injury* (pp. 17–39). New York, NY: Oxford University Press.

Bisiach, E., & Luzzatti, C. (1978). Unilateral neglect of representational space. *Cortex; A Journal Devoted to the Study of the Nervous System and Behavior, 14*(1), 129–133.

Bisiach, E., Rusconi, M. L., & Vallar, G. (1991). Remission of somatoparaphrenic delusion through vestibular stimulation. *Neuropsychologia, 29*(10), 1029–1031.

Bloom, P. (2004). *Descartes' baby.* New York, NY: Basic Books.

Bogen, J. E. (1997). Some neurophysiologic aspects of consciousness. *Seminars in Neurology, 17*(2), 95–103.

Boly, M., Massimini, M., & Tononi, G. (2009). Theoretical approaches to the diagnosis of altered states of consciousness. *Progress in Brain Research, 177*, 383–398.

Boly, M., Phillips, C., Tshibanda, L., Vanhaudenhuyse, A., Schabus, M., Dang Vu, T. T., . . . Laureys, S. (2008). Intrinsic brain activity in altered states of consciousness. *Annals of the New York Academy of Sciences, 1129*(1), 119–129.

Bonhomme, V., Boveroux, P., Hans, P., Brichant, J. F., Vanhaudenhuyse, A., Boly, M., & Laureys, S. (2011). Influence of anesthesia on cerebral blood flow, cerebral metabolic rate, and brain functional connectivity. *Current Opinion in Anesthesiology, 24*(5), 474–479.

Boveroux, P., Bonhomme, V., Boly, M., Vanhaudenhuyse, A., Maquet, P., & Laureys, S. (2008). Brain function in physiologically, pharmacologically, and pathologically altered states of consciousness. *International Anesthesiology Clinics, 46*(3), 131–146.

Bovill, J. G. (2007). *Anaesthesia—A medical and pharmacological revolution.* Leiden, Netherlands: Leiden University.

Bremer, F. (1935). Cerveau "isolé" et physiologie du sommeil. *Comptes Rendus des Séances et Mémoires de la Société de Biologie, 118*, 1235–1241.

Brodbeck, V., Kuhn, A., von Wegner, F., Morzelewski, A., Tagliazucchi, E., Borisov, S., . . . Laufs, H. (2012). EEG microstates of wakefulness and NREM sleep. *Neuroimage, 62*(3), 2129–2139.

Brown, H., Friston, K., & Bestmann, S. (2011). Active inference, attention, and motor preparation. *Frontiers in Psychology, 2,* 218.

Burgess, N., Maguire, E. A., Spiers, H. J., & O'Keefe, J. (2001). A temporoparietal and prefrontal network for retrieving the spatial context of lifelike events. *Neuroimage, 14*(2), 439–453.

Butter, C. M., Buchtel, H. A., & Santucci, R. (1989). Spatial attentional shifts: Further evidence for the role of polysensory mechanisms using visual and tactile stimuli. *Neuropsychologia, 27*(10), 1231–1240.

Buxbaum, L., Ferraro, M., Veramonti, T., Farne, A., Whyte, J., Ladavas, E., . . . Coslett, H. (2004). Hemispatial neglect: Subtypes, neuroanatomy, and disability. *Neurology, 62*(5), 749–756.

Chawla, D., Lumer, E. D., & Friston, K. J. (1999). The relationship between synchronization among neuronal populations and their mean activity levels. *Neural Computation, 11*(6), 1389–1411.

Chong, S. C., Tadin, D., & Blake, R. (2005). Endogenous attention prolongs dominance durations in binocular rivalry. *Journal of Vision, 5*(11), 1004–1012.

Cohen, M. R., & Maunsell, J. H. (2009). Attention improves performance primarily by reducing interneuronal correlations. *Nature Neuroscience, 12*(12), 1594–1600.

Constantinidis, C., Franowicz, M. N., & Goldman-Rakic, P. S. (2001). Coding specificity in cortical microcircuits: A multiple-electrode analysis of primate prefrontal cortex. *Journal of Neuroscience, 21*(10), 3646–3655.

Coull, J. T., Frith, C. D., Buchel, C., & Nobre, A. C. (2000). Orienting attention in time: Behavioural and neuroanatomical distinction between exogenous and endogenous shifts. *Neuropsychologia, 38*(6), 808–819.

Coull, J. T., & Nobre, A. C. (1998). Where and when to pay attention: The neural systems for directing attention to spatial locations and to time intervals as revealed by both PET and fMRI. *The Journal of Neuroscience: The Official Journal of the Society for Neuroscience, 18*(18), 7426–7435.

Courchesne, E., Hillyard, S. A., & Galambos, R. (1975). Stimulus novelty, task relevance and the visual evoked potential in man. *Electroencephalography and Clinical Neurophysiology, 39*(2), 131–143.

Crick, F., & Mitchison, G. (1983). The function of dream sleep. *Nature, 304*(5922), 111–114.

Critchley, H. D., Mathias, C. J., Josephs, O., O'Doherty, J., Zanini, S., Dewar, B. K., . . . Dolan, R. J. (2003). Human cingulate cortex and autonomic control: Converging neuroimaging and clinical evidence. *Brain: A Journal of Neurology, 126*(Pt. 10), 2139–2152.

Davis, S., Renaudineau, S., Poirier, R., Poucet, B., Save, E., & Laroche, S. (2010). The formation and stability of recognition memory: What happens upon recall? *Frontiers in Behavioral Neuroscience, 4,* 177.

Dehaene, S., & Naccache, L. (2001). Towards a cognitive neuroscience of consciousness: Basic evidence and a workspace framework. *Cognition, 79*(1), 1–37.

Dehaene, S., Naccache, L., Cohen, L., Bihan, D. L., Mangin, J. F., Poline, J. B., & Riviere, D. (2001). Cerebral mechanisms of word masking and unconscious repetition priming. *Nature Neuroscience, 4*(7), 752–758.

Descartes, R. (1996). *Descartes: Meditations on first philosophy: With selections from the objections and replies.* Cambridge, UK: Cambridge University Press.

Domich, L., Oakson, G., & Steriade, M. (1986). Thalamic burst patterns in the naturally sleeping cat: A comparison between cortically projecting and reticularis neurones. *The Journal of Physiology, 379*(1), 429–449.

Downar, J., Crawley, A. P., Mikulis, D. J., & Davis, K. D. (2002). A cortical network sensitive to stimulus salience in a neutral behavioral context across multiple sensory modalities. *Journal of Neurophysiology, 87*(1), 615–620.

Doyle, P., & Matta, B. (1999). Burst suppression or isoelectric encephalogram for cerebral protection: Evidence from metabolic suppression studies. *British Journal of Anaesthesia, 83*(4), 580–584.

Driver, J., & Vuilleumier, P. (2001). Perceptual awareness and its loss in unilateral neglect and extinction. *Cognition, 79*(1), 39–88.

Farah, M. J., Wong, A. B., Monheit, M. A., & Morrow, L. A. (1989). Parietal lobe mechanisms of spatial attention: Modality-specific or supramodal? *Neuropsychologia, 27*(4), 461–470.

Farb, N. A., Segal, Z. V., Mayberg, H., Bean, J., McKeon, D., Fatima, Z., & Anderson, A. K. (2007). Attending to the present: Mindfulness meditation reveals distinct neural modes of self-reference. *Social Cognitive and Affective Neuroscience, 2*(4), 313–322.

Ferrarelli, F., Massimini, M., Sarasso, S., Casali, A., Riedner, B. A., Angelini, G., . . . Pearce, R. A. (2010). Breakdown in cortical effective connectivity during midazolam-induced loss of consciousness. *Proceedings of the National Academy of Sciences of the United States of America, 107*(6), 2681–2686.

Frackowiak, R. S., Friston, K. J., Frith, C. D., Dolan, R. J., Mazziotta, J. C., & Hallett, M. (1997). *Human Brain Function.* Waltham, MA: Academic Press USA.

Gitelman, D. R., Nobre, A. C., Parrish, T. B., LaBar, K. S., Kim, Y. H., Meyer, J. R., & Mesulam, M. (1999). A large-scale distributed network for covert spatial attention: Further anatomical delineation based on stringent behavioural and cognitive controls. *Brain: A Journal of Neurology, 122* (Pt. 6), 1093–1106.

Grill-Spector, K., Henson, R., & Martin, A. (2006). Repetition and the brain: Neural models of stimulus-specific effects. *Trends in Cognitive Sciences, 10*(1), 14–23.

Haines, R. F. (1991). A breakdown in simultaneous information processing. In G. Obrecht & L. Stark (Eds.), *Presbyopia research* (pp. 171–175). New York, NY: Plenum.

Halligan, P. W., & Marshall, J. C. (1998). Neglect of awareness. *Consciousness and Cognition, 7*(3), 356–380.

Hayhoe, M. M., Bensinger, D. G., & Ballard, D. H. (1998). Task constraints in visual working memory. *Vision Research, 38*(1), 125–137.

Heilman, K. M., & Valenstein, E. (1979). Mechanisms underlying hemispatial neglect. *Annals of Neurology, 5*(2), 166–170.

Hobson, J. A., & Pace-Schott, E. F. (2002). The cognitive neuroscience of sleep: Neuronal systems, consciousness and learning. *Nature Reviews: Neuroscience, 3*(9), 679–693.

Horovitz, S. G., Braun, A. R., Carr, W. S., Picchioni, D., Balkin, T. J., Fukunaga, M., & Duyn, J. H. (2009). Decoupling of the brain's default mode network during deep sleep. *Proceedings of the National Academy of Sciences of the United States of America, 106*(27), 11376–11381.

Hugdahl, K., & Nordby, H. (1994). Electrophysiological correlates to cued attentional shifts in the visual and auditory modalities. *Behavioral and Neural Biology, 62*(1), 21–32.

Ingle, D. (1975). Focal attention in the frog: Behavioral and physiological correlates. *Science, 188*(4192), 1033–1035.

Jackson, F., & Pettit, P. (1988). Functionalism and broad content. *Mind, 97*(387), 381–400.

James, W. (1890). *The principles of psychology*. London, UK: MacMillan.

John, E. R., & Prichep, L. S. (2005). The anesthetic cascade: A theory of how anesthesia suppresses consciousness. *Anesthesiology*, 102(2), 447–471.

Jones, E. G. (2002). Thalamic circuitry and thalamocortical synchrony. *Philosophical Transactions of the Royal Society of London. Series B, Biological Sciences*, 357(1428), 1659–1673.

Jonides, J., & Irwin, D. E. (1981). Capturing attention. *Cognition*, 10(1–3), 145–150.

Kajimura, N., Uchiyama, M., Takayama, Y., Uchida, S., Uema, T., Kato, M., . . . Takahashi, K. (1999). Activity of midbrain reticular formation and neocortex during the progression of human non-rapid eye movement sleep. *The Journal of Neuroscience*, 19(22), 10065–10073.

Kanwisher, N., McDermott, J., & Chun, M. M. (1997). The fusiform face area: A module in human extrastriate cortex specialized for face perception. *The Journal of Neuroscience*, 17(11), 4302–4311.

Karnath, H.-O. (1988). Deficits of attention in acute and recovered visual hemi-neglect. *Neuropsychologia*, 26(1), 27–43.

Kastner, S., & Ungerleider, L. G. (2000). Mechanisms of visual attention in the human cortex. *Annual Review of Neuroscience*, 23, 315–341.

Kinomura, S., Larsson, J., Gulyás, B., & Roland, P. E. (1996). Activation by attention of the human reticular formation and thalamic intralaminar nuclei. *Science*, 271(5248), 512–515.

Kuhn, G., Tatler, B. W., Findlay, J. M., & Cole, G. G. (2008). Misdirection in magic: Implications for the relationship between eye gaze and attention. *Visual Cognition*, 16(2–3), 391–405.

Laureys, S. (2005). Science and society: Death, unconsciousness and the brain. *Nature Reviews: Neuroscience*, 6(11), 899–909.

Laureys, S., Faymonville, M. E., Degueldre, C., Fiore, G. D., Damas, P., Lambermont, B., Janssens, N., Aerts, J., Franck, G., Luxen, A., Moonen, G., Lamy, M., Maquet, P. (2000). Auditory processing in the vegetative state. *Brain*. 123(8),1589–601.

Laureys, S., Faymonville, M. E., Peigneux, P., Damas, P., Lambermont, B., Del Fiore, G., . . . Maquet, P. (2002). Cortical processing of noxious somatosensory stimuli in the persistent vegetative state. *Neuroimage*, 17(2), 732–741.

Laureys, S., Owen, A. M., & Schiff, N. D. (2004). Brain function in coma, vegetative state, and related disorders. *The Lancet Neurology*, 3(9), 537–546.

Lee, D., Port, N. L., Kruse, W., & Georgopoulos, A. P. (1998). Variability and correlated noise in the discharge of neurons in motor and parietal areas of the primate cortex. *Journal of Neuroscience*, 18(3), 1161–1170.

Leibniz, G. W. (1896). *New essays concerning human understanding*. New York, NY: Macmillan.

Limb, C. J., & Braun, A. R. (2008). Neural substrates of spontaneous musical performance: An FMRI study of jazz improvisation. *PloS One*, 3(2), e1679.

Linden, D. E., Prvulovic, D., Formisano, E., Vollinger, M., Zanella, F. E., Goebel, R., & Dierks, T. (1999). The functional neuroanatomy of target detection: An fMRI study of visual and auditory oddball tasks. *Cerebral Cortex*, 9(8), 815–823.

Llinas, R., & Ribary, U. (1993). Coherent 40-Hz oscillation characterizes dream state in humans. *Proceedings of the National Academy of Sciences of the United States of America*, 90(5), 2078–2081.

Lumer, E. D., Friston, K. J., & Rees, G. (1998). Neural correlates of perceptual rivalry in the human brain. *Science*, 280(5371), 1930–1934.

Mack, A., & Rock, I. (1999). Inattention blindness: An overview. *Psyche*, 5(3).

MacKinnon, F. I. (1928). Behaviorism and metaphysics. *The Journal of Philosophy*, 25(13), 353–356.

Macknik, S. L., King, M., Randi, J., Robbins, A., Teller, Thompson, J., & Martinez-Conde, S. (2008). Attention and awareness in stage magic: Turning tricks into research. *Nature Reviews: Neuroscience*, 9(11), 871–879.

Magoun, H. (1952). An ascending reticular activating system in the brain stem. *Archives of Neurology and Psychiatry*, 67(2), 145–154.

Maquet, P., Péters, J.-M., Aerts, J., Delfiore, G., Degueldre, C., Luxen, A., & Franck, G. (1996). Functional neuroanatomy of human rapid-eye-movement sleep and dreaming. *Nature*, 383(6596), 163–166.

Marken, R. S. (2002). Looking at behavior through control theory glasses. *Review of General Psychology*, 6(3), 260–270.

Marois, R., Chun, M. M., & Gore, J. C. (2000). Neural correlates of the attentional blink. *Neuron*, 28(1), 299–308.

Mashour, G. A. (2004). Consciousness unbound: Toward a paradigm of general anesthesia. *Anesthesiology*, 100(2), 428–433.

Massimini, M., Ferrarelli, F., Huber, R., Esser, S. K., Singh, H., & Tononi, G. (2005). Breakdown of cortical effective connectivity during sleep. *Science*, 309(5744), 2228–2232.

McAdams, C. J., & Maunsell, J. H. (1999). Effects of attention on orientation-tuning functions of single neurons in macaque cortical area V4. *The Journal of Neuroscience: The Official Journal of the Society for Neuroscience*, 19(1), 431–441.

Mesulam, M. M. (1998). From sensation to cognition. *Brain: A Journal of Neurology*, 121(Pt. 6), 1013–1052.

Mesulam, M. M. (1999). Spatial attention and neglect: Parietal, frontal and cingulate contributions to the mental representation and attentional targeting of salient extrapersonal events. *Philosophical Transactions of the Royal Society of London. Series B, Biological Sciences*, 354(1387), 1325–1346.

Momose, T., Nishikawa, J., Watanabe, T., Ohtake, T., Sasaki, Y., Sasaki, M., & Mii, K. (1992). Clinical application of 18F-FDG-PET in patients with brain death. *Kaku Igaku: The Japanese Journal of Nuclear Medicine*, 29(9), 1139–1142.

Moran, J., & Desimone, R. (1985). Selective attention gates visual processing in the extrastriate cortex. *Science*, 229(4715), 782–784.

Moruzzi, G. (1972). The sleep-waking cycle. In *Neurophysiology and neurochemistry of sleep and wakefulness* (pp. 1–165). New York, NY: Springer.

Murray, S. O., Olshausen, B. A., & Woods, D. L. (2003). Processing shape, motion and three-dimensional shape-from-motion in the human cortex. *Cerebral Cortex*, 13(5), 508–516.

Murthy, V. N., & Fetz, E. E. (1996). Synchronization of neurons during local field potential oscillations in sensorimotor cortex of awake monkeys. *Journal of Neurophysiology*, 76(6), 3968–3982.

Nobre, A. C. (2001). The attentive homunculus: Now you see it, now you don't. *Neuroscience and Biobehavioral Reviews*, 25(6), 477–496.

Nordqvist, C. (2007, August 4). Deep brain stimulation rouses man in minimally conscious state. *Medical News Today*. Retrieved from http://www.medicalnewstoday.com/articles/78799.php/

O'Regan, J. K. (2000). Perception, attention and the grand illusion. *Psyche*, 6(15).

O'Regan, J. K., Rensink, R. A., & Clark, J. J. (1999). Changeblindness as a result of "mudsplashes." *Nature*, 398(6722), 34.

Opitz, B., Mecklinger, A., Friederici, A. D., & von Cramon, D. Y. (1999). The functional neuroanatomy of novelty processing: Integrating ERP and fMRI results. *Cerebral Cortex*, 9(4), 379–391.

Orbach, J., Ehrlich, D., & Heath, H. A. (1963). Reversibility of the Necker cube: I. An examination of the concept of "satiation of orientation." *Perceptual and Motor Skills, 17*(2), 439–458.

Pace-Schott, E. F. (2003). *Sleep and dreaming: Scientific advances and reconsiderations.* Cambridge, UK: Cambridge University Press.

Parvizi, J., & Damasio, A. R. (2003). Neuroanatomical correlates of brainstem coma. *Brain, 126*(Pt. 7), 1524–1536.

Pause, B. M., Sojka, B., Krauel, K., & Ferstl, R. (1996). The nature of the late positive complex within the olfactory event-related potential (OERP). *Psychophysiology, 33*(4), 376–384.

Posner, M. I., & Petersen, S. E. (1990). The attention system of the human brain. *Annual Review of Neuroscience, 13*, 25–42.

Posner, M. I., Snyder, C. R., & Davidson, B. J. (1980). Attention and the detection of signals. *Journal of Experimental Psychology, 109*(2), 160–174.

Rees, G., Russell, C., Frith, C. D., & Driver, J. (1999). Inattentional blindness versus inattentional amnesia for fixated but ignored words. *Science, 286*(5449), 2504–2507.

Rees, G., Wojciulik, E., Clarke, K., Husain, M., Frith, C., & Driver, J. (2000). Unconscious activation of visual cortex in the damaged right hemisphere of a parietal patient with extinction. *Brain: A Journal of Neurology, 123*(Pt. 8), 1624–1633.

Rensink, R. A., O'Regan, J. K., & Clark, J. J. (1997). To see or not to see: The need for attention to perceive changes in scenes. *Psychological Science, 8*(5), 368–373.

Reynolds, J. H., & Chelazzi, L. (2004). Attentional modulation of visual processing. *Annual Review of Neuroscience, 27*, 611–647.

Reynolds, J. H., Pasternak, T., & Desimone, R. (2000). Attention increases sensitivity of V4 neurons. *Neuron, 26*(3), 703–714.

Ries, C. R., & Puil, E. (1999). Mechanism of anesthesia revealed by shunting actions of isoflurane on thalamocortical neurons. *Journal of Neurophysiology, 81*(4), 1795–1801.

Rode, G., Charles, N., Perenin, M.-T., Vighetto, A., Trillet, M., & Aimard, G. (1992). Partial remission of hemiplegia and somatoparaphrenia through vestibular stimulation in a case of unilateral neglect. *Cortex, 28*(2), 203–208.

Roelfsema, P. R., Engel, A. K., Konig, P., & Singer, W. (1997). Visuomotor integration is associated with zero time-lag synchronization among cortical areas. *Nature, 385*(6612), 157–161.

Ronan, M. (1989). Origins of the descending spinal projections in petromyzontid and myxinoid agnathans. *Journal of Comparative Neurology, 281*(1), 54–68.

Rosenthal, D. M. (2000). Metacognition and higher-order thoughts. *Consciousness and Cognition, 9*(2 Pt. 1), 231–242.

Saper, C. B., Chou, T. C., & Scammell, T. E. (2001). The sleep switch: Hypothalamic control of sleep and wakefulness. *Trends in Neurosciences, 24*(12), 726–731.

Schiff, N. D., Giacino, J. T., & Fins, J. J. (2009). Deep brain stimulation, neuroethics, and the minimally conscious state: Moving beyond proof of principle. *Archives of Neurology, 66*(6), 697–702.

Schiff, N. D., Giacino, J. T., Kalmar, K., Victor, J. D., Baker, K., Gerber, M., . . . Rezai, A. R. (2007). Behavioural improvements with thalamic stimulation after severe traumatic brain injury. *Nature, 448*(7153), 600–603.

Schiff, N. D., Rodriguez-Moreno, D., Kamal, A., Kim, K. H., Giacino, J. T., Plum, F., & Hirsch, J. (2005). fMRI reveals large-scale network activation in minimally conscious patients. *Neurology, 64*(3), 514–523.

Servan-Schreiber, D., Printz, H., & Cohen, J. D. (1990). A network model of catecholamine effects: Gain, signal-to-noise ratio, and behavior. *Science, 249*(4971), 892–895.

Simons, D. J., & Chabris, C. F. (1999). Gorillas in our midst: Sustained inattentional blindness for dynamic events. *Perception, 28*(9), 1059–1074.

Simons, D. J., & Levin, D. T. (1997). Change blindness. *Trends in Cognitive Sciences, 1*(7), 261–267.

Simons, D. J., & Levin, D. T. (1998). Failure to detect changes to people during a real-world interaction. *Psychonomic Bulletin & Review, 4*, 501–506.

Spoormaker, V. I., Schroter, M. S., Gleiser, P. M., Andrade, K. C., Dresler, M., Wehrle, R., . . . Czisch, M. (2010). Development of a large-scale functional brain network during human non-rapid eye movement sleep. *The Journal of Neuroscience: The Official Journal of the Society for Neuroscience, 30*(34), 11379–11387.

Steinmetz, P. N., Roy, A., Fitzgerald, P. J., Hsiao, S. S., Johnson, K. O., & Niebur, E. (2000). Attention modulates synchronized neuronal firing in primate somatosensory cortex. *Nature, 404*(6774), 187–190.

Steriade, M. (2001). Active neocortical processes during quiescent sleep. *Archives Italiennes de Biologie, 139*(1–2), 37–51.

Strauman, T. J., Detloff, A. M., Sestokas, R., Smith, D. V., Goetz, E. L., Rivera, C., & Kwapil, L. (2012). What shall I be, what must I be: Neural correlates of personal goal activation. *Frontiers in Integrative Neuroscience, 6*, 123.

Sukhotinsky, I., Zalkind, V., Lu, J., Hopkins, D. A., Saper, C. B., & Devor, M. (2007). Neural pathways associated with loss of consciousness caused by intracerebral microinjection of GABA A-active anesthetics. *The European Journal of Neuroscience, 25*(5), 1417–1436.

Swick, D., & Knight, R. T. (1998). Lesion studies of prefrontal cortex and attention. In R. Parasuraman (Ed.), *The attentive brain* (pp. 143–162). Cambridge, MA: MIT Press.

Takashima, M., Fujii, T., & Shiina, K. (2012). Face or vase? Areal homogeneity effect. *Perception, 41*(11), 1392–1394.

Tassi, P., & Muzet, A. (2001). Defining the states of consciousness. *Neuroscience & Biobehavioral Reviews, 25*(2), 175–191.

Tommasi, G., Lanotte, M., Albert, U., Zibetti, M., Castelli, L., Maina, G., & Lopiano, L. (2008). Transient acute depressive state induced by subthalamic region stimulation. *Journal of the Neurological Sciences, 273*(1–2), 135–138.

Tononi, G. (2008). Consciousness as integrated information: A provisional manifesto. *The Biological Bulletin, 215*(3), 216–242.

Treue, S., & Martinez Trujillo, J. C. (1999). Feature-based attention influences motion processing gain in macaque visual cortex. *Nature, 399*(6736), 575–579.

Vallar, G., & Ronchi, R. (2009). Somatoparaphrenia: A body delusion. A review of the neuropsychological literature. *Experimental Brain Research, 192*(3), 533–551.

Varela, F., Lachaux, J.-P., Rodriguez, E., & Martinerie, J. (2001). The brainweb: phase synchronization and large-scale integration. *Nature Reviews: Neuroscience, 2*(4), 229–239.

Wager, T. D., Phan, K. L., Liberzon, I., & Taylor, S. F. (2003). Valence, gender, and lateralization of functional brain anatomy in emotion: A meta-analysis of findings from neuroimaging. *Neuroimage, 19*(3), 513–531.

Waroux, O., Massotte, L., Alleva, L., Graulich, A., Thomas, E., Liégeois, J. F., . . . Seutin, V. (2005). SK channels control the firing pattern of midbrain dopaminergic neurons in vivo. *European Journal of Neuroscience, 22*(12), 3111–3121.

Wheatstone, C. (1838). Contributions to the physiology of vision—Part the first. On some remarkable, and hitherto unobserved, phenomena of binocular vision. *Philosophical Transactions of the Royal Society of London, 128*, 371–394.

White, N. S., & Alkire, M. T. (2003). Impaired thalamocortical connectivity in humans during general-anesthetic-induced unconsciousness. *Neuroimage, 19*(2 Pt. 1), 402–411.

Womelsdorf, T., Fries, P., Mitra, P. P., & Desimone, R. (2005). Gamma-band synchronization in visual cortex predicts speed of change detection. *Nature, 439*(7077), 733–736.

Worrell, G. A., Parish, L., Cranstoun, S. D., Jonas, R., Baltuch, G., & Litt, B. (2004). High-frequency oscillations and seizure generation in neocortical epilepsy. *Brain, 127*(Pt. 7), 1496–1506.

Yamaguchi, S., & Knight, R. T. (1991). Anterior and posterior association cortex contributions to the somatosensory P300. *The Journal of Neuroscience: The Official Journal of the Society for Neuroscience, 11*(7), 2039–2054.

Zepelin, H., & Rechtschaffen, A. (1974). Mammalian sleep, longevity, and energy metabolism. *Brain, Behavior, and Evolution, 10*(6), 447–470.

Chapter 9

Allison, T., Puce, A., & McCarthy, G. (2000). Social perception from visual cues: Role of the STS region. *Trends in Cognitive Sciences, 4*(7), 267–278.

Alvarez-Buylla, A. (1990). Mechanism of neurogenesis in adult avian brain. *Experientia, 46*(9), 948–955.

Amaral, D. G. (1993). Emerging principles of intrinsic hippocampal organization. *Current Opinion in Neurobiology, 3*(2), 225–229.

Baars, B. J., & Franklin, S. (2003). How conscious experience and working memory interact. *Trends in Cognitive Sciences, 7*(4), 166–172.

Barbas, H., Zikopoulos, B., & Timbie, C. (2011). Sensory pathways and emotional context for action in primate prefrontal cortex. *Biological Psychiatry, 69*(12), 1133–1139.

Bartlett, F. (1932). *Remembering: A study in experimental and social psychology.* Cambridge, UK: Cambridge University Press.

Bliss, T. V., & Lomo, T. (1973). Long-lasting potentiation of synaptic transmission in the dentate area of the anaesthetized rabbit following stimulation of the perforant path. *Journal of Physiology, 232*(2), 331–356.

Boddaert, N., Chabane, N., Gervais, H., Good, C., Bourgeois, M., Plumet, M., . . . Samson, Y. (2004). Superior temporal sulcus anatomical abnormalities in childhood autism: A voxel-based morphometry MRI study. *Neuroimage, 23*(1), 364–369.

Brodin, A., & Lundborg, K. (2003). Is hippocampal volume affected by specialization for food hoarding in birds? *Proceedings of the Royal Society of London. Series B: Biological Sciences, 270*(1524), 1555–1563.

Buckner, R. L., & Carroll, D. C. (2007). Self-projection and the brain. *Trends in Cognitive Sciences, 11*(2), 49–57.

Burgess, N., Barry, C., & O'Keefe, J. (2007). An oscillatory interference model of grid cell firing. *Hippocampus, 17*(9), 801–812.

Burgess, N., Maguire, E. A., & O'Keefe, J. (2002). The human hippocampus and spatial and episodic memory. *Neuron, 35*(4), 625–641.

Burgess, P. W. (1996). Confabulation and the control of recollection. *Memory, 4*(4), 359–412.

Byrne, P., Becker, S., & Burgess, N. (2007). Remembering the past and imagining the future: A neural model of spatial memory and imagery. *Psychological Review, 114*(2), 340–375.

Cabeza, R., Rao, S. M., Wagner, A. D., Mayer, A. R., & Schacter, D. L. (2001). Can medial temporal lobe regions distinguish true

from false? An event-related functional MRI study of veridical and illusory recognition memory. *Proceedings of the National Academy of Sciences of the United States of America, 98*(8), 4805–4810.

Chung, S., Li, X., & Nelson, S. B. (2002). Short-term depression at thalamocortical synapses contributes to rapid adaptation of cortical sensory responses in vivo. *Neuron, 34*(3), 437–446.

Clark, R. E., & Squire, L. R. (2010). An animal model of recognition memory and medial temporal lobe amnesia: History and current issues. *Neuropsychologia, 48*(8), 2234–2244.

Clayton, N. S., & Dickinson, A. (1998). Episodic-like memory during cache recovery by scrub jays. *Nature, 395*(6699), 272–274.

Clayton, N. S., Salwiczek, L. H., & Dickinson, A. (2007). Episodic memory. *Current Biology, 17*(6), R189–R191.

Cohen, N. J., Eichenbaum, H., Deacedo, B. S., & Corkin, S. (1985). Different memory systems underlying acquisition of procedural and declarative knowledge. *Annals of the New York Academy of Sciences, 444*(1), 54–71.

Corbetta, M., Kincade, J. M., Ollinger, J. M., McAvoy, M. P., & Shulman, G. L. (2000). Voluntary orienting is dissociated from target detection in human posterior parietal cortex. *Nature Neuroscience, 3*(3), 292–297.

Corbetta, M., & Shulman, G. L. (2002). Control of goal-directed and stimulus-driven attention in the brain. *Nature Reviews Neuroscience, 3*(3), 201–215.

Corkin, S., Amaral, D. G., González, R. G., Johnson, K. A., & Hyman, B. T. (1997). HM's medial temporal lobe lesion: Findings from magnetic resonance imaging. *The Journal of Neuroscience, 17*(10), 3964–3979.

Correia, S. P., Dickinson, A., & Clayton, N. S. (2007). Western scrub-jays anticipate future needs independently of their current motivational state. *Current Biology, 17*(10), 856–861.

Cowan, N., Morey, C. C., & Chen, Z. (2007). The legend of the magical number seven. In S. Della Sala (Ed.), *Tall tales about the brain: Things we think we know about the mind, but ain't so.* Oxford, UK: Oxford University Press.

Debiec, J., LeDoux, J. E., & Nader, K. (2002). Cellular and systems reconsolidation in the hippocampus. *Neuron, 36*(3), 527–538.

Dehaene, S., Naccache, L., Cohen, L., Le Bihan, D., Mangin, J.-F., Poline, J.-B., & Rivière, D. (2001). Cerebral mechanisms of word masking and unconscious repetition priming. *Nature Neuroscience, 4*(7), 752–758.

Deng, W., Aimone, J. B., & Gage, F. H. (2010). New neurons and new memories: How does adult hippocampal neurogenesis affect learning and memory? *Nature Reviews Neuroscience, 11*(5), 339–350.

DiMattia, B. V., & Kesner, R. P. (1988). Spatial cognitive maps: Differential role of parietal cortex and hippocampal formation. *Behavioral Neuroscience, 102*(4), 471.

Dolcos, F., LaBar, K. S., & Cabeza, R. (2004). Interaction between the amygdala and the medial temporal lobe memory system predicts better memory for emotional events. *Neuron, 42*(5), 855–863.

Doll, B. B., Shohamy, D., & Daw, N. D. (2014). Multiple memory systems as substrates for multiple decision systems. *Neurobioy of Learning and Memory, 117*:4–13.

Downar, J., Crawley, A. P., Mikulis, D. J., Davis, K. D. (2001). The effect of task relevance on the cortical response to changes in visual and auditory stimuli: An event-related fMRI study. *Neuroimage, 14*(6), 1256–1257.

Eagleman, D. M. (2009). The objectification of overlearned sequences: A new view of spatial sequence synesthesia. *Cortex, 45*(10), 1266–1277.

Eichenbaum, H., & Cohen, N. J. (2001). *From conditioning to conscious recollection: Memory systems of the brain.* Oxford, UK: Oxford University Press.

Eichenbaum, H., Yonelinas, A. P., & Ranganath, C. (2007). The medial temporal lobe and recognition memory. *Annual Review of Neuroscience, 30,* 123–152.

Eriksson, P. S., Perfilieva, E., Björk-Eriksson, T., Alborn, A.-M., Nordborg, C., Peterson, D. A., & Gage, F. H. (1998). Neurogenesis in the adult human hippocampus. *Nature Medicine, 4*(11), 1313–1317.

Ernst, M. O., & Bülthoff, H. H. (2004). Merging the senses into a robust percept. *Trends in Cognitive Sciences, 8*(4), 162–169.

Foster, D. J., & Wilson, M. A. (2006). Reverse replay of behavioural sequences in hippocampal place cells during the awake state. *Nature, 440*(7084), 680–683.

Gasbarri, A., Pompili, A., Packard, M. G., & Tomaz, C. (2014). Habit learning and memory in mammals: Behavioral and neural characteristics. *Neurobioy of Learning and Memory, 114C,* 198–208.

Gazzaniga, M. S. (2004). *The cognitive neurosciences.* Cambridge, MA: MIT Press.

Ghaem, O., Mellet, E., Crivello, F., Tzourio, N., Mazoyer, B., Berthoz, A., & Denis, M. (1997). Mental navigation along memorized routes activates the hippocampus, precuneus, and insula. *Neuroreport, 8*(3), 739–744.

Gilboa, A., Alain, C., Stuss, D. T., Melo, B., Miller, S., & Moscovitch, M. (2006). Mechanisms of spontaneous confabulations: A strategic retrieval account. *Brain, 129*(Pt. 6), 1399–1414.

Gilboa, A., Winocur, G., Grady, C. L., Hevenor, S. J., & Moscovitch, M. (2004). Remembering our past: Functional neuroanatomy of recollection of recent and very remote personal events. *Cerebral Cortex, 14*(11), 1214–1225.

Goldstein, L. E., Rasmusson, A. M., Bunney, B. S., & Roth, R. H. (1996). Role of the amygdala in the coordination of behavioral, neuroendocrine, and prefrontal cortical monoamine responses to psychological stress in the rat. *The Journal of Neuroscience, 16*(15), 4787–4798.

Gould, E., Beylin, A., Tanapat, P., Reeves, A., & Shors, T. J. (1999). Learning enhances adult neurogenesis in the hippocampal formation. *Nature Neuroscience, 2*(3), 260–265.

Gould, E., & Gross, C. G. (2002). Neurogenesis in adult mammals: Some progress and problems. *The Journal of Neuroscience, 22*(3), 619–623.

Grutzendler, J., Kasthuri, N., & Gan, W.-B. (2002). Long-term dendritic spine stability in the adult cortex. *Nature, 420*(6917), 812–816.

Guedj, E., Barbeau, E. J., Didic, M., Felician, O., De Laforte, C., Ranjeva, J.-P., . . . Ceccaldi, M. (2009). Effects of medial temporal lobe degeneration on brain perfusion in amnestic MCI of AD type: Deafferentation and functional compensation? *European Journal of Nuclear Medicine and Molecular Imaging, 36*(7), 1101–1112.

Hafting, T., Fyhn, M., Molden, S., Moser, M.-B., & Moser, E. I. (2005). Microstructure of a spatial map in the entorhinal cortex. *Nature, 436*(7052), 801–806.

Haijima, A., & Ichitani, Y. (2008). Anterograde and retrograde amnesia of place discrimination in retrosplenial cortex and hippocampal lesioned rats. *Learning & Memory, 15*(7), 477–482.

Hassabis, D., Kumaran, D., Vann, S. D., & Maguire, E. A. (2007). Patients with hippocampal amnesia cannot imagine new experiences. *Proceedings of the National Academy of Sciences of the United States of America, 104*(5), 1726–1731.

Hassabis, D., & Maguire, E. A. (2009). The construction system of the brain. *Philosophical Transactions of the Royal Society of London. Series B, Biological Sciences, 364*(1521), 1263–1271.

Hebb, D. O. (1949). *The organization of behavior.* New York, NY: Wiley.

Heinrich, S. U., & Lindquist, S. (2011). Protein-only mechanism induces self-perpetuating changes in the activity of neuronal Aplysia cytoplasmic polyadenylation element binding protein (CPEB). *Proceedings of the National Academy of Sciences of the United States of America, 108*(7), 2999–3004.

Herrick, C. J. (1930). Localization of function in the nervous system. *Proceedings of the National Academy of Sciences of the United States of America, 16*(10), 643.

Hodges, J. R., Patterson, K., Oxbury, S., & Funnell, E. (1992). Semantic dementia progressive fluent aphasia with temporal lobe atrophy. *Brain, 115*(6), 1783–1806.

Hodos, W. (1982). Some perspectives on the evolution of intelligence and the brain. In D. R. Griffin (Ed.), *Animal mind—Human mind* (pp. 33–55). New York, NY: Springer-Verlag.

Hoke, K. L., & Pitts, N. L. (2012). Modulation of sensory–motor integration as a general mechanism for context dependence of behavior. *General and Comparative Endocrinology, 176*(3), 465–471.

Hollup, S. A., Molden, S., Donnett, J. G., Moser, M.-B., & Moser, E. I. (2001). Accumulation of hippocampal place fields at the goal location in an annular watermaze task. *The Journal of Neuroscience, 21*(5), 1635–1644.

Hopfield, J. J. (1982). Neural networks and physical systems with emergent collective computational abilities. *Proceedings of the National Academy of Sciences of the United States of America, 79*(8), 2554–2558.

Hoppe, C. (2006). Controlling epilepsy. *Scientific American Mind, 17*(3), 62–67.

Horn, G. (1981). Review lecture: Neural mechanisms of learning: An analysis of imprinting in the domestic chick. *Proceedings of the Royal Society of London. Series B. Biological Sciences, 213*(1191), 101–137.

Hudmon, A., & Schulman, H. (2002). Neuronal CA2+/calmodulin-dependent protein kinase II: The role of structure and autoregulation in cellular function. *Annual Review of Biochemistry, 71*(1), 473–510.

Hyman, I. E., & Pentland, J. (1996). The role of mental imagery in the creation of false childhood memories. *Journal of Memory and Language, 35,* 101–117.

Ingvar, D. H. (1985). "Memory of the future": An essay on the temporal organization of conscious awareness. *Human Neurobiology, 4*(3), 127–136.

Isaac, C., Holdstock, J., Cezayirli, E., Roberts, J., Holmes, C., & Mayes, A. (1998). Amnesia in a patient with lesions limited to the dorsomedial thalamic nucleus. *Neurocase, 4*(6), 497–508.

Jacobs, L. F., & Schenk, F. (2003). Unpacking the cognitive map: The parallel map theory of hippocampal function. *Psychological Review, 110*(2), 285.

Johnson, A., & Redish, A. D. (2007). Neural ensembles in CA3 transiently encode paths forward of the animal at a decision point. *Journal of Neuroscience, 27*(45), 12176–12189.

Kahn, I., Davachi, L., & Wagner, A. D. (2004). Functional-neuroanatomic correlates of recollection: Implications for models of recognition memory. *Journal of Neuroscience, 24*(17), 4172–4180.

Kaplan, P. S., Werner, J. S., & Rudy, J. W. (1990). Habituation, sensitization, and infant visual attention. In C. Rovee-Collier (Ed.), *Advances in infancy research*. Norwood, NJ: Ablex.

Karney, B. R., & Coombs, R. H. (2000). Memory bias in long-term close relationships: Consistency or improvement? *Personality and Social Psychology Bulletin, 26*(8), 959–970.

Kjelstrup, K. B., Solstad, T., Brun, V. H., Hafting, T., Leutgeb, S., Witter, M. P., . . . Moser, M.-B. (2008). Finite scale of spatial representation in the hippocampus. *Science, 321*(5885), 140–143.

Klaver, J. R., Lee, Z., & Rose, V. G. (2008). Effects of personality, interrogation techniques and plausibility in an experimental false confession paradigm. *Legal and Criminological Psychology, 13*(1), 71–88.

Knutson, B., Wimmer, G. E., Rick, S., Hollon, N. G., Prelec, D., & Loewenstein, G. (2008). Neural antecedents of the endowment effect. *Neuron, 58*(5), 814–822.

Kolcz, A., & Allinson, N. M. (1999). Basis function models of the CMAC network. *Neural Networks, 12*(1), 107–126.

Korzus, E., Rosenfeld, M. G., & Mayford, M. (2004). CBP histone acetyltransferase activity is a critical component of memory consolidation. *Neuron, 42*(6), 961–972.

Kullmann, D., Asztely, F., & Walker, M. (2000). The role of mammalian ionotropic receptors in synaptic plasticity: LTP, LTD and epilepsy. *Cellular and Molecular Life Sciences CMLS, 57*(11), 1551–1561.

Lattal, K. M., & Abel, T. (2004). Behavioral impairments caused by injections of the protein synthesis inhibitor anisomycin after contextual retrieval reverse with time. *Proceedings of the National Academy of Sciences of the United States of America, 101*(13), 4667–4672.

Lavenex, P., Steele, M. A., & Jacobs, L. F. (2000). The seasonal pattern of cell proliferation and neuron number in the dentate gyrus of wild adult eastern grey squirrels. *European Journal of Neuroscience, 12*(2), 643–648.

Lavenex, P. B., Amaral, D. G., & Lavenex, P. (2006). Hippocampal lesion prevents spatial relational learning in adult macaque monkeys. *The Journal of Neuroscience, 26*(17), 4546–4558.

Levine, L. J., Lench, H. C., & Safer, M. A. (2009). Functions of remembering and misremembering emotion. *Applied Cognitive Psychology, 23*(8), 1059–1075.

Loftus, E. F., & Pickrell, J. E. (1995). The formation of false memories. *Psychiatric Annals, 25*(12), 720–725.

Lubin, F. D., Roth, T. L., & Sweatt, J. D. (2008). Epigenetic regulation of BDNF gene transcription in the consolidation of fear memory. *The Journal of Neuroscience, 28*(42), 10576–10586.

Lynch, M. A. (2004). Long-term potentiation and memory. *Physiological Review, 84*(1), 87–136.

Maguire, E. (2001). The retrosplenial contribution to human navigation: A review of lesion and neuroimaging findings. *Scandinavian Journal of Psychology, 42*(3), 225–238.

Maguire, E. A., Gadian, D. G., Johnsrude, I. S., Good, C. D., Ashburner, J., Frackowiak, R. S., & Frith, C. D. (2000). Navigation-related structural change in the hippocampi of taxi drivers. *Proceedings of the National Academy of Sciences of the United States of America, 97*(8), 4398–4403.

Maguire, E. A., Valentine, E. R., Wilding, J. M., & Kapur, N. (2003). Routes to remembering: The brains behind superior memory. *Nature Neuroscience, 6*(1), 90–95.

McGaugh, J. L. (2000). Memory—A century of consolidation. *Science, 287*(5451), 248–251.

Miller, G. A. (1956). The magical number seven plus or minus two: Some limits on our capacity for processing information. *Psychological Review, 63*(2), 81–97.

Miller, R. R., & Matzel, L. D. (2000). Commentary—Reconsolidation: Memory involves far more than "consolidation." *Nature Reviews Neuroscience, 1*(3), 214–216.

Momose, T., Nishikawa, J., Watanabe, T., Ohtake, T., Sasaki, Y., Sasaki, M., & Mii, K. (1992). [Clinical application of 18F-FDG-PET in patients with brain death]. *Kaku Igaku. The Japanese Journal of Nuclear Medicine, 29*(9), 1139–1142.

Morris, R. (1984). Developments of a water-maze procedure for studying spatial learning in the rat. *Journal of Neuroscience Methods, 11*(1), 47–60.

Moscovitch, M., & Melo, B. (1997). Strategic retrieval and the frontal lobes: Evidence from confabulation and amnesia. *Neuropsychologia, 35*(7), 1017–1034.

Mummery, C. J., Patterson, K., Price, C., Ashburner, J., Frackowiak, R., & Hodges, J. R. (2000). A voxel-based morphometry study of semantic dementia: Relationship between temporal lobe atrophy and semantic memory. *Annals of Neurology, 47*(1), 36–45.

Murray, E. A., & Mishkin, M. (1998). Object recognition and location memory in monkeys with excitotoxic lesions of the amygdala and hippocampus. *The Journal of Neuroscience, 18*(16), 6568–6582.

Nadel, L., Samsonovich, A., Ryan, L., & Moscovitch, M. (2000). Multiple trace theory of human memory: Computational, neuroimaging, and neuropsychological results. *Hippocampus, 10*(4), 352–368.

Nader, K., Schafe, G. E., & Le Doux, J. E. (2000). Fear memories require protein synthesis in the amygdala for reconsolidation after retrieval. *Nature, 406*(6797), 722–726.

Nairne, J. S., VanArsdall, J. E., Pandeirada, J. N., & Blunt, J. R. (2012). Adaptive memory: Enhanced location memory after survival processing. *Journal of Experimental Psychology: Learning, Memory, and Cognition, 38*(2), 495.

Naqshbandi, M., & Roberts, W. A. (2006). Anticipation of future events in squirrel monkeys (*Saimiri sciureus*) and rats (*Rattus norvegicus*): Tests of the Bischof–Kohler hypothesis. *Journal of Comparative Psychology, 120*(4), 345–357.

Nishizawa, K., Izawa, E.-I., & Watanabe, S. (2011). Neural-activity mapping of memory-based dominance in the crow: Neural networks integrating individual discrimination and social behaviour control. *Neuroscience, 197*, 307–319.

Nottebohm, F. (2002). Neuronal replacement in adult brain. *Brain Research Bulletin, 57*(6), 737–749.

Nyberg, L., McIntosh, A., Houle, S., Nilsson, L.-G., & Tulving, E. (1996). Activation of medial temporal structures during episodic memory retrieval. *Nature, 380*(6576), 715–717.

O'Keefe, J., & Burgess, N. (1996). Geometric determinants of the place fields of hippocampal neurons. *Nature, 381*(6581), 425–428.

O'Keefe, J., & Dostrovsky, J. (1971). The hippocampus as a spatial map. Preliminary evidence from unit activity in the freely-moving rat. *Brain Research, 34*(1), 171–175.

O'Keefe, J., & Nadel, L. (1978). *The hippocampus as a cognitive map* (Vol. 3). Oxford, UK: Oxford University Press.

Okado, Y., & Stark, C. E. (2005). Neural activity during encoding predicts false memories created by misinformation. *Learning and Memory, 12*(1), 3–11.

Olton, D. S., Collison, C., & Werz, M. A. (1977). Spatial memory and radial arm maze performance of rats. *Learning and Motivation, 8*(3), 289–314.

Orton, S. (2011). *World memory statistics.* Retrieved from http://www.world-memory-statistics.com/discipline.php?id=dates5

Papez, J. (1937). A proposed mechanism of emotion. *Archives of Neurology & Psychiatry, 38*(4), 725–743.

Parker, E. S., Cahill, L., & McGaugh, J. L. (2006). A case of unusual autobiographical remembering. *Neurocase, 12*(1), 35–49.

Parmeggiani, P., Azzaroni, A., & Lenzi, P. (1971). On the functional significance of the circuit of Papez. *Brain Research, 30*(2), 357–374.

Paton, J. J., Belova, M. A., Morrison, S. E., & Salzman, C. D. (2006). The primate amygdala represents the positive and negative value of visual stimuli during learning. *Nature, 439*(7078), 865–870.

Pavlov, I. P. (1927). *Conditioned reflexes: An investigation of the physiological activity of the cerebral cortex* (G. V. Anrep, trans.). London, UK: Oxford University Press.

Perry, R. J., Watson, P., & Hodges, J. R. (2000). The nature and staging of attention dysfunction in early (minimal and mild) Alzheimer's disease: Relationship to episodic and semantic memory impairment. *Neuropsychologia, 38*(3), 252–271.

Poppenk, J., McIntosh, A. R., Craik, F. I., & Moscovitch, M. (2010). Past experience modulates the neural mechanisms of episodic memory formation. *The Journal of Neuroscience, 30*(13), 4707–4716.

Ptak, R., Birtoli, B., Imboden, H., Hauser, C., Weis, J., & Schnider, A. (2001). Hypothalamic amnesia with spontaneous confabulations: A clinicopathologic study. *Neurology, 56*(11), 1597–1600.

Quiroga, R. Q., Kreiman, G., Koch, C., & Fried, I. (2008). Sparse but not "grandmother-cell" coding in the medial temporal lobe. *Trends in Cognitive Sciences, 12*(3), 87–91.

Ramón y Cajal, S. (1894). La fine structure des centres nerveux. *Proceedings of the Royal Society of London, 55*, 444–468.

Ramón y Cajal, S. (1899/1995). *Histology of the nervous system of man and vertebrates* (N. Swanson & L. Swanson, Trans.). New York, NY: Oxford University Press.

Richardson, M. P., Strange, B. A., & Dolan, R. J. (2004). Encoding of emotional memories depends on amygdala and hippocampus and their interactions. *Nature Neuroscience, 7*(3), 278–285.

Roberson, E. D., & Sweatt, J. D. (1999). A biochemical blueprint for long-term memory. *Learning and Memory, 6*(4), 381–388.

Rolls. E. T. (2004). The functions of the orbitofrontal cortex. *Brain and Cognition, 55*, 11–29.

Roth, T. L., Lubin, F. D., Funk, A. J., & Sweatt, J. D. (2009). Lasting epigenetic influence of early-life adversity on the BDNF gene. *Biological Psychiatry, 65*(9), 760–769.

Roux, F., Boulanouar, K., Ibarrola, D., Tremoulet, M., Chollet, F., & Berry, I. (2000). Functional MRI and intraoperative brain mapping to evaluate brain plasticity in patients with brain tumours and hemiparesis. *Journal of Neurology, Neurosurgery & Psychiatry, 69*(4), 453–463.

Ryan, L., Nadel, L., Keil, K., Putnam, K., Schnyer, D., Trouard, T., & Moscovitch, M. (2001). Hippocampal complex and retrieval of recent and very remote autobiographical memories: Evidence from functional magnetic resonance imaging in neurologically intact people. *Hippocampus, 11*(6), 707–714.

Schacter, D. L. (1996). *Searching for memory.* New York, NY: Basic Books.

Schacter, D. L. (1999). The seven sins of memory. Insights from psychology and cognitive neuroscience. *American Psychologist, 54*(3), 182–203.

Schacter, D. L., Addis, D. R., & Buckner, R. L. (2008). Episodic simulation of future events: Concepts, data, and applications. *Annals of the New York Academy of Sciences, 1124*, 39–60.

Schiller, D., Monfils, M. H., Raio, C. M., Johnson, D. C., LeDoux, J. E., & Phelps, E. A. (2010). Preventing the return of fear in humans using reconsolidation update mechanisms. *Nature, 463*(7277), 49–53.

Schnider, A. (2001). Spontaneous confabulation, reality monitoring, and the limbic system—A review. *Brain Research Reviews, 36*(2), 150–160.

Schnider, A. (2003). Spontaneous confabulation and the adaptation of thought to ongoing reality. *Nature Reviews Neuroscience, 4*(8), 662–671.

Schnider, A. (2013). Orbitofrontal reality filtering. *Frontiers in Behavioral Neuroscience 7*, 67.

Schnider, A., & Ptak, R. (1999). Spontaneous confabulators fail to suppress currently irrelevant memory traces. *Nature Neuroscience, 2*(7), 677–681.

Schnider, A., von Daniken, C., & Gutbrod, K. (1996). The mechanisms of spontaneous and provoked confabulations. *Brain, 119*(Pt. 4), 1365–1375.

Scoville, W. B., & Milner, B. (1957). Loss of recent memory after bilateral hippocampal lesions. *Journal of Neurology, Neurosurgery, and Psychiatry, 20*(1), 11.

Silva, A. J., Kogan, J. H., Frankland, P. W., & Kida, S. (1998). CREB and memory. *Annual Review of Neuroscience, 21*, 127–148.

Simonsson, S., & Gurdon, J. (2004). DNA demethylation is necessary for the epigenetic reprogramming of somatic cell nuclei. *Nature Cell Biology, 6*(10), 984–990.

Skinner, B. F. (1938). *The behavior of organisms: An experimental analysis.* New York, NY: Appleton–Century–Crofts.

Spence, S. A. (2008). Playing devil's advocate: The case *against* fMRI lie detection. *Legal and Criminological Psychology, 13*(1), 11–25.

Spreng, R. N., & Grady, C. L. (2010). Patterns of brain activity supporting autobiographical memory, prospection, and theory of mind, and their relationship to the default mode network. *Journal of Cognitive Neuroscience, 22*(6), 1112–1123.

Squire, L. R., van der Horst, A. S., McDuff, S. G., Frascino, J. C., Hopkins, R. O., & Mauldin, K. N. (2010). Role of the hippocampus in remembering the past and imagining the future. *Proceedings of the National Academy of Sciences of the United States of America, 107*(44), 19044–19048.

Stern, C. E., Corkin, S., Gonzalez, R. G., Guimaraes, A. R., Baker, J. R., Jennings, P. J., . . . Rosen, B. R. (1996). The hippocampal formation participates in novel picture encoding: evidence from functional magnetic resonance imaging. *Proceedings of the National Academy of Sciences of the United States of America, 93*(16), 8660–8665.

Stern, S. A., & Alberini, C. M. (2013). Mechanisms of memory enhancement. *Wiley Interdisciplinary Reviews. Systems Biology and Medicine, 5*(1), 37–53.

Söderlund, H., Moscovitch, M., Kumar, N., Mandic, M., & Levine, B. (2012). As time goes by: Hippocampal connectivity changes with remoteness of autobiographical memory retrieval. *Hippocampus, 22*(4), 670–679.

Takashima, A., Nieuwenhuis, I. L., Jensen, O., Talamini, L. M., Rijpkema, M., & Fernandez, G. (2009). Shift from hippocampal to neocortical centered retrieval network with consolidation. *Journal of Neuroscience, 29*(32), 10087–10093.

Thompson, R. F., Thompson, J. K., Kim, J. J., Krupa, D. J., & Shinkman, P. G. (1998). The nature of reinforcement in cerebellar learning. *Neurobiology of Learning and Memory, 70*(1), 150–176.

Thorndike, E. L. (1898). Animal intelligence: An experimental study of the associative processes in animals. *Psychological Monographs: General and Applied, 2*(4), i–109.

Toulouse, G. (1992). *Views of a theoretical physicist: Information Processing in the Cortex* (pp. 461–472). New York, NY: Springer.

Trachtenberg, J. T., Chen, B. E., Knott, G. W., Feng, G., Sanes, J. R., Welker, E., & Svoboda, K. (2002). Long-term in vivo imaging of experience-dependent synaptic plasticity in adult cortex. *Nature, 420*(6917), 788–794.

Tsujimoto, S., Genovesio, A., & Wise, S. P. (2011). Frontal pole cortex: Encoding ends at the end of the endbrain. *Trends in Cognitive Sciences, 15*(4), 169–176.

Tulving, E. (1985). Memory and consciousness. *Canadian Psychology, 26*, 1–12.

Tulving, E. (2005). Episodic memory and autonoesis: Uniquely human? In H. S. Terrace & J. Metcalfe (Eds.), *The Missing Link in Cognition* (pp. 4–56). New York, NY: Oxford University Press.

Turner, M. S., Cipolotti, L., Yousry, T. A., & Shallice, T. (2008). Confabulation: Damage to a specific inferior medial prefrontal system. *Cortex, 44*(6), 637–648.

van der Meulen, J. A., Bilbija, L., Joosten, R. N., de Bruin, J. P., & Feenstra, M. G. (2003). The NMDA-receptor antagonist MK-801 selectively disrupts reversal learning in rats. *Neuroreport, 14*(17), 2225–2228.

Van Strien, N., Cappaert, N., & Witter, M. (2009). The anatomy of memory: An interactive overview of the parahippocampal–hippocampal network. *Nature Reviews Neuroscience, 10*(4), 272–282.

Veena, J., Rao, B. S., & Srikumar, B. (2011). Regulation of adult neurogenesis in the hippocampus by stress, acetylcholine and dopamine. *Journal of Natural Science, Biology, and Medicine, 2*(1), 26.

Wheeler, M. E., & Buckner, R. L. (2003). Functional dissociation among components of remembering: Control, perceived oldness, and content. *The Journal of Neuroscience, 23*(9), 3869–3880.

Wickelgren, W. A. (1968). Sparing of short-term memory in an amnesic patient: Implications for strength theory of memory. *Neuropsychologia, 6*(3), 235–244.

Witter, M. P., Naber, P. A., van Haeften, T., Machielsen, W., Rombouts, S. A., Barkhof, F., . . . Lopes da Silva, F. H. (2000). Cortico-hippocampal communication by way of parallel parahippocampal–subicular pathways. *Hippocampus, 10*(4), 398–410.

Wolters, A., Sandbrink, F., Schlottmann, A., Kunesch, E., Stefan, K., Cohen, L. G., . . . Classen, J. (2003). A temporally asymmetric Hebbian rule governing plasticity in the human motor cortex. *Journal of Neurophysiology, 89*(5), 2339–2345.

Woollett, K., & Maguire, E. A. (2011). Acquiring "the Knowledge" of London's layout drives structural brain changes. *Current Biology, 21*(24), 2109–2114.

Yates, F. (1966). *The art of memory.* Chicago, IL: University of Chicago.

Yin, J. C., Wallach, J. S., Del Vecchio, M., Wilder, E. L., Zhou, H., Quinn, W. G., & Tully, T. (1994). Induction of a dominant negative CREB transgene specifically blocks long-term memory in Drosophila. *Cell, 79*(1), 49–58.

Chapter 10

Allen, R. P., Walters, A. S., Montplaisir, J., Hening, W., Myers, A., Bell, T. J., & Ferini-Strambi, L. (2005). Restless legs syndrome prevalence and impact: Rest general population study. *Archives of Internal Medicine, 165*(11), 1286–1292.

Ancoli-Israel, S., & Roth, T. (1999). Characteristics of insomnia in the United States: results of the 1991 National Sleep Foundation Survey. I. *Sleep. 22*:S347–53.

Angellis, V. (2007). *Zoologica.* Bloomington, IN: AuthorHouse.

Aschoff, J., Daan, S., & Honma, K.-I. (1982). Zeitgebers, entrainment, and masking: Some unsettled questions. In J. Aschoff, S. Daan, & G. A. Groos (Eds.), *Vertebrate circadian systems* (pp. 13–24). New York, NY: Springer.

Askenasy, J., & Rahmani, L. (1987). Neuropsycho-social rehabilitation of head injury. *American Journal of Physical Medicine & Rehabilitation, 66*(6), 315–327.

Backer, A. (1994.) To sleep, perchance to dream. *The Harvard Brain, 1*(1). Retrieved from http://www.hcs.harvard.edu/~hsmbb/BRAIN/vol1/sleep.html/

Basner, M., Rubinstein, J., Fomberstein, K. M., Coble, M. C., Ecker, A., Avinash, D., & Dinges, D. F. (2008). Effects of night work, sleep loss and time on task on simulated threat detection performance. *Sleep, 31*(9), 1251.

Baylor, G. W. (2001). What do we really know about Mendeleev's dream of the periodic table? A note on dreams of scientific problem solving. *Dreaming, 11*(2), 89–92.

Berlin, H. A. (2007). Antiepileptic drugs for the treatment of post–traumatic stress disorder. *Current Psychiatry Reports, 9,* 291–300.

Bes, F., Schulz, H., Navelet, Y., & Salzarulo, P. (1991). The distribution of slow-wave sleep across the night: A comparison for infants, children, and adults. *Sleep, 14*(1), 5–12.

Bluthé, R.-M., Dantzer, R., & Kelley, K. W. (1997). Central mediation of the effects of interleukin-1 on social exploration and body weight in mice. *Psychoneuroendocrinology, 22*(1), 1–11.

Boeve, B. F. (2010). REM sleep behavior disorder. *Annals of the New York Academy of Sciences, 1184*(1), 15–54.

Bonnet, M. H., & Arand, D. L. (1996). The consequences of a week of insomnia. *Sleep, 19*(6), 453–461.

Bonnet, M. H., & Arand, D. L. (2000). Activity, arousal, and the MSLT in patients with insomnia. *Sleep, 23*(2), 205–212.

Born, C., Costantini, M., Naegeli, K., & Rolfes, L. (2007). *Madeira city schools planning commission "balanced school year" study April 12, 2007.* Retrieved from http://www.madeiracityschools.org/docs/BSY41207.pdf/

Braun, A. R., Balkin, T. J., Wesensten, N. J., Gwadry, F., Carson, R. E., Varga, M., . . . Herscovitch, P. (1998). Dissociated pattern of activity in visual cortices and their projections during human rapid eye movement sleep. *Science, 279*(5347), 91–95.

Breslau, N., Roth, T., Rosenthal, L., & Andreski, P. (1996). Sleep disturbance and psychiatric disorders: A longitudinal epidemiological study of young adults. *Biological Psychiatry, 39*(6), 411–418.

Broughton, R. J. (1998). SCN controlled circadian arousal and the afternoon "nap zone." *Sleep Research Online, 1*(4), 166–178.

Broughton, R., Billings, R., Cartwright, R., Doucette, D., Edmeads, J., Edwardh, M., . . . Turrell, G. (1994). Homicidal somnambulism: A case report. *Sleep, 17*(3), 253–264.

Brown, S. A., Kunz, D., Dumas, A., Westermark, P. O., Vanselow, K., Tilmann-Wahnschaffe, A., . . . Kramer, A. (2008). Molecular insights into human daily behavior. *Proceedings of the National Academy of Sciences, 105*(5), 1602–1607.

Butler, B. (2011). *Nothing: A memoir of insomnia*: New York, NY: HarperCollins.

Campbell, S. S., & Murphy, P. J. (2007). The nature of spontaneous sleep across adulthood. *Journal of Sleep Research, 16*(1), 24–32.

Campbell, S. S., & Tobler, I. (1984). Animal sleep: A review of sleep duration across phylogeny. *Neuroscience & Biobehavioral Reviews, 8*(3), 269–300.

Cho, K. (2001). Chronic "jet lag" produces temporal lobe atrophy and spatial cognitive deficits. *Nature Neuroscience, 4*(6), 567–568.

Cline, J. (2011). Do later school start times really help high school students? *Psychology Today*. Retrieved from http://www.psychologytoday.com/blog/sleepless-in-america/201102/do-later-school-start-times-really-help-high-school-students/

Colin, J., Timbal, J., Boutelier, C., Houdas, Y., & Siffre, M. (1968). Rhythm of the rectal temperature during a 6-month free-running experiment. *Journal of Applied Physiology, 25*(2), 170–176.

Collin de Plancy, J. A. S. (1818). *Dictionnaire infernal*. Paris, France: Mongie.

Cox, J., King, J., Hutchinson, A., & McAvoy, P. (Eds.). (2006). *Understanding doctors' performance*. London, UK: Radcliffe.

Crick, F., & Mitchison, G. (1983). The function of dream sleep. *Nature, 304*(5922), 111–114.

Crick, F., & Mitchison, G. (1995). REM sleep and neural nets. *Behavioural Brain Research, 69*(1–2), 147–155.

Czeisler, C. A., Duffy, J. F., Shanahan, T. L., Brown, E. N., Mitchell, J. F., Rimmer, D. W., . . . & Kronauer, R. E. 1999. Stability, precision, and near-24-hour period of the human circadian pacemaker. *Science, 284*(5423), 2177–2181.

Dagan, Y. 2002. Circadian rhythm sleep disorders (CRSD). *Sleep Medicine Reviews, 6*(1), 45–54.

Dave, A. S, & Margoliash, D. (2000). Song replay during sleep and computational rules for sensorimotor vocal learning. *Science, 290*(5492), 812–816.

De Bellis, M. D., & Thomas, L. A. (2003). Biologic findings of post–traumatic stress disorder and child maltreatment. *Current Psychiatry Reports, 5*(2), 108–117.

Dement, W., & Kleitman, N. (1957a). Cyclic variations in EEG during sleep and their relation to eye movements, body motility, and dreaming. *Electroencephalography and Clinical Neurophysiology, 9*(4), 673–690.

Dement, W., & Kleitman, N. (1957b). The relation of eye movements during sleep to dream activity: An objective method for the study of dreaming. *Journal of Experimental Psychology, 53*(5), 339.

Detre, T., Himmelijoch, J., & Swartzburg, M. (1972). Hypersomnia and manic-depressive disease. *Sleep, 3*, 2.

Difrancesco, M. W., Holland, S. K., & Szaflarski, J. P. (2008). Simultaneous EEG/functional magnetic resonance imaging at 4 Tesla: Correlates of brain activity to spontaneous alpha rhythm during relaxation. *Journal of Clinical Neurophysiology, 25*(5), 255–264.

Domhoff, G. W. 1996. *Finding meaning in dreams: A quantitative approach*. New York, NY: Plenum.

Domhoff, G. W. (2001). A new neurocognitive theory of dreams. *Dreaming, 11*, 13–33.

Domhoff, G. W. (2002). *The scientific study of dreams: Neural networks, cognitive development, and content analysis*. Washington, DC: APA.

Domhoff, G. W., & Schneider, A. (2008). Similarities and differences in dream content at the cross-cultural, gender, and individual levels. *Consciousness and Cognition, 17*(4), 1257–1265.

Duffy, J., Dijk, D., Hall, E., & Czeisler, C. (1999). Relationship of endogenous circadian melatonin and temperature rhythms to self-reported preference for morning or evening activity in young and older people. *Journal of investigative Medicine: The Official Publication of the American Federation for Clinical Research, 47*(3), 141.

Durmer, J. S., & Dinges, D. F. (2005). *Neurocognitive consequences of sleep deprivation*. Paper presented at the Seminars in Neurology.

Dymaxion sleep. (1943). *Time*. Retrieved from http://content.time.com/time/magazine/article/0,9171,774680,00.html/

Eddy, R. (2005). Sleep deprivation among physicians. *British Columbia Medical Journal, 47*(4), 176.

Ekirch, A. R. (2005). *At day's close: Night in times past*. New York, NY: Norton.

Eppler, M. J., & Mengis, J. (2004). The concept of information overload: A review of literature from organization science, accounting, marketing, MIS, and related disciplines. *The Information Society, 20*(5), 325–344.

Epstein, A. W., & Hill, W. (1966). ICtal phenomena during REM sleep of a temporal lobe epileptic. *Archives of Neurology, 15*(4), 367–375.

Ezenwanne, E. (2013). Current concepts in the neurophysiologic basis of sleep; A review. *Annals of Medical and Health Sciences Research, 1*(2), 173–180.

Fenik, V. B., Davies, R. O., & Kubin, L. (2005). REM sleep-like atonia of hypoglossal (XII) motoneurons is caused by loss of noradrenergic and serotonergic inputs. *American Journal of Respiratory and Critical Care Medicine, 172*(10), 1322–1330.

Ferini-Strambi, L. (2009). Treatment options for restless legs syndrome. *Expert Opinion on Pharmacotherapy, 10*(4), 545–554.

Flanagan, O. (2000). *Dreaming souls: Sleep, dreams, and the evolution of the conscious mind*. New York, NY: Oxford University Press.

Foer, J., & Siffre, M. (2008). Caveman: An interview with Michel Siffre. *Cabinet*, (30).

Foulkes, D. (1999). *Children's dreaming and the development of consciousness*. Cambridge, MA: Harvard University Press.

Franken, P., Malafosse, A., & Tafti, M. (1999). Genetic determinants of sleep regulation in inbred mice. *Sleep: Journal of Sleep Research & Sleep Medicine, 22*(2), 155–169.

Freud, S. (1965). *New introductory lectures on psycho-analysis* (Vol. 24). New York, NY: Norton.

Fuller, R. B., Brattinga, P., & de Jong, S. (1958). *Buckminster Fuller*. Hilversum, the Netherlands: Steendrukkerij de Jong.

Gordon, R. M. (1992). The simulation theory: Objections and misconceptions. *Mind & Language, 7*(1–2), 11–34.

Hall, C. S., Domhoff, G. W., Blick, K. A., & Weesner, K. E. (1982). The dreams of college men and women in 1950 and 1980: A comparison of dream contents and sex differences. *Sleep, 5*(2), 188–194.

Hallmayer, J., Faraco, J., Lin, L., Hesselson, S., Winkelmann, J., Kawashima, M., . . . Mignot, E. (2009). Narcolepsy is strongly associated with the T-cell receptor alpha locus. *Nature Genetics, 41*(6), 708–711.

Hardeland, R. (2008). Melatonin, hormone of darkness and more—Occurrence, control mechanisms, actions and bioactive metabolites. *Cellular and Molecular Life Sciences, 65*(13), 2001–2018.

Hartley, D. (1749). *Observations on man, his frame, his deity, and his expectations*. Gainesville, FL: Scholars Facsimile Reprints.

Herxheimer, A., & Petrie, K. (2002). Melatonin for the prevention and treatment of jet lag. *Cochrane Database Syst Rev, 2*.

Hobson, J. Allan. (1987). *States of brain and mind*. Boston, MA: Birkhaeuser.

Hobson, J. Allan. (1988). *The dreaming brain*. New York, NY: Basic Books.

Hobson, J. A., & McCarley, R. W. (1977). The brain as a dream state generator: An activation-synthesis hypothesis of the dream process. *The American Journal of Psychiatry, 134*(12), 1335–1348.

Hopfield, J. J., Feinstein, D. I., & Palmer. R. G. (1983). "Unlearning" has a stabilizing effect in collective memories. *Nature, 304*(5922), 158–159.

Horne, J. A., & Ostberg, O. (1976). A self-assessment questionnaire to determine morningness–eveningness in human circadian rhythms. *International Journal of Chronobiology, 4*(2), 97–110.

Huber, R., Ghilardi, M. F., Massimini, M., & Tononi, G. (2004). Local sleep and learning. *Nature, 430*(6995), 78–81.

Huber, R., Ghilardi, M. F., Massimini, M., Ferrarelli, F., Riedner, B. A., Peterson, M. J., & Tononi, G. (2006). Arm immobilization causes cortical plastic changes and locally decreases sleep slow wave activity. *Nature Neuroscience, 9*(9), 1169–1176.

Hunter, P. (2008). To sleep, perchance to live. *EMBO Reports, 9*(11), 1070–1073.

Ibuka, N., & Kawamura, H. (1975). Loss of circadian rhythm in sleep–wakefulness cycle in the rat by suprachiasmatic nucleus lesions. *Brain Research, 96*(1), 76–81.

Johnson, L. C., Slye, E. S., & Dement, W. (1965). Electroencephalographic and autonomic activity during and after prolonged sleep deprivation. *Psychosomatic Medicine, 27*(5), 415–423.

Jung, C. G., & von Franz, M.-L. (1968). *Man and his symbols* (Vol. 5183). New York, NY: Random House Digital.

Jus, A., Jus, K., Villeneuve, A., Pires, A., Lachance, R., Fortier, J., & Villeneuve, R. (1973). Studies on dream recall in chronic schizophrenic patients after prefrontal lobotomy. *Biological Psychiatry, 6*(3), 275–293.

Kahn-Greene, E. T., Killgore, D. B., Kamimori, G. H., Balkin, T. J., & Killgore, W. D. (2007). The effects of sleep deprivation on symptoms of psychopathology in healthy adults. *Sleep Medicine, 8*(3), 215–221.

Karni, A., Tanne, D., Rubenstein, B. S., Askenasy, J. J., & Sagi, D. (1994). Dependence on REM sleep of overnight improvement of a perceptual skill. *Science, 265*(5172), 679–682.

Klein, D. C., Moore, R. Y., & Reppert, S. M. (1991). *Suprachiasmatic nucleus: The mind's clock*. New York, NY: Oxford University Press.

Kleitman, N. (1963). *Sleep and wakefulness*. Chicago, IL: University of Chicago Press.

Kopasz, M., Loessl, B., Hornyak, M., Riemann, D., Nissen, C., Piosczyk, H., & Voderholzer, U. (2010). Sleep and memory in healthy children and adolescents—A critical review. *Sleep Medicine Reviews, 14*(3), 167–177.

Kopell, N., Ermentrout, G. B., Whittington, M. A., & Traub, R. D. (2000). Gamma rhythms and beta rhythms have different synchronization properties. *Proceedings of the National Academy of Sciences of the United States of America, 97*(4), 1867–1872.

Kornhauser, J. M., Nelson, D. E., Mayo, K. E., & Takahashi, J. S. (1990). Photic and circadian regulation of c-fos gene expression in the hamster suprachiasmatic nucleus. *Neuron, 5*(2), 127–134.

Kramer, M., Roth, T., & Trinder, J. (1975). Dreams and dementia: A laboratory exploration of dream recall and dream content in chronic brain syndrome patients. *International Journal of Aging and Human Development, 6*, 169–178.

LaBerge, S. (2000). Lucid dreaming: Evidence and methodology. *Behavioral and Brain Sciences, 23*(6), 962–964.

LaBerge, S. (2009). *Lucid dreaming: A concise guide to awakening in your dreams and in your life: Easyread large edition*: ReadHowYouWant. com.

Lentz, M. J., Landis, C., Rothermel, J., & Shaver, J. (1999). Effects of selective slow wave sleep disruption on musculoskeletal pain and fatigue in middle aged women. *The Journal of Rheumatology, 26*(7), 1586–1592.

Louie, K., & Wilson, M. A. (2001). Temporally structured replay of awake hippocampal ensemble activity during rapid eye movement sleep. *Neuron, 29*(1), 145–156.

Lu, J., Greco, M. A., Shiromani, P., & Saper, C. B. (2000). Effect of lesions of the ventrolateral preoptic nucleus on NREM and REM sleep. *The Journal of Neuroscience: The Official Journal of the Society for Neuroscience, 20*(10), 3830–3842.

Lugaresi, E., & Provini, F. (2007). Fatal familial insomnia and agrypnia excitata. *Reviews in Neurological Diseases, 4*(3), 145–152.

Luppi, P.-H., Gervasoni, D., Verret, L., Goutagny, R., Peyron, C., Salvert, D., . . . Fort, P. (2006). Paradoxical (REM) sleep genesis: The switch from an aminergic–cholinergic to a GABAergic-glutamatergic hypothesis. *Journal of Physiology–Paris, 100*(5), 271–283.

Mahowald, M. W., & Schenck, C. H. (2005). Insights from studying human sleep disorders. *Nature, 437*(7063), 1279–1285.

Malcolm-Smith, S., Solms, M., Turnbull, O., & Tredoux, C. (2008). Threat in dreams: An adaptation? *Consciousness and Cognition, 17*(4), 1281–1291.

McCarley, R. W., Nelson, J. P., & Hobson, J. A. (1978). Pontogeniculo-occipital (PGO) burst neurons: Correlative evidence for neuronal generators of PGO waves. *Science, 201*(4352), 269–272.

Meddis, R. (1975). On the function of sleep. *Animal Behaviour, 23*, 676–691.

Mednick, S., Nakayama, K., & Stickgold. R. (2003). Sleep-dependent learning: A nap is as good as a night. *Nature Neuroscience, 6*(7), 697–698.

Mendelson, W. B. (2002). Melatonin microinjection into the medial preoptic area increases sleep in the rat. *Life Sciences, 71*(17), 2067–2070.

Mieda, M., Willie, J. T., Hara, J., Sinton, C. M., Sakurai, T., & Yanagisawa, M. (2004). Orexin peptides prevent cataplexy and improve wakefulness in an orexin neuron-ablated model of narcolepsy in mice. *Proceedings of the National Academy of Sciences of the United States of America, 101*(13), 4649–4654.

Minkel, J. D., Banks, S., Htaik, O., Moreta, M. C., Jones, C. W., McGlinchey, E. L., . . . Dinges, D. F. (2012). Sleep deprivation and stressors: Evidence for elevated negative affect in response to mild stressors when sleep deprived. *Emotion, 12*(5), 1015–1020.

Montplaisir, J., Boucher, S., Poirier, G., Lavigne, G., Lapierre, O., & Lespérance, P. (1997). Clinical, polysomnographic, and genetic characteristics of restless legs syndrome: A study of 133 patients diagnosed with new standard criteria. *Movement Disorders, 12*(1), 61–65.

Moorcroft, W. H. (1993) *Dreaming & sleep disorders: An introduction* (2nd ed.). Lanham, MD: University Press of America.

Moruzzi, G., & Magoun, H. W. (1949). Brain stem reticular formation and activation of the EEG. *Electroencephalography and Clinical Neurophysiology, 1*(1–4), 455–473.

Mouret, J., Lemoine, P., Minuit, M., Benkelfat, C., & Renardet, M. (1988). Effects of trazodone on the sleep of depressed subjects—A polygraphic study. *Psychopharmacology, 95*(1), S37–S43.

Mukhametov, L. M. (1987). Unihemispheric slow-wave sleep in the Amazonian dolphin, Inia geoffrensis. *Neuroscience Letters, 79*(1–2), 128–132.

Muller, J. E., Tofler, G., & Stone, P. (1989). Circadian variation and triggers of onset of acute cardiovascular disease. *Circulation, 79*(4), 733–743. National Institutes of Health. (2005). State of the Science Conference statement on Manifestations and Management of Chronic Insomnia in Adults, June 13–15, 2005. *Sleep, 28*(9), 1049–1057.

National Sleep Foundation. (2005). *Summary of findings: 2005 sleep in America® poll.* Retrieved from http://www.sleepfoundation.org/article/sleep-america-polls/2005-adult-sleep-habits-and-styles/

National Sleep Foundation. (2011). *Summary of findings 2011 sleep in America® poll: Communications technology in the bedroom.* Retrieved from http://sleepfoundation.org/sites/default/files/sleepinamericapoll/SIAP_2011_Summary_of_Findings.pdf/

National Sleep Foundation. (2013). *Summary of findings 2013 international bedroom poll.* Retrieved from http://sleepfoundation.org/sites/default/files/RPT495a.pdf/

Nelson, J. P., McCarley, R. W., & Hobson, J. A. (1983). REM sleep burst neurons, PGO waves, and eye movement information. *Journal of Neurophysiology, 50*(4), 784–797.

Neubauer, D. N. (2007). The evolution and development of insomnia pharmacotherapies. *Journal of Clinical Sleep Medicine, 3*(5 Suppl.), S11–S15.

Nishino, S., & Kanbayashi, T. (2005). Symptomatic narcolepsy, cataplexy and hypersomnia, and their implications in the hypothalamic hypocretin/orexin system. *Sleep Medicine Reviews, 9*(4), 269–310.

Nofzinger, E. A., Mintun, M. A., Wiseman, M., Kupfer, D. J., & Moore, R. Y. (1997). Forebrain activation in REM sleep: An FDG PET study. *Brain Research, 770*(1), 192–201.

Notturno, M. A., & McHugh, P. R. (1987). Is Freudian psychoanalytic theory really falsifiable? *Metaphilosophy, 18*(3–4), 306–320.

Okawa, M., & Uchiyama, M. (2007). Circadian rhythm sleep disorders: Characteristics and entrainment pathology in delayed sleep phase and non-24-h sleep–wake syndrome. *Sleep Medicine Reviews, 11*(6), 485–496.

Opstad, K. (2000). Polyphasic sleep and napping strategies. DTIC document.

Opstad, P., Ekanger, R., Nummestad, M., & Raabe, N. (1978). Performance, mood, and clinical symptoms in men exposed to prolonged, severe physical work and sleep deprivation. *Aviation, Space, and Environmental Medicine, 49*(9), 1065–1073.

Pagel, J. (2000). Nightmares and disorders of dreaming. *American Family Physician, 61*(7), 2037.

Parvizi, J., & Damasio, A. R. (2003). Neuroanatomical correlates of brainstem coma. *Brain, 126*(Pt. 7), 1524–1536.

Pierce, O. (2008). The night-owl quandary? Society should give a hoot. *The Columbus Dispatch.* Retrieved from http://www.dispatch.com/content/stories/life_and_entertainment/2008/04/16/1a_night_owls.art_art_04-16-08_d1_lg9t672.html/

Pilcher, J. J., & Huffcutt, A. J. (1996). Effects of sleep deprivation on performance: A meta-analysis. *Sleep: Journal of Sleep Research & Sleep Medicine, 19*(4), 318–326.

Pinto, L. R., Jr., Pinto, M. C. R., Goulart, L. I., Truksinas, E., Rossi, M. V., Morin, C. M., & Tufik, S. (2009). Sleep perception in insomniacs, sleep-disordered breathing patients, and healthy volunteers—An important biologic parameter of sleep. *Sleep Medicine, 10*(8), 865–868.

Plante, D. T., & Winkelman, J. W. (2006). Parasomnias. *The Psychiatric Clinics of North America, 29*(4), 969–987; abstract ix.

Porter, N., Kershaw, A., & Ollerhead, J. (2000). R&D Report 9964.

Rado, R., Gev, H., Goldman, B. D., & Terkel, J. (1991). Light and circadian activity in the blind mole rat. In E. Riklis (Ed.), *Photobiology* (pp. 581–589). New York, NY: Springer.

Rechtschaffen, A., & Bergmann, B. M. (1995). Sleep deprivation in the rat by the disk-over-water method. *Behavioural Brain Research, 69*(1–2), 55–63.

Revonsuo, A. (2000). The reinterpretation of dreams: An evolutionary hypothesis of the function of dreaming. *The Behavioral and Brain Sciences, 23*(6), 877–901; discussion 904–1121.

Revonsuo, A., & Salmivalli, C. (1995). A content analysis of bizarre elements in dreams. *Dreaming, 5*(3), 169.

Reynolds, C. F., III, Kupfer, D. J., & Sewitch, D. E. (1985). Diagnosis and management of sleep disorders in the elderly. *Elderly Mentally Ill, 51.*

Richardson, G. S. (2005). The human circadian system in normal and disordered sleep. *The Journal of Clinical Psychiatry, 66*(Suppl. 9), 3–9; quiz 42–43.

Ridgway, P. (1996). Sleepwalking: Insanity or automatism. *E-Law: Murdoch University Electronic Journal of Law, 3.*

Rignaud, M. C., & Flynn, C. (1995). Fitness for duty (FFD) evaluation in industrial and military workers. *Psychiatric Annals, 25*, 246–250.

Röschke, J., & Aldenhoff, J. (1993). Estimation of the dimensionality of sleep-EEG data in schizophrenics. *European Archives of Psychiatry and Clinical Neuroscience, 242*(4), 191–196.

Ross, J. J. (1965). Neurological findings after prolonged sleep deprivation. *Archives of Neurology, 12*(4), 399–403.

Sanfilippo, L. (2005). FDA approves ramelteon (Rozerem): The first sleep medication of its kind. *News Analysis.*

Scheer, F. A., Wright, K. P., Jr., Kronauer, R. E., & Czeisler, C. A. (2007). Plasticity of the intrinsic period of the human circadian timing system. *PloS One, 2*(1), e721.

Schenck, C. H, Arnulf, I., & Mahowald, M. W. (2007). Sleep and sex: What can go wrong? A review of the literature on sleep related disorders and abnormal sexual behaviors and experiences. *Sleep, 30*(6), 683–702.

Shanmugam, V., Wafi, A., Al-Taweel, N., & Büsselberg, D. (2013). Disruption of circadian rhythm increases the risk of cancer, metabolic syndrome and cardiovascular disease. *Journal of Local and Global Health Science, 2013.*

Shapiro, C. M., Bortz, R., Mitchell, D., Bartel, P., & Jooste, P. (1981). Slow-wave sleep: A recovery period after exercise. *Science, 214*(4526), 1253–1254.

Sharpley, A. L., Walsh, A. E., & Cowen, P. J. (1992). Nefazodone—a novel antidepressant—may increase REM sleep. *Biological Psychiatry, 31*(10), 1070–1073.

Shaw, P. J., Cirelli, C., Greenspan, R. J., & Tononi, G. (2000). Correlates of sleep and waking in *Drosophila melanogaster. Science, 287*(5459), 1834–1837.

Siegel, J. M. (2001). The REM sleep–memory consolidation hypothesis. *Science, 294*(5544), 1058–1063.

Smith-Spark, L. (2005). How sleepwalking can lead to killing. *BBC News*. Retrieved from http://news.bbc.co.uk/2/hi/uk_news/4362081.stm

Smith, W. J. (1965). Message, meaning, and context in ethology. *American Naturalist*, 405–409.

Solms, M. (1997). *The neuropsychology of dreams: A clinico-anatomical study*. Mahwah, NJ: Erlbaum.

Solms, M. (2000). Dreaming and REM sleep are controlled by different brain mechanisms. *The Behavioral and Brain Sciences*, 23(6), 843–850; discussion 904–1121.

Stampi, C., & Davis, B. (1991). Forty-eight days on the "Leonardo da Vinci" strategy for sleep reduction: Performance behaviour with three hours polyphasic sleep per day. *Sleep Research, 20*, 471.

Steriade, M., McCormick, D. A., & Sejnowski, T. J. (1993). Thalamocortical oscillations in the sleeping and aroused brain. *Science, 262*(5134), 679–685.

Stickgold, R. (2005). Sleep-dependent memory consolidation. *Nature, 437*(7063), 1272–1278.

Stickgold, R., James, L., & Hobson, J. A. (2000). Visual discrimination learning requires sleep after training. *Nature Neuroscience, 3*(12), 1237–1238.

Stickgold, R., Malia, A., Maguire, D., Roddenberry, D., & O'Connor, M. (2000). Replaying the game: Hypnagogic images in normals and amnesics. *Science, 290*(5490), 350–353.

Suzuki, H., Uchiyama, M., Tagaya, H., Ozaki, A., Kuriyama, K., Aritake, S., ... Kuga, R. (2004). Dreaming during non–rapid eye movement sleep in the absence of prior rapid eye movement sleep. *Sleep, 27*(8), 1486–1490.

Tankersley, C. G., Irizarry, R., Flanders, S., & Rabold, R. (2002). Circadian rhythm variation in activity, body temperature, and heart rate between C3H/HeJ and C57BL/6J inbred strains. *Journal of Applied Physiology, 92*(2), 870–877.

Teacher, B. E. (2009). Sleepwalking used as a defense in criminal cases and the evolution of the Ambien defense. *Duquesne Criminal Law Journal, 1*, 127.

Tobler, I. (1995). Is sleep fundamentally different between mammalian species? *Behavioural Brain Research, 69*(1–2), 35–41.

Toh, K. L., Jones, C. R., He, Y., Eide, E. J., Hinz, W. A., Virshup, D. M., ... Fu, Y.-H. (2001). An hPer2 phosphorylation site mutation in familial advanced sleep phase syndrome. *Science, 291*(5506), 1040–1043.

Uchida, S., Maehara, T., Hirai, N., Okubo, Y., & Shimizu, H. (2001). Cortical oscillations in human medial temporal lobe during wakefulness and all-night sleep. *Brain Research, 891*(1), 7–19.

Wagner, U., Gais, S., Haider, H., Verleger, R., & Born, J. (2004). Sleep inspires insight. *Nature, 427*(6972), 352–355.

Walker, M. P., & Stickgold, R. (2004). Sleep-dependent learning and memory consolidation. *Neuron, 44*(1), 121–133.

Walker, M. P., & Stickgold, R. (2006). Sleep, memory, and plasticity. *Annual Review of Psychology, 57*, 139–166.

Watson, N. F., Dikmen, S., Machamer, J., Doherty, M., & Temkin, N. (2007). Hypersomnia following traumatic brain injury. *Journal of Clinical Sleep Medicine: JCSM: Official Publication of the American Academy of Sleep Medicine, 3*(4), 363.

Wehr, T. A. (2001). Photoperiodism in humans and other primates: Evidence and implications. *Journal of Biological Rhythms, 16*(4), 348–364.

Welsh, D. K., Logothetis, D. E., Meister, M., & Reppert, S. M. (1995). Individual neurons dissociated from rat suprachiasmatic nucleus express independently phased circadian firing rhythms. *Neuron, 14*(4), 697–706.

Wilson, M. A. (2002). Hippocampal memory formation, plasticity, and the role of sleep. *Neurobiology of Learning and Memory, 78*(3), 565–569.

Wilson, M. A., & McNaughton, B. L. (1994). Reactivation of hippocampal ensemble memories during sleep. *Science, 265*(5172), 676–679.

Xu, M. (2008). Sexsomnia: A valid defense to sexual assault. *Journal of Gender, Race & Justice, 12*, 687.

Zepelin, H., & Rechtschaffen, A. (1974). Mammalian sleep, longevity, and energy metabolism. *Brain, Behavior and Evolution, 10*(6), 447–470.

Chapter 11

Allen, M. (1983). Models of hemispheric specialization. *Psychological Bulletin, 93*(1), 73.

American Academy of Pediatrics. (2013). Media and children. *AAP Health Initiatives*. Retrieved from http://www.aap.org/en-us/advocacy-and-policy/aap-health-initiatives/Pages/Media-and-Children.aspx?nfstatus=401/

Baumann, N., & Kuhl, J. (2002). Intuition, affect, and personality: Unconscious coherence judgments and self-regulation of negative affect. *Journal of Personality and Social Psychology, 83*(5), 1213–1223.

Beal, D. S., Gracco, V. L., Lafaille, S. J., & De Nil, L. F. (2007). Voxel-based morphometry of auditory and speech-related cortex in stutterers. *Neuroreport, 18*(12), 1257–1260.

Berwick, R. C., Pietroski, P., Yankama, B., & Chomsky, N. (2011). Poverty of the stimulus revisited. *Cognitive Science, 35*(7), 1207–1242.

Bickerton, D. (1981). *Roots of language*. Ann Arbor, MI: Karoma.

Bloom, L., & Capatides, J. B. (1987). Expression of affect and the emergence of language. *Child Development, 58*, 1513–1522.

Bonilha, L., & Fridriksson, J. (2009). Subcortical damage and white matter disconnection associated with non-fluent speech. *Brain, 132*(Pt. 6), e108.

Bornstein, M. H., Cote, L. R., Maital, S., Painter, K., Park, S. Y., Pascual, L., ... Vyt, A. (2004). Cross-linguistic analysis of vocabulary in young children: Spanish, Dutch, French, Hebrew, Italian, Korean, and American English. *Child Development, 75*(4), 1115–1139.

Bossy, J., Godlewski, G., & Maurel, J. C. (1976). [Study of right–left asymmetry of the temporal planum in the fetus]. *Bulletin de l'Association des Anatomistes, 60*(169), 253–258.

Cardin, V., Orfanidou, E., Ronnberg, J., Capek, C. M., Rudner, M., & Woll, B. (2013). Dissociating cognitive and sensory neural plasticity in human superior temporal cortex. *Nature Communications, 4*, 1473.

Carlson, N. R. (2011). *Foundations of behavioral neuroscience* (8th ed.). Boston, MA: Allyn & Bacon.

Chomsky, N. (1965). *Aspects of the theory of syntax*. Cambridge, MA: MIT Press.

Clark, A., & Lappin, S. (2011). *Linguistic nativism and the poverty of the stimulus*. Somerset, NJ: Wiley–Blackwell.

Corina, D. P., Lawyer, L. A., Hauser, P., & Hirshorn, E. (2013). Lexical processing in deaf readers: An fMRI investigation of reading proficiency. *PLoS One, 8*(1), e54696.

Damasio, A., Bellugi, U., Damasio, H., Poizner, H., & Van Gilder, J. (1986). Sign language aphasia during left-hemisphere amytal injection. *Nature, 322*(6077), 363–365.

Damasio, H., Grabowski, T. J., Tranel, D., Hichwa, R. D., & Damasio, A. R. (1996). A neural basis for lexical retrieval. *Nature, 380*(6574), 499–505.

Damasio, A. R., & Tranel, D. (1993). Nouns and verbs are retrieved with differently distributed neural systems. *Proceedings of the National Academy of Sciences of the United States of America, 90*(11), 4957–4960.

Darwin, C. (1891). *The descent of man, and selection in relation to sex* (2nd ed., Vol. I). London, UK: John Murray.

Davis, G. A. (2007). Appendix: Common classifications of aphasia. Adapted from *Aphasiology: Disorders and clinical practice* (pp. 33–39). Boston, MA: Allyn & Bacon. Retrieved from http://www.asha.org/Practice-Portal/Clinical-Topics/Aphasia/Common-Classifications-of-Aphasia/

DeCasper, A. J., & Fifer, W. P. (1980). Of human bonding: Newborns prefer their mothers' voices. *Science, 208*(4448), 1174–1176.

Dehaene-Lambertz, G., Montavont, A., Jobert, A., Allirol, L., Dubois, J., Hertz-Pannier, L., & Dehaene, S. (2010). Language or music, mother or Mozart? Structural and environmental influences on infants' language networks. *Brain and Language, 114*(2), 53–65.

Demb, J. B., Boynton, G. M., & Heeger, D. J. (1997). Brain activity in visual cortex predicts individual differences in reading performance. *Proceedings of the National Academy of Sciences, USA, 94*, 13363–13366.

Dorsaint-Pierre, R., Penhune, V. B., Watkins, K. E., Neelin, P., Lerch, J. P., Bouffard, M., & Zatorre, R. J. (2006). Asymmetries of the planum temporale and Heschl's gyrus: Relationship to language lateralization. *Brain, 129*(Pt. 5), 1164–1176.

Dowling, C. F. (1994). Differentiating normal speech dysfluency from stuttering in children. *The Nurse Practitioner, 19*(2), 30, 34–35.

Dronkers, N. F., Plaisant, O., Iba-Zizen, M. T., & Cabanis, E. A. (2007). Paul Broca's historic cases: High resolution MR imaging of the brains of Leborgne and Lelong. *Brain, 130*(Pt. 5), 1432–1441.

Eckert, M. A., Leonard, C. M., Possing, E. T., & Binder, J. R. (2006). Uncoupled leftward asymmetries for planum morphology and functional language processing. *Brain and Language, 98*(1), 102–111.

Fedorenko, E., Behr, M. K., & Kanwisher, N. (2011). Functional specificity for high-level linguistic processing in the human brain. *Proceedings of the National Academy of Sciences of the United States of America, 108*(39), 16428–16433.

Finn, E. (2011, 30 August). *Localizing language in the brain.* Retrieved from http://www.mit.edu/newsoffice/2011/language-brain-0830.html/

Foundas, A. L., Bollich, A. M., Feldman, J., Corey, D. M., Hurley, M., Lemen, L. C., & Heilman, K. M. (2004). Aberrant auditory processing and atypical planum temporale in developmental stuttering. *Neurology, 63*(9), 1640–1646.

Fridriksson, J., Bonilha, L., & Rorden, C. (2007). Severe Broca's aphasia without Broca's area damage. *Behavioural Neurology, 18*(4), 237–238.

Gazzaniga, M. S. (2005). Forty-five years of split-brain research and still going strong. *Nature Reviews Neuroscience, 6*(8), 653–659.

Gentner, E. (1982). Why nouns are learned before verbs: Linguistic relativity versus natural partitioning. In S. Kuczag (Ed.), *Language Development* (Vol. 2: *Language, Thought and Culture*, pp. 301–334). Hillsdale, NJ: Erlbaum.

Geschwind, N. (1970). The organization of language and the brain. *Science, 170*(3961), 940–944.

Goldstein, M. H., Schwade, J. A., & Bornstein, M. H. (2009). The value of vocalizing: Five-month-old infants associate their own noncry vocalizations with responses from caregivers. *Child Development, 80*(3), 636–644.

Golinkoff, R. M., & Alioto, A. (1995). Infant-directed speech facilitates lexical learning in adults hearing Chinese: Implications for language acquisition. *Journal of Child Language, 22*(3), 703–726.

Hackett, J. (2012). Roger Bacon. *The Stanford Encyclopedia of Philosophy.* Retrieved from http://plato.stanford.edu/

Hickok, G., Bellugi, U., & Klima, E. S. (2001). Sign language in the brain. *Scientific American, 284*(6), 58–65.

Jansen, A., Floel, A., Deppe, M., van Randenborgh, J., Drager, B., Kanowski, M., & Knecht, S. (2004). Determining the hemispheric dominance of spatial attention: A comparison between fTCD and fMRI. *Human Brain Mapping, 23*(3), 168–180.

Jusczyk, P. W., Cutler, A., & Redanz, N. J. (1993). Infants' preference for the predominant stress patterns of English words. *Child Development, 64*(3), 675–687.

Kim, K. H., Relkin, N. R., Lee, K. M., & Hirsch, J. (1997). Distinct cortical areas associated with native and second languages. *Nature, 388*(6638), 171–174.

Knecht, S., Drager, B., Deppe, M., Bobe, L., Lohmann, H., Floel, A., . . . Henningsen, H. (2000). Handedness and hemispheric language dominance in healthy humans. *Brain, 123*(Pt. 12), 2512–2518.

Kuhl, P. K. (2004). Early language acquisition: Cracking the speech code. *Nature Reviews Neuroscience, 5*(11), 831–843.

Kuhl, P. K., Andruski, J. E., Chistovich, I. A., Chistovich, L. A., Kozhevnikova, E. V., Ryskina, V. L., . . . Lacerda, F. (1997). Cross-language analysis of phonetic units in language addressed to infants. *Science, 277*(5326), 684–686.

Kuhl, P. K., Coffey-Corina, S., Padden, D., & Dawson, G. (2005). Links between social and linguistic processing of speech in preschool children with autism: Behavioral and electrophysiological measures. *Developmental Science, 8*(1), F1–F12.

Kuhl, P. K., Tsao, F. M., & Liu, H. M. (2003). Foreign-language experience in infancy: Effects of short-term exposure and social interaction on phonetic learning. *Proceedings of the National Academy of Sciences of the United States of America, 100*(15), 9096–9101.

Leung, A. K., & Kao, C. P. (1999). Evaluation and management of the child with speech delay. *American Family Physician, 59*, 3121–3128.

Liberman, A. M., & Mattingly, I. G. (1985). The motor theory of speech perception revised. *Cognition, 21*(1), 1–36.

Lidz, J., Gleitman, H., Gleitman, L.. (2003). Understanding how input matters: verb learning and the footprint of universal grammar. *Cognition, 87*(3), 151–178.

Lieberman, P. (1968). Primate vocalizations and human linguistic ability. *Journal of the Acoustical Society of America, 44*(6), 1574–1584.

Lundgren, K., Helm-Estabrooks, N., & Klein, R. (2010). Stuttering following acquired brain damage: A review of the literature. *Journal of Neurolinguistics, 23*(5), 447–454.

Lyn, H., & Savage-Rumbaugh, E. S. (2000). Observational word learning in two bonobos (*Pan paniscus*): Ostensive and non-ostensive contexts. *Language & Communication, 20*(3), 255–273.

Marler, P. (1991). Differences in behavioural development in closely related species: Birdsong. In P. Bateson (Ed.), *The development and integration of behaviour* (pp. 41–70). Cambridge, UK: Cambridge University Press.

Marshall, R. C. (2001). Management of Wernicke's aphasia: A context-based approach. In R. Chapey (Ed.), *Language intervention strategies in aphasia and related neurogenic communication disorders* (4th ed., pp. 513–521). Baltimore, MD: Lippincott Williams & Wilkins.

Martin, A., & Chao, L. L. (2001). Semantic memory and the brain: Structure and processes. *Current Opinion in Neurobiology, 11*(2), 194–201.

Martin, A., Wiggs, C. L., Ungerleider, L. G., & Haxby, J. V. (1996). Neural correlates of category-specific knowledge. *Nature, 379*(6566), 649–652.

McDonald, S., & Ramscar, M. (2001). *Testing the distributional hypothesis: The influence of context on judgements of semantic similarity.* Paper presented at the Proceedings of the 23rd Annual Conference of the Cognitive Science Society, Edinburgh, Scotland.

Milner, B. (1974). Functional recovery after lesions of the nervous system. 3. Developmental processes in neural plasticity. Sparing of language functions after early unilateral brain damage. *Neurosciences Research Program Bulletin, 12*(2), 213–217.

Minagar, A., Ragheb, J., & Kelley, R. E. (2003). The Edwin Smith surgical papyrus: Description and analysis of the earliest case of aphasia. *Journal of Medical Biography, 11*(2), 114–117.

Mitchell, L. (1999). Earliest Egyptian glyphs. *Archaeology, 52*(2).

Moon, C., Panneton-Cooper, R., & Fifer, W. P. (1993). Two-day-olds prefer their native language. *Infant Behavior and Development, 16,* 495–500.

Morseley, C. (Ed.). (2010). *Atlas of the world's languages in danger* (3rd ed.). Paris, France: UNESCO.

Mufwene, S. S. (1996). The founder principle in creole genesis. *Diachronica, 13*(1), 83–134.

Neumann, K., Euler, H. A., von Gudenberg, A. W., Giraud, A. L., Lanfermann, H., Gall, V., & Preibisch, C. (2003). The nature and treatment of stuttering as revealed by fMRI A within- and between-group comparison. *Journal of Fluency Disorders, 28*(4), 381–409; quiz 409–410.

Ojemann, G. A., & Whitaker, H. A. (1978). The bilingual brain. *Archives of Neurology 35*(7), 409–412.

Pan, B. A., & Snow, C. E. (1999). The development of conversational and discourse skills. In M. Barrett (Ed.), *The development of language* (pp. 229–249). Boca Raton, FL: Psychology Press.

Patterson, F. G. (1981). Ape language. *Science, 211*(4477), 87–88.

Petitto, L. A., Katerelos, M., Levy, B. G., Gauna, K., Tetreault, K., & Ferraro, V. (2001). Bilingual signed and spoken language acquisition from birth: Implications for the mechanisms underlying early bilingual language acquisition. *Journal of Child Language, 28*(2), 453–496.

Petitto, L. A., & Marentette, P. F. (1991). Babbling in the manual mode: Evidence for the ontogeny of language. *Science, 251*(5000), 1493–1496.

Pinker, S. (1994). *The language instinct: How the mind creates language.* New York, NY: Morrow.

Rihs, F., Sturzenegger, M., Gutbrod, K., Schroth, G., & Mattle, H. P. (1999). Determination of language dominance: Wada test confirms functional transcranial Doppler sonography. *Neurology, 52*(8), 1591–1596.

Rochat, P., Querido, J. G., & Striano, T. (1999). Emerging sensitivity to the timing and structure of protoconversation in early infancy. *Developmental Psychology 35*(4), 950–957.

Ross, E. D., & Mesulam, M. M. (1979). Dominant language functions of the right hemisphere? Prosody and emotional gesturing. *Archives of Neurology, 36*(3), 144–148.

Roy, D. (2009). *New horizons in the study of child language acquisition.* Paper presented at Interspeech 2009, Brighton, England.

Roy, D., Patel, R., DeCamp, P., Kubat, R., Fleischman, M., Roy, B., . . . Gorniak, P. (2006). *The Human Speechome Project.* Paper presented at the Twenty-eighth Annual Meeting of the Cognitive Science Society, Vancouver, Canada.

Sacks, O. (1970). The president's speech. In *The man who mistook his wife for a hat* (pp. 80–84). New York, NY: Simon & Schuster.

Saffran, J. R., Aslin, R. N., & Newport, E. L. (1996). Statistical learning by 8-month-old infants. *Science, 274*(5294), 1926–1928.

Sakai, K. L. (2005). Language acquisition and brain development. *Science, 310*(5749), 815–819.

Sakai, K. L., Noguchi, Y., Takeuchi, T., & Watanabe, E. (2002). Selective priming of syntactic processing by event-related transcranial magnetic stimulation of Broca's area. *Neuron, 35*(6), 1177–1182.

Savage-Rumbaugh, S., McDonald, K., Sevcik, R. A., Hopkins, W. D., & Rubert, E. (1986). Spontaneous symbol acquisition and communicative use by pygmy chimpanzees (*Pan paniscus*). *Journal of Experimental Psychology: General, 115*(3), 211–235.

Schwartz, M. F., & Linebarger, M. C. (1985). The status of the syntactic deficit theory of agrammatism. In M. L. Kean (Ed.), *Agrammatism* (pp. 83–124). New York, NY: Academic Press.

Sebastian, R., Schein, M. G., Davis, C., Gomez, Y., Newhart, M., Oishi, K., Hillis, A. E. (2014) Aphasia or neglect after thalamic stroke: the various ways they may be related to cortical hypoperfusion. *Front Neurol. 19,* 5:231.

Shapiro, K. A., Moo, L. R., & Caramazza, A. (2006). Cortical signatures of noun and verb production. *Proceedings of the National Academy of Sciences of the United States of America, 103*(5), 1644–1649.

Shaywitz, S. E., & Shaywitz, B. A. (2005). Dyslexia (specific reading disability). *Biological Psychiatry, 57*(11), 1301–1309.

Simonyan, K., & Horwitz, B. (2011). Laryngeal motor cortex and control of speech in humans. *Neuroscientist, 17*(2), 197–208.

Simos, P. G., Castillo, E. M., Fletcher, J. M., Francis, D. J., Maestu, F., Breier, J. I., . . . Papanicolaou, A. C. (2001). Mapping of receptive language cortex in bilingual volunteers by using magnetic source imaging. *Journal of Neurosurgery, 95*(1), 76–81.

Sperry, R. W. (1961). Cerebral organization and behavior: The split brain behaves in many respects like two separate brains, providing new research possibilities. *Science, 133*(3466), 1749–1757.

Temple, E., Deutsch, G. K., Poldrack, R. A., Miller, S. L., Tallal, P., Merzenich, M. M., Gabrieli, J. D. (2003). Neural deficits in children with dyslexia ameliorated by behavioral remediation: evidence from functional MRI. *Proc Natl Acad Sci U S A. 100*(5), 2860–2865.

Wada, J., & Rasmussen, T. (1960). Intracarotid injection of sodium amytal for the lateralization of cerebral speech dominance: Experimental and clinical observations. *Journal of Neurosurgery, 17*(2), 266–282.

Wan, C. Y., Ruber, T., Hohmann, A., & Schlaug, G. (2010). The therapeutic effects of singing in neurological disorders. *Music Perception: An Interdisciplinary Journal, 27*(4), 287–295.

Wildgruber, D., Ackermann, H., Kreifelts, B., & Ethofer, T. (2006). Cerebral processing of linguistic and emotional prosody: fMRI studies. *Progress in Brain Research, 156,* 249–268.

Yarlett, D. (2008). *Language learning through similarity-based generalization.* Ph.D. diss., Stanford University, Stanford, CA.

Chapter 12

Ainslie, G. W. (1974). Impulse control in pigeons. *Journal of the Experimental Analysis of Behavior, 21*(3), 485–489.

Ainslie, G., & Haslam, N. (1992). Hyperbolic discounting. In G. Loewenstein & J. Elster (Eds.), *Choice over Time* (pp. 57–92). New York, NY: Russell Sage Foundation.

Almashat, S., Ayotte, B., Edelstein, B., & Margrett, J. (2008). Framing effect debiasing in medical decision making. *Patient Education and Counseling, 71*(1), 102–107.

Ariely, D. (2008). *Predictably irrational*. New York, NY: HarperCollins.

Barmack, N. H. (2003). Central vestibular system: Vestibular nuclei and posterior cerebellum. *Brain Research Bulletin, 60*(5–6), 511–541.

Bateson, M., & Kacelnik, A. (1996). Rate currencies and the foraging starling: The fallacy of the averages revisited. *Behavioral Ecology, 7*(3), 341–352.

Bechara, A., Damasio, H., Damasio, A. R., & Lee, G. P. (1999). Different contributions of the human amygdala and ventromedial prefrontal cortex to decision-making. *The Journal of Neuroscience, 19*(13), 5473–5481.

Bhatti, T., Gillin, J. C., Seifritz, E., Moore, P., Clark, C., Golshan, S., . . . Kelsoe, J. (1998). Effects of a tryptophan-free amino acid drink challenge on normal human sleep electroencephalogram and mood. *Biological Psychiatry, 43*(1), 52–59.

Bizot, J., Le Bihan, C., Puech, A. J., Hamon, M., & Thiebot, M. (1999). Serotonin and tolerance to delay of reward in rats. *Psychopharmacology, 146*(4), 400–412.

Burman, K. J., Reser, D. H., Yu, H. H., & Rosa, M. G. (2011). Cortical input to the frontal pole of the marmoset monkey. *Cerebral Cortex, 21*(8), 1712–1737.

Camerer, C. F., Loewenstein, G., & Rabin, M. (2011). *Advances in behavioral economics*. Princeton, NJ: Princeton University Press.

Campbell-Meiklejohn, D. K., Woolrich, M. W., Passingham, R. E., & Rogers, R. D. (2008). Knowing when to stop: The brain mechanisms of chasing losses. *Biological Psychiatry, 63*(3), 293–300.

Chiappori, P.-A., & Rochet, J.-C. (1987). Revealed preferences and differentiable demand. *Econometrica, 55*(3), 687–691.

Chib, V. S., Rangel, A., Shimojo, S., & O'Doherty, J. P. (2009). Evidence for a common representation of decision values for dissimilar goods in human ventromedial prefrontal cortex. *The Journal of Neuroscience, 29*(39), 12315–12320.

Clark, L., Bechara, A., Damasio, H., Aitken, M. R., Sahakian, B. J., & Robbins, T. W. (2008). Differential effects of insular and ventromedial prefrontal cortex lesions on risky decision-making. *Brain: A Journal of Neurology, 131*(Pt. 5), 1311–1322.

Coleman, J. S., & Fararo, T. J. (1992). *Rational choice theory: Advocacy and critique*. Thousand Oaks, CA: Sage.

Craig, A. D. (2002). How do you feel? Interoception: The sense of the physiological condition of the body. *Nature Reviews: Neuroscience, 3*(8), 655–666.

De Martino, B., Kumaran, D., Seymour, B., & Dolan, R. J. (2006). Frames, biases, and rational decision-making in the human brain. *Science, 313*(5787), 684–687.

de Wit, H. (2009). Impulsivity as a determinant and consequence of drug use: A review of underlying processes. *Addiction Biology, 14*(1), 22–31.

de Wit, H., Crean, J., & Richards, J. B. (2000). Effects of D-amphetamine and ethanol on a measure of behavioral inhibition in humans. *Behavioral Neuroscience, 114*(4), 830–837.

de Wit, H., Enggasser, J. L., & Richards, J. B. (2002). Acute administration of D-amphetamine decreases impulsivity in healthy volunteers. *Neuropsychopharmacology, 27*(5), 813–825.

Deakin, J. B., Aitken, M. R., Dowson, J. H., Robbins, T. W., & Sahakian, B. J. (2004). Diazepam produces disinhibitory cognitive effects in male volunteers. *Psychopharmacology, 173*(1–2), 88–97.

Desmurget, M., & Sirigu, A. (2009). A parietal-premotor network for movement intention and motor awareness. *Trends in Cognitive Sciences, 13*(10), 411–419.

Dohmen, T., Falk, A., Huffman, D., & Sunde, U. (2010). Are risk aversion and impatience related to cognitive ability? *American Economic Review, 100*(3), 1238–1260.

Dreher, J. C., Koechlin, E., Tierney, M., & Grafman, J. (2008). Damage to the fronto-polar cortex is associated with impaired multitasking. *PloS One, 3*(9), e3227.

Evans, J. S. (2008). Dual-processing accounts of reasoning, judgment, and social cognition. *Annual Review of Psychology, 59*, 255–278.

Fehr, E., Fischbacher, U., & Kosfeld, M. (2005). Neuroeconomic foundations of trust and social preferences: Initial evidence. *American Economic Review, 95*(2), 346–351.

Figner, B., Knoch, D., Johnson, E. J., Krosch, A. R., Lisanby, S. H., Fehr, E., & Weber, E. U. (2010). Lateral prefrontal cortex and self-control in intertemporal choice. *Nature Neuroscience, 13*(5), 538–539.

Flegal, K. M., Carroll, M. D., Ogden, C. L., & Johnson, C. L. (2002). Prevalence and trends in obesity among US adults, 1999–2000. *JAMA, 288*(14), 1723–1727.

Forstmann, B. U., Brass, M., Koch, I., & von Cramon, D. Y. (2006). Voluntary selection of task sets revealed by functional magnetic resonance imaging. *Journal of Cognitive Neuroscience, 18*(3), 388–398.

Frederick, S., Loewenstein, G., & O'Donoghue, T. (2002). Time discounting and time preference: A critical review. *Journal of Economic Literature, 40*, 350–401.

Fried, I., Katz, A., McCarthy, G., Sass, K. J., Williamson, P., Spencer, S. S., & Spencer, D. D. (1991). Functional organization of human supplementary motor cortex studied by electrical stimulation. *The Journal of Neuroscience, 11*(11), 3656–3666.

Gilbert, D. T., & Malone, P. S. (1995). The correspondence bias. *Psychological Bulletin, 117*(1), 21–38.

Greene, J. D., Nystrom, L. E., Engell, A. D., Darley, J. M., & Cohen, J. D. (2004). The neural bases of cognitive conflict and control in moral judgment. *Neuron, 44*(2), 389–400.

Greene, J. D., Sommerville, R. B., Nystrom, L. E., Darley, J. M., & Cohen, J. D. (2001). An fMRI investigation of emotional engagement in moral judgment. *Science, 293*(5537), 2105–2108.

Haggard, P. (2008). Human volition: Towards a neuroscience of will. *Nature Reviews: Neuroscience, 9*(12), 934–946.

Hare, T. A., Camerer, C. F., & Rangel, A. (2009). Self-control in decision-making involves modulation of the vmPFC valuation system. *Science, 324*(5927), 646–648.

Hariri, A. R., Mattay, V. S., Tessitore, A., Kolachana, B., Fera, F., Goldman, D., . . . Weinberger, D. R. (2002). Serotonin transporter genetic variation and the response of the human amygdala. *Science, 297*(5580), 400–403.

Hayashi, T., Ko, J. H., Strafella, A. P., & Dagher, A. (2013). Dorsolateral prefrontal and orbitofrontal cortex interactions during self-control of cigarette craving. *Proceedings of the National Academy of Sciences of the United States of America, 110*(11), 4422–4427.

Haynes, J. D., Sakai, K., Rees, G., Gilbert, S., Frith, C., & Passingham, R. E. (2007). Reading hidden intentions in the human brain. *Current Biology: CB, 17*(4), 323–328.

Heilbronner, S. R., Rosati, A. G., Stevens, J. R., Hare, B., & Hauser, M. D. (2008). A fruit in the hand or two in the bush? Divergent risk preferences in chimpanzees and bonobos. *Biology Letters, 4*(3), 246–249.

Hilgard, E. R. (1980). The trilogy of mind: Cognition, affection, and conation. *Journal of the History of the Behavioral Sciences, 16*(2), 107–117.

Hoffman, W. F., Moore, M., Templin, R., McFarland, B., Hitzemann, R. J., & Mitchell, S. H. (2006). Neuropsychological function and delay discounting in methamphetamine-dependent individuals. *Psychopharmacology, 188*(2), 162–170.

Hoffman, W. F., Schwartz, D. L., Huckans, M. S., McFarland, B. H., Meiri, G., Stevens, A. A., & Mitchell, S. H. (2008). Cortical activation during delay discounting in abstinent methamphetamine dependent individuals. *Psychopharmacology, 201*(2), 183–193.

Jensen, L. R. (2013, July 11). *"Take Care of Your Health" initiative announced ahead of open enrollment.* Retrieved from http://news.psu.edu/story/281346/2013/07/11/administration/%E2%80%98take-care-your-health%E2%80%99-initiative-announced-ahead-open/

Johnson, M. K., Raye, C. L., Mitchell, K. J., Touryan, S. R., Greene, E. J., & Nolen-Hoeksema, S. (2006). Dissociating medial frontal and posterior cingulate activity during self-reflection. *Social Cognitive and Affective Neuroscience, 1*(1), 56–64.

Jones, E. E., & Harris, V. A. (1967). The attribution of attitudes. *Journal of Experimental Social Psychology, 3*, 1–24.

Kable, J. W., & Glimcher, P. W. (2007). The neural correlates of subjective value during intertemporal choice. *Nature Neuroscience, 10*(12), 1625–1633.

Kahneman, D., Knetsch, J. L., & Thaler, R. H. (1990). Experimental tests of the endowment effect and the Coase theorem. *Journal of Political Economy, 98*(6), 1325–1348.

Kahneman, D., Knetsch, J. L., & Thaler, R. H. (1991). Anomalies: The endowment effect, loss aversion, and status quo bias. *Journal of Economic Perspectives, 5*(1), 193–206.

Kahneman, D., & Tversky, A. (1979). Prospect theory: An analysis of decision under risk. *Econometrica, 47*(2), 263–292.

Knetsch, J. L. (1989). The endowment effect and evidence of nonreversible indifference curves. *The American Economic Review, 79*(5), 1277–1284.

Knutson, B., & Bossaerts, P. (2007). Neural antecedents of financial decisions. *The Journal of Neuroscience, 27*(31), 8174–8177.

Knutson, B., Taylor, J., Kaufman, M., Peterson, R., & Glover, G. (2005). Distributed neural representation of expected value. *The Journal of Neuroscience, 25*(19), 4806–4812.

Knutson, B., Wimmer, G. E., Rick, S., Hollon, N. G., Prelec, D., & Loewenstein, G. (2008). Neural antecedents of the endowment effect. *Neuron, 58*(5), 814–822.

Koechlin, E., Corrado, G., Pietrini, P., & Grafman, J. (2000). Dissociating the role of the medial and lateral anterior prefrontal cortex in human planning. *Proceedings of the National Academy of Sciences of the United States of America, 97*(13), 7651–7656.

Koechlin, E., & Hyafil, A. (2007). Anterior prefrontal function and the limits of human decision-making. *Science, 318*(5850), 594–598.

Krakauer, J. (1997). *Into thin air.* New York, NY: Anchor Books.

Kuhtz-Buschbeck, J. P., van der Horst, C., Pott, C., Wolff, S., Nabavi, A., Jansen, O., & Junemann, K. P. (2005). Cortical representation of the urge to void: A functional magnetic resonance imaging study. *The Journal of Urology, 174*(4 Pt. 1), 1477–1481.

Kuhtz-Buschbeck, J. P., van der Horst, C., Wolff, S., Filippow, N., Nabavi, A., Jansen, O., & Braun, P. M. (2007). Activation of the supplementary motor area (SMA) during voluntary pelvic floor muscle contractions—An fMRI study. *Neuroimage, 35*(2), 449–457.

Laibson, D. (1997). Golden eggs and hyperbolic discounting. *Quarterly Journal of Economics, 112*(2), 443–477.

Lakshminaryanan, V., Chen, M. K., & Santos, L. R. (2008). Endowment effect in capuchin monkeys. *Philosophical Transactions of the Royal Society of London. Series B, Biological Sciences, 363*(1511), 3837–3844.

Lau, H. C., Rogers, R. D., Ramnani, N., & Passingham, R. E. (2004). Willed action and attention to the selection of action. *Neuroimage, 21*(4), 1407–1415.

Laureiro-Martinez, D., Canessa, N., Brusoni, S., Zollo, M., Hare, T., Alemanno, F., & Cappa, S. F. (2013). Frontopolar cortex and decision-making efficiency: Comparing brain activity of experts with different professional background during an exploration–exploitation task. *Frontiers in Human Neuroscience, 7*, 927.

MacLean, P. D. (1990). *The triune brain in evolution: Role in paleocerebral functions.* New York, NY: Plenum.

Malenka, D. J., Baron, J. A., Johansen, S., Wahrenberger, J. W., & Ross, J. M. (1993). The framing effect of relative and absolute risk. *Journal of General Internal Medicine, 8*(10), 543–548.

McClure, S. M., Ericson, K. M., Laibson, D. I., Loewenstein, G., & Cohen, J. D. (2007). Time discounting for primary rewards. *The Journal of Neuroscience, 27*(21), 5796–5804.

McClure, S. M., Laibson, D. I., Loewenstein, G., & Cohen, J. D. (2004). Separate neural systems value immediate and delayed monetary rewards. *Science, 306*(5695), 503–507.

McClure, S. M., Li, J., Tomlin, D., Cypert, K. S., Montague, L. M., & Montague, P. R. (2004). Neural correlates of behavioral preference for culturally familiar drinks. *Neuron, 44*(2), 379–387.

McDonald, J., Schleifer, L., Richards, J. B., & de Wit, H. (2003). Effects of THC on behavioral measures of impulsivity in humans. *Neuropsychopharmacology, 28*(7), 1356–1365.

Mitz, A. R., & Wise, S. P. (1987). The somatotopic organization of the supplementary motor area: Intracortical microstimulation mapping. *The Journal of Neuroscience, 7*(4), 1010–1021.

Montague, P. R., & Berns, G. S. (2002). Neural economics and the biological substrates of valuation. *Neuron, 36*(2), 265–284.

Morecraft, R. J., Geula, C., & Mesulam, M. M. (1992). Cytoarchitecture and neural afferents of orbitofrontal cortex in the brain of the monkey. *The Journal of Comparative Neurology, 323*(3), 341–358.

Moxey, A., O'Connell, D., McGettigan, P., & Henry, D. (2003). Describing treatment effects to patients. *Journal of General Internal Medicine, 18*(11), 948–959.

Paulus, M. P., & Stein, M. B. (2006). An insular view of anxiety. *Biological Psychiatry, 60*(4), 383–387.

Peters, J., & Buchel, C. (2009). Overlapping and distinct neural systems code for subjective value during intertemporal and risky decision making. *The Journal of Neuroscience, 29*(50), 15727–15734.

Pine, A., Shiner, T., Seymour, B., & Dolan, R. J. (2010). Dopamine, time, and impulsivity in humans. *The Journal of Neuroscience, 30*(26), 8888–8896.

Powers, L. (2013, September 18). *Penn State suspends fee for employees who don't take health care survey.* Retrieved from http://news.psu.edu/story/288132/2013/09/18/administration/penn-state-suspends-fee-employees-who-dont-take-health-care/

Prentice, A. M. (2006). The emerging epidemic of obesity in developing countries. *International Journal of Epidemiology, 35*(1), 93–99.

Putman, P., Antypa, N., Crysovergi, P., & van der Does, W. A. (2010). Exogenous cortisol acutely influences motivated decision making in healthy young men. *Psychopharmacology, 208*(2), 257–263.

Rabin, M. (2000). Risk aversion and expected-utility theory: A calibration theorem. *Econometrica, 68*(5), 1281–1292.

Read, D. (2007). Experienced utility: Utility theory from Jeremy Bentham to Daniel Kahneman. *Thinking & Reasoning, 13*(1), 45–61.

Reynolds, B., & Schiffbauer, R. (2004). Measuring state changes in human delay discounting: An experiential discounting task. *Behavioural Processes, 67*(3), 343–356.

Rilling, J. K., Sanfey, A. G., Aronson, J. A., Nystrom, L. E., & Cohen, J. D. (2004). The neural correlates of theory of mind within interpersonal interactions. *Neuroimage, 22*(4), 1694–1703.

Rodrigues, S. M., LeDoux, J. E., & Sapolsky, R. M. (2009). The influence of stress hormones on fear circuitry. *Annual Review of Neuroscience, 32*, 289–313.

Roiser, J. P., de Martino, B., Tan, G. C., Kumaran, D., Seymour, B., Wood, N. W., & Dolan, R. J. (2009). A genetically mediated bias in decision making driven by failure of amygdala control. *The Journal of Neuroscience, 29*(18), 5985–5991.

Rolls, E. T., & Grabenhorst, F. (2008). The orbitofrontal cortex and beyond: From affect to decision-making. *Progress in Neurobiology, 86*(3), 216–244.

Rosati, A. G., Stevens, J. R., Hare, B., & Hauser, M. D. (2007). The evolutionary origins of human patience: Temporal preferences in chimpanzees, bonobos, and human adults. *Current Biology: CB, 17*(19), 1663–1668.

Roy, J. E., Buschman, T. J., & Miller, E. K. (2014). PFC neurons reflect categorical decisions about ambiguous stimuli. *Journal of Cognitive Neuroscience, 26*(6), 1283–1291.

Sanfey, A. G., & Chang, L. J. (2008). Multiple systems in decision making. *Annals of the New York Academy of Sciences, 1128*, 53–62.

Sanfey, A. G., Rilling, J. K., Aronson, J. A., Nystrom, L. E., & Cohen, J. D. (2003). The neural basis of economic decision-making in the Ultimatum Game. *Science, 300*(5626), 1755–1758.

Sapolsky, R. M. (2005). The influence of social hierarchy on primate health. *Science, 308*(5722), 648–652.

Schoemaker, P. J. H. (1982). The expected utility model: Its variants, purposes, evidence and limitations. *Journal of Economic Literature, 20*(2), 529–563.

Schwartz, B. (2009). *The paradox of choice.* New York, NY: Harper-Collins.

Schweighofer, N., Bertin, M., Shishida, K., Okamoto, Y., Tanaka, S. C., Yamawaki, S., & Doya, K. (2008). Low-serotonin levels increase delayed reward discounting in humans. *The Journal of Neuroscience, 28*(17), 4528–4532.

Small, D. M., Zatorre, R. J., Dagher, A., Evans, A. C., & Jones-Gotman, M. (2001). Changes in brain activity related to eating chocolate: From pleasure to aversion. *Brain: A Journal of Neurology, 124*(Pt. 9), 1720–1733.

Stevens, J. R., Hallinan, E. V., & Hauser, M. D. (2005). The ecology and evolution of patience in two New World monkeys. *Biology Letters, 1*(2), 223–226.

Thaler, D., Chen, Y. C., Nixon, P. D., Stern, C. E., & Passingham, R. E. (1995). The functions of the medial premotor cortex. I. Simple learned movements. *Experimental Brain Research, 102*(3), 445–460.

Thaler, R. (1980). Toward a positive theory of consumer choice. *Journal of Economic Behavior and Organization, 1*(1), 39–60.

Thaler, R. H. (2000). From *Homo economicus* to *Homo sapiens*. *Journal of Economic Perspectives, 14*(1), 133–141.

Tremblay, L., & Schultz, W. (1999). Relative reward preference in primate orbitofrontal cortex. *Nature, 398*(6729), 704–708.

Tversky, A., & Kahneman, D. (1981). The framing of decisions and the psychology of choice. *Science, 211*(4481), 453–458.

van den Bos, W., McClure, S. M., Harris, L. T., Fiske, S. T., & Cohen, J. D. (2007). Dissociating affective evaluation and social cognitive processes in the ventral medial prefrontal cortex. *Cognitive, Affective & Behavioral Neuroscience, 7*(4), 337–346.

Venkatraman, V., Payne, J. W., Bettman, J. R., Luce, M. F., & Huettel, S. A. (2009). Separate neural mechanisms underlie choices and strategic preferences in risky decision making. *Neuron, 62*(4), 593–602.

Wansink, B., & Sobal, J. (2006). Mindless eating: The 200 daily food decisions we overlook. *Environment & Behavior, 39*(1), 106–123.

Weber, B. J. (2005). Playing for peanuts: Why is risk seeking more common for low-stakes gambles? *Organizational Behavior and Human Decision Processes, 97*(1), 31–46.

Weiss, M., & Hechtman, L. (2006). A randomized double-blind trial of paroxetine and/or dextroamphetamine and problem-focused therapy for attention-deficit/hyperactivity disorder in adults. *The Journal of Clinical Psychiatry, 67*(4), 611–619.

Wiedman, D. W. (1989). Adiposity or longevity: Which factor accounts for the increase in type II diabetes mellitus when populations acculturate to an industrial technology? *Medical Anthropology, 11*(3), 237–253.

Wogar, M. A., Bradshaw, C. M., & Szabadi, E. (1993). Effect of lesions of the ascending 5-hydroxytryptaminergic pathways on choice between delayed reinforcers. *Psychopharmacology, 111*(2), 239–243.

World Health Organization. (2006). *Working together for health: The World Health Report 2006.* Geneva, Switzerland: World Health Organization.

Xu, P., Gu, R., Broster, L. S., Wu, R., Van Dam, N. T., Jiang, Y., . . . Luo, Y. J. (2013). Neural basis of emotional decision making in trait anxiety. *The Journal of Neuroscience, 33*(47), 18641–18653.

Yacubian, J., Glascher, J., Schroeder, K., Sommer, T., Braus, D. F., & Buchel, C. (2006). Dissociable systems for gain- and loss-related value predictions and errors of prediction in the human brain. *The Journal of Neuroscience, 26*(37), 9530–9537.

Zacny, J. P., & de Wit, H. (2009). The prescription opioid, oxycodone, does not alter behavioral measures of impulsivity in healthy volunteers. *Pharmacology, Biochemistry, and Behavior, 94*(1), 108–113.

Zald, D. H., Boileau, I., El-Dearedy, W., Gunn, R., McGlone, F., Dichter, G. S., & Dagher, A. (2004). Dopamine transmission in the human striatum during monetary reward tasks. *The Journal of Neuroscience, 24*(17), 4105–4112.

Chapter 13

Adams, D. B. (2006). Brain mechanisms of aggressive behavior: An updated review. *Neuroscience and Biobehavioral Reviews, 30*(3), 304–318.

Adams, D. B., Boudreau, W., Cowan, C. W., Kokonowski, C., Oberteuffer, K., & Yohay, K. (1993). Offense produced by chemical stimulation of the anterior hypothalamus of the rat. *Physiology & Behavior, 53*(6), 1127–1132.

Addis, D. R., Wong, A. T., & Schacter, D. L. (2007). Remembering the past and imagining the future: Common and distinct neural substrates during event construction and elaboration. *Neuropsychologia, 45*(7), 1363–1377.

Azmitia, E. C., & Segal, M. (1978). An autoradiographic analysis of the differential ascending projections of the dorsal and median raphe nuclei in the rat. *The Journal of Comparative Neurology, 179*(3), 641–667.

Bard, P. (1934). On emotional expression after decortication with some remarks on certain theoretical views: Part I. *Psychological Review, 41*(4), 309–329.

Bechara, A., Damasio, A. R., Damasio, H., & Anderson, S. W. (1994). Insensitivity to future consequences following damage to human prefrontal cortex. *Cognition, 50*(1–3), 7–15.

Bechara, A., Tranel, D., & Damasio, H. (2000). Characterization of the decision-making deficit of patients with ventromedial prefrontal cortex lesions. *Brain: A Journal of Neurology, 123*(Pt. 11), 2189–2202.

Bechara, A., Tranel, D., Damasio, H., & Damasio, A. R. (1996). Failure to respond autonomically to anticipated future outcomes following damage to prefrontal cortex. *Cerebral Cortex, 6*(2), 215–225.

Beckmann, M., Johansen-Berg, H., & Rushworth, M. F. (2009). Connectivity-based parcellation of human cingulate cortex and its relation to functional specialization. *The Journal of Neuroscience, 29*(4), 1175–1190.

Bejjani, B. P., Houeto, J. L., Hariz, M., Yelnik, J., Mesnage, V., Bonnet, A. M., . . . Agid, Y. (2002). Aggressive behavior induced by intraoperative stimulation in the triangle of Sano. *Neurology, 59*(9), 1425–1427.

Benazzouz, A., Gao, D. M., Ni, Z. G., Piallat, B., Bouali-Benazzouz, R., & Benabid, A. L. (2000). Effect of high-frequency stimulation of the subthalamic nucleus on the neuronal activities of the substantia nigra pars reticulata and ventrolateral nucleus of the thalamus in the rat. *Neuroscience, 99*(2), 289–295.

Beric, A., Kelly, P. J., Rezai, A., Sterio, D., Mogilner, A., Zonenshayn, M., & Kopell, B. (2002). Complications of deep brain stimulation surgery. *Stereotactic and Functional Neurosurgery, 77*(1–4), 73–78.

Bewernick, B. H., Hurlemann, R., Matusch, A., Kayser, S., Grubert, C., Hadrysiewicz, B., . . . Schlaepfer, T. E. (2010). Nucleus accumbens deep brain stimulation decreases ratings of depression and anxiety in treatment-resistant depression. *Biological Psychiatry, 67*(2), 110–116.

Binder, D. K., Rau, G. M., & Starr, P. A. (2005). Risk factors for hemorrhage during microelectrode-guided deep brain stimulator implantation for movement disorders. *Neurosurgery, 56*(4), 722–732; discussion 722–732.

Blier, P., & de Montigny, C. (1994). Current advances and trends in the treatment of depression. *Trends in Pharmacological Sciences, 15*(7), 220–226.

Bonne, O., Vythilingam, M., Inagaki, M., Wood, S., Neumeister, A., Nugent, A. C., . . . Charney, D. S. (2008). Reduced posterior hippocampal volume in posttraumatic stress disorder. *The Journal of Clinical Psychiatry, 69*(7), 1087–1091.

Booker, H. E., & Celesia, G. G. (1973). Serum concentrations of diazepam in subjects with epilepsy. *Archives of Neurology, 29*(3), 191–194.

Bruhl, A. B., Jancke, L., & Herwig, U. (2011). Differential modulation of emotion processing brain regions by noradrenergic and serotonergic antidepressants. *Psychopharmacology, 216*(3), 389–399.

Bruhl, A. B., Kaffenberger, T., & Herwig, U. (2010). Serotonergic and noradrenergic modulation of emotion processing by single dose antidepressants. *Neuropsychopharmacology, 35*(2), 521–533.

Cai, X. J., Widdowson, P. S., Harrold, J., Wilson, S., Buckingham, R. E., Arch, J. R., . . . Williams, G. (1999). Hypothalamic orexin expression: Modulation by blood glucose and feeding. *Diabetes, 48*(11), 2132–2137.

Campbell-Meiklejohn, D. K., Woolrich, M. W., Passingham, R. E., & Rogers, R. D. (2008). Knowing when to stop: The brain mechanisms of chasing losses. *Biological Psychiatry, 63*(3), 293–300.

Cannon, W. B. (1927). The James–Lange theory of emotions: A critical examination and an alternative theory. *American Journal of Psychology, 39*(1/4), 106–124.

Canteras, N. S., Chiavegatto, S., Ribeiro do Valle, L. E., & Swanson, L. W. (1997). Severe reduction of rat defensive behavior to a predator by discrete hypothalamic chemical lesions. *Brain Research Bulletin, 44*(3), 297–305.

Cardinal, R. N., Parkinson, J. A., Hall, J., & Everitt, B. J. (2002). Emotion and motivation: The role of the amygdala, ventral striatum, and prefrontal cortex. *Neuroscience and Biobehavioral Reviews, 26*(3), 321–352.

Carson, A. J., MacHale, S., Allen, K., Lawrie, S. M., Dennis, M., House, A., & Sharpe, M. (2000). Depression after stroke and lesion location: A systematic review. *Lancet, 356*(9224), 122–126.

Carter, C. S., & van Veen, V. (2007). Anterior cingulate cortex and conflict detection: An update of theory and data. *Cognitive, Affective & Behavioral Neuroscience, 7*(4), 367–379.

Cassell, E. J. (2000). The principles of the Belmont report revisited. How have respect for persons, beneficence, and justice been applied to clinical medicine? *The Hastings Center Report, 30*(4), 12–21.

Craig, A. D. (2002). How do you feel? Interoception: The sense of the physiological condition of the body. *Nature Reviews: Neuroscience, 3*(8), 655–666.

Craig, M. C., Catani, M., Deeley, Q., Latham, R., Daly, E., Kanaan, R., . . . Murphy, D. G. (2009). Altered connections on the road to psychopathy. *Molecular Psychiatry, 14*(10), 946–953.

Critchley, H. D., Mathias, C. J., & Dolan, R. J. (2001). Neuroanatomical basis for first- and second-order representations of bodily states. *Nature Neuroscience, 4*(2), 207–212.

Cullinan, W. E., Herman, J. P., & Watson, S. J. (1993). Ventral subicular interaction with the hypothalamic paraventricular nucleus: Evidence for a relay in the bed nucleus of the stria terminalis. *The Journal of Comparative Neurology, 332*(1), 1–20.

Dalgleish, T. (2004). The emotional brain. *Nature Reviews: Neuroscience, 5*(7), 583–589.

Damasio, A. R. (1994). *Descartes' error: Emotion, reason, and the human brain.* New York, NY: Grosset/Putnam.

Damasio, H., Grabowski, T., Frank, R., Galaburda, A. M., & Damasio, A. R. (1994). The return of Phineas Gage: Clues about the brain from the skull of a famous patient. *Science, 264*(5162), 1102–1105.

Del-Ben, C. M., Ferreira, C. A., Alves-Neto, W. C., & Graeff, F. G. (2008). Serotonergic modulation of face-emotion recognition. *Brazilian Journal of Medical and Biological Research, 41*(4), 263–269.

Di Simplicio, M., Massey-Chase, R., Cowen, P. J., & Harmer, C. J. (2009). Oxytocin enhances processing of positive versus negative emotional information in healthy male volunteers. *Journal of Psychopharmacology, 23*(3), 241–248.

Downar, J., & Daskalakis, Z. J. (2013). New targets for rTMS in depression: A review of convergent evidence. *Brain Stimulation, 6*(3), 231–240.

Dunn, B. D., Dalgleish, T., & Lawrence, A. D. (2006). The somatic marker hypothesis: A critical evaluation. *Neuroscience and Biobehavioral Reviews, 30*(2), 239–271.

Dutton, D. G., & Aron, A. P. (1974). Some evidence for heightened sexual attraction under conditions of high anxiety. *Journal of Personality and Social Psychology, 30*(4), 510–517.

Ellenbogen, J. M., Hurford, M. O., Liebeskind, D. S., Neimark, G. B., & Weiss, D. (2005). Ventromedial frontal lobe trauma. *Neurology, 64*(4), 757.

Elliott, R., Rees, G., & Dolan, R. J. (1999). Ventromedial prefrontal cortex mediates guessing. *Neuropsychologia, 37*(4), 403–411.

Ellison-Wright, I., & Bullmore, E. (2010). Anatomy of bipolar disorder and schizophrenia: A meta-analysis. *Schizophrenia Research, 117*(1), 1–12.

Fanselow, M. S., & Dong, H. W. (2010). Are the dorsal and ventral hippocampus functionally distinct structures? *Neuron, 65*(1), 7–19.

Feinstein, J. S., Adolphs, R., Damasio, A., & Tranel, D. (2011). The human amygdala and the induction and experience of fear. *Current Biology: CB, 21*(1), 34–38.

Fosse, R., & Read, J. (2013). Electroconvulsive treatment: Hypotheses about mechanisms of action. *Frontiers in Psychiatry, 4*, 94.

Frey, B. N., Andreazza, A. C., Nery, F. G., Martins, M. R., Quevedo, J., Soares, J. C., & Kapczinski, F. (2007). The role of hippocampus in the pathophysiology of bipolar disorder. *Behavioural Pharmacology, 18*(5–6), 419–430.

Gonon, F., Msghina, M., & Stjarne, L. (1993). Kinetics of noradrenaline released by sympathetic nerves. *Neuroscience, 56*(3), 535–538.

Griffiths, P. E. (2003). Basic emotions, complex emotions, Machiavellian emotions. *Royal Institute of Philosophy Supplement, 52*, 39–67.

Hadreas, P. (2010). Husserlian self-awareness and selective serotonin reuptake inhibitors. *Philosophy, Psychiatry, & Psychology, 17*(1), 43–51.

Hajos, M., Hajos-Korcsok, E., & Sharp, T. (1999). Role of the medial prefrontal cortex in 5-HT1A receptor-induced inhibition of 5-HT neuronal activity in the rat. *British Journal of Pharmacology, 126*(8), 1741–1750.

Harding, S. M., & McGinnis, M. Y. (2004). Androgen receptor blockade in the MPOA or VMN: Effects on male sociosexual behaviors. *Physiology & Behavior, 81*(4), 671–680.

Harlow, J. M. (1868). Recovery from the passage of an iron bar through the head. *Publications of the Massachusetts Medical Society, 2*, 327–347.

Harmer, C. J. (2008). Serotonin and emotional processing: Does it help explain antidepressant drug action? *Neuropharmacology, 55*(6), 1023–1028.

Harmer, C. J., Bhagwagar, Z., Perrett, D. I., Vollm, B. A., Cowen, P. J., & Goodwin, G. M. (2003). Acute SSRI administration affects the processing of social cues in healthy volunteers. *Neuropsychopharmacology, 28*(1), 148–152.

Harmer, C. J., Mackay, C. E., Reid, C. B., Cowen, P. J., & Goodwin, G. M. (2006). Antidepressant drug treatment modifies the neural processing of nonconscious threat cues. *Biological Psychiatry, 59*(9), 816–820.

Harmer, C. J., Shelley, N. C., Cowen, P. J., & Goodwin, G. M. (2004). Increased positive versus negative affective perception and memory in healthy volunteers following selective serotonin and norepinephrine reuptake inhibition. *The American Journal of Psychiatry, 161*(7), 1256–1263.

Hayman, L. A., Rexer, J. L., Pavol, M. A., Strite, D., & Meyers, C. A. (1998). Kluver–Bucy syndrome after bilateral selective damage of amygdala and its cortical connections. *The Journal of Neuropsychiatry and Clinical Neurosciences, 10*(3), 354–358.

Hjorth, S. (1993). Serotonin 5-HT1A autoreceptor blockade potentiates the ability of the 5-HT reuptake inhibitor citalopram to increase nerve terminal output of 5-HT in vivo: A microdialysis study. *Journal of Neurochemistry, 60*(2), 776–779.

Horvath, F. (1978). An experimental comparison of the psychological stress evaluator and the galvanic skin response in detection of deception. *The Journal of Applied Psychology, 63*(3), 338–344.

Hoyer, D., Clarke, D. E., Fozard, J. R., Hartig, P. R., Martin, G. R., Mylecharane, E. J., . . . Humphrey, P. P. (1994). International Union of Pharmacology classification of receptors for 5-hydroxytryptamine (serotonin). *Pharmacological Reviews, 46*(2), 157–203.

Ikemoto, S., Witkin, B. M., & Morales, M. (2003). Rewarding injections of the cholinergic agonist carbachol into the ventral tegmental area induce locomotion and c-Fos expression in the retrosplenial area and supramammillary nucleus. *Brain Research, 969*(1–2), 78–87.

Isnard, J., Guenot, M., Sindou, M., & Mauguiere, F. (2004). Clinical manifestations of insular lobe seizures: A stereoelectroencephalographic study. *Epilepsia, 45*(9), 1079–1090.

James, W. (1890). *The principles of psychology*. London, UK: MacMillan.

Johnson, R. H., & Nelson, D. R. (1973). Agonistic display in the gray reef shark, *Carcharhinus menisorrah*, and its relationship to attacks on man. *Copeia, 1973*(1), 76–84.

Johnstone, T., van Reekum, C. M., Urry, H. L., Kalin, N. H., & Davidson, R. J. (2007). Failure to regulate: Counterproductive recruitment of top-down prefrontal–subcortical circuitry in major depression. *The Journal of Neuroscience, 27*(33), 8877–8884.

Kenney, C., Simpson, R., Hunter, C., Ondo, W., Almaguer, M., Davidson, A., & Jankovic, J. (2007). Short-term and long-term safety of deep brain stimulation in the treatment of movement disorders. *Journal of Neurosurgery, 106*(4), 621–625.

Kluver, H., & Bucy, P. C. (1939/1997). Preliminary analysis of functions of the temporal lobes in monkeys. 1939. *Journal of Neuropsychiatry and Clinical Neurosciences, 9*(4), 606–620.

Koenigs, M., & Grafman, J. (2009). Prefrontal asymmetry in depression? The long-term effect of unilateral brain lesions. *Neuroscience Letters, 459*(2), 88–90.

Koenigs, M., Huey, E. D., Calamia, M., Raymont, V., Tranel, D., & Grafman, J. (2008). Distinct regions of prefrontal cortex mediate resistance and vulnerability to depression. *The Journal of Neuroscience, 28*(47), 12341–12348.

Kringelbach, M. L., & Berridge, K. C. (2009). Towards a functional neuroanatomy of pleasure and happiness. *Trends in Cognitive Sciences, 13*(11), 479–487.

LeDoux, J. (2007). The amygdala. *Current Biology: CB, 17*(20), R868–R874.

Lieberman, A., & Benson, D. F. (1977). Control of emotional expression in pseudobulbar palsy. A personal experience. *Archives of Neurology, 34*(11), 717–719.

Lin, D., Boyle, M. P., Dollar, P., Lee, H., Lein, E. S., Perona, P., & Anderson, D. J. (2011). Functional identification of an aggression locus in the mouse hypothalamus. *Nature, 470*(7333), 221–226.

Ling, M. H. , Perry, P. J. , Tsuang, M. T. (1981). Side effects of corticosteroid therapy. Psychiatric aspects. *Archives of General Psychiatry. 38*(4):471–477.

Low, K., Crestani, F., Keist, R., Benke, D., Brunig, I., Benson, J. A., . . . Rudolph, U. (2000). Molecular and neuronal substrate for the selective attenuation of anxiety. *Science, 290*(5489), 131–134.

Maglione-Garves, C. A., Kravitz, L., & Schneider, S. (2005). Cortisol connection: Tips on managing stress and weight. *ACSM's Health & Fitness Journal, 9*(5), 20–23.

Maguire, E. A., Gadian, D. G., Johnsrude, I. S., Good, C. D., Ashburner, J., Frackowiak, R. S., & Frith, C. D. (2000). Navigation-related structural change in the hippocampi of taxi drivers. *Proceedings of the National Academy of Sciences of the United States of America, 97*(8), 4398–403.

Maguire, E. A., Valentine, E. R., Wilding, J. M., & Kapur, N. (2003). Routes to remembering: The brains behind superior memory. *Nature Neuroscience, 6*(1), 90–95.

Maickel, R. P., Matussek, N., Stern, D. N., & Brodie, B. B. (1967). The sympathetic nervous system as a homeostatic mechanism. I. Absolute need for sympathetic nervous function in body temperature maintenance of cold-exposed rats. *The Journal of Pharmacology and Experimental Therapeutics, 157*(1), 103–110.

Marañon, G. (1924). Contribution a l'etude de l'action emotive de l'adrenaline. *Revue Francaise d'Endocrinologie, 2*, 301–325.

Martinez, R. C., Carvalho-Netto, E. F., Amaral, V. C., Nunes-de-Souza, R. L., & Canteras, N. S. (2008). Investigation of the hypothalamic defensive system in the mouse. *Behavioural Brain Research, 192*(2), 185–190.

Mathias, C. J., & Bannister, R. (1999). Investigation of autonomic disorders. In C. J. Mathias & R. Bannister (Eds.), *Autonomic failure: A textbook of clinical disorders of the autonomic nervous system* (pp. 169–195). Oxford, UK: Oxford University Press.

Mazzola, L., Isnard, J., Peyron, R., Guenot, M., & Mauguiere, F. (2009). Somatotopic organization of pain responses to direct electrical stimulation of the human insular cortex. *Pain, 146*(1–2), 99–104.

McEwen, B. S. (1999). Stress and hippocampal plasticity. *Annual Review of Neuroscience, 22*, 105–122.

Mesulam, M. M. (1998). From sensation to cognition. *Brain: A Journal of Neurology, 121*(Pt. 6), 1013–1052.

Miller, J. M., Vorel, S. R., Tranguch, A. J., Kenny, E. T., Mazzoni, P., van Gorp, W. G., & Kleber, H. D. (2006). Anhedonia after a selective bilateral lesion of the globus pallidus. *The American Journal of Psychiatry, 163*(5), 786–788.

Mogensen, F., Muller, D., & Valentin, N. (1986). Glycopyrrolate during ketamine/diazepam anaesthesia. A double-blind comparison with atropine. *Acta Anaesthesiologica Scandinavica, 30*(4), 332–336.

Mora, C. T., Torjman, M., & White, P. F. (1989). Effects of diazepam and flumazenil on sedation and hypoxic ventilatory response. *Anesthesia and Analgesia, 68*(4), 473–478.

Morgan, H. (1990). Dostoevsky's epilepsy: A case report and comparison. *Surgical Neurology, 33*(6), 413–416.

Moser, M. B., & Moser, E. I. (1998). Functional differentiation in the hippocampus. *Hippocampus, 8*(6), 608–619.

Naccache, L., Dehaene, S., Cohen, L., Habert, M. O., Guichart-Gomez, E., Galanaud, D., & Willer, J. C. (2005). Effortless control: Executive attention and conscious feeling of mental effort are dissociable. *Neuropsychologia, 43*(9), 1318–1328.

Okun, M. S., Fernandez, H. H., Wu, S. S., Kirsch-Darrow, L., Bowers, D., Bova, F., . . . Foote, K. D. (2009). Cognition and mood in Parkinson's disease in subthalamic nucleus versus globus pallidus interna deep brain stimulation: The COMPARE trial. *Annals of Neurology, 65*(5), 586–595.

Olds, J., & Milner, P. (1954). Positive reinforcement produced by electrical stimulation of septal area and other regions of rat brain. *Journal of Comparative and Physiological Psychology, 47*(6), 419–427.

Ostrowsky, K., Magnin, M., Ryvlin, P., Isnard, J., Guenot, M., & Mauguiere, F. (2002). Representation of pain and somatic sensation in the human insula: A study of responses to direct electrical cortical stimulation. *Cerebral Cortex, 12*(4), 376–385.

Pacherie, E. (2008). The phenomenology of action: A conceptual framework. *Cognition, 107*(1), 179–217.

Papez, J. (1937). A proposed mechanism of emotion. *Archives of Neurology & Psychiatry, 38*(4), 725–743.

Pardo, J. V., Pardo, P. J., Janer, K. W., & Raichle, M. E. (1990). The anterior cingulate cortex mediates processing selection in the Stroop attentional conflict paradigm. *Proceedings of the National Academy of Sciences of the United States of America, 87*(1), 256–259.

Park, I. H., Kim, J. J., Chun, J., Jung, Y. C., Seok, J. H., Park, H. J., & Lee, J. D. (2009). Medial prefrontal default-mode hypoactivity affecting trait physical anhedonia in schizophrenia. *Psychiatry Research, 171*(3), 155–165.

Paulus, M. P., Feinstein, J. S., Castillo, G., Simmons, A. N., & Stein, M. B. (2005). Dose-dependent decrease of activation in bilateral amygdala and insula by lorazepam during emotion processing. *Archives of General Psychiatry, 62*(3), 282–288.

Pecina, S., Smith, K. S., & Berridge, K. C. (2006). Hedonic hot spots in the brain. *The Neuroscientist, 12*(6), 500–511.

Pessoa, L. (2010). Emotion and cognition and the amygdala: from "what is it?" to "what's to be done?" *Neuropsychologia, 48*(12), 3416–3429.

Pessoa, L., & Engelmann, J. B. (2010). Embedding reward signals into perception and cognition. *Frontiers in Neuroscience, 4*.

Petrovic, P., Dietrich, T., Fransson, P., Andersson, J., Carlsson, K., & Ingvar, M. (2005). Placebo in emotional processing—Induced expectations of anxiety relief activate a generalized modulatory network. *Neuron, 46*(6), 957–969.

Pfaff, D. W., & Sakuma, Y. (1979). Deficit in the lordosis reflex of female rats caused by lesions in the ventromedial nucleus of the hypothalamus. *The Journal of Physiology, 288*, 203–210.

Phillips, R. G., & LeDoux, J. E. (1992). Differential contribution of amygdala and hippocampus to cued and contextual fear conditioning. *Behavioral Neuroscience, 106*(2), 274–285.

Picard, F., & Craig, A. D. (2009). Ecstatic epileptic seizures: A potential window on the neural basis for human self-awareness. *Epilepsy & Behavior: E&B, 16*(3), 539–546.

Pickens, C. L., Saddoris, M. P., Setlow, B., Gallagher, M., Holland, P. C., & Schoenbaum, G. (2003). Different roles for orbitofrontal cortex and basolateral amygdala in a reinforcer devaluation task. *The Journal of Neuroscience, 23*(35), 11078–11084.

Pochon, J. B., Levy, R., Fossati, P., Lehericy, S., Poline, J. B., Pillon, B., . . . Dubois, B. (2002). The neural system that bridges reward and cognition in humans: An fMRI study. *Proceedings of the National Academy of Sciences of the United States of America, 99*(8), 5669–5674.

Rainville, P., Bechara, A., Naqvi, N., & Damasio, A. R. (2006). Basic emotions are associated with distinct patterns of cardiorespiratory activity. *International Journal of Psychophysiology, 61*(1), 5–18.

Reeves, A. G., & Plum, F. (1969). Hyperphagia, rage, and dementia accompanying a ventromedial hypothalamic neoplasm. *Archives of Neurology, 20*(6), 616–624.

Rogan, M. T., & LeDoux, J. E. (1995). LTP is accompanied by commensurate enhancement of auditory-evoked responses in a fear conditioning circuit. *Neuron, 15*(1), 127–136.

Rowe, J. W., Young, J. B., Minaker, K. L., Stevens, A. L., Pallotta, J., & Landsberg, L. (1981). Effect of insulin and glucose infusions on sympathetic nervous system activity in normal man. *Diabetes, 30*(3), 219–225.

Sainani, M. P., Muralidhar, R., Parthiban, K., & Vijayalakshmi, P. (2011). Lipoid proteinosis of Urbach and Weithe: Case report and a brief review of the literature. *International Ophthalmology, 31*(2), 141–143.

Schachter, S., & Singer, J. E. (1962). Cognitive, social, and physiological determinants of emotional state. *Psychological Review, 69*, 379–399.

Scoville, W. B., & Milner, B. (1957). Loss of recent memory after bilateral hippocampal lesions. *Journal of Neurology, Neurosurgery, and Psychiatry, 20*(1), 11–21.

Scoville, W. B., & Milner, B. (2000). Loss of recent memory after bilateral hippocampal lesions. 1957. *The Journal of Neuropsychiatry and Clinical Neurosciences, 12*(1), 103–113.

Simons, F. E. (2004). First-aid treatment of anaphylaxis to food: Focus on epinephrine. *The Journal of Allergy and Clinical Immunology, 113*(5), 837–844.

Small, D. M., Zatorre, R. J., Dagher, A., Evans, A. C., & Jones-Gotman, M. (2001). Changes in brain activity related to eating chocolate: From pleasure to aversion. *Brain: A Journal of Neurology, 124*(Pt. 9), 1720–1733.

Sower, S. A., Freamat, M., & Kavanaugh, S. I. (2009). The origins of the vertebrate hypothalamic–pituitary–gonadal (HPG) and hypothalamic–pituitary–thyroid (HPT) endocrine systems: New insights from lampreys. *General and Comparative Endocrinology, 161*(1), 20–29.

Stefurak, T., Mikulis, D., Mayberg, H., Lang, A. E., Hevenor, S., Pahapill, P., . . . Lozano, A. (2003). Deep brain stimulation for Parkinson's disease dissociates mood and motor circuits: A functional MRI case study. *Movement Disorders, 18*(12), 1508–1516.

Stewart, R. D., Hake, C. L., & Peterson, J. E. (1974). "Degreasers' flush": Dermal response to trichloroethylene and ethanol. *Archives of Environmental Health, 29*(1), 1–5.

Stuss, D. T., Floden, D., Alexander, M. P., Levine, B., & Katz, D. (2001). Stroop performance in focal lesion patients: Dissociation of processes and frontal lobe lesion location. *Neuropsychologia, 39*(8), 771–786.

Synofzik, M., & Schlaepfer, T. E. (2011). Electrodes in the brain—Ethical criteria for research and treatment with deep brain stimulation for neuropsychiatric disorders. *Brain Stimulation, 4*(1), 7–16.

Terzian, H., & Ore, G. D. (1955). Syndrome of Kluver and Bucy; Reproduced in man by bilateral removal of the temporal lobes. *Neurology, 5*(6), 373–380.

Tolle, V., Bassant, M. H., Zizzari, P., Poindessous-Jazat, F., Tomasetto, C., Epelbaum, J., & Bluet-Pajot, M. T. (2002). Ultradian rhythmicity of ghrelin secretion in relation with GH, feeding behavior, and sleep–wake patterns in rats. *Endocrinology, 143*(4), 1353–1361.

van der Veen, F. M., Evers, E. A., Deutz, N. E., & Schmitt, J. A. (2007). Effects of acute tryptophan depletion on mood and facial emotion perception related brain activation and performance in healthy women with and without a family history of depression. *Neuropsychopharmacology, 32*(1), 216–224.

Vas, J., Topal, J., Gacsi, M., Miklosi, A., & Csanya, V. (2005). A friend or an enemy? Dogs' reaction to an unfamiliar person showing behavioural cues of threat and friendliness at different times. *Applied Animal Behaviour Science, 94*(1), 99–115.

Veendrick-Meekes, M. J., Verhoeven, W. M., van Erp, M. G., van Blarikom, W., & Tuinier, S. (2007). Neuropsychiatric aspects of patients with hypothalamic hamartomas. *Epilepsy & Behavior: E&B, 11*(2), 218–221.

Velando, A., Beamonte-Barrientos, R., & Torres, R. (2006). Pigment-based skin colour in the blue-footed booby: An honest signal of current condition used by females to adjust reproductive investment. *Oecologia, 149*(3), 535–542.

Wager, T. D., Davidson, M. L., Hughes, B. L., Lindquist, M. A., & Ochsner, K. N. (2008). Prefrontal–subcortical pathways mediating successful emotion regulation. *Neuron, 59*(6), 1037–1050.

Wager, T. D., Waugh, C. E., Lindquist, M., Noll, D. C., Fredrickson, B. L., & Taylor, S. F. (2009). Brain mediators of cardiovascular responses to social threat: Part I: Reciprocal dorsal and ventral sub-regions of the medial prefrontal cortex and heart-rate reactivity. *Neuroimage, 47*(3), 821–835.

Wilent, W. B., Oh, M. Y., Buetefisch, C. M., Bailes, J. E., Cantella, D., Angle, C., & Whiting, D. M. (2010). Induction of panic attack by stimulation of the ventromedial hypothalamus. *Journal of Neurosurgery, 112*(6), 1295–1298.

Wise, R. G., Lujan, B. J., Schweinhardt, P., Peskett, G. D., Rogers, R., & Tracey, I. (2007). The anxiolytic effects of midazolam during anticipation to pain revealed using fMRI. *Magnetic Resonance Imaging, 25*(6), 801–810.

Young, E. (2010, December 16). Meet the woman without fear. *Not exactly rocket science.* Retrieved from http://blogs.discovermagazine.com/notrocketscience/2010/12/16/meet-the-woman-without-fear/

Zald, D. H. (2003). The human amygdala and the emotional evaluation of sensory stimuli. *Brain Research. Brain Research Reviews, 41*(1), 88–123.

Chapter 14

Adi, Y., Juarez-Garcia, A., Wang, D., Jowett, S., Frew, E., Day, E., . . . Burls, A. (2007). Oral naltrexone as a treatment for relapse prevention in formerly opioid-dependent drug users: A systematic review and economic evaluation. *Health Technology Assessment, 11*(6), iii–iv, 1–85.

Bergson, C., Mrzljak, L., Smiley, J. F., Pappy, M., Levenson, R., & Goldman-Rakic, P. S. (1995). Regional, cellular, and subcellular variations in the distribution of D1 and D5 dopamine receptors in primate brain. *Journal of Neuroscience, 15*(12), 7821–7836.

Biebermann, H., Kuhnen, P., Kleinau, G., & Krude, H. (2012). The neuroendocrine circuitry controlled by POMC, MSH, and AGRP. In H. G. Joost (Ed.), *Handbook of Experimental Pharmacology* (Vol. 209, pp. 47–75). New York, NY: Springer.

Bodnar, R. J., Glass, M. J., Ragnauth, A., & Cooper, M. L. (1995). General, mu and kappa opioid antagonists in the nucleus accumbens alter food intake under deprivation, glucoprivic and palatable conditions. *Brain Research, 700*(1-2), 205–212.

Brickman, P., Coates, D., & Janoff-Bulman, R. (1978). Lottery winners and accident victims: Is happiness relative? *Journal of Personality and Social Psychology, 36*(8), 917–927.

Brundin, P., Strecker, R. E., Lindvall, O., Isacson, O., Nilsson, O. G., Barbin, G., . . . et al. (1987). Intracerebral grafting of dopamine neurons. Experimental basis for clinical trials in patients with Parkinson's disease. *Annals of the New York Academy of Sciences, 495*, 473–496.

Chugh, P. K., & Sharma, S. (2012). Recent advances in the pathophysiology and pharmacological treatment of obesity. *Journal of Clinical Pharmacy and Therapeutics, 37*(5), 525–535.

Clement, K., Vaisse, C., Lahlou, N., Cabrol, S., Pelloux, V., Cassuto, D., . . . Guy-Grand, B. (1998). A mutation in the human leptin receptor gene causes obesity and pituitary dysfunction. *Nature, 392*(6674), 398–401.

Csikszentmihalyi, M. (1997). *Finding flow: The psychology of engagement with everyday life.* New York, NY: Basic Books.

Davis, C. A., Levitan, R. D., Reid, C., Carter, J. C., Kaplan, A. S., Patte, K. A., . . . Kennedy, J. L. (2009). Dopamine for "wanting" and opioids for "liking": A comparison of obese adults with and without binge eating. *Obesity, 17*(6), 1220–1225.

Dietis, N., Rowbotham, D. J., & Lambert, D. G. (2011). Opioid receptor subtypes: Fact or artifact? *British Journal of Anaesthesia, 107*(1), 8–18.

Dreher, J. C., Kohn, P., & Berman, K. F. (2006). Neural coding of distinct statistical properties of reward information in humans. *Cerebral Cortex, 16*(4), 561–573.

Dreyer, J. K., Herrik, K. F., Berg, R. W., & Hounsgaard, J. D. (2010). Influence of phasic and tonic dopamine release on receptor activation. *Journal of Neuroscience, 30*(42), 14273–14283.

D'Souza, M. S., & Markou, A. (2011). Neuronal mechanisms underlying development of nicotine dependence: Implications for novel smoking-cessation treatments. *Addiction Science & Clinical Practice, 6*(1), 4–16.

Eagleman, D. M. (2013). *Brain food.* New York, NY: Pantheon.

Eagleman, D. M., Correro, M. A., & Singh, J. (2010). Why neuroscience matters for a rational drug policy. *Minnesota Journal of Law, Science and Technology, 11*(1), 7–26.

Edwards, S., Kenna, G. A., Swift, R. ., & Leggio, L. (2011). Current and promising pharmacotherapies, and novel research target areas in the treatment of alcohol dependence: A review. *Current Pharmaceutical Design, 17*(14), 1323–1332.

Fenu, S., Spina, L., Rivas, E., Longoni, R., & Di Chiara, G. (2006). Morphine-conditioned single-trial place preference: Role of nucleus accumbens shell dopamine receptors in acquisition, but not expression. *Psychopharmacology (Berl), 187*(2), 143–153.

Fields, H. L., Hjelmstad, G. O., Margolis, E. B., & Nicola, S. (2007). Ventral tegmental area neurons in learned appetitive behavior and positive reinforcement. *Annual Review of Neuroscience, 30*, 289–316.

Fletcher, B. W., & Chandler, R. K. (2012, January). *Principles of drug abuse treatment for criminal justice populations: A research-based guide.* Retrieved from http://www.drugabuse.gov/publications/principles-drug-abuse-treatment-criminal-justice-populations

Friedman, J. M., & Halaas, J. L. (1998). Leptin and the regulation of body weight in mammals. *Nature, 395*(6704), 763–770.

Fudge, J. L., & Haber, S. (2001). Bed nucleus of the stria terminalis and extended amygdala inputs to dopamine subpopulations in primates. *Neuroscience, 104*(3), 807–827.

Gardner, E. L. (2011). Addiction and brain reward and antireward pathways. *Advances in Psychosomatic Medicine, 30*, 22–60.

Geake, J., & Cooper, P. (2003). Cognitive neuroscience: Implications for education? *Westminster Studies in Education, 26*(1), 7–20.

Giuliano, C., Robbins, T. W., Nathan, P. J., Bullmore, E. T., & Everitt, B. J. (2012). Inhibition of opioid transmission at the mu-opioid receptor prevents both food seeking and binge-like eating. *Neuropsychopharmacology, 37*(12), 2643–2652.

Griffin, G. D., & Flanagan-Cato, L. M. (2011). Ovarian hormone action in the hypothalamic ventromedial nucleus: Remodelling to regulate reproduction. *Journal of Neuroendocrinology, 23*(6), 465–471.

Guyenet, P. G., & Aghajanian, G. K. (1978). Antidromic identification of dopaminergic and other output neurons of the rat substantia nigra. *Brain Research, 150*(1), 69–84.

Hall, H., Sedvall, G., Magnusson, O., Kopp, J., Halldin, C., & Farde, L. (1994). Distribution of D1- and D2-dopamine receptors, and dopamine and its metabolites in the human brain. *Neuropsychopharmacology, 11*(4), 245–256.

Hatsukami, D. K., Stead, L. F., & Gupta, P. C. (2008). Tobacco addiction. *Lancet, 371*(9629), 2027–2038.

Higgins, M., Zampogna, G., Pergolizzi, J. V., & LeQuang, J. A. (2014). *The evolving demographics of opioid addiction.* Paper presented at the PainWeek, Las Vegas, NV.

Hoelen, D. W., Spiering, W., & Valk, G. D. (2009). Long-QT syndrome induced by the antiaddiction drug ibogaine. *New England Journal of Medicine, 360*(3), 308–309.

Iversen, S., Iversen, L., & Saper, C. B. (2000). The autonomic nervous system and the hypothalamus. In E. R. Kandel, J. H. Schwartz & T. M. Jessell (Eds.), *Principles of neural science* (4th ed., pp. 960–981). New York, NY: McGraw–Hill.

Jequier, E. (2002). Leptin signaling, adiposity, and energy balance. *Annals of the New York Academy of Sciences, 967*, 379–388.

Kabat-Zinn, J. (1994). *Wherever you go, there you are: Mindfulness meditation in everyday life.* New York, NY: Hyperion.

Kalk, N. J., & Lingford-Hughes, A. R. (2014). The clinical pharmacology of acamprosate. *British Journal of Clinical Pharmacology, 77*(2), 315–323.

Katsuura, Y., Heckmann, J. A., & Taha, S. A. (2011). mu-Opioid receptor stimulation in the nucleus accumbens elevates fatty tastant intake by increasing palatability and suppressing satiety signals. *American Journal of Physiology—Regulatory, Integrative and Comparative Physiology, 301*(1), R244–R254.

Kelley, A. E., Bless, E. P., & Swanson, C. J. (1996). Investigation of the effects of opiate antagonists infused into the nucleus accumbens on feeding and sucrose drinking in rats. *Journal of Pharmacology and Experimental Therapeutics, 278*(3), 1499–1507.

Kendall, P. (2009, October 19). Can drugs for Parkinson's disease cause uncontrollable desires? *The Telegraph.* Retrieved from http://www.telegraph.co.uk/news/health/6350921/Can-drugs-for-Parkinsons-Disease-cause-uncontrollable-desires.html

King, D. P., Paciga, S., Pickering, E., Benowitz, N. L., Bierut, L. J., Conti, D. V., … Park, P. W. (2012). Smoking cessation pharmacogenetics: Analysis of varenicline and bupropion in placebo-controlled clinical trials. *Neuropsychopharmacology, 37*(3), 641–650.

Kovar, M., Koenig, X., Mike, A., Cervenka, R., Lukacs, P., Todt, H., … Hilber, K. (2011). The anti-addictive drug ibogaine modulates voltage-gated ion channels and may trigger cardiac arrhythmias. *BMC Pharmacology, 11*(Suppl. 2), A1.

Lacey, M. G., Mercuri, N B., & North, R. A. (1989). Two cell types in rat substantia nigra zona compacta distinguished by membrane properties and the actions of dopamine and opioids. *Journal of Neuroscience, 9*(4), 1233–1241.

Laviolette, S. R., Nader, K., & van der Kooy, D. (2002). Motivational state determines the functional role of the mesolimbic dopamine system in the mediation of opiate reward processes. *Behavioral Brain Research, 129*(1–2), 17–29.

Le Merrer, J., Becker, J. A., Befort, K., & Kieffer, B. L. (2009). Reward processing by the opioid system in the brain. *Physiological Reviews, 89*(4), 1379–1412.

Maciulaitis, R., Kontrimaviciute, V., Bressolle, F. M., & Briedis, V. (2008). Ibogaine, an anti-addictive drug: Pharmacology and time to go further in development. A narrative review. *Human & Experimental Toxicology, 27*(3), 181–194.

Malivert, M., Fatseas, M., Denis, C., Langlois, E., & Auriacombe, M. (2012). Effectiveness of therapeutic communities: A systematic review. *European Addiction Research, 18*(1), 1–11.

Mantzoros, C. S. (1999). The role of leptin in human obesity and disease: A review of current evidence. *Annals of Internal Medicine, 130*(8), 671–680.

Margolis, E. B., Hjelmstad, G. O., Bonci, A., & Fields, H. L. (2003). Kappa-opioid agonists directly inhibit midbrain dopaminergic neurons. *The Journal of Neuroscience, 23*(31), 9981–9986.

Margolis, E. B., Lock, H., Hjelmstad, G. O., & Fields, H. L. (2004). *Direct kappa opioid action on ventral tegmental area dopaminergic neurons is dependent on projection target*. Paper presented at the Society for Neuroscience, San Diego, CA.

Margolis, E. B., Toy, B., Himmels, P., Morales, M., & Fields, H. L. (2012). Identification of rat ventral tegmental area GABAergic neurons. *PLoS One, 7*(7), e42365.

Mayberg, H. S., Lozano, A. M., Voon, V., McNeely, H. E., Seminowicz, D., Hamani, C., … Kennedy, S. H. (2005). Deep brain stimulation for treatment-resistant depression. *Neuron, 45*(5), 651–660.

McAdams, C. J., & Maunsell, J. H. (1999). Effects of attention on orientation-tuning functions of single neurons in macaque cortical area V4. *The Journal of Neuroscience, 19*(1), 431–441.

McEwen, B. S. (1999). Stress and hippocampal plasticity. *Annual Review of Neuroscience, 22*, 105–122.

McKinley, M. J., Allen, A. M., Burns, P., Colvill, L. M., & Oldfield, B. J. (1998). Interaction of circulating hormones with the brain: The roles of the subfornical organ and the organum vasculosum of the lamina terminalis. *Clinical and Experimental Pharmacology & Physiology, 25*, S61–S67.

Mochon, E., Norton, M. I., & Ariely, D. (2008). Getting off the hedonic treadmill, one step at a time: The impact of regular religious practice and exercise on well-being. *Journal of Economic Psychology, 29*(5), 632–642.

Moreno, A. Y., & Janda, K. D. (2009). Immunopharmacotherapy: Vaccination strategies as a treatment for drug abuse and dependence. *Pharmacology Biochemistry and Behavior, 92*(2), 199–205.

Mutschler, J., Grosshans, M., Koopmann, A., Hermann, D., Diehl, A., Mann, K., & Kiefer, F. (2010). Supervised disulfiram in relapse prevention in alcohol-dependent patients suffering from comorbid borderline personality disorder: A case series. *Alcohol and Alcoholism, 45*(2), 146–150.

Nader, K., Majidishad, P., Amorapanth, P., & LeDoux, J. E. (2001). Damage to the lateral and central, but not other, amygdaloid nuclei prevents the acquisition of auditory fear conditioning. *Learning and Memory, 8*(3), 156–163.

Naqvi, N. H., & Bechara, A. (2009). The hidden island of addiction: The insula. *Trends in Neuroscience, 32*(1), 56–67.

Naqvi, N. H., Rudrauf, D., Damasio, H., & Bechara, A. (2007). Damage to the insula disrupts addiction to cigarette smoking. *Science, 315*(5811), 531–534.

O'Doherty, J. P., Dayan, P., Friston, K., Critchley, H., & Dolan, R. J. (2003). Temporal difference models and reward-related learning in the human brain. *Neuron, 38*(2), 329–337.

Olds, J., & Milner, P. (1954). Positive reinforcement produced by electrical stimulation of septal area and other regions of rat brain. *Journal of Comparative and Physiological Psychology, 47*(6), 419–427.

Paredes, R. G. (2009). Evaluating the neurobiology of sexual reward. *ILAR Journal, 50*(1), 15–27.

Pessiglione, M., Seymour, B., Flandin, G., Dolan, R. J., & Frith, C. D. (2006). Dopamine-dependent prediction errors underpin reward-seeking behaviour in humans. *Nature, 442*(7106), 1042–1045.

Phillips, P. E., Stuber, G. D., Heien, M. L., Wightman, R. M., & Carelli, R. M. (2003). Subsecond dopamine release promotes cocaine seeking. *Nature, 422*(6932), 614–618.

Pradhan, A. A., Befort, K., Nozaki, C., Gaveriaux-Ruff, C., & Kieffer, B. L. (2011). The delta opioid receptor: An evolving target for the treatment of brain disorders. *Trends in Pharmacological Sciences, 32*(10), 581–590.

Quirk, G. J., Repa, C., & LeDoux, J. E. (1995). Fear conditioning enhances short-latency auditory responses of lateral amygdala neurons: Parallel recordings in the freely behaving rat. *Neuron, 15*(5), 1029–1039.

Rehm, J., Taylor, B., & Room, R. (2006). Global burden of disease from alcohol, illicit drugs and tobacco. *Drug and Alcohol Review, 25*(6), 503–513.

Rescorla, R. A. (1972). "Configural" conditioning in discrete-trial bar pressing. *Journal of Comparative and Physiological Psychology, 79*(2), 307–317.

Rescorla, R. A., & Wagner, A. R. (1972). A theory of Pavlovian conditioning: Variations in the effectiveness of reinforcement and nonreinforcement. In A. H. Black & W. F. Prokasy (Eds.), *Classical conditioning II* (pp. 64–99). New York, NY: Appleton–Century–Crofts.

Robinson, T. E., & Berridge, K. C. (1993). The neural basis of drug craving: An incentive-sensitization theory of addiction. *Brain Research Brain Research Review, 18*(3), 247–291.

Rodriguez-Arias, M., Aguilar, M. A., Manzanedo, C., & Minarro, J. (2010). Preclinical evidence of new opioid modulators for the treatment of addiction. *Expert Opinion on Investigational Drugs, 19*(8), 977–994.

Roiser, J. P., Stephan, K. E., den Ouden, H. E., Friston, K. J., & Joyce, E. M. (2010). Adaptive and aberrant reward prediction signals in the human brain. *Neuroimage, 50*(2), 657–664.

Rollnick, S., Miller, W. R., & Butler, C. C. (2007). *Motivational interviewing in health care: Helping patients change behavior*. New York, NY: Guilford Press.

Schultz, W. (2000). Multiple reward signals in the brain. *Nature Reviews: Neuroscience, 1*(3), 199–207.

Schultz, W. (2006). Behavioral theories and the neurophysiology of reward. *Annual Review of Psychology, 57*, 87–115.

Schultz, W. (2010). Dopamine signals for reward value and risk: Basic and recent data. *Behavioral and Brain Functions, 6*, 24.

Seymour, B., O'Doherty, J. P., Dayan, P., Koltzenburg, M., Jones, A. K., Dolan, R. J., . . . Frackowiak, R. S. (2004). Temporal difference models describe higher-order learning in humans. *Nature, 429*(6992), 664–667.

Shaikh, M. B., & Siegel, A. (1994). Neuroanatomical and neurochemical mechanisms underlying amygdaloid control of defensive rage behavior in the cat. *Brazilian Journal of Medical and Biological Research, 27*(12), 2759-2779.

Shen, X. Y., Orson, F. M., & Kosten, T. R. (2012). Vaccines against drug abuse. *Clinical Pharmacology and Therapeutics, 91*(1), 60–70.

Stamford, J. A. (1990). Fast cyclic voltammetry: Measuring transmitter release in "real time." *Journal of Neuroscience Methods, 34*(1–3), 67–72.

Stead, L. F., & Lancaster, T. (2012a). Behavioural interventions as adjuncts to pharmacotherapy for smoking cessation. *Cochrane Database of Systematic Reviews (CDSR), 12*, CD009670.

Stead, L. F., & Lancaster, T. (2012b). Combined pharmacotherapy and behavioural interventions for smoking cessation. *Cochrane Database of Systematic Reviews, 10*, CD008286.

Stephen, J. H., Halpern, C. H., Barrios, C. J., Balmuri, U., Pisapia, J. M., Wolf, J. A., . . . Stein, S. C. (2012). Deep brain stimulation compared with methadone maintenance for the treatment of heroin dependence: A threshold and cost-effectiveness analysis. *Addiction, 107*(3), 624–634.

Stephenson-Jones, M., Floros, O., Robertson, B., & Grillner, S. (2012). Evolutionary conservation of the habenular nuclei and their circuitry controlling the dopamine and 5-hydroxytryptophan (5-HT) systems. *Proceedings of the National Academy of Sciences of the United States of America, 109*(3), E164–E173.

Tobler, P. N., O'Doherty, J. P., Dolan, R. J., & Schultz, W. (2007). Reward value coding distinct from risk attitude-related uncertainty coding in human reward systems. *Journal of Neurophysiology, 97*(2), 1621–1632.

Turner, B. H., & Herkenham, M. (1991). Thalamoamygdaloid projections in the rat: A test of the amygdala's role in sensory processing. *Journal of Comparative Neurology, 313*(2), 295–325.

Tyacke, R. J., Lingford-Hughes, A., Reed, L. J., & Nutt, D. J. (2010). GABAB receptors in addiction and its treatment. *Advances in Pharmacology, 58*, 373–396.

Veening, J. G., Swanson, L. W., & Sawchenko, P. (1984). The organization of projections from the central nucleus of the amygdala to brainstem sites involved in central autonomic regulation: A combined retrograde transport-immunohistochemical study. *Brain Research, 303*(2), 337–357.

Vitaliano, P. P., Scanlan, J. M., Zhang, J., Savage, M. V., Hirsch, I. B., & Siegler, I. C. (2002). A path model of chronic stress, the metabolic syndrome, and coronary heart disease. *Psychosomatic Medicine, 64*(3), 418–435.

Wanat, M. J., Willuhn, I., Clark, J. J., & Phillips, P. E. (2009). Phasic dopamine release in appetitive behaviors and drug addiction. *Current Drug Abuse Reviews, 2*(2), 195–213.

Wasserman, E. A. (1994). Common versus distinctive species: On the logic of behavioral comparison. *The Behavior Analyst, 17*(2), 221–223.

Wee, S., & Koob, G. F. (2010). The role of the dynorphin-kappa opioid system in the reinforcing effects of drugs of abuse. *Psychopharmacology (Berl), 210*(2), 121–135.

Zac-Varghese, S., Tan, T., & Bloom, S. R. (2010). Hormonal interactions between gut and brain. *Discovery Medicine, 10*(55), 543–552.

Zhang, M., & Kelley, A. E. (1997). Opiate agonists microinjected into the nucleus accumbens enhance sucrose drinking in rats. *Psychopharmacology (Berl), 132*(4), 350–360.

Zhang, M., & Kelley, A. E. (2000). Enhanced intake of high-fat food following striatal mu-opioid stimulation: Microinjection mapping and fos expression. *Neuroscience, 99*(2), 267–277.

Chapter 15

Allison, T., Puce, A., & McCarthy, G. (2000). Social perception from visual cues: Role of the STS region. *Trends in Cognitive Sciences, 4*(7), 267–278.

Allman, J. M., Watson, K. K., Tetreault, N. A., & Hakeem, A. Y. (2005). Intuition and autism: A possible role for Von Economo neurons. *Trends in Cognitive Sciences, 9*(8), 367–373.

Alvares, G. A., Hickie, I. B., & Guastella, A. J. (2010). Acute effects of intranasal oxytocin on subjective and behavioral responses to social rejection. *Experimental and Clinical Psychopharmacology, 18*(4), 316–321.

Amodio, D. M., & Frith, C. D. (2006). Meeting of minds: The medial frontal cortex and social cognition. *Nature Reviews: Neuroscience, 7*(4), 268–277.

Baier, B., & Karnath, H. O. (2008). Tight link between our sense of limb ownership and self-awareness of actions. *Stroke; A Journal of Cerebral Circulation, 39*(2), 486–488.

Ballew, C. C., 2nd, & Todorov, A. (2007). Predicting political elections from rapid and unreflective face judgments. *Proceedings of the National Academy of Sciences of the United States of America, 104*(46), 17948–17953.

Baron-Cohen, S. (2004). The cognitive neuroscience of autism. *Journal of Neurology, Neurosurgery, and Psychiatry, 75*(7), 945–948.

Barrash, J., Tranel, D., & Anderson, S. W. (2000). Acquired personality disturbances associated with bilateral damage to the ventromedial prefrontal region. *Developmental Neuropsychology, 18*(3), 355–381.

Barton, J. J., Press, D. Z., Keenan, J. P., & O'Connor, M. (2002). Lesions of the fusiform face area impair perception of facial configuration in prosopagnosia. *Neurology, 58*(1), 71–78.

Baumgartner, T., Heinrichs, M., Vonlanthen, A., Fischbacher, U., & Fehr, E. (2008). Oxytocin shapes the neural circuitry of trust and trust adaptation in humans. *Neuron, 58*(4), 639–650.

Belin, P., Fecteau, S., & Bédard, C. (2004). Thinking the voice: Neural correlates of voice perception. *Trends in Cognitive Sciences, 8*(3), 129–135.

Belin, P., Zatorre, R. J., Lafaille, P., Ahad, P., & Pike, B. (2000). Voice-selective areas in human auditory cortex. *Nature, 403*(6767), 309–312.

Berti, A., Bottini, G., Gandola, M., Pia, L., Smania, N., Stracciari, A., . . . Paulesu, E. (2005). Shared cortical anatomy for motor awareness and motor control. *Science, 309*(5733), 488–491.

Bester-Meredith, J. K., Young, L. J., & Marler, C. A. (1999). Species differences in paternal behavior and aggression in Peromyscus and their associations with vasopressin immunoreactivity and receptors. *Hormones and Behavior, 36*(1), 25–38.

Blair, K., Geraci, M., Devido, J., McCaffrey, D., Chen, G., Vythilingam, M., . . . Pine, D. S. (2008). Neural response to self- and other referential praise and criticism in generalized social phobia. *Archives of General Psychiatry, 65*(10), 1176–1184.

Blair, R. J., & Cipolotti, L. (2000). Impaired social response reversal. A case of "acquired sociopathy." *Brain: A Journal of Neurology, 123*(Pt. 6), 1122–1141.

Blair, R. J. R. (2001). Neurocognitive models of aggression, the antisocial personality disorders, and psychopathy. *Journal of Neurology, Neurosurgery and Psychiatry, 71*(6), 727–731.

Bloom, P., & German, T. P. (2000). Two reasons to abandon the false belief task as a test of theory of mind. *Cognition, 77*(1), B25–B31.

Breen, N., Caine, D., & Coltheart, M. (2001). Mirrored-self misidentification: Two cases of focal onset dementia. *Neurocase, 7*(3), 239–254.

Campbell, A. (2008). Attachment, aggression and affiliation: The role of oxytocin in female social behavior. *Biological Psychology, 77*(1), 1–10.

Carrington, S. J., & Bailey, A. J. (2009). Are there theory of mind regions in the brain? A review of the neuroimaging literature. *Human Brain Mapping, 30*(8), 2313–2335.

Carter, C. S., Braver, T. S., Barch, D. M., Botvinick, M. M., Noll, D., & Cohen, J. D. (1998). Anterior cingulate cortex, error detection, and the online monitoring of performance. *Science, 280*(5364), 747–749.

Carter, C. S., DeVries, A. C., & Getz, L. L. (1995). Physiological substrates of mammalian monogamy: The prairie vole model. *Neuroscience and Biobehavioral Reviews, 19*(2), 303–314.

Carter, J., Lyons, N. J., Cole, H. L., & Goldsmith, A. R. (2008). Subtle cues of predation risk: Starlings respond to a predator's direction of eye-gaze. *Proceedings. Biological Sciences/The Royal Society, 275*(1644), 1709–1715.

Castelli, F., Frith, C., Happe, F., & Frith, U. (2002). Autism, Asperger syndrome and brain mechanisms for the attribution of mental states to animated shapes. *Brain: A Journal of Neurology, 125*(Pt. 8), 1839–1849.

Charman, T., Pickles, A., Simonoff, E., Chandler, S., Loucas, T., & Baird, G. (2011). IQ in children with autism spectrum disorders: Data from the Special Needs and Autism Project (SNAP). *Psychological Medicine, 41*(03), 619–627.

Cohen, J. (2011). *Almost chimpanzee: Searching for what makes us human, in rainforests, labs, sanctuaries, and zoos.* New York, NY: St. Martin's Griffin.

Cohen, J. D., & Servan-Schreiber, D. (1992). Context, cortex, and dopamine: A connectionist approach to behavior and biology in schizophrenia. *Psychological Review, 99*(1), 45–77.

Craig, M. C., Catani, M., Deeley, Q., Latham, R., Daly, E., Kanaan, R., . . . Murphy, D. G. (2009). Altered connections on the road to psychopathy. *Molecular Psychiatry, 14*(10), 946–953.

Croft, K. E., Duff, M. C., Kovach, C. K., Anderson, S. W., Adolphs, R., & Tranel, D. (2010). Detestable or marvelous? Neuroanatomical correlates of character judgments. *Neuropsychologia, 48*(6), 1789–1801.

Damasio, A. R., Damasio, H., & Van Hoesen, G. W. (1982). Prosopagnosia: Anatomic basis and behavioral mechanisms. *Neurology, 32*(4), 331–331.

Damasio, H., Maurer, R. G., Damasio, A. R., & Chui, H. C. (1980). Computerized tomographic scan findings in patients with autistic behavior. *Archives of Neurology, 37*(8), 504–510.

Damasio, H., Tranel, D., Grabowski, T., Adolphs, R., & Damasio, A. (2004). Neural systems behind word and concept retrieval. *Cognition, 92*(1–2), 179–229.

De Dreu, C. K., Greer, L. L., Handgraaf, M. J., Shalvi, S., Van Kleef, G. A., Baas, M., . . . Feith, S. W. (2010). The neuropeptide oxytocin regulates parochial altruism in intergroup conflict among humans. *Science, 328*(5984), 1408–1411.

De Dreu, C. K., Greer, L. L., Van Kleef, G. A., Shalvi, S., & Handgraaf, M. J. (2011). Oxytocin promotes human ethnocentrism. *Proceedings of the National Academy of Sciences of the United States of America, 108*(4), 1262–1266.

de Vries, G. J. (2008). Sex differences in vasopressin and oxytocin innervation of the brain. *Progress in Brain Research, 170*, 17–27.

de Waal, F. B., Dindo, M., Freeman, C. A., & Hall, M. J. (2005). The monkey in the mirror: Hardly a stranger. *Proceedings of the National Academy of Sciences of the United States of America, 102*(32), 11140–11147.

Devinsky, O., Morrell, M. J., & Vogt, B. A. (1995). Contributions of anterior cingulate cortex to behaviour. *Brain, 118*(1), 279–306.

Dolan, M., & Fullam, R. (2004). Theory of mind and mentalizing ability in antisocial personality disorders with and without psychopathy. *Psychological Medicine, 34*(6), 1093–1102.

Donaldson, Z. R., & Young, L. J. (2008). Oxytocin, vasopressin, and the neurogenetics of sociality. *Science, 322*(5903), 900–904.

Eberhardt, J. L., Davies, P. G., Purdie-Vaughns, V. J., & Johnson, S. L. (2006). Looking deathworthy: Perceived stereotypicality of black defendants predicts capital-sentencing outcomes. *Psychological Science, 17*(5), 383–386.

Eisenberger, N. I., Lieberman, M. D., & Williams, K. D. (2003). Does rejection hurt? An fMRI study of social exclusion. *Science, 302*(5643), 290–292.

Ellison-Wright, I., & Bullmore, E. (2010). Anatomy of bipolar disorder and schizophrenia: A meta-analysis. *Schizophrenia Research, 117*(1), 1–12.

Emery, N. J., & Clayton, N. S. (2009). Comparative social cognition. *Annual Review of Psychology, 60*, 87–113.

Enticott, P. G., Kennedy, H. A., Zangen, A., & Fitzgerald, P. B. (2011). Deep repetitive transcranial magnetic stimulation associated with improved social functioning in a young woman with an autism spectrum disorder. *The Journal of ECT, 27*(1), 41–43.

Ernst, T., Chang, L., Melchor, R., & Mehringer, C. M. (1997). Frontotemporal dementia and early Alzheimer disease: Differentiation with frontal lobe H-1 MR spectroscopy. *Radiology, 203*(3), 829–836.

Feinberg, T. E., Venneri, A., Simone, A. M., Fan, Y., & Northoff, G. (2010). The neuroanatomy of asomatognosia and somatoparaphrenia. *Journal of Neurology, Neurosurgery, and Psychiatry, 81*(3), 276–281.

Ferris, C. F., Meenan, D. M., Axelson, J. F., & Albers, H. E. (1986). A vasopressin antagonist can reverse dominant/subordinate behavior in hamsters. *Physiology & Behavior, 38*(1), 135–138.

Frith, U. (2001). Mind blindness and the brain in autism. *Neuron, 32*(6), 969–979.

Fusar-Poli, P., Placentino, A., Carletti, F., Landi, P., Allen, P., Surguladze, S., . . . Politi, P. (2009). Functional atlas of emotional faces processing: A voxel-based meta-analysis of 105 functional magnetic resonance imaging studies. *Journal of Psychiatry & Neuroscience: JPN, 34*(6), 418–432.

Gallup, G. G. (1970). Chimpanzees: Self-recognition. *Science, 167*(3914), 86–87.

Gallup, G. G., Jr. (1997). On the rise and fall of self-conception in primates. *Annals of the New York Academy of Sciences, 818,* 72–82.

Gallup, G. G., Jr., Anderson, J. R., & Shillito, D. J. (2002). The mirror test. In M. Bekoff, C. Allen & G. M. Burghardt (Eds.), *The cognitive animal: Empirical and theoretical perspectives on animal cognition.* Cambridge, MA: MIT Press.

Gamer, M., Zurowski, B., & Buchel, C. (2010). Different amygdala subregions mediate valence-related and attentional effects of oxytocin in humans. *Proceedings of the National Academy of Sciences of the United States of America, 107*(20), 9400–9405.

Garrett-Peters, R. (2009). "If I don't have to work anymore, who am I?": Job loss and collaborative self-concept repair. *Journal of Contemporary Ethnography, 38*(5), 547–583.

Glannon, W. (1997). Psychopathy and responsibility. *Journal of Applied Philosophy, 14*(3), 263–275.

Greene, J. D., Nystrom, L. E., Engell, A. D., Darley, J. M., & Cohen, J. D. (2004). The neural bases of cognitive conflict and control in moral judgment. *Neuron, 44*(2), 389–400.

Greene, J. D., & Paxton, J. M. (2009). Patterns of neural activity associated with honest and dishonest moral decisions. *Proceedings of the National Academy of Sciences of the United States of America, 106*(30), 12506–12511.

Guastella, A. J., Mitchell, P. B., & Dadds, M. R. (2008). Oxytocin increases gaze to the eye region of human faces. *Biological Psychiatry, 63*(1), 3–5.

Gusnard, D. A., Akbudak, E., Shulman, G. L., & Raichle, M. E. (2001). Medial prefrontal cortex and self-referential mental activity: Relation to a default mode of brain function. *Proceedings of the National Academy of Sciences of the United States of America, 98*(7), 4259–4264.

Hadjikhani, N., Joseph, R. M., Manoach, D. S., Naik, P., Snyder, J., Dominick, K., . . . de Gelder, B. (2009). Body expressions of emotion do not trigger fear contagion in autism spectrum disorder. *Social Cognitive and Affective Neuroscience, 4*(1), 70–78.

Hammock, E. A. D., & Young, L. J. (2005). Microsatellite instability generates diversity in brain and sociobehavioral traits. *Science, 308*(5728), 1630–1634.

Harrison, N. A., Singer, T., Rotshtein, P., Dolan, R. J., & Critchley, H. D. (2006). Pupillary contagion: Central mechanisms engaged in sadness processing. *Social Cognitive and Affective Neuroscience, 1*(1), 5–17.

Heatherton, T. F. (2011). Neuroscience of self and self-regulation. *Annual Review of Psychology, 62,* 363–390.

Heinrichs, M., & Domes, G. (2008). Neuropeptides and social behaviour: Effects of oxytocin and vasopressin in humans. *Progress in Brain Research, 170,* 337–350.

Heinrichs, M., von Dawans, B., & Domes, G. (2009). Oxytocin, vasopressin, and human social behavior. *Frontiers in Neuroendocrinology, 30*(4), 548–557.

Herwig, U., Kaffenberger, T., Jancke, L., & Bruhl, A. B. (2010). Self-related awareness and emotion regulation. *Neuroimage, 50*(2), 734–741.

Heschl, A., & Fuchsbichler, C. (2009). Siamangs (*Hylobates syndactylus*) recognize their mirror image. *International Journal of Comparative Psychology, 22,* 221–233.

Hess, U., & Blairy, S. (2001). Facial mimicry and emotional contagion to dynamic emotional facial expressions and their influence on decoding accuracy. *International Journal of Psychophysiology, 40*(2), 129–141.

Hobson, R. P. (1985). Piaget: On the ways of knowing in childhood. In M. Rutter & L. Hersov (Eds.), *Child and adolescent psychiatry: Modern approaches* (pp. 191–203). Oxford, UK: Blackwell.

Homer-Dixon, T. F., Boutwell, J. H., & Rathjens, G. W. (1993). Environmental change and violent conflict. *Scientific American, 268,* 38–38.

Hooker, C., & Park, S. (2005). You must be looking at me: The nature of gaze perception in schizophrenia patients. *Cognitive Neuropsychiatry, 10*(5), 327–345.

Hutchison, W. D., Davis, K. D., Lozano, A. M., Tasker, R. R., & Dostrovsky, J. O. (1999). Pain-related neurons in the human cingulate cortex. *Nature Neuroscience, 2*(5), 403–405.

Iacoboni, M., Molnar-Szakacs, I., Gallese, V., Buccino, G., Mazziotta, J. C., & Rizzolatti, G. (2005). Grasping the intentions of others with one's own mirror neuron system. *PLoS Biology, 3*(3), e79.

Iacoboni, M., Woods, R. P., Brass, M., Bekkering, H., Mazziotta, J. C., & Rizzolatti, G. (1999). Cortical mechanisms of human imitation. *Science, 286*(5449), 2526–2528.

Insel, T. R. (1992). Oxytocin—A neuropeptide for affiliation: Evidence from behavioral, receptor autoradiographic, and comparative studies. *Psychoneuroendocrinology, 17*(1), 3–35.

Insel, T. R. (2003). Is social attachment an addictive disorder? *Physiology & Behavior, 79*(3), 351–357.

Izuma, K., Saito, D. N., & Sadato, N. (2008). Processing of social and monetary rewards in the human striatum. *Neuron, 58*(2), 284–294.

Izuma, K., Saito, D. N., & Sadato, N. (2010a). Processing of the incentive for social approval in the ventral striatum during charitable donation. *Journal of Cognitive Neuroscience, 22*(4), 621–631.

Izuma, K., Saito, D. N., & Sadato, N. (2010b). The roles of the medial prefrontal cortex and striatum in reputation processing. *Social Neuroscience, 5*(2), 133–147.

Johnson, M. K., Raye, C. L., Mitchell, K. J., Touryan, S. R., Greene, E. J., & Nolen-Hoeksema, S. (2006). Dissociating medial frontal and posterior cingulate activity during self-reflection. *Social Cognitive and Affective Neuroscience, 1*(1), 56–64.

Kanwisher, N., McDermott, J., & Chun, M. M. (1997). The fusiform face area: A module in human extrastriate cortex specialized for face perception. *The Journal of Neuroscience, 17*(11), 4302–4311.

Kaplan, J. T., Aziz-Zadeh, L., Uddin, L. Q., & Iacoboni, M. (2008). The self across the senses: An fMRI study of self-face and self-voice recognition. *Social Cognitive and Affective Neuroscience, 3*(3), 218–223.

Karim, A. A., Schneider, M., Lotze, M., Veit, R., Sauseng, P., Braun, C., & Birbaumer, N. (2010). The truth about lying: Inhibition of the anterior prefrontal cortex improves deceptive behavior. *Cerebral Cortex, 20*(1), 205–213.

Keenan, J. P., Wheeler, M. A., Gallup, G. G., Jr., & Pascual-Leone, A. (2000). Self-recognition and the right prefrontal cortex. *Trends in Cognitive Sciences, 4*(9), 338–344.

Keeney, A., & Hogg, S. (1999). Behavioural consequences of repeated social defeat in the mouse: Preliminary evaluation of a potential animal model of depression. *Behavioural Pharmacology, 10*(8), 753–764.

Kennedy, D. P., & Courchesne, E. (2008). Functional abnormalities of the default network during self- and other-reflection in autism. *Social Cognitive and Affective Neuroscience, 3*(2), 177–190.

Keverne, B., & Kendrick, K. (1994). Maternal behaviour in sheep and its neuroendocrine regulation. *Acta Paediatrica, 83*(s397), 47–56.

King-Casas, B., Tomlin, D., Anen C., Camerer, C. F., Quartz, S. R., & Montague, P. R. (2005). Getting to know you: reputation and trust in a two-person economic exchange. *Science, 308*(5718), 78–83.

Kirsch, P., Esslinger, C., Chen, Q., Mier, D., Lis, S., Siddhanti, S., . . . Meyer-Lindenberg, A. (2005). Oxytocin modulates neural circuitry for social cognition and fear in humans. *The Journal of Neuroscience, 25*(49), 11489–11493.

Kloeppel, K. M. (2005). *Pesky critters.* Maxwell AFB, AL: Air University, Air War College, Center for Strategy and Technology.

Kosfeld, M., Heinrichs, M., Zak, P. J., Fischbacher, U., & Fehr, E. (2005). Oxytocin increases trust in humans. *Nature, 435*(7042), 673–676.

Krach, S., Paulus, F. M., Bodden, M., & Kircher, T. (2010). The rewarding nature of social interactions. *Frontiers in Behavioral Neuroscience, 4*, 22.

Kriegstein, K. V., & Giraud, A.-L. (2004). Distinct functional substrates along the right superior temporal sulcus for the processing of voices. *Neuroimage, 22*(2), 948–955.

Kuzmanovic, B., Bente, G., von Cramon, D. Y., Schilbach, L., Tittgemeyer, M., & Vogeley, K. (2012). Imaging first impressions: Distinct neural processing of verbal and nonverbal social information. *Neuroimage, 60*(1), 179–188.

Liddle, B., & Nettle, D. (2006). Higher-order theory of mind and social competence in school-age children. *Journal of Cultural and Evolutionary Psychology, 4*(3), 231-244.

Lilley, R. (2008, October 28). Dolphin saves stuck whales, guides them back to sea. *National Geographic News.* Retrieved from http://news.nationalgeographic.com/news/2008/03/080312-AP-dolph-whal.html/

Lim, M. M., & Young, L. J. (2004). Vasopressin-dependent neural circuits underlying pair bond formation in the monogamous prairie vole. *Neuroscience, 125*(1), 35–45.

Lombardo, M. V., Chakrabarti, B., Bullmore, E. T., Sadek, S. A., Pasco, G., Wheelwright, S. J., . . . Baron-Cohen, S. (2010). Atypical neural self-representation in autism. *Brain: A Journal of Neurology, 133*(Pt. 2), 611–624.

Lombardo, M. V., Chakrabarti, B., Bullmore, E. T., Wheelwright, S. J., Sadek, S. A., Suckling, J., & Baron-Cohen, S. (2010). Shared neural circuits for mentalizing about the self and others. *Journal of Cognitive Neuroscience, 22*(7), 1623–1635.

Mendez, M. F., Chen, A. K., Shapira, J. S., & Miller, B. L. (2005). Acquired sociopathy and frontotemporal dementia. *Dementia and Geriatric Cognitive Disorders, 20*(2–3), 99–104.

Miller, B. L., Darby, A., Benson, D., Cummings, J., & Miller, M. (1997). Aggressive, socially disruptive and antisocial behaviour associated with fronto-temporal dementia. *The British Journal of Psychiatry, 170*(2), 150–154.

Monk, C. S., Peltier, S. J., Wiggins, J. L., Weng, S. J., Carrasco, M., Risi, S., & Lord, C. (2009). Abnormalities of intrinsic functional connectivity in autism spectrum disorders. *Neuroimage, 47*(2), 764–772.

Montague, P. R., & Berns, G. S. (2002). Neural economics and the biological substrates of valuation. *Neuron, 36*(2), 265–284.

Morris, J. S., Frith, C. D., Perrett, D. I., Rowland, D., Young, A. W., Calder, A. J., & Dolan, R. J. (1996). A differential neural response in the human amygdala to fearful and happy facial expressions. *Nature, 383*(6603), 812–815.

Mukamel, R., Ekstrom, A. D., Kaplan, J., Iacoboni, M., & Fried, I. (2010). Single-neuron responses in humans during execution and observation of actions. *Current Biology: CB, 20*(8), 750–756.

Murray, L., & Cooper, P. J. (1997). The role of infant and maternal factors in postpartum depression, mother–infant interactions, and infant outcome. In L. Murray & P. J. Cooper (Eds.), *Postpartum depression and child development* (pp. 111–135). New York, NY: Guilford Press.

Nachev, P., Rees, G., Parton, A., Kennard, C., & Husain, M. (2005). Volition and conflict in human medial frontal cortex. *Current Biology: CB, 15*(2), 122–128.

Ng, W., & Lindsay, R. C. L. (1994). Cross-race facial recognition: Failure of the contact hypothesis. *Journal of Cross-Cultural Psychology, 25*, 217–232.

Nitsche, M. A., Cohen, L. G., Wassermann, E. M., Priori, A., Lang, N., Antal, A., . . . Pascual-Leone, A. (2008). Transcranial direct current stimulation: State of the art 2008. *Brain Stimulation, 1*(3), 206–223.

Olson, I. R., Plotzker, A., & Ezzyat, Y. (2007). The enigmatic temporal pole: A review of findings on social and emotional processing. *Brain: A Journal of Neurology, 130*(Pt. 7), 1718–1731.

Oosterhof, N. N., & Todorov, A. (2008). The functional basis of face evaluation. *Proceedings of the National Academy of Sciences of the United States of America, 105*(32), 11087–11092.

Ozonoff, S., Pennington, B. F., & Rogers, S. J. (1991). Executive function deficits in high-functioning autistic individuals: Relationship to theory of mind. *Journal of Child Psychology and Psychiatry, 32*(7), 1081–1105.

Parker, S. T., Mitchell, R. W., & Boccia, M. L. (Eds.). (1994). *Self-awareness in animals and humans: Developmental perspectives.* New York, NY: Cambridge University Press.

Pelphrey, K. A., Viola, R. J., & McCarthy, G. (2004). When strangers pass: Processing of mutual and averted social gaze in the superior temporal sulcus. *Psychological Science, 15*(9), 598–603.

Perlman, L. (2000). Adults with Asperger disorder misdiagnosed as schizophrenic. *Professional Psychology: Research and Practice, 31*(2), 221–225.

Perrett, D. I., Harris, M. H., Mistlin, A. J., Hietanen, J. K., Benson, P. J., Bevan, R., . . . Brierly, K. (1990). Social signals analyzed at the single cell level: Someone is looking at me, something moved! *International Journal of Comparative Psychology, 4*(1), 25–55.

Peyron, R., García-Larrea, L., Grégoire, M.-C., Costes, N., Convers, P., Lavenne, F., . . . Laurent, B. (1999). Haemodynamic brain responses to acute pain in humans: Sensory and attentional networks. *Brain, 122*(9), 1765–1780.

Phillips, M. L., Young, A. W., Senior, C., Brammer, M., Andrew, C., Calder, A., . . . Williams, S. (1997). A specific neural substrate for perceiving facial expressions of disgust. *Nature, 389*(6650), 495–498.

Platek, S. M., Loughead, J. W., Gur, R. C., Busch, S., Ruparel, K., Phend, N., . . . Langleben, D. D. (2006). Neural substrates for functionally discriminating self-face from personally familiar faces. *Human Brain Mapping, 27*(2), 91–98.

Povinelli, D. J., & Vonk, J. (2003). Chimpanzee minds: Suspiciously human? *Trends in Cognitive Sciences, 7*(4), 157–160.

Premack, D., & Woodruff, G. (1978). Does the chimpanzee have a theory of mind? *Behavioral and Brain Sciences, 1*(4), 515–526.

Priori, A. (2003). Brain polarization in humans: A reappraisal of an old tool for prolonged non-invasive modulation of brain excitability. *Clinical Neurophysiology, 114*(4), 589–595.

Priori, A., Mameli, F., Cogiamanian, F., Marceglia, S., Tiriticco, M., Mrakic-Sposta, S., . . . Sartori, G. (2008). Lie-specific involvement of dorsolateral prefrontal cortex in deception. *Cerebral Cortex, 18*(2), 451–455.

Rapson, R. L., Hatfield, E., & Cacioppo, J. T. (1994). *Emotional contagion*. Cambridge, UK: Cambridge University Press.

Rilling, J., Gutman, D., Zeh, T., Pagnoni, G., Berns, G., & Kilts, C. (2002). A neural basis for social cooperation. *Neuron, 35*(2), 395–405.

Rizzolatti, G., & Craighero, L. (2004). The mirror-neuron system. *Annual Review of Neuroscience, 27*, 169–192.

Rizzolatti, G., Fadiga, L., Gallese, V., & Fogassi, L. (1996). Premotor cortex and the recognition of motor actions. *Brain Research. Cognitive Brain Research, 3*(2), 131–141.

Schlicht, E. J., Shimojo, S., Camerer, C. F., Battaglia, P., & Nakayama, K. (2010). Human wagering behavior depends on opponents' faces. *PloS One, 5*(7), e11663.

Servais, V. (2005). Enchanting dolphins: An analysis of human–dolphin encounters. In J. Knight (Ed.), *Animals in person: Cultural perspectives on human–animal intimacies* (pp. 211–229). Oxford, UK: Berg.

Shamay-Tsoory, S. G. (2011). The neural bases for empathy. *The Neuroscientist, 17*(1), 18–24.

Shamay-Tsoory, S. G., Aharon-Peretz, J., & Perry, D. (2009). Two systems for empathy: A double dissociation between emotional and cognitive empathy in inferior frontal gyrus versus ventromedial prefrontal lesions. *Brain: A Journal of Neurology, 132*(Pt. 3), 61–627.

Shultz, S., & McCarthy, G. (2012). Goal-directed actions activate the face-sensitive posterior superior temporal sulcus and fusiform gyrus in the absence of human-like perceptual cues. *Cerebral Cortex, 22*(5), 1098–1106.

Simmons, W. K., & Martin, A. (2009). The anterior temporal lobes and the functional architecture of semantic memory. *Journal of the International Neuropsychological Society, 15*(5), 645–649.

Singer, T., & Lamm, C. (2009). The social neuroscience of empathy. *Annals of the New York Academy of Sciences, 1156*, 81–96.

Singer, T., Seymour, B., O'Doherty, J., Kaube, H., Dolan, R. J., & Frith, C. D. (2004). Empathy for pain involves the affective but not sensory components of pain. *Science, 303*(5661), 1157–1162.

Singer, T., Seymour, B., O'Doherty, J. P., Stephan, K. E., Dolan, R. J., & Frith, C. D. (2006). Empathic neural responses are modulated by the perceived fairness of others. *Nature, 439*(7075), 466–469.

Spreng, R. N., Mar, R. A., & Kim, A. S. (2009). The common neural basis of autobiographical memory, prospection, navigation, theory of mind, and the default mode: A quantitative meta-analysis. *Journal of Cognitive Neuroscience, 21*(3), 489–510.

Stagg, C. J., & Nitsche, M. A. (2011). Physiological basis of transcranial direct current stimulation. *The Neuroscientist, 17*(1), 37–53.

Starkstein, S. E., Fedoroff, J. P., Price, T. R., Leiguarda, R., & Robinson, R. G. (1992). Anosognosia in patients with cerebrovascular lesions. A study of causative factors. *Stroke, 23*(10), 1446–1453.

Stern, D. N. (2000). *Interpersonal world of the infant: A view from psychoanalysis and development psychology*. New York, NY: Basic Books.

Suddendorf, T., & Collier-Baker, E. (2009). The evolution of primate visual self-recognition: Evidence of absence in lesser apes. *Proceedings. Biological Sciences/The Royal Society, 276*(1662), 1671–1677.

Sugiura, M., Watanabe, J., Maeda, Y., Matsue, Y., Fukuda, H., & Kawashima, R. (2005). Cortical mechanisms of visual self-recognition. *Neuroimage, 24*(1), 143–149.

Tager-Flusberg, H., & Sullivan, K. (1994). A second look at second-order belief attribution in autism. *Journal of Autism and Developmental Disorders, 24*(5), 577–586.

Thomas, J. A., & Birney, E. C. (1979). Parental care and mating system of the prairie vole, *Microtus ochrogaster. Behavioral Ecology and Sociobiology, 5*(2), 171–186.

Thompson, R., Gupta, S., Miller, K., Mills, S., & Orr, S. (2004). The effects of vasopressin on human facial responses related to social communication. *Psychoneuroendocrinology, 29*(1), 35–48.

Thompson, R. R., George, K., Walton, J. C., Orr, S.P., & Benson, J. (2006). Sex-specific influences of vasopressin on human social communication. *Proceedings of the National Academy of Sciences of the United States of America, 103*(20), 7889–7894.

Tiedens, L. Z., & Fragale, A. R. (2003). Power moves: Complementarity in dominant and submissive nonverbal behavior. *Journal of Personality and Social Psychology, 84*(3), 558–568.

Tiihonen, J., Rossi, R., Laakso, M. P., Hodgins, S., Testa, C., Perez, J., . . . Frisoni, G. B. (2008). Brain anatomy of persistent violent offenders: More rather than less. *Psychiatry Research, 163*(3), 201–212.

Todorov, A., Mandisodza, A. N., Goren, A., & Hall, C. C. (2005). Inferences of competence from faces predict election outcomes. *Science, 308*(5728), 1623–1626.

Todorov, A., & Olson, I. R. (2008). Robust learning of affective trait associations with faces when the hippocampus is damaged, but not when the amygdala and temporal pole are damaged. *Social, Cognitive, and Affective Neuroscience, 3*(3), 195–203.

Tranel, D. (2009). The left temporal pole is important for retrieving words for unique concrete entities. *Aphasiology, 23*(7), 867.

Tsukiura, T., Suzuki, C., Shigemune, Y., & Mochizuki-Kawai, H. (2008). Differential contributions of the anterior temporal and medial temporal lobe to the retrieval of memory for person identity information. *Human Brain Mapping, 29*(12), 1343–1354.

Uddin, L. Q., Kaplan, J. T., Molnar-Szakacs, I., Zaidel, E., & Iacoboni, M. (2005). Self-face recognition activates a frontoparietal "mirror" network in the right hemisphere: An event-related fMRI study. *Neuroimage, 25*(3), 926–935.

Vallar, G. (1993). The anatomical basis of spatial hemineglect in humans. In I. H. Robertson & J. C. Marshall (Eds.), *Unilateral neglect: Clinical and experimental studies* (pp. 27–59). Hove, UK: Erlbaum.

Vallar, G., & Ronchi, R. (2009). Somatoparaphrenia: A body delusion. A review of the neuropsychological literature. *Experimental Brain Research, 192*(3), 533–551.

Van Overwalle, F. (2009). Social cognition and the brain: A meta-analysis. *Human Brain Mapping, 30*(3), 829–858.

Van Overwalle, F., & Baetens, K. (2009). Understanding others' actions and goals by mirror and mentalizing systems: A meta-analysis. *Neuroimage, 48*(3), 564–584.

Venkatesh, B., Si-Hoe, S. L., Murphy, D., & Brenner, S. (1997). Transgenic rats reveal functional conservation of regulatory controls between the Fugu isotocin and rat oxytocin genes. *Proceedings of the National Academy of Sciences of the United States of America, 94*(23), 12462–12466.

Villarejo, A., Martin, V. P., Moreno-Ramos, T., Camachho-Salas, A., Porta-Etessam, J., & Bermejo-Pareja, F. (2011). Mirrored-self misidentification in a patient without dementia: Evidence for right hemispheric and bifrontal damage. *Neurocase, 17*(3), 276–284.

Wagner, U., N'Diaye, K., Ethofer, T., & Vuilleumier, P. (2011). Guilt-specific processing in the prefrontal cortex. *Cerebral Cortex, 21*(11), 2461–2470.

Wakusawa, K., Sugiura, M., Sassa, Y., Jeong, H., Horie, K., Sato, S., . . . Kawashima, R. (2007). Comprehension of implicit meanings in social situations involving irony: A functional MRI study. *Neuroimage, 37*(4), 1417–1426.

Weder, N. D., Aziz, R., Wilkins, K., & Tampi, R. R. (2007). Frontotemporal dementias: A review. *Annals of General Psychiatry, 6*(15), 1–10.

Wersinger, S., Ginns, E. I., O'carroll, A., Lolait, S., & Young Iii, W. (2002). Vasopressin V1b receptor knockout reduces aggressive behavior in male mice. *Molecular Psychiatry, 7*(9), 975–984.

Wicker, B., Keysers, C., Plailly, J., Royet, J. P., Gallese, V., & Rizzolatti, G. (2003). Both of us disgusted in my insula: The common neural basis of seeing and feeling disgust. *Neuron, 40*(3), 655–664.

Willis, J., & Todorov, A. (2006). First impressions: Making up your mind after a 100-ms exposure to a face. *Psychological Science, 17*(7), 592–598.

Wood, J. N., Glynn, D. D., Phillips, B. C., & Hauser, M. D. (2007). The perception of rational, goal-directed action in nonhuman primates. *Science, 317*(5843), 1402–1405.

Yamaguchi, M. K. (2000). Discriminating the sex of faces by 6- and 8-mo.-old infants. *Perceptual and Motor Skills, 91*(2), 653–664.

Young, L., Camprodon, J. A., Hauser, M., Pascual-Leone, A., & Saxe, R. (2010). Disruption of the right temporoparietal junction with transcranial magnetic stimulation reduces the role of beliefs in moral judgments. *Proceedings of the National Academy of Sciences of the United States of America, 107*(15), 6753–6758.

Young, L. J., Nilsen, R., Waymire, K. G., MacGregor, G. R., & Insel, T. R. (1999). Increased affiliative response to vasopressin in mice expressing the V1a receptor from a monogamous vole. *Nature, 400*(6746), 766–768.

Young, L. J., & Wang, Z. (2004). The neurobiology of pair bonding. *Nature Neuroscience, 7*(10), 1048–1054.

Zahn, R., Moll, J., Iyengar, V., Huey, E. D., Tierney, M., Krueger, F., & Grafman, J. (2009). Social conceptual impairments in frontotemporal lobar degeneration with right anterior temporal hypometabolism. *Brain, 132*(Pt. 3), 604–616.

Zahn, R., Moll, J., Krueger, F., Huey, E. D., Garrido, G., & Grafman, J. (2007). Social concepts are represented in the superior anterior temporal cortex. *Proceedings of the National Academy of Sciences of the United States of America, 104*(15), 6430–6435.

Zahn, R., Moll, J., Paiva, M., Garrido, G., Krueger, F., Huey, E. D., & Grafman, J. (2009). The neural basis of human social values: Evidence from functional MRI. *Cerebral Cortex, 19*(2), 276–283.

Zilbovicius, M., Meresse, I., Chabane, N., Brunelle, F., Samson, Y., & Boddaert, N. (2006). Autism, the superior temporal sulcus and social perception. *Trends in Neurosciences, 29*(7), 359–366.

Chapter 16

Abi-Jaoude, E., & Gorman, D. A. (2013). Tourette syndrome. *CMAJ: Canadian Medical Association Journal, 185*(3), 236.

Amaducci, L., Grassi, E., & Boller, F. (2002). Maurice Ravel and right-hemisphere musical creativity: Influence of disease on his last musical works? *European Journal of Neurology, 9*(1), 75–82.

Andreasen, N. C., & Glick, I. D. (1988). Bipolar affective disorder and creativity: Implications and clinical management. *Comprehensive Psychiatry, 29*(3), 207–217.

Angst, J., & Marneros, A. (2001). Bipolarity from ancient to modern times: Conception, birth and rebirth. *Journal of Affective Disorders, 67*(1–3), 3–19.

Apter, A., Pauls, D. L., Bleich, A., Zohar, A. H., Kron, S., Ratzoni, G., . . . et al. (1993). An epidemiologic study of Gilles de la Tourette's syndrome in Israel. *Archives of General Psychiatry, 50*(9), 734–738.

Ballard, C., Gauthier, S., Corbett, A., Brayne, C., Aarsland, D., & Jones, E. (2011). Alzheimer's disease. *Lancet, 377*(9770), 1019–1031.

Benes, F. M., & Berretta, S. (2001). GABAergic interneurons: Implications for understanding schizophrenia and bipolar disorder. *Neuropsychopharmacology, 25*(1), 1–27.

Berlim, M. T., Van den Eynde, F., & Daskalakis, Z. J. (2013). Clinical utility of transcranial direct current stimulation (tDCS) for treating major depression: A systematic review and meta-analysis of randomized, double-blind and sham-controlled trials. *Journal of Psychiatric Research, 47*(1), 1–7.

Berman, R. M., Narasimhan, M., Miller, H. L., Anand, A., Cappiello, A., Oren, D. A., . . . Charney, D. S. (1999). Transient depressive relapse induced by catecholamine depletion: Potential phenotypic vulnerability marker? *Archives of General Psychiatry, 56*(5), 395–403.

Berrios, G. E. (1997). The scientific origins of electroconvulsive therapy: A conceptual history. *History of Psychiatry, 8*(29 Pt. 1), 105–119.

Blackwood, D. H., & Muir, W. J. (2004). Clinical phenotypes associated with DISC1, a candidate gene for schizophrenia. *Neurotoxicity Research, 6*(1), 35–41.

Blomstedt, P., Sjoberg, R. L., Hansson, M., Bodlund, O., & Hariz, M. I. (2013). Deep brain stimulation in the treatment of obsessive–compulsive disorder. *World Neurosurgery, 80*(6), e245–e253.

Boksa, P. (2012). Abnormal synaptic pruning in schizophrenia: Urban myth or reality? *Journal of Psychiatry & Neuroscience, 37*(2), 75–77.

Booij, L., Van der Does, W., Benkelfat, C., Bremner, J. D., Cowen, P. J., Fava, M., . . . Van der Kloot, W. A. (2002). Predictors of mood response to acute tryptophan depletion. A reanalysis. *Neuropsychopharmacology, 27*(5), 852–861.

Bora, E., Fornito, A., Pantelis, C., & Yucel, M. (2012). Gray matter abnormalities in major depressive disorder: A meta-analysis of voxel based morphometry studies. *Journal of Affective Disorders, 138*(1–2), 9–18.

Bora, E., Fornito, A., Yucel, M., & Pantelis, C. (2012). The effects of gender on grey matter abnormalities in major psychoses: A comparative voxelwise meta-analysis of schizophrenia and bipolar disorder. *Psychological Medicine, 42*(2), 295–307.

Bostwick, J. M., & Pankratz, V. S. (2000). Affective disorders and suicide risk: A reexamination. *The American Journal of Psychiatry, 157*(12), 1925–1932.

Bowden, C. L., Schatzberg, A. F., Rosenbaum, A., Contreras, S. A., Samson, J. A., Dessain, E., & Sayler, M. (1993). Fluoxetine and desipramine in major depressive disorder. *Journal of Clinical Psychopharmacology, 13*(5), 305–311.

Boxer, A. L., & Miller, B. L. (2005). Clinical features of frontotemporal dementia. *Alzheimer Disease and Associated Disorders, 19*(Suppl. 1), S3–S6.

Breitner, J. C., Jarvik, G. P., Plassman, B. L., Saunders, A. M., & Welsh, K. A. (1998). Risk of Alzheimer disease with the epsilon4 allele for apolipoprotein E in a population-based study of men aged 62–73 years. *Alzheimer Disease and Associated Disorders, 12*(1), 40–44.

Brown, A. S., & Patterson, P. H. (2011). Maternal infection and schizophrenia: Implications for prevention. *Schizophrenia Bulletin, 37*(2), 284–290.

Buckner, R. L., Sepulcre, J., Talukdar, T., Krienen, F. M., Liu, H., Hedden, T., . . . Johnson, K. A. (2009). Cortical hubs revealed by intrinsic functional connectivity: Mapping, assessment of stability, and relation to Alzheimer's disease. *The Journal of Neuroscience, 29*(6), 1860–1873.

Cade, J. F. (1949). Lithium salts in the treatment of psychotic excitement. *The Medical Journal of Australia, 2*(10), 349–352.

Cannon, M., Jones, P. B., & Murray, R. M. (2002). Obstetric complications and schizophrenia: Historical and meta-analytic review. *The American Journal of Psychiatry, 159*(7), 1080–1092.

Carmin, C. N., Wiegartz, P. S., Yunus, U., & Gillock, K. L. (2002). Treatment of late-onset OCD following basal ganglia infarct. *Depression and Anxiety, 15*(2), 87–90.

Carr, D. B., & Sesack, S. R. (2000). Projections from the rat prefrontal cortex to the ventral tegmental area: Target specificity in the synaptic associations with mesoaccumbens and mesocortical neurons. *The Journal of Neuroscience, 20*(10), 3864–3873.

Case, B. G., Bertollo, D. N., Laska, E. M., Price, L. H., Siegel, C. E., Olfson, M., & Marcus, S. C. (2013). Declining use of electroconvulsive therapy in United States general hospitals. *Biological Psychiatry, 73*(2), 119–126.

Caspi, A., Sugden, K., Moffitt, T. E., Taylor, A., Craig, I. W., Harrington, H., . . . Poulton, R. (2003). Influence of life stress on depression: Moderation by a polymorphism in the 5-HTT gene. *Science, 301*(5631), 386–389.

Cattaneo, E., Rigamonti, D., Goffredo, D., Zuccato, C., Squitieri, F., & Sipione, S. (2001). Loss of normal huntingtin function: New developments in Huntington's disease research. *Trends in Neurosciences, 24*(3), 182–188.

Cattaneo, E., Zuccato, C., & Tartari, M. (2005). Normal huntingtin function: An alternative approach to Huntington's disease. *Nature Reviews: Neuroscience, 6*(12), 919–930.

Cepeda, C., Wu, N., Andre, V. M., Cummings, D. M., & Levine, M. S. (2007). The corticostriatal pathway in Huntington's disease. *Progress in Neurobiology, 81*(5–6), 253–271.

Chacko, R. C., Corbin, M. A., & Harper, R. G. (2000). Acquired obsessive–compulsive disorder associated with basal ganglia lesions. *The Journal of Neuropsychiatry and Clinical Neurosciences, 12*(2), 269–272.

Charney, D. S. (1998). Monoamine dysfunction and the pathophysiology and treatment of depression. *The Journal of Clinical Psychiatry, 59*(Suppl. 14), 11–14.

Chassagnon, S., Minotti, L., Kremer, S., Hoffmann, D., & Kahane, P. (2008). Somatosensory, motor, and reaching/grasping responses to direct electrical stimulation of the human cingulate motor areas. *Journal of Neurosurgery, 109*(4), 593–604.

Chaste, P., & Leboyer, M. (2012). Autism risk factors: Genes, environment, and gene–environment interactions. *Dialogues in Clinical Neuroscience, 14*(3), 281–292.

Chengappa, K. N., Kupfer, D. J., Frank, E., Houck, P. R., Grochocinski, V. J., Cluss, P. A., & Stapf, D. A. (2003). Relationship of birth cohort and early age at onset of illness in a bipolar disorder case registry. *The American Journal of Psychiatry, 160*(9), 1636–1642.

Clarke, M. C., Kelleher, I., Clancy, M., & Cannon, M. (2012). Predicting risk and the emergence of schizophrenia. *The Psychiatric Clinics of North America, 35*(3), 585–612.

Clayton, A. H., Croft, H. A., Horrigan, J. P., Wightman, D. S., Krishen, A., Richard, N. E., & Modell, J. G. (2006). Bupropion extended release compared with escitalopram: Effects on sexual functioning and antidepressant efficacy in 2 randomized, double-blind, placebo-controlled studies. *The Journal of Clinical Psychiatry, 67*(5), 736–746.

Corlett, P. R., Honey, G. D., & Fletcher, P. C. (2007). From prediction error to psychosis: Ketamine as a pharmacological model of delusions. *Journal of Psychopharmacology, 21*(3), 238–252.

D'Souza, D. C. (2007). Cannabinoids and psychosis. *International Review of Neurobiology, 78*, 289–326.

De Hert, M., Dobbelaere, M., Sheridan, E. M., Cohen, D., & Correll, C. U. (2011). Metabolic and endocrine adverse effects of second-generation antipsychotics in children and adolescents: A systematic review of randomized, placebo controlled trials and guidelines for clinical practice. *European Psychiatry, 26*(3), 144–158.

den Dunnen, W. F., Brouwer, W. H., Bijlard, E., Kamphuis, J., van Linschoten, K., Eggens-Meijer, E., & Holstege, G. (2008). No disease in the brain of a 115-year-old woman. *Neurobiology of Aging, 29*(8), 1127–1132.

DeRubeis, R. J., Siegle, G. J., & Hollon, S. D. (2008). Cognitive therapy versus medication for depression: Treatment outcomes and neural mechanisms. *Nature Reviews: Neuroscience, 9*(10), 788–796.

Dhaenen, H. (2001). Imaging the serotonergic system in depression. *European Archives of Psychiatry and Clinical Neuroscience, 251*(Suppl. 2), II76–II80.

Disner, S. G., Beevers, C. G., Haigh, E. A., & Beck, A. T. (2011). Neural mechanisms of the cognitive model of depression. *Nature Reviews: Neuroscience, 12*(8), 467–477.

Dougherty, D. D., Baer, L., Cosgrove, G. R., Cassem, E. H., Price, B. H., Nierenberg, A. A., . . . Rauch, S. L. (2002). Prospective long-term follow-up of 44 patients who received cingulotomy for treatment-refractory obsessive–compulsive disorder. *The American Journal of Psychiatry, 159*(2), 269–275.

Downar, J., & Daskalakis, Z. J. (2013). New targets for rTMS in depression: A review of convergent evidence. *Brain Stimulation, 6*(3), 231–240.

Drevets, W. C., Savitz, J., & Trimble, M. (2008). The subgenual anterior cingulate cortex in mood disorders. *CNS Spectrums, 13*(8), 663–681.

Dwivedi, Y., Rizavi, H. S., Conley, R. R., Roberts, R. C., Tamminga, C. A., & Pandey, G. N. (2003). Altered gene expression of brain-derived neurotrophic factor and receptor tyrosine kinase B in postmortem brain of suicide subjects. *Archives of General Psychiatry, 60*(8), 804–815.

Eichstedt, J. A., & Arnold, S. L. (2001). Childhood-onset obsessive–compulsive disorder: A tic-related subtype of OCD? *Clinical Psychology Review, 21*(1), 137–157.

Ellison-Wright, I., & Bullmore, E. (2010). Anatomy of bipolar disorder and schizophrenia: A meta-analysis. *Schizophrenia Research, 117*(1), 1–12.

Erickson, K. I., Weinstein, A. M., & Lopez, O. L. (2012). Physical activity, brain plasticity, and Alzheimer's disease. *Archives of Medical Research, 43*(8), 615–621.

Fahim, C., Yoon, U., Sandor, P., Frey, K., & Evans, A. C. (2009). Thinning of the motor-cingulate–insular cortices in siblings concordant for Tourette syndrome. *Brain Topography, 22*(3), 176–184.

Faridi, K., & Suchowersky, O. (2003). Gilles de la Tourette's syndrome. *The Canadian Journal of Neurological Sciences, 30*(Suppl. 1), S64–S71.

Farrer, L. A. (1986). Suicide and attempted suicide in Huntington disease: Implications for preclinical testing of persons at risk. *American Journal of Medical Genetics, 24*(2), 305–311.

Feighner, J. P. (1999). Mechanism of action of antidepressant medications. *The Journal of Clinical Psychiatry, 60*(Suppl. 4), 4–11; discussion 12–13.

Fink, M. (1984). Meduna and the origins of convulsive therapy. *The American Journal of Psychiatry, 141*(9), 1034–1041.

Fried, I., Katz, A., McCarthy, G., Sass, K. J., Williamson, P., Spencer, S. S., & Spencer, D. D. (1991). Functional organization of human supplementary motor cortex studied by electrical stimulation. *The Journal of Neuroscience, 11*(11), 3656–3666.

Fujihara, H., Sei, H., Morita, Y., Ueta, Y., & Morita, K. (2003). Short-term sleep disturbance enhances brain-derived neurotrophic factor gene expression in rat hippocampus by acting as internal stressor. *Journal of Molecular Neuroscience, 21*(3), 223–232.

Fujii, T., Otsuba, Y., Suzuki, K., Endo, K., & Yamadori, A. (2005). Improvement of obsessive–compulsive disorder following left putaminal hemorrhage. *European Neurology, 54*(3), 166–170.

Giuffrida, M. L., Caraci, F., Pignataro, B., Cataldo, S., De Bona, P., Bruno, V., . . . Copani, A. (2009). Beta-amyloid monomers are neuroprotective. *The Journal of Neuroscience, 29*(34), 10582–10587.

Glantz, L. A., & Lewis, D. A. (2000). Decreased dendritic spine density on prefrontal cortical pyramidal neurons in schizophrenia. *Archives of General Psychiatry, 57*(1), 65–73.

Greenberg, P. E., Kessler, R. C., Birnbaum, H. G., Leong, S. A., Lowe, S. W., Berglund, P. A., & Corey-Lisle, P. K. (2003). The economic burden of depression in the United States: How did it change between 1990 and 2000? *The Journal of Clinical Psychiatry, 64*(12), 1465–1475.

Grigoryev, Y. (2012, December 18). Depression has become leading cause of disability burden amongst US and Canadian teens. *Spoonful of Medicine*. Retrieved from http://blogs.nature.com/spoonful/2012/12/depression-has-become-leading-cause-of-disability-burden-amongst-us-and-candian-teens.html/

Haggard, P. (2008). Human volition: Towards a neuroscience of will. *Nature Reviews: Neuroscience, 9*(12), 934–946.

Hamani, C., Mayberg, H., Stone, S., Laxton, A., Haber, S., & Lozano, A. M. (2011). The subcallosal cingulate gyrus in the context of major depression. *Biological Psychiatry, 69*(4), 301–308.

Harrison, P. J. (1999). The neuropathology of schizophrenia. A critical review of the data and their interpretation. *Brain: A Journal of Neurology, 122*(Pt. 4), 593–624.

Harvey, C. A., Jeffreys, S. E., McNaught, A. S., Blizard, R. A., & King, M. B. (2007). The Camden Schizophrenia Surveys. III: Five-year outcome of a sample of individuals from a prevalence survey and the importance of social relationships. *The International Journal of Social Psychiatry, 53*(4), 340–356.

Healy, D. (1997). *The antidepressant era.* Cambridge, MA: Harvard University Press.

Hennah, W., Thomson, P., McQuillin, A., Bass, N., Loukola, A., Anjorin, A., . . . Porteous, D. (2009). DISC1 association, heterogeneity and interplay in schizophrenia and bipolar disorder. *Molecular Psychiatry, 14*(9), 865–873.

Henry, T. R. (2003). The history of valproate in clinical neuroscience. *Psychopharmacology Bulletin, 37*(Suppl. 2), 5–16.

Hirschfeld, R. M. (2000). History and evolution of the monoamine hypothesis of depression. *The Journal of Clinical Psychiatry, 61*(Suppl. 6), 4–6.

Hoff, P. (2012). Eugen Bleuler's concept of schizophrenia and its relevance to present-day psychiatry. *Neuropsychobiology, 66*(1), 6–13.

Holmes, C., Boche, D., Wilkinson, D., Yadegarfar, G., Hopkins, V., Bayer, A., . . . Nicoll, J. A. (2008). Long-term effects of Abeta42 immunisation in Alzheimer's disease: Follow-up of a randomised, placebo-controlled phase I trial. *Lancet, 372*(9634), 216–223.

Honjo, K., Black, S. E., & Verhoeff, N. P. (2012). Alzheimer's disease, cerebrovascular disease, and the beta-amyloid cascade. *The Canadian Journal of Neurological Sciences, 39*(6), 712–728.

Howes, O. D., Egerton, A., Allan, V., McGuire, P., Stokes, P., & Kapur, S. (2009). Mechanisms underlying psychosis and antipsychotic treatment response in schizophrenia: Insights from PET and SPECT imaging. *Current Pharmaceutical Design, 15*(22), 2550–2559.

Huang, Y. (2006). Apolipoprotein E and Alzheimer disease. *Neurology, 66*(2 Suppl. 1), S79–S85.

Huang, Y., & Mucke, L. (2012). Alzheimer mechanisms and therapeutic strategies. *Cell, 148*(6), 1204–1222.

Huntington, G. (1872). On cholera. *The Medical and Surgical Reporter, 26*(15), 4.

Jamison, K. R. (1993). *Touched with fire: Manic–depressive illness and the artistic temperament.* New York: Free Press.

Jamison, K. R. (1995). *An unquiet mind.* New York, NY: Vintage Books.

Javitt, D. C. (2007). Glutamate and schizophrenia: phEncyclidine, N-methyl-D-aspartate receptors, and dopamine–glutamate interactions. *International Review of Neurobiology, 78*, 69–108.

Jefferies, E., & Lambon Ralph, M. A. (2006). Semantic impairment in stroke aphasia versus semantic dementia: A case-series comparison. *Brain: A Journal of Neurology, 129*(Pt. 8), 2132–2147.

Johnson, C. N., & Wellman, H. M. (1982). Children's developing conceptions of the mind and brain. *Child Development, 53*(1), 222–234.

Johnstone, T., van Reekum, C. M., Urry, H. L., Kalin, N. H., & Davidson, R. J. (2007). Failure to regulate: Counterproductive recruitment of top-down prefrontal–subcortical circuitry in major depression. *The Journal of Neuroscience, 27*(33), 8877–8884.

Joseph, P. G., Pare, G., & Anand, S. S. (2013). Exploring gene–environment relationships in cardiovascular disease. *The Canadian Journal of Cardiology, 29*(1), 37–45.

Jostins, L., & Barrett, J. C. (2011). Genetic risk prediction in complex disease. *Human Molecular Genetics, 20*(R2), R182–R188.

Kanat, A., Kayaci, S., Yazar, U., & Yilmaz, A. (2010). What makes Maurice Ravel's deadly craniotomy interesting? Concerns of one of the most famous craniotomies in history. *Acta Neurochirurgica, 152*(4), 737–742.

Kapur, S., & Mamo, D. (2003). Half a century of antipsychotics and still a central role for dopamine D2 receptors. *Progress in Neuro-Psychopharmacology and Biological Psychiatry, 27*(7), 1081–1090.

Kapur, S., Mizrahi, R., & Li, M. (2005). From dopamine to salience to psychosis—Linking biology, pharmacology and phenomenology of psychosis. *Schizophrenia Research, 79*(1), 59–68.

Karno, M., Golding, J. M., Sorenson, S. B., & Burnam, M. A. (1988). The epidemiology of obsessive–compulsive disorder in five US communities. *Archives of General Psychiatry, 45*(12), 1094–1099.

Kaufman, J., Yang, B. Z., Douglas-Palumberi, H., Houshyar, S., Lipschitz, D., Krystal, J. H., & Gelernter, J. (2004). Social supports and serotonin transporter gene moderate depression in maltreated children. *Proceedings of the National Academy of Sciences of the United States of America, 101*(49), 17316–17321.

Kawohl, W., Bruhl, A., Krowatschek, G., Ketteler, D., & Herwig, U. (2009). Functional magnetic resonance imaging of tics and tic suppression in Gilles de la Tourette syndrome. *The World Journal of Biological Psychiatry, 10*(4 Pt. 2), 567–570.

Kennedy, S. H., Giacobbe, P., Rizvi, S. J., Placenza, F. M., Nishikawa, Y., Mayberg, H. S., & Lozano, A. M. (2011). Deep brain stimulation for treatment-resistant depression: Follow-up after 3 to 6 years. *The American Journal of Psychiatry, 168*(5), 502–510.

Kessler, R. C., Chiu, W. T., Demler, O., Merikangas, K. R., & Walters, E. E. (2005). Prevalence, severity, and comorbidity of 12-month DSM-IV disorders in the National Comorbidity Survey Replication. *Archives of General Psychiatry, 62*(6), 617–627.

Khashan, A. S., Abel, K. M., McNamee, R., Pedersen, M. G., Webb, R. T., Baker, P. N., . . . Mortensen, P. B. (2008). Higher risk of offspring schizophrenia following antenatal maternal exposure to severe adverse life events. *Archives of General Psychiatry, 65*(2), 146–152.

Kieseppa, T., Partonen, T., Haukka, J., Kaprio, J., & Lonnqvist, J. (2004). High concordance of bipolar I disorder in a nationwide sample of twins. *The American Journal of Psychiatry, 161*(10), 1814–1821.

Kim, K. W., & Lee, D. Y. (2002). Obsessive–compulsive disorder associated with a left orbitofrontal infarct. *The Journal of Neuropsychiatry and Clinical Neurosciences, 14*(1), 88–89.

Kinney, D. K., & Richards, R. L. (1986). Creativity and manic depressive illness. *Science, 234*(4776), 529.

Kirsch, I., Deacon, B. J., Huedo-Medina, T. B., Scoboria, A., Moore, T. J., & Johnson, B. T. (2008). Initial severity and antidepressant benefits: A meta-analysis of data submitted to the Food and Drug Administration. *PLoS Medicine, 5*(2), e45.

Klunk, W. E., Engler, H., Nordberg, A., Wang, Y., Blomqvist, G., Holt, D. P., . . . Langstrom, B. (2004). Imaging brain amyloid in Alzheimer's disease with Pittsburgh Compound-B. *Annals of Neurology, 55*(3), 306–319.

Knight, T., Steeves, T., Day, L., Lowerison, M., Jette, N., & Pringsheim, T. (2012). Prevalence of tic disorders: A systematic review and meta-analysis. *Pediatric Neurology, 47*(2), 77–90.

Kraft, J. B., Peters, E. J., Slager, S. L., Jenkins, G. D., Reinalda, M. S., McGrath, P. J., & Hamilton, S. P. (2007). Analysis of association between the serotonin transporter and antidepressant response in a large clinical sample. *Biological Psychiatry, 61*(6), 734–742.

Kreitzer, A. C. (2009). Physiology and pharmacology of striatal neurons. *Annual Review of Neuroscience, 32,* 127–147.

Lam, R. W., Kennedy, S. H., Grigoriadis, S., McIntyre, R. S., Milev, R., Ramasubbu, R., . . . Ravindran, A. V. (2009). Canadian Network for Mood and Anxiety Treatments (CANMAT) clinical guidelines for the management of major depressive disorder in adults. III. Pharmacotherapy. *Journal of Affective Disorders, 117*(Suppl. 1), S26–S43.

Lanska, D. J. (2000). George Huntington (1850–1916) and hereditary chorea. *Journal of the History of the Neurosciences, 9*(1), 76–89.

Launer, L. J., Andersen, K., Dewey, M. E., Letenneur, L., Ott, A., Amaducci, L.A., . . . Hofman, A. (1999). Rates and risk factors for dementia and Alzheimer's disease: Results from EURODEM pooled analyses. EURODEM Incidence Research Group and Work Groups. European Studies of Dementia. *Neurology, 52*(1), 78–84.

Leckman, J. F., Bloch, M. H., Smith, M. E., Larabi, D., & Hampson, M. (2010). Neurobiological substrates of Tourette's disorder. *Journal of Child and Adolescent Psychopharmacology, 20*(4), 237–247.

Lenz, J. D., & Lobo, M. K. (2013). Optogenetic insights into striatal function and behavior. *Behavioural Brain Research, 255,* 44–54.

Lepine, J. P., & Briley, M. (2011). The increasing burden of depression. *Neuropsychiatric Disease and Treatment, 7*(Suppl. 1), 3–7.

Lesage, A., & Steckler, T. (2010). Metabotropic glutamate mGlu1 receptor stimulation and blockade: Therapeutic opportunities in psychiatric illness. *European Journal of Pharmacology, 639*(1–3), 2–16.

Leucht, S., Corves, C., Arbter, D., Engel, R. R., Li, C., & Davis, J. M. (2009). Second-generation versus first-generation antipsychotic drugs for schizophrenia: A meta-analysis. *Lancet, 373*(9657), 31–41.

Lichtenstein, P., Yip, B. H., Bjork, C., Pawitan, Y., Cannon, T. D., Sullivan, P. F., & Hultman, C. M. (2009). Common genetic determinants of schizophrenia and bipolar disorder in Swedish families: A population-based study. *Lancet, 373*(9659), 234–239.

Limb, C. J., & Braun, A. R. (2008). Neural substrates of spontaneous musical performance: An fMRI study of jazz improvisation. *PLoS One, 3*(2), e1679.

Lisman, J. E., Coyle, J. T., Green, R. W., Javitt, D. C., Benes, F. M., Heckers, S., & Grace, A. A. (2008). Circuit-based framework for understanding neurotransmitter and risk gene interactions in schizophrenia. *Trends in Neurosciences, 31*(5), 234–242.

Lopera, F., Ardilla, A., Martinez, A., Madrigal, L., Arango-Viana, J. C., Lemere, C. A., . . . Kosik, K. S. (1997). Clinical features of early-onset Alzheimer disease in a large kindred with an E280A presenilin-1 mutation. *JAMA, 277*(10), 793–799.

Lopez-Munoz, F., & Alamo, C. (2009). Monoaminergic neurotransmission: The history of the discovery of antidepressants from 1950s until today. *Current Pharmaceutical Design, 15*(14), 1563–1586.

Malhi, G. S., Tanious, M., Das, P., Coulston, C. M., & Berk, M. (2013). Potential mechanisms of action of lithium in bipolar disorder. Current understanding. *CNS Drugs, 27*(2), 135–153.

Marwaha, S., Johnson, S., Bebbington, P., Stafford, M., Angermeyer, M. C., Brugha, T., . . . Toumi, M. (2007). Rates and correlates of employment in people with schizophrenia in the UK, France and Germany. *The British Journal of Psychiatry, 191,* 30–37.

Mataix-Cols, D., Wooderson, S., Lawrence, N., Brammer, M. J., Speckens, A., & Phillips, M. L. (2004). Distinct neural correlates of washing, checking, and hoarding symptom dimensions in obsessive–compulsive disorder. *Archives of General Psychiatry, 61*(6), 564–576.

Mathews, D. C., & Zarate, C. A., Jr. (2013). Current status of ketamine and related compounds for depression. *The Journal of Clinical Psychiatry, 74*(5), 516–517.

Maurer, K., Volk, S., & Gerbaldo, H. (1997). Auguste D and Alzheimer's disease. *Lancet, 349*(9064), 1546–1549.

Mayberg, H. S. (1997). Limbic–cortical dysregulation: A proposed model of depression. *The Journal of Neuropsychiatry and Clinical Neurosciences, 9*(3), 471–481.

Mayberg, H. S. (2003). Modulating dysfunctional limbic–cortical circuits in depression: Towards development of brain-based algorithms for diagnosis and optimised treatment. *British Medical Bulletin, 65*, 193–207.

Mayberg, H. S., Lozano, A. M., Voon, V., McNeely, H. E., Seminowicz, D., Hamani, C., . . . Kennedy, S. H. (2005). Deep brain stimulation for treatment-resistant depression. *Neuron, 45*(5), 651–660.

Mendez, M. F. (2009). Frontotemporal dementia: Therapeutic interventions. *Frontiers of Neurology and Neuroscience, 24*, 168–178.

Menezes, N. M., Arenovich, T., & Zipursky, R. B. (2006). A systematic review of longitudinal outcome studies of first-episode psychosis. *Psychological Medicine, 36*(10), 1349–1362.

Merikangas, K. R., Akiskal, H. S., Angst, J., Greenberg, P. E., Hirschfeld, R. M., Petukhova, M., & Kessler, R. C. (2007). Lifetime and 12-month prevalence of bipolar spectrum disorder in the National Comorbidity Survey replication. *Archives of General Psychiatry, 64*(5), 543–552.

Merikangas, K. R., Jin, R., He, J. P., Kessler, R. C., Lee, S., Sampson, N. A., . . . Zarkov, Z. (2011). Prevalence and correlates of bipolar spectrum disorder in the world mental health survey initiative. *Archives of General Psychiatry, 68*(3), 241–251.

Millar, J. K., Wilson-Annan, J. C., Anderson, S., Christie, S., Taylor, M. S., Semple, C.A., . . . Porteous, D. J. (2000). Disruption of two novel genes by a translocation co-segregating with schizophrenia. *Human Molecular Genetics, 9*(9), 1415–1423.

Moussavi, S., Chatterji, S., Verdes, E., Tandon, A., Patel, V., & Ustun, B. (2007). Depression, chronic diseases, and decrements in health: Results from the World Health Surveys. *Lancet, 370*(9590), 851–858.

Muller-Vahl, K. R., Kaufmann, J., Grosskreutz, J., Dengler, R., Emrich, H. M., & Peschel, T. (2009). Prefrontal and anterior cingulate cortex abnormalities in Tourette syndrome: Evidence from voxel-based morphometry and magnetization transfer imaging. *BMC Neuroscience, 10*, 47.

Murphy, G. M., Jr., Hollander, S. B., Rodrigues, H. E., Kremer, C., & Schatzberg, A. F. (2004). Effects of the serotonin transporter gene promoter polymorphism on mirtazapine and paroxetine efficacy and adverse events in geriatric major depression. *Archives of General Psychiatry, 61*(11), 1163–1169.

Murray, C. J., Vos, T., Lozano, R., Naghavi, M., Flaxman, A. D., Michaud, C., . . . Memish, Z. A. (2012). Disability-adjusted life years (DALYs) for 291 diseases and injuries in 21 regions, 1990–2010: A systematic analysis for the Global Burden of Disease Study 2010. *Lancet, 380*(9859), 2197–2223.

Myers, R. H., Schaefer, E. J., Wilson, P. W., D'Agostino, R., Ordovas, J. M., Espino, A., . . . Wolf, P. A. (1996).

Apolipoprotein E epsilon4 association with dementia in a population-based study: The Framingham study. *Neurology, 46*(3), 673–677.

Nelson, P. T., Alafuzoff, I., Bigio, E. H., Bouras, C., Braak, H., Cairns, N. J., . . . Beach, T. G. (2012). Correlation of Alzheimer disease neuropathologic changes with cognitive status: A review of the literature. *Journal of Neuropathology and Experimental Neurology, 71*(5), 362–381.

Neumann, M., Tolnay, M., & Mackenzie, I. R. (2009). The molecular basis of frontotemporal dementia. *Expert Reviews in Molecular Medicine, 11*, e23.

Nibuya, M., Morinobu, S., & Duman, R. S. (1995). Regulation of BDNF and trkB mRNA in rat brain by chronic electroconvulsive seizure and antidepressant drug treatments. *The Journal of Neuroscience, 15*(11), 7539–7547.

Ochsner, K. N., Ray, R. D., Cooper, J. C., Robertson, E. R., Chopra, S., Gabrieli, J. D., & Gross, J. J. (2004). For better or for worse: Neural systems supporting the cognitive down- and up-regulation of negative emotion. *Neuroimage, 23*(2), 483–499.

Ogai, M., Iyo, M., Mori, N., & Takei, N. (2005). A right orbitofrontal region and OCD symptoms: A case report. *Acta Psychiatrica Scandinavica, 111*(1), 74–76; discussion 76–77.

Olney, J. W., & Farber, N. B. (1995). Glutamate receptor dysfunction and schizophrenia. *Archives of General Psychiatry, 52*(12), 998–1007.

Onstad, S., Skre, I., Torgersen, S., & Kringlen, E. (1991). Twin concordance for DSM-III-R schizophrenia. *Acta Psychiatrica Scandinavica, 83*(5), 395–401.

Paschou, P. (2013). The genetic basis of Gilles de la Tourette syndrome. *Neuroscience and Biobehavioral Reviews, 37*(6), 1026–1039.

Patterson, K., Nestor, P. J., & Rogers, T. T. (2007). Where do you know what you know? The representation of semantic knowledge in the human brain. *Nature Reviews: Neuroscience, 8*(12), 976–987.

Peterson, B. S., & Cohen, D. J. (1998). The treatment of Tourette's syndrome: Multimodal, developmental intervention. *The Journal of Clinical Psychiatry, 59*(Suppl. 1), 62–72; discussion 73–64.

Picard, N., & Strick, P. L. (1996). Motor areas of the medial wall: A review of their location and functional activation. *Cerebral Cortex, 6*(3), 342–353.

Poon, L. H., Kang, G. A., & Lee, A. J. (2010). Role of tetrabenazine for Huntington's disease–associated chorea. *The Annals of Pharmacotherapy, 44*(6), 1080–1089.

Radua, J., & Mataix-Cols, D. (2009). Voxel-wise meta-analysis of grey matter changes in obsessive–compulsive disorder. *The British Journal of Psychiatry, 195*(5), 393–402.

Raichle, M. E. (2006). Neuroscience. The brain's dark energy. *Science, 314*(5803), 1249–1250.

Raichle, M. E., MacLeod, A. M., Snyder, A. Z., Powers, W. J., Gusnard, D. A., & Shulman, G. L. (2001). A default mode of brain function. *Proceedings of the National Academy of Sciences of the United States of America, 98*(2), 676–682.

Rapoport, J. L., Addington, A. M., Frangou, S., & Psych, M. R. (2005). The neurodevelopmental model of schizophrenia: Update 2005. *Molecular Psychiatry, 10*(5), 434–449.

Richards, R., & Kinney, D. K. (1989). Compelling evidence for increased rates of affective disorder among eminent creative persons. *Comprehensive Psychiatry, 30*(3), 272–273.

Risch, N., Herrell, R., Lehner, T., Liang, K. Y., Eaves, L., Hoh, J., . . . Merikangas, K. R. (2009). Interaction between the serotonin transporter gene (5-HTTLPR), stressful life events, and risk of depression: A meta-analysis. *JAMA, 301*(23), 2462–2471.

Rotge, J. Y., Guehl, D., Dilharreguy, B., Cuny, E., Tignol, J., Bioulac, B., . . . Aouizerate, B. (2008). Provocation of obsessive–compulsive symptoms: A quantitative voxel-based meta-analysis of functional neuroimaging studies. *Journal of Psychiatry & Neuroscience, 33*(5), 405–412.

Sackeim, H. A., Prudic, J., Nobler, M. S., Fitzsimons, L., Lisanby, S. H., Payne, N., . . . Devanand, D. P. (2008). Effects of pulse width and electrode placement on the efficacy and cognitive effects of electroconvulsive therapy. *Brain Stimulation, 1*(2), 71–83.

Santosa, C. M., Strong, C. M., Nowakowska, C., Wang, P. W., Rennicke, C. M., & Ketter, T. A. (2007). Enhanced creativity in bipolar disorder patients: A controlled study. *Journal of Affective Disorders, 100*(1–3), 31–39.

Schneider, L. S., Dagerman, K. S., Higgins, J. P., & McShane, R. (2011). Lack of evidence for the efficacy of memantine in mild Alzheimer disease. *Archives of Neurology, 68*(8), 991–998.

Seeley, W. W., Matthews, B. R., Crawford, R. K., Gorno-Tempini, M. L., Foti, D., Mackenzie, I. R., & Miller, B. L. (2008). Unravelling Bolero: Progressive aphasia, transmodal creativity and the right posterior neocortex. *Brain: A Journal of Neurology, 131*(Pt. 1), 39–49.

Seeman, P., & Lee, T. (1975). Antipsychotic drugs: Direct correlation between clinical potency and presynaptic action on dopamine neurons. *Science, 188*(4194), 1217–1219.

Selemon, L. D., & Goldman-Rakic, P. S. (1999). The reduced neuropil hypothesis: A circuit based model of schizophrenia. *Biological Psychiatry, 45*(1), 17–25.

Seminowicz, D. A., Mayberg, H. S., McIntosh, A. R., Goldapple, K., Kennedy, S., Segal, Z., & Rafi-Tari, S. (2004). Limbic-frontal circuitry in major depression: A path modeling metanalysis. *Neuroimage, 22*(1), 409–418.

Serretti, A., Kato, M., De Ronchi, D., & Kinoshita, T. (2007). Meta-analysis of serotonin transporter gene promoter polymorphism (5-HTTLPR) association with selective serotonin reuptake inhibitor efficacy in depressed patients. *Molecular Psychiatry, 12*(3), 247–257.

Sidor, M. M., & MacQueen, G. M. (2012). An update on antidepressant use in bipolar depression. *Current Psychiatry Reports, 14*(6), 696–704.

Singer, H. S. (2005). Tourette's syndrome: From behaviour to biology. *The Lancet. Neurology, 4*(3), 149–159.

Sleegers, K., Lambert, J. C., Bertram, L., Cruts, M., Amouyel, P., & Van Broeckhoven, C. (2010). The pursuit of susceptibility genes for Alzheimer's disease: Progress and prospects. *Trends in Genetics, 26*(2), 84–93.

Sloman, L., Gilbert, P., & Hasey, G. (2003). Evolved mechanisms in depression: The role and interaction of attachment and social rank in depression. *Journal of Affective Disorders, 74*(2), 107–121.

Smith, K. A., Fairburn, C. G., & Cowen, P. J. (1997). Relapse of depression after rapid depletion of tryptophan. *Lancet, 349*(9056), 915–919.

Spreng, R. N., Mar, R. A., & Kim, A. S. (2009). The common neural basis of autobiographical memory, prospection, navigation, theory of mind, and the default mode: A quantitative meta-analysis. *Journal of Cognitive Neuroscience, 21*(3), 489–510.

Stahl, S. M. (1998). Basic psychopharmacology of antidepressants, part 1: Antidepressants have seven distinct mechanisms of action. *The Journal of Clinical Psychiatry, 59*(Suppl. 4), 5–14.

Stein, D. J. (2002). Obsessive–compulsive disorder. *Lancet, 360*(9330), 397–405.

Stern, Y. (2012). Cognitive reserve in ageing and Alzheimer's disease. *The Lancet. Neurology, 11*(11), 1006–1012.

Sullivan, P. F., Neale, M. C., & Kendler, K. S. (2000). Genetic epidemiology of major depression: Review and meta-analysis. *The American Journal of Psychiatry, 157*(10), 1552–1562.

Swedo, S. E., Leonard, H. L., Garvey, M., Mittleman, B., Allen, A. J., Perlmutter, S., . . . Dubbert, B. K. (1998). Pediatric autoimmune neuropsychiatric disorders associated with streptococcal infections: Clinical description of the first 50 cases. *The American Journal of Psychiatry, 155*(2), 264–271.

Swedo, S. E., Schrag, A., Gilbert, R., Giovannoni, G., Robertson, M. M., Metcalfe, C., . . . Gilbert, D. L. (2010). Streptococcal infection, Tourette syndrome, and OCD: Is there a connection? PANDAS: Horse or zebra? *Neurology, 74*(17), 1397–1398; author reply 1398-1399.

Taylor, S. (2011). Early versus late onset obsessive–compulsive disorder: Evidence for distinct subtypes. *Clinical Psychology Review, 31*(7), 1083–1100.

Todd, S., Barr, S., Roberts, M., & Passmore, A. P. (2013). Survival in dementia and predictors of mortality: A review. *International Journal of Geriatric Psychiatry, 28*(11), 1109–1124.

Torres, A. R., Ramos-Cerqueira, A. T., Ferrao, Y. A., Fontenelle, L. F., do Rosario, M. C., & Miguel, E. C. (2011). Suicidality in obsessive–compulsive disorder: Prevalence and relation to symptom dimensions and comorbid conditions. *The Journal of Clinical Psychiatry, 72*(1), 17–26; quiz 119–120.

Traskman-Bendz, L., Asberg, M., Bertilsson, L., & Thoren, P. (1984). CSF monoamine metabolites of depressed patients during illness and after recovery. *Acta Psychiatrica Scandinavica, 69*(4), 333–342.

Tremblay, C. H., Grosskopf, S., & Yang, K. (2010). Brainstorm: Occupational choice, bipolar illness and creativity. *Economics and Human Biology, 8*(2), 233–241.

van Haren, N. E., Hulshoff Pol, H. E., Schnack, H. G., Cahn, W., Brans, R., Carati, I., . . . Kahn, R. S. (2008). Progressive brain volume loss in schizophrenia over the course of the illness: Evidence of maturational abnormalities in early adulthood. *Biological Psychiatry, 63*(1), 106–113.

van Haren, N. E., Hulshoff Pol, H. E., Schnack, H. G., Cahn, W., Mandl, R. C., Collins, D. L., . . . Kahn, R. S. (2007). Focal gray matter changes in schizophrenia across the course of the illness: A 5-year follow-up study. *Neuropsychopharmacology, 32*(10), 2057–2066.

van Os, J., & Kapur, S. (2009). Schizophrenia. *Lancet, 374*(9690), 635–645.

Venuto, C. S., McGarry, A., Ma, Q., & Kieburtz, K. (2012). Pharmacologic approaches to the treatment of Huntington's disease. *Movement Disorders, 27*(1), 31–41.

Vita, A., De Peri, L., Silenzi, C., & Dieci, M. (2006). Brain morphology in first-episode schizophrenia: A meta-analysis of quantitative magnetic resonance imaging studies. *Schizophrenia Research, 82*(1), 75–88.

Walker, F. O. (2007). Huntington's disease. *Lancet, 369*(9557), 218–228.

Watts, B. V., Groft, A., Bagian, J. P., & Mills, P. D. (2011). An examination of mortality and other adverse events related to electroconvulsive therapy using a national adverse event report system. *The Journal of ECT, 27*(2), 105–108.

Wilhelm, K., Mitchell, P. B., Niven, H., Finch, A., Wedgwood, L., Scimone, A., ... Schofield, P.R. (2006). Life events, first depression onset and the serotonin transporter gene. *The British Journal of Psychiatry, 188*, 210–215.

Wolozin, B., Manger, J., Bryant, R., Cordy, J., Green, R. C., & McKee, A. (2006). Re-assessing the relationship between cholesterol, statins and Alzheimer's disease. *Acta Neurologica Scandinavica. Supplementum, 185*, 63–70.

Wong, D. T., Horng, J. S., Bymaster, F. P., Hauser, K. L., & Molloy, B. B. (1974). A selective inhibitor of serotonin uptake: Lilly 110140, 3-(*p*-trifluoromethylphenoxy)-*N*-methyl-3-phenylpropylamine. *Life Sciences, 15*(3), 471–479.

The World Health Organization. (2004). *The World Health Report 2004: Changing history.* Geneva: World Health Organization.

Yaryura-Tobias, J. A., & Neziroglu, F. (2003). Basal ganglia hemorrhagic ablation associated with temporary suppression of obsessive–compulsive symptoms. *Revista brasileira de psiquiatria, 25*(1), 40–42.

Yatham, L. N., Kennedy, S. H., O'Donovan, C., Parikh, S., MacQueen, G., McIntyre, R., ... Gorman, C. P. (2005). Canadian Network for Mood and Anxiety Treatments (CANMAT) guidelines for the management of patients with bipolar disorder: Consensus and controversies. *Bipolar Disorders, 7*(Suppl. 3), 5–69.

Zou, K., Kim, D., Kakio, A., Byun, K., Gong, J. S., Kim, J., ... Michikawa, M. (2003). Amyloid beta-protein (Abeta)1-40 protects neurons from damage induced by Abeta1-42 in culture and in rat brain. *Journal of Neurochemistry, 87*(3), 609–619.

CREDITS

Chapter 1

Figure 1.1: X-ray: NASA/CXC/NCSU/M.Burkey et al; Optical: DSS. **Figure 1.2:** Image provided courtesy of Jeff W. Lichtman, M.D., Ph.D. Harvard University. Department of Molecular and Cellular Biology. **Figure 1.3:** Image provided courtesy of Profs. Alan Evans (Montreal Neurological Institute, McGill University) and Katrin Amunts (Institute for Neuroscience and Medicine, Juelich Research Centre). **Figure 1.4:** Photo Credit of the San Diego Convention Center. **Figure 1.5b:** John Hay Library, Brown University Library. **Figure 1.6:** Petra Stoerig/Frontiers in Psychology. **Figure 1.7:** AFP/Stringer/Getty Images. **Figure 1.8:** Fiber Pathways of the Brain by Shmahmann and Pandya (2006), Fig. 10-2. By permission of Oxford University Press, USA. **Figure 1.9:** Courtesy of the Laboratory of Neuro Imaging and Martinos Center for Biomedical Imaging, Consortium of the Human Connectome Project: www.humanconnectomeproject.org. **Figure 1.10:** Hank Morgan/Science Source. **Figure 1.11a:** istock/©selimaksan. **Figure 1.11b:** Image courtesy of Jonathan Downar, Read Montague, and Meghan Bhatt. **Figure 1.12a:** Medoc Ltd. **Figure 1.12b:** Image courtesy of Irene Tracey, MA (Oxon), D.Phil (PhD), FRCA Nuffield Professor Anaesthetic Science & Director, Oxford Centre for FMRI of Brain Nuffield Department of Clinical Neurosciences. **Figure 1.13a:** N. F. Dronkers, O. Plaisant, M. T. Iba-Zizen, E. A. Cabanis, Paul Broca's historic cases: high resolution MR imaging of the brains of Leborgne and Lelong, *Brain* (2007) 130 (5): 1432–1441, Figure 3 A & C. Reprinted with permission by Oxford University Press Journals. **Figure 1.13b:** Reprinted from Generating predictions: Lesion evidence on the role of left inferior frontal cortex in rapid syntactic analysis by Maria Jakuszeit, Sonja A. Kotz, Anna S. Hasting, with permission from Elsevier. **Figure 1.14:** Reprinted from: A parietal-premotor network for movement intention and motor awareness. Michel Desmurget, Angela Sirigu, with permission from Elsevier. **Figure 1.17b:** Willem van de Kerkhof/Shutterstock. **Figure 1.17c:** Nigel J. Dennis/Science Source. **Figure 1.17d:** Sharon Morris/Shutterstock. **Figure 1.21:** Regulation of Postsynaptic Structure and Function by an A-Kinase Anchoring Protein–Membrane-Associated Guanylate Kinase Scaffolding Complex. Holly R. Robertson, Emily S. Gibson, Timothy A. Benke, and Mark L. Dell'Acqua. *The Journal of Neuroscience*, 17 June 2009, 29(24):7929–7943; doi:10.1523/JNEUROSCI.6093-08.2009. Reprinted with permission from the authors. **Figure 1.22:** © Octavio Ocampo. **Figure 1.23:** nunosilvaphotography/Shutterstock. **Figure 1.24:** Alex Norton/EyeWire. **Figure 1.25:** Adapted by permission from Macmillan Publishers Ltd. **Figure 1.26a:** Photo Researchers. **Figure 1.26b:** Photo Researchers. **Figure 1.26c:** Photo Researchers. **Figure 1.26d:** Photo Researchers. **Figure 1.26e:** Photo Researchers. **Figure 1.26f:** Photo Researchers. **Figure 1.27:** FEREX/Associated Press. **Figure 1.28a:** Reprinted from Gray matter abnormalities in Major Depressive Disorder: A meta-analysis of voxel based morphometry studies. Emre Bora, Alex Fornito, Christos Pantelis, Murat Yücel. *Journal of Affective Disorders*, April 2012, with permission from Elsevier. **Figure 1.28b:** The effects of gender on grey matter abnormalities, in major psychoses: a comparative voxel-wise meta-analysis of schizophrenia and bipolar disorder, E. Bora, A. Fornito, M. Yücel and C. Pantelis. August, 2011. Reprinted with permission from Cambridge University Press. **Figure 1.28c:** Reprinted from Gray Matter Correlates of Posttraumatic Stress Disorder: A Quantitative Meta-Analysis. Simone Kühn, Jürgen Gallinat. *Biological Psychiatry*, January 2013, with permission from Elsevier.

Figure 1.29: © 2010 Ankur Garg et al. **Figure 1.30a:** Picture provided courtesy of Cochlear Americas, © 2015 Cochlear Americas. **Figure 1.30b:** The Retinal Implant. First Bionic Eye For US Market Awaits Approval From FDA by Jennifer Hicks. Forbes/Tech, 2013. **Figure 1.30c:** Braingate2.0rg. **Figure 1.30d:** BrainGate, Brown University/Matt McKee Photography. **Figure 1.31:** Felix Miozioznikov/Shutterstock.

Chapter 2

Figure 2.1a: Merlin D. Tuttle/Science Source. **Figure 2.1b:** Shane Gross/Shutterstock. **Figure 2.1c:** Tom McHugh/Science Source. **Figure 2.1d:** Betty Shelton/Shutterstock. **Figure 2.2a:** Pete Spiro/Shutterstock. **Figure 2.2b:** pierre_j/Shutterstock. **Figure 2.3a:** Image courtesy of Dr. Timothy Cox, SANTA, Seattle Children's Research Institute. **Figure 2.3b:** Xiao Wei Wendy Gu. **Figure 2.4a:** Halder, G., Callaerts, P. and Gehring, W. J. (1995), Induction of ectopic eyes by targeted expression of the eyeless gene in Drosophila. *Science*, New Series, Volume 267, 1788–1792. **Figure 2.4b:** Halder, G., Callaerts, P. and Gehring, W. J. (1995), Induction of ectopic eyes by targeted expression of the eyeless gene in Drosophila. *Science*, New Series, Volume 267, 1788–1792. **Figure 2.7b1:** Copyright ©1993–2004 Louis Collins, McConnell Brain Imaging Centre, Montreal Neurological Institute, McGill University. **Figure 2.7b2:** Copyright ©1993–2004 Louis Collins, McConnell Brain Imaging Centre, Montreal Neurological Institute, McGill University. **Figure 2.7b3:** Copyright ©1993–2004 Louis Collins, McConnell Brain Imaging Centre, Montreal Neurological Institute, McGill University.

Chapter 3

Figure 3.1: Beth Swanson/Shutterstock. **Figure 3.2a:** Clark University, 1889–1899, decennial celebration (1899). Page 310. Worcester, Mass.: Printed for the University. **Figure 3.2b:** Santiago Ramón y Cajal. **Figure 3.4:** Information Processing Dendritic Trees, Bartlett W. Mel. Copyright © 1994, Massachusetts Institute of Technology. Reprinted by permission of MIT Press Journals. **Figure 3.5b:** Manfred Kage/Science Source. **Figure 3.6b:** CNRI/Science Source. **Figure 3.10a:** Martin M. Rotker/Science Source. **Figure 3.10b:** Biophoto Associates/Science Source. **Figure 3.10c:** Autoradiographic and histological evidence of postnatal hippocampal neurogenesis in rats by Joseph Altman and Gopal D. Das, Copyright © 1965, The Wistar Institute of Anatomy and Biology. Reprinted with permission from Wiley and Sons. **Figure 3.10d:** Image provided courtesy of Abcam Inc. Image copyright © 2013 Abcam. **Figure 3.10e:** Cell-type-specific consequences of reelin deficiency in the mouse neocortex, hippocampus, and amygdala. Maureen P. Boyle, Amy Bernard, Carol L. Thompson, Lydia Ng, Andrew Boe, Marty Mortrud, Michael J. Hawrylycz, Allan R. Jones, Robert F. Hevner, Ed S. Lein. *Journal of Comparative Neurology*, Volume 519, Issue 11, pages 2061–2089, 1 August 2011. Reprinted with permission from John Wiley and Sons. **Figure 3.11c:** Don W. Fawcett/Science Source. **Figure 3.12a:** C. J. Guerin, PhD, MRC Toxicology Unit/Science Source. **Figure 3.12b:** R. BICK, B. POINDEXTER, UT MEDICAL SCHOOL/SCIENCE PHOTO LIBRARY. **Figure 3.13a:** New York Public Library/Science Source. **Figure 3.14b:** © Dr. Kristen M. Harris. **Figure 3.20b:** KU Medical Center. The University of Kansas. **Figure 3.22b:** Photo courtesy of

Chapter 4

Chapter 5

Chapter 6

Chapter 7

Chapter 8

kind permission from Springer Science and Business Media. Photo courtesy of Daniel J. Simons. **Figure 8.4c:** Failure to detect changes to people during a real-world interaction by DANIEL J. SIMONS and DANIEL T. LEVIN. *Psychonomic Bulletin & Review,* volume 5, issue 4, January 1, 1998. Reprinted with kind permission from Springer Science and Business Media. Photo courtesy of Daniel J. Simons. **Figure 8.4d:** Failure to detect changes to people during a real-world interaction by DANIEL J. SIMONS and DANIEL T. LEVIN. *Psychonomic Bulletin & Review,* volume 5, issue 4, January 1, 1998. Reprinted with kind permission from Springer Science and Business Media. Photo courtesy of Daniel J. Simons. **Figure 8.5:** Simons, D. J., & Chabris, C. F. (1999). Gorillas in our midst: Sustained inattentional blindness for dynamic events. *Perception,* 28, 1059–1074. Figure provided by Daniel Simons, www.dansimons.com. **Figure 8.8:** New York Public Library/Science Source. **Figure 8.9:** Reprinted by permission from Macmillan Publishers Ltd. Neural correlates of change detection and change blindness, Diane M. Beck, Geraint Rees, Christopher D. Frith and Nilli Lavie. *Nature Neuroscience,* volume 4, issue 6, Jun 1, 2001. **Figure 8.10:** Neural Correlates of Perceptual Rivalry in the Human Brain. Erik D. Lumer, Karl J. Friston, Geraint Rees. *The American Association for the Advancement of Science.* Volume 280, Issue 5371, June 19, 1998. Reprinted with permission from AAAS. **Figure 8.13:** Geraint Rees, Ewa Wojciulik, Karen Clarke, Masud Husain, Chris Frith, Jon Driver, Unconscious activation of visual cortex in the damaged right hemisphere of a parietal patient with extinction, *Brain* (2000) 123 (8) 1624–1633, Figure 2. Reprinted with permission from Oxford University Press. **Figure 8.16:** Tyler Olson/Shutterstock. **Figure 8.23:** Steven Laureys. Death, unconsciousness and the brain. SCIENCE AND SOCIETY, *Nature Reviews: Neuroscience,* 6(11), 899–909. **Figure 8.24:** Brain function in coma, vegetative state, and related disorders by Steven Laureys, Adrian M Owen, Nicholas D Schiff. *The Lancet Neurology,* Volume 3, Issue 9, pp. 537–546, September 2004. With permission from Elsevier. **Figure 8.25a:** Steven Laureys, Marie-Elisabeth Faymonville, Christian Degueldre et al. Auditory processing in the vegetative state, *Brain* (2000) 123 (8) 1589–1601, Figure 1. Reprinted with permission from Oxford University Press Journals. **Figure 8.25b:** Steven Laureys, Marie-Elisabeth Faymonville, Christian Degueldre et al. Auditory processing in the vegetative state, *Brain* (2000) 123 (8) 1589–1601, Figure 1. Reprinted with permission from Oxford University Press Journals. **Figure 8.34:** Dehaene, S., Changeux, J. P., & Naccache, L. (1998). The Global Neuronal Workspace Model of Conscious Access: From Neuronal Architectures to Clinical Applications. In S. Dehaene & Y. Christen (Eds.), Characterizing Consciousness: From Cognition to the Clinic? (pp. 55–84). Heidelberg: Springer-Verlag. With kind permission from Springer Science and Business Media.

Chapter 9

Figure 9.1: Dan Tuffs/Contributor/Getty Images. **Figure 9.9:** Published originally by Whitlock, JR, Sutherland, RJ, Witter MP, Moser MB, Moser EI. (2008) Proceedings of the National Academy of Sciences USA, 105(39):14755–62. **Figure 9.10:** Copyright © 2000 National Academy of Sciences, U.S.A. **Figure 9.13:** Reprinted by permission from Macmillan Publishers Ltd: *Nature Neuroscience,* 6(1), 90–95. Routes to remembering: the brains behind superior memory. Maguire, E. A., Valentine, E. R., Wilding, J. M., & Kapur, N. (2003). **Figure 9.14:** Reprinted by permission from Macmillan Publishers Ltd: *Nature,* 440(7084), 680–683. Reverse replay of behavioural sequences in hippocampal place cells during the awake

state. Foster, D. J., & Wilson, M. A. (2006). **Figure 9.18:** Reprinted by permission from Macmillan Publishers Ltd: *Nature Reviews Neuroscience,* 4(8), 662–671. doi: 10.1038/nrn1179. Spontaneous confabulation and the adaptation of thought to ongoing reality. Schnider, A. (2003). **Figure 9.19:** Yoko Okado and Craig E.L. Stark. Neural activity during encoding predicts false memories created by misinformation. Departments of Psychological and Brain Sciences and Neuroscience, Johns Hopkins University. **Figure 9.21:** Bliss, T. V., & Lomo, T. (1973). Long-lasting potentiation of synaptic transmission in the dentate area of the anaesthetized rabbit following stimulation of the perforant path. *Journal of Physiology,* 232(2), 331–356. Reprinted with permission from Wiley and Sons Ltd. **Figure 9.25:** Epp, J. R., Chow, C., & Galea, L. A. (2013). Hippocampus-dependent learning influences hippocampal neurogenesis. Frontiers in *Neuroscience,* 7, 57. **Figure 9.26:** Trachtenberg, J. T., Chen, B. E., Knott, G. W., Feng, G., Sanes, J. R., Welker, E., & Svoboda, K. (2002). Long-term in vivo imaging of experience-dependent synaptic plasticity in adult cortex. *Nature,* 420(6917), 788–794. **Figure 9.31:** Markram, H., Gerstner, W., & Sjostrom, P. J. (2011). A history of spike-timing-dependent plasticity. *Frontiers in Synaptic Neuroscience,* 3, 4. doi: 10.3389/fnsyn.2011.00004. Photo courtesy of the authors. **Figure 9.33:** Chin, S. (2005). A canonical face based virtual face modeling. In J. Tao, T. Tan & R. W. Picard (Eds.), Affective Computing and Intelligent Interaction: First International Conference, ACII 2005, Beijing, China, October 22–24, 2005. Proceedings. New York: Springer. With kind permission from Springer Science and Business Media.

Chapter 10

Figure 10.1: Frank Lennon/Contributor/Getty Images. **Figure 10.2:** © Corbis. **Figure 10.3a:** © Agencja Fotograficzna Caro/Alamy. **Figure 10.11:** © Bettmann/CORBIS. **Figure 10.12a:** AP Photo/Bill Ingraham. **Figure 10.12b:** Georgios Kollidas/Shutterstock. **Figure 10.12c:** Getty Images/UniversalImagesGroup/Contributor. **Figure 10.13a:** EcoPrint/Shutterstock. **Figure 10.13b:** Darren Foard/Shutterstock. **Figure 10.13c:** Sergey Uryadnikov/Shutterstock. **Figure 10.13d:** aldorado/Shutterstock. **Figure 10.13e:** Leena Robinson/Shutterstock. **Figure 10.13f:** Jearu/Shutterstock. **Figure 10.13g:** davemhuntphotography/Shutterstock. **Figure 10.13h:** Igor Chernomorchenko/Shutterstock. **Figure 10.13i:** Martin Maun/Shutterstock. **Figure 10.13j:** Lenkadan/Shutterstock. **Figure 10.14:** Adapted from: Sleep-dependent learning: a nap is as good as a night, Sara Mednick, Ken Nakayama & Robert Stickgold. *Nature Neuroscience* 6, 697–698 (2003). **Figure 10.15:** Reprinted from: Temporally Structured Replay of Awake Hippocampal Ensemble Activity during Rapid Eye Movement Sleep by Kenway Louie and Matthew A. Wilson. *Neuron:* Volume 29, Issue 1, January 2001, Pages 145–156. Reprinted with permission from Elsevier. **Figure 10.16:** THPStock/Shutterstock. **Figure 10.19:** Getty Images/Mondadori/Contributor. **Figure 10.20:** Photo credit: Lucidity.com. **Figure 10.23:** Getty Images/Don Cravens/Contributor. **Figure 10.26:** © Louie Psihoyos/Corbis.

Chapter 11

Figure 11.1: Getty Images/Popperfoto/Contributor. **Figure 11.3b:** N. F. Dronkers, O. Plaisant, M. T. Iba-Zizen, E. A. Cabanis, Paul Broca's historic cases: high resolution MR imaging of the brains of Leborgne and Lelong, *Brain* (2007) 130 (5): 1432–1441, Figure 3 A & C. Reprinted with permission from Oxford University Press. **Figure 11.3c:** N. F. Dronkers, O. Plaisant, M. T. Iba-Zizen, E. A.

Cabanis, Paul Broca's historic cases: high resolution MR imaging of the brains of Leborgne and Lelong, *Brain* (2007) 130 (5): 1432–1441, Figure 3 A & C. Repritned with permission from Oxford University Press. **Figure 11.8:** Shapiro, K. A., Moo, L. R., & Caramazza, A. (2006). Cortical signatures of noun and verb production. *Proc Natl Acad Sci USA*, 103(5), 1644–1649. doi: 10.1073/pnas.0504142103. Copyright © 2006 National Academy of Sciences, U.S.A. **Figure 11.10:** From Sakai, K. L. (2005). Language acquisition and brain development. *Science*, 310(5749), 815–819. Reprinted with permission from AAAS. **Figure 11.18a:** Ghonim et al/UNSW. **Figure 11.20a:** Andrew Durick/Shutterstock. **Figure 11.20b:** Photo courtesy of Dr. Irene Pepperberg: www .alexfoundation.org. **Figure 11.20c:** Photo courtesy of Friends of Washoe. http://www.friendsofwashoe.org/. **Figure 11.22:** © Brandon Roy. **Figure 11.23a:** Philip DeCamp and Deb Roy, MIT Media Lab. **Figure 11.23b:** Philip DeCamp and Deb Roy, MIT Media Lab.

Chapter 12

Figure 12.1: Getty Images/mage Source. **Figure 12.4a:** Sebastian Kaulitzki/Shutterstock. **Figure 12.4b:** Foto by M/Shutterstock. **Figure 12.4c:** Ivan Kruk/Shutterstock. **Figure 12.9:** Copyright © 2008 The Royal Society. **Figure 12.10a:** FloridaStock/Shutterstock. **Figure 12.10b:** Marketa Mark/Shutterstock. **Figure 12.11:** Getty Images/Sean Gallup/Staff. **Figure 12.12:** From McClure, S.M., Laibson, D.I., Loewenstein, G., & Cohen, J.D. (2004). Separate neural systems value immediate and delayed monetary rewards. *Science*, 306 (5695), 503–507. doi: 10.1126/science.1100907. Reprinted with permission from AAAS. **Figure 12.14:** L. Clark , A. Bechara , H. Damasio , M. R. F. Aitken , B. J. Sahakian , T. W. Robbins. Differential effects of insular and ventromedial prefrontal cortex lesions on risky decision-making, *Brain* (2008) 131 (5): 1311–1322, Figures 1 & 2. Reprinted with permission from Oxford University Press. **Figure 12.15:** Reprinted from Knutson, B., Wimmer, G.E., Rick, S., Hollon, N.G., Prelec, D., & Loewenstein, G. (2008). Neural antecedents of the endowment effect. *Neuron*, 58(5), 814–822. doi: 10.1016/j.neuron.2008.05.018, with permission from Elsevier. **Figure 12.17a:** Monkey Business Images/Shutterstock. **Figure 12.17b:** nito/Shutterstock. **Figure 12.18:** Reprinted by permission from Macmillan Publishers Ltd: from Kable, J.W., & Glimcher, P.W. (2007). The neural correlates of subjective value during intertemporal choice. *Nature Neuroscience*, 10(12), 1625–1633. doi: 10.1038/nn2007. **Figure 12.31:** Reprinted by permission from Macmillan Publishers Ltd: Acute Administration of d-Amphetamine Decreases Impulsivity in Healthy Volunteer by: Harriet de Wit, Justin L Enggasser and Jerry B Richards. *Neuropsychopharmacology*, November 2002, Nature Publishing Group. **Figure 12.32:** *Ulysses and the Sirens*, 1909 (oil on canvas), Draper, Herbert James (1864–1920)/Ferens Art Gallery, Hull Museums, UK/Bridgeman Images.

Chapter 13

Figure 13.2a: MindStorm/Shutterstock. **Figure 13.2b:** Russ Beinder/Shutterstock. **Figure 13.2c:** Andrea Izzotti/Shutterstock. **Figure 13.3a:** © PhotoAlto sas/Alamy Stock Photo. **Figure 13.3b:** wavebreakmedia/Shutterstock. **Figure 13.3c:** Ryan Jorgensen—Jorgo/Shutterstock. **Figure 13.3d:** Rommel Canlas/Shutterstock. **Figure 13.3e:** © Michael Clement/Masterfile/Corbis. **Figure 13.3f:** © Sergio Azenha / Alamy Stock Photo. **Figure 13.5:** Living Art Enterprises, LLC/Science Source. **Figure 13.6:** Associated Press. **Figure 13.8:** Eugene Buchko/Shutterstock. **Figure 13.14:**

Dr. Reeder. **Figure 13.17:** Images are from the Iowa Neurological Patient Registry at the University of Iowa. **Figure 13.21:** Reprinted from Bewernick, B.H., Hurlemann, R., Matusch, A., Kayser, S., Grubert, C., Hadrysiewicz, B., . . . Schlaepfer, T.E. (2010). Nucleus accumbens deep brain stimulation decreases ratings of depression and anxiety in treatment-resistant depression. *Biological Psychiatry*, 67(2), 110–116. doi: 10.1016/j.biopsych.2009.09.013, with permission from Elsevier. **Figure 13.27:** Elliott, R., Rees, G., & Dolan, R.J. (1999). Ventromedial prefrontal cortex mediates guessing. *Neuropsychologia*, 37(4), 403–411. **Figure 13.29:** © MoreISO/iStock. **Figure 13.34:** Koenigs, M., Huey, E.D., Calamia, M., Raymont, V., Tranel, D., & Grafman, J. (2008). Distinct regions of prefrontal cortex mediate resistance and vulnerability to depression. *The Journal of Neuroscience: the official journal of the Society for Neuroscience*, 28(47). **Figure 13.36:** Reprinted by permission from Macmillan Publishers Ltd. From Harmer, C.J., Bhagwagar, Z., Perrett, D.I., Vollm, B.A., Cowen, P.J., & Goodwin, G.M. (2003). Acute SSRI administration affects the processing of social cues in healthy volunteers. Neuropsychopharmacology: official publication of the American College of Neuropsychopharmacology, 28(1), 148–152. doi: 10.1038/sj.npp.1300004. **Figure 13.40:** Stefurak, T., Mikulis, D., Mayberg, H., Lang, A.E., Hevenor, S., Pahapill, P., . . . Lozano, A. (2003). Deep brain stimulation for Parkinson's disease dissociates mood and motor circuits: a functional MRI case study. Movement disorders: official journal of the Movement Disorder Society, 18(12), 1508–1516. doi: 10.1002/mds.10593. Reprinted with permission from Wiley and Sons Ltd.

Chapter 14

Figure 14.1: Shira Raz/Shutterstock. **Figure 14.2a:** Susan McKenzie/Shutterstock. **Figure 14.2a:** bheath03/Shutterstock. **Figure 14.2c:** Malivan_Iuliia/Shutterstock. **Figure 14.5:** Getty Images/Remi BENALI/Contributor. **Figure 14.10:** Getty Images/Hulton Archive/Stringer. **Figure 14.11a:** Aureus Virid/Shutterstock. **Figure 14.11b:** pogonici/Shutterstock. **Figure 14.13:** nevenm/Shutterstock. **Figure 14.14a:** B.erne/Shutterstock. **Figure 14.15:** Merrer et al, Reward Processing by the Opioid System in the Brain, *Physiol Rev* 89: 1379–1412, 2009; doi:10.1152/physrev.00005.2009. **Figure 14.16:** Inhibition of Opioid Transmission at the [mu]-Opioid Receptor Prevents Both Food Seeking and Binge-Like Eating. Chiara Giuliano, Trevor W Robbins, Pradeep J Nathan, Edward T Bullmore and Barry J Everitt. *Neuropsychopharmacology*, July 2012, Nature Publishing Group. **Figure 14.20a:** dwphotos/Shutterstock. **Figure 14.20b:** Iakov Kalinin/Shutterstock. **Figure 14.21a:** wavebreakmedia. **Figure 14.21b:** Press Association via AP Images. **Figure 14.25:** Reprinted from the World Health Organization: http://www.who.int/substance_abuse/facts/en/page39new.jpg. **Figure 14.27b:** Cordelia Molloy/Science Source. **Figure 14.28:** © Sue Cunningham Photographic/Alamy.

Chapter 15

Figure 15.1: Laurent Cipriani/Associated Press. **Figure 15.2a:** doglikehorse/Shutterstock. **Figure 15.2b:** Endless Traveller/Shutterstock. **Figure 15.4:** Schlicht EJ, Shimojo S, Camerer CF, Battaglia P, Nakayama K (2010) Human Wagering Behavior Depends on Opponents' Faces. *PLoS ONE* 5(7): e11663. doi:10.1371/journal.pone.0011663. **Figure 15.5:** Oosterhof, N.N., & Todorov, A. (2008). The functional basis of face evaluation. Proceedings of the National Academy of Sciences of the United States of America, 105(32), 11087–11092. Copyright © 2008 National Academy of

Sciences, U.S.A. **Figure 15.6b:** Everett Collection/Shutterstock. **Figure 15.6c:** © MARKA/Alamy. **Figure 15.6d:** Debby Wong/ Shutterstock. **Figure 15.6e:** Featureflash/Shutterstock. **Figure 15.6f:** s_bukley/Shutterstock. **Figure 15.7b:** Hurst Photo/Shutterstock. **Figure 15.14:** © Xinhua/Alamy. **Figure 15.16:** © PAINTING/Alamy. **Figure 15.17:** Farah Abdi Warsameh/Associated Press. **Figure 15.18a:** Neil A. Harrison, Tania Singer, Pia Rotshtein, Ray J. Dolan, and Hugo D. Critchley. Pupillary contagion: central mechanisms engaged in sadness processing, *Soc Cogn Affect Neurosci* (2006) 1 (1): 5–17, Figure 1A. Reprinted with permission of Oxford University Press. **Figure 15.20:** Singer, T., Seymour, B., O'Doherty, J., Kaube, H., Dolan, R.J., & Frith, C.D. (2004). Empathy for pain involves the affective but not sensory components of pain. *Science*, 303(5661), 1157–1162. doi: 10.1126/science.1093535 Reprinted with permission from AAAS. **Figure 15.21:** Reprinted by permission from Macmillan Publishers Ltd: Empathic neural responses are modulated by the perceived fairness of others. Tania Singer, Ben Seymour, John P. O'Doherty, Klaas E. Stephan, Raymond J. Dolan et al. *Nature*, January 2006, Nature Publishing Group. **Figure 15.22a/b:** Simone G. Shamay-Tsoory, Judith Aharon-Peretz, Daniella Perry. Two systems for empathy: a double dissociation between emotional and cognitive empathy in inferior frontal gyrus versus ventromedial prefrontal lesions, *Brain* (2009) 132 (3): 617–627, Figure 4 (adapted). Reprinted with permission from Oxford University Press. **Figure 15.22c:** Simone G. Shamay-Tsoory, Judith Aharon-Peretz, Daniella Perry. Two systems for empathy: a double dissociation between emotional and cognitive empathy in inferior frontal gyrus versus ventromedial prefrontal lesions, *Brain* (2009) 132 (3): 617–627, Figure 4 (adapted). Reprinted with permission from Oxford University Press. **Figure 15.25:** R. J. R. Blair, L. Cipolotti. Impaired social response reversal, *Brain* (2000) 123 (6) 1122–1141, Figure 1 (adapted). Reprinted with permission from Oxford University Press. **Figure 15.33a:** Barcroft Media/Getty Images. **Figure 15.33b:** © Rick & Nora Bowers/ Alamy. **Figure 15.36:** Oxytocin, Vasopressin, and the Neurogenetics of Sociality. Zoe R. Donaldson, Larry J. Young, *Science*. Reprinted with permission from AAAS. **Figure 15.37:** Vitalinka/ Shutterstock. **Figure 15.38:** Dick Hanley/Science Source. **Figure 15.41:** Berti, A., Bottini, G., Gandola, M., Pia, L., Smania, N., Stracciari, A., . . . Paulesu, E. (2005). Shared cortical anatomy for motor awareness and motor control. *Science*, 309(5733), 488–491. doi: 10.1126/science.1110625 http://www.sciencemag.org/content/309/5733/488.full. Reprinted with permission from AAAS.

Figure 15.42: Villarejo, A., Martin, V.P., Moreno-Ramos, T., Camachho-Salas, A., Porta-Etessam, J., & Bermejo-Pareja, F. (2011). Mirrored-self misidentification in a patient without dementia: evidence for right hemispheric and bifrontal damage. *Neurocase*, 17(3), 276–284.Taylor & Francis Ltd.

Chapter 16

Figure 16.1: Getty Images/DEA/A. DAGLI ORTI/Contributor. **Figure 16.4b:** Thomas Deerinck, NCMIR/Science Sou. **Figure 16.6:** The Lancet: from Holmes, C., Boche, D., Wilkinson, D., Yadegarfar, G., Hopkins, V., Bayer, A., Nicoll, J.A. (2008). Long-term effects of Abeta42 immunisation in Alzheimer's disease: follow-up of a randomised, placebo-controlled phase I trial. *Lancet*, 372(9634), 216–223. Reprinted with permission from Elsevier. **Figure 16.7:** Buckner, R.L., Sepulcre, J., Talukdar, T., Krienen, F.M., Liu, H., Hedden, T. et al. (2009). Cortical hubs revealed by intrinsic functional connectivity: mapping, assessment of stability, and relation to Alzheimer's disease. The Journal of Neuroscience : the official journal of the Society for Neuroscience, 29(6), 1860–1873. **Figure 16.8:** Corticobasal ganglionic degeneration and/or frontotemporal dementia? A report of two overlap cases and review of literature. P Mathuranath, J. Xuereb, T. Bak, and J. Hodges. *J Neurol Neurosurg Psychiatry*. 2000 Mar; 68(3): 304–312 doi: 10.1136/jnnp.68.3.304, with permission from BMJ Publishing Group Ltd. **Figure 16.10:** Bolero, Ravel/ Hal Leonard MGB. **Figure 16.14:** Wellcome Library, London Portrait of George Gilles de la Tourette. **Figure 16.16:** National Tourette Syndrome Association. **Figure 16.17:** Neuroskeptic Blog/blogs.discovermagazine.com/neuroskeptic/2011/04/07/neurology-vs-psychiatry/. **Figure 16.21:** Prometheus72/Shutterstock. **Figure 16.23:** Mapping adolescent brain change reveals dynamic wave of accelerated gray matter loss in very early-onset schizophrenia. Paul M. Thompson, Christine Vidal, Jay N. Giedd, Peter Gochman, Jonathan Blumenthal, Robert Nicolson, Arthur W. Toga, and Judith L. Rapoport. © 2001 National Academy of Sciences, U.S.A. **Figure 16.30A:** © Everett Collection Inc/Alamy. **Figure 16.30b:** © Everett Collection Historical/Alamy. **Figure 16.30c:** © Peter Barritt/Alamy. **Figure 16.31:** Getty Images/Robert Sherbow/Contributor. **Figure 16.32:** Burden of Depressive Disorders by Country, Sex, Age, and Year: Findings from the Global Burden of Disease Study 2010. Alize J. Ferrari, Fiona J. Charlson, Rosana E. Norman, Scott B. Patten, Greg Freedman, Christopher J.L. Murray, Theo Vos, Harvey A. Whiteford. PLOS Medicine, November 5, 2013. **Figure 16.39:** Aisha Dar.s

Note: page numbers in *italics* refer to figures.